INTERNATIONAL HUMAN RIGHTS LAW IN AFRICA

International Human Rights Law in Africa

FRANS VILJOEN

OXFORD
UNIVERSITY PRESS

OXFORD
UNIVERSITY PRESS

Great Clarendon Street, Oxford OX2 6DP

Oxford University Press is a department of the University of Oxford.
It furthers the University's objective of excellence in research, scholarship,
and education by publishing worldwide in

Oxford New York

Auckland Cape Town Dar es Salaam Hong Kong Karachi
Kuala Lumpur Madrid Melbourne Mexico City Nairobi
New Delhi Shanghai Taipei Toronto

With offices in

Argentina Austria Brazil Chile Czech Republic France Greece
Guatemala Hungary Italy Japan Poland Portugal Singapore
South Korea Switzerland Thailand Turkey Ukraine Vietnam

Oxford is a registered trade mark of Oxford University Press
in the UK and in certain other countries

Published in the United States
by Oxford University Press Inc., New York

British Library Cataloguing in Publication Data
Data available

Library of Congress Cataloging in Publication Data
Data available

Typeset by Newgen Imaging Systems (P) Ltd., Chennai, India
Printed in Great Britain
on acid-free paper by
Biddles Ltd., King's Lynn

ISBN 978–0–19–921858–5

1 3 5 7 9 10 8 6 4 2

Foreword

The heart of our problems in Africa are the problems which confront human rights: poverty, hunger and malnutrition, gender equality, discrimination on ethnic differences, diseases, wars, arbitrary detention, extra judicial executions, unemployment and exploitation of children, to name some of them. Limited knowledge of international human rights law, disregard and disrespect of the subject, as well as a low level of commitment by African states to the implementation of their obligations under human rights treaties to which they are parties account significantly in making rights and freedoms appear esoteric to many: the reality of human rights comes out of their enjoyment. Admittedly, in bringing pressure to bear on governments to ratify human rights treaties, neither the need for compatibility study of national law and international law nor the obligations to be undertaken by states parties to such instruments is brought to the fore, or up at all.

Deserving of serious attention because it touches everybody, the issues of concern in human rights, for some time, have been addressed, with varying degree of specificity and depth at the national, regional, and global or universal levels, bringing in its trail multiple international human rights systems with various institutions, norms and processes, all of which are considered by Frans Viljoen. At the sub regional level, the potential to advance human rights by the eight economic institutions, recognised by the African Union, makes the inclusion of an overall picture of these institutions in this study desirable. International human rights law need to be made part of municipal law, implemented and enforced in all African countries for it to be effective; and the route to this goal is set out clearly in this work. A background to international human rights law and an explanation of the basic terms within it make for greater understanding of, and clarity of thought about the subject. In this context, an explanation of 'human rights', 'human rights law' and 'international human rights law', for instance, is welcome. It is given to a commentator to introduce a new term for a crisp and sharper focus on a problem; therein lies the justification for the appearance of 'rightoric' which is derived from 'rhetoric' and rights, or the credibility gap between the proclamation of 'rights' and their enforcement. The nature of the subject compels a primary responsibility to be placed on governments to respect, protect, fulfil and promote human rights. To aid in the performance of these obligations, the justiciability of international human rights law is amply demonstrated.

While rightly concentrating on the regional body African Union, formerly Organisation of African Unity, its human rights instruments notably African Charter on Human and Peoples' Rights, institutions, the main one being the African Commission on Human and Peoples' Rights, and processes; a work on international human rights law in Africa must of necessity assess the impact of the United Nations human rights system on African countries on account of African states being part of this global system. United Nations Charter-based human rights mechanisms such as Country Rapporteurs, Thematic Rapporteurs and Working Groups of Experts, as well as the seven treaty bodies Human Rights Committee, Committee on Economic, Social and Cultural Rights which was created by a resolution of the Economic and Social Council in 1985, Committee on Elimination of Racial Discrimination, Committee on the Elimination of Discrimination against Women, Committee against Torture, and its Subcommittee on Prevention, Committee on the Rights of the Child, Committee on the Protection of the Rights of All Migrant Workers and Members of Their Families are equally assessed for a similar purpose. Relatedly, in considering the human rights functions of United Nations organs and agencies and the specialised financial institutions World Bank, International Monetary Fund and World Trade Organisation and their impact on African states, Frans Viljoen presents an appropriate measure of international human rights law in Africa. By parity of treatment, other institutions with responsibility for human rights protection under the African Union, Assembly of Heads of State and Government, Permanent Representative Committee, Pan-African Parliament, Executive Council, Peer Review Mechanism, African Commission and Peace and Security Council are examined. To a lesser extent, because of its limited impact on international human rights in Africa, three inter-governmental organisations Commonwealth of Nations, Organisation de la Francophone and Community of Portuguese Speaking Countries find a place in this work. In sum, no institution either in or outside Africa whose functions have a bearing on international human rights in Africa escapes the scrutiny of Frans Viljoen.

Ten years ago, in his doctoral (LLD) thesis which was presented to University of Pretoria, South Africa: 'Realisation of Human Rights in Africa through Inter-Governmental Institutions', Frans Viljoen approached the subject with such depth and breadth that, as an external examiner, I recommended its publication. In the intervening period, sober reflection and hard work have resulted in updates, published articles, and contributions in books, unpublished research papers and reports, as well as interactions with students, colleagues and others in the area of the subject. He has also taken into account the extant commentaries and literature on the subject. Not an arm-chair critic, wherever and whenever it matters, Frans Viljoen is likely to be found on the ground, and his activist trait has enriched the work. Enlightenment is likely to accompany even disagreements which readers may have with any aspect of this work, because of the thoroughness and comprehensive nature of the work.

If we pay heed to the lessons in this book, we shall come closer to solving the core problems in Africa: the satisfaction of the basic needs of our people in an atmosphere of peace and security. This book must be read by all: politicians, scholars, human rights activists, the unitiated for it is so intelligible, and all others, especially those in Africa, because there is much to be gained in so doing.

E.V.O. Dankwa
Former Chair, African Commission on
Human and Peoples' Rights

Summary Contents

PART VI: CONCLUSION

Contents

Introduction

My interest in international human rights law dates from the time when, as a law student at the University of Pretoria in the mid-1980s, I came to appreciate its importance to the struggle against apartheid, and its role in discrediting apartheid locally and abroad. Not only was it pivotal in the birth and growth of the African National Congress, but human rights law also provided the window through which I, a white South African, could critically assess myself and the society in which I was living. International human rights served as the basis for the 'shame' that was mobilized around the world, and which impacted nationally in South Africa.

The immediate inspiration for this book was the 20-year celebration of the entry into force of the African Charter on Human and Peoples' Rights on 21 October 2006. Occasionally attending sessions of the African Commission on Human and Peoples' Rights since 1994 as representative of the Centre for Human Rights, University of Pretoria, I became a keen observer of the Commission's activities and at times participated in its sessions. I also had the privilege of being involved in a communication submitted to the African Commission, in the state reporting process, and in consultations concerning and assessment of the working methods of the Commission, and of one of its special mechanisms, the Special Rapporteur on Prisons and Conditions of Detention in Africa. The insights that I gained as a result of these academic and activist activities no doubt left their imprint on the book.

International human rights law, which is the main focus of this book, has infiltrated the spaces inhabited by humanity. Starting with the global human rights system, and progressing to the regional and subregional levels, the study describes and critically discusses these international human rights law systems with respect to their various *institutions, norms*, and *processes*.

Three cross-cutting themes are emphasized as part of the discussion: national implementation and enforcement, integration, and poverty.

National implementation and enforcement: International human rights law must be made to matter nationally. Throughout, the work foregrounds the pre-eminence of the national level of human rights protection in relation to the international level. Going beyond theories of 'monism' and 'dualism', an awareness of the importance of the national arena inevitably shifts the searchlight to follow-up (implementation or 'enforcement') of human rights.

An important axis along which I explore national implementation and enforcement is that of commitment-compliance. Although international human rights laws norms are still evolving, increasingly towards the inclusion of subaltern groups such as persons living with disabilities, migrant workers, and indigenous peoples, over the last decade mechanisms and procedures to improve implementation and enforcement measures have received more attention than before. By dealing with human rights in the abstract, scholarly publications on the topic often reinforce the commitment-compliance divide by limiting their focus to 'commitments'. If norms are continuously discussed in separation from the reality of their application, it should not be surprising that the impression is created that the human rights system is not 'real'. In this book, efforts are made to view standards in the context of their supervision. Using concrete examples from the application and implementation of international human rights law in Africa, and relying on the insights of the American Realists that it is 'law-in-action' that matters most, I endeavour as far as possible to explain and shed light on the status of national compliance.

I try to capture this dichotomy by the neologism 'rightoric' ('rightorical'; 'rightorics'), composed of two roots: *rights* and *rhetoric*. 'Rhetoric' is used in a pejorative sense, denoting the practice of persuasion in order to misinform, to obfuscate, and to serve public relations purposes (to 'spin'). When employing this discursive approach in the context of human rights, a state engages in *rightoric*. For example, a state uses *rightoric* when it ratifies a treaty without conducting a prior compatibility study, without domesticating it, and without accepting all the complaints mechanisms available under that treaty.

Integration: The integration of human rights has many dimensions. The question is posed whether human rights are sufficiently and effectively integrated into the norms, institutions, and processes of the UN, the AU, and African subregional organizations, and at the national level. To what extent are the actions and activities of international organizations informed by human rights? To what extent are institutions at each level, and between the different levels, attuned to cooperate and coordinate their activities towards a human rights-directed common goal? To what extent do the four levels overlap with, supplement, and reinforce each other? What is the role of human rights in processes of regional integration, for example in 'moving' institutions from an 'international' to a 'supra-national' character?

Against the background of the inevitable inroads of human rights into state sovereignty, the weakness of African states, and the negative consequences of the principle of *uti possidetis*, the prospects of and problems associated with economic and legal integration in Africa are considered. Specific attention is paid to the role of the regional human rights system in this process.

Poverty: Many human rights violations may in one way or another be traced to poverty and impoverishment. In a book such as this, there is a need to engage with this aspect of overriding importance in Africa, and the potential of the law, and in particular international human rights law, by asking the question: Can international human rights law make a difference? Thus far, human rights discourse has placed its hope in justiciable socio-economic rights. These efforts are traced and analysed.

The book is divided into five parts. Part I, consisting of Chapter 1, provides basic background information about international human rights law to the uninitiated reader.

Part II, comprising Chapters 2 and 3, deals with international human rights law at the global level, operating under the auspices of the United Nations.

Part C, which makes up the bulk of the book, concerns itself with the African regional human rights system: its location and functioning within the African Union (Chapters 4 and 5); its substantive norms (Chapter 6); the quasi-judicial application of these norms by the African Commission on Human and Peoples' Rights (Chapters 7, 8, 9, and 10); and the prospects of judicial application by the African Court on Human and Peoples' Rights (Chapter 11).

In Part IV, Chapter 12 focuses on the subregional level, and investigates the realized and potential role of African Regional Economic Communities (RECs) in advancing human rights on the continent.

Part V locates the discussion at the national level as a space in which international human rights law is (or should be) implemented and enforced (Chapter 13). It further directs its attention to the role of the national legal order in supplementing deficiencies in the international regime, particularly when it comes to the justiciability of socio-economic rights (in Chapter 14) and HIV/AIDS (in Chapter 15).

Part VI contains a conclusion (Chapter 16).

The aim of this book is to present a comprehensive, systematic and holistic overview of African states' obligations under, and realization of international human rights law. It tries to steer a middle course between the two extremes of being a basic introductory text for students of international human rights law, and an encyclopaedic source of reference on the topic. Inevitably, some important aspects are left out. I choose a few random examples: the ILO Convention 182 (Prohibition and Immediate Action for the Elimination of the Worst Forms of Child Labour), the Hague Convention on Protection of Children and Co-operation in respect of Inter-country Adoption, and in-depth discussions of the right to development and cultural relativism. As far as possible, I include concrete examples and actual practices.

The accomplishment of human rights is a shifting target. A study of its realization inevitably provides a picture that is limited by various factors, one of which is a set time-frame. In this book, as far as available sources allow, the position is set out as it was on 31 December 2006. However, this date line is sometimes shifted backward, because updated data was not available as at the end of 2006, and forward, to incorporate some crucial developments that took place in early 2007. Still, the limitation of a cut-off mark caused the neglect of important developments, such as the African Charter on Democracy, Elections and Governance. A discussion of this treaty, adopted on 30 January 2007, is consequently not included in Chapter 6 of this book.

The book is partly composed of updates of published articles, contributions in books, and unpublished research papers and reports, as well as my doctoral (LL D) thesis ('The Realization of Human Rights in Africa through Inter-Governmental

Institutions', unpublished, University of Pretoria, 1997, <http://upetd.up.ac.za>), all of which I have rethought and reworked. Where applicable, these sources are referenced in the work—not to create a space of self-reference, but in acknowledgement of my reliance on these sources.

In the past, one of the problems facing researchers on international human rights law in Africa has been the dearth of material. The Internet and a number of publications that appeared over the last decade or so have filled much of the gap. To avoid referencing these sources throughout the book, I provide a list here: On the United Nations human rights system, the web-site of the Office of the High Commissioner for Human Rights is an invaluable source of information (see <http://www.ohchr.org>). The web-sites of the African Union (<http:www.africa-union.org>) and African Commission on Human and Peoples' Rights (<http://www.achpr.org>) are valuable sources on the African regional institutions and human rights system, but in some respects they need to be supplemented by those of the Institute for Security Studies (<http://www.iss.co.za>) and the Centre for Human Rights (www.chr.up.ac.za). As far as primary sources that have been collated and reprinted are concerned, see R Murray and M Evans (eds), *Documents of the African Commission on Human and Peoples' Rights* (Oxford: Hart, 2001) (for African Commission documents between 1987 and 1999); C Heyns (ed), *Human Rights Law in Africa* (Leiden: Martinus Nijhoff, 2004) (vol 1 containing documents of AU organs, the African Commission, and other relevant bodies; vol 2 containing the constitutional provisions related to human rights of all African states); and C Heyns and M Killander (eds), *Compendium of Key Human Rights Documents of the African Union* (Pretoria: PULP, 2006) (containing key AU human rights documents and decisions of the African Commission).

In the absence of an official 'law reports series' published by the African Commission, reference to decisions of the Commission is to the African Human Rights Law Reports (AHRLR) (Cape Town: Juta) and the Commission's Activity Reports.

My thanks go to all who directly and indirectly contributed to the final product:

• The students of the LL M (Human Rights and Democratization in Africa) programme, presented by the Centre for Human Rights since 2000, with whom I—as academic coordinator—exchanged ideas, by whom I was challenged on substantive issues, and from whom I learnt in class and through their written assignments and dissertations;

• The tutors of the programme, and LL D students at the Centre;

• Christof Heyns, who was my doctoral supervisor and academic mentor, Michelo Hansungule, and other colleagues at the Centre;

• Contributors to the *African Human Rights Law Journal*, of which I am the coeditor;

- Annelize Nienaber, whose editing and language skills significantly improved the book;

- Magnus Killander (who gave very insightful comments on chapters 4, 5, and 7 to 10); and Mianko Ramaroson, Mary Crewe, Karen Stefiszyn, Waruguru Kaguongo, Julius Mengot, Susan Precious, Nyasha Chingore, Babatunde Fagbayibo, David Padilla, Hye-Young Lim, Solomon Ebobrah, Tarisai Mutangi, George Mukundi, Solomon Dersso and Siegfried Wiessner, who all made useful comments on substantive issues contained in various parts of the work;

- Sunét Slabbert and Isabeau de Meyer, who typed parts of the manuscript;

- Simon Weldehaimanot, Tsegay Tesfemicael, Tebogo Mogosoana, Isolde de Villiers, Matilda Lasseko, Lizette Bezaans, Maria Nassali, Gus Waschefort, and Patricia Bako, who helped to proofread, and to create and compile the tables and the bibliography;

- The staff of the OR Tambo Library, Faculty of Law, University of Pretoria;

- Members of the African Commission with whom I interacted over the years, in particular Commissioners Umozurike, Dankwa, Chigovera, Chirwa, Pityana, Nyanduga and Malila; and

- Members of the Commission's Secretariat, in particular the Documentalist until 2006, Jan Jallow.

Pretoria
31 January 2007

Table of Cases

International Criminal Tribunal for Rwanda

Special Court for Sierra Leone

United Nations CAT Committee

United Nations CERD Committee

United Nations Human Rights Committee

United Nations Working Group on Arbitrary Detention

NATIONAL COURTS

Benin

Botswana

Nigeria

Senegal

Seychelles

South Africa

List of Abbreviations

ACHPR	African Commission on Human and Peoples' Rights
ACJ	African Court of Justice (AU Court of Justice)
AEC	African Economic Community
AFLAQ	*African Legal Aid Quarterly*
AFRC	Armed Forces Revolutionary Council
AG	Attorney General
AHG	AU/OAU Assembly of Heads of State and Governments
AHRLJ	*African Human Rights Law Journal*
AHRLR	African Human Rights Law Reports
AIR	All Indian Reports
AJIL	*American Journal of International Law*
ALADI	Latin American Integration Association
AMIS	African Mission in Sudan
ANPPCAN	African Network for the Prevention and Protection against Child Abuse and Neglect
APRM	African Peer Review Mechanism
APR Forum	African Peer Review Forum
ARV	anti-retroviral
ASEAN	Association of Southeast Asian Nations
ASICL Proc	*Proceedings of the African Society of International and Comparative Law*
AU	African Union
AYBIL	*African Yearbook of International Law*
BCLR	Butterworths Constitutional Law Reports
BnCC	Benin Constitutional Court
BLR	Botswana Law Reports
BwCA	Botswana Court of Appeal
CACM	General Treaty on Central American Integration
CAO	Office of the Compliance Advisor/Ombudsman
CAR	Central African Republic
CARICOM	Caribbean Community and Common Market
CAT	Convention against Torture and Other Cruel, Inhuman or Degrading Treatment or Punishment
CCAR	Commission on Refugees and the Coordinating Committee on Assistance to Refugees
CDF	Civil Defence Forces
CEDAW	Convention on the Elimination of All Forms of Discrimination against Women

CEMAC	Central African Economic and Monetary Community
CEMIRIDE	Centre for Minority Rights Development
CEN-SAD	Community of Sahel-Saharan States
CEPGL	Economic Community of Great Lakes Countries (*Communauté Economique des Pays des Grands Lacs*)
CERD	Convention on the Elimination of All Forms of Racial Discrimination
CESCR	Committee on Economic, Social and Cultural Rights
CEWARN	Conflict Early Warning and Response Mechanism
CHOGM	Commonwealth Heads of Government Meetings
CHRD	Commonwealth Human Rights Digest
CIDO	African Citizen (Civil Society and Diaspora) Directorate
CILSA	*Comparative and International Law Journal of Southern Africa*
CKGR	Central Kalahari Game Reserve
CMW	Convention on the Protection of the Rights of All Migrant Workers and Members of their Families
CODESRIA	Council for the Development of Social Science Research in Africa
COI	Indian Ocean Commission (*Commission de l'Océan Indien*)
COMESA	Common Market for Eastern and Southern Africa
COPAX	*Conseil de Paix, de Sécurité et de Stabilité de l'Afrique Centrale*
COREPER	EU Committee of Permanent Representatives
CPLP	Community of Portuguese Speaking Countries
CRC	Convention on the Rights of the Child
CRC-AC	Option Protocol to CRC on the Involvement of Children in Armed Conflict
CRC-SC	Option Protocol to CRC on the Sale of Children, Child Prostitution and Child Pornography
CRM	APRM Country Review Mission
CSO	Civil Society Organizations
CSSDCA	Conference on Security, Stability, Development and Cooperation in Africa
DANIDA	Danish International Development Agency
Doc	Document
DPSP	Directive Principles of State Policy
DRC	Democratic Republic of Congo
EAC	East African Community
EACJ	East African Court of Justice
EACSO	East African Common Services Organization
EALA	East African Legislative Assembly
ECCAS	Economic Community of Central African States

ECHR	European Court of Human Rights
ECHM	European Commission of Human Rights
ECOMOG	ECOWAS Cease-Fire Monitoring Group
ECOSOC	UN Economic and Social Council
ECOSOCC	AU Economic, Social and Cultural Council
ECOWAS	Economic Community of Western African States
EIDSNet	East African Integrated Diseases Surveillance Network
ESR	Economic and Social Rights in South Africa
EU	European Union
EU-MEFTA	Euro-Mediterranean Free Trade Area
FAO	Food and Agricultural Organization
FDI	foreign direct investment
FGM	female genital mutilation
FHRI	Foundation for Human Rights Initiative
FIDH	International Federation of Human Rights
FNL	Algerian National Liberation Front
FOMAC	Central African Multinational Force
G-8	Group of Eight
GATS	General Agreement on Trade in Services
GIS	Group of Interested States
GNI	Gross National Income
GNP	Gross National Product
HARDP	Humanitarian Affairs, Refugees, and Displaced Persons
HIPC	Highly Indebted Poor Countries Initiative
HRC	UN Human Rights Committee
HRLJ	*Human Rights Law Journal*
HRLRA	Human Rights Law Reports of Africa
HRQ	*Human Rights Quarterly*
IBRD	International Bank for Reconstruction and Development
ICC	International Criminal Court
ICCPR	International Covenant on Civil and Political Rights
ICCPR (OPI)	First Optional Protocol to the ICCPR
ICED	International Convention for the Protection of All Persons from Enforced Disappearance
ICESCR	International Covenant on Economic, Social and Cultural Rights
ICHRL	Interights Commonwealth Human Rights Law
ICJ	International Court of Justice
ICJ-Geneva	International Commission of Jurists
ICLQ	*International and Comparative Law Quarterly*
ICTR	International Criminal Tribunal for Rwanda
ICTY	International Criminal Tribunal for the Former Yugoslavia
IDA	International Development Association

IDP	Internally Displaced Person
IFC	International Finance Corporation
IFDH	International Federation of Human Rights
IFI	International Financial Institutions
IGAD	Intergovernmental Authority on Development
IGLHRC	International Gay and Lesbian Human Rights Committee
ILO	International Labour Organization
IMF	International Monetary Fund
INGO	International Non-Governmental Organization
IOC	Indian Ocean Commission
IWGIA	International Working Group for Indigenous Affairs
JAL	*Journal of African Law*
JEM	Justice and Equality Movement
LAC	Legal Assistance Centre
LesH	Lesotho High Court
LRA	Lord's Resistance Army
LRC	Commonwealth Law Reports
MARAC	Central African Early Warning Mechanism
MDGs	Millennium Development Goals
MDRI	Multilateral Debt Relief Initiative
MERCOSUR	Common Market of the Southern Cone
MIGA	Multilateral Investment Guarantee Agency
MINURSO	UN Mission for the Referendum in Western Sahara
MOSOP	Movement for the Survival of the Ogoni People
MOU	APRM Memorandum of Understanding
MPs	Members of Parliaments
MRU	Mano River Union
MSM	men who have sex with men
NEPAD	New Partnership for Africa's Development
NGO	Non-Governmental Organization
NgSC	Nigerian Supreme Court
NHRIs	National Human Rights Institutions
NILR	*Netherlands International Law Review*
NPFL	National Patriotic Front of Liberia
NQHR	*Netherlands Quarterly of Human Rights*
NR	Namibian Law Reports
NWLR	Nigerian Weekly Law Reports
NYBIL	*Netherlands Yearbook of International Law*
OAS	Organization of American States
OAU	Organization of African Unity
OHADA	*Organisation pour l'Harmonisation en Afrique du Droit des Affaires*
OHCHR	UN Office of the High Commissioner for Human Rights

OIC	Organization of Islamic Conference
OIF	International Organization of the *Francophonie*
ONUC	Operation of the United Nations in Congo *(Operation des Nations Unies en Congo)*
ONUS	United Nations Peace Keeping to the Congo
OP	Optional Protocol
OP-CAT	Optional Protocol to CAT
OP-CEDAW	Optional Protocol to CEDAW
OPI	(First) Optional Protocol to ICCPR
OPII	Second Optional Protocol to ICCPR
OPDS	(SADC) Organ on Politics, Defence and Security Cooperation
OPDS Protocol	Protocol on Politics Defence and Security Cooperation
OSCE	Organization for Security and Cooperation
PAP	Pan-African Parliament
PMTCT	Prevention of Mother-to-Child Transmission (of HIV)
PRC	AU Permanent Representatives' Committee
PRSP	Poverty Reduction Strategy Papers
PSC	AU Peace and Security Council
PTA	Preferential Trade Area of Eastern and Southern African States
PWG	AU Provisional Working Group
RADDHO	*Rencontre africaine pour la défense des droits de l'Homme*
RADIC	*African Journal of International and Comparative Law (Revue africaine de Droit International et Comparé)*
REC	Regional Economic Community
Res	Resolution
RESEFAC	*Réseau pour les femmes de l'Afrique Centrale*
RPF	Rwandan Patriotic Front
SA	South African Law Reports
SACR	South African Criminal Reports
SACU	Southern African Customs Union
SADC	Southern African Development Community
SADCC	Southern African Development Coordination Conference
SADC PF	SADC Parliamentary Forum
SADR	Saharawi Arab Democratic Republic
SAHRINGON	Southern African Human Rights NGO Network
SAHRIT	Human Rights Trust of Southern Africa
SALJ	*South African Law Journal*
SAPs	Structural Adjustment Programmes
SAYIL	*South African Yearbook of International Law*
SCSL	Special Court for Sierra Leone
SeCC	Senegalese *Conseil Constitutionnel*
SERAC	Social and Economic Rights Action Centre
SLA	Sudan Liberation Army

SRH	UN Special Rapporteur on Health
SRP	Special Rapporteur on Prisons and Conditions of Detention in Africa
STD	sexually transmitted disease
TNC	transnational corporation
UK	United Kingdom
UEMOA	West African Economic and Monetary Union (*l'Union économique et monétaire de l'Afrique de l'ouest*)
UMA	Arab Maghreb Union (*Union du Maghreb Arabe*)
UN	United Nations Organization
UNAIDS	UN Programme on HIV/AIDS
UNAMIR	UN Assistance Mission for Rwanda
UNCHR	UN Commission on Human Rights
UNDP	United Nations Development Programme
UNEP	United Nations Environmental Programme
UNESCO	United Nations Educational, Scientific and Cultural Organization
UNGA	United Nations General Assembly
UNICEF	United Nations Children's Fund
UNHCR	United Nations High Commissioner for Refugees
UNHRC	United Nations Human Rights Council
UNMIL	UN Mission in Liberia
UNMIS	United Nations Mission in Sudan
UNOMIL	United Nations Observer Mission in Liberia
UNOSOM	United Nations Observer Mission in Somalia
UNITAF	Unified Task Force
UNSC	UN Security Council
UNSG	UN Secretary-General
UNTAG	United Nations Transitional Assistance Group
UNTS	United Nations Treaty Series
UOBDU	United Organization for Batwa Development in Uganda
USA	United States of America
VCLT	Vienna Convention on the Law of Treaties
VCT	voluntary counselling and testing
WAMZ	West African Monetary Zone
WEOG	Western European and Others Group
WHO	World Health Organization
WILDAF	Women in Law and Development in Africa
WTO	World Trade Organization

PART I
BACKGROUND

1

An Introduction to International Human Rights Law

This chapter clarifies some of the concepts used in the book;[1] it provides an introduction to the 'four levels' at which international human rights law operates; and it acknowledges the limitations inherent in an overly legalistic approach to the subject-matter.

A What is 'International Human Rights Law'?

1 'Human Rights', 'Human Rights Law', and 'International Human Rights Law'

The term 'human rights' may be used either in an abstract and philosophical sense, as denoting a 'special kind of moral claim'[2] that all humans may invoke; or, more pragmatically, as the manifestation of these claims in positive law, for example as constitutional guarantees that serve as the basis to hold governments accountable under national legal processes. To avoid confusion, the first understanding of the term will be referred to as 'human rights', and the second as 'human rights law'.

Because the concept 'human rights' presupposes the existence of 'humans', it finds application in human interaction, and is thus relational in nature. Sustained human

---

[1] To some extent, much of this chapter approximates a brief 'International Human Rights Law 101' course. Although there is a wealth of literature on the subject (see RM Smith, *Textbook on International Human Rights* (Oxford: Oxford University Press, 2003), M Nowak, *Introduction to the International Human Rights Regime* (Leiden: Martinus Nijhoff, 2003) and similar sources cited below), the most important concepts are integrated into the study to enable anyone not well-versed in this field to follow the discussion without referring to other sources. More complete information on some of the issues is found in these sources.

[2] S Meckled-García and B Çali, 'Lost in Translation: The Human Rights Ideal and International Human Rights Law' in S Meckled-García and B Çali (eds), *The Legalization of Human Rights: Multidisciplinary Perspectives on Human Rights and Human Rights Law* (London: Routledge, 2006) 11.

contact and community requires mutual respect—respect of the other's life, of the child's needs, of the elder's age and wisdom, and so on. In a closely knit society, such as 'traditional' African communities often lacking a centralized structure, the reciprocity of expectations is taken for granted, and need not be formally determined—members of society are socialized into their roles. In these contexts, non-compliance carries the risk of social exclusion, and even expulsion—a life outside the group. These relationships could have been formally conceptualized as 'rights and duties', but there was no need to do so, as they were already intricately tied to one's very identity and social role. Understood in this way, there is little doubt that 'human rights' (but perhaps not 'human rights law') existed in traditional (pre-colonial) Africa. Although the position in pre-colonial Africa should not be romanticized, and was far from homogenous, there clearly were established ways and means of marshalling custom and wise leadership that led to effective consensus and legitimate dispute resolution.

As colonialism, urbanization, and industrialization ruptured traditional African societies, the bonds of immediacy and reciprocity grew weaker; people became alienated and isolated, and formed new communities. Formalized state structures were instituted to organize social interaction on the basis of pre-determined expectations of roles, referred to as 'rights' and 'duties'. The idea of *Gemeinschaft*, a community based on relationships, made place for the notion of *Gesellschaft*, a society based on rights.[3] The state set up a legal system to mediate rights-based claims. With time, state power became increasingly intrusive, exemplified by the use of a criminal justice systems to arrest, interrogate, search and seize, imprison and execute.

Although majoritarianism legitimates legislation and the increasingly bureaucratized functioning of the executive, majorities sometimes get it wrong. They may have little regard for 'numerical' minorities such as sentenced criminals, linguistic or religious minorities, non-nationals, 'indigenous peoples', and the socially stigmatized. It therefore becomes necessary to guarantee the existence and rights of numerical minorities, of the vulnerable, and the powerless. This is done by agreeing on the rules governing society in the form of a constitutionally entrenched and justiciable Bill of Rights, containing the basic human rights of 'everyone'. Through a Bill of Rights, human rights become integral to the legal system—become 'human rights law'—superior to ordinary law and executive action.

From the discussion above it emerges that 'human rights law' is closely linked to the emergence of the nation state. The implication of this state-centredness is that states are the primary duty-bearers in respect of these rights.[4] A fundamental

---

[3] See eg N Luhmann, *A Sociological Theory of Law* (London: Routledge and Kegan Paul, 1985), relying on the 'abstract version' of this formulation by Talcott Parsons (242–3). On the concept of human rights in Africa see eg the sources quoted in ch 6. J below.

[4] It is accepted that the provisions of national and human rights instruments may be applied against states (that is, 'vertically'). It is more exceptional for these instruments to bind individuals, or non-state actors (that is, to apply 'horizontally'). The constitutional guarantees under both the South African 1996 Constitution (s 8(2) (the Bill of Rights 'binds a natural person . . .') and s 9(4) ('no person may

paradox is therefore introduced: individuals depend on states to guarantee their rights, but they also need to defend their rights against these very states as the principal violators of their rights.[5] In a particular state, 'human rights law' represents the state's obligations at a given time, while 'human rights' serve as a yardstick against which the nature and extent of these obligations may be assessed, an ideal towards which to strive, and an inspiration for struggles to improve the current state of affairs.[6]

The preceding discussion may easily be transferred to the international level, where the same two notions play themselves out in debates concerning human rights. 'International human rights law' differs from national human rights law as to its source, in that its concretized content is found mainly in provisions of international human rights treaties. It is in this sense that the term 'international human rights law' is used in this book.

1.1 'Three Generations' of International Human Rights Law

The traditional categorization of three 'generations' of rights, used in both national and international human rights discourse, traces the chronological evolution of human rights as an echo to the three-dimensional call of the French revolution: *liberté* ('freedoms', 'civil and political' or 'first generation' rights),[7] *equalité* (equality, 'socio-economic', or 'second generation' rights),[8] and *fraternité* (solidarity, 'collective' or 'third generation' rights).[9]

During the period of the Cold War, 'first generation civil and political' rights were prioritized in Western democracies, while 'second generation socio-economic' rights were resisted as socialist notions. In the developing world, economic growth

---

unfairly discriminate')), and Ugandan 1995 Constitution (art 137(3) (the Constitutional Court may adjudicate an allegation that 'any act or omission by any person' violated the Constitution)) provide for 'horizontal application'. The Convention on the Elimination of Discrimination against Women imposes the obligation on states to eliminate discrimination at the horizontal level (art 2(e): states must take 'all appropriate measures to eliminate discrimination against women by any person...').

[5] See eg C Douzinas, *The End of Human Rights* (Oxford: Hart, 2000) 100–7, 115–22.

[6] See eg CH Heyns, 'A "Struggle Approach" to Human Rights' in C Heyns and K Stefiszyn (eds), *Human Rights, Peace and Justice in Africa: A Reader* (Pretoria: PULP, 2006) 15–35.

[7] These rights, invoking and obtaining guarantees from autocratic governments that the individual should be 'left alone', were first contained in the English Bill of Rights (1689), the Virginia Declaration of Rights (1776), and the *Déclaration des Droits de l'Homme et du Citoyen* (Declaration of Man and Citizen (1789)).

[8] These rights, inspired by socialist philosophy and responding to increasing urbanization and poverty in the rapidly industrializing world at the beginning of the 20th century, were first included in the 1917 Mexican Constitution. Under the heading 'Of Personal Guarantees' (Title I, Chapter I), it is provided that '[p]rimary instruction in public institutions shall be gratuitous' (art 3). These provisions generally are not formulated as claims against the government (see eg the reconceptualization of property as being 'vested originally in the Nation' (art 27), combined with the guarantee that property 'shall not be expropriated except for reasons of public utility and by means of indemnification'). See also the 1918 Constitution of the former Soviet Republic, and the 1919 Weimar Constitution of Germany.

[9] With growing globalization and a heightened awareness of overlapping global concerns, especially due to extreme poverty in some parts of the world, rights such as the right to a healthy environment, to self-determination, and to development have been developed.

and development were often regarded as goals able to trump 'civil and political' rights. The discrepancy between the two sets of rights was also emphasized: 'civil and political' rights were said to be of immediate application, while 'second generation' rights were understood to be implemented only in the long term or 'progressively'. Another axis of division was the supposed notion that 'first generation' rights place 'negative obligations' on states, and 'second generation' rights impose 'positive obligations'. In the post-Cold War era, it became generally accepted that such a dichotomy does not do justice to the extent to which these rights are interrelated and interdependent.[10] The dichotomy of positive/negative obligations also no longer holds water, as even a classical 'civil and political' right such as the right to vote is now understood to require the state to use resources to organize regular elections, for example by printing ballot papers, installing voting booths, and so on.[11]

It has therefore become more acceptable not to distinguish between rights with reference to their 'nature' or 'generation', but to differentiate between the various forms of government obligations imposed by rights, thereby directing the focus to government action that is required to give effect to a particular right under specific circumstances. Governments have four major tiers of obligation—they must 'respect', 'protect', 'fulfil' and 'promote' human rights. These obligations apply equally to all rights, depending on the circumstances.[12] States must *respect* rights by refraining from interfering with the enjoyment of these rights, for example by not evicting people who have nowhere to go. This obligation is understood to be 'negative', in that it does not require government action or resource allocation. States must *protect* bearers of rights from intrusions by third parties, by way of legislating or by adopting other measures, for instance, by prohibiting exploitative child labour by private employers. States have to *fulfil* rights when they are required to take positive measures to ensure the direct enjoyment of a right by, for example, building and equipping clinics and by providing medication. A fourth obligation, to *promote* rights, has subsequently been devised,[13] and requires states to enable people to exercise rights in the longer term, for instance by education and awareness-raising about rights.

Still, in this book the terms 'civil and political' and 'socio-economic' rights are used from time to time, as this distinction is maintained under current international

---

[10] In fact, the general consensus expressed in the Vienna Declaration and Programme of Action (1993) (Vienna Declaration) was that all rights are indivisible.

[11] The 1918 Soviet Constitution had already recognized this reality by spelling out the resource implications of a 'civil' right protected under that Constitution: 'To ensure for the workers effective liberty of opinion', the state 'transfers to the working class and to the peasants all the technical and material resources necessary for the publication of newspapers, pamphlets, books...' (Ch V, 14).

[12] H Shue, *Basic Rights: Subsistence, Affluence and US Foreign Policy* (New Jersey: Princeton University Press, 1980) 52–3 (distinguishing the state's duty to 'avoid', 'protect', and 'aid'.

[13] See GJH van Hoof, 'The Legal Nature of Economic, Social and Cultural Rights: A Rebuttal of Some Traditional Views' in P Alston and K Tomasevski (eds), *The Right to Food* (Utrecht: Martinus Nijhoff, 1984) 97, 106.

human rights law,[14] and in the approaches of states. The term 'socio-economic rights' is used here to refer to rights 'whose purpose is to assure that human beings have the ability to obtain and maintain a minimum decent standard of living consistent with human dignity'.[15] These rights, which are principally the right to education, health care, food, work, social security, water, and shelter, give rise to the perception that they are programmatic and that their realization requires resource allocation (or at least greater allocation than other rights).[16]

1.2 The 'Justiciability' of International Human Rights Law

Given their legal (or 'juridical') character, the 'justiciability' of rights is central to international human rights law. 'Juridical' rights serve as authoritative sources of claims, aimed at holding violator-states accountable, provide a normative yardstick for acceptable behaviour, and supply a basis for persuasion and lobbying.

Referring to human rights claims as 'justiciable' implies something about the *claim* (or case), about the *setting* in which it may be resolved, and about the *consequences* of successfully invoking it. A justiciable claim is based on the alleged infringement of a subjective (human) right (invoked by an individual or collectivity). This claim has to be determined by a court or other tribunal or judicial body, or by a quasi-judicial body sharing the main features of a court.[17] If a violation of the subjective right is found, a court (or quasi-judicial body) must be able to find a remedy to redress the violation,[18] and the finding should set a form of precedent or at least embody an authoritative interpretation of that right.[19]

Even though the judicialization of rights has become increasingly the norm in international human rights law (as demonstrated by an increase in complaints mechanisms, the overly judicial nature of the procedures of treaty bodies, and the establishment of numerous international judicial institutions), its acceptance in reality remains, on the whole, restricted to 'civil and political' rights. States' differential treatment of 'civil and political' and 'socio-economic' rights in respect of justiciability is another reason why I maintain that duality in parts of this book.

---

[14] As exemplified in the division between the two 'categories' of rights in the International Covenant on Civil and Political Rights (ICCPR) and the International Covenant on Economic, Social and Cultural Rights (ICESCR).

[15] VH Condé, *A Handbook of International Human Rights Terminology* (Lincoln, Nebr: University of Nebraska, 2004) 55.

[16] C Scott and P Macklem, 'Constitutional Ropes of Sand or Justiciable Guarantees? Social Rights in a New South African Constitution' (1992) 141 *U of Pennsylvania L Rev* 1, 9, categorize these rights as 'social rights'.

[17] E Vierdag, 'The Nature of the Rights Granted by the International Covenant on Economic, Social and Cultural Rights' (1987) 9 *NYBIL* 69, 78 (violations are justiciable if they 'can be judged to have occurred, or to be occurring, by courts of law or similar bodies').

[18] Vierdag (n 17 above) 78 (justiciable claims are 'able to afford redress: The violation will consist of actions or omissions by officials or private persons which can be cancelled, rectified, declared void, or lead to the payment of compensation for damage').

[19] K Arambulo, *Strengthening the Supervision of the International Covenant on Economic Social and Cultural Rights: Theoretical and Procedural Aspects* (Oxford: Hart, 1999) 55.

B International Human Rights—The Four Levels

Human rights protection functions at four levels. The inner layer, forming the core of protection, is the national (domestic, or municipal) level. Subregional arrangements, which bring together a number of states in a relatively restricted region (such as a part of a continent), form the second tier. The next layer is the regional level, comprising the states situated on a particular continent or in a hemisphere. The global level, functioning under the auspices of the UN, forms the outer ring. Viewed from the perspective of the state, the subregional, regional, and global tiers together comprise the international level. The terms 'international', 'global', 'regional', and 'subregional' bear corresponding meanings in this book.

International human rights law was established as a normative beacon, beckoning states to an internationally agreed upon minimum standard of behaviour, and as a 'safety net' for individuals who are denied their rights under the domestic system, or who fall through the cracks of the national legal system. International complaints mechanisms provide a last hope when all other recourse fails. The relative advantage of the subregional and regional levels, compared to the global level, is the higher level of convergence and coherence between states, allowing for greater norm-specification in the regional and subregional spheres; and the immediacy of interlocking interests, opening the possibility for faster response and improved implementation when states are closely bound by economic and political ties. Reaching agreement on standards at the global level is time-consuming and necessarily entails striking compromises in the interest of universal acceptance. Greater coherence at the regional and subregional levels favours specificity and a concern for regional problems over vagueness and universal or 'Western' values.[20] Closer economic, cultural, and political ties and common loyalties are further likely to ensure better implementation and more immediate and effective 'mobilization of shame'.[21] Communities sharing bonds of mutuality ('common loyalties') are more likely to be attuned to each other than those separated by vast geographical and psychological divides.[22]

1 National Level

Given the dominant role of the state at the national level, it is self-evident that it carries the primary responsibility for human rights. To become meaningful, international

[20] In Africa, in particular, the African Charter on Human and Peoples' Rights (African Charter) embodies a more collective 'African conception' of human rights consistent with the 'historical tradition and the values of African civilization' (Preamble to the African Charter) by providing for 'peoples' rights' and individual duties. Implementation and enforcement are weak at the global level.

[21] See eg RF Drinan, *Mobilization of Shame: A World View of Human Rights* (New Haven: Yale University Press, 2001), who traces the origins of the term 'mobilization of shame' to early Amnesty International campaigns.

[22] IL Claude, *Swords into Plowshares: The Problems and Progress of International Organization* (New York: Random House, 4th edn, 1971) 103.

human rights law has to be brought 'home'. When states ratify international human rights treaties, they undertake to domesticate and comply with their provisions. Implementation and enforcement of international human rights law have to take place domestically, where rights are protected most effectively. In an ideal world, their ratification would be preceded by a compatibility study, thereby creating a perfect overlap between national law and international law. In the real world, however, some states do not become party to international human rights treaties; many do not conduct compatibility studies; and all states violate their treaty obligations from time to time. Civil society (comprising NGOs, lawyers, the media, churches, labour organizations, and so on) therefore plays an essential role domestically to raise awareness and to hold governments accountable; and to exhort external pressure in reinforcing and supplementing national protection.

2 Subregional Level

Usually, subregional arrangements are primarily directed at economic integration, and not at the promotion and protection of human rights. Given that they function at a level at which inter-country bonds may be assumed to be relatively strong, the potential of these arrangements for human rights is evident. Although no subregional human rights system exists in Africa, there are a number of subregional intergovernmental groupings that include a concern for human rights within their mandates.[23]

3 Regional Level

At the regional level, three fully-fledged human rights regimes and two fledgling systems may be identified. In one region, Asia, no human rights system has yet been established.

3.1 *Three Existing Systems in Europe, the Americas, and Africa*

Three regional human rights regimes, in the sense of 'a set of norms and institutions that is accepted by states as binding',[24] have been established.[25] Each of these systems operates under the auspices of an intergovernmental organization, or international political body. In the case of the European system—the best developed of the three—this is the Council of Europe. The Council of Europe was founded in 1949 by 11 Western European states to promote human rights and the rule of law in post-World War II Europe, to avoid a regression into totalitarianism and to

---

[23] In Africa, eg the Economic Community of West African States (ECOWAS) and the Southern African Development Community (SADC). See Ch 12 below.

[24] M Freeman, *Human Rights: An Interdisciplinary Approach* (Cambridge: Polity, 2002) 53.

[25] For a comparison of the three systems, see C Heyns, D Padilla, and L Zwaak, 'A Schematic Comparison of Regional Human Rights Systems' in F Gómez Isa and K de Feyter (eds), *International Protection of Human Rights: Achievements and Challenges* (Bilbao: University of Deusto, 2006) 545.

serve as a bulwark against Communism.[26] By 31 December 2006, the Council of Europe had 46 members. The Organization of American States (OAS) was founded in 1948 to promote regional peace, security, and development,[27] and its membership includes all 35 states in the Americas. In Africa, a human rights system was adopted under the auspices of the Organization of African Unity (OAU), which in 2002 transformed itself into the African Union (AU).[28] The AU comprises 53 members—all African states with the exception of Morocco.

In each of the three systems the substantive norms are set out in one principal treaty. The Council of Europe adopted its primary human rights treaty, the European Convention on Human Rights and Fundamental Freedoms (European Convention), in 1950.[29] The European Convention, incorporating 14 Protocols adopted thereto, includes mainly 'civil and political' rights. All 47 Council of Europe members have become party to the European Convention. The OAS adopted the American Convention on Human Rights (American Convention) in 1969.[30] It has now been ratified by 25 states.[31] The American Convention contains rights similar to those in the European Convention, but goes further by providing for a minimum of 'socio-economic' rights.[32] In contrast to these two treaties, the African Charter, adopted by the OAU in 1981,[33] contains justiciable 'socio-economic' rights, and elaborates on the duties of individuals and the rights of peoples. All AU member states are parties to the African Charter.

There is a difference in the way in which the principal treaty is implemented or enforced in each region. In an evolution spanning many decades, the European system of implementation developed from a two-tiered system consisting of a Commission and a Court, to a single judicial institution, the European Court of Human Rights, based in Strasbourg, France. This Court deals with individual and inter-state cases. A dual model is still in place in the Americas, consisting of the Inter-American Commission, based in Washington DC, and the Inter-American Court of Human Rights, based in San José, Costa Rica. Individual petitioners have to submit complaints first to the Inter-American Commission; thereafter the case may proceed to the Inter-American Court. The Commission also has the function of conducting on-site visits. After some recent institutional reforms, the African system resembles the two-tiered Inter-American system.[34]

---

[26] <http://www.coe.int> (30 November 2006). A distinction should be drawn between the Council of Europe, with 47 members, and the European Union (EU) with only 27 member countries. Disputes about the process of European economic integration are adjudicated by the Court of Justice of the European Communities, based in Luxembourg. While the EU and its Court of Justice were not established with a human rights mandate, in practice there is some convergence between EU and European Convention law. The increasing influence of human rights in the EU has led to the adoption of an EU Charter of Fundamental Rights.   [27] <http://www.oas.org> (30 November 2006).

[28] Web-site <http://www.africa-union.org>; see Ch 4.B.4 below.

[29] It entered into force in 1953.   [30] It entered into force in 1978.

[31] The two major economic powers in the region, the USA and Canada, are not party to the American Convention.   [32] American Convention, art 26.

[33] It entered into force in 1986; see further Ch 6.A below.   [34] See Ch 11 below.

The substantive basis of each of the systems goes beyond the main instruments. In Europe, two additional human rights regimes exist under the Council of Europe, each with its separate set of legal norms and implementation body. Filling the vacuum left by the omission of 'socio-economic' rights from the European Convention, the Council of Europe adopted the European Social Charter in 1961. The Council of Europe further adopted the European Convention for the Prevention of Torture and Inhuman or Degrading Treatment or Punishment.[35] Each of these treaties establishes a separate institutional mechanism independent from the European Court of Human Rights. Without establishing any new structures, the OAS has extended human rights norms in the Americas beyond the American Convention.[36] Three main treaties supplement the African Charter: the OAU Convention governing the Specific Aspects of Refugee Problems in Africa, the African Charter on the Rights and Welfare of the Child (African Children's Charter), and the Protocol to the African Charter on the Rights of Women in Africa. In respect of one of these supplementing standards, the African Children's Charter, a separate treaty body, the African Committee of Experts on the Right of the Child, has been created.

3.2 *Fledgling Systems in the Arab and Muslim Worlds*

Fledgling Arab and Muslim regional systems have also emerged. Without delving into the depths of difference in the conception of human rights between the Arab and Western worlds, the following is noted: according to the Islamic world-view, the Quh'ran and other religious sources play a dominant role in the regulation of social life. All Muslims are 'perpetually bound to other believers in a code of life conduct' based on the will of Allah.[37] In the classical view, there is no need for a constitution, as people are bound equally to each other through their 'oath of allegiance to their Lord'.[38] Legislation is exceptional, and is reserved for areas not covered by religious prescription. A religion-based scepticism of codified ('human') law, in general, and constitutionalism, in particular, no doubt finds its way to the international law sphere.

African states feature prominently among the members of the two major Arabic and Islamic organizations, the League of Arab States (Arab League) and the Organization of Islamic Conference (OIC). Ten African states (Algeria, Comoros, Djibouti, Egypt, Libya, Mauritania, Morocco, Somalia, Sudan, and Tunisia) are members of both. The role of human rights under these two regimes is therefore discussed in some depth.[39]

---

[35] Adopted in 1987, entered into force in 1989.

[36] Eg the Additional Protocol to the American Convention on Human Rights in the Area of Economic, Social and Cultural Rights, the Inter-American Convention on the Prevention, Punishment and Eradication of Violence Against Women and the Protocol to the American Convention on Human Rights to Abolish the Death Penalty, the Inter-American Convention to Prevent and Punish Torture, and the Inter-American Convention on the Elimination of Discrimination against Persons with Disabilities.

[37] MH Syed (ed), *Human Rights in Islam: The Modern Approach* (New Delhi: Anmol, 2003) 140.

[38] ibid.

[39] See generally on these and other instruments in the Arab and Islamic worlds, T Koraytem, 'Arab Islamic Developments on Human Rights' (2001) 16 *Arab L Q* 256.

The League of Arab States was founded in terms of the Pact of the League of Arab States of 1945.[40] Its overriding aim is to strengthen unity among Arab states by developing closer links between its members.[41] The Pact emphasizes the independence and sovereignty of its members. No mention is made in its founding document of either the contents or principles of human rights.

At an international conference on human rights held in Tehran in 1968, some Arab states, with the assistance of the secretariat of the Arab League, managed to have the position of Arabs in the territories occupied by Israel included in the agenda. This successful invocation of 'human rights' issues, in the aftermath of a number of defeats at the hands of Israel in 1967, created an awareness of human rights among the Arab states. However, at the Tehran Conference, and thereafter, the commitment of the Arab League to human rights was primarily 'a means of censuring Israel over its treatment of the inhabitants of the occupied territories'.[42] Soon after the conference, in 1968, a regional conference on human rights was held in Beirut, where the Permanent Arab Commission on Human Rights was established. From its inception, this was a highly politicized body. The political nature of the Commission is accentuated by the method of appointment. The Commission does not consist of independent experts, as in many other international human rights bodies, but of government representatives. The Commission may only submit recommendations and suggestions to the Council of the Arab League, another political body.[43]

On 15 September 1994, the Council adopted the Arab Charter on Human Rights.[44] The requirement for the entry into force of the Arab Charter, seven ratifications, has not yet been reached. The Charter invokes the Shari'ah in conjunction with 'other divinely-revealed religions', to underline the 'eternal principles of brotherhood and equality among all human beings'.[45] Tolerance of religious and cultural diversity is guaranteed unequivocally.[46] According to its Preamble, the Arab Charter reaffirms the principles of the two UN Covenants. The Charter enshrines the principle of non-discrimination in its application, including on grounds of sex and religion.[47] Using the limitations clauses found in some of the ICCPR provisions as basis,[48] the Arab Charter contains a single clear limitation provision, allowing 'restrictions' only if they are provided by 'law' and are 'deemed necessary' to serve the same societal goals as under the ICCPR. Similar to the ICCPR, the Arab Charter contains a derogation clause, stipulating circumstances under which rights may be derogated from and listing non-derogable rights. While mirroring most of the non-derogable grounds in the ICCPR, the Arab Charter omits some (such as slavery and freedom of conscience), but adds other grounds (such as 'return to one's country' and

---

[40] RW MacDonald, *The League of Arab States* (Princeton: Princeton University Press, 1965).
[41] Pact of the League of Arab States, art 2.
[42] AH Robertson and JG Merrils, *Human Rights in the World* (Manchester: Manchester University Press, 1977) 198.   [43] ibid 198–9.
[44] Reprinted in C Heyns (ed), *Human Rights Law in Africa* (vol 1) (Leiden: Martinus Nijhoff, 2004) 733.   [45] Preamble.
[46] Arab Charter, arts 27 and 37.   [47] ibid, art 2.   [48] eg ICCPR, art 12.

'asylum'). The Arab Charter contains a number of fair trial rights, and although it does not outlaw the death penalty, it allows capital punishment only for 'the most serious crimes'.[49] The Arab Charter does not emulate the ICESCR in the same way. Rights associated with employment, the right to 'own private property', the right to education and to participate in cultural life are guaranteed, but no 'socio-economic' rights relevant to health, housing, and nutritional needs are included.

Once established, supervision will take the form of a Committee of Human Rights Experts.[50] Seven human rights experts, serving in their personal capacities, are to be elected from candidates proposed by member states to the Charter.[51] The Committee's only function is the examination of state reports.[52]

For those states that are members of both the AU and the Arab League, the African system provides for more effective implementation in the form of an individual complaints mechanism. The global human rights regimes also contemplate a higher level of protection for those states that have ratified such international instruments. A number of Arab states have ratified the ICESCR, ICCPR, the Convention on the Rights of the Child (CRC) and the Convention on the Elimination of All Forms of Discrimination against Women (CEDAW). However, many of these states have entered far-reaching reservations at ratification, especially in the case of CEDAW. The assumption that the African members of the Arab League take formal adherence to human rights instruments more seriously than other League members is confirmed by the fact that the four League members that by 31 July 2006 have adhered to the Optional Protocol to the ICCPR (OPI), are all African.[53]

Two approaches to the evaluation of the Arab system are possible. One may regard its establishment as a positive development. Although it has obvious deficiencies, it must be viewed as part of a gradual process. Seen from this perspective, it is better to have a weak system in place, than having nothing at all. One may, on the other hand, regard the system as meaningless and mere make-belief. Viewed from an African perspective, the argument for gradual evolution should find little favour, as Africa is at present moving beyond this phase to improve the effective functioning of its human rights system.

The OIC, established in 1969, aims at the promotion of Islamic solidarity among member states. It works towards cooperation in the economic, cultural, and political spheres.[54] Of its 57 members by mid-2006, 27 states were African.[55]

---

[49] Again, echoing the ICCPR, art 6(2).

[50] M Rishmawi, 'The Arab Charter of Human Rights: A Comment' (1996) 10 *Interights Bulletin* 8, 9–10.   [51] Arab Charter, art 40(B).

[52] Arab Charter, art 41(1).

[53] These states were Algeria, Djibouti, Libya, and Somalia. Complaints have been directed against the government of at least two of these countries, Algeria and Libya, see Ch 3.B.4 below.

[54] The OIC is also seized with matters such as unconstitutional changes of government, see eg Report of the Pan-African Parliament Mission to Mauritania from 10–16 October 2005, Ch 5.A.3 below.

[55] Algeria, Benin, Burkina Faso, Cameroon, Chad, Comoros, Côte d'Ivoire, Djibouti, Egypt, Gabon, Gambia, Guinea, Guinea-Bissau, Libya, Mali, Mauritania, Morocco, Mozambique, Niger, Nigeria, Senegal, Sierra Leone, Somalia, Sudan, Togo, Tunisia, and Uganda.

The major human rights document under this framework, the Cairo Declaration on Human Rights in Islam, adopted by members of the OIC in Cairo in 1990, is of a declamatory nature only.[56] As its title indicates, and given the aims of the OIC, the declaration is closely based on the principles of the Shari'ah.[57] In a concluding provision it is stipulated that all 'rights and freedoms . . . are subject to the Islam Shari'ah'.[58] Many rights are explicitly limited by the provisions of the Shari'ah. Examples are the right to life,[59] regulation of punishment,[60] and the right to assume public office.[61] These deviations are extreme to the extent of threatening the international project to attain a core consensus on human rights across cultural barriers. An Intergovernmental Group of Experts Entrusted with undertaking follow-up on the Cairo Declaration was established, and meets regularly.[62]

In 2004, the OIC adopted a binding instrument with a specific thematic focus, the Covenant on the Rights of the Child in Islam (Islamic Children's Covenant).[63] This Covenant is open for ratification and will enter into force once 20 OIC member states have ratified it. No state has done so yet, prompting the OIC Conference of Foreign Ministers to urge member states to sign and ratify the Covenant.[64] Compared to other international instruments dealing with children's rights, the Islamic Children's Covenant is more restrictive in scope and application. Its 'principles' include the observance by state parties of 'domestic legislations' and of the principle of non-interference in the internal affairs of states. Although the Covenant includes some socio-economic rights, they are either framed in a very particular Islamic context,[65] or made contingent on 'national laws'.[66] Although the Covenant provides for a monitoring mechanism, the Islamic Committee on the Rights of the Child, its mandate is only vaguely drafted.[67]

As with the Arab League, membership of the OIC has not contributed in any significant sense to the improvement of human rights in these countries. African countries also generally perform better than other OIC states as far as the ratification of international human rights instruments is concerned. A cause for disappointment is the inability of the sizeable African bloc within the OIC to steer that

---

[56] The Cairo Declaration was 'proclaimed' on 5 Aug 1990, by the OIC Conference of Foreign Ministers (Resolution 49/19-P) (see also UN Doc A/45/421/5/21797 at 199).

[57] Generally on human rights and Islam, see AA An Na'im, 'Human Rights in the Muslim World: Socio-political Conditions and Scriptural Imperatives' (1990) 3 *Harvard Human Rights J* 13.

[58] Cairo Declaration, art 24.   [59] Cairo Declaration, art 2.

[60] Cairo Declaration, art 19(d).   [61] Cairo Declaration, art 23(b).

[62] See eg speech by the Secretary-General of the OIC at the Group's seventh meeting, <http://www.oic-oic.org/press/english/old/january2003/HumanR.htm>.

[63] OIC/9-IGGE/HRI/2004/Rep.Final.

[64] Resolution 1/33—LEG on the Coordination among Member States in the field of Human Rights, <http://www.oic-oic.org/baku2006/english>.

[65] Islamic Children's Covenant, art 12(1) (the right to 'free basic education' is qualified by its aim of 'learning the principles of Islamic education').

[66] ibid, art 14(2) (the right to social security 'in accordance with their national laws').

[67] ibid, art 24(1) ('to examine the progress made in the implementation of the Covenant').

organization towards a human rights regime more in tune with the African regional system. Instead, at the first sessions of the Human Rights Council, the African Group became conscripted into the OIC cause of ensuring that the situation in Israel/the occupied territories and the Middle East more generally take centre stage, at the expense of attention being devoted to the situation in Darfur. The OAU/AU has also routinely devoted valuable discussion time to, and adopted lengthy resolutions on, the Middle East,[68] while neglecting pressing human rights concerns on the continent.

3.3 No System Yet: Asia

Overlapping to some extent with the Muslim world, the heterogeneous Asian region stretches from Indonesia to Japan, comprising a diverse group of nations. Despite some efforts by the UN, no binding regional human rights treaty or body has been established in the Asia-Pacific region. In the absence of an intergovernmental organization serving as a regional umbrella uniting the diverse states in this region, a regional human rights system remains unlikely. The emergence of such a human rights system is further curtailed by deep-seated 'disinterest or hostility shown by many governments in the region towards domestic or international concern about human rights',[69] and the notion that 'Asian' understandings of human rights are at odds with the 'universal' discourse. Promising developments towards subregional human rights protection, especially in the framework of the Association of Southeast Asian Nations (ASEAN), bringing together states such as Indonesia, Singapore, Malaysia, and Thailand, have as yet not culminated in standard-setting or the establishment of institutional arrangements at the subregional level.[70]

4 Global Level

The growth of a global human rights system depends on the existence of a global organization with the promotion and protection of human rights as part of its aims. Dedicated to the maintenance of international peace and security, but also including the promotion of a respect for human rights, the UN, founded in 1945, provides such a vehicle. Human rights protection under the UN derives either from the UN Charter, or from human rights treaties.[71]

---

[68] For a recent exponent, see AU Doc EX.CL/Dec.326(X), Decision on Palestine and the Middle East (January 2007).

[69] S Jones, 'Regional Institutions for Protecting Human Rights in Asia' (1996) 50 *Australian J of Intl Affairs* 269, 271.

[70] At its 11th Summit, ASEAN took a first step by adopting the Kuala Lumpur Declaration on the Establishment of an ASEAN Charter. An Eminent Persons Group has been set up, and it is guided by, amongst other principles, the promotion of democracy and human rights. A factor that has inhibited progress towards the establishment of a regional human rights body is the fact that some of the countries in the region, such as Myanmar (Burma), Laos, Vietnam, and Cambodia, fall in the category of 'Non Free' states, identified by Freedom House (see Freedom House, 'Human Rights Must Become a Priority for ASEAN' <http://www.freedomhouse.org> (8 January 2007)).   [71] See Chs 2 and 3 below.

C Relationship between the International and National Levels

International human rights law has obvious implications for national 'state sovereignty' and national legal systems. Before one rushes to judgment about international law as outright imposition, the principle of 'subsidiarity', aimed at mediating the effect of the international regime on the national level, should be considered.

1 Erosion of Sovereignty

All states in the world are formally recognized as equals and have international and national independence. International independence means that they may freely enter into agreements with other states. National independence means that they may regulate their internal affairs (the territory and the persons constituting the state) without foreign interference. Although the UN is based on the principles of the 'sovereign equality of all its members' and 'non-interference in the domestic affairs',[72] over the last decades the absolute nature of sovereignty has been eroded, especially through the working of international human rights law. By adhering to multilateral treaties, states voluntarily allow inroads into their own sovereignty. A state can thus not simultaneously become a party to a treaty under which it undertakes to outlaw torture, and argue that it has the sovereign right to torture its nationals. Under many human rights treaties, states accept the competence of an independent UN body to supervise their compliance with the treaty, and sometimes states even allow nationals to bring complaints against it to an external, international body of independent experts.

All UN members also accept the competence of the UN Security Council to order military intervention in a state to 'maintain or restore international peace and security'.[73] Similarly, the highest organ of the African Union (AU), the Assembly, may decide to intervene in a member state when genocide, war crimes or crimes against humanity take place in that state.[74] It is questionable whether there is a general 'right' to humanitarian intervention outside the UN Charter or specific regional security arrangement as set out in the AU Constitutive Act. Humanitarian intervention consists of the use of military force against a state (the 'target state') without the consent of such a state, to protect the nationals of the target state from flagrant violations of their human rights. Its application in practice has revealed the inherent problem of selective application, and of the potential for abuse when leaders mask their 'true' intentions with the rhetoric of humanitarian intervention.

---

[72] UN Charter, arts 2(2) and 2(7) respectively.   [73] UN Charter, art 42.
[74] AU Constitutive Act, art 4(h).

2 Domestic Legal Effect: Monism and Dualism

The relationship between international and national law poses two major questions: Can international law norms be invoked as part of the municipal legal system? If so, what is the relative weight of the international and municipal systems? The question whether international law may be 'invoked' begs the question of what such 'invocation' entails, as the term may refer to the use of international law as a guide to interpretation, or as the substantive basis of a legal remedy.

Two approaches concerning the relationship between international law and national law are usually juxtaposed: dualism and monism.[75] For the dualists, international law and national law are fundamentally different, and domestic law-making (enabling legislation) is required to 'transform' or 'incorporate' ('domesticate') international law into national law. 'Transformation' entails amendment to existing laws or the adoption of new domestic legislation in line with the treaty; 'incorporation' is the wholesale inclusion of the treaty in national law. For the monists, the two legal orders are inextricably linked, and international law becomes part of national law upon ratification. Increasingly, as the fallacy of this dichotomy is revealed, other approaches, such as those having regard to the 'self-executing' nature of particular treaties, emerge.[76]

Should international law be considered part of national law, questions of a hierarchy of norms arise. International law may enjoy a position inferior to national law (both legislation and the constitution); international law may be given a status superior to that of *national legislation* (but not the constitution); or international law may enjoy a status superior to *all national law* (including the constitution). National constitutions should stipulate which ranking applies, but often do not cover this aspect.

3 The Principle of Subsidiarity

As a system that is subsidiary to the national system, international human rights law does not replace national law, but co-exists with and supplements it. States are primarily responsible for securing the rights of those under their jurisdiction in line with international law, and therefore have primacy in the determination of the precise form in which to shape open-ended international norms. However, their discretion to do so is constrained by the minimum threshold of international law. The principle of subsidiarity is evidenced in the development by the European Court of Human Rights of the concept 'margin of appreciation', in terms of which states are granted a degree of latitude in matters related to the

---

[75] See eg I Brownlie, *Principles of Public International Law* (Oxford: Oxford University Press, 6th edn, 2003) 31–4.   [76] See Ch 13 below.

balancing of individual rights and public interest, especially when moral issues are involved.[77]

Subsidiarity as 'complementarity' is reflected in the requirement of the 'exhaustion of local remedies': if a treaty allows an individual to complain against a state, the state must be given notice of the violation, so that it may have an opportunity to live up to its treaty undertakings. Only when it clearly fails to do so, may the individual approach an international body. However, if there is no effective local remedy, or if domestic processes are unduly prolonged, an individual may be exempted from first exhausting domestic recourse. Another illustration is found in the Statute of the International Criminal Court (ICC), which stipulates that the ICC does not have jurisdiction over cases that are 'being investigated or prosecuted' by a state that has jurisdiction over the case,[78] thus enshrining the principle that the state must have the 'first bite of the cherry'.

However, when there is a very limited possibility of protection at the national level, or serious violations occur, it does not make logical sense to defer to the domestic courts. International criminal tribunals such as the International Criminal Court for Rwanda (ICTR) have primacy over national courts. Only if the ICTR does not prosecute will the national courts be given an opportunity to do so.

D Sources of International Human Rights Law

Traditionally, the sources of international human rights law, the 'places' where it originates and where it may be found,[79] are divided into those that are binding and those that are non-binding. International law, also of the human rights variety, binds states on the basis of the explicit acceptance by specific states (by becoming parties to treaties), or by the implicit acceptance by the community of states generally (giving rise to customary international law, *jus cogens*, and obligations *erga omnes*). Declarations, resolutions, and other recommendatory instruments, often categorized under the umbrella term 'soft law', are considered non-binding. However, the growing importance of 'soft law' as a source of international human rights law increasingly calls into question the rigid distinction between 'binding' and 'non-binding' sources. Together, treaties and written products of 'soft law' are referred to as 'human rights instruments', an umbrella term that combines all 'human rights documents'.

---

[77] So, for example, did the Court allow the UK a 'margin of appreciation' in determining whether its restriction of free speech was justifiable in order to protect public morals (*Handyside v UK* ECHR Series A No 2 (7 December 1976)).

[78] Art 17(1) of the Rome Statute; see however the exceptions to this rule—when the state itself is unwilling or unable to prosecute.

[79] This discussion of sources of international human rights law is located within the sources of international law, more generally, which are set out in art 38(1) of the Statute of the International Court of Justice (ICJ).

1 Treaties

1.1 Definition and Terminology

A treaty is a written agreement to which a party may consent to be bound. With reference to the number of parties, a distinction may be drawn between 'bilateral' treaties (between two states) and 'multilateral' treaties (between more than two states). The human rights treaties under discussion are all multilateral treaties. Treaties may be 'tagged' in a variety of ways, so one should not be blinded by the terminology used. Mostly, treaties are called 'conventions' (such as the 'Convention on the Rights of the Child'), but they may also bear the title 'covenant' (as in 'International Covenant on Civil and Political Rights') or 'charter' (for example, the 'African Charter on Human and Peoples' Rights'). These terms are used interchangeably, and the legal weight of each of these instruments is equal.

Protocols are instruments adopted to supplement or amend an aspect or aspects of existing treaties, often creating new rights and obligations, thereby allowing treaties to evolve with time. Protocols have the same legal force as the treaties they supplement. Usually, state parties to the main treaty have the option of becoming a party to a protocol to that treaty, thereby extending the scope of their substantive obligations or accepting a procedural amendment. One of the oldest human rights treaties, the European Convention, has seen the addition of numerous Protocols since its adoption in 1950. The existence of protocols means that a two-tier system exists at times, with some states accepting, for example, an individual complaints mechanism, provided for in a protocol, while others do not. A similar duality exists in the African system after the adoption of two Protocols to the African Charter, one establishing the African Human Rights Court, and the other supplementing the substantive scope of the Charter by cataloguing women's rights.

1.2 Phases in the Life of a Treaty

Seven phases in the life of a treaty may be distinguished:[80] elaboration, adoption, adherence, entry into force, operationalization, domestication, and internalization.

Elaboration: What eventually may become a 'treaty' starts with a process of discussion, elaboration, and drafting, which Maluwa refers to as 'initiation' and 'formulation'.[81] The process starts when a need for reform is identified, for example by organs of the political umbrella body, states, or NGOs. More discussions follow, initially mostly informally, but gradually becoming more formalized. The basis of formal discussion is usually a preliminary draft. Negotiations and discussions may involve numerous parties, and usually culminate in a meeting of experts within the framework of the political or policy-making body that aims to adopt the treaty.

---

[80] See also T Maluwa, 'International Law-Making in the Organisation of African Unity: An Overview' (2000) 12 *RADIC* 201, who distinguishes four phases: 'initiation', 'formulation', 'adoption', and 'entry into force'.   [81] ibid, 207–8.

At some stage, matters proceed to a diplomatic conference, consisting of government representatives of the states making up the political body. Numerous drafts
may be prepared, discussed, and redrafted as part of this process, which may last
from months to decades. Together, all these drafts and records of deliberations are
referred to as the '*travaux préparatoires*' (drafting history).

Adoption: The finalized draft is placed before the political body or policy-making
organ for its adoption. Under the OAU/AU, the Assembly of Heads of State and
Government usually adopts the text of treaties. Consensus is usually sought,[82] but
may have negative consequences in cases where states that are unlikely to ratify the
draft cause it to be watered down.[83] Upon adoption of the final version of the text,
the treaty is not immediately legally binding on the adopting parties, but instead
is opened for signature and ratification.

Adherence: It is important to distinguish between signature, on the one hand, and
ratification or accession, on the other. A state becomes a 'state party' to a human
rights treaty only by ratification, and not by signature. Signature ('initializing') of
a human rights treaty is a formal recognition of the authenticity of the adopted
text. As all multinational human rights treaties require ratification by states as an
expression of their consent to be bound, signature is not a definitive indication to
be bound, but provides evidence of the state's intention to be bound in the future.
However, signatory states have the obligation not to undermine the object and
purpose of the signed treaty.[84] Both ratification and accession bind states to a treaty.
States that had not participated in the drafting or negotiation of the treaty, and
had not signed it, become state parties by way of accession.[85] (In this book, the
term 'ratification' is sometimes used to refer to both ratification and accession.)
Acceptance has an external dimension (playing itself out at the international level)
and an internal aspect (which is dependent on national processes). On the international plane, ratification takes place when a state deposits an 'instrument of
ratification' with an appropriate body (the depository). Such an action binds the
state as a matter of international law, and applies between it and other state parties.
A national process of 'ratification' or approval should precede external ratification.
Although the national process varies from one state to another, parliamentary

---

[82] VCLT, art 9.

[83] See eg the numerous 'reservations' made by Sudan during the drafting of the Protocol to the
African Charter on the Rights of Women in Africa, Report of the Meeting of Experts on the Draft
Protocol on the Rights of Women in Africa, 12–16 December 2001 (AU Doc DOC/OS(XXXI)/
INF.47). Sudan has not yet become a state party to the Protocol.   [84] VCLT, art 18(a).

[85] See generally eg Council of Europe, *Treaty Making: Expression of Consent to be Bound by a Treaty*
(The Hague: Kluwer International, 2001). The case of South Africa acceding to the African Charter
provides an example. The African Charter was negotiated in the late 1970s, and was formally adopted
by the OAU Assembly in 1981. Due to its apartheid policies, South Africa was at that stage not a member of the OAU. When it became a member in 1994, South Africa became a state party to the Charter
by way of accession.

approval is often required.[86] Domestic approval should ideally be preceded by a compatibility study between treaty provisions and national law, leading to legislative amendments before ratification or accession, or prompting narrowly circumscribed reservations.

Entry into force: Once it has been ratified by the required number of states, the treaty enters into force. From this moment on, the treaty is an internationally binding legal instrument, and state parties are bound to observe its provisions in accordance with the principle of *pacta sunt servanda* ('agreements must respected'). A distinction should be drawn between a treaty's entry into force, and the point in time it becomes binding upon a particular state. The entry into force of a treaty, generally, takes place a specified number of days after the required number of ratifications has been secured. The number of required ratifications and accessions differs from treaty to treaty.[87] If a state is among those that have ratified the treaty before its entry into force, the treaty enters into force for that particular state on the date the treaty takes effect. For each state that subsequently formally accepts the treaty, the entry into force of the treaty is on a different date, usually a fixed time period after ratification by that state.

Operationalization: When a treaty monitoring mechanism is provided for, as is the case in most human rights instruments, an important phase following entry into force is operationalization, that is, establishing the conditions to ensure the treaty body's effective functioning. This process cannot and does not happen overnight. Once in force, the members of the treaty body may need to be nominated and elected; a seat may have to be determined; a secretariat may need to be established; supporting staff appointed; a budget adopted; buildings let; and rules of procedure prepared and adopted. This process inevitably causes some delay before the treaty becomes operational.[88]

Domestication: To maximize its effect at the national level, an international human rights treaty has to be made part of domestic law, either by way of 'incorporation' or 'transformation'. Even if this is not formally done, the treaty's influence should still be brought to bear on domestic law, policy, and judicial decisions.

---

[86] See the Constitution of the USA, art II, s 2(2): The requirement that the President may enter into treaties only on the advice and with the consent of two-thirds of the Senate. The role of the Senate Committee on Foreign Relations, and of Senators Bricker and Helms, in particular, delayed for many years the formal acceptance of the ICCPR, which took place in 1992, with numerous ratifications, and caused the USA to be one of two countries globally still outside the fold of the CRC.

[87] Acceptance by a simple majority of African states was required for the entry into force of the African Charter. For the Protocol thereto establishing an African Court on Human and Peoples' Rights, the required number is 15 states.

[88] The African Commission, for example, had its first session only in November 1987, more than a year after the African Charter had entered into force.

Internalization: The greatest challenge is to bring about compliance with the treaty provisions by government officials, and nationals alike. International legal norms only become truly effective if compliance is not motivated by coercion or self-interest, but flows from personal motivation brought about by an internal process of norm-acceptance ('internalization').

1.3 Interpretation of Treaties

The laws governing the interpretation of treaties have themselves become the subject-matter of a treaty, the Vienna Convention on the Law of Treaties (VCLT), which entered into force in 1980.[89] The general rule of treaty interpretation requires a 'good faith' interpretation in accordance with 'the ordinary meaning' of words, but placed 'in context' and taking into account the 'object and purpose' of the treaty.[90] When such an interpretation is uncertain, or ambiguous, 'obscure' or leads to a manifestly absurd or unreasonable result, other 'means of interpretation' may be used to complement the treaty. The *travaux préparatoires* of a treaty is an example of supplementary means of interpretation.[91] Numerous other aspects, such as the general rule of the 'non-retroactive' application of treaties,[92] are also regulated by the VCLT.

1.4 Reservations and 'Interpretive Declarations' to Treaties

A reservation is a unilateral statement by a state party to a treaty through which it 'excludes' or 'modifies' in respect of that state the 'legal effect of certain provisions' of the treaty.[93] This is an avenue through which international human rights law acknowledges that states may have legitimate justifications for insulating parts of the culture practised in that country from the homogenizing effect of supra-national normativity.[94] A reservation must be entered at the time of accession or ratification, and not during negotiations, as part of signature, or after ratification.

[89] Signed at Vienna, 23 May 1969, entered into force 27 January 1980, embodying rules already accepted as customary international law. African states have been slow in ratifying the VCLT—of the 108 states party to it as at 31 December 2006, only 23 were from Africa (Algeria, Burkina Faso, Cameroon, Central African Republic, Congo, DRC, Egypt, Gabon, Guinea, Lesotho, Liberia, Malawi, Mali, Mauritius, Morocco, Niger, Nigeria, Rwanda, Senegal, Sudan, Tanzania, Togo, and Tunisia) <http://untreaty.un.org> (31 January 2007).

[90] VCLT, art 31(1); the 'object and purpose' of treaties are by no means self-evident. For a discussion on the complexities eg of ascertaining this, as well as the question whether there is a difference between 'object' and 'purpose' see J Klabbers, 'Some Problems regarding the Object and Purpose of Treaties' (1997) 8 *Finnish Ybk of Intl L* 138.

[91] In resolving the uncertainty about the definition of genocide, the ICTR for example relied on the drafting history of the Convention on the Prevention and Punishment of the Crime of Genocide (*The Prosecutor v Akayesu*, ICTR-96-4-T, 2 September 1988, para 516: 'The Chamber relies on the drafting history to extend the four groups at which genocidal acts need to be directed (national, ethnic, racial and religious groups) to all other stable and permanent groups'). [92] VCLT, art 28.

[93] VCLT, art 2(1)(d).

[94] The following is an example of a reservation in respect of CEDAW: 'The Government of the Kingdom of Lesotho declares that it does not consider itself bound by article 2 to the extent that it conflicts with Lesotho's constitutional stipulations relative to succession to the throne of the Kingdom of Lesotho and law relating to succession to chieftainship'.

An answer to the question whether these reservations are acceptable under international law must be sought first in the treaty itself.[95] If the treaty prohibits it, no state party may enter a reservation; if the treaty allows for the possibility of entering reservations, state parties may do so.[96] When the treaty is silent, the fall-back position is that which is set out in the VCLT: a state may only enter reservations that are not 'incompatible with the object and purpose of the treaty'.[97] Even if reservations are allowed in principle, it is only logical that there should be a limit to the degree to which the treaty is 'excluded' by way of the reservation. A boundless discretion could result in the absurd situation where a state ratifies a treaty, but then enters reservations to just about every important aspect thereof. For this reason, many treaties provide for the possibility of reservations, but only to the extent that they are compatible with the 'object and purpose' of that treaty. It is generally understood that universal ratification is an ideal. If states participate in the human rights system, gradually the weight of human rights ideas will be brought to bear on them. Allowing for reservations is the price of this quest. More substantially, reservations allow states to opt out of a treaty to the extent that cultural specificity clashes with universality, on condition that the integrity of the very system is not being undermined.

States may enter 'interpretive declarations' when ratifying a treaty. Such declarations aim to make publicly known a particular interpretation or 'understanding' of a provision by a state, or, in the words of the International Law Commission, 'purports to specify or clarify the meaning or scope attributed by the declarant to a treaty or to certain of its provisions'.[98] The wording of these terms already hints at the possibility of conflation between 'reservations' and 'interpretative declarations'. The terms 'interpretive declaration' may thus be used merely as a cloak behind which to hide a 'reservation'.[99]

The Human Rights Committee adopted General Comment 24, in response to a rising number of reservations, in which it set out its view on the matter as follows[100]

It is desirable for a State entering a reservation to indicate in precise terms the domestic legislation or practices which it believes to be incompatible with the Covenant obligation

---

[95] On this issue, see also the ICJ's advisory opinion in *Reservations to the Convention on the Prevention and Punishment of the Crime of Genocide* [1951] ICJ Reports 15, in which the ICJ held that a state may enter a reservation to a multilateral treaty if such reservation is compatible with the object and purpose of the treaty. [96] VCLT, art 19(a).
[97] VCLT, art 19(c).
[98] See 'Report of the International Law Commission on the Work of its Fifty-Second Session, (2000); Chapter vii, Reservations to Treaties', para 649, available at <http://www.un.org/law/ilc/reports/2000/english/chp7.pdf> (31 January 2007) para 622.
[99] Morocco entered the following 'declaration' to art 2 of CEDAW: 'The Government of the Kingdom of Morocco express (*sic*) its readiness to apply the provisions of this article provided that they are without prejudice to the constitutional requirement that regulate the rules of succession to the throne of the Kingdom of Morocco; [and] they do not conflict with the provisions of the Islamic Shariah'. See also *Belilos v Switzerland* ECHR Series A No 132 (29 April 1988) para 49.
[100] General Comment 24, para 20.

reserved; and to explain the time period it requires to render its own laws and practices compatible with the Covenant, or why it is unable to render its own laws and practices compatible with the Covenant. States should also ensure that the necessity for maintaining reservations is periodically reviewed, taking into account any observations and recommendations made by the Committee during examination of their reports. Reservations should be withdrawn at the earliest possible moment. Reports to the Committee should contain information on what action has been taken to review, reconsider or withdraw reservations.

The consequence of an incompatible reservation remains uncertain, though, leaving open the possibility that ratification is nullified, that the whole reservation is void, that a reservation is severable from ratification, or that a particular term therein is severable from other parts of the reservation. Questions about the effect of incompatible reservations may arise during the examination of state reports, or as part of considering communications. During the examination of the initial state report of the USA, the Human Rights Committee pronounced a reservation to article 6(5) of the ICCPR (allowing for the imposition of capital punishment on juveniles) to be incompatible with the object and purpose of that treaty. However, the Committee did not declare it to be void, but examined the report as if the reservation was not in place.[101] Dealing with an 'interpretative declaration' entered by France (to the effect that article 27 of the ICCPR 'is not applicable' in France 'in the light of article 2' of the French Constitution), the Human Rights Committee considered it to be a 'reservation' because the 'effect' of the statement rather than the 'formal designation' was decisive.[102] Consequently, the Committee's competence to consider a complaint based on article 27 was precluded.[103]

State parties to treaties may, and do, formally object to reservations by other state parties.[104] In practice it has been accepted that raising objections does not preclude the treaty from entering into force between the relevant states.[105]

1.5 Withdrawal from and Denunciation of Treaties

May a state party withdraw from or denounce a treaty? If the treaty explicitly provides for such an eventuality, there seems to be little room for debate. But what about treaties without any provision dealing with such a possibility? As states have

---

[101] UN Doc CCPR/C/SR.1406, 24 April 1995.

[102] See Communication 220/1987, *T K v France*, UN Doc A/45/40, vol II, (8 November 1989) 252.

[103] See, however, the dissenting view of Committee member Higgins in this and similar matters against France.

[104] An example is the objection by Norway against numerous reservations, including the one by Lesotho. 'In the view of the Government of Norway, a reservation by which a State party limits its responsibilities under the Convention by invoking general principles of internal law may create doubts about the commitments of the reserving State to the object and purpose of the Convention and, moreover, contribute to undermine the basis of international treaty law. It is in the common interest of States that treaties to which they have chosen to become parties also are respected, as to their object and purpose, by all parties. Furthermore, under well established international treaty law, a State is not permitted to invoke internal law as justification for its failure to perform its treaty obligations.'

[105] See also VCLT, art 20, which finds uneasy application in the context of multilateral human rights treaties.

consented to be bound by a treaty, it may be argued that they may also withdraw that consent. In this regard, the VCLT embodies the general rule—a treaty that does not provide for this eventuality is not subject to withdrawal or denunciation, unless 'it is established that the parties intended to admit the possibility' or that such a right is implied by 'the nature of the treaty'.[106] In any event, states must give 12 months' notice of such an intention.[107]

For many years this issue did not seem to pose a problem. At the end of the last century, some instances nevertheless occurred that seem to threaten the international human rights regime.[108] North Korea withdrew from the ICCPR in August 1997. Trinidad and Tobago, having withdrawn from the First Optional Protocol in 1998, immediately re-acceded, but with a reservation excluding from the competence of the Human Rights Committee any communication 'relating to any prisoner who is under sentence of death'.[109] In the course of dealing with a communication submitted notwithstanding this reservation, the Committee declared that the reservation was incompatible with the object and purpose of the Protocol, and proceeded to consider the merits of the case.[110] As a result of the decision, Trinidad and Tobago denounced the Optional Protocol in 2000,[111] thereby casting doubt on the wisdom of the HRC's 'all or nothing' approach. In response, the Human Rights Committee adopted General Comment 26, in which it expresses the view that the omission of this possibility from the ICCPR is deliberate and that it therefore does not allow for withdrawal or denunciation. The Committee adds that the rights in the Covenant 'belong to the people living in the territory of the state' and that these rights 'devolve with territory' rather than with the whims of or changes in government.[112]

2 Customary International Law

As long as international human rights treaties do not enjoy universal ratification, treaties will be an incomplete means of attaining the goal of universal respect for

---

[106] VCLT, art 56(1).   [107] VCLT, art 56(2).

[108] See also the 'un-signing' of the Statute of the International Criminal Court by the USA (see US Ambassador for War Crimes, stating that the USA 'does not intend to become a state party' to the ICC Statute and 'accordingly has no obligation as a result of' its signature of the Statute: <http://fpc.gov> (31 December 2006)).

[109] Communication 845/1999, *Kennedy v Trinidad and Tobago*, UN Doc CCPR/C/67/845/1999, 31 December 1999, para 6.3.

[110] On the basis that the Committee 'cannot accept a reservation which singles out a certain group of individuals for lesser procedural protection than that which is enjoyed by the rest of the population' (para 6.7). But also see the view of a minority of four Committee members in this case.

[111] T Buergenthal, 'The UN Human Rights Committee' (2001) 5 *Max Planck Ybk of United Nations L* 341, 385. The unfortunate effect of the Committee's 'all-or-nothing' approach, that of removing the right of individual petition to all the country's nationals, has been criticized as undermining the objects of the Protocol (G McGrory, 'Reservations of Virtue? Lessons from Trinidad and Tobago's Reservation to the First Optional Protocol' (2001) 23 *HRQ* 769, 815). Trinidad and Tobago subsequently also denounced the American Convention with effect from 29 May 1999.

[112] General Comment 26, para 4.

human rights. Customary international law fills this gap, as it binds those states not party to a treaty—provided that the relevant norm has become a rule of customary international law. A norm attains that status if it is a 'general practice accepted as law'.[113] This means that the existence of such a rule has to be proven by demonstrating two elements: state practice and *opinio juris*. There has to be widespread evidence of consistent practice by states conforming to a certain norm.[114] To obviate the possibility that states only observe the rule owing to political convenience or even compulsion by other states, there must also be proof that they observe these norms because of '. . . a belief that this practice is rendered obligatory by the existence of a rule of law requiring it'.[115] Support for the notion that a state that has 'consistently objected' to the development of such a norm is not bound by the rule of custom, has waned away, reiterating that 'general' (and not 'universal') state practice constitutes custom.[116]

The crystallization of a norm into a rule of customary international law needs to be determined (or confirmed) in concrete cases. Compared to treaties, customary rules are fluid, uncertain, and less readily accessible. Still, there seem to be strong arguments that the prohibition of at least the following has attained that status:[117] genocide,[118] slavery, racial discrimination, murder or 'disappearing' a person, torture,[119] prolonged arbitrary detention, returning refugees to a country where they would be exposed to persecution ('*non-refoulement*');[120] and in the *Restatement*'s formulation, 'a consistent pattern of gross violations of internationally recognized human rights'. Custom has been less important in the field of human rights, because empirical proof of 'the way that states behave in their dealings with individual citizens' makes ascertaining custom problematic.[121]

3 *Jus Cogens* and Obligations *Erga Omnes*

Some rules or norms tower above other sources of international law. They are norms that 'cannot be set aside by treaty or acquiescence but only by the formation of a subsequent customary rule of contrary effect',[122] and are referred to as rules of

---

[113] ICJ Statute, art 38(1)(b).

[114] For a general application of these requirements, see *US Military and Paramilitary Activities in and against Nicaragua* [1986] ICJ Rep 14, paras 183–215.

[115] *North Sea Continental Shelf* [1969] ICJ Rep 3, para 77.

[116] *North Sea Continental Shelf* cases, above, para 63, in which the ICJ observes that custom 'cannot . . . be subject of any right of unilateral exclusion'.

[117] Most of these are contained in the American Law Institute's *Restatement of the Law, the Third, the Foreign Relations Law of the United States* (*Restatement*), 1987, cited in Brownlie (n 75 above) 537.

[118] *Reservation to the Convention on the Prevention and Punishment of the Crime of Genocide* (Advisory Opinion) [1951] ICJ Rep 15.

[119] R Higgins, *Problems and Process: International Law and How to Use It* (Oxford: Clarendon, 1994) 20.

[120] M Kjárum, 'Article 14' in G Alfredsson and A Eide (eds), *The Universal Declaration of Human Rights: A Common Standard of Achievement* (The Hague: Kluwer Law International, 1999) 279, 285.

[121] C Tomuschat, *Human Rights between Idealism and Realism* (Oxford: Oxford University Press, 2003) 34.   [122] Brownlie (n 75 above) 488.

jus cogens, or 'peremptory norms'. How do norms attain this status and who decides what status they have? A peremptory norm is a norm 'accepted and recognized by the international community of states as a whole' to be of that nature.[123] As the 'international community' is a nebulous concept, the content of *jus cogens* is the subject of continuous debate. However, there is general agreement among writers that at least the prohibition of the use of force by states has become *jus cogens*.[124] As for human rights-related standards, the most eligible candidates are the prohibition against slavery, the right (of peoples under colonial rule or foreign domination) to self-determination, the prohibition against massive and serious human rights violations in the form of genocide and crimes against humanity, the principle of non-discrimination on racial grounds, and the prevention of torture.[125] Others have added to the list the right to life, and liberty and security of the person.[126]

Peremptory norms largely overlap (are 'virtually coexistent')[127] with 'obligations *erga omnes*' and non-derogable rights. Norms become peremptory when they have an *erga omnes* character, that is, when they impose an obligation owed to the international community as a whole. Put another way: The breach of peremptory norms gives rise to obligations *erga omnes*. The International Court of Justice accepted that the right to self-determination,[128] and protection from slavery and racial discrimination constitute obligations *erga omnes*.[129]

4 Non-binding 'Soft Law'

Although the term 'soft law' is understood to refer to rules of conduct that do not create legal obligations, non-compliance may nonetheless have serious consequences for states, for instance in their international relations. 'Soft law' takes the form of declarations and resolutions of international organizations or bodies such as the UN General Assembly. Declarations are statements of intent, and are not as such legally binding under international law, although they may (even if just partially) evolve into customary international law. It is generally accepted that some parts of the Universal Declaration of Human Rights have attained the status of customary international law.[130] A declaration may also be a step in the process towards a binding treaty, as in the case of the Declaration on the Rights and Welfare of the African Child,[131] predating the African Charter on the Rights and Welfare of the Child. Other declarations, such as the UN Declaration on the Right to

---

[123] VCLT, art 53.   [124] Brownlie (n 75 above), 490.
[125] J Dugard, *International Law: A South African Perspective* (Cape Town: Juta, 3rd edn, 2005) 43–4.
[126] J Rehman, *International Human Rights Law. A Practical Approach* (London: Longman, 2003) 23.
[127] J Crawford, Third Report on State Responsibility UN Doc A/CN.4/507, 10 March 2000, para 106(a).   [128] *East Timor Case (Portugal v Australia)* [1995] ICJ Rep 90.
[129] *Barcelona Traction, Light and Power Co* [1970] ICJ Rep 3, 32.
[130] T Buergenthal, *International Human Rights in a Nutshell* (St Paul, Minn: West Publishing, 2nd edn, 1995) 36–7.
[131] Resolution AHG/ST.4(XVI), adopted by the OAU Assembly, Monrovia, Liberia, July 1979.

Development,[132] have not been transformed into binding treaties. Some resolutions constitute codes of conduct that are often invoked and applied, such as the United Nations Standard Minimum Rules for the Administration of Juvenile Justice ('The Beijing Rules').[133] 'Soft law' standards may also be elaborated by non-governmental organizations or structures, such as in the case of the Maastricht Guidelines.[134]

To this may be added numerous other non-binding statements or 'decisions' by human rights treaty bodies, such as 'General Comments', 'opinions' or 'views', and 'Concluding Observations'. In 'General Comments' (or 'General Recommendations') and 'resolutions', treaty bodies give voice to their understanding of substantive treaty provisions.[135] Being the product of compromise, treaty provisions are often formulated in vague and open-ended terms, and are in need of clarification. The ICESCR, for example, provides in article 2(1) that state parties are required to 'take steps' to ensure the progressive realization of the Covenant rights. Elaborating on the nature of the obligation of state parties in its General Comment 3, the ICESCR Committee in 1990 gave the following elucidation of the phrase 'take steps':[136] '[W]hile the full realization of the relevant rights may be achieved progressively, steps towards that goal must be taken within a reasonably short time after the Covenant's entry into force for the States concerned. Such steps should be deliberate, concrete and targeted as clearly as possible towards meeting the obligations recognized in the Covenant'.

In this context one may mention the numerous human rights conferences and gatherings that take place and often end in the formulation of a statement, declaration, or programme of action. The weight of the concluding document may depend on the stature of the organization and participants, or subsequent action. Twenty and fifty-five years, respectively, after the adoption of the Universal Declaration, the UN organized two World Conferences on Human Rights; the first in Tehran (1968), and the second in Vienna (1993). Subsequent to its adoption at the end of the 1993 conference, the Vienna Declaration and Plan of Action has become an important persuasive source.

As is the case with the UN and other regional quasi-judicial human rights treaty bodies, these statements are not legally binding on states. However, depending on a number of factors, such as their quality, dissemination, and subsequent use by, for example, domestic courts,[137] they may have great persuasive force. Much criticism has been levelled against the term 'soft law', amongst others for postulating a post-modern paradox by conjoining with 'law', a term used to indicate obligation,

---

[132] UN Doc A/41/53 (1986).

[133] Adopted by General Assembly Resolution 40/33 of 29 November 1985.

[134] See eg the discussion by EVO Dankwa, C Flinterman, and S Leckie, 'Commentary to the Maastricht Guidelines on Violations of Economic, Social and Cultural Rights' (1998) 20 *HRQ* 705.

[135] See 'Compilation of the General Comments and General Recommendations of the Human Rights Treaty Bodies', UN Doc HRI/GEN/1/Rev 6, 12 May 2003, available on the web-site of the OHCHR. [136] General Comment 3, dated 14 December 1990.

[137] See eg *Government of the Republic of South Africa v Grootboom and Others* (2001) 1 SA 46 (CC), paras 29 and 45, for an example of domestic reliance on General Comment 3.

the 'soft'-ness of nothing more than moral persuasion. Others argue that 'soft law' takes the form of law, thus constituting legal rules that are not binding.

5 Relationship between Sources

Treaties and custom are both based on consent, but differ in that treaties are written and custom is not. Custom may and does often develop into and serve as the basis for treaties. Treaties, for their part, may also constitute an important factor indicating (and proving) the existence of custom. The apparent contradiction that this leads to (namely, that states which have explicitly opted out of the treaty regime are bound by those very treaty provisions on the basis of their implied consent) seems to question the coherence of the notion that both these sources derive from consent.[138]

Multilateral treaties constitute the major source of international human rights law. Compared to custom, treaties are clearer in content, more orderly, and develop more quickly. However, treaties may be inflexible, requiring very complicated and lengthy processes for amendment; their drafting may be cumbersome due to attempts at accommodating as many views as possible; and the quest for consensus often associated with multilateral treaties may lead to the adoption of the 'least common denominator'.

Although the content of *jus cogens* and customary law norms may coincide, their foundations differ. *Jus cogens*, giving rise to obligations *erga omnes*, binds states notwithstanding their consent to these norms. Custom becomes binding if the requirements of *usus* and *opinio juris* have been met. The question may accordingly be posed whether there is a hierarchy of norms, in terms of which some sources are more important than others. While some protest that a hierarchy of sources would detract from the ideal of the interdependence and indivisibility of rights,[139] others argue that it has indeed already happened. In as much as the creation of a hierarchy of human rights norms aims to improve human rights protection, the abstract discussion of nebulous superior norms (such as *jus cogens*) should be converted into the legally more certain and significant category of non-derogable rights.[140]

6 Convergence between International Human Rights, Humanitarian, and Criminal Law

Although distinctions have traditionally been drawn between international human rights law, international humanitarian law, and international criminal law, this book does not observe a watertight division between the three, in line with a growing trend to acknowledge the link between these different bodies of international law.

---

[138] See on this and other contradictions between consensual and non-consensual elements in the requirements for custom, M Koskenniemi, *From Apology to Utopia* (Helsinki: Finnish Lawyers' Publishing, 1989) 342–421.

[139] P Weil, 'Towards Relative Normativity in International Law?' (1983) 77 *AJIL* 413.

[140] T Meron, 'On a Hierarchy of International Human Rights' (1986) 80 *AJIL* 1, 12–13.

The traditional distinction between international human rights law and international humanitarian law is that the former applies in peacetime, and the latter in wartime. While this is broadly correct, such a statement does not allow for the frequent difficulty of distinguishing between peace and war, and for the increasing application of human rights in internal conflicts. Although there still are clear differences,[141] the overlap between human rights and humanitarian law becomes most apparent during situations of armed conflict of a non-international nature. In such situations, humanitarian law operates through the 1977 Geneva Protocol II, and common article 3 of the 1949 Conventions. Since those in the territory of a state are also entitled to the rights in, for example, the African Charter, the ICCPR, and CAT, these and other human rights treaties also find application. In time of conflict of an internal nature, the state may declare a state of emergency, formally marking a threat to the life of the nation. Under such circumstances, some rights may be suspended or derogated from in order to deal with the emergency. However, an important core of non-derogable rights remains, playing an even more important role than before.[142] The overlap between the international humanitarian and criminal law also appears from the definition of crimes that may be prosecuted by ad hoc criminal tribunals such as the International Criminal Tribunal for Rwanda (ICTR) and the ICC.

Although international criminal law and international human rights law direct themselves at different conduct (the first aims at punishing individual perpetrators; the second holds states accountable for human rights violations), there is a significant degree of normative overlap between the two regimes. Both systems uphold the values of human life and dignity. The distinction is often one of degree, as international criminal law concerns itself only with serious violations that amount to international crimes.

In this respect, reference should be made to the concept of 'universal jurisdiction'. Traditionally, states establish criminal jurisdiction over individuals on the basis of (active) nationality (the alleged perpetrator is a national of the state), passive nationality (the victims are nationals of the state concerned), or on the basis of territoriality (the alleged crimes have been committed within the territory of the state). This implied that there would be impunity for those responsible for gross human rights violations who have been given a safe haven in another state, such as Idi Amin (who was given refuge in Saudi Arabia), or Mengistu Haile Miriam (residing in Zimbabwe), if the state of nationality did not prosecute. In terms of

---

[141] The two legal orders are, for example, founded on different sources—human rights treaties on the one hand, and the four Geneva Conventions of 1949, with the two 1977 Protocols thereto, on the other hand. Implementation also differs—under the international human rights system, treaty bodies have been established to supervise state obligations, and to consider individual complaints. No such system exists under humanitarian law, although some suggestions have been made for the establishment of a 'humanitarian law committee' (See J Kleffner and L Zegveld, 'Establishing an Individual Complaints Procedure for Violations of International Humanitarian Law' (2000) 3 *Ybk of Intl Humanitarian L* 384).

[142] See *Legality of the Use of Nuclear Weapons* (Advisory Opinion) [1996] ICJ Rep 226, 240.

universal jurisdiction, the national courts can exercise jurisdiction in the absence of any link to nationality or territory. In other words, the person tried need not be a national of the prosecuting state, the victims need not be its nationals, and the offence need not have been committed in the territory of the state. What is required, though, is a serious human rights violation, such as genocide, war crimes, crimes against humanity, or torture. In these instances, the national courts apply international criminal law 'on behalf of the international legal order', and not 'their own domestic legal system'.[143] They also only do so when the principle has been concretized into national legislation, such as the Belgian law of universal jurisdiction of 1993, amended in 2003; and the Canadian Crimes Against Humanity and War Crimes Act of 2000.

E Implementation and Enforcement of International Human Rights Law

Human rights violations persist—also in countries that have ratified international human rights instruments. The question has consequently been posed whether the international human rights system makes any difference,[144] and is being posed with increasing frequency. In a study comparing the human rights situation in states that had ratified treaties with those that had not, Hathaway found that the mere fact of ratification did not seem to have a demonstrably positive effect.[145] When assessing the impact of international human rights law, a distinction should be drawn between 'direct' and 'indirect' impact. The former is clearly demonstrable, for example when a decision of a treaty body is complied with under domestic law. Assessment of the latter is more complex, as it involves impact upon less tangible aspects such as policies, attitudes, and general behaviour.

Different understandings of the meaning of 'impact' have a bearing on the way in which the terms 'enforcement' and 'implementation' are used in the study. 'Direct' impact is linked to 'enforcement', as understood in the study. 'Enforcement' of international human rights law is used here in a restricted sense, denoting the conversion into an effective domestic remedy of an international decision ('view' or 'finding'). Under a 'monist' legal system, 'enforcement' in this sense takes place when a provision of international human rights law is applied as the basis for a remedy under national law—when there is proof that these norms have reached their ultimately targeted 'recipient': the individual. 'Implementation' is used to refer to all other means of 'giving effect' to treaty provisions and pronouncements by

---

[143] MT Kamminga, 'Lessons Learned from the Exercise of Universal Jurisdiction in respect of Gross Human Rights Violations' (2001) 23 *HRQ* 940, 964. See also the discussion of the prosecution of the former Chadian President Habré, who fled to Senegal, in Ch 5 below.

[144] C Heyns and F Viljoen, *The Impact of the United Nations Human Rights Treaties on the Domestic Level* (The Hague: Kluwer Law International, 2002).

[145] OA Hathaway, 'Do Human Rights Treaties Make a Difference?' (2002) 111 *Yale L J* 1935.

treaty bodies in domestic policies and legislation. The term also includes compliance with obligations to report, consent to visits of special mechanism, and reaction to reports. Together, 'enforcement' and 'implementation' constitute compliance.

Three main (groups of) theories have been forwarded to explain (non-)compliance.[146] According to *realist theories*, pragmatism prevails. States ratify treaties and abide by their obligations when it is in their 'national interest' to do so. From this perspective, one of the important factors influencing compliance is the power of a state relative to the other states party to a particular human rights regime. For weaker states, reliance on donor funding may be an important factor in assessing the cost and benefits of a particular course of action. Sanctions, or the fear of sanctions, by other states or by a collectivity of states such as the UN or AU may also exert leverage towards compliance. In direct contrast, *normative theories* elevate principle above pragmatism. According to these approaches, the normative force of treaties inspires an ethical obligation on states to comply. From this viewpoint, the 'compliance pull' of a treaty depends on the legitimacy of the norms and the process of their application. Factors that enhance compliance are therefore inclusion in the creation of the relevant norms, and a transparent, fair, and credible system of implementation. *Institutional theories*, constituting the third group, postulate that membership of an institutional arrangement, which states join as rational actors with the aim of setting a common standard of behaviour, creates an incentive to comply. It should be clear, though, that the mere 'belonging to a like-minded brotherhood' is not enough to ensure compliance. Under these theories, institutional strength and willingness to prod states towards enforcement and implementation will have a significant bearing on the compliance by individual states.

1 Implementing Bodies

'Implementing' or 'monitoring' bodies at the international level, responsible for applying treaty provisions, may be divided into three categories: judicial, quasi-judicial, and political bodies.

As much as ours is an era of rights, it is also an era of courts. At the domestic level, the post-World War II world saw the rise of the constitutional court, and an increased judicialization of political life. The internal constitutional order largely determines which domestic courts may apply international human rights law, and what form that 'application' may take. As was mentioned above, domestic courts have an important role in the application of international human rights law— either as a source of a remedy, or as interpretive guide to the proper understanding of national law. Usually, someone seeking redress under tort law (or the 'law of delict') for violation of international human rights law needs to approach a

---

[146] See M Burgstaller, *Theories of Compliance with International Law* (Leiden: Martinus Nijhoff, 2005) (summarizing the theories, 95–102), on which the discussion here relies heavily.

domestic court.[147] Exceptionally, as in the USA, courts may adjudicate civil claims based on human rights violations that took place outside the particular country— provided they qualify as violations of 'the law of nations'.[148]

Four courts of an international character potentially play a role in human rights— the International Court of Justice, the European Court of Human Rights, the Inter-American Court of Human Rights, and the African Court of Human and Peoples' Rights. Each has a contentious and advisory jurisdiction. Contentious jurisdiction refers to the competence to decide on the merits of disputes between parties. An advisory opinion does not lead to a solution of a dispute, and does not bind the parties thereto, but gives an interpretation in the form of an advice or recommendation.

The main characteristic of a judicial decision that distinguishes it from other mechanisms is its unequivocal adversarial nature and the legally binding force of findings. In order to judge a case, a court has to have the competence (jurisdiction) over the material issue at hand (jurisdiction *ratione materiae* (what?)), over the parties involved (*ratione personae* (who?)), over the relevant place (*ratione loci* (where?)), and over the time when the relevant events occurred (*ratione temporis* (when?)). If one of these conditions is not met, the Court does not have jurisdiction to decide the matter.

At the national level, 'quasi-judicial' mechanisms such as national human rights institutions ('Commissions') mostly play a promotional role, although some, such as the Ugandan Human Rights Commission, also have a protective mandate. Truth and reconciliation commissions (for example in South Africa, Rwanda, Sierra Leone, Morocco, and Liberia) have been established to rebuild and heal divisions in post-conflict societies.

Lacking the competence to give binding decisions, some of the seven monitoring bodies established under UN human rights treaties, as well as the Inter-American and African Commissions, also consider cases (called 'communications' or 'petitions') and adopt findings (or 'views'). Although the procedure before these bodies has become increasingly judicialized, their findings formally remain non-binding. This competence, as well as other aspects of their mandates such as the examination of state reports, makes these bodies 'quasi-judicial' in nature.

At both the national and international levels, political bodies, such as national parliaments and executives, the Committee of Ministers of the Council of Europe, and the AU Executive Council play a role in monitoring the implementation of treaties (including the 'execution' of judgments). On the international plane, implementation or enforcement depends largely on the 'mobilization of shame', but may also take the form of multilateral sanctions against members of an intergovernmental organization.

---

[147] See eg attempts to institute civil proceedings against Charles Taylor in Nigeria, which a federal High Court allowed in principle, despite the asylum granted to Taylor by the Nigerian government (Open Society Justice Initiative, 'Nigerian Court Paves the Way for War Crimes Victims' Suit against Charles Taylor', <http://www.justiceinitiative.org>, 2 November 2005 (11 January 2006).

[148] Under the US Alien Tort Claims Act, see eg Tomuschat (n 121 above) 311–12.

2 Mechanisms of Application

Human rights procedures or mechanisms are usually divided into the functions of 'promotion' or 'protection'. Promotional functions are directed at non-confrontational measures that usually take place in public, and are aimed at raising awareness and consciousness. Protective activities are confrontational, directed either by one state against another, or by individuals against states. These proceedings are usually dealt with in private. However, this dichotomy cannot be rigidly adhered to, as 'promotional' activities often overlap with 'protection' and the other way round. Four of the main implementing mechanisms are discussed below.

2.1 Inter-state (or State-to-State) Complaints

Most human rights treaty bodies are competent to deal with inter-state complaints (or 'communications'). Acceptance of inter-state complaints procedures is mostly optional.[149] In terms of this procedure, one state party directs a complaint to the treaty body against another state party. In principle, the complaining state does so, not on the basis of the nationality of the victims or because there is some threat to the complaining state, but merely to ensure that the other state abides by its treaty obligations. As far as its motivation is concerned, a state making use of this mechanism acts in a way similar to that of a state undertaking humanitarian intervention—it undertakes bona fide action in the common interest of upholding the integrity of the treaty. It may be argued that Tanzania's invasion of Uganda in 1979, as far as it was motivated by humanitarian reasons, could have been prevented if an effective inter-state complaints mechanism had been in place.

Very few states have made use of this mechanism, underlining the notion that the inter-state complaints procedure assumes too much concern for human rights on the part of states, and accords too small a role to the reality of international relations between states. No inter-state communication has been submitted under any of the UN human rights treaties. With 13 inter-state communications decided so far, the European human rights system provides some illustration of the use of the inter-state procedure.[150] The single inter-state communication (*DRC v Burundi, Rwanda and Uganda*)[151] submitted thus far under the African system relates to a situation where relations between the states involved have deteriorated steadily due to conflict in the 'Great Lakes' area.

---

[149] Under arts 11 of CERD (mandatory), 41 of ICCPR (optional), 21 of CAT (optional), and 76 of the CMW (optional). The ICESCR, CEDAW, and CRC do not provide for this possibility.

[150] In a celebrated case, four parties to the Europe Convention (Denmark, Norway, Sweden, and the Netherlands) brought a complaint against Greece for gross human rights violations under the military junta that took office. This case confirms the underlying philosophy that this procedure is best used in situations of large-scale or systematic violations. The submission and decision in the case were part of the economic and political pressure that was brought to bear on Greece; eventually—in 1974—leading to a change of government and the return of democratic government and the rule of law.

[151] See Ch 8.B below.

2.2 Individual Complaints

Individual complaints mechanisms allow individuals (and sometimes groups of individuals, or NGOs) to complain against a state to a treaty body for having violated the treaty. This is a much more intrusive mechanism than state reporting, as states may be embarrassed by an unequivocal finding by a court or court-like (quasi-judicial) body that it had fallen short of its commitments. For this reason, this mechanism is often not a necessary consequence of treaty ratification, but is available as an optional extra. States have to 'opt into' these 'voluntary' mechanisms by explicitly expressing their choice to do so. Examples are OPI and the possibility of making a declaration in terms of article 22 to CAT. Other treaties, such as CESCR and CRC, have dispensed with this possibility altogether.[152]

The treaty body considers the communication in two, and sometimes three, phases. First, it decides on the admissibility of the communication. Should the case be admissible, it proceeds to its merits. If a violation is found, the question of an appropriate remedy arises. A pre-admissibility phase, entrusted to the body's secretariat and aimed at distilling 'communications' from a vast volume of correspondence, usually precedes consideration by the treaty body.

Every treaty stipulates the requirements that need to be fulfilled for complaints to be heard by the body, that is, to be admissible. The most important requirement, and the one most often at issue, is that domestic remedies must first be exhausted (the 'exhaustion of local remedies'-requirement). Not everyone who feels that their rights have been violated can approach the international body directly. If this were the case, the body would be flooded with cases and this would make for an unmanageable workload. More fundamentally, the state must be given an opportunity to live up to its obligations under the treaty—it must be given 'notice' of the violation. The individual has to show that attempts to use available and effective remedies have been futile. Only then will the international body agree to deal with the case. Other admissibility requirements differ from treaty to treaty, but will mostly include the substantive prerequisite that a provision (right) in the treaty must have been violated. Sometimes there are time periods within which a case has to be submitted, or a need to be directly affected by the measure complained about (the 'victim'-requirement). Both sides are given an opportunity to send submissions to the treaty body on issues.

If a case is declared admissible, the matter proceeds to a consideration of the substantive issue, during which the body must decide whether a right in the applicable treaty has been violated. This finding is contained in an opinion, referred to as a 'view'. Most of the quasi-judicial bodies decide this issue on written submissions only. In this respect the African Commission is different in that it allows witnesses to be called and oral submissions to be made. In courts, oral testimony and argument

---

[152] There is a process under way to establish individual complaints under ICESCR, see Ch 3. C. 1 below.

always supplement the written documents. Again, the basic rule of *audi alteram partem* (literally, also hear the other side) applies, except when the state does not respond, in which case 'default' proceedings are followed. Should a violation be found, a third phase often comes into play—the 'remedies' stage. The body sets out its finding in a 'view' or 'opinion' or 'decision'. There is some debate about whether these 'views' are legally binding. It should be accepted that they are not, although their status may be enhanced by careful reasoning and follow-up.

The procedure before these bodies and courts is time-consuming and usually takes years to be finalized. It may happen that the complainant's rights are threatened in the period between submission and decision. For this reason, most bodies make use of interim, precautionary, or preliminary measures to 'order' the state to refrain from harming the complainant or victim. Courts and quasi-judicial bodies both may order interim measures, usually aimed at avoiding irreparable harm to the person who submitted a complaint (or on whose behalf a complaint was lodged), before the body is in a position to pronounce on the substance of the matter. This may for example be invoked where the complainant is awaiting the execution of a death sentence and complains to the Human Rights Committee (HRC) about the fairness of his or her trial. By executing the person before the complaint could be assessed, the state not only undermines the procedure to which it has become a party, but also commits a 'grave breach' of its obligations under OPI.[153]

2.3 State Reporting

Under most human rights treaties, states have the obligation to submit reports to treaty monitoring bodies at prescribed intervals.[154] The aim of this process is to ensure 'introspection' nationally and to facilitate 'inspection' internationally. Reporting is an opportunity for stock-taking at governmental level by all those responsible for the implementation of the treaty. To be most effective, such introspection should not be once-off, but should be part of a continuous engagement with questions about the extent of the realization of the rights in the treaty. A state report is an assessment of how well the state, in its own opinion, is living up to its treaty obligations. Because the treaty bodies cannot visit all the state parties to the treaty, it has to rely on the self-assessment as set out in the report, which therefore serves as the basis for 'inspection' by an independent treaty monitoring body.

State representatives are invited to attend the session of the body where the report is tabled and discussed ('examined'). During open session, questions are put to the representatives, who then respond. This process of questions and answers is best seen as a 'constructive dialogue' aimed at identifying problems and obstacles to the realization of the rights in a particular state. During a subsequent private session,

---

[153] See Communication 869/1999, *Piandiong and Others v The Philippines*, UN Doc A/56/40, Vol II, 19 October 2000.

[154] These intervals range from months to years. A distinction is also drawn between initial and periodic reports. Initial reports have to be submitted within a shorter period of time than later reports.

the body adopts 'concluding observations'. These observations usually contain three main parts: positive developments, areas of concern, and recommendations arising from those concerns. These recommendations should not only be implemented by the state, but should also serve as the starting point for the next discussion in the continuing dialogue between the state and the treaty body.

Governments are likely to paint a relatively positive picture of the situation for which they bear responsibility. Some state reports even blatantly distort facts. To ensure the legitimacy of the process of examination, the treaty body needs to be informed of discrepancies between reports and present circumstances. While it is possible that members of treaty bodies obtain this information themselves, or with secretarial assistance, over the years the practice of allowing NGOs to submit shadow or parallel reports has developed. Although NGOs may not participate in the examination, these reports often serve as the basis of questions put to the state delegation. In the practice of some bodies, NGOs even meet with treaty bodies before the examination of a state report.

Numerous problems afflict the state reporting system. The worst is non-submission of reports or only very irregular reporting, which defeats the aim of the process. Particularly plagued by non-compliance, the CERD Committee has adopted a special 'review of implementation' procedure in such instances, thus examining the state's record on the basis of available information even in the absence of a report. All the treaty bodies allow states with more than one overdue report to submit a single combined report, thus with one sweep extinguishing the state's record of overdue reports. Although each of the treaty bodies has adopted a set of guidelines to assist states in the preparation of these reports, some state reports are not drafted in conformity with the guidelines.[155] If the report is totally unacceptable due to deficiencies or lack of information, the practice is to return the report, pointing out the reason to the government. At the other end of the scale, some reports have been extremely long, prompting the CRC Committee to request states to limit reports to 120 pages.

2.4 Fact-finding Missions or On-site Visits

There are a number of drawbacks to the state reporting and complaints procedures. For one, it leaves the treaty body passive, in principle dependent on the submission of reports or complaints. Once submitted, reports and complaints require the bodies to examine and make a finding on the basis of past events, restricting their role to commenting on past compliance. These procedures, usually requiring a long time to be finalized, are also not suitable to address urgent situations. To this may be added the geographic inaccessibility and relative invisibility of these procedures.

---

[155] These guidelines are consolidated in UN Doc HRI/GEN/2/Rev 1, but also see UN Doc HRI/GEN/2/Rev 1 Add and Doc/HRI/GEN/2/Rev 1 Add 2, see <http://www.unhchr.ch> (30 November 2006).

Human rights fact-finding, that is, collecting information about alleged human rights violations, eliminates (or at least mitigates) many of these problems. Fact-finding missions usually take place in the state under investigation (thus termed 'on-site' visits or missions or investigations), giving the fact-finder the opportunity to assess the situation from close by, and to interact with government officials and other nationals, including NGOs. Under such a procedure, there is a much greater opportunity to intervene with high government officials and to make recommendations required by the urgency of the situation. Preventing or halting rather than redressing violations is the focus of concern in fact-finding.

On-site visits only take place with the consent of the state. Visits are usually followed by a report and recommendations to the state. The UN Special Rapporteur for Rwanda, appointed in 1994 to investigate human rights violations in that country, is an example of a fact-finding mechanism. At the African regional level, the Special Rapporteur of the African Commission on Prisons and Conditions of Detention in Africa, established to study and make recommendations about the position of detainees in AU member states, is another. On a number of occasions the African Commission, itself, undertook 'on-site missions' to states (such as Nigeria and Sudan) against which a large number of communications had been received. The aims of fact-finding can range from being an immediate intervention in an urgent situation, to dissemination and awareness-raising.

F Intergovernmental Organizations, Integration, and International Human Rights Law

This book starts from the premise that intergovernmental arrangements are important vehicles for the realization of human rights. While the focus falls on the UN, AU, and regional economic communities ('subregional organizations' or 'RECs') in Africa, other intergovernmental organizations also have an important role to play.

Following the contours of the previous colonial empires, three intergovernmental organizations have been set up to bolster cooperation between erstwhile colonial powers and post-colonial states: the Commonwealth, *l'Organisation Internationale de la Francophonie*, and the Community of Portuguese Speaking Countries. Adherence to democratic values and human rights is an important part of each of their agendas. Built on the intimacy of a common cultural and linguistic heritage, these groupings have significant potential to ensure that their members remain in or return to the fold of human rights.

1 The Commonwealth of Nations

The Commonwealth of Nations (Commonwealth) is the longest standing and most influential of the three. It is a loose association bringing together 53 states from different ethnic and cultural backgrounds from all corners of the globe.[156] Membership of the Commonwealth is based on an unacknowledged link with the British Monarch as unifying head, and a past of direct or indirect British rule or administration in most—but not all—Commonwealth members.[157] At present, seventeen African states, all from the sub-Saharan region, are members of the Commonwealth.[158] Although it extends worldwide, African states clearly make up a significant part of the Commonwealth's membership.

The principal decision-making organ of the Commonwealth is the Commonwealth Heads of Government Meeting (CHOGM), which takes place every two years. The CHOGM has not adopted a coherent or consistent approach to human rights violations in member states.[159] The Commonwealth is built on consensus and informal means of persuasion. An exception to this approach is the condemnation of massive human rights violations in Uganda at the 1977 meeting. A clear indication that human rights standards form one of the cornerstones of the organization was the adoption in 1991 of the Harare Declaration. At the 1995 meeting in Auckland, Nigeria was suspended because of its serious violation of the Harare Declaration.[160] Zimbabwe withdrew from the Commonwealth in 2003, after it had been suspended in 2002 over concerns with the electoral and land reform policies of the Mugabe government.

The Commonwealth Secretariat provides administrative support to further the human rights agenda of the Commonwealth. It has adopted a pro-active role by organizing training workshops on human rights for public officials. The Secretariat's Legal and Constitutional Division is active in various fields, such as the publication of law reports and the *Commonwealth Law Bulletin*. One of its major contributions (with the NGO Interights) to the improvement of human rights in member states has been a series of colloquia on the domestic application of international human rights norms.[161] The outcome of the first of these, the Bangalore Principles, endeavours to get Commonwealth judiciaries to give greater recognition to the importance and potential of international human rights norms. Although the Principles concede that the dualist tradition followed in the Commonwealth precludes international treaties from being 'directly enforceable in national courts' in the absence of incorporating legislation, they encourage judiciaries to seek judicial guidance in these norms when national law is 'uncertain or incomplete'.

The Secretariat is further involved in the monitoring of elections in numerous countries, most recently in The Gambia and Zambia. Set up in 1985, the Human

---

[156] <http://www.thecommonwealth.org> (30 September 2006).

[157] In Africa, Mozambique does not share this British colonial experience.

[158] These 17 states are Botswana, Cameroon, The Gambia, Ghana, Kenya, Lesotho, Malawi, Mauritius, Mozambique, Namibia, Seychelles, Sierra Leone, South Africa, Swaziland, Tanzania, Uganda, and Zambia. Zimbabwe's membership has been suspended.

[159] A Duxbury, 'Rejuvenating the Commonwealth—The Human Rights Remedy' (1977) 46 *ICLQ* 344, 361.

[160] The Ministerial Action Group has subsequently followed a process of continued dialogue.

[161] See Commonwealth Secretariat (1988–93) *Developing Human Rights Jurisprudence* (vols 1–6).

Rights Unit of the Secretariat has been involved in human rights promotion and training,[162] and the development of two 'accession kits' to assist states ratifying CEDAW and the two UN Covenants.[163]

The Commonwealth has given a prominent role to human rights, especially through standard-setting and promotion. This engagement has been described as a tidal wave which must be ridden.[164] In fact, it has used the human rights debate 'to reaffirm and reform its role as an international organisation'.[165] However, the effective supervision of standards has been almost non-existent. The Secretariat has consistently denied that it has any role in investigating the human rights-related conduct of member states.[166]

Membership of the Commonwealth does not require members to accept the possibility of a final appeal to the Judicial Committee of the Privy Council. Although Privy Council appeals have been in place for a number of African countries, today they exist only in Mauritius.[167] The Privy Council applies the Constitution and legislation of a particular state, but may give important interpretative guidance. For example, in a case from The Gambia, where cases up until July 1998 could go on final appeal to the Privy Council,[168] the Privy Council underscored the need for a 'generous and purposive construction' of the Constitution.[169] With the entry into force in 2000 of the Human Rights Act of 1998 in the UK, the question was posed whether this Act binds the Privy Council to observe the European Convention in its decisions.[170] This may be of particular relevance when the death penalty, outlawed for all offences in Protocol 13 to the European Convention, is at stake. As Mauritius still retains the death penalty,[171] this issue may yet arise.

2 *Organisation Internationale da la Francophonie* (OIF)

The International Organization of the *Francophonie* (OIF) is centred more pertinently around a common language.[172] The OIF is rooted in attempts by leaders in African French-speaking post-colonial countries to create an agency to facilitate closer cultural and technical cooperation. As more states became involved, the more formal structure of the OIF was established in 1995. Under its Charter and the Bamako Declaration of 2000, the *Francophonie* has made support for the rule of law and human rights part of the cement that holds the members together. Since

---

[162] Duxbury (n 159 above) 344, 359.   [163] ibid 344, 358.

[164] R Chongwe, 'The Commonwealth and the New World Order—Safeguarding Civil Society' (1992) 4 *RADIC* 962.   [165] Duxbury (n 159 above) 344, 345.

[166] ibid 344, 348.

[167] In 2004, three cases were referred, and in 2005, nine cases. <http://www.privy-council.org/uk> (30 September 2006).   [168] <http://www.privy-council.org/uk/> (30 September 2006).

[169] *A-G of the Gambia v Jobe* [1985] LRC (Const) 556, 565.

[170] R Murray, 'The Human Rights Act: The End of the Privy Council and Death Penalty Cases?' (2001) 6 *J Civil Liberties* 35.   [171] Constitution of Mauritius 1968, art 4.

[172] See P Tavernier, 'International Organisation of the Francophonie: Profile of the Francophonie' in C Heyns (ed), *Human Rights Law in Africa* (vol 1) (Leiden: Martinus Nijhoff, 2004) 746; and <http://www.francophonie.org> (30 September 2006).

1992, it has undertaken more than a hundred electoral observation missions. It also brings together judges and members of other judicial bodies in French-speaking countries in 'associations'. Conflict in countries such as the DRC and Côte d'Ivoire and unconstitutional changes of government[173] feature on the OIF's agenda. With 29 out of 55 members, African states form the majority within the OIF.

3 Community of Portuguese Speaking Countries (CPLP)

With five out of eight members,[174] African states have the potential to form a majority in the Community of Portuguese Speaking Countries (CPLP), but one country, Brazil, dominates the grouping in geographic and population size. Going beyond its starting point as a linguistic community, the CPLP has acted as mediator in Guinea-Bissau,[175] and conducted electoral missions to numerous African countries, including Mozambique,[176] in pursuance of its mandate to 'ensure respect for human rights at national and international levels'. Linking the CPLP to global efforts towards human rights realization, its Constitutive Declaration also calls on members to specifically comply with the CRC.

G The Limits of International Human Rights Law

International human rights, understood primarily as judicial or quasi-judicial claims, have dominated the human rights discourse. In line with prevailing reality, codified human rights serve as the main sources of rights in this book, and judicial and quasi-judicial procedures are the main areas of investigation. However, based on the premise that law is an important and necessary—but certainly not a sufficient—means of realizing rights and improving peoples' lives, an attempt will be made to break the legal deadlock, by adopting a modest interdisciplinary approach.

Traditional, 'purely legal' approaches are aimed primarily at textual analysis of norms, and an analysis of their case-by-case application.[177] In the main, international

---

[173] In its report on its mission to Mauritania, the Pan-African Parliament noted the role of the *Francophonie* in the process towards transition (Report of the Pan-African Parliament Mission to Mauritania from 10–16 October 2005).

[174] The African states are Angola, Cape Verde, Guinea-Bissau, Mozambique, and São Tomée Príncipe; <http://www.cplp.org> (30 September 2006).

[175] In his report on the situation in Guinea-Bissau, the AU Chairperson noted the role of the CPLP, and suggested that the AU follows its example of setting up a 'Liaison Office' in Bissau; he also stressed the importance of working with the CPLP in a campaign to sensitize International Financial Institutions (IFIs) and other donors 'with a view to establishing a disarmament programme' (AU Doc PSC/PR/2(XXXI) 8 June 2005, paras 13 and 27).

[176] MJM Pires, 'Profile of the Community of Portuguese Speaking Countries', in Heyns (n 44 above) 744.

[177] For a profound critique of the African human rights discourse, see I Shivji, *The Concept of Human Rights in Africa* (London: CODESRIA, 1989) 50: 'African writers, particularly lawyers, have uncritically embraced the methodology of positivism and its prescriptions. Law is seen as a self-contained system of

human rights law adopts a reactive position to human rights violations, ending in a judgment call after the event, ascribing responsibility, and granting a remedy. Legal analysis focuses on the judicial setting, where courts or quasi-judicial bodies are the primary sites under investigation. As they do not concern themselves with the social, political, or cultural causes of violations, these analyses are weak on prevention and fall short on insight about systemic or structural causes of violations. As they often shun the political and social context of the application or findings, their inquiries do not extend sufficiently to implementation and enforcement in practice.

Legal analyses should be supplemented by insights from disciplines that address some of these limitations and omissions.[178]

(i) International human rights law is applied and implemented by state officials, institutional bureaucracies, courts, and treaty bodies. Principles used in public administration and business management may be useful in shedding light on issues such as the functioning of institutions; financial and human resource management; leadership, supervision, and institutional accountability; office organization and procedures; and information management and dissemination.[179] As some of the weaknesses of the African regional system are for instance linked to these issues, a purely legal analysis of that system would be inadequate.

(ii) The social sciences, especially the 'investigative' disciplines of anthropology and parts of sociology,[180] and political science, are essential in understanding that international human rights law is an expression of power and ideology. These disciplines also seek insight into the cultural, social, and political contexts that generate violations, to question the legitimacy of the norms and institutions, and to account for social movements and the role of civil society in advancing rights. They are also better equipped than the legal discourse to assess the role of law and legal institutions in effecting social transformation (such as 'inculcating a human rights culture' or forging 'real' regional integration between individuals and states[181]).

---

norms complete in itself, separate and abstracted from both state and society. The ills of society are seen as inconsistencies in the existing rules or lack of appropriate rules'. On the need for an interdisciplinary approach, he notes that the 'whole debate that has taken place in the social sciences about inter-disciplinary approaches and the associated critique of the compartmentalisation of knowledge' has 'by-passed the discourse in human rights'.

[178] Freeman (n 24 above) ch 5.

[179] See eg F Fukuyama, *State Building. Governance and World Order in the Twenty-First Century* (London: Profile Books, 2005), who emphasizes the role of public administration in reaching an understanding of state capacity.

[180] For a socio-legal approach to the implementation of international human rights law, see H Hydén, 'Implementation of International Conventions as a Socio-Legal Enterprise: Examples from the Convention on the Rights of the Child' in J Grimheben and R Ring (eds), *Human Rights Law: From Dissemination to Application* (Leiden: Martinus Nijhoff, 2006) 375.

[181] See eg PT Zeleza, 'The Struggle for Human Rights' in PT Zeleza and PJ McConnaughay (eds), *Human Rights, the Rule of Law, and Development in Africa* (Philadelphia: University of Philadelphia Press, 2004) 1.

(iii) International human rights law is not only a subset of international law, but is also firmly embedded in international relations (or 'international politics'). As intergovernmental organizations, composed of states, the institutions under review (the UN, AU, subregional groupings) function in a context where sovereignty and national interest are important determinants of foreign policy and state (and therefore, also institutional) behaviour. Particularly when it comes to the implementation and 'enforcement' of international human rights law, it would be myopic to disregard the 'real politics' of inter-state relations.[182]

(iv) In recent times, international political economy has gained much ground as a discipline taking stock of the structural, economic causes of human rights violations in the context of globalized capitalism. Discussion about poverty and socio-economic rights will remain anaemic if this perspective is disregarded.

Let me be clear: in what follows, these disciplines are inadequately accounted for. I write as someone trained in international law, and not in other disciplines. In the main, my writing joins the dominant 'legal' discourse, but it does so self-consciously, while making modest efforts to broaden and supplement that approach.

---

[182] For a contribution bridging this gap, see DP Forsythe, *Human Rights in International Relations* (Cambridge: Cambridge University Press, 2nd edn, 2006).

PART II
THE GLOBAL LEVEL

2

The Role of United Nations Organs and Agencies in Realizing Human Rights in Africa

The gravitational pull of international human rights grew ever stronger towards the end of the last century, as globalization increasingly accentuated the common causes of humanity, and neo-liberal ideologies positioned themselves in an apparently unassailable hegemony. Significant advances have been made since World War II in expanding the normative reach of international human rights law. However, over the last decade attention has shifted to the implementation of human rights norms, the development of more secure safety nets, and to a critical appraisal of the impact of the norms.[1] In this chapter, the multiple layers constituting the 'gravitational pull' and the 'safety nets' provided by United Nations (UN) organs and agencies are assessed, with specific reference to their role in and effect on human rights in African countries (in Section A). The increasingly important role in the protection of human rights of the UN specialized financial agencies (the World Bank, and the International Monetary Fund (IMF)) and of the World Trade Organization (WTO) is then discussed, with specific attention again devoted to Africa (in Section B).

When the UN was formed in 1945, the then independent states in Africa (Egypt, Ethiopia, Liberia, and the Union of South Africa) joined the new global organization. As more African states became independent, a seat at the UN became one of the foremost manifestations affirming their 'flag independence'. A preoccupation with 'UN-recognized' independence ('seat independence') became a contributing factor in the elevation of colonial borders to intangible national frontiers—a requirement for international recognition.[2] It was in the interest of the West, which largely controlled international law, that the newly independent African states did not become radically reconfigured.[3] By colluding with the uncritical succession of colonial states, the UN contributed to the establishment of states that lacked moral legitimacy. The lack of internal moral legitimacy arguably predisposed the independent African states, 'the instruments of narrow elites and their international backers', to using sovereign statehood as a shield against accusations of immoral domestic practices, including human rights violations.

In an attempt to reduce international conflict and widespread human rights violations, the UN embraces the principles of development, peaceful settlement of disputes, and respect for human rights.[4] All UN member states pledge to 'take joint and separate action' in pursuit of achieving 'universal respect for, and observance of, human rights and fundamental freedoms without distinction as to race, sex, language, or religion'.[5]

The core system of human rights promotion and protection under the UN has a dual basis: the UN Charter, adopted in 1945; and a network of treaties subsequently adopted by UN members. The current membership of the UN is 192,[6] of which 53

---

[1] Also see Ch 1.B above.

[2] On the 'validation of the colonial state in international law', see M Wa Mutua, 'Why Redraw the Map of Africa: A Moral and Legal Inquiry' (1994–5) 16 *Michigan J of Intl L* 113, 137–42. Departing from the premise that the post-colonial African state lacks moral legitimacy due to the fact that it was imposed through colonization, and not by 'the African peoples', Mutua proposes a radical reconfiguration of the continent. In some way, his vision is being realized through the consolidation of RECs in Africa (see Ch 12 below).

[3] See eg SR Ratner, 'Drawing a Better Line: *Uti Possidetis* and the Borders of New States' (1996) 90 *AJIL* 590, 595–6.   [4] UN Charter, art 1.

[5] UN Charter, art 55(c).

[6] When calculating adherence, the figure of 194 states is used (Table 3.2 in Ch 3 below), to reflect the fact that two state entities (the Cook Islands and the Holy See) ratified some UN instruments (eg CERD and CRC) despite not being UN members.

are African states.[7] A major implication of this duality is that, by virtue of their UN membership, *all* UN member states fall under the ambit of the Charter-based system, while only those states that have ratified or acceded to particular treaties are bound to observe that part of the treaty-based (or 'conventional') system which they have explicitly agreed to. By becoming members of the UN, states cede a substantial part of their sovereignty; however, the voluntary acceptance of further treaty obligations has the potential to erode state sovereignty much more profoundly. In Section A of this chapter, the Charter-based system is discussed, while the treaty-based system is the topic of the following chapter.

A The UN Charter-based System and Human Rights in Africa

Under the UN Charter, responsibility for protecting human rights is assigned to the Economic and Social Council (ECOSOC), which is entitled to undertake studies and make relevant recommendations.[8] Under the UN policy of 'mainstreaming' human rights, not only ECOSOC, but all principal organs of the UN (in particular the General Assembly, the Security Council, and the International Court of Justice) have significant roles to play. These organs are discussed below, with reference to their relevance for Africa.

Although numerous UN specialized agencies and programmes have contributed to the realization of human rights in Africa, the restricted scope of this discussion requires the focus to be limited to those entities within the UN with a clear 'legal' mandate with respect to human rights, either in norm-setting or in norm-implementation. Deriving their existence from the UN Charter, and functioning under the UN, these specialized agencies and programmes have an important bearing on human rights. At the forefront is the Office of the High Commissioner for Human Rights (OHCHR), the secretariat from where the UN's human rights efforts are coordinated and managed. Specialized agencies such as the International Labour Organization (ILO), the Food and Agriculture Organization (FAO), the UN Educational, Scientific and Cultural Organization (UNESCO), and the World Health Organization (WHO) all play a significant role in protecting and promoting

---

[7] This total includes Morocco, a member of the UN but not of the African Union (AU), but excludes the Sahrawi Arab Democratic Republic (SADR), a member of the AU but not of the UN. The AU membership currently numbers 53, which excludes Morocco, who withdrew from the OAU when the SADR was admitted and took its seat at the OAU Assembly of Heads of State and Government in 1984. Morocco remains a member of the UN, though, while the Saharawi Democratic Republic has not been recognized as a member state (GJ Naldi, *The Organization of African Unity: An Analysis of its Role* (London: Mansell, 1989) 49, also on the UN General Assembly's 'low-key' approach to this issue). The question of the statehood of the SADR is not canvassed here. Naldi argues that the four requirements of a permanent population, a defined territory, a stable and effective government, and capacity to enter into international relations, are met (62). The SADR was established by a unilateral declaration of independence by the Polisario Front on 27 February 1976.

[8] UN Charter, art 62.

human rights in Africa. The UN also established various programmes and funds, such as the UN Development Programme (UNDP), the UN High Commissioner for Refugees (UNHCR), UN Children's Fund (UNICEF), and the Joint UN Programme on HIV/AIDS (UNAIDS). These programmes and funds either focus on some particular aspect related to human rights or include human rights in their development agendas.

1 The General Assembly

Assigned the responsibility of assisting in the 'realisation of human rights and fundamental freedoms for all',[9] the main contribution of the United Nations General Assembly (UNGA) to human rights lies in the field of standard-setting.[10] General Assembly debates and discussions have, over the years, resulted in numerous resolutions, declarations and binding treaties.[11] The first of these was the landmark Universal Declaration of Human Rights in 1948.[12] The following resolutions serve as examples of the sustained significance of the General Assembly's role: in 1990, the Assembly adopted the resolution deciding to convene a World Conference on Human Rights. In 1993, it established the post of UN High Commissioner for Human Rights. In 1994, it resolved to proclaim the UN Decade of Human Rights Education.[13]

Before political decisions are taken, human rights matters are usually referred to the UNGA's Third Committee, which is responsible for social, humanitarian, and cultural affairs, for an often intensive, yet protracted process of technical and legal debate. Initially, African voices have not been sufficiently audible in this forum, but increasingly, this trend is being reversed.

The role of the General Assembly extends much further. It not only plays a legislative role, but also serves as a forum for various other human rights oversight activities. For example, it receives annual reports from the various human rights treaty bodies, from thematic and country rapporteurs, and from the High Commissioner for Human Rights.[14]

[9] UN Charter, art 13.

[10] On the involvement of the General Assembly in the field of human rights, see in general A Cassese, 'The General Assembly: Historical Perspectives 1945–1989' in P Alston (ed), *The United Nations and Human Rights: A Critical Appraisal* (Oxford: Clarendon Press, 1992) 25, and J Quinn, 'The General Assembly into the 1990s' in P Alston (ed), *The United Nations and Human Rights: A Critical Appraisal* (Oxford: Clarendon Press, 1992) 55.

[11] General Assembly resolutions are generally only recommendatory, but may become binding if they are proof of pertinent contemporary international community standards (*South West Africa Cases (Second Phase)* [1966] ICJ Rep 6, 50–1).

[12] While the other three African members of the UN voted in favour of the Universal Declaration's adoption, the Union of South Africa joined the Soviet bloc states and Saudi Arabia in abstaining.

[13] For a full list of resolutions dealing with human rights matters, see United Nations, *The United Nations and Human Rights 1945–1995* (New York: UN Department of Public Information, 1995).

[14] Quinn (n 10 above).

African scepticism towards the UN changed in the 1960s, due mainly to the role newly independent African states started playing in the UNGA, where the Afro-Asian bloc now constitutes a majority. African states used the Assembly as a forum to address the issues of self-determination, decolonization, and racism. The adoption by the General Assembly, in 1960, of the Declaration on the Granting of Independence to Colonial Countries and Peoples, accentuated the right to self-determination of peoples in the colonial sphere.[15] The UNGA also established a Special Committee on the Situation regarding the Implementation of the Declaration on the Granting of Independence to Colonial Countries and Peoples.

Although African states did not play a significant role in the initial proposals for the incorporation of the right to self-determination of peoples in the International Covenant on Economic, Social and Cultural Rights (ICESCR) and the International Covenant on Civil and Political Rights (ICCPR) of 1966, their support ensured its eventual inclusion in these treaties.[16] To some extent, African states have been instrumental in the adoption of the first binding treaty adopted by the UN in 1965, the Convention on the Elimination of All Forms of Racial Discrimination. Also, African opposition against South Africa's racial policies helped inspire the adoption of the Convention on the Suppression and Punishment of the Crime of Apartheid.[17]

The South African minority government, especially, became a frequent target, leading to the first significant encroachment on state sovereignty by the UN,[18] as the UNGA rejected South Africa's reliance on the principle of non-interference in its domestic affairs as a reason to disallow international inspection and criticism. In this way the South African precedent has, perhaps ironically, paved the way for more effective human rights scrutiny by the General Assembly in later years.[19]

The majority of African states have not been equally prepared for inspection and criticism of their internal affairs. For example, when the General Assembly raised the issue of the execution by Nigeria of Ken Saro-Wiwa and eight other Ogoni activists in 1995,[20] it adopted a resolution on the general situation of human rights in Nigeria. This resolution condemned arbitrary executions and expressed concern about the human rights situation in Nigeria.[21] However, with

[15] A Cassese, 'Political Self-Determination—Old Conceptions and New Developments' in A Cassese (ed), *UN Law/Fundamental Rights: Two Topics in International Law* (Alphen aan den Rijn: Sijthoff and Noordhoff, 1979) 141.

[16] See ICESCR and ICCPR, art 1; Cassese (n 15 above) 140–3, M Nowak, *UN Covenant on Civil and Political Rights (CCPR) Commentary* (Kehl: NP Engel, 2nd edn, 2005) 6–13.

[17] Cassese (n 10 above) 39–40.

[18] See eg NM Stultz, 'Evolution of the United Nations Anti-Apartheid Regime' (1991) 13 *HRQ* 1.

[19] The new doctrine was consolidated in 1974, when the Assembly 'intervened' in the case of Chile (Cassese (n 10 above) 43).

[20] The Security Council would not consider the matter (SP Marks, 'Social and Humanitarian Issues' in J Tessitore and S Woolfson (eds), *A Global Agenda: Issues before the 51st General Assembly of the United Nations* (Boulder, Colo: Rowman & Littlefields Publishers, 1996) 203.

[21] UN Doc A/Res/50/199.

African states, in particular, responsible for toning down the operative sections of this resolution in order to counter a perceived trend of resolutions critical of African states, the UNGA stopped short of recommending economic measures against Nigeria.[22]

As a concrete signal that it views the eradication of poverty, which is one of Africa's gravest concerns, as a matter of urgency and an attainable ideal, the UNGA in 2000 adopted the Millennium Declaration, from which the Millennium Development Goals (MDGs) are derived.[23] The eight MDGs cover poverty and hunger; primary education; gender equality; infant child mortality; maternal health; HIV/AIDS, malaria, and other diseases; environmental sustainability; and global partnerships. Measurable 'targets', most of which have to be reached by 2015, accompany these goals. Alston points to the limited and selective nature of the MDGs, but also notes that the time-bound and measurable targets set by the goals suggest accountability, and that an 'extensive institutional apparatus' for their promotion departs from a 'business-as-usual' approach.[24] Although the MDGs are of obvious relevance to human rights, they fail adequately to 'mainstream' human rights into the development agenda and, by omitting many 'civil and political' rights, do not refer to the 'full human rights framework'.[25] Socio-economic rights are included by implication only.

Lamenting the disjuncture between development and human rights approaches and discourses, Alston shows the limited extent to which both the UN's Charter-based and treaty-based human rights systems have attempted to implement and promote the MDGs. He proposes that special mechanisms and treaty bodies should support the 'mainstreaming' agenda by making the MDGs an explicit and consistent part of its activities. Citing state reporting as an example, Alston shows how the recurring criticism that concluding observations are often 'not sufficiently precise or targeted' can be addressed by focusing on 'individual MDGs, combined with explicit recommendations as to what needs to be done'.[26]

In 2005, the UN General Assembly held a Special Session to review the progress made towards the accomplishment of the MDGs. As the UN's 2006 Millennium Report shows, it is extremely unlikely that sub-Saharan Africa will attain these goals within the stipulated time-frame. Some small gains have been made.[27] In respect of MDG 2, aimed at achieving universal access to primary education by 2015, the net

---

[22] The Security Council refused to consider the matter (Marks (n 20 above) 203).

[23] UN Doc A/Res/55/2 (2000).

[24] P Alston, 'Ships Passing in the Night: The Current State of the Human Rights and Development Debate Seen through the Lens of the Millennium Development Goals' (2005) 27 *HRQ* 755, 756.   [25] ibid 758.

[26] 'A Human Rights Perspective on the Millennium Development Goals', paper prepared as a contribution to the work of the Millennium Project Task Force on Poverty and Economic Development, <http://www.ohchr.org/english/issues/millenium-development/docs/alston.doc> (30 September 2006).

[27] United Nations, 'The Millennium Development Goals Report 2006' (2006 Millennium Report), <http://mdgs.un.org/unsd/mdg/Resources/Static/Products/Progress2006/MDGReport2006.pdf> (30 September 2006).

enrolment in primary education increased from 53 per cent in 1990/1 to 64 per cent in 2003/4.[28] There also was slight progress towards MDG 1, which aims at halving the proportion of the population living on less than US$1 per day: the proportion of people in sub-Saharan Africa living on less that US$1 per day decreased slightly over the period from 1990 to 2002, from 44.6 to 44 per cent.[29]

MDG 4, aiming to reduce, by 2015, infant mortality rates by two-thirds, will certainly not be accomplished. Despite a reduction of infant mortality from 185 per 1,000 live births in 1990 to 168 in 2004, sub-Saharan Africa still lags far behind other regions and the target of 62 infant deaths per 1,000 live births.[30] One of the targets under MDG 6 is to halt and start decreasing the incidence of malaria and other major diseases by 2015. Between 1999 and 2003, a tenfold increase in the distribution of mosquito nets in the region had been recorded, but over the same period the incidence of tuberculosis (excluding HIV positive people) had risen alarmingly from 148 to 281 per 100,000 of the population.[31] Goal 7 aims to reverse the loss of environmental resources. The 2006 Millennium Report notes that in Africa, as in many other regions of the world, the percentage of land covered by forests is still declining.[32]

A cursory glance at the resolutions adopted at some recent General Assembly sessions reveals that numerous issues of relevance to the developing world, and in particular to Africa, are now firmly part of the matters under constant review before the Assembly.[33]

2 The Security Council

Although the UN Security Council (UNSC) does not have an explicit mandate to involve itself in human rights matters, its mandate of maintaining 'international peace and security'[34] has been extended to include human rights-related issues. The Security Council functions as the only body in the UN able to take executive decisions and 'call on' member states to carry out decisions. At present, the Security Council consists of 15 members,[35] of which five are permanent. They are the USA,

---

[28] 2006 Millennium Report (n 27 above) 6; see also NEPAD's African Peer Review Mechanism, Country Review Report of Kenya, May 2006, <http://www.aprmkenya.org/downloads/Kenyareport.pdf> (30 September 2006), which notes that progress has been made in respect of this objective in particular, but that Kenya is not on track to achieve most others, due to factors such as 'poor infrastructure, weak service-delivery mechanisms, poor governance and a weak science and technology base' (231).

[29] 2006 Millennium Report (n 27 above) 15 (over the period 1990 to 2004); however, the number in North Africa (measured together with West Asia) actually increased.

[30] 2006 Millennium Report (n 27 above) 6.   [31] ibid 10.

[32] In Africa, the decline was from 29% of all land surface in 1990 to 27% in 2005 (2006 Millennium Report (n 27 above) 16).

[33] See eg the items on the agenda of its 61st session (<http://www.un.org/ga>), which includes the situation in the DRC, the situation of refugees, the ICTR, malaria in Africa, a follow-up to the Declaration of Commitment on HIV/AIDS, and the inclusion of reports of the New Partnership for Africa's Development (NEPAD).   [34] UN Charter, art 24(1).

[35] On its composition, see <http://www.un.org/Overview/Organs/sc.html>.

Britain, France, Russia, and China (all victors of World War II). The ten non-permanent members are elected by the General Assembly for two-year terms. The current ten non-permanent members comprise three African states: Congo (with a term expiring on 31 December 2007); Ghana (with a term also expiring at the end of 2007); and South Africa (with a term ending at the end of 2008). The Security Council meets on a continuous basis, usually in New York. A peculiar feature of its operations is the veto power of the five permanent members; one of these states opposed to a course of action is able to render the Council powerless.

The Security Council is empowered to take 'measures not involving the use of force' when a 'threat to the peace' exists.[36] This power was used for the first time in 1968 when mandatory sanctions were imposed on Southern Rhodesia.[37] South Africa became the next target, when the Security Council imposed a mandatory arms embargo against that country in 1977.[38] These two instances were groundbreaking in that they were 'self-evidently based upon *internal situations*' and served as precedents for sanctions imposed by the Security Council in the post-Cold War era.[39] These precedents make South Africa's voting record as UNSC member all the more disappointing. Basing its arguments more on geopolitical pragmatism than on a principled respect for human rights, in votes on the human rights situation in Myanmar and Zimbabwe, South Africa sided with those members of the UNSC, such as China, who define 'threat to peace' very narrowly, and 'non-interference' very broadly.

In the build-up towards the 50-year celebrations of the birth of the UN, in 1995, its institutions and functions were scrutinized. Since then, calls have increasingly been heard for an end to the way in which the five permanent members dominate the Security Council, and, in effect, the United Nations as a whole.[40] Questions that arose were:[41] Why should the victors of World War II remain in a dominant position in international affairs? Do the mechanisms in the Security Council reflect the democratic ideals of the organization? Is the collective authority as exercised by the Security Council legitimate?

---

[36] UN Charter, arts 39 and 41.

[37] Resolution 232 (1966), *SCOR Resolutions and Decisions* at 7, adopted by 11 votes to zero, with four members abstaining.

[38] Resolution 418 (1977), *SCOR Resolutions and Decisions* at 5, adopted unanimously; see also EY Benneh, 'The United Nations and Economic Sanctions: Towards a New World Order?' (1993) 5 *ASICL Proc* 241, 243. In 1985, the Security Council adopted a further resolution, calling for the following comprehensive measures against South Africa: (a) suspension of investments; (b) prohibition of the sale of Krugerrands; (c) restrictions on sport and cultural relations; (d) suspension of guaranteed export loans; (e) prohibition of new nuclear contracts; and (f) prohibition of the sale of computers that may be used by the army or police.   [39] See Benneh (n 38 above).

[40] This unease is not novel, though. Since its founding, in 1963, the OAU insisted that 'Africa as a geographical region should have equitable representation in the principal organs of the United Nations, particularly the Security Council' (Resolutions adopted by the First Conference of Independent African Heads of State and Government held in Addis Ababa, Ethiopia, 22–5 May 1963 (CIAS/Plen.2/Rev.2)).

[41] See H Koechler, 'The United Nations Security Council and the New World Order' in F Barnaby (ed), *Building a More Democratic United Nations* (New York: Frank Cass, 1991) 238, DD Caron, 'The Legitimacy of the Collective Authority of the Security Council' (1993) 87 *AJIL* 552 and K Hüfnerk, *Agenda for Change: New Tasks for the United Nations* (Opladen: Leske and Bundrich, 1995).

Possible ways of addressing the problem were identified: the veto system should be reformed, either through its abolition[42] or extension; the membership of the Council may be increased; and the influence of the General Assembly in the work of the Security Council should be enhanced. Whatever form the eventual reforms take, it is accepted that at least some African representation should be allowed in order to make the Security Council more legitimate.[43]

The tension between African interests and the right to veto came to a head when Boutros-Ghali (an Egyptian) stood for election to a second term as Secretary-General in 1996. In the initial round of voting he was accepted by all the permanent members of the Security Council, except the USA. The three African countries that served as temporary members at the time expressed their support for his re-appointment. Despite this unanimity, the USA persisted in vetoing the candidature. It is accepted UN practice that the Secretary-General serves for two consecutive terms. It was generally agreed among members, including the USA, that another candidate from Africa should be elected in Boutros-Ghali's place. With the election of Kofi Annan, a career-diplomat from Ghana who had previously served as under-Secretary-General for peace-keeping, the first sub-Saharan African was elevated to the highest position in the UN. He served for two five-year terms (1997–2006) and has been succeeded by Ban Ki-moon of South Korea.[44]

The UN Charter does not specifically provide for peace-keeping. Such operations are justified under the general rubric of its aim to 'maintain peace and security'.[45] The UN's involvement in this regard may take different forms. On one end of the scale lies monitoring, allowing for minimal UN involvement. On the other end lies 'peace-enforcement', with the UN becoming actively involved in conflicts.[46] The middle ground consists of numerous forms of peace-keeping, ranging from technical and humanitarian assistance, to overseeing cease-fires.

The UN's peace-keeping operations started off as 'simply observation and interposition missions'.[47] The peace-keeping mission to the Congo (ONUC) in 1960 was the first UN operation of its kind. Initially welcomed by most African states, ONUC came to be regarded as 'an imperialistic instrument to subvert African independence'.[48] This mission was a precursor to the UN's increasing involvement

---

[42] The South African President Mandela expressed his preference for its abolition: see 'Scrap UN Veto—Mandela' (29 March 1997) *Pretoria News* 4.

[43] The AU position is that it opposes in principle the existence of a veto power; however, as long as that exists, Africa should be represented by two permanent members with veto powers, and by five non-permanent members (The Common African Position on the Proposed Reforms of the UN: 'The Ezulwini Consensus', AU Doc Ext/EX.CL/2(VII), March 2005). The strongest candidates are Egypt and Nigeria, see DJ Whittaker, *United Nations in Action* (London: UCL Press, 1995) 18. Since its return as an esteemed member of the international community, South Africa has positioned itself as the third major African regional power with similar ambitions.

[44] Ki-moon was elected for a five-year term, ending on 31 December 2011 (UN Doc S/RES/1715(2006)), 9 October 2006.   [45] UN Charter, art 1(1).

[46] This is justified in terms of Ch VI of the UN Charter.

[47] B Boutros-Ghali, 'Introduction' in United Nations (n 13 above) 112.

[48] JOC Jonah, 'The Organization of African Unity: Peace-keeping and Conflict Resolution' in Y El-Ayouty, *The Organization of African Unity after Thirty Years* (Westport, Conn: Praeger, 1994) 1, 4.

in internal conflicts, as opposed to inter-state wars. The United Nations Transitional Assistance Group (UNTAG) to Namibia marked the advent of more active UN participation in multidisciplinary peace-building, rather than attaining military objectives as part of peace-keeping. UN missions gradually became involved in the protection of human rights, providing humanitarian relief, and the supervision of elections. More importantly, also for the purpose of this study, this marks a shift away from the conference room to the reality of the situation.[49] After the end of the Cold War the link between peace-keeping and human rights was increasingly highlighted. In 1995, the UN Secretary-General wrote that 'any process whose goal is one of peace-keeping must take into account the human rights situation and aim to ensure the promotion and protection of those rights'.[50] By that time, at least seven UN operations worldwide included an essential human rights component.[51] UN involvement in Namibia and Rwanda in previous years paints a different picture.

The UN Security Council approved the establishment of UNTAG in 1978.[52] Its main function was to implement the provisions of Security Council Resolution 435, calling for free elections as the only way of resolving the dispute in Namibia. Martti Athisaari was appointed as the Secretary-General's Special Representative, and more than 8,000 UN personnel were deployed. UNTAG oversaw the transition and elections which culminated in Namibia becoming an independent state on 21 March 1990. The Namibian experience, in which the UN successfully acted as midwife in the birth process of a new state, indicated a new direction of involvement for the UN. In essence, it was a decolonization operation, but it extended to a wide range of aspects to become 'a highly successful process of peace-keeping, constitution making, and election (management)'.[53]

Even prior to the violence of April 1994, the UN was involved in Rwanda. Its involvement took the form of the UN Assistance Mission for Rwanda (UNAMIR).[54] Its function was to oversee a cease-fire agreement between the interim government of Rwanda and the Rwandan Patriotic Front (RPF). UNAMIR was woefully inadequate in preventing ethnic violence, or in intervening. In fact, its size was reduced. The UN's main contribution was made after the event, with the establishment of the International Criminal Tribunal for Rwanda (ICTR). This followed upon a request by the Security Council in 1994 that the Secretary-General establish an

---

[49] See R Brody, 'UN Peace-Keeping and Human Rights' (1994) 53 *The Review: International Commission of Jurists* 1, 1–2. According to him, the appointment of the UN's High Commissioner for Human Rights (UNHCR) as the first human rights 'executive' is another signal of this shift in emphasis.
[50] Boutros-Ghali (n 47 above) 113.
[51] Boutros-Ghali (n 47 above) 113 cites UNTAG (Namibia), ONUSAL (El Salvador), UNTAC (Cambodia), ONUMOZ (Mozambique), UNPROFOR, UNCRO (former Yugoslavia), and MINUGUA (Guatemala).   [52] Whittaker (n 43 above) 204–13.
[53] B Andemicael, 'Organisation of African Unity—UN Relations in a Changing World' in El-Ayouty (n 48 above) 119, 123.
[54] See M Sinjela, 'The UN and Internal Conflicts in Africa: A Documentary Survey' (1995) 3 *AYBIL* 318–62, and M Mubiala, 'L'Operation des Nations Unies pour les Droits de l'Homme au Rwanda' (1995) 3 *AYBIL* 277.

impartial Commission of Experts to investigate violations of human rights committed after 6 April 1994.[55] Independent from UNAMIR, the UN also launched a human rights operation. A few human rights observers were deployed in August 1994, and grew to some 90 by January 1996.[56] Their mandate included investigations into the human rights violations that occurred between April and July 1994.[57] In this respect, it assisted the work of the ICTR and also provided assistance to the Commission of Experts.

In addition, the data gathered by the human rights mission served as a source of information to the Special Rapporteur on Rwanda, Réné Degni-Sègui, and thematic rapporteurs concerned with the situation in Rwanda. The UN's involvement in Rwanda has undergone a shift in its approach. Initially, military objectives, such as peace-keeping and cease-fires, were the aim. These objectives were replaced by longer-lasting, prospective objectives, such as peace-building and the promotion of human rights. This illustrates a general shift in the UN away from 'peacekeeping' to a 'field approach', which entails continuous involvement at grassroots level.

Over the last decade or so, the Security Council's involvement in Africa has focused on Côte d'Ivoire, DRC, Liberia, Somalia, Western Sahara, and Sudan. Security Council-mandated missions employed in four of these countries are discussed below, indicating their relevance to the realization of human rights.[58]

After Siad Barré was ousted in 1991, a severe civil war erupted in Somalia. The UN dispatched an observer mission, the United Nations Observer Mission in Somalia (UNOSOM). After conditions necessitated its active involvement in providing a secure environment for humanitarian relief, the mission was strengthened and converted into the Unified Task Force (UNITAF). This changed the UN's role into peace-keeping. UNOSOM II was later established to assist in the process of reconciliation,[59] but inter-clan fighting persisted. UN peacekeepers were threatened and even attacked. This force was a failure, and withdrew in 1999. The Somali experience shows that the UN is powerless in situations where a state's infrastructure has broken down, and where the parties actively oppose its actions.

In Liberia, for the first time, the UN coordinated its efforts with that of a regional force already involved in a conflict. A number of West African states, under the auspices of the subregional economic community, the Economic Community of West African States (ECOWAS), established ECOWAS Cease-Fire Monitoring Group (ECOMOG). The ECOWAS intervention was arguably a result of reluctance on the part of the UNSC to become involved.[60] In 1993 the UN established the UN

---

[55] Resolution 935 (1994).   [56] Mubiala (n 54 above) 281.   [57] ibid.
[58] On the Security Council's general involvement in human rights, see SD Bailey, *The United Nations Security and Human Rights* (London: St Martin's, 1994).   [59] Sinjela (n 54 above) 195.
[60] M Weller (ed), *Regional Peacekeeping and International Enforcement: The Liberian Crisis* (Cambridge: Cambridge University Press, 1994) foreword (ix) (pointing out that the UNSC intervened only after ECOWAS, and contrasting its actions in respect of Liberia with greater vigour demonstrated in the ex-Yugoslavia).

Observer Mission in Liberia (UNOMIL) to work with ECOMOG towards the implementation of the Cotonou Peace Agreement signed between the Liberian parties.[61] Initially, the parties failed to abide by the agreement between them. The mandate of UNOMIL was extended time and again. By 1995 the parties had installed the Council of State and had re-established a cease-fire which appeared to be holding.

After a bloody relapse into violence in April 1996, democratic elections were eventually held in July 1997, leading to the discontinuation of UNOMIL. One of the 'ex-war lords', Charles Taylor, won the Presidential election when he secured more than 75 per cent of the vote.[62] The UN remained involved in subsequent developments, which required a second mission (UN Mission in Liberia (UNMIL)) to be established in 2003,[63] principally to oversee a cease-fire agreement. With the exile of Taylor to Nigeria in August 2003, the table was set for the return of stability and the election of Ellen Johnson-Sirleaf as the first female African head of state. Although gradually phased out, UNMIL remained involved in key aspects of consolidating state authority by, for example, ensuring the reintegration of former combatants and the restoration of effective government control over the country's natural and mineral resources.[64]

The aim of United Nations Mission for the Referendum in Western Sahara (MINURSO) is to assist in a referendum in which the inhabitants of the Western Sahara will be able to choose between independence and Moroccan rule. Its main activity, which is to identify and register potential voters, is being delayed by various technical and political factors, and this has resulted in the mandate of MINURSO being extended time and again. The referendum, initially planned for 1992, has not yet taken place.[65] The Security Council over the years has adopted numerous resolutions on, and remains seized with this situation.[66]

In response to the attacks on civilians by the government-backed militia called Janjaweed in the Darfur region of Sudan, the Security Council condemned 'all acts of violence and violations of human rights and international humanitarian law by all parties to the crisis, in particular by the Janjaweed, including indiscriminate attacks on civilians, rapes, forced displacements, and acts of violence especially those with an ethnic dimension', and expressed its utmost concern at the consequences of the conflict in Darfur on the civilian population, including women, children,

---

[61] For background information see F Ouguergouz, 'Liberia' (1994) 2 *AYBIL* 210 and Sinjela (n 54 above) 299–300.

[62] See 'At Last, Liberia has a President' (September 1997) *New African* 14–15.

[63] UN Doc SC Resolution 1509 (2003).

[64] UN Doc S/Resolution/1712 (2006), 29 September 2006.

[65] In April 1997, James Baker, newly appointed head of the UN mission, undertook a mission to the area. He cautioned that a final decision about the fate of the former Spanish colony is still far off ((1997) 34 *Africa Research Bulletin* 12635).

[66] In its most recent resolution, the UNSC reiterated its previous calls to 'the parties and states of the region to continue to cooperate fully with the UN to end the current impasse and to achieve progress towards a political solution' (UN Doc S/RES/1720 (2006) (31 October 2006).

internally displaced persons, and refugees.[67] It followed up this resolution with calls for strict compliance with its initial resolution.

The UN set up a mission, UNMIS, which was not deployed to Darfur. Although the African Union (AU) deployed a cease-fire observation mission in the form of the AU Mission in the Sudan (AMIS), its accomplishments were limited due to financial and logistical constraints. After the AU called for the transition of AMIS into a UN operation, the UNSC, acting under Chapter VII of the UN Charter, authorized the deployment of UNMIS to Darfur by 31 December 2006.[68] UNMIS would constitute a significant enlargement of forces (from just over 7,000 to more than 17,000) and is authorized to 'use all necessary means' among others, to protect civilians and to prevent the disruption of the Darfur Peace Agreement. Although it accepted the presence of AMIS, the Sudanese government did not consent to the deployment of a UN force.

Under article 39 of the UN Charter, the Security Council may invoke 'measures not involving the use of force' to ensure compliance with its decisions. Before 1990, sanctions were imposed on the white minority regimes in Southern Rhodesia and South Africa.[69] Since the end of the Cold War, sanctions have been imposed with greater regularity. Although the aim of these sanctions was related to the protection of human rights, sanctions themselves may also cause human rights violations.[70] For this reason, sanctions are usually specifically targeted at economic activity (such as an embargo on the import of oil from Sierra Leone, in 1997), or on travel (for example, in 1997 restrictions were imposed on UNITA flights, and on travel by members of the Sierra Leonean military junta and their families).[71] In the case of Sierra Leone, the Security Council responded to a request by ECOWAS,[72] underscoring the link between security at the global and regional levels.

Going beyond being passive recipients of the UN's peace-keeping and peace-building efforts, states themselves are increasingly regarded as having the 'duty to protect' people under their authority. The acceptance of this responsibility marks a shift away from *state* security to *human* security, and 'further qualifies' the notion of 'non-interference' in the 'domestic affairs' of states.[73]

---

[67] UN Doc SC Resolution 1556/2004 (30 July 2004).

[68] UN Doc SC Resolution 1706/2006 (31 August 2006).

[69] FAM Alting van Geusau, 'Recent and Problematic: The Imposition of Sanctions by the UN Security Council' in WJM van Genugten and GA de Groot (eds), *United Nations Sanctions: Effectiveness and Effects, Especially in the Field of Human Rights: A Multidisciplinary Approach* (Antwerp: Intersentia, 1999) 1, 7.

[70] See in this regard, General Comment 8 of the Committee on Economic, Social and Cultural Rights ('The Relationship between Economic Sanctions and Respect for Economic, Social and Cultural Rights' (1997)).

[71] DC Cotright and GA Lopez, *Sanctions and the Search for Security* (Boulder, Colo: Lynne Rienner, 2002) chs 4, 5, and 8.   [72] ibid 81.

[73] See NJ Schrijver, 'The Future of the Charter of the United Nations' (2006) 10 *Max Planck Ybk of United Nations L* 1, 23–5.

3 Economic and Social Council (ECOSOC)

One of the central institutions created by the Charter is the Economic and Social Council (ECOSOC). It consists of representatives from 54 UN member states[74] and may make recommendations to the UN General Assembly on a wide range of topics, including human rights matters.[75] ECOSOC was instructed to set up commissions to further the promotion of human rights.[76] These commissions include the UN Commission on Human Rights (UNCHR), the Sub-Commission on the Prevention of Discrimination and Protection of Minorities (later renamed the Sub-Commission on the Promotion and Protection of Human Rights), the Commission on the Status of Women, and the High Commissioner for Human Rights.

3.1 The UN Commission on Human Rights (UNCHR)/Human Rights Council (UNHRC)

One of the first actions undertaken by ECOSOC was setting up the UNCHR, as mandated by article 68 of the UN Charter.[77] The UNCHR did not consist of independent experts, but was made up of 54 'instructed governmental representatives' elected by ECOSOC irrespective of the human rights record of the states concerned.[78] As a consequence, states earmarked as some of the worst human rights violators served as members of the Commission.[79] The main accomplishment of the UNCHR was the elaboration and near-universal acceptance of the three major international human rights instruments: the Universal Declaration of Human Rights (1948), the ICCPR and ICESCR (1966).[80] The Commission was also instrumental in the process of drafting other human rights instruments, such as the Convention on the Elimination of All Forms of Racial Discrimination (CERD).

While the UNCHR initially worked primarily towards human rights promotion, it became increasingly involved in efforts to deal with human rights violations. On the basis of the 1235 procedure, its approach started off as country-oriented, with

---

[74] UN Charter, art 61(1). By the end of 2006, the following 14 African states served on ECOSOC; their terms end on 31 December of the year indicated in brackets: Angola (2008), Benin (2008), Chad (2007), Democratic Republic of the Congo (2007), Guinea (2007), Guinea-Bissau (2008), Madagascar (2008), Mauritania (2008), Mauritius (2006), Namibia (2006), Nigeria (2006), South Africa (2007), Tunisia (2006), Tanzania (2006). Retiring members are eligible for immediate re-election (UN Charter, art 61(2)).   [75] In terms of the UN Charter, art 62(2).

[76] UN Charter, art 68.

[77] In terms of this article, ECOSOC 'shall set up commissions in economic and social fields and for the promotion of human rights...' This was done in respect of the UNCHR in 1946.

[78] H Boekle, 'Western States, the UN Commission on Human Rights, and the "1235 Procedure": The "Question of Bias" Revisited' (1995) 13 *NQHR* 367, 368.

[79] In 2005, for example, the African members of the UNCHR included the 'human rights violators' Eritrea, the Sudan, and Zimbabwe, joining others in that category (China and Saudi Arabia) (H Scanlon, 'The Human Rights Council: From Human Rights to Responsibility?' in A Adebajo and H Scanlon (eds), *A Dialogue of the Deaf: Essays on Africa and the United Nations* (Auckland Park: Centre for Conflict Resolution, 2006) 131, 135).

[80] Sometimes referred to as the 'International Bill of Rights'.

the appointment of ad hoc rapporteurs, called 'Special Rapporteurs'. In the 1980s it broadened its approach to make provision for thematic rapporteurs, such as the Special Rapporteurs on religious intolerance and mercenarism. An 'ever expanding network' of working groups and rapporteurs serves as an important vehicle in the process of human rights realization.[81] Africa features prominently in the activities of most of these mechanisms. In the 1990s, the Commission started to emphasize a field approach, through the deployment of human rights 'field officers' in areas where human rights are under threat, thereby helping to restore faith in and rebuild state institutions.[82]

In his 2005 report, *In Larger Freedom*,[83] the Secretary-General called for the replacement of the UNCHR by a smaller, permanent, and human rights-compliant Council, able to fill the credibility gap left by states that used their Commission membership 'to protect themselves against criticism and to criticise others'.[84] The major reason for replacing the UNCHR is the very selective way in which it exercised its country-specific mandate, due mainly to the political bias of representatives and the ability of more powerful countries to deflect attention away from themselves and those enjoying their support.

In 2006, the General Assembly decided to follow the Secretary-General's recommendation, causing the Human Rights Council to replace the Commission on Human Rights.[85] There are some important differences between the UNCHR and the Human Rights Council. As a subsidiary organ of the UNGA, the Council enjoys an elevated status compared to the UNCHR, which was a functional commission of ECOSOC.

A discussion of the UNHRC is, therefore, better placed under the UNGA. It has a slightly smaller membership of 47, and its members are elected by an absolute majority of the UNGA (97 states). To avoid prolonged dominance by a few states, members may only be elected for two consecutive three-year terms. The Council serves as a 'standing' or permanent body,[86] and does not only meet for annual 'politically charged six week sessions', as the UNCHR did.[87] By 30 March 2007, the Council had held four sessions. Following the more human rights-sensitive selection criteria,[88] the list of states elected by the UNGA contrasts with the list of countries that, in 2006, served on the UNCHR. The UNGA may, by a two-thirds majority vote,

---

[81] T Buergenthal, *International Human Rights in a Nutshell* (St Paul, Minn: West Publishing, 2nd edn, 1995) 81. [82] Mubiala (n 54 above) 277.

[83] *In Larger Freedom: Towards Development, Security and Human Rights for All*, Report of the Secretary-General, UN Doc A/49/2005, 21 March 2005 (*In Larger Freedom*). [84] ibid 45.

[85] UN Doc A/RES/60/251, 3 April 2006, recommending to ECOSOC to 'abolish' the UNHRC on 16 June 2006, para 13.

[86] It 'shall meet regularly throughout the year and schedule no fewer than three sessions per year' (UN Doc A/RES/60/251, para 10).

[87] Explanatory note of the UNSG on the Human Rights Council, attached to *In Larger Freedom* (UN Doc A/59/205/Add.1, 23 May 2005).

[88] The UNGA is guided in the election process by the contribution of states to human rights and 'their voluntary pledges and commitments made thereto'; the UNGA may also suspend a state's membership for gross and systematic human rights violations by a two-thirds majority vote (UN Doc A/RES/60/251, para 8).

suspend a member that engages in 'gross and systematic human rights violations'. Reflecting 'equitable geographic distribution', the African and Asian regions together form a majority on the Council. Whether the Council will be able to exercise its mandate with greater 'objectivity and non-selectivity' than the UNCHR,[89] for example by initiating a system of universal periodic peer review, remains to be seen.

As far as African states are concerned, serving members of the UNCHR such as Mauritania, Sudan, and Zimbabwe, countries characterized by serious human rights violations, especially over the last few years, were not elected to the Council. The African membership, which stands at 13, comprises states with a relatively good human rights record and level of engagement with the UN treaty bodies: Algeria, Cameroon, Djibouti, Gabon, Ghana, Mali, Mauritius, Morocco, Nigeria, Senegal, South Africa, Tunisia, and Zambia.

At its first meeting in 2006, the Council decided to extend the mandates of the special mechanism and the Sub-Commission on the Promotion and Protection of Human Rights for one year, pending a comprehensive review. It also took two bold standard-setting steps. Without voting, the Council adopted the International Convention for the Protection of All Persons from Enforced Disappearance (ICED) and recommended its adoption by the General Assembly.[90] Once it has entered into force, this treaty will see the establishment of an eighth treaty body, the Committee on Enforced Disappearance.[91] Similar to existing treaty bodies, this Committee will have the mandate to examine state reports, to consider individual and inter-state communications against states accepting these optional procedures, and to undertake country visits. Its mandate to investigate and act upon requests 'that a disappeared person should be sought and found' represents an innovation as far as treaty bodies are concerned,[92] reflecting the practice of the Working Group on Enforced and Involuntary Disappearances.

The second standard-setting accomplishment of the Council is the adoption, after years of discussion, of the UN Declaration on the Rights of Indigenous Peoples, by a vote of 30 in favour, two against, and 12 abstentions. A minority of African states on the UNHRC (Cameroon, Mauritius, South Africa, and Zambia) voted in favour, while another six abstained. The remaining three states (Djibouti, Gabon, and Mali) were absent. However, when this matter was taken up by the UNGA's Third Committee, the African Group proposed that discussion of the Declaration should be deferred 'to allow time for further consultations'.[93] Even those African states that supported the adoption of the Declaration in the Council formed part of the majority in favour of deferral.

3.2 Complaints under ECOSOC Resolutions

As far as human rights violations are concerned, two different routes were used to approach the UNCHR: the 1235 and 1503 procedures. Through its special

---

[89] Guidance to the Council in UN Doc A/RES/60/251, para 4.
[90] Resolution 2006/1, 29 June 2006.   [91] ICED, art 26.   [92] ICED, art 30(1).
[93] UN Doc A/C.3/61/L.57/Rev.1. See also Ch 6.E.1 below.

procedures and country-specific discussions and resolutions, the Human Rights Council continues with the 1235 mandate; it also mandated the continuation of the confidential 1503 procedure.[94] Despite their weaknesses, the major strength of these procedures is that all member states of the UN are subject to scrutiny by the Commission, notwithstanding the fact that they may not have ratified any international human rights instruments.[95] Since its inception, the Council has been preoccupied with the situation in the Middle East, provoking criticism that it is neglecting human rights violations in other regions of the world,[96] especially in Africa. African support for this preoccupation reinforced the impression that AU member states have been taken in tow by the agenda of the Organization of Islamic Conference.

The 1235 Procedure

Despite the fact that large numbers of communications requesting UN intervention in human rights matters have been received since 1945, the UNCHR decided in 1947 that it had 'no power to act' on the basis of such complaints.[97] This position changed in 1967, when ECOSOC adopted resolution 1235, permitting the Commission to examine gross human rights violations.[98] The role that the situation of racial discrimination in South Africa played in the adoption of this resolution is immediately apparent from its wording. It provides that the Commission and its Sub-Commission is empowered to 'examine information relevant to gross violations of human rights and fundamental freedoms, as exemplified by the policy of *apartheid* as practised in the Republic of South Africa'.[99]

The 1235 procedure does not require the initiative of an individual complainant. In terms of this procedure, which is public and non-confidential, the Commission conducts country-based investigations of gross human rights violations. The approach taken could be confrontational, with the situation included as a 'violation' on the Commission's agenda; and may be taken one step further when a country-specific rapporteur is appointed; or it could be conciliatory, with the situation included on its agenda as part of 'technical support'.

The first African-specific investigations concerned situations of racial discrimination, colonial oppression, and the denial of self-determination. South Africa, setting the whole procedure in motion, was also the first African country to be investigated, and remained on the Commission's agenda from 1967 to 1995.[100] The

---

[94] Decision 2006/102, UN Doc A/HRC/1/L.10/Add.1 (30 June 2006).

[95] See eg J Kokott, 'The Protection of Fundamental Rights under German and International Law' (1996) 8 *RADIC* 347, 375.

[96] Human Rights Watch criticized the Council for not conducting public scrutiny of the situation in Uzbekistan, following the 'massacre of hundreds of unarmed protesters' in May 2005 (Human Rights Watch, 'UN: Rights Council Misses Opportunity on Uzbekistan', 3 October 2006).

[97] Buergenthal (n 81 above) 87; and I Nifosi, *The UN Special Procedures in the Field of Human Rights* (Antwerp: Intersentia, 2005) 8–10. [98] Adopted on 6 June 1967.

[99] Quoted Buergenthal (n 81 above) 89 (emphasis in original).

[100] Boekle tabulates 37 instances in which the UNCHR adopted 1235 procedure measures between 1967 and 1995, 14 of them involving African countries (Boekle (n 78 above) 378).

other two pre-1980 investigations also targeted countries in Southern Africa that still suffered under colonialism or its aftermath—Rhodesia and the Portuguese colonies—Angola and Mozambique. The Commission treated these situations as 'violations', and it appointed a country-specific special procedure for South Africa. A first attempt to discuss violations by independent African states was thwarted when the situation in Uganda was moved to a closed session in 1977.[101] Severe atrocities and human rights violations in a number of African countries, particularly the Central African Republic (CAR), Equatorial Guinea, and Uganda during the late 1970s and early 1980s caused the UNCHR to place these countries on its 1235 agenda. However, although they were treated as 'violations', no measures were taken in any of these instances.[102]

When the impasse of the Cold War was broken in the early 1990s, the situation in many more African states came to be discussed, leading to the adoption of country-specific special mechanisms in respect of Sudan (since 1993), DRC/Zaïre (since 1994), Rwanda (1995–2001), Burundi (since 1995), and Nigeria (1997–9).[103] African states reacted markedly differently to resolutions introduced by other African countries than to those initiated by Western states. Africa-initiated resolutions, dealing with 'less difficult situations', are usually adopted without a vote, and mostly lead to a greater willingness to cooperate on the part of the target state.[104]

In 2004, EU initiatives to have Zimbabwe's human rights record scrutinized were met by the African Group's resistance, expressed as disappointment at the 'non-consensual, confrontational, politically motivated' proposal.[105] Bolstered by China's warning that interference in the affairs of Africa should be avoided on the ground that African states 'know what was best for Africa',[106] the EU draft was rejected. As a result, the UNCHR did not adopt any resolution or take any other action related to Zimbabwe. Perceptions that these country-specific resolutions were biased and overly politicized were important justifications informing the reform of the UNCHR.

The 1503 Procedure

The other possibility is the 1503 procedure, established by ECOSOC Resolution 1503.[107] An individual complaining of a violation of his or her rights sets this process in motion. The Commission may act by conducting a thorough study or by appointing an ad hoc committee to investigate. Two factors minimize the role

---

[101] M Lempinen, *The United Nations Commission on Human Rights and the Different Treatment of Governments* (Abo: Abo Akademi Forlag, 2005) 148.

[102] ibid, Annex 9.

[103] See (June–July 1997) 18 *African Topics* 32. In the vote on the appointment of a Special Rapporteur on Nigeria, only two African states were amongst the 28 members in favour of the appointment. These states were South Africa and Uganda. Ten African states abstained, while three more or less neighbouring states (Benin, Gabon, and Zaire) joined China, Cuba, and Indonesia in voting against it.

[104] Lempinen (n 101 above) 174.

[105] ibid 153 (the South African representative speaking on behalf of the African Group).

[106] Quoted in Lempinen (n 101 above) 153.   [107] Adopted on 27 May 1970.

of the UNCHR in this regard. First, the procedure is shrouded in secrecy. Only the names of the relevant countries are announced after deliberations, without any details given. Secondly, the procedure comes into play only after domestic remedies have been exhausted and procedures prescribed in international or regional instruments, available to the individual, have been followed.

This procedure found application in the dictatorships of the Central African Empire/Republic, Equatorial Guinea, and Uganda, during the later 1970s, indirectly contributing to the adoption of an African regional human rights treaty in 1981.[108] In the 1970s and 1980s, the 1503 procedure was also applied to Benin, Burundi, Ethiopia, Gabon, Mali, Mozambique, Tanzania, and Zaire.[109] In the post-1990 era, the following African states featured on the UNCHR's 1503 agenda: Botswana, Chad, Congo, Djibouti, the Gambia, Kenya, Liberia, Mali, Nigeria, Rwanda, Sierra Leone, Somalia, Togo, Uganda, Zaire/DRC, Zambia, and Zimbabwe.[110]

The continuation of this procedure, under the Human Rights Council, has been dominated by debates about the conflict in the Middle East. During these discussions the African Group joined the Organization of the Islamic Conference (OIC) in condemning Israel. Arguably, as a consequence of their close association with the OIC agenda, African members do not sufficiently pursue Council involvement in urgent situations on the African continent. The Council first engaged with an African human rights situation when it devoted its fourth special session, in December 2006, to the situation in Darfur. Responding to the initiative of European and WEOG states,[111] the African Group proposed amendments to a proposed resolution omitting the word 'gross' from the description of human rights violations in Darfur; and inserting a call to the international community (including the donor countries) to 'provide urgent and adequate financial and technical assistance' to the Sudanese government.[112] After an intensive debate, including differences of view about the composition of a high-level mission to assess the human rights situation in Darfur, unanimity was reached about a final text. In the adopted resolution, the Council expresses its concern about 'the seriousness of the human and humanitarian situation', and decides to 'dispatch' a High-Level Mission to assess the human rights situation and the needs of Sudan, comprising 'five highly qualified persons', to be appointed by the President of the Council.[113] Unfortunately, Sudan did not allow the mission to enter its territory. At its fourth

---

[108] With respect to Equatorial Guinea, see 'Commentaries' (1980) 24 *The Review: International Commission of Jurists* 34.

[109] <http://www.ohchr.org/english/bodies/chr/stat1.htm> (30 November 2006).

[110] ibid.

[111] Draft resolution, 'The Human Rights Situation in Darfur' (UN Doc A/HRC/S-4/L.1 (4 December 2006)).

[112] 'La situation des droits de l'homme au Darfur: Algeria (au nom du Groupe africaine): amendements au projet de résolution A/HRC/S-4/L.1' (UN Doc A/HRC/S-4/L.3 (11 December 2006)); and 'Algeria (on behalf of the African Group): draft resolution' (UN Doc A/HRC/S-4/L.2 (6 December 2006)).

[113] Human Rights Council, Decision S-4/101 (Situation of Human Rights in Darfur).

session, the UNHRC expressed regret about this lack of cooperation, and called on the Special Rapporteur on Sudan to continue efforts, together with other UN mechanisms, the Sudanese government, and the AU's 'appropriate human rights mechanisms', to work towards a solution.

3.3 Special Mechanisms

A first fact-finding body, the ad hoc Working Group of Experts on Human Rights in Southern Africa, was appointed in 1967.[114] Following its successful use in focusing attention on the phenomenon of 'disappeared' persons, especially under the Chilean dictatorship during the 1970s, the 1980s saw a multiplication of fact-finding mechanisms mandated to investigate country situations and thematic issues of broader concern. As these mechanisms developed incrementally, and do not form part of a holistic design, there is no standard fact-finding procedure or format. Attempts to formalize such a uniform code have bent the knee to the reality of the diversity of institutions and aims, as well as the need for flexibility. Special mechanisms are divided into two broad categories: country-specific and thematic rapporteurs. In general terms, these mechanisms ensure that the UN's radar screen of concern focuses on pertinent places and issues of concern. The mechanisms may receive and react to complaints; they may undertake visits to countries; and they conduct studies and report to the UNHRC/UNHRC. Country visits require an invitation of consent from the state to be visited. Although agreements may be reached on an ad hoc basis, visits are easier to organize and more likely in respect of states that have issued a 'standing invitation', allowing visits by all special mechanisms. By 31 July 2006, only two African states (Sierra Leone and South Africa) had issued a 'standing invitation'.[115] The lack of 'standing invitations' by African states reinforces the perception of their *rightorical* commitment to international scrutiny. However, special mechanisms are not completely dependent on invitations, as they may rely on other sources of information to investigate a particular theme or situation in a specific state.

Country Rapporteurs

Over the years, the UNCHR appointed numerous individuals (called Special Rapporteurs or Independent Experts) to study and report on the human rights situation in specific countries. The decision to expose a particular state to this mechanism has become extremely politicized, and the exclusion of states with significant international clout was one of the recurring criticisms against the Commission. Usually, a country rapporteur's mandate is for one year. According to the most recent information available, five of the 13 UN country rapporteurs are assigned

---

[114] See K Herndl, 'Recent Developments concerning United Nations Fact-Finding in the Field of Human Rights' in M Nowak, D Steurer, and H Tretter (eds), *Progress in the Spirit of Human Right: Festschrift für Felix Ermacora* (Kehl: Engel, 1988) 9.

[115] A total of 55 states had done so, see <http://www.ohchr.org/english/bodies/chr/special/invitations.htm> (30 November 2006).

to African states, namely, Burundi, the DRC, Liberia, Somalia, and Sudan. There can be little doubt that each of these situations merits international concern.

Thematic Rapporteurs and Working Groups

Most of the 28 UN special thematic mechanisms reflect pertinent African preoccupations. Even if most African states did not issue 'standing invitations' to the special mechanism, a number of states have allowed visits by thematic rapporteurs. In 2005, for example, nine such visits took place: the Special Rapporteur on the Right to Education went to Botswana;[116] the Special Rapporteur on Migrants visited Burkina Faso;[117] the Independent Expert on Economic Reform Policies and Foreign Debt undertook a visit to Mozambique;[118] the Special Rapporteur on the Right to Food undertook a visit to Niger;[119] Nigeria received visits by no fewer than three special mechanisms, by the Special Rapporteur on Freedom of Religion or Belief, the Special Representative of the Secretary General on Human Rights Defenders, and the Special Rapporteur on Extrajudicial, Summary or Arbitrary Executions; Sudan hosted the Representative of the Secretary-General on Internally Displaced Persons (IDPs);[120] and the Special Rapporteur on the Right to Health (SRH) visited Uganda. Two further visits took place to South Africa under its 'standing invitation'.[121]

In an earlier visit of the SRH to Mozambique, in December 2003, the link between poverty, discrimination, and stigma was highlighted. As part of the recommendations, and demonstrating the overlap of these issues, the SRH requested that the Mozambican Ministry of Health set up an independent review of user fees, with technical support from WHO, 'to determine whether user fees impede access, especially for those living in poverty, women and other disadvantaged groups'.[122] The SRH's report contains some encouraging indications of better integration within the UN system, not only by making a link to the WHO, but also by referring to cooperation with the UNDP and OHCHR. As this report deals mainly with obstacles at the 'national level', the report of the subsequent visit by the Independent Expert on Economic Reform Policies and Foreign Debt provides a commendable supplementary focus on the obstacles at the 'international level'.[123]

The UN Independent Expert on the Question of Human Rights and Extreme Poverty studies best practices to combat poverty.[124] In the exercise of her mandate, the Independent Expert has so far visited five African countries: Algeria, Benin, Burundi, the DRC, and Sudan.[125] Drawing on her experience of these visits, she

---

[116] 26 September–4 October.   [117] 2–9 February.   [118] 25–29 July.

[119] UN Doc E/CN.4/2006/44; the visit took place 8–12 July 2005.

[120] 27 February–7 March, 3–12 May, and 27 June–8 July 2005, respectively.

[121] The Working Group on Arbitrary Detention (4–19 September 2005) and the Special Rapporteur on the Human Rights of Indigenous People (28 July–8 August 2005).

[122] UN Doc E/CN.4/2005/51/Add.2 (4 January 2005) para 52.

[123] UN Doc E/CN.4/2005/51/Add.2, para 2.

[124] Established in 1988 (Human Rights Commission Resolution 1998/25).

[125] UN Doc E/CN.4/2004/43; 29 February 2004.

recommended the following seven measures to guide governments in their efforts to eradicate poverty: (1) Infrastructure is required to realize socio-economic rights. Budgets have to be redirected from military spending towards education and health,[126] allowing access to schools and health care, which is identified as 'essential'.[127] (2) Legislation has to be put in place to create a social security system covering health risks, loss of employment, and retirement,[128] and to guarantee a minimum income.[129] (3) Weak state structures, and 'sometimes the complete absence of such a structure',[130] are major contributors to extreme poverty. It is at the internal level of state restructuring, ensuring a functional civil service, that the solution lies, and not at the global level of free trade and open markets.[131] (4) Women's 'capacity to act in society' must be enhanced at all levels.[132] (5) Micro-credit schemes should be an essential component of policies to combat poverty.[133] (6) Governance should be decentralized, as it presents the 'only effective administrative arrangement that allows the poorest to express themselves'.[134] (7) The individual's right 'to existence', as manifested in birth registration and the issuing of identity cards, should be ensured as part of recognizing the civil status of everyone.[135]

Formally forming part of the UN Charter-based thematic special mechanisms, the Working Group on Arbitrary Detention 'adopts a methodology more akin to that of treaty bodies with competence over individual communications',[136] and has interpreted its mandate to become a 'fully-fledged supervisory mechanism outside the specific human rights treaties'.[137] Adopting 'quasi-judicial' working methods similar to those of corresponding treaty bodies, the Working Group on Arbitrary Detention has finalized a huge number of complaints, euphemistically termed 'opinions', and has made many 'urgent appeals' to states. In 2005 alone, it adopted 48 'opinions' concerning 115 persons in 30 countries; and transmitted a total of 181 urgent appeals concerning 565 individuals to 56 governments.[138]

Two communications considered against African governments in 1994 illustrate the functioning and potential effect of the Working Group. Two citizens of the then Zaire addressed a communication to the Working Group concerning their detention without trial because of their opposition to the Mobutu regime.[139] When the government failed to respond to a request for information, the Working Group was left with no option but to proceed on the available information. After investigating the facts, the Working Group found that the detention was arbitrary, in contravention of articles 19 and 20 of the Universal Declaration and of articles 19 and 22 of the ICCPR. It then requested the government of Zaire to 'take the

---

[126] Para 20.   [127] Para 25.   [128] Para 21.   [129] Para 24.   [130] Para 22.
[131] Para 22.   [132] Para 26.   [133] Para 27.   [134] Para 31.   [135] Para 42.
[136] J Fitzpatrick, 'Human Rights Fact-Finding' in AF Bayefsky (ed), *The UN Human Rights Treaty System in the 21st Century* (The Hague: Kluwer Law International, 2000) 65, 77; F Viljoen, "Fact-Finding by UN Human Rights Complaints Bodies—Analysis and Suggested Reforms' (2004) 8 *Max Planck Ybk of United Nations L* 49, 76–80.
[137] B Rudolf, 'The Thematic Rapporteurs and Working Groups of the United Nations Commission on Human Rights' (2000) 4 *Max Planck Ybk of United Nations L* 297, 319.
[138] UN Doc E/CN.4/2006/7/Add.1 (19 October 2005).
[139] See Decision 4/1994 (Zaire), UN doc E/CN.4/1995/31/Add.1, 59–60.

necessary steps to remedy the situation in order to bring it into conformity with'
the principles and provisions of the Universal Declaration and the ICCPR.[140] In a
decision taken in September 1994, the Working Group found that two senior
members of the South African National Congress (ANC) had been arbitrarily
detained prior to the formation of the 'popular Government'.[141] It requested the
new government to 'take note of this decision' and to 'take such appropriate steps
as it considers necessary to remedy the situation in order to bring it into conformity' with the provisions of the above-mentioned human rights instruments.[142]

Since 2000, 'opinions' have been issued mostly against China and the USA. In
Africa, countries in the North, in particular Algeria, Egypt, Libya, Morocco, and
Tunisia, featured prominently, although arbitrary detention in some other coun-
tries also led to the adoption of 'opinions'.[143]

The intensity and persistence of the Working Group's follow-up procedure
make it one of the best examples of a special mechanism that secures results, also in
respect of African states. In a number of cases against African states, the Working
Group not only noted compliance with its request to provide it with information
within 90 days of its 'opinion',[144] but also noted the release of the 'victims'.[145] The
only exception seems to be Libya, from which the Working Group did not receive
any information.

With the consent of states, the Working Group undertakes country visits.
Disappointingly, only one of the 21 visits so far has been to an African state—South
Africa. In its report on that visit, the Working Group noted advances in the criminal justice system, but expressed its concerns about the high rate of incarceration;
the fact that the 'situation of pretrial detainees is worse than that for convicts,
particularly when they are held in police cells'; the high rate of police brutality,
including the deaths of suspects in custody; and the detention of foreigners in the
Lindela Repatriation Centre, which does not meet international standards.[146]

The Working Group of Experts on People of African Descent was established
in 2002.[147] Its establishment is an acknowledgement of the manifestation of racial

---

[140] Para 9 of Decision 4/1994 (Zaïre) (18 May 1994).
[141] Decision 15/1994 (South Africa), UN doc E/CN.4/1995/31/Add. 2, 14–15.
[142] Para 8 of Decision 15/1994 (28 September 1994).
[143] Other African states that featured during this period are Cameroon, CAR, Chad, Djibouti,
Eritrea, Ethiopia, Equatorial Guinea, Madagascar, Nigeria, and Rwanda.
[144] See eg Opinion 5/2005, *El-Derini v Egypt*, 24 May 2005, UN Doc E/CN.4/2006/7/Add.1
(19 October 2005) paras 2 and 4; Opinion 36/2005, *Samaali v Tunisia*, 2 September 2005, UN Doc
E/CN.4/2006/7/Add.1 (19 October 2005) para 2.
[145] See eg Opinion 23/2004, *El Ghoul v Algeria*, 26 November 2004, para 3, where the Working
Group noted that 'the Government has informed it that on 24 November 2004 the Djelfa court ordered
the release of the above-mentioned person and that this order was carried out on the same day.' (UN
Doc E/CN.4/2006/7/Add.1 (19 October 2005)); see also the *note verbale* dated 8 November 2005, in
which the Permanent Mission of Egypt to the United Nations Office at Geneva reported, in connection
with Opinion 5/2005 (Egypt), that Mr Mohamed Ramadan Mohamed Hussein El-Derini had been
released on 19 June 2005 (UN Doc E/CN.4/2006/7/Add.1, 19 October 2005, 'Government Reactions
to Opinions', para 15).
[146] UN Doc E/CN.4/2006/7/Add.3 (29 December 2005) paras 84 and 85.
[147] Established by Commission on Human Rights Resolution 2002/68 (25 April 2002).

discrimination against people of African descent, as highlighted in the Durban Declaration and Programme of Action.[148] Paragraph 7 of the Durban Programme of Action specifically 'requests the Commission on Human Rights to consider establishing a working group or other mechanism of the United Nations to study the problems of racial discrimination faced by people of African descent living in the African Diaspora and make proposals for the elimination of racial discrimination against people of African descent'. Its reports so far reveal an engagement with racism and access to education, administration of justice, employment, housing and health, particularly in Western European countries and the USA.[149]

4 Judicial Organs: Ending Individual Impunity for Grave Human Rights Violations

The increasing judicialization of international law forms part of ongoing efforts to improve the implementation of international law standards.[150] Although there is no international human rights court,[151] concerns for human rights, especially gross human rights violations, have found their way into the jurisprudence of courts with a more general mandate, such as the International Court of Justice (ICJ), and led to the establishment of courts specifically targeting impunity for gross human rights violations (such as the International Criminal Tribunal for Rwanda (ICTR), Special Court for Sierra Leone (SCSL) and the International Criminal Court (ICC)). The SCSL and the ICC are included in the discussion, despite not officially being part of the UN, because they have come about and operate in close collaboration with the UN.

4.1 International Court of Justice (ICJ)

The UN's principal judicial organ, the ICJ, to a limited extent involves itself in human rights matters in the exercise of its advisory and contentious mandates generally,[152] but also with respect to Africa, specifically.[153] Three Africans also

---

[148] Adopted at the Conference on Racism, Racial Discrimination, Xenophobia and Related Intolerance, which took place in Durban in 2001.

[149] UN Docs E/CN.4/2003/21; E/CN.4/2004/21; E/CN.4/2005/21.

[150] See generally eg T Buergenthal, 'Proliferation of International Courts and Tribunals: Is it Good or Bad?' (2001) 14 *Leiden J of Intl L* 267.

[151] Some see the establishment of such a court as an end-development of current trends, or as an ideal (T Buergenthal, 'A Court and Two Consolidated Treaty Bodies' in AF Bayefsky, *The UN Human Rights Treaty System in the 21st Century* (The Hague: Kluwer Law International, 2000) 299, 301.

[152] See eg on its advisory mandate, *Difference relating to Immunity from Legal Process of Special Rapporteur of the Commission on Human Rights* [1999] ICJ Rep 62 (29 April 1999); and *Legal Consequences of the Construction of a Wall in the Occupied Palestinian Territory*, judgment of 9 July 2004; and on its contentious mandate, *Barcelona Traction, Light and Power Company, Limited (New Application: 1962) (Belgium v Spain)* [1970] ICJ Rep 3 (5 February 1970) (human rights obligations *erga omnes*), and *Application of the Convention on the Prevention and Punishment of the Crime of Genocide (Bosnia and Herzegovina v Serbia and Montenegro)*, judgment of 26 February 2007.

[153] See, in general, TO Elias, *Africa and the Development of International Law* (Dordrecht: Martinus Nijhoff, 2nd edn, 1988) (2nd edn ed and rev by R Akinjibe) ch 5.

serve among the 15 ICJ judges: Mohamed Bennouna (Morocco) (whose term ends on 5 February 2015); Abdul G Koroma (Sierra Leone) (whose term ends in 2012); Raymond Ranjeva (Madagascar) (whose term ends in 2009).

Although the ICJ does not individualize findings of violations (either as far as the violator or the victim is concerned), and notwithstanding its dependence on states (rather than individual 'victims') for the submission of cases, ICJ judgments may have a close bearing on human rights. Two advisory opinions, in particular, affirmed the right of self-determination of the people of the Western Sahara,[154] and Namibia.[155] However, as far as its decisions in territorial disputes are concerned,[156] the ICJ's application of the *uti possidetis* principle amounts to the 'settlement' of people within fixed territories, rather than the 'seeking of territorial settlement'.[157] Differently stated, it amounts to the territory determining the 'fate of the people', rather than the people determining the 'fate of the territory'.[158]

As far as the Court's contentious jurisdiction regarding human rights is concerned, three cases are highlighted. In *Arrest Warrant of 11 April 2000 (Democratic Republic of the Congo v Belgium)*,[159] the Court accepted the argument by the DRC that Belgium's attempts at prosecuting Mr Yerodia Ndombasi under the Geneva Conventions and Protocols thereto, violated international law because he was at the time of the indictment the incumbent Minister of Foreign Affairs. In the second case, the conflict in the DRC gave rise to a finding by the ICJ not only that Uganda violated international human rights law (including the African Charter)[160] and international humanitarian law on Congolese territory, particularly in the Ituri province,[161] but also that the DRC violated the Vienna Convention on Diplomatic Relations when its forces attacked the Ugandan Embassy at Ndjili International Airport.[162] Although cloaked as an application for 'diplomatic protection', in the third case, Guinea instituted what amounts to an inter-state complaint on the basis of human rights violations against the DRC.[163] Guinea claims that its national, Diallo, was unjustly imprisoned for two-and-a-half months, and 'despoiled' of his property and bank accounts.

---

[154] *Advisory Opinion on Western Sahara* [1975] ICJ Rep 12.

[155] *Legal Consequences for States of the Continued Presence of South Africa in Namibia (South West Africa) Notwithstanding Security Council Resolution 276 (1970)* [1971] ICJ Rep 16.

[156] See eg *Case concerning the Frontier Dispute (Burkina Faso/Mali)* [1986] ICJ Rep 554.

[157] J Castellino and S Allen, *Title to Territory in International Law: A Temporal Analysis* (Aldershot: Ashgate, 2003) 114.

[158] Dillard J, separate opinion in the *Western Sahara* case [1975] ICJ Rep 12, 116.

[159] Judgment of 14 February 2002.

[160] African Charter, arts 4 and 5; *Armed Activities on the Territory of the Congo (DRC v Uganda)* (19 December 2005) para 219.

[161] *Armed Activities on the Territory of the Congo (DRC v Uganda)* (19 December 2005) paras 205–21.   [162] ibid, finding on Uganda's second counter-claim, paras 306–44.

[163] *Ahmadou Sadio Diallo (Republic of Guinea v Democratic Republic of the Congo)*, instituted in 1998, but not yet finalized.

4.2 International Criminal Tribunal for Rwanda (ICTR)

On 8 November 1994, acting under Chapter VII of the UN Charter, the UN
Security Council established an international tribunal, the ICTR, to prosecute
and punish individuals responsible for genocide and other serious violations of
international humanitarian law committed in Rwanda between 1 January and
31 December 1994.[164] The ICTR had by early 2007 finalized 27 trials in the first
instance, while 36 accused persons were either being tried or awaited trials.[165] The
Court's completion strategy envisages that all current and other outstanding cases
will be finalized by the end of 2008.[166] Cases that cannot be dealt with are transferred to states that express a willingness to prosecute suspects. In identifying which
cases to transfer, the ICTR has adopted the yardstick of prosecuting those bearing
the 'greatest responsibility',[167] in that respect mirroring the Special Court for
Sierra Leone. The fact that some cases are also transferred to Rwanda is problematic, given the possibility of imposing the death penalty in Rwanda, the delay in
trying suspects in that jurisdiction, and the relative unpredictability of the *gacaca*
process.[168]

   This Tribunal followed in the footsteps of, and was institutionally linked to, the
International Criminal Tribunal for the Former Yugoslavia (ICTY), established in
1993.[169] Although the ICTY was the first truly international tribunal to prosecute
serious violations of international humanitarian law, the ICTR extends the ambit
of the ICTY's protection. While the ICTY covers violations arising from an international armed conflict, the ICTR was created to deal with violations arising from
internal (non-international) conflict.[170]

   Not only the creation of the ICTR, but also its functioning, has contributed
to enriching international humanitarian and human rights law.[171] The ICTR
became, in *The Prosecutor v Jean Kambanda*,[172] the first court to find an individual

---

[164] UN Doc S/RES/955 (1994), adopted by 13 votes to 1 (Rwanda), with 1 abstention. The Statute
of the ICTR is annexed to the Resolution. The Statute provides that Rwandan citizens responsible for
violations 'committed in the territory of neighbouring states' may also be subjected to the jurisdiction of
the ICTR (ICTR Statute, art 1).

   [165] Letter to the President of the ICTR to the President of the Security Council, 1 June 2006, UN
Doc S/2066/358.

   [166] The SC extended the terms of the 11 permanent and the *ad litem* judges to 31 December 2008
(UN Docs S/RES/1684(2006), 13 June 2006; S/RES/1717(2006), 13 October 2006).

   [167] See 'Completion strategy of the ICTR', attached to the letter of the President of the ICTR to
the Security Council, UN Doc S/2006/358 (1 June 2006), para 35.

   [168] See eg IP Gaparayi, 'Justice and Social Reconstruction in the Aftermath of the Genocide in
Rwanda: An Evaluation of the Possible Role of the *Gacaca* Tribunals' (2001) 1 *AHRLJ* 78.

   [169] UN Doc S/RES/827 (1993).

   [170] Art 3 common to the 1949 Geneva Conventions and the 1977 Additional Protocol II is included
in the jurisdiction of the ICTR (art 4 of the Statute of the ICTR) and not in that of the ICTY. See also
RS Lee, 'The Rwanda Tribunal' (1996) 9 *Leiden J of Intl L* 37, 38.

   [171] M Mubiala, *Le Système Régional Africain de Protection des Droits de l'Homme* (Brussels: Bruylant,
2005) 199.

   [172] Case ICTR-97-23-S (4 September 1998); (1998) 37 ILM 1411; <http://www.ictr.org>
(1 February 2001).

(and a head of government, at that) guilty of the crime of genocide. This decision brought to life the Convention on the Prevention and Punishment of the Crime of Genocide,[173] which had remained largely a dead letter since 1948. It should be recalled that it was proposed during the deliberation of this Convention that a court be created to implement its provisions. As a result of a compromise, no implementing mechanism was brought into existence. This judgment could serve as an important precedent for the International Criminal Court (ICC). In *The Prosecutor v Jean-Paul Akayesu*,[174] an international court for the first time applied the crime of rape in an international context. Initially, the indictment against Jean-Paul Akayesu did not contain specific charges of sexual crimes. An amendment to the indictment, in 1997, added a count of a crime against humanity (rape),[175] setting out allegations that displaced Tutsi women, who had sought refuge at the *bureau communal*, were repeatedly subjected to sexual violence. Jean-Paul Akayesu, it was further alleged, knew of and encouraged the commission of these crimes. When these allegations were proven, the ICTR Chamber found Akayesu guilty of a crime against humanity. However, the Court went even further by finding, of its own accord, that the same acts also constituted genocide.[176] Article 2(2) of the ICTR Statute does not refer explicitly to sexual crimes, but makes reference to acts 'deliberately inflicting on the group conditions of life calculated to bring about its physical destruction in whole or in part'.[177] The Tribunal concluded that the rapes met this requirement.[178] This decision has been singled out for its 'immense factual and jurisprudential importance'.[179] It stands as the first instance of rape being included as part of the definition of genocide. Stated differently, it has now been established that rape may be committed with genocidal intent.

4.3 Special Court for Sierra Leone (SCSL)

Established by an Agreement between the United Nations and the Government of Sierra Leone pursuant to a Security Council resolution,[180] the SCSL is a hybrid 'international-national' court. The SCSL may prosecute crimes both under international law, such as crimes against humanity and violations of international humanitarian law,[181] and crimes under domestic Sierra Leonean law.[182] The mixed nature of the Court is further reflected in the appointment of judges to both trial courts

---

[173] Adopted on 9 December 1948 and entered into force on 12 January 1951.

[174] ICTR 96–4-T (2 September 1998), <http://www.ictr.org> (1 February 2001). Summary of case (1998) 37 ILM 1399; (1999) 11 *RADIC* 336.

[175] PJ Magnarella, 'Some Milestones and Achievements at the International Criminal Tribunal for Rwanda: The 1998 *Kambanda, Akayesu* Cases' (1998) 11 *Florida J of Intl L* 517, 532.

[176] Paras 731, 734 of the judgment.　　[177] ICTR Statute, art 2(2)(c).

[178] Paras 731, 734 of the judgment ('Sexual violence was an integral part of the process of destruction, specifically targeting Tutsi women and specifically contributing to their destruction and to the destruction of the Tutsi group as a whole').　　[179] Magnarella (n 175 above) 537.

[180] Resolution 1315 (2000), 14 August 2000.　　[181] Statute of the SCSL, arts 2 and 3.

[182] Such as offences under the Prevention of Cruelty to Children Act, 1926 (Cap 31) and the Malicious Damage Act, 1861 (Statute of the SCSL, art 5).

and the Appeals Chamber,[183] and in the composition of Court staff.[184] Imprisonment shall be served in Sierra Leone.[185] In all these respects, aimed at ensuring a more immediate and visible process resonating with the Sierra Leonean people, the SCSL differs from the ICTR and builds on some of the lessons learnt from it. The UN's involvement is illustrated in the appointment by the Secretary-General of the majority of judges, the Prosecutor and Registrar, and in the obligation on the SCSL to submit an annual report to the SG.[186] A Group of Interested States (GIS) appoints a Management Committee, consisting of a group of states and members of the UN Secretariat to oversee the non-judicial operations of the Court. The SCSL is financed by these interested states, with the greatest contributions coming from the USA, the Netherlands, and the UK.[187]

The Court may indict suspects who 'bear the greatest responsibility for serious violations of international humanitarian law and Sierra Leonean law committed in the territory of Sierra Leone since 30 November 1996'.[188] Interpreting the term 'greatest responsibility' narrowly to refer only to those political leaders who masterminded, caused, and sustained the war, the Prosecutor issued a limited number of indictments.[189] By 30 April 2007, the trials of nine suspects are ongoing in four separate trials. In one trial, three leaders of the Armed Forces Revolutionary Council (AFRC) are prosecuted together, in another, two leaders of the Civil Defence Forces (CDF) (down from three after the death by natural causes of Hinga Norman), in a third, three leaders of the Revolutionary United Front (RUF). The fourth trial, which has been transferred to The Hague, is that of former Liberian President Charles Taylor. Although Taylor was indicted in 2003 on counts of war crimes, crimes against humanity, and other serious violations of international humanitarian law, he was only arrested in 2006. Following authorization to this effect by the President of the Court,[190] his trial was transferred to The Hague. An eleventh person, who also was a leader of the AFRC, Johnny Paul Koroma, has been indicted. Although his whereabouts and fate are unknown, the indictment against him remains in force.

Although no case had been finalized by 31 December 2006, the SCSL gave numerous judgments on a plethora of motions. In a notable example dealing with an important element of human rights,[191] the SCSL had to decide whether the

---

[183] Statute of the SCSL, art 12(1): 'the government of Sierra Leone appoint 1 of 3 trails judges and 2 of 5 members of the Appeals Chamber. At present, Justice King, a Sierra Leonean, serves as president of the Court'.

[184] The UN SG appoints the Court's Prosecutor, who is assisted by a 'Sierra Leonean Deputy-Prosecutor' (Statute of the SCSL, art 15(4)).

[185] Statute of the SCSL, art 22. However, an undertaking has been given that Taylor will serve any term of imprisonment in the UK.   [186] Statute of the SCSL, arts 12(1), 16(3) and 26.

[187] First Annual Report of the President of the Special Court for Sierra Leone for the period 2 December 2002–1 December 2003, 37.   [188] Statute of the SCSL, art 1(1).

[189] <www.sc-sl.org> (30 September 2006).

[190] The Security Council took note of and welcomed this development, UN Doc S/RES/1688 (2006).

[191] Decision on Preliminary Motion Based on the Lack of Jurisdiction (Child Recruitment), SCSL-2004–14-AR72(E), 31 May 2004.

recruitment of children under 15 into the armed forces was a crime under customary international law by November 1996.[192] The defence argued that, because the Rome Statute criminalized child recruitment for the first time only in 1998,[193] the charge against the accused should be struck from the indictment as its inclusion violates the *nullum crimen sine lege* principle. Observing that a norm does not need to be expressly included in an international treaty for it to 'crystallize as a crime under international customary law',[194] the majority found sufficient national legislation and state practice of child recruitment being criminalized prior to 1996, to justify a finding that dismissed the defence's challenge.[195]

Drawing a distinction between 'child enlistment', for which the accused had been indicted, and child 'recruitment',[196] which had been removed from the charge sheet, Justice Robertson was not persuaded by any of the material before the Court that a majority of states explicitly criminalized child enlistment or instituted any prosecutions on that charge.[197] He therefore concluded, in a dissenting judgment, that 'non-forcible enlistment did not enter international criminal law until the Rome Statute in July 1998'.[198] In a sparsely veiled critical nudge at the majority, Justice Robertson reiterated that the principle of *nullum crimen sine lege* must be upheld most stringently in respect of deeply shocking acts, so as to ensure that 'a defendant is not convicted out of disgust rather than evidence, or of a non-existent crime'.[199] The majority judgment has been welcomed for aligning 'international humanitarian law with more general human rights protections'.[200]

4.4 International Criminal Court (ICC)

Although it was established by a United Nations conference (the UN Diplomatic Conference of Plenipotentiaries on the Establishment of an International Criminal Court), the ICC is not a UN organ. Its existence is derived from a separate legal instrument, the Rome Statute of the International Criminal Court,[201] which binds only those states that formally ratify or accede to the Statute. As of 31 December 2006, of the 104 state parties, 29 were from Africa.[202] Despite being distinct and independent institutions, the links between the ICC and the UN are well-developed.[203]

---

[192] Statute of the SCSL, art 4(c).   [193] Statute of the ICC, art 8(xxvi).
[194] Judgment, para 38.   [195] Judgment, paras 45–51.
[196] Dissenting Opinion of Justice Robertson, para 1.   [197] ibid, para 22.
[198] ibid, para 47.   [199] ibid, para 12.
[200] N Novogrodsky and M Goldstein, 'Small Steps: Prosecuting the Recruitment of Child Soldiers—The Case of *Sam Hinga Norman*' (2006) 15 *Interights Bulletin* 148, 149.
[201] Adopted in Rome, Italy on 17 July 1998; entered into force on 1 July 2002.
[202] These states are, in order of acceptance of the Statute: Burkina Faso, Senegal, Ghana, Mali, Lesotho, Botswana, Sierra Leone, Gabon, South Africa, Nigeria, CAR, Benin, Mauritius, DRC, Niger, Uganda, Namibia, Gambia, Tanzania, Malawi, Djibouti, Zambia, Guinea, Congo, Burundi, Liberia, Kenya, Comoros, and Chad.
[203] See the Relationship Agreement between the United Nations and the International Criminal Court, UN Doc A/58/874, annex; and the annual report of the ICC to the UN General Assembly.

The ICC Statute entered into force on 1 July 2002. So far, Africa has dominated the Court's agenda.[204] The Office of the Prosecutor has investigated three situations referred to the Court by African states (the CAR, DRC, and Uganda), and the first situation referred to it by the UN Security Council under article 13(b) of the Statute (Darfur, Sudan).[205] Due to the lack of cooperation by the Sudanese government, investigations have been hampered. It has become clear that the Security Council will have to strengthen the Court's efforts to ensure that the referral does not become a dead letter.[206]

The first arrest warrants, issued on 8 July 2005, were for five members of the Lord's Resistance Army (LRA), who for many years terrorized the civilian population of Northern Uganda: Joseph Kony, Vincent Otti, Okot Odhiambo, Dominic Ongwen, and Raska Lukwiya. They are charged with crimes against humanity and war crimes, including murder, sexual enslavement, intentionally attacking civilians, pillaging, rape, cruel treatment of civilians, and the forced enlistment of child soldiers, but have not been arrested. In an attempt to include the LRA in the ongoing Ugandan peace process, the immediate objectives of security and reconciliation may have a stronger appeal than the more indirect and long-term goals that the international criminal justice system holds, such as deterrence and justice.[207] A rebel leader in the DRC,[208] Thomas Lubanga Dyilo, in March 2006 became the first accused to be arrested and to appear before the Court.[209]

4.5 Conclusion

Endowed with limited resources and restricted in their mandates, the international criminal courts have prosecuted, and are likely in the future to prosecute, only a small number of human rights violators. In the first place symbolizing an end to impunity, the existence of these courts does not absolve states from taking action domestically. As international and national prosecutions mostly become a possibility after violations have ceased, when a new political dispensation has already been put in place, it may not be overly problematic to secure collaboration by the 'new' government. However, difficulties may arise if the government disagrees with the mandate of the international tribunal, or if a judicial approach is at odds with the imperatives of national peace-building. A change of government does not

---

[204] Report of the International Criminal Court to the UN General Assembly, UN Doc A/61/217, 3 August 2006.

[205] UN Doc Security Council Resolution 1593 (2005) <http://www.icc-cpi.int> (30 September 2006).

[206] M Du Plessis and C Gevers, 'Into the Deep End—The International Criminal Court and Sudan' (2006) *African Ybk on Int Humanitarian L* 88, 111–17.

[207] While the peace process may require 'amnesty' guarantees to rebel leaders, the ICC insists that the arrest warrants remain in place (see eg C Maddux, 'International Court Wants Ugandan Rebel Leader Despite Amnesty Offer' <http://www.voanews.com/english/archives/2006–07/2006–07–05> (31 July 2006).

[208] He allegedly founded and is the leader of the *Union des Parties Congolais* (UPC).

[209] Case ICC-01/04–01/06, indicted for conscripting and enlisting children under 15 into the armed forces since July 2002.

play the same role in the acceptance of the ICJ's jurisdiction. Despite the unease of African states that the jurisdiction of the ICJ in respect of disputes arising from human rights treaties would apply without their explicit consent, as is reflected in their reluctance to subject themselves on a permanent basis to the ICJ's jurisdiction,[210] these states have been prepared to accept the jurisdiction of the Court in disputes involving them. African participation in the activities of the four Courts discussed here defies sentiments that judicial approaches to conflict and human rights resolution are 'un-African'.

B The UN Financial and Trade Institutions and Human Rights in Africa

In Africa, poverty and economic development are inextricably linked to economic globalization and its main institutional actors. Globalization appears on many fronts, including the cultural, social, environmental, and political, but it is nowhere more far-reaching than in its economic manifestation. Economic globalization may be portrayed as the process of 'breaking down State borders in order to allow the free flow of finance, trade, production and at least in theory, labour'.[211] Although it could have evolved into any one of many possible forms, for example being associated with welfare economics or socialist policies, global economic forces dictated that economic globalization took on a singular, neo-liberal agenda.[212] It is against this dominant form of economic globalization that many of this century's protests have been aimed, and to which this discussion on the human rights implications for Africa of international financial institutions and the WTO is directed.[213] Within the UN framework, the World Bank, the International Monetary Fund (IMF), and the World Trade Organization (WTO) are closely involved with the process of economic globalization.[214] Even if these institutions do not make reference to human rights as part of their mandates, their operations inevitably comprise 'socio-economic' rights, and even 'civil and political' rights (such as participation in

[210] Twenty-two African states have by 31 December 2006 accepted the compulsory jurisdiction of the Court (Botswana, Cameroon, Côte d'Ivoire, DRC, Egypt, Djibouti, The Gambia, Guinea, Guinea-Bissau, Kenya, Lesotho, Liberia, Madagascar, Malawi, Mauritius, Nigeria, Senegal, Somalia, Sudan, Swaziland, Togo, and Uganda) (Report of the International Court of Justice 1 August 2005–31 July 2006, <http://www.icj-cij.org> (12 November 2006)).

[211] K De Feyter and F Gómez Isa, 'Privatisation and Human Rights: An Overview' in K De Feyter and F Gómez Isa (eds), *Privatisation and Human Rights in the Age of Globalisation* (Antwerp: Intersentia, 2005) 1, 7.

[212] F Gómez Isa, 'Globalisation, Privatisation and Human Rights' in De Feyter and Gómez Isa (n 211 above) 9, 10.

[213] This discussion omits many international arrangements and institutions impacting on Africa, such as the Lomé and Cotonou Agreements.

[214] The World Bank and IMF are specialized UN agencies. While the WTO does not have a similar official status, it is regarded as an organization 'related' to the UN, and is often treated as part of the UN specialized agencies (see eg M Nowak, *Introduction to the International Human Rights Regime* (Leiden: Martinus Nijhoff, 2003) 144–7).

decision-making) in the achievement of their 'developmental' objectives. Arising from insights about the human rights impact of their activities and their dominance of global financing and trade, the relevance of human rights to these institutions has increasingly been placed under the spotlight,[215] and forms the basis for the survey below. Although multinational corporations play a very important role in the global economy and are its major beneficiaries, they are not included in the discussion.[216]

1 The Bretton Woods Institutions

In 1944, a meeting to address the material devastation of World War II, especially in Europe, at Bretton Woods, New Hampshire, saw the creation of the two major international financial institutions (IFIs): the International Bank for Reconstruction and Development (IBRD), and the IMF.[217] The first, which subsequently became part of the World Bank Group (World Bank),[218] was set up as a specialized agency within the UN system. Initially aimed at rebuilding Europe, it later became the channel for the international community's development efforts. The second, the IMF, had the immediate aim of preventing a recurrence of a global depression, as was experienced in the 1930s, and is more generally geared towards global economic stability.[219] Together, the IMF and World Bank are referred to as the Bretton Woods institutions.

1.1 Negative Effect of Structural Adjustment Programmes

In the 1960s and 1970s, most African economies started declining. Some of the factors responsible for the decline were overly centralized economies with excessive government intervention in the market, badly controlled and expansive government spending, closed and tightly controlled markets, burgeoning civil service bureaucracies that often served patrimonial interests, and 'poor governance'.[220]

As free market ideologies blossomed under conservative governments in two main global economies, the USA and UK, during the 1980s, the World Bank and

---

[215] SI Skogly, 'The Position of the World Bank and the International Monetary Fund in the Human Rights Field' in R Hanski and M Suksi (eds), *An Introduction to the International Protection of Human Rights: A Textbook* (Turku: Abo Akademi University, 2nd edn, 1999) 231, 232.

[216] This omission is due to the lack of space, the 'institutional' (UN) focus of this study, and the limits of international human rights law, which has been viewed as non-binding on TNCs; see, however, A Clapham, *Human Rights Obligations of Non-State Actors* (Oxford: Oxford University Press, 2006) ch 6, arguing that international law already applies to corporations, and that there is a 'paradigm shift' towards placing responsibilities on them under international human rights law.

[217] J Stiglitz, *Globalization and its Discontents* (London: Penguin, 2002) 11.

[218] The World Bank Group consists of the IBRD, the International Development Association (IDA), which provides loans to poorer countries that may not otherwise qualify for support, the International Finance Corporation (IFC), the Multilateral Investment Guarantee Agency (MIGA) and the International Centre for Settlement of Investment Disputes (see eg B Ghazi, *The IMF, the World Bank Group and the Question of Human Rights* (Ardsley: Transnational Publishers, 2005) 19).

[219] On the human rights mandate of these institutions, see D Bradlow, 'The World Bank, the IMF, and Human Rights' (1996) 6 *Transnational L and Contemporary Problems* 47.

[220] J Sachs, *The End of Poverty* (London: Penguin, 2005) 81.

IMF took on a more prominent role in the developing world. The World Bank broadened its focus beyond isolated projects (such as the building of dams), to include more extensive loan schemes, and the IMF increasingly provided funds to declining and developing economies. However, the assistance was accompanied by structural adjustment programmes (SAPs) and conditionalities such as trade liberalization, privatization, and the downscaling of the civil service. Especially after the end of the Cold War, and with the collapse of the communist economies, the neo-liberal approach, referred to as the 'Washington Consensus',[221] gained a very strong foothold. In addition to the conditionalities mentioned above, the Washington Consensus recommended fiscal discipline, interest rate liberalization, trade liberalization, liberalization of foreign direct investment (FDI), and deregulation.[222]

Although well-intended, these conditionalities and elements of SAPs had a negative effect on development and lower income countries, particularly in Africa.

Trade liberalization often occurred before 'safety nets' were put into place. As Stiglitz argues, forcing developing countries to allow in imported products exposed local industries to competition from much stronger counterpart industries in other countries.[223] Small-scale farmers in developing countries were unable to compete with highly subsidized goods from Europe and the USA. The major consequence of rapid trade liberalization was therefore a loss of jobs in the industrial and agricultural sectors of the poorer countries. In this context, the IMF's insistence on tight monetary policies, for example by requiring states to maintain or raise interest rates, impeded growth possibilities and job creation.

Structural adjustment negated the structural causes of poverty that lie beyond economic management styles and priorities, such as pervasive illness, geography, and climate. Focusing on factors internal to the country, the role of foreign financial assistance declined. Reviewing 20 years of SAPs, the Independent Expert of the Human Rights Commission in 1999 concluded that they are 'not consistent with long-term development needs of developing countries'.[224] The UN Special Rapporteur also noted the adverse effect of SAPs on the realization of the right to food, particularly in Africa.[225] Dissatisfaction with the effects of these policies

---

[221] This term, coined by J Williamson ('The Progress of Policy Reform in Latin America', quoted in Ghazi (n 218 above) 46), refers to the 'think-tank' set up between the US administration and the IFIs, dictating their collective will in the form of a 'Consensus' strategy.

[222] Ghazi (n 218 above) 46.   [223] Stiglitz (n 217 above) 59–61.

[224] F Cheru, 'Effects of Structural Adjustment Policies on the Full Enjoyment of Human Rights', UN Doc E/CN.4/1999/50 (24 February 1999) 16.

[225] Report of the UN Special Rapporteur on the Right to Food, UN Doc A/60/350 (12 September 2005) para 42: 'Many NGOs and civil society organizations claim that the economic policies advocated by the World Bank and IMF through programmes such as structural adjustment programmes or poverty reduction strategies have had negative impacts on the right to food of large sections of the populations of many countries, particularly in Africa . . . Far from improving food security for the most vulnerable populations, these programmes have often resulted in a deterioration of food security among the poorest. The strong advocacy pursued by the World Bank and IMF for the drastic reduction of public spending, the privatization of public enterprises, trade liberalization and the flexibilization of financial, labour and land markets has had negative impacts on the right to food and other economic, social and cultural rights. In Zambia, after a programme of rapid structural adjustment was

gave rise to civil unrest and concomitant violations of 'civil and political' human rights.[226]

Privatization is justified by the claim that it would enhance 'the efficiency of a country's economy by reducing public spending'.[227] Where privatization of some of the most basic services such as water, sanitation, health, and education results in hardship, it is always that part of the population most marginalized and most at risk that suffers, not least because of the introduction of 'user fees' and weak state structures that do not effectively discharge their obligation to protect.

FDI is a key part of the new global economy. Theoretically, FDI is aimed at increasing growth by providing technical expertise, employment opportunities, and access to foreign markets, but in practice it often threatens local entrepreneurship, and does not promote growth. In fact, it may have the opposite effect of creating a 'dual economy', where small 'pockets of wealth' accentuate the economic exclusion of the majority.[228]

1.2 *World Bank Inspection Panel*

To address these—and many other—concerns, the Bretton Woods institutions have set policies in place to monitor and soften the social impact of its activities, and have created the World Bank Inspection Panel (Panel).[229] However, only one of the Bank's Operational Directives mentions human rights explicitly, namely, as part of a yardstick to assess the impact of programmes on 'indigenous peoples'.[230] By contrast, as far as the environment is concerned, another directive stipulates that the Bank 'does not finance projects that contravene applicable international environmental agreements'.[231] One must, with De Feyter, question the omission of a similar statement requiring conformity of Bank policies with international human rights law.[232] The Panel, aimed at ensuring a greater role for human rights and the principle of accountability in the management of the Bank,[233] may be

introduced in the 1990s, an evaluation made by IMF itself recognized that the liberalization in agriculture had caused hardship for poor Zambians, with maize consumption falling by 20 per cent between 1990 and 1997 as the poorest could not afford enough to eat. In most cases, the World Bank and IMF have not required that prior to introducing rapid adjustment measures safety nets be put in place that would support the poorest and most vulnerable populations'.

[226] Ghazi (n 218 above) 49.   [227] ibid 50.   [228] Stiglitz (n 217 above) 72.

[229] See generally on the Panel, G Alfredsson and R Ring (eds), *The Inspection Panel of the World Bank: A Different Complaints Procedure* (The Hague: Martinus Nijhoff, 2001).

[230] World Bank's Operational Manual: Operational Directive 4.20 on Indigenous Peoples (January 2007), committing the Bank to design and implement projects in a way that fosters full respect for indigenous peoples' dignity, human rights, and cultural uniqueness, so that they (a) receive culturally compatible social and economic benefits; and (b) do not suffer adverse effects during the development process.

[231] Operational Directive 4.15 on Environmental Assessment (January 1999) para 2.

[232] K De Feyter, 'The International Financial Institutions and Human Rights: Law and Practice' in F Gómez Isa and K De Feyter (eds), *International Protection of Human Rights: Achievements and Challenges* (Bilbao: University of Deusto, 2006) 561, 572.

[233] On the World Bank and human rights, see eg R Daňň, 'The Legal Aspects of the World Bank's Work on Human Rights: Some Preliminary Thoughts' in P Alston and M Robinson (eds), *Human Rights and Development: Towards Mutual Reinforcement* (Oxford: Oxford University Press, 2005) 509.

approached by individuals or groups alleging that they are (or are likely to be) adversely affected by the Bank's failure to follow its own procedures and policies in the course of a Bank-financed project. Even if 'requesters' (as complainants are called) may invoke national and international human rights law to substantiate claims that Bank policies and directives have been violated, the Panel is not concerned with the application or interpretation of international human rights law as such. The Panel makes recommendations to the Bank's decision-making body, the Board of Executive Directors, which disposes of the matter in an administrative process characterized by pragmatism rather than by way of a principled judicial process.[234] One of the greatest weaknesses of the Panel is its inability to oversee the implementation of any remedial measures that would emanate from the inspection process.[235]

At the outset, the Bank drew a rigid dividing line between 'socio-economic' rights, which fell inside its mandate as part of the economic consequences of projects, and 'civil and political' rights, which by virtue of the Bank's Articles of Agreement were excluded from its mandate because of their 'political' nature.[236] The Bank's Operational Directive on Poverty Reduction, which underscores the centrality to sustained poverty reduction of 'improved access to education, health care, and other social services',[237] manifests the Bank's concern for socio-economic development. Although the distinction later became blurred, for example when the Bank included rights of affected populations to consultation and participation,[238] the Chad–Cameroon Oil and Pipeline Project (the Chad Pipeline Project) illustrates the persistence of this tension.

For many years, due to civil war and dictatorship, oil reserves—and their potential to ordinary Chadians—lay unexploited under the dry earth of one of the world's poorest countries. In the Chad Pipeline Project, aimed at oil drilling and pipeline construction, the Bank acted as 'lender and moral guarantor' to an international consortium consisting of three private companies: Exxon, Petronas, and Chevron.[239] The Bank became involved in the project on the basis of its potential benefit to the extremely impoverished people of Chad. Under media and civil society pressure, the private investors undertook to abide by a 'certain set of standards', provided for in the Bank's operational policies.[240]

The government of Chad was also forced to adopt sound revenue management measures. Rejecting the government's initial plan as not clear enough on the management of the oil revenues, the Bank recommended the adoption of a domestic

---

[234] De Feyter (n 232 above) 580.
[235] DL Clark, 'The World Bank and Human Rights: The Need for Greater Accountability' (2002) 15 *Harvard Human Rights J* 205, 218.   [236] World Bank Articles of Agreement, art IV, 10.
[237] Operational Directive 4.15 on Poverty Reduction (December 1991) para 3.
[238] See also the Panel's Report on the Chad Pipeline, in which the Panel accepts that it had to examine the possibility that 'proper governance' and human rights violations in the country had 'impeded the implementation of the Project in a manner incompatible with the Bank's policies' (quoted in Clapham (n 216 above) 154).
[239] GH Uriz, 'To Lend or Not to Lend: Oil, Human Rights, and the World Bank's Internal Contradictions' (2001) 14 *Harvard Human Rights J* 197, 198.   [240] ibid.

Oil Revenue Management Law. The Law, which stipulated that 80 per cent of oil revenues would be spent to alleviate urgent socio-economic needs, was lauded as an 'unprecedented landmark' demonstrating Chad's 'commitment to a fair and transparent distribution, of profits'.[241] According to the Law, 5 per cent of the revenue would be ploughed back into the producing region, and 10 per cent would go into a 'Future Generations Fund'. A supervisory body, the Oil Revenues Control and Monitoring Board, would be set up to vet government spending. Informally, the Chadian President also undertook that the government would manage the $25 million 'bonus', to be received on signature of the final agreement, in the same way as other revenue.[242]

However, the Bank failed to view the Law through a human rights lens, as is apparent from three aspects. The first is the process of legislative adoption, which took place in the absence of the only vocal parliamentary opponent of the Project, who at the time had been imprisoned.[243] Secondly, the composition of the body that would oversee the disbursing process was heavily weighted in the government's favour. Lastly, scant regard was paid to allowances in the Law providing for changes to the allocation formula by decree. In addition, the Project's impact upon rural communities and indigenous peoples was not addressed adequately either by the government concerned or the Panel.[244]

After the approval of the Chad Pipeline Project, the incumbent President (Deby) manipulated elections, and displayed no qualms about deviating from his previously stated intentions: contrary to its undertaking, the government channelled the 'bonus' payment clandestinely to include the purchase of arms.[245] This caused the World Bank to postpone Chad's access to debt relief. In an attempt to assert its sovereignty, and in denial of the spirit of the agreement with the Bank, the executive-controlled Chadian Parliament on 29 December 2005 amended the Law, 'increasing the portion of revenues that flow directly to state coffers, by-passing the government-civil society oversight body charged with controlling petroleum revenue expenditures; and including security spending among the "priority sectors" to which oil funds can be allocated'.[246] The Bank reacted by suspending loans, but was quick to resume payment after it had entered into a Memorandum of Understanding with the government in 2006, in terms of which the government would spend 70 per cent of its 2007 budget on poverty reduction programmes.[247]

Lagos, Nigeria, provided the setting for the Panel's second African involvement. In 1993, a few days after a presidential election had taken place in Nigeria, but before the annulment of the elections and the coup bringing Abacha to power, the

---

[241] ibid.
[242] R Calderisi, *The Trouble with Africa: Why Foreign Aid is Not Working* (New Haven: Yale University Press, 2006) 190.   [243] Uriz (n 239 above) 222.
[244] K Horta, 'Rhetoric and Reality: Human Rights and the World Bank' (2002) 15 *Harvard Human Rights J* 227, 234.   [245] Calderisi (n 242 above) 190–1.
[246] Bank Information Centre, 'BIC Discusses Chad Oil Pipeline on NPR: Collapse of Bank's "model" project Offers Lessons and Exposes Risks to the Poor', Book Information Centre, <http://www.bicusa.org/en/Article.2668.aspx> (30 September 2006).
[247] Book Information Centre, <http://www.bicusa.org/en/Article.2892.aspx> (30 September 2006).

IDA approved the financing of a drainage and sanitation project in Lagos.[248] In retrospect, the wisdom of this decision has been seriously called into question. However, it represents the Bank's 'traditional position that political circumstances are irrelevant to decisions on loans'.[249] In implementing the project, the Bank's staff relied heavily on government officials to secure community participation. This consultative process, as was the case with life in Nigeria generally, played itself out in a context of political repression and massive human rights violations. When political circumstances changed with the death of Abacha, in 1998, the Lagos-based NGO Social and Economic Rights Action Centre (SERAC) and others filed a 'request' to the Panel. Because the allegations of massive violations in the request were not sufficiently linked to the sanitation project, and because they were targeted at the Nigerian government, many of the allegations contained in the request were found to be irrelevant to the Bank's conduct and operations. Although the Panel criticized the consultation with communities as being tainted by the collusion of Bank staff with the Abacha government, it did not recommend a further investigation. One may accept that this deferential course of action was at least in part a motion of confidence in the new government.

The essence of the lessons learnt from this narrative is that the Bank must include a more pronounced and consistent human rights policy, which should integrate the reinforcement of government capacity, the strengthening of democratic institutions, and the improvement of a country's human rights record. The Bank should eschew the 'political rights'/socio-economic rights dichotomy,[250] and should move towards a 'rights-based political economy where development means support for national and local-level decision-making to create sustainable livelihoods'.[251]

1.3 Office of the Compliance Advisor/Ombudsman

Another mechanism, the IFC/MIGA Office of the Compliance Advisor/ Ombudsman (CAO), was established in 1999 to ensure greater accountability in relation especially to the social dimension of projects by two other members of the World Bank Group, the International Finance Corporation (IFC) and the Multilateral Investment Guarantee Agency (MIGA). As its name indicates, the CAO oversees compliance by conducting audits, advises the Bank President, and investigates complaints with respect to IFC and MIGA projects. It reports directly to the Bank's President. The basis of its role is a set of environmental and social standards. Sub-Saharan Africa accounted for 32 per cent of its total portfolio of complaints related to 19 projects between 1999 and 2005.[252] The CAO has had limited

---

[248] See De Feyter (n 232 above) 583–86, which serves as the basis for the discussion that follows.
[249] ibid 585.
[250] Uriz (n 242 above) refers to the Bank's 'internal contradictions', pointing to instances where broader human rights concerns have permeated the Bank's activities (such as its encouragement of political 'decentralization' and its cancellation of a loan to Nigeria after the execution of Ken Saro-Wiwa and other Ogoni activists) (207, 210).   [251] Horta (n 244 above) 243.
[252] 'A Retrospective Analysis of CAO Interventions Trends, Outcomes and Effectiveness', May 2006, <http://www.cao-ombudsman.org> (30 September 2006).

impact and its decisions do not demonstrate great sensitivity to human rights. In the audit of the Dikulushi Copper-Silver Mining Project in Katanga, DRC, the CAO found in rather vague terms that MIGA did not adequately assess whether the project would indirectly have an adverse impact on the community. In the Botswana–Kalahari Diamonds complaint, indigenous San people in November 2004 alleged that they had been illegally evicted from their traditional hunting grounds because of a diamond mining project. The CAO found that 'the San people were displaced due to a policy by the Government of Botswana unrelated to the diamond exploration activities' and that the mine was not 'invasive or disruptive to the San's traditional hunting and gathering way of life'.[253]

1.4 Debt Relief

The IFIs have also been engaged in debt relief involving many African countries. In 1996, the Bank and the IMF together endorsed the Highly Indebted Poor Countries Initiative (HIPC), aimed at cutting 'debt service payments within a sustainable development strategy'.[254] In 2005, at Gleneagles, the G-8 leaders committed themselves to writing off the debt of these countries. Under the Multi-lateral Debt Relief Initiative (MDRI), HIPC are eligible for 100 per cent debt relief to the IMF, IDA, and the African Development Fund, provided they have completed the 'HIPC process'. One of the prerequisites to gaining access to debt relief is the drafting of Poverty Reduction Strategy Papers (PRSP), devised at the national level with the participation of civil society. To qualify, countries also have to establish a 'track-record of reform and sound policies'.[255] By the end of September 2006, 16 African countries had qualified;[256] nine were in an interim phase,[257] and eight in the pre-decision phase.[258] The IMF noted that debt cancellation had a positive effect on spending on basic social services.

2 The World Trade Organization (WTO)

The third institution in the triad forming the helm of economic globalization, the World Trade Organization (WTO), was already envisaged at Bretton Woods, but was only established in 1985. Aimed at fostering international trade relations, the WTO provides a forum where states can negotiate trade agreements. It also provides mechanisms through which these agreements may be implemented. Forty-one

---

[253] <http://www.cao-ombudsman.org/html-english/complaint_botswana.htm> (30 September 2006).
[254] World Bank, *Development and Human Rights: The Role of the World Bank* (Washington, DC: World Bank, 1998) 9.
[255] IMF, *Debt Relief under the HIPC Initiative: A Fact-sheet* (September 2006) <http://www.imf.org>.
[256] Benin, Burkina Faso, Cameroon, Ethiopia, Ghana, Madagascar, Malawi, Mali, Mauritania, Mozambique, Niger, Rwanda, Senegal, Tanzania, Uganda, and Zambia,
[257] Burundi, Chad, Congo, DRC, The Gambia, Guinea, Guinea-Bissau, São Tomé e Príncipe, and Sierra Leone.   [258] CAR, Comoros, Côte d'Ivoire, Eritrea, Liberia, Somalia, Sudan, and Togo.

African states have become members of the WTO, while a further eight have observer status.[259] Despite having opened their economies and markets, the continent's share in 'international merchandise trade' has actually decreased by 4 per cent since 1980.[260] Instead, the increasing appetite for raw materials of ever-enlarging global markets saw the colonization of African resources, often to the detriment of indigenous peoples.[261]

Equality in trade is undermined by Western hypocrisy, exemplified by advocacy for trade liberalization in some sectors (in which Western countries are net exporters) and the opposition to free trade in others (in which developing economies stood a chance of competing with local products). Subsidies, in particular, have become a bone of contention. Africa's trade has been influenced negatively; especially by the agricultural subsidies in developed countries. These subsidies give farmers in developed countries an unfair advantage when they export to global—including the African—markets, exemplified by the subsidies to cotton farmers in the USA.[262] Some progress has been made during the Doha Round of negotiations, when the sixth WTO Ministerial Conference decided to ensure that the 'parallel elimination of all forms of agricultural export subsidies and disciplines on all exports with equivalent effect is completed by 2013', a step welcomed by the AU Assembly.[263] However, in July 2006, the AU Assembly expressed its concern about the limited progress and emphasized that the failure to 'incorporate Africa's needs' into the outcomes will 'undermine Africa's already limited trade opportunities' and erode its attempts at pursuing trade policies that serve the goal of development and sustained growth.[264]

It is impossible to divorce the WTO's programmes and policies from its decision-making structures. Increasingly, the dominance of the Western economic powers has come under scrutiny from non-dominant quarters, also Africa, whose 'poor representation' in these processes has been lamented.[265]

African members of the WTO are bound by the WTO Agreement on Trade-Related Aspects of Intellectual Property Rights (TRIPS). Designed to protect intellectual property rights, embodied, for example, in patents, TRIPS may be viewed as an instrument of monopoly. Transnational and multinational companies,

---

[259] <http://www.wto.org>.

[260] HB Hammouda *et al*, 'Africa's (Mis)fortunes in Global Trade and the Country's Diversification Regimes' (2006) 7 *J of World Investment and Trade* 587, 588.

[261] J Oloka-Onyango, 'Who's Watching "Big Brother"? Globalization and the Protection of Cultural Rights in Present Day Africa' (2005) 27 *HRQ* 1245, 1259, citing the examples of the Bakyeli people affected by oil exploration in Cameroon; logging affecting the Batwa living in Central African countries; and tourism dislocating the San of Botswana.

[262] Oloka-Onyango (n 261 above) 1259. Farmers in some of Africa's poorest countries, such as Mali, are seriously threatened by the 'dumping' of US cotton on the world market.

[263] Declaration on the Outcome of the Sixth WTO Ministerial Conference held in Hong Kong, China, 13–18 December 2005, AU Doc Assembly/AU/Decl.1(VI).

[264] Decision on WTO Negotiations, AU Doc Assembly/AU/Dec.119(VII).

[265] Decision on Strengthening Africa's Representation in the Bretton Woods Institutions, AU Doc Assembly/AU/Dec.126(VII).

almost exclusively based in developing countries, are favoured by the global application of 'developed country standards'.[266] Traditional knowledge, an expression
of intellectual property of great importance to Africa, is omitted from TRIPS.
Although this aspect is covered in the Convention on Biological Diversity, that
treaty lacks an implementation arm comparable to that of the WTO.

The potential and actual negative impact of TRIPS on the right to health is
partly mitigated by the 'flexibilities' within TRIPS, such as parallel importation
and compulsory licensing. Responding to the dire need for affordable AIDS medication in Africa, and propelled into action by the insistence of the African group,
the WTO ministers at the Doha meeting in 2001 agreed that 'the TRIPS Agreement does not and should not prevent Members from taking measures to protect
public health'.[267] On 30 August 2003, the WTO Council of Ministers agreed that
countries facing a public health emergency may issue compulsory licences to local
manufacturers to produce patent-protected medicines (compulsory licensing),
or may issue licences allowing for the importation of generic medicines (parallel
importation). 'Compulsory licensing' is of limited use to countries that lack a
pharmaceutical manufacturing sector. It may therefore depend on imported drugs
from other countries where generic drugs are manufactured under 'compulsory
licence'. However, TRIPS allows for the production of drugs without the patent
holder's consent only if it is directed primarily at the domestic market of that
country.[268] Under a relaxation of this rule, developing countries may import drugs
from countries that manufacture them under compulsory licences, provided the
export is not part of a commercial or industrial policy.[269]

Few African states have made use of these possibilities, presumably due to a lack
of legal-technical expertise. Zimbabwe is an exception: in 2002, the government
of Zimbabwe declared HIV/AIDS an emergency under its Patents Act, and allowed
a third party (other than the government) to produce anti-retroviral medicines.[270]
Despite having legal provisions allowing for similar possibilities,[271] the South
African government has not implemented domestic flexibilities.

Whatever protection and possibilities TRIPS provides are seriously eroded by
bilateral 'TRIPS plus' agreements, whereby developed countries impose obligations
on developing countries to provide for more stringent domestic requirements than
those set out in TRIPS itself. An example would be when a state provides for legal

---

[266] ibid.
[267] 'Declaration on the TRIPS Agreement on Public Health', Doha Ministerial Conference, 9–14
November 2001, WTO Doc WT/MIN/(01)/DEC/W/2 (20 November 2001).
[268] TRIPS, art 31(f).
[269] WTO General Council, 'Implementation of Paragraph 6 of the Doha Declaration on the
TRIPS Agreement and Public Health', WTO Doc WT/L/540 and Corr.1 (1 September 2003) (also
referred to as the '30 August Decision').
[270] See s 35 of the Zimbabwe Patents Act, and the discussion by S Sacco, 'A Comparative Study of
the Implementation in Zimbabwe and South Africa of the International Law Rules that Allow
Compulsory Licensing and Parallel Importation of HIV/AIDS Drugs' (2005) 5 *AHRLJ* 105.
[271] See s 56(2) of the Patents Act and s 15C of the Medicines and Related Substances Control Act.

protection of biotechnological innovations. The UN Special Rapporteur on the Right to Health warned against the enactment of such legislation, and urged 'wealthy countries not [to] pressure a developing country to implement "TRIPS plus" legislation' unless it is reliably established that the legislation will enhance the enjoyment of the right to health in that country.[272]

The WTO also developed the General Agreement on Trade in Services (GATS). As Stiglitz argues,[273] the selection of included 'services' are skewed in favour of developed economies. Selective liberalization of trade in services (including, for example, financial services but not agriculture and construction, from which African and other developing countries stand to benefit more) often works against the interests of Africa.

C Conclusion

Citizens of the twenty-first century may find it difficult to imagine a world without the UN. The UN's influence has been particularly pervasive in Africa: its efforts supplemented those of weak state institutions; it used its moral authority to confront and curb serious and persistent human rights violations; and it promoted adherence to human rights.

The UN system as a whole and its role in Africa are assessed along three headings: the UN's main aims (development–security–human rights); the gradual strengthening of the human rights regime (promotion–protection–prevention); and compliance with international human rights law (none–partial–full).

Although particular UN bodies bear major responsibility for each particular aim, it is immediately apparent that much overlap exists. 'Development' may be the primary responsibility of specialized programmes such as the UNDP, but the General Assembly, various special mechanisms, and treaty bodies have all highlighted poverty in Africa (and elsewhere) and the need to realize 'socio-economic' rights. Financial and trade arrangements have taken tentative steps to integrate human rights into their development agendas, but increasing integration of human rights is required. Efforts to address poverty should be guided by the CESCR Committee's elaboration of the 'minimum core content' of 'socio-economic' rights and the MDGs. Even though the World Bank Inspection Panel has been created, it remains largely inaccessible[274] in the absence of efforts at the national level to educate, inform, and sensitize those who are affected by World Bank projects. Despite these efforts, the UN Charter system and the myriad of agencies and institutions have not served as an adequate catalyst to jerk the global consciousness into

---

[272] Report of the Special Rapporteur on the Right to Health: Mission to the WTO, UN Doc E/CN.4/2004/49/Add.1 (1 March 2004) para 82.   [273] n 217 above, 387.
[274] M Hansungule, 'Access to Panel: The Notion of Affected Party, Issues of Collective and Material Interest' in Alfredsson and Ring (n 229 above) 143, 155–6.

action, and have not succeeded in making a marked difference to the material realities on the African continent.

While 'peace and security' is the main responsibility of the Security Council, judicial mechanisms and treaty bodies have also played a part. However, the inability of these mechanisms and bodies to be effective in prevention has been starkly illustrated in their response to conflict and serious human rights violations in countries such as Burundi and Rwanda. Both state reporting and the complaints procedure should be better integrated with the activities of the UN's political bodies, to ensure improved prevention and compliance. While the UN has played an important part in this domain, the impasse in Darfur has detracted from its record on human security in Africa.

Going beyond promotion, human rights bodies are playing an increasingly important role in prevention. Compliance by African states has improved, as illustrated in the reaction of states to findings of the Working Group on Arbitrary Detention and the Human Rights Committee. However, the number of complaints and their impact remain 'negligible',[275] and follow-up procedures often focus on the information supplied by states, rather than on substantive compliance.

As the UNHRC considers its future role amidst a resurgence of the 'non-interference' principle, supported by China, the African bloc, and others, human rights protection under the UN Charter seems precariously poised. Greater engagement of African civil society is called for to ensure that African political elites—even of 'progressive' countries such as South Africa—do not derail a system that is precariously on course towards realizing human development, human security, and human rights of everyone on the planet, including in Africa.

---

[275] See J Donelly, 'The Virtues of Legalization' in S Meckled-García and B Çali (eds), *The Legalization of Human Rights: Multidisciplinary Perspectives on Human Rights and Human Rights Law* (London: Routledge, 2006) 67, 73: 'Although these procedures have brought a few demonstrable changes in state practice and occasional remedies for individual victims, to call their impact negligible would be extremely charitable'.

3

The United Nations Treaty-based Human Rights System and Africa

Since the adoption of the Universal Declaration of Human Rights on 10 December 1948, seven major human rights treaties have been adopted under UN auspices. The first, adopted in 1965, is the International Convention on the Elimination of All Forms of Racial Discrimination (CERD).[1] Soon thereafter, in 1966, it was followed by the ICCPR[2] and the ICESCR.[3] The international human rights regime was further supplemented by human rights treaties with a focus on specific groups or themes: The Convention on the Elimination of All Forms of Discrimination against Women (CEDAW) (adopted in 1979),[4] the Convention against Torture and Other Cruel, Inhuman or Degrading Treatment or Punishment (CAT) (of 1984),[5] followed in 1989 by the Convention on the Rights of the Child (CRC),[6] and most recently by the Convention on the Protection of the Rights of All Migrant Workers and Members of their Families (CMW), adopted in 1990.[7] Each of these treaties, with the exception of the ICESCR, establishes a treaty monitoring body (or 'committee') in the form of a supervisory quasi-judicial institution.[8]

These seven treaties are by no means the only human rights instruments adopted under UN auspices. Other human rights treaties include the following: the

---

   [1] 660 UNTS 195 (GA Res 2106A (1965)), adopted 21 December 1965, entered into force 4 January 1969.
   [2] 999 UNTS 171, adopted 16 December 1966, entered into force 23 March 1976.
   [3] 993 UNTS 3, adopted 16 December 1966, entered into force 3 January 1976.
   [4] UNGA Res 34/180, UN Doc A/34/46, adopted 18 December 1979, entered into force 3 September 1981.
   [5] UNGA Res 39/46, UN Doc A/39/51, adopted 10 December 1984, entered into force 26 June 1987.
   [6] UNGA Res 44/25, adopted 20 November 1989, entered into force 2 September 1990.
   [7] UNGA Res, adopted 18 December 1990, entered into force 1 July 2003.
   [8] A 'treaty body' also exists to monitor ICESCR, but was established by ECOSOC.

Convention on the Prevention and Punishment of the Crime of Genocide,[9] the Convention relating to the Status of Refugees[10] and the Protocol thereto,[11] the Convention on the Political Rights of Women,[12] the Convention on the Nationality of Married Women,[13] the Convention on Consent to Marriage, Minimum Age for Marriage and Registration of Marriages,[14] and the Convention on the Suppression and Punishment of the Crime of Apartheid.[15] The difference is that treaty bodies have not been established to supervise any of these human rights instruments. The number human rights treaty bodies is set to increase to nine after the UNGA at the end of 2006 adopted two further treaties. Each setting up its own treaty monitoring body, these treaties deal with the rights of people living with disabilities,[16] and with those who have been foricibly 'disappeared'.[17]

The adherence of African states to the seven major treaties, as at 31 December 2006, is set out in Table 3.2 below. To form a better impression of Africa's formal adherence to these instruments, in comparison with that of other continents or regions of the world, one must keep in mind that African states constitute nearly a quarter of the total number of states in the world. African states represent 27 per cent of the total number of state parties to the UN. When ratifications by region are considered, the division of UN members into five regional units, as grouped together mainly for lobbying and electoral purposes, is adopted in this study. The five regions are the 'African', 'Asian', 'Eastern European', 'Latin American and Caribbean', and the 'Western and Other' (WEO) blocs.[18] The discussion now turns to the role in and importance to Africa of these seven treaties and their monitoring mechanisms.

[9] 78 UNTS 277, adopted 9 December 1948, entered into force 12 January 1951.
[10] 189 UNTS 137, adopted 28 July 1951, entered into force 22 April 1954.
[11] 606 UNTS 267, adopted 31 January 1967, entered into force 4 October 1967.
[12] 193 UNTS 135, adopted 20 December 1952, entered into force 7 July 1954.
[13] 309 UNTS 65, adopted 20 February 1957, entered into force 11 August 1958.
[14] 521 UNTS 231, adopted 10 December 1962, entered into force 9 December 1964.
[15] 1015 UNTS 243, adopted 30 November 1973, entered into force 18 July 1976.
[16] Convention on the Rights of Persons with Disabilities, adopted on 13 December 2006, will enter into force when 20 states have formally accepted it, when the Committee on the Rights of Persons with Disabilities will be established. States may declare themselves willing to accept individual and inter-state communities against them by ratifying or acceding to the Optional Protocol on the Rights of Persons with Disabilities, which will enter into force after ten states have done so.
[17] International Convention for the Protection of All Persons from Enforced Disappearence, adopted on 20 December 2006, will enter into force after 20 states have formally accepted it, when the Committee on Enforced Disappearences will be established. States may make a declaration to accept this Committee's competence to consider individual and inter-state complaints (arts 31 and 32).
[18] While the first four geographical groupings are more or less self-explanatory, the last is quite a diverse conglomerate of nations The full list of WEO states is provided by AF Bayefsky, 'Making the Human Rights Treaties Work' in L Henkin and JL Hargrove (eds), *Human Rights: An Agenda for the Next Century* (Washington, DC: The American Society of International Law, 1994) 269 n 43: They are Australia, Austria, Belgium, Canada, Denmark, Finland, France, Germany, Greece, Iceland, Ireland, Italy, Liechtenstein, Luxembourg, Malta, Netherlands, New Zealand, Norway, Portugal, San Marino, Spain, Sweden, Turkey, and the United Kingdom. The USA is considered to be a member of this group only for electoral purposes. Israel is not a member of any regional grouping of the UN.

A The Convention on the Elimination of All Forms of Racial Discrimination (CERD)

The first comprehensive and binding multilateral treaty concluded under UN auspices is CERD.[19] Its adoption in 1965 was preceded by a declaration on the same subject in 1963.[20] African states took the initiative on both occasions.[21] CERD was ratified by a sufficient number of states and entered into force in just over three years.

State parties to CERD undertake to pursue all appropriate means to eliminate racial discrimination.[22] In terms of the definition, distinctions, restrictions, or exclusions on the basis of 'colour, descent, or national or ethnic origin' are included under 'racial discrimination'. From its inception, however, states have tended to regard CERD more as a policy than a human rights instrument, more attuned to rhetoric than compliance, and concerned primarily with racial discrimination as manifested in *apartheid* South Africa—based on 'colour' and not on other differences.[23] As a result, the impact of CERD has remained very limited. The substantive scope of CERD was extended by 'General Recommendations', adopted by the CERD Committee, and the Durban Declaration and Programme of Action.

1 Mandate and Composition of the CERD Committee

Three main functions are entrusted to the CERD Committee: the examination of periodic state reports, and the consideration of inter-state, and individual, communications. The latter two competences are optional.

The CERD Committee consists of 18 independent experts, nominated and elected by member states.[24] State parties elect Committee members for terms of four years.[25] In the establishment of the Committee, three factors should be given consideration: 'equitable geographical distribution', representation of 'different forms of civilization', and the representation of 'the principal legal systems'.[26] By

---

[19] See the general discussion by KJ Partsch, 'The Committee on the Elimination of Racial Discrimination' in P Alston (ed), *The United Nations and Human Rights* (Oxford: Calrendon Press, 1992) 339 and sources listed by M O'Flaherty, *Human Rights and the UN* (London: Sweet & Maxwell, 1996) 83.

[20] The Declaration on the Elimination of All Forms of Racial Discrimination, adopted by the General Assembly by resolution 1904 (IXVIII) on 20 November 1963.

[21] E Schwelb, 'The International Convention on the Elimination of All Forms of Racial Discrimination' (1966) 15 *ICLQ* 996, 998; and N Lerner, *The UN Convention on the Elimination of All Forms of Racial Discrimination* (Alphen aan den Rijn: Sijthoff and Noordhoff, 1980) 2 (mentioning the role of CAR, Chad, Dahomey (later, Benin), Guinea, Côte d'Ivoire, Mali, Mauritania, and Upper Volta (later, Burkina Faso) in proposing that an international convention on the elimination of racial discrimination be adopted).   [22] CERD, art 2.

[23] See eg Lerner (n 21 above) 10.   [24] CERD, art 8.   [25] CERD, art 8(2) and 8(5).

[26] CERD, art 8(1).

31 December 2006, the African membership had grown to its highest level, with five members from Africa serving on the Committee.[27]

2 Ratifications and Reservations

At the time CERD entered into force, a substantial number of ratifying states were from Africa.[28] By 31 December 2006, 49 African states had acceded to or ratified the Convention, while two states had signed it. This means that 92 per cent of all African UN members have become party to CERD, a percentage surpassed by this group of states only in relation to the UN treaties on women, children, and refugees. The total number of ratifications globally on that date was 173, or 89 per cent of all potential ratifying states. The likelihood of an African state having ratified CERD is thus slightly greater than the chance of states around the globe having done so. Some 50 countries worldwide have entered reservations or have made declarations on accession or ratification, including seven African states (Egypt, Equatorial Guinea, Libya, Madagascar, Morocco, Mozambique, and Rwanda).[29] Where some of the other states raised concerns about substantive provisions of CERD, the seven African states raised procedural reservations.[30]

3 State Reporting

Initially, African states reported reasonably regularly, but, associating CERD with 'apartheid', tended consistently to negate or underplay the existence of discrimination on the basis of ethnicity within their own borders. A Libyan report, combining its 15th to 17th reports, examined in 2004, illustrates the persistent problem of states denying the presence of any ethnic groups, thus foreclosing potential allegations of racism. In its conclusions on the report, the CERD Committee noted the 'discrepancy between the assessment of the state party, according to which Libyan society is ethnically homogenous, and information indicating that Amazigh, Tuareg

---

[27] Abdoul-Nasr (Egypt); Amir (Algeria); Dah (Burkina Faso, serving as one of three Vice-Chairpersons); January-Bardill (South Africa); and Ewomsan (Togo).

[28] Of the 27 states that had ratified the instrument when it entered into force in January 1969, a majority (19) were from the 'third world' (Partsch (n 19 above) 339).

[29] ibid, information on declarations and reservations. A number of states (22) worldwide formally objected to reservations and declarations entered by other states. Ethiopia's objection is quite unique, as African states as a rule do not object to reservations or declarations by other states. Ethiopia's objection was not directed at the substance of the Convention, but is clearly politically motivated. In its objection, Ethiopia declared that the *ratification* by the 'Government of Democratic Kampuchea' was, as far as it was concerned, null and void. This 'objection' was based on the fact of ratification, rather than on a reservation or declaration.

[30] They all declared themselves not to be bound by art 22 of the Convention, in terms of which disputes between parties not settled by negotiation shall be referred to the ICJ 'at the request of any of the parties to the dispute'. Article 22 represents a departure of the normal procedure in relation to the ICJ. As a rule, both parties to a dispute have to agree to accept the ICJ's jurisdiction. The six states mentioned above (as well as others, such as the USA) declared that the consent of all the parties in each individual case will still be required before they would submit to the jurisdiction of the ICJ.

and Black African populations live in the country'.[31] As is often the case—especially with African states—information on the ethnic composition of the population was lacking. The same denial and subsequent omission appear in respect of non-citizens and indigenous peoples, two groups that the Committee had explicitly included within the scope of CERD through its General Recommendations.[32] With time, reporting by African states declined, as it became clearer that 'racial discrimination' under CERD went beyond the racial divide between black and white (that is, the issue of 'apartheid'), to include the grounds of ethnicity, nationality, and even indigeneity.

The issue of respect for the rights of indigenous peoples was high on the Committee's agenda when it examined Botswana's combined 16th and 17th reports in 2006.[33] Recalling its General Recommendations on self-identification (no 8) and on Indigenous Peoples (no 23), it urged Botswana to 'respect and protect the existence and cultural identity of all ethnic groups within its territory'.[34] Referring to indigenous people as 'some residents of the Central Kalahari Game Reserve', the 'non-Tswana' tribes, and the 'San/Basarwa groups', the Committee highlighted issues such as their forced removal, lack of access to courts, and lack of access to education.

The role of state reporting under CERD is examined below with reference to three African countries in which discrimination on grounds of ethnicity has been a pervasive issue: Rwanda, Mauritania, and the Sudan.

Some sobering lessons can be learnt from the Rwandan reporting experience.[35] At the time of the genocide in Rwanda, in 1994, Rwanda was one of the state parties to CERD that had established a good reporting record. It submitted state reports regularly between 1976 and 1989. When it examined Rwanda's third periodic report in 1979, the Committee expressed its general satisfaction with Rwanda's reporting since 1976, and the Committee described the report as 'a praiseworthy attempt by a small country to continue the dialogue with the Committee'.[36] At the examination of the fourth report, the Committee not only 'expressed satisfaction' with the report and government action, but went as far as describing the report as 'exemplary', as refuting the general opinion that developing countries were not able to submit satisfactory reports, and as a 'model'.[37] During the examination, the government representative painted a very favourable picture of a society

---

[31] UN Doc A/59/18, para 99.

[32] See General Recommendation 30, in which the CERD Committee asserts that 'State parties are under an obligation to guarantee equality between citizens and non-citizens in the enjoyment of these rights to the extent recognized under international law'; and General Recommendation 23, in which the CERD Committee affirms the position that 'discrimination against indigenous peoples falls under the scope of the Convention and that all appropriate means must be taken to combat and eliminate such discrimination'.   [33] UN Doc CERD/C/BWA/CO/16, 4 April 2006.

[34] ibid, para 9.

[35] See also F Viljoen, 'Hate Speech in Rwanda as a Test Case for International Human Rights Law' (2005) 38 *CILSA* 1.   [36] UN Doc A/36/18, para 306.

[37] UN Doc CERD/C/SR.657, paras 51 and 52.

in which the Hutus, Tutsis, and the Twa 'had become practically indistinguish-able'.[38] Answering questions posed in respect of the single political party system during the examination of the fifth state report, the government representative remarked that there was 'freedom of expression and the government press co-existed with a growing private press'.[39] Rwanda's last two reports before the genocide (the sixth and seventh) were considered together in 1989.[40] The crux of these reports was that the CERD formed part of national law,[41] and that racial discrimination was 'totally prohibited under Rwandese law'.[42]

Some 14 years of regular reporting then abruptly came to a halt, roughly coin-ciding with the 'invasion' of Rwanda by the Rwandan Patriotic Front (RPF) in October 1990. The CERD Committee applied its preventive procedure (termed 'prevention of racial discrimination, including early warning and urgent pro-cedures') of considering the situation in the absence of a state report. The Committee met with a government representative, who 'beg[ged] the Committee's indulgence for his Government's shortcomings',[43] and undertook to present a written reply.[44] A short question-and-answer session covered issues such as the failure to implement the 1993 Arusha Peace Accord, and the abolition of identity cards. The answers left much in the air, exemplified by the following response: 'The previous Government had decided to print new identity cards that did not mention ethnic origin, but, owing to the political vacuum, that decision had not yet been implemented'.[45] Subsequent to the interaction, on 9 March 1994, the Committee adopted con-cluding observations, in which it regretted that the information requested was not supplied. It further noted with concern the impunity for ethnically motivated murders, recommending that 'steps should be taken immediately at the inter-national level to investigate the crimes against humanity which have been com-mitted in Rwanda and to collect systematically evidence which could eventually be submitted to an international tribunal with competence on this question'.[46] This recommendation, predating the unleashing of the genocide on 6–7 April 1994 by about two weeks, demonstrates the seriousness with which the CERD Committee viewed the matter. However, quite clearly the recommended steps were not taken. Its further recommendation that Rwanda provide the Committee with additional information by 30 June 1994 also did not prove to have any impact.

Rwanda remained on the CERD Committee's agenda during and after the 1994 genocide. Between 1994 and 1998, Rwanda was the subject of no fewer than seven

[38] UN Doc A/39/18, para 165.
[39] UN Doc A/42/18, para 91. According to the representative, dissent could be expressed within the party, adding that the 'fact that no one was currently doing so merely indicated that there was general satisfaction with the way the country was being run' (UN Doc CERD/C/SR.568, para 19).
[40] UN Doc CERD/C/SR.839.
[41] 'Under the Rwandese constitutional system, an international convention takes full effect intern-ally as soon as it is ratified, without any need for any legal or administrative measure' (seventh periodic report, UN Doc CERD/C/169/Add.1, dated 17 January 1989, para 9).
[42] UN Doc CRD/C/SR.839, para 5.
[43] UN Doc CERD/C/SR.1027 (Summary Record) (15 March 1994) para 33.
[44] ibid, para 42.   [45] ibid, para 52.   [46] ibid, para 69.

Committee decisions.[47] In 1998, again applying its early warning and urgent procedure, the Committee's comments shifted its concern to the lengthy detention of
accused persons, the slowness of rebuilding the judiciary, and also the slowness of
'action to combat ethnic prejudice in accordance with article 7 of the Convention'.[48]
In 1999, Rwanda submitted its eighth to twelfth reports as a consolidated report,[49]
which the Committee considered in 2000.[50] In its conclusions, the Committee
noted issues such as the persistent impunity of security forces, the deplorable prison
conditions of mostly Hutu prisoners, and alarming evidence of civil defence units
being set up, but it is silent about the role of ethnicity in the law and practice of
the post-genocide state.

Mauritania has also been a regular reporter under CERD. In its concluding
observations adopted after its examination of the latest Mauritanian report in 2004
(its combined sixth and seventh),[51] the Committee expressed its continued concern about the inferior position of black Africans (Moors) in Mauritanian society,
and 'about information on the persistence of slavery-like practices, which constitute serious instances of discrimination based on descent', despite the abolition of
slavery in 1981.[52] In particular, it noted the lack of demonstrable implementation
of the 1981 law and the absence of any criminal law provision that expressly pun-
ishes slavery. These observations informed the recommendation that a detailed
study of this issue should be included in the state party's next report, that it should
launch a wide-ranging information and public-awareness campaign to put an end
to slavery-like practices, and that perpetrators should be systematically prosecuted.

These observations elicited a barrage of criticism from the government.[53] In its
response, the government conceded that 'some individuals who descended from
former feudal strata still consider themselves more noble than others and may, for
example, refuse marriage on this basis' but insisted that such attitudes do not constitute 'slavery-like practices'.[54] It considered the recommendations 'redundant' as
the integration of 'citizens who are descendants of former slaves provides a model
of integration and social advancement'.[55] Emphasizing the discrepancy between
the formal law and its practical application, the Committee noted that 'the information on the adoption of practical measures designed specifically to combat slavery-like practices remains inadequate', and recommended that actions specifically
targeting the populations concerned, besides general anti-poverty programmes,
should be taken.[56] This recommendation met with the government's disavowal
of measures intent on 'reopening past divisions or making the slightest distinction
between citizens below the poverty line'.[57] A recommendation that a detailed study
of the situation of Mauritanian refugees still in exile and of those who have returned

---

[47] See eg UN Doc A/50/18, para 25(7), in 1995, A/53/18, para IIA4 in 1998.
[48] Decision 4(52) on Rwanda, UN Doc A/53/18, para IIA4 (20 March 1998) para 4.
[49] UN Doc CERD/C/335/Add.1 (28 June 1999).
[50] UN Doc CERD/C/304/Add.97 (19 April 2001).   [51] UN Doc A/59/18, paras 328–57.
[52] ibid, para 342.   [53] UN Doc A/59/18, 115–20.   [54] ibid, 116.   [55] ibid.
[56] UN Doc A/59/18, para 343.   [57] ibid, 117.

should be provided in the next periodic report met with the response that 'today no Mauritanian can be described as a refugee under the relevant conventions'.[58]

Much of the government's response dwells on the 'divergence between the fruitful interactive dialogue between its delegation . . . and the concluding observations adopted by the Committee'.[59] The Committee is taken to task for not noting 'the progress made' after the examination of the previous report. Despite the 'progress made over the past five years in the legal, political, economic, and social spheres, . . . certain conclusions adopted contradict those adopted in 1999, whereas others refer to "concerns" going back 10 years but not commented on at the time of the Committee's consideration of the previous report'. While there may well be room for a perception that the concluding observations were much more pointed and less conciliatory than the dialogue during the presentation of the report, the challenge of discontinuity between recommendations emanating from the present and the last report do not withstand closer scrutiny. On the most pertinent issue, that of the actual implementation of formal guarantees, the Committee in its previous recommendation urged the State to 'include information in its next report on legislative measures and practices introduced by the authorities . . . with a view to promoting the struggle against discrimination affecting the most vulnerable groups of the population, in particular the black communities, and to eradicating vestiges of practices of slavery and involuntary servitude'.[60] An assessment of all the verbiage reveals that this aspect remains as pertinent as ever. While these comments indicate serious engagement with the reporting process, they seem to depart from a premise of infallibility and are revealing in their sensitivity to the issues addressed.[61]

When the CERD Committee examined the last Sudanese state report (combining its ninth to eleventh reports) in 2001, it expressed general concern about the lack of information concerning the demographic composition of the population.[62] Noting the seriousness of the situation, it remarked that 'massive loss of life, destruction of property, abductions and a decline in financial and material resources and political conflict overshadow all efforts made by the State party to implement the Convention'.[63] The primary focus of its concluding observations was on the Nuer and Dinka ethnic groups in the upper Nile region, omitting any reference to the western region of Darfur. Unsurprisingly, no reports were submitted at the height of the Darfur crisis.

Faced with a huge volume of overdue reports, the CERD Committee adopted the procedure of 'reviewing' the situation in states from which reports were seriously overdue, in the absence of a state report.[64] Numerous African countries

---

[58] ibid, 118.   [59] ibid, 115, 119.

[60] UN Doc CERD/C/304/Add.82 (12 April 2001) para 12.

[61] ibid, 116: 'Neither these individuals nor anyone else can cite the slightest evidence to corroborate the allegations on which the Committee has based its concluding observations'.

[62] UN Doc CERD/C/304/Add.116 (27 April 2001) para 9.

[63] UN Doc CERD/C/304/Add.116, para 8.

[64] W Vandenhole, *The Procedure before the UN Human Rights Treaty Bodies* (Antwerp: Intersentia, 2004) 83.

have been at the receiving end of this procedure.[65] In 1999, for example, the Committee considered the implementation of CERD in Congo, as Congo's initial report had been overdue since August 1989. Basing itself on UN and 'other' information sources, the Committee highlighted some of the problematic aspects, especially arising from the conflict in Congo during 1997. In one instance, the Committee not only conducted a review, but decided to remain seized of the situation under its urgent action and early-warning procedure.[66]

4 Early-warning Measures and Urgent Procedure

As was mentioned, the CERD Committee established early-warning measures and urgent procedures, which are directed at preventing existing problems from escalating into conflicts.[67] Since then, the Committee has taken action in respect of more than 20 state parties. As part of this practice, the CERD adopts decisions and may undertake country visits. Examples of the application of this procedure include action in respect of the Sudan. In 1998, the Committee highlighted some serious concerns arising from the ethnic and racial dimension of the conflict between the southern and northern regions of the country. Amongst other things, it called on the state to guarantee the freedom of religion of all Sudanese. In its 2004 decision, it supported the deployment in Darfur of an adequately reinforced African Union-led protection force with the support of the League of Arab States and the logistic and financial assistance of the European Union and the USA.[68] Overtaken by events, the Committee again recommended to the Secretary-General, and through him, to the Security Council, the deployment, without further delay, of a sufficiently enlarged African Union force in Darfur with a Security Council mandate to protect the civilian population, including those in camps, displaced persons, and refugees returning to their homes in Darfur, against war crimes, crimes against humanity, and the risk of genocide.[69]

5 Individual Communications

Complaints by individuals may be considered by the Committee in respect of those states that have made a declaration under article 14 of the Convention.[70] As

[65] Some of the states in the category of 'worst reporters', such as Côte d'Ivoire, Ethiopia, Equatorial Guinea, Somalia, and Sierra Leone, have all undergone such reviews.

[66] This concerns Liberia, which did not report for 25 years after ratification: UN Doc A/56/18, paras 429 and 480.

[67] See paras 14 to 19 of the Report of the Committee on the Elimination of Racial Discrimination, UN Doc A/52/18.

[68] Decision 1 (65), Situation in Darfur, 14 August 2004, UN Doc A/59/18, para 17.

[69] Decision 2 (66), Situation in Darfur, CERD/C/DEC/SDN/1 (27 April 2005).

[70] The provisions of this article entered into force for those states that made a declaration in terms thereof in 1982.

at 31 December 2006, a total of 47 such declarations had been made.[71] Only three of these declarations came from African states: Algeria, Senegal, and South Africa.[72] The Durban Declaration, which urges state parties to CERD to 'consider making the declaration envisaged under article 14',[73] set the standard for the subsequent formulation in concluding observations adopted after the examination of state reports, as exemplified in its concluding observations to the Libyan report in 2004.[74] Expressed as a percentage, the three acceptances represent 6 per cent of the total number of African states parties.

Although CERD entered into force in 1969, its complaints procedure, requiring acceptance by ten states, only started functioning in 1982. By 31 December 2003, 27 communications had been submitted to the Committee. Of these, 11 were declared inadmissible; the CERD Committee found violations in only six cases—a 'dismal' record, indeed.[75] By 31 December 2006, the number of cases had grown to 34. None of these complaints has emanated from the three African states that have accepted the right of individual petition. The states complained against were Australia, Denmark, France, Norway, the Netherlands, Serbia Montenegro, Slovakia, and Sweden. On a number of occasions, complaints were submitted by persons of African nationality residing in these states,[76] or nationals of these states of African origin.[77]

6 Realization

Discrimination based on ethnic difference is not only pervasive in much of Africa, it is a major source of conflict and the erosion of security. Despite the initial enthusiasm on the part of African countries about CERD and ratification by most, it has not become a vehicle for the elimination of racial discrimination in Africa. As long as 'racial discrimination' could be equated with 'apartheid', African states were united in their condemnation. The unequivocal African support in the drafting

---

[71] The analysis here is based on the data at <http://www.un.org/Depts/Treaty/final/ts2/newfiles/> (30 November 2006).

[72] South Africa's declaration states that communications may be directed to the CERD Committee after all domestic remedies have been exhausted. By specifically 'indicating' the South African Human Rights Commission under art 14(2) of CERD, this statement seems to indicate that a complaint first has to be submitted to this national human rights institution.   [73] Para 75.

[74] A/59/18, para 111: 'The Committee further notes that the State party has not made the optional declaration provided for in article 14 of the Convention, and recommends that it consider the possibility of making such a declaration'.

[75] T van Boven, 'The Petition System under the International Covenant on the Elimination of All Forms of Racial Discrimination: A Sobering Balance Sheet' (2000) 4 *Max Planck Ybk of United Nations L* 271, 275–7.

[76] See eg Communication 2/1989, *Diop v France*, UN Doc CERD/C/39/D/2/1989 (10 May 1991) (Senegalese citizen residing in Monaco) and Communication 4/1991, *LK v Netherlands*, UN Doc CERD/C/42/D/4/1991 (16 March 1993) (Moroccan citizen residing in Utrecht).

[77] See eg Communication 34/2004, *Gelle v Denmark*, UN Doc CERD/C/68/D/34/2004 (15 March 2006) (Danish national of Somali origin).

and adoption phases may be ascribed to the common ideal to eradicate systematic racial discrimination from the continent. This also explains the inclusion of the 'duty' on states to 'condemn racial segregation and *apartheid*',[78] a duty most Organization of African Unity (OAU) member states fulfilled. Perhaps blinded by the scale and extent of racial discrimination in South Africa, African states unfortunately did not take CERD seriously as far as their domestic situations were concerned. Few states complied fully with their primary 'visible' duty under the Convention, the submission of state reports. In the light of the non-compliance with this obligation, the extent to which states comply with other, 'unsupervised'[79] duties, such as the duty to encourage 'integrationalist multiracial organizations', remains an open question.[80] Even where states have submitted reports, they have largely failed to provide information on aspects related to ethnicity. This omission is symptomatic of the failure of most governments to accept and accommodate diversity. Because so few African states have allowed individuals to lodge complaints with the Committee, this avenue never became a viable route of redressing racial discrimination.[81] The CERD Committee has also not done enough to address the root causes of ethnic conflict or to respond when racially based violence erupted, particularly in Central Africa. Although the Committee has gradually adopted a more pro-active approach, this approach has not translated into reality in Africa.

B International Covenant on Civil and Political Rights (ICCPR)

The ICCPR contains the most important civil and political rights, mostly of individuals, but in one respect also of peoples, as far as a 'peoples' right to self-determination' is concerned.[82] By providing for the right to join trade unions as part of the right of freedom of association, the Covenant goes beyond typical civil and political rights.[83] A unique feature of the ICCPR is the right of 'persons belonging to' minorities to 'enjoy their own culture' in community with other members of a minority group.[84] Although it guarantees the right to life, the ICCPR does not abolish the death penalty, but restricts its imposition to the 'most serious crimes'.[85] The Second Protocol to the ICCPR (OPII), aimed at the abolition of the death penalty in ratifying states,[86] extends the substantive scope of the Covenant to capital punishment.

---

[78] CERD, art 3.   [79] That is, not dependent on state reports.   [80] CERD, art 2(1)(e).
[81] For an example of a South African court finding interpretative guidance in CERD, see *Ex p Gauteng Legislature* (1996) 3 SA 163 (CC), para 71 n 53 and para 82.
[82] ICCPR, art 1, overlapping with ICESCR, art 1.   [83] ICCPR, art 22.
[84] ICCPR, art 27.   [85] ICCPR, art 6.
[86] OPII, art 1 provides that no person 'shall be executed' in a ratifying state, and that state parties 'shall take all necessary measures to abolish the death penalty within its jurisdiction' (adopted in 1989, and entering into force in 1991).

1 Mandate and Composition of the Human Rights Committee (HRC)

The monitoring body established under ICCPR is the Human Rights Committee (HRC).[87] The HRC has four functions: In the case of all state parties, it considers periodic reports submitted by them.[88] In respect of those states that have made declarations under article 41 of the Covenant, the HRC considers inter-state communications. So far, no state has made use of this procedure. In respect of states that have accepted the First Optional Protocol to the Covenant (OPI), it considers communications submitted by individuals against those states.[89] In respect of states parties that have accepted the HRC's competence to consider inter-state and individual communications, other states and individuals may base communications against ratifying states on the provisions of OPII.[90]

The HRC is composed of 18 members who are elected by the states parties to ICCPR for renewable terms of four years.[91] They serve in their personal capacity. At its inception, African states were underrepresented on the HRC.[92] By 30 June 1999, Rajsoomer Lallah (Mauritius) and Abdelfattah Amor (Tunisia) were serving on the HRC. By 31 December 2006, the African membership had increased to four: Amor, whose term expires at the end of 2006, and Lallah, Ahmed Tawfik Khalil (Egypt), and Maurice Glèlè-Ahanhanzo (Benin), whose terms run to the end of 2008. The situation improved even further subsequent to the election by ICCPR state parties on 17 September 2006: as from 2007, five Africans will be serving on the HRC, with the re-election of Amor and the election of Zonke Majodina (South Africa).

2 Ratifications, Reservations, and Derogations

By 31 December 2006, 50 African states had ratified the ICCPR.[93] The global number of ratifications of ICCPR on the same date was 160, or 82 per cent of the

---

[87] Not to be confused with the Commission on Human Rights.

[88] In terms of ICCPR, art 40.

[89] This Protocol ('OPI') entered into force on 23 March 1976, simultaneously with the ICCPR. The Preamble of the Optional Protocol states that it is aimed at further achieving the purpose of the ICCPR and at improving the implementation thereof. Art 1 provides that state parties to the Protocol recognize the competence of the HRC 'to receive and consider communications from individuals subject to its jurisdiction'.

[90] See OPII, arts 4 and 5; however, a state may make a statement to the contrary at the moment of ratification or accession.   [91] ICCPR, arts 28(1) and 32(1).

[92] Of the 18 members elected in 1993–4, three were African, one each from Egypt, Mauritius, and Senegal (UN Docs A/48/40, A/49/40). Of the three female members of the HRC, none was from an African state. From 1977 to 1993, eight Africans were part of the group of 48 people who had served on the HRC (see M Nowak, *UN Covenant on Civil and Political Rights (CCPR) Commentary* (Kehl: NP Engel, 2nd edn, 2005) 1227–8. The states represented were Egypt, Kenya, Mauritius, Rwanda, Senegal, and Tunisia. The last two countries had twice had members serving on the Committee. From 1 January 1995 to 31 December 1996 only two Africans served on the Committee. They are El Shafei (Egypt) and Lallah (Mauritius). (The member from Senegal (Ndiaye) retired, and was not replaced by an African: see M Nowak, 'The Activities of the UN Human Rights Committee: Developments from 1 August 1992 through 31 July 1995' (1995) 16 *HRLJ* 377, 378.) Africa's clear underrepresentation is to an extent palliated by the fact that El Shafei served as the body's Vice-Chairperson for two successive terms.

[93] See Table 3.2 below.

total number of potential ratifying states.[94] For the African states, the average was 94 per cent.[95] By 31 December 2006, only 57 states, seven of them from Africa, have become state parties to OPII.[96]

Seven African countries entered reservations or made interpretative declarations when they ratified or acceded to the ICCPR. This is a small proportion of the total number of state parties that entered some form of reservation, undertaking, or declaration.[97] The reservations of African states are not very detailed or comprehensive, when compared to, for example, the five reservations, five undertakings, and three declarations made by the USA on accession.[98] The reservations by African states may be grouped as follows:

• Guinea and Libya raised concerns of an explicit political nature in their reservations. Guinea objected that article 48(1) is contrary to the democratization of international relations. Libya clarified that its acceptance of the treaty obligations did not imply acceptance of the Israeli state.

• Congo and The Gambia raised substantive conflicts between domestic law and provisions of ICCPR. Article 11 of the ICCPR stipulates that no one 'shall be imprisoned merely on the ground of inability to fulfil a contractual obligation'. Congo's reservation left its private law intact in so far as it allows for civil imprisonment.[99] The Gambia reserved the right of its nationals to invoke the right to free legal assistance 'where the interests of justice so require'[100] only when charged with a capital offence.

• Egypt made a declaration intent on infusing the interpretation of ICCPR with the spirit of Shari'ah: It accepted ICCPR, but 'taking into consideration the

---

[94] That is, 156 out of the total of 194.

[95] Calculated as 50 out of the 53 UN African members.

[96] The acceptance of Protocol II by most of the African states confirms a constitutional guarantee against the death penalty, included in post-1989 Constitutions (Cape Verde 1992 Constitution, art 27(2); Mozambique 1990 Constitution, art 70(2), Namibia 1990 Constitution, art 6; Seychelles 1993 Constitution, art 15(2)). This matter was left open in the 1994 South African Constitution, leaving it to the Constitutional Court to declare capital punishment unconstitutional (*S v Makwanyane* 1995 (3) SA 391 (CC)). Despite this finding, the subsequent 1996 Constitution did not explicitly outlaw the death penalty. Despite ongoing debates and popular support for the death penalty, South Africa eventually acceded to Protocol II (in 2002). In the other two states (Djibouti and Liberia), acceptance of Protocol II also followed upon domestic abolition.

[97] R Higgins, 'Africa and the Convenant on Civil and Political Rights during the First Five Years of the *Journal*: Some Facts and Some Thoughts' (1993) 5 *RADIC* 55, 59 described the African record in respect of reservations as 'very good indeed'.

[98] See information contained at web-site <http://www.un.org/Depts/Treaty/funal/newfiles/frontboo/tocgen.html>.

[99] Belgium entered an objection to this reservation. On the basis of an analysis of the Congolese law, Belgium observed that the reservation was unnecessary and should not be regarded as setting a precedent. In terms of the Congolese law, imprisonment will only follow if a creditor is due more than 20,000 CFA, and in bad faith became insolvent. Imprisonment can only be imposed for those between 18 and 60 years of age. Higgins (n 97 above) expressed the view that it 'certainly cannot be said to be contrary to the entire purpose of the Covenant'. See also the South African Constitutional Court's decision in *Coetzee v Government of RSA* 1995 (4) SA 631 (CC).   [100] ICCPR, art 14(3)(d).

provisions of the Islamic Shari'ah and the fact that it does not conflict with the text...'.

- Botswana entered two reservations aimed at subordinating the interpretation by the HRC of the relevant provisions to that given under the Botswana Constitution. One reservation has the effect of equating the prohibition against torture in article 7 with Botswana's domestic constitutional level of protection. It also accepted only those restrictions to freedom of movement, exile, and return that are 'compatible with' the corresponding provisions of the Botswana Constitution.

- Algeria made a number of what it termed 'interpretative declarations'. The reference in article 1 to 'Non-Self-Governing and Trust Territories' prompted Algeria to state that article 1 cannot in any way imply the impairment of the right to self-determination. Article 22, dealing with freedom of association, does not impair the right to organize, but makes 'law the framework for action by the State'. The last reference is to the position of women. Article 23(4) requires state parties to ensure equality of spouses in marriage. The declaration that this provision shall in no way impair the 'essential foundations of the Algerian legal system' in relation to entering into marriage, the situation during marriage, and the dissolution of the marriage, is very drastic.[101]

Mainly Western European states raised objections against a number of these reservations.[102] Objections were also directed against the reservations entered by the USA. No African state raised any objection against any of the reservations or declarations.

As was stated, the ICCPR also provides for the optional acceptance of inter-state complaints.[103] By 31 December 2006, a total of 48 states globally had accepted the competence of the HRC to consider communications of this nature. Eight African states have accepted this optional provision.[104] Article 4(3) allows state parties to notify other parties of temporary derogations from the Convention. Only two state parties from the African continent have as yet provided such information.[105] They are Algeria[106] and Sudan. In the case of Sudan, the continuous conflict between the north and south provides the explanation for a continued state of emergency.[107]

---

[101] Germany and the Netherlands raised objections to the Algerian 'declaration'.

[102] See eg the objections of most West European States (including Denmark, France, Ireland, the Netherlands, Portugal, Spain, and Sweden) against the reservations entered by Botswana, on the basis that they invoke the internal law of Botswana and may cast doubts on the commitment of the state to fulfil its obligations under the ICCPR.   [103] ICCPR, art 41.

[104] See Table 3.2 below.

[105] Information contained on web-site <http:/www.un.org/Depts/Treaty/final/ts2/newfiles/frontboo /tocgen.html>.

[106] In 1991, and again in 1992, in respect of a state of emergency of 12 months.

[107] Higgins (n 97 above) 69, 61.

3 State Reporting

The primary duty of ratifying states is to present an initial report (within two years of ratification) and periodic reports (every five years thereafter, or as required by the HRC). Initial reporting is required by article 40 of ICCPR; periodic reporting was introduced by the HRC.[108] The non-compliance of states has become a major obstacle to the effective functioning of the system. By 31 December 2006, of the 24 states from which at least one report was due for ten years or longer, 13 were from Africa. These states are, in descending order of dereliction: The Gambia, Equatorial Guinea, Somalia, Rwanda, Côte d'Ivoire, the Seychelles, Angola, Niger, Ethiopia, Guinea, Mozambique, Cape Verde, and Malawi.[109]

Not only were reports submitted late, but they mostly also suffered from a lack of detail.[110] Where details of legislative provisions and administrative regulations were provided, there was a lack of information on the 'implementation of the Convention in practice',[111] and on the difficulties experienced in securing enjoyment of the rights in the Convention.[112] Also disappointing is the fact that many of the reports were not the first to be presented by the state and to be considered by the HRC. Despite previous advice, states have still not followed the guidelines for reporting and have not complied with the spirit required for meaningful reporting. However, as in the case of Morocco, the problematic aspects of the report were sometimes rectified by frank answers, even admitting to some difficulties in implementing the Covenant.[113]

The timely submission of reports should not be regarded as a goal in itself, and guarantees very little. Burundi had, for example, submitted its periodic report on time.[114] When it was considered in 1992, the delegation supplemented the report with more updated information. The HRC expressed its concern about the lack of protection of minorities, ethnic dominance of one ethnic group of the armed forces, the declaration of and power to declare states of emergency, detentions, and the lack of investigation of past atrocities. Not long after the report was considered, renewed ethnic violence broke out in Burundi. In 1994, the HRC requested the Burundi government to submit a report about the local human rights conditions. This request was made in terms of the obligation of states to submit reports 'whenever the Committee so requests'.[115] Although the report lacked information on the situation in Burundi, the HRC used all information at its disposal to examine the situation. By

---

[108] See M Nowak, 'The Activities of the UN-Human Rights Committee: Developments from 1 August 1989 through 31 July 1992' (1993) 14 *HRLJ* 9.

[109] UN Doc A/60/40 (Vol I) para 71.

[110] The report of Niger was described as 'extremely succinct' (UN Doc CCPR/C/79/Add 17 (1993)) and that of Cameroon as 'summary and rather theoretical' (UN Doc CCPR/C/79/Add. 33 (1994)).

[111] See the Moroccan report (UN Doc CCPR/C/79/Add. 44 (1994)) and the report submitted by Senegal, described by the HRC as lacking in attention to actual implementation (UN Doc CCPR/C/79/Add. 10 (1992)).

[112] See eg HRC report on Egypt's report (UN Doc CCPR/C/79/Add. 23 (1993)).

[113] UN Doc CCPR/C/79/Add. 44 (1994) para A.

[114] UN Doc CCPR/C/79/Add. 9 (1992).   [115] ICCPR, art 40(1).

that time, the violence had abated. The HRC repeated, formulated in greater detail, the observations and recommendations contained in its previous comments.[116] The HRC emphasized that these human rights violations must be addressed within the greater framework of working towards national reconciliation.

Since 1991, the HRC requested special reports in exceptionally serious situations, such as in respect of Rwanda (1994). Rwanda submitted its initial report under the ICCPR, which it had acceded to five years earlier, in 1981,[117] and it was examined in 1982.[118] Members of the HRC expressed dissatisfaction with the delay in submission and the brevity of the report.[119] Its second report, submitted and considered in 1987,[120] was also its last. The HRC's examination relating to freedom of the press reflected the need for less media restriction, more multiplicity and accessibility to foreign print media,[121] but did not address the crucial issue of hate propaganda. Not commenting on the substance of report, the HRC praised the delegation for being well-prepared and for engaging in a 'genuine dialogue'.[122] All subsequent reports are overdue, despite a 'special decision', taken after the genocide, on 27 October 1994, in which the HRC requested the submission of Rwanda's third report 'without delay',[123] so that it could be discussed during 1995. One has to agree with Buergenthal that it is 'by no means certain that by seeking special reports from Rwanda [and other countries], the Committee had any meaningful impact on the human rights situation in those countries or effectively complemented the actions of other UN bodies'.[124] For the rest, it seems the HRC has washed its hands of Rwanda and the conflict there.

But there is also a ray of hope. The HRC in 2002 started to address the problem of long overdue reports by scheduling the examination of the situation in a country in the absence of a report or even in the absence of both a report and a representative (as in respect of The Gambia).[125] Emerging African democracies also seem more likely to submit reports.[126] It is significant that these states submit themselves to international scrutiny. Viewed in the context of democratization, the reporting obligation takes on new meaning, and becomes a vehicle for establishing and guarding democratic institutions. Non-reporting is one feature that distinguishes *de facto* from *de iure* democracies. A review of African state reporting since 2000 reveals that the HRC increasingly notes encouraging developments in legislative enactment and judicial application.[127] Some of its main concerns are: states which

116 UN Doc CCPR/C/79/Add. 41 (1994).   117 UN Doc CCPR/C/1/Add. 54.
118 UN Doc A/37/40, para 214.   119 UN Doc A/37/40, para 216.
120 UN Doc CCPR/C/46/Add. 1; A/43/40, paras 200–40.
121 UN Doc A/43/40, para 232.   122 UN Doc A/43/40, para 239.
123 UN Doc A/50/40 (dated 4 February 1996) para 55.
124 T Buergenthal, 'The UN Human Rights Committee' (2001) 5 *Max Planck Ybk of United Nations L* 341, 359.   125 UN Doc CCPR/CO/75/GMB (12 August 2004).
126 This is of particular relevance in the case of Algeria (UN Doc CCPR/C/97/Add. 1 (1992)), Niger (UN Doc CCPR/C/97/Add. 17 (1993)), Tanzania (UN Doc CCPR/C/97/Add. 12 (1992)) and Togo (UN Doc CCPR/C/97/Add. 36 (1994)).
127 Concluding observations on Congo's second periodic report, UN Doc CCPR/C/79/Add.118 (Conclusions: Congo), 27 March 2000; Concluding observations on Mali's second periodic report,

set up national human rights institutions, but do not allow them to operate effectively.[128] Some 'civil and political' rights are constantly under serious threat, consistently due to torture and deplorable prison conditions, and often as a result of arbitrary detention and extrajudicial killings.[129] The HRC criticized the reinstatement in 1996 of the death penalty in The Gambia, where it was abolished in 1993;[130] it expressed concern that ratification of OPII did not follow upon a *de facto* moratorium on the death penalty in Benin;[131] and it urged states to ensure that the death sentence is imposed only for the 'most serious crimes' and should not be mandatory.[132] Anti-terrorism legislation in African states, as elsewhere, is too vague.[133] Other issues receiving attention include the rights especially of 'ethnic'[134] and homosexual minorities,[135] and the persistence of slave-like practices.[136] Country-specific issues include the lack of security measures to protect the civilian population of Northern Uganda against the Lord's Resistance Army attacks, and children against abduction.[137] In respect of Namibia, the HRC recommended a domestic mechanism to implement the Committee's decisions under OPI.[138]

An analysis of the HRC's concluding observations reveals extensive overlap with other UN human rights treaties. As far as women (also covered in CEDAW) are concerned, for example, recurrent themes are domestic and other forms of violence against women;[139] discriminatory and harmful cultural practices such as genital mutilation and the *levirat*;[140] and the importance of registering marriages to ensure the prohibition of child marriages.[141] In its recommendations relating to maternal and infant mortality in Mali, the HRC did not make any reference to the MDGs,[142] which speak pertinently to these issues. Although the HRC does not treat issues with the same amount of specificity as specific treaty bodies would, its 'general mandate' is interpreted to cover the most important aspects relating to women and children, and occasionally extends to socio-economic rights as well.[143]

UN Doc CCPR/CO/77/MLI (Conclusions: Mali), 16 April 2003; Concluding observations on Uganda's initial report, UN Doc CCPR/CO/80/UGA, 4 May 2004 (Conclusions: Uganda); Concluding observations on Namibia's initial report, UN Doc CCPR/CO/81/NAM, 30 July 2004 (Conclusions: Namibia); Concluding observations on Benin's initial report, UN Doc CCPR/CO/82/BEN, 1 December 2004 (Conclusions: Benin).

[128] Conclusions: Benin, para 8; Conclusions: Mali, para 8; Conclusions: Uganda, para 7.
[129] Conclusions: Benin, para 17; Conclusions: Congo, paras 8, 13, and 15; Conclusions: The Gambia, para 7; Conclusions: Mali, para 15; Conclusions: Uganda, para 18;
[130] Conclusions: The Gambia, para 8.   [131] Conclusions: Benin, para 13.
[132] Conclusions: The Gambia, para 8; Conclusions: Uganda, para 13.
[133] Conclusions: Benin, para 12; Conclusions: Uganda, para 8.
[134] The HRC criticized the Gambia for denying the existence of ethnic minorities (Conclusions: The Gambia, para 24); see also Conclusions: Congo, para 21 (relating to the Pygmies).
[135] Conclusions: Namibia, para 22.   [136] Conclusions: Mali, para 16.
[137] Conclusions: Uganda, paras 12 and 15.   [138] Conclusions: Namibia, para 8.
[139] Conclusions: Congo, para 10; Conclusions: Mali, para 12; Conclusions: Namibia, para 20; Conclusions: Uganda, para 9.   [140] Conclusions: Benin, para 11; Conclusions: Mali, para 10.
[141] Conclusions: Namibia, para 9.
[142] Conclusions, Mali, para 14; on the MDGs, see Section A.1 above.
[143] On a limited number of occasions, the HRC addressed the right to anti-retroviral (ARV) treatment of people with AIDS, see Conclusions: Namibia, para 10; Conclusions: Uganda, para 14.

Underscoring the indivisibility of human rights, and ensuring that major concerns are covered when a state reports under the ICCPR and not under other treaties, such an approach supports arguments for the consolidation of reporting under the seven UN human rights treaties.

4 Individual Complaints under the First Optional Protocol (OPI)

As at 31 December 2006, 32 of the 50 African state parties to ICCPR had become a party to OPI.[144] This means that more than half (60 per cent) of all African UN member states were party to both the Covenant and its optional complaints procedure. By comparison, the percentage globally stood at slightly lower than 56 per cent.

Communications may, in principle, only be submitted by 'victims'. In terms of the HRC's jurisprudence,[145] it lacks competence to hear matters brought under article 1 ('peoples' right to self-determination'), because it can only be approached by *individuals*. The HRC has received by far the most communications of any of the UN human rights treaty bodies. Given its experience, productivity and the quality of its work, the HRC is regarded as the UN's primary human rights body.

At the end of each session the HRC publishes its 'views'. An analysis is now made of the views and decisions issued from 1981, when the HRC adopted its first 'view' in respect of an African country, up to the end of 2006, in order to establish to what extent individuals in African states have utilized the OPI procedure.[146] The first view adopted in relation to an African state was done in a case from Mauritius.[147] By the end of 2006, the HRC had made public a total of 59 findings against African states: 48 findings of 'violations', ten of inadmissibility, and one finding disclosing 'no violation'. The Democratic Republic of the Congo (DRC) accounted for the highest number of cases submitted against a single state, with 13 cases from that state having led to findings of violations by the HRC, while another two communications against it had been declared inadmissible. The other states complained against most frequently were Zambia (eight cases, seven findings of violation) and Madagascar (four cases, all ending in findings of a violation). With the exception of one case against Togo,[148] the HRC found

---

[144] See Table 3.2 below.

[145] Communication 167/1984, *Ominayak v Canada*, UN Doc CCPR/C/38/D/167/1984 (10 May 1990) para 32.1: 'The Optional Protocol provides a procedure under which individuals can claim that their individual rights have been violated. These rights are set out in part III of the Covenant, articles 6 to 27, inclusive. There is, however, no objection to a group of individuals, who claim to be similarly affected, collectively to submit a communication about alleged breaches of their rights.'

[146] The fourth session is the starting point, as the Committee issued views for the first time at the end of this session, when it began 'consideration of communications in accordance with the Protocol'. See UN Doc A/32/40, 37/40, para 147.

[147] Communication 35/1978, *Aumeeruddy-Cziffra and Others v Mauritius*, UN Doc CCPR/C/12/D/35/1978 (9 April 1981) (*Aumeeruddy-Cziffra* case). Mauritius became the second African state to accede to or ratify the Optional Protocol by acceding to it in 1973 (after Madagascar ratified it in 1971).

[148] Communication 910/2000, *Rudolph v Togo*, UN Doc CCPR/C/79/D/910/2000 (15 December 2003) (*Rudolph* case).

violations on the merits in all instances. Although five communications were submitted against Mauritius, four of them were declared inadmissible. The views expressed on the merits of communications against African governments[149] are as follows:

Table 3.1: HRC views in respect of African states

Year	African state complained against	HRC finding
1981	Mauritius[150]	violation
1983	Madagascar[151]	violation
	Zaire (2)[152]	violation
1984	Zaire[153]	violation
1985	Madagascar (2)[154]	violation
1986	Zaire (2)[155]	violation
1897	Madagascar[156]	violation
1988	Zaire[157]	violation
1990	Mauritius[158]	inadmissible
	Zaire (2)[159]	violation
1991	Libya[160]	inadmissible
	Zaire[161]	inadmissible

[149] Since states undertake to 'respect and to ensure to all individuals within its territory and subject to its jurisdiction' the rights set out in the ICCPR (art 2(1) of the ICCPR), citizens of African countries are sometimes complainants in cases against non-African governments, especially in Europe.

[150] *Aumeeruddy-Cziffra* case (n 145 above).

[151] Communication 49/1979, *Marais v Madagascar*, UN Doc CCPR/C/18/D/49/1979 (24 March 1983) (*Marais* case).

[152] Communication 16/1997, *Mbenge v Zaire*, UN Doc CCPR/C/18/D/16/1997 (25 March 1983) and Communication 90/1981, *Luyeye v Zaire*, UN Doc CCPR/C/19/D/90/1981 (21 July 1983).

[153] Communication 124/1982, *Muteba v Zaire*, UN Doc CCPR/C/22/D/124/1982 (24 July 1984).

[154] Communication 115/1982, *Wight v Madagascar*, UN Doc CCPR/C/22/D/115/1982 (1 April 1985); and Communication 132/1982, *Jaona v Madagascar*, UN Doc CCPR/C/24/D/132/1982 (1 April 1985).

[155] Communication 138/1983, *Mpandanjila et al v Zaïre*, UN Doc CCPR/C/27/D/138/1983 (26 March 1986); and Communication 157/1983, *Mpaka-Nsusu v Zaire*, UN Doc CCPR/C/27/D/157/1983 (26 March 1986).

[156] Communication 155/1983, *Hammel v Madagascar*, UN Doc CCPR/C/29/D/155/1983 (3 April 1987).

[157] Communication 194/1985, *Muiyo v Zaire*, UN Doc CCPR/C/31/D/194/1985 (27 October 1987).

[158] Communication 354/1989, *Gooriah v Mauritius*, UN Doc CCPR/C/40/D/354/1989 (28 November 1990) (inadmissible).

[159] Communication 241/1987, *Birindiwa v Zaire*, CCPR/C/37/D/241/1987 (29 November 1989); and Communication 242/1987, *Tshisekedi v Zaire*, UN Doc CCPR/C/37/D/242/1987 (29 November 1989).

[160] Communication 457/1991, *AIE v Libya*, UN Doc CCPR/C/43/D/457/1991 (15 November 1991) (inadmissible).

[161] Communication 463/1991, *B-B v Zaire*, UN Doc CCPR/C/43/D/463/1991 (5 December 1991) (inadmissible).

Table 3.1 (*cont.*)

Year	African state complained against	HRC finding
1993	Zambia (2)[162]	violation
1994	Cameroon[163]	violation
	CAR[164]	violation
	Equatorial Guinea (2)[165]	violation
	Libya[166]	violation
	Mauritius[167]	inadmissible
	Senegal[168]	violation
	Zaire (2)[169]	violation (1) inadmissible (1)
1995	Zambia[170]	violation
1996	Togo (2)[171]	violation
	DRC[172]	violation
1999	Zambia[173]	violation
2000	Angola[174]	violation

[162] Communication 314/1988, *Bwalya v Zambia;* UN Doc CCPR/C/48/D/314/1988 (27 July 1993) (*Bwalya* case); and Communication 326/1988, *Kalenga v Zambia*, UN Doc CCPR/C/48/D/326/1988 (2 August 1993) (*Kalenga* case).

[163] Communication 458/1991, *Mukong v Cameroon*, UN Doc CCPR/C/51/D/458/1991 (10 August 1994).

[164] Communication 428/1990, *M'Boissona on behalf of Bozize v CAR*, UN Doc CCPR/C/50/D/428/1990 (26 April 1994).

[165] Communication 468/1991, *Bahamonde v Equatorial Guinea*, UN Doc CCPR/C/49/D/468/1991 (10 November 1993) (*Bahamonde* case); and Communication 414/1990, *Mika Miha v Equatorial Guinea*, UN Doc CCPR/C/51/D/414/1990 (10 August 1994).

[166] Communication 440/1990, *Youssef on behalf of Bashir El-Megreisi v Libya*, UN Doc CCPR/C/50/D/440/1990 (24 March 1994).

[167] Communication 567/1993, *Poongavanam v Mauritius*, UN Doc CCPR/C/51/D/567/1993 (9 August 1994) (inadmissible).

[168] Communication 386/1989, *Koné v Senegal*, UN Doc CCPR/C/52/D/386/1989 (27 October 1994).

[169] Communication 366/1989, *Tshiongo a Minanga v Zaire*, UN Doc CCPR/C/49/D/366/1989 (8 November 1993); Communication 497/1992, *Amisi v Zaire*, UN Doc CCPR/C/51/D/497/1992 (27 July 1994) (inadmissible).

[170] Communications 390/1990, *Lubuto v Zambia*, UN Doc CCPR/C/55/D/390/1990 (17 November 1995) (*Lubuto* case).

[171] Communications 422–44/1990 (joined), *Aduayom and Others v Togo*, UN Doc CCPR/C/57/D/422–4/1990 (19 August 1996); and Communication 505/1992, *Ackla v Togo*, UN Doc CCPR/C/51/D/505/1992 (10 April 1996) (*Ackla* case).

[172] Communication 542/1993, *N'Goya v DRC*, UN Doc CCPR/C/56/D/542/1993 (16 April 1996).

[173] Communication 768/1997, *Mukunto v Zambia*, UN Doc CCPR/C/66/D/768/1997 (2 August 1999).

[174] Communication 711/1996, *Dias v Angola*, UN Doc CCPR/C/681/D/711/1996 (18 April 2000).

Table 3.1 (*cont.*)

Year	African state complained against	HRC finding
	Namibia[175]	violation
	Zambia[176]	violation
2001	Cameroon[177]	violation
	Mauritius[178]	inadmissible
	Sierra Leone[179]	violation
2002	Côte d'Ivoire[180]	inadmissible
	DRC[181]	violation
	Namibia[182]	violation
	Zambia[183]	inadmissible
2003	DRC[184]	violation
	Mauritius[185]	inadmissible
	Togo[186]	no violation
	Zambia[187]	violation
2004	DRC[188]	violation
	Libya[189]	violation
2005	Angola[190]	violation

[175] Communication 760/1997, *Diergaardt and Others v Nambia*, UN Doc CCPR/C/69/D/760/1997 (6 September 2000).

[176] Communication 821/1998, *Chongwe v Zambia*, UN Doc CCPR/C/70/D/821/1998 (9 November 2000).

[177] Communication 630/1995, *Mazou v Cameroon*, UN Doc CCPR/C/72/D/630/1995 (3 August 2001).

[178] Communication 787/1997, *Gobin v Mauritius*, UN Doc CCPR/C/72/D/787/1997 (20 August 2001) (inadmissible).

[179] Communications 839, 840, and 841/1998, *Mansaraj and Others v Sierra Leone*, UN Docs CCPR/C/72/D/839–841/1998 (three identical views, 30 July 2001) (*Masaraj* case). The state party did not comply with the HRC's interim measures, but went ahead and executed the complainants. The HRC expressed its 'indignation' at the state's failure in a 'Decision': UN Doc CCPR/C/64/D/839–41/1998 (4 November 1998).

[180] Communication 940/2000, *Bi v Côte d'Ivoire*, UN Doc CCPR/C/75/D/940/2000 (26 July 2002) (inadmissible).

[181] Communication 641/1995, *Gedumbe v DRC*, UN Doc CCPR/C/75/D/641/1995 (26 July 2002).

[182] Communication 919/2000, *Müller and Another v Namibia*, UN Doc CCPR/C/74/D/919/2000 (28 June 2002) (*Müller* case).

[183] Communications 825–8/1998 (joined), *Silva and Others v Zambia*, UN Doc CCPR/C/75/D/825–8/1998 (26 July 2002) (inadmissible).

[184] Communication 933/2000, *Busyo v DRC*, UN Doc CCPR/C/78/D/933/2000 (19 September 2003).

[185] Communication 980/2001, *Hussain v Mauritius*, UN Doc CCPR/C/77/D/980/2001 (17 April 2003) (inadmissible).   [186] *Rudolph* case (n 148 above).

[187] Communication 856/1999, *Cambala v Zambia*, UN Doc CCPR/C/78/D/856/1999 (30 July 2003).

[188] Communication 962/2001, *Mulezi v DRC*, UN Doc CCPR/C/81/D/962/2001 (23 July 2004).

[189] Communication 1107/2002, *El Ghar v Libya*, UN Doc CCPR/C/82/D/1107/2002 (15 November 2004) (*El Ghar* case).

[190] Communication 1128/2002, *De Morais v Angola*, UN Doc CCPR/C/83/D/1128/2002 (18 April 2005).

Table 3.1 (*cont.*)

Year	African state complained against	HRC finding
	Cameroon[191]	violation
	Equatorial	
	Guinea[192]	violation
	Zambia[193]	violation
2006	Algeria (5)[194]	violations (4) inadmissible (1)
	Burkina Faso[195]	violation
	DRC[196]	violation

The following three cases illustrate the potential role of the HRC in the African context. In the first, the HRC in 1993 decided a case following a complaint by Angel Bahamonde, an outspoken opponent of the Equatorial regime, against Equatorial Guinea.[197] His allegations were as follows: Before he fled the country in 1991, he was the victim of numerous human rights violations. His passport was confiscated, he was arbitrarily detained, and his lands were expropriated. The government argued that local remedies had not been exhausted, as Bahamonde had not filed any action before local courts. The complainant gave detailed information of numerous attempts to obtain judicial redress, which had all failed. The authorities and the President himself systematically blocked his attempts at redress. In the communication, the applicant added that the judiciary in the country could not act independently as all judges and magistrates were nominated directly by the President.

The HRC declared the communication admissible, finding that the applicant could not under the circumstances have been expected to exhaust local remedies. The government had asserted, but only in very general terms, that the complainant could have involved at least four laws or regulations before local tribunals. The failure of the state 'to link its observations to the specific circumstances of the

---

[191] Communication 1134/2002, *Gorji-Dinka v Cameroon*, UN Doc CCPR/C/83/D/1134/2002 (10 May 2005).

[192] Communications 1152/2003 & 1190/2003 (joined), *Bee and Others v Equatorial Guinea*, UN Doc CCPR/C/85/D/1152 & 1190/2003 (30 November 2005).

[193] Communication 11132/2002, *Chisanga v Zambia*, UN Doc CCPR/C/85/D/1132/2002 (18 November 2005).

[194] Communication 992/2001, *Bousroual v Algeria*, UN Doc CCPR/C/86/D/992/2001 (24 April 2006); Communication 1085/2002, *Taright and Others v Algeria*, UN Doc CCPR/C/86/D/1085/2002 (16 May 2006); Communication 1196/2003, *Boucherf v Algeria*, UN Doc CCPR/C/86/D/1196/2003 (27 April 2006); Communication 1297/2002, *Medjnoune v Algeria*, UN Doc CCPR/C/87/D/1297/2004 (9 August 2006); and Communication 1424/2005, *Anton v Algeria*, UN Doc CCPR/C/88/D/1424/2005 (20 December 2006).

[195] Communication 1159/2003, *Sankara and Others v Burkina Faso*, UN Doc CCPR/C/86/D/1159/2003 (11 April 2006).

[196] Communication 1177/2003, *Ilombe and Another v DRC*, UN Doc CCPR/C/86/D/1177/2003 (16 May 2006). [197] *Bahamonde* case (n 165 above).

author's case'[198] prompted the Committee to find that the applicant had met all admissibility requirements.

As to the merits, the HRC found that the complainant had been arbitrarily arrested, that his right to security of the person had been violated, that he was denied the right to leave his country, and that he was discriminated against. As an appropriate remedy the government was urged to 'guarantee the security of his person, to return confiscated property to him or to grant him appropriate compensation, and that the discrimination to which he has been subjected be remedied without delay'.[199] The Committee requested to receive, within 90 days, information on steps subsequently adopted by the government.

In the first of a series of cases against Zambia, *Lubuto v Zambia*,[200] the HRC dealt with article 6(2) of the ICCPR, which allows for the imposition of the death penalty 'only for the most serious crimes'. In terms of Zambian legislation, the imposition of the death sentence was mandatory where a firearm had been used in the course of a robbery. Capital punishment had to follow, irrespective of whether the firearm was used to injure or kill anyone. The HRC held this position to be in violation of article 6(2), as the courts could not take into account whether the use of the firearm had resulted in death or injury, or not. In Lubuto's case, gunshots were fired during the course of the robbery, but no one was injured. The Committee regarded the commutation of Lubuto's sentence as an appropriate and effective remedy in the circumstances. The HRC also found that Lubuto was not tried without undue delay,[201] as the period that had expired between his arrest and the final decision dismissing the appeal was excessive. Although the Committee took into account the difficult economic conditions faced by the Zambian government, it had to implement the minimum standards contained in the ICCPR.

A subsequent case, *Chisanga v Zambia*,[202] not only indicates that the relevant legislation did not change, but also illustrates how a person falling through the cracks of the criminal justice system may find recourse to the HRC. Like Lubuto, Chisanga was convicted of aggravated robbery and sentenced to death. The HRC reiterated its previous finding that mandatory capital punishment for all armed robbery convictions, involving the use of firearms, deprives Chisanga 'of the benefit of the most fundamental of rights, the right to life, without considering whether this exceptional form of punishment could be appropriate in the circumstances of his case'.[203] As in the *Lubuto* case, the HRC found a violation of article 6(2). After Chisanga had been convicted, the President commuted the death sentences of all prisoners who had been on death row for longer than ten years. However, due to some confusion about his sentence, Chisanga was transferred from death row to the long-term section of the prison for two years. During that time, he was left under the impression that his death sentence was commuted to 18 years imprisonment, only to find out that it was in fact not the case and that he

---

[198] ibid, para 6.1.   [199] At para 11 of HRC's views.   [200] n 170 above.
[201] ICCPR, art 4(3)(c).   [202] n 193 above.   [203] ibid, para 7.4.

was to be returned to death row. The HRC found that these circumstances, which had such a 'negative psychological impact' on him and 'left him in such continuing uncertainty, anguish and mental distress', amounted to cruel and inhuman treatment and therefore violated article 7.[204] His exclusion from the ambit of the general commutation, to which he too was eligible,[205] constituted a violation of the right to an effective remedy.[206] A 'necessary prerequisite' of a remedy, the HRC found, was 'the commutation of the author's death sentence'.[207]

In a third case involving Zambia, the HRC in 1994 found violations of the ICCPR, committed under the Kaunda government.[208] The case originated when Bwalya ran for a parliamentary seat in 1983, and was arrested and detained for 31 months on charges that he belonged to an organization considered illegal under Zambia's (then) one-party Constitution. The HRC found a violation of article 25, which allows for free participation in the conduct of public affairs, and to 'be elected at genuine periodic elections'.[209] The Committee observed that the restriction on political activity 'amounts to an unreasonable restriction on the right to participate in the conduct of public affairs'.[210] Other rights of the author of the communication had also been violated, the Committee concluded. In a brief note, the state informed the HRC that the complainant had been released. As if to suggest that the matter should be laid to rest, the state failed to cooperate any further. However, the HRC found that the release of the complainant is not the only 'remedy' appropriate in the circumstances, and it urged the state to grant compensation to Bwalya, and to ensure that similar violations do not occur in the future.[211]

In *Diergaardt v Namibia*,[212] a cultural minority invoked the ICCPR for the first time in an African context. On behalf of the Rehoboth community, its leader, Diergaardt, alleged that a government circular prohibiting the use of Afrikaans language in any written or oral communication between civil service and the Namibian citizenry discriminated against this Afrikaans-speaking community. After its independence in 1990, in a quest for nation-building and to undo its colonial history, English was made the only official language of Namibia. The communication states that the Rehoboth are Afrikaans-speaking, and that according to the 1991 census, English was the mother tongue of only 0.8 per cent of the Namibian population.[213] In its majority opinion, the HRC found a violation of article 26 on the basis that the government circular 'intentionally targeted against the possibility to use Afrikaans when dealing with public authorities'[214] and recommends

---

[204] ibid, para 7.3.
[205] The HRC refers to the period of his 'detention' as 11 years, which places him in the ambit of the ten-year period of the general commutation (para 7.5). This calculation is not clear: He was arrested in 1993, and convicted in 1995, constituting 12 and ten years respectively.
[206] ICCPR, art 6(4), read with art 2.   [207] ibid, para 9.
[208] *Bwalya* case (n 162 above).   [209] ICCPR, art 25(b).
[210] Committee's views, para 6.6.   [211] At para 8 of the HRC's views.
[212] n 175 above.   [213] ibid, para 3.4.
[214] ibid, para 10.10. In the view of the minority members (dissenting opinions of HRC members Amor, Ando, and, joining in a dissenting opinion, Bhagwati, Colville, and Yalden), it is more appropriate

that the government must allow its officials 'to respond in other languages than the official one in a non-discriminatory manner'.[215]

Comparatively few cases against African states have been declared inadmissible.[216] However, the HRC's general generous attitude to complainants contrasts with the finding in one case against Mauritius, in which it seems to bend backwards to find the communication inadmissible. In a slender majority decision (nine to seven), the HRC held that it constitutes an abuse of the right of submission if a communication is submitted five years after the alleged violation occurred. In the view of the minority, the majority finding introduced 'a preclusive time limit' into Protocol I, which 'does not set any time limit for the submission of a communication'.[217] The issue at stake, namely 'affirmative action' measures favouring members of certain ethnic groups, seems to have influenced the majority to introduce this new restriction without any reference to supporting jurisprudence.

5 Realization

Against the above background, questions may be asked as to the effectiveness of the domestic implementation of the ICCPR and the HRC's views in the African context.

State reporting suffers from numerous drawbacks. As was pointed out above, in the case of Burundi, subsequent events have revealed the ineffectiveness of the reporting procedure in the reality of a state caught up in cycles of ethnically based violence. It also shows the limitations of the inherent effectiveness of the reporting system in the face of massive violations during large-scale civil disturbance. However, other cases emanating from Africa show the potential of the mechanism to strengthen democratic governance. State reporting cannot uproot repressive regimes and cannot redress massive violations, but it can bolster fledgling democracies already in place, and it can improve the protection of human rights, if states are, in principle, committed to the advancement of human rights.

Increasingly, instances are noted in which concluding observations are acted upon. Where states submitted second and further periodic reports, the extent of progress between their different reports can be gauged.[218] Senegal and Tunisia have, for example, been praised for progress in a number of respects. After the consideration of its last report, the HRC observed with approval that Senegal had taken

that deference be given to the language policy adopted by a sovereign state. One of the consequences of designating one language as official is that non-official languages are treated differently. Although the Circular only prohibits the use of Afrikaans, it should not be understood as singling Afrikaans out for less favourable treatment, but as an indication that all non-official (tribal) languages are dealt with on the same footing.

[215] ibid, para 12.   [216] See Table 3.1 above.

[217] Minority view by HRC members Chanet, Henkin, Scheinin, Shearer, Yalden, and Klein (the latter in a separate dissenting view).

[218] This is indeed regarded as the method by which follow-up would be effected.

the following steps:[219] The State Security Court was abolished; the position of a Mediator was created; a new, improved Electoral Code was adopted; the provisions of ICCPR were applied by domestic courts for the first time; the state enacted legislation providing for easier movement out of the country; and the Constitution was amended to abolish all restrictions on political parties, at least in part in response to concluding observations.[220] Although Tunisia had generally seen a deterioration of human rights in the period between the submission of its reports, certain reforms had also been implemented. These included new provisions in the Penal Code which provide for heavy sanctions in respect of violence against women, and changes to the Personal Status Code liberalizing women's access to child custody and divorce.[221]

In 2006, an encouraging reaction came from the Kenyan government. After examining Kenya's second periodic report, in 2005 the HRC issued its concluding observations.[222] In its subsequent 'Comments', issued in July 2006, the government at the outset stated that it 'has given serious consideration' to the concluding observations.[223] It held a 'number of intra-agency consultations', culminating in a workshop co-sponsored by the Ministry of Justice and Constitutional Affairs, at which an implementation plan was drawn up. Some examples of the response are as follows: In response to the recommendation that Kenya should take 'urgent steps to address the absence of constitutional protection against discrimination in relation to women and gender disparities',[224] the government lists a number of legislative projects, amongst which is the Sexual Offences Bill, adopted on 30 May 2006.[225] However, in reply to the recommended abolition of polygamy, it stated that it 'sees no possibility of prohibiting polygamy at the present time without a lot of negotiations and advocacy', but added that the 'foundation' of an education and sensitization programme was 'currently being laid down'.[226] Following the HRC's recommendation for the establishment of an independent civilian body to investigate complaints against the police,[227] the President appointed a Task Force to review this issue as part of a process of 'overhauling the whole national concept of law enforcement'.[228] The government also responded unequivocally to a recommendation that it should 'enforce the law' allowing the Kenya Human Rights Commission access to places of detention by issuing a firm and clear 'Ministerial

[219] UN Doc CCPR/C/79/ Add. 10 (1992) para 3.
[220] C Heyns and F Viljoen, *The Impact of the United Nations Human Rights Treaties on the Domestic Level* (The Hague: Kluwer Law International, 2002) 532.
[221] UN Doc CCPR/C/97/Add. 43 (1994).
[222] UN Doc CCPR/CO/83/KEN, 29 April 2005.
[223] UN Doc CCPR/C/KEN/CO/2/Add.1, dated 17 July 2006, 2.
[224] UN Doc CCPR/CO/83/KEN, para 10.
[225] UN Doc CCPR/C/KEN/CO/2/Add.1, 2.
[226] UN Doc CCPR/C/KEN/CO/2/Add.1, 6 (para 20).
[227] UN Doc CCPR/CO/83/KEN, para 16.
[228] UN Doc CCPR/C/KEN/CO/2/Add.1, 6 (paras 22, 23).

Statement' in Parliament reiterating its 'commitment to facilitate the Kenya Human Rights Commission and its agents in the execution of its legal mandate'.[229]

This response is different to that of most other states, including those in Africa. By not adopting a defensive posture aimed at denial and deferral, this self-critical and detailed government response provides a model of constructive engagement with the Committee's concluding observations. The ultimate proof of good faith will be put to the test when the next report is submitted, though, as many steps are still ongoing. A reference to attendance by senior judicial officers of the Nairobi Judicial Colloquium on Domestic Application of International Norms, held under the auspices of the OHCHR earlier in 2006,[230] suggests that this event served as an impetus for the government's positive response.

The question arises to what extent individuals have in fact benefited from the procedure provided for especially in the OPI. Even in respect of the African states that have ratified the OPI, few communications have been brought against African states. From 1976 to 1 June 1993 the HRC issued a total of 291 final views and findings on admissibility.[231] At that stage, less than 5 per cent (16) of these were issued in respect of African states.[232] By the end of 1992, when 17 African states had accepted the Committee's competence to receive individual communications, eight of these states had not been the subject of any such complaints. These states were Algeria, Angola, Benin, Congo, Gambia, Niger, Seychelles, and Somalia.[233] By the end of 2006, the position had changed only marginally, with complaints being directed also against Algeria and Angola. Despite its meagre contribution of cases, Odinkalu *et al* concluded that the views adopted on African communications significantly enriched the jurisprudence of the Committee.[234] The likelihood of a communication emanating from Africa being declared admissible is greater than those emanating from any other region.[235] When communications were in fact considered on the merits, the HRC found violations in all but one of the cases against African states.[236]

McGoldrick, in analysing the effectiveness of the OPI for individuals, compiled two lists of states: one of those that usually cooperate and comply, and one of those

---

[229] UN Doc CCPR/C/KEN/CO/2/Add.1, 9 (para 37).

[230] UN Doc CCPR/C/KEN/CO/2/Add.1, 11 (para 44).

[231] Nowak (n 90 above) gives a list of these views and findings in an addendum. Although the last case mentioned was registered as 491, the smaller total (291) represents the number of cases in which views were expressed or findings were made.

[232] Communications 16/1977 (against Zaire), 35/1978 (against Mauritius), 49/1979 (against Madagascar), 90/1981 (against Zaire), 115/1982 (against Madagascar), 124/1982 (against Zaire), 132/1982 (against Madagascar), 138/1983 (Zaire), 155/1983 (Madagascar), 157/1983 (Zaire), 194/1985 (Zaire), 241/1987 (Zaire), 242/1987 (Zaire), 354/1989 (Mauritius), 457/1991 (Libya), and 463/1991 (Zaire).   [233] Bayefsky (n 18 above) 292, Table J.

[234] CA Odinkalu, Y Tadesse, and P Lumumba, 'The Work of the UN Human Rights Committee on Individual Communucations from Africa: An Overview' (1994) 8 *Interights Bulletin* 67.

[235] Based on figures as from February 1993, see Bayefsky (n 18 above) 294, Table M. Of the African communications, 82% were declared admissible, as against 50% from Eastern Europe, 71% from Latin America, and 32% from the WEO states.

[236] See Bayefsky (n 18 above) 294, Table M. The African percentage at that stage (1992) (100%) should be contrasted with the 30% violations found in respect of communications from WEO states.

that do not. This list of states identified as willing to cooperate with the Committee and abide by its final views includes Canada, a number of West European states, and Jamaica. Only one African state, Mauritius, is included. The *Mauritian Women* case in fact provides, in his view, 'the clearest example of a State party taking measures in consequence of the HRC's final views'.[237] The Mauritius legislature amended two pieces of legislation found by the HRC to be discriminatory against women. When it considered a similar issue,[238] the Zimbabwean Supreme Court cited this decision with approval.

However, without doubt, most African states do not comply with the views issued by the HRC. In the *Marais* case, for example, Madagascar did not adhere to the Committee's statement that it would 'welcome a decision by the State party to release Mr Marais, prior to completion of his sentence, in response to his petition for clemency'. Marais was only released after he had completed his sentence.[239] The decision in the *Mpandanjila* case was not only rejected by the Zairian government, but also resulted in retaliatory measures by the government. In response to the HRC's views, the authors of the communication were arbitrarily detained and subjected to internal banishment and inhuman treatment, against which two of them complained in a subsequent communication to the HRC. In that decision, *Birindiwa and Tshisekedi v Zaire*,[240] the government was again found to be in violation of the ICCPR.

The HRC should bear some of the blame for the ineffective implementation and lack of compliance. Inevitable time delays contribute to inhibiting the impact of the HRC's views. For example, views were adopted in two cases against Zambia in July 1993.[241] Both communications related to the restraint of free political activity and a delay in giving reasons for arrest. The circumstances in both had a close link to the one-party system prevailing at the time. Although numerous violations were found and compensation was ordered, some five years had already lapsed by then. The intervening years saw the one-party system dismantled. It fell to the new, democratically elected government to redress the wrongs of the past.

In all its findings emanating in violations, the HRC requests that states provide information about the 'measures taken to give effect' to the findings and to publish the Committee's views. To track this process, the HRC has developed the most sophisticated system of follow-up to communications of all the treaty bodies. Since 1991, a specifically appointed Special Rapporteur has been requesting information from states and has been following up on their failure to respond. Currently, each annual report of the HRC sets out the status of follow-up responses to every communication in which a violation had been found, categorizing them as 'satisfactory',

[237] D McGoldrick *The Human Rights Committee: Its Role in the Development of the International Covenant on Civil and Political Rights* (Oxford: Clarendon Press, 1991) 203, para 4.132.

[238] See *Rattigan v Chief Immigration Officer, Zimbabwe* 1995 (2) SA 182 (ZSC) 189–90.

[239] McGoldrick (n 237 above) 223 n 325.   [240] n 159 above.

[241] *Bwalya* case, n 162 above, and *Kalenga* case, n 162 above.

'not satisfactory', or 'no follow-up'. Some states, such as Equatorial Guinea, Zairian/
DRC, before and after the regime and name change,[242] and Libya have been categorized as 'no response' states.[243]

At the same time, a surprising number of states have engaged with the follow-up
process. Three states, Mauritius, Namibia, and Senegal, have a record of 'satisfactory' responses. Some of these instances are now highlighted. In the *Koné* case, the
HRC requested an explanation from the Senegalese government for the protracted
pre-trial detention of the party concerned and recommended that the victim be
paid compensation. Senegal reported that Koné had been offered CFAF 300,000,
'which he viewed as insufficient under the circumstances'. The government added
that the 'President of the Republic had asked the Senegalese Human Rights Committee to look into the matter and as a result Mr Kone had been given a plot of land
to build a home, the compensation had been increased to CFAF 500,000 and his
medical problems were being treated free of charge by the President's personal
physician'.[244] In the *Müller* case, Namibian law was found to violate the ICCPR for
not allowing a man to take his wife's surname. The state informed the HRC that 'it
had informed the authors, through their counsel, that they could, under the terms
of the Aliens Act 1937, assume as family name the surname of the wife', but added
that 'it could not dictate to the Namibian courts, including the Supreme Court, as
regards cost awards in matters before them'.[245] The matter was thus resolved in
respect of the author, but the underlying and more systemic legal defect was not
corrected. In response to the *Diergaardt* case, Namibia provided some background
information that is not pertinent to the HRC's finding, such as the following: The
Namibian Constitution does not prohibit the use of languages other than English
in schools; persons appearing before the official English-speaking courts are provided with state-paid interpreters in any of the 12 state languages, and proceedings
do not go ahead if interpreters are unavailable. More pertinent to the substance of
the communication, it observed as follows: 'If a civil servant speaks a non-official
language, she or he will endeavour to assist a person using that language. The state
party refers to a Minister of Justice circular of 9 July 1990 to the effect that civil servants may receive and process non-English correspondence, but should respond in
writing in English.'[246]

---

[242] On the Special Rapporteur's futile efforts, see the following narrative report: 'No follow-up
reply has been received in respect of any of the above cases, in spite of repeated reminders addressed to
the State party. During the fifty-third and fifty-sixth sessions, the Committee's Special Rapporteur
could not establish contact with the Permanent Mission of the State party, with a view to discussing
follow-up action. On 3 January 1996, he addressed a note verbale to the Permanent Mission of the
State party to the United Nations, requesting a follow-up meeting with the State party's Permanent
Representative during the fifty-sixth session. There was no reply. On 29 October 2001, during the
Committee's seventy-third session, the Special Rapporteur met with representatives of the Permanent
Mission, who agreed to transmit the Special Rapporteur's concerns to the capital and provide a written
response. No replies have been received.' (UN Doc A/58/40 (Vol I, Ch VI, 111).

[243] Report of the Human Rights Committee, UN Doc A/60/40 (Vol I) Ch VI.

[244] UN Doc CCPR/C/SR.1619, para 35.   [245] UN Doc A/58/40 (Vol I) para 242.

[246] UN Doc A/57/40 (Vol I) para 244.

Other states, including Cameroon, Sierra Leone, Togo, and Zambia, have responded satisfactorily in at least some instances. In the *Mansaraj* case against Sierra Leone, for example, the state reported that the six persons who had not been executed were released and that a right of appeal from courts martial had been reinstated.[247] There is no indication that the next-of-kin of the 12 executed men had been compensated, as the Committee required.[248] With regard to the *Mukonto* case against Zambia, the author informed the Committee by a letter dated 2 April 2002 that the state party had paid him US$5,000 compensation. The author regarded this payment as insufficient satisfaction of his claim for US$80,000, and further pointed out that the state party had not published the Committee's views nationally. By a *note verbale* of 12 June 2002, the state party indicated that both parties had agreed that the sum of $5,000 compensation was a full and final settlement, and supplied a signed undertaking of full satisfaction by the author of a sum of 20 million Kwacha.[249]

The 2005 Annual Report of the HRC gives insight into African responses to requests for follow-up. Some states use this opportunity to contest the findings of the HRC. In response to the Special Rapporteur's requests in respect of the *Dias* case, the Angolan representative, for example, contested both the admissibility and finding on the merits, by reiterating the view that the author had not exhausted domestic remedies and that the Committee should not have declared the case admissible. Furthermore, the representative stated that 'it was not true that the Angolan authorities were unable to guarantee the author's security should he return to Angola and file a claim'.[250] Explaining the lack of a response to requests in the *De Morais* case,[251] the Angolan representative 'indicated that the State had limited capacity to deal with all human rights issues before it'.[252] With respect to the *Ackla* case, Togo insisted that the allegations of state restrictions upon his movement and the confiscation of his house were demonstrably false and that a mission was invited to confirm this. As to the *Aduayom* case, the state party contended that the withdrawal of the charges did not indicate that the acts charged had not taken place, and accordingly it was not possible to pay any compensation.[253]

Other states do not take issue with the HRC's findings, but pledge to cooperate, yet never do. In discussions on the *El Ghar* case, the Libyan representative, for example, informed the Special Rapporteur that the Libyan Embassy in Morocco had 'once again been instructed to issue a passport to the author' and expressed 'confidence that a passport would be issued to Ms El Ghar within weeks'.[254] However, this pledge rings hollow in the light of the fact that similar undertakings had

[247] UN Doc A/57/40 (Vol I) para 249.   [248] *Mansaraj* case (n 179 above) para 6.3.
[249] UN Doc A/57/40 (Vol I) para 235.
[250] Report of the Human Rights Committee, UN Doc A/60/40 (Vol II) Annex VII, 490.
[251] n 190 above.
[252] Report of the Human Rights Committee, UN Doc A/60/40 (Vol II) Annex VII, 491.
[253] UN Doc A/57/40 (Vol I) para 251.
[254] Report of the Human Rights Committee, UN Doc A/60/40 (Vol II) Annex VII, 510.

been made even at the time the communication had been considered. In response
to requests for information about cases decided against Madagascar, the representative confirmed that she 'would relay the request for information in relation to
these cases to her capital and request a written response' to the HRC's views, but
no response has been forthcoming.[255]

The cases brought and findings reached by the HRC reinforce the interdependence of the rights in the ICCPR and those in the ICESCR. The socio-economic
implications of detention have been raised on numerous occasions. In *Mukongo v
Cameroon*,[256] for example, the Cameroon government argued that harsh prison
conditions were a result of the persistent underdevelopment of that country. The
HRC referred to the UN Standard Minimum Rules for the Treatment of Prisoners
and held that those minimum requirements had to be met by all states, regardless
of possible 'economic justifications'.[257] Two other cases, *M'Boissona v CAR*[258] and
Koné v Senegal,[259] are examples of states invoking resource constraints as a justification for trial delay. Securing expeditious trials, as required by the HRC, will
only be attained through better resource allocation.

If the verification of domestic 'enforcement' of the HRC's views is problematic,
it is even more difficult to gauge the more indirect influence of the ICCPR. It has
come to be accepted as one of the primary international human rights instruments,
and has served as a role model for human rights standard-setting in the domestic
sphere, for example forming judicial reliance on ICCPR provisions as interpretative guides by domestic courts.[260]

C International Covenant on Economic, Social and Cultural Rights (ICESCR)

The ICESCR is one of the two human rights treaties that converted the lofty
ideals elaborated in the Universal Declaration into binding state obligations. In its
attempt to realize social justice, the document covers a wide scope of rights, ranging
from education, employment and the family, to minority languages and cultures.
Article 2 of the Covenant compels states to 'take steps' 'to the maximum of its
available resources, with a view to achieving progressively the full realization of
the rights' in the Covenant. In its General Comment 3, the ICESCR Committee
reiterated that the formulation of article 2 does not detract from the obligation of

---

[255] Report of the Human Rights Committee, UN Doc A/60/40 (Vol II) Annex VII, 511.
[256] Communication 458/1991.   [257] See para 9.3 of the HRC's views.
[258] Communication 428/1990. The Committee also noted the extremely poor prison conditions
in this case, and found a violation of art 7. Redress of such conditions will clearly have 'economic'
implications.   [259] Communication 386/1989.
[260] See eg *Nyambirai v National Social Security Authority* (1996) 1 SA 636 (ZS) 6471; *Ex p Gauteng
Legislature* (1995) 3 SA 165 (CC) para 71; *S v Makwanyane*, paras 63–7; and *S v Williams*, paras 21
n 24 and 26.

states to take immediate action. First, the obligation not to discriminate has immediate effect. Secondly, the state must take at least some immediate action, in the form of deliberate, concrete, and targeted steps, towards the goal of progressively realizing the rights 'fully'.[261]

1 Mandate and Composition of the Committee on Economic, Social and Cultural Rights (CESCR)

As the ICESCR does not provide for a specific treaty monitoring body, ECOSOC itself was left with the responsibility of implementation. This ECOSOC did in an ad hoc way until 1985, when it established a body of independent experts, similar to the HRC, by way of a resolution.[262] The main function of the body, which may be considered as a 'subsidiary body' of the ECOSOC Council,[263] is to examine state reports. As the ICESCR does not stipulate that reports should be submitted periodically, another ECOSOC resolution sets the reporting interval at five years.[264] In 1990, the CESCR became the first treaty body to develop the practice of adopting 'concluding observations' at the end of these examinations, in which the views of the Committee as a whole were systematically set out.[265]

Individual or inter-state complaints were not foreseen, due to the prevailing view that socio-economic rights were not directly justiciable. By the time of the Vienna Conference in 1993, the possibility of adopting an optional protocol establishing a complaints procedure had been under ongoing investigation. The call adopted in the Vienna Declaration and Programme of Action for the continuation of 'the examination of optional protocols' (without referring to 'complaints' as such)[266] was heeded when first an independent expert and then an open-ended working group were set up to discuss this matter. Despite these efforts, the reluctance of especially Western governments to recognize a complaints-based implementation of 'second' generation rights still stalls the process. At its first meeting, the Human Rights Council renewed the mandate of the open-ended working group, requesting it to elaborate a draft optional protocol.[267]

The 18 members of the CESCR are elected by all the members of ECOSOC.[268] In the process of electing members, 'due consideration' is to be given to 'equitable geographical distribution and to the representation of different forms of social and

[261] General Comment 3, The Nature of States Parties' Obligations, para 2.
[262] UN Doc E/1998/22, para 22. [263] Vandenhole (n 64 above) 47.
[264] UN Doc E/12/RES/1988/4; before 1988 the reporting cycle was two years for a third of the rights, adding up to a six-year cycle. (P Alston, 'The Committee on Economic, Social and Cultural Rights' in Alston (n 17 above) 473, 504.)
[265] See Alston's report ('Effective Functioning of Bodies Established pursuant to United Nations Human Rights Instruments'), UN Doc E/CN.4/1997/74, 27 March 1997, para 109.
[266] Vienna Declaration and Programme of Action, para 75.
[267] Resolution 2006/3, Open-Ended Working Group on an Optional Protocol to the ICESCR, UN Doc A/HRC/1/L.10, 73.
[268] See P Alston, 'The Committee on Economic, Social and Cultural Rights' in Alston (n 264 above) 488.

legal systems'.[269] This was interpreted as allowing each of the five regional group-ings three members to the Committee, with the additional three being divided between Latin America, Africa, and the WEO states.[270] In accordance with this formula, the following four members from African states were serving on the Committee by 30 June 1999: Mahmoud Ahmed Ahmed (Egypt), Clement Antanga (Cameroon), Abdesattar Grissa (Tunisia), and Ariranga Pillay (Mauritius). By 31 December 2006, Antanga and Pillay were still serving, together with Azzouz Kerdoum (Algeria) and Mohamed Abdel-Moneim (Egypt).

2 Ratifications and Reservations

Writing in 1995, Oloka-Onyango analysed the state of African ratification of ICESCR.[271] As of 15 July of that year, over 30 per cent of African states had not ratified the instrument. Using the analogy of the CRC, he argued that universal African ratification of the ICESCR is the 'necessary first step for all African states that claim to uphold the ideals contained in the instrument'.[272] Serious observance will only follow once a 'benchmark from which standards in the area can be crit-ically and universally assessed', is in place.[273] Oloka-Onyango singled out Ghana as a state that purports to be a proponent of the need to address socio-economic inequalities at the international level and domestically, but which had not ratified the ICESCR. Revealing a greater willingness to hold their record up to international scrutiny, Ghana later joined seven other African states (Sierra Leone, Burkina Faso, Eritrea, Djibouti, Swaziland, Mauritania, and Liberia) who have become party to the ICESCR since 1995.

By 31 December 2006, 48 African UN member states (91 per cent of the total) had ratified the ICESCR.[274] All but two states (Comoros and São Tomé e Príncipe) had become party to at least one of the Covenants. One African state, Guinea-Bissau, had ratified ICESCR, but not ICCPR, while three, Botswana, Mozambique, and South Africa, had ratified ICCPR, but not ICESCR.

Nine African state parties entered reservations or made interpretative declar-ations when accepting their obligations in terms of the treaty. The Covenant obliges state parties to respect the liberty of parents to choose schools, other than public schools, for the education of their children 'in conformity with their own convic-tions'.[275] In this respect, Algeria, Congo, and Rwanda raised objections. Algeria made an interpretative declaration to the effect that the relevant provision 'can in no way impair its right freely to organise its educational system'.[276] Congo declared

---

[269] ESC Res 1985/17, para B, quoted by Alston (n 264 above) 487.

[270] See Alston (n 264 above) 488.

[271] J Oloka-Onyango, 'Beyond the Rhetoric: Reinvigorating the Struggle for Economic and Social Rights in Africa' (1995) 26 *California Western Intl L J* 1.   [272] ibid, 16.

[273] ibid, 15.   [274] Table 3.2 below.   [275] ICCPR, art 13(3).

[276] Both the Netherlands and Portugal characterized this as a 'reservation' and objected thereto, stating that it is inconsistent with the objects and purpose of the treaty.

that the article does not give parents the right to establish private schools contrary to the monopoly of the State in the 'nationalisation of education'.[277] Rwanda stated that it is, in respect of education, only bound by its own Constitution. On 21 March 2001, Congo informed the Secretary-General that it withdrew its reservation.

Algeria, Guinea, and Libya made reservations of a political nature similar to those entered in relation to the ICCPR.[278] Egypt made an interpretative declaration of a religious nature, similar to the one entered in relation to the ICCPR.[279]

Reservations made by Kenya, Madagascar, and Zambia are indicative of an honest appraisal of the implications of the obligations under the Covenant. Reserving its adherence to the obligation to ensure paid leave or adequate social security to women before and after childbirth,[280] Kenya observed that 'the present circumstances obtaining in Kenya do not render necessary and expedient the imposition of those principles by legislation'. Both Madagascar and Zambia declared that the full implementation of the right to free primary education for all cannot be realized at the time.[281]

Only the Algerian reservation to article 13 elicited an objection. Factors such as their curtailed incision into the treaty and their application only for a limited period make it likely that the other substantive reservations are not incompatible with the object and purpose of ICESCR. However, a vaguely framed time limitation invites vigilant and continuous scrutiny.

3 State Reporting

African states have been even more reluctant to meet their obligation to report under ICESCR than under other treaties.[282] As only 14 African state parties to ICESCR have submitted at least one report, non-submission stands at a staggering high of 71 per cent.[283] Although the lack on the part of African governments of 'appropriate data of good quality for this type of analysis'[284] may have inhibited reporting, that factor alone cannot explain the dismal reporting record of African

---

[277] This must be understood in the context of the time of accession, 1983.

[278] See Section B.2 above.

[279] Egypt prefaced its ratification with the statement that Islamic Shari'ah does not conflict with the ICESCR.   [280] ICESCR, art 10(2).

[281] ICESCR, art 13(2)(a). The Zambian reservation refers to the postponement of the application of the provision due to its 'financial implications'. Madagascar undertook 'to take the necessary steps to apply' the provision 'at the earliest possible date, the problems of implementation, and particularly the financial implications, are such that full application of the principles in question cannot be guaranteed at this stage'.

[282] See in general on reporting MCR Craven, *The International Covenant on Economic, Social and Cultural Rights: A Perspective on its Development* (Oxford: Clarendon Press, 1995).

[283] The 14 states that have reported at least once are Algeria, Benin, Cameroon, Egypt, Kenya, Libya, Mauritius, Morocco, Nigeria, Senegal, Sudan, Tunisia, Zambia, and Zimbabwe. Some of the African states that have never reported under ICESCR include states that have a relatively good reporting record under other treaties, such as Gabon and Ethiopia.

[284] AR Chapman, 'A New Approach to Monitoring the International Covenant on Economic, Social and Cultural Rights' (1995) 55 *The Review: International Commission of Jurists* 23, 28.

states. African compliance with the obligation to report is also at odds with that of other parties to ICESCR.[285]

It is therefore no wonder that the ICESCR Committee decided at its seventh session, in 1992, to consider the 'state of implementation' of the Covenant in states that were long overdue with the submission of their initial reports. In 2000, using available information from intergovernmental and non-governmental sources, it conducted such a review in respect of Congo.[286] On the scheduled date, a high-level government delegation was present to engage in a dialogue with the Committee. The fate of the majority of Congolese, as set out in the Committee's concluding observations, starkly illuminates the link between unrest, civil war, and other forms of political instability and the negation of socio-economic rights such as health care, a constant supply of food, and access to education. Given the overwhelming economic collapse, the Committee's major recommendations direct themselves at the present political situation, in particular the abrogation of the Constitution. Clearly linking 'civil and political' rights and 'socio-economic' rights, the Committee recommends that the government adopts a Constitution, 'in order to ensure that the people of the Republic, and particularly the most vulnerable and marginal-ized groups of society, enjoy their economic, social and cultural rights'.[287] In line with its jurisprudence, the Committee also highlighted the importance of non-discrimination (against women and ethnic minorities, for example) as a non-negotiable threshold requirement even in dire circumstances.[288] However, none of these circumstances absolves the government from taking immediate and targeted actions, for example to restore basic health services and facilitate access to food through small-scale low-cost agricultural projects. In all these endeavours, the state is encouraged to work with relevant UN agencies.

The examination of the initial report of Zambia, one of the world's poorest coun-tries, provides an opportunity to observe the Committee's approach to a severely resource-constrained country. In some instances, the Committee focuses on con-crete measures that should be taken, such as 'legislative and other measures and to improve its monitoring mechanisms so as to address effectively the persistent prob-lem of child labour'.[289] Confronted with deep-rooted problems related to the denial of basic socio-economic rights, the Committee reminds the state to prioritize the 'most disadvantaged and marginalized groups',[290] invites it to 'set both intermediate goals and concrete and measurable benchmarks',[291] and places the situation in a global context by urging the state to take all its obligations under the Covenant into account 'in all aspects of its negotiations with international financial institutions, such as the International Monetary Fund and the World Bank'.[292]

---

[285] Of the 106 non-African state parties to ICESCR, 86 (or 81%) have submitted at least one report.   [286] UN Doc E/C.12/1/Add.45, 23 May 2000.
[287] UN Doc E/C.12/1/Add.45, para 25.   [288] UN Doc E/C.12/1/Add.45, paras 26 and 27.
[289] UN Doc E/C.12/1/Add.106, 23 June 2005, para 47.   [290] ibid, para 48.
[291] ibid, para 54.   [292] ibid, para 36.

On numerous other occasions, the Committee highlighted the potential or actual negative impact of globalization and global inequalities, such as the role of the international financial institutions, the state's debt servicing obligations, structural adjustment programmes and privatization, on the realization of socio-economic rights, especially of the most vulnerable sectors of society.[293]

Less frequently, the Committee put the spotlight on the important issue of budgetary allocation. The second periodic report of Algeria provides an example where the Committee engaged the state on this aspect. Noting a 'significant decrease' during the 1990s in spending on health and education at the expense of military expenditure,[294] the Committee urged Algeria to 'allot a large share of the national budget surplus' to the struggle against poverty, and to 'increase its expenditures for health and education'.[295]

The submission and examination of second periodic reports by some countries provide an opportunity to gauge the impact of the Committee's concluding observations. In the concluding observations adopted on Morocco's second periodic report, for example, the Committee on three occasions explicitly 'reiterated' the recommendations issued on the initial report,[296] and concluded with the recommendation that the next report should include information about the implementation of the present concluding observations.[297] Similarly, the Committee in its observations on Algeria's second periodic report referred back to its recommendations on the initial report, and recommended that the next report should provide details about compliance.[298]

4 Realization

A few positive developments may be cited in juxtaposition to the bleak picture painted so far. After a long period of non-reporting, Mauritius became the subject of a review of implementation in 1994. This review was followed by the submission, in the same year, of the state's second periodic report containing a 'statistical profile of socio-economic indicators'.[299] In its relatively favourable assessment of the socio-economic situation in Mauritius, the Committee noted at least two pertinent examples of compliance with its previous recommendations.[300] Evidencing another positive development, Congo withdrew its reservation to article 13 on 21 March 2001 in line with the Committee's recommendation, issued on 23 May 2000.[301] On the one hand, this suggests that Congo is taking concrete steps to

---

[293] See eg concluding observations on Morocco's second periodic report, UN Doc E/C.12/1/ Add.55, paras 10, 38, and 39 and those on Algeria's second report, UN Doc E/CN.12/1/Add.71, paras 9, 36, and 43. [294] UN Doc E/CN.12/1/Add.71, para 23.

[295] UN Doc E/CN.12/1/Add.71, paras 34 and 40.

[296] UN Doc E/C.12/1/Add.55, paras 39, 47, and 50.

[297] ibid, para 59. [298] UN Doc E/CN.12//Add.71, paras 14 and 46.

[299] UN Doc E/C.12/1995/14, para 8. [300] UN Doc E/C.12/1995/14, para 5.

[301] UN Doc E/C.12/1/Add.45, 23 May 2000, para 29: 'The Committee urges the State party to pay due attention to the rehabilitation of the educational infrastructure by allocating the necessary

give effect to the Committee's concluding observations. On the other hand, withdrawing a reservation remains a formal act, not requiring the redirection of resources, but perhaps directed at earning the government international goodwill.

Continent-wide conditions of poverty, illiteracy, and general underdevelopment testify to the failure of African states to secure viable socio-economic conditions for their nationals. Ratifying the ICESCR might exert some gravitational pull, but as yet its promise lies unfulfilled. Reporting obligations have been insufficient in securing the improved realization of these rights. In future, the gravest breaches of socio-economic rights may, at least in isolated cases, be redressed through a violations-based approach.

D Convention on the Elimination of All Forms of Discrimination against Women (CEDAW)

Numerous human rights instruments have been adopted to deal with aspects of the precarious position of women around the globe. The most comprehensive of these is CEDAW, which was adopted in 1979, and entered into force in 1981. Others include the Convention on the Political Rights of Women,[302] the Convention on Consent to Marriage,[303] and the Convention on the Nationality of Married Women.[304]

1 Mandate and Composition of the CEDAW Committee

The Committee on the Elimination of Discrimination against Women (CEDAW Committee) is made up of 23 independent experts, elected by the state parties to CEDAW.[305] They meet yearly to consider state reports submitted in terms of CEDAW.[306] The CEDAW Committee may 'make suggestions and general recommendations based on the examination of reports and information received from the states parties'.[307] These suggestions and recommendations are contained in the Committee's annual report to the General Assembly.[308]

On 30 June 1999, six of the 23 Committee members were from African states.[309] They were all female and are more or less representative of the African continent, although Central, Eastern, and Southern Africa are underrepresented. Around this time, Byrnes described the performance of African members of the Committee

---

funds for teachers' salaries, teaching materials and school building repairs. It also recommends that the State party withdraw its reservation to article 13, paragraphs 3 and 4, of the Covenant.'

[302] 193 UNTS 135, adopted 20 December 1952, entered into force 7 July 1954.

[303] ILO Convention no 100, 165 UNTS 303, adopted 29 June 1951, entered into force 23 May 1953.   [304] 309 UNTS 65, adopted 20 February 1957, entered into force 11 August 1958.

[305] CEDAW, art 17.   [306] CEDAW, art 20.   [307] CEDAW, art 21(1).

[308] This report is submitted through ECOSOC: see art 21(1) of CEDAW.

[309] See web-site <http://gopher://gopher.un.org: 70/00/ga/CEDAW/REP>.

as 'varied': 'some have been among the most active members of the Committee, while others have been relatively passive'.[310] He also noted that 'rigorous scrutiny of developing countries appears to have been tempered by the perception of difficulties they face in the promotion of the equality for women'.[311] By 31 December 2006, the number of CEDAW Committee members from African countries stood at five: Mohamed Gabr (Egypt), Meriem Belmihoub-Zerdani (Algeria), Dorcas Coker-Appiah (Ghana), Huguette Bokpe Gnacadja (Benin), and Pramila Patten (Mauritius).

2 Ratifications and Reservations

As at 31 December 2006, CEDAW had been ratified by 51 African states.[312] The two non-ratifying states, Somalia and Sudan, are Muslim countries, but have also been undergoing periods of social turmoil. This represents 96 per cent of all African members of the UN. The percentage of states globally that had become state parties then stood at 95 per cent.

States may enter reservations when ratifying or acceding to CEDAW. The general rule that reservations may not be incompatible with the object and purpose of a treaty,[313] is spelt out explicitly in the Convention.[314] Eleven African states ratified or acceded to CEDAW with reservations. One of these was subsequently withdrawn: Malawi entered a general and over-broad reservation to the effect that, in cases of conflict, traditional customary practice rather than CEDAW is to be upheld.[315] However, in October 1991, the newly instated democratic government withdrew the reservation.

Algeria, Ethiopia, Mauritius, Morocco, and Tunisia declared themselves not bound by article 29(1). That provision creates the possibility of doing away with the requirement of mutual consent of state parties in order to seize the ICJ.

Upon ratification in 1995, Lesotho entered a reservation that covered three aspects.[316] Two of these were subsequently withdrawn, on 25 August 2004. One of the withdrawn reservations was framed as an 'understanding' that Lesotho would not apply CEDAW's provisions (particularly article 2(e)), which requires state parties to take measures so as to eliminate discrimination against women by any person, organization, or enterprise. The effect of this provision would not be extended to affairs of religious groups.[317] The other withdrawn reservation restricted CEDAW's

---

[310] AC Byrnes, 'The "Other" Human Rights Treaty Body: The Work of the Committee on the Elimination of Discrimination against Women' (1989) 14 *Yale J of Intl L* 1, 11.   [311] ibid.
    [312] See Table 3.2 below.   [313] VCLT, art 19.   [314] CEDAW, art 28(2).
    [315] See web-site <http://www.un.org/Depts/Treaty/final/ts2/newfiles/part_boo/iv_boo/iv_8.html>. The formulation of the reservation referred to the 'deep-rooted nature of some traditional customs and practices'. Malawi considered itself not bound to 'eradicate' such customs and practices 'for the time being'.
    [316] For a more general discussion of the significance of CEDAW for women in Lesotho, see MP Mamashela, 'The Significance of the Convention on the Elimination of All Forms of Discrimination against Women for a Mosotho Woman' (1993) 5 *ASICL Proc* 153.   [317] CEDAW, art 2(e).

effect by equating it to the Constitution of Lesotho. It declared that 'it shall not take any legislative measures under the Convention where those measures would be incompatible with the Constitution of Lesotho'.[318] The third aspect of the original reservation, which was retained, reads as follows:[319]

> The Government of the Kingdom of Lesotho declares that it does not consider itself bound by article 2 to the extent that it conflicts with Lesotho's constitutional stipulations relative to succession to the throne of the Kingdom of Lesotho and law relating to succession to chieftainship.

Article 11 of CEDAW deals with equality in employment. A number of state parties made reservations about the full realization of the rights contained in this article. The 'most blunt' of these reservations comes from Mauritius,[320] who declared itself not bound by articles 11(1)(b)[321] and 11(1)(d), which guarantees equal remuneration for work of equal value. Lijnzaad has described the terms of these reservations as 'highly questionable'.[322]

Algeria, Egypt, Libya, Mauritania, Morocco, Niger, and Tunisia entered reservations on the basis of the Islamic Shari'ah. These reservations mainly relate to the rights of women to inherit, their choice of residence, the status of children, and women's rights during marriage and at its dissolution. An Algerian reservation, for example, requires that the Convention may not contradict provisions of the Algerian Family Code in respect of rights in marriage.[323] The Egyptian reservation also invokes the Shari'ah.[324] Libya made it clear that the principle of equality may not be invoked in contradiction of Shari'ah.[325] In 1995 Libya notified the Secretary-General of a 'new formulation', which 'replaces the formulation contained in the instrument of accession'. According to the new formulation, its accession is 'subject

---

[318] Noting that these reservations 'are covering central provisions of the Convention' and that 'internal law may not be invoked as justification for failure to perform treaty obligations', the Netherlands and Norway (in 1996) and Denmark (in 1997) formally objected to the reservations as being incompatible with the object and purpose of CEDAW. Finland objected to the Lesotho reservation stating that it was 'devoid of legal effect'. Its reasoning was that the reservation was of such a general nature and did not give specifics and that other state parties would be uncertain as to what extent CEDAW would apply to Lesotho. Finland was of the view that the reservation created 'serious doubts' about Lesotho's commitment to CEDAW and as a result the reservation undermined the treaty. Finland, the Netherlands, and Norway were united in their objection to Lesotho's attempt to invoke its national law as a justification for its failure to abide by its obligations under the treaty and they indicated that this was contrary to international law governing treaties. Denmark held the same view as that held by Finland, Netherlands, and Norway about the principle of not invoking national law.

[319] See <http://untreaty.un.org/ENGLISH/bible/englishinternetbible/partI/chapterIV/treaty10.asp> (22 December 2005). Morocco, like Lesotho a 'kingdom', entered a similar reservation, noting that its ratification is 'without prejudice to the constitutional requirement that regulate the rules of succession to the throne of the Kingdom of Morocco'.

[320] As L Lijnzaad, *Reservations to UN-Human Rights Treaties: Ratify and Ruin* (Dordrecht: Martinus Nijhoff, 1995) observed (314).

[321] This sub-article grants women equality in employment opportunity.

[322] Lijnzaad (n 320 above) 314. See also the objections by eg Germany and Sweden.

[323] See eg the objection of Germany hereto.

[324] See the objections of eg Germany and Sweden.

[325] See the objections of eg Denmark, Finland, Germany, Norway, and Sweden.

to the general reservation that such accession cannot conflict with the laws on personal status derived from the Islamic *Shariah*'. By not replacing the initial text, and by keeping the 1995 modification in a footnote, the UN signals that the initial reservation is still valid, because the 1995 text is not a modification, but is an inadmissible extension of the scope of the reservation. Mauritania's very broad reservation states that it approves of CEDAW 'in each and every one of its parts which are not contrary to Islamic Sharia and are in accordance with our Constitution'.[326] By contrast, Niger made a series of reservations to specific provisions, all inspired by Shari'ah, but framed as being 'contrary to existing customs and practices'. Invoking by implication the tenets of cultural relativism, Niger justified these reservations on the basis that they form part of deep-seated historical cultural patterns. By their nature, Niger asserted, these practices 'can be modified only with the passage of time and the evolution of society and cannot, therefore, be abolished by an act of authority'.

Several non-African states objected formally to reservations entered by states parties. All of them objected to Libya's reservation. In my view the reservations entered by both Libya and Malawi are too vague and general. If a state enters a reservation, it must at least be precise about what aspect it reserves.[327] All-inclusive reservations, like those of Libya and Malawi, dilute all the rights in CEDAW. They reduce the state's obligation to existing local law, either in the form of Shari'ah or traditional law. This is clearly incompatible with the principal objective of the Convention, which is to eliminate all forms of discrimination against women.[328] Subjecting international human rights law to national law conflicts with the Vienna Convention on the Law of Treaties, which provides that local legislation may not be invoked as a ground to dilute treaty obligations.[329]

The Committee's reaction has been to recommend to states, in its concluding observations, to withdraw these reservations.[330]

3 State Reporting

African states have maintained a relatively good state reporting record under CEDAW.[331] By the end of 2006, only 11 of the African state parties had never submitted reports. This list includes states that have, for various reasons, a history of disengagement with the UN treaty bodies, such as Botswana, CAR, Chad, Côte d'Ivoire, Comoros, Djibouti, Guinea-Bissau, Liberia, the Seychelles, and Sierra Leone.

In the two-year period between 1995 and 1997, reports from Ethiopia, Morocco, and Namibia were considered:[332] In its examination of Ethiopia's combined first,

---

[326] France and Ireland objected.
[327] See Lijnzaad (n 320 above) 305, pointing out that the Malawian reservation encompasses all spheres of society.   [328] CEDAW, Preamble and art 2.
[329] VCLT, art 27.
[330] See eg the concluding observations on the second Algerian report, UN Doc E/CN.12/1/Add.71, para 30.   [331] See <http://www.un.org/womenwatch/daw/cedaw/reports.htm>.
[332] UN Docs A/51/38 and A/52/38/Rev.1.

second, and third reports the Committee identified poverty, unemployment, illiteracy, high birth rates, deep-rooted customs and traditions as problematic aspects.[333] The Committee recommended that the government should seek 'international support for poverty alleviation', that awareness be created so that female genital mutilation may be abolished, and that women should be given access to health care services and family planning. In its examination, the Committee expressed grave concern about reservations entered by Morocco, especially its reservation to article 2.[334] The Committee made the observation that any reservation to that article is incompatible with the object and purpose of CEDAW. The Committee identified and condemned considerable discrimination in both the public and private spheres in Morocco. Blatant inequalities still exist in women's access to employment. In its concluding comments, the Committee highlighted the dismal position of rural women in respect of health and education. Namibia's initial report provoked many favourable comments from the Committee.[335] However, concerns were raised about aspects of customary law (such as the prevalence of polygamous marriages and an inability of women to own rural land), the low level of female participation in higher education, discrimination against women in the labour market, and the high rate of maternal mortality.

An analysis of more recent reports reveals that advances are being made, exemplified by the increase in women's enrolment in higher education in Algeria;[336] and legal reform prohibiting sexual harassment and a successful campaign against female genital mutilation in Burkina Faso.[337] Despite advances, many recommendations set out in previous concluding observations remain unimplemented. In a state such as the DRC, which is recovering from the effects of civil war, the much more precarious position of women gave rise to recommendations of a more fundamental nature, such as the inclusion of gender in reconstruction programmes, a comprehensive legislative review, and the increase of women in decision-making positions.[338]

4 Individual Communications

The lack of an individual complaints mechanism was rectified when the Optional Protocol to the CEDAW (OP-CEDAW) was adopted in 1999, and entered into force in 2000.[339] States who become party to this Protocol accept the right of individual petition. By 31 December 2006, 12 African states had accepted OP-CEDAW. None of the three cases finalized by the end of 2006 had been submitted against an African state.[340]

---

[333] UN Doc A/51/38.   [334] UN Doc A/52/38/Rev.1, 11–15.
[335] UN Doc A/52/38/Rev.1, 82–87.
[336] Un Doc CEDAW/C/DZA/CC/2, 15 February 2005, para 14.
[337] Un Doc CEDAW/C/BFA/CO/4–5, 22 July 2005, paras 16 and 19.
[338] UN Doc CEDAW/C/COD/CO/5, 25 August 2005.
[339] <http://www.ohchr.org> (30 September 2006).
[340] The communications were directed at Hungary, Germany, and Turkey.

5 Inquiry Procedure

OP-CEDAW also allows for an inquiry or investigation procedure. However, states may opt out of this procedure when they ratify the Protocol by making a declaration to that effect.[341]

The inquiry procedure is initiated when the Committee 'receives reliable information indicating grave or systematic violations' in a particular state.[342] After examining the information, the CEDAW Committee may designate one or more of its members to conduct an inquiry. The ideal of a visit to the state party may be thwarted by the state, as such a visit is contingent upon state consent.[343] Follow-up to recommendations emanating from an inquiry is twofold: the state should include details of the measures taken in response to the inquiry in its next periodic report;[344] and the CEDAW Committee may seek information about compliance with its recommendations six months after they have been communicated to the state.[345]

One inquiry has so far been undertaken, to Mexico, after three NGOs had submitted the information that more than 230 young women and girls, most of them *maquiladora* workers, had been killed in or near Ciudad Juárez, Mexica. The Committee organized a visit of inquiry in 2003, and presented its conclusions to both the state and the NGOs concerned.[346] Its final findings have not yet been made public.[347]

6 Realization

CEDAW has played a significant role in African states, by bringing women's issues and gender equality into the open and making them part of national dialogue. Strong and vocal civil society gender movements are developing in many African states, where their efforts are strengthened by the state's ratification of CEDAW. Some gains are increasingly observed in the reporting process. The potential of the individual complaints mechanism and inquiry procedures still needs to be explored, although it is unlikely that these procedures will break the hold of custom and culture in most of Africa.

E Convention against Torture and Other Cruel, Inhuman or Degrading Treatment or Punishment (CAT)

State parties to the CAT, adopted by the UN General Assembly in 1984, and entering into force in 1987, undertake to take 'effective legislative, administrative,

---

[341] OP-CEDAW, art 10.   [342] ibid, art 8.
[343] CEDAW Committee's Rules of Procedure, r 86.
[344] UN Doc A/57/38, Annex (Reporting Guidelines) F.2.   [345] OP-CEDAW, art 9.
[346] UN Doc 38 (A/59/38), 2004, paras 393–408.
[347] UN Doc 60/38 (Part I), 18 March 2005, para 40. For a brief discussion, see A Byrnes and M Graterol, 'Violence against Women: Private Actors and the Obligation of Due Diligence' (2006) 15 *Interights Bulletin* 156.

judicial' and other measures to combat torture.[348] These measures must at least include adherence to the principle of non-expulsion of anyone likely to be subjected to torture (the principle of *non-refoulement*).[349] In addition, CAT enshrines the principle of universal jurisdiction, in terms of which anyone suspected of having committed torture must either be prosecuted in the state where he or she is, or be extradited to another state that has jurisdiction (either on the basis of territoriality—the torture was committed there—or on the grounds of nationality—that of the suspect or the victim).[350] (This is the principle of *aut dedere aut judicare*.)

On 22 June 2006, the Optional Protocol to CAT (OP-CAT) entered into force, strengthening the protection of detainees against torture by allowing for on-site investigative visits. States accepting OP-CAT allow periodic and ad hoc visits to places of detention by the newly established Sub-Committee on Prevention, and by national preventive mechanisms. If such a national mechanism does not exist, the state must set it up; where it already exists, it should be strengthened and supported.[351] However, state parties may at ratification (or accession) make a declaration postponing either the visits of the Sub-Committee or the national preventive mechanism for up to three years. By 31 December 2006, five African states had become party to OP-CAT.

1 Mandate and Composition of the CAT Committee

An international supervising body, the Committee against Torture (CAT Committee), is established to implement the provisions of CAT.[352] Four functions are accorded to the CAT Committee: it considers state reports, which states parties have to submit within one year of ratification or accession, and again every four years thereafter;[353] it may initiate a confidential inquiry on the basis of reliable information meeting certain threshold criteria; and it may finalize complaints by or on behalf of individuals, and between state parties.

The state parties to CAT elect ten experts as Committee members for renewable terms of four years.[354] Consideration is given to equitable geographical distribution and the usefulness of the participation of persons having legal experience.[355] Those elected perform their functions in their personal capacities.[356] The first CAT Committee was elected in 1987. Of the ten members, one (or 10 per cent of the membership), Alexis Mouelle, from Cameroon,[357] was from an African state. At that stage, 27 states had ratified CAT. Of these, four (or 7 per cent of the ratifying states) were African.[358] Before the meeting an informal agreement had

[348] CAT, art 2(1).   [349] ibid, art 3.   [350] ibid, art 5(2).
[351] CAT Protocol, art 24.   [352] CAT, arts 17 and 18.   [353] ibid, art 19.
[354] ibid, art 17(1) and 17(5).   [355] ibid, art 17(1).   [356] ibid.
[357] JH Burgers and H Danelius, *The United Nations Convention against Torture* (Dordrecht: Martinus Nijhoff, 1988) 111. At the end of 1997 Mouelle chaired the CAT Committee.
[358] These four states were Egypt, Senegal, Cameroon, and Togo (see Burgers and Danelius (n 357 above) 109).

been worked out by the state parties. In terms thereof, two members would be from Africa, one from Asia, two from Eastern Europe, two from Latin America, and three from the WEO states. The end-result did not reflect this informal agreement, as the WEO states were 'overrepresented' in relation to the agreement, with four representatives and Africa 'underrepresented', with only one. The African states, and the Philippines, expressed their concern about this departure from the informal agreement.[359] However, at 7 per cent of the ratifying states, and 10 per cent of the Committee membership, Africa had in fact been overrepresented on the Committee.[360] On 30 June 1999, two Africans were represented on the CAT Committee. They were Guibril Camara (Senegal) and Sayed El Masry (Egypt). By 31 December 2006, Camara still served, while Essadia Belmir (also from Egypt) replaced El Masry.

2 Ratifications and Reservations

Nineteen African states had ratified CAT by 1 January 1996.[361] By 30 June 1999, nine more African states (Côte d'Ivoire, Malawi, and Zaire in 1996, Kenya in 1997, Niger, South Africa, and Zambia in 1998, and Burkina Faso and Mali in 1999) had ratified CAT, increasing the African total to 23. This is proportionately less than the global average: 53 per cent of states worldwide had ratified,[362] compared to only 43 per cent of African states.[363] By 31 December 2006, the number stood at 42 (representing well over three-quarters of the potential number of ratifying states).

Two African states, Equatorial Guinea and Mauritania, of eight states globally,[364] made declarations to exclude the competence of the CAT Committee in terms of article 20(1) of CAT.[365] This is disappointing, as article 20(1) provides one of the most significant mechanisms for preventative and pro-active implementation of CAT. It provides the Committee with the power to 'invite' a state party to 'co-operate in the examination' of reliable information about systematic practices of torture received by the CAT Committee in respect of that state. The 'invitation' needs not entail a visit to the state party, as visits are dependent on state consent.[366] By excluding the competence of the Committee *ab initio*, these states have given a very clear indication of their reluctance to subject their penitentiary systems to international scrutiny. This conclusion is consistent with both states' non-acceptance of the CAT Committee's other optional competencies. In a

---

[359] See Burgers and Danelius (n 357 above) 111.

[360] From 1992–93 two Africans served on the Committee: Moulle and El Ibrashi from Egypt, whose terms expired at the end of 1995 (Annex II to UN Doc A/48/44, Supplement 44).

[361] See table in C Heyns (ed), *Human Rights Law in Africa 1996* (The Hague: Kluwer Law International, 1996) 2–3.   [362] 102 of the total of 191 states.

[363] 23 of the 53 African UN member states.

[364] The other states are Afghanistan, Belarus, China, Indonesia, Israel, and Kuwait.

[365] See web-site <http://www.un.org/Depts/Treaty/final/ts2/newfiles/part_boo/iv_boo/iv_9.html>.

[366] CAT, art 20(3).

significant move towards greater openness and engagement with the treaty body system, Zambia withdrew its declaration in February 1999.

Botswana entered a substantive reservation, in which the meaning of 'torture' under CAT is equated to its domestic constitutional law interpretation. Three states objected to this reservation.[367]

3 State Reporting

As is the case with reporting to other treaty bodies, many states lag behind with their reports.[368] The general problem of duplication of information contained in different reports is accentuated by the high degree of overlap between CAT and ICCPR. This factor may impact significantly on states that already find it difficult to comply with reporting obligations. Institutional and financial constraints accentuate these difficulties in most African countries.

The danger of formulaic compliance to serve *rightorics* may be gauged from the experience in relation to two states that have submitted more than one report, Libya and Tunisia. The Committee examined Libya's initial report in 1991.[369] The Committee referred the report back for supplementary information on the way in which CAT was implemented in Libya. In November 1992, the Committee examined the additional report. Although the report, and the answers of the Libyan representative, gave details about the Libyan legal system and its formal conformity with the Convention, the report still lacked information about the practical application of the instrument.[370] When it considered Libya's third report in 1999, the Committee—almost in desperation—regretted that neither the report nor the responses of the delegation 'addressed substantially' the concerns raised in the concluding observations issued previously. Unfortunately, it then proceeded to make a recommendation so general that it cannot be of much value in the increasingly fruitless 'dialogue' with the state.[371]

The examination by the Committee of Tunisia's second periodic report in 1998 met with a response from the government, in which almost all its findings and recommendations were challenged. The Committee, for example, expressed concern over the 'wide gap that exists between law and practice with regard to the protection of human rights', pointing to 'reported widespread practice of torture and other cruel and degrading treatment perpetrated by security forces and the police, which, in certain cases, resulted in death in custody'.[372] The government's response questioned the accuracy and reliability of the Committee's fact-finding, and

---

[367] Denmark, Norway, and Sweden.   [368] See Bayefsky (n 18 above) 229, 287 (table C).

[369] See paras 181–207 of Report of the Committee against Torture, UN Doc A/48/44.

[370] The Committee concluded as follows: 'The Committee also stated that it was awaiting with impatience the second periodic report…due in June 1994, and that it would be grateful if that report would describe the application of the Convention article by article' (para 205 of UN Doc A/48/44).

[371] The state 'should send a clear message to all its law-enforcement personnel that torture is not permitted under any circumstances'.

[372] UN Doc A/54/44, paras 88–105, 19 November 1998, para 96.

dismissed the allegations as having 'no basis in fact'.[373] However, this statement is contradicted by communications submitted to the Committee, as is highlighted below. The Committee also noted 'the abuses directed against female members of the families of detainees and exiled persons' as a cause for anxiety on its part.[374] Again, the response was one of denial, dismissing the observations as 'so obviously biased as to be absurd'.[375]

4 Confidential Inquiry

CAT was the first treaty to provide its treaty body with the competence to undertake an inquiry to a state party if the Committee has received 'well-founded indications that torture is being systematically practised' in that state.[376] However, states may opt out of this procedure by making a specific declaration to this effect at the time of its formal acceptance.[377] As stated above, by 31 December 2006 two African states had such declarations in place.[378]

A visit to the state concerned may only take place with the state's consent.[379] Once the inquiry is completed, its results are communicated to the state party. The state may then comment. Thereafter, the CAT Committee may publish the summarized report in its annual report. The Committee embarked on its first investigation of this kind at its fourth session,[380] and by the end of 2006 has undertaken six such inquiries: in respect of Mexico, Serbia, Sri Lanka, Peru, Egypt, and Turkey.

In the one case involving an African state party, Egypt, the CAT Committee undertook its confidential enquiry between 1991 and 1994.[381] Some of the problems encountered in the course of applying article 20 are illustrated by this inquiry. Although the CAT Committee targeted Egypt for an article 20 inquiry, the Committee never managed to visit Egypt, and had to rely on NGO reports (mainly provided by Amnesty International, the Egyptian Organization for Human Rights, and the World Organization against Torture) and the UN Special Rapporteur on Torture. Concluding its inquiry in May 1996 with the finding that torture is 'systematically practiced by the security forces in Egypt, in particular by State Security Intelligence',[382] the Committee recommended that Egypt reinforces its legal and judicial infrastructure 'in order to combat the phenomenon of torture in an effective way'.[383]

Although the Egyptian government provided detailed information about efforts to combat torture, it did not address the main issue raised by the NGOs' reports, which consistently describe the 'State Security Intelligence premises and military

---

[373] UN Doc A/54/44, paras 88–105, government's response, para 105.
[374] UN Doc A/54/44, paras 88–105, para 99.
[375] UN Doc A/54/44, paras 88–105, para 105.   [376] CAT, art 20.   [377] ibid, art 28.
[378] See Sect E.2 above.   [379] CAT, art 20(3).
[380] A Byrnes, 'The Committee against Torture' in Alston (n 19 above) 509, 532.
[381] Report of the CAT Committee, UN Doc A/51/44.
[382] UN Doc A/51/44, dated 3 May 1996, para 220.   [383] ibid, para 22.

camps of the Central Security Forces as places where torture allegedly occurs'.[384] Instead, the Egyptian government adopted the formalistic stance that 'State Security premises are administrative buildings and that Central Security camps are military installations and, that, therefore these places are not among those where people may be detained'.[385] Given that the two parties have essentially spoken past each other, the Committee's finding that 'there is a clear contradiction between the allegations made by non-governmental sources and the information provided by the Government with regard to the role of the Egyptian security forces and the methods they use' comes as no surprise.[386] In addition to making use of NGO sources, the Committee relied on written information presented by Egypt, as well as meetings with Egyptian delegations in Geneva. However, in the light of the contradictions, it reiterated its 'conviction that a visiting mission to Egypt would have been extremely useful to complete the inquiry'.[387]

In another example of speaking-past-each-other, the acceptance by Egypt of a visit also became the object of a factual dispute. Formally, the Egyptian government continuously expressed its commitment to engage in dialogue with the Committee. It never expressly declined permission for a visit, but drew attention to the need to discuss 'the framework through which the visit could take place'.[388] However, the Egyptian government never responded to two explicit invitations to visit within a specified time,[389] thus rendering unconvincing the argument by Egypt that 'at no stage of its dialogue with the Committee did it protest against the request for a visiting mission to Egypt'.[390] The extended nature of these deliberations is one of the main reasons why the investigation took three years to be finalized (from November 1991 to 1994).

In the end, the Committee accepted that the allegations appear to be 'well founded'. Its conclusion is based on the quantity of (the 'existence of a great number of allegations'), variety in ('which came from different sources'), consistency between ('allegations largely coincide and describe in the same way the methods of torture, the places where torture is practiced . . .'), and consistent reliability of sources ('sources that have proved to be reliable in connection with other activities of the Committee').[391] There can be little doubt that the government's objection to the publication of the inquiry report is just as much about a denial of the factual basis of the finding as it is about the reasons stated, namely the implicit support of terrorism.[392]

---

[384] ibid, para 208. [385] ibid, para 209. [386] ibid, para 209.
[387] ibid, para 209. [388] ibid, para 216. [389] ibid, paras 185 and 186.
[390] ibid, para 216. [391] ibid, para 219.
[392] See the following statement, contained in a letter by the Egyptian government to the Committee, pre-empting post-11 September 2001 USA rhetoric: 'If a summary account of the results of the confidential proceedings concerning Egypt were published in the Committee's annual report, this might be interpreted as signifying support for terrorist groups and would encourage the latter to proceed with their terrorist schemes and to defend their criminal members who engage in acts of terrorism by resorting to false accusations of torture. In other words, it might ultimately be interpreted as signifying that the Committee is indirectly encouraging terrorist groups not only in Egypt but worldwide. This is definitely not one of the objectives specified in the Committee's mandate'.

5 Individual Complaints

A declaration in terms of article 21 allows the CAT Committee to consider inter-state complaints, and one made in terms of article 22 allows individuals to complain to the Committee. By 31 December 2006, eight African states, namely Algeria, Ghana, Senegal, the Seychelles, South Africa, Togo, Tunisia, and Uganda had made declarations, all of them in terms of both articles. This means that 15 per cent of the African states parties to CAT have accepted the Committee's broader competence, as opposed to 28 per cent of all the states party to CAT taken together.[393] So far, two African states have been the subject of communications—four have been submitted against Tunisia; and one against Senegal.

The first case against Tunisia, submitted in 1994,[394] concerned the arrest and death in detention of a Tunisian student, Faïsal Barakat. On the facts presented to the Committee, including medical reports, a case of torture seemed to have been established. The application was, however, declared inadmissible. The Committee had to interpret article 22(1) of the Convention, stipulating that state parties may recognize the Committee's competence to receive communications 'from or on behalf of individuals'. This article should be read with rule 107(1)(b) of the Committee's Rules of Procedure. This rule provides that the communication must be submitted by: 'the individual himself'; or 'by his relatives or designated representative'; or 'by others on behalf of an alleged victim when it appears that the victim is unable to submit the communication himself, and the author of the communication justifies his acting on the victim's behalf'.

The third of these categories was at issue in the communication. The victim was dead and therefore obviously unable to complain personally. Provided that he 'justifies' his acting on the deceased's behalf, the author would be allowed to bring the communication. The author in this case was a political refugee, residing in France, but he did not establish that he was duly authorized by the deceased's family to submit the communication. The Committee arguably accepted the allegations that the victim's and author's family were threatened by the Tunisian government, as it requested the government to ensure that no harm was done to them. Given this context, it seems overly restrictive and technical for the Committee to have accepted the government's contention that the author had not been 'duly authorised by the family'. Having declared the communication inadmissible, the Committee left the door open for a subsequent communication properly establishing standing on behalf of the victim. When this indeed happened, the communication was declared admissible, and the CAT Committee found a violation.[395]

---

[393] The total number of state parties to CAT that have made declarations is 37, expressed as a percentage of the total number of state parties, this is 36% (<http:www.ohchr.org> (30 April 2007)).

[394] Communication 14/1994, *Faïsal Bakarat and Family v Tunisia*, UN Doc CAT/C/14/D/1994 (1995).

[395] Communication 60/1996, *M'Barek v Tunisia*, UN Doc CAT/C/23/D/60/1996 (2000).

In three subsequent communications against the same country,[396] the CAT Committee found Tunisia in violation of article 13 of CAT, which requires state parties to ensure that allegations of torture are promptly and impartially investigated. The three communications reveal a similar pattern: all three complainants alleged that they were tortured by the Tunisian authorities after being arrested and detained on suspicions related to their membership of an Islamist organization. The allegations cover the period between 1987 and 1995, and were contained in communications submitted from Switzerland, where the alleged victims have settled after fleeing Tunisia. Although the communications read like a litany of torture techniques,[397] and despite individual allegations being substantiated by extraneous sources,[398] the Committee, under persuasion from the Tunisian government, declined to find that torture in fact occurred. However, because complaints to judicial authorities in all three instances (to a military court, ordinary courts, and an examining magistrate respectively) fell on deaf ears and did not lead to any investigation, the Committee found a violation only of article 13. These decisions, which placed a heavy burden of persuasion on the complainants, water down the Committee's general stance that no circumstances—including the threat of 'terrorism'—may justify torture.[399]

The communication submitted against Senegal has its origin in Chad, where systematic acts of torture were allegedly committed between 1982 and 1990. The Chadian President at the time, Hissène Habré, sought refuge in Senegal when he was ousted as President of Chad in 1990. A group of Chadian nationals, alleging to be victims of acts of torture for which Habré had political responsibility, approached the Senegalese courts to ensure that their former President be tried for these acts. In 2001, the highest Senegalese court (the Court of Cassation) decided that Habré could not be tried in Senegal because no domestic legislation vested the Senegalese courts with 'universal jurisdiction'. Based on Senegal's failure to comply with its obligations under articles 5(2) and 7 of CAT, the complainants approached the CAT Committee.[400] Before the Committee finalized the matter, Belgium made a request to Senegal for the extradition of Habré after a Belgian judge had issued an arrest warrant, charging him, amongst other crimes, with torture.

The CAT Committee found Senegal in violation of both provisions of CAT: Senegal's failure to enact legislation domesticating the principle of 'universal jurisdiction' for perpetrators of torture amounts to a violation of its duty to take the

[396] Communication 187/2001, *Thabti v Tunisia*, UN Doc CAT/C/31/D/187/2001; Communication 188/2001, *Abdelli v Tunisia*, UN Doc CAT/C/31/D/188/2001; Communication 189/2001, *Ltaief v Tunisia*, UN Doc CAT/C/31/D/189/2001 (all 20 November 2003).

[397] Details of the 'roast chicken', 'upside-down' and 'scorpion' positions, immersion techniques, and 'table torture' are provided in the three communications.

[398] See eg Communication 187/2001, para 2.9, in which the evidence of a physiotherapist, a neurological surgeon, and a visit by the International Federation of Human Rights are cited in support of the veracity of the torture allegations.

[399] CAT, art 2(2), reiterated in numerous concluding observations.

[400] Communication 181/2001, *Guengueng and Others v Senegal*, UN Doc CAT/C/36/D/181/2001 (10 May 2006).

'necessary' measures to establish jurisdiction over non-nationals who have allegedly committed torture elsewhere but find themselves on its territory.[401] Senegal's failure either to prosecute or extradite Habré to Belgium violated its obligation under article 7 to do exactly that.[402]

As was the case with CERD, the complaints procedure under CAT was of significance to African nationals who brought communications against non-African state parties to CAT. In the first of these cases, *Mutombo v Switzerland*,[403] the subject-matter was torture and consistent mass violations of human rights in Zaire (now the DRC). Mutombo, a Zairian citizen who was involved in activities opposed to the Mobutu regime, was allegedly detained and exposed to torture in Zaire/ DRC. When he was released, he fled the country, and eventually ended up in Switzerland. His entry into Switzerland was illegal, and consequently, he applied for refugee status. However, his application was rejected, his appeal to the Commission of Appeal in Refugee Matters was unsuccessful, and he faced expulsion. The CAT Committee concluded that his expulsion would constitute a violation of article 3[404] of CAT.[405] As Zaire was not a party to CAT, Mutombo would no longer be under CAT's legal protection from expulsion. The Committee concluded that Switzerland was under an obligation not to expel him to Zaire/DRC, or to a country where he would face a real risk of being expelled to Zaire/DRC.[406] Since then, numerous communications involving African nationals have been directed against state parties. However, many of these communications have been declared inadmissible.[407]

6 Realization

The most promising aspect of implementation under CAT, the article 20 investigation, has not taken off yet. It is encouraging, though, that only two African state parties to CAT have declared themselves unwilling to recognize this competence

---

[401] CAT, art 5(2). The Committee explicitly rejected the state's argument that the 'complexity' of its legal system in some way exonerated it from its obligations under CAT. It also considered that Senegal had had an adequate opportunity to react to the judgment of the Court of Cassation, which was decided on 20 March 2001.

[402] On the AU's involvement in this matter, see Ch 5.B below; and on the arguments about the 'self-executing' nature of CAT, see Ch 13 below.

[403] Communication 13/1993, *Mutombo v Switzerland*, UN Doc CAT/C/12/D/13/1993 (27 April 1994).

[404] Art 3(1) reads: 'No State Party shall expel, return (*refouler*) or extradite a person to another State where there are substantial grounds for believing that he would be in danger of being subjected to torture'.

[405] At para 9.7 of its views.   [406] At para 10 of its views.

[407] See eg Communication 23/1995, *X v Spain*, UN Doc CAT/C/15/D/23/1995 (15 November 1995), involving an Algerian national; Communication 26/1995, *X v Canada*, UN Doc CAT/C/15/ D/26/1995 (20 November 1995), involving a Zaïrian citizen; Communication 30/1995, *PMPK v Sweden*, UN Doc CAT/C/15/D/30/1995 (20 November 1995), involving a Zaïrian national; Communication 32/1995, *ND v France*, UN Doc CAT/C/15/D/32/1995 (20 November 1995), involving a Zaïrian national; Communication 35/1995, *KKH v Canada*, UN Doc CAT/C/15/D/35/1995 (22 November 1995), involving a Ghanaian national.

of the CAT Committee. Of the total number of parties (144), eight have made declarations excluding the Committee's competence under article 20,[408] compared with two African states. In the absence of an effectively functional judicial system, CAT provides important redress possibilities in individual cases. A similar tendency as in the case of the ICCPR and its OP1 is noted: The African percentage drops strikingly when the percentage of states that have made declarations in terms of articles 21 and 22 of CAT is compared with the number of states that have ratified the Convention.

Some states do not allow individual complaints even when domestic redress is in place,[409] probably out of ignorance or out of fear for greater publicity at the international level. Few cases have been filed with the Committee, though. In time, this avenue may become better known and may be more effectively utilized. At the moment a very limited number of complaints have been brought under CAT.

F Convention on the Rights of the Child (CRC)

After its adoption in 1989, the CRC secured the required 20 ratifications, causing the Convention to enter into force in record time, in September 1990, less than a year after its adoption. African involvement in the drafting process was limited. A maximum of three African states participated for the first nine years that the working group took to draft a final proposal.[410] This is the lowest percentage of all the continents, contrasting sharply with Western Europe (61 per cent of the total number of participants) and even Latin American (with 29 per cent) participation over a similar period.[411] The fact that, by 1989, nine African states had been participating in the activities of the working group[412] hardly justifies a conclusion that the goal of the drafting process—'consensus over the need for setting international standards to protect the interests and well-being of children globally'— was not impeded by 'cross-cultural barriers'.[413]

Some lacunae in the substantive ambit of the CRC have subsequently been filled by two Optional Protocols. Resulting from a compromise during its drafting, the CRC sets the minimum age for conscription and direct participation in armed conflict at 15.[414] This provision was criticized, among other reasons because it contradicts International Labour Organization Convention 182 on the Prohibition

---

[408] See CAT, art 28, which earmarks such a declaration as a reservation.

[409] See eg Uganda, where more than 20% of the significant caseload of the Uganda Human Rights Commission usually deals with allegations of torture (Uganda Human Rights Commission, Annual Report 2005, Table 2.6, Graph B (<http://www.uhrc.org>) (11 November 2006)).

[410] See table in LJ LeBlanc, *The Convention on the Rights of the Child: United Nations Lawmaking on Human Rights* (Lincoln, Nebr: University of Nebraska Press, 1995) 30.   [411] ibid.

[412] See table in LeBlanc (n 410 above) 48.

[413] D Johnson, 'Cultural and Regional Pluralism in the Drafting of the UN Convention on the Rights of the Child' in M Freeman and P Veerman (eds), *The Ideologies of Children's Rights* (Dordrecht: Martinus Nijhoff, 1992).   [414] CRC, art 38(2) and 38(3).

and Immediate Action for the Elimination of the Worst Forms of Child Labour, which prohibits, *inter alia*, forced or compulsory recruitment of children for use in armed conflict.[415] Under the Optional Protocol on Children in Armed Conflict (CRC-AC), adopted in 2000 and entering into force in 2002, state parties undertake to ensure that children (everyone under the age of 18) do not take part in direct hostilities nor are conscripted into the armed forces. The Optional Protocol on the Sale of Children, Child Prostitution and Child Pornography (CRC-SC) (also adopted in 2000, entered into force in 2002) extends the protection of the CRC to the areas mentioned in its title.

1 Mandate and Composition of the CRC Committee

The Committee on the Rights of the Child (CRC Committee), which met for the first time in 1991, is the implementing mechanism under this Convention. Individual communications are not provided for. Self-reporting by state parties is the main method of ensuring compliance with the provisions of the Convention.[416]

The Committee initially consisted of ten members, each with recognized competence in the field of children's rights. They are elected by state parties, and serve in their personal capacity.[417] Members are elected for terms of four years, but they may be re-elected.[418] In electing members to the Committee, state parties should consider 'equitable geographical distribution, as well as . . . the principal legal systems'.[419] On 30 June 1999, the CRC Committee comprised three members from African state parties: Amina El Gidi (Egypt), Esther Mokhuane (South Africa), and Awa Ouedraogo (Burkina Faso). This means that 30 per cent of the membership of the Committee was African, a figure that deviates slightly from the African percentage of the total number of state parties (which stood at 37 per cent). The West European region was 'overrepresented'. LeBlanc justifies this overriding of strict geographical considerations with reference to the fact that 'states in that region were the most active and constructive'[420] in drafting the Convention. They also carry 'the heaviest financial burdens' in supporting the UN.[421] By 31 December 2006, the position had changed slightly. Based on an increased membership of 18, Africans by then made up a third of the Committee, with three members from North Africa, and three from sub-Saharan Africa.

2 Ratifications and Reservations

As at 31 December 2006, 193 states were party to the Convention, including 52 African states.[422] Only one state on the continent, Somalia, has neither signed nor ratified the Convention. Simultaneously, however, the number of states entering

---

[415] Adopted in June 1999.   [416] CRC, art 44.   [417] ibid, art 43(2).
[418] ibid, art 43(b).   [419] ibid, art 43(2).   [420] LeBlanc (n 410 above) 210.
[421] ibid.
[422] See web-site <http://www.un.org/Depts/Treaty/final/t52/newfiles/part-600/iv-600/iv-11.html>.

reservations is very high. Ten African states entered reservations or declarations. These relate to the Islamic religion,[423] the age of majority,[424] religion and traditional values,[425] the provisions of national legislation,[426] the state's inability to ensure free primary education,[427] and children seeking refugee status.[428]

A total of 28 African states have ratified CRC-SC, while 22 have ratified CRC-AC. No African state party to any of the two Optional Protocols to CRC entered a reservation. Although CRC-AC obliges states to 'raise' the minimum age for voluntary recruitment into the armed forces above the 15-year limit provided for in the 'mother' convention, it does not fix a minimum age of recruitment.[429] To oversee 'progressive' adherence to this obligation, the Protocol sets up an internal accountability mechanism requiring states to make 'binding' declarations about the minimum recruitment age at the time of becoming a party.[430] All the states complied, and Senegal even went beyond the minimum requirement by stipulating a minimum age of 20. Only one state, Cape Verde, declared that its minimum age of recruitment was 17, but added that legislation allowing a reduction of this age in times of war will not be applied to reduce the age of recruitment below 17 years.[431] Under the same provision, states must declare what steps they have taken to ensure that recruitment is *in fact* voluntary. African states complied, although some— such as Chad and the DRC—provided sparse details.

3 State Reporting

On 30 June 1995, a total of 86 reports were overdue by African state parties to CRC.[432] It should be noted that of the three African state parties represented on the Committee on the Rights of the Child at the time, two (Burkina Faso and Egypt) complied with their obligations to report. Over the last decade, the situation improved considerably. By 31 December 2006, all African state parties to CRC had submitted at least one report, and most of them had no overdue reports. No doubt, the CRC Committee's practice of allowing combined reports and of setting deadlines beyond the scheduled reporting time contributed to reducing overdue reports.[433]

In general, governments cooperated with the Committee by drafting adequate reports, by sending high profile delegations, and by answering queries. Madagascar presents an example. It ratified the Convention on 19 December 1990, and

---

[423] Reservation by Algeria, Egypt, Mauritania, and Morocco.
[424] Reservation by Botswana.   [425] Reservation by Djibouti.
[426] Reservations by Mali and Tunisia.   [427] Declaration by Swaziland.
[428] Reservation by Mauritius.   [429] CRC-AC, art 3(1).   [430] CRC-AC, art 3(2).
[431] This statement amounts to an 'interpretative declaration'.
[432] See UN Doc HRI/MC/1995/3 at 3–9. The following African state parties had one report overdue: Algeria, Angola, Benin, Burundi, Cameroon, Cape Verde, CAR, Chad, Côte d'Ivoire, Djibouti, Equatorial Guinea, Ethiopia, Gambia, Ghana, Guinea, Guinea-Bissau, Kenya, Lesotho, Liberia, Libya, Malawi, Mali, Mauritania, Mauritius, Niger, Nigeria, São Tomé Príncipe, Seychelles, Sierra Leone, Togo, Uganda, Tanzania, Zaire, Zambia, Zimbabwe.   [433] Vandenhole (n 64 above) 143–4.

submitted its first periodic report on 20 July 1993.[434] The 65-page report is an excellent example of serious compliance with reporting obligations. The richness of detail and the inclusion of statistical data (on the percentage of children attending school, and on technical education) made the examination of the report meaningful. State compliance is not taken as a *fait accompli*, but is sometimes criticized in the country report.[435] One problematic aspect in terms of the preparation of reports is the provision of statistics on the realization of especially socio-economic rights of children. The Committee requested that such information be included in subsequent reports.[436] As more states submit second periodic reports, the CRC Committee often points to the failure of states to implement concluding observations.[437]

This does not mean that the Committee did not in its comparatively expansive observations identify areas in which the protection granted by states fell short of the guarantees in the CRC. Some of these areas, identified over the last decade or so, are:

- Discrimination against girls is rife in most states. This is especially the case when cultural practices indigenous to parts of Africa, such as female genital mutilation, conflict with the provisions of the CRC. Other forms of discrimination and violation of the dignity of the girl-child are the practice of forced marriage, the incidence of domestic violence,[438] and sexual exploitation.[439] In some states, patterns of disparity in access to education have been criticized.[440]

- Education has been targeted as a cause for concern. The absence of compulsory and free education at the primary level,[441] the quality of education,[442] and the high drop-out rate before pupils finish primary school,[443] have been brought to the attention of states.

- Alarmingly low rates of birth registration are noted in many countries. Departing from the premise that the consequence of non-registration often is exclusion from basic services, the Committee recommends that this issue be prioritized, for example by using mobile birth registration units in the rural areas of Angola.[444]

[434] See UN Doc CRC/C/8/Add 5 (13 September 1993).

[435] eg para 79: 'The provisions are not always observed by those required to apply them' (on problems with the implementation of civil registration of births) and para 309: 'provisions on sexual abuse and exploitation are not always effectively applied'.

[436] See eg the Egyptian report, and the Committee's comments.

[437] See eg the second periodic report of Libya, UN Doc CRC/C/15/Add.209 (4 July 2003) para 4, and that of Morocco, UN Doc CRC/C/15/Add.211 (10 July 2003) para 5.

[438] See the Committee's evaluation of the report by Burkina Faso (see UN Doc CRC/C/15/Add. 19 (1994) (paras 8 and 14) and that of Sudan (para 13 of the Committee's concluding observations).

[439] See eg the Committee's views in respect of the Madagascar report (para 15).

[440] See the Committee's comments on the Egyptian report, UN Doc CRC/C/15/Add. 5 (1993), also at web-site <http://www.umn.edu/humanrts/crc/EGYPT.htm> (para 6).

[441] See the Committee's views on the report of Senegal (para 14).

[442] See the Committee's concluding observations in respect of Egypt's report UN Doc CRC/C/14.145: (1995) (para 47).

[443] See eg the Madagascar report, and the Committee's concluding observations (para 13).

[444] UN Doc CRC/C/15/Add.246 (3 November 2004) para 27.

- Socio-economic issues, such as birth rates, health, and welfare have been raised consistently. In addressing these issues, the CRC Committee more regularly than some other treaty bodies focuses on budgetary allocations,[445] but it too does not factor in the MDGs in issues such as maternal and infant mortality.[446]
- A recurring concern has also been the position of working children. In many instances this amounts to child labour.[447] The Committee drew the attention of states to the ILO Convention on minimum age requirements for employment.[448]
- The position of the juvenile offender has also elicited unfavourable comments from the Committee.[449]

The examination of reports under the two Protocols started in 2005, but no report from an African state party has yet been considered. No report has been submitted under CRC-AC; only Morocco has submitted a report under OP-SC.[450]

4 Realization

The CRC enjoys near-universal ratification in Africa. This contrasts with only partial adherence to the regional pendant, the African Charter on the Rights and Welfare of the Child (African Children's Charter). After a hesitant start, states are now much more engaged with the reporting system. As appears more fully below, the compliance of African states under the CRC has far surpassed that under the African Children's Charter. A sizeable portion of African states also ratified the two Protocols. However, reservations to the CRC, incomplete domestication, and a lack of implementation of concluding observations still detract from giving the CRC its full effect in most states.

G Convention on the Protection of the Rights of All Migrant Workers and Members of their Families (CMW)

It took many years for the CMW, adopted in 1990, to reach the required number of ratifications (20) to secure its entry into force. When this target was reached in 2003, the CMW Committee was set up. The Convention aims at preventing the exploitation of migrant workers through a set of binding international standards

---

[445] See eg Angola's initial report, UN Doc CRC/C/15/Add.246, 3 November 2004, para 13; Sudan's second periodic report, UN Doc CRC/C/15/Add.190 (9 October 2002) para 53.

[446] See eg Sudan's second periodic report, UN Doc CRC/C/15/Add.190 (9 October 2002) paras 43 and 44.

[447] See the reference to 'forced labour and slavery' in the Committee's concluding observations on the Sudanese report (para 12).

[448] See eg comments on the report of Zimbabwe UN Doc CRC/C/15/Add. 55 (1995) para 32.

[449] See eg paras 11 and 20 of the Committee's observations on the otherwise almost uncriticized Namibian report UN Doc CRC/C/15/Add. 14 (1994).

[450] By 31 July 2006, 18 reports have been submitted under OP-AC and 17 under OP-SC.

to address the treatment, welfare, and human rights of both documented and undocumented migrants. It further seeks to prevent the illegal recruitment and trafficking of migrant workers and to discourage the irregular or undocumented employment of migrant workers.

1 Mandate and Composition of the CMW Committee

Under its mandate, the CMW Committee examines periodic state reports,[451] and considers inter-state and individual communications. The ten-member Committee comprises two Africans, Ahmed El-Borai from Egypt and Abdelhamid El Jamri from Morocco.

2 Ratifications and Reservations

Being responsible for 13 of the 34 ratifications and accessions by 31 December 2006, African states have shown much greater enthusiasm to become party to this Convention than the rest of the world.[452] Most of the ratifying states are predominantly 'countries of origin' ('sending countries') rather than 'countries of employment' ('receiving countries').[453] None of the European Union members or WEO group countries is amongst the 34. As long as industrialized states, where most migrant workers find themselves, do not ratify the CMW, its effect will remain limited.

Four African states have entered reservations: two (Algeria and Morocco) on the procedural matter of mutual consent for the submission of a dispute; one (Egypt) entered 'reservations' on articles 4 and 18(6) that read more like interpretative declarations; and one (Uganda) stated that it 'cannot guarantee at all times to provide free legal assistance' in accordance with article 18(3)(d).

3 State Reporting

Setting an example to Africa and the world, Mali was the first country to submit its state report. By the end of 2006, it was joined by only two more states—Egypt and Mexico. What gave Mali the confidence to take this bold step is partly the promulgation of Act 04-058 of 25 November 2004 on 'the entry, stay and residence of foreigners' in Mali, which 'replaces legislation and regulations dating from the colonial period'.[454] In its examination of the report, the CMW Committee raised issues that are likely to recur in the concluding observations on the reports of other states. The issues raised relate primarily to the sufficiency and specificity of information about measures the state has taken to implement the Convention,

---

[451] CMW, art 73.

[452] Translated into percentages, this means that Africa accounts for 38% of CMW acceptances, while it holds only 27% of UN membership. [453] CMW, art 1.

[454] Concluding observation, UN Doc CMW/C/MLI/CO/1 (31 May 2006) para 6.

including the need for a 'sound database, with data disaggregated by sex'.[455] As with other treaties and treaty bodies, the Committee reiterates that reports have to go beyond citing formal legal provisions, by including examples of and problems encountered in the actual application of those provisions. As was the case with Mali, all other member states are likely to be encouraged to accept the optional complaints mechanism under CMW, to provide free access by migrant workers to information about their rights, and to 'institute a participatory procedure' to allow the involvement of NGOs in the state reporting process.[456]

4 Individual Communications

Individual complaints are allowed against states that have made a declaration under article 77 of CMW. Of the ten declarations accepting the CMW Committee's competence to consider individual communications required before this mechanism will enter into force, none has been deposited by 30 April 2007.

5 Realization

Although it is too early to gauge the impact of the CMW, it appears that, inspired by the relevance of the subject-matter of CMW to them, African states are more enthusiastic about this treaty than other regions of the world. More cynically, one may point to the perception that this Convention does not impose onerous obligations on African states, because they are mostly 'sending' rather than 'receiving' states. However, as the examination of the Egyptian report in April 2007 shows, African states also violate the rights of migrants who settle in or are transiting through their territories.[457] However, as trans-border employment takes root as a result of increasing regional and subregional integration in Africa, states' commitment to upholding CMW may yet be put to more stringent tests.

H Conclusion

Questions should be posed whether the seven treaties and their monitoring mechanisms have had any significant impact in African states. If the UN human rights treaty system 'is one of the Organization's great achievements',[458] there must be some evidence of this 'achievement' in Africa.

---

[455] ibid, paras 12–14.   [456] ibid, paras 10, 16, and 17.
[457] In its 'advanced unedited' concluding observations, the CMW Committee for example urged the Egyptian government to investigate fully the events on 31 December 2005 that led to the death of Sudanese migrants, and to review its policy of testing foreign migrants for HIV.
[458] Plan of action of the UNHCHR, reported to the UNSG, UN Doc A/59/20045/Add.3 (26 May 2005) para 95.

Table 3.2. Ratification of major United Nations human rights treaties in Africa as at 31 December 2006

	ICESCR	ICCPR	Art 41	OPI	OPII	CERD	Art 14	CRC	CRC-SC	CRC-AC	CEDAW	OP-CEDAW	CAT	OP-CAT	Arts 21 and 22	CMW
Algeria	X	X	X	X		X	X	X	X		X		X		X	X
Angola	X	X		X				X	X		X					X
Benin	X	X		X		X		X	X	X	X	s	X	X		s
Botswana		X				X		X	X		X		X			
Burkina Faso	X	X		X		X		X	X	X	X	X	X	X		X
Burundi	X	X				X		X		s	X		X			
Cameroon	X	X		X		X		X	s	s	X	s	X			
Cape Verde	X	X		X	X	X		X	X	X	X	X	X			X
Central African Republic	X	X		X		X		X			X					
Chad	X	X		X		X		X	X	X	X		X			
Comoros						X		X			X		s			s
Congo	X	X	X	X		X		X			X		X			
Côte d'Ivoire	X	X		X		X		X			X		X			
Democratic Republic of the Congo	X	X		X		X		X	X	X	X		X			
Djibouti	X	X			X			X	s	s	X		X			
Egypt	X	X				X		X	X	X	X		X			X
Equatorial Guinea	X	X		X		X		X			X		X			
Eritrea	X	X				X		X	X	X	X					
Ethiopia	X	X				X		X	s		X		X			
Gabon	X	X				X		X	s	s	X	X	X	s		s

Table 3.2. (*cont.*)

	ICESCR	ICCPR	Art 41	OPI	OPII	CERD	Art 14	CRC	CRC-SC	CRC-AC	CEDAW	OP-CEDAW	CAT	OP-CAT	Arts 21 and 22	CMW
Gambia	X	X	X	X		X		X	s	s	X	s	s	s		X
Ghana	X	X	X	X		X		X	s	s	X		X	s	X	X
Guinea	X	X		X	s	X		X			X	s	X			s
Guinea-Bissau	X	s		s		s		X	s	s	X		s			
Kenya	X	X				X		X	s	X	X	X	X			X
Lesotho	X	X		X		X		X	s	X	X	s				s
Liberia	X	X		s	X	X		X	s	s	X	X	X	X		X
Libyan Arab Jamahiriya	X	X		X		X		X	X	X	X	X	X			
Madagascar	X	X		X		X		X	X	X	X	s	X			
Malawi	X	X		X		X		X	s	s	X	s	X			X
Mali	X	X		X	X	X		X	X	X	X	X	X			X
Mauritania	X	X			X	X		X	s	s	X		X	s		
Mauritius	X	X		X		X		X	X	X	X	s	X	X		X
Morocco	X	X				X		X	X	X	X		X	X		
Mozambique									X	X						
Namibia	X	X		X	X	X		X	X	X	X	X	X			X
Niger	X	X		X	X	X		X	X	X	X	X	X			
Nigeria	X	X		X		X		X	s	s	X	X	X			

Table 3.2. (*cont.*)

Rwanda	X	X		X		X		X	X	X	X		X		s	
São Tomé e Príncipe	s	s		s	s	s		X			s	X	s		X	X
Senegal	X	X	X	X		X	X	X	X	X	X	X	X	X	X	X
Seychelles	X	X		X	X	X		X	s	s	X	s	X			s
Sierra Leone	X	X		X		X		X		s	X	s	X	s		
Somalia	X	X		X		X		s	s	s	X		X			
South Africa	s	X	X	X	X	X	X	X	X	X	X	X	X	s	X	
Sudan	X	X				X		X	X	X	s		X			
Swaziland	X	X				X		X			X		s			
Togo	X	X	X	X		X		X	X	X	X		X	s	X	s
Tunisia	X	X				X		X	X	X	X		X		X	
Uganda	X	X	X	X		X		X	X	X	X		X		X	X
United Republic of Tanzania	X							X	X	X	X					
Zambia	X	X		X		X		X		X	X		X			
Zimbabwe	X	X	X			X		X		X	X					
Total Number of African State Parties	48	50	8	32	7	49	3	52	28	22	51	12	42	5	8	13
Percentage of African State Parties	*91%*	*94%*	*13%*	*60%*	*13%*	*92%*	*6%*	*98%*	*53%*	*42%*	*96%*	*23%*	*79%*	*9%*	*15%*	*25%*
Total State Parties Globally	155	160	48	109	60	173	47	193	115	110	185	83	144	30	55	34
Percentage of Total States	*80%*	*82%*	*25%*	*56%*	*31%*	*89%*	*24%*	*99%*	*59%*	*57%*	*95%*	*43%*	*74%*	*15%*	*28%*	*18%*

Note. X: ratification or accession; s: signature.

The formal 'first step' of ensuring universal ratification is further advanced in Africa than in the rest of the world. With the exception of CMW, at least 75 per cent of African states have formally accepted each of the treaties. The highest acceptance has been achieved for CRC (98 per cent), followed by CEDAW (96 per cent), ICCPR (94 per cent), CERD (92 per cent), ICESCR (91 per cent), and CAT (79 per cent). These figures represent significant advances since 1997, when the corresponding formal acceptance percentage rates for CRC stood at 98, for CEDAW at 85, ICCPR at 77, CERD at 81, ICESCR at 77, and CAT at 43.[459] Compared to the percentage of states that have acceded to and ratified these treaties globally, the African percentage is higher with respect to all treaties,[460] with the exception of the CRC and its Protocols, where African states lag behind by a small margin.

Although cynicism is expressed about the factors motivating states to ratify treaties, the acceptance of international human rights standards is an important anchor that may help stabilize the gains of democratization. In the 1960s, 'flag independence' meant a UN seat; in the 1990s and early 2000s, breaking with a past of one-party rule, brutality, and civil war came to be symbolized by adherence to international human rights treaties. Numerous African states, such as Benin, South Africa, and Zambia, embraced international human rights as part of the process of consolidating democracy. Two recent examples stand out. On 22 September 2004, after Charles Taylor had left the country in August 2003 for exile in Nigeria and during a two-year transitional government, Liberia acceded to three of these treaties (CAT, OP-CAT, ICESCR), ratified one (ICCPR), and signed another five (OPI, OP-CEDAW, CMW, CRC-SC, and CRC-AC). It followed this up in 2005 by becoming the seventh African state party to OPII, aimed at the abolition of the death penalty. Similarly, in one go, on 5 November 2002, Djibouti acceded to four of the UN instruments (ICCPR, OPI, OPII, ICESCR). What may be interpreted as a sign to the international community of a changing of the guards came in the aftermath of the first multi-party democratic elections in 1999 and a peace agreement between the Afar rebels and the Issa-dominated government in 2001. Both these states had long been party to CEDAW and CRC. Although the trend towards universal ratification should be welcomed, multiple ratifications without prior assessment of their implications for domestic law reinforce the impression that states accept international human rights law lightly, and mainly for symbolic reasons.

However, when it comes to the acceptance of optional individual complaints mechanisms, allowing for much closer scrutiny and allowing for case-based governmental embarrassment, the inverse applies. Only 6 per cent of African states accept individual complaints under CERD, compared to a global percentage of 24 per cent; in respect of the CAT complaints procedure, the percentages are

---

[459] F Viljoen, 'The Realisation of Human Rights in Africa through Inter-Governmental Institutions', LL D thesis, University of Pretoria, unpublished LL D thesis, 1997.

[460] Sometimes the difference is significant, as with ICCPR (African rate 94%, global rate 80%), see Table 3.2 above.

28 per cent (globally), and 15 per cent (for Africa). For OPI, Africa's acceptance stands at 55 against 54 per cent. One explanation for the general trend could be that, in Africa, a commitment is easily secured at the more rhetorical level. Mechanisms that could publicly embarrass states are less easily accepted. Peter's opinion that 'most states, and in particular those from the developing world, have constantly avoided signing or ratifying the Optional Protocol' because it is an 'enforcement mechanism' no longer holds water.[461]

There is growing evidence that the limited possibilities for individual complaints are being exploited. Although none of the handful of communications before the CERD Committee involved an African state, some of them came from Africans living in other state parties. It often takes one case to set off the more frequent submission of complaints. An initial complaint against Tunisia under CAT, which was declared inadmissible, was followed by three others, in which the state was found in violation. The 59 communications against African states finalized by the HRC almost universally concluded with a finding of violation. Most of these cases emanated from the DRC, allowing the HRC to provide an independently scrutinized record of violations. There is an inevitable trend towards greater judicialization of the treaty bodies, leading some even to suggest the establishment of an International Human Rights Court.[462] As part of this trend, complaints are now also possible under CEDAW and CMW, and foreseen under ICESCR.

Due to the focus on state obligations, the role of civil society in the UN system has not been elaborated upon. Especially in the reporting procedure, this silence needs to be broken, to acknowledge the importance of NGOs in supplying the treaty bodies with information about the situation in reporting states, often in the form of 'shadow reports'.[463] The Committee on the Rights of the Child, in particular, has developed a very close relationship with NGOs. Supported by UNICEF, the NGO Group for the Convention on the Rights of the Child keeps NGOs informed, and assists a small group of national NGOs to attend the session where the state report from their country is examined.[464] State compliance with state reporting under CRC is partly explained by the role of UNICEF and NGOs.

African state parties have entered a number of reservations, especially in respect of CEDAW. The single African objection was of a political nature. A number of, particularly WEO, states have objected to African reservations, especially in

[461] CM Peter, 'Enforcement of Fundamental Rights and Freedoms in Tanzania: Matching Theory and Practice' in CM Peter and IH Juma (eds), Fundamental Rights and Freedoms and Public Order in Tanzania (unpublished report of workshop held in Dar es Salaam, 3–7 April 1995) (copy of original on file with author) (1996) 52, 54.

[462] T Buergenthal, 'A Court and two Consolidated Treaty Bodies' in A Bayefsky (ed), *The UN Human Rights Treaty System in the 21st Century* (The Hague: Kluwer Law International, 2000) 299, 301.

[463] In a notable example, Japanese NGOs submitted 23 'shadow reports' to Japan's second periodic report to the HRC, and about 80 delegates attended the examination, eliciting some criticism about the lack of coordination between civil society organizations (Heyns and Viljoen (n 220 above) 409).

[464] AF Bayefsky, *The UN Human Rights Treaty System: Universality at the Crossroads* (The Hague: Kluwer Law International, 2001) 45.

respect of CEDAW. However, the withdrawal of some of these is another positive development.

The examination of state reports by treaty bodies is the main supervisory mechanism provided for under these treaties. In the light of the experience gained from years of state reporting, Bayefsky concluded that the number of overdue reports brought the system into disrepute.[465] Over the last decade or so, there has been a reversal of trends owing to a more pro-active stance taken by treaty bodies and improved compliance with states. The reporting record of African states under the seven treaties that were investigated varies considerably. It is a good sign that all 52 African state parties to CRC have submitted at least an initial report and that most have no overdue reports under CRC. Reporting under CEDAW has been relatively frequent and thorough. The reasons for these exceptions should be investigated more closely, but some of the relevant factors may be state perceptions of the content matter of the CRC and CEDAW, which is perceived as 'non-political', the role of UNICEF, and the emergence of a strong women's movement and civil society organizations dealing with women's and children's rights in many African states. Less impressive reporting has been accomplished under CAT, the most 'political' of the treaties, and by far the worst under ICESCR, which places the most onerous obligation on states, namely to 'fulfil' socio-economic rights. Examples of fruitful follow-up to concluding observations are also more frequent, as is an engagement with states. The response by Kenya to the HRC's concluding observations to its second periodic report stands as a precedent worthy of emulation.

Greater inclusion in decision-making bodies by African states may also be a factor in strengthening perceptions of legitimacy. At 30 June 1999, 20 African representatives served on the six treaty bodies. By 31 July 2006, this number had increased to 26. Two Africans also served on the CMW Committee. However, on all these bodies, Northern American countries are overrepresented and dominant, skewing the potential role of treaty body membership. With a representative on each of the seven treaty bodies, Egypt, in particular, stands out. The disproportionate representation of countries in the North may be ascribed to the membership of these countries of not only the AU (or the 'African Group'), but also to the Arab League and OIC (and thus of the 'Asian Group'). Viewed from an African perspective, it seems that these states get a double bite at the cherry. A better geographic distribution should be achieved, so that the majority of African states do not perceive themselves as sidelined by decision-making institutions.

The main problem remains that of securing the involvement of consistently disengaged countries, of which many are in Africa. Treaty bodies have started taking innovative steps, such as the review of long overdue reports and urgent procedures, to target these states. A lack of compliance with treaty obligations may be deliberate, but often results from a lack of information and knowledge associated with weak governance structures and systems, and from the fact that these obligations

---

[465] See data in tables A, D, E, gathered by Bayefsky (n 18 above) nn 286–9.

are overshadowed by more immediate and pressing concerns related to conflict or the disintegration of the state. While technical assistance, in the form of training programmes aimed at government officials and assistance with reporting, may go some distance to securing the greater involvement of these states, the ultimate answer lies in a radical overhaul of political governance and prospects for development. It must be acknowledged that the breakdown of state authority, the pressure of civil war, and external aggression make it extremely difficult to maintain security, domestic law and order, and essential basic services. States in which effective government, essential to statehood, is severely under strain, should be treated differently from other states. Merely citing non-compliance by non-functional states serves little purpose if technical and other assistance is not provided.

PART III

THE REGIONAL LEVEL

4

The African Regional Architecture and Human Rights

A Pan-Africanism, Colonial Borders, and the Contested Form of African Unity

Africa's continental architecture of the independence period and of the new millennium did not come about in an ideological vacuum, but was forged from the tension between different understandings of pan-Africanism, which are linked to contending visions of state sovereignty. The evolution of pan-African institutions reflects changing notions of what African unity and solidarity entail, and may be charted on the intergovernmental–supranational continuum. While the OAU Charter of 1963 does not identify its pan-Africanist roots by name, it locates itself in the 'aspirations of peoples for brotherhood and solidarity'.[1] The legal framework of two of the present institutions with African-wide ambitions, the AU and the APRM of NEPAD, make explicit reference to this ancestry.[2]

Pan-Africanism is not a one-dimensional concept that allows for an easy and finite definition. The term may be understood from a 'cultural' (people-centred) or from a 'political' (state-centred) perspective.[3] Culturally, it is the affirmation of a

---

[1] OAU Charter, Preamble.

[2] AU Constitutive Act, Preamble: 'Inspired by...generations of Pan-Africanists'; see also the African Peer Review Mechanism Base Document (2003) (<http://www.nepad.org/2005/files/documents/49.pdf>) (para 6 requires the members of the Panel of Eminent Persons to be committed to the ideals of pan-Africanism). On the pan-African background to the AU, see T Murithi, *The African Union: Pan-Africanism, Peacebuilding and Development* (Aldershot: Ashgate, 2005) 7–38.

[3] See I Geiss, *The Pan-African Movement* (London: Methuen, 1974) 7.

common ancestry of members of 'the black race' with their real or perceived 'origin' in Africa,[4] wherever they find themselves. Politically, it is a movement aimed at closer unity between African states. As the movement towards African independence unfolded in the last century, the contested nature of the term's political implications was starkly revealed.

The origins of pan-Africanism as an intellectual movement may be traced to early advocates in Africa and in the African Diaspora. One of its earliest exponents, Edward Wilmot Blyden, who first settled in Liberia, the haven in Africa for freed slaves that became independent in 1847, and later in Sierra Leone, initiated campaigns for West African unity. Under the inspirational guidance of leaders in the Diaspora, such as Marcus Garvey (from Jamaica), WEB Du Bois (an African-American living in the USA), George Padmore (from Trinidad), and Sylvester Williams (a London barrister born in Trinidad), a tentative movement started in the nineteenth century, loosely aimed at giving a common voice to Africans and people of African descent.[5] There is some irony in the fact that the descendants of African slaves, gained from and made use of educational opportunities provided in the 'new world' to verbalize their experience and to advocate solidarity between Africans.[6]

Africans' suffering, oppression, and exploitation can be traced back to a shared history of slavery, followed by colonialism and institutionalized discrimination.[7] This initial focus on membership of the 'black race' caused the term 'pan-Negroism' to be used to describe the form of solidarity among Africans in the Diaspora and those living in Africa.[8] In its most radical form, pan-Africanism may thus be defined as unity based on affiliation with the 'black race', based on the ideal of a common patria or motherland.

As support and interest grew, the movement became institutionalized. A first pan-African conference was organized when a small group met in 1900, at the start of the new century, in London.[9] At this meeting and the subsequent five 'Pan-African Congresses', starting in 1919 with the 'First Pan-African Congress' of Paris, people from Africa were not well represented. The situation changed at the 'Fifth Pan-African Congress', held in Manchester in 1945, soon after the end of World War II. After their participation in the two world wars, Africans and people of African descent experienced their social and legal exclusion and the colonial domination as more hurtful and oppressive than ever before. Allowing Africans to take control and leading to the Africanization of pan-Africanism, Manchester was a turning point as the torch was handed to a new generation of Africans, such as Kwame Nkrumah and Jomo Kenyatta. The momentum of the movement strengthened the

---

[4] A Ajala, *Pan-Africanism: Evolution, Progress and Prospects* (London: André Deutsch, 1974) 93.
    [5] See KA Appiah, 'Pan-Africanism' in KA Appiah and HL Gates (eds), *Africana: The Encyclopedia of the African and African American Experience* (New York: Basic Civitas Books, 1999) 1484.
    [6] Geiss (n 3 above) 5.
    [7] Geiss (n 3 above) 8 n 14 (pan-Africanism described as 'a delayed boomerang from the time of slavery').   [8] B Davidson, *Modern Africa* (New York: Longman, 1987) 28.
    [9] Ajala (n 4 above) 4.

hands of African politicians and liberation leaders in their struggle against colonial rule and in favour of attaining independence.

Although inspired by a common ideology, in each colonial entity the struggle for independence relied heavily on a particularized discourse of nationalism. Pragmatism—and the target of the anti-colonial struggle—dictated that colonially imposed demarcations should define the various 'nationalisms'. As independence was gained, it became almost inevitable that this image of the nationhood would be invoked to legitimate the new state. The problem is that this conception of 'nation' was an artificial and temporary construct that relied on the border lines invented by European powers and formalized at the Berlin Conference.[10] Serving colonial interests rather than those of the people defined 'in' or 'out', these boundaries were mostly arbitrary and did not take into account the composition of the resulting population.[11] The colonial period and concomitant anti-colonial struggles were too brief to ensure the emergence of a centripetal and unifying concept of community within the new territories. 'Nation-building' campaigns to contain competing identities of entities constituting the 'state', which often followed independence, could not ensure 'enduring stability, cultural identity and national development'.[12]

In 1957, Ghana became the first state with a majority black ('African') population to gain its independence from its colonial master.[13] Nkrumah, who became the first independence President, campaigned under the slogan 'Seek ye first the political kingdom', and explained that it requires 'resolute leadership' 'to subordinate the understandable desire of the people for better living conditions' to the 'achievement of the primary aim of the abolition of colonial rule'.[14] Unfortunately, this sentiment was carried over into the independence era, where it manifested itself in a preoccupation with political power at the expense of the sustainable development of the people.

Soon after independence, Nkrumah brought together the eight states that had at that stage achieved independence together for the first Conference of Independent African states of 1958, which 'marked the formal launching of the pan-African movement on African soil'.[15] Pan-Africanism itself became the filter through which newly independent states would organize their relationships and co-existence. At the end of the same year, Nkrumah hosted another conference, the All African

---

[10] T Pakenham, *Scramble for Africa: 1876–1912* (New York: Random House, 1991) part III.

[11] Forty-four per cent of modern African boundaries follow meridian parallels; 30% follow mathematical lines such as arcs and curves and 26% follow geographical features (J Castellino and S Allen, *Title to Territoriality in International Law: A Temporal Analysis* (Aldershot: Ashgate, 2003) sources cited at 113; see also C Clapham, 'Boundaries and States in the New African Order' in DC Bach (ed), *Regionalism in Africa: Integration and Disintegration* (Oxford: James Currey, 1999) 53, 55–6).

[12] Castellino and Allen (n 11 above) 118.

[13] States in northern Africa attained their independence earlier (Libya, in 1951; and Sudan, Morocco, and Tunisia in 1956). Strictly speaking, Sudan is the first 'sub-Saharan state' to obtain independence, and Ghana the first 'black' African state. However, in the literature, Ghana is often identified as the first 'sub-Saharan' state to gain its independence, indicating that the term 'sub-Sahara' may sometimes be given more than merely a geographic content.

[14] K Nkrumah, *Africa Must Unite* (New York: Praeger, 1963) 51, which appeared just in time for the Addis Ababa Conference in 1963.   [15] Ajala (n 4 above) 14.

Peoples' Organization, a meeting of African political parties. During these events, Nkrumah propagated his vision that 'Africa must unite' to form a supranational 'United States of Africa'.[16] In his view, the gains of freedom could only be secured if Africa formed a bulwark against the pressures of 'neo-colonialism'.[17] The form of this 'Union' cannot clearly be discerned from his writings: on the one hand he models his thinking on states where smaller units have ceded their sovereignty to a central political entity;[18] on the other hand he refers to separate states with common policies within an elaborate political framework.

At two further conferences of independent states and political parties, as well as at other conferences (held at Brazzaville, Casablanca, and Monrovia), the idea of continental unity grew, but three conflicts accentuated the fault lines among participants in the debate about the form that unity should take. The first was the armed struggle of the Algerian National Liberation Front (FNL) in pursuit of independence from France;[19] the second was the situation in Congo, including the Katangese attempt at secession, the overthrow of Lumumba's government, and the UN's reaction to these events;[20] and the third was Morocco's challenge to Mauritania's claim to UN membership. The last two situations were especially intimately linked to the issue of territory and existing borders. Fearing the fragmentation of the territorial borders of their states, most leaders found recourse in the notion of *uti possidetis* (the principle of intangible borders).[21]

These and other complex and overlapping factors saw the emergence of perceived 'groupings': the 'Brazzaville' group (associated with former French colonies—except Guinea—that had a sustained reliance on the French economic, military, and administrative presence, and did not want to be part of a radical unitary Africa loose from France); the 'Casablanca' group (associated with a radical transformative and integrationist agenda driven by Ghana and Guinea); and the 'Monrovia' group (associated with attempts by more 'moderate' states such as Ethiopia, Nigeria, and Liberia to find a compromise position).

The hand of the 'Casablanca' group was strengthened by developments in West Africa, where attempts were made to forge a political union, first between Ghana and Guinea, which later extended to Mali.[22] Threatened by these attempts, other states in the region disapproved, notably the leaders of Liberia and Nigeria. Benjamin Nnamdi Azikiwe, the first Nigerian President, stated that 'if for many years certain parties have fought for their sovereignty, it is unlikely that they will surrender that sovereignty to a nebulous organisation simply because we feel it necessary to work together'.[23]

---

[16] Nkrumah (n 14 above) 142.

[17] B Davidson, *Africa in History: Themes and Outlines* (London: Paladin, 1974) 317.

[18] Under the Ghanaian Constitution, the independence of Ghana may be diminished only on grounds of the 'furtherance of African Unity' (Nkrumah, n 14 above, 85).

[19] Ajala (n 4 above) 16.   [20] ibid 28–30.

[21] OAU Doc AHG/Res.16(I), July 1964, 'Border Disputes among African States', declaring the commitment of all member states 'to respect the borders existing on their achievement of national independence' (para 2).

[22] Ajala (n 4 above) 32–3.   [23] Quoted in ibid 23.

As the movement became firmly rooted in African soil, two further major challenges to 'true' pan-Africanism emerged: ensuring the inclusion of Arabs and French-speaking Africans.

The initial 'cultural' focus on the 'black race' of Africa had to be adapted if the 'political' dimension of pan-Africanism were to include Arab-North Africa. After establishing himself as the Egyptian leader through the 1952 Revolution, Nasser supported nationalist movements in sub-Saharan Africa.[24] Nasser saw Egypt as the centre of three overlapping worlds: the Arab, Muslim, and African. To some extent, though, Nasser's aspirations in the Arab and African worlds were conflicting. In 1945, the Arab League had been established, with its headquarters in Cairo, suggesting primary concern with the Arab world. Only when Nasser's radical pan-Arabism failed in the early 1960s, with the dissolution of the political union between Egypt and Syria (the 'United Arab Republic'), was he able more fully to embrace political pan-Africanism.

Pan-Africanism was predominantly a movement of English-speakers. Its parallel, Léopold Senghor's *Négritude* movement, was concerned much more with the cultural implications of being African. Subsequent developments also saw the recently independent French states clinging on to colonial skirts. Based at least in principle on a policy of assimilation, the relationship between France and its subjects was different from that of the ex-British colonies. In the 1920s, Blaise Diagne, a Senegalese Member of the French Parliament, for example opposed Garvey's pan-African campaign in Africa by stating that 'we French natives wish to remain French, since France has given us every liberty and since she has unreservedly accepted us'.[25] With the exception of Guinea, where Sékou Touré opted for an early independence, close ties persisted between the French-speaking states and France.[26] As a result of their eventual independence, states previously under French rule also came around to accepting the importance of some form of unity of newly independent states.

Discussions among newly independent African states about the possibilities of regional cooperation and unity thus brought together sub-Saharan states, including the 'French states', and Arab-North African states. In this context, pan-Africanism changed its hue, and achieved an inclusive yet mythical trans-Saharan character.

As more states, including Mauritania, gained independence and membership of the UN, the question turned to the practical manifestation of unity of the newly independent states. Two major models served as points of reference: the USA inspired the notion of a closely knit 'United States of Africa'; and the UN, providing the model for a loose association in the form of a 'United Africa of (independent) states'. Moderate leaders such as President Senghor and Emperor Haile Selassie supported the second option. On behalf of the French-speaking

---

[24] On Nasser, see AA Mazrui and M Tidy, *Nationalism and New States in Africa from about 1935 to the Present* (Nairobi: Heinemann, 1984) 51–5.   [25] Quoted in Ajala (n 4 above) 99.
[26] Davidson (n 17 above) 317.

states, Senghor articulated a gradualist view: 'If we wish to succeed we must put the stress on cultural, technical and economic co-operation, rather than on the co-operation of political parties. We must progress step by step, keeping our feet firmly on the ground.'[27] Selassie questioned the existence of 'hard-and-fast groupings', mentioned above, and pointed out that 'we Africans have been misled into pigeonholing one another', and proclaimed that Ethiopia considered itself member of only one group—'the African group'.[28] Another factor working against the acceptance of Nkrumah's vision was the suspicion by some fellow leaders that he was bidding for the 'leadership of Africa'.[29] Bridging all previous divides, Selassie succeeded in securing the presence of all 32 African independent states at the Addis Ababa conference, held in May 1963. The Organization of African Unity (OAU) came about on 25 May 1963 as the first pan-African intergovernmental organization taking the form of a loose association (a 'United Africa of independent states').

Having largely defined both the anti-colonial struggle and post-colonial statehood resulting from the struggle's eventual success, it seemed inevitable that colonial borders would also determine the form of a pan-African institution. At the time the OAU came into being, no dispute brought the contested nature of existing borders more clearly into relief than the Somali attempts to re-open discussions about its colonially determined borders in order to unite Somalis who were artificially separated from each other. Supporting these sentiments, Nkrumah contended that 'only African Unity can heal this festering sore of boundary disputes'.[30] However, the majority argued in favour of maintaining the borders drawn by 'the former colonizers', 'in the interest of Africa',[31] or out of 'respect for the legacy that we have received from the colonial system'.[32]

Despite its prominence, *uti possidetis*[33] did not feature explicitly in the OAU Charter. By demanding respect for 'sovereignty' and 'territorial integrity', the Charter lends support to this general trend of thinking, though. If there was any room for ambiguity, it was removed when the first Assembly of Heads of State and Government, in July 1964, 'solemnly declared' that 'all Member States pledge themselves to respect the borders existing on their achievement of national independence'.[34] Border disputes and simmering conflicts did not provoke discussions about the artificial nature of many of these borders, which came about through colonial fiat and not, as in the colonial states themselves, through protracted processes of

[27] Quoted in Ajala (n 4 above) 35.   [28] Quoted in ibid 48.
[29] C Chime, *Integration and Politics among African States* (Uppsala: Scandinavian Institute for African Studies, 1977) 178.
[30] S Touval, *The Boundary Politics of Independent Africa* (Cambridge, Mass: Harvard University Press, 1972) 85.   [31] View of the Ethiopian Prime Minister, cited in ibid 84.
[32] View of the President of Mali, cited in ibid 85.
[33] Defined as 'a principle which upgraded former administrative delimitations, established during the colonial period, to international frontiers' (T Maluwa, 'International Law-Making in the Organisation of African Unity: An Overview' (2000) 12 *RADIC* 201, 215).
[34] OAU Doc AHG/Res.16(I). The OAU affirmed 'a pre-existing principle of international law', which first emerged among newly independent Latin American states in the early 19th century.

consolidating 'nations' and territories. Obsessions with enlarging and supporting a continental 'political kingdom' of independent leaders and consolidating domestic political power blindfolded the OAU to the importance of economic development and human rights violations in the newly independent states.[35] In the years that followed, the geographical dimension of intangible frontiers colluded with the ideology of national sovereignty to insulate national interest, as defined by a narrow elite. The two main role players in the Cold War, the USA and the Soviet Union, also supported the territorial basis of the post-1945 world order as stable means to 'seek clients through the recruitment of state administrations rather than by challenging principles of state sovereignty'.[36]

B From OAU to African Union (AU)

The subsequent evolution of the OAU may be charted through four phases, along the two axes of political and economic integration. The engagement with human rights forms the central prism through which these periods are briefly viewed.

1 Foundation and Stagnation (1963–1978)

In many respects the 1963 OAU Charter was the antithesis of Nkrumah's ideal of sovereignty ceded to a form of overarching African governance. By prioritizing the 'sovereign equality' and 'respect for the sovereignty and territorial integrity' of the new member states,[37] the OAU Charter provided a very heavy anchor to stabilize and solidify the position of fledgling African states in the sea of international relations. To this should be added the principle of 'non-interference in the internal affairs of states'.[38]

It should come as no surprise that the Charter did not explicitly include human rights as part of the OAU's mandate.[39] The OAU member states were only required to have 'due regard' for the human rights set out in the Universal Declaration.[40] Bolstered by the principle of 'non-interference', the OAU in subsequent years turned a blind eye to allegations of human rights violations in member states. In one

---

[35] The lack of attention to economic development may in part be explained by the fact that much of Africa enjoyed relatively favourable economic growth rates at the time of independence. A period of drastic decline started in the early 1970s. The average per capita gross national product (GNP) for Africa declined from $546 to $525 (excluding South Africa, the decline is from $525 to $336) (see World Bank, *Can Africa Claim the 21st Century?* (Washington, DC: World Bank, 2000) table 1.1). The average African gross national income (GNI) declined by a further almost 10% from 1980 to 2004 (African Development Bank, 'Gender, Poverty, and Environmental Indicators on African Countries', 2006, <http://www.afdb.org>).   [36] Clapham (n 11 above) 56.

[37] OAU Charter, arts 3(1) and 3(3).   [38] OAU Charter, art 3(2).

[39] The OAU Charter was adopted by a Conference of Heads of States and Governments in Addis Ababa on 25 May 1963. The Charter was signed by 23 states. It is reprinted in (1964) 3 ILM 1116.

[40] OAU Charter, art 2(1)(e); the Preamble of the OAU Charter also recognizes the Universal Declaration and the UN Charter as the foundation of peaceful and positive cooperation between states.

commentator's view, the OAU could be regarded as functioning 'as a club of presidents, engaged in a tacit policy of not inquiring into each other's practices'.[41] The lacuna was not only substantive, but also institutional. None of the specialist commissions provided for under article 20 of the OAU Charter, or established later, was devoted to human rights.[42]

Despite the lack of a clear human rights mandate, the OAU in the period between 1963 and 1978 addressed two major issues of human rights concern. Predominantly concerned with issues external to the state, these developments did not provide for rights of nationals that could be enforced against their own states, and did not allow the domestic human rights record of post-colonial states to be scrutinized.

First, the OAU campaigned strongly for the self-determination of 'peoples' still under colonial domination. Decolonization implied the recognition of a whole range of basic rights that had been denied during colonialism. It also aimed at the removal of repressive regimes, most blatantly illustrated in the last days of Portuguese rule in Angola and Mozambique. Self-determination of African peoples enjoyed a high priority, but again within the context of decolonization.[43] In conformity with the 1964 resolution on respect for existing borders,[44] the OAU rejected post-independence claims to self-determination in Biafra, Katanga, southern Sudan, Shaba, and Eritrea.[45] Regarding the Western Sahara, the OAU admitted the Saharawi Arab Democratic Republic (Western Sahara) as a member, resulting in Morocco's withdrawal from the organization in 1984. However, the OAU did not recognize the Sahrawi people's right to self-determination.[46] A related area on which the OAU focused was the collective effort to rid Africa of apartheid in South Africa and white minority rule in Rhodesia (now Zimbabwe). The OAU dedicated itself to the full liberation of southern Africa, through its endorsement of the 'Lusaka Manifesto' in

[41] CE Welch, *Protecting Human Rights in Africa: Strategies and Roles of Non-governmental Organizations* (Philadelphia: University of Pennsylvania, 1995) 151; see also 288, where the OAU's policy of non-interference is criticized.

[42] The Charter established five 'Specialized Commissions': (i) Economic and Social; (ii) Educational and Cultural; (iii) Health, Sanitation, and Nutrition; (iv) Defence; (v) Scientific, Technical and Research Commission. At the first ordinary session of the OAU in 1964, a Commission on Transport and Communications, and one on Jurists, were added. The last was designed as an instrument for legal research (KB M'Baye and B Ndiaye, 'The Organization of African Unity' in K Vasak and P Alston (eds), *The International Dimension of Human Rights* (Westport, Conn: Greenwood Press, 1982) 583, but was disbanded after only one year (AE El-Obaid and A Appiagyei-Atua, 'Human Rights in Africa—A New Perspective on Linking the Past to the Present' (1996) 41 *McGill LJ* 819–27)).

[43] Denoted 'pigmentational self-determination' by Mazrui, quoted by SKN Blay, 'Changing African Perspectives on the Right to Self-Determination in the Wake of the Banjul Charter on Human and Peoples' Rights' (1985) 29 *JAL* 143, 157.

[44] OAU Doc AHG/Res.16(1). Also see A Chanda, 'The Organization of African Unity: An Appraisal' (1989–92) 21–4 *Zambian LJ* 1, 13.

[45] Eritrea won its independence in 1991, despite the OAU's lack of support for the application of the principle of self-determination in its case (Blay, n 43 above, 152–3).

[46] G Naldi, 'The Organization of African Unity and the Sahara Arab Democratic Republic' (1982) 26 *JAL* 152–7.

1969. It also played an influential role in the UN to ensure an arms embargo, economic sanctions, condemnation of South Africa's main trade partners, and the non-recognition of the 'homelands'.[47] The OAU Liberation Committee, established to ensure the elimination of colonialism from Africa, in particular assisted in forging an international consensus against apartheid.[48]

Secondly, the OAU had to deal with the problem of refugees, arising from the numerous conflicts in Africa. In 1964, the OAU set up the Commission on Refugees to work with the UN High Commission for Refugees.[49] In response to an increasing awareness of the vulnerability of a growing number of refugees in Africa, the OAU Assembly in 1969 adopted the OAU Convention Governing the Specific Aspects of Refugee Problems in Africa.[50] Although this development had positive implications for human rights, it was principally aimed at addressing friction between states arising from 'subversive activities' of refugees.[51] The absence of a monitoring body also detracted from the potential of this Convention as an agent of changing domestic laws and practices.

As was to be expected, border disputes were often on the OAU's agenda. Some superficial success in this area over these years include involvement in the settlement of border disputes between Algeria and Morocco, between Somalia and Ethiopia, Somalia and Kenya and between Niger and Dahomey (now Benin), as well as the improvement of inter-state relations.[52] However, none of these conflicts led to a reintroduction of a debate about the *uti possidetis* principle.

With the dissolution of the Ghana–Guinea–Mali Union soon after the formation of the OAU,[53] and after Nkrumah and Azikiwe had been overthrown in 1966, pan-Africanism as a political movement fell into abeyance.[54] In so far as it continued, it was in a much more pragmatic form, exemplified by ideologies such as Nyerere's 'African socialism'.

On the economic front, the OAU presided over a continent of unrelentingly declining growth rates and seemingly unstoppable increases in levels of poverty.[55] Instead of adopting inclusive people-oriented policies, most leaders tried to consolidate power by imposing state-driven developmentalist drives. One of the few early moves of significance was the establishment in 1964 of the African Development Bank, which is aimed at 'channelling investment of African capital into a wide variety of enterprises'.[56]

[47] See eg B Andemicael, *The OAU and the UN: Relations between the Organization of African Unity and the United Nations* (New York: Africana Publishing, 1976) 133–7 and WJ Foltz and J Widner, 'The OAU and Southern African Liberation' in Y El-Ayouty and IW Zartman (eds), *The OAU after Twenty Years* (New York: Praeger, 1984) 249, 263–9.
[48] See eg Z Cervenka, *The Unfinished Quest for Unity: Africa and the OAU* (New York: Africana, 1977) 45.   [49] Davidson (n 8 above) 217.
[50] OAU Doc CAB/LEG/24.3.   [51] Ajala (n 4 above) 174–5.   [52] ibid 148–76.
[53] KC Kotecha and RW Adams, *African Politics: The Corruption of Power* (Washington, DC: University Press of America, 1981) 341.   [54] Geiss (n 3 above) 422.
[55] On the decline in food production in independent Africa, see A Adedeji, 'Comparative Strategies of Economic Decolonization in Africa' in AA Mazrui (ed), *General History of Africa VIII: Africa since 1935* (Glosderry: New Africa Books, 2003) 401.   [56] Davidson (n 8 above) 216.

2 Shaking the Baobab (1979–1989)

By the 1970s, the principle of non-interference in the domestic affairs of OAU members had become as firmly rooted in African soil as an unwavering baobab. The adoption in 1981 of the first set of continental human rights standards, in the form of the African Charter on Human and Peoples' Rights (African Charter), presents a drastic curtailment of the non-interference principle. Numerous writers have described and discussed political and other factors that created an enabling environment for the Charter's adoption.[57]

Most commentators regard the drafting and adoption of the African Charter as Africa's response to the human rights abuses of the 1970s in Amin's Uganda,[58] Nguema's Equatorial Guinea, and Bokassa's Central African Empire. All three dictators were overthrown in 1979, bringing some pressure to bear on the baobab. The 'back-lash to these atrocities', Umozurike wrote, 'had their impact on Africa and the OAU'.[59] The need to review the principle of non-interference was enforced by the fact that the OAU raised no criticism against these dictators, while at the same time condemning South Africa's internal policies, giving rise to the criticism that African states had been applying 'double standards'.[60] The invasion by Tanzania of Uganda in 1978–9 also served as a precedent for the *de facto* erosion of the doctrine of non-interference in the domestic affairs of other OAU member states.[61] As for the rest of the leaders, there was no changing of the guard, as in the three countries mentioned above, raising question marks about the sincerity of their involvement in the subsequent process of elaborating the Charter, to which the discussion now turns.

During the 1970s, human rights also became of more prominent concern in international politics, especially as an ideological tool in the West's Cold War armoury.[62] Other regional human rights regimes, which only started flexing their muscles in the

[57] E Kannyo, 'The Banjul Charter on Human and Peoples' Rights: Genesis and Political Background' in CE Welch and RI Meltzer (eds), *Human Rights and Development in Africa* (Albany, NY: State University of New York, 1984) 128.

[58] For an account of Tanzanian opposition against the regime, see United Republic of Tanzania, *Tanzania and the War against Amin's Uganda* (Dar es Salaam: Government Printer, 1979). This 'war' led to an important debate at the 16th summit of the OAU Assembly of Heads of State and Government in Liberia, touching on the question about the extent to which human rights violations may be regarded as matters of domestic concern only; see eg G Naldi, *The Organization of African Unity: An Analysis of its Role* (London: Mansell, 1989) 108–9.

[59] U Umozurike, *Five Years of the African Commission on Human and Peoples' Rights* (Ile-Ife: Obafemi Awolowo University, 1992) 3.

[60] RF Weisfelder, 'Human Rights and Majority Rule in Southern Africa: The Mote in Thy Brother's Eye' in Welch and Meltzer (eds), n 57 above, 90.

[61] The Constitutive Act of the African Union reflects this shift, as it provides for 'the right of the Union to intervene in a Member state pursuant to a decision of the Assembly in respect of grave circumstances, namely: war crimes, genocide and crimes against humanity' (art 4(h)).

[62] On President Carter's foreign policy, see H Hartmann, 'US Human Rights Policy under Carter and Reagan, 1977–1981' (2001) 23 *HRQ* 402.

1970s, provided a clear benchmark. The greater involvement of the UN in human rights questions also played its part. Throughout the 1970s, the UN promoted the idea of a regional human rights mechanism in Africa.[63] Although the two International Covenants were adopted in 1966, they only entered into force in 1976 and the Human Rights Committee only really started functioning in 1977.[64] Other developments on the international scene further favoured the adoption of the Charter. These include the emphasis placed on human rights by the then USA President, Jimmy Carter, the adoption of the Helsinki Final Act in 1975, and the media exposure of the suffering of the Vietnamese refugees ('boat people') in Southeast Asia. While critical of human rights abuses in some parts of Africa, the West (and particularly the USA) found it convenient to support dictators such as Mobutu in Zaire.

Democratization in some African states also facilitated discussion on a regional human rights instrument. Young identifies three 'waves of democratization' in Africa.[65] The first was embodied in the constitutional changes dictated by departing colonial powers. This 'wave' had little momentum. Soon after independence, democratic governance largely ceased to exist, being replaced by the doctrines of one-party rule, military dictatorship, and Afro-Marxism. Botswana, Mauritius, and Senegal were notable exceptions.[66] The 'second wave' came in the period just prior to the adoption of the African Charter. The defining cases of this wave were Ghana and Nigeria. In 1979 the military in Ghana agreed to 'full democratization'.[67] Sometimes the gains were short-lived. In Nigeria, Obasanjo in 1979 handed power to a democratically elected government. Broad public participation in establishing the Second Nigerian Republic, which culminated in the adoption of the 1979 Constitution,[68] soon had to make room for a return to military rule, first under Buhari, and then under Babangida.

The role of individuals should not go unnoticed. The OAU Secretary-General at the time, Edem Kodjo, used his influence to promote human rights. Other influential voices inside the OAU were those of the Senegalese President, Léopold Senghor, and the Gambian President, Jawara, as appears from a brief detour to the *travaux préparatoires* of the African Charter.

Senghor started the process within the OAU officially, at the OAU Assembly of Heads of State and Government in 1979,[69] when he, on behalf of Senegal, and the

---

[63] Some of these conferences and seminars are listed in Kannyo (n 57 above) 338.

[64] W Vandenhole, *The Procedure before the UN Human Rights Treaty Bodies* (Antwerp: Intersentia, 2004) 19.

[65] C Young, 'Africa: An Interim Balance Sheet' (1996) 7 *J of Democracy* 53, 54, following SP Huntington, *The Third Wave: Democratization in the Late Twentieth Century* (Norman: University of Oklahoma Press, 1991).

[66] By and large, multi-party elections took place uninterrupted in these countries since independence (see the country discussions in C Heyns (ed), *Human Rights Law in Africa* (vol 2) (Leiden: Martinus Nijhoff, 2004) 904; 1311–13; 1444–6.　　　　　　　　　　[67] Young (n 65 above) 56.

[68] Akende described it as Nigeria's first 'autochthonous Constitution' (JO Akende, *Introduction to the Nigerian Constitution* (London: Sweet and Maxwell, 1982) at intro).

[69] Meeting in Monrovia, Liberia; according to Welch (n 41 above) 165, Senghor's involvement was secured through the persuasion of Kéba M'Baye, the principal drafter of the African Charter.

representative of Mauritius, supported by Nigeria and Uganda, proposed that the OAU Assembly adopt a resolution to set in motion the process towards adopting an African human rights instrument. The resolution that was adopted called on the Secretary-General to 'organise as soon as possible, in an African capital, a restricted meeting of highly qualified experts to prepare a preliminary draft of an "African Charter on Human and Peoples' Rights" providing *inter alia* for the establishment of bodies to promote and protect human and peoples' rights'.[70]

Despite the presence of these favourable winds, progress on the journey towards a final draft was not always swift. The back-peddling oarsmen of the old guard delayed the process at every turn. After an initial draft was prepared in Dakar, it was to be submitted to a group of governmental experts, which never took place for want of a quorum.[71] According to some, this was due to deliberate attempts by states that were not prepared to openly oppose the creation of a Charter to silently derail the process.[72] After this failure, the Secretary-General changed tactics. Rather than referring the issue to an ad hoc meeting of governmental experts, he initiated a ministerial conference.[73] At his initiative, the president of one of the very few consistently democratic African countries at the time, President Jawara of The Gambia, invited the ministers to meet in Banjul.

This meeting of ministers of justice of OAU member states took place from 9 to 16 June 1980 in Banjul. Still, the baobab held firm. The meeting was also only partially successful, as the participants managed to finalize deliberations on the Preamble and only 11 of the more than 60 articles. Never opposing the process, but delaying it at every turn, delegations made 'general statements' about the realization of human rights in their countries,[74] and asked questions about the size of the 'small Committee of Experts requested to prepare the Preliminary Draft Charter on Human and Peoples' Rights' instead of getting on with the drafting.[75]

After some prodding by the OAU Council of Ministers and Assembly, the ministerial group managed to finalize a draft at a further meeting, also held in Banjul, early in 1981. Two factors caused the ministerial meeting to accelerate into action when it met for the second time. The first was the fact that some members of the delegation of Upper Volta (now Burkina Faso) were politically victimized after the Banjul meeting of June 1980, putting in a new light 'the necessity not only to insist on human rights but also the importance of their effectiveness'.[76] The second factor was the result of political pressure of a different nature: At the 17th Ordinary Session of the Assembly of Heads of State and Government, the ministerial

---

[70] OAU DOC AHG/Dec.115(XVI) Rev.1.

[71] K M'Baye, *Les Droits de l'Homme en Afrique* (Paris: Pedone, 1992) 153.   [72] ibid.

[73] Almost without exception, African states regularly attend OAU meetings (see M'Baye (n 71 above) 153.

[74] Rapporteur's Report OAU Doc CAB/LEG/67/3/Draft Rapt.Rpt (11) Rev.4, para 9.

[75] Rapporteur's Report, para 32.

[76] ML Balanda, 'African Charter on Human and Peoples' Rights' in K Ginther and W Benedek (eds), *New Perspectives and Conceptions of International Law: An Afro-European Dialogue* (Vienna: Springer-Verlag, 1983) 134, 136.

meeting was urged to 'exert efforts to complete its work'.[77] Instrumental in this resolution was the initiative of the OAU Secretary-General Kodjo, who persuaded President Jawara to table the resolution at the Assembly session following the first meeting in Banjul.[78]

When the African Charter was eventually adopted in 1981, it happened with little fanfare, close to midnight on the last day of the Assembly's session, with no debate or even a formal vote.[79] With the adoption event carrying clear insignia of a *rightorical* commitment—a formal resignation to the inevitable—it should come as no surprise that enthusiasm once again made room for stagnation. It took more than five years for a simple majority of states to ratify the Charter, allowing it to enter into force on 21 October 1986. The implementing arm of the Charter, the African Commission on Human and Peoples' Rights (African Commission) was established in 1987, but did not have a permanent Secretariat after its inauguration and only became fully functional in June 1989. Very little was known of the Commission's work in its early years. Only in 1994 did it start to make public its decisions on communications brought before it.[80]

3 The Winds of Change (1990–2000)

In the 1990s, the effects of the end of the Cold War also reverberated through Africa. Multi-party democratic elections took place all over the continent, starting with Benin, Zambia,[81] and South Africa. Constitutions were redrafted, and civil and political rights were mostly restored. In some instances the progress to democracy was incomplete, as in Nigeria, where Abacha forcibly took over power and presided over a regime of terror and human rights abuses. In other countries, such as Côte d'Ivoire, Uganda, and Zambia, election disputes marred the consolidation of democracy.

Showing keen awareness of the changed political landscape, the OAU in 1990 adopted the Declaration on Political and Socio-Economic Situation in Africa and the Fundamental Changes Taking Place in the World (the Algiers Declaration).[82] This Declaration notes that the era of focusing mainly on 'political liberation and nation building' should make way for a new era of greater emphasis on economic

---

[77] OAU Doc CH/1148(XXXVII).   [78] M'Baye (n 71 above) 158.

[79] AM Akiwumi, 'The United Nations International Covenant on Economic, Social and Cultural Rights and the African Charter on Human and Peoples' Rights', unpublished paper, cited in F Ouguergouz, *The African Charter on Human and Peoples' Rights: A Comprehensive Agenda for Human Rights and Sustainable Democracy in Africa* (The Hague: Kluwer Law International, 2003) 47–8.

[80] See Ch 8 on this and other aspects of the African Commission's work.

[81] M Bratton, 'Zambia Starts Over' (1992) 3 *J of Democracy* 81 (noting that Zambia was the first country in Anglophone Africa to hold multi-party elections, which resulted in the ousting of the ruling party).

[82] OAU Doc AHG/Decl.1(XXVI). The Declaration is firmly rooted in Africa's economic malaise, as appears from the acknowledgement that between 1980 and 1989 Africa's external debt rose from US$60 billion to 275 billion, and that the number of Least Developed Countries in Africa rose from 21 to 28 (para 6).

development and integration.[83] The heads of state also committed themselves to stronger unity and solidarity as part of reviving the ideals of pan-Africanism.[84] Two key preconditions for economic growth are identified: a political environment in which popular participation, human rights, and the rule of law are observed; and effective resolution of disputes to ensure lasting peace and stability.[85] Displaying an acknowledgement of the importance of the role of ordinary citizens in the processes of democratization and development, the OAU in 1999 adopted the 'Decision on the Right of Political Participation', as well as the 'Decision on Unconstitutional Changes of Government'.[86]

In this era of possibilities, the OAU adopted two of its most progressive human rights instruments. The first of these, the African Charter on the Rights and Welfare of the Child (African Children's Charter), was adopted in 1990. Disappointingly, the spirit of the times did not change the *rightorical* stance of most OAU leaders, who did not come forward to accept as binding the new OAU instrument. The small target of 15 ratifying states was only reached at the close of the decade of promise, in 1999.

The process towards the second of these, the Protocol to the African Charter on the Establishment of an African Court on Human and Peoples' Rights, began in 1994. Pioneered by NGOs, supported by the Commission, and benefiting from some high-level political support,[87] the movement for the creation of an African Court received the cautious support of the OAU Assembly in 1994. At its meeting in Tunis, the Assembly requested 'the OAU Secretary-General to convene a meeting of government experts to ponder in conjunction with the African Commission ... over the means to enhance the efficiency of the Commission in considering in particular the establishment of an African Court'.[88] Driven initially by NGOs and the African Commission, the OAU took ownership by adopting the Protocol on the Establishment of an African Court on Human and Peoples' Rights in 1998.

The establishment of an increasing number of regional economic communities (RECs) reflected growing concern that the OAU had failed to provide a framework for economic integration and development in Africa. Although the idea for the establishment of an African Economic Community was raised as early as 1977, it came to fruition only in 1991, with the adoption of the Treaty establishing the African Economic Community (AEC) in Abuja, Nigeria.[89] Its primary objective is to 'promote economic, social and cultural development and the integration of

---

[83] ibid, para 12.   [84] ibid.   [85] ibid, paras 10 and 11.

[86] OAU Doc AHG/Dec.141(XXXV); OAU Doc AHG/Dec.142(XXXV).

[87] The then Secretary-General of the OAU, Salim Ahmed Salim, stated at the Commission's 14th session, in 1993, that the time had come for an African Human Rights Court: see E Ankumah, *The African Commission on Human and Peoples' Rights: Practice and Procedures* (The Hague: Martinus Nijhoff, 1996) 70.   [88] OAU Doc AHG/Res.230(XXX).

[89] For a comprehensive discussion see B Thompson, 'Economic Integration Efforts in Africa: A Milestone—The Abuja Treaty' (1993) 5 *RADIC* 743.

African economies' in order to 'raise the standard of living in African peoples'.[90] One of its guiding principles is the 'recognition, promotion and protection of human and peoples' rights in accordance with the provisions of the African Charter'.[91] The link to human rights is thus both implicit and explicit. The envisaged process of integration is a gradual one, comprising six stages over 34 years. Subregional economic communities are to form the building blocks of the larger integrated union. The AEC Treaty entered into force on 12 May 1994 as an integral part of the OAU Charter for those states that had become party to both the AEC and the OAU. However, little progress has subsequently been made towards its implementation.[92]

The OAU took other steps relevant to human rights in this period. Departing from the realization that the aims of the AEC Treaty would not be fulfilled as long as war, civil strife, and insecurity beset the continent, the OAU finally, in 1993, created a mechanism to address conflicts in and between states, by adopting the Cairo Declaration establishing the OAU Mechanism for Conflict Prevention, Management and Resolution (Cairo Declaration), eroding somewhat the principle of non-interference.[93] Inspired by the accomplishments of the Conference on Security and Cooperation in Europe (CSCE),[94] and premised on the link between human rights and security, the Mechanism was set up to anticipate and prevent conflict in Africa. Suggesting an inroad into state sovereignty by allowing the Mechanism's involvement in intra-state conflicts, the Cairo Declaration acknowledges that no single factor 'has contributed more to the present socio-economic problems on the continent than the scourge of conflicts *within* and between our countries'.[95] Although the stipulation that it should be 'guided' by the principles of non-interference and state sovereignty introduced some ambiguity,[96] the Mechanism's Central Organ decided to be seized with situations of internal conflict, such as those in Angola, Burundi, Rwanda, and Somalia.[97] The Mechanism served as progenitor to the AU Peace and Security Council, by which it was replaced, and its fledgling efforts culminated in an explicit AU mandate with respect to humanitarian intervention.[98]

---

[90] AEC Treaty, art 4(1)(a) and (c).   [91] ibid, art 3(g).   [92] See Ch 7 below.
[93] G Naldi *The Organisation of African Unity: An Analysis of its Role* (London: Mansell, 2nd edn, 1999) 32–3.
[94] In 1994 redefined and renamed as the Organization for Security and Cooperation in Europe (OSCE) (see M Nowak, *Introduction to the International Human Rights Regime* (Leiden: Martinus Nijhoff, 2003) 223).   [95] Cairo Declaration, para 9 (emphasis added).
[96] ibid, para 14.
[97] SBO Gutto, 'The New Mechanism of the Organisation of African Unity for Conflict Prevention, Management and Resolution, and the Controversial Concept of Humanitarian Intervention in International Law' (1996) 113 *South African LJ* 314, 321.
[98] AU Constitutive Act, art 4(h); see MD Wembou, 'A Propos du Nouveau Mécanisme de l'OUA sur les Conflits' (1993) 5 *RADIC* 725, 729, indicating that with the exception of Sudan, states agreed that the OAU may intervene in extraordinary circumstances (of extreme suffering, total disregard for human rights indicating the disintegration of the state) without first appealing to the international community.

The OAU Assembly also lent its institutional support to the drafting of a protocol to the African Charter on the rights of women,[99] setting in motion a process
that culminated in the adoption of a final text in 2003. For the first time, in 1999, an
OAU Ministerial Conference on Human Rights was held in Grand Baie, Mauritius,
culminating in the adoption of the Grand Baie Declaration and Plan of Action.
Another milestone was also reached in the same year, when Eritrea became a state
party to the Charter, marking universal regional acceptance of the Charter by all
53 AU members. At its summit in 2000, the OAU took a clear stand in favour of
democratic pluralism when it adopted the 'Declaration on the Framework for an
OAU Response to Unconstitutional Government'.[100] Under this Declaration, the
'perpetrators' of an 'unconstitutional change' are given six months to 'restore constitutional order'.[101] Should the new regime 'stubbornly' refuse to 'restore constitutional order', 'limited and targeted sanctions' may be imposed, in addition to
suspension from participation in OAU policy organs.

Not all African leaders favoured the gradualist approach adopted in the Abuja
Treaty. The first steps towards a radical acceleration of African unification in the
new millennium were taken on the initiative of the Libyan President, Moummar
al-Qadhafi. Meeting at his birthplace, Sirte, the OAU held the third extraordinary
summit in its existence, to discuss the lack of progress in the process of African integration. In the Sirte Declaration, adopted on 9 September 1999, the OAU leaders
committed themselves to form an African Union on the basis of accelerated implementation of the AEC timetable and the speedy establishment of the institutions
envisaged in the AEC Treaty.[102] The persistence of ambivalence about the meaning
of pan-Africanism appears from the Declaration, which proclaims to be 'inspired by
the ideals which guided the Founding Fathers of our organisation and Generations
of Pan-Africanists' to forge on the one hand 'unity, solidarity and cohesion' and
'co-operation between African peoples', and among 'African States' on the other.

4 A New Institution for a New Millennium (2001–2006)

Ushering in the new millennium, the OAU leaders adopted the AU Constitutive
Act on 11 July 2000 as a culmination of the Sirte Declaration. The Constitutive
Act entered into force on 26 May 2001, replacing the OAU Charter, and incorporating within the AU the AEC Treaty in so far as there are no inconsistencies
between the two treaties.[103] The AU, which was eventually inaugurated in 2002, is
thus essentially a merger of the largely political ambitions of the OAU and the
mainly economically minded AEC,[104] with the addition of some organs and with
an acceleration of pace towards economic integration.

---

[99] OAU Doc AHG/Res.240(XXXI).   [100] OAU Doc AHG/Decl.5(XXXVI).
[101] ibid.   [102] OAU Doc EAHG/Draft/Decl.(IV)Rev.1.
[103] AU Constitutive Act, art 33(2).
[104] See CAA Packer and D Rukare, 'The New African Union and its Constitutive Act' (2002) 96
AJIL 365, 372 (although the AEC and its functions are 'subsumed' by the AU, its Treaty remains

The AU Constitutive Act presents its reader with the paradox between a quest for greater unity,[105] inspired by generations of pan-Africanists who promoted solidarity and cohesion, and unwavering reverence for the borders imposed in colonial times and sanctified by post-colonial governments.[106] Reiterating the 1964 OAU declaration referred to above, which was absent from the OAU Charter, the AU places 'respect for borders existing on achievement of independence' very high on its list of founding principles.[107]

Reflecting major shifts in the intervening period of almost 20 years, the AU Constitutive Act contrasts sharply with the 1963 OAU Charter. It provides extensively for human rights in its Preamble, objectives, and founding principles.[108] 'Human rights', 'good governance', and 'the rule of law' are some of the most important recurring concepts in the Constitutive Act. Explicit reference is made to the African Charter: one of the objectives of the AU is the promotion and protection of human and peoples' rights in accordance with the Charter and other relevant human rights instruments.[109] Six of the 16 guiding principles of the AU make reference to human rights either implicitly or explicitly. The most far-reaching is the right of the Union to intervene in a member state pursuant to a decision of the Assembly in respect of grave circumstances, namely: war crimes, genocide, and crimes against humanity.[110] Collective AU action, which is dependent on an Assembly decision, should be distinguished from the right of individual members 'to request intervention from the Union in order to restore peace and security'.[111]

Other references to human rights-related issues include the promotion of gender equality;[112] respect for democratic principles, human rights, the rule of law, and good governance;[113] the promotion of social justice to ensure balanced economic development;[114] respect for the sanctity of human life, the condemnation and rejection of impunity and political assassination, acts of terrorism, and subversive activities;[115] as well as the condemnation and rejection of unconstitutional changes of government.[116] The possibility of suspending a member state if its seat

---

legally binding). The 1999 Sirte Declaration (OAU Doc EAHG/Draft/Decl.(IV) Rev.1, 8–9 September 1999, para 8) proposes the establishment of the AU 'in conformity with' the ultimate objectives of the OAU Charter and AEC Treaty by 'accelerating' the process of implementing the AEC Treaty and by shortening the 'implementation periods of the Abuja Treaty'. On the achievement of this objective, see Ch 7 below.

[105] One of its stated objectives is to 'accelerate the political and socio-economic integration of the continent' (AU Constitutive Act, art 3(c)).

[106] See NJ Udombana, 'A Harmony or a Cacophony? The Music of Integration in the African Union Treaty and the New Partnership for Africa's Development' (2002) 13 *Indiana International and Comparative LR* 185, 228 ('The paradox is that while the OAU is striving at regional co-operation and integration, it is simultaneously rigidly adhering to the colonial borders drawn in imperial European capitals').   [107] AU Constitutive Act, art 4(b).

[108] See in general E Baimu, 'The African Union: Hope for Better Protection of Human Rights in Africa?' (2001) 1 *AHRLJ* 299, 311–12.   [109] AU Constitutive Act, art 3(h).

[110] ibid, art (h).   [111] ibid, art 4(j).   [112] ibid, art 4(l).   [113] ibid, art 4(m).
[114] ibid, art 4(n).   [115] ibid, art 4(o).   [116] ibid, art 4(p).

of power has been usurped unconstitutionally presents a further significant inroad into the paramount importance of state sovereignty. The fact that the AU not only sets out to attain human rights *objectives* but also intends to use human rights-based means (or *principles*) to achieve those objectives evidences its resolve to make a clean break from the OAU's *modus operandi*.

However, from a human rights perspective the AU Constitutive Act falters in three respects. First, the principle of non-interference by any member state in the internal affairs of another has been retained.[117] Secondly, the Constitutive Act does not require observance of human rights as a prerequisite for admission to the AU.[118] It should be conceded, though, that this approach allowed states into the fold of an organization that should—in principle—have steered them towards ever-increasing observance of human rights. Thirdly, the Constitutive Act is vague on enforcement and the imposition of sanctions in cases where states do not conform to AU norms.[119] For example, unlike the UN Charter, the Act does not explicitly provide for expulsion of a member state that persistently violates the principles, including those relating to human rights, set out in the Act.[120] However, the Constitutive Act does provide for sanctions against states that fail to comply with the principles and policies of the AU.[121] Although the only specific instances mentioned are the denial of 'transport' and 'communication' links with other members, the Assembly may decide on potentially far-reaching 'other measures of a political and economic nature'.

Compared with the OAU Charter, the socio-economic well-being of Africa's people is accorded much more prominence in the AU Constitutive Act. Among other things, the AU aims at promoting 'co-operation in all fields of human activity to raise the living standards of African peoples',[122] and hopes to 'work with relevant international partners in the eradication of preventable diseases and the promotion of good health on the continent'.[123] In their formulation, however, these aspects are portrayed as being part of international cooperation efforts rather than as obligations of AU member states.

The post-2000 phase also saw the adoption of important new normative standards relevant to human rights, such as the Protocol to the African Charter on the

---

[117] AU Constitutive Act, art 4(g). The principle has, however, been diluted by another principle which gives the Union the right to intervene in a member state pursuant to a decision of the Assembly in respect of war crimes, genocide, and crimes against humanity (Constitutive Act, art 4(h)).

[118] In other regional and subregional bodies membership is conditional on demonstration of commitment to, among other things, respect of human rights, see for example arts 3 and 4 of the Statute of the Council of Europe which state that the membership of the Council of Europe is open only to those states that are deemed able and willing *inter alia* to accept the principles of the rule of law and of the enjoyment of all persons within its jurisdiction of human rights and fundamental freedoms. See also art 3(b) of the Treaty for the Establishment of the East African Community, reprinted in (1999) 7 *AYBIL* 421.

[119] One should note though that, unlike the OAU Charter, the Act has put in place a mechanism to ensure that states pay their financial contribution, see the AU Constitutive Act, art 23(1).

[120] UN Charter, art 6.   [121] AU Constitutive Act, art 23(2).

[122] UN Charter, art 3(k).   [123] ibid, art 3(n).

Rights of Women in Africa (Women's Protocol), the AU Convention on Prevention and Combating Corruption and related offences,[124] and the African Charter on Democracy, Elections and Governance.[125] In this period, also, a sufficient number of states ratified the African Human Rights Court Protocol to ensure its entry into force.[126]

Greater integration of the economic and political agendas, which was the order of the day in the period around the millennium, further gave rise to the New Partnership for Africa's Development (NEPAD). The omission from the AU Constitutive Act of an economic blueprint left an opening, and perhaps a need, for a continental economic and development framework. NEPAD, which resulted from two independent plans for Africa's economic development, the Millennium Africa Recovery Plan and the OMEGA Plan,[127] provides this framework. Tabled together at the Sirte Summit in March 2001, the obvious synergy between the two projects prompted a decision for their integration. The result, NEPAD, is a 'pledge by African leaders' to 'eradicate poverty' and to pursue 'sustainable growth'.[128]

In the NEPAD 'Programme of Action', the conditions for sustainable development are identified as peace and security, economic and political governance, and subregional and regional approaches to development. Sectoral priorities for their achievement include bridging the gaps in infrastructure, investing in people, the development of agriculture, and the protection of the environment. One of its components, 'democracy and political governance', is most relevant to human rights, and reinforces the premise that democracy, respect for human rights, peace, and good governance are prerequisites for economic development.[129] A number of implementation plans aimed at social and economic development have been launched, including strategic plans on health and agriculture.[130]

NEPAD differs from the AEC Treaty and its predecessors in important respects. NEPAD departs from a bleak reality of socio-economic deprivation, and targets specifically the eradication of poverty.[131] The goal of the AEC was economic coordination and development, but its founding Treaty did not articulate the crux of its existence from a people-centred perspective and it was largely silent on human rights issues. While the AEC Treaty was premised on collective self-reliance,[132] NEPAD embraces neo-liberal capitalist models of development,

---

[124] Adopted in Maputo, Mozambique, July 2003.

[125] Adopted at the Assembly's eighth session, January 2007 (AU Doc Assembly/AU/Dec.147(VIII)).

[126] See Ch 11 below.

[127] See eg E Baimu, 'Human Rights in NEPAD and its Implications for the African Human Rights System' (2002) 2 *AHRLJ* 301, 302.

[128] The New Partnership for Africa's Development (NEPAD Declaration) (2001), <http://www.issafrica.org/AF/RegOrg/nepad/nepaddoc.pdf>, para 1.

[129] Baimu (n 127 above) 301.

[130] See eg NEPAD, Main Report (Draft) Short-Term Action Plan Infrastructure (<http://www.nepad.org>), highlighting proposed projects for regional integration and infrastructure development in the areas of energy, transport, water, information and communications technology, and public–private partnerships.   [131] See eg NEPAD Declaration (2001) para 4.

[132] AEC Treaty, arts 3(b) and 4(1)(a).

where an emphasis on 'self-reliance' makes place for 'partnerships' with global, especially Western, economic powers.[133]

Scepticism has been expressed that the NEPAD agenda is 'more tailored to commit African leaders to undertake the twin projects of political and economic liberalization in the anticipation that the flood-gates of developed country assistance and credit would suddenly open'.[134] This view may be overstated, but the NEPAD Declaration does not hide the nature of African leaders' commitment: It is as much a pledge to hold 'each other accountable' as it is to forge partnerships with 'the world to work together in rebuilding the continent'.[135] Despite the references to 'human rights' in the NEPAD Declaration, concerns have also been aired about the lack of a rights-based approach to development,[136] and the limited extent to which NEPAD is integrated into and coordinated with pre-existing human rights procedures and mechanisms.[137] For those states that accept NEPAD's African Peer Review Mechanism (APRM), voluntary peer review adds to the erosion of the doctrine of non-interference in internal affairs already brought about by acceptance of the African human rights regime. The APRM framework also represents a significant expansion on NEPAD's provisions related to human rights.

The Sirte Declaration also called for a conference on security, stability, development, and cooperation in Africa. Reviving an initiative dating back to the early 1990s, prodded by Nigerian President Obasanjo, the OAU in 2000 adopted the Conference on Security, Stability, Development and Cooperation in Africa (CSS-DCA) Solemn Declaration.[138] As its name indicates, the CSSDCA encompassed four major areas, called 'calabashes': security, stability, development, and cooperation. The Solemn Declaration departs from the view that both security and stability are intimately entangled with and dependent on human rights. Security 'should be seen in its wholesomeness and totality', which includes socio-economic rights ('access to the basic necessities of life'), enjoyment of the rights in the African Charter, and unfettered participation in all societal affairs.[139] 'Strict adherence to the rule of law', 'good governance', public participation in politics, and 'respect for human rights and fundamental freedoms' are all prerequisites for stability.[140] Providing for a 'Standing Conference' to meet every two years and for review meetings, and geared towards the elusive ideal of an integrated response, the CSSDCA held much initial promise. A CSSDCA Unit was established and made part of the AU Commission. Overtaken by other institutional developments,

---

[133] NEPAD Declaration (2001) paras 183 and 184.

[134] J Gathii, 'A Critical Appraisal of the NEPAD Agenda in Light of Africa's Place in the World Trade Regime in an Era of Market Centred Development' (2003) 13 *Transnational L and Contemporary Problems* 179, 183; S Gumedze, 'The NEPAD and Human Rights' (2006) 22 *South African J on Human Rights* 144, 151.   [135] NEPAD Declaration (2001) para 202.

[136] B Manby, 'The African Union, NEPAD and Human Rights: The Missing Agenda' (2004) 26 *HRQ* 983, 1002.   [137] Gumedze (n 134 above) 158–64.

[138] OAU Doc CM/Dec.520(LXXII) Rev1.   [139] CSSDCA Solemn Declaration, para 10.

[140] ibid, para 11.

most importantly the Peace and Security Council (PSC), the CSSDCA was soon consigned to the rubbish heap of lofty declarations without implementation. Only its initiative of country reviews was taken up by the APRM.

Debates about the extent and form of African unification, integration, and harmonization did not come to an end with the adoption of the AU Constitutive Act. To the contrary, soon after the AU was formed, for example, Qadhafi introduced a proposal for a common defence policy and an 'African army', effectively reviving Nkrumah's call for an 'African High Command'.[141] The outcome was the adoption of the AU Non-aggression and Common Defence Pact,[142] while the idea of a single pan-African military force was shelved. Even if, as a matter of principle, African states agree to the pan-African vision that the 'ultimate objective of the African Union is the political and economic integration of the continent leading to the creation of the United States of Africa',[143] the form of 'Union government' and the powers of a supranational 'United States of Africa' remain matters of continuous debate within the AU.[144]

[141] Chime (n 29 above) 186.

[142] AU Doc Assembly/AU/Dec.71(IV), adopted by the Assembly at its fourth ordinary session, 31 January 2005.

[143] AU Doc Assembly/AU/Dec.156(VIII), adopted by the Assembly at its eighth session, January 2007, para 2.

[144] AU Doc Assembly/AU/Dec.123(VII), Decision on the Union Government, reporting on the progress of the 'Committee of Seven' on an 'African Union Government towards the United States of Africa'. See generally E Maloka (ed), *A United States of Africa?* (Pretoria: Africa Institute of South Africa, 2001), and also AU Doc Assembly/AU/Dec.99(VI), Decision on the Report of the Committee of Seven Heads of State and Government Chaired by the President of the Federal Republic of Nigeria, reaffirming that 'the ultimate goal of the African Union is the full political and economic integration of the continent leading to the United States of Africa' (para 3).

5

The African Union and Human Rights

On the occasion of the celebration of 25 years since the adoption of the African Charter (and 20 years since its entry into force) in 2006, a brainstorming meeting was held on the strengthening of the African Commission.[1] African Union (AU) policy organs with competence in the promotion and protection of human rights participated. Resulting from these discussions, the Executive Council adopted a decision stressing 'the need for closer collaboration between various policy organs with competence in human rights as well as with national human rights bodies'.[2] This is an important official acknowledgement that human rights do not fall exclusively under the African Commission's mandate, and that all the AU organs have to integrate human rights into their mandate and functioning.

---

[1] Held in Banjul, May 2006. See AU Doc EX.CL/Dec. 306 (IX), Decision on the Strengthening of the Africa Commission on Human and Peoples' Rights, see also Report of the Brainstorming Meeting on the African Commission on Human and Peoples' Rights: 9–10 May 2006, Banjul, The Gambia, 20th Activity Report, Annex II (Brainstorming Meeting).

[2] AU Doc Ex.CL/Dec.306(IX) (June 2006).

With the proliferation of institutions and mechanisms within the AU, some with their own specific human rights mandate, the need for coordination is even greater than in the past. A promising start at improving coordination was made in 2003 when a retreat of the African Commission brought together not only Commissioners, but also members of the African Peer Review Mechanism (APRM) Panel of Eminent Persons, the African Children's Rights Committee, the African Coordinating Committee of National Human Rights Institutions, and the Conference on Security, Stability, Development and Cooperation in Africa (CSSDCA). The Retreat Report noted the 'lack of coordination' and the need to develop working relationships with AU structures such as the APRM process, the Peace and Security Council (PSC), and Economic, Social and Cultural Council (ECOSOCC).[3]

The CSSDCA is not discussed here. This project did not leave the ground, and became effectively amalgamated into the PSC and two other initiatives. Its normative benchmarks and fledgling system of review now fall within the mandate of NEPAD and its APRM. The CSSDCA Unit within the AU Commission has been transformed into the African Citizens Directorate (CIDO), which also functions as ECOSOCC's secretariat.[4]

Although NEPAD is not provided for under the AU Constitutive Act and is therefore not an official AU organ, it has *de facto* become an integral part of the AU, and its *de jure* integration into the AU structures and processes is under way.[5] At one of its last meetings, the OAU Assembly 'adopted' it,[6] and at its first meeting, the AU Assembly expressed its support for NEPAD,[7] and took decisions pertaining to its functioning.[8] The highest NEPAD organ, the Heads of State and Government Implementation Committee, regularly reports to the AU Assembly.[9] By the end of 2006, the NEPAD structures were in the process of being integrated into the AU Commission.[10] Even if NEPAD does not create binding legal obligations on them, it has come to be 'owned' by all AU member states.

Although it functions as a system of intergovernmental governance, the AU's institutional structure increasingly reflects the *trias politica* of national governments. In the past, human rights were too often 'detached from the mainstream OAU bodies',[11] leading to the isolation of the African Commission from the AU as a whole. The greatest challenge to the AU is to explore the possibilities of a combined and united response to human rights from its different organs and 'branches' of its

---

[3] Report of the Retreat of Members of the African Commission on Human and Peoples' Rights, facilitated by the OHCHR, Addis Ababa, 24–6 September 2003 (Retreat Report) para IV.
[4] See Section D below.   [5] See eg AU Doc Assembly/AU/Dec.153(VIII).
[6] OAU Doc AHG/Decl.1(XXXVII) (July 2001) (it was then called the 'New Africa Initiative').
[7] AU Doc ASS/AU/Decl.1(I) (July 2002).   [8] ibid, para 14.
[9] See eg AU Doc Assembly/AU/Dec.70(IV) (January 2005) and AU Doc Assembly/AU/Dec.104(VI) (January 2006).
[10] Decision on the Integration of NEPAD into the Structure and the Processes of the African Union, AU Doc Assembly/AU/Dec.124(VII) (June 2006).
[11] A Lloyd and R Murray, 'Institutions with Responsibility for Human Rights Protection under the African Union' (2004) 48 *JAL* 165, 167.

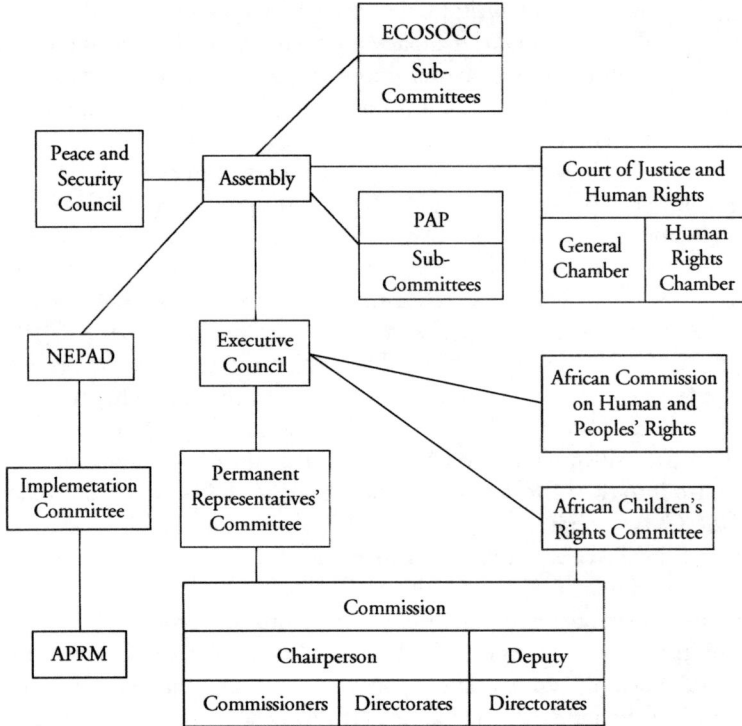

Fig. 5.1. African regional architecture

authority. To some extent, all AU organs, performing functions in all three spheres, have a potential role to play in the promotion and protection of human rights on the continent. As the AU's authoritative and overriding normative beacon, the Constitutive Act guides all its organs towards the accomplishment of human rights in all their activities.[12] Integration of efforts and coordination of activities are key ingredients for a recipe to ensure improved human rights realization under the AU. To accomplish this aim, the establishment of a Working Group on the AU and the Future of Human Rights has been suggested.[13]

In the time of the OAU, the dominance of the Assembly as single source of authority would have made such a three-layered analysis impossible. Evidencing structural democratization, as setout in Figure 5.1, the AU decentralizes authority to three main seats of power: the Assembly, as executive arm; the Pan-African Parliament (PAP), as legislative branch (when it has become a binding law-making organ); and when it is ultimately established, the African Court of Justice and Human Rights as seat of judicial authority. It remains to be seen to what extent the

---

[12] AU Constitutive Act, arts 3(h) and 4(m).   [13] Lloyd and Murray (n 11 above) 186.

ideal of functional independence of these three branches, in particularly non-dominance by the executive of the other two branches, will be achieved. In addition to these three principal organs, other organs and bodies also function at the three levels. A 'fourth branch', that of civil society,[14] for which ECOSOCC is responsible, is added as a necessary supplement to the three traditional branches of authority.

The remainder of this chapter is devoted to the human rights mandate of these AU bodies and the possible integration between them.[15] Although the activities of AU organs and bodies do not always fit neatly into one of the four 'branches', this division is used to emphasize the decentralized nature of authority under the AU—even though it is mostly still in its infancy.

A Legislative Role

In this chapter, the AU's 'legislative role' is understood in an extended sense as referring to both the adoption of binding standards ('law-making') and to the expression of 'advisory' views and recommendations (elaboration of 'soft law' norms).[16] The organs principally responsible for 'legislation' in this sense are the AU Assembly and the Pan-African Parliament (PAP), while other organs, such as the PRC (Permanent Representatives' Committee), also play a role. In the future, an African Law Commission may stimulate and guide law-making under the AU.

1 AU Assembly of Heads of State and Government (AU Assembly)

The AU Assembly is the 'supreme organ' of the AU.[17] It consists of the heads of state and governments, and usually meets twice annually in ordinary session.[18] One of these leaders usually serves as Chairperson for a term of one year. The rule that a head of state or government of a country hosting the Assembly 'shall have the right' to act as AU Chairperson until the next summit[19] came under severe stress when the AU met in Khartoum, in January 2006, amidst allegations of

---

[14] On civil society involvement in the AU, see T Murithi, The *African Union: Pan-Africanism, Peacebuilding and Development* (Aldershot: Ashgate, 2005) 112–36.

[15] For a comprehensive and detailed analysis of human rights under the OAU/AU at the end of the OAU's life span and as the AU emerged, see R Murray, *Human Rights in Africa: From the OAU to the African Union* (Cambridge: Cambridge University Press, 2004). My discussion deals with the AU organs as they subsequently emerged and started to function, focusing on their interrelationship in the field of human rights. For the status of ratification of the relevant treaties, see Table 5.1 at the end of this chapter.

[16] Although the African Human Rights Court and the African Commission may adopt advisory opinions interpreting the African Charter, and the African Commission adopts resolutions, these bodies are treated as 'judicial' and 'quasi-judicial' bodies respectively, in line with their core competencies.

[17] AU Constitutive Act, art 6(2).

[18] AU Doc Assembly/AU/Dec.53(III), Decision on the Periodicity of the Ordinary Sessions of the Assembly. The January summit is usually held in Addis Ababa, the headquarters of the AU Commission.

[19] AU Doc ASS/AU/Dec.2(I) Rules of Procedure of the Assembly of the African Union, first ordinary session, 9–10 July 2002, Durban, South Africa (Assembly Rules of Procedure), r 15(2).

involvement by the Sudanese government in fomenting civil strife and of perpe-
trating crimes against humanity in the Darfur region. In a lukewarm solution, the
Assembly agreed that Sudan could not hold the Chair—at least for the time
being.[20] The decision, allowing President Al-Bashir of Sudan to assume the position of Chair of the Union in 2007, may have looked like a pragmatic solution,
but proved not only to be unprincipled, but also unworkable. Although the 'postponement of his [Bashir's] term' had not been made conditional on any improvement in the Sudanese situation, when the matter came up for discussion in
January 2007, the persistence of human rights violations caused the AU to award
the position of Chairperson to President Kofuor of Ghana. In its decision, the
Assembly justified this choice in the light of the 50-years celebration of Ghanaian
independence during 2007, and postponed East Africa's turn for another year.[21]

Decisions of the Assembly should preferably be taken by consensus, or, if that is
not possible, by a two-thirds majority of the 53 members.[22] Under its Rules and
Procedure, the two-thirds requirement is confirmed for the Assembly's decisions
on substantive issues, while questions of procedure only require a simple majority
of the member states.[23] 'Decisions' are subdivided into three categories: (1) 'regulations', which are applicable in all states; (2) 'directives', which may be addressed
to one or more member state, 'undertakings', or individuals; and (3) 'recommendations, declarations, resolutions and opinions'.[24] 'Regulations' and 'directives' are
binding on member states, AU organs, and the RECs,[25] although national authorities are allowed some leeway to determine the 'form and the means' of implementation. Non-compliance is dealt with under article 23 of the AU Constitutive
Act.[26] The third category of 'decisions' is not binding, and aims to 'guide and har-
monise the viewpoints' of member states.[27] In its practice, the Assembly has not
made use of the terms 'regulation' or 'directive', and opted instead for the term
'decision' to denote its binding findings or views.

As the highest AU organ, the Assembly is mandated to 'determine the common
policies' of the AU.[28] Under similar authority, the OAU Assembly adopted numerous human rights treaties, such as the OAU Convention Governing the Specific
Aspects of Refugee Problems in Africa, the African Charter, and the African
Children's Charter.[29] The first human rights treaty adopted by the AU Assembly,
in 2003, is the Protocol to the African Charter on the Rights of Women in Africa.
Although the AU Assembly adopts the final texts of these treaties, their drafting
depends on numerous other role players. Especially the *travaux préparatoires* of the

---

[20] AU Doc Assembly/AU/Decl.2(VI), Declaration by the Assembly of the African Union.
[21] AU Doc Assembly/AU/Dec.150(VIII).   [22] AU Constitutive Act, art 7.
[23] Assembly Rules of Procedure, r 18.   [24] ibid, r 33(1).   [25] ibid, r 34.
[26] ibid, r 33(2).   [27] ibid.   [28] AU Constitutive Act, art 9(1)(a).
[29] See T Maluwa, 'International Law-Making in the Organisation of African Unity: An Overview'
(2000) 12 *RADIC* 201, 207–10 on the drafting of the Protocol to the African Charter on the
Establishment of an African Court on Human and Peoples' Rights, especially highlighting the role of
civil society.

African Human Right's Court Protocol and the Woman's Protocol demonstrate the influential role of NGOs.[30] At some stage in the drafting process, however, the pendulum shifts back to the states and the political organs.

It is not only by adopting potentially binding legal instruments that the Assembly is able to provide normative guidance. Examples of non-binding instruments adopted by the AU Assembly are the Maputo Declaration on Malaria, HIV/AIDS, Tuberculosis, and Other Related Infectious Diseases,[31] and the Solemn Declaration on Gender Equality in Africa,[32] aimed at the promotion of gender equality at all levels. Displaying an increased acknowledgement of the urgency of the socio-economic situation in Africa, the Assembly adopted the Declaration on Employment and Poverty Alleviation at its third extraordinary session in 2004, which was devoted to that topic.[33]

The exclusion of the African Commission from the process of drafting these and many other AU declarations not only demonstrates the marginalization of the African Commission, but also deprives the AU organs of its expertise and demonstrates the lack of an integrated approach to human rights within the AU.

2 Permanent Representatives' Committee (PRC)

To a great extent, the PRC is the most active of the AU institutions. Consisting of the 'ambassadors' (or 'permanent representatives') of member states to the AU headquarters in Addis Ababa, the PRC is a 'hands-on' body, engaged continuously in negotiations on a variety of issues.[34] The broad involvement of the PRC also extends to standard-setting. An example of the role of the PRC in preparing drafts of new instruments appears from its involvement in the process of drafting a protocol merging the African Human Rights Court and the AU Court of Justice. After a meeting of a working group in Algiers made some progress, states were invited to submit comments on the draft single instrument prepared by the Algiers working group. The responsibility of 'finalization and submission' of a final draft fell to a joint meeting of the PRC and legal experts from member states.[35] The PRC Sub-Committee on Refugees, Returnees, and Internally Displaced Persons

---

[30] See Chs 6 and 10 below.   [31] AU Assembly/AU/Decl.6(II).

[32] Adopted in Ethiopia, July 2004. The Assembly oversees its implementation (see AU Doc Assembly/AU/Dec.143(VIII) (Decision on the Reports on the Implementation of the AU Solemn Declaration on Gender Equality in Africa), listing the following ten countries that have (by early 2007) submitted their baseline reports: Algeria, Burundi, Ethiopia, Lesotho, Namibia, Mauritius, Rwanda, Senegal, South Africa, and Tunisia.

[33] AU Doc EXT/ASSEMBLY/AU/3(111); held in Ouagadougou, 8–9 September 2004.

[34] AU Constitutive Act, art 21. The PRC is 'where the political deals are made that turn technical drafting into formal policy' (African Network on Debt and Development, Open Society Initiative for Southern Africa and Oxfam GB, 'Towards a People-Driven African Union: Current Obstacles and New Opportunities' (2007) <http://www.afrimap.org> (31 January 2007) (hereinafter 'Toward a People-Driven African Union') 14).

[35] AU Doc EX.CL/Dec.237(VIII) Decision on the merger of the African Court on Human and People's Rights and the Court of Justice of the African Union.

has also taken a leading role in the elaboration of a 'legal framework for the protection and assistance of internally displaced persons in Africa'.[36]

3 Pan-African Parliament (PAP)

Although the Pan-African Parliament (PAP) currently acts only as an organ for deliberation and oversight, its evolution into a legislative organ is anticipated as regional integration is strengthened and the need for the harmonization of laws across Africa increases. The PAP is premised on the 'firm conviction' that it 'will ensure effectively the full participation of the African peoples in the economic development and integration of the continent'.[37] Under its first term of five years, from March 2004 to 2009, the PAP only has consultative and advisory powers.[38] When the first term comes to an end, the Conference of state parties must review the PAP's functioning.[39] At that stage, as well as during the subsequent ten-yearly review processes, the Conference of state parties may decide that the time is ripe for the PAP to attain its 'ultimate aim' of becoming a continental legislature with full legislative powers.[40] For the time being, though, the PAP provides a space for deliberation rather than legislation.

The PAP is one of the institutions envisaged under the Treaty establishing the African Economic Community (AEC).[41] However, between 1994, when the AEC Protocol entered into force, and 2001, when the AU Constitutive Act attained the same status, the evolution of the AEC did not encompass the adoption of a legal instrument to create a Parliament. As the AEC continued to co-exist with the AU, the PAP was established in terms of a Protocol to the AEC Treaty.[42] Although the legal basis of the PAP is thus located in both the AEC Treaty and the AU Constitutive Act,[43] its detailed composition and functioning is spelt out in the PAP Protocol to the AEC Treaty, to which 46 states had become party by 31 December 2006. The PAP was inaugurated in 1994, with Ms Gertrude Mongella from Tanzania as its first President.[44] Its subsequent sessions took place at its seat in Midrand, South Africa.

The PAP is an attempt to 'provide a common platform for African peoples and their grass-roots organisations to be more involved in discussions and decision-making on the problems and challenges facing the continent'.[45] The PAP is the AU's principal answer to criticism about the lack of popular inclusion and democratic

---

[36] AU Doc EX.CL/Dec.284(IX) para 9.   [37] PAP Protocol to the AEC Treaty, Preamble.
[38] PAP Protocol, art 2(3)(i).   [39] PAP Protocol, art 25.   [40] PAP Protocol, art 2(3).
[41] AEC Treaty, art 7(1)(c). See Table 5.1 below for status of ratification of the PAP Protocol.
[42] Protocol to the Treaty Establishing the African Economic Community Relating to the Pan-African Parliament, AU Doc CM/2198(LXXIII), Annex I.
[43] AU Constitutive Act lists the PAP as an AU organ, art 5(1)(c); AU Constitutive Act allows the AU to 'establish any organ of the Union', art 9(1)(d).   [44] AU Doc Assembly/AU/Dec.39(III).
[45] PAP Protocol, Preamble.

legitimacy of the AU project.[46] Unfortunately, its formation has been and its functioning is mainly in the hands of a political elite.[47]

Despite proclamations to the contrary, the membership of the PAP does not represent Africa's people in any meaningful sense. This is most obviously the case when a state without a democratically elected parliament, such as Libya, assigns members to PAP, as the Protocol allows.[48] In line with the principle of sovereign equality of states, each state party is represented by five members.[49] This principle, which for example accords Djibouti as much of a say as Nigeria, may be easy to observe while the stakes are low, but the position is bound to change if the PAP becomes more than a deliberative forum.

The PAP Protocol further stipulates that PAP membership should be at least 20 per cent female and that state representation should 'reflect the diversity of political opinion' within national parliaments.[50] It goes against the spirit of this provision if 'diversity' is made up of one or two very small parties rather than a clearly identifiable opposition grouping in the national parliament.[51] In states dominated by one political party, representation at the PAP inevitably reflects only the views of the dominant political elite.

Members of the PAP are not directly elected to the PAP, but are appointed or elected from among sitting members of national parliaments. The potential problem of contending demands from national and supranational constituencies has not really arisen, due mainly to the fact that the PAP sits only for two short terms of two weeks per year. Future amendments to the PAP Protocol may provide for continent-wide universal adult suffrage, thereby ensuring that the peoples of Africa are directly represented in the PAP. It should be recalled that the members of the European Parliament only became directly elected from 1979. Subsequent developments in Europe, where the minimal role of the Parliament never kindled enthusiasm for direct elections, do not support the notion that direct elections to the PAP will endow the AU with more popular legitimacy.[52]

[46] See generally, J Cilliers and P Mashele, 'The Pan-African Parliament: A Plenary of Parliamentarians' (2004) 13 *African Security Review* 78.

[47] This is also true for the process of European integration, see J Smith, 'Legitimacy and Democracy in the EU' in J Gower (ed), *The European Union Handbook* (London: Fitzroy Dearborn, 2002) 64, 66: 'European integration began as a profound elitist process, in which the support of the citizenry was simply assumed'. Direct elections to the European Parliament did not change much. However, each member state has to accept reform of the founding treaties in line with its national procedures, which may be approval of Parliament or through a referendum. Rejection by the majority, as was the case when the Danish voters said 'no' to the Maastricht Treaty in 1992, and the Dutch and French rejected the EU Constitution, exposes the fallacy of assumed popular support.

[48] PAP Protocol, art 5(1), allowing PAP members to be 'designated' by 'deliberative organs' other than parliaments.   [49] PAP Protocol, art 4(2).

[50] ibid.

[51] The South African Parliament for example sidelined the official opposition party, the Democratic Alliance, in its representation.

[52] Smith (n 47 above) 67 remarks that direct elections in Europe 'highlight the failure to engage the people in the integration process and to cast a shadow over the legitimacy of the integration process— quite the inverse of what was expected'.

The PAP has a clear human rights mandate. Its aim of consolidating democracy and good governance and to promote and protect human rights 'in accordance with the African Charter' and 'other relevant human rights instruments' is foregrounded in its founding treaty.[53] Similarly, its main competence, that of examining, discussing, and expressing opinions on 'any matter', is illustrated by a list of specific substantive issues that include human rights, democracy, good governance, and the rule of law.[54]

At its second session, the PAP has accepted that it has an 'oversight' role and requested the Committee on Rules, Privileges, and Discipline to make 'specific recommendations' about the ways in which the PAP should oversee the AU 'executive'.[55] Although PAP members mostly raised administrative and financial matters when the Chairperson of the AU Commission appeared at the PAP, this engagement could serve as a precedent for oversight on more substantive issues, including human rights, in future.

Serving mainly as an ineffectual 'talk-shop', the PAP has accumulated a number of resolutions and recommendations. Often very brief, insufficiently substantiated, and poorly drafted, the quality of these outcomes of PAP's deliberations leaves much room for improvement.[56] Examples of human rights-related resolutions adopted so far are: (i) an appeal to all countries that have not done so to ratify the Protocol on Women's Rights in Africa;[57] (ii) an appeal that the merger of the African Court of Justice and the African Court on Human and Peoples' Rights should not 'compromise the immediate establishment' of the latter;[58] (iii) an encouragement to states to sign on to the APRM;[59] (iv) a resolution to conduct an audit of the constitutions of member states, working closely with 'the AU Commission on People's and Human Rights' (*sic*);[60] and (v) a call that detained Ugandan opposition leader Dr Kizza Besigye be released.[61] Especially the latter resolution, with its country-targeted focus and immediate political relevance, provides an example

[53] PAP Protocol, Preamble.
[54] PAP Protocol, art 11(1); see also the inclusion of human rights in its objectives (PAP Protocol, art 3(2)).   [55] Resolution on Oversight (AU Doc PAP-Res 004/04).
[56] See eg the reference to 'the African Union Protocol on Human Rights and Peoples Freedoms' (for 'the African Charter on Human and Peoples' Rights') in Res 005/05, n 207 below. The fact that the original of the resolution was in English excludes translation as a source of the inaccuracy.
[57] Resolution on Ratification of Protocol on Women's Rights in Africa (AU Doc PAP-Res 006/04).
[58] Recommendation on the Role of the PAP (AU Doc PAP-Res 005/04).
[59] Resolution on Signing of Adherence to the African Peer Review Mechanism (AU Doc PAP-Res 0001/05).
[60] Audit of Constitutions of Member States of the AU (AU Doc PAP-Res 002/06). Although the link with the African Commission (on Human and Peoples' Rights) is to be welcomed, the confusing and incorrect reference to its name provides an example of regrettable drafting.
[61] Resolution on the Unconditional Release of Dr Kizza Besigye Leader of the Opposition in Uganda (AU Doc PAP-Res 005/05), adopted at the PAP's fourth session, December 2005, under arts 3, 11, and 18 of the Protocol, which mandates it to promote and ensure respect for human rights. In its critical response, the government (through its Minister of Information) relied on the principle of non-interference in Uganda's domestic governance (P Nyazi, 'Uganda: African Parliament has no Mandate on Besigye Says Government' (12 February 2005) *The Monitor* (Uganda) (see <http://www.afrika.no/Detailed/10970.html>) (30 November 2006).

of the PAP's potential role in holding governments publicly accountable and of raising awareness about specific human rights violations. The PAP has not applied this potentially powerful tool in other instances, underscoring the important role of civil society advocacy in setting the PAP's agenda.[62]

Soon after its establishment, the conflict and major human rights crisis in the Darfur region of Sudan provided the PAP with an opportunity to extend its mandate. Invoking its power to examine 'any matter' and to make recommendations aimed at the attainment of the AU's objectives, the PAP in 2004 decided to deploy a fact-finding mission to the region to 'acquaint itself with the realities on the ground and to report to the PAP'.[63] Seven PAP members visited Sudan in late 2004. They reported that they were 'free to interact with the population and many officials in Darfur'.[64] Their report analyses the causes and consequences of the conflict and makes a number of recommendations. When this report was tabled at its third session in April 2005, the PAP updated and adopted some of these recommendations.[65] In one of these recommendations, the PAP recommended that the Joint Commission mentioned in the Humanitarian Cease-Fire Agreement should be established, and should forge a 'close relationship' with the African Commission effectively to address allegations of human rights violations.[66] However, there is no indication that such a 'close relationship' was ever established.[67] At its fifth session, the PAP resolved to send a mission of the Committee on Gender, Family, Youth, and People with Disability to Darfur to conduct a gender assessment.[68]

Following this precedent, 'peace missions' to Côte d'Ivoire,[69] the DRC,[70] and Mauritania were mandated. The mission report of the Mauritanian visit reveals an ambiguity in the AU's stance on 'unconstitutional changes of government'.[71]

---

[62] It was reported that 'placard-waving protesters' were outside the PAP and handed a memorandum to the PAP (*Business Day* (Johannesburg) (<http://mathaba.net/0_index.shtml?x=496313>) (30 November 2006)). In the preamble to its resolution, the PAP also notes that a demonstration by Ugandans resident in South Africa had taken place 'at the precincts of the PAP', and that they handed a petition to the President of the PAP.

[63] Resolution on Conflict Resolution (AU Doc PAP-Res 002/04).

[64] Report on the PAP Fact-Finding Mission on Darfur, the Sudan (AU Doc AU/PAP/RPT/CIRCR.CTTEE), 23 February 2005.

[65] The debate of the report took place on 5 April 2005, see Official Report of the Debates of the PAP (Hansard), No 1–2005: third ordinary session, PAP. Contributors to the debate, which included five Sudanese PAP members, did not focus much on the specific recommendations, but opted to make general declarations invoking for example slogans about 'African solutions to African problems'.

[66] Recommendation on Pan-African Parliament Peace Mission to Darfur (AU Doc PAP Rec 001/05), paras g and h.

[67] This does not, for example, transpire from any of the African Commission's subsequent resolutions on Darfur.

[68] Resolution on the Violation of Human Rights on Women and Children in the Darfur Region of the Sudan (*sic*) (AU Doc PAP-Res 003/06).

[69] Resolution on the Dispatch of the PAP Parliamentary Peace Mission to Côte d'Ivoire at the Beginning of May 2005 (AU Doc PAP-Res 006/05).

[70] Resolution on the Dispatch of a PAP Peace Mission during the First Fortnight of 2005 (AU Doc PAP-Res 007/05).

[71] Report of the Pan-African Parliament Mission to Mauritania 10–16 October 2005.

Although the mission supports the PSC request for a rapid return to constitutional order, it recommends that the AU Assembly should 'draw lessons' from the 'realities' so as to 'save' the AU 'from being placed in as complex and uncomfortable a situation'. This complexity and discomfort apparently arises from the practical reality that 'it is the violations of commitments' (by the previous regime) 'which make anti-constitutional change inevitable'. Alluding to the paradox that human rights violations are perpetrated to rectify human rights violations by an intransigent incumbent government, the mission seems to sympathize with the coup plotters. This matter should be the subject of debate in the AU, including the African Commission, without compromising the principles of human rights or eroding the legal framework on unconstitutional changes of government. One of the ways out of the paradox is that the AU should be much more engaged in ensuring that the conditions giving rise to situations such as that in Mauritania are pre-emptively addressed. To accomplish this objective, the AU Assembly, PSC, PAP, the African Commission, and other AU bodies need to devise clearer human rights-informed strategies.

The PAP functions through a number of committees. One of these, the Justice and Human Rights Committee, can play an important role in galvanizing PAP's human rights mandate into action. It may for example undertake a review of the status of ratification of AU human rights instruments, and should raise the failure of states to ratify these instruments on a continuous basis. It could go one step further, though, to monitor the state of implementation and compliance with these obligations by developing a human rights accountability index.[72] It should also analyse the African Commission's activity reports and prepare resolutions for adoption by PAP. A functional relationship between this PAP sub-committee and the African Commission should be worked out in order to enhance their mutual effectiveness. Their joint activities could for example inform the PAP's impact at the national level by informing the PAP's efforts 'towards the harmonisation or co-ordination of the laws of member states'.[73] The PAP also provides a valuable link to national Parliaments, with whom the African Commission should forge better links. Together with the PAP, the Commission could make specific recommendations to national Parliaments about the domestication of the African Charter and other international treaties.[74]

As long as its deliberations do not lead to binding 'law', the PAP should consider other avenues to enhance its impact, and should ensure greater publicity about its activities.[75] One possibility is to approach the African Human Rights Court for

---

[72] The Committee may rely on work submitted to it by students on the 2006 LL M (Human Rights and Democratization in Africa) programme, presented at the Centre for Human Rights, University of Pretoria (see JO Ambani, GW Maindi, and GT Mirugi-Mukundi, 'Suggestions on the Mandate of the Justice and Human Rights Committee of the Pan-African Parliament', June 2006, on file with author).

[73] PAP Protocol, art 11(3).   [74] See Brainstorming Meeting (n 1 above) para 48(f).

[75] This should begin within the AU family: It may be noted that the AU's web-site is not linked to that of the PAP (<http://www.pan-african-parliament.org>), and only contains outdated information about the PAP.

an advisory opinion.[76] Other possibilities are to direct its recommendations to the AU Assembly and Executive Council for their action, and to put into effective operation the relationship with the PSC provided for in the PSC Protocol.[77]

The potential for the PAP to become a crucial forum on human rights issues is vast. Following the practice of the European Parliament, the PAP may for example become involved in the process of appointing members of human rights treaty bodies and the African Human Rights Court. By scrutinizing the records of candidates and publicly debating their compliance with the criteria set out in the relevant legal instruments, the PAP may make suitable recommendations to the Assembly. Such a process will be a vast improvement on the political trade-offs inherent in appointments on the basis of geopolitical considerations. The African Commission should ensure that its Activity Reports are tabled and discussed in the PAP, and that appropriate recommendations are made to AU organs for their action.

As one of its organs, the PAP depends on the AU for its budget. Limited budgetary allocation has hampered the effectiveness of the PAP, and has led to an acrimonious exchange between the PAP President and the AU Chairperson. The AU Assembly and Executive Council decided that member states bear financial responsibility for the participation of their PAP members. Due to financial constraints, the PAP Bureau will in the first five years not reside at the PAP headquarters, and PAP sessions were 'reviewed downwards'.[78] The PAP objected to the devolution of the power to authorize its budget to the Permanent Representatives' Committee.[79] Although the PAP Protocol provides the PAP with the role of 'discussing' and making recommendations not only on its own, but also on the 'budget of the Community', the PAP was not 'actively involved' in this process.[80]

The output of the PAP so far does not justify its budgetary allocation,[81] and does not bode well for its evolution into a fully-fledged continental parliament. Problematic areas include the number, focus, and quality of its resolutions; the lack of implementation of follow-up; the nature of debates; the lack of web-based accessibility to its documents; and the publication of its *Hansard* without translation.

B Executive Role

The executive function of implementing programmes, policies, and laws lies with the AU Assembly of Heads of State and Government, the Executive Council, the

---

[76] African Human Rights Court Protocol, art 4(1), any AU organ may request an advisory opinion from that Court.   [77] PSC Protocol, art 18.

[78] AU Docs Assembly/AU/Dec.39(III)Rev.1; EX.CL/Dec.98(V).

[79] Recommendation on the Budget for the PAP (AU Doc PAP-Res 004/04).

[80] PAP Protocol, art 11(2).

[81] Its 2005 allocation was US$6.2 million; its 2006 budgetary request was close to US$12 million (<http://www.pan-african-parliament.org>), but only some US$ 6.4 million was allocated for 2007 (AU Doc Assembly/AU/Res.154(VIII)).

AU Commission, the Permanent Representatives' Committee, and the Peace and Security Council.[82]

1 AU Assembly

As the highest AU organ, the AU Assembly monitors implementation of policies and decisions and ensures compliance by member states.[83] It oversees the activities of all AU organs and gives effect to their recommendations. It also has the final say about budgetary allocations. The 2007 budget of the AU stood at just under $US133 million.[84]

The AU Assembly may impose sanctions of a 'political and economic nature' on states that fail to comply with AU decisions and policies.[85] It may also sanction states that fall into arrears with their contributions to the AU. At its June 2006 session, the Executive Council affirmed that the following states remain under sanction:[86] Cape Verde, Central African Republic, Democratic Republic of the Congo, Eritrea, Guinea-Bissau, Liberia, Mauritania, São Tomé e Príncipe, and the Seychelles.

As far as human rights are concerned, the AU Assembly fulfils numerous crucial executive functions.

First, as they operate within its ambit, the AU Assembly is responsible for the funding and effective functioning of the African human rights treaty bodies. In the African Charter, explicit provision is made for the AU to bear the 'cost of the staff and services'.[87] Similarly, the African Human Rights Court Protocol provides that the AU bears responsibility for 'emoluments and allowances for judges and the budget of its registry'.[88] One of the reasons for the status of the African Children's Rights Committee as neglected stepchild as far as resources are concerned, is the omission of a comparable provision in the African Children's Charter.[89]

Budgetary allocation to the African Commission has been sparse. In one of the most spectacular examples of a *rightorical* commitment to human rights, the concern for limited resource allocation to the African Commission, repeated recurrently but manifestly never properly addressed,[90] should be juxtaposed against

---

[82] The NEPAD and the APRM institutions (such as the NEPAD Implementation Committee, the APRM Forum, the NEPAD Secretariat, and the APRM Secretariat) may, to the extent that NEPAD has been integrated into the AU, also be considered as forming part of the AU's 'executive' branch.   [83] AU Constitutive Act, art 9(1)(e).

[84] Of this amount, member states contribute some $US97 million, and 'partners' some $US36 million (AU Doc AU/Assembly/Dec.154(VIII)). In 2005, the total budget of US$158 million was approved ('Towards a People-Driven African Union', n 34 above, 10).

[85] AU Constitutive Act, art 23(2); Rules of Procedure, r 36, also mentioning 'denial of transport and communication links' as a possible form of sanction.   [86] AU Doc EX. CL/Dec. 279 (IX).

[87] African Charter, art 41.   [88] African Human Rights Court Protocol, art 32.

[89] However, it should be noted that the AU Commission (Social Affairs Department) serves as the secretariat of the African Children's Rights Committee; see further Section C.2 below.

[90] The call for financial and other support to the Commission is the most consistently recurring theme in the resolutions and decisions of both the OAU and AU Assembly. See Resolution on the First Annual Activity Report of the African Commission (OAU Doc AHG/Res.188(XXV)(1989)

the OAU/AU Assembly's praise for the accomplishments and encouragement of the Commission.[91] Read together, the resolutions and decisions in effect note the accomplishments *despite* the limited resources. Reasons for this financial neglect are manifold. Evidently, the AU and member states were aware of the need, but lacked the will to act. Partly, the deplorable state of affairs may be ascribed to the Commission. Due to the part-time status of Commissioners, the responsibility of submitting budgets fell to the Secretary of the African Commission. However, as an AU functionary, the Secretary has limited authority and room for manoeuvre. In respect of the African Human Rights Court, budgetary allocations require prior 'consultation' with the Court.[92]

Secondly, the AU elects members of various human rights bodies: the African Commission, the African Children's Rights Committee, and the African Human Rights Court. This power is vested in the treaties setting up these bodies,[93] and not in the AU Constitutive Act. As the membership of these human rights treaties

para 5): the OAU Assembly 'requests the Secretary-General . . . to find, prior to the next financial year, appropriate solutions to the budgetary, financial and personnel problems raised by the African Commission'; Resolution on the Seventh Annual Activity Report of the African Commission (OAU Doc AHG/Res.240(XXXI)(1995) para 8): the OAU Assembly 'calls on the OAU Secretary-General to take all the necessary measures to provide the African Commission . . . with all the human, material and financial resources it needs to accomplish its mission, and to report on the implementation of this to the 33rd ordinary session'; Decision on the Tenth Annual Activity Report of the African Commission (OAU Doc AHG/Res.123(XXXIII)(1997) para 4): the OAU Assembly 'acknowledges the inadequate resources at the disposal of the African Commission and calls on the competent organs of the OAU to take the necessary measures, as appropriate, to provide the African Commission as quickly as possible with adequate human and financial resources to ensure its smooth functioning'; Decision on the 17th Annual Activity Report of the African Commission (AU Doc Assembly/AU/Dec.49(III) (2004) para 2): the AU Assembly 'requests all the organs concerned to take the necessary steps to provide the Commission with the human, financial and material resources needed for its smooth functioning in keeping with article 41 of the African Charter and submit a report thereon to the 7th ordinary session'; Decision on the 19th Annual Activity Report of the African Commission (AU Doc Assembly/AU/Dec.101(VI)(2006) para 6): the AU Assembly 'reiterates its request to the AU Commission to allocate adequate resources from its operational budget to the African Commission as provided for in article 41 of the Charter to enable the African Commission [to] discharge independently its mandate under the Charter'.

[91] See eg Resolution on the Fifth Annual Activity Report of the African Commission (OAU Doc AHG/Res.207(XVIII)(1992) para A.1): the OAU Assembly 'underlines the importance of ensuring respect for human and peoples' rights with the view of enhancing peace, stability and development in Africa; Decision on the Tenth Annual Activity Report of the African Commission (OAU Doc AHG/Res.123(XXXIII)(1997) para 2): the OAU Assembly 'commends the African Commission for the excellent work done and exhorts it to persevere in its efforts to promote and protect human and peoples' rights in member states in keeping with its mandate'; Decision on the Tenth Annual Activity Report of the African Commission (OAU Doc AHG/Res.153(XXXVI)(2000) para 1): the OAU Assembly 'commends the Commission for the quality of work accomplished during the period under review'; Decision on the 16th Annual Activity Report of the African Commission (AU Doc Assembly/AU/Dec.11(III)(2003) para 1): the AU Assembly 'commends' the African Commission 'for the excellent work accomplished during the past year'; Decision on the 16th Annual Activity Report of the African Commission (AU Doc Assembly/AU/Dec.77(V)(2005) para 2): the AU Assembly 'commends the African Commission for the work accomplished and urges it to pursue its efforts in this regard'.   [92] African Human Rights Court Protocol, art 32.
[93] African Charter, art 33; African Children's Committee, art 34; African Human Rights Court Protocol, art 14(1).

does not necessarily correspond with that of the AU, it is noteworthy that the power to elect is not granted to a conference of state parties to specific treaties, but to the AU Assembly. This position derives from the fact that these bodies function as AU organs and because the AU, rather than state parties, bears the responsibility for the funding and functioning of these bodies.

One of the perennial criticisms of the OAU Assembly has been the election of individuals holding political office and diplomatic positions as members of the Commission.[94] This criticism was addressed when the AU issued a circular (*note verbale*), advising state parties as follows:[95]

As a guide for states Parties in interpreting the question of incompatibility or impartiality, the Advisory Committee of Jurists in the establishment of the Permanent Court of International Justice (now the International Court of Justice (ICJ)) had pointed out that '(A) member of government, a Minister or under-secretary of State, a diplomatic representative, a director of a ministry, or one of his subordinates, or the legal adviser to a foreign office, though they would be eligible for appointment as arbitrators to the Permanent Court of Arbitration of 1899, are certainly not eligible for appointment as judges upon our Court.' (See PCIJ/Advisory Committee of Jurists, *Procès-Verbaux of the Proceedings of the Committee.* June 16–July 24 1920, 693, 715–716 (1920)). States Parties are also reminded to ensure adequate gender representation in their nominations and to bear in mind the need to continue to enhance the independence and operational integrity of the African Commission in the spirit of the Grand Bay Declaration of 1999 and the Kigali Declaration of 8 May 2003.

This directive seems to have had a noticeable effect.[96] Although the current membership still includes diplomats and government officials,[97] the four Commissioners who took up their oath as new members to the African Commission in November 2005 all fit the required profile.[98] Gender representation has also improved. At first, the Commission was an all male body. The first female Commissioner, Vera Duarte Martins, of Cape Verde, was elected in 1993. By 1995, the female composition had grown to two, with the addition of Julienne Ondziel-Gnelenga. The 1999 elections increased the female complement to four, and by 2004 the number had grown to five. As at 31 July 2006, the number still stood at five.[99] The *note verbale*, as well as the Rules of Procedure of the African Children's Committee, played a part in the request by the AU that caused two members to leave the Committee and another to resign when they took up potentially compromising positions.[100]

With the exception of one judge of the African Human Rights Court, who served as legal advisor to the President of Burkina Faso, the newly elected judges comply

[94] See Ch 7.A below.
[95] AU Doc BC/OLC/66/Vol. XVIII (April 2005); first issued in relation to the nomination of judges to the African Human Rights Court.
[96] See also Brainstorming Meeting (n 1 above) para 17(a).
[97] The current Chair (Sawadogo) of the Commission is the Ambassador of Burkina Faso to Senegal.
[98] F Viljoen, 'Promising Profiles: An Interview with the Four New Members of the African Commission on Human and Peoples' Rights' (2006) 6 *AHRLJ* 237. However, although Commissioner Malila has subsequently been appointed as Attorney-General of Zambia, he did not resign from the Commission.
[99] The current female Commissioners are: Salamata Sawadogo, Angela Melo, Sanji Monageng, Reine Alapini-Gansou, and Faith Pansy Tlakula.   [100] See Murray (n 15 above) 168–9.

with the guidelines of the *note verbale*. However, only two of the 11 judges elected to the Court are women, indicating that 'adequate gender representation' is still not 'equal' representation. It should be noted that even if the Assembly retained its formal role of 'electing' members to these bodies, the Executive Council now effectively performs this function.[101]

Thirdly, the AU Assembly oversees the activities of these bodies and takes action on the basis of their reports.[102] Since the findings of the two quasi-judicial bodies are 'recommendatory', the question arises whether the adoption by the AU of their recommendations bestows binding legal status on them.[103] While it remains arguable that the mere adoption of reports does not confer such status, the position is different when the AU founds one of its decisions on the content of such a report.

Before the OAU reinvented itself as the AU, the OAU Assembly authorized the publication of the African Commission's report without any significant discussion or debate. Its resolutions and decisions on the Commission's Annual Activity Reports sound formulaic, and with a few exceptions,[104] did not engage with substantive issues arising from the reports. Under the AU, the Assembly delegated the authority to examine the Commission's activity reports to the Executive Council.[105] Although the consequent position apparently conflicts with the stipulations of the African Charter,[106] the AU Constitutive Act mandates this delegation of functions.[107] In any event, since this function has been performed by the Executive Council, the time devoted to and intensity of debate about the Commission's reports increased dramatically.[108]

Fourthly, as the political organ responsible for quasi-judicial and judicial bodies, the AU Assembly is responsible for the implementation or enforcement of their findings and decisions.[109] This competence is backed up by the threat of sanctions for failure to comply with decisions and policies.[110] The Assembly, to

[101] See Section B.2 below.

[102] African Charter, arts 58 and 45(2); in respect of communications and African Children's Charter, art 45(3); African Human Rights Court Protocol, art 31.

[103] See F Viljoen and L Louw, 'The Status of the Findings of the African Commission: From Moral Persuasion to Legal Obligation' (2004) 48 *JAL* 1.

[104] See Resolution on the Fifth Annual Activity Report of the African Commission (OAU Doc AHG/Res.207(XXVIII)(199)) and Resolution on the Sixth Annual Activity Report of the African Commission (OAU Doc AHG/Res.227(XXIX)(1993)), where the Assembly lists states that have submitted reports under art 62 of the Charter, refers to overdue reports, and calls on states to implement art 26 of the Charter.

[105] AU Doc Assembly/AU/Dec.6(II), July 2003. This development was already recommended in the Grand Baie Declaration and Plan of Action, OAU Doc CONF/HRA/DEC 1, para 24, where the Ministerial Conference called on the Assembly to 'consider delegating' this task to the then Council of Ministers.

[106] African Charter, art 54, stipulating that the Commission 'shall submit' a report to 'each ordinary session of the Assembly'. African Charter, arts 58 and 59 also clearly assume that the Assembly will take decisions arising from the consideration of the Commission's report. However, as long as the Assembly takes the final political responsibility, the role of the Executive Council is not necessarily excluded.

[107] AU Constitutive Act, art 9(2): the AU Assembly may 'delegate any of its powers and functions to any organ of the Union'.   [108] See the discussion under 'Executive Council' below.

[109] AU Constitutive Act, art 9(1)(e).   [110] ibid, art 23(2).

which the exercise of this competence falls, may for example restrict transport and communication links between AU members and an offending state, and may impose other sanctions of a political and economic nature.[111] Under the African Charter and African Children's Charter, no mention is made of implementation or follow-up of recommendations, presumably on the basis of the distinction between the quasi-legal role of the Commission (of 'interpreting' the law) and the political role of the Assembly (of 'ensuring compliance' with findings).[112] To a great extent, then, implementation and enforcement of findings of these bodies, including the African Human Rights Court, depend on the political backing they receive to ensure the effective implementation of their findings.[113]

The Assembly's enforcement powers go much wider, though. Although the Constitutive Act does not prescribe the modalities of suspending governments that 'come to power through unconstitutional means',[114] it is up to the Assembly to give effect to this provision.[115] Questions of interpretation may arise, such as whether 'means' are 'unconstitutional' and at what stage the suspension may be revoked in the light of a return to constitutionalism. In deciding on such issues, the Assembly should be guided by the OAU Declaration on Unconstitutional Changes of Government,[116] the African Commission's resolution on Electoral Processes and Participatory Government,[117] and the African Charter on Democracy, Elections and Governance. Madagascar was suspended when Marc Ravalomanana claimed to be head of state after the 2001 disputed presidential elections and was only readmitted in 2003.[118] The coup in Mauritania posed a further challenge to the AU Assembly. The African Charter on Democracy, Elections and Governance sets out in more detail the ground for sanctions and interventions under these circumstances, and the procedure to be followed.[119]

Fifthly, the Assembly takes decisions and adopts resolutions relevant to human rights. The Assembly for example decided to appoint a Committee of Eminent African Jurists to advise it on the prosecution of former Chadian president Hissène Habré.[120] Accepting the Committee's report, the Assembly 'mandated' Senegal to

---

[111] On other possible sanctions see art 23 of the Constitutive Act.

[112] See Ch 8.A.9 below.

[113] On an early occasion, the OAU Assembly called on states to take 'concrete measures' to give 'effective implementation' to the African Charter (OAU Doc AHG/Res.230(XXX) para 4) (June 1994, Tunis, Tunisia). Declarations by the AU Assembly may also serve to enhance human rights by bringing moral pressure to bear on role players—in particular, on states. In the Banjul Declaration on the 25th Anniversary of the African Charter on Human and Peoples' Rights, for example, the AU Assembly took the bold step of urging member states to 'take the necessary steps to fulfill their obligations under the African Charter and other human rights instruments to which they are parties, in particular, the implementation of decisions and recommendations of human rights treaty-bodies' (AU Doc Assembly/AU/Decl.3(VII), July 2006).   [114] AU Constitutive Act, art 30.

[115] See Rules of Procedure, r 37.   [116] Adopted in Lomé, Togo, in July 2000.

[117] Adopted in 1996; one of the principles in the Declaration on Unconstitutional Changes of Government is the values set out in the African Charter.

[118] AU Doc Assembly/AU/Dec.6(II), July 2003.   [119] Arts 27–34.

[120] AU Doc Assembly/AU/Dec.103(VI), at the Summit of African Union Heads of State and Government in Khartoum, Sudan, in January 2006.

prosecute Habré and to 'ensure' that he is tried 'on behalf of Africa', and called on the Chairperson of the AU Commission to provide Senegal with the necessary assistance for the effective conduct of the trial.[121] Even if the choice of the word 'mandate' may suggest otherwise, it is contended that the decision is binding on Senegal. For one, it has been included in the category earmarked 'decisions' (and not as one of the 'declarations') adopted at the seventh ordinary Assembly session. In addition, the use of the word 'ensure' in the phrase 'mandates Senegal to ensure that Habré is tried', provides support for an interpretation that the Habré decision is a 'directive' that binds Senegal. If this interpretation is correct, the Habré decision represents a significant step towards eroding the sanctity of state sovereignty on the basis of human rights-related concerns, and sets a precedent for future binding decisions ensuring state compliance with human rights norms.[122] Senegal's willingness to implement this decision has effectively foreclosed debate about the legal force of the Assembly's decision.[123]

Sixthly, the AU Assembly inherited the power to request in-depth studies when the African Commission draws its attention to the situations of 'a series of serious or massive violations' of human rights.[124] Due to the OAU Assembly's failure to act in situations brought to its attention, this procedure has fallen into abeyance.[125] As a result of political inaction, the African Commission has developed a practice of refraining from invoking this measure as part of its findings.[126]

Seventhly, the Assembly is mandated to order military intervention of a member state in order to respond to very serious and massive human rights violations amounting to 'war crimes, genocide and crimes against humanity'.[127] Neither the consent of the targeted state, nor prior authorization of the UN Security Council is required.[128] When the drafting of the AU Constitutive Act started, memories of

---

[121] AU Doc Assembly/AU/Dec.127(VII), Decision on the Hissène Habré case and the African Union (Habré decision).

[122] Habré decision, para 3 (referring to AU Constitutive Act, art 4(h); para 5 (invoking the UN Convention against Torture)).

[123] In January 2007, some seven months after its initial decision, the AU Assembly noted the efforts that Senegal 'has already deployed to speed up the implementation' of the decision (AU Doc Assembly/AU/Dec.157(VIII) para 3).   [124] African Charter, art 58.

[125] R Murray, 'Massive or Serious Violations under the African Charter on Human and Peoples' Rights: A Comparison with the Inter-American and European Mechanisms' (1999) 17 *NQHR* 109, 128.

[126] See eg Communication 155/96, *SERAC v Nigeria* (2001) AHRLR 60 (ACHPR 2001) (15th Annual Activity Report), in which the Commission refrains from finding the existence of serious or massive violations, despite the massive scale and systematic nature of the violations (see eg para 59, where the Commission makes reference to these facts).   [127] AU Constitutive Act, art 4(h).

[128] This flies in the face of UN Charter, art 53, which stipulates that 'no enforcement action' may be undertaken by regional arrangements without the authorization of the Security Council (SC); but see also the OAU Solemn Declaration on Security, Stability, Development and Co-operation in Africa, OAU Doc AHG/Dec.14(XXXVI) para 9(9), recognizing the 'primary' responsibility of the SC for security in Africa, and K Kindiki, 'The Normative and Institutional Framework of the African Union relating to the Protection of Human Rights and the Maintenance of International Peace and Security: A Critical Appraisal' (2003) 3 *AHRLJ* 97, 108–10, who argues that the AU position reflects concern with SC inaction, and should serve as a sufficient mandate for action when the SC fails to intervene.

the lamentable inaction on the part of the OAU and the UN in response to the 1994 genocide in Rwanda were still acutely felt. It is therefore hardly surprising that the AU became the first international organization to include such a provision in its founding treaty.[129] Under an amendment to the Constitutive Act, adopted in 2003 but not yet in force, the grounds for intervention have been extended to encompass also a 'serious threat to legitimate order'.[130] This amendment invites the fear that the new ground may be invoked as an excuse to violate the human rights of those engaged in legitimate civil strife or struggles for self-determination against repressive governments.

Much depends on the Assembly's application of such a provision. Should 'legitimate order' be interpreted to serve the sacred cow of the status quo at all costs, the new version of article 4(h) will uphold regimes that have lost their popular appeal and deny their nationals the possibility of constitutional change. A historical tendency for solidarity among African leaders increases the likelihood of such an interpretation. However, the provision may also be interpreted in a way that favours human rights. Article 4(i) already allows for 'requests' from members for intervention to 'restore peace and security' in their countries. The same fears alluded to above may arise in respect of the application of this provision. The new article 4(h) should therefore allow the Assembly to intervene in instances where the government does *not* request intervention, where there is no functional government in place, and human rights violations amount to 'grave circumstances', as required in the wording of the provision.

Given the opportunity to use article 4(h) in Darfur, the Assembly opted not to 'wait to investigate reports of genocide', but took a 'proactive role in convincing the Sudanese government to accept African Union mediation'.[131] Although the AU later sent an African Union Military Observation Mission to Sudan (AMIS), its mandate was very limited and detracted little from a largely mediatory approach. By not taking more decisive action in Darfur, the AU showed remnants of the inaction and deference to states that characterized the OAU.

Eighthly, the Assembly has taken numerous steps to improve the realization of socio-economic rights on the continent. Two issues stand out: food security and poverty alleviation.

Departing from the grim reality that some 30 per cent of Africa's population is 'chronically and severely undernourished', the Assembly called for the adoption and implementation of special policies and strategies targeted at small-scale and

---

[129] See E Baimu and K Sturman, 'Amendments to the African Union's Right to Intervene: A Shift from Human Security to Regional Security?' (2003) 12 *African Security Review* 37, 40 and T Maluwa, 'Reimagining African Unity: Some Preliminary Reflections on the Constitutive Act of the African Union' (2002) 8 *AYBIL* 28.

[130] See Protocol on Amendments to the Constitutive Act of the African Union, adopted 11 July 2003, partially reprinted in C Heyns and M Killander (eds), *Compendium of Key Human Rights Documents of the African Union* (Pretoria: PULP, 2006) 12.

[131] Report of the Pan-African Parliament Fact-Finding Mission on Darfur, the Sudan, AU Doc AU/PAP/RPT/CIRC.CTTEE, 23 February 2005, para 1.5.

traditional farmers.[132] The most tangible commitment on states in this regard is to allocate 10 per cent of their budgets to agricultural and rural development.[133] When the heads of state met some three years after this commitment was made, at the Abuja Summit on Food Security in Africa, it was still necessary to call on states to 'formalize' this commitment.[134] The Abuja Summit resolution further reiterated the need for intra-regional trade, and made concrete proposals to states, the RECs, and NEPAD. It called, in particular, for the expansion of the NEPAD Home-Grown School feeding initiative.[135]

The Assembly devoted its third extraordinary session, in September 2004, to alleviate 'pervasive poverty' and 'rampant unemployment' in Africa. In the Plan of Action for Promotion of Employment and Poverty Alleviation,[136] it identified the creation of an enabling environment of good governance; human and institutional capacity-building; fair and equitable globalization; and interregional trade as some of the key priorities. Acknowledging that previous declarations and commitments often went unheeded, the Assembly established a Follow-Up Mechanism,[137] under which member states and the RECs bear the primary responsibility to implement the Plan.

More so than UN organs, the AU Assembly has inserted the Millennium Development Goals (MDGs) into its activities. On numerous occasions it expressed concern that African states are unlikely to meet the MDGs, and urged its development arms, NEPAD and the RECs, to step up efforts to develop and implement programmes to achieve the MDG targets.[138]

2 Executive Council

Meeting more frequently than the AU Assembly, actively involved in preparing the agenda, and adopting decisions to be considered by the Assembly, the Executive Council is in many ways more influential than the Assembly. The Executive Council (previously the OAU Council of Ministers) is composed of the Ministers of Foreign Affairs (or other designated Ministers) of AU member states.[139] Like the Assembly, it may take decisions in the form of binding 'regulations' and 'directives', and non-binding 'recommendations, declarations, resolutions and opinions'.[140] It coordinates and takes decisions on 'policies in areas of common interest' of members.[141]

---

[132] AU Doc Assembly/AU/Decl.7(II) (July 2003) (Declaration on Agriculture and Food Security in Africa). [133] ibid, para 2.
[134] AU Doc FS/Res(I) (December 2006) (Resolution of the Abuja Food Security Summit) para 2.
[135] AU Doc FS/Decl(I) (December 2006) (Declaration of the Abuja Food Security Summit) para 9.
[136] AU Doc EXT/Assembly/AU/4(III)Rev.3 (September 2004).
[137] AU Doc EXT/Assembly/AU/5(III) (Follow-Up Mechanism for Implementation, Monitoring and Evaluation). [138] See eg AU Doc Assembly/AU/Dec.38(III) (July 2004) esp paras 18 and 20.
[139] AU Constitutive Act, art 10.
[140] See A.1 above; and Rules of Procedure of the Executive Council of the AU (AU Doc Assembly/AU/2(I)b), r 34(1)). As with Assembly decisions, their non-compliance may be addressed in terms of art 23 of the AU Constitutive Act (rr 34(1) and 35). [141] AU Constitutive Act, art 13(1).

It is 'responsible' to the Assembly and monitors the implementation of policies formulated by the Assembly.[142]

As their mandates and world-views are heavily dependent on international relations and geopolitics, ministers of foreign affairs, who usually make up the Executive Council, are not necessarily attuned to human rights. Departing from the premise that ministers of justice, or, where they exist, ministers of human rights, are better suited to deal with and should become more involved in human rights within continental structures, it is suggested that these ministers should represent member states in the Executive Council when the African Commission's reports are considered. Other AU ministers already come together from time to time for ministerial meetings on topics related to human rights.[143]

The role of the ministers of justice and human rights has already been enhanced through the organization of ministerial conferences. The first of these was held in 1999, as the OAU's life span neared its end, and concluded in the Grand Baie Declaration and Plan of Action.[144] This Declaration emphasizes the responsibility of states to give effect to the African Charter in their national legislation, and to submit reports as required under the Charter. It also recognized the need for mainstreaming human rights in the OAU's programmes. Under the AU, a similar conference was held, this time in Rwanda, culminating in the Kigali Declaration of 2003.[145] Echoing many of the affirmations of the first conference, the Kigali Declaration goes further by calling on the Chairperson of the AU Commission to coordinate the follow-up of the two Declarations, and by recommending that such conferences should become a regular feature with intervals of no more than four years.[146]

The Executive Council also adopts decisions on matters of human rights interest, such as the Decision on the Situation of Refugees, Returnees and Displaced Persons,[147] in which it expressed concern about 'the persistence and the magnitude of the phenomenon of refugees and displaced persons in Africa'.[148] In its decision, it further requested the AU Commission to 'formulate a policy that will facilitate access of refugees and displaced persons to education, including at the post-primary level'.[149]

As was explained above, in 2003 the Assembly extended the Executive Council's expanding mandate to include consideration of the African Commission's activity

---

[142] Seven special technical committees have been established under the AU Constitutive Act to bring together ministers and senior civil servants in designated areas of competence (AU Constitutive Act, art 14). These committees assist the Executive Council in preparing and implementing AU programmes and projects (art 15). The mandate of two of these, the Committee on Health, Labour and Social Affairs and the Committee on Education, Culture and Human Resources, seem particularly attuned to the promotion and protection of human rights. The Assembly should consider adding a committee on legal and human rights (under art 14(2)).

[143] See eg the Ministerial Conference on Refugees, Returnees and Displaced Persons in Africa, held 29–30 May 2006, Ouagadougou, Burkina Faso (AU Doc AU/MIN/HARDP/Decl.1).

[144] n 105 above.   [145] AU Doc MIN/CONF/HRA/Decl.1(I)   [146] ibid, para 34.

[147] AU Doc EX.CL/Dec.240(VIII)   [148] ibid, para 1.   [149] ibid, para 5.

report.[150] At its meeting in June 2006, the Executive Council adopted the 20th Activity Report of the Commission without a recommendation to the Assembly for its decision. As a much more deliberative organ with much more time allocated for debate and discussion, the Executive Council was always going to take the obligation of considering the African Commission's report in more depth than the AU Assembly. However, greater engagement by the Executive Council not only brought the advantages of closer scrutiny, but also had the downside of increasing attempts at bedevilling and thwarting scrutiny. As a consequence, some of the Charter guarantees and long-standing practices have been eroded.

These encroachments relate to (i) the authorization of the Commission's report (allowing it to be 'published'), and (ii) the extent of consultation in which the Commission is required to engage before adopting measures for inclusion in its report. Under article 59(1) of the Charter, all 'measures' taken within chapter III, dealing with inter-state and individual communications, remain 'confidential' until the Assembly decides that they may be made public. On no occasion did the OAU Assembly exercise this discretion to stall the publication of the Commission's report. It refrained from using its article 59 powers despite the inclusion of numerous findings of serious violations by member states—most probably motivated more by disinterest than by considerations of contrition. A technical interpretation of the provision suggests that the Commission's activities may be categorized neatly as either 'promotional' or 'protective'. Article 59(1) principally covers the latter category, which comprises findings on communications, as well as reports of protective fact-finding missions or visits undertaken under article 46, which also fall within chapter III. Excluded from the possibility of withholding publication are all other measures, broadly described as 'promotional', which include the adoption of resolutions, reports of Special Rapporteurs, and the conclusions adopted at the end of examining state reports.

The inroads into established practice came in three phases.[151]

The first step backwards relates to the Commission's competence to issue reports as a result of fact-finding missions. In the past, the Commission undertook such missions and included reports on them in its activity reports after the state had been provided with an opportunity to provide its views on the mission report.[152]

At the first session where the Executive Council considered the Commission's activity report, in June 2004, the Zimbabwean Minister of Foreign Affairs raised an objection to the publication of the report on the basis that the Zimbabwean government did not have an opportunity to respond to the Commission's fact-finding

---

[150] See Section B.1 above; Decision on the 16th Annual Activity Report of the African Commission on Human and Peoples' Rights, AU Doc Assembly/AU/Dec.11(II).

[151] See M Killander, 'Confidentiality versus Publicity: Interpreting Article 59 of the African Charter on Human and Peoples' Rights' (2006) 6 *AHRLJ* 572.

[152] See eg Report on the Mission of Good Offices to Senegal of the African Commission on Human and Peoples' Rights, 1–7 June 1996, Annex VIII to the Commission's Tenth Activity Report.

report to Zimbabwe, contained in the Commission's 17th Activity Report.[153] After an acrimonious debate, involving the Chair of the African Commission, the Executive Council decided to withhold its authority for the publication of the report until the Zimbabwean government (and other states) had an opportunity to reply.[154] At the subsequent session, the 17th Activity Report, which by then included the Zimbabwean response, was approved.[155] However, an unfortunate consequence was that the *whole* activity report was withheld from public scrutiny for a period of some six months, pending the inclusion of the state's comments. In principle, Zimbabwe was entitled to raise the *audi alteram partem* argument, but in the specific circumstances, where there were clear indications that the government had already been granted an opportunity to respond, the Executive Council's decision to suspend publication allowed too much deference and leeway to the state.

The second inroad relates to the Commission's mandate to adopt resolutions.[156] In the past, the Commission routinely included both thematic[157] and country-specific[158] resolutions in its activity reports. State representatives similarly raised objections to the publication of these resolutions contained in the African Commission's 19th Activity Report due to the fact that they were not given an opportunity to express their 'views' on them. Confirming the decision of the Executive Council that accepted the state representatives' arguments, the Assembly decided to authorize publication of everything contained in the activity report, with the exception of the resolutions on Eritrea, Ethiopia, Sudan, Uganda, and Zimbabwe.[159] These states were given three months to provide their views on the resolutions; and the African Commission was required to 'submit a Report thereon to the next Ordinary Session of the Executive Council'.[160] Going one step further, the decision called on the African Commission to 'ensure that in future, it enlists the responses of all states parties to its Resolutions and Decisions before submitting them to the Executive Council and/or Assembly for consideration'.[161]

With one sweep, the Assembly, following the advice of the Council,[162] obliterated the carefully drawn distinction in article 59(1) between 'promotional' activities (such as resolutions) and 'protective' measures (decisions and protective missions). Resolutions are in principle adopted on matters of urgency, informed by circumstances and the available information, to focus attention on a matter of immediate

[153] F Viljoen, 'Recent Developments in the African Regional Human Rights System' (2004) 4 *AHRLJ* 344.

[154] AU Doc EX.CL/Dec.155(V).

[155] AU Doc Assembly/AU/Dec.56(IV), Decision on 17th Annual Activity Report of the African Commission on Human and Peoples' Rights.   [156] African Charter, art 45(1).

[157] See eg Resolution on the HIV/AIDS Pandemic—Threats against Human Rights and Humanity, adopted at the Commission's 29th session, 23 April–7 May 2001.

[158] See eg Resolution on the Situation of Human Rights Defenders in Tunisia, adopted at the Commission's 29th session, 23 April–7 May 2001, in which the Commission expresses the 'problem' of the suspension of the *Ligue Tunisienne de Défense des Droits de l'Homme*.

[159] AU Doc Assembly/AU/Dec.101(VI), Decision on the 19th Activity Report of the African Commission on Human and Peoples' Rights, para 1.   [160] ibid, para 2.

[161] ibid, para 3.   [162] AU Doc EX.CL/Dec.257(VIII).

concern. Their adoption does not amount to findings of violation. The mere fact that NGOs lobbied the Commission to adopt a particular resolution, or that the Commission relied on a draft resolution adopted at the NGO Forum preceding the Commission's session, does not detract from the Commission's role as independent expert body assessing the human rights situation in Africa. Obtaining the views of states prior to the adoption and publication of resolutions runs counter to the established procedure of the Commission, comparative practice of other international human rights bodies, and undermines the purpose of adopting resolutions.

However, it may be argued that some country-specific resolutions go further than being merely 'promotional' in nature. When they amount to 'decisions' on the merits of a specific country-situation, resolutions correspond closely with the Commission's protective mandate, even if they masquerade as part of the promotional mandate. As such, states argue that they are entitled to a hearing before these 'resolution-communications' are adopted, on the basis of the *audi alteram partem* principle. This line of argument is bolstered when such resolutions purport to make specific findings about human rights violations,[163] and when such resolutions are based very closely on recommendations adopted at NGO workshop or otherwise submitted to Commissioners by civil society organizations.[164] As a way of ensuring adherence to this principle, the African Commission could use the public sessions to solicit the views of states. So far, states have in any event used this opportunity, but usually to deny blankly all allegations against them.

Very elaborate government responses were attached to these resolutions in the Commission's 20th Activity Report, which was adopted in June 2006.[165] One state, Eritrea, did not make use of the opportunity to respond. As a consequence, the resolution in respect of Eritrea is effectively still under embargo, as it was not included with the others in the 20th Activity Report. This omission illustrates how states may manipulate the additional leeway granted to them. It is not clear what the reason was for omitting the Eritrean resolution. Once the time limit to respond has expired—as it has in this instance—the resolution should have been made public.

The third encroachment came when the Executive Council tabled the Commission's 20th Activity Report in June 2006, and Zimbabwe objected to the inclusion of a 'decision' on the merits of a case. Not making the same mistake of throwing out the baby with the bath-water, the Executive Council authorized the publication of the 20th Activity Report of the African Commission, with the exception of the decision on communication 245/2002 against Zimbabwe.[166] The period

---

[163] See Resolution on the Situation of Human Rights in Ethiopia, Annex III to the Commission's 20th Activity Report, which 'deplores the killing of civilians during confrontation with security forces'.

[164] See eg the Response by the Government of Zimbabwe to the Resolution adopted by the Commission at its 38th session (Annex III to the Commission's 20th Activity Report), in which the government argues that the Commission's resolution echoes and is 'an improper reproduction' of a proposal by Amnesty International (para 3.6).

[165] AU Doc EX.CL/Dec.310(IX), Decision on the Activity Report of the African Commission on Human and Peoples' Rights.   [166] ibid, para 1.

given to Zimbabwe to provide its 'observations' was reduced to two months. Disconcertingly, the Executive Council went one step further, by instituting a rule that all states against whom a violation had been found, should within two months 'following the reception of African Commission's notification' submit their observations on the decisions to the Executive Council or the Assembly.[167]

This step represents the clearest inroad yet, and is certainly illustrative of a regressive tendency. The requirement that states have to provide their observations on decisions flies in the face of the communications procedure developed under the African Charter. Under the Commission's Rules of Procedure, states are given two opportunities to respond during the consideration of communications: once on the issue of admissibility,[168] and once on the merits of the allegations.[169] In addition, a practice has been institutionalized of allowing both the complainant and the respondent state to be present at the Commission's hearing and to present oral arguments. The failure of states to make use of these opportunities has been a frequent cause of disquiet on the part of the Commission. In the absence of a response from the state, the Commission follows the approach, adopted by similar bodies, of proceeding to make a finding on the facts before it. The Executive Council's decision, which nullifies this well-established and fair procedure by providing states with yet another chance for comment, only serves to duplicate opportunities available to states and will lead to further delay in bringing an already protracted process to finality.

The Commission should engage the Executive Council on this issue. If it is left unchallenged, it is possible that similar obstacles may also be put in the way of the African Human Rights Court. The Commission should use the greater engagement of the Executive Council as an opportunity to involve the Council in the follow-up to its findings, for instance by devoting part of its activity reports to directing the Council's attention to the substantive issues at stake and to recommending 'decisions it would like to see the Executive Council take concerning the promotion and protection of human rights'.[170] This approach could lead to the Executive Council breaking the formulaic mould of decisions taken on the basis of the Commission's activity reports.

The Executive Council's involvement with the African Commission has not been all doom and gloom, though. Its involvement in the election of members of the African Commission and African Children's Rights Committee improved the independence of these bodies.[171] Its initial decision on the Commission's 17th

---

[167] ibid, para 3.

[168] Rules of Procedure, r 119(2): states must within three months, 'submit in writing to the Commission, explanations or statements elucidating the issue under consideration'.

[169] Rules of Procedure, r 120(1).

[170] I Kane, 'The African Commission on Human and Peoples' Rights and the New Organs of the African Union' in L Wohlgemuth and E Sall (eds), *Human Rights, Regionalism and the Dilemmas of Democracy in Africa* (Dakar: CODESRIA, 2006) 160.

[171] Under r 5(f) of its Rules of Procedure, the Executive Council is responsible for electing the members to these bodies (see Kane (n 170 above) 157).

Activity Report represents 'the first time that a political organ of the AU urged the member states to comply with the decisions of the Commission'.[172] In its decision on the Commission's 20th Activity Report, the Council urged states to ratify the Protocol to the African Charter on Human and Peoples' Rights Relating to the Rights of Women in Africa, emphasized the need for the AU Commission to allocate adequate human and financial resources to the African Commission, and urged states which have not yet done so, to submit and present their state reports to the African Commission.[173]

Clearly concerned with the lack of action taken in response to its decisions concerning resource-allocation to the African Commission, the Council requested the Chairperson of the AU Commission to report on the implementation of its decision on the Commission's 21st Activity Report at the Council's next session.[174] In this decision, the Council once more called on the AU Commission 'to allocate adequate resources' to the Commission, and to set up a voluntary human rights fund.[175]

3 Permanent Representatives' Committee

Aimed at establishing common positions and areas of disagreement, the PRC's detailed discussions serve to ease the burden on the Executive Council, to which it usually reports. The PRC also provides an important link between the AU and member states. It is through the PRC that members may place national concerns onto continental agendas. In the European Union (EU), the Committee of Permanent Representatives (COREPER) plays a similar role. At any given time, approximately 300 sub-committees report to the EU Council of Ministers through the filter of COREPER.[176] Many decisions affecting human rights that are finally taken by the Executive Council or Assembly are initially debated by the PRC.

4 AU Commission

Previously the OAU Secretariat, the AU Commission operates as the functional heart of the AU and is responsible for the day-to-day operations of the AU. The AU Commission is headed by a Chairperson, who is elected by the Assembly. Even if the position of the Chairperson of the AU Commission is not given prominence in the AU Constitutive Act, the Chairperson's constant presence in Addis Ababa and involvement in almost all AU activities make this position immeasurably important—also as far as human rights are concerned. The first Chairperson was the former President of Mali, Alpha Konaré, and the Deputy-Chairperson was Patrick Mazimhaka, from Rwanda.[177]

---

172 Killander (n 151 above) 575.   173 AU Doc EX.CL/Dec.310(IX) para 4.
174 AU Doc EX.CL/Dec.344(X) para 2(x).   175 ibid, paras iii and vi.
176 TC Salmon, 'The Structure, Institutions, and Powers of the EU' in Gower (n 47 above) 16, 24.
177 Elections for these two positions, as well as those of the AU Commissioners, are held in July 2007.

The AU Commission further consists of eight Commissioners, also appointed by the Assembly, each in control of a Department. Regional and gender representation guide the appointment of Commissioners.[178] This requirement resulted in the appointment of five female Commissioners, making the Commission the 'first AU organ to achieve gender parity'.[179] The subregional allocation was as follows: one Commissioner each from western and eastern Africa; and two from each of the northern, central, and southern regions.[180] Taking into account that the Chairperson and Deputy Chairperson hail from western and eastern Africa, it appears that a formal (two-regions-each) rather than a substantive approach (weighted according to countries per region) was followed. Elections of new members of the AU Commission take place in July 2007.[181]

Two AU Commissioners are of particular significance to human rights. They are the Commissioner for Political Affairs (under whom the African Commission falls) and the Commissioner for Social Affairs (responsible for the African Children's Rights Committee).[182] The Political Affairs Department concerns itself with democratization, governance, the rule of law, and human rights. The Commissioner for Political Affairs manages the African Commission administratively and financially at the level of the AU. In her capacity as Commissioner for Political Affairs, Ms Julia Joiner regularly attended the African Commission's sessions. The Political Affairs Department is divided into branches (or 'Divisions'), including the following: the Democracy, Governance, Human Rights, and Elections Division; the Humanitarian Affairs, Refugees, and Displaced Persons Division (HARDP); and the African Commission on Human and Peoples' Rights. The Social Affairs Department concerns itself with issues relating to social welfare. The objective of the department is to promote and intensify collective efforts for sustained development. Issues of disability, the elderly, health, shelter, reproductive, and employment rights and responsibilities fall within the remit of this department.

The relationship between the African Commission and the Commissioner for Political Affairs requires a delicate balancing act. On the one hand, the Commission's independence in proposing a budget and executing its activities should be respected; on the other hand, the Commissioner has to take political responsibility for the Commission within the AU Commission, while taking into account the demands

---

[178] Statutes of the AU Commission, art 6(2) and 6(3).

[179] K Stefiszyn, 'The African Union: Challenges and Opportunities for Women' (2005) 5 *AHRLJ* 358, 365.

[180] The countries comprising each of Africa's five regions are as follows: *Western Africa—16 members:* Benin, Burkina Faso, Cape Verde, Côte d'Ivoire, The Gambia, Ghana, Guinea, Guinea-Bissau, Liberia, Mali, Mauritania, Niger, Nigeria, Senegal, Sierra Leone, Togo; *Central Africa—nine members:* Burundi, Cameroon, Central African Republic, Chad, DRC, Equatorial Guinea, Gabon, Republic of Congo, São Tomé e Príncipe; *Eastern Africa—13 members:* Comoros, Djibouti, Eritrea, Ethiopia, Kenya, Madagascar, Mauritius, Seychelles, Somalia, Sudan, Tanzania, Uganda, Rwanda; *Northern Africa—five members:* Algeria, Egypt, Libya, Saharawi Arab Democratic Republic, Tunisia; *Southern Africa—ten members:* Angola, Botswana, Lesotho, Malawi, Mozambique, Namibia, South Africa, Swaziland, Zambia, Zimbabwe.   [181] AU Doc EX.CL/Dec.281(IX).

[182] See also Lloyd and Murray (n 11 above) 175.

of other issues under her portfolio. So far, the political control by and involvement of the Political Affairs Department in human rights, generally, and the work of the African Commission, in particular, have been minimal. In 2006, there was only one AU Commission staff member, seconded by the OHCHR, who dealt with human rights matters. More 'professional human rights officers with appropriate experience' should be recruited to the Political Affairs Department.[183]

Human rights-related issues are by no means the preserve of only two departments. The intersection between human rights and conflict prevention highlights the role of the Peace and Security Department. Socio-economic rights feature in the mandate of the Labour and Social Affairs Department. Refugee issues fall under the remit of the Directorate of Humanitarian Affairs, where the Commission on Refugees and the Coordinating Committee on Assistance to and Protection to Refugees, Returnees and Internally Displaced Persons in Africa (CCAR) are located.[184] The Legal Affairs Department plays a supporting role, especially in drafting legal documents and other texts. It was crucial in setting up the African Children's Rights Committee. Previously, as the Legal Division, this Department was part of the Political Affairs Department. Institutionally located directly under the Chairperson, the Women, Gender and Development Directorate coordinates all gender-related programmes of the AU Commission.[185] The mandates and activities of other departments and directorates within the AU Commission that also deal with human rights should be integrated into a comprehensive human rights response. One of the weaknesses of the division of competences is that no department is devoted to human rights. In theory, human rights may be 'cross-cutting', but in practice the division of competences among departments inevitably occasions further fragmentation of human rights.

5 Peace and Security Council (PSC)

Very soon after the AU Constitutive Act entered into force, the Peace and Security Council (PSC) became the first organ to be added to those already listed in the Act.[186] States ratified its founding Protocol with greater urgency than those of the AU organs, securing its entry into force on 26 December 2003. By 31 December 2006, 41 states had become members of the PSC. (See Table 5.1 below.) The PSC

[183] Retreat Report (n 3 above) para IV.
[184] The African Commission should enhance the 'cooperation already established between the Special Rapporteur on Refugees, IDPs and Asylum Seekers in Africa and the Division on Refugees, IDPs and Humanitarian Affairs of the AU' (Brainstorming meeting (n 1 above), para 66(i)).
[185] Statutes of the AU Commission, art 12(3); see Stefiszyn (n 179 above) 365.
[186] Under art 5(2) of the AU Constitutive Act; by the Protocol relating to the establishment of the Peace and Security Council, adopted at the first AU Assembly session, on 9 July 2002, Durban, South Africa, AU Doc ASS/AU/Dec.3(I), para 3: Decision on the Establishment of the Peace and Security Council of the African Union. See generally J Cilliers and K Sturman, 'Challenges Facing the AU's Peace and Security Council' (2004) 13 *African Security Review* 97. The AU Constitutive Act will only reflect the existence of the PSC as an AU organ once the Protocol on Amendments to the AU Constitutive Act has entered into force (see art 5 of the amending protocol, n 130 above).

replaces the Mechanism for Conflict Prevention, Management and Resolution in Africa, which was set up in 1993 under the Cairo Declaration.

The PSC is a 'standing decision-making organ for the prevention, management and resolution of conflicts'.[187] It is supplemented by a Panel of the Wise, a Continental Early Warning System, an African Standby Force and a Special Fund. Some of these institutions have not yet been made fully functional.[188] Rooted in traditional African culture's respect for the authority and wisdom of elders, the Panel of the Wise is made up of five 'highly respected African personalities'.[189] Its function is to provide an advisory voice to the PSC. Prevention of conflict depends on accurate and timely information. For this reason, an observation and monitoring centre is set up within the AU Commission to collect and analyse data on the basis of indicators.[190] Members must designate part of their military force to be on 'standby' to join PSC peace missions. Once deployed, these contingents make up the African Standby Force. To defray the cost of such missions, a Peace Fund is set up. It depends on contributions from the AU budget, voluntary contributions, and fund-raising.

The PSC functions at four levels. Meeting most frequently, the Permanent Representatives of each member based at the AU headquarters form the nerve centre of the PSC. One level higher, the relevant ministers of members meet less frequently. At the highest level, and meeting at least once per year, members are represented by their heads of state or government. Acting in an advisory capacity, senior military officers of members make up the last level, the Military Staff Committee.

To ensure its effective functioning, it was decided that the membership of the PSC should be smaller than that of the AU. Inspired no doubt by the number of seats on the UN Security Council, the membership was set at 15: ten members elected for two years, and five for three years. Members may be immediately re-elected. The AU Assembly (and not states party to the PSC Protocol) elects these members. The factors guiding this electoral process may lead to conflict and contradiction. On the one hand, the principles of 'equitable regional representation' and 'rotation' have to be observed. Rigid adherence to the first of these principles would entail that each of the five regions in Africa is represented by three states. However, as often in the past, representation is based on the 3-3-3-2-4 principle, with the

[187] PSC Protocol, art 2(1).
[188] See AU Doc Assembly/AU/Dec.120(VII), in which the Assembly requests the Peace and Security Council to ensure 'the establishment and the effective functioning of the Panel of the Wise as well as the establishment of the Continental Early-Warning System and the African Defense Force with a view to giving the Continent the required structure and means to meet the challenge of peace and security in Africa'.
[189] PSC Protocol, art 11(2). The members who were elected in January 2007 (AU Doc Assembly/AU/Dec.152(VIII)) comprise respected elderly statesmen (Salim Ahmed Salim, former Secretary-General of the Organization of African Unity (East Africa), Ahmed Ben Bella, former President of Algeria (North Africa), and Miguel Trovoada, former President of São Tomé e Príncipe (Central Africa)); and respected women who head reputable domestic institutions (Brigalia Bam, Chairperson of the Independent Electoral Commission of South Africa (Southern Africa), and Elisabeth K Pognon, President of the Constitutional Court of Benin (West Africa)).　　　　[190] PSC Protocol, art 12(4).

more populous West Africa entitled to representation above the mean at the expense of the Northern region. On the other hand, the Assembly is guided by substantive considerations, most importantly the prospective members' track-record of respect for constitutionalism, the rule of law, and human rights.[191] This requirement is revolutionary, as it provides the first normative gate-keeping measure for membership of an AU organ. Other factors relate to the capacity of aspirant states to function effectively as a member and are based on prior involvement in African peace-keeping processes.

The first 15 states that were intially elected were Lesotho, Mozambique, and South Africa (Southern Africa); Ethiopia, Kenya, and the Sudan (East Africa); Cameroon, the DRC, and Gabon (Central Africa); Ghana, Nigeria, Senegal, and Togo (West Africa); and Algeria and Libya (North Africa).[192] When the two-year terms of ten members expired,[193] Botswana and Malawi replaced Lesotho and Mozambique; Congo replaced the DRC; Rwanda and Uganda replaced Kenya and Sudan; Burkina Faso replaced Togo; and Egypt replaced Libya.[194] While the respect for human rights and constitutionalism of some of these states may be questioned, the majority of states are generally viewed relatively favourably.[195]

Departing from the premise that there is an important link between peace, security, and human rights, the PSC Protocol in numerous respects stresses the importance of human rights. Included among the PSC's objectives and principles is the protection of human rights and fundamental freedoms and respect for human life.[196] Human rights must also be part of the training of PSC civilian and military personnel.[197] As part of its peace-building activities, the PSC must assist member states with 'social and economic reconstruction', demobilization and reintegration especially of child soldiers, resettlement of refugees and internally displaced persons, and must provide assistance to 'vulnerable persons, including children, the elderly, women and other traumatized groups'.[198] However, the African Charter is not referred to by name among the PSC's 'guiding principles', despite the fact that the Universal Declaration of Human Rights is mentioned.[199] This is not only surprising because the African Charter is the main continental human rights treaty, but also because the Universal Declaration is not binding, as such, while the African

---

[191] PSC Protocol, art 5(2)(g).

[192] Wikipedia <http://en.wikipedia.org/wiki/African_Union> (31 July 2006).

[193] AU Doc Assembly/AU/Dec.106(VI), Decision on Election of Ten (10) Members of the Peace and Security Council of the African Union following the results of the election conducted by the Executive Council.

[194] South Africa (South), Ethiopia (East), Gabon (Central), Nigeria (West), and Algeria (North) served for three-year terms. As of March 2007, South Africa will be replaced by Angola, while the other states will again serve for a three-year term (AU Doc Assembly/AU/Dec.149(VIII)).

[195] Six of the ten African members of the UN Human Rights Council are represented on the PSC: Algeria, Cameroon, Ghana, Nigeria, Senegal, and South Africa.

[196] PSC Protocol, arts 3(f) and 4(c).   [197] ibid, art 13(13).   [198] ibid, art 14(3).

[199] ibid, art 4: the PSC 'shall be guided' by the AU Constitutive Act, the UN Charter, and the Universal Declaration of Human Rights.

Charter binds all AU members. In terms similar to those of the AU Constitutive Act, the PSC Protocol reiterates principles that may occasionally conflict with international human rights, such as respect for territorial integrity, non-interference in the domestic affairs of states, and respect for borders achieved at independence.[200]

A reciprocal relationship between the PSC and the African Commission on Human and Peoples' Rights is envisaged,[201] reinforcing the role of human rights as a 'key tool for promoting collective security, durable peace and sustainable development',[202] on the one hand, and the need for peace and stability as a necessary condition for sustainable realization of especially socio-economic rights, on the other.

The PSC must seek to involve the African Commission in its activities.[203] It may, for example, invite the Commission to take part in its discussions or may request the Commission to undertake studies or on-site missions on its behalf. In 2004, when a deadlock occurred in the implementation of the Linas-Marcoussis Agreement and the situation in Côte d'Ivoire continued to deteriorate, the PSC, meeting at the level of heads of state and government, 'reiterated' its request to the African Commission to 'carry out an investigation into human rights violations' in the conflict-torn country.[204] In the same communiqué, the PSC 'endorsed' the initiative of the UN Commission on Human Rights 'to set up a Commission to investigate the human rights violations perpetrated since the beginning of the crisis'.[205] It is a cause for regret that the African mechanism needed to be prodded into action on a matter of grave concern to the continent, while a UN body had already initiated action.

For its part, the African Commission must bring relevant information to the attention of the PSC.[206] This information may be sourced from the initial and periodic state reports, reports by the Commission's thematic Special Rapporteurs after visits to AU member states, on-site promotional and protective missions, statements made during its public sessions, and from communications submitted to the Commission, while bearing in mind the confidentiality requirement. At the very least, the Commission should on a consistent basis submit its activity report, in which relevant information and possible steps are foregrounded, before the PSC. When issues of conflict, peace and security are addressed in concluding observations to state reports, in resolutions, in the text of finalized communications, and

[200] PSC Protocol, art 2(e), (f), (g), and (i).   [201] ibid, art 19.

[202] Grand Baie Declaration, n 105 above, Preamble.

[203] ibid: it must 'seek close cooperation' with the African Commission 'in *all* matters relevant to its objectives and mandate' (emphasis added).

[204] AU Doc PSC/AHG/Comm.(X), 25 May 2004, para 4. See also the Report of the Chairperson of the AU Commission on the Situation in Côte d'Ivoire, AU Doc PSC/PR/3(V), para 40 (indicating the Chairperson's intent to request the African Commission to 'join the ongoing efforts to determine what contribution it can make in combating impunity and promoting human rights').

[205] ibid.

[206] PSC Protocol, art 19: the African Commission must 'bring to the attention' of the PSC 'any information relevant to its objectives and mandate'.

in other pertinent reports, these should immediately be brought to the attention of the PSC.

The African Commission's activities most clearly overlap with those of the PSC when dealing with massive or serious human rights violations. Under the African Charter, the African Commission is mandated to bring such cases to the attention of the AU Assembly.[207] However, given the evolution of the AU organs, the PSC should become the first port of call on these issues.[208] Information obtained in the course of undertaking promotional visits should be communicated to the PSC in order to work out joint strategies to forestall the escalation of human rights violations into more serious conflict. The African Commission is also best placed to inform a decision of the PSC, and ultimately the Assembly, about possible intervention in a member state on the basis of 'grave circumstances'.[209] Such a decision needs to be justified on reliable information and an informed analysis indicating whether the human rights violations amount to 'war crimes, genocide and crimes against humanity'.

In cases of great urgency, the Commission may recommend provisional measures to 'avoid irreparable damage being caused to the victim of the alleged violation'.[210] In order to enhance compliance with these measures, the PSC should become the Commission's political arm, exerting pressure to improve compliance.[211] When these measures relate to the substantive issues under the mandate of the PSC, the Commission should communicate their terms to the PSC. Non-compliance with these orders may be a root cause of conflict in a society, and should be addressed by the PSC.

The half-hearted embrace of civil society characteristic of the AU's attempts at including 'the African people' in its activities also transpires from the PSC Protocol. Civil society involvement is not alluded to in either the PSC's objectives or principles. As an afterthought, participation of civil society—particularly women—is encouraged, and provided for in theory. However, an 'invitation' by the PSC is required before such organizations may 'address' the Council.[212]

The PSC has been actively exercising its assigned mandate. Apprised of an unconstitutional change of government in Togo, the PSC for the first time declared its determination to impose sanctions under article 7(g) of the PSC Protocol,[213] and later suspended the *de facto* authorities from 'participation in the activities of all the organs of the AU until such a time when constitutional legality is restored'.[214]

---

[207] African Charter, art 58(1).   [208] See Kindiki (n 128 above) 115.
[209] AU Constitutive Act, art 4(h).   [210] African Commission's Rules of Procedure, r 111(1).
[211] See also Brainstorming Meeting (n 1 above), para 48(a) (The African Commission should 'explore the possibility' of the PSC enforcing the decisions of the Commission 'within the framework of' art 19 of the PSC Protocol).   [212] PSC Protocol, art 20.
[213] See DL Tehindrazanarivelo, 'Les sanctions de l'Union africaine contre les coups d'état et autres changements anticonstitutionels de gouvernement: potentialités et mesures de renforcement' (2004) 12 *AYBIL* 255, 277.
[214] AU Doc PSC/PR/Comm(XXV), 25 February 2005, para 3. Communiqué of the 25th meeting of the PSC.

After the Constitutional Court had proclaimed the official results of a subsequent democratic election, the PSC decided that the conditions for Togo's resumption had been fulfilled and mandated the lifting of the suspension.[215] The PSC has also been involved in Burundi, Comoros, Liberia, the Democratic Republic of Congo (DRC), Guinea-Bissau,[216] Sudan, and Côte d'Ivoire,[217] 'in spite of the delay in the implementation of the Roadmap adopted by the Ivorian Government in February 2006'.[218] It has been credited for its contributions towards the reconciliation process in the Comoros (which contributed to the holding of the April–May 2006 presidential elections), for its role in the elections in the DRC as part of the transition period, for its involvement in Mauritania,[219] leading to the Constitutional Referendum of 25 June 2006 and multi-party elections for the National Assembly in November 2006, generally regarded as free and fair; and for positive developments in Burundi, with the signing on 18 June 2006 of the Dar-es-Salaam Principles of Agreement.

The situation in Darfur posed the biggest challenge to the PSC. After the adoption of the 8 April 2004 Humanitarian Ceasefire Agreement, which includes commitments not to attack civilians, by the government of Sudan, the Sudan Liberation Army (SLA) and the Justice and Equality Movement (JEM), in N'Djamena, an AU Ceasefire Commission of 60 officers, later protected by a force of 350 soldiers essentially from Nigeria and Rwanda, started to monitor violations of the ceasefire. This was followed by a decision to employ the African Mission in Sudan (AMIS), consisting of observers, military personnel, and police officers, mandated to protect civilians under 'imminent threat and in the immediate vicinity' and 'within resources and capability'.[220] At 1 September 2006, the strength of AMIS stood at 7,200 personnel, 541 short of its authorized strength.[221] In the light of especially logistical and financial limitations, the PSC decided that AMIS should by 30 September 2006 be replaced by a UN peace-keeping operation.[222] Due to reluctance on the part of the Sudanese government to accept a UN operation on

---

[215] AU Doc PSC/PR/Comm(XXX), 27 May 2005, para 3, Communiqué of the 30th meeting of the PSC.

[216] Concern for human rights transpire from the AU Chairperson's report to the PSC on this situation, noting for example 'numerous cases of human rights violations' (AU Doc PSC/PR/2(XXXI), 8 June 2005); this observation could have been brought to the attention of and should have been the subject of a recommendation to the African Commission.

[217] See eg AU Doc Assembly/AU/Decl.3(VI), Declaration on the Activities of the Peace and Security Council of the African Union and the State of Peace and Security in Africa.

[218] AU Doc Assembly/AU/Dec.120(VII), Decision on the Activities of the Peace and Security Council of the African Union on the Peace and Security Situation in Africa.

[219] Acting immediately after the coup d'état, the PSC suspended the participation of Mauritania in AU activities 'until the reinstatement of constitutional order in that country' (AU Doc PSC/PR/Stat.(XXXVI), 4 August 2004).

[220] AU Doc Communiqué PSC/PR/Comm(XVII), 20 October 2004.

[221] Report of the Chairperson of the Commission on the Situation in Darfur, AU Doc PSC/MIN/2(LXIII), 18 September 2006, para 23.

[222] AU Doc PSC/MIN/Comm(LXV), 10 March 2006, para 3, Communiqué of the 46th meeting of the PSC.

the basis that the UN mission would undermine Sudanese sovereignty, the mandate of AMIS was extended to the end of 2006.[223] Even when a UN operation is in place, the AU would retain the lead role in the overall Darfur peace process.[224] Within its limitations, AMIS has undeniably been the 'largest and most demanding peace support operation' in the AU's history and has to some extent contributed to 'further the cause of peace, security and stability' in Darfur.[225]

6 African Peer Review Mechanism (APRM)

NEPAD's APRM is a voluntary process of submission to review by 'peers' (fellow heads of state) of a country's record in political, economic, and corporate governance. Its substantive basis is the Declaration on Democracy, Political, Economic and Corporate Governance (Democracy and Governance Declaration),[226] an aspirational and not a legally binding instrument, which sets out the principles to which the participating states agree to adhere. Primarily a codification of existing standards adopted by the OAU/AU and other international organizations such as the UN, the Democracy and Governance Declaration accords 'an importance and urgency all of its own' to human rights.[227] Its ideological basis is neo-liberal and free market-oriented;[228] and it is premised on the notion that good governance and democracy will lead to the alleviation of poverty. The philosophy of 'peer review' is aimed at a 'constructive dialogue' between equals, and derives from the self-imposed commitment of states to take 'national ownership' of a rigorous process of 'self-assessment'.[229] The process allows participating states to identify weaknesses in governance and to benefit from shared experience in devising strategies to overcome these weaknesses, set out in a national Programme of Action.[230] States voluntarily accept the APRM process by signing a Memorandum of Understanding on the APRM (MOU).[231] By 31 December 2006, 25 states had signed the MOU.[232]

Taking ultimate political responsibility for the APRM process, the participating Heads of State and Government (known as the APRM Forum) discuss reports and take a final decision at the end of a review.[233] The 'peer review' is preceded by a

---

[223] AU Doc PSC/MIN/Comm(LXIII).
[224] AU Doc PSC/MIN/Comm(LXV), 10 March 2006, para 6, Communiqué of the 46th meeting of the PSC.
[225] AU Doc PSC/MIN/2(LXIII), 18 September 2006, para 98, Report of the Chairperson of the Commission on the Situation in Darfur.   [226] OAU/AU Doc AHG/235(XXXVIII), Annex I.
[227] Democracy and Governance Declaration, para 10
[228] K Appiagyei-Atua, 'Bumps on the Road: A Critique of How Africa Got to NEPAD' (2006) 6 *AHRLJ* 524, 545.
[229] APRM, Country Review Report of Ghana, June 2005, <http://www.nepad.org/aprm/>, 12.
[230] Communiqué of the 15th meeting of the APRM Panel of Eminent Persons, 19–29 January 2006, Sudan.
[231] Memorandum of Understanding on the African Peer Review Mechanism, NEPAD Doc NEPAD/HSGIC/03-2003/APRM/MOU, adopted by the NEPAD HSGIC, 9 March 2003.
[232] See Table 5.1 below. São Tomé e Príncipe signed the MOU in 2007.
[233] NEPAD: The African Peer Review Mechanism, OAU/AU Doc AHG/235(XXXVIII), Annex II (APRM Base Document) para 23.

technical assessment, undertaken by a member of the Panel of Eminent Persons,[234] with the assistance of an ARPM Secretariat based in Midrand, South Africa, and 'African experts', which oversee the running of the review process.

The review process, which is set out in detail in the APRM Base Document,[235] is not a one-off event, but extends over five stages. As at December 2006, four states (Ghana, Rwanda, South Africa, and Kenya) have either been reviewed or were in the process of being reviewed. Ghana was the first country to be reviewed, and in this discussion serves as the principal illustration of the rather protracted APRM process, although insights gained from other countries are also included.

A precondition for the APR process is the existence of a national APRM coordinating structure.[236] A 'support mission' is undertaken to a state that prepares itself for review. Ghana created a Ministry of Regional Cooperation and NEPAD in May 2003. This Ministry became the designated APRM focal point.[237] Dr Stals, one of the members of the Panel of Eminent Persons, coordinated the Ghana review process and led a preparatory visit to Ghana in May 2004.

The review proper starts with two studies of the situation in the country (stage 1), aimed at assessing how the country measures up to the Democracy and Governance Declaration: one by the state itself (the self-assessment); and one by the APRM Secretariat, relying on appropriate experts (the background paper).[238] A very detailed questionnaire (entitled 'Country Self-Assessment for the African Peer Review Mechanism') was developed to guide the process.[239] As far as the part on Democracy and Good Political Governance (section 1), parts of Corporate Governance (section 2), and Socio-Economic Development (section 4) are concerned, the potential overlap with state reporting under the African Charter and numerous UN human rights instruments is evident. Compliance with a long list of human rights instruments, including the African Charter and UN instruments under which states already have reporting obligations, is measured by indicators that outline legislative, policy, or institutional frameworks that have been put in place to give effect to these treaties.[240]

Ghana established a local team of esteemed and qualified experts to form a National APRM Governing Council.[241] This Council appointed four local research institutes as think-tanks, each tasked with conducting the assessment in its area of

---

[234] See APRM Base Document, paras 6–12. The Panel consists of Adebayo Adedeji (Nigeria), Marie-Angelique Savane (Senegal), Bethuel Kiplagat (Kenya), Dorothy Njeuma (Cameroon), Graça Machel (Mozambique), Mohammed Segir Babes (Algeria).   [235] APRM Base Document.

[236] See APRM, Country Review of Ghana June 2005 (n 229 above) 5–6.   [237] ibid.

[238] APRM Base Document (2003), para 18.

[239] Country Self-Assessment for the African Peer Review Mechanism (2004), which is based on 'Objectives, Standards, Criteria and Indicators for the APRM', NEPAD/HSGIC-03-2003/APRM/Guidelines/OSCI (9 March 2003).

[240] Country Self-Assessment for the African Peer Review Mechanism (2004), section I, para 3.

[241] APRM, Country Review Report of Ghana, June 2005, 5. This process may be contrasted with that followed in Rwanda, where the review team expressed concern about the number of government officials on the APRM National Commission, as well as the exclusion of civil society and other stakeholders and the lack of national ownership of the report (APRM, Country Review Report of the Republic of Rwanda, June 2006, <http://www.devpartners.gov.rw/docs/documents> (31 December 2006).

expertise.[242] A National Stakeholders' Forum, aimed at creating national ownership and at fostering national dialogue was also organized.[243] The final self-assessment, containing more than 1,200 pages, accompanied by a Draft Plan of Action, was submitted in May 2005.

The next phase (stage 2) is the Country Review Mission (CRM).[244] Armed with an Issue Paper prepared by the APRM Secretariat, as well as the country's self-assessment and Plan of Action, and assisted by independent technical consultants,[245] the APRM visit to Ghana took place from 4 to 16 April 2005. During the country review mission, the team met numerous stakeholders, including MPs, and travelled to regional capitals. The CRM satisfied itself that Ghana's self-assessment had been done autonomously and independently, and commended efforts to ensure 'broad-based participation'.[246] The quality of information was also a cause for praise, as concrete and specific country-issues were captured, resulting from 'in-depth surveys reflecting the view of ordinary Ghanaians'.[247]

In the next step (stage 3), the CRM's report is drafted, after which an opportunity for initial verification of factual accuracy is given to the government. Any such responses are attached to the report,[248] together with the revised Plan of Action. Following this process, the Country Review Report of the Republic of Ghana was finalized in June 2005. Attached to it as appendices were the Comments of the Government of Ghana, as well as four separate Programmes of Action, one for each of the four thematic areas. Each of the Programmes of Action was 'costed', together adding up to some \$5.6 billion, of which Democracy and Good Political Governance actions require by far the smallest proportion.

The CRM report on Kenya provides an example of the significance of human rights in the review process.[249] Not only is the status of UN and AU human rights reviewed and the realization of 'civil and political' and 'economic, social and cultural' rights analysed, but considerable attention is also devoted to the rights of particularly vulnerable groups (women, children, refugees, IDPs, and people living with disabilities). The report notes, amongst other findings, the lack of domestication of international norms, exemplified by the delay in adopting the Family and Domestic Violence Bill, and the lack of enforcement of these norms.[250] Recommendations pertaining to human rights are appropriately embedded in, but to some extent overshadowed by, broader concerns that impact on their realization, such as the rule of law, the independence of the judiciary, and corruption.

---

[242] APRM, Country Review Report of Ghana, June 2005, 6.

[243] APRM, Country Review Report of Ghana, June 2005, 7.

[244] APRM Base Document (2003) para 19.

[245] The team to Ghana consisted of 16 persons: seven independent technical experts, members from partner institutions, and staff from both the NEPAD and APRM Secretariats accompanied Dr Stals (Ghana Review Report, n 229 above, 8).

[246] APRM, Country Review Report of Ghana, June 2005, 10.   [247] ibid.

[248] APRM Base Document (2003) paras 20–2.

[249] APRM, Country Review Report of the Republic of Kenya, May 2006, <http://www. aprmkenya.org/downloads/Kenyareport.pdf> (30 September 2006).   [250] ibid 67–8.

The next phase (stage 4) is the actual peer-review process by the APRM Forum.[251] The Forum reviews the Mission Report, including the recommendations for future action, as well as the government reaction as it appears in its Programme of Action. The participating governments must take measures to assist the state if it 'shows a demonstrable will to rectify the identified shortcomings'.[252] Should the opposite be the case, the Forum members have to engage the recalcitrant state in 'constructive dialogue', and if that fails, unidentified 'appropriate measures' of 'last resort' may be utilized. In this way, the APRM integrates 'the political level of the AU/NEPAD in a way that other parts of the African human rights system have not done'.[253]

The final Ghanaian report was presented at the Forum meeting of June 2005. The participating leaders declined to undertake the 'peer review' there and then, as they first needed to study the Mission Report. When they met again, in January 2006, the report was discussed in the presence of Ghanaian President Kufuor. With little media interest, and no record of any pertinent insights shared or queries raised,[254] the final discussion appears—at least to an outside observer—largely to have been a non-event. An explanation for this state of affairs is that the 'peers' are engaged in 'implementation', away from the public eye, while the CRM report is made public. The Rwanda report was reviewed in June 2006, and the Kenyan report was presented at the same meeting.

Once the 'peer review' has been conducted, the report should be widely disseminated (stage 5).[255] Up to that point, the report remains a confidential document. The report must also be 'formally and publicly tabled' in the REC to which the state belongs, the African Commission, the PAP, the Peace and Security Council, and ECOSOCC. It is not clear why this should only happen 'six months after the report has been considered'. The use of the passive voice ('it should be tabled') also leaves the question open as to who bears the responsibility of 'tabling'. The reports on Ghana, Kenya, and Rwanda were tabled before the PAP in November 2006.

To some extent, the APRM overlaps with the African Commission's state reporting procedure. Both serve the underlying aim of ensuring a culture of adherence by African states with their commitments under internationally recognized standards. Both procedures allow the state an opportunity for 'introspection' (either in the form of the APRM self-assessment, or in the form of the state report submitted

---

[251] APRM Base Document (2003) paras 23–4.   [252] APRM Base Document (2003) para 24.
[253] C Heyns and M Killander, 'The African Regional Human Rights System' in F Gómez Isa and K De Feyter (eds), *International Protection of Human Rights: Achievements and Challenges* (Bilbao: University of Deusto, 2006) 509, 537.
[254] The Communiqué issued at the end of the Fourth Summit of the Committee of Participating Heads of State and Government in the APRM, 22 January 2006, Khartoum, Sudan (<http://www.nepad.org/2005/files/aprm/PressRelease05042006.pdf>) does not provide any evidence of critical engagement with the report; it notes only in very vague terms that Ghana presents many best practices from which other African states could benefit. It further underscores the importance of the financing the Programme of Action, and the potential role of 'development partners' (para 13).
[255] APRM Base Document (2003) para 25.

under article 62 of the African Charter); and both also provide for an independent assessment or 'inspection' (either by the Country Review Team, or the African Commission). Human rights may feature prominently in parts of the APRM review, but it constitutes the core of the African Commission's evaluation. There are important differences in the basis for the appraisal; the substantive content and scope of the review; and the nature and aim of the review process prevent the degree of overlap from becoming unacceptable.

The basis of the APR is the voluntary acceptance of the Declaration and the MOU, while state reporting is compulsory, resulting from the formal acceptance of binding treaty obligations. The scope of the APR process is much wider than that of the state reporting procedure under the African Charter. Even if the Women's Protocol is added to the Charter, the APRM process extends far wider than the review of the African Commission, by including the country's broader political structure, economic and corporate governance, and socio-economic development.[256]

The APRM 'review' itself, which also forms the public record of the process, is not undertaken by 'peers', but by the panel of independent technical experts. This stands in contrast to the peer-review *implementation* phase, where the situation in one country is ultimately reviewed by the heads of state of other countries. It is not qualities that are respected in African culture, such as wisdom and age, which qualify someone as a 'peer'—it is the fact of holding a particular political office. Although this aspect makes the APR process overtly political, it also ensures involvement at the highest government level, with a greater likelihood of 'political will' than state reporting, which often involves lower-ranking government officials. The APRM is also more flexible, and takes much longer and is more intensive than the state reporting procedure.

Although the APRM foresees the involvement of the African Commission, this has not happened in the first few reviews. Even if the aim and scope of the two exercises differ, the APRM should have engaged with the African Commission to seek synergies and to enhance the human rights aspect of its mandate. Ideally, a member of the African Commission (for example, the one to which the particular country has been assigned for 'promotional purposes') should form part of the Country Review Team.

Unnecessary overlap in the two processes should be avoided and cooperation should be improved.[257] As far as human rights are concerned, the state reporting process provides a more profound and better informed analysis, based on long-standing practice and an extensive legally binding basis. The African Commission's

---

[256] In its Declaration on Employment and Poverty Alleviation in Africa (n 33 above) para 14, the AU Assembly called for inclusion indicators on poverty alleviation and employment creation under the APRM.

[257] See Brainstorming Meeting (n 1 above) para 66(g) (The African Commission and APRM 'should formalise modalities of cooperation with the view to enabling' the African Commission to participate in the APRM process).

state reporting process does not include most aspects related to economic governance, management, and corporate governance.[258] One possibility of synergizing the two processes is to encourage 'simultaneous' reporting under the APRM and African Charter. This would allow for a holistic view and an integrated approach, and better coordination. To this end, states could be required to submit their reports under article 62 of the Charter as part of the APRM process. The Commission's examination, including its concluding observations, could then form part of the 'information package' of the Country Review Team. Such an integration of the African Commission's role would also require it to raise the level of its own performance and to issue concrete, meaningful, and timely concluding observations. Another possibility is to substitute article 62 state reporting in respect of APRM-participating countries with the 'tabling' of the Country Review Report, by adopting a similar process of questions to a high-level delegation, followed by concluding observations, on the basis of the APRM report.

One of the deficiencies of NEPAD and the APRM process is the lack of integration between the invocation of 'human rights' and the realization of development goals. As Manby argues, the objectives of development are not understood as being dependent on the existence of 'legally enforceable entitlement'.[259] This is particularly true of the goal of improving access to socio-economic 'services', such as health care and education. Building on the African Charter and the African Commission's jurisprudence, the social objectives should be defined as 'entitlements to services', framed as justiciable socio-economic rights. At the same time, the APRM provides a useful mechanism to hold participating states accountable for their lack of achieving sustainable development and to eradicate poverty in line with the MDGs.[260]

C Quasi-judicial and Judicial Functions

In a dramatic departure from the OAU Charter, the AU Constitutive Act introduced a judicial organ, the Court of Justice, alongside the African Human Rights Court, which was already established under the OAU to supplement the protective

---

[258] There is some overlap between 'corporate governance', as understood under NEPAD, and the African Charter, in respect of workers' rights and the protection of the environment (see Country Self-Assessment for the APRM, section 3, objective 2, dealing with 'human rights', 'social responsibility', and 'environmental sustainability', and in particular questions 1 and 3)

[259] B Manby, 'The African Union, NEPAD and Human Rights: The Missing Agenda' (2004) 4 *HRQ* 983, 1002. This is particularly true of the goal of improving access to socio-economic 'services', such as health and education. Building on the African Charter and the African Commission's jurisprudence, these social objectives should be defined as 'entitlements to these services', that is, as justiciable socio-economic rights. See also C Mbazira, 'A Path to Realising Economic, Social and Cultural Rights in Africa? A Critique of the New Partnership for Africa's Development' (2004) 4 *AHRLJ* 35.

[260] See eg Country Self-Assessment (n 239 above) section 4, Socio-Economic Development, objective 2.

mandate of the African Commission. The African Commission has been functioning as a quasi-judicial institution since 1987. In 2002, another quasi-judicial body, the African Children's Rights Committee, was inaugurated. The human rights mandates of these institutions should be coordinated to minimize overlaps and conflicts.

1 African Commission

The African Commission is the primary body responsible for human rights in the AU.[261] The Executive Council underlined this fact when it reaffirmed the 'primordial role' that the African Commission plays in promoting and protecting human rights on the continent.[262] Details about the mandate and functioning of the Commission are provided in Chapter 7.

In the aftermath of the AU's inauguration, some uncertainty arose about the relationship between the AU and the African Commission. The persistence of the confusion appears from a public disagreement on this issue between the Chairperson of the AU Commission and the Commissioner for Political Affairs during the AU's January 2006 Summit meeting in Khartoum. In response to a communication submitted against it under the African Charter, Botswana also relied on these perceived uncertainties to question the legality of the Commission's existence.[263] The root of the confusion is the impression created by the omission of the African Commission from the 'AU organs' listed in the AU Constitutive Act,[264] and the failure of the AU Assembly subsequently to 'establish' the Commission as one of its organs.[265]

It should be easy to clarify the confusion, though. Including the African Commission on the list of AU organs would have contradicted the prior establishment of the African Commission as a separate entity within the OAU. The Commission's legal existence was not derived from the OAU Charter, but from a separate legal instrument, the African Charter. Although it had a separate legal foundation and source of legitimacy, the African Commission functioned as an OAU body within the OAU structure.[266] According to its Constitutive Act, the AU must promote and protect human rights 'in accordance with the African Charter'.[267] The principle way in which the AU can comply with this injunction is to support the African Commission to comply with its mandate under the Charter. It is the situation existing under the Charter that the AU Constitutive Act retains and supports. Listing

---

[261] For a full discussion, see Chs 8 and 9 below.
[262] AU Doc Ex.CL/Dec.306(IX).
[263] Communication 313/2005, *Kenneth Good v Botswana*, 'Further Submissions against Admissibility' (Filed on Behalf of the Respondent in terms of art 51(2) of the Charter) (on file with author).
[264] AU Constitutive Act, art 5.
[265] Under the AU Constitutive Act, art 9(1)(d); see also the submissions by Botswana (n 263 above) para 3.
[266] African Charter, art 30: 'The African Commission . . . shall be established within the OAU . . .'.
[267] AU Constitutive Act, art 3(h).

the African Commission as an AU organ would have suggested a change in the status of the Commission, and could have suggested a more subservient relationship to the AU, compared to the position prevailing under the OAU.

Since its establishment in 1987, the OAU did not merely passively allow the African Commission to function—it or its functionaries actively facilitated the Commission's functioning by electing its members,[268] budgeting for its functioning,[269] appointing its Secretary, and approving its reports.[270] This interrelationship does not prove that the African Commission was 'an organ', but provides adequate proof that the Commission has a special relationship with the OAU and was given support to function as an organ within the OAU.

In 2001, the AU Constitutive Act formally replaced the OAU Charter, not the African Charter. The African Commission had no place under the 1963 OAU Charter; it owes its existence to a subsequent legal instrument, the 1981 African Charter. The transformation of the OAU into the AU left the African Charter and its Commission intact. It is therefore impossible for the AU to 'establish' the Commission as one of its organs, as it already had and continues to have a separate legal existence.

Members of the Commission owe their legitimacy first to the OAU, and now to the AU Assembly. Those members elected before 2002 did not lose their seats on the Commission. There is also no doubt that the AU has accepted the African Commission subsequent to 2002. At its 2003 session in Maputo, the AU Assembly confirmed the appointment of three new members of the African Commission on Human and Peoples' Rights.[271] It also congratulated the Commission on the last year's work, encouraged all AU organs concerned to provide the Commission with the 'requisite human, financial, and material resources for its smooth functioning', and adopted its Activity Report.[272] Emphasizing these interlinkages, the Assembly went even further by asking the African Commission to continue, in concert with the AU Commission, to enhance interaction and coordination with the different organs of the AU in order to strengthen the African mechanism for the promotion and protection of human and peoples' rights and report to Council at its next session.[273]

In any event, the AU Assembly in Durban already pre-empted this debate and took the decision, as part of its 'Decision on the Interim Period',[274] that 'the

---

[268] African Charter, arts 35 and 36.

[269] ibid, art 41, and the OAU's annual budget.

[270] Submitted under African Charter, art 54. In its decision on the Commission's first Activity Report, the Assembly approved the Commission's Rules of Procedure, and endorsed the Commission's recommendations on its headquarters, the financial rules governing the functioning of the Commission, and its periodic reports (OAU Doc AHG/Res.176(XXIV) (1988)).

[271] AU Doc Assembly/AU/Dec.23(II), Decision on the Appointment of Members of the African Commission on Human and Peoples' Rights.

[272] AU Doc Assembly/AU/Dec.11(II) paras 2 and 4, Decision of the African Commission on Human and Peoples' Rights.   [273] ibid, para 3.

[274] AU Doc ASS/AU/Dec.1(I) xi.

African Commission on Human and Peoples' Rights . . . shall henceforth operate within the framework of the African Union'.

Others view the matter differently. Gutto's view is that the African Charter and other African human rights instruments ought to be incorporated into the AU Constitutive Act by way of a Protocol in the same way that the Statute of the defunct Permanent Court of International Justice was incorporated into the UN during the transformation of the League of Nation into the UN in 1945.[275] This would in his view make the African human rights instruments an integral part of the AU Constitutive Act.

Even if it is recognized as 'functioning as' an AU organ, the problem of the Commission's functional isolation from other AU organs has to be addressed.

It should 'systematically participate' in the activities of relevant AU organs.[276] At this stage, the African Commission's Chairperson appears before the Executive Council to 'defend' the Commission's report. Going beyond this occasional formal appearance, the Commission—at least at the level of the Chairperson—should meet regularly or on pertinent issues with the AU Chairperson, the relevant Commissioners, the PRC, the PAP, and the PSC. Where the legal framework of an organ or entity already endows the Commission with a role, as in the case of the PSC and APRM processes, the Commission should develop a formal working relationship with these AU structures.[277] It should do the same where its role is not explicitly recognized, as in the case of the PAP and ECOSOCC. Numerous areas of potential cooperation, highlighted in the discussion above, should be implemented and form part of an articulation by the African Commission of an integrated and coherent policy clarifying its own role and its operational relationship with the AU organs and entities dealt with in this chapter. The imperative of closer cooperation underlines the need for an improvement in the availability and flow of information about the work of the African Commission.

2 African Children's Rights Committee

Both the UN Convention on the Rights of the Child, and its African pendant, the African Charter on the Rights and Welfare of the Child (African Children's Charter), provide for a supervisory body:[278] the CRC Committee and the African Committee of Experts on the Rights and Welfare of the Child (African Children's Committee). State parties nominate and the OAU/AU Assembly of Heads of State and Government elects the 11 members of the African Children's Committee.[279] The members must have 'competence in matters of the rights and welfare of the child' and serve in their personal capacities.[280]

---

[275] S Gutto, 'The Reform and Renewal of the African Regional Human and Peoples' Rights System' (2001) 1 *AHRLJ* 175, 183–4. According to Gutto, this would create legal, institutional, and operational certainty.　　　　　　　　　　　　　　　　　　[276] Kane (n 170 above) 164.

[277] Retreat Report (n 3 above) para IV.　　　[278] See further Ch 6 below.

[279] African Children's Charter, arts 33–6.　　　[280] ibid, art 33.

The mandate of the African Children's Committee mirrors that of the 'mother' institution, the African Commission, in that the African Children's Committee can receive individual and inter-state communications, is implicitly mandated to examine state reports[281] and to undertake fact-finding missions.[282] The initial uncertainty that arose under the African Charter about which body should examine the state reports should not be repeated, as the African Children's Charter provides that reports must be submitted 'to the Committee'.[283] These reports have to be submitted more regularly than is the case with the CRC—initially, two years after entry into force of the African Children's Charter, and thereafter every three years.[284] As in the case of the African Commission, emphasis is also placed on the importance of the promotional mandate of the African Children's Committee.[285] Compared to the CRC Committee, the African Children's Committee has much wider powers. By ratifying the African Children's Charter, states for example automatically accept the competence of the African Children's Committee to 'receive' individual and inter-state communications.[286]

The African Children's Charter does not provide for a detailed procedure about submission and examination of communications. It does not, for example, state any admissibility requirements, such as that domestic remedies have to be exhausted before submitting a communication to the African Children's Committee. It is argued here that the relevant provisions in the African Charter should apply to fill that gap. Such an approach makes sense in the light of the African Children's Committee's general mandate to 'ensure protection of the rights' in the African Children's Charter,[287] the injunction that the African Children's Committee must 'draw inspiration' particularly from the African Charter,[288] and the broad power to 'resort to any method of investigation'.[289] A specific provision allows for the adoption of Rules of Procedure.[290] The consideration of communications and conduct of investigations were not dealt with in the Rules of Procedure, but were left to be clarified in future 'guidelines'.[291]

More than a year after the entry into force of the African Children's Charter, the OAU Assembly in July 2001 elected the 11-member African Children's Committee.[292] Delay was caused when state parties nominated an insufficient number of candidates due to their lack of awareness about or interest in this new body, especially in the context of the institutional proliferation of the time.[293] The eventual 11 members were scraped together from a pool of 12 nominees. For some time, only ten members serve on the Committee. With the election of a member from

---

[281] ibid, arts 43 and 44.
[282] ibid, art 45(1), mirroring the African Charter, art 46, which served as the basis for the Commission's fact-finding.   [283] African Children's Charter, art 43(1).
[284] ibid, art 43(1).   [285] ibid, art 42.   [286] ibid, art 44.   [287] ibid, art 42(b).
[288] ibid, art 46.   [289] ibid, art 45(1).   [290] ibid, art 38(1).
[291] Committee's Rules of Procedure, r 74 (Cmtee/ACRWC/II.Rev. 2), adopted at the Committee's second ordinary session, February 2003.
[292] See A Lloyd, 'The First Meeting of the African Committee of Experts on the Rights and Welfare of the Child' (2002) 2 *AHRLJ* 320.   [293] ibid.

Egypt in 2006, this issue, and the problem that there was no representation from Northern Africa despite formal acceptance of the African Children's Charter by three states from that area, were addressed.

In more than five years since then, this Committee has accomplished very little, and enjoys very limited visibility. Its major formal achievements are that it held eight sessions (meetings), totalling some 35 days; it adopted Rules of Procedure and guidelines for the submission of state reports; it selected themes for the Day of the African Child; it undertook promotional ('lobbying') visits to four countries (Burundi, Madagascar, Namibia, and Sudan);[294] and in August 2005 undertook a fact-finding mission to Uganda. But during these five years it did not adopt final guidelines on the consideration of communications, although a draft had been prepared and discussed. It could not deal with the first communication submitted to it in 2005.[295] It did not get around to ensuring translated versions of the two submitted state reports or to examining these reports.[296] It did not undertake any of the further promotional visits it had planned. It arrived at guidelines for observer status to NGOs only by the end of 2006. And it did not invoke its competence to investigate the situation of African children by way of any 'appropriate method of investigation'. What makes the Committee's failings all the more disappointing is the fact that it was in a position to benefit from the precedents and practice established by the African Commission on most (if not all) of these matters. The failure of the Committee so far may to a great extent be ascribed to a lack of coordination and experience-sharing.

What the Committee did was to engage in discussions on issues of form rather than on anything substantive.[297] One reason for the lackadaisical attitude could be that the members were just not competent to perform these functions. Effectively performing the work of the Committee requires more than enthusiasm and empathy. The Committee's quasi-judicial nature makes some expertise not only in law, but particularly in international human rights law, more than just recommended. However, there is no requirement that any member of the Committee should have legal expertise. At the same time, it should be acknowledged that a legal background does not guarantee improved performance, especially when lawyers trained under national law transpose strict adherence to formalities and technicalities from the domestic to the regional system.

The AU is also—perhaps principally—to blame for the lacklustre performance of the Committee. Institutionally, the Committee is located in the Department of

---

[294] See the Committee's web-site, <http://www.africa-union.org/child/home.htm> (which was up to date as at February 2004 with some of its information) (31 July 2006).

[295] Submitted by the Centre for Human Rights, University of Pretoria, against Uganda, in respect of the fate of children in Northern Uganda.

[296] The agenda of the Committee's eighth meeting (27 November–1 December 2006) contains an item entitled 'Procedure for analyzing country reports received from State Parties', but no indication that the reports were in fact to be examined.

[297] See A Lloyd, 'Report of the Second Ordinary Session of the African Committee of Experts on the Rights and Welfare of the Child' (2003) 3 *AHRLJ* 329.

Social Affairs, causing a separation between it and the main human rights body of the AU, the African Commission.[298] It is the AU's responsibility to support the Committee financially and to ensure its effective functioning. In the first five years, the level of assistance has been negligible. Not even a one-person secretariat has been established.[299] The core minimum capacity to organize and coordinate the Committee's activities was patently absent.[300] A lack of financial resources explains the inability to have the two state reports translated into the Committee's working languages. More promotional visits also failed to be undertaken due to a lack of material resources.[301] Implicitly acknowledging its failure to provide adequate resources, the Executive Council in 2005 urged the AU Commission 'to strengthen the Committee and to urgently ensure the full and effective functioning of its Secretariat'.[302]

For reasons largely similar to those in respect of the African Commission, the African Children's Committee was also not listed in the AU Constitutive Act as an AU organ. The arguments that it is an entity 'functioning within the AU' are even stronger than in respect of the African Commission, because of its location in Addis Ababa, the lack of an independently functional secretariat, and the greater reliance on the assistance of AU organs such as the AU Commission and the AU Legal Counsel.[303] As with the African Commission, the AU Assembly in 2003 resolved that the African Children's Committee 'shall henceforth operate within the framework of the African Union'.[304]

Some problems also arose from the legal framework of the Children's Charter. For example, the Charter provides that Committee members may not be re-elected.[305] By disqualifying members who only served for two years from re-election, this requirement impeded continuity.

Member states must also shoulder some of the blame for the chasm that developed between the promise of the African Children's Charter and its actual realization.[306] The primary obligation of states is to submit state reports to the Committee.[307] By 31 December 2006, only four states (Egypt, Mauritius, Nigeria and Rwanda) had submitted reports.[308] Even if other states arguably took note that the two submitted reports were not being examined, they were not as a consequence exempted from submission. On the contrary, it may be contended that if the Committee had been

---

[298] See also Lloyd and Murray (n 11 above) 175.   [299] Retreat Report (n 3 above) para IV.

[300] This resulted in poor communication, delays, and other logistical problems (Lloyd, n 292 above, 322).

[301] See A Lloyd, 'The Third Ordinary Session of the African Committee of Experts on the Rights and Welfare of the Child' (2004) 4 *AHRLJ* 139, 144, 149.

[302] AU Doc EX.CL/Dec.233(VII), Decision on the African Committee of Experts on the Rights and Welfare of the Child.   [303] Lloyd (n 292 above) 324.

[304] AU Doc ASS/AU/Dec.1(I) xi.   [305] African Children's Charter, art 37(1).

[306] See eg the Executive Council decision in 2005, calling—euphemistically—on member states to 'continue to support the Committee to carry out its mandate efficiently' (AU Doc EX.CL/Dec. 233(VII)) para 7.   [307] African Children's Charter, art 43.

[308] BD Mezmur, 'The African Committee of Experts on the Rights and Welfare of the Child: An Update' (2006) 6 *AHRLJ* 549, 561.

faced with many more reports, the urgency of dealing with them would have been greater. Two states showed even more lethargy than others, when they omitted to nominate replacement members to the Committee when elected members from those countries vacated their seats.[309] It therefore still remains to be seen if the procedure allowing states undemocratically to nominate replacements who will not be required to undergo any 'vetting procedure'[310] would be a real cause of concern.

Although civil society involvement has been minimal,[311] NGOs played a pivotal role in propelling the African Commission forward. Uncertainty about observer status and a lack of publicity are factors that inhibit NGO engagement with the Committee's activities. A number of workshops on the procedures of the Committee were organized by two of the NGOs most prominently involved with the work of the Committee, the Institute for Human Rights and Development in Africa and Save the Children Sweden. Personal experience as a facilitator at one of these workshops alerted me to the risk of raising expectations about an institution that struggles to find its feet.

Unless the Committee's record soon improves, an amendment to the African Children's Charter should be adopted, allowing the African Commission to take over the responsibility to monitor the substantive provisions of the African Children's Charter. Alternatively, a Protocol to the African Children's Charter, a decision by an AU political organ, or resolution of the Committee should be adopted, allowing the African Commission to fulfil the functions designated to the Committee.[312] Four reasons in support of both these rather bold steps are advanced.[313]

First, the existence of the Committee unnecessarily splits the allocation of limited resources. The African Commission has now been functioning since 1987. It is still restricted in its functioning due to a lack of resources. The Secretariat of the Commission is under-resourced and understaffed. The Commission relies very heavily on funding by donors. It should be the AU's priority to consolidate and further strengthen the existing mechanism, the African Commission. So far, the African Children's Committee has barely been functional. Revamping this moribund body is bound to detract from the budgetary allocations and institutional energy that could be devoted to further reinforce the African Commission. With

---

[309] These countries are Chad and Senegal.

[310] A Lloyd, 'How to Guarantee Credence: Recommendations and Proposals for the African Committee of Experts on the Rights and Welfare of the Child' (2004) 12 *Intl J of Children's Rights* 21, 35.

[311] See eg Lloyd (n 292 above) 322, who mentions the presence of only three NGOs at the Committee's inaugural meeting.

[312] The African Children's Charter provides for the following procedure in case of amendments: A state party must submit a written request to this effect to the Chair of the AU Commission. All state parties must be 'duly notified' about the proposed amendment. The Committee must give its opinion on the proposed amendment. The proposed amendment is then submitted to the AU Assembly, who may approve it by a simple majority (African Children's Charter, art 48).

[313] For a previous articulation of these arguments, see F Viljoen, 'The African Charter on the Rights and Welfare of the Child' in CJ Davel (ed), *Introduction to Child Law in South Africa* (Cape Town: Juta, 2000) 214, 227–9.

the establishment of the African Human Rights Court, it is of even greater importance that the African Commission functions effectively, as the Court in many
respects acts as a supplement to the Commission.

Secondly, the Commission is well placed to perform the Committee's mandate.
The mandate and functions of the African Commission and the African Children's
Committee are substantially similar. This means that, functionally, the African
Commission is an appropriate mechanism to replace the Committee. The provisions of the African Children's Charter could merely be added to the substance of
the African Charter to enlarge the Commission's existing substantive ambit. The
African Charter already provides that every state must ensure the protection of the
rights of the child as stipulated in international declarations and conventions.[314]
Adding the substance of the African Children's Charter to the African Charter
would therefore be a legitimate extension without including anything unrelated
to the African Commission's initial mandate. The African Commission has established a number of Special Rapporteurs.[315] The appointment of one of the members of the Commission as Special Rapporteur on Children in Africa will go a long
way towards ensuring that the rights set out in the African Children's Charter are
not neglected in the Commission's work.

Thirdly, developments subsequent to the creation of the Committee support its
abolition. It must be assumed that the motivation to create a new human rights
institution in Africa was influenced by a contemporaneous context that has subsequently changed. In 1989/90, when the African Children's Charter was drafted
and adopted, the African Commission had hardly started functioning and maintained a cloak of secrecy. No information about its activities and possibilities
was available. No complaints had been decided. In sum, there was little faith in
the African Commission, and it enjoyed very limited visibility. Since then, it has
established itself as a much more visible and important institution championing
human rights promotion and protection in Africa.[316] Implicit mistrust of the
African Commission has been overtaken by subsequent events, thereby weakening the reasoning used at the time when a separate institution was founded to deal
with children's rights in Africa. In the interim, the AU also adopted the Protocol to
the African Charter on the Rights of Women in Africa, which entered into force in
2005. The African Commission has been given the additional mandate to monitor
compliance with this new normative framework. Applying similar logic, the African
Children's Charter could effectively be treated as a 'Protocol' to the African Charter,
to be supervised by the existing Charter organs. This contention should not imply
that the African Commission will necessarily be overburdened, as the advent of the
African Human Rights Court may, at least in the longer term, as more states accept
direct individual access to the Court, lighten the communications workload of the
Commission. In any event, the argument that it makes more institutional sense to

---

314 African Charter, art 18(3).   315 See Ch 9.B.1 below for a discussion.
316 See Chaps 7–10 below.

strengthen one body, rather than two, should still apply even if a case is made out that the Commission is indeed overburdened.

Fourthly, consolidated state reporting is likely to lead to improvements. Member states have widely neglected the duty to report under both the African Charter and the African Children's Charter. Consolidating the provisions of the African Children's Charter (as well as the Women's Protocol) with those of the African Charter for the purpose of a single report also makes more sense in this context. Even at the UN level, much effort is now focused on the consolidation, rather than the further proliferation, of the work of human rights treaty bodies.[317]

If the Committee is retained, the coordination of activities of the African Commission and the African Children's Committee should at least be assured, for example by ensuring a presence at each other's meetings; coordinating meeting dates to allow NGOs to attend both sessions; an annual meeting of Chairpersons, as is done in the UN system; sharing of staff, information, and experience; and inviting states to present combined or simultaneous state reports.

3 Judicial Institutions

When the AU Constitutive Act was adopted, the AU landscape was set to accommodate two new courts.[318] The history that followed is one of confusion and delay, suggesting at best that the implications of moving from zero to two judicial institutions was not thought through properly, and, at worst, signifying some institutional resistance to the judicialization of disputes.

Conceptualized as two separate courts with clearly distinct mandates, a decision was subsequently taken to merge the two institutions into one. The African Court on Human and Peoples' Rights, set up under the African Charter, was devised to deal with allegations of human rights against AU members. The AU Court of Justice, instituted under the AU Constitutive Act, was expected to deal mainly with contentious matters of a political and economic nature. The mandate of the AU Court of the Justice related to disputes about the common policies of the AU,[319] and issues arising from accelerated political and socio-economic integration.[320] Although its jurisdiction did not explicitly include human rights, the possibility of overlap could not be excluded. However, not long after the Protocol of the African Court of Justice was adopted, setting out its detailed functioning, the AU Assembly decided that there had to be a merger between the judicial institutions. The reasons for and implications of the merger are discussed in Chapter 11, and the status of ratification of the Protocols establishing the two Courts is set out in Table 5.1 below.

---

[317] See also CA Odinkalu, 'Back to the Future: The Imperative of Prioritizing for the Protection of Human Rights in Africa' (2003) 47 *JAL* 1, 25, who comments as follows about the multiplicity of bodies and institutions under the AU, and in particular the two under discussion: 'One is tempted to suggest that there is a deliberate strategy to bring the notion of supra-national legality into disrepute through the creation of a multiplicity of under-resourced and deliberately ineffectual institutions'. See Ch 2 above.   [318] For a discussion of these courts, see Ch 10 below.
[319] AU Constitutive Act, art 9(1)(a).   [320] ibid, art 3.

D Civil Society: The Fourth Branch

African integration will remain superficial as long as it is viewed and managed as the closer cooperation between states and political elites, and not as the forging of closer bonds between Africa's peoples towards the exploration of a common identity and citizenship. In an apparent attempt to reverse decades of excluding civil society voices from OAU activities, the last years of the OAU saw a surge in activities aimed at working out modalities and developing mechanisms for improved collaboration between African civil society organizations and the OAU. Two OAU-Civil Society Conferences were held, in June 2001,[321] and in June 2002.[322] A Provisional Working Group (PWG), a forerunner of the Economic, Social and Cultural Council (ECOSOCC), was elected in 2002, to steer the process of closer collaboration.[323] Its selection process, by governments and embassies, has been criticized.[324] After the establishment of the AU, the PWG continued meeting as the 'AU-Civil Society PWG', amongst others to discuss the structure of ECOSOCC.[325] In 2004, an AU-Civil Society Organization Forum was held.[326]

Although the AU Constitutive Act provides for the establishment of ECOSOCC as an 'advisory organ' to give a voice to civil society,[327] its composition and functioning were left to be determined by the Assembly.[328] Reinforcing perceptions that the AU accorded a low priority to the inclusion of ordinary African people in its structures, ECOSOCC was the last of the series of organs established. Formally in operation since March 2005, the establishment of ECOSOCC threatens to become a largely symbolic gesture if this new body does not start to function effectively in this important fledgling phase. By the end of 2006, ECOSOCC members had not been elected. An Interim Assembly of ECOSOCC, mandated to facilitate the election of members to the ECOSOCC Assembly, and launched in 2005 with Professor Wangari Maathai as Interim Presiding Officer, has been constrained by lack of funds.[329] With the Interim ECOSOCC's mandate extended to the end of 2007,[330] meaningful civil society participation for the time being remains an unfulfilled ideal.

---

[321] 'OAU-Civil Society Conference General Report of the Conference (11–15 June 2001)'.
[322] OAU Doc OAU/CIVIL SOCIETY.3(II)Rev.1, General Report Second OAU/Civil Society Conference, 11–14 June 2002.   [323] AU Doc AU/Civil Society/PWGM/1.
[324] AU Doc EX.CL/118(V)vii, para 6. Report on the Activities of the CSSDCA Proposed to be CIDO.   [325] AU Doc AU/Civil Society/PWGM/1.
[326] See The Civil Society Declaration (26–7 June 2004).
[327] Statutes of ECOSOCC, art 3(1).   [328] AU Constitutive Act, art 22.
[329] See MG Waiko, 'The African Union's Economic, Social and Cultural Council: An Evaluation of its Mandate of Facilitating Civil Society Participation in the African Union' (unpublished LL M dissertation, University of Pretoria, 2006, <https://www.up.ac.za/dspace/handle/2263/1260>). The 15-member Interim Standing Committee, which met for the first time in April 2005, is mandated to oversee the election of national representatives ('Towards a People-Driven African Union', n 34 above).
[330] AU Doc EX.CL/Dec.338(X).

ECOSOCC has been established to give African civil society and the African Diaspora a voice in the AU structures.[331] The establishment of ECOSOCC thus aims at fostering a partnership between the AU and civil society. It is not treated as a 'legislative' organ in this discussion, because the outcomes of this partnership will only take the form of 'advice' to the organs with decision-making powers, and there is no stated intention that the AU will ever change this position.

A small ECOSOCC secretariat is based in the African Citizen (Civil Society and Diaspora) Directorate (CIDO).[332] CIDO falls under the Office of the Chairperson of the African Union. Renaming and replacing the CSSDCA Coordinating Unit, the new name reflects the shift away from the broad original mandate of the CSSDCA to 'focus more explicitly on critical areas of concern such as the civil society agenda, the Diaspora, civil society and private sector forums etc . . . that are required to promote a wider sense of African citizenship'.[333] However, this statement shows that, by embracing the aim of cultivating a common African identity, the re-definition of CSSDCA as CIDO goes further than a mere name change. Because each of the AU Commission's departments has a civil society component, there may be some duplication and the need for coordination.

Having been excluded from any meaningful debate about the formation of the AU, ECOSOCC provides African civil society with an opportunity to participate in dialogues and debates about AU policies and programmes. However, its Statutes are silent on how the outcomes of debates may be brought to the attention of other AU organs, or what the relationship is between ECOSOCC and other AU organs. What is clear is that it has only advisory powers. Its counsel 'may or may not be heeded', because it is not 'a decision-making body' and therefore does not 'detract from the powers and ability of Member States to make decisions'.[334]

ECOSOCC will consist of 150 civil society organs (CSOs):[335] two from each member state (106 in total); ten with a subregional and eight with a regional (continent-wide) focus; 20 representing the Diaspora; and another six nominated by the AU Commission. The category 'CSO' is made up of a very wide array of groups, and goes much further than NGOs and Community-Based Organizations (CBOs), by also embracing social groups (such as youth groups), professional groups (such as workers' associations (trade unions)) and cultural organizations. CSOs represent diverse interest groups that lack centralized structures. In the absence of

---

[331] ECOSOCC Statutes, AU Doc Experts/PRC/ECOSOCC Statutes/Rev.5, June 2004, art 2(1) (ECOSOCC must 'promote continuous dialogue between all segments of the African people on issues concerning Africa and its future'); art 2(2) specifically mentions the Diaspora. The AU Assembly amended the AU Constitutive Act in 2003 by inserting as an objective of the AU the following: 'invite and encourage the full participation of the African Diaspora as an important part of our continent, in the building of the African Union'. This amendment is not yet in force.

[332] AU Doc ADM.HRD/26A/Vol.I/8290, Revised Maputo Structure of the AU Commission.

[333] AU Doc EX.CL/118(V)vii, para 19, Report on the Activities of the CSSDCA Proposed to be CIDO.   [334] ibid, para 8.

[335] ECOSOCC Statutes, art 4.

an umbrella body covering all the interest groups, states may easily usurp this role and manipulate the process to exclude critical voices.

The ECOSOCC Statutes provide that 'competent CSO authorities' in each state must oversee the process for 'election'.[336] This formulation leaves too much room for uncertainty and manipulation. Similarly, the Diaspora membership is to be determined by the amorphous 'African Diaspora organisations'.[337] Elections at all levels must result in 50 per cent women and 50 per cent youths (between 18 and 35) being elected.[338] Apart from the possibility of governments dictating elections, the criteria for eligibility may also exclude civil society dissent. As only organizations that have been registered for at least three years in an AU member qualify,[339] states may silence dissenting voices by refusing them registration. Sources of funding may also disqualify an organization from ECOSOCC membership. At least half of the 'basic resources' of a CSO must come from membership contributions.[340] It would appear that government or even foreign funding is allowed, provided that these sources are declared and do not exceed 50 per cent of the total resources.

The 150 ECOSOCC members make up the 'General Assembly'. Its role is likely to be very limited, as its regular meetings take place only on a two-yearly basis.[341] ECOSOCC's functioning will depend much more on the 'standing committee' of 18 members and its ten sectoral cluster committees.

It is not surprising that ECOSOCC, as the *vox populi* of the AU, is mandated to concern itself with human rights. The promotion of good governance, popular participation, human rights, gender equality, children's rights, and social justice feature among its objectives and functions.[342] A number of sectoral cluster committees are provided for, such as the Political Affairs Committee, with a mandate including human rights, the Women and Gender Committee, and a Cross-Cutting Programmes Committee, amongst other things responsible for HIV and AIDS.[343] These Committees should harmonize their activities, and forge linkages with other AU bodies with powers going beyond that of ECOSOCC and its constituent parts.[344] In the field of gender, for example, the ECOSOCC Women and Gender Committee should collaborate with the Commission-based Women, Gender and

---

[336] ibid, art 5.

[337] The concept of 'African Diaspora' is in need of definition. A technical workshop was convened and proposed that the definition should 'refer to the geographic dispersion of peoples whose ancestors, without historic memory, originally came from Africa, but who are currently domiciled, or claim residence or citizenship, outside the continent' (Report on the Definition of the African Diaspora, AU Doc EX.CL/164(VI)).　　　　　　　　　　　　　[338] ECOSOCC Statutes, art 4(2).

[339] ibid, art 6(3). See also the criticism that 'a large proportion of . . . human rights organisations, think tanks and other groups likely to be critical of AU activities' are likely to be excluded from membership ('Towards a People-Driven African Union', n 34 above).

[340] ECOSOCC Statutes, art 6(6).　　　　[341] ibid, art 9(3).　　　　[342] ibid, arts 2(5) and 7(5).

[343] ibid, art 11.

[344] See Waiko (n 329 above) and EA Bekele, 'Implications of ECOSOCC's Mandate for the Promotion and Protection of Human Rights in Africa: Inquiry into the Relationship between ECOSOCC and the Human Rights Organs of the African Union' (unpublished LL M dissertation, University of Pretoria, 2006, <https://www.up.ac.za/dspace/handle/2263/1260>).

Development Directorate, the African Commission, the Executive Council, and the PAP.[345]

The danger looms large that ECOSOCC may not constitute a vibrant 'fourth branch' in which the participation of African citizens will be secured, due mainly to its limited advisory powers and the possibility of state elites controlling its membership. Perhaps a leaf could be taken from the book of NGOs involved with the African Commission, who carved out an important role for civil society in the Commission's activities.[346] In any event, the voice of these NGOs should be heard in ECOSOCC, to provide its members with information about the activities of the African Commission, the human rights situation in Africa, and insights into ECOSOCC's potential role in supporting the African Commission. A similar approach should also be taken in respect of the African Children's Committee and the African Human Rights Court.

E Conclusion

Improved coordination and integration of human rights are required among the political organs of the AU, and in the functioning of the AU as a whole.

If the African Commission has been sidelined in the era of the AU, it has mostly itself to blame. Already in 2001, the OAU Assembly,[347] and later, the AU organs, repeatedly called on the Commission to reflect and report upon its relationship with AU organs and its position within the AU.[348] Not much came of the Commission's decision to set up a working group to 'initiate an in-depth discussion on all the implications' of the entry into force of the AU Constitutive Act in 2001.[349] A brainstorming session, which eventually took place in 2006, is a first stage in this process, but was to be completed by January 2007.[350] At the very least, the African Commission should invite representatives of the AU organs to attend its sessions, and these organs should extend similar invitations, 'in order to reinforce mutual cooperation'.[351] Any recommendations are likely to be informed by the

[345] Stefiszyn (n 179 above) 370. Women's organizations have 'probably been the most successful in engaging the African Union' (see 'Towards a People-Driven African Union', n 34 above).
[346] See Ch 9.H.1 below.
[347] Decision on the 14th Activity Report of the Commission, OAU Doc AHG/Dec.3(XXXVII) para 2.
[348] See eg Declaration of the AU Assembly, AU Doc Assembly/AU/Dec.7(II); AU Doc EX.CL/ Dec.220(VII).
[349] Resolution on the African Union and the African Charter on Human and Peoples' Rights, 29th session of the African Commission, 23 April–7 May 2001. This working group was to submit its final report at the Commission's 31st session.
[350] AU Doc EX.CL/Dec.303(IX): The Executive Council requests the African Commission to complete, as early as possible, the brainstorming it has initiated on its relations with the various organs and institutions of the African Union, including the African Court of Human and Peoples' Rights, and submit appropriate recommendations to Council in January 2007.
[351] Brainstorming Meeting (n 1 above) para 66(c).

report of the Commission's ad hoc Working Group on Specific Issues relevant to the Work of the African Commission, which was set up in 2005.[352]

The need for coordination and reflection is all the more urgent when it comes to the Commission's future co-existence with the African Human Rights Court. The Assembly has reiterated the importance of the African Commission's active participation in the process for the effective establishment of the African Court of Human and Peoples' Rights and the need for cooperation between the two institutions.[353] So far, the Commission has not taken proactive steps to provide its vision of the co-existence of the two institutions. In 2006, the Executive Council requested the African Commission to 'take part in the process of operationalization' of the African Human Rights Court.[354]

With the advent of the African Human Rights Court, which supplements the African Commission's protective human rights mandate, there is a danger that too much reliance will be placed on the judicial and even quasi-judicial dimensions of human rights. Important as this aspect is, there are many factors, such as illiteracy, ignorance, and lack of resources, that render enforceable human rights illusory, especially in Africa. Excessively focusing on individual recourse as re-active remedial strategy will lead to a 'negative integration' of human rights.[355]

Instead, the AU as a whole must send a message that it takes integration of human rights seriously. Given their inherently expansive scope, human rights are not exclusive to the matters covered in the mandate of the Political Affairs Department. However, the option of inserting human rights into the mandates of other departments under the Commissioners for Peace and Security and Social Affairs is likely to lead to further fragmentation.[356] Preferable options are the creation of a separate Human Rights Department,[357] with a designated Commissioner, or the establishment of a 'cross-cutting' human rights unit (or 'Directorate') within the office of the Chairperson, similar to the Directorate for Women, Gender and Development. Either of these options will demonstrate a high level of political commitment and will ensure improved integration in the management of human rights bodies by providing a forum where all AU organs with a responsibility for human rights could meet with the human rights-specific 'organs'.

Concern for human rights should also translate to the very foundation of the AU as a continental institution, by focusing on the involvement of the African

[352] Resolution on the Creation of a Working Group on Specific Issues relevant to the Work of the African Commission, ACHPR/Res.77(XXXVII)05; at the end of 2005, its mandate was renewed for another year (ACHPR/Res.80(XXXVIII)05).

[353] See eg Executive Council decision AU Doc EX.CL/Dec.306(IX).

[354] AU Doc EX.CL/Dec. 257(VIII) para 6.

[355] For a similar argument in the European context, see P Alston and JHH Weler, 'An "Ever Closer Union" in Need of a Human Rights Policy: The European Union and Human Rights' in P Alston (ed), *The EU and Human Rights* (Oxford: Oxford University Press, 1999) 3, 13.

[356] Kane (n 170 above) 159.

[357] See GW Mugwanya, *Human Rights in Africa. Enhancing Human Rights through the African Regional Human Rights System* (Ardsley: Transnational, 2003) 407–10, who argues for a 'permanent specialized human rights department within the Legal Division'.

Table 5.1. Staus of Ratifications: AU Documents and Treaties, position as at 31 December 2006

Country	Constitutive Act of the African Union	Protocol on Amendments to the AU Constitutive Act	Protocol on the Establishment of an African Court on Human and Peoples' Rights	Protocol on the Court of Justice of the AU	Protocol Relating to the Establishment of the Peace and Security Council of the AU	Protocol to the Treaty establishing the AEC relating to the Pan-African Parliament	NEPAD's APRM
	Ratified/acceded	Ratified/acceded	Ratified/acceded	Ratified/acceded	Ratified/acceded	Ratified/acceded	Signed
Algeria	23/05/01	—	22/04/03	—	29/01/03	22/04/03	9/03/03
Angola	19/09/01	—	—	—	30/08/04	29/10/03	8/07/04
Benin	3/07/01	1/12/05	—	—	10/05/04	11/11/03	31/04/04
Botswana	1/03/01	—	—	—	21/06/05	10/07/01	—
Burkina Faso	27/02/01	5/04/05	31/12/98	—	1/12/03	23/06/03	9/03/03
Burundi	28/02/01	12/12/06	2/04/03	—	4/11/03	4/11/03	—
Cameroon	9/11/01	—	—	—	4/11/03	4/11/03	3/04/03
Cape Verde	21/06/01	—	—	—	—	17/02/04	—
Central African Republic	16/02/01	—	—	—	—	12/03/04	—
Chad	16/01/01	—	—	—	7/04/04	7/01/04	—
Comoros	16/02/01	2/04/04	23/12/03	2/04/04	26/07/03	13/03/04	—
Congo	18/02/02	—	—	—	23/02/04	23/02/04	9/03/03
Côte d'Ivoire	27/02/01	—	7/01/03	—	—	—	—
Democratic Republic of Congo	7/07/02	—	—	—	—	—	—
Djibouti	14/12/00	—	—	—	18/10/05	10/03/04	—
Egypt	5/07/01	—	—	6/07/06	1/02/05	8/10/03	9/04/04
Equatorial Guinea	26/12/00	11/05/06	—	—	29/01/03	3/02/04	—

Table 5.1. (*Cont.*)

Country	Constitutive Act of the African Union	Protocol on Amendments to the AU Constitutive Act	Protocol on the Establishment of an African Court on Human and Peoples' Rights	Protocol on the Court of Justice of the AU	Protocol Relating to the Establishment of the Peace and Security Council of the AU	Protocol to the Treaty establishing the AEC relating to the Pan-African Parliament	NEPAD's APRM
	Ratified/acceded	Ratified/acceded	Ratified/acceded	Ratified/acceded	Ratified/acceded	Ratified/acceded	Signed
Eritrea	1/03/01	—	—	—	—	—	—
Ethiopia	8/03/01	—	—	—	29/05/03	29/05/03	9/03/03
Gabon	17/05/01	—	14/08/00	—	29/12/03	29/12/03	13/04/03
The Gambia	22/02/01	—	30/06/99	—	19/11/03	4/07/03	—
Ghana	11/05/01	—	25/08/04	—	4/07/03	15/09/03	9/03/03
Guinea	23/04/02	—	—	—	—	15/03/04	—
Guinea-Bissau	14/01/01	—	—	—	—	—	—
Kenya	4/07/01	—	4/02/04	—	19/12/03	19/12/03	—
Lesotho	16/02/01	26/10/04	28/10/03	26/10/04	30/06/03	16/04/03	8/07/04
Liberia	26/02/01	—	—	—	—	—	—
Libya	25/10/00	23/05/04	19/11/03	4/05/05	24/06/03	10/08/02	—
Madagascar	5/06/03	—	—	—	28/06/04	9/02/04	—
Malawi	3/02/01	—	—	—	7/07/23	3/07/02	8/07/04
Mali	11/08/00	7/05/04	10/05/00	17/12/04	28/02/03	26/05/01	28/05/03
Mauritania	20/11/01	—	19/05/05	—	—	22/12/03	—
Mauritius	13/04/01	—	3/03/03	23/02/04	16/06/03	9/02/04	9/03/04
Mozambique	17/05/01	17/07/04	17/07/04	17/07/04	20/05/03	20/05/03	9/03/04
Namibia	28/02/01	—	—	—	19/11/03	13/08/02	—
Niger	26/01/01	—	17/05/04	15/02/06	7/08/03	7/08/03	9/04/04

Table 5.1. (*Cont.*)

Country	Constitutive Act of the African Union	Protocol on Amendments to the AU Constitutive Act	Protocol on the Establishment of an African Court on Human and Peoples' Rights	Protocol on the Court of Justice of the AU	Protocol Relating to the Establishment of the Peace and Security Council of the AU	Protocol to the Treaty establishing the AEC relating to the Pan-African Parliament	NEPAD's APRM
	Ratified/acceded	Ratified/acceded	Ratified/acceded	Ratified/acceded	Ratified/acceded	Ratified/acceded	Signed
Nigeria	29/03/01	—	20/05/04	—	23/12/03	23/12/03	9/04/04
Rwanda	16/04/01	25/10/04	5/05/03	25/06/04	19/05/03	22/08/01	9/04/04
Sahrawi Arab Democratic Rep.	27/12/00	—	—	—	10/05/04	04/06/01	—
São Tomé Príncipe	27/02/01	—	—	—	22/09/03	—	—
Senegal	28/08/00	14/02/06	29/09/98	—	9/09/03	14/10/03	9/04/04
Seychelles	20/03/01	—	—	—	—	24/03/03	—
Sierra Leone	9/02/01	—	—	—	16/06/03	16/06/03	8/07/04
Somalia	26/02/01	—	—	—	—	—	—
South Africa	3/03/01	16/03/04	3/07/02	17/12/04	15/05/03	3/07/02	9/04/04
Sudan	22/11/00	—	—	19/01/06	5/07/03	16/10/02	22/01/06
Swaziland	8/08/01	—	—	—	30/12/05	11/03/04	—
Tanzania	6/04/01	14/04/04	7/02/06	7/02/06	3/09/03	4/07/02	8/07/04
Togo	30/08/00	—	23/06/03	—	23/02/04	3/01/03	—
Tunisia	13/03/01	—	—	—	—	1/03/04	—
Uganda	3/04/01	—	16/02/01	—	10/03/04	9/07/03	9/04/04
Zambia	21/02/01	—	—	—	4/07/03	21/11/03	22/01/06
Zimbabwe	3/03/01	—	—	—	2/02/04	7/07/03	—
Total no. of states	53	13	23	12	41	46	25

people at all levels of the AU's functioning. Decisions of national Parliaments and the outcomes of referendums should steer the future evolution of the AU to ensure that it has not only legal legitimacy, but also social legitimacy and acceptance. This form of legitimacy is a prerequisite to justifying the AU's evolution from an inter-governmental present to a federalist future—the ultimate realization of the ideals of pan-Africanism and a 'better prospect of economic well-being, a healthy envi-ronment, and freedom from threats to . . . security'.[358] Only if it is able to allow for a truly deliberative and inclusive culture will the AU become an institution of the African people, by them and for them, and not an institution of, by, and for African heads of state.[359]

Integration would still be isolation if it remains restricted to the AU structures. As much as there needs to be better coordination and cooperation within the AU, the AU organs and entities must also build alliances at the global level, with the UN, and subregionally, with the RECs.

[358] J Pinder, 'The EU of the Future: Federal or Intergovernmental?' in Gower (n 7 above) 369, 375.
[359] For the use of this formulation in a different context, see K Mathews, 'The Organization of African Unity' in D Mazzeo (ed), *African Regional Organizations* (Cambridge: Cambridge University Press, 1984) 49.

6

Substantive Human Rights Norms in the African Regional System

In this chapter, human rights and human rights-related instruments functioning under the aegis of the African Union (AU) are outlined. The discussion starts with the principal instrument, the African Charter on Human and Peoples' Rights (African Charter),[1] and proceeds to sketch the framework for the protection of the

---

[1] OAU Doc CAB/LEG/67/3/Rev.5, adopted 27 June 1981, entered into force 21 October 1986.

rights of refugees, children, women, indigenous peoples, and the environment. Finally, the threats to rights posed by corruption, mercenaries, and terrorism are briefly examined.

With the exception of the Cultural Charter for Africa, the discussion incorporates all the binding human rights-related instruments adopted by the Assembly of Heads of State and Government of the OAU and AU (OAU/AU Assembly),[2] questioning the extent to which they co-exist, overlap, and mutually reinforce one another. Building on the previous chapter, which presented the argument that institutional collaboration within the AU is crucial to more effective human rights protection, this chapter aims to position the African Charter and the other human rights treaties as part of a normative network, instead of isolated loose threads. An attempt is also made to assess the 'Africanness' of this regional human rights network.

The omission from this survey of declarations and other non-binding standards providing for the promotion and protection of human rights in Africa should not be interpreted as a negation of their role and potentially persuasive normative value.[3] Where relevant, for each instrument or right a brief background is provided; its drafting history is reviewed; a comparison is drawn with pre-existing (or later) UN standards; its normative content is explored in the light of the relevant jurisprudence, state reporting practice, or resolutions; and finally, the right or normative framework is located against the background of domestic 'principles of law recognized by African states' and within the broader AU context.

A African Charter on Human and Peoples' Rights

A detailed analysis of all 29 substantive provisions of the African Charter is not attempted here.[4] Instead, the focus falls on four of its features that, to varying

---

[2] The Cultural Charter for Africa, adopted 5 July 1976, entered into force 19 September 1990, <http://www.dfa.gov.za> and <http://www.africa-union.org> (accessed 31 December 2006), has not had any significant impact due to its framing (imposing obligations on states and making lofty commitments without providing for individual human rights to culture) and its lack of an implementation mechanism. A total of 33 states have at the end of 2006 become party to the Cultural Charter for Africa. The instrument's stagnation and lack of relevance appear from the fact that the last ratification, that of Chad, dates back to 15 August 1990.

[3] The African Commission eg adopted the Resolution Urging States to Envisage a Moratorium on the Death Penalty, at its 26th session, 1–15 November 1999, Commission's 13th Annual Activity Report, Annex IV. On the rights of prisoners, see eg Resolution on Guidelines and Measures for the Prohibition and Prevention of Torture, Cruel, Inhuman or Degrading Treatment or Punishment in Africa (Robben Island Guidelines), adopted at the 14th session of the Commission (16th Annual Activity Report); on the rights of people living with HIV and AIDS, see eg Resolution on the HIV/AIDS Pandemic—Threat against Human Rights and Humanity, adopted at the Commission's 29th session, 23 April–7 May 2001 (14th Annual Activity Report, Annex IV).

[4] Of the numerous sources that do exactly that, F Ouguergouz, *The African Charter on Human and Peoples' Rights: A Comprehensive Agenda for Human Dignity and Sustainable Democracy in Africa* (The Hague: Martinus Nijhoff, 2003) stands out. See also eg F Viljoen, 'Introduction to the African Commission and the Regional Human Rights System' in C Heyns (ed), *Human Rights Law in Africa* (vol 1) (Leiden: Martinus Nijhoff, 2004) 385, 399–410.

degrees, reflect a particularly African 'fingerprint',[5] namely, the indivisibility of rights; the concept of 'peoples' rights'; individual duties; and the lack of a derogation clause.

1 Indivisibility of 'Three Generations' of Rights

Sometime before the traditional tripartite division of rights into 'first', 'second', and 'third' 'generations' became discredited,[6] the African Charter had already undone this categorization by including rights from all three 'generations' in one document.[7] 'First generation' rights in the African Charter are, for example, the right to equality before the law,[8] the right to have one's case heard,[9] and the right to freely associate.[10] Socio-economic (or 'second generation') rights include the right 'to work under equitable and satisfactory conditions',[11] the right to 'enjoy the best attainable state of physical and mental health',[12] and the right to education.[13] The right to a generally satisfactory environment[14] and the right to international peace and security,[15] included in the Charter as 'peoples' rights', have been characterized as 'third generation' rights.[16]

One of the most far-reaching consequences of this development is that socio-economic rights are as unequivocally justiciable as any of the other rights in the Charter. Even if the drafters did not specifically refer to these conditions, the justiciability of socio-economic rights stands as a response to the prevailing situation of dire poverty and exploitation by kleptocratic elites. The justiciability of socio-economic rights was not only an exhortation for things to be different, but also an acknowledgement that accountability through the law was part of the solution. This position was not contained in the initial draft of the Charter. Based on the American Convention and the ICESCR, the initial draft of the Charter not only differentiated

---

[5] UO Umozurike, *The African Charter on Human and Peoples' Rights* (The Hague: Martinus Nijhoff, 1997) 46; E Bondzie-Simpson, 'A Critique of the African Charter of Human and Peoples' Rights' (1988) 31 *Howard Law Journal* 643; M Mutua, 'The Banjul Charter and the African Cultural Fingerprint: An Evaluation of the Language of Duties' (1995) 35 *Virginia J of Intl L* 339.

[6] The alternative typology of 'respect', 'protect', and 'fulfil' can be traced back to H Shue, *Basic Rights: Subsistence, Affluence and US Foreign Policy* (New Jersey: Princeton University Press, 1980) and gained prominence in the late 1980s and in the 1990s; see also Ch 1 above.

[7] See also the Preamble, which proclaims that 'civil and political rights cannot be dissociated from economic, social and cultural rights'. This situation can be distinguished from the dichotomy at the global level (between 'civil and political' rights in the Covenant on Civil and Political Rights (ICCPR) and 'socio-economic rights' in the International Covenant on Economic, Social and Cultural Rights (ICESCR)) and at the regional level (in the European Convention of Human Rights and Fundamental Freedoms and the European Social Charter, as well as the American Convention of Human Rights (American Convention) and the Protocol of San Salvador).　　　　　[8] African Charter, art 3.

[9] ibid, art 7.　　　　[10] ibid, art 10.

[11] ibid, art 15. This provision does not grant a 'right to work'. Rather, it deals with conditions of work and introduces the principle of 'equal pay for equal work'. As pointed out by Umozurike (n 5 above), it is doubtful whether this right 'involves protection against unemployment or unemployment benefits in the absence of a job'.　　　　　　　　[12] African Charter, art 16(1).

[13] ibid, art 17(1).　　　　[14] ibid, art 24.　　　　[15] ibid, art 23(1).

[16] See eg Umozurike (n 5 above) 51.

between 'economic, social and cultural rights' in its first chapter, and 'civil and political rights', in its second, but also between the implementation of these two categories. The first chapter ended with a provision on state reporting, relating to 'progress made' in realizing rights,[17] while the second chapter ended with a guarantee of judicial recourse.[18] Bringing together the two 'categories' of rights under the same heading ('Human and Peoples' Rights'), a later draft did away with this distinction, thus lending support to the view that socio-economic rights in the Charter, in particular the right to education and the right to health, place obligations on state parties to fulfil them and not merely to respect and protect them.[19]

Due to a 'minimalist' approach adopted during its drafting, only a limited number of socio-economic rights were included in the African Charter. The most important omissions are the right to social security,[20] the right to an adequate standard of living, including 'adequate food, clothing and housing, and the right to the continuous improvement of living conditions'.[21] Although they were included in some initial drafts, none of these rights are contained in the final version of the African Charter. During the drafting deliberations, the Chairman of the Committee of Experts explained that the concise and general conception in respect of economic, social, and cultural rights is 'in line with the concern to spare our young states too many but important obligations'.[22] Even if it was aimed at appeasing states, this statement may be read as reinforcing the justiciable ('obligation'-based) nature *of a limited set of* socio-economic rights. Still, the Charter remained silent on some of the most pressing socio-economic needs of Africa's predominantly rural impoverished communities, such as safe and accessible drinking water, adequate housing or shelter, and sustained food supplies.

Most of the communications submitted to the Commission so far dealt with the right to a fair trial,[23] and touched on issues such as the ousting of courts' jurisdiction by military decrees,[24] access to legal counsel,[25] the presumption of

[17] M'Baye Draft African Charter on Human and Peoples' Rights, OAU Doc CAB/LEG/67/1, prepared for the Meeting of Experts, Dakar, Senegal, 28 November–8 December 1979, reprinted in C Heyns (ed), *Human Rights Law in Africa 1999* (The Hague: Kluwer Law International, 2002) 65–77 (M'Baye proposal) art 14.   [18] M'Baye proposal (n 17 above) art 32.
   [19] Dakar Draft, OAU Doc CAB/LEG/67/3/Rev.1, repr in Heyns (n 17 above) 81–91.
   [20] This right contained in the M'Baye proposal (n 17 above) art 7.
   [21] Also this right was contained in the M'Baye proposal (n 17 above) art 10.
   [22] Rapporteur's Report on the Draft African Charter on Human and Peoples' Rights, OAU Doc CAB/LEG/67/Draft Rapt.Rpt.(II) Rev.4, para 13, repr in Heyns (n 17 above) 94.
   [23] See eg C Heyns, 'Civil and Political Rights in the African Charter' in MD Evans and R Murray (eds), *The African Charter on Human and Peoples' Rights: The System in Practice, 1986–2000* (Cambridge: Cambridge University Press, 2002) 137; and M Killander, 'Communications before the African Commission on Human and Peoples' Rights 1988–2002' (2006) 10(1) *Law, Democracy and Development* 101, 103 (noting that a violation of art 7 (right to fair trial) was found in 32 of the 42 finalized cases).
   [24] See eg Communications 105/93, 128/94, 130/94, 152/96 (joined), *Media Rights Agenda and Others v Nigeria* (2000) AHRLR 200 (ACHPR 1998) (12th Annual Activity Report) (*Nigerian Media* case) paras 63 and 78–82; and Communications 143/95, 150/96 (joined), *Constitutional Rights Project and Another v Nigeria* (2000) AHRLR 235 (ACHPR 1999) (13th Annual Activity Report) (*Nigerian Habeas Corpus* case) paras 30 and 34.
   [25] See eg Communication 87/93, *Constitutional Rights Project (in respect of Lekwot and Others) v Nigeria* (2000) AHRLR 183 (ACHPR 1995) (8th Annual Activity Report) (*Lekwot* case) para 13; and

innocence,[26] and the right to a trial within a reasonable time.[27] Findings on the right to personal liberty and security and the prohibition against torture and cruel, inhuman, degrading treatment or punishment also featured regularly.[28]

By finding violations of both the legal causes and socio-economic implications of detention, the Commission provides jurisprudential evidence of the indivisibility and co-existence of rights. In the *Nigerian Media* case,[29] for example, the Commission found the government wanting in respect of its obligation to respect the right to liberty and security (by detaining the victims without charge) and its obligation to respect the right to health (by denying them access to medical care).[30]

Although the Commission never used 'generational' labels to guide its jurisprudence, it dealt a final blow to the tripartite division of rights by introducing the four-layered conceptualization of government obligations to 'promote', 'respect', 'protect', and 'fulfil' rights in the *Ogoniland* case against Nigeria.[31] In that case, the Commission found that the killing and destruction by government forces and agents of the state-controlled oil company violated Nigeria's duty to 'respect' the right to life and dignity, and the right to health, property, the 'implied' rights to shelter and food,[32] and the right to economic, social, and cultural development of the Ogonis. Clearly spelling out the implications of its finding, the Commission reiterated that 'there is no right in the African Charter that cannot be made effective'.[33]

Going beyond the duty to 'respect', the Commission also interpreted rights in the Charter to entail a 'positive obligation' to 'protect' and 'fulfil'. A communication resulting from massive violations during a civil war in Chad exemplifies the duty (or 'positive obligation') of the state to 'protect' civilians against violations by non-state actors.[34] A government cannot absolve itself from responsibility when it failed to prevent and took no action to investigate assassinations and other killings, even if its own forces were not responsible for the atrocities. The impact on resources

---

Communications 54/91, 61/91, 98/93, 164–96/97, 310/98 (joined), *Malawi African Association and Others v Mauritania* (2000) AHRLR 149 (ACHPR 2000) (13th Annual Activity Report) (*Mauritanian Widows* case) para 96.

[26] Communications 37/94, 139/94, 154/96, 161/97 (joined), *International PEN and Others (on behalf of Saro-Wiwa) v Nigeria* (2000) AHRLR 212 (ACHPR 1998) (12th Annual Activity Report) (*Saro-Wiwa* case) para 96; and Communication 224/98, *Media Rights Agenda v Nigeria* (2000) AHRLR 262 (ACHPR 2000) (14th Annual Activity Report) (*Malaolu* case) paras 47 and 48.

[27] See eg Communication 103/93, *Abubakar v Ghana* (2000) AHRLR 124 (ACHPR 1996) (10th Annual Activity Report) (*Abubakar* case) paras 11 and 12; and Communication 225/98, *Huri-Laws v Nigeria* (2000) AHRLR 273 (ACHPR 2000) (14th Annual Activity Report) (*Huri-Laws* case) paras 45 and 46.

[28] Violations of art 6 (personal liberty and security) were found in 24 of the 42 cases finalized up to 2002 (Killander, n 23 above, 103).   [29] n 24 above.

[30] As above, paras 83–6 and 89–91. See also *Huri-Laws* case (n 27 above) para 41 and the *Saro-Wiwa* case (n 26 above) paras 111 and 112.

[31] Communication 155/96, *Social and Economic Rights Action Centre and Another v Nigeria* (2001) AHRLR 60 (ACHPR 2001) (15th Annual Activity Report) (*Ogoniland* case).

[32] See Ch 8.A.7.5 below for the 'implied rights' basis of this finding.

[33] *Ogoniland* case (n 31 above) para 68.

[34] Communication 74/92, *Commission Nationale des Droits de l'Homme et des Libertés v Chad* (2000) AHRLR 66 (ACHPR 1995) (9th Annual Activity Report) (*Chad Mass Violations* case) para 22.

of the duty to 'fulfil' is further illustrated in two cases dealing with the right to
health. In the first,[35] the Commission found that detainees' lack of drinking water
and medicine constituted a violation, thus implying a duty to make resources
available to this end. In the second finding,[36] the Commission not only found
that the insufficient medical and material care of persons detained in a mental
health facility constituted a violation of the right to health, but in its recommendations also placed an explicit duty on the state to 'fulfil' that obligation as part of
its minimum obligation to 'take concrete and targeted steps' towards the realization of that right. In as much as both these findings deal with persons to whom the
state owes a special duty of care, due to their detention, they may be interpreted as
reinforcing the principle that detainees should not be deprived of rights to a greater
extent than their incarceration necessitates. However, there seems to be no sound
reason to restrict the duty to 'fulfil' the right to health, and other socio-economic
rights, to narrow categories of people such as prisoners.

The Charter does not make the 'fulfilment' of any of its provisions dependent on 'available resources' or 'progressive realization'. In this respect—as far as
'socio-economic' rights are concerned—the Charter deviates from the ICESCR. It
appears that the Commission, acutely conscious of the prevalence of the 'problem
of poverty',[37] entertained some doubt about the feasibility of altogether dispensing
with those elements, though. It therefore decided to 'read into' the right to health
the qualification of 'available resources'.[38] At the same time, it imported from the
Committee in Economic, Social and Cultural Rights the notion that states retain
the 'core' obligation to take concrete, targeted, and non-discriminatory steps.[39] It
may be argued that this interpretation is influenced by the wording of article 16,
which provides for the 'best attainable' state of health and 'necessary measures',
and is therefore not a general statement about the duty to 'fulfil' rights. The qualification of 'available resources' should therefore not, on the basis of this decision,
be applied to the 'unqualified' right to education.

The Commission's very elaborate Guidelines for state reporting shed some
(contradictory) light on these issues.[40] Mirroring the guidelines under the ICESCR,
the Commission's guidelines do not make reference to the justiciability of socio-
economic rights. Instead, they seem to require targeted steps such as legislation, and
give some indication that socio-economic rights have to be realized 'progressively':
states have to report on how social security benefits are extended to 'further groups

[35] *Ogoniland* case (n 31 above).
[36] Communications 25/89, 47/90, 56/91, 100/93 (joined), *Free Legal Assistance Group and Another v
Zaire* (2000) AHRLR 74 (ACHPR 1995) (*Zairian Mass Violations* case) para 47.
[37] Communication 241/2001, *Purohit and Another v The Gambia* (2003) AHRLR 96 (ACHPR
2003) (16th Annual Activity Report) (*Gambian Mental Health* case) para 84.   [38] ibid.
[39] General Comment 3 of the Committee on Economic, Social and Cultural Rights on the nature
of states parties obligations, 14 December 1990, para 2; see also C Mbazira, 'Enforcing the Economic,
Social and Cultural Rights in the African Charter on Human and Peoples' Rights: Twenty Years of
Redundancy, Progression and Significant Strides' (2006) 6 *AHRLJ* 333, 353.
[40] See Ch 9.A.2 below.

of the population';[41] and even in respect of education, which is framed without qualification,[42] states are required to report about measures 'for the progressive implementation of the principle of compulsory education free of charge'.[43]

Anticipating the Commission's decision in the *Ogoniland* case (that the rights in the Charter 'imply' other rights,[44] such as the right to food and shelter or housing) the Guidelines require states to report on rights not expressly included in the Charter. One of these is the 'right to an adequate standard of living', which encompasses food production, distribution, and improved 'food consumption levels'.[45] Another is the right to social security, in respect of which states are to provide information about, among other schemes, old-age benefits, unemployment benefits, and 'family benefits'.[46]

States have generally followed the Charter provisions when reporting on socio-economic rights,[47] although they have also taken into account the more expansive reporting guidelines.[48] Some states have made reference to statistics and budgetary allocations,[49] but this data is mostly insufficient and too general,[50] and legislative or policy provisions take up too much of the reports.[51] In some instances, as in the case of Mauritania, states subsequently submitted more detailed and informative reports.

Although numerous African domestic legal systems provide for at least some justiciable socio-economic rights, there is—with the exception of South Africa—little indication of indivisibility in the jurisprudence of domestic courts.[52] By relegating socio-economic rights to non-justiciable directive principles of state policy, states contradict one of the core principles of the African Charter. It is particularly disappointing that the list of culprits includes states that generally have a relatively favourable reputation for observance of human rights, such as Ghana, and also includes Nigeria, the only state to have expressly domesticated the Charter.[53]

Other major AU treaties have followed the lead of the African Charter by including rights of all three 'generations'. The African Charter on the Rights and Welfare of the Child (African Children's Charter) provides for the right to education and to

---

[41] Guidelines for National Periodic Reports, para II.19.
[42] African Charter, art 17(1): 'Everyone shall have the right to education'.
[43] Guidelines for National Periodic Reports, para II.B.58.   [44] See Ch 7.A.7.5 below.
[45] Guidelines for National Periodic Reports, paras II.A.31–4.
[46] Guidelines for National Periodic Reports, para II.18.
[47] See eg *Rapport Initial de la Republique Islamique de Mauritanie*, OAU Doc DOC/OS(XXXI)/269d, dated October 2001, considered at the Commission's 31st session, 2–16 May 2002 (Initial Mauritanian Report), part II, ch II.
[48] See eg Initial Mauritanian Report, n 47 above, which includes data on the right to social security (26).
[49] See eg Initial Mauritanian Report, n 47 above, which showed that the education budget increased from 20% of the total expenditure in 1992 to 25% in 1998 (30); and that the adult illiteracy rate decreased from 72% in 1985 to 50% in 1995 (33).
[50] See eg Uganda's Second Periodic Report, <http://www.achpr.org/english/state_reports/40_Uganda%20periodic%20report_Eng.pdf> (31 October 2006) para 5.
[51] Initial Mauritanian Report (n 47 above) 27; see also 29, where an unsubstantiated statement is made that 75% of the population has access to medications against respiratory infections.
[52] See Ch 14 below.   [53] ibid.

health, making them in principle justiciable. However, elements of 'progressive real-ization' have also crept into this text: while compulsory and free primary education is guaranteed as a right, secondary education must 'progressively' be made free and accessible to all.[54] In respect of the right to health, states must 'pursue' its 'full imple-mentation' by, for example, 'reducing' infant mortality rates.[55] The immediacy of state obligations is more apparent in the Protocol to the African Charetr on the Rights of Women in Africa (Women's Protocol). Building on the '*Ogoniland* rights', the Protocol requires that states take measures to 'provide women with access to clean drinking water' and to 'acceptable living conditions'.[56]

At least in theory, the NEPAD APRM echoes the indivisibility and 'implied' rights doctrine. One of the objectives to be kept in mind in the Country Self-Assessment is the 'promotion of economic, social, cultural, civil and political lib-erties'.[57] An 'indicator' of the realization of these rights is the 'capacity of the state' to provide 'an adequate standard of living, education, housing and health care'.

2 The Concept of 'Peoples' Rights'

As its title stresses, the African Charter recognizes not only individual rights, but also those of 'peoples'.[58] According to the Charter, peoples have the right to existence, to self-determination, to freely dispose of their natural resources, to development, to international peace and security, and to a generally satisfactory environment.[59]

Despite its omission from Senghor's initial proposal,[60] the concept 'peoples' was mentioned in the resolution of the OAU Assembly calling for the elaboration of the Charter.[61] Two states with socialist inclinations at the time, Guinea and Madagascar, pressed for the inclusion of the term 'peoples' rights' alongside 'human rights' as part of the mandate for the experts' meeting.[62] Through their insistence, the African human rights instrument was guaranteed one of its distinctly 'African' characteristics. During his address to the Dakar meeting, Senghor added a cultural justification to the ideological one, explaining the reference to peoples' rights as follows: 'We simply meant . . . to show our attachment to economic, social and cul-tural rights, to collective rights, in general, rights which have a particular importance in our situation in a developing country'.[63] He added that, in Africa, 'the individual and his rights are wrapped in the protection of the family and other communities'. However, the principal reliance placed on the ICESCR and American Convention

---

[54] African Children's Charter, art 11(3)(b).   [55] ibid, art 14(2)(a).
[56] Women's Protocol, arts 15 and 16.
[57] Country Self-Assessment for the APRM (2004) para 1.1.3 (Objective 3).
[58] On this, see the early view expressed by RN Kiwanuka, 'The Meaning of "People" in the African Charter on Human and Peoples' Rights' (1988) 82 *AJIL* 80.   [59] African Charter, arts 19–24.
[60] K M'Baye, *Les Droits de l'Homme en Afrique* (Paris: Pedone, 1992) 150.   [61] Ch 4 above.
[62] M'Baye (n 60 above) 150.
[63] Address delivered by Leopold Sedar Senghor, President of the Republic of Senegal, at the opening of the Meeting of Africa Experts preparing the Draft African Charter in Dakar, Senegal 28 November–8 December 1979 (Senghor's speech), reprinted in Heyns (n 17 above) 78–80, 79.

meant that the rights bearers were predominantly phrased as 'individuals' and 'every person'. During the drafting of the Charter, the concept 'peoples' was deliberately left undefined, so as to avoid controversy.[64]

Morphologically, the terms 'people' and 'a people' are distinguishable. On the one hand, the term 'people', used with a definite article ('the') but not with an indefinite article ('a'), has no plural form; in a given context it always denotes an inclusive plurality of all human beings, such as 'the people of Congo'.[65] On the other hand, 'a people' (and its plural, 'peoples', the term used in the African Charter),[66] is a term with a more restricted scope, and may be demarcated by factors other than territorial boundaries or nationality. However, this morphological distinction is often overlooked. In the Ethiopian Constitution, for example, the right to sustainable development is guaranteed to both 'the *peoples* of Ethiopia as a whole' and to 'each Nation, Nationality and People in Ethiopia'.[67]

Three ways of understanding the term 'peoples' in the context of the Charter may therefore be suggested. First, following the most common understanding of the term 'people', that of essentially encompassing 'everyone', the term 'people' has been interpreted to denote 'everyone within a state', that is, all the inhabitants of any member state, also in the post-colonial context. The problem with this interpretation is that 'people' in this sense does not allow for the use of the plural 'peoples' ('the peoples of Egypt'). However, the Commission often uses the term 'peoples' in this sense. Despite the interchangeable use of the terms 'Congolese peoples' rights' and 'the rights of the people' of Congo in *DRC v Burundi, Rwanda and Uganda*,[68] the Commission clearly refers to the right of all (affected) Congolese—the 'people' of Congo. Even if the Charter's term, 'peoples', is used, it essentially denotes 'the people' of Congo. By equating state with 'peoples', a state-centred interpretation of the term, following the territorial demarcation of the state, has been adopted. This interpretation of the concept is closest to that of the proponents of including 'peoples' rights' in the Charter for ideological reasons. Against a background of strict adherence to the principles of *uti possidetis* and the centrality of territoriality to notions of statehood, it is more than likely that the majority of African states supported—and still support—this status quo-serving interpretation of the term.

Secondly, the term 'peoples' (or 'a people') may denote distinct minority groups, such as linguistic, ethnic, religious, or other groups sharing common characteristics, consisting of individuals who are usually—but not necessarily—inhabitants of the

---

[64] Report of the Draft African Charter presented by the Secretary-General at the 37th ordinary session of the OAU Council of Ministers, Kenya, 15–21 June 1981, OAU Doc CM/1149(XXXVII), Annex II: Rapporteur's Report OAU Doc CAB/LEG/67/Draft.Rept(II) Rev.4 (Rapporteur's Report), reprinted in Heyns (n 17 above) 94–105, 96.

[65] See 2001 Constitution of Congo, art 3 ('sovereignty belongs to the people'); in French, the equivalent is '*la peuple*', which does not allow for a plural.

[66] In French, '*une peuple*', with the plural form of '*peuples*'.

[67] 1994 Constitution, art 43(1) (emphasis added: here, 'peoples' is used to refer to the nation as a whole (the 'people' of Ethiopia).

[68] Communication 227/1999, 20th Annual Activity Report, paras 87 and 95.

same state. Such an interpretation is most in line with the linguistic analysis above, and goes the furthest in extending the potential benefits of the Charter. The Commission steered towards this interpretation in a number of cases.

Thirdly, should the meaning of the term be placed in its historical context, 'peoples' may denote the inhabitants of an African territory under colonial rule, as 'oppressed peoples', or as groups under alien domination. However, if this interpretation is accepted as the single correct interpretation of the term, the question arises whether the end of colonial rule in Africa has not rendered the term obsolete. The omission of the eradication of colonialism from Africa from the objectives set out in the AU Constitutive Act lends some support to this line of reasoning.[69]

Ouguergouz has aptly described the word 'people' as a 'chameleon-like term' that 'varies in nature according to the right which is to be implemented'.[70] For this reason, a search for a single meaning of 'people' should be abandoned. A further contextual exploration of the meaning of the term is therefore embarked upon with reference to the interpretation by the Commission of three provisions (articles 19 to 21).

In *Legal Resources Foundation v Zambia*,[71] a violation of article 19, the right of peoples to be treated equally, was alleged. Reliance was placed on this right on behalf of 'the entire population' (all Zambian citizens) in support of a contention that a constitutional amendment (restricting potential presidential candidates to persons whose parents were Zambian by birth or descent) violated the African Charter. Finding violations on other grounds, the Commission found that article 19, as a provision 'dealing with "peoples" cannot apply'. Success on that basis, the Commission reasoned, depends on evidence that 'an identifiable group of Zambian citizens by reason of their common ancestry, ethnic origin, language and cultural habits' was adversely affected.[72] By adopting this approach, at least in that particular instance, the Commission gives a clear indication that a linguistic or ethnic sub-set of the population may qualify as a 'people'.[73] Similarly, the finding in the *Mauritanian Widows* case,[74] although unsuccessful on the facts, could be read as allowing groups such as 'black Mauritanians' to rely on this right to launch a Charter-based attack against Arab domination.

Article 20(1) provides that 'all peoples' have the right to 'self-determination'. When the Katangese Peoples' Congress requested that the Commission recognizes the right of the 'Katangese people' to complete sovereign independence, the complex issue of secession was introduced before the Commission.[75] The Commission found that the claim as such did not amount to a violation of article 20(1), because

---

[69] In contrast with the OAU Charter, art 2(1)(d).   [70] Ouguergouz (n 4 above) 211.

[71] Communication 211/98, *Legal Resources Foundation v Zambia* (2001) AHRLR 84 (ACHPR 2001) (14th Annual Activity Report) (*Zambian Presidential Candidates* case) para 73.   [72] ibid.

[73] See also SA Dersso, 'The Jurisprudence of the African Commission on Human and Peoples' Rights with Respect to Peoples' Rights' (2006) 6 *AHRLJ* 358, 375, who notes that the Commission, in applying the concept 'peoples' to groups in Africa, does not seem to consider as relevant whether the group is a 'minority, an indigenous group or a nation'.   [74] n 25 above, para 142.

[75] Communication 75/92, *Katangese Peoples' Congress v Zaire* (2000) AHRLR 72 (ACHPR 1995) (8th Annual Activity Report) (*Katangese Secession* case).

the claimants had not shown that they had made efforts to exercise this right in accordance with constitutional options open to them, ranging from confederalism to self-government. As the Commission is 'obliged to uphold' the territorial integrity and sovereignty of Zaire,[76] there is a strong presumption that all nationals who happen to find themselves in a particular state will be able to express their 'right to self-determination' within the boundaries of that state. However, the Commission left the door open that the right may be extended to groups within a state who are persecuted, whose rights are consistently violated and who are denied a meaning-ful say in government.[77] Like everyone else, these groups qualify as 'peoples' with a 'right to self-determination'. Exceptionally, when the stated conditions of exclu-sion and persecution have been met, this right may entitle them to secede from the state of which they are nationals. Part of the problem with the Katangese com-munication was that it lacked a factual or evidentiary basis indicative of oppres-sion or human rights abuses by the Zairian government directed at the Katangese people. Ankumah advises that oppressed groups 'within sovereign African States should be entitled to seek redress from the Commission'.[78] The *Katangese Secession* case thus seems to lend support to an interpretation of 'peoples' which includes minority groups within a state.

After examining South Africa's initial state report,[79] the Commission expressed its anxiety about the 'preservation of unity and stability' of the country in light of the right to self-determination of 'people' provided for under the South African Constitution, fearing that it may be interpreted to undermine the country's terri-torial integrity.[80] In the Constitution, the right to self-determination is granted to the 'South African people as a whole', without precluding 'recognition of the notion' of this right by groups sharing a common cultural and language heritage. Echoing the sentiments in the *Katanga Secession* case, the Commission favoured an approach by which the rights of these minority communities would be guaranteed 'through constant improvement of democratic participation of all the citizens'.[81]

When article 20 was invoked in the *Gambian Coup* case,[82] the Commission found that the coup of 11 November 1994 brought a military government to power by forceful means, depriving the 'Gambian people' of their right to 'freely determine

---

[76] ibid, para 5.

[77] ibid, para 6: '*In the absence of concrete evidence* of violations of human rights to the point that the territorial integrity of Zaire should be called to question and *in the absence of* evidence that the people of Katanga are denied the right to participate in government . . . , Katanga is obliged to exercise a vari-ant of self-determination that is compatible with the sovereignty and territorial integrity of Zaire' (emphasis added).

[78] EA Ankumah, *The African Commission on Human and Peoples' Rights: Practice and Procedures* (The Hague: Martinus Nijhoff, 1996) 165.

[79] Examined at the Commission's 25th session, April 1999, emanating in 'concluding observations' entitled 'Initial Report of South Africa' (on file with author).

[80] South African Constitution 1996, s 235.

[81] Concluding observations on Initial Report of South Africa (n 79 above) para III.1.

[82] Communications 147/95, 149/96 (joined), *Jawara v The Gambia* (2000) AHRLR 107 (ACHPR 2000) (13th Annual Activity Report) (*Gambian Coup* case).

their political status', guaranteed by article 20(1).[83] The Commission again did not seek to define the concept 'people', but uses it to refer to all Gambians eligible to vote, seemingly favouring the 'state-centred' understanding of 'peoples'.

Article 21 guarantees 'peoples' the right to freely 'dispose of their wealth and natural resources'. Finding that Nigeria had violated that right by giving the green light to oil companies to operate and keep operating in Ogoniland, despite the destruction of resources, the Commission in the *Ogoniland* case traces the origin of the provision to colonialism.[84] It adds that the 'aftermath of colonial exploitation has left Africa's precious resources and people still vulnerable to foreign misappropriation'.[85] The Commission passed by the opportunity to clarify the concept 'peoples', accepting uncritically and without justification that groups of individuals constitute 'peoples' under the Charter. In this case, the Commission refers to the victims as the 'Ogonis', the 'Ogoni people', 'individuals in Ogoniland', 'the whole of the Ogoni Community as a whole' (*sic*) and 'the people of Ogoniland',[86] without examining what the constituent elements of a 'people' are. The Commission concludes as follows:[87] 'The *drafters of the Charter obviously* wanted to remind African governments of the continent's painful legacy and restore co-operative economic development to its traditional place at the heart of African society'.

This interpretation ties the right to colonial exploitation, and its reverberating effect on the present. While colonialism accounts for some of the current forms of resource depletion, it tends to obscure the continuing role of corrupt and preying African governments. This is also the only instance found in which the Commission invokes the 'drafting history' of the Charter, by referring to the 'origin' of the provision and to what the 'drafters ... wanted'. As original intent is considered to be self-evident ('obviously'), no attempt is made to substantiate it on the strength of the *travaux préparatoires* or any other source.

Article 23 provides for the right to 'national and international peace and security'. Unfortunately, the Commission's finding in the *Mauritanian Widows* case, that Mauritania violated this provision by attacking 'Mauritanian villages' without provocation, does not advance our quest for interpretative clarity.[88] The Commission merely found that the attacks constituted a 'denial of the right to live in peace and security',[89] without exploring the 'peoples' dimension.

The Commission's cautiously progressive approach does not find support in other international human rights law instruments to which African states are party. The Human Rights Committee made it clear that, notwithstanding the guarantee to 'peoples' of the right to self-determination, only individual communications are allowed under the OPI to the ICCPR.[90] In its concluding observations in respect

---

[83] ibid, para 73.   [84] n 31 above.   [85] ibid, para 56.
[86] ibid, paras 1, 67, and 69.   [87] ibid, para 56 (emphasis added).   [88] n 25 above.
[89] ibid, para 140.
[90] See Communication 760/1997, *Diergaardt v Namibia*, UN Doc CCPR/C/69/D/760/1997 (6 September 2000), in which the Human Rights Committee observed that, 'as stipulated in article 1 of the Covenant, the question whether the community to which the authors belong is a "people" is not an issue for the Committee to address under the Optional Protocol to the Covenant' (para 10.3).

of the Congolese state report, the Human Rights Committee equated 'people' in article 1 of the ICCPR with the population as a whole, when it noted 'with concern that the Congolese people have been unable, owing to the postponement of general elections, to exercise their right to self-determination'.[91]

One looks in vain for guidance to the state reports of Senegal, from where the idea of 'peoples' rights' partially originated.[92] Containing a comprehensive discussion, the Burkinabe state report represents at least a concerted attempt to report on 'peoples' rights'.[93] Still, the concept of 'peoples' is not clarified, and the report mostly refers to provisions of the Constitution. Sometimes, as in the case of Egypt's third submitted report,[94] Commissioners criticized this silence. On that occasion, the Commissioner-rapporteur's concern that Egypt's previous reports had also 'made nothing of' peoples' rights did not inspire any response from the government delegation.[95] In three more recent reports, submitted by Nigeria, Uganda, and Zambia, very little discussion is devoted to peoples' rights under the Charter.[96] While Nigeria provided some superficial details, Uganda omitted all reference, and Zambia avoids the issue by referring back to the 'core information' in the report.

The omission of 'peoples' rights' from national constitutions explains the inability of state reports to shed light on the meaning of 'peoples'. When national constitutions invoke the concept of 'people', they seem to project their voice to an external international audience, mostly as a rhetorical device to legitimate the state ('national sovereignty belongs to the people'),[97] in the context of representative government,[98] or in support of 'peoples' fighting for self-determination elsewhere,[99] and not to the plurality that makes up their states. These invocations align themselves closely with the first interpretation alluded to above. Opting to designate as right-bearers 'everyone', 'every person', or 'every national', very few constitutions domesticated the notion of justiciable 'peoples' rights'. The notable exception is the 1994 Ethiopian Constitution, which not only grants to 'every people in Ethiopia' the 'unquestionable right to self-determination, including the right to secession',[100] but also unequivocally defines a 'people' as 'a group of people who have or share a large measure of a common culture or similar customs,

---

[91] UN Doc CCPR/C/79/Add.118 (27 March 2000) para 20.

[92] *Deuxième Rapport Périodique de la République du Sénégal en Application des Dispositions de l'Article 62 de la Charte Africaine des Droits de l'Homme et des Peuples*, January–February 1992, in African Commission on Human and Peoples' Rights, *Examination of State Reports: 12th Session October 1992* (1995) Appendix II (merely reciting the provisions of the Charter and Preamble to the Senegalese Constitution).

[93] Periodic Report of Burkina Faso to the African Commission on the Implementation of the African Charter, October 1998–December 2002, July 2003 (on file with author).

[94] Combining Egypt's seventh and eighth periodic reports, examined at the Commission's 37th session, 27 April–11 May 2005.   [95] Notes on file with author.

[96] <http://www.achpr.org/english/state_reports> (30 November 2006).

[97] See eg 2001 Constitution of Congo, art 3; 1990 Constitution of Guinea, art 2; 1977 Constitution of Tanzania (as amended) art 8.

[98] See eg 2001 Constitution of Congo, art 2; 1990 Constitution of Guinea, art 1; 1993 Constitution of Mali, art 25.   [99] 1976 Constitution of Algeria, art 27.

[100] 1994 Constitution of Ethiopia, art 39(1).

mutual intelligibility of language, belief in a common or related identities, a common psychological make-up, and who inhabit an identifiable, predominantly contiguous territory'.[101] This right, which follows the second line of interpretation suggested above, has not found application in practice. By avoiding the terminology of 'peoples' rights', but still providing a space for collective claims based on language, ethnicity, and so on, the Ugandan Constitution opts instead to provide for the right of 'minorities' to participate in national decision-making processes.[102]

Further evidence that the concept 'peoples' has largely become outdated—or is in need of a radically renewing overhaul—is found in the omission of this concept from human rights treaties adopted subsequent to the African Charter. However, given their focus on two particular groups—children and women—it is perhaps understandable that the African Children's Charter and the Women's Protocol do not include the concept 'peoples'. None of the rights of peoples was found appropriate for inclusion in the African Children's Charter, as they do not deal with issues that are pertinent to children. In so far as the Women's Protocol deals with rights designated as 'peoples' rights' under the Charter,[103] it does not use this terminology, instead restricting the rights-bearers to the group of its concern—women. Confirming its neo-liberal globally directed positioning, NEPAD and the APRM do not even pay lip-service to the idea of 'peoples' rights'.

3 Individual Duties

Another distinguishing feature of the Charter is the emphasis placed on individual 'duties'.[104] The individual has duties towards other individuals, his or her family, towards the community, towards the state whose national he or she happens to be, and to the African and international community.[105]

One of the factors inspiring the committee of experts drafting the African Charter was President Senghor's speech, calling for the inclusion of 'individual duties', 'contrary to what has been done so far in other regions of the world'.[106] Senghor emphasized the interrelated nature of traditional African society, where 'the individual and his rights are wrapped in the protection the family and other communities ensure everyone'.[107] This is contrasted with the European tradition,

---

[101] Art 39(5).

[102] 1995 Constitution of Uganda, art 36. See also 1996 Constitution of South Africa, s 31(1), providing cautiously that persons 'belonging to a cultural, religious or linguistic community may not be denied the right' to practice elements of their culture together.

[103] Women's Protocol, arts 10 (peace) and 19 (sustainable development).

[104] As in other international human rights treaties, the primary duty under the Charter is the duty of state parties to 'recognize' the rights therein, and to 'adopt legislative or other measures to give effect to them'. Except for the mention in art 10, individual duties are not included in the European Convention, and are barely mentioned in the American Convention, making the African Charter the first to 'elaborate' the duties of individuals (Umozurike (n 6 above) 64). On this concept, see Mutua (n 5 above) 339.

[105] African Charter, arts 27–9.   [106] Senghor's speech (n 63 above) 78, 80.

[107] ibid.

allowing human rights to be used as a 'weapon' with which the individual can defend 'himself against the group or entity representing it'.[108] By accepting that rights in Africa *in the form of rites* 'must be obeyed' because they 'command', and by insisting that rights-as-rites cannot be separated from duties to family and 'other communities',[109] Senghor fuses the dividing lines between legal enforcement and moral obligation. However, painting with a philosopher's brush, Senghor does not suggest ways in which this tension may be settled.

So far, the Commission has not dealt with this tension, either in its communications or in its state reporting procedures. No cases involving individual duties have been submitted to the Commission. The Guidelines for National Periodic Reports shed some light on the content of these duties by indicating that states should provide particulars about legislative measures, administrative regulations, and court decisions 'establishing the atmosphere for enforcement and effectuation of these duties'.[110] This corresponds with Umozurike's view that these duties require states to 'instil [them] in their subjects'.[111] Indeed, these duties by themselves cannot confer upon state parties jurisdiction over individuals. Complaints against individuals also cannot be brought to the African Commission, for the simple reason that the Charter is open for ratification only to states. The inclusion of duties should also not serve as a pretext for the curtailment of individual rights by repressive governments.[112]

In the reports they submit, states often omit any discussion of articles 27 to 29 of the Charter,[113] and go no further than citing the inclusion of individual duties in their Constitutions as proof of domestic adherence.[114] Without any indication what the significance or practical application is of constitutionalized individual

---

[108] Senghor's speech (n 63 above) 79.   [109] ibid 80.

[110] Para IV.7 of the Guidelines, Second Activity Report, Annex XII. See also para IV. 8 of the Guidelines, noting the need to establish programmes because some of these 'valuable traditional duties might have been treated lightly . . . because of the overwhelming Western influence in the past colonial days'.

[111] Umozurike (n 6 above) 65. See eg Rwanda Penal Code, art 380, imposing penalties on men and women (equally) for deserting the family, which may be linked to the duty to preserve the cohesion of the family (art 29(1) of the Charter) (UN Doc A/43/40, para 227, examination of Rwanda's Second State Report under ICCPR).

[112] See eg art 29(4), requiring the individual to 'preserve and strengthen national security'.

[113] See eg Implementation of the African Charter on Human and Peoples' Rights by the Republic of Senegal: Third to Seventh Periodic Reports (Senegalese 3rd–7th reports) (trans and unpub, on file with author); Uganda's Second Periodic Report <http://www.achpr.org/english/state_reports/40_Uganda%20periodic%20report_Eng.pdf> (30 November 2006); Nigeria's Second Periodic Report <http://www.achpr.org/english/state_reports/40_Nigeria%20periodic%20report_Eng.pdf> (30 November 2006).

[114] eg the Initial Zambian Report, para 537, citing art 113 of the Constitution, sets out the duties of a citizen as follows: '(a) be patriotic and loyal to Zambia and promote its well-being; (b) contribute to the well-being of the community where that citizen lives, including the observance of health controls; (c) foster national unity and live in harmony with others; (d) promote democracy and the rule of law; (e) vote in national and local government elections; (f) provide defense and military service when called upon; (g) carry out with discipline and honesty legal public functions; (h) pay all taxes and duties legally due and owing to the State; and (i) assist in the enforcement of the law at all times'.

duties, the references to constitutions are circular as they merely refer back to an undefined concept of 'individual duty', even if the catalogue of individual duties contained in constitutions is different from that in the Charter. Further insights into this concept are to be gained from isolated references to legislation, laws, and policies.[115]

While the concept of peoples did not find its way into domestic constitutions, individual duties did.[116] Their inclusion in domestic Constitutions underscores the reciprocity of rights and duties, an aspect that is hailed as a part of the African understanding of rights. States are much more likely to entertain the notion of individual duties, as they do not pose any threat to state sovereignty—to the contrary, they may serve as a counterbalance to civil and political rights, and may even be used by repressive states to undermine individual rights.

Even if the constitutionalization of individual duties is the exception rather than the rule, all legal systems are to a significant extent premised on the reciprocity of rights and duties. Domestic legislation routinely imposes individual duties on individuals. Sometimes this is done explicitly, for example in the Ugandan Children's Act, which provides that it is 'the duty of a parent or guardian to maintain a child and every parent shall have parental responsibility for his or her child'.[117] More frequently, this is done implicitly, for instance in laws requiring payment of tax or child maintenance, and in measures criminalizing certain conduct.

The notion of individual duties has on occasion been the subject of litigation in domestic courts. In an illustration of the deep-seated nature of duties in a traditional society, a Nigerian community-based women's association imposed and forcibly effected a service levy for a community development project on a woman who refused to contribute on the basis of her religious beliefs.[118] The obligation to pay was justified as a customary practice requiring members of the Igbo community to fulfil their 'civil obligations' towards the well-being of the community. A refusal to perform a civic duty was regarded as 'anti-social' behaviour.[119] Finding this levy to be arbitrarily imposed and illegally enforced, the Nigerian Court of Appeal held that recourse to self-help to impose a customary practice was unconstitutional. Levies could only be imposed by law; and the community could 'encourage the people to participate in community development',[120] but the decision to contribute remained voluntary.

[115] See eg Human Rights, Poverty Alleviation and Social Integration Commission, '8th and 9th Periodic Reports of the Islamic Republic of Mauritania on the Implementation of the Provisions of the African Charter' (January 2005) (trans), where the code of personal status and legislation curbing human trafficking are cited as part of an 'appropriate framework' to protect the family (64).
[116] See C Heyns, 'Where is the Voice of Africa in Our Constitution?' Centre for Human Rights, Pretoria, Occasional Paper 8 <http://www.chr.up.ac.za/centre_publications/occ_papers/occ8.html> (accessed 30 September 2006), citing the Constitutions of Algeria (art 60), Cape Verde (art 80(2)), Congo (art 56), Ghana (art 41), São Tomé e Príncipe (art 20), Sierra Leone (art 13(e)), Tanzania (arts 29(5), 30(1) and (2)) and Zimbabwe (art 11).　　　　　[117] Ch 50 (of the Laws of Uganda), s 6.
[118] *Nkpa v Nkume* (2003) AHRLR 208 (NgCA 2000) Nigerian Court of Appeal (Port Harcourt Division) 6 April 2000, reversing the decision of the trial Court.　　　　　[119] ibid, para 28.
[120] ibid, para 26.

More pertinent to the duties in the African Charter, the Constitutional Court of Benin found a husband and father who 'ceased without grounds to ensure the upkeep and education of his children' to be in violation of his duty under the African Charter to 'preserve the harmonious development of the family and to work for the cohesion and respect of his family'.[121] It is not clear if this duty is also contained in domestic legislation, and why mention was not made of such a provision. A parental duty was also invoked in the following Kenyan case—not as an individual constitutional obligation, but as part of domestic legislation: A divorced father paid maintenance for his daughter's education until she reached the age of 18, when she completed her secondary schooling.[122] The daughter then enrolled at the university where her father was employed, and without his consent applied for a 50 per cent fee reduction to which family relations of staff members were entitled. The father, whose signature was required, refused to sign the application. The daughter brought a suit to compel her father to uphold his 'parental responsibility' under the Child Act 2001.[123] Giving effect to a moral obligation by requiring that maintenance be paid under the Act, the Court found the father's refusal unreasonable.

4 Derogation

The African Charter is silent on the effect of the suspension or derogation of rights. Unlike other international human rights treaties, the Charter does not contain a derogation clause, in terms of which rights, or certain selected rights, may be suspended temporarily during times of national emergency. This omission may constitute a normative innovation, but it also puts the Charter at odds with the domestic constitutional law of many sub-Saharan African states,[124] as well as with some of their international law obligations. Under the ICCPR, to which 45 African states are party, derogations are allowed, but states are also required to immediately inform the UN Secretary-General of the provisions from which they have derogated and the reasons for their derogation.[125] A similar communication must be made when the derogation ends. However, certain rights, such as the right to life; the prohibition on torture, slavery, forced labour, and on retroactive penal laws; as well as freedom of conscience and religion, may under no circumstances be suspended or derogated from.[126]

---

[121] *Okpeitcha v Okpeitcha* (2001) AHRLR 33 (BnCC 2001), Decision DCC 96-024 of 26 April 1996, para 10, applying African Charter, art 29(1).

[122] *Wambua v Wambua* (2004) AHRLR 189 (KeHC 2004).

[123] Under s 28 of the Act, the Court has the power to extend parental responsibility in respect of a child beyond the date of the child's 18th birthday if 'special circumstances' exist.

[124] A significant number of African Constitutions allow for derogation under circumscribed circumstances: see eg the following examples, representing the main regions and legal traditions in Africa: 1973 Constitution of Angola, art 52; 1966 Constitution of Botswana, art 16; 1994 Constitution of Ethiopia, art 93; 1992 Constitution of Ghana, art 31; 1990 Constitution of Mozambique, art 828. No such clauses were observed in the Constitutions of North African states. [125] ICCPR, art 4(3).

[126] ibid, art 4(2).

Confronted with the 'derogation defence' by states during the communications procedure to justify human rights violations, the Commission took the position that derogations are never allowed. In the *Chad Massive Violations* case, an issue to be decided was whether a country could derogate from the Charter during emergency situations. The Commission made the following clear statement: 'The African Charter, unlike other human rights instruments, does not allow for state parties to derogate from their treaty obligations during emergency situations. Thus, even a civil war in Chad cannot be used as an excuse by the State violating or permitting violations of rights in the African Charter'.[127]

The *Gambian Coup* case provides an example of the indirect suspension of the African Charter. In 1992, the Gambian state report to the African Commission indicated that chapter 3 of the 1970 Gambian Constitution (the Bill of Rights) provided for most of the rights in the Charter. After the coup, the new government suspended chapter 3 of the Constitution. The Commission found that such a suspension restricted the enjoyment of the rights in the Bill of Rights, and by implication, also of the rights in the African Charter. Holding that the suspension constituted a violation of articles 1 and 2 of the Charter, the Commission reiterated that 'the suspension of the Bill of Rights does not *ipso facto* mean the suspension of the domestic effect of the Charter'.[128]

It has been argued that it is perhaps an unrealistically high standard to expect from states never to derogate from rights, even during legitimately declared states of emergency, occasioned by, for example, flooding. Through its non-derogability jurisprudence, the Commission elevated all Charter rights to the level of regional *jus cogens*, while, under international law it is accepted that only a few rights, such as the prohibition on torture, slavery and servitude, and non-discrimination, have attained the status of peremptory norms.

However, the Commission has made it clear that it treats attempts at derogation as just another form of limitation. In *Constitutional Rights Project and Others v Nigeria*,[129] the Commission noted that the African Charter does not contain a derogation clause and that, 'therefore', limitations may not be justified by mere reliance on a declared state of emergency or other 'special circumstances'. As with other limitations, the only basis on which to justify a 'derogation' is article 27(2) of the Charter. If such derogation is proportionate and necessary to achieve the protection of the rights of others, collective security, morality, or common interest, and does not erode the right to render it illusory, it may be Charter-compliant. It is important to state that the source of the 'derogation-limitation' should be a lawfully declared state of emergency of limited duration.

However, two factors point to the danger that derogation—even under tight and clearly-defined conditions—may be abused in the African context.

---

[127] Communication 74/92, *Commission Nationale des Droits de l'Homme et des Libertés v Chad*, para 21.   [128] *Gambian Coup* case (n 82 above) para 49.
[129] Communications 140/94, 141/94, 145/94 (joined) (2000) AHRLR 227 (ACHPR 1999) (13th Annual Activity Report) para 41; see also the *Nigerian Media* case (n 24 above) paras 67 and 68.

The first is the fact that African states have mostly failed to abide by the 'notification' requirement under the ICCPR. In this respect, African practice contrasts sharply with that of states in other regions plagued by emergencies, such as Latin America. Despite the numerous states of emergency across the continent, only three African states have ever made the required notifications.[130] Algeria made such a notification in 1991 and 1992, when a state of emergency was declared after disrupted elections. A rational and circumscribed list of rights, namely the rights to a prompt trial, freedom of movement, privacy, freedom of expression, and freedom of assembly, were derogated from. The rights Sudan derogated from in 1992 included the prohibition on discrimination. Namibia also provided the required information when a state of emergency was declared in 1992, and when aspects of the right to a fair trial were derogated from.

The second is the regularity with which domestic provisions allowing for states of emergency have been invoked across Africa. When governments are faced with threats, the general tendency is to declare national emergencies. In 1973, the King of Swaziland declared a state of emergency, suspending the Constitution in its totality. In Egypt, a state of emergency has been in force since 1981, when Islamic militants assassinated President Anwar Sadat. For Khamil, an Egyptian official who submitted the state's report to the 11th session of the African Commission in 1992,[131] a declaration of a state of emergency is not an unusual measure since it is expressly provided for in other international human rights instruments, such as the ICCPR.[132] The concerns and request for information from the UN Special Rapporteur on the Promotion and Protection of Human Rights and Fundmanatal Freedoms while Countering Terrorism did not elicit any government response.[133] Despite an indication that the 'current state of emergency regime' would be replaced by counter-terrorism legislation,[134] the Egyption Parliament in April 2006 extended the state of emergency for a further two years.[135]

B Refugees

Some of the consequences of the solidification of African colonial borders in line with the principle of *uti possidetis* were internal strife, large-scale dislocation, and the movement of people across these borders. Although national wars of liberation accounted for a substantial number of refugees in the 1960s, many more fled

---

[130] See OHCHR <http://www.ohchr.org> (31 July 2006).

[131] African Commission on Human and Peoples' Rights, Examination of State Reports, 11th session, March 1992 (Egypt–Tanzania) 21 and 23.   [132] ibid, reference to art 4 of the ICCPR.

[133] UN Doc E/CN.4/2006/98/Add.1 (23 December 2005) paras 1 and 2.

[134] ibid, para 1.

[135] 'Egypt's Parliament Extends State of Emergency', 30 April 2006, <http://www.voanews.com/english/archive/2006-04/2006-04-30-voa10.cfm?CFID=34831920&CFTOKEN=63097152> (31 January 2007).

'explosive internal, social and political situations', which predated independence but reached a climax 'when the internal forces were no longer controlled by the straht-jacket [*sic*] of colonial domination'.[136] At the time it was not uncommon to find frequent references to the word 'problem' in any discourse on 'refugees'. By 1964, the influx of refugees from Rwanda into Burundi, the DRC, and Uganda had spurred the OAU into action, first leading to the establishment of a ten-member Refugee Commission to investigate the refugee 'problem' in Africa,[137] and later setting in motion the drafting of a regional treaty.[138]

This process culminated in the adoption by the OAU Assembly in 1969 of the OAU Convention Governing the Specific Aspects of Refugee *Problems* in Africa (OAU Refugee Convention).[139] With the exception of the right not to be sent back or expelled (the *non-refoulement* principle),[140] the OAU Refugee Convention does not provide explicitly for the 'rights' of refugees. Still, entitlements (or 'indirect rights') are implied by the imposition of obligations on states, thus rendering the OAU Refugee Convention a 'human rights-related' treaty.

At the time, the comparable instrument under the UN, the UN Refugee Convention, had long been adopted and entered into force (in 1951 and 1954, respectively).[141] Three of the most important limitations of the UN Refugee Convention may be traced to the socio-political context of its adoption, which was dominated by the effects of the aftermath of World War II and the beginning of the Cold War. First, the basis of qualification for refugee status was limited to a 'well-founded fear of being persecuted for reasons of race, religion, nationality, membership of a particular social group or political opinion'.[142] 'Fear' is a subjective requirement, which needs to be assessed individually for its 'well-foundedness'. Apart from the individualistic focus, the list of grounds on which one could earn the status of 'refugee' is very restrictive and also does not take into account other factors (such as natural disasters or internal wars) which may be just as instrumental in persons becoming refugees. Secondly, a time-limit was included in the UN Refugee Convention. The 'fear' had to be 'as a result of events occurring before 1 January 1951'.[143] This cut-off date underlines the close link between the UN Refugee Convention and the war that preceded it, leaving its ripple effect across different populations. A third limitation, geographical in nature, was included as an option to be adopted at ratification (or accession). By making a declaration, states were able to specify

---

[136] S Hamrell, 'Introduction' in S Hamrell (ed), *Refugee Problems in Africa* (Uppsala: Scandinavian Institute of African Studies, 1967) 9.   [137] OAU Doc CCM/Res.19(II).

[138] OAU Doc CC/Res.36(III), Cairo, 13–17 July 1964; see further M Mubiala, *Le Système Régional Africain de Protection des Droits de l'Homme* (Brussels: Bruylant, 2005) 128–30.

[139] OAU Doc CAB/LEG/24.3, adopted 10 September 1969, entered into force 20 June 1974 (emphasis added). For a general discussion, see J Oloka-Onyango, 'Human Rights, the OAU Convention and the Refugee Crisis in Africa: Forty Years after Geneva' (1991) 3 *International J of Refugee L* 453; and M Rwelamira, 'The 1969 Convention on the Specific Aspects of Refugee Problems in Africa' (1989) 1 *International J of Refugee L* 557.   [140] OAU Refugee Convention, art II(3).

[141] For the UN Refugee Convention text, and ratification status, see <http://www.ohchr.org>.

[142] UN Refugee Convention, art 1(A)(2).   [143] ibid.

that the 'events' referred to above should be understood to mean 'events occurring in Europe'.[144] Few states made such a declaration, though.[145]

In the light of the above, it is not surprising that African states saw the Convention as a 'European instrument'.[146] The perception of exclusion was exacerbated in the 1960s, when it became clear that, in Africa, refugee problems continued and, most often, started well after 1951. Massive problems arose due to internal conflicts. For example, soon after independence, many refugees fled conditions in Zaïre[147] and Nigeria, mostly because divergent identity-based groupings took issue with the imposition of colonial borders as markers of national identity. Due in the main to Africa's criticism and its efforts to adopt a separate convention, the UN in 1966 adopted a brief Protocol to the 1951 Convention, which entered into force in 1967. The Protocol dispensed with the temporal and geographic limitations of the 1951 Convention. In the Protocol's Preamble, 'consideration' was given to the fact that 'refugee situations have arisen since the Convention was adopted'. From 1967 on, then, the Convention applied equally to all who qualified for refugee status. However, the restrictive definition of 'refugee' was left intact.

After the adoption of the 1967 Protocol, African efforts to elaborate a separate UN instrument dealing with refugees were channelled into the adoption of a complementary regional instrument,[148] eventually resulting in the OAU Refugee Convention of 1969. By 31 December 2006, the OAU Refugee Convention had been ratified by 45 AU member states.[149] In an attempt to understand why an 'African supplement'[150] to existing international refugee law was added, one should differentiate between the global and regional systems of refugee protection.

The OAU Refugee Convention, on the whole, mirrors exactly the wording of the UN Convention, but expands the definition of the term 'refugee'. The global instrument requires a 'well-founded fear of being persecuted' as a fundamental precondition for refugee status. In contrast, the OAU Refugee Convention extends the term to include anyone who is compelled to flee a country of residence 'owing to external aggression, occupation, foreign domination or events seriously disturbing public order in either part or the whole of his country of origin or nationality'.[151] It is no longer the subjective fear of the individual alone, but also objectively ascertainable circumstantial compulsion that may give rise to 'refugee' status. This expansion of the term was necessitated to overcome the restrictive nature of the initial approach to refugees. 'Fear of persecution' places the emphasis on a person's beliefs, and not on the socio-political context. The omission of reference to the socio-political context in the UN definition has led Oloka-Onyango to conclude that 'the overall ideology of those grounds...are rooted in the philosophy that accords primacy of place to

---

[144] ibid, art 1(B)(1).

[145] P Weis, 'The Convention of the Organization of African Unity Governing the Specific Aspects of Refugee Problems' (1970) 3 *Revue des Droits de l'Homme* 449.   [146] ibid, 449, 452.

[147] Now, the Democratic Republic of the Congo.   [148] Weis (n 145 above) 449, 453.

[149] Table 6.1 below.

[150] The OAU Refugee Convention recognizes the UN Convention and Protocol as 'the basic and universal instrument' on the topic (Preamble).   [151] OAU Refugee Convention, art I(2).

political and civil rights over economic, social, and cultural rights'.[152] The broadened definition of the OAU Convention allows for many more factors to be considered when evaluating refugee status, including serious natural disasters (such as famine, which has become prevalent in Africa).

The UN Refugee Convention's definition presupposes that refugees will be screened individually in order to establish whether they have a 'well-founded fear of persecution'. Such a system is obviously only manageable when persons flee on their own or in small groups. However, in the case of mass migrations, the application of such an individualized test becomes impossible. This is exactly the situation that prevailed, and continues to prevail, in Africa. Mass migrations necessitate an approach which uses cumulative and objective factors to determine refugee status. Such factors are events 'seriously disrupting' public order and 'foreign domination'.[153]

The grounds in the OAU Convention on which refugees lose their status ('cessation of status') or on which they are barred from qualifying as refugees ('exclusion from status') are once more derived from the UN document. In this, also, the OAU Refugee Convention adds to the list, and consequently narrows down the widened scope created by the expanded definition of 'refugee status' by adding grounds of exclusion and cessation of refugee status.[154] Three additional categories of exclusion or cessation are included in the OAU document: anyone guilty of acts contrary to the purpose and principles of the OAU; anyone who has seriously infringed the purposes and objectives of the OAU Refugee Convention; and anyone who has committed a serious non-political crime outside his country of refuge after his admission to that country.[155]

The OAU Refugee Convention is explicit about the obligation of states to grant asylum to refugees,[156] in contrast to the UN Convention which is silent on the issue. The duty on states under the OAU Refugee Convention is 'to use their best endeavours ... to receive all refugees'.[157] The way in which this duty was phrased led Weis to conclude that the requirement is recommendatory, rather than binding.[158] Also, because these endeavours must be 'consistent with their respective legislation',[159] states need merely to comply with internal laws, whatever their content. This provision may be viewed as a precursor to the inclusion of 'claw-back' clauses in the African Charter.[160]

---

[152] J Oloka-Onyango, 'The Plight of the Larger Half: Human Rights, Gender Violence and the Legal Status of Refugee and Internally Displaced Women in Africa' (1995–6) 24 *Denver J of Intl L and Policy* 349, 364.

[153] See OAU Refugee Convention, art I(2). Nigeria entered a reservation to the term 'events seriously disturbing public order' (repr in C Heyns (ed), *Human Rights Law in Africa* (vol 1) (Leiden: Martinus Nijhoff, 2004) 108).

[154] See generally the articles in the Special Supplementary Issue (2000) 12 *International J of Refugee L*.   [155] OAU Refugee Convention, arts I(4) and I(5).

[156] ibid, art II(2).   [157] ibid, art II(1).

[158] Weis (n 145 above) 457. However, see African Charter, art 12(3), which provides for the right 'when persecuted, to seek and obtain asylum'.   [159] OAU Refugee Convention, art II.

[160] An example of such a clause is the phrase 'provided he abides by the law' in African Charter, art 10.

Highlighting the fact that its adoption resulted rather from the inter-state ramifications of refugee movements than from a concern for the 'rights' of refugees, the OAU Refugee Convention reinforces notions of state security and sovereignty. It determines that a refugee has to conform to the law in the state of refuge, and that he or she has a duty to 'abstain from any subversive activities against any Member State of the OAU'.[161] In this regard, states have the obligation to prohibit refugees from attacking other OAU member states through acts of armed aggression or by using the mass media.[162] Although the basis of the prohibition on the use of force and on disseminating propaganda for war has its roots in international law, the OAU Refugee Convention is unique in placing a duty on the host state to ensure compliance.

An interesting innovation is the duty placed by the OAU Refugee Convention on the country of origin in relation to returning refugees: states must grant full rights and privileges to returning nationals, and must refrain from any sanctions or punishment against them.[163]

The regional specificities of the OAU Convention have rightly been linked to the nature of refugee problems in Africa.[164] It presents a clear example of how a regional instrument can supplement an international regime by addressing problems specific to that region. The restrictive definition of a 'refugee' under the UN Refugee Convention has made the application of the Convention difficult; also in regions other than Africa. For example, mass migrations due to political violence and instability in Latin America highlighted the inadequacy of the UN Convention definition. As part of its practice, the Inter-American Commission granted refugee protection to 'persons who have fled their country because their lives, safety, or freedom has been threatened by generalized violence, foreign aggression, internal conflicts, massive violations of human rights or other circumstances which have seriously disrupted public order'.[165] This broadened working definition of 'refugee' status, which also formed the basis of the 1984 Cartagena Declaration on Refugees,[166] incorporates much of the African instrument, but does not grant refugee status merely because persons had to leave their country due to disturbed public order.

The African refugee 'problem' is not a thing of the past, but continues to challenge the humanitarianism and hospitality traditionally associated with 'African Civilizations'.[167] Five of the countries from which most refugees emanate are in Africa.[168] The practical implementation of both the UN and OAU Conventions

[161] OAU Refugee Convention, art III(1).   [162] ibid, art III(2).
[163] ibid, art III(3) and III(4); and Weis (n 145 above) 463.
[164] Mubiala (n 138 above) 130.
[165] *Annual Report of Inter-American Commission 1984–1985.*
[166] See E Arboleda, 'Refugee Definitions in Africa and Latin America: The Lessons of Pragmatism' (1991) 3 *Intl J of Refugee L* 185.
[167] P Noble, 'Refugees, Law and Development in Africa' [1982] *Michigan YB of Intl Legal Studies* 255.
[168] UNHCR, 'Refugees by Numbers 2006 Edition' <http://www.unhcr.org> (accessed 30 September 2006: Sudan, 693, 300; Burundi, 438, 700; DRC, 430, 600; Somalia, 394, 800; Liberia, 231, 100). By mid-2006, the estimated number of refugees in Africa stood at more than 2.5 million.

has been plagued with difficulties. Both Conventions provide that a person considered for valid reasons to have committed a 'crime against peace, a war crime, or a crime against humanity' must be excluded from protection as a refugee.[169] This provision was seriously challenged when refugees poured out of Rwanda during and after the 1994 genocide.[170]

Although the OAU Refugee Convention creates an impressive normative framework, serious violations of this treaty have occurred and continue. Examples dating from the 1990s are the following: Nigeria expelled refugees (in conflict with the principle of *non-refoulement*) from Chad,[171] Kenya and Zimbabwe neglected their duty to protect Somali and Mozambican refugees, respectively[172] and Senegal refused to recognize Mauritanian expellees as refugees.[173] One of the problems is the lack of domestic legislation incorporating international standards. The OAU Refugee Convention inspired limited domestic legislation, especially after the Pan-African Conference on Refugees of 1979, at which a model for drafting refugee legislation was adopted.[174]

In one of the clearest manifestations of collaboration between the African regional human rights system and the UN, the African Commission and the UN High Commissioner for Refugees (UNHCR) entered into a Memorandum of Understanding.[175] A joint mechanism for implementation has been established, which should involve the UN Division of Humanitarian Affairs, Refugees and Displaced Persons and the AU Commission. Some of the areas of interaction envisaged are joint field missions and bi-annual meetings between the African Commission and the UNHCR. The UNHCR will also provide the African Commission with information on refugees, asylum-seekers, and IDPs to inform the examination of state reports and other discussions.

The OAU and UN Refugee Conventions should not be considered in isolation from other international norms. In addition to the protection under the OAU Refugee Convention, every refugee—as part of the category 'every individual'—is also entitled to all the rights in the African Charter, such as the rights to dignity, property, and health. The provision of the Charter that deals with freedom of movement is of particular importance to refugees. It guarantees to non-nationals

---

[169] OAU Refugee Convention, art I(5)(a).

[170] W O'Neill, B Rutinwa, and G Verdirame, 'The Great Lakes: A Survey of the Application of the Exclusion Clause in the Central African Republic, Kenya and Tanzania' (2000) 12 *Intl J of Refugee L* 135.

[171] Lawyers Committee for Human Rights, *African Exodus: Refugee Crisis, Human Rights and the 1969 OAU Refugee Convention* (New York: Lawyers Committee for Human Rights, 1995) 87–9.

[172] ibid, 64–71, 78–80.   [173] ibid, 54.

[174] National legislation includes the 1983 Zimbabwean Refugee Act; the Nigerian National Commission for Refugees Act, No 52 of 1989 Cap 244 Laws of the Federation of Nigeria (see NS Okogbule, 'The Legal Dimensions of the Refugee Problem in Africa' (2004) 10 *East African J of Peace and Human Rights* 176, 187); and the 1989 Refugee Act of Malawi (see T Maluwa, 'The Domestic Implementation of International Refugee Law: A Brief Note on Malawi's Refugee Act of 1989' (1991) 1 *Intl J of Refugee L* 503).

[175] Modalities for the Operationalization of the Memorandum of Understanding between the African Commission and the UNHCR (17th Annual Activity Report, Annex IV).

who have been 'legally admitted' to a country the right not to be expelled without a legal decision to that effect.[176] Additionally, 'mass expulsions' on the basis of nationality, race, ethnicity, and religion are explicitly prohibited.[177] Subsequent to the Commission's establishment of a Special Rapporteur on Refugees, Asylum Seekers and Displaced Persons in Africa,[178] the rights of refugees and internally displaced persons (IDPs) were integrated into the examination of state reports.

The treatment by Guinea of Sierra Leonean refugees within its borders brought these guarantees and the link between the African Charter and the OAU Refugee Convention into the spotlight.[179] Due to civil war and conflict in its two neighbours, Liberia and Sierra Leone, Guinea has become the largest host to refugees on the continent. In September 2000, 'rebel' groups launched surprise attacks against Guinea from Liberia and Sierra Leone. Invoking the constitutional obligation to guarantee Guinea's territorial integrity, the President of Guinea ordered that refugees be 'quartered' in 'secured areas'. When it appeared that these measures had a limted effect, he proceeded to deliver a speech in a local language which incited soldiers and civilians to harass Sierra Leoneans in Guinea in order to unmask the attackers. His speech unleashed large-scale looting, sexual violence against Sierra Leonean women, mass expulsions, and killings.

The Commission rejected the government's contention that it acted legitimately in the interests of national security and that it did not discriminate against Sierra Leoneans, but treated all refugees, including those from Liberia and Equatorial Guinea, the same. Although the Commission recognized that Guinea is entitled to prosecute anyone suspected of threatening state security, it faulted the government for not distinguishing between 'rebels' and refugees. The Commission found that massive violations causing a group of refugees to flee *en masse* constitute a violation of article 14(5) of the Charter. Illustrating the integration of legal regimes, the Commission further held that sexual violence against female refugees violated the right to inherent human dignity, guaranteed under the Charter,[180] and that Guinea was in breach of its undertaking to apply the OAU Refugee Convention 'to all refugees without discrimination as to . . . nationality'.[181]

To address the plight of female refugees, highlighted on numerous previous occasions, regard should also be had to the Women's Protocol. In response to circumstances such as those in which the Sierra Leonean refugee women found themselves, the Women's Protocol obliges state parties to protect asylum-seeking women, refugees, returnees, and internally displaced persons against 'all forms of violence, rape and other forms of sexual exploitation'.[182] By including the category 'internally

---

[176] African Charter, art 12(4).   [177] ibid, art 12(5).

[178] Terms of reference adopted at the Commission's 36th session, 23 November–7 December 2004, Banjul, 18th Activity Report of the Commission, para 28.

[179] Communication 249/2002, *African Institute for Human Rights and Development (on behalf of Sierra Leonean Refugees in Guinea) v Guinea* (2004) AHRLR 57 (ACHPR 2004) (20th Activity Report).   [180] African Charter, art 5.

[181] OAU Refugee Convention, art IV.   [182] Women's Protocol, art 11(3).

displaced persons',[183] the Women's Protocol builds on the precedent of the African Childrens' Charter, which was the the first binding legal instrument to provide protection to this vulnerable group.[184] The word 'persons' introduces some ambiguity as it seems to extend the Women's Protocol's protective ambit beyond women. Although the Women's Protocol generally deals with women's rights, this provision—and others similarly phrased—exposes the Women's Protocol to the criticism of inconsistency: sometimes it deals with women, and sometimes with women and men. By requiring that states ensure women's participation in decision-making to secure better legal protection for the categories of persons mentioned above, and the management of camps and settlement processes, the Women's Protocol goes beyond situations of sexual violence.[185]

NEPAD's APRM places not only refugees, but also IDPs in the category of 'vulnerable groups' about whose rights participating states have to report.[186] The review of Ghana acknowledges the existence of a comprehensive legal framework in the form of the Refugee Act, and notes the high number of IDPs and the influx of refugees arising from the perception of Ghana as a 'haven of peace and security'.[187] In line with one of the overarching objectives of the NEPAD process—to forge 'partnerships' with developed countries to financially assist African states—the report calls on the 'international community' to support Ghana to cope with the problem of refugees.[188]

The numbers, as well as the situation of IDPs, especially in the Sudan, Somalia, and Liberia, remain grave.[189] Efforts to address their situation have so far not filled the normative gap relating to their situation, exposing IDPs as the Achilles' heel of international refugee law.[190]

C Children

With some 44 per cent of its population under the age of 15, the adage that 'children are the future' rings more true in Africa than anywhere else.[191] The protection of children's rights is not only an investment in the future, but also an imperative of

---

[183] Women's Protocol, art 11(3).

[184] African Children's Charter, art 23(4). See also T Kaime, 'From Lofty Jargon to Durable Solutions: Unaccompanied Refugee Children and the African Charter on the Rights and Welfare of the Child' (2004) 16 *Inl J of Refugee L* 336.   [185] Women's Protocol, art 10(2)(c) and (d).

[186] Country Self-Assessment for the APRM (n 57 above) para 1.3.3 (Objective 9).

[187] APRM, Country Review Report of Ghana 41.   [188] ibid, 42.

[189] UNHCR (n 155 above). By the end of 2005, the number of IDPs in Africa, though difficult to establish, was estimated at 1.5 million (UNHCR, 2005 Statistical Yearbook, Annexes, <http://www.unhcr,org>).

[190] These efforts are continuing, see eg AU EX.CL/Dec.319(X) (Decision on the Situation of Refugees, Returnees and Displaced Persons in Africa).

[191] This figure contrasts sharply with the global percentage, which at the corresponding time stood at 28.9%: UNDP, Human Development Report 2005, Human Development Indicators, Table 5, <http:www.undp.org> (31 December 2006).

the present, which is characterized by children's exploitation as soldiers, labourers, and sex-workers, and in human trafficking; the neglect of orphans, especially due to AIDS deaths; the prevalence of street-children; early marriages and other harmful cultural practices; and the disproportionate impact of conflict on children.[192] An authoritarian mindset, justified by cultural tradition, often exacerbates the precarious position of children in Africa.

Children's rights first featured on the OAU's agenda in 1979, the UN-declared International Year of the Child, when the Assembly adopted the Declaration on the Rights and Welfare of the African Child.[193] Although not legally binding, this Declaration provided a moral compass for legal reform. Among other measures, the Declaration urged states to adopt 'legal and educational measures' to abolish cultural practices that are harmful to children, such as child marriage and female circumcision.[194]

On 11 July 1990, very soon after the adoption of the Convention on the Rights of the Child (CRC) by the UN, the OAU Assembly adopted a regional pendant, the African Charter on the Rights and Welfare of the Child (African Children's Charter).[195] One may identify political and legal reasons for the adoption of this document. On a political level, the OAU reacted against a perception of exclusion or marginalization of African states in the drafting process of the CRC.[196] It is true that African involvement in the drafting process was initially limited,[197] but by 1989 nine African states had been participating in the activities of the working group.[198] The first vocal opposition to the UN process in Africa was raised at a workshop co-organized by the African Network for the Prevention and Protection against Child Abuse and Neglect (ANPPCAN) and UNICEF on Children in Situations of Armed Conflicts in Africa, which took place in 1988 in Nairobi. Pursuant to the meeting, the OAU, in collaboration with ANPPCAN and UNICEF, set up a working group of African experts. This group produced a draft Charter, forming the basis of the eventual African Children's Charter,[199] adopted in 1990, and entering into force almost a decade later, on 29 November 1999.

An attempt should therefore be made to determine the 'unique' features of the African Children's Charter in comparison to the CRC. As a global instrument, the

---

[192] See UNICEF, 'State of the World's Children 2006: Excluded and Invisible', <http://www.unicef.org> (31 December 2006), highlighting the dire position of children particularly in West and Central Africa.   [193] OAU Doc AHG/st.4(XVI)Rev.1(1979).

[194] ibid, para 3.

[195] OAU Doc CAB/LEG/24.9/49(1990); adopted 11 July 1990; entered into force 29 November 1999.

[196] See generally F Viljoen, 'The African Charter on the Rights and Welfare of the Child' in CJ Davel (ed), *Introduction to Child Law in South Africa* (Cape Town: Juta, 2000) 214–31.

[197] R Barsh, 'The Draft Convention on the Rights of the Child: A Case of Eurocentrism in Standard Setting' (1989) 58 *Nordic J of Intl L* 24 (citing the fact that only three African states participated for at least five of the nine years that the working group took to draft a final proposal).

[198] See LJ LeBlanc *The Convention on the Rights of the Child* (Lincoln, Nebr: University of Nebraska Press, 1995) 30.

[199] N Muhindi, 'A Proposal for an African Draft Charter on the Rights of the Child' (unpublished, on file with the author).

CRC is the product of numerous compromises. Regional specificities often are the victims in processes of universal consensus-seeking. From a legal point of view, therefore, there was a need to adopt a regional human rights instrument dealing with issues of particular interest and importance to children in Africa. Some of the omissions from the CRC, identified by those involved in the drafting process of the African Children's Charter, are the following:[200]

- The situation of children living under apartheid was not addressed.
- Factors disadvantaging the female child were not sufficiently considered.
- Practices prevalent in African society, such as female genital mutilation and circumcision, were not explicitly outlawed.
- Socio-economic conditions such as illiteracy and low levels of sanitary conditions which threaten the survival of and pose specific problems in Africa have not been addressed.
- The community's inability to engage in meaningful participation in the planning and management of basic programmes for children was not taken into account.[201]
- The African conception of the community's responsibilities and duties had been neglected.
- As children in Africa are used as soldiers, a compulsory minimum age for military service is of great importance.
- The CRC negates the role of the family (also in its extended sense) in the upbringing of the child and in matters of adoption and fostering.

All these concerns were—at least partly—addressed by the African Children's Charter. Compared to the CRC, the African Children's Charter raises the level of children's protection in three important respects:[202] First, while the CRC allows child soldiers to be recruited and to be used in direct hostilities,[203] the African Children's Charter completely outlaws the use of child soldiers.[204] Secondly, in terms of the CRC, child marriages are allowed, because article 1 stipulates that childhood ends at 18 years, unless majority is acquired at an earlier age. The African Children's Charter is explicit in its prohibition of child marriages;[205] in fact, it adds that legislation must be adopted to specify the age of marriage to be 18 years. Thirdly, in its protection of child refugees, the African Children's Charter extends its ambit to 'internally displaced children',[206] something the CRC does not do.[207]

---

[200] These grounds have been forwarded by LG Muthoga, 'Introducing the African Charter on the Rights and Welfare of the African Child and the Convention on the Rights of the Child', paper delivered at the International Conference on the Rights of the Child, Community Law Centre, University of the Western Cape (1992) and SA Wako, 'Towards an African Charter on the Rights of the Child', paper delivered at a workshop on the Draft Convention on the Rights of the Child, Nairobi (9–11 May 1988).

[201] Muthoga (n 200 above) 4.

[202] See F Viljoen, 'Supra-National Human Rights Instruments for the Protection of Children in Africa: The Convention on the Rights of the Child and the African Charter on the Rights and Welfare of the Child' (1998) 31 *CILSA* 199, 207–11.   [203] CRC, art 38(2) and 38(3).

[204] African Children's Charter, art 22(2).   [205] ibid, art 21(2).   [206] ibid, art 23(4).

[207] CRC, art 22.

The causes for internal displacement are also all-inclusive. In these three respects, the African Children's Charter has succeeded in addressing concerns of particular relevance to Africa. It has therefore fulfilled the objective of supplementing the CRC with regional specificities.

By placing duties (or 'responsibilities') on children, the African Children's Charter also mirrors the African Charter and deviates further from the CRC.[208] This aspect may be identified as one of the 'African' features of the African Children's Charter, in that it gives effect to the subordinate role of children within the strict age-based hierarchy of traditional African societies.

Some of these duties may, at first glance, look controversial. However, they should be interpreted in the light of the Children's Charter as a whole and in light of international human rights law.[209] Duties, even the rather extreme one of obeying a parent 'at all times', must not be read out of context. These duties are made subject to the 'age and ability' of the child,[210] and are further subject to 'such limitations as may be contained in the present Charter'.[211] The duty to obey, for example, must be counterbalanced with the child's right to freedom of expression and protection of privacy, to name but a few possibilities, as well as parents' duty to 'ensure that the best interests of the child are their basic concern at all times'.[212]

The inclusion of these duties cannot be enforced against children, as no complaints mechanism allows complaints *against* individuals (only *by* individuals). As complaints may be directed against states only, they alone have enforceable obligations under the African Children's Charter. The inclusion of duties, therefore, places an obligation on states to 'instil these duties in their subjects'.[213] Understood in this way, this aspect seems less problematic and should certainly not be used as a justification for non-ratification, or to erode rights.

In any event, the overriding consideration in resolving interpretive disputes should be the guideline that 'the best interest of the child shall be the primary consideration'.[214] This is a powerful statement, and again differs in an important respect from the CRC, which refers to the best interest of the child as 'a' (rather than 'the')[215] primary consideration in all actions concerning children.

By placing duties also on parents, the African Children's Charter emphasizes the relational character of children's rights which are, to some extent, enjoyed in reliance on adult support and guidance. In this respect, another comparison with the CRC may be apposite. Under the CRC, a child is accorded the right to freedom of religion, while the state must 'respect the rights and duties of the parents . . . to provide direction to the child' in the exercise of the rights 'in a manner consistent with the evolving capacities of the child'.[216] Invoking the example of an 8-year-old Cameroonian child challenging his or her traditional religion, Nkot criticizes this provision as placing parents and children in a situation of inevitable conflict, and for being so far removed from the 'imagined universe' of most Africans that it is

---

[208] African Children's Charter, art 31. [209] ibid, art 46.   [210] ibid, art 31.
[211] ibid.   [212] ibid, art 29(1)(a).   [213] Umozurike (n 6 above) 65.
[214] African Children's Charter, art 4(1).   [215] CRC, art 3(1).   [216] ibid, art 14.

inoperable.[217] He then questions the reasons for the inclusion of a provision so unrelated to African realities in an instrument that has Africa as one of its main targets.[218] Had Nkot turned his gaze to the African Children's Charter, to which Cameroon is also a state party, he would have found that the African instrument echoes the language of the CRC when it provides for the right to freedom of religion.[219] There the only difference is that the implicit duty on parents to give guidance and direction is made explicit.[220] Despite this subtle shift of focus, his conclusion that the complete negation of African realities in the CRC is a result of the political use of international law by 'Western powers',[221] seems equally applicable to the corresponding provision in the African Children's Charter.

One of the prominent features of the African Charter, the inclusion of peoples' rights, is not reflected in the African Children's Charter. In my view, this was done because it is not appropriate specifically to entitle children to most collective rights, such as the right to self-determination.[222] In addition, it should be kept in mind that children are included in the terms 'every individual' and 'peoples' (whatever its meaning) as used in the African Charter.[223] This indicates that children are also bearers of all the rights in the African Charter (including as members of a 'people'). As a consequence, there was no need to restate the concept of 'peoples' rights' in the African Children's Charter.

Like the CRC Committee, the supervisory body established under the African Children's Charter, the African Children's Rights Committee, is mandated to examine state reports. Providing a commendable but all too rare example of international-regional cooperation, the reporting procedures under the African Children's Charter have been harmonized with those under the CRC. All states party to the African Children's Charter have submitted at least an initial report to the UN Committee on the Rights of the Child.[224] When state parties report under the African Children's Charter, they are required to 're-submit' reports already submitted under the UN system, together with a 'supplementary report' devoted to those provisions of the African Children's Charter 'not duplicated in the CRC'.[225] State parties are thus required to provide information only about those provisions that are unique to the African Children's Charter. Reporting under the African system also serves as a mechanism for following up on the concluding observations of the CRC Committee, as 'action taken' in this regard also has to be included in a state's 'supplementary report'.[226] In this respect, too, the regional system reinforces the global human rights sytem.

---

[217] PF Nkot, *Usages Politiques du Droit en Afrique: Le Cas du Cameroon* (Brussels: Bruylant, 2000) 167–71.　　[218] ibid, 172.
[219] African Children's Charter, art 9(1).
[220] ibid, art 9(2): 'Parents... shall have the duty to provide guidance and direction...'
[221] Nkot (n 217 above) 173.　　[222] African Charter, art 20.
[223] ibid, arts 2, 3, 5, 6, and 7.　　[224] See Ch 3 above.
[225] Guidelines for initial reports of state parties to the African Charter on the Rights and Welfare of the Child, AU Doc Cttee/ACRWC/2.II.Rev.2, adopted pursuant to African Children's Charter, art 43, February 2003; repr in (2003) 3 *AHRLJ* 347–53, paras 24 and 25.　　[226] ibid, para 25.

However, the African Children's Rights Committee may also consider individual communications and conduct on-site investigations.[227] The initial reluctance of African states to ratify the home-grown, 'African' treaty on children's rights was as much due to these invasive procedural mechanisms as to the African Children's Charter's progressive substantive provisions. A further explanation as to why African states ratified CRC, but not its African pendant, was the lack of publicity and awareness about the African instrument, compared to the global sensitization campaigns about the CRC, supported by UNICEF. Despite having delayed its entry into force, the strict standards of the African Children's Charter are increasingly being accepted and domesticated.[228] The African Children's Charter therefore not only succeeded in addressing particular African concerns, but also, eventually, in progressively raising the bar in respect of children's rights in Africa.

The African Children's Charter intimately co-exists with the African Charter and Women's Protocol. Although the African Charter mentions children only once, in the context of the protection of the family and women's rights, as 'individuals' they also are right-bearers under the Charter. By their very nature, some Charter provisions, such as the right to education, is of greater relevance to children. Notwithstanding this possibility, no communication alleging a violation of children's rights has been submitted to the Commission. Although the initial reporting guidelines do not devote much attention to children's rights—probably because they predate the adoption of the CRC's guidelines—some states have included information about children's rights in their reports.[229] The brief 1998 revised guidelines for reporting ask states to report on steps undertaken to 'improve the condition of children'.[230] During the examination of state reports, questions are now often being posed particularly about the female child. Devoted not only to the rights of women over the age of 18,[231] the Women's Protocol never uses the term 'girl' or 'girl-child', but some rights are clearly applicable particularly to this category of 'women'.[232]

The promotion and protection of the rights of children and young persons are prominently included as objectives to be addressed in countries' self-assessment for the APRM.[233] In line with this requirement, both Ghana and Kenya dealt extensively with this aspect, as is reflected in the Country Review Reports. Some of the recommendations to Ghana include a review of the Children's Act to 'mirror more closely international standards on the rights of the child', and the conversion of the

---

[227] African Children's Charter, arts 44 and 45.

[228] By the end of 2006, 39 AU member states had become party to the African Children's Charter.

[229] See eg South Africa's Initial Country Report 1998, 3.2.5.A (on file with author).

[230] Reprinted in C Heyns and M Killander (eds), *Compendium of Key Human Rights Documents of the African Union* (Pretoria: PULP, 2nd edn, 2006) 129.

[231] Women's Protocol, art 1(k), defining 'women' as 'persons of female gender, including girls'.

[232] See eg Women's Protocol, arts 5, 6(b), and 14; see further the discussion on 'women' immediately below.

[233] Country Self-Assessment for the APRM (n 57 above) Objective 8 under 'Democracy and Good Political Governance'.

Ghana National Commission on Children into 'an independent autonomous organ within the government'.[234] Children's rights, especially those of disabled and orphaned children, form a recurrent theme in the Kenyan report. In the section on socio-economic rights, for example, the government is urged to provide 'alternative education models appropriate for children of nomadic groups'.[235] One of the major recommendations of the Country Review Mission is the need for greater resource allocation to children at all levels.[236]

D Women

African public life has been and is being dominated by men. The negotiations resulting in the OAU Charter and the African Charter were characterized by the absence of any meaningful contribution by women. Until recently, all the decisions of the OAU/AU Assembly of Heads of State and Government have been taken by men. The first female head of state, former senator Ruth Perry, was appointed Head of the Council of State of Liberia by an ECOWAS summit in August 1996.[237] On 16 January 2005, Ellen Johnson-Sirleaf became the first elected female head of state when she took office as President of the same country, joining a number of female African Deputy-Presidents.[238] In many other parts of the continent, women increasingly enter the public domain and occupy positions of authority,[239] and the percentage of women represented in parliaments has grown steadily.[240] Progress has also been made at the AU and UN levels.[241] Although the achievement of equal female representation in the AU Commission is significant,

---

[234] Ghana's Review Report, 40.   [235] Kenya's Review Report, 228.

[236] ibid, 274–5.

[237] See K Tuttle, 'Perry, Ruth' in KA Appiah and HL Gates (eds), *Africana: The Encyclopedia of the African and African American Experience* (New York: Basic Civitas Books, 1999) 32: 'She has given new content to the position of head of state, by eg converting part of her home into a feeding centre for displaced people'.

[238] In eg The Gambia ('President Jammeh of the Gambia to Appoint a Woman, Isatou Saidy, as his Deputy' (June–July 1997) *African Topics* 33, although one may not help but feel some scepticism; such a step may have been aimed at securing the female vote) and in Mozambique; the Namibian Prime Minister is also a woman (*The Official SADC Trade, Industry and Investment Review 2006*, 33).

[239] Examples of the increasing number of women holding high judicial office are Justice Lady Effie Owuor (High Court judge in Kenya), Justice Anastasia Msosa (Malawi's only High Court judge, who previously was Chairperson of the Electoral Commission), and Justices O'Regan and Mokgoro (on the South African Constitutional Court); women also increasingly hold positions as Speakers (eg in South Africa) and Deputy Speakers in national parliaments, and even as Attorney-General (eg in Botswana).

[240] The highest percentage in the world has been achieved in Rwanda, where women occupy 49% of the seats in the lower house (APRM, Country Review Report of the Republic of Rwanda, para 138, see Ch 3 above).

[241] See eg the appointment as UN Deputy Secretary-General of the Tanzanian Minister of Foreign Affairs, Asha Rose Mashigo. See also the Protocol on Amendments to the AU Constitutive Act, adopted in July 2003, but not yet in force (replacing the word 'founding fathers' with 'founders' in the Preamble; and 'Chairman' with 'Chairperson'; and adding to the AU's objectives the 'effective participation of women in decision-making').

and improves on the position in other international organizations, one should note that the two highest office bearers during the first term of appointment were still male. Under the AU, a 'Solemn Declaration on Gender Equality in Africa' was adopted,[242] which calls for the expansion of the 'gender parity principle' to all AU organs, NEPAD, the RECs, and national Parliaments.

To effectively address the marginalization of women in Africa, a female perspective and presence is essential. The male perspective inherent in the following statement reminds one of that fact: 'It is almost embarrassing for me to have to question the Gambian delegate, not just because she is a woman, but because of the debt we owe to Gambia'.[243] In a later interview, the first female member of the African Commission was asked how she had been received by her male colleagues. Her response underlies the role of stigmatization: 'In principle I have been treated as an equal. But people are used to seeing a woman in different roles. Sometimes some unexpected comments have been made'.[244]

NGOs working in the field of women's rights have over many years expressed concern about the pervasive abuses of women's rights by state parties and have campaigned for a study on ways of improving women's rights, including the possibility of an African treaty of women's rights. In 1995, Commissioners Duarte-Martins and Dankwa were entrusted with the task of initiating work on a protocol additional to the African Charter on the rights of women, and later in the same year, the OAU Assembly endorsed a recommendation by the African Commission on the elaboration of such a protocol.[245] In 1997, a group of experts used a document prepared by Commissioner Dankwa to prepare a draft Protocol.[246] The subsequent appointment of Commissioner Ondziel-Gnelenga as Special Rapporteur on Women's Rights accelerated the process. Preparatory meetings, attended by Commissioners and representatives of the International Commission of Jurists (ICJ-Geneva), Women in Law and Development in Africa (WILDAF), and the African Centre for Democracy and Human Rights Studies, were held in Banjul, Dakar, and Kigali. At each of these meetings a new draft was adopted, the last being the Kigali draft.[247]

In the meantime, and manifestly attesting to the failure to coordinate women's rights issues and the elaboration of new norms within the OAU, the Gender Unit within the OAU Education, Science, Culture and Social Affairs Department, in collaboration with the Inter-African Committee on Traditional Practices, had drafted an OAU Convention on Harmful Traditional Practices Affecting the Fundamental

---

[242] AU Doc Assembly/AU/Decl.12(III)Rev.1(III) (July 2004).

[243] Examination of State Reports (vol 3) (1995) 24 (Commissioner Umozurike, prefacing his remarks about the examination of the Gambian state report).

[244] Interview reported in October–December (1996) *AFLAQ* 15.

[245] OAU Doc AHG/Res.240(XXXI). On the drafting process, see F Banda, *Women, Law and Human Rights: An African Perspective* (Oxford: Hart, 2005) 66–79.

[246] See, for background, <http://www.wildaf.org.zw.news.html> (accessed 30 November 2006) and MS Nsibirwa, 'A Brief Analysis of the Draft Protocol to the African Charter on Human and Peoples' Rights on the Rights of Women' (2001) 1 *AHRLJ* 40.

[247] DOC/OS(XXVI)/125, adopted in November 1999.

Rights of Women and Girls. As there was significant overlap between the two drafts, the OAU Legal Counsel advised that the Commission merge the two documents.[248] As the African Commission expressed reluctance to restart the work,[249] the OAU Secretariat produced a draft (the OAU Secretariat draft) that merged the two documents.[250] At the conclusion of a meeting of government experts, held in Addis Ababa during 2001, a new version of the Protocol, the Draft Protocol to the African Charter on the Rights of Women in Africa (the Addis Ababa draft) was adopted.[251] In July 2003, the AU Assembly adopted the Protocol to the African Charter on the Rights of Women in Africa,[252] which entered into force on 25 November 2005.

The 'mischief' that the Protocol seeks to correct is not the normative deficiency of international human rights law dealing with women's rights, but its lack of implementation.[253] In 2003, when the Women's Protocol was adopted, the two main instruments in existence (the African Charter and CEDAW) both enjoyed near-universal ratification in Africa. Covering only persons under 18, and enjoying more limited acceptance,[254] the African Children's Charter is perhaps less relevant.[255] To overcome the apparent paradox of creating another *legal instrument* to undo the defects of existing *legal instruments*, the Protocol adopts three strategies: it extends the substantive scope of the existing law; it aims to improve quasi-legal and legal means of ensuring compliance; and it seeks to extend the use of non-legal forms of implementation.

1 Expanding the Existing Law

To assess the normative expansion brought about by the Protocol, the pre-existing normative framework ('the existing law') has to be reviewed and contrasted with the Protocol. Before the Protocol's adoption, African states were already bound to (at least some) provisions affecting women's rights under the African Charter, CEDAW, and the African Children's Charter.

The African Charter is not blind to the split personality of a society that remains poised between tradition and modernity.[256] In traditional Africa, the role of women was predominantly restricted to the private sphere of the family. Women were, and

---

[248] Letter by OAU Legal Counsel to the Chair of the African Commission, OAU Doc CAB/LEG/72.20/27/Vol II, dated 7 March 2000.   [249] 13th Annual Activity Report, para 33.

[250] OAU Doc CAB/LEG/66.6, dated 13 September 2000, and marked 'Final Version'.

[251] OAU Doc CAB/LEG/66.6/Rev.1.

[252] Adopted 11 July 2003, entered into force 25 November 2005.

[253] See F Banda, 'Blazing a Trail: The African Protocol on Women's Rights Comes into Force' (2006) 50 *JAL* 72; Women's Protocol, Preamble: 'Concerned that despite the ratification of the African Charter on Human and Peoples' Rights and other international human rights instruments by the majority of state parties . . . women in Africa still continue to be victims of discrimination and harmful practices'.

[254] At the end of 2003, 32 states had become party to the African Children's Charter.

[255] As far as the 'girl-child' is concerned, its most important provisions are those prohibiting child marriage and harmful and discriminatory practices (African Children's Charter, art 21).

[256] See, generally F Ouguergouz, *La Charte Africain des Droits de l'Homme et des Peuples* (Paris: Presses Universitaires de France, 1993) 84–91.

still are, regarded as fulfilling functions of childbearing, child care, and sustaining a family, which by necessity subordinate them to men. These sentiments are prevailing in much of Africa today. In many respects, though, the role of women has changed, leading to greater acceptance of their role in public life and their equality as partners in the family sphere. Although the Charter incorporates traditional values inherited from 'ancient African civilizations',[257] these values find their counterweight in the duty of states not to discriminate, in any form, on the basis of a person's sex.[258] Male dominance and female subordination (bordering on disregard) are suggested by the language of the Charter. Male pronouns[259] and words such as 'chairman' are used throughout the document. However, any fear that the rights in the Charter are in fact reserved for men only, are immediately dispelled. These rights, we are assured, are the entitlements of all individuals, irrespective of their sex.[260] Article 3 reinforces the approach of ensuring equality by providing for equality before the law. In this discourse, women are no different from men. For example, the right of 'every individual' to dignity[261] may be invoked by women in their struggle against demeaning cultural practices, and the general prohibition on inhuman treatment may be raised as the basis of a positive obligation on states to criminalize female circumcision.

However, the Charter also moves outside the rhetoric of formal equality by singling out women for special treatment and specific measures. This is done in article 18, which characterizes women and children together as groups deserving of 'protection'. This is followed, in the next sub-article, by the provision that the aged and disabled 'shall *also* have the right to special measures of protection'.[262] One may easily form the impression that women are viewed only within the context of the family, and are deserving of special protective measures, in the same sense as are children, the aged, and disabled.

The special measures that should be directed at protecting women (and at ensuring the elimination of discrimination against them)[263] are not delineated. They are to be found in 'international declarations and conventions'[264] on the elimination of discrimination against and the protection of women. Immediately, the major international human rights instrument on women's rights, CEDAW—a comprehensive codification of various rights dealing with aspects as diverse as voting, nationality, gender stereotyping, cultural practices, and ownership—comes to mind.

---

[257] See the Preamble: all human rights in the Charter are inspired by 'virtues of their historical tradition and values of African civilization'. Also refer to the duty (in art 29(1)) to preserve the harmonious development of the family and the emphasis on respect in the family environment.

[258] Again, in the Preamble: states proclaim that they are conscious of their duty to dismantle all forms of discrimination, 'particularly those based on ... sex ...' Art 2 converts this into a legal obligation on states: '[e]very individual shall be entitled to the rights in the Charter without distinction of sex, among others'.

[259] See eg art 9(2) ('his opinions'); art 12(1) ('provided he abides by the law'); and art 17(2) ('his community'). [260] Art 2.

[261] African Charter, art 5. [262] ibid, art 18(4) (emphasis added).

[263] See ibid, art 18(3). [264] ibid.

CEDAW was passed two years prior to the adoption of the Charter. This fact is only 'obliquely apparent'[265] from the wording of the Charter. Oloka-Onyango and Tamale[266] argue that the drafters of the African Charter were 'only minimally influenced by CEDAW's provisions',[267] because there is only one article in the Charter dealing with women's rights. The authors are also critical of the wording of that article, which incorporates CEDAW 'by inference and not by name'.[268] They find evidence of the lack of African leaders' enthusiasm for CEDAW in the fact that they did not initiate a regional duplication. In this, they argue, the response was markedly different from those following the adoption of the Universal Declaration, the 1966 Covenants, and the international conventions on refugees and children. Langley acknowledges, but is less critical of, the incorporation by reference.[269] If all the conventions referred to had explicitly been included in the Charter, it would have been 'overly complicated'.[270] On the other hand, had only some of these rights been incorporated specifically, it would have created the impression that other rights have in fact been excluded.[271]

Does article 18(3) imply that all state parties to the African Charter have become bound to implement all the provisions of CEDAW? To answer this question, a distinction has to be drawn between those state parties that have ratified CEDAW, and those that have not.

As for the states that have ratified CEDAW, the provision in the African Charter serves to reiterate their obligations under CEDAW. It reminds the state and individuals of the supplement to the Charter contained in the international instrument. In a sense it is an unnecessary duplication. The implication that state reports on the realization of rights in CEDAW must be presented to both the African Commission and the CEDAW Committee was indeed factored into the Guidelines for state reporting. These Guidelines go even further in requiring *all* state parties to the Charter to report to the African Commission on 'each provision' of CEDAW.[272]

As for the second group of states, those that have not formally undertaken the CEDAW obligations, it is submitted that these states also become bound to observe the provisions of CEDAW when ratifying the Charter. Article 18(3) of the African Charter refers to the elimination of discrimination and the protection of the rights of women 'as stipulated in international declarations and conventions'. No mention is made of any requirement to ratify the applicable conventions. In this respect, the provisions in article 18(3) should be contrasted with those in article 60. Article 60 refers to international law on human and peoples' rights from which the Commission may 'draw inspiration'. Particular mention is made of UN instruments

---

[265] Oloka-Onyango (n 152 above) 349, 372.

[266] J Oloka-Onyango and S Tamale, ' "The Personal is Political", or Why Women's Rights are Indeed Human Rights: An African Perspective on International Feminism' (1995) 17 *HRQ* 691.

[267] ibid, 719.   [268] ibid.

[269] W Langley, 'The Rights of Women, the African Charter, and the Economic Development of Africa' (1987) 7 *Boston College Third World L J* 215.   [270] ibid, 220.

[271] ibid.   [272] Guidelines for National Periodic Reports, part VII, para 4.

'of which the parties to the present Charter are members'. Prior ratification may enter into discussion on article 60, but not on article 18(3). CEDAW was adopted by the UN in 1979, and entered into force on 3 September 1981. As the adoption of the African Charter (on 21 October 1981) post-dates the adoption of CEDAW, it must be presumed that reference to 'international conventions' includes CEDAW. In any event, the Charter only took effect in 1986, when CEDAW was already well established and ratified by numerous African states. This argument also finds support in the Guidelines for reporting, which require all state parties to the Charter to report on obligations set out in CEDAW, which are not explicitly provided for, in the Charter. In any event, as AU member states increasingly become party to CEDAW, the importance of this argument has diminished.

The African Children's Charter is also part of the 'existing law'. As indicated above, the African Children's Charter provides for important rights of the girl-child, in particular the prohibition on children marrying under the age of 18.

Given the scope of protection under the three treaties discussed above, what then is the 'added normative value' of the Protocol? As a supplement to the African Charter, the Protocol primarily brings into the open the Charter's shrouded premise that women are included in its protective scope. Compared to CEDAW, the Protocol speaks in a clearer voice about issues of particular concern to African women, locates CEDAW in African reality, and returns some casualties of quests for global consensus into its fold. The perception that the Protocol is superfluous because CEDAW already 'accords women the protection' provided for under the Women's Protocol is therefore incorrect.[273]

The Women's Protocol is the first treaty to place 'medical abortion',[274] HIV/AIDS,[275] polygamy,[276] and domestic violence[277] in a binding human rights framework. It provides in detail for the protection of women in armed conflict,[278] and reiterates the need to accord women refugees protection under international law.[279] The Women's Protocol incorporates clear and expansive definitions of 'discrimination against women',[280] 'harmful practices', and 'violence against women'. 'Harmful practices' such as female genital mutilation are specifically prohibited.[281] The Protocol provides specificity where vagueness prevailed, for example when it clarifies

[273] See the remarks by the Kenyan government in response to the APRM Country Review Team's recommendation that it ratify the Protocol (APRM, Country Review Report of the Republic of Kenya, May 2006, 256, <http://www.nepad.org/2005/files/aprm/APRMKenyareport.pdf>).
[274] Art 14(2)(c) requires states to authorize abortion in cases of sexual assault, rape, incest, and where a continued pregnancy threatens the health of the mother or the life of the foetus.
[275] Under art 14(1)(d) states have to ensure that women are protected against sexually transmitted diseases, including HIV/AIDS, and art 14(1)(e) requires that states ensure that women are informed of the HIV status of their partners 'in accordance with internationally recognized standards'.
[276] Women's Protocol, art 6(c) (the rights of women in polygamous marital relationships must be promoted and protected). In previous drafts, polygamy was totally outlawed; in the final Protocol a watered-down compromise was adopted, allowing polygamy to persist, with a guarantee of women's protection, combined with an 'encouragement' of monogamy as the preferred form of marriage.
[277] Art 4(2).   [278] Art 11.   [279] Art 4(2)(k).
[280] Art 1(j) eg includes 'economic harm' in its definitional scope.   [281] Art 5.

that 'positive African values'[282] are those 'based on the principles of equality, peace, freedom, dignity, justice, solidarity and democracy'.[283] It also spells out the scope of socio-economic rights in greater detail than CEDAW, which limited some socio-economic rights to 'rural women',[284] and goes beyond the scope of the rights provided for under the African Charter by spelling out the content of rights and by including the right to food security and adequate housing.[285] A necessary implication of targeting violence against women and 'unwanted or forced sex' in the private sphere is that the Protocol requires domestic violence legislation and the criminalization of 'rape in marriage'. Also in this respect, the Women's Protocol is much more specific and throws its protective mantle wider than CEDAW. The precarious position of groups of women that have been rendered particularly vulnerable due to the loss of a spouse, overlap with old age, disability, and poverty which also receive the Protocol's attention.[286] As far as the African Children's Charter is concerned, the Protocol reiterates the general stipulation of 18 as the minimum age of marriage.[287]

Adopting a distinctly transformative stance, the Protocol emphasizes 'corrective' and 'specific positive' (or 'affirmative') action. While CEDAW contains a generic provision allowing for 'temporary special measures aimed at accelerating *de facto* equality between men and women',[288] the Protocol reiterates the need for 'positive' measures by locating them in different contexts. Pre-empting arguments based on formal equality, the Protocol requires states to adopt measures that may favour women above men, such as electoral quotas for women, in order to ensure substantive ('in fact') equality.[289] Positive action is also specifically required with regard to 'discrimination in law',[290] illiteracy, and education.[291]

It may be argued that the differences between the Protocol, CEDAW and the African Charter are more apparent than real, because the CEDAW Committee and African Commission have in general comments, resolutions, concluding observations, and findings expanded the scope of the relevant treaties. However, even if these clarifications have considerable persuasive weight, they do not constitute binding obligations. By making those 'clarifications' unequivocally binding and by supplementing them, the Women's Protocol takes an undeniable normative step forward.

Although the Women's Protocol significantly advances standard-setting, it could have gone further in a number of respects, and suffers from inelegant and unfortunate drafting deficiencies. The disproportionate effect of HIV and AIDS on women in Africa is not adequately reflected in the text. In any event, the right to be informed of one's own and one's partner's HIV status (*in accordance with internationally recognised standards and best practices*),[292] is ambiguous, and should not form the

---

[282] African Charter, art 29(7).   [283] Women's Protocol, Preamble.
[284] CEDAW, art 14.   [285] See eg arts 12, 13, 14, 15, and 16.
[286] Women's Protocol, arts 204.   [287] ibid, art 6(b).   [288] CEDAW, art 4(1).
[289] Women's Protocol, art 9(1).   [290] ibid, art 2(1)(d).
[291] ibid, art 12(2).   [292] Art 14(1)(e) (emphasis added).

basis for the erosion of rights.[293] The feminization of poverty, especially in rural Africa, is also not adequately reflected. As for its drafting, there is some inconsistency in the 'rights-bearers' in the Protocol, with men sometimes specifically included in the scope of rights, and sometimes not. The Protocol's lack of a 'clear vision' about its status as 'supplement' to both CEDAW and the African Charter has resulted in the Protocol restating some but not all existing relevant state obligations, and not systematically expanding upon the Charter's provisions.[294]

The benefits of these treaty provisions may be lost if reservations exclude the application of some of its important provisions. Similar to the instrument that it supplements, the African Charter, the Women's Protocol does not have a provision on reservations, thus bringing the VCLT into play. Three states (Namibia, South Africa, and The Gambia) entered reservations upon ratification of the Women's Protocol.[295] Both Namibia and South Africa entered a reservation in relation to article 6(d), which requires marriages to be recorded in writing and registered in order for them to be valid. Namibia's reservation applies 'until legislation regarding the recording and registration of customary marriages is enacted'. Given its specificity and limited temporal application, this reservation is most probably not contrary to the object and purpose of the Protocol. South Africa's reservation to article 6(d) differs from that of Namibia in that it is not temporary in nature.[296] The text of the reservation argues that according to the law governing customary marriages in South Africa,[297] failure to register customary marriages does not render them invalid, and that 'it is considered to be a protection for women married under customary law'. It may, however, be argued that the non-registration of marriage facilitates the marriage of girl-children, and therefore strikes at a core provision of the Protocol.[298]

The Gambia entered a blanket reservation to articles 5, 6, 7, and 14.[299] It appears that the Gambian government did not undertake a careful compatibility study

---

[293] See Ch 15.C.1 below.
[294] R Murray, 'Women's Rights and the Organization of African Unity and African Union: The Protocol on the Rights of Women in Africa' in D Buss and A Manji (eds), *International Law: Modern Feminist Approaches* (Oxford: Hart, 2005) 252, 269.
[295] See <http://www.chr.up.ac.za/hr_docs/themes/theme39.html>(31 January 2007).
[296] South Africa entered further 'reservations', but they aim to extend rather than restrict protection, and are not discussed here. [297] Recognition of Customary Marriages Act 120 of 1998, s 4(9).
[298] See also CEDAW General Recommendation 21 (of 1994), para 36, stating that the Committee 'considers that the minimum age for marriage should be 18 years for both man and woman'; para 39: 'States parties should also require the registration of all marriages whether contracted civilly or according to custom or religious law. The State can thereby ensure compliance with the Convention and establish equality between partners, a minimum age for marriage, prohibition of bigamy and polygamy and the protection of the rights of children.'
[299] Art 5 deals with the elimination of harmful cultural practices. Art 6, dealing with marriage, includes the requirement of full consent to marriage, the stipulation that 18 years is the minimum age of marriage, and the right of married women to acquire and manage their own property. Art 7 requires states to adopt laws to ensure equality between men and women in separation, divorce, and annulment of marriage. Under art 14, states are required to ensure various aspects of women's health and reproductive health, including the right to family planning education and allowing for 'authorised medical abortion', for example in cases of rape and incest.

to ascertain which aspects of the four provisions are in conflict with its current law. The reservations fell far short of indicating the specific domestic legal rules that necessitates reservation. The Gambia also provided no indication of the rationale for the reservations. Insulating all harmful cultural practices from the normative pull of the Protocol considerably weakens its effect and renders the reservation of article 5 against the object and purpose of the Protocol. Due to the width of their scope, and absent any bona-fide attempt to engage with the transformative possibilities of the Protocol, the reservations to articles 6, 7, and 14 should also be regarded as against the spirit and purport of the Protocol.[300] Resulting from a sensitization campaign by civil society, in collaboration with the parliamentary committee on women's rights, and profiting from the prospect of the upcoming AU summit meeting to be held in June 2006, the Gambian Parliament decided to withdraw the reservations in March 2006.[301]

All 20 African states that have become state parties to the Protocol are also parties to CEDAW. Two of them (Lesotho and Libya) reserved part of CEDAW, but did not enter similar reservations when ratifying the Protocol. Lesotho did not repeat its reservation in respect of succession to the throne and to chieftainship, even though the Protocol is quite explicit on this issue.[302] In the generally framed article 2, states are called upon to commit themselves to 'modify the social and cultural patterns of conduct of women and men through public education', to eliminate practices that are 'based on the inferiority' of women or on the 'stereotyped roles for women and men'. Given the centrality of article 2 in the framework of the Protocol, and the overriding importance of the King and chiefs in Lesotho, where traditional structures still have much currency, I contend that a reservation similar to that under CEDAW would have been incompatible with the object and purpose of the Protocol.[303] One may interpret the omission of a reservation as amounting to a change from the previous position that Lesotho held when it was ratifying CEDAW. This is particularly the impression given because both instruments deal with women's rights and specifically address the principles of equality and political participation.[304] Libya entered reservations related to Islamic Shari'ah law in respect of articles 2 and 16(c) and (d) of CEDAW. Despite

---

[300] This view was shared by numerous speakers, who made interventions during the day of celebrations for the entry into force of the Protocol, which was—ironically—held in Banjul, The Gambia, as part of the African Commission's 38th session.

[301] Interview with Ms Sainabou Jaye (Programme Officer, Centre for Democracy and Human Rights Studies, based in Banjul, The Gambia), conducted in Banjul, 15 November 2006 (notes on file with author).

[302] In art 9, the Protocol requires of state parties to ensure 'increased and effective representation and participation of women at all levels of decision-making'. As the Protocol contains no exemption for traditional or non-democratic structures, it appears that the exclusion of women from succession to the throne or from the position of chief falls foul of the Protocol.

[303] For a contrary view, namely that exclusive male claims to chieftaincy do not constitute gender discrimination, see B Ibhawoh, 'Between Culture and Constitution: Evaluating the Cultural Legitimacy of Human Rights in the African State' (2000) 22 *HRQ* 856.

[304] CEDAW, arts 2 and 7 and the Protocol, arts 2 and 9.

provisions in the Protocol with an effect similar to those to which it made reservations under CEDAW,[305] Libya did not make any reservations to the Protocol. Some of the non-ratifying states—especially those with a majority Muslim population—may have second thoughts about ratifying the Women's Protocol in the light of their experience with reservations under CEDAW.[306]

2 Improving Compliance

Even before the Protocol was put in place, both the African Commission and the CEDAW Committee were empowered to implement women's rights in African states.[307] As was stated above, the African Commission's reporting guidelines, requiring states to report on aspects pertaining to women's rights, extend far beyond the stipulations of the African Charter. Even if they did not follow the Guidelines, almost all reporting states included at least some information about the domestic protection of women's rights. Questions and comments related to sex and gender formed an integral part of the examination of these reports, especially subsequent to the appointment of a Special Rapporteur on the Rights of Women in Africa. Even though it was possible to do so, women's rights NGOs have not utilized the possibility of submitting parallel reports to state reports. Although the communications procedure has always been open to women and women's rights activists, women have brought very few cases, and matters pertinent to women have only been raised as 'secondary or indirect' issues.[308] Numerous African states have reported under CEDAW, but no communications have been brought against any of them under CEDAW-OP.[309]

The main reasons for the deficiencies in the supervisory procedures under the Charter and CEDAW—lack of compliance with reporting obligations; the failure to domesticate treaty provisions and implement concluding observations; and the limited use of the complaints mechanism—are likely to affect the implementation of the Women's Protocol, too. The Women's Protocol does not create new mechanisms or procedures to improve implementation. As a supplement to the African Charter, the Protocol is monitored by the same mechanism as the Charter (the African Commission) and through the same procedures (state reporting, explicitly provided for;[310] and individual communications, by necessary implication). Not only was no attempt made in the Women's Protocol to address the weaknesses besetting state reporting, but the possibility that an additional reporting requirement may lead to further duplication and fragmentation has been introduced.

---

[305] Arts 6 and 7 of the Protocol state that men and women shall be equal during marriage and its dissolution and this would therefore mean even in terms of rights and responsibilities towards their children. [306] See Ch 2 above.

[307] Due to the lack of concrete implementation, the African Children's Committee is omitted from this discussion. [308] Murray (n 294 above) 259.

[309] See Ch 3 above. [310] Women's Protocol, art 26(1).

However, by strengthening domestic judicial enforcement, the Women's Protocol may become increasingly accessible to women. The Protocol goes further than CEDAW and the Charter by requiring states to ensure women's 'effective access' to the law, amongst others by providing legal aid schemes for women.[311] It also fills a gap in the Charter by stipulating that 'appropriate remedies' must be provided.[312] The legal basis of implementation is further enhanced in that it is not only compulsory that some measures are enacted, but their enforcement is explicitly required by the Women's Protocol.[313] However, these measures are unlikely to improve treaty monitoring if there is no greater awareness and activism about the state reporting, communication, and other procedures. It is as an unambiguous symbol, on which greater awareness may be built and social movements mobilized, that the Women's Protocol will strengthen compliance. Still, effective domestication and domestic legal action remain the best ways of ensuring implementation.

3 Non-legal Implementation

The Protocol's privileging of non-legal forms of implementation or 'realization' (the third and most pertinent of the strategies to bridge the ratification–realization divide) attempts to undo the paradox of non-compliance with the law by creating more law. States have to go beyond adopting legislation to ensure that the Protocol's promises will reverse deeply engrained patterns and practices.[314] To this end, a golden thread of political empowerment, education, sensitization, outreach, public awareness, and resource-allocation is interwoven with the legal guarantees of the Protocol.[315] The principle of 'mainstreaming' gender into processes of decision-making, policy-formulation, and implementation also features prominently.[316] The Protocol acknowledges that violence against women can be eradicated not only by legislation, but also through 'social and economic measures'.[317] States are further required to go beyond legislative processes by identifying and addressing the 'causes' of violence against women.[318] Governments, the Protocol warns, cannot succeed alone, but must support 'initiatives' at all levels.[319] Psychological support services and vocational training complement the legal prohibition of harmful practices.[320] The justiciability of socio-economic rights is enhanced by and closely linked to adequate budgetary allocation.[321] In this respect, the Protocol gives considerable importance to prioritizing available resources, exemplified by the obligation on states to 'reduce military expenditure significantly in favour of spending on social development'.[322]

---

[311] Art 8(a) and (b).   [312] Art 25(a).   [313] Art 4(2)(a).
[314] See eg CAA Packer, *Using Human Rights to Change Tradition: Traditional Practices Harmful to Women's Reproductive Health in Sub-Saharan Africa* (Antwerp: Intersentia, 2002) 170, who notes that introduction of legislation against cultural practices without public support led to polarization and a firmer entrenchment of the practice.   [315] See eg arts 2(2), 4(2)(f), 5(a), and 14(2)(a).
[316] See eg arts 10(2)(e), 17(2), 19(a), and 19(b).   [317] Art 4(2)(b).   [318] Art 4(2)(c).
[319] Art 2(1)(e).   [320] Art 5(c).   [321] See eg arts 4(2)(i) and 26(2).
[322] Art 10(3).

It is in its deliberate fusion of legal and non-legal means of implementation that the Protocol makes its most significant contribution to address the frustration of unrealized treaty promises, and it is on the further pursuit of this approach that the improvement of women's rights through the African regional system depends.

Within the AU, women's rights and gender issues are by no means the exclusive preserve of the African Commission. Located prominently under the Chairperson of the AU Commission, the Directorate for Women, Gender and Development is mandated to ensure gender mainstreaming in all AU activities. The 'promotion and protection of the rights of women and the mainstreaming of gender equality' also feature as an important part of the APRM under NEPAD,[323] and were extensively covered in both the Ghanaian and Kenyan reports.[324] The AU Executive Council contributed to the gender-sensitive evolution of the APRM when it called on states to develop national policies for the economic empowerment of women, and decided that these policies should be included in the APRM assessment criteria.[325]

E Indigenous Peoples

1 A Contested Concept

The term 'indigenous' in 'indigenous peoples' rights' is a result of significant population movements spearheaded by colonial conquest, mass murder, dispossession, and displacement, particularly in the Americas and Australasia.[326] After international law had allowed the settler states to be fully established,[327] the pendulum of international concern slowly swung back towards those groups that had became excluded from the mainstream of public life and had been consigned to neglect in the 'new' states. When these groups started raising arguments for recognition and redress, they did so in the name of the morally compelling claim of being 'first' peoples. Thus, 'indigenous' came to be defined in opposition to those who came later ('second peoples'), who dislocated 'first peoples' through conquest

---

[323] Country Self-Assessment for the APRM (n 54 above) para 1.3.1 (Objective 7), which reiterates some of the crucial features of the Women's Protocol, such as access to and control over reproductive services, women's role on decision-making and conflict resolution. See also para 1.1.3 (Objective 3) as far as socio-economic rights are concerned.

[324] On Ghana, see APRM, Country Review Report of Ghana, June 2005 <http://www.adb.org> (accessed 30 September 2006) eg para 37: 'The Affirmative Action Policy of 1998 stipulated a 40% representation of women at all levels of governance, on public boards, commissions, councils, committees, the Cabinet and Council of State'. The fact that this goal, on the whole, has not been achieved is attributed to a lack of political will or commitment to gender equality by the political class. It is also attributed to the lack of clear affirmative action policies by most constitutionally created bodies and their failure to mainstream gender; see also paras 85–96; on Kenya, see Ch 5 above.

[325] AU Doc EX.CL/Dec.114(V) (July 2004).

[326] On this 'legacy of conquest', see S Wiessner, 'Rights and Status of Indigenous Peoples: A Global Comparative and International Legal Analysis' (1999) 12 *Harvard Human Rights J* 57, 58–93.

[327] See eg B Bowden, 'The Colonial Origins of International Law. European Expansion and the Classical Standard of Civilization' (2005) 7 *J of the History of Intl L* 1, 13.

and colonialism.[328] Juxtaposing the 'culture' or lifestyle of settler societies with that of 'indigenous' communities, the 'primitive' cultural distinctiveness of a particular group emerged as a further defining feature denoting indigeneity.[329]

As greater international visibility and acceptance of the importance of indigenous issues increased over the years, the International Labour Organization (ILO) in 1989 adopted Convention 169, concerning Indigenous and Tribal Peoples in Independent Countries.[330] Echoing the 'first peoples' and 'primitiveness' elements, this Convention applies to peoples who descended from populations 'which inhabited the country . . . at the time of conquest or colonisation', and whose 'status is regulated . . . by their own customs or traditions'.[331] However, the ILO Convention also introduced 'self-identification' as a fundamental factor determining whether a group falls within the protective ambit of the Convention.[332] The basic obligation of state parties is to guarantee to these groups 'the full measure of human rights and fundamental freedoms'.[333] Partly because so few states ratified this Convention, the UN developed other institutional mechanisms—a Working Group on Indigenous Populations,[334] a Permanent Forum on Indigenous Issues,[335] and a Special Rapporteur for Indigenous Peoples[336]—to ensure that this issue features adequately on its agenda.[337] As the potential benefits of the UN system became clear to them, representatives of African 'indigenous communities' in independent

---

[328] See eg SJ Anaya, *Indigenous Peoples in International Law* (Oxford: Oxford University Press, 2nd edn, 2004) 4; P Keal, *European Conquest and the Rights of Indigenous Peoples: The Moral Backwardness of International Society* (Cambridge: Cambridge University Press, 2003).

[329] See eg the use of the word 'tribal' in ILO Conventions 107 and 169; and see A Kuper, 'The Return of the Native' (2003) 44 *Current Anthropology* 389.

[330] Adopted 27 June 1989, entered into force 5 September 1991, deviating from the assimilationist approach of its predecessor, ILO Convention 107. As its title indicates, ILO Convention 169 employs two interrelated categories, 'indigenous peoples' and 'tribal peoples'. The most important element associated with the former is their 'descent', while the latter group is distinguishable on the grounds of its 'customs and traditions'.   [331] ILO Convention 169, art 1(a) and (b).

[332] As above, art 1(2).   [333] As above, art 3(1).

[334] The Working Group on Indigenous Populations was established pursuant to Economic and Social Council Resolution 1982/34 as a subsidiary organ of the Sub-Commission on the Promotion and Protection of Human Rights. Its mandate is to review developments pertaining to the promotion and protection of human rights and fundamental freedoms of indigenous peoples and to give attention to the evolution of international standards concerning indigenous rights. Its five members are experts from the Sub-Commission representing the geopolitical regions of the world, and included one African, El Hadjè Guissé, from Senegal, who was elected as one of the first 11 judges of the African Court on Human and Peoples' Rights (see Ch 11.C.1 below).

[335] The Permanent Forum is an advisory body to ECOSOC; it consists of 16 independent experts, of which only one—the South African, William Langeveldt, patron and founder member of the National Land Khoe-San African Movement and a Commissioner of a statutory body, the Commission for the Promotion and Protection of the Rights of Cultural, Religious and Linguistic Communities—is from an African country, <http://www.un.org/esa/socdev/unpfii/en/members.html> (accessed 30 September 2006). The terms of the current members expire at the end of 2007.

[336] Established in 2001, this Special Rapporteur studies issues impacting on the human rights of indigenous peoples, and undertakes visits to countries; only one such visit has taken place to an African country (South Africa, see UN Doc E/CN.4/2006/78/Add.2).

[337] See also the World Bank Operational Directive 4.20, discussed more fully in Ch 2 above.

states started attending the Working Group on Indigenous Populations in growing numbers.[338] Their presence at the sessions of the Working Group has contributed much to give prominence to African indigenous concerns, but, due to the non-attendance of African governments, has not led to a deeper engagement with national authorities. Other UN multilateral treaties, in particular CERD and ICCPR, have also proven to be of relevance to indigenous peoples in Africa.[339]

After a long drafting process within the UN, the Human Rights Council in June 2006 approved the UN Declaration on the Rights of Indigenous Peoples.[340] This Declaration discards the notion of 'tribalism', and introduces the right to self-determination of indigenous peoples.[341] Underscoring their reluctance to acknowledge the presence of indigenous peopels, no African state has ratified ILO Convention 169, and of the 13 African members of the Human Rights Council, only four voted in favour of the UN Declaration on the Rights of Indigenous Peoples.[342] Subsequently proposing and supporting a proposal that discussion of the Declaration be deferred, African states were instrumental in thwarting its adoption by the UNGA.[343]

African resistance to accepting the rights of 'indigenous peoples' is due in part to the association of the term with colonialism, informing uneasiness about the determination of who 'first peoples' are, and fears that recognition and the right to 'self-determination' of 'indigenous peoples' will expose the fragility of the artifice of the African nation state.[344] Governments' overly sensitive stance on self-determination may thus be traced back to their uncritical acceptance of colonially demarcated territorial boundaries.[345] Establishing the hegemony of the post-colonial state depended on silencing counter-hegemonic voices and on submerging

---

[338] Report of the African Commission's Working Group of Experts on Indigenous Populations/Communities, adopted at the Commission's 34th session, November 2003, 90.

[339] See eg the Human Rights Committee's finding in Communication 760/1997, *Diergaardt and Others v Namibia*, UN Doc CCPR/C/69/D/760/1997, discussed in Ch 3.3.4 above; and the CERD Committee's Concluding Observations on Botswana (UN Doc CERD/C/BWA/CO/16 (4 April 2006) paras 12–14), Mauritania (UN Doc CERD/C/65/CO/5 (10 December 2004) para 22), and South Africa (UN Doc CERD/C/ZAF/CO/3 (19 October 2006) paras 11,19, and 22).

[340] See Ch 2 above.

[341] Declaration on the Rights of Indigenous Peoples (UN Doc A/C.3/61/L.18/Rev.1), arts 3 and 4. While art 3 guarantees that right in general terms, seemingly allowing it to be invoked in pursuance of secessionist claims, art 4 limits the 'exercising' of this right to claims that do not threaten territorial integrity ('autonomy or self-government in matters relating to their internal and local affairs'). It should be noted that indigenous peoples 'seldom aspire to independent statehood, but claim rights to territory and to self-determination in order to secure their own existence' (H Veber and E Waehle, '...Never Drink From the Same Cup' in H Veber, J Dahl, F Wilson, and E Waehle (eds), ... *Never Drink From the Same Cup: Proceedings of the Conference on Indigenous Peoples in Africa, Tune, Denmark, 1993* (Copenhagen: IWGIA and Centre for Development Research, 1993) 9, 15).

[342] See Ch 2.B above.   [343] See Ch 2 above.

[344] Veber and Waehle (n 341 above) 10–11.

[345] ibid, 10: 'When Europeans were forced to relinquish political control, the artificial colonial borders became the borders of the post-colonial states... The indigenous "movement" in Africa has grown as a response to the policies adopted by independent post-colonial African states'.

divergent cultures and identities into the new construct of the 'nation'.[346] Sadly, the post- and neo-colonial state mostly privileged one ethnic community and caused the neglect of and marginalized other ethnic communities.[347] On the basis of numerical superiority, or a position of power secured through collusion with colonial governments, the neo-colonial state became another illegitimate imposition on many Africans. The consequence of this 'imposition' was a lack of tolerance for diversity, leaving numerous communities excluded and exploited.

In January 2007, the AU Assembly welcomed the deferral of discussion on the UN Declaration on the Rights of Indegenous Peoples, and mandated the African Group at the UN to guard Africa's interests and concerns about the 'political, economic, social and constitutional implications' of the Declaration.[348] By reiterating the principle of *uti possidetis*, and by explicitly referring not only to the OAU Assembly resolution of 1964, in which all OAU members pledged to respect borders existing at the time of independence, but also to the 1960 UN General Assembly Declaration on the granting of independence to colonial countries and peoples,[349] the AU underlined its salient (but arguably unfounded) concern about the Declaration—its destabilizing effect on national territories.[350]

Most African states and a number of academics have questioned the conceptual and strategic applicability of the concept to the African context.[351] These criticisms have foregrounded the complexity of applying the concept 'indigenous' to the postcolonial African state. Arguably, in Africa, most nationals are to varying degrees 'indigenous' in the original sense of the term.[352] Attaching the term to only one particular group would therefore be an unacceptable privileging of a part of the nation and would undermine nation-building. African inclusion in the international indigenous rights discussion thus highlighted the implications of the 'global interpretation' of 'Western-originated' concepts,[353] and the need to refocus the term

---

[346] This sentiment persists into the present; see eg the statement by President Festus Mogae of Botswana: 'While it is perfectly legitimate for tribes to promote their individual cultures, we should avoid setting up exclusive organisations whose membership is drawn from one tribe... Our goal of nation-building needs to prevail over narrow tribal sentiment' ('Botswana Minorities Defend the Right to Organise' 24 October 2006 <http://www.andnetwork> (accessed 25 October 2006)).

[347] See eg AG Selassie, 'Ethnic Identity and Constitutional Design for Africa' (1992–3) 29 *Stanford J of Intl L* 1, 8–13.   [348] AU Doc Assembly/AU/Dec.141(VIII), para 3.

[349] ibid, paras 2 and 4.

[350] The complete list of the AU's concerns, to be addressed during further discussions, reads as follows: the definition of indigenous peoples; self-determination; ownership of land and resources; establishment of distinct political and economic institutions; and national and territorial integrity (ibid, para 6).

[351] R Hitchcock and D Vinding, 'Indigenous Peoples' Rights in Southern Africa: An Introduction' in R Hitchcock and D Vinding (eds), *Indigenous Peoples' Rights in Southern Africa* (Copenhagen: IWGIA, 2004) 8 (stating that most African governments either deny the existence of indigenous groups or claim that all their nationals are indigenous); see also Kuper (n 329 above).

[352] In its January 2007 decision (n 348 above) para 7, the AU Assembly indeed 'affirmed' that the 'vast majority of the peoples of Africa' are indigenous to the African continent.

[353] This is also a consequence of the extrapolation of the term to Asia, see B Kingsbury, '"Indigenous Peoples" in International Law: A Constructivist Approach to the Asian Controversy' (1998) 92 *AJIL* 414, 455.

'indigenous' to refer to 'marginality',[354] and 'self-identification',[355] rather than 'priority of time'.

Indeed, the term 'indigenous' is not static and rigid, but should be reconceptualized as a context-dependent concept, to be given meaning in relation to the politically dominant group in society.[356] Even when the governing elite is an ethnically African (and, in the original understanding of the term, also 'indigenous') group within a multi-ethnic state, indigenous groups may still be identified, mainly on the basis of their lifestyle and the ethical imperative of their marginality and vulnerability. It is the confluence of a historical dependence for survival on the land, exemplified, in Africa, by a life of hunter-gatherers and pastoralists, and a present-day neglect and exploitation that constitute an 'indigenous' group. It is precisely their traditional lifestyles that left indigenous groups unprepared for life in a modernizing state, eroding the basis of their survival, increasing their vulnerability, and exposing them to the real risk of extinction. Even if they become absorbed in the modernist state, theirs is a counter-hegemonic citizenship, claiming respect for their ancestral land, language, and culture.

Different from 'minority' groups, the claims of indigenous peoples are almost always collective in nature, are mostly linked to spiritual ties to and dependence on land, and are rooted in extreme forms of marginalization and subjugation that go beyond 'mere' non-dominance. Self-identification, which is also an important marker, is saved from the trap of subjectivity by the requirement that the factors elucidated above (such as marginality threatening extinction) have to accompany such a claim. Claims of 'indigenous peoples' should, on the basis of the definitional focus proposed above, not be understood as an attempt to gain special privileges,[357] but as an effort to secure survival and equal treatment 'based on an acceptance of the legitimacy of the economic and social basis of their ways of life'.[358]

2 The African Charter as a Basis for Protection

Even if the African Charter does not expressly include indigenous peoples within its ambit, there is no reason why they should not benefit from the Charter's guarantees—either as individuals, or, more importantly, as members of a collectivity.[359] It is inconceivable that a person will be disqualified as a rights-bearer of,

[354] Wiessner (n 326 above) 115 (defining indigenous peoples as those who suffered 'a pervasive pattern of subjugation, marginalization, dispossession, exclusion and discrimination').
[355] Wiessner (ibid) adds an external element to self-definition (by defining indigenous peoples as 'peoples traditionally regarded, and self-defined' as 'descendants of the original inhabitants of lands'.
[356] J Kenrick and J Lewis, 'Indigenous Peoples' Rights and the Politics of the Term "Indigenous"' (2004) 20 *Anthropology Today* 4, 6 and 9.
[357] See the legitimate concerns raised by B Kingsbury, 'Reconciling Five Competing Conceptual Structures of Indigenous Peoples' Claims in International and Comparative Law' in P Alston (ed), *Peoples' Rights* (Oxford: Oxford University Press, 2001) 69, 107.
[358] Kenrick and Lewis (n 356 above) 4, 9, taking issue with Kuper's arguments (n 329 above).
[359] See also the extension of CERD to cover indigenous peoples: General Recommendation 23: Indigenous Peoples, 18 August 1997 (UN Doc A/52/18, Annex V), and the application of the ICCPR (art 27, rights of minorities) to indigenous claims.

say, the right to a fair trial, just because he or she is 'indigenous'. In line with the Commission's interpretation of the concept 'peoples' discussed above, indigenous groupings should as a matter of principle be eligible to claim, as 'peoples', the right to an existence; to economic, social, and cultural development; and to peace and security.[360] The mere fact that indigenous 'peoples' would also be entitled to invoke the 'right to self-determination' does not detract from this logic. As was clarified in the *Katangese Secession* case,[361] various constitutional models may suffice to give effect to this right—including autonomy taking the form of meaningful involvement in local government. The most problematic Charter-based 'peoples' right' to apply to 'indigeous peoples' may be the right to 'freely dispose of their wealth and natural resources'.[362] If it is accepted that both nationals-as-people (comprising a nation state) and an indigenous-group-as-a-people within that nation state may rely on this provision, the Commission (or African Human Rights Court) will have to strike a balance between competing claims to resources, supported by different concepts of 'peoples', as required by the particular circumstances.

The potential application of the Charter to 'indigenous peoples' lay unexplored, until civil society started to prod and urge on the Commission. Spearheaded by the INGO, International Work Group for Indigenous Affairs (IWGIA),[363] and following a first conference on indigenous issues in Africa, African-based NGOs advocating for indigenous rights increasingly succeeded in obtaining observer status with the Commission.[364] In 2000, the Commission provided an institutional foothold for the concerns of indigenous peoples when it established the Working Group on Indigenous Populations or Communities in Africa (Working Group on Indigenous Communities), composed of two Commissioners and members of civil society.[365] Acting upon its mandate to examine the concept of 'indigenous populations/communities in Africa', the Working Group on Indigenous Communities prepared a report, which the Commission adopted in 2003.[366] In this very

---

[360] African Charter, arts 19–24.   [361] n 75 above.   [362] African Charter, art 21(1).

[363] See Ch 9.H below. The successful collaboration between IWGIA and African-based NGOs is the 'product both of Euro-American interests in empowering marginal groups and of the success of certain minority groups in strategically representing and promoting their identities to defend rights' (DL Hodgson, 'Introduction: Comparative Perspectives on the Indigenous Rights Movement in Africa and the Americas' (2002) 104 *American Anthropologist* 1037, 1040).

[364] The following NGOs with a specific mandate related to indigenous peoples' rights obtained observer status: Survival International (23 April–7 May 2001, 29th Ordinary Session, Tripoli, Libya); Minority Rights Group (13–27 October 2001, 30th Ordinary Session. Banjul, The Gambia); Mainyoito Pastoralist, Indigenous Peoples of Africa, Centre for Minority Rights Development (Kenya), Indigenous Peoples' Association Coordinating Committee (South Africa) (15–29 May 2003, 33rd Ordinary Session, Niamey, Niger).

[365] Resolution on the Rights of Indigenous Populations/Communities in Africa, establishing a Working Group of Experts on Indigenous Populations/Communities, adopted at the Commission's 28th session, 23 October–November 2000. The omission of the word 'peoples' from the Working Group's title reflects the Commission's reluctance to 'entitle' indigenous 'communities' to the benefits under the Charter, in particular the right to self-determination (art 20(1)).

[366] Report of the African Commission's Working Group of Experts on Indigenous Populations/ Communities. See also Resolution on the adoption of the 'Report of the African Commission's

significant report, the Commission takes the view that indigenous peoples are present in many African countries,[367] that the African Charter guarantees their rights as individuals and 'peoples', and that state parties to the Charter routinely violate these rights.[368]

To some extent, indigenous rights have featured in the Commission's two main procedures: state reporting and individual communications. NGOs also used the forum provided by the Commission's public sessions to raise concerns about indigenous rights issues, often eliciting responses from government representatives. It is the real possibility of entering into some form of debate with governments during the African Commission's sessions that prompted representatives of African indigenous communities to present their case in this forum.

Predating the debates before the Commission, the Guidelines for state reporting make passing reference to 'indigenous sectors' of African states in the context of states' obligation to report about steps taken to promote cultural identity.[369] Initially, this call went unheeded, and the Commissioners did not prompt state representatives to provide any information related to indigenous 'sectors'. Following the establishment of the Working Group on Indigenous Communities, the Commission at its 29th session, in 2001, posed questions about the situation of indigenous peoples in reporting states.[370] Since then, this aspect has featured consistently during the examination of state reports, and sometimes even as part of concluding observations. Following the consideration of its first periodic report at that session, Namibia became the first state to be targeted with concluding observations relating to indigenous peoples.[371] In another example, the concluding observations, adopted after examining South Africa's second report in 2005, recommended that

Working Group on Indigenous Populations/Communities', 20 November 2003, 17th Activity Report of the Commission, annex IV. For an analysis of the report, see KN Bojosi and GM Wachira, 'Protecting Indigenous Peoples in Africa: An Analysis of the Approach of the African Commission on Human and Peoples' Rights' (2006) 6 *AHRLJ* 382, 393–406.

[367] The Working Group Report (n 366 above) includes reference to the Batwa/Pygmy (Central Africa), Hadzabe (Tanzania), Ogiek (Kenya), San (Southern Africa), Masaai (East Africa), Himba (Namibia), Tuareg (West and North Africa), Ogoni (Nigeria), and the Berbers (North Africa), based on self-identification and traditional lifestyle (categorizing the groups above into 'hunter-gatherers' and 'pastoralists') as primary indicia.   [368] Working Group Report (n 366 above) para 42.

[369] Guidelines for National Periodic Reports, para III(14)(b)(iv), calling for an indication of measures promoting the cultural heritage of 'national ethnic groups and minorities and of indigenous sectors of the population'.

[370] Report of the Working Group on Indigenous Communities (2005) 78.

[371] The Commission took note of the government's 'commitment to promoting national unity within an environment where there is a multi-cultural, multi-lingual and multi-ethnic society'; the Commission emphasized that 'a commitment to human rights will help the state to manage tension particularly in the Caprivi strip affected by the Secessionist Movement and the protection of the under privileged peoples such as the Himba and the San'; it further noted the 'inadequate measures to address the special needs of the vulnerable groups such as the Himba and San'; and it recommended that the Namibian government 'urgently introduce measures that adequately address the situation of vulnerable groups such as the San and Himba so as to enable such groups to enjoy the rights under the Charter on the basis of equality with other groups in the country' (Concluding Observations for the Report of Namibia, issued after examination at the 29th session, on file with author).

South Africa 'undertake all appropriate measures to ensure that the rights of children belonging to minority groups, including the Khoi-Khoi and San, are guaranteed, particularly those rights concerning culture, religion, language and access to information'.[372] States still devote minimal attention to this aspect in their state reports, though, as exemplified by the recent Ugandan report, which merely states that Uganda is 'composed of 56 different indigenous communities', which are 'segregated under four major ethnicities', the Bantu, the Nilotics, the Nilo Hamites, and the Luo.[373]

Although no communication dealing with indigenous peoples' rights has as yet been finalized on its merits, the African Commission declared inadmissible two communications involving indigenous peoples. The first case, *Bakweri Land Claims Committee v Cameroon*,[374] instituted on behalf of an 'indigenous minority' in Cameroon, was declared inadmissible due to the non-exhaustion of local remedies. Even if the complaint alleged the violation of individual and *peoples'* rights, the admissibility decision does not reveal an attempt to define the Bakweri as an 'indigenous people'. This approach underscores the fact that indigenous groups may bring individual and collective claims under the Charter, irrespective of whether the tag of indigenousness is placed around their necks. In the second case, *Anuak Justice Council v Ethiopia*,[375] the Anuak, who describe themselves as members of an 'indigenous minority group', principally claimed violations resulting from massacres, disappearances, detentions without charge, and destruction of property. Based on allegations that individual rights have been violated—even if they are invoked cumulatively and on a massive scale, the claim does not rely on any of the peoples' rights in the Charter. Mention is made of the entitlement of the Anuak to oil resources, but the drafters of the communication (the International Human Rights Clinic, Washington College of Law) did not locate arguments about this entitlement in the indigeneity of the Anuak as a 'people'.

A third communication, *Centre for Minority Rights Development (CEMIRIDE) (on behalf of the Endorois Community) v Kenya*,[376] submitted in 2003 and still pending, is more clearly linked to the alleged victims' membership of an indigenous people. The Endorois, a pastoralist group in Kenya numbering some 60,000, claim that their eviction from ancestral land to make room for a wildlife reserve (the Lake Bogoria Game Reserve) violates their rights as individuals (for example, their right to practise their religion) and their 'peoples' rights' (such as the right to dispose of wealth and to development).

---

[372] Conclusions and Recommendations on the First Periodic Report of the Republic of South Africa, 38th session of the Commission, 21 November–5 December 2005 (on file with author) para 34.

[373] Uganda's second Periodic Report, <http://www.achpr.org/english/state_reports/40_Uganda%20periodic%20report_Eng.pdf> (accessed 30 November 2006) para 3.

[374] Communication 260/02, decided at the Commission's 36th session, November–December 2004, not yet contained in an Activity Report of the Commission.

[375] Communication 299/03, 20th Activity Report.   [376] Communication 276/2003.

3 Other AU Standards

Other AU instruments also show an awareness of the rights of indigenous peoples. In the Revised African Nature Convention, for example, the imperative is introduced that states must respect the 'traditional rights and intellectual property rights of local communities including farmers' rights'; and that 'indigenous knowledge' may be accessed only with the consent of concerned communities and that they have to be compensated for the 'economic value' of that knowledge.[377] To ensure sustainable resource use, local communities have to be actively involved in the 'planning and management of natural resources' upon which they depend.[378] As state parties to the Cultural Charter for Africa, the majority of African states should be reminded that they have committed themselves to develop 'national languages', 'peoples' culture' and 'cultural' diversity, and not to impoverish or 'subject' minority cultures to the 'assertion of national identity'.[379] Although this Charter does not mention indigenous peoples by the name, its relevance to many of the claims of indigenous peoples is clear.

The APRM does not expressly require participating states to report on the protection of indigenous peoples. Objective 9, dealing with the rights of 'vulnerable groups', is the most appropriate heading under which this important aspect should be covered. The Country Review Report of Ghana does not do so explicitly, restricting instead its focus to groups such as people living with HIV and the aged. The Kenyan report contains a brief discussion in which it avoids using the term 'indigenous'. Although it notes the existence of 'groups that seemed to qualify as indigenous tribes who retain their cultural identity, such as pastoralists, hunters and gatherers', it observes that stakeholders use the terms 'vulnerable', 'marginalized', and 'minority' interchangeably, 'describing their plight in an often confusing and misleading manner'.[380] The Country Review Mission did not 'find evidence of any legal or policy document indicating which groups were at risk in any of the aforementioned categories'.[381] It expressed criticism against the 'isolationist view and approach' of the different groups, who displayed no 'consciousness of the problems faced by other groups or how to collectively address the overarching issues that cut across the structural difficulties faced by individual groups'.[382] The Country Mission's insight that the problem is mainly resource-based, led it to recommend to the government that it 'prioritise basic infrastructure projects targeted at improving the lives of vulnerable groups, including tribal minorities'.[383]

---

[377] Revised African Nature Convention, art XVII(1) and (2).
[378] ibid, art XVII(3).
[379] Cultural Charter for Africa, arts 3, 5, 6(1)(a), and 9.
[380] Kenya's APRM Review Report, 112.   [381] ibid.   [382] ibid.
[383] ibid, 114. See also Country Review Report of the Republic of Rwanda, November 2005, paras 15 and 156: the vulnerability and assimilation of the Batwa are noted, and dialogue between the government and this minority community is recommended. The concept of 'indigenousness' is not specifically mentioned in the Report.

4 Domestic Law

Although almost all African constitutions prohibit discrimination on the basis of ethnicity or ethnic origin, and a small number of African constitutions provide for the rights of minorities,[384] only the Constitution of Burundi of 2004 includes a specific guarantee to members of an indigenous group, the Twa. In terms of the Constitution, the Twa is represented by three 'deputies' in the National Assembly,[385] and by the same number of 'delegates' in the Senate.[386] Even if it did not extend the same guarantee to other levels or branches of government, the Burundi Constitution sets a promising precedent recognizing the need to include indigenous peoples in political institutions.

In instances where the constitution does not provide for indigenous or minority rights, as in Botswana, other constitutional provisions and domestic law have been used to address the violation of indigenous peoples' rights. Members of the Basarwa, an indigenous group of Botswana, settled in an area that in 1961 was proclaimed as the Central Kalahari Game Reserve (CKGR). Despite numerous attempts to resettle them in 'viable sites' for 'economic and social development', they were allowed to continue living there. Finally, in 2002, the government took decisive steps to relocate them.[387] In a case brought by members of the Basarwa, the Botswana High Court held that their forced relocation amounted to an unlawful dispossession of their land, and that the refusal to grant them game licences and to allow them to enter the CKGR was not only unlawful,[388] but also unconstitutional.[389] While one of the three judges clearly acknowledged the Basarwa as an 'indigenous' group,[390] another managed *not* to use the word 'indigenous' in his entire judgment.[391] Although one judge placed reliance on a General Recommendation of the Committee on the Elimination of Racial Discrimination,[392] the judgment does not mention the

---

[384] See eg the Constitution of Uganda 1995, art 36 ('Minorities have a right to participate in decision-making processes and their views and interests shall be taken into account in the making of national plans and programmes').

[385] Art 164. See also Constitution of South Africa 1996, ss 6(5) and 31.   [386] Art 180(2).

[387] See also the report of the UN Special Rapporteur on Indigenous Peoples (UN Doc E/CN.4/2002/97/Add.1, and the government's response (*note verbale* contained in UN Doc E/CN.4/2002/181, 18 April 2002), in which the Botswana government denied that it had engaged in 'assimilationist' practices, and underscored that the Basarwa were 'not forced but persuaded to relocate' (*note verbale*, para 10). However, the government's own explanation that it terminated services to this community contradicts the assertion about voluntariness. See also *Alexkor and Another v Richtersveld Community and Others* (2003) 12 BCLR 1301 (CC).

[388] *Sesana and Others v Attorney General*, Case Msca No 52 of 2002, High Court of Botswana at Lobatse, judgment of 13 December 2005 (on file with author), the Court finding that the exercise of discretion allowed for under the Wild Conservation and National Parks Act 28 of 1992 was unlawful.

[389] By a majority of two to one, the Court found that the denial of special gaming licences constituted a violation of the right to life; and that the restrictions on the Basarwa's movements violated their right to freedom of movement. Both these rights are contained in Botswana's Constitution (arts 4 and 14).   [390] Dow J, 160 of the typed judgment.

[391] Dibotelo J.

[392] General Recommendation 23 (1997), on indigenous peoples, para 4(d).

African Charter or its Working Group on Indigenous Communities. This judgment illustrates that the redress of indigenous peoples' rights is not dependent on them being identified as such, or on legal provisions aimed at their protection, but on appropriate legal argument, judicial activism, and social mobilization.

With its adapted focus on the present exclusion and marginalization of groups who have relied and still predominantly rely for their survival on their relationship with the land, the concept of 'indigenousness' may be of strategic use in lobbying and advocacy for legal reform domestically and internationally. However, the analysis of instruments, and the communications before the African Commission, in particular, illustrate that the exercise of tagging a group or claim as 'indigenous' should not take up all our time and energy. Instead of the conceptual strait-jacket of a meta-narrative of indigeneity, the focus should be on the claims of all marginalized groups, as they arise in a particular context. The diversity of these claims and their resolutions further belie a one-size-fits-all approach. Being indigenous should not be a threshold requirement for protection, but should inform, as an indication of the extent and degree of marginalization and subjugation of a particular group, the substance of the claim and the form of redress, irrespective of the legal basis on which it is raised.[393] As more empirical evidence is provided that proves the forced removal and exploitation of indigenous groups, it will be increasingly difficult for governments to escape with blanket denials, as they managed to do when the discourse on 'indigeneity' was closely tied to priority in time and colonialism.

F Environment

In recent times, the influence of relentless development on the well-being of individuals and the environment in which they live has become a cause for increasing alarm. Although the protection of the environment is primarily dependent on non-legal factors (such as government policy, local and international economic forces, demographics, and natural elements), international treaties may also play a role in creating or stimulating an appropriate (legal) framework to improve environmental protection.

Establishing the first binding international human rights-based approach to environmental protection,[394] the African Charter goes further than any previous instrument by providing for the right of 'all peoples' to a general satisfactory environment 'favourable to their development'.[395] This formulation, which encompasses the elements of 'environment' and 'development', pre-empts the tension between

---

[393] See also Kingsbury (n 353 above) 457, calling for a flexible approach in which requirements and indicia of indigeneity are applied in combination to particular circumstances in an ad hoc way.

[394] M Van der Linde and L Louw, 'Considering the Interpretation and Implementation of Article 24 of the African Charter on Human and Peoples' Rights in the Light of the *SERAC* Communication' (2003) 3 *AHRLJ* 167, 169–70.   [395] African Charter, art 24.

the 'right to an environment' and the right to development—another area in which the Charter first elaborated an issue of international concern in a binding human rights framework.[396] The sustainable growth and development of Africa feature prominently in the discourse of African economic integration.[397] Progress and development, requiring the exploitation and use of resources, are viewed as the keys to approximate the gains of the idealized 'developed' world, to overcome underdevelopment, and to eradicate poverty.[398] There seems to be little place in this discourse for the negative impact on the environment of the concrete manifestations of development: the disrupting and displacing of communities as a result of building dams, highways, and railway lines, extracting minerals and oil, felling of trees, pollution, and so on.

The same tension also underlies the *Ogoniland* case, the only communication concluded by the Commission in which the right to an environment played a pertinent role. Intent on development and short-term benefits, the Nigerian government-controlled oil company engaged in activities causing the contamination of air, water, and soil. For the first time giving effect to a binding international environmental right, the Commission observed that article 24 of the Charter imposes an obligation on the state to take reasonable measures 'to prevent pollution and ecological degradation, to promote conservation, and to ensure an ecologically sustainable development and use of natural resources'.[399] In addition to addressing itself to the substantive aspect of the right, the Commission also gave effect to its procedural aspects by, for example, requiring that the state ensure that appropriate impact assessments are conducted before future oil 'developments' are embarked upon, and that communities likely to be affected are made part of relevant decision-making processes.[400]

Article 24, seen as a move towards a human rights-based approach to the environment, should be viewed in conjunction with the first OAU treaty on the environment, the Convention on the Conservation of Nature and Natural Resources, which predates the African Charter, and another instrument adopted subsequently, the Bamako Convention. These treaties are therefore discussed briefly. Moreover, in the Treaty Establishing the African Economic Community (AEC), which co-exists with the AU Constitutive Act, specific provision is also made for the environment and the ban on the import of hazardous waste into Africa and across African borders.[401] Apart from listing 'environmental protection' as one of the functions of the Executive Council,[402] and adding it onto the mandate of one of the specialized technical committees,[403] the AU Constitutive Act is silent on the environment.

[396] African Charter, art 22.
[397] See eg AU Constitutive Act, arts 3(j) and 4(n); NEPAD Declaration (2001) para 1.
[398] NEPAD Declaration, paras 1–7.   [399] *Ogoniland* case (n 31 above) para 52.
[400] ibid, para 71.   [401] Abuja Treaty, arts 58 and 59.
[402] AU Constitutive Act, art 13(1)(e).
[403] ibid, art 14(1)(d): the Committee on Industry, Science and Technology, Energy, Natural Resources and the Environment.

1 The African Convention on the Conservation of Nature and Natural Resources

In 1968 the OAU Heads of State and Government adopted an African instrument on the environment, the African Convention on the Conservation of Nature and Natural Resources (African Nature Convention) in Algiers.[404] It entered into force on 16 June 1969. This Convention concerns itself primarily with wildlife, but also deals with many other aspects, including the use of resources such as soil and water. It has been described (in 1985) as the 'most comprehensive multilateral treaty for the conservation of nature yet negotiated',[405] in which environmental concerns and development are linked.[406] As is the case with many other treaties on the environment, no administrative structure is created to ensure implementation. As a result, the Convention's provisions have largely remained neglected. Still, the Convention 'has stimulated useful conservation measures in some countries and remains the framework on which a substantial body of national legislation is based'.[407] By 1985, 28 states had become party to the Convention. A further 14 had at that stage signed the treaty, without ratifying it.[408] Between 1985 and 1997, the number of ratifications had only risen by one;[409] indicating that the Convention has lost some of its initial appeal.

Numerous conferences, such as the UN 1992 Conference on Environment and Development, culminating in the adoption of the Rio Declaration on Environment and Development, and the elaboration of a variety of standards necessitated the adaptation and updating of the African Nature Convention. Although attempts to revise the African Nature Convention may be traced back to 1983, they gained momentum when a series of inter-agency meetings was launched in 2000.[410] The process led to the adoption, under AU auspices, of a revised African Convention on the Conservation of Nature and Natural Resources (Revised African Nature Convention).[411]

In its Preamble, the Revised African Nature Convention 'recalls' the African Charter, as well as other instruments such as the AEC Treaty and the Rio Declaration, and reiterates its aim to include 'elements related to sustainable development'. The amended text updates the African Nature Convention and adds new provisions. In a significant departure from its predecessor, the Revised African Nature

---

[404] OAU Doc CAB/LEG/24.1, adopted on 15 September 1968.

[405] S Lyster, *International Wildlife Law: An Analysis of International Treaties Concerned with the Conservation of Wildlife* (Cambridge: Grotius Publications, 1985) 115.

[406] African Nature Convention, art 7.   [407] Lyster (n 405 above) 115.

[408] For a list of these states, see Lyster (n 405 above) 115.

[409] Only Gabon became a party after 1985—in 1988. For ratifications as at the end of 2006, see Table 6.1 below.

[410] M Van der Linde, 'A Review of the African Convention on Nature and Natural Resources' (2002) 2 *AHRLJ* 33, 44–56.

[411] Adopted by the AU Assembly on 11 July 2003; it will enter into force after 15 states have ratified it. By 31 December 2006, only five states (Comoros, Lesotho, Libya, Mali, and Rwanda) have done so. Of these states, two (Lesotho and Libya) have never become party to the 1968 Convention.

Convention locates its implementation in the context of articles 22 (the right to development) and 24 (the right to a satisfactory environment) of the Charter.[412] It also provides for 'procedural rights', requiring states to adopt legislation and other measures to ensure dissemination and public access to 'environmental information', to ensure public participation in environmentally sensitive decision-making, and to allow for 'access to justice' in matters related to the environment.[413]

Some of the other innovations in the revised treaty are: (i) the obligation on states to take 'every practical measure' to protect the environment during times of armed conflict,[414] (ii) the acceptance in principle of state liability for damages related to the Convention,[415] and (iii) the establishment of a Conference of State Parties as decision-making body with powers to review the implementation of the Convention.[416] Deviating from the African Charter, the Revised African Nature Convention allows for 'precisely defined' derogation from its provisions during 'declared emergencies arising from disasters' and 'for the protection of public health'.[417]

2 The Bamako Convention

As the human suffering caused by the dumping of petrochemical material in Côte d'Ivoire during 2006 illustrates,[418] trade in toxic waste remains an important human rights issue. Earlier, the issue attracted international concern when dumping of toxic waste in many parts of the world, and particularly in Africa, was revealed. In response, the UN adopted the Basel Convention on the Control of Transboundary Movements of Hazardous Wastes and their Disposal (Basel Convention) on 22 March 1989.[419] It entered into force in 1992.[420] The dissatisfaction of African states with the Basel Convention's major premise (that hazardous waste may be exported from industrialized to developing countries, but that its movement needs to be regulated and controlled) spurred the drafting of a multilateral African treaty. This treaty is the Bamako Convention on the Ban of the Import into Africa and the Control of Transboundary Movement and Management of Hazardous Wastes within Africa (Bamako Convention), which was adopted on 30 January 1991 by a conference of Ministers of the Environment from 51 OAU states,[421] and entered into force on 22 April 1998.

Adopted after the African Charter had already signalled a human rights-based approach to the environment, the Bamako Convention does not expressly embrace

---

[412] Revised African Nature Convention, art III.   [413] ibid, art XVI(1).

[414] ibid, art XV(1).   [415] ibid, art XXIV.   [416] ibid, art XXVI.

[417] ibid, art XXV(2).

[418] See eg UNEP, 'Côte d'Ivoire: UN Environmental Arm Probes Dumping of Deadly Toxic Wastes', 8 September 2006, <http://www.un.org/apps/news/story.asp?NewsID=19764&Cr=ivoire&Cr1=> (31 January 2007).   [419] See text in (1989) 28 ILM 656.

[420] See F Ouguergouz, 'The Bamako Convention on Hazardous Waste: A New Step in the Development of the African Environmental Law' (1993) 1 *AYBIL* 195, 196.

[421] See text in (1993) 1 *AYBIL* 268–93. Neither the Assembly nor the then Council of Ministers adopted the Bamako Treaty (T Maluwa, 'International Law-Making in the Organisation of African Unity: An Overview' (2000) 12 *RADIC* 201, 206 n 13).

human rights terminology, but does position itself as an 'effective way' of protecting 'the human health of the African population'.[422] Given the high degree of specialization and uniformity due to standardized technical terminology, it should hardly be surprising that the regional treaty borrows extensively from its international predecessor. Not only the sequence of issues dealt with, but also the wording of articles corresponds very closely in the two instruments.[423] However, the Bamako Convention can hardly be described as a 'supplement' to the Basel Convention.[424] As its title suggests, the Bamako Convention places a total ban on the import of waste *into* the continent, and regulates the movement of waste generated in Africa itself. The Basel Convention, in contrast, contains no ban, but is regulatory in that it permits and controls transboundary movement of hazardous waste.[425] There are further differences between the two instruments: The scope of the Bamako document is more extensive, as it broadens the definition of 'hazardous waste',[426] for example by including artificially created radioactive waste in the list of controlled waste streams.[427]

In a very significant development, essentially adopting the position in the Bamako Convention, the Conference of State Parties to the Basel Convention in 1994 adopted a decision placing a ban on the exportation of hazardous waste from Organization of Economic Development (OECD) countries to non-OECD countries.[428] When a number of state parties argued that such a 'decision' was not binding, the Basel Convention itself was amended to reflect the change.[429] This development shows that, despite initial misgivings, the innovative and principled approach of the Bamako Convention was later followed by the international community.[430]

Although these treaties have caused a reduction in the flow of hazardous waste, millions of tons continue to be produced yearly, especially in the developed world. Due to the rising cost of waste disposal and the introduction of more stringent environmental control standards in the developed world, the developing world (and particularly Africa) remains an attractive destination for waste disposal.[431] African leaders should resist any short-term benefits—of 'recyclable waste' to economical development, and especially of incentives to themselves—at the expense

---

[422] Bamako Convention, Preamble.

[423] Both envisage implementation primarily through national institutions, with trans-national institutions in the form of a secretariat and conference (see arts 5, 15, and 16 of the Bamako Convention). See in general Ouguergouz (n 420 above) 195 and D Tladi, 'The Quest to Ban Hazardous Waste Import into Africa: First Bamako and Now Basel' (2000) 33 *CILSA* 210.

[424] AO Akinnusi, 'The Bamako and Basel Conventions on the Transboundary Movement and Disposal of Hazardous Waste: A Comparative and Critical Analysis' (2001) *Stellenbosch L Rev* 306, 309–13 discusses differences between the two treaties.

[425] See I Cheyne, 'Africa and the International Trade in Hazardous Waste' (1994) 6 *RADIC* 493, 499.

[426] See Ouguergouz (n 420 above) 201.

[427] This aspect has probably inhibited ratification by a country like South Africa.

[428] Decision II/12; see <http://www.ban.org> (accessed 30 September 2006); Akinnusi, (n 424 above) 314.   [429] And is to enter into force in the very near future.

[430] Akinuusi (n 424 above) 315.   [431] ibid, 306.

of the rights of their people, including the right to life and to live in a satisfactory environment.

Despite its uneasy course between the imperatives of 'development' and the 'right to a satisfactory environment', the African human rights system provides a framework that is more favourable to the individual, and more restrictive to the developmentalist state than most other international human rights regimes and regional arrangements. Yet, it is at the national level that the rights discourse has to be invoked to ensure a clean environment. Partly inspired by the African Charter and other international law developments, 33 African constitutions include a related right.[432] As the following cases illustrate, the inclusion of such a right is not a prerequisite for a favourable judicial outcome, though.

In finding that gas flaring in the course of oil exploration and production activities in the Delta region of Nigeria constitutes a violation of the rights to life and to dignity, the Nigerian High Court used article 24 to 'reinforce' provisions of the Nigerian Constitution.[433] Article 24 thus served as an aid in interpreting (justiciable) rights as including a 'healthy environment'. Surprisingly, though, the Court did not make any reference to the *Ogoniland* case, or to the 'Fundamental Objectives and Directive Principles of State Policy'.[434] Although the Tanzanian Constitution of 1984 does not contain a provision on environmental protection, in a case resulting from dumping and burning of refuse that polluted the air, the High Court interpreted the right to life[435] to mean that the state must 'not deliberately... expose anyone's life to danger'.[436] In arriving at a finding that the dumping posed a threat to human lives and the environment and therefore violated the right to life, the Court found support in domestic law criminalizing the voluntary pollution of the environment by making it 'noxious' to the 'health of persons'.[437]

G Corruption

Corruption is a pervasive problem in Africa,[438] not only hindering progress towards 'good governance', but also undermining the protection of human rights. The links

---

[432] C Heyns and W Kaguongo, 'Constitutional Human Rights Law in Africa' (2006) 22 *South African J on Human Rights* 673, 707, noting that some of these constitutions even make damage to the environment punishable.

[433] *Jonah Gbemre v Shell Petroleum Development Company Nigeria Ltd and Others*, suit FHC/B/CS/53/05, Hugh Court of Nigeria Benin Judicial Division, 14 November 2005 (on file with author), see Ch 8 below; see also Constitution of Nigeria 1999, art 33(1) (right to life), and 34(1) (right to dignity of the human person).   [434] See Ch 14.C.2 below.

[435] Constitution 1984, art 14.   [436] At 448.

[437] *Kessy and Others v City Council of Dar es Salaam*, High Court of Tanzania, Dar es Salaam, International Environmental Law Reports (vol 4) (9 September 1991) (Cambridge: Cambridge University Press, 2004) 445.

[438] See eg the 2006 Corruption Perception Index of Transparency International, which places 163 countries in order of perceptions about corruption, with the least corrupt country at number One. African countries generally feature at the bottom of this list: Guinea (160); Sudan, Chad, DRC (at 156); Equatorial Guinea and Côte d'Ivoire (at 151), and Sierra Leone, Nigeria, Kenya, Congo, and

between corruption and human rights are manifold. All the potential gains of human rights may be squandered if corruption stifles entrepreneurship, constrains economic development, and ultimately becomes the yeast from which political dissent is brewed. Enrichment of dominant elites exacerbates poverty,[439] as it depends on the appropriation of funds and resources destined for the public good. Military takeovers, which may spill over into protracted periods of insecurity and massive human rights violations, are often justified in the name of purging the incumbent regime's corrupt practices.

Taking the commitment to 'good governance' of its founding treaty to a more concrete level, the AU Assembly at its 2003 meeting adopted the AU Convention on Preventing and Combating Corruption (AU Anti-Corruption Convention).[440] Although the AU Anti-Corruption Convention is not framed in the language of human rights instruments, it recognizes the link between corruption and human rights when it stipulates that one of its aims is to 'promote socio-economic development by removing obstacles to the enjoyment of economic, social and cultural rights as well as civil and political rights'.[441] Having entered into force only in August 2006 when the target of 15 ratifications had been reached,[442] it is still too early to assess the impact of the Convention.

The Anti-Corruption Convention consists of legislative commands requiring state action, and not of self-executing provisions immediately giving rise to 'subjective rights'. The Convention may be abridged to a checklist of four main issues: Did the state criminalize private and public-sphere corruption in the required format? Did the state set up and does it maintain national anti-corruption agencies? Did it set up and does it maintain credible accounting and auditing of public funds? Did it enact laws to enable and safeguard 'whistle-blowers'? The answer to each of these questions depends on the extent to which the instrument has been domesticated, and not on the 'monist' or 'dualist' nature of the relationship between national and international law.

The UN Convention against Corruption (UN Anti-Corruption Convention) was adopted after the AU instrument—in October 2003[443]—but entered into force sooner, on 14 December 2005. The UN Anti-Corruption Convention currently enjoys ratification by 70 states, of which 28 are from Africa.[444] There are many

Angola (at 142). The highest-ranking African countries are Botswana (at 37); Mauritius (at 42); and South Africa and Tunisia (at 51) <http:www.transparency.org> (accessed 12 November 2006).

[439] See also the 2005 Global Corruption Barometer, which indicates that the impoverished are disproportionately affected, with between a third and a fifth of per capita income reportedly being spent by people in Cameroon, Ghana, and Nigeria on paying 'bribes' <http://www.transparency.org> (accessed 12 November 2006)).

[440] See <http://www.africa-union.org> (accessed 30 September 2006), adopted 11 July 2003, entered into force 5 August 2006.   [441] AU Anti-Corruption Convention, art 2(4).

[442] ibid, art 23(1). See also Table 6.1 below for updated status.   [443] UN Doc A/58/422.

[444] The following African states are parties: Algeria, Angola, Benin, Burkina Faso, Burundi, Cameroon, CAR, Congo, Djibouti, Egypt, Kenya, Lesotho, Liberia, Madagascar, Libya, Mauritius, Namibia, Nigeria, Rwanda, São Tomé e Príncipe, Seychelles, Senegal, Sierra Leone, South Africa, Togo, Uganda, and Tanzania.

substantive similarities between the AU and UN instruments: both address themselves to states and confer no rights as such. Because it devotes more attention to the element of prevention, to asset recovery, and to corruption in the private sphere, the UN Anti-Corruption Convention provides a more elaborate normative framework. As in the case of the AU instrument, the implementation of the UN Convention depends on its domestication. In its establishment of a Conference of State Parties to review and make recommendations on implementation,[445] the UN system has a better supervisory mechanism in place than its AU equivalent.

As has been stated, the efficacy of both Conventions depends on domestication. Increasingly, domestic legislation is enacted as part of a move from a policy-based approach to a rights-based approach to corruption. An example is the Nigerian Corrupt Practices and Other Related Offences Act.[446] Providing some evidence that a compatibility study has been undertaken before ratifying the UN Anti-Corruption Convention, the South African Parliament enacted the Prevention and Combating of Corrupt Activities Act,[447] 'in the light' of the fact that South Africa 'desires to be in compliance with and to become party to the UN Convention against Corruption'.[448] As South Africa had at that stage not become party to either the UN or the AU instruments, the reference to the UN treaty represents an unjustifiable privileging of a UN over an AU instrument, which was rendered immaterial only because South Africa later became a party to both these instruments.

Of all the instruments in the AU family, NEPAD speaks most pertinently to the issue of corruption. The AU Anti-Corruption Convention reinforces NEPAD's commitment to take 'targeted capacity-building initiatives' aimed at adopting 'effective measures to combat corruption and embezzlement'.[449] Under the heading 'Democracy and Good Political Governance', the Democracy and Governance Declaration requires states to undertake to combat and eradicate corruption, 'which both retards economic development and undermines the moral fabric of society'.[450] In its focus on the legal dimension of corruption, the Declaration reiterates the importance of an effective and independent judicial system to prevent corruption.[451] The APRM also requires participating states to include measures taken to combat corruption in their self-assessment reports.[452]

The first peer review, conducted on Ghana, confirmed the pervasiveness of corruption in the public service notwithstanding the introduction of legislative measures (such as the criminal law), the creation of institutions (the Commission for Human Rights and Administrative Justice and the Serious Fraud Office), and a

---

[445] UN Anti-Corruption Convention, art 63(4)(e) and (f).   [446] Of 2000, Cap 359.
[447] Act 12 of 2004.   [448] ibid, Preamble.   [449] NEPAD Declaration (2001) para 83.
[450] Declaration on Democracy, Political, Economic and Corporate Governance (2002) (Declaration) para 8.   [451] ibid, para 14.
[452] See eg Objective 6 of 'Democracy and Political Governance' ('Fighting corruption in the political sphere'), where questions are posed such as 'Are there independent and effective institutions, mechanisms, and processes for combating corruption?' and 'Are there precedents for dealing effectively with proven cases of corruption?' (Objectives, Standards, Criteria, and Indicators for the APRM, see Ch 3 above).

presidential commitment (Declaration of Zero Tolerance for Corruption).[453] Inadequate human resources and infrastructural capacity hampering the implementation of laws and the operation of institutions prompted the recommendation that more resources be devoted to the fight against corruption in Ghana.[454]

To increase the significance of legislative guarantees against corruption, impediments in the way of access to justice have to be removed. Civil society has to play a significant role in ensuring that the norms are implemented, that transgressors are brought to book, and that government is sensitized. A successful campaign against corruption obviously has to go beyond mere legislative solutions, as legislative steps are but part of the solution to corruption. At the highest political level the unequivocal condemnation of corruption is required, supported by exemplary action. Also, corruption cannot be isolated from the problems of a lack of good governance. As the list of the most corrupt countries shows,[455] there is a strong correlation between corruption and ruptured or weak state institutions. An effective 'right' against government corruption (arguably comprising rights such as those to an effective remedy, to meaningful participation in government, and to access to information) depends on factors such as the elimination of conflict, stronger state institutions, and better governance.

H Mercenarism

Mercenaries pose threats to human security and human rights because of their involvement in conflicts. Perversely privatizing state security, undemocratic leaders have bankrolled foreign forces to subvert democracy and good governance, thus securing their own survival and undermining their peoples' right to self-determination.

Although mercenarism has existed from time immemorial,[456] it only really became an issue in international humanitarian law during the twentieth century. The first comprehensive codification of humanitarian law—the Hague Convention of 1907—prohibited the recruitment of mercenaries.[457] When the UN was formed in 1945, the single provision prohibiting the recruitment of mercenaries in the Hague Convention was the only reference to mercenarism in international law. The UN Charter added little, stating in general that states should refrain from the use of force against 'the territorial integrity or political independence'[458] of

---

[453] APRM, Country Review Report of Ghana, June 2005.   [454] ibid, 34–5.

[455] n 438 above (especially eg Sudan, Sierra Leone, Angola, Côte d'Ivoire).

[456] During the 16th century, for example, the use of mercenaries was the unquestioned norm (C Botha, 'Soldiers of Fortune or Whores of War: The Legal Position of Mercenaries with Specific Reference to South Africa' (1993) 15 *Strategic Rev of Southern Africa* 75, 78).

[457] 1907 Convention (V) Respecting the Rights and Duties of Neutral Powers and Persons in Case of War on Land, art 4 ('recruiting agencies' may not be formed on the territory of 'neutral states').

[458] UN Charter, art 2(4).

another state. Viewed against the background of the realities of World War II and the ideological conflicts flaring up immediately thereafter, mercenaries hardly merited any attention.[459]

Africa's independence from colonial rule coincided with an increase in, and a changing attitude towards, the use of mercenaries, making mercenarism a focus of attention—also in Africa. Concerns were first raised about mercenary intervention in the Congo when the Katangese secessionist forces of Moise Tshombe were assisted by mercenaries from Europe and South Africa.[460] Subsequent examples of mercenaries being conscripted to oust African leaders include the *coup d'état* by the French national Bob Denard in the Comoros, and the attempted *coup d'état* in the Seychelles by mercenaries under the leadership of Mike Hoare.[461]

Gradually, mercenarism was raised as an issue of concern in international political fora. At the regional level, the OAU Council of Ministers and the Assembly of Heads of State and Government denounced these activities.[462] At the global level, the UN General Assembly in 1968 declared the use of mercenaries against national liberation movements in colonial territories a criminal act.[463]

On the legal plane, Africa took the lead. The first treaty dealing specifically with mercenaries—the OAU Convention on the Elimination of Mercenarism in Africa (OAU Anti-Mercenarism Convention)—was adopted under OAU auspices in 1977.[464] After the required number of states (17) had ratified the Convention, it entered into force in 1985.[465] Its current membership stands at 27. The OAU Anti-Mercenarism Convention defines a mercenary as a non-national of the state against which he is employed, who 'links himself willingly', for 'private gain', to groups or organizations aiming to overthrow or undermine the 'stability or the territorial integrity' of another state, or aiming to obstruct the activities of any liberation movement recognized by the OAU.[466] Because there is no requirement related to legitimacy, even undemocratic governments of state parties are allowed to conscript non-nationals to thwart threats in order to ensure their political stability and survival. Undemocratic leaders who have themselves relied on mercenary forces to keep them in power include Mobutu Sese Seko, in Zaire,

---

[459] JL Taulbee, 'Myths, Mercenaries and Contemporary International Law' (1985) 15 *California Western Intl L J* 339, 345.

[460] PW Mourning, 'Leashing the Dogs of War: Outlawing the Recruitment of and Use of Mercenaries' (1981–2) 22 *Virginia J of Intl L* 589, 599.

[461] On their prosecution in South Africa for contraventions of the Civil Aviation Offences Act 10 of 1972, see *S v Hoare* (1982) 4 SA 865 (N).

[462] See eg OAU Doc ECM/Res.17(VII) (1970) (condemning mercenary activity in Guinea); and OAU Doc AHG/Res.49(IV) (1967).

[463] Resolution 2465 (1968) 'Implementation of the Declaration on the Granting of Independence to Colonial Countries and Peoples'.

[464] OAU Doc CM/817(XXIX)Annex II Rev. Text of substantive provisions reproduced in (1981–2) 22 *Virginia J of Intl L* 613–18, and the International Convention Against the Activities of Mercenaries, 619–25.

[465] GJ Naldi, *The Organization of African Unity: An Analysis of its Role* (London: Mansell, 1989) gives a list of state parties in 1989 (40 n 20).   [466] OAU Anti-Mercenarism Convention, art 1.

against the armed forces led by Laurent-Desiré Kabila.[467] However, the OAU Anti-Mercenarism Convention has to be interpreted in light of changed circumstances, reflected most strikingly in the OAU Declaration on Unconstitutional Changes of Government, of 2000.[468] By defining intervention by mercenaries 'to replace a *democratically elected* government' as an 'unconstitutional change of government',[469] this Declaration incorporates an important qualification, and implies that an undemocratic government's use of mercenaries to hold on to power is unacceptable.

The African initiative was 'seminal' in the development of international law.[470] It partly inspired the inclusion of a provision on the issue in the 1977 Geneva Protocol I Additional to the Geneva Convention of 1949,[471] which stipulates that a mercenary 'shall not have the right to be a combatant or a prisoner of war'.[472] A product of compromise, this provision stopped short of the OAU Convention which criminalized mercenarism and detailed the obligations of states to secure its elimination. It also served as a precedent for an international treaty by the UN General Assembly in 1989, namely the Convention against the Recruitment, Use, Financing and Training of Mercenaries.[473] The limited impact of the UN Anti-Mercenarism Convention, which has the same number of ratifications as its African equivalent, was one of the reasons why the UN Commission on Human Rights in 2005 established a Working Group on the Use of Mercenarism as a Means of Impeding the Exercise of the Right of Peoples to Self-Determination. None of its seven visits so far has been to Africa.

Still, the foregrounding of mercenarism on the international stage is an African achievement, reflecting the increasing prominence of Africa in the UN. However, this development had more to do with securing the sovereignty of the fragile post-colonial state than with a concern for human rights. The African response may be explained primarily with reference to the fact that mercenaries have become 'the

[467] The 1990s saw the emergence of a corporate army, Executive Outcomes, which played an active role in numerous African conflicts, especially in Angola and Sierra Leone. Obvious concerns have been raised: leaders with little popular support remain in power despite national disintegration (also of the military forces), only because they control state finances. In the process, democracy may be thwarted, and national resources may become directed at the survival of a leader rather than the improvement of citizens' quality of life. On the other hand, Executive Outcomes has served as a 'private Pan-African peace-keeping force of a kind which the international community has long promised, but failed to deliver' ('Africa's New-Look Dogs of War' (24–30 January 1997) *Mail and Guardian* 24). In both Angola and Sierra Leone its intervention has contributed to an eventual peace process. The absence of any meaningful role played by the OAU or the UN has created the room for the involvement of Executive Outcomes in internal African conflicts.

[468] For an earlier condemnation of such action, see OAU Doc ECM/Res.5(III) (1964) (condemning the recruitment by the then Democratic Republic of Congo, under Presdient Kasavubu, of mercenaries from South Africa and Southern Rhodesia to uphold his regime).

[469] Repr in Heyns and Killander (n 230 above) 85, 87, emphasis added. See also at the subregional level, the ECOWAS Protocol Relating to the Mechanism for Conflict Prevention, Management, Resolution, Peace-Keeping and Security (discussed in Ch 7 below).

[470] JC Zarate, 'The Emergence of a New Dog of War: Private International Security Companies, International Law, and the New World Disorder' (1998) 34 *Stanford J of Int L* 75, 128.

[471] Signed on 12 December1977, some five months after the OAU instruments had been adopted.

[472] Geneva Protocol I, art 47(1).   [473] It entered into force on 20 October 2001.

symbol of racism and neo-colonialism within the Afro-Asian bloc',[474] because the recurring scenario was one of 'white soldiers of fortune fighting black natives'.[475] Given the repeated involvement of South African mercenaries in African conflicts,[476] the cohesiveness in Africa's approach becomes all the more understandable. One must also not lose sight of the context. The sovereignty of the newly independent African states was easily threatened, especially in the absence of a loyal citizenry and a loyal and well-trained armed force. Seen from this perspective, the outlawing of mercenaries had little to do with the protection of human rights but was intertwined with a movement to consolidate power in the hands of African rulers.

More recently, in 2004, this perception was strengthened when a plot involving a group of mainly South African-based mercenaries to overthrow the government in Equatorial Guinea was thwarted.[477] After their arrest in Zimbabwe, a number of these men petitioned the South African Constitutional Court to prevent their extradition to Equatorial Guinea for fear that they might be executed following trials that were, according to them, likely to be unfair.[478] Even though South Africa is not a party to the Anti-Mercenarism Convention, the Court observed that it would be a breach of South Africa's 'international obligations, in particular to other African states, to frustrate a criminal prosecution instituted there simply because the accused persons are South African nationals'.[479] Although some of those involved with the planning of the coup were prosecuted under existing South African legislation, a process for the adoption of new legislation was also launched.[480]

I Terrorism: Balancing Human Rights and State Security in a State of Fear

The current overview will be incomplete without a discussion of terrorism as a manifold threat to human rights in Africa. Although the events of 11 September 2001

---

[474] Taulbee (n 459 above) 342.   [475] ibid.

[476] In the 1990s Executive Outcomes played a prominent role in eg Angola and Sierra Leone. In both these instances they were on the payroll of the government in the countries concerned. Newly elected President of Sierra Leone, Ahmed Tejan Kabbah, relied on the presence of Executive Outcomes to keep rebel forces at bay and ensure stability. In 1996, Executive Outcomes was paid $1.2 million per month, making up a considerable percentage of state expenditure ('Kabbah Strikes Back' November/December (1996) *Africa Today* 43–4).

[477] See also AU Doc Assembly/AU/Dec.37(III), in which the AU condemned the planned overthrow in March 2004, and expressed its concern about the recurrence of the phenomenon of mercenarism in Africa (para 1); the Assembly also requested that its decision be brought to the attention of the UN Security Council, for that body to take a resolution on this matter (para 6).

[478] See also *Thatcher v Minister of Justice and Constitutional Development* [2005] 1 All SA 373 (C), in which the South African government's assistance in issuing a subpoena to compel Thatcher, a South African resident alleged to have been involved in the coup, to answer questions of the government of Equatorial Guinea.

[479] *Kaunda and Others v President of South Africa* (2005) 4 SA 235 (CC) para 125.

[480] Prohibition of Mercenary Activities and Prohibition and Regulation of Certain Activities in Areas of Armed Conflict Bill [B 42-2005] will ban those South African citizens who are not serving in

and the subsequent US-initiated 'war on terror' led to the portrayal of terrorism as a common threat to humanity, African countries such as Algeria, Egypt, Kenya, Tanzania, and Tunisia had before that date experienced terrorist-related incidents and threats. At one level, terrorism violates human rights in its assault on human life, bodily integrity and security, and property. At another level, the reaction against terrorist acts or anticipatory steps directed at alleged terrorist threats may undermine human rights such as freedom of association and fair trial rights. Often, counter-terrorism not only undermines human rights, but also erodes people's quality of life when terrorism, for example, is used as a smokescreen to justify increased budgetary allocations to the military at the expense of social spending.

On the whole, counter-terrorist measures pose a much greater risk to Africa's people than terrorism itself. Already in 1992 the OAU adopted a resolution calling on members to refrain from supporting groups 'that could disrupt the stability and the territorial integrity of member States by violent means', and encouraged cooperation and coordination among OAU members to combat the 'phenomenon of extremism and terrorism'.[481] This resolution was taken a step further when the Assembly adopted a Declaration on a Code of Conduct for Inter-African Relations, condemning as 'criminal' all terrorist attacks.[482] The prominence of 'territorial integrity' in both these resolutions, and the inclusion alongside 'terrorism' of 'destabilization activities' give some indication that the prevailing concern was the preservation of political power in 'third wave' post-1990 African democracies. After 11 September 2001, the fear always loomed large that states would exploit the mood of the time to cloak the stifling and criminalization of internal dissent as 'terrorism'.

The August 1998 bombing of the USA Embassy buildings in Kenya and Tanzania brought home to Africa the threat of terrorism. In a resolution expressing its condolences, the UN Security Council called upon states to adopt 'effective and practical measures for security co-operation, for the prevention of such acts of terrorism, and for the prosecution and punishment of their perpetrators'.[483] Within a year, the OAU Assembly had adopted the OAU Convention on the Prevention and Combating of Terrorism (Anti-Terrorism Convention),[484] which went beyond existing UN treaties.[485] An initiative by the OAU Secretary-General, a draft prepared

---

the national armed forces from participating in foreign conflicts in any capacity, be it as soldiers, security personnel, pilots, or other security-orientated professions. The South African National Assembly has approved the Bill but it will have to pass through the second chamber of Parliament before being signed into law by South African President Thabo Mbeki. <http://www.mg.co.za/articlePage.aspx?articleid=282388&area=/breaking_news/breaking_news__national/> (accessed 29 August 2006).

[481] Resolution on the Strengthening of Co-operation and Coordination among African States, OAU Doc AHG/Res.213(XXVIII), 28 June–1 July 1992, para 2.

[482] OAU Doc AHG/Decl.2(XXX) 13–15 June 1994. For status of ratification, see Table 6.1 below.　　　　　　　　　　　　　　　　　　　　　　　　[483] UN Doc SC Res 1189 (1998).

[484] Adopted in Algiers, 14 July 1999 and entered into force 6 December 2002.

[485] Under UN auspices, the most important instruments are the 1997 International Convention for the Suppression of Terrorist Explosive Bombs; the 1999 International Convention for the Suppression of the Financing of Terrorism; and the only relevant instrument adopted after

by a sub-committee of the Central Organ of the OAU Mechanism for Conflict
Prevention, Management and Resolution, and an offer by the Algerian President to
host a ministerial meeting all contributed to the uncharacteristic swiftness of the
process of adoption.[486]

The Anti-Terrorism Convention requires states to criminalize 'terrorism' and to
cooperate with other states in information exchange, extradition, extra-territorial
investigations and legal assistance. The crux of the Convention, as of almost any
discussion on this topic, lies in the definition of the term 'terrorism'.[487] In its very
broad definition of a 'terrorist act', the Convention stipulates three elements: formally, the act must constitute a 'violation of the criminal laws'. Its effect may range
from endangering 'life, physical integrity or freedom', to causing 'damage to public or private property, natural resources, environmental or cultural heritage'. The
act must be committed with the intention to 'intimidate, put in fear, force, coerce
or induce any government, body, institution, the general public or any segment
thereof, to do or abstain from doing any act, or to adopt or abandon a particular
standpoint, or to act according to certain principles'; or to disrupt an essential
public service; or to 'create general insurrection'. Not only such actions, but also
their promotion, aid, and incitement are 'terrorist acts'.

This definition unfortunately provides too broad a brush with which states may
colour legitimate political opposition and civil dissent as acts of terrorism. An
exclusionary clause, which removes struggles for liberation and self-determination
from the definition, is of scant relevance to situations of legitimate domestic dissent, as the acts covered in its ambit need to be directed against colonialism and
'foreign forces'. In fact, the clause has a qualification of its own, which states that
'political, philosophical, ideological, racial, ethnic, religious or other motives' cannot justify 'terrorist acts'. However, the interpretation in particular circumstances
may constrain the seemingly over-broad definition, if the injunction is heeded
that the Convention's interpretation should not allow 'derogating from the general
principles of international law, in particular the principles of international humanitarian law, as well as the African Charter on Human and Peoples' Rights'.[488]

Displaying a lack of political will, African states were slow to ratify the Anti-
Terrorism Convention. Only four states (Algeria, Angola, Egypt, and Eritrea) became
state parties before 11 September 2001. Thereafter, despite the fact that the threat
of terrorism to Africa did not increase, the pace accelerated significantly, with some
states ratifying the Convention almost immediately after the events of September
2001, causing the Convention to enter into force on 6 December 2002.

Responding to the events of 11 September 2001, further standard-setting actions
were taken in Africa. On 17 October 2001, a summit of African leaders adopted a

---

11 September 2001, the 2005 International Convention for the Suppression of Acts of Nuclear
Terrorism.

[486] See OAU Doc CM/Dec.441(LXIX) March 1999.

[487] Anti-Terrorism Convention, art 2.   [488] ibid, art 22(1).

Declaration against Terrorism,[489] and an intergovernmental high level meeting in 2002 drafted a 'Plan of Action for the Prevention and Combating of Terrorism' (Anti-Terrorism Plan of Action).[490] To a significant extent, the Anti-Terrorism Plan of Action, 'a handbook... of strategies for African anti-terrorism endeavours',[491] overlaps with the Anti-Terrorism Convention. The Plan of Action resonates with 'war on terror' imperatives, for example in its premise that 'poverty and deprivation experienced by large sections of the African population provide a fertile breeding ground for terrorist extremism'.[492] While the AU Commission is given an elaborate mandate, the African Commission does not feature, despite its potentially crucial role in ensuring human rights observance in an age of counter-terrorism. A second high level meeting in 2004 established the African Centre for the Study and Research on Terrorism, in Algiers, Algeria, as a 'structure' of the AU Commission and the Peace and Security Council (PSC) to conduct studies and provide training related to terrorism in Africa.[493]

In line with the AU's principles,[494] the AU Assembly adopted a Protocol to the Anti-Terrorism Convention.[495] The aim of this Protocol, which is not yet in force, is to ensure the 'effective implementation' of the Convention.[496] Elaborating upon its mandate to 'co-ordinate and harmonize continental efforts in the prevention and combating of international terrorism',[497] the PSC is given the primary responsibility to monitor not only the Anti-Terrorism Convention,[498] but also the Anti-Terrorism Plan of Action. Again, human rights feature as both a justification for terrorism measures, and as a potential casualty of the very same measures: states are required to implement the Convention in order to 'protect the fundamental human rights of their populations against all acts of terrorism',[499] but they also undertake to 'outlaw torture and other degrading and inhuman treatment, including discrimination and racist treatment of terrorist suspects, which are inconsistent with international law'.[500] Many other rights may also be at stake, however, such as the right to be presumed innocent and to have access to legal representation.

Influenced by global trends, domestic efforts in Africa have not always attained a balance between human security and humane counter-terrorism. In Algeria, where the USA strengthened anti-terrorist efforts, it has been noted that the number of arrests and secret detentions has increased, no efforts have been made to review the over-broad definition of 'terrorism', and the 'crushing of armed groups' in the

---

[489] M Ewi and K Aning, 'Assessing the Role of the African Union in Preventing and Combating Terrorism in Africa' (2006) 15(3) *African Security Rev* 32, 38.

[490] AU Doc Mtg/HLIG/Conv.Terror/Plan.(I), 11–14 September 2002.

[491] Ewi and Aning (n 489 above) 39.   [492] ibid, para 6.

[493] Mtg/HLIG/Conv.Terror/Decl.(II) Rev.2, 13–14 October 2004, para I.

[494] AU Constitutive Act, art 4(o) (condemning acts of terrorism and 'subversive activities').

[495] Protocol to the OAU Convention on the Prevention and Combating of Terrorism (Anti-Terrorism Protocol), adopted in Addis Ababa, 8 July 2004.   [496] Anti-Terrorism Protocol, Preamble.

[497] PSC Protocol, art 3(d).   [498] See also ibid, art 7(1)(i).

[499] Anti-Terrorism Protocol, art 3(1)(a).   [500] ibid, art 3(1)(k).

state is justified as action against al-Qa'ida.[501] Various other states either already
have legislation or are in the process of adopting legislation, eliciting concern that
such legislation may be used to stifle legitimate opposition or otherwise be inimical
to human rights. Examples are the Zimbabwean Suppression of Foreign and
International Terrorism Bill, the Tanzanian Preventative Detention Act,[502] the
Swaziland Internal Security Act, and legislative enactments or proposals in Egypt,
Kenya, Nigeria, Tunisia, Uganda,[503] and South Africa.[504]

The quest for an appropriate symmetry between counter-terrorism and human
rights also informs the most conspicuous step the African Commission has taken
in this area. In its resolution on the Protection of Human Rights and the Rule
of Law in the Fight against Terrorism, the Commission calls on states to 'reinforce
their activities of co-operation' in the fight against terrorism, but also emphasizes
that states must 'fully comply' with their obligations to respect of the African
Charter and other international law treaties.[505] Rights that are highlighted as cause
for special concern are the right to life, the right to a fair hearing, the right to seek
asylum, and the prohibitions against arbitrary detention and against torture and
cruel, inhuman, and degrading treatment or punishment.

The NEPAD and APRM texts do not specifically link terrorism to the protection of human rights.

J Conclusion

The global proliferation of human rights instruments has also manifested itself in
Africa. As most African treaties in one way or another are region-specific revisions
and supplements to UN treaties, it may be expected that they express a particular
'Africanness'. Before one assesses the 'Africanness' of these treaties, one should first
clarify what that concept entails.

[501] Amnesty International, 'Unrestrained Powers: Torture by Algeria's Military Security' 10 July 2006
<http://web.amnesty.org/library/Index/ENGMDE280042006?open&of=ENG-313> (accessed 30
September 2006). See also Ch 2 above for cases brought against Algeria to the UN Working Group on
Arbitrary Detention.
[502] Eminent Jurist Panel on Terrorism, Counter-Terrorism and Human Rights of the International
Commission of Jurists (ICJ) <http://ejp.icj.org/IMG/pdf/Press_release_Kenya_hearing-2.pdf>
(accessed 30 September 2006).
[503] See Constitutional Petition 18 of 2005, *Uganda Law Society v A-G of Uganda*, judgment of 31
January 2006, in which the Constitutional Court of Uganda (by four to one) held that the indictment of Besigye and others before a court martial on charges under the 2002 Anti-Terrorism Act was
unconstitutional.
[504] See the Report of the UN Special Rapporteur on the promotion and protection of human rights
and fundamental freedoms while countering terrorism, Addendum: Communications with Governments, UN Doc E/CN.4/2006/98/Add.1, 23 December 2005; and the South African Protection of
Constitutional Democracy against Terrorism and Related Activities Act (Act 33 of 2004).
[505] Adopted at the Commission's 38th session, 21 November–5 December 2005, Commission's
19th Activity Report, Annex II.

On the one hand, as a political concept, 'Africanness' may relate to the process of adoption and 'ownership' of the instruments. Using the term in this sense, as denoting a geographic or demographic rootedness, it is incontrovertible that the treaties under discussion are 'African'. They have been initiated, elaborated, and adopted in Africa, by Africans, for Africans, often to correct the real or perceived exclusion and marginalization of African voices during UN drafting processes. In the domain of human rights law, it is therefore incorrect to state that Africa has been 'a recipient of, rather than a contributor to, the development of international law'.[506]

No doubt questions may be posed about the representativity of these processes, also in Africa. Although limited African inclusion in the elaboration of the UN treaties has led to questions being asked about their legitimacy, Africa's response is open to similar criticism. Elaborated by technical experts and adopted by politicians, the African instruments have resulted from a top-down approach that lacks the legitimation that national and pan-African institutional involvement and debate could have provided. In addition, treaties are sometimes adopted more in response to international pressure or developments than domestic African concerns. However, as identified in this chapter and elsewhere in this book, ordinary Africans, represented by civil society organizations, have at least in respect of the African Children's Charter, the African Human Rights Court Protocol, and the African Women's Protocol played a crucial role in initiating and elaborating regional standards. Yet, even if regional pendants of international treaties essentially serve as a means of appropriating (or 'taking ownership of')[507] international human rights standards, this 'appropriation' may be an important step towards more meaningful domestication (and eventual internalization) of these standards.

On the other hand, because the 'geographic' understanding of 'Africanness' is overly procedural and formalistic, one's attention should also be directed to the substantive content of these norms. In doing so, the first step is to compare the regional and the global standards, identifying what is omitted from and added into African human rights-related treaties. While such an approach has the disadvantage of not treating African treaties 'on their own terms', but in reference to other instruments, it allows for a focused and specific analysis. Earlier in this chapter, I attempted to highlight some of the differences between global and regional manifestations of the human rights-related norms under discussion. It transpired that, in some instances, for example when it comes to mercenaries, Africa has taken the lead in adopting standards that had not been articulated in binding global instruments; and that, in others, such as the African Charter, the OAU Refugee Convention, the African Children's Charter, and the Bamako Convention, African treaties contain significant innovations or shifts in focus.

---

[506] As has been argued by PM Mutharika, 'The Role of International Law in the Twenty-First Century: An African Perspective' (1994–5) 18 *Fordham Intl L J* 1706, 1719.

[507] See Murray (n 294 above) 271, who sees this aspect as the main motivation for the adoption of the African Women's Protocol.

Having identified some omissions and additions, the question must be posed to what extent they constitute 'Africanness'. Two possibilities are introduced, the one linked to the 'real needs' of Africa; the other to the notion of African 'civilization'.[508]

First, at the level of pragmatism, the identified norms may be assessed for their adequacy as a response to the most pressing and specific human rights violations in Africa. The question is: Do they address the peculiar and historically contextualized needs of people on the African continent? To be sure, the 'needs' of Africans are not homogeneous, but it is possible to discern trends and identify priorities. African supplements have addressed some pervasive violations, such as those resulting from cultural practices (for example, child marriages and female genital mutilation), armed conflict (for example, child soldiers and refugees), the importation of hazardous waste, and the denial of identity (of indigenous peoples, most prominently). However, critical 'African' problems such as HIV/AIDS and poverty do not feature meaningfully in these 'African' human rights frameworks.

Even when innovative aspects are added to African treaties, these additions are superimposed on, and integrated into, existing frameworks. In many respects, OAU/AU treaties merely borrowed or adapted formulations from UN instruments. One may thus conclude that African states have 'bought into' the existing rights-based framework. African treaties may indeed insert some peculiarities, but they do not contest the major contours of existing human rights law. This observation fits with Maluwa's view of OAU law-making as 'complementary to, rather than in competition with, the universal processes undertaken within the wider UN system'.[509]

Secondly, on a more philosophical level, the extent to which the identified norms resonate with 'African cultural values' or world-views has to be accounted for, to assess the likelihood of their 'internalization'. In some sense, the question is: What kind of human being or society do these norms presuppose? I used 'values' and world-views' deliberately, cognizant of the differences across the vast continent, between urbanized and rural communities, and over time. Philosophers have identified various aspects of traditional African values and world-views that are of relevance to human rights, of which I highlight three: (i) Arising from the importance given to the 'collective' or group in African society, 'African traditional systems are likely to see individual rights in the context of group solidarity, with mutual support entailing rights and duties'.[510] (ii) Because 'rights' in indigenous political systems 'tended to emphasize cooperative support in the social and economic spheres of life', a rigid distinction between 'civil and political' and 'socio-economic' rights is an anomaly.[511] (iii) 'African jurisprudence' concerns itself not only with living human beings and ancestors, but also with inanimate objects, which are all part of 'what is'. Environmental law is therefore not 'extraneous' to 'African jurisprudence', but is a matter 'of the recognition and affirmation of the kinship of what is

---

[508] See the speech made by President Senghor when he launched the drafting of the African Charter (n 63 above).   [509] Maluwa (n 421 above) 204.
[510] FM Deng, 'Human Rights in the African Context' in K Wiredu (ed), *A Companion to African Philosophy* (Oxford: Blackwell, 2004) 499, 502.   [511] ibid.

not human with what is human'.[512] As has been pointed out in the chapter, all three aspects of substantive 'cultural' 'Africanness' mentioned above are to some extent reflected in the normative landscape of the African regional human rights system.

Pointing to the reverberation of these conceptions with African human rights treaties does not necessarily entail a regress into cultural relativism. Communitarianism and the idea that rights have reciprocal duties are not unique to Africa.[513] If a broader historical time-frame is adopted, 'Western' societies at some stage of their development also largely conformed to these notions. There has also been a revival of 'Western' communitarian thinking as a critique of the liberal ideology of individualism. By allowing for 'limitations' of rights, almost all constitutions and international instruments accept that rights are not invoked in a vacuum where the individual's rights are applied and interpreted in isolation from communal considerations.

It has also been argued that (at least aspects of) the 'African' manifestation of international human rights law are fundamentally at odds with the values of African 'civilization'. Arguments that some provisions of African human rights treaties are not reflective of African values underscore the contested nature of culture. One of the explanations for the adoption of norms that are arguably at odds with African tradition and that are characterized by non-compliance is the largely symbolical (or 'cosmetic') role that law generally, and international law specifically, often play in the African state. The inclusion of these norms in African instruments follows the dictates of liberal political ideologies, and of international politics which require African states to be seen as 'good international citizens', and the AU as a 'good regional arrangement', acceptable internationally, and particularly to the West.

However, as some of the experiences of the African Charter demonstrate, an independent and progressive implementing body may defy the *rightorical* roots of these instruments by applying them contextually and to the benefit of the people of Africa. One of the marked features of at least some interpretations has been the introduction of an element of fluidity. Defying an overly restrictive notion of legal certainty and reification of norms, concepts such as 'peoples' rights' and individual duties have been approached with an openness to circumstances, and in avoidance of rigid legal reductionism.

These efforts will be enhanced further if the instruments discussed above are treated holistically. It is important that the plurality of instruments and institutions should not lead to fragmentation. To some extent, this can be achieved through NEPAD's APRM. With its broad substantive jurisdiction, the African Court may also play an important role in enhancing the synergy between the different normative frameworks.

---

[512] J Murungi, 'The Question of an African Jurisprudence: Some Hermeneutical Reflections' in Wiredu (n 510 above), 519 525.

[513] DA Masolo, 'Western and African Communitarianism: A Comparison' in Wiredu (n 510 above) 483.

Table 6.1. Chart of Ratifications of AU Human Rights-related Treaties (as at 31 December 2006)

COUNTRY	OAU/AU Convention on the Conservation of Nature and Natural Resources (Ratified/Acceded)	AU Convention Governing the Specific Aspects of Refugee Problems in Africa (Ratified/Acceded)	Convention for the Elimination of Mercenarism in Africa (Ratified/Acceded)	African Charter on Human and Peoples' Rights (Ratified/Acceded)	Bamako Convention on the Ban of the Import of Hazardous Wastes into Africa (Ratified/Acceded)	African Charter on the Rights and Welfare of the Child (Ratified/Acceded)	Protocol to the African Charter on the Rights of Women (Ratified/Acceded)	AU Convention on Preventing and Combating Corruption (Ratified/Acceded)	African Convention on the Prevention and Combating of Terrorism (Ratified/Acceded)
Algeria	5/09/68	24/05/74	—	1/03/87	—	8/07/03	—	23/05/06	16/09/00
Angola	—	30/04/81	—	2/03/90	—	11/04/92	—	—	20/08/99
Benin	—	26/02/73	17/01/79	20/01/86	30/01/91	17/04/97	30/09/05	—	1/03/04
Botswana	—	4/05/95	—	17/07/86	—	10/07/01	—	—	—
Burkina Faso	16/08/69	19/03/74	6/07/84	6/07/84	31/01/91	8/06/92	6/09/06	29/11/05	23/06/03
Burundi	—	31/10/75	—	28/07/89	30/01/91	28/06/04	—	18/01/05	4/11/03
Cameroon	18/07/77	7/09/85	11/04/87	20/06/89	1/03/91	5/09/97	—	—	—
Cape Verde	—	16/02/89	—	2/06/87	—	20/07/93	21/06/05	—	3/05/02
Central African Republic	16/03/70	23/07/70	—	26/04/86	30/01/91	—	—	—	—
Chad	—	12/08/81	—	9/10/86	27/01/92	30/03/00	—	—	—
Comoros	18/03/04	2/04/04	18/03/04	1/06/86	26/02/04	18/03/04	18/03/04	2/04/04	13/09/02
Congo	4/04/81	16/01/71	1/04/88	9/12/82	—	8/09/06	—	31/01/06	8/09/06
Côte d'Ivoire	15/09/68	26/02/98	—	6/01/92	30/01/91	—	—	—	—
Democratic Republic of Congo	29/05/76	14/02/73	13/07/79	20/07/87	—	—	—	—	—
Djibouti	11/04/78	—	—	11/11/91	20/12/91	—	2/02/05	—	16/05/04
Egypt	6/03/72	12/06/80	10/05/78	20/03/84	30/01/91	9/05/01	—	—	8/02/01

Table 6.1. (cont.)

	OAU/AU Convention on the Conservation of Nature and Natural Resources	AU Convention Governing the Specific Aspects of Refugee Problems in Africa	Convention for the Elimination of Mercenarism in Africa	African Charter on Human and Peoples' Rights	Bamako Convention on the Ban of the Import of Hazardous Wastes into Africa	African Charter on the Rights and Welfare of the Child	Protocol to the African Charter on the Rights of Women	AU Convention on Preventing and Combating Corruption	African Convention on the Prevention and Combating of Terrorism
Equatorial Guinea	—	8/09/80	20/12/02	7/04/86	—	20/12/02	—	—	20/12/02
Eritrea	—	—	—	14/01/99	—	22/12/99	—	—	22/12/99
Ethiopia	15/10/73	—	7/02/82	15/06/98	—	2/10/02	—	—	24/02/03
Gabon	9/05/88	21/03/86	—	20/02/86	—	—	—	—	25/02/05
The Gambia	—	12/11/80	—	8/06/83	—	14/12/00	25/05/05	—	—
Ghana	17/05/69	19/06/75	20/07/78	24/01/89	2/07/04	10/06/05	—	—	30/08/02
Guinea	—	18/10/72	14/03/03	16/02/82	30/01/91	27/05/99	—	—	20/06/03
Guinea-Bissau	—	27/06/89	—	4/12/85	1/03/91	—	—	—	—
Kenya	12/05/69	23/06/92	—	23/01/92	17/12/03	25/07/00	—	—	28/11/01
Lesotho	—	18/11/88	29/10/82	10/02/92	1/06/91	27/09/99	26/10/04	26/10/04	6/03/02
Liberia	21/09/78	1/10/71	31/03/82	4/08/82	16/12/03	—	—	—	—
Libya	—	25/04/81	25/01/05	19/07/86	30/01/91	23/09/00	23/05/04	23/05/04	16/01/02
Madagascar	2/09/71	—	31/08/05	9/03/92	17/03/04	30/03/05	—	6/10/04	12/09/03
Malawi	6/03/73	4/11/87	—	17/11/89	—	16/09/99	20/05/05	—	23/06/03
Mali	3/06/74	10/10/81	25/09/78	21/12/81	30/01/91	3/06/98	13/01/05	17/12/04	11/03/02
Mauritania	—	22/07/72	—	14/06/86	—	21/09/05	21/09/05	—	3/03/04
Mauritius	—	—	—	19/06/92	—	14/02/92	—	—	27/01/03
Mozambique	28/02/81	22/02/89	—	22/02/89	—	15/07/98	9/12/05	2/08/06	21/10/02
Namibia	—	—	—	30/07/92	—	23/07/04	11/08/04	5/08/04	—
Niger	10/01/70	16/09/71	11/07/80	15/07/86	30/01/91	11/12/99	—	15/02/06	14/09/05
Nigeria	2/04/74	23/05/86	14/05/86	22/06/83	—	23/07/01	16/12/04	—	28/04/02
Rwanda	19/11/79	19/11/79	8/05/79	15/07/83	26/08/91	11/05/01	25/06/04	25/06/04	29/04/02

Table 6.1. (cont.)

	OAU/AU Convention on the Conservation of Nature and Natural Resources	AU Convention Governing the Specific Aspects of Refugee Problems in Africa	Convention for the Elimination of Mercenarism in Africa	African Charter on Human and Peoples' Rights	Bamako Convention on the Ban of the Import of Hazardous Wastes into Africa	African Charter on the Rights and Welfare of the Child	Protocol to the African Charter on the Rights of Women	AU Convention on Preventing and Combating Corruption	African Convention on the Preventionan and Combating of Terrorism
Sahrawi Arab Democratic Rep	—	—	—	2/05/86	—	—	—	—	9/01/02
São Tomé e Príncipe		—	—	23/05/86					
Senegal	3/02/72	1/04/71	2/10/81	13/08/82	30/01/91	29/09/98	27/12/04	—	21/01/02
Seychelles	31/08/77	11/09/80	15/10/79	13/04/92	—	13/02/92	9/03/06	—	17/07/03
Sierra Leone	—	28/12/87	—	21/09/83	9/12/03	13/05/02	—	—	—
Somalia	—	—	—	31/07/85	1/06/91	—	—	—	—
South Africa	—	15/12/95	—	9/07/96	—	7/01/00	17/12/04	11/11/05	7/11/02
Sudan	9/10/73	24/12/72	26/08/78	18/02/86	—	—	—	—	15/04/03
Swaziland	25/03/69	16/01/89		15/09/95	29/06/92	—	—	—	—
Tanzania	7/09/74	10/01/75	4/03/85	18/02/84	26/11/91	16/03/03	—	22/02/05	3/09/03
Togo	24/10/79	10/04/70	30/03/87	5/11/82	30/01/91	5/05/98	12/10/05	—	3/01/03
Tunisia	21/12/76	17/11/89	24/04/84	16/03/83	20/05/91	—	—	—	13/11/01
Uganda	15/11/77	24/07/87	—	10/05/86	—	17/08/94	—	30/08/04	17/10/03
Zambia	29/03/72	30/07/73	21/01/83	10/01/84	3/08/05	—	2/05/06	—	—
Zimbabwe	—	28/09/85·	27/01/92	30/05/86	—	19/01/95	—	—	—
Total no of states	**30**	**45**	**27**	**53**	**22**	**39**	**20**	**16**	**27**

The strengthening of implementing bodies cannot be the sole responsibility of states. African states have shown that they are much better at making supportive statements, declarations, and recommendations than they are at providing material support and giving effect to the treaties they so readily adopt and ratify. Civil society's support and commitment have to be secured in order to supplement the inadequate efforts of states. Their contribution should be directed at the national level, where these norms have to be domesticated. It is in the national legal system that the meaning of 'peoples', of individual duties, of Africa-specific obligations, the justiciability of socio-economic rights, and measures to curb the erosion of human rights should be debated and applied. This challenge is immense, as it often requires a paradigm shift in the legal system as a whole, away from a discretionary tradition-based system to a principled rights-based approach.

Most of the instruments discussed here are relatively unknown in Africa, even among human rights NGOs and lawyers. A greater awareness and knowledge of these norms—prerequisites for improved international and national implementation—necessitate their inclusion in educational programmes and academic curricula, and call for the greater involvement of the African media in disseminating these norms.

7

The African Commission: An Introduction

Even if one accepts the conclusion of the previous chapter that states mostly draft and ratify human rights treaties for purposes of external relations and domestic appeasement, it is also true that these treaties do not remain static or necessarily tied to the intentions of their founders. In fact, the previous chapter demonstrates advances in the interpretation of these treaties which went beyond their original intent. The following two chapters investigate the realized and potential contribution of the African Commission on Human and Peoples' Rights (African Commission) in chiselling away at the edifice of the African Charter, revealing cracks and openings that may be used to advance the cause of human rights and undo state reliance on *rightorical* commitments. Serving as a background to Chapters 8 and 9, this brief chapter sketches the salient features of the African Commission's composition and functioning.

Displaying advances as well as regression, the course taken by the Commission has not been linear.[1] Deliberately adopting a minimalist approach, and leaving little public record of their deliberations, the drafters of the Charter founded the African regional human rights system on grounds which were particularly open-ended. The indeterminacy of the text is exacerbated by the fluctuation in the Commission's membership (causing it, among other things, to hover between 'civil' and 'common' law approaches to adjudication), by the lack of a system of precedent, and by its weak institutional memory. These factors underscore the important role of individual Commissioners and of NGOs. What is required is a much more transparent and participatory selection process for members of the Commission—within the AU and in domestic systems—to ensure that Commissioners are elected who will

---

[1] There has most certainly been significant progress since the early years of the Commission, requiring a revision of the views expressed by M Wa Mutua, 'The African Human Rights System in a Comparative Perspective' (1993) 3 *Review of the African Commission on Human and Peoples' Rights* 5, 11 ('What we have is a *façade*, a yoke that Africa leaders have put around our necks. We must cast it off and reconstruct a system that we can proudly proclaim as ours').

interpret the Charter in defiance of pressure by governments. It is up to NGOs, activists, lawyers, and other members of civil society to support the Commission and further explore ways in which international human rights may become a reality in the lives of the people of Africa.

A Composition

Eleven Commissioners, elected by the Assembly of Heads of State and Government, serve part-time and in their personal capacity.[2] They are nominated by state parties from amongst 'African personalities of the highest reputation' and known for their 'competence in matters of human and peoples' rights'.[3] These members are elected for six-year terms, and may be re-elected indefinitely.[4] The Commission elects a Chairperson and Deputy-Chairperson (together referred to as the 'Bureau') from among their members for two-year terms.[5] The first 11 Commissioners met for their inaugural session in Addis Ababa on 2 November 1987.

With no provision in the Charter governing geographic or gender representation in the composition of the Commission, regional imbalances in its membership have arisen from time to time. Initially, the membership of the Commission was all-male and the average age was relatively advanced. As was pointed out earlier,[6] female representation improved gradually, reaching the present position of five female Commissioners. The average age has also decreased over the years.

A problem that persists is the close link between certain Commissioners and their nominating governments. The Charter requires Commissioners to be 'impartial' and they swear a solemn oath to that effect.[7] While this requirement may cover a Commissioner's subjective state of mind, questions have arisen about the institutional 'independence' of Commissioners.[8] In accordance with its own jurisprudence, membership of the Commission should be incompatible with positions that create

---

[2] African Charter, art 31(2).

[3] African Charter, art 31(1). Despite the absence of any formal requirement that they should hold legal qualifications, thus far all commissioners have had legal training. Art 31 does state that 'particular consideration' should be given to persons 'having legal experience'.   [4] African Charter, art 36.

[5] The current Bureau's term expires in November 2007. The Chairperson is Commissioner Sawadogo (a national of Burkina Faso) and the Deputy-Chairperson is Commissioner El Hassan (a national of Sudan). Both were elected in November 2005 for second two year terms (18th Activity Report, para 7).   [6] Ch 5 above.

[7] African Charter, art 38; see also Rules of Procedure, r 110, which allows for the recusal of a member 'for any reason', but does not require that members recuse themselves when communications against their own countries are considered; in practice such members are not allowed to participate in deliberations or to 'vote' on such issues. During the examination of state reports, Commissioners who are nationals of reporting states remain present, but do not usually participate in the dialogue (see eg the examination of South Africa's second periodic report at the Commission's 38th session, in which Commissioner Tlakula did not participate).

[8] The Kigali Declaration of the AU Ministerial Conference on Human Rights in Africa (2003), para 24 called on the AU to strengthen the 'independence and operational integrity' of the African Commission.

the appearance of bias or political dependence.[9] Indicators of incompatibility are the degree of dependence on the nominating government, as exemplified by the relationship of institutional dependence, and the degree of authority a government exerts over a person. It is submitted that positions linking Commissioners too closely to the incumbent government of a state party are, at a minimum, membership of the executive, holding the position of ambassador as well as the offices of other members of the diplomatic service, and high-ranking civil servants, appointed by the executive and exercising political power, such as the office of Attorney-General.[10] These positions should be regarded as incompatible with membership on the Commission because the Commission's promotional and protective functions are compromised by an appearance of partiality. A promotional visit by a Commissioner who is an ambassador or high-ranking civil servant of another country may be perceived as a visit by a representative of that country, rather than by the Commission. Despite some recent progress,[11] a number of Commissioners remain closely linked to the governments of the countries of which they are nationals.[12]

B Seat

Banjul, the slumbering capital of one of Africa's micro-states, The Gambia, is the seat of the Secretariat. After a hosting agreement was signed between the OAU and the Gambian government, the headquarters of the Commission was inaugurated on 12 June 1989. Two views on the selection of Banjul as seat are supported by the contemporaneous context of the Charter's drafting:[13] either this inaccessible and

---

[9] Regarding a domestic tribunal consisting of a judge, a military officer, and a member of the police force, the Commission in Communication 60/91, *Constitutional Rights Project (in respect of Akamu and Others) v Nigeria (Nigerian Judicial Independence* case) (2000) AHRLR 180 (ACHPR 1995) (Eighth Annual Activity Report) para 12 observed as follows: 'Regardless of the character of the individual members of such tribunals, its composition alone creates the appearance, if not actual lack, of impartiality'.

[10] Examples of past Commissioners holding such positions are Ben Salem (who was Ambassador of his country (Tunisia) to Senegal); and Commissioner Chigovera (before he resigned, he was the Attorney-General of Zimbabwe; the Attorney-General is the Chief Legal Officer and is separate and independent from the Minister of Legal and Parliamentary Affairs). See Ch 5 above.

[11] In 2005, the AU Commission issued a *note verbale* to states, mirroring the one sent to states on the eve of nominations to the African Human Rights Court (see ch 5 above), in which states were advised that membership of 'government, a Minister or under-secretary of state, a diplomatic representative, a director of a ministry, or one of his subordinates, or the legal adviser to a foreign office' renders a candidate ineligible for appointment as member of the African Commission (AU Doc BC/OLC/66/Vol XVIII (5 April 2005)). States are also invited to encourage civil society participation and transparency in the domestic selection process.

[12] Of the present Commissioners, Rezag-Bara (Algerian Ambassador to Libya), and Sawadogo (Ambassador of Burkina Faso to Senegal) are similarly compromised; see also F Viljoen, 'Promising Profiles: An Interview with the Four New Members of the African Commission on Human and Peoples' Rights' (2006) 6 *AHRLJ* 237.

[13] See further F Viljoen, 'Introduction to the African Commission and the Regional Human Rights System' in C Heyns (ed), *Human Rights Law in Africa* (vol 1) (Leiden: Martinus Nijhoff, 2004) 426–7.

remote outpost was chosen as a safe haven, located in one of Africa's long-standing democracies, and as a symbol of the Commission's independence from the Addis Ababa institutions and pressures;[14] or it was chosen as a way of consigning the Commission to neglect, a struggle against the odds, and possible oblivion.

Although the Commission may meet in other places on the continent,[15] the great majority of its sessions take place in Banjul. A trend to alternate sessions between Banjul and another African capital has been reversed since the AU came into being, with all four sessions in 2005 and 2006 taking place in Banjul. As the state hosting a session is expected to contribute financially, a disproportionate burden has been placed on the 'Gambian tax payer'.[16] This means that The Gambia has hosted every session since the AU Executive Council started putting obstacles in the way of making the Commission's reports public, suggesting that states have become less willing to be seen (by other states) as supporting the Commission. The Gambia, itself, protested against the high financial burden, and refused to bear expenses for the 40th session, in November 2006, almost causing the session to be cancelled.[17]

With the OAU Assembly like clockwork approving all the Commission's Activity Reports, the Commission was left to function independently—by default. However, 'approval' should be ascribed a very narrow meaning, because there are clear indications that the Assembly paid negligible attention to the content of these reports, and merely adopted a formulaic resolution never preceded by any substantive discussion. The tabling of reports, the existence of the Commission, and the language of resolutions brought all the advantages of *rightorics* without in any way encroaching on state sovereignty.

The illusionist's web spun by the OAU's practice came under some strain when the rationale for the choice of Banjul as a long-standing democracy fell away in 1994. On 22 July of that year, a young military officer, Yahya Jammeh, seized power from President Jawara, who had been democratically elected in 1970 and in five subsequent consecutive elections. Although Jammeh adorned himself with a civilian cloak and won subsequent elections, persistent allegations of electoral manipulation and other human rights violations in The Gambia have emerged. Some of the human rights concerns relate to the independence of the judiciary, the elimination of political opponents and journalists, and the banning of newspapers.[18] During a

---

[14] In this regard, see the Commission's 'Recommendation on the Headquarters of the African Commission', adopted at its third session (First Annual Activity Report, Annex VI), recommending that the headquarters be in a country 'other than the one hosting the political and administrative organs of the OAU' which had ratified the Charter and 'which offers to the Commission substantial material and human resource facilities for its establishment, work and researches'.

[15] Rules of Procedure, r 4 ('The sessions shall normally be held at the Headquarters of the Commission. The Commission may, in consultation with the [Chairperson of the AU Commission], decide to hold a session elsewhere').

[16] Keynote Speech of the representative of the Gambian Deputy-President, Dr Njie-Saidy, at the opening ceremony of the 40th session of the African Commission, 15 November 2006, 5 (Keynote Speech, on file with author).   [17] Keynote Speech (n 16 above).

[18] See eg International Bar Association, 'Under Pressure: A Report on the Rule of Law in The Gambia', August 2006; and sustained allegations about government involvement in the killing of

press conference after his re-election in 2006, a defiant Jammeh made the following statement: 'The whole world can go to hell. If I want to ban any newspaper, I will, with good reason.'[19]

At the first session after the unconstitutional change of government had taken place, the Commission adopted a resolution condemning the coup as a 'flagrant and grave violation of the right of the Gambian people to freely choose their government',[20] and called on the military government to observe international human rights standards. However, short of finding a violation of the Charter in a communication submitted by ex-President Jawara,[21] the Commission seemed to have settled comfortably into life under the new regime. As will be discussed below in more detail, the Commission on a number of occasions bent over backwards to avoid a detrimental finding against the Gambian state, and did not express criticism against or follow up on indications of flagrant disregard for the law emerging from the report of the Special Rapporteur on Prisons in Africa on prison conditions in The Gambia.

Another consequence of the change in government is that permanent headquarters for the Commission have not yet been built. In terms of the hosting agreement, the Gambian government undertook to provide rent-free and adequate accommodation for the Commission's Secretariat, including basic furniture, translation and interpretation equipment, and typewriting, duplicating, and photocopying machines. In 1992, the process to construct for the Commission a building of its own was set in motion.[22] The Commission argued that considerable construction costs make sense in the long run, as the Gambian government would save on renting headquarters and facilities for Commission sessions. Dormant during the time of political upheaval, since 1996 the idea has slowly been revived. Political commitment at the highest level and numerous consultative meetings culminated in the setting aside of a plot of land which the Commission, however, deemed to be inappropriate. On 21 October 2001, the foundation stone was laid at a more suitable site. Limited further progress has been made due to the government's inadequate financial resources.[23] When the Commission was later relocated to smaller and inadequate premises, relations actually deteriorated.

Gambian journalist Deyda Hydara (Reporters Without Borders, 'Deyda Hydara: The Murder of a Journalist under Surveillance', <http://www.rsf.org> (17 May 2005).

[19] N Tattersall, 'Gambia Leader Signals Firm Rule after Election Win', Reuters, <http://www.alertnet.org/thenews/newsdesk/L24811983.htm> (24 September 2006).

[20] Resolution on the Gambia, adopted at the Commission's 17th session, 22 March 1995, Eighth Annual Activity Report, Annex VIII.

[21] Communications 147/95, 149/95 (joined), *Jawara v The Gambia* (2000) AHRLR 107 (ACHPR 2000) (13th Annual Activity Report) (*Gambian Coup* case).

[22] Note on the construction of the Headquarters of the African Commission, AU Doc ACHPR/BS/01/005, prepared for the 2006 Brainstorming Meeting.

[23] The budget of the construction process was estimated at approximately US$3.8 million; which was later reduced to US$3 million.

C Functioning

As a part-time, eleven-member body, meeting twice annually for 10 to 15 days to monitor state compliance with the Charter,[24] the Commission has clearly been programmed to accomplish very little.[25] Calls to have at least the Chairperson of the African Commission serve on a full-time basis and to increase the number of Commissioners have fallen on deaf ears.[26] This state of affairs increases the importance of the Commission's Secretariat. That body, headed by a Secretary appointed by the Chairperson of the AU Commission without consulting the Commission, consists of a small administrative staff. The number of legal officers fluctuates, but averages around five. Human and other resource constraints seriously impair the efficiency and professionalism of the Secretariat.[27]

Despite repeated calls by the Assembly,[28] the Commission and its Secretariat remain under-resourced, and are forced to rely on outside funds for most of its promotional work and for the appointment of at least a bare minimum of legal officers. Despite making lofty declarations and commitments of support to the Commission, especially on the occasion of the 20-year commemoration of the adoption of the Charter, the AU allowed the Commission's staffing situation to deteriorate into an unprecedented crisis. The position of Secretary to the Commission had been vacant since late 2005;[29] during 2006 the position of Documentation Officer became and still remains vacant;[30] and three experienced legal officers left the Commission due to financial uncertainty.[31] One of the reasons for the neglect of the Commission was that its budget was subsumed under that of the Political Affairs Department. From the financial year 2008 onwards,

---

[24] The period of 10 days was extended as from October 1999, see R Murray, *The African Commission on Human and Peoples' Rights and International Law* (Oxford: Hart, 2000) 13.

[25] The Commission may also meet for 'extraordinary sessions', and did so on three occasions: the first, on 13–14 June 1989 (on working methods, in Banjul); the second, on 18–19 December 1995 (on Nigeria, in Kampala); the third, on 18–19 September 2004 (on Sudan, in Pretoria). In this chapter, 'session' refers to the Commission's ordinary sessions.

[26] The call to increase the members of the Commission from 11 to between 15 and 18 was reiterated at the 2006 Brainstorming Meeting between the African Commission and the AU (Report of the Brainstorming Meeting on the African Commission: 9–10 May 2006, Banjul, The Gambia (AU Doc ACHPR/BS/01/010, 9 May 2006) (20th Annual Activity Report, Annex II) (Brainstorming Report) para 18.

[27] C Heyns, D Padilla, and L Zwaak, 'A Schematic Comparison of Regional Human Rights Systems' in F Gómez Isa and K de Feyter (eds), *International Protection of Human Rights: Achievements and Challenges* (Bilbao: University of Deusto, 2006) 545, 552–5, for a comparison between the three regional systems in respect of staff, budget, and facilities.   [28] See Ch 4 above.

[29] An acting Secretary served the Commission for a few months, but with her departure, the position of Secretary was filled by one of the senior legal officers who acted as 'officer in charge'.

[30] 20th Activity Report, para 23.

[31] Brainstorming Report (n 26 above) para 32: 'Only 2 legal officers are presently paid by the AU. Legal officers have always been paid from extra-budgetary resources and the funding of these staff is running out by end of 2006'.

the situation will change, as the African Commission will present and defend its own budget before the AU's Permanent Representatives' Committee.[32]

The lack of funding from the OAU/AU has caused the Commission to be reliant on 'extra-budgetary' sources,[33] especially 'Western' donors,[34] thereby opening the Commission to the criticism that its agenda is dictated by non-African governments.[35] Stepping into the void left by the AU's failure to give effect to the call in the Kigali Declaration for the establishment of a voluntary human rights fund,[36] the Commission in November 2006 recommended that the AU Commission prepare a draft decision for adoption by the AU Executive Council.[37] In its subsequent decision, drafted in line with the African Commission's recommendation, the AU Executive Council requested the AU Commission to put in place an effective 'Voluntary Contribution Fund for African Human Rights institutions'.[38]

Although the Commission's mandate is provided for in the Charter, its detailed functioning is regulated by Rules of Procedure. A first set of Rules of Procedure was adopted in 1988,[39] and was amended in 1995.[40] In recent years, especially in anticipation of the Commission's co-existence with the African Court on Human and Peoples' Rights, a number of studies have been done and consultations conducted to review the procedures of the Commission.[41] The results of these processes should inform the work of the Commission's Working Group on Specific Issues Relevant to the Work of the African Commission, which has been reviewing the Rules of Procedure.[42]

[32] AU Doc EX.CL/Dec.344(X), para 2(iv).
[33] The budget allocated to the African Commission for the year 2002/3 was around $760,000, about 2.5% of the total AU budget (S Yonaba and F Viljoen, 'Review of the Procedures of the African Commission and Peoples' Rights' (conducted in September 2002) (on file with author). This amount contrasts sharply with the amount of US$2,373,750 allocated to the African Court on Human and Peoples' Rights for 2007 (AU Doc Assembly/AU/Dec.154(VIII)).
[34] The donors consistently acknowledged in the last few Activity Reports are the Danish Institute for Human Rights, the Danish International Development Agency (DANIDA), the government of the Netherlands, the Canadian-based NGO, Rights and Democracy, and the OHCHR.
[35] See eg the comments of the Zimbabwean Minister of Information in reaction to a resolution adopted by the Commission on Zimbabwe: 'What do you expect from them? They are looking for money and what better way to make money than to vilify Zimbabwe' ('Mugabe Trashes New AU Resolution on Human Rights' <http://www.wmnews.com>, 8 January 2006 (9 January 2006)).
[36] Kigali Declaration, n 8 above, para 23.
[37] AU Doc ACHPR/Res.96(XXXX)06, 'Resolution on the Establishment of a Voluntary Contribution Fund for the African Human Rights System', adopted at its 40th session, 29 November 2006, proposing that a seven-member Board of Directors be set up, comprising, among other members, the Commission's Bureau and Secretary, and representatives of the African Human Rights Court and the African Children's Committee.
[38] AU Doc EX.CL/Dec.344(X), Decision on the 21st Activity Report of the African Commission, para 2(vi).
[39] Adopted at the Commission's second session (First Annual Activity Report, Annex V), reprinted in R Murray and M Evans (eds), *Documents of the African Commission on Human and Peoples' Rights* (Oxford: Hart, 2001) 136–64.
[40] Adopted at the Commission's 18th session, reprinted in Heyns (n 13 above) 540–56.
[41] See eg Retreat of the Commission, facilitated by the Office of the High Commissioner for Human Rights (OHCHR), 24–6 September 2003.
[42] This Working Group was established at the Commission's 37th session, 23 November–7 December 2004.

The Commission's mandate is typically divided into 'protective' and 'promotional' roles.[43] The protective mandate consists mainly of the consideration of complaints ('communications'); the promotional mandate of the examination of state reports. The former is exercised in closed sessions, while the latter takes place in public. However, it is not possible to draw a watertight dividing line between the Commission's 'promotional' and 'protective' activities. Strictly speaking, only the communications procedure and on-site investigative missions are 'protective'. Nevertheless, other mechanisms, such as the Special Rapporteurs and the adoption of resolutions, may also aim to 'protect' rights. State reporting may be regarded as mainly 'promotional', but also aims to 'protect' rights, especially when the Commission requires reporting on the implementation of communications. These aspects of the Commission's mandate are touched upon in the discussion that follows in Chapters 8 and 9.

[43] On the Commission's exercise of its mandate, see EA Ankumah, *The African Commission: Practice and Procedures* (The Hague: Martinus Nijhoff, 1996); UO Umozurike, *The African Charter on Human and Peoples' Rights* (The Hague: Kluwer Law International, 1997); CA Odinkalu, 'The Individual Complaints Procedures of the African Commission on Human and Peoples' Rights: A Preliminary Assessment' (1998) 8 *Transnational L and Contemporary Problems* 359; Murray (n 24 above); I Österdahl, *Implementing Human Rights in Africa* (Uppsala: Iustus Förlag, 2002); MD Evans and R Murray (eds), *The African Charter on Human and Peoples' Rights. The System in Practice 1986–2000* (Cambridge: Cambridge University Press, 2002); F Ouguergouz, *The African Charter on Human and Peoples' Rights: A Comprehensive Agenda for Human Dignity and Sustainable Democracy in Africa* (The Hague: Martinus Nijhoff, 2003); F Viljoen, 'Introduction to the African Commission and the Regional Human Rights System' in Heyns (n 13 above) 385; M Mubiala, *Le Système Régional Africain de Protection des Droits de l'Homme* (Brussels: Bruylant, 2005); C Heyns and M Killander, 'The African Regional Human Rights System' in F Gómez Isa and K de Feyter (eds), *International Protection of Human Rights: Achievements and Challenges* (Bilbao: University of Deusto, 2006) 509.

8

The African Commission:
Protective Mandate

Three aspects of the Commission's protective mandate are discussed: individual communications; inter-state communications; and 'on-site' or 'fact-finding' missions.

A Individual Communications

1 Forging an Individual Communications Procedure

The communications procedure provides the clearest possibility of holding states accountable to their commitments under the Charter. Before embarking on a step-by-step overview of the communications procedure, it should be noted that the drafters of the Charter would most probably be surprised to see how this procedure had developed. At the time of the Charter's drafting, international human rights law provided two divergent options for dealing with 'communications': the ECOSOC 1503 procedure,[1] on the one hand, and those of the Convention on the Elimination of All Forms of Racial Discrimination (CERD),[2] and the First Optional Protocol to the ICCPR (OPI), on the other hand. The different drafts and the final text of the African Charter demonstrate an uneasy balancing act. Following the ECOSOC procedure would have seen a mechanism dealing only with a series of violations, shrouded in secrecy, and leading to a political decision (for example, the appointment of a country-specific Special Rapporteur). Building on the precedent of the OPI would have secured an unequivocal individual communications procedure.

These opposing models play themselves out in the Charter's *travaux préparatoires*. The ECOSOC model seems to have informed the Monrovia proposal for the setting-up of an African Commission on Human Rights, aimed at providing the Commission with 'the power of initiative to take action in response to serious violations of human rights'.[3] No reference is made to the possibility of submitting or considering complaints. In terms of the Monrovia proposal, the Commission would have been entitled to 'study situations of alleged violations', provide 'good offices', and make reports with recommendations to the OAU.[4] A perusal of the M'Baye proposal,[5] which set the drafting of the African Charter in motion, and the subsequent Dakar and the final Banjul draft is revealing: the M'Baye proposal aligns itself with OPI by explicitly including in the Commission's mandate the power to 'take action on petitions and other communications pursuant to its authority under the provisions of the Charter'.[6] This should be read with clause 49 of that draft, which allows 'persons or groups of persons, or any non-governmental entity legally recognised' in a member state to 'lodge petitions' alleging violations by a state party. The Dakar draft omits this aspect from the article delineating the mandate of

---

[1] See Ch 2 above; and I Österdahl, *Implementing Human Rights in Africa* (Uppsala: Iustus Förlag, 2002) 34–43.   [2] CERD, art 14.

[3] BG Ramcharan, 'The *Travaux Préparatoires* of the African Commission on Human Rights' (1992) 13 *HRLJ* 307, 308.   [4] Cited in Ramcharan (n 3 above) 312.

[5] OAU Doc CAB/LEG/67/1, repr in C Heyns (ed), *Human Rights Law in Africa 1999* (The Hague: Kluwer Law International, 2002) 65–80.

[6] M'Baye Draft African Charter on Human and Peoples' Rights, OAU Doc CAB/LEG/67/1, prepared for the Meeting of Experts, Dakar, Senegal, 28 November–8 December 1979, repr in Heyns (n 5 above) clause 46(f).

the Commission, and contains no equivalent to clause 49. It does admit the possibility of communications 'other' than those against state parties, but chiefly incorporates a new scheme of referral to the OAU Assembly, who may order in-depth studies.[7] Apparently trying to set at ease the minds of those who feared an intrusive Commission, M'Baye gave the assurance in Banjul that the Commission's 'terms of reference' are 'essentially technical', with the Assembly as final decision-maker.[8] The restrictive effect of these in-depth studies, as foreseen by the drafters, is highlighted when contrasting the Dakar and Banjul drafts. In the latter, a phrase enabling the Commission to report, and the Assembly to 'take such measures intended to protect human and peoples' rights', was omitted.[9]

As a result, in-depth studies are left in the air, seemingly without any purpose. The Secretary-General could therefore report as follows to the Council of Ministers: 'This Commission will gather information, establish facts, draw necessary conclusions and make recommendations to the Assembly of Heads of State and Government'.[10] This lack of clarity may have played a role in the fact that no 'Chairman' of the OAU Assembly ever referred such a matter to the Commission for its study, and took no further action when the Commission brought the existence of a series of serious or massive violations to the Assembly's attention.

Writing in 1991 as one of the first Chairs of the Commission, Commissioner Umozurike gives some insight into the approach adopted by the Commission to these strictures:[11] 'It appears that a single breach is not enough, it must be massive and serious. The Commission is likely to break out of this close confinement and make a report on every case that is reported to it provided it relates to a denial or violation of a right. Otherwise it [the Charter] should not be talking of individual rights but the rights of the masses or peoples. The wrongful detention of citizen A cannot be regarded as massive and serious in the strict language of the Charter but offends modern notions of human rights.'

To its credit, the Commission adopted an approach allowing for findings on individual communications,[12] integrated it into its Rules of Procedure,[13] and confirmed it in its 'case-law'.[14]

[7] OAU Doc CAB/LEG/67/3/Rev.1 (Dakar draft), repr in Heyns (n 5 above) 81–91, clause 56.

[8] OAU Doc CAB/LEG/67/DraftRaptRpt(III)Rev.4, repr in Heyns (n 5 above) 94–105 (Rapporteur's Report) para 13.

[9] Dakar draft, art 56(3); Rapporteur's Report, para 103; and Banjul draft (African Charter) art 58(3).

[10] OAU Doc CM/1149(XXXVII), repr in Heyns (n 5 above) 92–3 (Secretary-General's Report), under the heading 'Measures of Safeguard'.

[11] UO Umozurike 'The African Commission on Human and Peoples' Rights: An Introduction' (1991) 1 *Review of the African Commission on Human and Peoples' Rights* 5, 11.

[12] See also the argument of CA Odinkalu and A Christensen, 'The African Commission on Human and Peoples' Rights: The Development of its Non-state Communications Procedures' (1998) 20 *HRQ* 235, 237–9.

[13] This was in fact already the case in 1988, when the Commission adopted its first Rules of Procedure (First Annual Activity Report of the African Commission, Annex V).

[14] In Communications 147/95, 149/96 (joined), *Jawara v The Gambia* (2000) AHRLR 107 (ACHPR 2000) (13th Annual Activity Report) (*Gambian Coup* case), an individual communication brought after the military coup in 1995, by the deposed head of state, the Gambian government

2 Registration of Communications

Each communication (or 'case')[15] received by the Commission is registered. In this respect, the issue of 'naming' the parties to the case needs to be considered. A confusing practice in the naming of cases has developed. It is suggested that individual lawyers or institutions (NGOs) *acting as legal representatives* should not be regarded as 'authors' or 'complainants', and that cases should be registered (or 'named') accordingly.[16] So, for example, the case of *Zegveld and Another v Eritrea*[17] should have been registered as *Fissehastion and 10 Others v Eritrea*. In Communication 240/2001, registered as *Interights and Another (on behalf of Bosch) v Botswana*,[18] the 'victim' clearly is Ms Bosch, while Interights and the law firm involved merely acted as legal representatives. The case should most appropriately have been registered and cited as *Bosch v Botswana*.

There are a number of reasons for this suggestion: where lawyers act in that capacity, or NGOs act *in the capacity of representatives*, they are not the 'victims' of alleged human rights violations.[19] Calling the case *Bosch v Botswana* would have given a clearer indication of whose interests were at stake, and would have ensured that the 'victim' would not be marginalized in the process. Such a citation or case name also has the benefit of simplicity, making a reference to and discussion of these cases much easier. If a certain NGO or lawyer frequently acts as legal representative of victims, there will soon be numerous case citations making reference to that NGO or lawyer, not only creating the (erroneous) impression that the NGO or lawyer has been the victim of numerous human rights violations, but also making it increasingly difficult to distinguish one case from another. The approach that is proposed is also in line with the practice of other international human rights treaty bodies.

---

raised an objection at the admissibility stage that 'the Commission is allowed under the Charter to take action only on cases that reveal a series of serious or massive violations of human rights' (para 41). Dismissing this proposition as 'erroneous', the Commission refers to art 55 of the Charter and remarks that the Commission's practice has 'in any event' been 'to consider communications even if they do not reveal a series of serious or massive violations' (para 42).

[15] Formally, the Commission does not 'decide' 'cases'—it rather issues 'findings' in respect of 'communications'. In line with terminology often adopted, reference in this chapter is made to 'cases' or 'decisions', as a shorthand for 'communications'. However, the use of the words 'case', 'decision', and, 'case-law' does not imply that these 'findings' are 'judicial decisions' in the true sense of those phrases.

[16] The name of the specific person acting on behalf of an NGO should also be avoided in the case 'name' (See eg Communication 39/90, *Pagnoulle (on behalf of Mazou) v Cameroon* (2000) AHRLR 57 (ACHPR 1997) (Tenth Annual Activity Report) (*Mazou* case). Ms Pagnoulle acted on behalf of Amnesty International, who acted as the legal representative. That case should thus have been registered as *Mazou v Cameroon*.

[17] Communication 250/2002 (2003) AHRLR 85 (ACHPR 2003) (17th Annual Activity Report) (*Eritrean Detention* case)

[18] (2003) AHRLR 55 (ACHPR 2003) (17th Annual Activity Report) (*Botswana Death Penalty* case).

[19] If it is considered imperative to make reference to the legal representative, the case name could be framed as *Fissehastion and 10 Others (represented by Zegveld) v Eritrea*, or as *Bosch (represented by Interights and Another) v Botswana*. In my view, this is not necessary, as such phrases are not included in case names or citations in the national jurisdictions or in the practice of other international treaty bodies.

The name of an NGO (or an individual) who is not the actual 'victim' of a violation may have to appear in instances where the *actio popularis* is invoked, and there is no clearly identifiable 'victim'. An example would be a case that is brought on behalf of a 'people'. Still, when the collective (the 'people') is clearly identifiable, it should be possible to frame the case in its name. So, for example, *SERAC v Nigeria*[20] could have been cited as *Ogoni People v Nigeria*. However, when the group is difficult to define or not clearly demarcated, the situation may be different. It is only in instances where individuals and NGOs do not *merely submit the case and act as legal representatives* of specific individuals or groups, and where there is *no identifiable victim and the matter is brought in the public interest* (as an *actio popularis*), that the name of the individual lawyer or NGO should appear in the case 'name' as registered and cited.

According to the numbering system adopted by the Secretariat, each new communication is assigned a number. Going strictly by the last number given to a communication registered by the Secretariat, and thus including communications that were submitted against non-state parties, the Commission received 328 communications over the almost two decades of its existence (1987 to the end of 2006). Considering the nature and extent of violations over these years, an average of some 16 communications per year does not represent even the tip of the iceberg of violations on the continent. Over the corresponding period, the Commission finalized 147 cases.[21] Excluding the communications (especially initially) submitted against non-state parties, the number shrinks to 124 (an average of some six cases per year). Of these, 48 (or 39 per cent) were declared inadmissible, mostly due to a lack of exhausting local remedies; six ended in a friendly settlement; and 13 were closed, withdrawn, or postponed *sine die*.[22] In the remaining 57 cases, violations were found in all but four instances (that is, in 93 per cent of the decisions on the merits). The countries against which most of these finalized cases were directed are Nigeria (30 cases), The Gambia (nine cases), DRC/Zaire (eight cases), Cameroon (seven cases), and Kenya and Sudan (four cases each).[23] Although not entirely

---

[20] Communication 155/96, *Social and Economic Rights Action Centre (SERAC) and Another v Nigeria* (2001) AHRLR 60 (ACHPR 2001) (15th Annual Activity Report) (*Ogoniland* case).

[21] These figures are based on F Viljoen, 'Introduction to the African Commission and the Regional Human Rights System' in C Heyns (ed), *Human Rights Law in Africa* (vol 1) (Leiden: Martinus Nijhoff, 2004) 426, 434–9, and subsequent Activity Reports. The apparent discrepancy between the two totals (328 and 147) can be explained as follows: (i) Numerous communications are still pending. (ii) In some instances, numerous communications that are closely linked in time and substance were taken as one communication. The two major instances are: Communications 109/93 to 126/93 (18 communications), one complaint submitted against a number of countries, found to be inadmissible, and Communications 54/91, 61/91, 98/93, 164–96/97, 210/98 (joined), *Malawi African Association and Others v Mauritania* (2000) AHRLR 149 (ACHPR 2000) (13th Annual Activity Report) (*Mauritanian Widows* case). (iii) The single inter-state communication finalized by the Commission (see below) is also not included in this analysis.

[22] The latter category has seen a significant increase in the last few years.

[23] Zimbabwe is about to ascend in this hierarchy, as numerous cases against it are pending before the Commission.

accurate, in that some parties only ratified the Charter sometime after 1986, these figures represent an average total of almost three cases submitted per country, over 19 years. Given the severity of human rights violations in Africa during this period, the question must be asked why so few communications found their way to the Commission, especially given that all AU member states have been state parties to the Charter since January 1999.

3 Standing (*Locus Standi*)

Once a 'case' is registered, the first question to be considered is whether the person or entity bringing the communication (the 'author' or 'complainant') has standing to do so. In answering this question, a clear distinction needs to be drawn between the requirements for standing, on the one hand, and those for admissibility (and merits), on the other. Standing is the 'right to appear as a party' before a judicial tribunal or quasi-judicial body.[24] This should be viewed as a threshold issue, an 'absolute precondition of all legal actions'.[25] The possibility that the substantive basis of the claim is lacking should be determined as part of the admissibility process, under article 56 of the Charter, and is not part of the standing inquiry.

The Commission's initial (1988) Rules of Procedure stipulated that communications could be submitted on behalf of (in the 'name of the victim'), but only when he or she is 'unable to submit the communication'.[26] This wording seems to suggest that a 'victim' requirement is in principle necessary, but that in exceptional cases a complaint may be brought by a non-affected party. Serious or massive violations were treated differently, in that no victim requirement featured in such circumstances, although the allegation of a violation had to be made 'with proofs in support'.[27] The Charter and current (1995) Rules of Procedure are silent on the issue of standing. The Charter does not stipulate a 'victim' requirement, noting only that communications should 'indicate their authors' even if they request anonymity.[28] In this respect, the Charter deviates from most domestic legal systems, which restrict standing to those individuals who are personally adversely affected by that which they complain about,[29] and from the position under most of the UN human rights treaty bodies.[30]

There is a difference between a 'victim' and an 'author' (or 'complainant'). The Commission does not always use these terms accurately and consistently, but it has been made clear that the person submitting the communication (the 'author' or 'complainant') need not be the victim. This position is put succinctly as follows by the Commission:[31]

Article 56(1) of the Charter demands that any persons submitting communications to the Commission relating to human and peoples' rights must reveal their identity. They do not

---

[24] *Encyclopedia of Public International Law*, vol IV, 594.   [25] ibid, 598.
[26] 1988 Rules of Procedure, r 114(1)(a).   [27] ibid, r 114(1)(b).
[28] African Charter, art 56(1).
[29] See eg *Cabinet of the Transitional Government of SWA v Eins* (1985) 2 SA 369 (A).
[30] See eg Ch 3.B.4 above.   [31] *Mauritanian Widows* case (n 21 above) para 78.

necessarily have to be the victims of such violations or members of their families. This characteristic of the African Charter reflects sensitivity to the practical difficulties that individuals can face in countries where human rights are violated. The national or international channels of remedy may not be accessible to the victims.

The Commission has also taken the position that the person, persons, or entity submitting the communication need not act with the express consent of the 'victim'. In this respect, African regional practice differs from that of other international bodies.[32] The communication may be submitted by another individual (including family members), or by a group of persons, or by an NGO.[33] An NGO may submit a communication on behalf of an individual, a group of individuals, or another NGO. The submitting NGO need not enjoy observer status with the Commission.[34] The person or NGO further need not be a national or be registered in the territory of the state against which the communication is directed. There is also no prerequisite that the person or NGO should be 'African', composed of people of African origin, or based in an African state or states.[35]

The Commission has accepted the submission of a communication in the public interest, as an *actio popularis*. In the *Ogoniland* case, the Commission observed as follows:[36]

In accordance with articles 60 and 61 of the African Charter, this communication is examined in the light of the provisions of the African Charter and the relevant international and regional human rights instruments and principles. The Commission thanks the two human rights NGOs which brought the matter under its purview: the Social and Economic Rights Action Centre (Nigeria) and the Centre for Economic and Social Rights (USA). This is a demonstration of the usefulness to the Commission and individuals of [the] *actio popularis*, which is wisely allowed under the African Charter.

Some link between the author or complainant and 'victim' in an *actio popularis* is still suggested by the requirement that the action must serve the public interest, as the 'victimized people' inevitably has a bearing on that determination. Although the author-complainant need not act with the explicit permission or consent of the group, it must be shown in what way the public interest is being served. Unease

[32] See eg Optional Protocol to the International Covenant on Civil and Political Rights, art 1 ('communications from individuals... who claim to be a victim of a violation'), and Convention against Torture and Other Cruel, Inhuman or Degrading Treatment or Punishment, art 22 ('communications from or on behalf of individuals... who claim to be victims of a violation').

[33] See eg Communication 241/2001, *Purohit and Another v Gambia* (2003) AHRLR 96 (ACHPR 2003) (16th Annual Activity Report) (*Gambian Mental Health* case); and Communication 135/94, *Kenya Human Rights Commission v Kenya* (2000) AHRLR 133 (ACHPR 1995) (18th Annual Activity Report).

[34] Such as Social and Economic Rights Action Centre in the *Ogoniland* case (n 20 above).

[35] See eg cases submitted by Amnesty International, Interights, and also Communication 31/98, *Baes v Zaire* (2000) AHRLR 72 (ACHPR 1995) (Eighth Annual Activity Report); the *Eritrean Detention* case (n 17 above); and the USA-based Center for Social and Economic Rights (which co-submitted the *Ogoniland* case, n 20 above).

[36] *Ogoniland* case (n 20 above) para 49.

about broad standing should be addressed by focusing on the strict application of this requirement, rather than dismissing a communication for lack of standing because there is no specific link between the complainant and the 'people' as such.[37]

The rationale for such an expansive standing requirement, which includes the *actio popularis*, is multifaceted.

By their very nature, human rights claims should be approached in a way that supports the meaning that most favours the individual. In line with the purpose of the African Charter, the Commission has followed a purposive approach to the interpretation of the rights under the Charter.[38] Such an approach often leads to a 'generous' reading of the provisions of a treaty, or a 'generous approach',[39] of which a broad approach to standing forms a part.

The African Charter not only protects the rights of individuals, as is done in most other human rights instruments, but also protects the rights of 'peoples'. Since a narrow individualized 'victim' requirement will pose an obstacle to bringing collective communications, the current approach of allowing broad standing in the public interest accords appropriate weight to the concept of 'peoples' rights' under the Charter.

As a matter of practical necessity, there are also numerous reasons why a broad standing regime needs to be in place to maximize the impact of the African Charter. These reasons relate to the presence of repressive forms of governance, making it very difficult for anyone in a state (even lawyers or NGOs) to submit communications. The current situation in Eritrea is a good example, inspiring the presentation of the communication by a Dutch lawyer, Elizabeth Zegveld. Other reasons are: a lack of technical expertise, a lack of information, legal illiteracy on the part of individuals and NGOs, and also the indigence of individuals and limited resources available for legal aid in many African states. An unfortunate consequence of these factors is that the broad standing requirement has mostly been utilized by NGOs based outside Africa, rather than local NGOs.[40]

Broadened standing is also in line with some domestic trends in Africa. In human rights matters, especially, courts observe that overly strict formalism should not be employed to undermine human rights or to restrict the scope of its protection. In *Attorney-General v Dow*,[41] for example, responding to arguments about *locus standi*, the Botswana Court of Appeal observed that 'constitutional rights should not be whittled down by principles derived from the common law, whether Roman-Dutch,

---

[37] Some disquiet arose due to a growing tendency of author-complainants to withdraw cases because they did not obtain sufficient information, or because links with 'victims' were severed. The discussion during its private meeting of a draft position paper on *locus standi* has been on the agenda of the Commission's 39th and 40th sessions. See also MP Pedersen, 'Standing and the African Commission on Human and Peoples' Rights' (2006) 6 *AHRLJ* 407, 412–15.

[38] See eg *Ogoniland* case (n 20 above) paras 37 and 38.

[39] See eg Communications 48/90, 50/91, 52/91, 89/93 (joined), *Amnesty International and Others v Sudan* (2000) AHRLR 297 (ACHPR 1999) (13th Annual Activity Report) para 80.

[40] See also the discussion in Ch 9.H.1 below.

[41] *Attorney-General v Dow* (2001) AHRLR 99 (BwCA 1992).

English or Botswana', and that standing should not be denied on 'purely technical grounds'.[42]

4 Provisional Measures

As a long period of time may elapse between the submission of a complaint and its resolution,[43] it may be necessary to safeguard the rights of the victim during the interim period. Although provisional measures are partly aimed at upholding the integrity of the body that will take the final decision (by not rendering its final decision meaningless), they also aim to secure the rights of the individual concerned pending finalization of the communication. Compliance with provisional measures therefore shows respect both for the body issuing those measures and for human rights—often the right to life.

The African Charter's silence on this issue may be understood as a by-product of its general ambiguous position on individual complaints. To its credit, the Commission inserted the possibility of provisional measures into its Rules of Procedure as a means of clarifying the communications procedure. In order to 'avoid irreparable damage being caused to the victim of the alleged violation', the Commission, or its Chairperson if it is not in session, may indicate to the state against which a communication is pending what 'provisional measures' it should take.[44] Provisional measures must be accompanied by an assurance to the state that the adoption of such measures does not imply 'a decision on the substance of the communication'.

On the few occasions that the Commission did issue provisional measures, states almost uniformly disregarded them.[45] In an infamous case, Ken Saro-Wiwa, the

---

[42] Para 117.

[43] Excessive delay for example occurred in the resolution of Communication 73/92, *Diakité v Gabon* (2000) AHRLR 98 (ACHPR 2000) (13th Annual Activity Report), which was received in April 1992, and finalized more than eight years later, in May 2000. The delay was due to efforts towards settling the matter amicably, involving Commissioner Nguema, a national of Gabon. During that period, Nguema served as Chair of the Commission (1994 to 1997). The inordinate period of delay underlines the risks involved if a national of a respondent becomes involved in a communication against that state, as one is left with the impression that Commissioner Nguema did not treat the case with the level of seriousness and resolve required. See also F Viljoen, 'Communications under the African Charter: Procedure and Admissibility' in MD Evans and R Murray (eds), *The African Charter on Human and Peoples' Rights: The System in Practice (1986–2006)* (Cambridge: Cambridge University Press, 2007) ch 3.   [44] Rules of Procedure, r 111(1).

[45] Baricako, the Secretary of the Commission until 2005, makes the unsubstantiated statement that states 'have taken into account' these measures in 'certain cases'. He proceeds to discuss one such case, Communication 239/2001, *Interights (on behalf of Sikunda) v Namibia* (2002) AHRLR 21 (ACHPR 2002) (15th Annual Activity Report) (*Sikunda* case), as an example of a government that complied with the directive—but only after a visit to Namibia by a member of the Commission (G Baricako, 'La Mise en Oeuvre des Décisions de la Commission Africaine des Droits de l'Homme et des Peuples par les Autorités Nationales' in J Flauss and E Lambert-Abdelgawad, *L'Application Nationale de la Charte Africaine des Droits de l'Homme et des Peuples* (Brussels: Bruylant, 2004) 207, 221–2. In fact, according to the text of the decision, a promotional visit was undertaken to Namibia in July 2001. Before that time, though, the local courts had also proceeded with the matter: after the Minister refused to execute an initial court order that Sikunda should be released, the Minister was found in contempt of court and

President of the Movement for the Survival of the Ogoni People (MOSOP), and other members of MOSOP were charged with murder following the death of four Ogoni leaders in 1994. Saro-Wiwa and eight co-accused were convicted and sentenced to death on 31 October 1995. The Commission on 1 November 1995 invoked Rule 111, pending not only the finalization of the communication before it, but also in light of the planned protective mission to Nigeria—to which the Nigerian government had agreed—which would provide an opportunity to discuss 'the case with the Nigerian authorities'.[46] The only response of the government was to proceed, with 'unseemly haste',[47] to secretly execute the convicted persons on 10 November 1995. Finding that the accused persons' right to a fair trial had been violated, the Commission's eventual decision in 1998 on the merits of this matter illustrates the rationale for interim measures. Applying general principles of international law, the unfairness of a trial taints the death sentence imposed as a result of that trial. At the *very least*, the government should have awaited and should have attached *some* weight to the Commission's decision in its final determination whether to execute the convicted persons. Carrying out a death sentence makes *restitutio in integrum* an impossibility, and displays bad faith.[48]

In a departure from prevailing international law,[49] and pre-empting the approach of the International Court of Justice in 2001,[50] and subsequent findings of the European Court of Human Rights and the UN Human Rights Committee,[51]

Sikunda was released. The local courts therefore seem to have played a more pertinent role in securing Sikunda's release: see *Sikunda v Government of Namibia* (3) 2001 NR 481 (SC); *Government of Namibia v Sikunda* 2002 NR 203 (SC).

[46] Communications 137/94, 139/94, 154/96, 161/97 (joined), *International PEN and Others (on behalf of Saro-Wiwa) v Nigeria* (2000) AHRLR 212 (ACHPR 1998) (12th Annual Activity Report) (*Saro-Wiwa* case), para 8, indicating that *notes verbales* were sent to the Ministry of Foreign Affairs of Nigeria, the Secretary-General of the OAU, the Special Legal Adviser to the Head of State, the Nigerian Ministry of Justice, and the Nigerian High Commission in The Gambia.

[47] GJ Naldi, 'Interim Measures of Protection in the African System for the Protection of Human and Peoples' Rights' (2002) 2 *AHRLJ* 1, 7. [48] VCLT, art 31(1).

[49] See eg the practice of the pre-Protocol 11 European Courts of Human Rights, holding in *Cruz Varas v Sweden* (ECHR Series A No 201) (20 March 1991) 35) that in the light of the absence of a specific provision in the European Convention on Human Rights, the relevant provision in the Rules of Procedure (as applied by the then European Commission on Human Rights) did not give rise to a binding obligation. (See the criticism of this approach in P Van Dijk and GJH Van Hoof, *Theory and Practice of the European Convention on Human Rights* (The Hague: Kluwer Law International, 3rd edn, 1998) 62).

[50] In *LaGrand (Germany v USA)* [2001] ICJ Rep 466 (27 June 2001), <http://www.cij-icj.org> (30 September 2006), the ICJ observed that an indication of provisional measures is not a mere exhortation; its basis in the ICJ Statute, art 41 (the 'Court shall have the power to indicate... any provisional measures') makes it binding in character and creates a legal obligation (para 94 of the judgment). In its order, the ICJ required the USA to take 'all measures at its disposal' to ensure that LaGrand was not executed (para 111); the USA fell short of this obligation by merely transmitting the order to the governor of Arizona without any comment, for example a plea for a temporary stay of execution and an indication that 'there is no general agreement on the position of the United States that orders of the International Court of Justice on provisional measures are non-binding' (para 112).

[51] See eg instances where the European Court effectively overruled its previous ruling (*Mamatkulov and Abdurasulovic v Turkey*, case nos 48827/99 and 46951/99, judgment of 6 February 2003, and *Mamatkulov and Askarov v Turkey* [GC] nos 46827/99 and 46951/99, 4 February 2005); and the view

the Commission further found that Nigeria was 'legally bound' to respect the provisional measures. Ignoring the request for provisional measures defeats the purpose of Rule 111 and constitutes a violation of article 1 of the Charter, which requires states to take legislative and 'other measures' to 'give effect to' the rights in the Charter.[52] Unfortunately, the finding lacks clear and substantiated reasoning.[53] It does not deal with the issue that the provisional measures are dealt with in the Commission's Rules, rather than in the Charter; neither does it expressly locate its reasoning in a holistic and teleological interpretation of the Charter.

However, in a subsequent case against Botswana, also involving a death sentence that was executed pending the finalization of a communication, the Commission did not find that a failure to abide by provisional measures amounted to a violation of article 1.[54] Without making any reference to the *Saro-Wiwa* decision, the Commission observed that the 'only instance' where a state could be found in violation of that provision would be an instance 'where the state does not enact the necessary legislative enactment'.[55] This finding not only contradicts the previous decision, but also ignores the phrase 'other measures' (which should for example include domestic judicial decisions and findings of the Commission) in article 1 of the Charter. Although the Commission does not follow a strict system of precedent, a clearer articulation of reasons in the *Saro-Wiwa* case might have ensured that greater persuasive authority be given to the finding in that case.

Although an order to stay an execution is the most dramatic manifestation of 'provisional measures',[56] the Commission applied interim measures in other cases

of the Human Rights Committee in Communication 840/1998, *Mansaraj and Others v Sierra Leone*, UN Doc CCPR/C/72/D/840/1998 (30 July 2001), finding that Sierra Leone 'committed a grave breach of its obligations under the Optional Protocol by putting 12 of the authors to death before the Committee had concluded its consideration of the communication' (para 6.3). Disregarding preliminary measures renders 'examination by the Committee moot and the expression of its Views nugatory and futile'.

[52] *Saro-Wiwa* case (n 46 above) para 122; see also para 115: 'That it is a violation of the Charter is an understatement'. See also 'Human Rights Report on the Situation in Nigeria', second extraordinary session, 18–19 December 1995, reprinted in R Murray and M Evans (eds), *Documents of the African Commission on Human and Peoples' Rights* (Oxford: Hart, 2001) 474.

[53] See eg Naldi (n 47 above) 8; and J Flauss, 'Notule sur les Mesures Provisoires devant la Commission Africaine des Droits de l'Homme et des Peuples' in G Cohen-Jonathan and J Flauss (eds), *Mesures Conservatoires et Droits Fondamentaux* (Brussels: Bruylant, 2005) 213, 237.

[54] *Botswana Death Penalty* case (n 18 above). It is not clear to what extent the decision turned on the particular circumstances of the case. According to the Commission, the request for a stay of execution was faxed to the President of Botswana on 27 March 2001 (see para 10 of the case, where this is stated as a matter of fact). The government averred that the President never received the fax. Tilting its fact-finding function squarely in the government's favour, the Commission observed that it was not 'in possession of any proof that the fax was indeed received' (para 49). The Commission's remark that art 1 of the Charter would not be violated by a failure to comply with an order for 'preliminary measures' may thus be regarded as an *obiter dictum* in the *Botswana Death Penalty* case (n 18 above).

[55] ibid, para 51.

[56] See also Communication 231/99, *Avocats sans Fontières (on behalf of Bwampamye) v Burundi* (2000) AHRLR 48 (ACHPR 2000) (14th Annual Activity Report) (*Bwampamye* case) para 15 (seemingly, this order was complied with).

as well.[57] However, in some instances the Commission did not respond to a request for such measures to be applied.[58]

5 Amicable Settlements

Because the African Commission was specifically established as a quasi-judicial body, it may seem surprising that it was not endowed with the classical function of amicably settling individual communications.[59] It is only when it deals with inter-state communications that the Commission is explicitly mandated to 'reach an amicable solution'.[60] The Charter's ambiguity about individual communications is the most likely explanation for the absence of an 'individual' friendly settlement procedure. Although it did not fill this gap by prescribing an individual amicable settlement process through its Rules of Procedure, the Commission has used these means to settle a number of individual communications. The basis of this practice is found in article 60 of the Charter, allowing the Commission to draw on the experience of other quasi-judicial human rights bodies. However, as a feature closely linked to the African conception of 'talking things out', or 'palaver',[61] the infrequency of its use is perhaps surprising.

Amicable settlements do not necessarily convey an acknowledgement of governmental wrongdoing, especially when the settlement coincides with a change of government or an alteration in political conditions. In two notable instances governments were prepared to settle disputes that arose and had been instituted under a previous government or before circumstances had changed. In the first,[62] the complaint was directed at voter-registration, allowed for under Gambian electoral laws enacted before the 1994 coup, which brought the Jammeh government to power. Calling the law 'inexcusable and indefensible', the new government undertook to 'review the current electoral law'. In what amounts to a *nisi* order, the Commission allowed a period of just over a month within which the complainant could indicate that the settlement was not acceptable. In the absence of any response,

---

[57] *Sikunda* case (n 45 above); Communication 133/94, *Association pour la Defense des Droits de l'Homme et des Libertés v Djibouti* (2000) AHRLR 80 (ACHPR 2000) (13th Annual Activity Report) (*Afar* case); and Communication 212/98, *Amnesty International v Zambia* (2000) AHRLR 325 (ACHPR 1999) (12th Annual Activity Report) (*Banda* case) paras 39 and 40 (although there seems to be a conflation of 'provisional measures' and 'remedies' in the last case).

[58] See eg Communication 220/98, *Law Offices of Ghazi Suleiman v Sudan* (2002) AHRLR 25 (ACHPR 2002) (15th Annual Activity Report) (*Sudanese Universities Closure* case) para 6.

[59] For a thorough discussion of the Commission's involvement in amicable settlement, more broadly understood, see R Murray, *The African Commission on Human and Peoples' Rights and International Law* (Oxford: Hart, 2000) 153–98; See also Viljoen (n 43 above) 115–20.

[60] African Charter, art 52.

[61] See eg UO Umozurike, *The African Charter on Human and Peoples' Rights* (The Hague: Kluwer Law International, 1997) 81: 'The African Commission has a quasi-judicial, quasi-diplomatic and recommendatory function aimed at bringing about good relations'.

[62] Communication 44/90, *Peoples' Democratic Organisation for Independence and Socialism v The Gambia* (2000) AHRLR 104 (ACHPR 1996) (Tenth Annual Activity Report) (*Gambian Voter Registration* case).

and without explicit agreement from the complainant, the case was concluded on the basis of the government's undertaking. In the second,[63] a complaint submitted in 1994, alleging the extra judicial killing, torture, and rape of unarmed civilians, was subsequently, according to the government, addressed as part of a peace agreement between the Issa-dominated government forces and the Afar nationalist or 'rebel movement'. However, because the Commission could not obtain confirmation from the complainant, it mandated one of its members to undertake a mission to Djibouti. After the mission had provided evidence confirming that an amicable settlement had in fact been reached, the Commission confirmed the settlement.

The Commission does not generally initiate amicable settlements. Its involvement mostly takes the form of transmitting a reconciliatory state response to complainants for their acceptance[64] on the basis of an evolving agreement between the parties. In *Mouvement Burkinabé des Droits de l'Homme et des Peuples v Burkina Faso*,[65] the Commission played a much more active role. During an initial oral hearing, the parties indicated their desire to settle the dispute amicably and asked the Commission for its assistance. When the Commission's offer to the parties of 'its good services' brought no results, it 'decided' that the state should take the initiative by inviting the complainant to a 'settlement', 'failing which, the Commission would proceed to consider the case on its merits'.[66] As the subsequent hearing illustrates, two parties may interpret events differently and may hold divergent views about the 'settled' nature of the dispute. At the hearing it transpired that the government viewed at least part of the dispute as having been settled, while the complainant stated that 'there had been no progress in so far as settling the dispute was concerned'.[67] The result was that the Commission proceeded to decide the matter on the merits, finding the state in violation of numerous provisions of the Charter, and recommending investigation, prosecution, and compensation.[68]

Perhaps grasping at an easy way of finalizing cases, the Commission has shown too much deference to states and too little regard for human rights in its amicable settlement practice. Its inconsistent or deficient practice further demonstrates the lack of a clear legal basis of operation. This is true of all three elements that should form part of an amicable settlement: it must be acceptable to both parties, it must be human rights-compliant, and the agreement should be a matter of public record. Acceptance by both parties should be explicit. It is insufficient to apply a default rule, in terms of which silence is understood as acceptance, as happened in the *Gambian Voter Registration* case.[69]

While the amicable settlement procedure fits well with the Commission's approach of engaging in a 'constructive dialogue' with states, and while the benefits to the 'victim' of amicable compliance are undeniable, the Commission has to ensure that the 'victim' consents to the agreement, that the settlement is in accordance

---

[63] *Afar* case (n 57 above).   [64] *Gambian Voter Registration* case (n 62 above) paras 15 and 16.
[65] Communication 204/97, (2001) AHRLR 51 (ACHPR 2001) (14th Annual Activity Report) (*Burkinabé Mass Violations* case).
[66] ibid, para 31.   [67] ibid, para 34.   [68] ibid, para 50.   [69] n 62 above.

with human rights principles, and that the settlement is as far as possible made part of the public record by including its text in the final decision.

6 Admissibility

Article 56 of the Charter sets out seven requirements for admissibility. All of these requirements have to be complied with before a complaint will be declared admissible.[70]

6.1 Communications must Indicate Authors, even if Anonymity may be Guaranteed

Article 56(1) stipulates that communications must indicate their authors, even if they 'request anonymity'. For administrative purposes, including correspondence between the Commission and the author, a communication must state the names of its author. If authors request that their identity be kept confidential, this information should not be revealed to the state concerned or otherwise become public. There seems to be some confusion between 'author' and 'victim', though, especially in case where the two are different entities or persons. While there may at times be reasons why authors would want to keep their anonymity, it is more likely that the victims of a violation would want to remain anonymous. Still, the communication must be sufficiently detailed to prevent the state from arguing that it is not in a position to answer or investigate the allegations. As most communications have been instituted by NGOs, no problem arose about the identity of the 'authors'. The Commission has maintained the anonymity of an author who was also the alleged victim of a violation,[71] and an author who submitted a communication on behalf of her father and others.[72]

6.2 Communications must be Compatible with the African Charter and the AU Constitutive Act

The wording of the African Charter requires that a communication must be compatible with the Charter *or* the AU Constitutive Act (previously, the OAU Charter).[73] However, the AU Constitutive Act does not contain 'rights' that need to be respected, or that may potentially be violated. It would therefore be inappropriate for the Commission to deal with communications that are compatible with the AU Constitutive Act, but *not* with the Charter. The 'or' in article 56(2) should

---

[70] *Ogoniland* case (n 20 above) para 35. All the complexities of these requirements are not canvassed here. For a more complete discussion, see F Viljoen, 'Admissibility under the African Charter' in MD Evans and R Murray (eds), *The African Charter on Human and Peoples' Rights; The System in Practice 1986–2000* (Cambridge: Cambridge University Press, 2002) 61, and also Viljoen (n 43 above).

[71] Communication 283/2003, *B v Kenya* (2004) AHRLR 67 (ACHPR 2004) (17th Annual Activity Report) Annex VII (withdrawn by author-complainant).

[72] Communication 258/2002, *Miss A v Cameroon* (2004) AHRLR 39 (ACHPR 2004) (17th Annual Activity Report) Annex VII (declared inadmissible). [73] Art 56(2).

thus be read conjunctively: the provision should be understood as requiring compatibility with the African Charter in all instances, and when applicable, with the AU Constitutive Act.[74]

The compatibility requirement relates to (i) the right-bearers by whom and duty-holders against which communications may be brought, (ii) the substantive issues that may be invoked, (iii) the time period within which, and (iv) the place where the alleged violation must have occurred.

As far as the 'personal requirement' is concerned, a communication may be brought by a wide array of persons,[75] alleging violations for which state parties to the Charter are allegedly responsible. During the first few years of its existence, the Commission wasted considerable time and effort in processing and taking decisions on communications submitted against non-state parties—not only African states that had not yet become party to the African Charter, but also against states in other parts of the world (such as the USA and Yugoslavia) and the OAU itself.[76] Relegating these communications to the procedural domain of the Secretariat, the 1995 Rules of Procedure prescribed that they should not be placed before the Commission.[77]

As far as the 'material requirement' is concerned, it is usually understood that a communication should allege a violation of the Charter. This interpretation is presumably based on the introductory sentence of article 56, which makes reference to 'communications relating to human and peoples' rights', on the reference to the 'African Charter' in article 56(2), and on the position of the Commission within the African regional system. A closer reading renders this interpretation suspect, though. None of these provisions require that the communication be based on the Charter—the communication must merely *relate to* 'human and peoples' rights', and *be compatible with* the African Charter.

Accepting that the Charter is the basis within which communications have to be anchored, the Commission does not require that the text of the communication should invoke a specific right in the Charter.[78] Still, it has been generally accepted that the substance of the complaint must be located within the Charter, and must make out a prima-facie case that a violation has occurred.[79] Broad allegations, for example that there is a 'corrupt state of affairs' present in a certain state, were found to be too general to constitute a specific violation, and were declared inadmissible.[80] However, in a few instances the Commission went even further, finding that instruments other than the Charter had been violated—even when the parties did not

---

[74] See also Odinkalu and Christensen (n 12 above) 251.   [75] See 'standing' above.

[76] See cases cited in Viljoen (n 21 above) 385, 441.   [77] Rules of Procedure, r 102(2).

[78] This approach corresponds with that of the UN Human Rights Committee (see eg *El Ghar* case, Ch 3 above, para 1.1).

[79] For this reason, a communication is declared inadmissible if it is incoherent and vague (see eg Communication 142/94, *Njoka v Kenya* (2000) AHRLR 132 (ACHPR 1995) (Eighth Annual Activity Report) (*Njoka* case) para 5).

[80] See eg Communication 1/88, *Korvah v Liberia* (2000) AHRLR 140 (ACHPR 1988) (Seventh Annual Activity Report).

specifically allege these violations.[81] Arguably, such an extended material basis, inspired by articles 60 and 61 of the Charter,[82] is in line with article 56, provided the extra-Charter provisions relate to 'human and peoples' rights' and are 'compatible with' the African Charter's provisions and with the AU Constitutive Act. In both the instances mentioned, this proviso seems to have been complied with.

In the absence of any specific provision on 'reservations' under the Charter, the general international law principle should be applied that reservations are acceptable as long as they are compatible with the 'object and purport' of a treaty.[83] Two states, Egypt and Zambia, entered reservations to the Charter.[84] Should a communication be directed at one of the few rights 'reserved' under the African Charter, the question of the compatibility of the reservation should be determined as part of the admissibility hearing. If the Commission finds that the reservation is acceptable, the communication should be declared inadmissible for lack of a material basis. Although the Commission has not made a specific pronouncement on reservations, questions raised during the examination of Egypt's third report (combining its seventh and eighth periodic reports) suggest that the state should withdraw its reservations to articles 8 and 18(3).[85]

As for the 'temporal requirement', the primary condition is that the respondent state had ratified the Charter by the time the alleged violation occurred. The Commission observed this principle,[86] but in line with other human rights treaty bodies, it allowed an exception when the violation started before the entry into force of the Charter, but continued thereafter.[87]

---

[81] Communication 224/98, *Media Rights Agenda v Nigeria* (2000) AHRLR 262 (ACHPR 2000) (14th Annual Activity Report) (*Malaolu* case) para 76, where the Commission found a violation of 'principle 5 of the UN Basic Principles on the Independence of the Judiciary'; and Communication 249/2002, *African Institute for Human Rights and Development (on behalf of Sierra Leonean Refugees in Guinea) v Guinea* (2004) AHRLR 57 (ACHPR 2004) (20th Activity Report) (*Sierra Leonean Refugees* case), where the Commission found that the state party had violated art 4 of the OAU Convention Governing the Specific Aspects of Refugees in Africa of 1969.

[82] By stipulating that the Commission may 'draw inspiration' from sources other than the Charter, article 60 seems to allow for an enlarged interpretative but not an extended substantive scope. Article 61 is more equivocal, though. Under that provision, the Commission's competence to establish 'subsidiary measures' to *determine* the 'principles of law' is probably worded widely enough to allow for substantive findings on instruments other than the Charter.

[83] Vienna Convention on the Law of Treaties, art 19(c).

[84] Repr in Heyns (n 5 above) 108–9. Reservations under the Women's Protocol will also fall under the Commission's purview.

[85] Questions posed by Commissioners Hassan and Dankwa, Commission's 37th session, 27 April–11 May 2005 (notes on file with author).   [86] See eg *Njoka* case (n 79 above) para 5.

[87] See the following remark in the *Mazou* case (n 16 above) para 15: 'If... irregularities... have consequences that constitute a continuing violation of any of the articles of the African Charter, the Commission must pronounce on these'. See, however, Communication 197/97, *Bah Ould Rabah v Mauritania* (2004) AHRLR 78 (ACHPR 2004) (17th Annual Activity Report) (*Mauritanian Dispossession* case), where (a majority of) the Commission found a violation arising from an eviction that took place in 1975, when the complainant and his family were forcibly evicted from their 'ancestral domicile' (para 1). The possibility of a 'continuing violation' was not addressed at all in the Commission's decision. In his minority opinion, Commissioner El Hassan noted that the 'events in question took place' before Mauritania became a state party to the Charter (in 1986), and pointed

As far as 'territoriality' is concerned, the general position is that the alleged violation must have occurred in the territory of the respondent state, or in an area over which or within a context in which it had effective control. So far, questions about the extra-territorial application of the Charter, for example when government agents perpetrate a human rights violation in another state, had not been raised in any individual communication. If full effect is to be given to the Charter, a state should be equally liable for such extra-territorial violations. In the only inter-state communication finalized by the Commission,[88] it was found that the respondent states had violated the Charter in the territory of the complainant state. However, as article 56 does not apply to inter-state communications, this finding does not shed light on its application with respect to individual communications.

6.3 Communications must not be Written in Disparaging Language

The African Charter is the only human rights instrument to require sanitized communications that are not 'disparaging' or 'insulting' towards the respondent state, its institutions, or the AU.[89] This provision, more than any other in the Charter, reveals an attempt to minimize embarrassment in the name of the sanctity of state sovereignty and in deference to political position. Seemingly, states wanted the luxury of a regional human rights instrument without the possibility of getting their reputations tainted. The potential that such a requirement may nullify an otherwise legitimate complaint and the deference to authority it implies are reasons why a similar requirement has not been included in other human rights treaties. At the very least, the Commission should be expected to interpret the term 'disparaging language' and its possible 'targets' as restrictively as possible.

Unfortunately, the Commission had on two occasions based a finding of inadmissibility, at least partly, on this ground. A communication against Cameroon[90] included statements such as 'Paul Biya must respond to crimes against humanity'; '30 years of the criminal neo-colonial regime incarnated by the duo Ahidjo/Biya'; 'regime of torturers' and 'government barbarism'.[91] The Commission's decision to declare the communication inadmissible is regrettable. At most, it should have struck out the offending phrases, or should have referred the matter back to the author, indicating that article 56(3) should be complied with in a resubmission. Although the author could have resubmitted the communication, he did not muster the determination to pursue the matter again. No wonder: the original communication was submitted in March 1992, and the admissibility decision was taken only in April 1997. It is unrealistic to expect a complainant to resume a process that has

out that this brings the 'principle of retroactivity of law' into play, which the Commission's decision did not discuss (para 49).

[88] Communication 227/1999, *DRC v Burundi, Rwanda and Uganda* (20th Activity Report) (*Congo* case).   [89] African Charter, art 56(3).

[90] Communication 65/92, *Ligue Camerounaise des Droits de l'Homme v Cameroon* (2000) AHRLR 61 (ACHPR 1997) (Tenth Annual Activity Report).

[91] Paul Biya is the current President of Cameroon, while Ahmadou Ahidjo was his predecessor.

proven unsuccessful after more than five years. The remarks in this communication should not have been viewed as 'insulting' to the state, but as part of a passionate plea to focus attention on the situation in Cameroon. The Commission should have adopted the narrowest possible meaning of the words 'disparaging', 'insulting', and 'state concerned'. It is something quite different to use insulting language towards a 'state', as the Charter requires, than to insult a head of state; yet this distinction is not referred to in the Commission's finding.

On a second occasion, in *Ilesanmi v Nigeria*,[92] the complainant alleged widespread smuggling and corruption, and mocked the effectiveness of the government's anti-smuggling and anti-corruption efforts. It was also alleged that the President was corrupt and had been bribed by drug smugglers. On the basis that 'every reasonable person would lose respect' for an institution or person that is alleged to be corrupt,[93] the Commission declared the communication inadmissible.[94] One must inevitably agree with Odinkalu's assessment that this sub-article provides 'an artifice for distraction, obfuscation, and subterfuge'.[95]

As in many other instances, the Commission's case-law on this issue lacks uniformity. In another communication against Cameroon, the Commission found that allegations that the President 'wielded extraordinary powers so as to influence the judiciary' and that the judiciary lacked independence, did not amount to 'disparaging' language.[96] In its finding, the Commission noted that the veracity of the allegations does not determine the issue, although it may play a role in an inquiry about the 'disparaging' nature of a remark.

6.4 The Communication must not be Based Exclusively on Media Reports

Given the broad standing requirement, it is appropriate to require that a communication should be based on more than just media reports. As the word 'exclusively' indicates, newspaper and other media may partially lay the factual basis of the complaint. Reiterating the importance of the news media in revealing human rights violations, the Commission in the *Gambian Coup* case in part relied on media reports.[97] Although it suggested as an additional threshold the requirement

---

[92] Communication 268/2003, *Ilesanmi v Nigeria* (18th Activity Report, Annex III).

[93] The Commission defined 'disparaging' to mean 'to speak slightingly of... or to belittle' and 'insulting' to mean 'to abuse scornfully or to offend the self respect or modesty of' (para 39).

[94] See, however, the Commission's observation that persons 'who assume highly visible public roles must necessarily face a higher degree of criticism than private citizens, otherwise public debate may be stifled altogether' in the Communications 105/93, 128/94, 130/94, 152/96 (joined), *Media Rights Agenda and Others v Nigeria* (2000) AHRLR 200 (ACHPR 1998) (12th Annual Activity Report) (*Nigerian Media* case) para 74. Although arising as part of the consideration on the merits of an alleged violation of art 9(2) of the Charter (right to express and disseminate opinions), the same sentiments should be applied to interpret the words 'disparaging' and 'insulting' in art 56(3).

[95] CA Odinkalu, 'The Individual Complaints Procedures of the African Commission on Human and Peoples' Rights: A Preliminary Assessment' (1998) 8 *Transnational L and Contemporary Problems* 359, 382.

[96] Communication 260/2002, *Bakweri Land Claims Committee v Cameroon* (2004) AHRLR 43 (ACHPR 2004) (decided at the Commission's 36th session, November–December 2004) para 48.

[97] n 14 above, para 27.

that the complainant must at least have made efforts to establish the veracity of the allegations, the Commission did not apply that requirement to the reports *in casu.*

6.5 Domestic Remedies must First be Exhausted

The purpose of requiring complainants to exhaust local remedies, provided for in article 56(5), is to allow the respondent state an opportunity to remedy the alleged violation before the matter is referred for international adjudication.[98] It has been suggested that the underlying rationale is that the state must have received notice of the alleged violation.[99] If a state is unaware of an alleged violation, it would not be in a position to live up to its obligation under the treaty by correcting the defect in national law and practice. As domestic courts are better situated to undertake fact-finding, it is preferable that they hear cases before their possible referral to an international body. The domestic remedies requirement prevents international bodies from becoming tribunals of first instance,[100] and reinforces the complementary relationship between the international and internal protective systems.[101] The requirement further emphasizes the primacy and greater immediacy of the national level,[102] in that local remedies are 'normally quicker, cheaper, and more effective'.[103]

As the African Charter is a legal text, the official notification of an allegation should come through a legal, as opposed to an extra-legal challenge. The term 'local remedies' has therefore been interpreted to refer to 'the ordinary remedies of common law that exist in jurisdictions and normally accessible to people seeking justice'.[104] Extra-judicial remedies such as recourse to quasi-judicial bodies,[105] executive pardon,[106] and a 'discretionary, extraordinary remedy of a non-judicial nature'[107] need not be exhausted.

Only domestic remedies that are available, effective, and adequate (sufficient) need to be exhausted.[108] A remedy is 'available' if it can be utilized as a matter of fact and without impediment; a remedy that offers a prospect of success is 'effective'; and it is 'sufficient' if it is capable of redressing the wrong complained against. When massive and serious violations are alleged, the complainant need not exhaust

---

[98] On the rationale for this requirement under international law, see CF Amerasinghe, *Local Remedies in International Law* (Cambridge: Cambridge University Press, 2nd edn, 2004) 71–4.

[99] Communications 25/89, 47/90, 56/91, 100/93 (joined), *Free Legal Assistance Group and Another v Zaire* (2000) AHRLR 74 (ACHPR 1995) (Ninth Annual Activity Report) (*Zairian Mass Violations* case) para 36.

[100] Communications 48/90, 50/91, 52/91, 89/93 (joined), *Amnesty International and Others v Sudan* (2000) AHRLR 297 (ACHPR 1999) (13th Annual Activity Report) para 32.

[101] Communication 299/2005, *Anuak Justice Council v Ethiopia* (20th Activity Report, Annex IV) (*Anuak* case) para 48.   [102] See Ch 13 below.

[103] *Anuak* case (n 101 above) para 48.

[104] Communication 242/2001, *Interights and Others v Mauritania* (2004) AHRLR 87 (ACHPR 2004) (17th Activity Report) (*Mauritanian Political Parties* case) para 27.

[105] Communication 221/98, *Cudjoe v Ghana* (2000) AHRLR 127 (ACHPR 1999) (12th Annual Activity Report) para 13.   [106] *Bwampamye* case (n 56 above) para 23.

[107] Communication 60/91, *Constitutional Rights Project (in respect of Akamu and Others) v Nigeria* (*Nigerian Judicial Independence* case) (2000) AHRLR 180 (ACHPR 1995) (Eighth Annual Activity Report) para 8.   [108] *Gambian Coup* case (n 14 above) paras 31–8.

local remedies if it would be 'impractical' to do so, or when the violations are so pervasive and ubiquitous that knowledge about and opportunity for redress on the part of the state may be assumed.[109] When 'ouster clauses' in national law exclude the jurisdiction of courts, local remedies are not regarded as being 'available'.[110] Complainants are also exempted from using local remedies if their exhaustion is 'unduly prolonged'.[111]

The question whether indigence is a ground for exemption brought one of the ambiguities of the domestic remedies requirement into the open: who is required to exhaust local remedies if the 'author' (or 'complainant') and the 'victim' are not the same person or entity? Logic dictates that it should be the author or complainant, because the victim needs not be involved in, or even consent to, the submission of the communication. However, in the *Gambian Mental Health* case,[112] a communication submitted by two 'mental health advocates' on behalf of patients detained in a psychiatric unit under the Gambian Lunatics Detention Act, the Commission examined the indigence of 'the *people being represented* in the present communication'.[113] As these people are likely to be from 'poor backgrounds' or would be 'picked up from the streets', it would be unrealistic to expect them to avail themselves of 'available' remedies without legal aid, the Commission held. Although these dicta may not be appropriate in this particular case as they were applied to the 'victims' rather than the 'authors/complainants', they should be persuasive in applicable analogous cases concerning indigent 'victims'. However, it may also be contended that it was indeed appropriate to direct the inquiry to the possibility of the *victim* exhausting local remedies, as restrictive standing requirements under domestic law would not have allowed the 'authors' to exhaust local remedies at all.

The procedure to determine whether local remedies had been exhausted is as follows:[114] The complainant must allege, but does not need to prove, that a particular local remedy is 'unavailable, ineffective or insufficient'. The onus then shifts to the respondent state to show that the remedy is indeed available, effective, and sufficient. If the state acquits itself of that burden, the complainant must demonstrate that the indicated remedy was indeed exhausted, or that, despite the general availability, effectiveness, and sufficiency of the remedy, it was not a real option under the specific circumstances. The standard of proof, based on a balance of probabilities, should not require a complainant to pursue a remedy if it has only 'the slightest likelihood to be effective', though.[115]

[109] *Zairian Mass Violations* case (n 99 above) para 37; *Ogoniland* case (n 20 above) paras 38–40.

[110] See eg Communications 105/93, 128/94, 130/94, 152/96 (joined), *Media Rights Agenda and Others v Nigeria* (2000) AHRLR 200 (ACHPR 1998) (12th Annual Activity Report) (*Nigerian Media* case n 94 above) paras 49 and 50.

[111] African Charter, art 56(5): exhaustion of local remedies is required 'unless it is obvious that this procedure is unduly prolonged'. [112] n 33 above.

[113] Emphasis added.

[114] Communication 268/2003, *Ilesanmi v Nigeria* (n 92 above), 18th Activity Report, Annex III, para 45. [115] As was observed in the *Anuak* case (n 101 above) para 58.

The case of *Anuak Justice Council v Ethiopia* serves as an illustration:[116] The complainant alleged that local remedies were generally unavailable because an independent and fair hearing would be impossible before Ethiopian courts due to executive interference, and because lawyers would not be able to present cases on the Council's behalf as their lives would be threatened. The state countered these allegations by providing a list of criminal cases related to the alleged violations that were pending before the Federal Circuit Court. In the absence of any attempt to approach the courts and due to the speculative and unsubstantiated nature of its allegations,[117] the complainant was unable to show that these remedies had been exhausted or were unavailable and insufficient in the particular case. The case was therefore found to be inadmissible on this ground.

Inconsistencies plaguing the Commission are on display in a series of decisions on the question of whether a complainant is required to exhaust domestic remedies in the country that he has fled to or if he or she went into hiding. In *Abubakar v Ghana*,[118] the facts were as follows: The complainant (Abubakar) escaped from prison in Ghana, where he had been held as a political detainee without having been tried, and fled to Côte d'Ivoire. Using the 'nature of the complaint' as its guiding principle, the Commission concluded that it would not be 'logical to ask the complainant to go back to Ghana in order to seek a remedy from national legal authorities'.[119] In a subsequent case, *Rights International v Nigeria*,[120] someone fleeing dictatorship in Nigeria was granted refugee status in the USA. On the basis that he had fled due to fear for his life, the 'victim' was not required to return to Nigeria to exhaust local remedies there.

Three further cases concerning this question were finalized at the Commission's 27th session, held in May 2000. The Commission observed its own precedents in two of these cases, but deviated from the established line of argument in the third. In one case,[121] the deposed Gambian head of state submitted a complaint after a *coup d'état* removed him from power. Finding that the complainant does not have to exhaust domestic remedies in The Gambia, the Commission held that it would be an affront to logic and common sense to require the ex-President to risk his life to return to The Gambia. In the second case,[122] the complainant's fear for his life also led to a finding that it would be improper to require him to ensure that local remedies had been exhausted. In the third case, *Legal Defence Centre v The Gambia*,[123]

---

[116] n 101 above.

[117] ibid, para 58: 'Apart from casting aspersions on the effectiveness of local remedies, the complainant has not provided concrete evidence or demonstrated sufficiently that these apprehensions are founded'.

[118] Communication 103/93, *Abubakar v Ghana* (2000) AHRLR 124 (ACHPR 1996) (Tenth Annual Activity Report).   [119] ibid, para 6.

[120] Communication 215/98, *Rights International v Nigeria* (2000) AHRLR 254 (ACHPR 1999) (13th Annual Activity Report).   [121] *Gambian Coup* case (n 14 above).

[122] Communication 205/97, *Aminu v Nigeria* (2000) AHRLR 258 (ACHPR 2000) (13th Annual Activity Report).

[123] Communication 219/98, *Legal Defence Centre v The Gambia* (2000) AHRLR 121 (ACHPR 2000) (13th Annual Activity Report).

the Commission deviated from its own jurisprudence by requiring exhaustion of local remedies by a complainant in a situation analogous to those in the first two cases. The complainant, a Nigerian journalist based in The Gambia, was ordered to leave his host country after his reporting had caused embarrassment to the Nigerian government. According to the government's version, the journalist was deported to 'face trials for crimes he committed in Nigeria'.[124] However, he was not arrested or prosecuted in Nigeria. Despite the uncontested allegation presented as part of his argument that he could not return to The Gambia because the deportation order was still valid, the Commission found that the complainant should have exhausted possible remedies in The Gambia. Declaring the communication inadmissible, the Commission for the first time required a complainant who had fled or was otherwise forced to leave a country to instruct counsel in the country that he had left. This requirement may often place an unreasonable financial and logistical burden on a person in such a position.

The finding also flies in the face of the Commission's jurisprudence dealing with deportation, according to which the exhaustion of local remedies was not required when a person was expelled from a country. Under circumstances of mass expulsion that did not allow a group of West Africans in Zambia and in Angola to challenge their expulsion, the Commission did not require that they exhaust local remedies in the country that had expelled them while present in the countries they had been expelled to.[125]

6.6 *The Communication must be Submitted within a Reasonable Period*

By not stipulating a fixed period within which a communication has to be submitted to the Commission after local remedies have been exhausted, the Charter displays a responsiveness to the African landscape's fluidity rather than an adherence to inflexible time standards.[126]

6.7 *The Matter must not have been Settled under other International Procedures*

The matter is not admissible if it has been 'settled' under an AU or UN dispute settlement procedure.[127] It is important to note that the matter must not have been 'settled'—it may thus still be 'under consideration' under an international dispute settlement procedure.[128] The reason behind this requirement is twofold.[129] By

---

[124] ibid, para 4; his deportation took place within a very short time and he had no opportunity to contest it.
[125] Communication 71/92, *Rencontre Africaine pour la Défense des Droits de l'Homme v Zambia* (2000) AHRLR 321 (ACHPR 1996) (Tenth Annual Activity Report) (*RADDHO* case); Communication 159/96, *Union Interafricaine des Droits de l'Homme and Others v Angola* (2000) AHRLR 18 (ACHPR 1997) (11th Annual Activity Report).
[126] See *Mauritanian Dispossession* case (n 87 above)   [127] African Charter, art 56(7).
[128] Under other treaties, some controversy arose over the use of the term 'being considered'.
[129] Communication 260/2002, *Bakweri Land Claims Committee v Cameroon*, decided at the Commission's 36th session, November–December 2004, paras 52 and 53.

lending support to the principle of *res judicata*, this requirement serves the aims of certainty and finality in international adjudication. Building on the analogy of the criminal justice principle that an accused person may not be indicted twice for the same offence arising from the same circumstances, this requirement further ensures that a state is not 'condemned' internationally twice for the same violation.

This issue may have a bearing on a complainant's selection of a forum. Should a complainant consider submitting a claim to more than one international body, such as the African Commission and the UN Human Rights Committee (HRC), it is clear that such a communication should be directed to the Commission first.[130] If the matter has already been finalized by the HRC, it cannot be instituted before the African Commission. As the HRC only requires that the matter should not be in the process of 'being considered' by another body, an unsuccessful complainant may direct a complaint to the HRC after the Commission has finalized the case.[131] It is not clear whether the question is whether the matter has been 'settled' at the time of submission of the communication, or at the time the Commission decides on admissibility.

7 Merits

7.1 Hearing and Evidence

Like other quasi-judicial international human rights bodies, the Commission lacks a well-developed fact-finding practice.[132] Although its Rules allow for a written procedure only, in line with UN treaty bodies, the Commission has developed the practice of allowing parties to present oral arguments during hearings, and even to call witnesses.[133] The Commission's practice in this regard is pragmatic

---

[130] See eg Communication 255/2002, *Prince v South Africa* (*Prince* case), finalized at the Commission's 36th session, partially reprinted in C Heyns and M Killander (eds), *Compendium of Key Human Rights Documents of the African Union* (Pretoria: PULP, 2006) 205, which was subsequently submitted to the HRC and is currently pending before that body.

[131] Although this aspect is not mentioned in either of the cases, and although there is no cross-reference from the one to the other, this was the position in respect of Communication 223/98, *Forum of Conscience v Sierra Leone* (2000) AHRLR 293 (ACHPR 2000), which the African Commission finalized in October–November 2000, and Communications 839/1998, 840/1998, 841/1998 (joined), *Mansaraj and Others v Sierra Leone*, which were subsequently decided by the HRC on 16 July 2001. Both these cases relate to the execution of a number of former members of the armed forces of Sierra Leone by firing squad on 19 October 1998. Both bodies found a violation of the right to life and the right to an appeal. See also the *Mazou* case (n 16 above), submitted to the African Commission in 1990, finalized by the Commission in April 1997. The same matter was also submitted to the HRC (see Ch 3.B.4 above) (according to the HRC's finding, the communication was submitted 'initially' on 31 October 1994). Although no mention is made of the proceedings before the African Commission, it appears that the HRC (or the complainant) awaited finalization by the African Commission before proceeding before the HRC. The HRC finalized the matter on 3 August 2001. Both bodies found the state in violation of the relevant provisions.

[132] R Murray 'Evidence and Fact-Finding by the African Commission' in Evans and Murray (n 70 above) 100.

[133] The decisive role of testimony of and sworn statements by witnesses is illustrated well in the *Sierra Leonean Refugees* case (n 81 above, paras 26 and 59), especially in the light of the fact that none of the parties provided a copy of an important speech by the President of Guinea, which was alleged to have incited violence against the Sierra Leonean refugees in Guinea (paras 46 and 73).

and ad hoc. As the issues of admissibility and the merits are considered separately, the parties often appear twice. In some instances, the parties appeared before the Commission three times.[134] Nevertheless, even though the Commission relies on personal accounts and oral submissions, the main source of its factual findings is written materials. These materials may take the form of copies of judgments (especially to prove exhaustion of domestic remedies),[135] letters,[136] government memoranda,[137] official post-mortem reports,[138] and a list of repatriated aliens, supplied by the government.[139] Reports and recorded interviews by NGOs,[140] a UN Special Rapporteur's report,[141] and even a video have also served to corroborate evidence before the Commission.[142]

The evidentiary basis of most findings is unclear. The Commission's guidelines for submission of communications and its practice do not generally require sworn statements or evidence under oath. The complainant is required to 'substantiate his claim'.[143] When conflicting factual versions are placed before it, the Commission has shown a reluctance to 'verify the authenticity' of alleged facts. Its case-law requires that a complainant furnishes 'concrete' evidence. When the Commission introduced the requirement that the statements of a complainant must be 'made under oath or corroborated by sworn affidavits', it not only adopted too inflexible a standard, but it also opened itself to the criticism of bias, as it accepted the mere statement by the state—without requiring sworn statements or statistical breakdowns—that 'in the bulk of the cases the perpetrators had been identified, arrested, tried, convicted or acquitted'.[144] The Commission accepted that the state sufficiently refuted allegations of extra-judicial killings when it provided 'official post-mortem reports' indicating the cause of death of the alleged victims.[145] In a long line of decisions, again in conformity with the practice of other international human rights adjudicatory bodies, the Commission held that it 'must decide on the facts as given' when allegations of violations go uncontested by the government concerned.[146] Allegations of massive violations do not require a list

---

[134] *Burkinabé Mass Violations* case (n 65 above) paras 25, 31, and 34.
[135] *Banda* case (n 57 above) para 26.   [136] *Gambian Coup* case (n 14 above) para 27.
[137] *Ogoniland* case (n 20 above) para 8.   [138] ibid, para 52.
[139] *RADDHO* case (n 125 above) para 24.
[140] *Sierra Leonean Refugees* case (n 81 above) para 40 (corroboration of oral testimony in interviews recorded by the Institute for Human Rights and Development in Africa, based in Banjul, and the Campaign for Good Governance, based in Sierra Leone; and in reports of Human Rights Watch and Amnesty International).
[141] Communications 48/90, 50/91, 52/91, 89/93 (joined), *Amnesty International and Others v Sudan* (n 39 above) para 48.   [142] *Ogoniland* case (n 20 above) para 8.
[143] Communication 232/99, *Ouko v Kenya* (2000) AHRLR 135 (ACHPR 2000) (14th Annual Activity Report) para 26.
[144] Communication 245/2002, *Zimbabwe Human Rights NGO Forum v Zimbabwe* (*Zimbabwean Political Violence* case) para 122. (This case was contained in the 20th Activity Report, but not published as part of that report due to objections by the government, see Ch 5 below.)
[145] *Gambian Coup* case (n 14 above) paras 52 and 53.
[146] See eg *Zairian Mass Violations* case (n 99 above) para 40 and *Zegveld and Another v Eritrea* (2000) AHRLR 84 (ACHPR 2003) (17th Annual Activity Report) para 46.

with the specific names of individuals who are affected. This is an appropriate deviation from the strictures usually followed with respect to 'class actions' in national courts.

One of the reasons for the domestic remedies requirement for admissibility is the reality that domestic courts are better placed than the Commission to establish the relevant facts. Decisions of domestic courts provide the best evidence that local remedies have been exhausted, and should mostly offer a sufficient basis for the Commission's findings. Mainly for pragmatic reasons, the Commission considers that it is 'not competent to substitute the judgments' of national courts, 'especially on matters of fact'.[147] The Commission may only substitute its own factual decision for that of local courts if 'it is shown that the courts' evaluation of the facts was manifestly arbitrary or amounted to a denial of justice'.[148] However, the exemption of the domestic remedies requirement has become more the rule than the exception, often leaving the Commission without the benefits of a factual basis carefully articulated in a domestic court's decision. This situation, which calls upon the Commission to make *de novo* factual findings, is at odds with the assumptions underlying international complaints systems.

7.2 Theory of Interpretation

The Commission has not shied away from adopting innovative interpretations of the Charter in its Rules of Procedure and its jurisprudence, especially in stopping the gaps and clarifying ambiguities in the African Charter. In response to one of the principal ambiguities, the lack of a clearly delineated individual complaints procedure, the Commission provided details of such a procedure in its Rules and proceeded to deal with communications submitted by individuals. By adopting numerous resolutions elucidating the rights in the Charter, the Commission provided clarity about vaguely formulated rights and expanded the normative scope of the Charter.[149]

To the extent that a coherent approach to interpretation has emerged from the Commission's jurisprudence, it first and foremost follows a textual approach, reflecting the requirement of the Vienna Convention on the Law of Treaties (VCLT) that interpretation should be guided by the 'ordinary meaning' of a treaty.[150] Still, the Commission does not use words very self-consciously or reflectively and mostly accepts their meaning as self-evident.[151] As far as 'wording' is concerned, reference

---

[147] Communications 64/92, 68/92, 78/92 (joined) *Achutan and Another (on behalf of Banda and Others) v Malawi* (2000) AHRLR 144 (ACHPR 1995) (Eighth Annual Activity Report) (*Chirwa* case) para 32.   [148] *Botswana Death Penalty* case (n 18 above) para 29.
[149] See eg the references to the Declaration of Principles on Freedom of Expression in Africa, in Communication 228/99, *Law Office of Suleiman v Sudan (II)* (2003) AHRLR 144 (ACHPR 2003) (16th Annual Activity Report) (*Suleiman* case) paras 40 and 46.
[150] VCLT, art 31(1). See also F Viljoen, 'The African Charter on Human and Peoples' Rights: The *Travaux Préparatoires* in the Light of Subsequent Practice' (2004) 25 *HRLJ* 313, 325.
[151] See eg the following statement in Communication 236/2000, *Doebbler v Sudan* (2003) AHRLR 153 (ACHPR 2003) (*Sudanese Picnic* case) (16th Annual Activity Report, Annex VII) ('Article 5 of the

is made not only to the Charter, but also to resolutions adopted by the Commission. Recourse is made very infrequently to the original intention of the drafters. On a number of occasions, case-law highlights the need to interpret provisions within a context, or 'holistically'.[152] Textual reliance is counter balanced by the need to make rights effective through interpretations that are 'responsive to African circumstances',[153] or taking into account 'the differing legal traditions of Africa'.[154]

A golden thread is the interpretation of rights *in favorem libertatis* (in favour of the individual and human rights),[155] or 'generously'.[156] Although this trend certainly contains the beginnings of a generous approach, as yet it is little more than a generous 'tendency'. In some admissibility findings, where the Commission distinguished clearly between the literal application of the admissibility requirements and the purpose they serve,[157] and in some other cases, including the *Ogoniland* case, the Commission adopted a purposive (or teleological) approach.[158]

Partly because the publicly accessible drafting history of the Charter is very patchy, consisting of three consecutive drafts and a single technical report, and partly because the political context of the drafting has been altered radically by events in the 1990s, there has been little attempt to import an original understanding of the Charter into the Commission's jurisprudence. On one occasion, though, the origin of a provision was traced back to 'colonialism, during which

Charter prohibits not only cruel but also inhuman and degrading treatment. This includes not only actions which cause serious physical or psychological suffering, but which humiliate or force the individual against his will or conscience' (para 36)).

[152] Also in accordance with VCLT, art 31(1); and see Communication 211/98, *Legal Resources Foundation v Zambia* (2001) AHRLR 84 (ACHPR 2001) (14th Annual Activity Report) (*Zambian Presidential Candidates* case) para 70: 'The Charter must be interpreted holistically and all clauses must reinforce each other'.   [153] *Ogoniland* case (n 20 above) para 68.

[154] Communications 143/95, 150/96 (joined), *Constitutional Rights Project and Another v Nigeria* (2000) AHRLR 235 (ACHPR 1999) (13th Annual Activity Report) (*Nigerian Habeas Corpus* case) para 26.   [155] See Justinian's *Digest* 29.2.71.pr.

[156] See eg Communication 225/98, *Huri-Laws v Nigeria* (2000) AHRLR 273 (ACHPR 2000) (14th Annual Activity Report) (*Huri-Laws* case) para 40; and Communications 48/90, 50/91, 52/91, 89/93 (joined), *Amnesty International and Others v Sudan* (n 39 above) para 80: 'Any restriction of rights should be the exception'.

[157] *Zairian Mass Violations* case (n 99 above) para 36: 'The requirement of exhaustion of local remedies is founded on the *principle* that a government should have notice of a human rights violation in order to remedy such violations before being called before an international body'; and para 37: 'The Commission has never held the requirement of local remedies to apply *literally* in cases where it is impractical and undesirable . . .' (emphasis added on both occasions). See also eg the *Ogoniland* case (n 20 above) paras 37 and 38, where the 'purpose' and the 'rationale' of the local remedies requirement are also identified, and Communication 48/90, 50/91, 52/91, 89/93 (joined), *Amnesty International and Others v Sudan* (n 39 above) para 38, where the admissibility requirements were held not to 'apply literally' in cases of serious and massive violations. See also *the Nigerian Media* case (n 94 above) para 59 (where the Commission rejected the 'literal, minimalist interpretation' advanced by the Nigerian government).

[158] See *Sudanese Picnic* case (n 151 above), where state conduct is contrasted with the 'very nature' of the Charter (para 42) and the *Zambian Presidential Candidates* case (n 152 above), where the Commission requires that the 'purpose or effect of any limitation must also be examined' (para 70). See also VCLT, art 31, which determines that a treaty should be interpreted in the light of 'its object and purpose'.

the human and material resources of Africa were largely exploited for the benefit of outside powers, creating tragedy for Africans themselves, depriving them of their birthright and alienating them from the land. The aftermath of colonial exploitation has left Africa's precious resources and people still vulnerable to foreign misappropriation. The drafters of the Charter obviously wanted to remind African governments of the continent's painful legacy and restore cooperative economic development to its traditional place at the heart of African society'.[159]

Made up of lawyers from both the civil law and common law traditions, the Commission is ambivalent about the '*stare decisis*' doctrine. Although it has not wholeheartedly embraced a system of precedent, it has on numerous occasions relied on its own precedents,[160] and has countered the argument that the Commission may only consider cases revealing serious or massive violations by relying on its contrary 'practice' of considering individual communications.[161] Some inconsistency in the Commission's findings underscores the fact that a rigid system of precedent does not exist. Even if a strict system of precedent does not apply, to bolster its legitimacy as an institution following a fair procedure, the Commission should not deviate from previous decisions without clear substantiation.[162]

7.3 Reliance on Comparative Sources

In terms of articles 60 and 61 of the African Charter, the Commission may draw inspiration from a wide range of international human rights sources. These two provisions were initially included in the Monrovia proposal, directed at setting up an African human rights body. The aim of their inclusion in that draft was primarily to ensure that the proposed Commission would have a substantive basis on which to operate, *in the absence of any African human rights convention or charter*. Despite the fact that the provisions establishing the Commission were subsequently, in the later drafts, supplemented by substantive provisions setting out rights and duties, the precursors of article 60 and 61 were retained.

From one point of view, these provisions are superfluous. The Commission must, in the first place, apply the African Charter. Other regional and international human rights instruments do not contain a similar 'interpretation' provision, but nonetheless use other international law as interpretive guides. However, this emphasis on the importance of international human rights instruments has assisted the

---

[159] *Ogoniland* case (n 20 above) para 56.

[160] See eg *Nigerian Media* case (n 94 above) paras 48 and 49; Communications 222/98, 229/99, *Law Offices of Suleiman v Sudan (I)* (2003) AHRLR 134 (ACHPR 2003) (16th Annual Activity Report) para 40: 'Supported by its earlier decisions, the African Commission has always treated communications by ruling on the alleged facts at the time of submission of the communication (see *Organisation Mondiale contre la Torture and Others v Rwanda* (n 202 below)).

[161] *Gambian Coup* case (n 14 above) para 42.

[162] In similar vein, the European Court of Human Rights had this to say: 'While the Court is not formally bound to follow its previous judgments, in the interests of legal certainty and foreseeability it should not depart, without good reason, from its own precedents' (*Mamatkulov and Abdurasulovic v Turkey* (n 51 above) para 105).

Commission to adopt a progressive interpretation of the Charter. These provisions open a wide array of possible sources that could give interpretative guidance, including African and UN human rights instruments, customary international law, judicial precedents, doctrine (academic writing), and general principles of law recognized by African states.

The Commission did not initially make extensive use of the possibilities provided for in articles 60 and 61. In fact, in one of the few early references found, the Commission does so merely to distinguish the African system from other international human rights systems.[163] This initial neglect may in part have been a deliberate attempt not to alienate states and to establish the Commission as an African institution, but in part also reflected the initial absence of reasoned and well-researched findings. This tendency has changed markedly since the publication of its 14th Annual Activity Report, covering the period 2000 to 2001. The Commission now refers to UN treaties and interpretations thereof, such as General Comments of the Committee on Economic, Social and Cultural Rights,[164] and General Comments and case-law of the Human Rights Committee.[165] It has also made numerous references to 'soft' law, for example in the form of the UN Basic Principles on the Independence of the Judiciary[166] and the Body of Principles for the Protection of All Persons under any Form of Detention or Imprisonment.[167] The Commission refers to regional human rights instruments and decisions rendered under these instruments. This includes the three main institutions operating in Europe and the Americas, the European Court of Human Rights,[168] the Inter-American Court of Human Rights,[169] and the Inter-American Commission of Human Rights.[170] The Commission also refers to authors. Examples are Eide,[171] on the issue of the distinction of the levels of protection and Franscioni, on the enforcement of international law domestically.[172] The Commission has also relied on and made reference to general principles of interpretation, as contained in the VCLT, to refute the reliance of states on national law as justification for non-compliance with international law.[173]

In the first inter-state communication it decided, the Commission went one step further by including international humanitarian law in the ambit of articles 60 and 61, on the strength of its principal embodiments, the four Geneva Conventions

[163] Communication 74/92, *Commission Nationale des Droits de l'Homme et des Libertés v Chad* (2000) AHRLR 66 (ACHPR 1995) (Ninth Annual Activity Report) (*Chad Mass Violations* case) para 21, where the African Charter is distinguished from eg the European Convention, the American Convention, and the ICCPR in not providing for derogation during emergencies.
[164] *Ogoniland* case (n 20 above) para 63.
[165] *Zimbabwean Political Violence* case (n 144 above) para 203.
[166] Communication 206/97, *Centre for Free Speech v Nigeria* (2000) AHRLR 250 (ACHPR 1999) (13th Annual Activity Report) para 13.   [167] *Malaolu* case (n 81 above) para 70.
[168] See eg the reliance on case-law in the *Ogoniland* case (n 20 above) para 57 (*X and Y v Netherlands*).
[169] See eg reliance on case-law in the *Ogoniland* case (n 20 above) para 57 (*Velásquez Rodríguez v Honduras*).   [170] See eg *Zambian Presidential Candidates* case (n 152 above) para 59.
[171] *Ogoniland* case (n 20 above) para 44.
[172] *Zambian Presidential Candidates* case (n 152 above) para 59.   [173] ibid.

and the two Optional Protocols thereto constituting 'general principles of law recognized by African states'.[174] The Commission remains clear that these norms are 'taken into consideration' to determine the case, but do not by themselves found the Commission's finding. The same is true for other non-human rights standards invoked in the determination of the issues in that case, such as the use of the UN Declaration on Principles of International Law concerning Friendly Relations and Cooperation among States.[175]

The Commission has paid little attention to the possibility of interpreting the reference to 'African practices' and 'legal precedents' in article 61 as allowing it to rely on the decisions of domestic African courts. While it may have been true at some stage that there is a serious shortage of case-law 'consistent with international norms', today there are numerous examples of progressive judicial interpretation of human rights on the continent.[176] In fact, there is some irony in the fact that in interpreting some of the distinctly 'African' features of the Charter, as in the *Ogoniland* case, the Commission only relied on non-African sources. Similar criticism may be levelled at the Commission's meagre reliance on African academic writing.

7.4 Doctrine of Implied Rights

One of the Commission's boldest moves has been the acceptance of the doctrine of 'implied rights' (or 'unenumerated rights'),[177] which entails that explicitly guaranteed rights in a legal text by necessary implication may 'imply' the existence of rights not explicitly guaranteed in that text. The doctrine gives concrete manifestation to the notion that rights are indivisible, in as much as one right may invoke another (previously invisible) right. Its potentially far-reaching implications derive from the underlying acceptance that the textualization of ('positive law') rights does not deny the continued existence of non-textual ('natural law') rights.

In the *Ogoniland* case,[178] the Commission held that the rights to shelter or housing, and the right to food, are implicit in the Charter. In this respect, the communication alleged that the Nigerian government destroyed houses and prevented people from rebuilding ruined houses. The Commission found that the 'combined effect' of three 'corollary' rights (the right to property, to health, and to the protection of the family) is to constitute the right to shelter or housing.[179] When these rights are, in combination, 'adversely affected', the right to shelter or housing is violated.

---

[174] *Congo* case (n 88 above) para 70, relying on the wording in art 61, taken over from the ICJ Statute, art 38(1)(c).

[175] *Congo* case, para 68. Art 23 guarantees the 'right to national and international peace', as is governed by the principles of 'solidarity and friendly relations' set out in the UN Charter and OAU Charter (AU Constitutive Act).

[176] G Bekker, 'The Social and Economic Rights Action Center and the Center for Economic and Social Rights/Nigeria' (2003) *JAL* 126, 132, who takes the Commission to task for not 'fruitfully' relying in the *Ogoniland* case on the South African Constitutional Court judgment of *Government of RSA v Grootboom and Others* (2000) 1 SA 46 (CC)); see also Ch 13 below.

[177] See the landmark case of *Griswold v Connecticut* 381 (US) 479 (1965) (*Griswold* case), in which the USA Supreme Court held that the unmentioned right to privacy was part of the 'penumbra' of the Ninth Amendment due process 'liberty' clause.   [178] n 20 above.

[179] ibid, para 60.

However, on the facts of the case, the violation related to shelter may be viewed as constituting essentially a violation of the right to property. The government was found in violation of its obligation to 'respect' and 'protect' the rights of persons not to have their houses (or shelters) 'wantonly destructed'.[180] The communication was also seemingly brought as a violation of article 14 of the Charter (the right to property). Caught in the fervour of progressive interpretation, the Commission went further by reading an implied right to privacy into the newly constituted right to shelter or housing, when it stated as follows: 'The right to shelter even goes further than a roof over one's head. It extends to embody the individual's right to be left alone and to live in peace—whether under a roof or not.'[181]

The communication further alleged that the Nigerian government destroyed food sources and allowed the destruction of food sources. According to the Commission, the right to food is 'inseparably linked' to the (right to) dignity, and 'therefore essential' for the enjoyment of other rights such as the right to life, health, development, education, work, and political participation.[182]

Most commentators have welcomed this approach,[183] which treats the Charter as a living document, allowing for its constant 'updating', thus underlining its adaptability and continuous relevance. Adopting a progressive interpretation of the Charter, the Commission enlarged the scope of substantive protection to the benefit of the individuals and groups concerned. The *Ogoniland* finding is also a concrete manifestation of the indivisibility of rights, showing the link between 'civil and political' and 'socio-economic' rights.

This approach was embraced despite the (implicit) arguments by state parties that international law is based on their consent, epitomized by the principle of *pacta sunt servanda*, and that the Commission's interpretation in the *Ogoniland* case goes beyond the ambit of the initial agreement (the African Charter), thereby allowing a quasi-judicial body to usurp 'legislative' powers, and to introduce uncertainty and unpredictability.[184] A counter-argument in response to this contention is that all treaties are living documents that need to be (re)interpreted continuously in the light of changing and contemporaneous circumstances.[185]

Perceptions matter, though, and the question must be asked if the Commission is not unnecessarily putting its legitimacy and many other interpretive gains at risk. No doubt, the burning of crops and destruction of houses in Ogoniland should have been earmarked as violations. However, it was not necessary to 'invent' new Charter rights to reach this result. To better insulate the system against challenges of illegitimate usurpation of power, the Commission should in future base its

---

[180] ibid.   [181] ibid, para 61.   [182] ibid, para 65.

[183] See eg P De Vos, 'A New Beginning? The Enforcement of Social, Economic and Cultural Rights under the African Charter on Human and Peoples' Rights' (2004) 8 *Law, Democracy and Development* 1, 24.

[184] See the dissenting opinions of Justices Black and Stewart in the *Griswold* case (n 177 above) 507, 527.

[185] This is the approach adopted by the European Court of Human Rights, see eg *Selmouni v France* (2000) 29 EHRR 403 (28 July 1999), para 101; and *Stafford v UK* (2002) 35 EHRR 32 (28 May 2002).

finding on an expansive interpretation of a specified right that is already provided for in the Charter, unless the required or desired meaning cannot be located in the scope of that right. In other words, the quest for absent (but 'implied') rights should only be embarked upon if a lacuna in the existing rights framework has in fact been established. In the *Ogoniland* case, this was not the case. The Commission could have arrived at the same result by engaging in an expansive interpretation of the right to property, in terms of which possession and control would be considered to be included within the ambit of 'property'. As far as the finding on the right to food is concerned, a number of explicit Charter rights were in any event found to have been violated, 'but also' the right to food.[186] The leap into 'implied rights' was, strictly speaking, superfluous.

Still, the *Ogoniland* case provides a useful precedent on which reliance should be placed if and when circumstances so require.[187] So far, the Commission has not found it necessary to rely on the doctrine in any subsequent case.

7.5 Limitation of Rights

Rights do not apply absolutely, but may be restricted in terms of legitimate 'limitations'. Such limitations are present in other regional human rights instruments such as the Council of Europe's Convention for the Protection of Human Rights and Fundamental Freedoms (European Convention), which for example provides that freedom of expression may be justifiably limited by 'law' that is 'necessary in a democratic society' to serve certain circumscribed interests such as 'the protection of health or morals' and 'the reputation or rights of others'.[188]

There are three types of limitations in the Charter: right-specific 'claw-back' clauses, right-specific norm-based limitations reminiscent of the European Convention, and a general limitations clause (article 27(2)). Initial disquiet about 'claw-back' provisions centred around the first of these categories.

Rights that are limited by 'claw-back' clauses are the right to liberty and security,[189] freedom of conscience,[190] the right to freedom of expression,[191] freedom of association,[192] and freedom of movement.[193] 'Claw-back' clauses take the form of formulations such as 'for reasons . . . previously laid down by law',[194] 'subject to law and order',[195] 'within the law',[196] and 'provided he abides by the law'.[197] The inclusion of these provisions, evoking the fear that the Charter guarantees would be equated with domestic law, without requiring any further enquiry, was one of the major reasons for derision and despair expressed by textual analysts of

---

[186] *Ogoniland* case (n 20 above) para 64.

[187] The right to privacy, seemingly deliberately omitted from the Charter, may arguably be 'implied' by the cumulative existence of the right to respect for life and 'the integrity' of a person (art 4); respect for dignity (art 5); and the right 'to liberty' of the person (art 6).

[188] European Convention, art 10(2).   [189] African Charter, art 6.   [190] ibid, art 8.

[191] ibid, art 9.   [192] ibid, art 10.   [193] ibid, art 12.   [194] ibid, art 6.

[195] ibid, art 8.   [196] ibid, art 9.   [197] ibid, arts 10(1) and 12(1).

the Charter.[198] However, in the absence of a definition of 'law', the Commission interpreted that term more broadly than merely meaning 'national legislation'.[199] Relying on articles 60 and 61 of the Charter, the Commission adopted a restrictive interpretation of the reach of claw-back clauses,[200] requiring that limitations conform to 'international human rights standards'.[201] An example of this approach follows: According to article 12(4) of the Charter, the expulsion of non-nationals may only take place 'by virtue of a decision taken in accordance with the law'. The expulsion of Burundian refugees from Rwanda in 1989 was found to violate this provision.[202] The Commission interpreted the phrase 'in accordance with law' as including international law on the subject, which prohibits the expulsion of refugees who would be subjected to persecution in their country of nationality.[203]

Requiring that the limiting 'law' must serve some stipulated objective, the second category ('norm-based limitations') does not allow states and the Commission the same boundless discretion. The right to freedom of movement to leave one's country may for example only be subject to law aimed at protecting 'national security, law and order, public health or morality'.[204] Other justificatory grounds for restricting rights are 'national security, health, ethics and rights and freedoms of others'.[205] The usefulness of these norm-based limitations is limited by their apparent haphazard inclusion in respect of some rights and not others, and by the variable standard of review (with 'necessity' being required in one provision, and not in others).

Treating them as 'claw-back' clauses, the Commission has not paid much heed to the norm-based nature of these restrictions. In *Amnesty International v Zambia*,[206] for example, the Zambian government in 1994 deported two leading politicians after serving deportation orders on them, stating that their continued

[198] E Bondzie-Simpson, 'A Critique of the African Charter on Human and Peoples' Rights' (1988) 31 *Howard L J* 643, 661; R Gittleman, 'The Banjul Charter on Human and Peoples' Rights: A Legal Analysis' in CE Welch and RE Meltzer (eds), *Human Rights and Development in Africa* (Albany, NY: State University of New York Press, 1984) 152, 158–9.

[199] See eg *Nigerian Media* case (n 94 above) para 66: 'According to Article 9(2) of the Charter, dissemination of opinions may be restricted by law. This does not mean that national law can set aside the right to express and disseminate one's opinions; this would make the protection of the right to express one's opinion ineffective. To allow national law to have precedent over the international law of the Charter would defeat the purpose of the rights and freedoms enshrined in the Charter. International human rights standards must always prevail over contradictory national law. Any limitation on the rights of the Charter must be in conformity with the provisions of the Charter.'

[200] *Banda* case (n 57 above) para 50.

[201] Communication 101/93, *Civil Liberties Organisation (in respect of Bar Association) v Nigeria* (2000) AHRLR 186 (ACHPR 1995) (Eighth Annual Activity Report) para 15.

[202] See Communications 27/89, 46/90, 49/90, 99/93 (joined), *Organisation Mondiale Contre la Torture and Others v Rwanda* (2000) AHRLR 282 (ACHPR 1996) (Tenth Annual Activity Report) (*Rwandan Mass Violations* case).

[203] The Commission observed as follows: 'This provision should be read as including a general protection of all those who are subject to persecution, that they may seek refuge in another state. Article ibid 12(4) prohibits the arbitrary expulsion of such persons from the country of asylum'.

[204] African Charter, art 12(2).   [205] ibid, art 11; see also art 8.

[206] *Banda* case (n 57 above).

presence in Zambia would likely 'be a danger to peace and good order in Zambia'. The complainants alleged, amongst other things, that their right to 'leave any country... and to return to this country' had been infringed.[207] The government invoked the limitation clause contained in the same provision, to the effect that the right may be subject to restrictions 'provided for by law for the protection of national security, law and order, public health and morality'. Rejecting the contention that the mere fact of a deportation order is sufficient to meet this standard, the Commission observed as follows: 'The Commission is of the view that the "claw-back" clauses must not be interpreted against the Charter. Recourse to them should not be used as a means of giving credence to violations of the express provisions of the Charter'.[208]

It is now accepted that all rights in the Charter may justifiably be limited in terms of article 27(2), which reads as follows: 'The rights and freedoms of each individual shall be exercised with due regard to the rights of others, collective security, morality and common interest'. Once the complainant has established that there is a prima facie violation of a right,[209] the respondent state may argue that the right has been legitimately encroached upon by 'law', by providing evidence that the encroachment serves one of the purposes set out in article 27(2).[210] The Commission has repeatedly remarked that the 'only legitimate reasons for limitations to the rights and freedoms of the African Charter', are found in article 27(2).[211]

The limitation must take the form of 'law' which does not 'apply specifically to one individual or legal personality', as illustrated in the following case: The Nigerian military government in 1994 issued three decrees proscribing *The Concord, The Guardian,* and *Punch* newspapers, each by name.[212] The complainants argued that these decrees violate article 9(2) of the Charter, amongst other provisions. In terms of this provision, every individual has the right to freedom of expression 'within the law'. The government argued that the decrees constituted 'law', as that term refers to the current Nigerian law and not to constitutional or international standards, and argued that the decrees were justified by special circumstances. The Commission accepted that the decrees constituted 'law', but remarked that legal regulation targeting 'one individual or legal personality raise the serious danger of discrimination'.[213] This reasoning seems to introduce a requirement that a limitation must take the form of 'law' of 'general application'.[214]

---

[207] African Charter, art 12(2).   [208] Para 50.

[209] See eg *Mauritanian Political Parties* case (n 104 above) para 80 ('closely linked' freedom of expression and right to association invoked together).

[210] Once the prima-facie violation (or 'limitation') has been established, the onus to justify the limitation falls to the respondent state (see eg *Nigerian Media* case (n 94 above) para 77 ('The government did not offer any explanation...')).

[211] *Nigerian Media* case (n 94 above) para 68; *Prince* case (n 130 above) para 43 (see, however, the unsubstantiated conclusion in the latter case that the limitation (criminalization of cannabis) is legitimately within the 'spirit' of art 27(2) 'cum' art 8).

[212] See eg The Punch Newspapers (Proscription and Prohibition from Circulation) Decree No 7 of 1994.   [213] Para 44. See also the *Prince* case (n 130 above) para 44.

[214] See eg South African Constitution of 1996, s 36(1).

After satisfying itself that a limitation constitutes 'law of general application', the Commission applies a proportionality test, in terms of which it weighs the impact, nature and extent of the limitation against the legitimate state interest serving a particular goal. The 'evil' of a limitation can only be outweighed by legitimate state interests that are 'strictly proportionate with and absolutely necessary for the advantages which are to be obtained'.[215] Even if a limitation is legitimate, it may not totally obliterate the right and render it illusory.[216] When there is more than one way of achieving an objective, the less invasive route has to be followed.[217]

In assessing what is in line with 'morality' and what constitutes the 'common interest', questions may arise about the weight that should be accorded to public opinion on a particular matter. Justifying constitutional amendments restricting eligibility for the office of president to persons whose parents were both Zambians, the Zambian government claimed that the amendments were in line with the 'popular will'.[218] Not commenting on the basis of this claim (namely, the recommendations of a Commission of Inquiry relied upon by Parliament), the Commission held that the justification of a limitation 'cannot be derived *solely* from the popular will, as this cannot be used to limit the responsibilities of the state in terms of the Charter'.[219] The ambiguity of according 'some' weight to public opinion, while simultaneously excluding its use categorically, is likely to persist as the Commission negotiates the tension between protecting minority interests from being burnt at the stake of populism, and retaining popular legitimacy. Failing to accommodate an exemption for Rastafarian users of cannabis on the basis that the values keeping 'the whole nation together' outweigh that of the adherents of a 'restricted practice of Rastafari culture',[220] the Commission in the *Prince* case unnecessarily posited the majority against a politically powerless minority. The matter may just as well have been framed as one involving tolerance and respect of diversity, which is certainly (also) a value—and arguably a majority value—that holds together the South African nation.

These tensions relate to the principle of subsidiarity, which requires that 'decisions should always be taken at the closest level to the citizen at which they can be taken effectively'.[221] However, this does not imply that the 'responsibility for matters dealing with human rights should remain at the national level', because subsidiarity is not a 'one-way street'.[222] Subsidiarity underlies the development by the

---

[215] *Malaolu* case (n 81 above) para 69; *Prince* case (n 130 above) para 43.

[216] *Malaolu* case (n 81 above) para 70; *Nigerian Media* case (n 94 above) para 65 ('No situation justifies the wholesale violation of human rights').

[217] *Mauritanian Political Parties* case (n 104 above) para 82 (the respondent state had a 'whole gamut of sanctions' short of dissolving the political party to which it could have resorted); and the *Nigerian Media* case (n 94 above) para 75 (a libel action is a more appropriate measure to deal with criticism than 'the seizure of a whole edition' of a magazine containing criticism of a head of state).

[218] *Zambian Presidential Candidates* case (n 152 above) para 69.

[219] ibid, para 70 (emphasis added).   [220] *Prince* case (n 130 above) para 48.

[221] P Alston and JHH Weler, 'An "Ever Closer Union" in Need of a Human Rights Policy: The European Union and Human Rights' in P Alston (ed), *The EU and Human Rights* (Oxford: Oxford University Press, 1999) 3, 27.   [222] ibid.

European Court of Human Rights of the 'margin of appreciation' doctrine, allowing states a 'margin' to determine issues that national institutions are better placed
to 'appreciate', such as the extent to which freedom of speech may be restricted to
protect public morals,[223] or whether the right to stand for political office may be
limited by national law disqualifying holders of certain government positions from
being candidates in a general election.[224] The doctrine finds application mostly in
matters calling for a clear value judgement on the part of national authorities. The
inconsistency in its application has given rise to calls that its area of application be
more clearly delineated. Detractors of this doctrine argue that its open-endedness
and its deference to context undermine the process of legal harmonization and
the principle of universality. Proponents argue that any text requires flexibility in
application, and that some deference to national authorities is required to uphold
the value of pluralism as one of the central virtues of liberal democracies.[225] Especially
in a continent with a religion-based cleavage as pronounced as that of Africa, com-
pounded by numerous other cultural variances, some judicial deference is called for
to respect plurality. However, its scope must be delineated to avoid using it as a
smokescreen for undemocratic and repressive practices.

One of Africa's leading 'liberal democracies', South Africa, invoked this doctrine
in the single case submitted against it. The question in this matter, *Prince v South
Africa*,[226] was whether the state should accommodate the bona fide use of cannabis
as an essential part of the religious practice by adherents to the Rastafari faith.
Prince's case was not aimed at the decriminalization of the use of cannabis. Rather,
the crux of the complainant's argument was that the administrative burden of
implementing a circumscribed exemption was a necessary consequence of his right
to freedom of religion. By deciding that the criminalization of the use of cannabis
is a legitimate limitation of the complainant's rights, and by not investigating the
reasonableness of the state's rejection of a tailor-made exemption, the Commission
implicitly deferred to the determination by national authorities on the question of
'reasonable accommodation'.

Although it did not (expressly) base its finding on the 'margin of appreciation',
the Commission did make remarks in passing as to its potential application in an
African context. It accepted that the principle of subsidiarity and the doctrine of
'margin of appreciation' underlie the Charter system, as evidenced in the fact that
states are primarily responsible for protecting the Charter rights.[227] What the African
Commission did not approve of, though, was a 'restrictive reading of these doctrines, like that of the respondent state, which advocates for the hands-off approach
by the African Commission on the mere assertion that its domestic procedures

---

[223] *Handyside v United Kingdom* ECHR Series A No 24 (7 December 1976) paras 48, 49.
[224] *Gitonas v Greece* (1998) 26 EHRR 691, (1 July 1999) para 39.
[225] Y Arakai-Takahashi, *The Margin of Appreciation Doctrine and the Principle of Proportionality in the Jurisprudence of the ECHR* (Antwerp: Intersentia, 2002) 249.   [226] *Prince* case (n 130 above).
[227] *Prince* case (n 130 above) para 51 (the state has 'direct and continuous knowledge of its society, its needs, resources, economic and political situation, legal practices, and the fine balance that needs to be struck between the competing and sometimes conflicting forces that shape its society').

meet more than the minimum requirements of the African Charter'.[228] These remarks emphasize that reliance on the 'margin of appreciation' does not preclude an assessment by the Commission of the reasonableness of the limitation of rights. In making that determination, the Commission applied its general approach to the limitation of rights under the Charter.

7.6 Finding on the Merits

The findings of the Commission, as 'measures taken within the provisions of the present *Chapter*' (Chapter III of the African Charter, dealing with protective functions), must remain confidential until the OAU/AU Assembly 'shall otherwise decide'.[229] Although authorization for publication is only required for the Commission's protective activities (its complaints procedure and measures taken under article 46, which falls in the same chapter), some confusion and controversy have arisen about this aspect,[230] in part due to the replacement of the word 'Chapter' (in article 59(1)) in some web-based and printed texts of the Charter with the word 'Charter'.[231]

The great majority of decisions on the merits of cases found a violation of at least one Charter provision. The Commission's decisions end in findings that the African Charter, and not national constitutions or legislation, was violated. In terms of style, the Commission's jurisprudence has come a long way since 1994 when exceedingly sparse 'details' of communications were first included in its Seventh Annual Activity Report.[232] On that occasion, the final decision was provided in no more than two sentences; or as a brief, one-line decision on the basis of a civil law-style preamble ('recalling' and 'considering' certain provisions), after which the conclusion followed. Some of the Commission's decisions date back to 1988, so for about six years the Commission did not approach the Assembly to obtain authorization under article 59 of the Charter to publish its decisions.

The reasons for the Commission's hesitation may be twofold. Partly, the Commission's omission of communications from its initial activity reports may reflect an attempt to allow the communications procedure to establish itself outside the leaders' gaze. With only two of the first 52 decided cases culminating in a finding that the respondent-states had violated the Charter,[233] the Commission may have

---

[228] *Prince* case (n 130 above) para 53.   [229] African Charter, art 59(1) (emphasis added).
[230] See Ch 3 above.
[231] See eg the AU's web-site (http://www.africa-union.org/root/au/Documents/Treaties/Text/Banjul%20Charter.pdf) (31 January 2007); Murray and Evans (n 52 above) 16; C Heyns (ed), *Human Rights Law in Africa 1996* (The Hague: Kluwer Law International, 1996) 15. See also W Benedek, 'The 9th Session of the African Commission on Human and Peoples' Rights' (1993) 12 *HRLJ* 216, 217 n 5, who traces the confusion to a 'printing error' in a publication of the UN Centre for Human Rights. The correct position is set out on the Commission's web-site (<http://www.achpr.org/english/_info/charter_en.html>) (31 January 2007).
[232] In 1993, the Sixth Annual Activity Report noted that 'the details of the...communications are contained in a *confidential* annex', in accordance with art 59 of the Charter (para 29) (emphasis added).
[233] These are the cases included in the Seventh Annual Activity Report: they were mostly instituted against non-state parties, or were declared inadmissible for a variety of other reasons.

been shielding itself from the embarrassing perception of inertia and irrelevance. In any event, the Commission had no choice but to include the two cases in which violations had been found, as they both contained findings of 'serious or massive' violations and needed to be referred to the Assembly. It is uncertain when these two decisions were taken. It seems likely, though, that the decision relating to Orton and Vera Chirwa may have been taken already in 1992.[234] It has been suggested that the 'unfortunate outcome' of the *Chirwa* case had the consequence of ensuring that from then on, the Commission 'would pursue communications about individuals with more dispatch and an enhanced sense of urgency'.[235] However, the delay to include the *Chirwa* case in the Activity Report shows that resistance against publicity continued to be a constraining factor.

Over the years, the Commission's findings became longer and its reasoning more elaborate. Generally, the common law style of formulating a judgment is followed.[236] This development, which is part of a trend towards increased judicialization of the Commission's complaints procedure, has been brought about by Commissioners who were prepared to articulate reasons more clearly, by better secretarial support, and through the improved contribution of pleadings by the parties, which stimulated more rigorous analysis. The greater and increasingly critical engagement of states also had the salutary consequence of more elaborate and closely reasoned decisions by the Commission. Another by-product of the closer attention to judicial reasoning, and the display of a greater maturity among the Commissioners, is the first articulation of a dissenting opinion by one of the Commissioners.[237]

There is some indication of a balance in the Commission's findings being upset in favour of states, though. In a recent case against Zimbabwe[238]—a state which has a tradition of challenging Commission findings—the Commission found that the state did not fail in its positive obligation to protect its nationals against violations by non-state actors. Despite finding that violations had occurred through violence by non-state actors, and that not all of these had been investigated by the Zimbabwean state, the Commission held that the measures taken by the state were sufficient to meet the 'due diligence' test. At the same time the Commission found that Clemency Order 1 of 2000, which granted pardon to everyone open to criminal prosecution for any politically-motivated crime committed in the relevant

[234] Final Communiqué of the 12th session of the Commission, 21 October 1992, para 18: 'The Commission learnt with consternation of the death of Mr Orton Chirwa whilst in detention together with his wife for their political beliefs. The Commission recalls that this regrettable incident occurred whilst it had been seized with this case and one of its members was carrying out on-the-spot investigations'. See n 147 above.

[235] CE Welch, *Protecting Human Rights in Africa: Strategies and Roles of Non-governmental Organizations* (Philadelphia: University of Pennsylvania Press, 1995) 161.

[236] See all the cases decided on the merits in eg the 17th to 20th Activity Reports.

[237] *Mauritanian Dispossession* case (n 87 above), dissenting opinion of Commissioner El Hassan (disagreeing with the finding of a violation, based, amongst other things, on his interpretation of the original documentation, in Arabic, of which he is a mother-tongue speaker).

[238] *Zimbabwean Political Violence* case (n 144 above).

period, constituted a violation of the Charter. Because the Order 'did not only prevent the victims from seeking redress, but also encouraged impunity', it violated articles 1 and 7(1) of the Charter.[239] However, in my view the Commission should not have treated the Order as a separate issue. The very basis of the finding that the Order violates the Charter indicates that the state did not comply with its 'due diligence' obligation to protect the rights of its nationals. Had the Order been considered together with the other factors, it should have been clear that by 'encouraging impunity', the state allowed human rights violations to escalate and, in fact, created the climate for subsequent lawlessness. The Commission also placed selective reliance on the fact-finding mission to Zimbabwe. While the Commission's finding that the state cannot be held accountable for the actions of 'non-state actors' is bolstered by the inability of the mission to conclude that there was 'an orchestrated policy' in this regard,[240] the finding overlooks the 'ruling' in the Zimbabwe mission report that the government 'cannot wash its hands from responsibility of all these happenings', and that it 'did not act soon enough and firmly enough against those guilty of gross criminal acts', and that it failed 'at critical moments' to uphold the rule of law.[241]

8 Remedies

Another consequence of the Charter's ambiguity about individual complaints and its preoccupation with 'serious or massive' violations is its silence on remedies for violations. This caused the Commission, especially in its initial practice, to make findings of violations without addressing the issue of an appropriate remedy.[242] In cases where the Commission found 'serious or massive violations', the absence of a remedy in most cases may have been justified in light of the Assembly's anticipated 'request to undertake an in-depth study'.[243] When it became clear that the Assembly was not exercising its article 58 mandate, the Commission's findings omitted explicit and implicit reference to article 58.[244]

The initial thinking apparently was that a remedial order in individual communications lay outside the mandate of the Commission, and had to be addressed— if at all—at the political level, by the Assembly. This approach, which assumes that the state ultimately retains discretion over the exact manner in which the violation

---

[239] ibid, para 215.
[240] Executive Summary of the Report of the Fact-Finding Mission to Zimbabwe 24–8 June 2002, 17th Activity Report, Annex II (Zimbabwe Mission Report) para 4, and *Zimbabwean Political Violence* case, para 163.   [241] Zimbabwe Mission Report (n 240 above) para 5.
[242] See the *Banda* case (n 57 above), in which the Commission in 1995 found Malawi in violation of a number of Charter provisions, but omitted any reference to a remedy. Examples of later instances where the Commission found violations of the Charter, but left the issue of an appropriate remedy totally open, are the *Huri-Laws* case (n 156 above) and *Forum of Conscience v Sierra Leone* (n 131 above).
[243] African Charter, art 58(2); see eg *Chad Mass Violations* case (n 163 above) paras 27 and 28; and *Zairian Mass Violations* case (n 99 above) para 49. Note, however, the detailed remedial 'order' in the *Mauritanian Widows* case (n 21 above) paras 144–9, where a finding of 'grave or massive violations' was made (para 143).   [244] See eg the *Ogoniland* case (n 20 above) para 70.

should be corrected, allows states too much leeway. A holistic reading of the Charter requires that violations should be rectified. A domestic remedy in response to a violation is one of the 'other measures' through which a state must 'give effect' to the Charter. It is the role of the Commission to assist states in this process by recommending a clearly specified remedy. To deny this interpretation would be to render the communications procedure an illusory technicality and would undermine its practical effectiveness.

Two further approaches to remedies have subsequently crystallized: open-ended remedies, and relatively clear and targeted remedies. Although a general trend towards greater clarity may be discerned as the Commission grew in stature and responded to a more favourable political climate, inconsistencies still prevail. This inconsistent practice not only reveals an unprincipled approach, but also impedes meaningful follow-up ensuring the implementation of decisions.

The Commission issues an 'open-ended' remedy when it for example urges the respondent state 'to bring its laws in conformity with the provisions of the African Charter'.[245] In other communications, the Commission merely stated that the state should 'adopt measures in conformity with' its decision.[246] Such remedies are unhelpful to both the state and the complainant, since the state does not know exactly what it is required to do, and the complainant does not know what he or she is entitled to.

The 'relatively clear and targeted' remedies may be grouped into three categories. (i) Some remedies are directed at executive conduct, and prescribe administrative measures to correct violations. An example is a recommendation that a government charges or releases detainees.[247] (ii) Other remedies pertain to legislative or other enactments, and may for example require the annulment of proclamations or decrees.[248] (iii) Recommendations that compensation be paid to the victim of a violation make up the third category.[249] The amount of compensation is never prescribed, leaving it either to the domestic legal system to follow the usual quantifying methods,[250] or to a commission specifically established for that purpose.[251] Examples of very detailed and specifically-targeted remedies are found in the *Ogoniland*[252] and *Mauritanian Widows* cases.[253]

---

[245] *Malaolu* case (n 81 above) para 93.

[246] *Rwandan Mass Violations* case (n 202 above) para 37.

[247] See eg Communication 153/96, *Constitutional Rights Project v Nigeria (II)* (2000) AHRLR 248 (ACHPR 1999) (13th Annual Activity Report) para 22.

[248] See eg Communication 251/2002, *Lawyers for Human Rights v Swaziland*, 18th Activity Report, Annex III (the Commission recommended that the Proclamation of 1973 and Decree 3 of 2001 be 'brought into conformity with the provisions of the African Charter').

[249] For a rare case in which this was part of the remedial order, see Communication 56/91 *Mekongo v Cameroon* (2000) AHRLR 56 (ACHPR 1995) (Eighth Annual Activity Report).

[250] As above, para 2: 'Being unable to determine the amount of damages, the Commission recommends that the quantum should be determined under the law of Cameroon'.

[251] See eg *Sierra Leonean Refugee* case (n 81 above), where the Commission recommended that a 'Joint Commission' of the Sierra Leonean and Guinea governments be established 'to assess the losses by various victims with a view to compensate the victims'.

[252] n 20 above, paras 71 and 72.   [253] n 21 above, paras 144–9.

9 Implementation of and Follow-up on Decisions

The ambition of the Charter and the Commission should be, and to some extent is stated to be,[254] to impact positively on the lives of Africans living in state parties. In respect of communications, the question of overriding importance is: have the findings of violations made any difference to the complainants? The energy devoted towards securing an effective African human rights system amounts to nothing if the system does not make a difference to nationals and others living in member states. A distinction should be drawn between the indirect and direct 'impact' (or 'effect') of the Charter. Its indirect impact of incrementally influencing law, policy, and practice is very difficult to assess.[255] Compliance by states with decisions of the Commission is an example of direct impact. Because it is to some extent clearly demonstrable, direct impact may be easier to assess, but this is by no means a simple exercise.[256]

Following-up on decisions is a means of assessing direct impact. However, no systematic follow-up exists at the level of the Secretariat or the Commission to find out whether states that have been ordered to remedy violations had in fact complied. When there is no empirical evidence of non-compliance, no consequences arise from a state's (sometimes even blatant) disregard for a decision taken and remedy 'ordered' by the Commission.

An empirical study of 44 communications in which the Commission found violations of the Charter between 1987 and mid-2003 reveals that the assumption is only partly correct that states fail to comply with the Commission's decisions.[257] Non-compliance seems to be the rule when one juxtaposes instances of 'full compliance' (recorded in six cases, or 14 per cent) against 'non-compliance' (recorded in 13 cases, or 30 per cent). However, in a significant number of cases (14 cases, or 32 per cent), 'partial' compliance was recorded, and 'situational' compliance, occasioned by a far-reaching change in circumstances, occurred in seven (or 16 per cent) of the cases. The study concludes that the most important variables responsible for compliance are political, rather than legal. 'Legal' factors, such as the nature of the

---

[254] African Charter, Preamble (reaffirming their pledge 'to achieve a better life for the peoples of Africa').

[255] See eg LC Keith, 'The United Nations International Covenant on Civil and Political Rights: Does it Make a Difference in Human Rights Behavior?' (1999) 36 *J Peace Research* 95; and OA Hathaway, 'Do Human Rights Treaties Make a Difference?' (2002) 112 *Yale L J* 1935.

[256] Assessing compliance depends on accurate fact-finding, which is rendered difficult by, amongst other factors, insufficient records, subjectivity, and the difficulties in accessing complainants and state representatives.

[257] L Louw, 'An Analysis of State Compliance with the Recommendations of the African Commission on Human and Peoples' Rights' unpublished LLD thesis, University of Pretoria, January 2005; and F Viljoen and L Louw, 'State Compliance with the Recommendations of the African Commission on Human and Peoples' Rights, 1993–2004' (2007) 101 *AJIL* 1. 'Full' compliance denotes the implementation of all aspects of the remedy indicated; 'non-compliance' is used if a state did not implement any of the recommendations; 'partial' compliance indicates that a state implemented some but not all elements of the recommended remedy; and 'situational' compliance came about as a result of changed circumstances and not from a government's response as such.

right concerned and the extent of legal reasoning in a decision, were not found to be predictive of compliance. Factors that were found to be most significant are the type of government in place and the level of stability within respondent states; and the involvement of NGOs in the case and in its follow-up. Because the political engagement in all of these decisions was equally limited, it was not possible to factor that aspect into the equation. However, as the primary regional political organ responsible for enforcing decisions regarding AU members, the AU (Assembly and Executive Council) has a crucial role to play in bringing pressure to bear on violator-states. As far as the Commission's decisions are concerned, the issue of their binding authority largely becomes a red herring, because compliance ultimately depends on political factors, including the possible application of sanctions for non-compliance to be enforced by the Assembly.[258]

The reasons for the Commission's long-standing inaction in respect of following up its decisions are related to two interrelated issues: the authority of its decisions, and its competence to undertake follow-up enquiries. There is some debate about the binding nature of the Commission's decisions.[259] States may argue that they are not legally bound to comply with 'decisions', as they are not decisions at all but merely 'recommendations'. However, once these 'recommendations' have been adopted as 'decisions' by the AU Assembly, states should have difficulty arguing convincingly that they need not comply. Denying an obligation to comply with recommendations would also stand in stark contrast to the principal undertaking of states to give effect to the Charter and to guarantee its provisions.

Neither the African Charter, nor the Commission's Rules of Procedure explicitly require follow-up. Questions may therefore be raised regarding the Commission's institutional competence to undertake follow-up measures or actions. A narrow reading of the word 'consider' in article 55 of the Charter would suggest that it does not have such competence. To 'consider'—such an argument would go—is to 'think carefully about' and to 'look attentively at', and not to 'implement' findings of communications.[260] In other words, the argument would be that the Charter does not mandate follow-up measures in respect of communications. Such an argument is reinforced by the complementarity between the African Commission and the Assembly. The drafting history of the Charter also indicates that the Commission is not to take decisions. The Commission's mandate is restricted to addressing reports that contain its conclusions and recommendations to the Assembly. It is for the Assembly to decide what needs to be done, in the sense of determining which action needs to be taken. However, the preferable view is that the Charter implicitly allows for, and in fact, requires, follow-up. Implicit in the concept 'consider' must be 'careful thoughts' and 'attention' given to the implementation of a decision. If implementation is not regarded as intrinsically part of the consideration

---

[258] See Ch 5.B.1 above.
[259] See eg F Viljoen and L Louw, 'The Status of Findings of the African Commission: From Moral Persuasion to Legal Obligation?' (2004) 48 *JAL* 1.   [260] *Concise Oxford Dictionary.*

of a decision, the following question arises: Why does the Commission consider communications in the first place, if it remains unconcerned about their implementation and effect? Adopting views is not a purposeless, formulaic exercise. Using a teleological approach, the aim of the communications procedure must be to grant relief (in the form of a remedy) to a complainant, or to change laws or practices. Follow-up is therefore integral to the process of individual communications, and making sense of the overarching duty of states to give effect to the rights in the Charter.[261] Because follow-up may be considered a form of investigation in the context of the communications procedure, the Commission's extensive competence to 'resort to any appropriate method of investigation'[262] also applies here. Furthermore, in terms of article 60, the Commission 'shall draw inspiration' from international human rights law. Drawing inspiration from the UN human rights treaty bodies that also deal with communications, and from the Inter-American human rights system, one observes a trend towards the use of institutionalized follow-up procedures.[263]

Despite these misgivings, the African Commission has shown a certain measure of concern about implementation and has started to engage in a limited follow-up of decisions, by utilizing the state reporting procedure, its own decisions, resolutions, promotional visits, and on-site missions.[264]

In theory at least, states submit reports at regular intervals. It follows that this provides an ideal opportunity for feedback about the implementation of findings on communications. Sometimes the Commission has inserted a condition into its recommendations to the violator-state, requiring the state to account, in its next periodic report, on its implementation of a decision.[265] When the state subsequently reports, the Commission reminds it of this obligation and asks for the required information. In this way a practice has evolved whereby Commissioners use the state reporting procedure to inquire about the implementation of decisions, even in the absence of a specific recommendation to the state to report on this issue.[266] This development suggests that the Commission considers non-compliance with its findings to be violations of the Charter.

In at least one instance, the Commission detached the requirement to provide information about the implementation of the state reporting procedure, when it

---

[261] African Charter, art 1.   [262] ibid, art 46.

[263] For example, initially the Human Rights Committee held that its role in the examination of communications comes to an end when it adopts a final decision, including a view on the merits of a case. By 1990, however, it had appointed a Special Rapporteur on the Follow-up of Views.

[264] At least in theory; see Communication 87/93, *Constitutional Rights Project (on behalf of Lekwot and Others) v Nigeria* (2000) AHRLR 183 (ACHPR 1995) (Eighth Annual Activity Report) (*Lekwot* case) para 16 (Commission deciding to 'bring the file to Nigeria for a planned mission in order to make sure that the violations have been repaired').

[265] *Zambian Presidential Candidates* case (n 152 above) para 76; and *Gambian Mental Health* case (n 33 above) para 85.

[266] As was done by Commissioner Johm in respect of the state reports of Mauritania, examined during the Commission's 31st session; see also objectives of the 'Report of the African Commission's Promotional Mission to Burkina Faso', 22 September–2 October 2001, DOC/OS(XXXIII)/324b/I.

recommended that the Swazi government inform it 'in writing within six months on the measures it has taken to implement' the remedies indicated.[267] Such an approach seems preferable, given the irregularity of state reporting. This decision, as well as the remedies ordered in the *Ogoniland* case,[268] implies a continuous monitoring role on the part of the Commission—something that the Commission has not yet done effectively.

Country-specific resolutions have also been used as a vehicle to encourage compliance with decisions. In response to Eritrea's failure to implement the finding in the *Eritrean Detention* case,[269] the Commission condemned the continued detention of the victims and called on the government to 'immediately free' the victims who 'have been arrested and detained without trial for many years'.[270] In this resolution, the Commission makes it clear that non-compliance with its finding and recommendations constitutes a breach of the state's obligations under the African Charter and the AU Constitutive Act.[271]

These developments culminated in the adoption by the Commission at its 40th session, in November 2006, of a 'Resolution on the Importance of the Implementation of the recommendations of the African Commission on Human and Peoples' Rights',[272] converting a previous 'discussion' document into clear normative guidance.[273] In this resolution, the Commission calls on states to 'respect without delay' its 'recommendations', and to indicate—within 90 days of being notified— the measures taken and 'obstacles' experienced in implementing them. The Commission further decided to attach an annex to future activity reports to the AU Executive Council, setting out the state of compliance with 'recommendations' by state parties. This is one of the most significant of the Commission's resolutions, and should form the basis of a much more rigorous future communications procedure. The new procedure also prepares the ground for the Commission to exercise

---

[267] Communication 251/2002, *Lawyers for Human Rights v Swaziland* (n 248 above) para 53.

[268] n 20 above, in which the Commission urged the government of Nigeria to keep it informed of the outcome of the work of the Ministry of the Environment addressing environmental issues, particularly in Ogoniland, and about the outcome of the Judicial Commission of Inquiry investigating human rights violations.

[269] n 17 above.

[270] Resolution on the Human Rights Situation in Eritrea, adopted at the Commission's 38th session, 21 November–5 December 2005, paras 1 and 4. (The resolution was contained in the 19th Activity Report submitted to the Executive Council. Apparently because Eritrea did not make use of the opportunity to respond, the resolution was omitted from the 20th Activity Report, in which the other resolutions were included to which state parties responded. This has the effect that this resolution has not (yet) been officially adopted by the AU Executive Council or Assembly.)

[271] ibid, para 2.

[272] Final Communiqué of the 40th session. See also the Executive Council's decision on the Commission's 21st Activity Report (AU Doc EX.CL/Dec.344(X)), in which this resolution was contained, calling on AU members to which the African Commission has made recommendations 'to work with the African Commission and other relevant national and organs of the African Union to ensure the effective implementation of these recommendations' (para 2(viii)).

[273] See the discussion document entitled 'Non-Compliance of State Parties to Adopted Recommendations of the African Commission: A Legal Approach', DOC/OS/50b(XXIV) (1998) (reprinted in Murray and Evans (n 52 above) 758).

its discretion of referring cases to the African Court in instances where states fail to comply with its recommendations within a stipulated period.[274]

B Inter-state Communications

As stated above, an amicable settlement is not a Charter-imposed requirement of the individual communications procedure. Neither is it a prerequisite for all inter-state communications. Two distinct possibilities for submitting inter-state communications are provided for: a conciliatory route,[275] requiring peaceful procedures to be exploited, and a non-conciliatory route of directly seizing the Commission,[276] to be followed when the chances of an amicable settlement are remote and need not be pursued.

In both instances, admissibility depends on three factors: a violation of the Charter must be alleged; local remedies must have been exhausted;[277] and information must be provided of any 'other procedure for the international investigation or international settlement to which the interested parties have resorted'.[278]

In the one inter-state communication decided so far,[279] the applicant state, the DRC, followed the non-conciliatory route. Against the background of an 'undeclared war' between the DRC and the respondent states prevailing at the time of submission, this was the most appropriate avenue as efforts to effect a reconciliation would neither have been 'effective' nor 'desirable'.[280] Although the applicant state invoked breaches of international humanitarian law, it linked these to violations of the Charter. With respect to an alleged siege of a hydroelectric dam, for example, the Commission found that this matter may 'be brought within the prohibition' of the relevant Hague Convention, but that by 'parity of reason' and in the light of articles 60 and 61, the respondent states are in violation of article 23 of the African Charter.[281]

---

[274] See Ch 11.E.1.2 below.   [275] African Charter, arts 47 and 48.   [276] ibid, art 49.

[277] ibid, art 50.   [278] Rules of Procedure, r 93(2)(c).

[279] Sometimes the dividing line between 'inter-state' and 'individual' communications becomes blurred, as in Communication 157/96, *Association pour la Sauvegarde de la Paix au Burundi v Kenya, Rwanda, Tanzania, Uganda, Zaire and Zambia* (2003) AHRLR 111 (ACHPR 2003) (17th Annual Activity Report) esp para 63, where the Commission observes as follows on the issue of *locus standi*: 'It would appear that the authors of the communication were in all respects representing the interests of the military regime of Burundi'. The fact that the Commission dealt with the communication as an 'individual communication' elicited the following criticism: 'If the Commission firmly concluded that ASP-Burundi, although formally an NGO, "represented" in all respects "the interests of the military regime of Burundi", then the logical conclusion ought to have been that it was Burundi directly that was the party instituting proceedings and not an under-cover NGO' (AD Olinga, 'The Embargo against Burundi before the African Commission on Human and Peoples' Rights, (Note on Communication 157/96, *Association pour la Sauvegarde de la Paix au Burundi v Kenya, Rwanda, Tanzania, Uganda, Zaire and Zambia*) (2005) 5 *AHRLJ* 424, 427). See also Communications 233/99, 234/99 (joined), *Interights (on behalf of Pan African Movement and Others) v Eritrea and Ethiopia* (2003) AHRLR 74 (ACHPR 2003) (16th Annual Activity Report).   [280] *Congo* case (n 88 above) para 61.

[281] ibid, para 84.

The other two prerequisites invited more interpretative difficulties. As far as domestic remedies are concerned, one of the issues is whether the applicant state, or the individuals concerned, is responsible for the exhaustion of such remedies. This question remained unanswered, as the Commission found that the issue of local remedies does not arise at all when the respondent state committed the violations in the territory of the applicant state.[282] Perhaps this conclusion was arrived at too glibly, as the possibility of redress by the individuals concerned was not raised. As for the issue of other international processes, it is not clear what legal value should be attached to the information that needs to be supplied. Although Uganda raised the argument that an inter-state complaint would be inadmissible if a similar procedure was pending before the ICJ at the time of its submission, the Commission did not pronounce on the issue.[283]

Having found the communication admissible, the Commission proceeded to a finding on the merits. The Commission's finding that the three respondent states had violated numerous Charter provisions, and its recommendation that these states abide by their obligations under international law, ring hollow in the light of their timing: although the matter was instituted in 1999, it was only 'resolved' in 2003, at a time when the armed forces of the respondent states had already withdrawn. The Commission's finding was only published in 2006.[284] The only recommendatory relief of significance in this case was that of 'reparations' to be paid by the respondent states for violations to individual rights.[285]

C On-site Protective and Fact-finding Missions

In addition to undertaking promotional visits, members of the Commission also undertake missions in response to specific allegations of human rights violations. These missions may be termed 'on-site investigative', 'protective', 'fact-finding', or 'high-level' missions.[286] The Commission has not yet clearly distinguished between the different types of missions, and is ambivalent about the aim of each of these. However, the following distinction seems to have guided the development of this procedure: (i) 'On-site investigative' or 'protective' missions were, at least initially,

---

[282] ibid, para 63.

[283] Uganda raised this matter, as the DRC had by the time of submitting the inter-state communication already submitted a case against Uganda to the ICJ. The likelihood of conflicting resolutions thus actually arose in this case, see Ch 11.H below.

[284] Although the decision was taken at the Commission's 33rd session, in 2003, it was—exceptionally—only contained in the 20th Activity Report, considered in mid-2006. The fact that the matter was pending before the ICJ, which took a decision on 19 December 2005, in all likelihood accounts for this delay.

[285] *Congo* case (n 88 above), concluding para, 'adequate reparations' are to be paid, 'for or on behalf of victims of the human rights by the armed forces . . . while the armed forces . . . were in effective control' and who 'suffered these violations'.

[286] See generally T Mutangi, 'Fact-Finding Missions or Omissions? A Critical Analysis of the African Commission on Human and Peoples' Rights' (2006) 12 *East African Jnl of Peace and Human Rights* 1.

undertaken to states against which a number of communications had been formally submitted. The legal basis of the Commission's mandate is found in article 46, which is located in the chapter dealing with 'protection', and allows the Commission to use 'any appropriate method of investigation'. The aim of these missions is to attempt amicable settlements and investigate the factual circumstances pertaining to communications submitted against the visited state. (ii) 'Fact-finding' and 'high-level' missions are undertaken to establish the veracity of allegations of a more general nature, independent of the prior submission of communications against the visited state.

The main reason why only a limited number of these missions have been undertaken is mainly that the consent of the state in question is required before such missions may be undertaken. For example, at its 16th session, towards the end of 1994, the Commission decided to send a protective mission to Zaire to investigate a number of communications.[287] This visit never took place for want of government consent. From 1990 to 1995 the Commission also attempted unsuccessfully to send an investigative mission to Rwanda to investigate cases pending before the Commission.[288] Initial enthusiasm for the use of this mechanism in this guise soon petered out.[289]

As was intimated above, the categorization of missions is problematic. Missions considered to be part of the first category—those to Senegal, Mauritania, Sudan, and Nigeria—are now analysed. As will be observed, the Commission downplayed the link to its communications procedure in these missions, thereby conflating the distinction drawn above.

The mission to Senegal, which was undertaken from 1 to 7 June 1996, dealt exclusively with the situation in the Casamance province of that country. It was undertaken following a communication received in 1992 by the Commission about clashes between the Senegalese army and Casamance rebels.[290] Having analysed the conflict in a historical context, the delegation recommended a number of steps to bring about 'constructive dialogue' between the Senegalese government and the Casamance separatists. However, the mission's status as a 'protective' mission (as defined above) is placed in doubt because neither the mission nor the mission's report reveals any connection to the two communications decided against Senegal.

A mission to Mauritania was undertaken from 19 to 27 June 1996. Although the Commission had received four communications prior to its visit to that country, no specific findings were made about these individual violations in the course of the Commission's report on its visit. Instead, the communications served as a basis for initiating an investigation into more systematic and pervasive violations

---

[287] *Zairian Mass Violations* case (n 99 above).

[288] *Rwandan Mass Violations* case (n 202 above).

[289] At its 19th session the Commission reaffirmed its decision to conduct missions to a number of states (Burundi, Mauritania, Nigeria, Rwanda, Senegal, and Sudan) in order to 'consider' communications brought against states which have already been declared admissible by the Commission (Ninth Annual Activity Report, para 20).

[290] See the country report, Annex VIII to the Tenth Annual Activity Report.

by the government of Mauritania. The communications relate to the massacre of black Mauritanians by the government, the torture of black Mauritanian prisoners, and the deportation and expulsion of black Mauritanians to Senegal and Mali. The Commission's mission investigated these allegations. In their concluding remarks the Commissioners deplored 'all the tragic events that have occurred in Mauritania and their consequences'.[291] The mission went further and analysed some of the systematic patterns of human rights violations, such as slavery and its remnants,[292] as well as the inferior position of women in Mauritanian society.[293] Although this mission may properly be described as a 'protective' mission, it poses questions about the relationship between the mission and the communications procedure.[294]

The first mission to Sudan was undertaken from 1 to 7 December 1996. In this instance,[295] the Commission's delegation[296] was given the opportunity to meet senior government officials[297] and even to visit prisons.[298] However, the Commission found these interviews less than helpful, and criticized government officials and even members of civil society for engaging in official propaganda. It is unfortunate that the report of the visit was not discussed publicly during the same session in which Sudan submitted its country report.[299] Although a subsequent decision against Sudan disclosed that the mission 'was able to verify on the ground elements of the four communications under consideration',[300] the Commission later on in the same decision concluded that the mission must be considered as part of its 'promotional activities' and that it did not form 'a part of the procedure of the communications'.[301]

---

[291] Para VI of the report, Annex IX to the Tenth Annual Activity Report.

[292] Despite the fact that slavery was formally abolished in 1981 (Ordinance 81–234 of 9 November 1981), many 'vestiges of slavery' are still prevailing in Mauritania (see para IV of the Commission report, Annex IX to the Tenth Annual Activity Report).

[293] The Commission found the promotion of women's rights to be 'deficient'. An example confirming this is the fact that no female was a member of the National Assembly or Senate.

[294] In the *Mauritanian Widows* case (n 21 above), the mission is described as a 'good-offices mission'; the Commission further reiterated that the decision is based on 'the written and oral declarations made before the Commission', as the mission 'did not gather any additional specific information on the alleged violations, except on the issue of slavery' (paras 86 and 87). In that case (para 134) and again in the *Mauritanian Dispossession* case (n 87 above), the Commission relied on the report to find that the vestiges of slavery still exist in Mauritania (para 29).

[295] 'Report of the Mission of Promotion and Protection of Human Rights in Sudan: 1–7 December 1996' (Report of the Secretariat). This 'report' is nothing more than a working draft, and is not the Commission's official mission report.

[296] The delegation consisted of Commissioners Dankwa, Kisanga, and Rezag-Bara, accompanied by the legal advisor of the Commission at the time (Essombé Edimo Joseph).

[297] Ranging from the Minister of Justice to spokespersons of the armed forces, the Attorney-General, the Chief of Police, and the Director of Prisons.

[298] In relation to allegations of 'ghost' prisons, the mission 'noted that the place specified was empty of any building' (*sic*). This rather ambiguous sentence seems to denote that the Commission had at least visited part of the prison.

[299] The Sudanese state report was examined at the 21st session, held in April 1997, in Nouakchott, Mauritania, and the report on the visit was considered at the 23rd session held in April 1998, in Banjul, The Gambia.   [300] *Amnesty International v Sudan* (n 39 above) para 26.

[301] ibid, para 46.

After many delays, a mission to Nigeria eventually took place from 7 to 14 March 1997.[302] The mission took place against the background of the nullification of the 1993 elections, the execution in 1995 of Ken Saro-Wiwa, a series of decrees which suspended the constitutional basis of the state, and a number of communications submitted to the Commission by Nigerian NGOs. The terms of reference of the mission were fourfold. They were aimed at gathering information about communications pending before the Commission and at finding amicable settlements to them; at visiting people in prison; at visiting Ogoniland to gather information about the dispute between the Ogonis and the oil companies; and at strengthening cooperation with Nigerian NGOs.

The mission managed to accomplish most of what it set out to do. However, the mission was criticized on a number of counts.[303] First, the mission's neutrality was compromised because it was hosted and accompanied by the Nigerian government and its officials. The mission was unable to meet with NGOs in the south (especially in Lagos). NGOs were not informed fully and in a timely way about its visit and the itinerary to be followed. The time allocated for the visit was too short to enable the members of the Commission to investigate the large number of communications pending against Nigeria. The mission was seen as counteracting the Nigerian government's refusal to allow two thematic UN rapporteurs to visit Nigeria.

The Commission's inability to finalize its report pursuant to the mission undertaken to Nigeria delayed the finalization of communications against Nigeria. For example: Communication 102/93, *Constitutional Rights Project and Another v Nigeria*, was received on 29 July 1993, and was finally decided only on 31 October 1998—a delay of five years and three months. This communication was first postponed awaiting the result of the mission to Nigeria, but thereafter pending the discussion (and adoption) of the mission report. This report was in fact never adopted, and the eventual decision on the merits does not make any reference whatsoever to the mission.

Although the Commission had in 2002 conducted a second mission to Sudan, followed by an extraordinary session, this report has not yet been published. In a resolution adopted at its 40th session in November 2006, the Commission urged the Sudanese government to 'acknowledge the 2004 Report of the African Commission Mission to Darfur and submit its response to the African Commission'.[304] This extended period of delay in making the mission findings public is clearly unacceptable.

'Fact-finding' missions (in the second category above) respond to allegations of a more general nature, for example the expulsion of sub-Saharan migrants by

---

[302] Pursuant to a resolution at the Commission's second extraordinary meeting in Kampala, in 1995, reiterated at its 20th session.

[303] 'Observations of the Nigerian Human Rights Community on the Mission of the African Commission on Human and Peoples' Rights to Nigeria in March 1997' (on file with author).

[304] AU Doc ACHPR/Res.102(XXXX)06, 'Resolution on the Situation in Darfur', adopted on 29 November 2006.

Morocco, in the context of African migration to Europe, and in response to human rights violations in Togo.[305]

Following 'widespread reports of human rights violations' arising from a constitutional referendum and parliamentary elections in 2000, a presidential election in 2002, and a programme of land reform, a mission to Zimbabwe took place in 2002. The report, of which only the 'executive summary' is contained in the Commission's 17th Annual Activity Report, concluded that human rights violations had occurred; nevertheless, the mission was unable to 'find definitively' that these violations were due to an 'orchestrated' government policy.[306] Steering clear of controversy, the mission observed that 'land reform has to be the prerogative of the government' and expressed the view that 'this policy matter' has been brought 'under the legal and constitutional system of the country'.[307] As has been noted previously, this report became the reason for the first-ever embargo on the Commission's Activity Report, causing it to be contained in the final version of the 17th Annual Activity Report together with the government's comments.[308]

Allowed the opportunity to respond, the government of Zimbabwe lodged a 28-page comment[309] in which it criticized the duration of the mission (four working days were too short to 'search for the truth'); its reach (the mission was restricted to Harare, the capital, and it met 'the same organizations who had made the initial complaints'); its failure to verify allegations; and its lack of 'specific detail'. The government also pointed out 'inaccuracies and inconsistencies' in the report. It conceded that it was given an opportunity to comment on the report after its adoption by the Commission at its 34th session, and prior to its being contained in the 17th Annual Activity Report, but objected to the fact that this was done only after the Commission had already adopted the report.[310] As for substantive issues, the Zimbabwean government devoted the largest part of its reply to providing a background to the 'land question in Zimbabwe', which it considers to be 'intricately related' to all the other allegations.[311] Its main response to the allegations of human rights violations seems to be to concede that 'violence and unsanctioned torture' took place between 2000 and 2002, but that the government was at the time of the mission 'thoroughly in charge of her people's affairs'.[312] Despite the concession just cited, the government claims to have investigated and 'brought to book' those responsible for assaults and injuries.[313] This statement is an example of a

---

[305] 'Fact-Finding Mission to the Sharawi Arab Democratic Republic', mission undertaken by Commissioner Rezag-Bara, 28 October–3 November 2005; report adopted at the Commission's 38th session; 'Fact-Finding Mission' to Togo (20th Activity Report, para 14).

[306] 'Executive Summary of the Report of the Fact-Finding Mission to Zimbabwe 24th to 28th June 2002' (17th Annual Activity Report, Annex II) (Zimbabwe Mission Report) para 3. The full version of the report has not been made public.   [307] Zimbabwe Mission Report (n 306 above) para 2.

[308] Ch 5 above.

[309] 'Comments by the Government of Zimbabwe on the Report of the Fact-Finding Mission' (17th Activity Report) Annex II (Zimbabwean Response).   [310] ibid, para 5.4.

[311] ibid, 10.1.   [312] ibid, para 9.3.

[313] ibid, para 9.3 (under the heading 'Torture at the Hands of State Agents').

government failing to provide sufficiently detailed information to make out a convincing case—one of its criticisms of the Commission's report.

Implementation and follow-up, highlighted in respect of individual communications, also need to be secured in respect of the recommendations in mission reports. Subsequently, during a public meeting at the Commission's 40th session, the Zimbabwean delegation indicated to what extent it had implemented the recommendations. Although it conceded that all recommendations had not (yet) been fully complied with, the government indicated that electoral laws were reformed in 2005, judicial reforms were launched, the Ombudsman Office reformed in 2006, and that two Bills (dealing with the interception of communication and regulating NGOs) had been withdrawn pursuant to the report.

Missions to state parties have highlighted the Commission's potential role in taking the initiative to visit a state in order to investigate problematic aspects pertaining to human rights protection and promotion. Initially clearly conceived under chapter 3 of the Charter, these types of missions have increasingly been dissociated from the Commission's protective mandate, and have been couched instead as part of its promotional activities. This tactical shift enabled the Commission to more readily obtain state consent, and to waive the strictures of confidentiality.

So far, this 'alternative system of reporting' has suffered from a number of disadvantages. Inadequate financial resources cause delays and allow brief visits only.[314] There has been no consistency in procedure—sometimes no reports were adopted after a visit (as in the case of the Nigerian mission). Finally, as in other areas of the Commission's work, there has been a great lack of publicity and of meaningful follow-up strategies. The integration of the findings of these visits in the finalization of communications has also been inconsistent.[315]

---

[314] The mission to Sudan was made possible by the Swedish International Development Agency (SIDA), through the Raoul Wallenberg Institute for Human Rights and Humanitarian Law, Sweden.

[315] See eg these rather confusing observations in respect of the *Mauritanian Widows* case (n 21 above) para 87: 'The mission was undertaken at the initiative of the Commission in its capacity as promoter of human and peoples' rights. It was not an enquiry mission; and while it permitted the Commission to get a better grasp of the prevailing situation in Mauritania, the mission did not gather any additional specific information on the alleged violations, except on the issue of slavery'.

9

The African Commission:
Promotional Mandate

The examination of state reports is the core of the Commission's 'promotional' mandate. In addition, special mechanisms, promotional visits, the adoption of resolutions, seminars and conferences, and publications are discussed. The relationship between the Commission, NGOs, and national human rights institutions is also highlighted.

A State Reporting

Reduced to its core, ratification of the African Charter requires states to 'give effect' to its provisions.[1] State reporting, which is aimed at assessing whether and to what extent states have adhered to this obligation, may therefore be regarded as the 'backbone of the mission' of the African Commission.[2]

1 Aim of State Reporting

When states proclaim that they undertake to observe the rights in the Charter, they direct themselves both to their own nationals and residents within their boundaries ('everyone') and to the international community (other state parties).[3] Through the interrelated processes of introspection and inspection, the state is held accountable to its treaty obligations at the national level, and before the international community.

At the national level, the reporting process provides a state with an opportunity to take stock of its achievements and failures in making the guarantees in the Charter a reality. Reviewing compliance with the Charter should not be regarded

---

[1] African Charter, art 1.

[2] Despite this fact (see Ex-Chairperson of the Commission, Badawi El-Sheikh, quoted in FD Gaer, 'First Fruits: Reporting by States under the African Charter on Human and Peoples' Rights' (1992) 10 *NQHR* 29), state reporting under the African Charter has received relatively little emphasis. The first reason for this state of affairs is a lack of access to primary sources—copies of state reports, the record of examinations, and concluding observations have long not been part of the public domain. They have not been accessible on the Commission's web-site, and are not contained in its Activity Reports. In a welcome recent development, country reports have been posted on the Commission's web-site. The best sources of some primary materials, covering the earlier period of the Commission, are A Danielsen and J Harrington (eds), *Examination of State Reports* (vols 1–5) (Denmark: Danish Centre for Human Rights and African Commission on Human and Peoples' Rights, 1995) (*Examination of State Reports*), containing full texts of reports and transcription of examinations from the 9th–14th sessions. See also A Danielsen, *The State Reporting Procedure under the African Charter* (Copenhagen: Danish Centre for Human Rights, 1994), who brought together further information (such as questionnaires sent to and other correspondence with states) covering the 9th–15th sessions. As I have attended many sessions at which subsequent reports were examined, I have obtained copies of most of these reports and kept notes of their examination by the Commission. These notes will thus be relied upon heavily. In addition to Gaer, further secondary sources include EA Ankumah, *The African Commission on Human and Peoples' Rights: Practice and Procedures* (The Hague: Martinus Nijhoff, 1996) ch 4; K Quashigah, 'The African Charter on Human and Peoples' Rights: Towards a More Effective Reporting Mechanism' (2002) 2 *AHRLJ* 261; M Evans, T Ige, and R Murray, 'The Reporting Mechanism of the African Charter on Human and Peoples' Rights' in MD Evans and R Murray (eds), *African Charter on Human and Peoples' Rights: The System in Practice, 1986–2000* (Cambridge: Cambridge University Press, 2002) 36–60; P Tigere, 'State Reporting to the African Commission: The Case of Zimbabwe' (1994) 38 *JAL* 64; F Viljoen, 'State Reporting under the African Charter on Human and Peoples' Rights: A Boost from the South' (2000) 44 *JAL* 110.

[3] On the aims of state reporting in general, see P Alston, 'The Purposes of Reporting' in United Nations, *Manual on Human Rights Reporting* (Geneva: United Nations, 1997) 19–24.

as an additional obligation, to be formally complied with only occasionally, but as an integral and continuous part of good governance. Involving high-ranking officials from all departments responsible for realizing aspects of the Charter (such as the departments of justice, health, education, environment, labour, and immigration),[4] the aim is critical introspection on the part of the state. There can thus be little doubt about the potential usefulness of this procedure, as full compliance with this obligation will give the government insight into, or will remind it about, the need to adapt laws, policies, and practices.

At the international level, the aim is to establish an objective and impartial inspection by an external body of the state's recent human rights record. At the same time, state reporting is not in the first place an adversarial process, but rather an opportunity for constructive dialogue between the government and the Commission. In an attempt not to alienate states, the Commission has emphasized the non-confrontational nature of this encounter.[5] Taking place during public sessions, the examination of state reports is not restricted to the Commission, but also involves other states. Since the examination of one state's report is an opportunity for other states to benefit from that state's experience, the examination of the report thus also has an educational goal. However, states may legitimately question the concrete benefits of the reporting process. When problems in the implementation of the Charter are revealed, the Commission—unlike UN treaty bodies—does not call upon states to make use of technical or other assistance.[6]

2 Introspection: Preparation of Reports

State reports may take two forms. An initial report, to be submitted two years subsequent to becoming a state party, should provide a background to the country and its laws, and is the starting point for future dialogue between the state party and the Commission. Thereafter, periodic reports must be submitted every two years, providing state parties with the opportunity to keep the Commission informed about human rights developments in that country.[7]

---

[4] An inter-ministerial committee on human rights may also be tasked with the responsibility to prepare a report.

[5] Commissioner Chirwa, at the Commission's 37th session, 27 April–11 May 2005, stated that the objective of state reporting is not to 'expose' state parties, but to 'assist' the Commission in finding out to which aspects it needs to pay attention in a particular state (notes on file with author).

[6] See eg the CERD Committee's recommendation that Madagascar should 'request technical assistance from the Programme of Advisory Services and Technical Assistance of the United Nations Centre for Human Rights' (UN Doc A/50/18, para 597); and the concluding observation of the CRC Committee that Ethiopia should 'consider seeking technical assistance from UNICEF and OHCHR' to embark on human rights awareness and information campaigns on the CRC (UN Doc CRC/C/15/Add.144, para 25). Although similar possibilities do not exist under the AU, the Commission may assist in linking states to NGO training programmes (see Section G below), and perhaps also refer them to eg the Capacity Building and Filed Operations Branch of the OHCHR.

[7] Some confusion may arise about the way reports are referred to. In the UN system, the first report is called an 'initial report', and the one following that, the 'second periodic report'. In its documentation about the status of reporting, the Commission refers to such reports as the 'second

Seen from the perspective of the state, the state report ideally is the product of inter-governmental reflection and input, and not the responsibility of one department, a single civil servant, or a consultant appointed for that purpose.[8] While one department (the department of human rights; and in its absence, the department of justice or foreign affairs) usually acts as the leading agency, all relevant departments should be called upon to undertake a process of assessing its activities and programmes against the yardstick of the Charter. The state report essentially represents a pooling together of contributions from different departments.

General ambivalence about the relationship between national human rights institutions (NHRIs) and their governments also manifests itself in the process of state reporting. In one approach, strictly following the Paris Principles and emphasizing the independence of NHRIs, these institutions should not be responsible for preparing the state's report. At most, they should fulfil the function of watch-dog, reminding states of their obligation to report, and may contribute partly to the report, for example by supplying information about its own activities, and on the accomplishment of its mandate related to human rights education. Following this approach, it would also be appropriate for NHRIs to submit 'shadow' reports. Another approach favours a much more central role for NHRIs in the process, departing from the premise that these institutions, being well-positioned to coordinate the reporting process, should share the responsibility of preparing the report with government departments. Under both approaches, NHRIs should in some way be involved in the process.[9] In respect of South Africa's second periodic report, the Commission noted its concern about 'the lack of involvement of various state institutions involved in the promotion and protection of civil, political and socio-economic rights'.[10] These state institutions are the South African Human Rights Commission, the Commission for Gender Equality, the Public Protector, and the Commission for the Promotion and Protection of the Rights of Cultural, Religious, and Linguistic Communities.

States are guided in their preparation of reports by a confusing array of guidelines. The official 'Guidelines for National Periodic Reports under the African Charter', adopted at the Commission's second session in 1989, are very elaborate,

---

report'. However, these reports really are 'first periodic reports'. In order to mediate between these possibilities, in this chapter the terminology of 'initial report' (or 'first report'), 'second report', third report', etc is used.

[8] The Commission praised the initial South African report for being written 'in consultation with the main government departments concerned' (document entitled 'Initial Report of South Africa', on file with author).

[9] See 2006 Brainstorming Meeting between the African Commission and the AU (Report of the Brainstorming Meeting on the African Commission, 9–10 May 2006, Banjul, The Gambia (AU Doc ACHPR/BS/01/010, 9 May 2006) (20th Annual Activity Report, Annex II) (Brainstorming Report) item 2 ('States should involve NGOs and NHRI in the preparation of their reports and should send shadow reports' to the Commission)).

[10] 'Concluding Observations and Recommendations on the First Periodic Report of the Republic of South Africa', 38th session, 21 November–December 2005, para 17 (using the terminology adopted here, this is South Africa's 'second report').

but also too lengthy and complicated, making compliance a matter of impossibility.[11] They are also not readily accessible. Two seminars were held to discuss and improve the existing guidelines, one in English for Anglophone state parties (Harare, August 1993), and another in French, for Francophone state parties (Tunis, April 1994). This process culminated in an 11-point amendment to the Guidelines (the Umozurike amendment).[12] The amendment highlights certain important issues, but is too brief and its provisions are too vague to function as a comprehensive guideline. A third set of guidelines, essentially an elaboration of the Umozurike amendment, prepared by Commissioner Dankwa (Dankwa document), also exists.[13] Although the status of the 'Dankwa document' is unclear, it is often sent out together with the original guidelines to prospective reporting states.

The Dankwa document draws a distinction between initial and periodic reports.[14] Periodic reports must contain the following: (1) particulars about ratification, domestication, and state reporting under the major human rights instruments to which the state is a party; (2) measures taken to implement the rights protected in the African Charter under the following headings: (a) civil and political rights; (b) socio-economic and cultural rights; (c) collective rights; (d) steps taken to implement the right to development; (e) steps taken to protect the following specific groups: women, children, the disabled, the aged, minorities, and other 'oppressed and/or disadvantaged groups'; (f) steps taken to 'protect the family and encourage its cohesion'; (g) any domestic protection that goes beyond the African Charter; (h) steps taken 'to ensure that individual duties are observed'; and (i) difficulties encountered in implementing the African Charter; (3) particulars about human rights teaching, education, and publication;[15] (4) the role of the Charter in the state's international relations.

In addition, state parties are given the extensive task of conducting a compatibility study 'of each piece of their national legislation with each article of the African Charter' as part of their reports. States found to have violated the Charter are required to report about follow-up measures taken 'to comply with the decisions of the African Commission'. As to formal requirements, reports have to be substantive,

---

[11] The Guidelines for State Reporting are reprinted in C Heyns (ed), *Human Rights Law in Africa* (vol 1) (Leiden: Martinus Nijhoff, 2004) 507–24; they are not available on the web-site of the Commission, but at <http://www.chr.up.ac.za/hr_docs/african/docs/achpr/achpr4.doc>.

[12] 'Guidelines to Periodic Reporting under Article 62 of the African Charter on Human and Peoples' Rights by UO Umozurike', apparently adopted at the Commission's 23rd session, in 1998, DOC/OS/27(XXIII); reprinted in C Heyns and M Killander (eds), *Compendium of Key Human Rights Documents of the African Union* (Pretoria: PULP, 2006) 129.

[13] 'Simplified Guidelines for State Reporting under Article 62 of the African Charter on Human and Peoples' Rights (printed in Viljoen (n 2 above) 112–13). These undated 'Guidelines' have apparently never been adopted officially by the Commission.

[14] The following vital information on the reporting state has to be included in initial reports (in addition to what is required for periodic reports): a brief history of the state concerned; its form of government; the legal system and the relationship between the three branches of government of the state. The following documents have to be annexed to initial reports: the state's constitution; the labour law, act, or code; the penal code and the code of criminal procedure; landmark decisions on human rights.

[15] African Charter, art 25.

accurate, and up to date. Reports, in English and French, should be submitted every two years.

These guidelines are a vast improvement on those that were originally adopted. They are much more concise, follow a more logical sequence, and do away with the misguided inclusion of the guidelines for the Convention on the Elimination of All Forms of Racial Discrimination and the Convention on the Elimination of All Forms of Discrimination against Women.[16] In the short term, it is recommended that states follow these revised guidelines in the preparation of their reports. In the longer term, the Commission should adopt updated, unified, and simplified Guidelines for State Reporting.[17] Subsequent practice of the Commission, questions posed consistently by the Commissioners during examination of state reports, resolutions, declarations, concerns related to the work of the Special Rapporteurs, the supplementary norms of the Women's Protocol,[18] the African Human Rights Court Protocol, and the threat posed by HIV and AIDS should all be incorporated into a new set of guidelines. Any process of revising the reporting guidelines should also take into account and be coordinated with the relevant questions and indicators devised under NEPAD's African Peer Review Mechanism.

Only in exceptional instances have state reports met the formal and substantive requirements set out in the guidelines.[19] Deficiencies relate to form, length, currency, and substance. On many occasions, states content themselves with merely listing legislative provisions and policies in their reports.[20] There is no fixed requirement as to the length of reports. A balance has to be struck between overly extensive and unacceptably brief reports. States often err on the side of brevity.[21] One may expect initial reports to surpass periodic reports in length, because initial reports provide a background to the country and its laws, and should serve as a starting point for future dialogue between the state party and the Commission. Unfortunately, some initial reports have been very brief.[22] The information in reports

---

[16] Parts V and VII of the Guidelines for State Reporting (n 11 above).

[17] See also Brainstorming Meeting of the African Commission (n 9 above) item 2 ('The guidelines on state reporting should be made user friendly to enable states to understand better what is required from them in their reports under article 62 of the Charter').

[18] Women's Protocol, art 26(1): States are required to indicate 'the legislative and other measures undertaken for the full realisation of the rights' provided for under the Charter 'in their periodic reports submitted in accordance with article 62 of the African Charter'. This formulation, which indicates that state parties to the Women's Protocol do not have to submit an additional report, gives rise to two consequences: (1) The existing Guidelines for National Periodic Reports have to be amended and updated by aligning them with the Women's Protocol; (2) There will be a dual system of reporting, as only state parties to the Women's Protocol will be required to comply with these new guidelines.

[19] Some 'best practice' models are the second report of Zimbabwe (combining its second and third reports); the initial report of South Africa 1998; the first report of Niger 1988–2002 (identifies as the 'initial and periodic' report); and the second report of Burkina Faso 1998–2002, dated July 2003.

[20] For a crude example, see Nigeria's initial report, dated 18 July 1990, which cites three pages of legislative provisions, before annexing the table of contents of the Constitution. Nigeria withdrew this report (see C E Welch, 'The African Commission on Human and Peoples' Rights: A Five Year Report and Assessment' (1992) 14 *HRQ* 43 and Tigere (n 2 above) 66).

[21] See eg the initial report of Swaziland, DOC/OS(XXVII)/154a (eight substantive pages).

[22] See, however, Rules of Procedure, r 85(2), allowing the Commission to request the reporting state to furnish it with additional information.

should be as up to date as possible. Time gaps between the compilation of information and the submission of reports should be avoided.[23] Reports should cover
all the substantive rights in the Charter, and should highlight the issues stipulated
in the amended guidelines. A recurrent concern raised during examinations is the
overly formalistic nature of reports.[24] States are frequently urged to explain how
legal provisions relate to practical reality, how they are applied, and what problems
are being experienced in their enforcement. Ideally, a report should be an honest
portrayal of the situation, and should reflect the obstacles and difficulties that have
been experienced.

A country's constitution, other legislation, and important case-law should
accompany the report as attachments. While this is particularly true for initial
reports,[25] attachments often also enhance the value of periodic reports.[26] In an
attempt to decrease overlap and repetition, states may incorporate and refer to reports
recently submitted to UN human rights treaty bodies.[27] However, the report should
still follow the structure of the Charter, and address all the rights in the Charter—
especially those aspects not covered in UN treaties. An exact copy of a report under
UN treaty can evidently not be submitted under article 62 of the Charter.[28]

The fact that states mostly submit reports in one language has caused numerous
problems. In earlier years, especially, the inability to have reports translated caused
delays in the examination of reports.[29] Often, reports were not translated, but
only summarized in one of the working languages of the Commission (which are
English and French).[30]

---

[23] The concluding observations issued after the examination of South Africa's second report note:
'The African Commission is concerned by the fact that the report was submitted almost four years
after it was prepared making most of the information and statistics therein outdated during the time
of examination by the African Commission' (para 16) (available at <http://www.chr.up.ac.za>).

[24] See eg the comment in the concluding observations on South Africa's second report: 'The
African Commission notes that in some sections of the Report, the State Party simply provides a general description of the provisions of the Charter and the legislation and/or policy put in place, without indicating how these measures have contributed in enhancing the rights of the persons under its
jurisdiction' (para 18).

[25] See eg South Africa's initial report of 1998, which contained the National Programme of Action
for Children in South Africa, the 1996 Constitution, other legislation, and judgments of the Constitutional Court.

[26] During the presentation and examination of Egypt's second report, the Commission requested
and the delegation promised to submit a copy of the report of the NHRI, the Egyptian National
Human Rights Council.

[27] See eg South Africa's initial report of 1998, to which South Africa's recently submitted reports
under the CRC and CEDAW were appended.

[28] Uganda's second report largely resembles its initial report submitted to the UN Human Rights
Committee under the ICCPR (see UN Doc CCPR/C/UGA/2003/1 (25 February 2003)). It was
pointed out during the examination at the 40th session (November 2006) that the report does not
follow the provisions of the Charter, but those of the ICCPR. Questioned about this aspect, the delegation did not provide any explanation.

[29] F Viljoen, 'Introduction to the African Commission and the Regional Human Rights System'
in Heyns (n 11 above) 426, 475.

[30] See Rules of Procedure, r 80: 'The Secretary shall endeavour to translate all reports and other
documents of the Commission into the working languages'.

3 Submission of Reports

No state has so far met the prescription of article 62,[31] which requires states to report every two years. Compared with other human rights treaties,[32] the period of two years is unrealistically short.[33] In any event, had states consistently complied with this requirement, the Commission would not have been able to examine all the submitted reports.[34] In an attempt to encourage states to report, and to make state reporting more realistic, the Commission in a *note verbale* communicated to all state parties that it may consolidate outstanding reports into a single report, thus making up any backlog in one go.[35] The implicit concession that the two-year period is too short and burdensome is at odds with the Commission's occasional criticism of states for non-compliance with the strict two-year reporting cycle. As 'consolidated' reports have now become the rule, the 'leap-frogging' measure can no longer be regarded as an emergency stop-gap measure, thereby leaving strict compliance with article 62 as a distant ideal. Non-submission, more than late submission, seriously erodes the effectiveness of the state reporting procedure.

Ignorance, inadequate internal governmental processes, bureaucratic bungling, and inefficiency often account more for non-submission of reports than a concerted lack of political will at a high political level. In its report on Ghana, the APRM Country Review Team noted the irregularity and tardiness of Ghana's reporting, and recommended that Ghana adopt a 'deliberate plan' to address overdue reporting, and 'institute a mechanism for automatic compliance' with reporting obligations.[36] Having identified a 'major weakness in the internal systems of the Ministries of Foreign Affairs and Justice', the APRM report suggested that the government strengthen these departments with a view to fulfilling their reporting obligations.[37]

With the number of reports submitted in the seven years since 2000 far exceeding the total number of reports submitted between 1991 and 1999, there are some indications of improvement.

---

[31] On the reporting procedure before the Commission, see State Reporting Procedure: Information Sheet No 4, prepared by the Secretariat, available at <http://www.achpr.org/english/information_sheets/ACHPR%20inf.%20sheet%20No.4.doc> and Rules of Procedure, rr 81–7.

[32] The reporting cycle under the ICCPR (art 40(1)) is open-ended, allowing the Human Rights Committee to set appropriate dates. African states have the best reporting record under CEDAW and the CRC, which respectively set the reporting period at four and five years (CEDAW (art 18(1) and CRC (art 44(1)).

[33] At the Commission's Brainstorming Meeting (n 9 above) it was recommended that the AU 'should consider a review of the Charter to render the submission and presentation of state reports under article 62 from 2 years to 4 years'.

[34] On average, the Commission examined two reports per session; the largest number of reports examined at a single session (the 27th) was five. At the same time, the Commission consistently complained that it did not have enough time to deal with many items on its agenda, especially communications.

[35] ACHPR/PR/A046, 30 November 1995. This allowed states to combine their initial and subsequent reports into a single report, see eg Niger's 'Initial and Periodic Report' (covering the period 1988–2002), consolidating seven overdue reports.

[36] APRM, Country Review Report of the Republic of Ghana, June 2005, ch 2, paras 12, 13, <http://www.nepad.org/2005/files/aprm/APRMGhanareport.pdf.> [37] ibid.

4 Inspection: Examination of Reports

The Commission had to request, and was granted, the mandate to examine state reports,[38] based on the *implied* power arising from article 62.[39] The examination

Table 9.1 Examination of state reports by the African Commission, 1991–2006

Date	Session	Country
1991	9th session	Libya, Rwanda, Tunisia
	10th session	none
1992	11th session	Egypt, Tanzania
	12th session	The Gambia, Senegal I and II,[40] Zimbabwe
1993	13th session	Nigeria, Togo
	14th session	Ghana
1994	15th session	none
	16th session	Benin, Cape Verde, The Gambia II
1995	17th session	none
	18th session	Tunisia II
1996	19th session	Algeria, Mozambique
	20th session	Mauritius
1997	21st session	Sudan, Zimbabwe II[41]
	22nd session	none
1998	23rd session	Guinea, Namibia
	24th session	Angola
1999	25th session	Burkina Faso, Chad, South Africa
	26th session	Mali
2000	27th session	Burundi, Libya II, Rwanda, Swaziland, Uganda
	28th session	Benin II, Egypt II
2001	29th session	Algeria II, Congo, Ghana II, Namibia II
	30th session	none
2002	31st session	Cameroon, Togo II, Lesotho, Mauritania
	32nd session	none
2003	33rd session	Saharawi Arab Democratic Republic
	34th session	DRC, Senegal III
2004	35th session	Burkina Faso II, Niger, Sudan II
	36th session	Rwanda II
2005	37th session	Mauritania II, Egypt III
	38th session	South Africa II
2006	39th session	Cameroon II, CAR, Libya III
	40th session	Nigeria II, Uganda II

[38] Recommendation on periodic reports (Annex IX to the First Annual Activity Report), adopted at the Commission's third session, held in April 1988, endorsed by the OAU Assembly (see the Commission's Second Annual Activity Report, para 31).

[39] The 'Recommendation on periodic reports' states in its Preamble that 'considering that the Charter has not specifically entrusted the Commission the responsibility to consider the periodic reports', the Assembly of Heads of State and Government should 'specifically entrust it with the task of examining the periodic reports'.

[40] The two reports were examined together, but were dated 1989 and 1992 respectively.

[41] This was presented as a single report, combining the second and third reports.

of state reports started during the Commission's ninth session, held in Banjul in October 1991. Since November 1995, almost all countries have combined their overdue reports into a single report. The state reports listed in Table 9.1 have since then been examined.

This table shows the reports examined by the Commission, rather than all those submitted by state parties. To complete the picture, it should be noted that the following reports are ready to be scheduled for examination at the Commission's 41st session: Algeria III, Angola II, Kenya, Zambia, and Zimbabwe III.

This data shows that 15 of the 53 member states have never submitted any state report. They are: Botswana, Comoros, Côte d'Ivoire, Djibouti, Equatorial Guinea, Ethiopia,[42] Eritrea, Gabon, Guinea-Bissau, Liberia, Madagascar, Malawi, São Tomé e Príncipe, Sierra Leone, and Somalia. Generally speaking,[43] these states have a much better record of reporting under UN human rights treaties. With the exception of Somalia, all the states have submitted at least one report (under the CRC). In fact, some of these states have reported very regularly: Madagascar has submitted reports under five UN treaties,[44] Gabon under four,[45] and Ethiopia under three.[46] Isolated reporting under one treaty—usually CEDAW—dispels the contention that non-reporting states lack the overall capacity to report.[47] A further seven countries are more than ten years overdue with the submission of reports to the Commission: Cape Verde, The Gambia, Mauritius, Mozambique, Tanzania, and Tunisia.

There are also some positive developments. Twenty states have reported more than once, and 14 states are up to date with their reporting obligations: Algeria, Angola, Cameroon, CAR, Egypt, Kenya, Mauritania, Rwanda, the Seychelles, South Africa, Sudan, Uganda, Zambia, and Zimbabwe.

According to the procedures of the Secretariat, a report is scheduled for a forthcoming session if it is received at least three months before that session. The legal officer in charge of the report studies the report, obtains supplementary information, and prepares a preliminary questionnaire on the report. The Commissioner responsible for the country concerned reviews the questionnaire. On some occasions, the Commissioner provides the state with questions before the examination, requesting the state to answer them in writing before the examination,[48] but this does not seem to be a consistent practice.

Reports are examined during public sessions. The following procedure is followed at these sessions: the state delegation is given an opportunity to introduce the report. The Commissioner who acts as rapporteur then starts posing questions

[42] Note, however, the elaborate response to the Commission's resolution by Ethiopia, canvassing numerous aspects of human rights in that country (20th Activity Report, Annex III).

[43] Except under ICESCR, see Ch 3 above.

[44] Madagascar submitted three reports under CCPR, an initial report under CEDAW, nine reports to CERD, one under CESCR, and two reports to CRC.

[45] Gabon submitted reports under CCPR, CEDAW, CERD, and CRC.

[46] Ethiopia had reported under CEDAW, CERD, and was up to date with reporting under CRC.

[47] See eg Equatorial Guinea, which had reports due under CAT, CCPR, CERD, and CESCR, but was up to date with its reporting obligations under CEDAW and CRC.

[48] See eg the questions prepared in respect of Tanzania's initial report (Danielsen (n 2 above) 95).

to the members of the delegation and makes comments about the report. Other Commissioners follow with their questions and comments. After being given an opportunity to prepare responses to questions and issues raised, the delegation delivers its oral response. In some instances, the opportunity for preparation is waived, or is very short (for example, the duration of a tea break). The Chair of the Commission thanks the delegation and the examination is closed.

The quality of responses depends on the quality of the government delegation. It has become standard practice for states to send a high-level government delegation, headed by a minister, and consisting of up to ten delegates.[49] As political head of the responsible department, it is appropriate that a minister should introduce the report. However, experience has underlined the need for experts to be present to answer technical and focused questions in a detailed and precise way.

Questions by Commissioners are part of a 'constructive dialogue' between the Commission and state. In practice, different Commissioners are bound to steer their inquiry between conciliation and confrontation. The dialogue between the Commissioners and state representatives initially tended to be subdued and overly 'correct'. The first two representatives to appear before the Commission at its ninth session were both ambassadors. According to Commissioner Nguema, the representatives were handled with too much deference and respect.[50] This point is obviously connected to the level of the delegation, as such dialogue depends on a high level of legal expertise as well as information about recent developments in the domestic legal system. Sometimes government delegates deflect pertinent issues raised by Commissioners. In examining the first Zimbabwean report, for example, Commissioner Buhedma raised concerns about a constitutional amendment to nullify the effect of a Supreme Court judgment on the treatment of convicts on death row.[51] The representative responded by contending that the government could not be blamed, because 'it is the issue of the legislature and it is a compromise sort of legislation'.[52] The examination has gradually become more vigorous since the 11th session, but no level of consistency has been reached.[53] Although the semblance of civility and 'constructive dialogue' is still securely in place, over time, the questioning by Commissioners has taken on a more combative tone and has become more incisive.

---

[49] See eg the presentation of the second periodic report of Mauritania, at the Commission's 37th session, by the Minister of Human Rights and Poverty Alleviation; the South African Minister of Justice and Constitutional Development presented its second periodic report at the 38th session; at the Commission's 40th session the Ugandan report was introduced by the Minister of Justice and Attorney-General. A diplomat (such as the Nigerian High Commissioner to The Gambia who tabled Nigeria's second periodic report at the 40th session) is less ideal.

[50] 'I have the feeling that the sitting was rather too diplomatic—we hear the one party and then the other and then we rise.... I thought we should engage in a dialogue, in other words we should not treat them as diplomats but rather as technicians of law that should be able on technical issues to elicit the responses' (*Examination of State Reports* (vol 1) (1995) 23).

[51] *Examination of State Reports* (vol 3) (1995) 97.   [52] ibid, 109.

[53] CE Welch, *Protecting Human Rights in Africa: Strategies and Roles of Non-Governmental Organizations* (Philadelphia: University of Pennsylvania, 1995) 156.

The procedure adopted by the Commission is also hardly conducive to true dialogue. A series of questions is posed in quick succession by each of the 11 Commissioners, followed by responses to some of these questions by an often-bewildered representative. The process is more akin to a series of critical statements, followed by a statement in defence of the report. Better results would be attained if definite replies to specific questions were required. A question-and-answer format would probably be more time-consuming, but would leave little room for ignoring pertinent issues. The level of examination by the Commission also varies. The rapporteur often sets the tone of the questioning. In instances where the Commissioner-rapporteur has visited the reporting country relatively recently, the questioning tends to be more incisive, detailed, and topical. Commissioner Dankwa, who had visited Uganda as part of his promotional activities, addressed the most important issues pertinently as rapporteur of the Ugandan initial report.[54] Commissioner Ondziel visited Burundi as part of her promotional visits.[55] Her questioning illustrated her awareness of the problems encountered when implementing the African Charter at ground level. She referred, for example, to the position of those recently condemned to death, the overcrowding of prisons, the long periods of detention of trial-awaiting youths in prison, the discrepancies between the conditions in camps for 'displaced' persons (predominantly Tutsis) and in camps for 'regrouped' people (mostly Hutus).

During the examination of state reports, Commissioners routinely ask questions that are not immediately apparent from the African Charter or the reporting guidelines. At most examinations, questions are posed about the process of drafting the report, including the participation of civil society and different government departments in the preparation of the state report. States are requested to clarify the domestic legal status of international law, in particular the African Charter, and to explain what that means in practice. Examination patterns also reveal the need for states to go beyond citing legal texts, and to report on their implementation. On almost every occasion, the Commission required more detailed information about the practical implementation of legislation and policies. Statistics are required, for example on levels of poverty,[56] the number of women represented in high-level government positions, and details about the composition and functioning of constitutional or other government bodies.[57]

Specific questions are directed at issues that are covered by the Commission's special mechanisms. Commissioners responsible for particular portfolios often focus their questions on issues related to the substantive scope of their mandate. So, for

---

[54] At the Commission's 27th session (27 April–7 May 2000), notes on file with author.

[55] In March 2000.

[56] See eg the questions by Commissioner Hassan to the Egyptian delegation during the examination of its third report, requesting statistics about levels of poverty and unemployment. It may be added that this information could be obtained from sources in the public domain, such as the websites of UN agencies.

[57] Commissioner Hassan also requested that the government provide the Commission with the Council's first report (notes on file with author).

example, does the Special Rapporteur on Prisons and Conditions of Detention in Africa usually inquire about the number, capacity, and occupancy of prisons; conditions of detention; and reliance on non-custodial sentences. The Special Rapporteur on Freedom of Expression may pose questions about awareness and adherence to the Commission's Declaration on Freedom of Expression. Irrespective of who is responsible for the portfolio at the time, the Chairperson of the Working Group on Indigenous Populations or Communities consistently directs queries about the presence, official recognition, and legal regime for the treatment of indigenous communities. Detailed questions about the situation of refugees, asylum-seekers, and internally displaced persons reflect the concerns of another Special Rapporteur. An area often neglected in the examination process, socio-economic rights, may receive more attention after the establishment of the Working Group on Economic, Social and Cultural Rights in Africa.[58] When preparing their reports states would therefore do well to take note of and include information on the concerns arising from all the Commission's special mechanisms in existence at the time of reporting.

The quality of responses to questions depends on the composition of the delegation. Some delegations have made considerable efforts to answer most of the Commission's questions. Others have avoided answering contentious questions, instead making general declaratory statements, or even deflecting attention by religious and populist ranting.[59]

The Commission's credibility relies on a fair and efficient procedure. Time management during the examination of state reports is of great importance. Generally, about three hours are devoted to each state report. The presentation of the report unfortunately takes a disproportionate percentage of this time. Rather, the presentation should concisely highlight the most prominent features of the report, and update the report by providing information about events that have occurred subsequent to its submission. Instead, regarding this as an opportunity for *rightorics*, governments often make general declarations and vague statements about the human rights position in their countries. There is also a disjuncture between the amount of time devoted to questioning and answering. Questioning by Commissioners should be focused on those issues that are of pertinent concern, so as not to flood the delegation with questions that could not possibly be answered in the allotted time. Generally, the Commissioners pose more than a hundred questions in roughly two hours. After an opportunity to prepare their answers, the delegation is given some 30 minutes in which to respond.[60] By placing such severe restrictions on the time allowed for answers to an extensive list of questions, delegates

---

[58] See Section B.2 below.

[59] Responding to questions on the Ugandan second report, at the 40th session, the Ugandan Minister of Justice and Attorney-General quoted biblical texts at length, and in response to questions about gays and lesbians, mispronounced that word as [lɛzəbiəns]' (transcribed phonetically).

[60] See eg the examination of Uganda's second report at the Commission's 40th session, where the head of the government delegation counted 95 questions, and was allowed 30 minutes to answer (which he managed to extend to 40 minutes).

are able to deal with issues in a superficial way, and omit answers on issues that are particularly problematic.[61]

5 The Role of NGOs in the Reporting Process

Reporting under the African Charter adds weight to the supposition that states are likely to paint a rosy picture under human rights treaties—no matter what. Because of many states' lack of honest self-reflection or introspection, civil society becomes an important source of supplementary information about the status of human rights in that state. Information and reports by non-governmental organizations are the most obvious potential source of information against which a state report can be evaluated.

The Commission has made it clear that, ideally, NGOs should be involved in the process of preparing a report, implying that the domestic process of drafting a report should be transparent and accessible.[62] Through the state reporting process, states are held accountable primarily to their own nationals. Adequate and timely notice should be given to NGOs, informing them of a report being prepared. Ideally, reporting should be part of a visible national debate. NGOs may from the outset be involved in the reporting process, or may be given the opportunity to comment on a draft state report. Such a report should be disseminated widely, it should be accessible, and the date for the presentation of the report should be communicated to the public.[63] Still, involvement in the 'official' state report does not disqualify NGOs from submitting their own 'shadow' reports.

Even in the absence of a formal avenue allowing alternative or 'shadow' reports to reach the Commission, NGOs have informally approached the Secretariat and Commissioners with information and questions. At its 11th session, the Commission started to refer publicly to documentation and other information presented to it by NGOs.[64] At its 23rd session in April 1998, for example, Commissioner

---

[61] The time allocation in respect of the Sudanese second report (examined at the Commission's 35th session, notes on file with author) illustrates this point. Allowing the delegate to introduce the report for about half an hour, and after questions by Commissioners lasting 2 hours and 15 minutes (135 minutes), the government was pressured to complete its response in 70 minutes.

[62] See eg the criticism of South Africa's second report: 'The African Commission is concerned at the lack of involvement of various state institutions involved in the promotion and protection of civil, political and socio-economic rights, and of civil society participation in the preparation of the report. The Commission notes in this regard that reports required under Article 62 should be shared with all sectors of the society to give them an opportunity to contribute in its preparation or to react thereto' (para 17).

[63] An example of a 'best practice' is the initial report of Namibia, presented at the Commission's 23rd session, which was compiled by the Ministry of Justice 'with inputs from members of the Interministerial Committee on Human rights whose membership is drawn from staff of government ministries and other agencies and from the University of Namibia'. The Human Rights and Documentation Centre, set up by the University of Namibia in collaboration with the Ministry, and an NGO, Legal Assistance Centre (LAC), received the original draft of the report 'for their comments' (Namibia's initial report, 36, on file with author).   [64] Welch (n 53 above) 156.

Pityana based some questions to the Namibian delegation on the reports of civil society organizations.[65]

Such efforts have been constrained by a lack of access to state reports.[66] Ideally, civil society should at the national level have access to a widely disseminated and accessible state report. If attempts to obtain the report domestically fail, NGOs enjoying observer status with the Commission should approach the Commission's Secretariat. As these reports are public documents,[67] there should be no constraint on their distribution, even before the examination of the report. The prominent display on the Commission's web-site of the three state reports prior to their examination at the Commission's 40th session is a welcome development, and may partly explain the high number and quality of 'shadow' reports submitted to, for example, Uganda's state report.[68]

Because NGOs are not allowed to participate in the examination of state reports, as such, they should devise other strategies to ensure that their critical voice reaches the ear of the Commission. NGOs may informally provide the necessary information to and 'lobby' individual Commissioners. Although an NGO intervention amounting to the presentation of a 'shadow report' was once allowed under the agenda item 'state reporting',[69] more recently the Commission nipped a similar attempt in the bud.[70] However, nothing prevents NGOs with observer status from taking the floor during public sessions under the item 'the human rights situation in Africa'. In this way, an NGO may supplement the informal submission of its information or 'shadow' report to Commissioners with an oral presentation concisely highlighting the issues arising from that report. By making the information part of the public discourse, pressure is increased on the Commission to address those issues during the examination of the report.

Recent examples of meaningful reliance by the Commission on NGO reports include the second reports of South Africa (examined at the 38th session), Cameroon

[65] He made specific reference to the Namibian National Society of Human Rights (notes on file with author).

[66] See eg the question posed to the Egyptian delegation during the Commission's 37th session as part of the examination of Egypt's third report (combining its seventh and eighth reports), by Commissioner Nyanduga (inquiring about the drafting process, he noted that NGO attempts to obtain copies of the state report were not successful) (notes on file with author).

[67] R 78: 'Periodic reports and other information submitted by state parties to the Charter as requested under article 62 . . . shall be documents for general distribution'.

[68] Four alternative NGO reports were submitted, a 'general' report by the Foundation for Human Rights Initiative (FHRI), with the support of the International Federation of Human Rights (FIDH), two reports highlighting indigenous rights issues (a joint report by the Centre for Minority Rights Development (CEMIRIDE) and International Working Group of Indigenous Affairs (IWGIA)), and another joint report by IWGIA, the Forest Peoples Programme, and United Organization for Batwa Development in Uganda (UOBDU)), and a joint report by the International Gay and Lesbian Human Rights Committee (IGLHRC) and Sexual Minorities of Uganda, concerning itself with the rights of gays, lesbians, and other 'sexual minorities' in Uganda.   [69] Ankumah (n 2 above) 95.

[70] Immediately preceding the examination of the second report of South Africa, a representative of a South African NGO was prevented from raising issues set out in a shadow report to the South African report.

(examined at the 39th session), and Uganda (considered at the 40th session). A group of seven NGOs, forming part of the South African NGO Forum (an ad hoc group meeting before and after sessions of the African Commission), submitted a 12-page 'shadow' report to South Africa's second report.[71] Some of the issues raised in the report were clearly reflected in the Commission's questions and conclusions.[72] Similarly, when the second report of Cameroon was examined at the Commission's 39th session (in May 2006), NGOs raised concerns about the treatment of 11 men who were arrested in a nightclub in Yaoundé, detained, exposed to invasive medical examination, and charged with sodomy under section 347(a) of Cameroon's Penal Code.[73] After being detained for almost a year, a court acquitted the men. However, upon their acquittal they were not released, but recharged.[74] Three Commissioners posed questions on the above-mentioned issues, which arose from 'shadow' reports and information supplied to them.[75]

6 Absence of Government Delegation

The African Commission has on one occasion, in the case of the Seychelles, examined a report in the absence of a government delegation, but only after numerous efforts had failed to ensure that the delegation presented its report. After the submission of the initial report of the Seychelles in 1994, its examination was on a number of occasions deferred due to the absence of a representative. For example, its report was scheduled for examination at the Commission's 17th session, held in March 1995, but postponed due to the absence of a representative. Due to the inaction of the Seychelles government, the report became outdated. For this reason,

---

[71] <http://www.chr.up.ac.za/hr_docs/countries/docs/Shadow%20report.doc> (30 November 2006).
[72] See eg Concluding Observations (para 35) ('The Commission notes the measures the State Party has taken to improve the conditions of persons deprived of their liberty. The Commission however recommends that the State Party should take the necessary measures to fully implement the recommendations of the Commission's Special Rapporteur on Prisons and Conditions of Detention in Africa') and Shadow Report (para 12), posing the question: 'How has South Africa implemented the recommendations of the African Commission's Special Rapporteur on Prisons and Conditions of Detention?'
[73] 'Whoever has sexual relations with a person of the same sex shall be punished with imprisonment for from six months to five years and a fine of from 20,000 to 200,000 francs.' See also International Gay and Lesbian Human Rights Commission (IGLHRC), 'Cameroon: Public Homophobia Increases on the Eve of Sodomy Trial' <http://www.iglhrc.org> (3 March 2006).
[74] Afrol News, 'Cameroon refuses to Release Acquitted Homosexuals', see <http://www.afrol.com/articles/19065> (17 June 2006).
[75] Commissioner Tlakula (from South Africa) asked the delegation whether the criminalization of sodomy under Cameroonian law was compatible with the Charter; Commissioner Malila (from Zambia, who is also the Special Rapporteur on Prisons and Conditions of Detention in Africa) asked questions related to the trial process, and wanted to know, amongst others, whether subjecting the suspects to invasive medical examinations did not contravene article 5 of the African Charter; Commissioner Alapini-Gansou (from Benin, Special Rapporteur on Human Rights Defenders) raised the lack of tolerance on the grounds of people's sexual orientation. (Notes of Judith Oder, Lawyer, Africa Programme, Interights, who attended the session, on file with the author; I thank her for allowing me to make use of her notes.)

and because it fell completely short of the reporting guidelines, this very brief report was returned to the state without the Commission examining it. Despite submitting a more complete and improved report in 2004, the Seychelles once again did not send a representative to present the report. The persistent appearance of this item on the Commission's agenda eventually prompted the adoption of a resolution, calling on the OAU Assembly to express its 'disapproval of such a persistent refusal that amounts to a deliberate violation of the Charter'.[76] The Commission further requested the Assembly to 'invite Seychelles to abide by the Charter' and to adopt appropriate measures against the Seychelles. When this too provoked no action, the Commission finally decided to examine the report in the absence of the government delegation. Commissioner Nyanduga, who had undertaken a promotional mission to the Seychelles in 2004, presented the report before the Commission.[77] Questions that arose formed the basis of written observations addressed to the government.

7 Non-submission of Reports

The fact that the state reporting procedure collapses if states fail to report leads to the question as to the most appropriate action against persistent non-reporting states. Thus far, the Commission sent out reminders, and in cases where states still did not submit a report, included this information in its activity reports.[78] In devising and implementing a strategy regarding this issue, the Commission has never applied Rule 81(2) of its Rules of Procedure, which provides as follows: 'If a state party fails to comply with article 62 of the Charter, the Commission shall fix the date for the submission of that state party's report'. The Commission should use this procedure to indicate to states that they must submit, by a specified date, their outstanding reports in the form of a single cumulative report.[79] Hopefully this will encourage states to submit reports. If reports remain overdue, the Commission must resort to proactive measures. A possibility is to schedule a 'review of implementation', even in the absence of a report, as has been done in the UN human rights system.[80] A state representative should be invited for a 'dialogue' with the Commission.

---

[76] ACHPR/Res.39(XXV)99: Resolution concerning the Republic of Seychelles' refusal to present its Initial Report, 25th session of the Commission, 5 May 1999 (12th Annual Activity Report, Annex IV).

[77] 20th Activity Report, para 13; and interview with Commissioner Nyanduga, 29 August 2006, Addis Ababa (notes on file with author).

[78] Rules of Procedure, r 84; see eg 19th Activity Report, para 13, and 20th Activity Report, para 9, where the status of state reporting, including non-submission, is detailed per state party.

[79] This is also the procedure adopted by UN human rights treaty bodies, such as the Human Rights Committee.

[80] This is in line with the procedure adopted by the Committee on the Elimination of Racial Discrimination. It had, for example, scheduled such a review in respect of Senegal for August 1999, after that country had not submitted its 11th to 14th reports. The 11th report was already due in 1993. See also Brainstorming Meeting of the African Commission (n 9 above) item 2 ('The African Commission should consider the human rights situation in states that do not comply with article 62, with the information available').

Beforehand, the Commission should obtain independent information about the implementation of the Charter in that country. NGOs, particularly those working in the country, must be invited to present information. Other sources, such as reports of that country to UN supervisory bodies and their subsequent comments; reports of UN and the Commission's own Special Rapporteurs; and the reports emanating from the African Peer Review Mechanism (APRM),[81] may also be used to obtain information. Another possibility is to undertake on-site missions or investigations to the states concerned.[82]

There is no doubt that such a course of action is not ideal, as the treaty body would have to rely on sources other than that of the official state records. It would also be deprived of a party with whom it could enter into a 'dialogue'. However, in my view, the advantages outweigh the disadvantages: Even in the absence of a report, the Commission should be able to subject the situation in that country to international scrutiny in an impartial setting, and would be in a position to make recommendations that may initiate reforms.[83] The experience of the UN also shows that in many instances notice about the treaty body's intention to take such drastic action galvanized states into action, either to submit reports, or at least to be present at the examination.[84]

8 Adoption of Concluding Observations

In order to gain the maximum benefit, the examination of state reports should result in an objective assessment of the state's performance, leading to recommendations to guide improvements. The adoption of such 'concluding observations' is a prerequisite for continuity in the dialogue between states and the Commission. Because the Commission's members rotate, it is likely that at least some Commissioners involved in the initial examination of a particular report, will no longer be present at the time of a subsequent examination. It is thus important that these observations be publicly accessible to improve the institutional memory of the Commission and of states. Lacking access to 'concluding observations', the reporting state is left in the dark as to how its performance had been assessed, and what steps, if any, it should take to improve the realization of the rights in the African Charter. Civil society is further unable to monitor or follow up any recommendations. Allowing these 'concluding observations' to enter the public domain will enable civil society

[81] See Ch 5 above.

[82] This has been done in a number of cases, see section D below. The competence of the Commission to undertake these missions is derived from art 46 of the Charter, which allows the Commission to resort to 'any method of investigation'. This provision seems to be broad enough to allow the measures proposed here as well.

[83] See eg AF Bayefsky, *The UN Human Rights Treaty System: Universality at the Crossroads* (The Hague: Kluwer Law International, 2001) 13.

[84] See eg M Banton, 'Decision-Taking in the Committee on the Elimination of Racial Discrimination' in P Alston and J Crawford (eds), *The Future of UN Human Rights Treaty Monitoring* (Cambridge: Cambridge University Press, 2000) 55, 73.

to assist with, lobby for, and monitor the steps that are taken to give effect to the Commission's recommendations. Wide dissemination will also provide a clear and accessible beacon against which the state and the Commission may measure the progress of a particular state. In short, concluding observations are essential to ensure international and national accountability.

Initially, the dialogue between state and Commission ended abruptly after the day of the examination. When Commissioners raised issues during their examination, government representatives made general and vague promises of answering questions in soon-to-be-presented further reports. For instance, at the 12th session the Gambian representative expressed the hope of answering the questions fully in a second report to be submitted at the next session.[85] However, The Gambia's second report was examined only at the 16th session. Similarly, at the 12th session the head of the Zimbabwean delegation remarked: 'We would like to take these observations and questions with us, and hope to come back in the next session . . . and answer those observations in a proper manner in the right place'.[86] This did not happen. When Zimbabwe's combined second and third reports were examined at the 21st session, no reference was made to observations arising from the initial report.

Due to time constraints and bad time-management on the part of the Commission, and the lack of expertise on the part of the state, government delegations are sometimes unable (or unwilling) to answer some questions, usually promising to supply answers on their return home. Lacking a follow-up mechanism and secretarial staff dedicated to following up on these answers, the Commission's practice has been erratic, inaccessible, or characterized by unfulfilled promises. In the absence of an official text indicating the 'findings' of the Commission, in the form of 'concluding observations', there is little possibility for follow-up and continuous dialogue.

Even if the Charter was silent on this issue, the Commission's 1988 Rules of Procedure provided for the possibility of adopting concluding observations.[87] Rule 85(3) allows the Commission to 'address all general observations to the state concerned as it may deem necessary' when it decides that the state 'has not discharged some of its obligations under the Charter'. Rule 86(1) of the current Rules takes the matter further:

The Commission shall, through the Secretary, communicate to states parties to the Charter for comments, its general observations made following the consideration of the reports and the information submitted by states parties to the Charter which shall be public documents. The Commission may, when necessary fix a time limit for the submission of the comments by the states parties to the Charter.

---

[85] *Examination of State Reports* (vol 3) (1995) 41.   [86] ibid, 107.

[87] These guidelines were confirmed in the amended Rules of Procedure, adopted in 1995. See also the 'Recommendation on Periodic Reports', also adopted in 1988, which makes preambular reference to the African Commission 'making pertinent observations to states parties'.

Disappointingly, this competence has been used only sporadically, in a rudimentary form (as general observations) in respect of Senegal's initial report,[88] and in a more extensive and detailed way, after South Africa's initial report had been examined at the Commission's 25th session in 1999.[89] On other occasions, the Commission at most included some of its ad hoc 'observations' in the final communiqué issued after sessions.[90] However, one should not despair at the Commission's inconsistent practice. The UN Human Rights Committee, which was established to examine state reports under the International Covenant on Civil and Political Rights, likewise did not adopt concluding observations from the outset.[91] Starting at the Commission's 29th session, in 2001, a more consistent practice seems to have developed when concluding observations were adopted in respect of the reports of Algeria, Congo, Ghana, and Namibia.[92]

This step was eventually taken for a number of reasons: the Commission may initially have shied away from adopting concluding observations as part of a strategy to avoid confrontation with states. As the Commission grew in confidence, and with states showing greater cooperation and NGOs exerting increasing pressure, the Commission generally extended its role and influence. The adoption of concluding observations may thus be seen as part of a trend in terms of which the Commission has been asserting its mandate more forcefully. As the Commission had by then been functional for about 14 years, an increasing number of states were submitting their second and later reports. The need to keep the dialogue (between Commission and state party) going from one report to another highlighted the

[88] This report was considered at the Commission's 12th session. Although neither the final communiqué of this session, nor Danielsen (n 2 above, 92) notes that any 'concluding observations' were adopted, the subsequent Senegalese report (its 'third report', combining its third to seventh reports) contains a part devoted to 'answers to the concerns expressed by the Commission after the presentation of the last report of Senegal, where specific reference is made to the Commission's 'comments and recommendations' (Implementation of the African Charter on Human and Peoples' Rights by the Republic of Senegal: third to seventh periodic reports (Senegalese Third–Seventh Report) (trans and unpub, on file with author) 27).

[89] The undated document is entitled simply 'South Africa's Initial Report', and consists of 'general observations', 'positive developments and factors of satisfaction', 'factors of concern', and 'recommendations' (on file with author).

[90] See eg Final Communiqué of the Commission's 16th session, 25 October–3 November 1994, para 38 (when examining its second report, the Commission expressed concern about the suspension by The Gambia of parts of the Constitution and requested that the rights of detained and arrested persons be respected). The Final Communiqué of the Commission's 19th session sketched the prevailing situation as follows: 'During discussions following the presentation of reports, the Commission urged countries to observe the provisions of the African Charter' (para 10).

[91] Such a practice evolved over a number of years. Initially, the HRC did not adopt concluding observations. Later it became common practice for HRC members to 'submit quasi-concluding personal statements on the human rights situation in the State concerned' (M Nowak, 'The International Covenant on Civil and Political Rights' in R Hanski and M Suksi (eds), *An Introduction to the International Protection of Human Rights: A Textbook* (Abo: Abo Akademi University, 1997) 79, 93). Eventually these country-specific comments were formulated into a comprehensive document, called 'concluding observations'.

[92] See eg Heyns and Killander (n 12 above) 130, where the concluding observations on Ghana's second report are reprinted.

necessity for a structured reminder of the earlier dialogue. Some state parties, such as South Africa, requested some tangible or concrete feedback from the Commission on the presentation and content of their reports. As states began to take their obligation to report more seriously, the need for a framework for evaluation became more pronounced. No continuous dialogue is possible in the absence of a record of the previous report. In fact, of the four reports examined at the 29th session, three were second or later reports.

The concluding observations that have been adopted generally provide a summary of the Commission's findings, and deal with 'positive factors', 'factors constituting obstacles to human rights as prescribed by the Charter', 'areas of concern', and 'recommendations'. Although the recommendations are sometimes formulated in a way that allows for later assessment,[93] many others are problematic because they are too vague, too deferential to the state, too idealistic, or too extensive. The recommendation to Ghana to amend 'its national laws' and to bring 'them in line with the Charter' is so wide-ranging that it becomes meaningless. The Namibian government is urged vaguely to 'continue cultivating a culture of respect for human rights in order to reduce tension in the conflict areas and among the vulnerable groups'. In similar vein, Ghana was required to 'continue working closely with NGOs'. If trends in a certain state are required to continue, there must be clarity about the starting point and some benchmarks to move towards. None of this is indicated in the Commission's observations. In respect of the Algerian report, the Commission recommended that 'questions relating to women's rights [be] paid more attention by the authorities', and that the government of Congo 'grant special attention to the rights of women and vulnerable groups such as ethnic minorities'. In respect of South Africa's second periodic report, the Commission was too deferential when it 'welcomed' South Africa's decision to provide free ARVs to HIV-positive expectant women, without devoting attention to the more pervasive issue of treatment to all who need it, and to the situation of orphans.[94] However, the 'concluding observations' did address pertinent issues such as xenophobia,[95] sexual violence,[96] asylum-seekers,[97] and indigenous peoples[98] more directly.

[93] A good example is the recommendation that Ghana amends article 270 of its Constitution and ratifies the Protocol on the Establishment of the African Court as well as the African Charter on the Rights and Welfare of the Child.   [94] Concluding observations, para 13.

[95] Consideration of Reports submitted by State Parties under Article 62 of the African Charter on Human and Peoples' Rights: Concluding Observations and Recommendations on the First Periodic Report of the Republic of South Africa, adopted at the 38th session of the African Commission, 21 November–5 December 2005, Banjul, The Gambia, para 19, where the Commission noted with concern the lack of details on the measures taken by the state party to eradicate the phenomenon of xenophobia directed towards African migrants in particular.

[96] As above, para 20: 'While noting the efforts of the State Party to implement legislation, policies and programmes to prevent and combat the sexual exploitation of children and violence against women, the African Commission remains concerned at the high incidence of sexual violence against women and children'.

[97] As above, para 32: 'The Commission urges the State Party to take appropriate administrative measures to ensure the speedy consideration of the applications for asylum seekers'.

[98] As above, para 34: 'The Commission notes the establishment of the Commission for the Protection and Promotion of the Rights of Cultural, Religious and Linguistic Communities and notes the steps

With some exceptions, the adoption of such conclusions seems to have become consistent practice. Although the Commission indicates that concluding observations are adopted, they have never become part of the Commission's official record in the form of either the session reports or Activity Reports.[99]

Not only publicity, but timing is of the essence. Concluding observations have to be made public immediately after the session at which the state report is examined. The requirement of confidentiality, as set by article 59 of the African Charter, is limited to 'measures taken' under the chapter dealing with communications. Observations adopted after the examination of state reports are not 'measures taken' in respect of the Commission's protective mandate, and, as such, need not be kept confidential. The Commission should therefore make its 'concluding observations' public by including them in the full text as part of the final communiqué adopted immediately after the session, by simultaneously placing them on the Commission's web-site, and by including them in the activity reports of the Commission to the AU Executive Council and Assembly.[100]

9 Follow-up

The Commission's practice regarding following up on reports has been inconsistent. On some occasions, the Commission followed up the examination of a report with a request that the answers or supplementary information be provided in writing before the next session, or that it be included in the next periodic report.[101] It has also written to the state, reminding it of its promise to submit written answers to the Commission's questions.[102]

It is to a great extent left to the reporting state to indicate whether it has complied with the Commission's recommendations. The submission of a subsequent state report is the best opportunity to do this. The inclusion of civil society in the reporting process and parallel NGO reports are required to ensure verification of the government's implementation report. Follow-up at subsequent examinations

taken by government to recognize the rights of indigenous populations. However, the Commission recommends that the State party undertake all appropriate measures to ensure that the rights of children belonging to minority groups, including the Khoi-Khoi and San, are guaranteed, particularly those rights concerning culture, religion, language and access to information'.

[99] See eg the Commission's 17th Activity Report, which states that the African Commission 'adopted Concluding Observations' on the five reports examined at the 34th and 35th sessions, 'which will be published together with the reports' (para 21). To date, these observations and reports have not been 'published'.

[100] The downside to this suggestion is that the AU Executive Council may, as a consequence of its consideration, further suspend or delay the publication of the Activity Reports (see Ch 5 above). This negative consequence has to be weighed against the opportunity for publicity and 'naming and shaming' that such an approach would allow for.

[101] See eg the questions addressed to the Tunisian government after the examination of its initial report (Danielsen (n 2 above) 98–9).

[102] In 1994, for example, following the examination of its initial report, the Secretary wrote to the Minister of Foreign Affairs of Ghana with a request that the government reply to the Commission's questions before the next session.

also depends on accessible concluding observations and an awareness of prior report-ing. So far, the Commission has made scant reference to reports or recommendations previously issued, although there are some exceptions.[103]

State reports should be contextualized within the reporting history of a report-ing state. In 2003, during the examination of Senegal's third (combined third to seventh) periodic report, concerns were expressed by the Commission about five issues raised by Senegal's initial report.[104] Unfortunately, Senegal's second report refers to and cites fully only one of the Commission's 'concluding observations' made during the previous examination. The Commission's other recommenda-tions, therefore, did not enter the public domain. Regarding the issue of prison conditions, the periodic report indicates targeted measures taken since 1992 to address the Commission's concerns.[105] The report highlights legislative reforms aimed at reducing the prison population, but neglects to provide details about their application. On the situation in Casamance, the Senegalese report indicates that the Commission, had previously recommended that the government attach 'priority to negotiations, rather than the use of force', and maintain 'absolute trans-parency'.[106] In response, the report expounds on the history of the region, and concludes that the Senegalese government is prepared to re-establish 'dialogue with a United Movement of Democratic Forces of Casamance that speaks with one voice'.[107]

The adoption by the Commission of a resolution on 'implementation of its rec-ommendations', discussed above,[108] should not only apply to the communications procedure, but also to recommendations contained in concluding observations. This means that states will have 90 days to respond to these recommendations, and that the Commission should also include information about compliance with concluding observations in its annual reports to the AU Executive Council. Even if this is the case, effective follow-up further depends on the integration of the state reporting process into the mandates and activities of other AU organs, such as the Peace and Security Council and the Pan-African Parliament, and the APRM.[109]

10 Importance and Potential Impact

The unimpressive record of state reporting under the Charter may be ascribed to the actions of states, the Commission, and the AU. Although there has been some improvement, the system of state reporting is poised delicately, and should receive continuous attention from all role players.

Although the compliance of states with their reporting obligations under the African Charter has improved gradually, it still falls short of the quality of their

---

[103] To a limited extent, in the case of the third Egyptian report, the Rapporteur-Commissioner noted that the report constituted an improvement on previous reports, and asked some specific ques-tions about developments subsequent to the last report (notes on file with author).
[104] n 88 above.   [105] Senegalese third report, 33–4.   [106] ibid, 27.
[107] ibid, 29.   [108] Ch 8.A.9.   [109] See Ch 5 above.

reporting under UN human rights treaties—particularly CEDAW and CRC. Too often, states approach reporting as a mere formality, and not as an honest and self-critical assessment of its efforts to realize Charter rights.

The Commission has not succeeded in establishing a continuous and construct-ive dialogue with reporting states. The key to improvement is the adoption, publi-cation, and wide dissemination of concluding observations. The Commission should amend its Guidelines on state reporting to require states to respond to con-cluding observations in their subsequent reports. Recommendations must require definite action and must allow for later assessment. States can only respond to rec-ommendations that are clear and directed. Steps should also be taken when a state fails to comply with recommendations. It is suggested that on-site investigations (country visits or missions) be undertaken to such states, with the specific mandate to follow up on recommendations made after the examination of state reports.

More should be done to engage non-reporting states. The Commission should schedule 'reviews of implementation', and should cooperate with NGOs involved in training on state reporting to ensure that states that lack the administrative and technical capacity to report are assisted and encouraged to report.[110] Although the AU Assembly has on numerous occasions called on states to submit their reports,[111] it has never singled out non-reporting states,[112] and has never engaged on substan-tive issues arising from the examination of reports. In the future, the Commission should not only include concluding observations in its Activity Reports, but should highlight serious instances of non-compliance with the Charter.

As a means of 'mobilizing shame', the effectiveness of state reporting depends on publicity. The Pan-African and local media must become more involved in the dissemination and discussion of information about state reporting. As it stands, criticism directed at a state during the 'event' of the Commission's public session may cause it a measure of embarrassment. However, the impact of this criticism will remain extremely limited if it is not made known beyond the hundred or so representatives of states and NGOs present at the session. Without greater expos-ure, state reporting will continue to support the *rightorical* stance of states by

---

[110] One such NGO is the Human Rights Trust of Southern Africa (SAHRIT), see <http://www.sahrit.org>.

[111] The OAU Assembly earlier on implored states to submit regular reports (eg its decision on the Commission's Fourth Annual Activity Report, OAU Doc AHG/Res.202(XXVII) (1991)); subsequently, on numerous occasions, it made more vaguely formulated calls on states to 'honour' or to 'fulfil' their obligations enshrined in the African Charter, without specifying the duty to report (see eg its decision on the 11th Annual Activity Report, OAU Doc AHG/Dec.126(XXXIV) (1998); and its decision on the 12th Annual Activity Report, OAU Doc AHG/Dec.133(XXXV) (1999)). Since it started examining the Commission's Activity Reports, the AU Executive Council has been more explicit with calls on non-reporting states to submit their reports under art 62 (see its decisions on the Commission's 18th and 20th Activity Reports, AU Doc EX.CL/Dec.220(VII) and AU Doc EX.CL/Dec.310(IX)).

[112] The OAU Assembly came closest to doing so when it listed the states that had complied with reporting obligations, see Resolution on the Fifth Annual Activity Report of the African Commission (OAU Doc AHG/Res.207(XXVIII)(1992) para B.2; and Resolution on the Sixth Annual Activity Report of the African Commission (OAU Doc AHG/Res.227(XXIX)(1993), para B.1).

providing them with the benefit of formal legitimacy, without any substantive accountability, either domestically or elsewhere on the continent.

B   Special Mechanisms

1   Special Rapporteurs

The very limited success of the state reporting procedure may be linked to the establishment by the Commission of the position of special rapporteur. While state reporting is almost exclusively dependent on the initiative of states to submit reports, the position of special rapporteur allows the Commission to take the initiative and to be more pro-active. Starting in 1994, the Commission established a number of Special Rapporteurs to provide focal points for the Commission on issues arising from the Charter.[113] Because the African Charter does not provide an explicit legal basis for the establishment of special mechanisms, the Commission had to adopt a progressive interpretation to find room for these mechanisms within its Charter mandate.[114]

Special Rapporteur on Extrajudicial, Summary or Arbitrary Executions in Africa

The mandate of the first Special Rapporteur (on Extrajudicial, Summary or Arbitrary Executions in Africa) was located in the substantive provisions of the Charter.[115] Procedurally, this extension of the Commission's mandate could be based on articles 45(1)(a), 46, and 66 of the Charter. The mandates of subsequent rapporteurs have been located in article 45, suggesting a preference for a legal basis not constrained by the confidentiality requirements of 'protective' measures applicable to article 46 investigations.

Despite protestations to the contrary,[116] the impression of a courageous Commission taking the initiative in establishing its first special mechanism is undermined by two factors in particular. The first is the pressure exerted by an international non-governmental organization (INGO),[117] Amnesty International. One of the

---

[113] See generally J Harrington, 'Special Rapporteurs of the African Commission on Human and Peoples' Rights' (2001) 1 *AHRLJ* 247; and M Evans and R Murray, 'The Special Rapporteurs in the African System' in Evans and Murray (n 2 above) 280.

[114] After a review of its mechanisms, the Commission adopted guidelines (17th Annual Activity Report, para 33).   [115] African Charter, art 4.

[116] Report on Extrajudicial, Summary and Arbitrary Executions, 10th Annual Activity Report, annex VI: 'Far from being the result of chance or circumstance, the decision of the African Commission was taken with courage and determination, taken in spite of paucity of means'.

[117] The term 'INGO' is used here to denote NGOs with headquarters based outside Africa, with a transnational scope and mandate. If only the latter part of the definition is applied, there are also 'INGOs' based in Africa, such as the Africa Institute for Human Rights and Development and the African Centre, both based in Banjul.

first three NGOs to obtain observer status with the Commission in 1988, Amnesty International has had a consistent presence at Commission sessions. Already in 1993, it proposed the creation of a Special Rapporteur on Extrajudicial Executions in Africa.[118] The Commission deferred a decision to its next session, but instructed one of its members to engage in discussions with the UN Special Rapporteur on Extrajudicial Executions. By the time the Commission's next session took place, the genocide in Rwanda had been unleashed, providing the second incentive for the Commission's action. Although these circumstances brought greater urgency, and the matter was discussed again, it was only at the next session that one of the Commissioners (Ben Salem) was designated as Special Rapporteur, and only two sessions later, in October 1995, that the Special Rapporteur's mandate was approved. However, already at the 15th session, in April 1994, he was requested to address the situation in Rwanda as a matter of urgency.[119]

Although the establishment of this position aimed to show the determination of the Commission to leave behind its failure to act in response to the genocide in Rwanda, the delays in the appointment of someone to the position and the lack of tangible results achieved the opposite result. With little relevant expertise and ill-fitted for this appointment due to his position as the Tunisian Ambassador to Senegal,[120] Ben Salem detracted from the credibility of the Commission. Despite assistance from the Banjul-based NGO, the African Institute for Human Rights and Development, the Special Rapporteur accomplished very little. Plagued further by the lack of cooperation from states and the shortage of resources, the position became defunct in 2001, when Commissioner Ben Salem resigned as Special Rapporteur.

Special Rapporteur on Prisions and Conditions of Detention in Africa

Nevertheless, the establishment of the position set a precedent for the appointment of further Special Rapporteurs and provided a checklist of obstacles to be avoided. To some extent, the establishment of the office of Special Rapporteur on Prisons and Conditions of Detention in Africa (SRP) overcame these difficulties. During the establishment of the office, arguments for appointing outside experts to the position, rejected in the past, were reintroduced. Following the practice of the UN Commission on Human Rights, and because of the time in attendance required of part-time Commissioners who hold full-time employment, a strong argument was advanced for appointing outside experts. However, resistance against those arguments prevailed, based on the apprehension that the Commission would not be able to 'control' outsiders and the impression it might create that the Commission was somehow inadequate.

---

[118] Harrington (n 113 above) 251.
[119] Final Communiqué of the 15th session, para 20; and Annexes VI and VII to the Commission's Tenth Annual Activity Report.   [120] Harrington (n 113 above) 256.

The initiative to establish the position also came from an INGO, Penal Reform International (PRI).[121] However, PRI's approach was very different from that of Amnesty International. It organized, with the African Commission and other international and Ugandan NGOs, the 'Pan-African Seminar on Prison Conditions in Africa', firmly positioning the hitherto neglected issue of prisoners' rights on the agenda of the Commission and African NGOs. The creation of a Special Rapporteur was legitimated further by a call for its establishment in the 'Kampala Declaration on Prison Conditions in Africa' adopted at the end of the conference. NGO support was garnered at the NGO Workshop preceding the Commission's 16th session, where a draft resolution was adopted that served as the basis for a Commission resolution on this topic. When it approached the Commission, PRI gave an undertaking of financial and institutional support and provided draft terms of reference, making it easy for the Commission to set the process in motion. The commitment and talents of the first two Commissioners who held this position, Commissioners Dankwa and Chirwa,[122] contributed to making the SRP one of the flagships of the Commission. As its longest-standing and most successful special mechanism, the SRP is discussed in some detail below.

Although its mandate encompasses other measures, the SRP mainly engaged in country visits, followed by reports containing recommendations to state parties. As the word 'detention' in its formal title suggests, not only sentenced but also trial-awaiting and other detainees fall under the mandate of the SRP. So far, the SRP has conducted 16 visits to 13 countries.[123] These visits resulted in nationwide exposure to issues related to the plight of detainees, as a large number of government officials in these countries, including ministers and heads of state, engaged with the SRP about its mandate.

States and the SRP contributed to—but also hindered—the full realization of the SRP's potential. State consent is required for visits. During country visits, states are required to grant unfettered access to all detention facilities. Thirteen states made it possible for the SRP to visit, and three follow-up visits took place. However, this requirement also meant that some of the states from which allegations

---

[121] On the SRP, see F Viljoen, 'The Special Rapporteur on Prisons and Conditions of Detention in Africa: Achievements and Possibilities' (2003) 27 *HRQ* 125.

[122] At the time when he became Special Rapporteur, Dankwa served as Deputy-Chairperson of the Commission; Chirwa brought to the position her personal experience as political prisoner under the Banda government, as is depicted in *Achutan and Another (on behalf of Banda and Others) v Malawi* (2000) AHRLR 144 (ACHPR 1995) (Eighth Annual Activity Report) (*Chirwa* case). Commissioner Malila (a national of Zambia) took over from Chirwa.

[123] The following visits have been undertaken: Zimbabwe: 23 February–3 March 1997; Mali: 20–30 August 1997; Mozambique: 4–24 December 1997; Madagascar: 10–20 February 1998; Mali: 27 November–8 December 1998 (second visit); The Gambia: 21–26 June 1999; Benin: 23–31 August 1999: Central African Republic: 19–29 June 2000; Mozambique: 4–14 April 2001 (second visit): Malawi: 17–28 June 2001; Namibia: 17–28 September 2001; Uganda: 11–22 March 2002; Cameroon: 1–14 September 2002; Benin: 23 January–5 February 2003 (second visit); Ethiopia: 15–29 March 2004; South Africa: 14–30 June 2004. The SRP visited more than 250 prisons and other places of detention in 13 countries.

of maltreatment of detainees regularly emanate (such as Algeria, Egypt, Libya, and Tunisia)[124] fell outside the purview of the SRP. For its part, the SRP could have undertaken more visits, and could have been more proactive about obtaining 'invitations'. The gradual disengagement of PRI also saw a decrease in visits, with the last visit taking place in June 2004.

A deficiency in the reports of the SRP is their concern mainly with the material, as opposed to the legal, conditions of detention, as is illustrated by the issue of overcrowding in prisons. Again and again, SRP reports highlight overcrowding as a central concern that gives rise to many unacceptable conditions such as a lack of space, inadequate nutrition, unhygienic sanitation, and the insufficiency of rehabilitation programmes. Of equal, if not greater, importance is to ensure that non-sentenced prisoners are detained on a sound legal basis, and the limited use of alternative sentencing options. Surprisingly, few of the SRP reports provide a clear indication of the percentage or number of un-sentenced detainees in a particular country. For example, data on this issue is absent from the Cameroon report. In other reports, information is provided only on the number of person 'on remand' who find themselves *in prisons*, and not in all detention facilities. Where information is available, it reveals that a very high percentage of detainees are still under investigation, awaiting the start of their trial, or are somewhere in the trial process. In Malawi, some prisoners have been detained pending trial for up to ten years.[125] According to the Ugandan report, a remand detainee in one prison had been detained in isolation for some eight years; in another prison the longest remand case was also eight years.[126]

The greatest irony of the situation in prisons is the fact that sentenced prisoners are detained in conditions that are, as a rule, far superior to those under which suspects (who are under investigation, awaiting trail, or who are being tried) are kept. This is ironic as the guilt of sentenced prisoners has been established, unlike that of suspects. As far as possible, the rights of suspects should be observed as if they are not guilty of the crime they are charged with. Under the African Charter[127] and the laws of each of these countries, suspects are presumed innocent until their guilt is established.[128] At least some of them will (one day) be found not guilty. The conditions of detention of suspects should also be conducive to the preparation of an effective defence. By discussing most of the aspects in the report separately in relation to prisons and police cells, the Namibian report illustrates this ironic dichotomy.[129] In a telling

---

[124] See Ch 3 above.   [125] Malawi report, 7.   [126] Ugandan report, 34.

[127] Art 7(1)(b) provides that the right of every individual to have his cause heard comprises 'the right to be presumed innocent until proven guilty by a competent court or tribunal'.

[128] The (justiciable) Preamble of the 1972 Constitution of Cameroon (as amended) provides that every 'accused person is presumed innocent until found guilty'; art 20(3) of the 1994 Constitution of Ethiopia reiterates that accused persons 'have the right to be presumed innocent until proved guilty according to law'; similar provisions are found in art 28(3)(a) of the 1995 Ugandan Constitution and s 35(3)(d) of the 1996 Constitution of South Africa.

[129] As far as prison cells are concerned, Namibian prisons are 'generally ventilated', 'well lit', 'most inmates sleep in a bed', each dormitory has 'an independent bathroom' and adequate sanitation. The

admission, the Uganda Prison Service acknowledges that deaths among remand prisoners account for 90 per cent of all deaths in prison.[130]

All international bodies that depend on the cooperation of recalcitrant states need to walk a tightrope between open confrontation and constructive dialogue. Especially if the mechanism relies upon state consent or invitation, an openly confrontational attitude may inhibit future cooperation and may cause apprehension on the part of other states. At the same time, the SRP must uphold the integrity of the normative regime and must seek to 'improve' the conditions of detention.[131] The fact that visits depend on a state's invitation and cooperation reinforces the consensual nature of a visit. The 'means of implementing the mandate' state that the SRP must 'seek and receive information from States Parties to the Charter' and that states should give 'the necessary assistance and co-operation to carry out on-site visits and receive information from individuals who have been deprived of their liberty, their families or representatives, from governmental or non-governmental organisations and individuals'. At the same time, and potentially confrontational, the SRP is also entitled to seek the views of 'individuals, national and international organisations and institutions as well as other relevant bodies on cases or situations which fall within the scope of the mandate'.

Sometime after its visit, the SRP adopts a report. Reports of visits were eventually published with the technical assistance of PRI and the financial assistance of NORAD.[132] In the spirit of dialogue, states were afforded an opportunity to respond to the SRP's report. Although the SRP's report will not be amended (unless, perhaps, the government points to some blatantly incorrect facts contained in the report), these comments are attached to the final version of the report. An example of this process is the response by the government of Malawi, who thanked the delegation for 'a comprehensive report' and assured the SRP that 'areas of concern have been noted for our necessary action where possible'. Another example of meaningful 'constructive dialogue' is the elaborate 11-page response of the Ugandan government. A recurring problem has been the lack of formal adoption of these reports by the Commission. On only one occasion was the SRP's report included in the Commission's Annual Activity Report.[133]

Efforts towards 'constructive dialogue' are thwarted when governments issue blanket denials of crucial factual findings in the reports. The SRP visited Gambian

most striking phrases and adjectives used to describe cells at Namibian police stations are 'lacked ventilation', 'crammed', 'dangerous', 'very uncomfortable', 'no sleeping facilities', 'toilets...no longer function', 'major unhygienic conditions', 'health hazard', and 'affront to dignity'.

[130] Uganda report, 22.   [131] Para 3.1 of SRP's mandate.

[132] Nine such reports have appeared, all in English and French, and on occasion also in Portuguese and Arabic. These reports deal with the SRP's visits to Zimbabwe, Mali, Mozambique, The Gambia, Benin, Central African Republic, and Malawi, as well as the follow-up visits to Mali and Mozambique (*Mali Revisited* and *Mozambique Revisited*).

[133] Tenth Annual Activity Report, Annex VII; even on this occasion, the Commission did not stipulate that it 'adopted' the report (para 19). Formal adoption by the Commission of Special Rapporteurs' (and other) reports is a more recent phenomenon, see eg 17th Activity Annual Activity Report, para 25. However, these reports are still not included in the Activity Reports.

prisons in June 1999. One of the major concerns of the SRP in respect of The Gambia was detention without being brought before a judge beyond the legal limit of 72 hours. Responding to the SRP's report in August 2000, the Gambian government denied that it ever transgressed the 72-hour rule. However, subsequent events demonstrate how untruthful and unhelpful these remarks are. In December 2000, the Gambian High Court decided the case of *Suwandi Camara v The Commissioner Mile II Prisons and Another.*[134] The facts of this case were uncontested: Suwandi Camara was detained in Mile II Prison in July 1997, apparently without charge. The National Intelligence Agency interrogated him once, in July 1997. Since then, no charges were brought against Camara. The High Court accepted that he had been detained without charge since July 1997, that is, for about three and a half years. Finding his detention unlawful, the Court ordered his immediate release. Such instances underline the limits of 'constructive dialogue', and the need for the SRP to be unequivocal about non-compliance by states. In appropriate cases, the Commission should adopt applicable resolutions condemning the lack of meaningful cooperation.

It is not easy to point to improvements and other positive changes resulting directly from the SRP's visits. However, 'follow-up' visits, especially, allow for some assessment of the impact consequent to the SRP's visit. In Mali, for example, the problem of overcrowding was addressed through an amendment to the criminal procedure code, reducing the period of detention legally permissible from one year to six months.[135] This legislative change was one of the reasons why the percentage of un-sentenced detainees in the country's biggest prison decreased from 90 per cent to 77 per cent of the total prison population between 1998 and 2002. Some improvement in material conditions has also been pointed out.[136] Deteriorating conditions, in other instances, indicate that the record remains uneven. In yet other instances, however, the follow-up visit concluded that very little had changed.

Special Rapporteur on the Rights of Women in Africa

NGOs such as Women in Law and Development in Africa (WILDAF) have for a number of years advocated the creation of a special mechanism dealing with the rights of women. Established at the Commission's 23rd session, in April 1998, the mandate of the Special Rapporteur on the Rights of Women in Africa was not so much directed at visits, resulting in reports, but rather at general studies and collaboration with NGOs and governments.[137] Specifically the mandate called for the elaboration of guidelines to assist states in improving their reporting on the situation of women, and for the finalization of the Protocol on the Rights of Women.

---

[134] Case MA 72/2000 (14 December 2000), decided by Kabalata J.
[135] *Loi* 01-080 of 20 August 2001, see also Viljoen (n 121 above) 164.
[136] See Viljoen (n 121 above) 163–7.
[137] As at 31 December 2006 the position was held by Commissioner Melo (a national of Mozambique).

One of the major accomplishments of this Special Rapporteur is the adoption of the Protocol to the African Charter on the Rights of Women in Africa (Women's Protocol). After the adoption of the Women's Protocol, the attention of the Special Rapporteur shifted to the speedy ratification and domestication of the instrument.[138] Perhaps profiting from her position in the Mozambican Ministry of Justice, the Special Rapporteur was successful in persuading Mozambique to ratify the Women's Protocol.[139] During the examination of state reports, the Special Rappporteur has been raising questions pertinent to the position of women, and about the status of ratification of and reservations to the Women's Protocol. Although numerous visits have been undertaken, followed by the preparation of reports, there were often delays in the adoption of these reports and delays in their dissemination.

The Special Rapporteur also issues 'urgent appeals' in response to specific situations affecting women. For the first time, at the Commission's 40th session in November 2006, the inaction of a government to which an appeal was directed led to the adoption of a resolution by the Commission.[140] In this resolution, the state in question, the DRC, was urged to guarantee the right to security of young women in the country who were allegedly suffering sexual abuse, to ratify and domesticate the African Women's Protocol, and effectively to implement a new law on sexual violence. By noting that similar appeals have also been sent to UN Special Rapporteurs, the Commission shows a welcome sign of greater awareness of the co-existence and potential collaboration between its special mechanism and those of the UN.

Special Rapporteur on Human Rights Defenders in Africa

The Special Rapporteur on Human Rights Defenders in Africa functions on the substantive basis of the UN Declaration on the Rights and Responsibilities of Individuals, Groups and Organs of Society to Promote and Protect Universally Recognized Human Rights and Fundamental Freedoms (Declaration on Human Rights Defenders).[141] In addition to its promotional mandate, it also receives, examines, and 'acts upon' information about human rights defenders, and engages governments in dialogue.[142] Responding to information supplied to her, the Special Rapporteur sent urgent appeals to heads of states.[143]

---

[138] The Special Rapporteur in 2005 addressed a communication to the Chairperson of the Pan-African Parliament, urging her to set in motion a process of domesticating the Women's Protocol in national laws (20th Activity Report, para 30).

[139] In July 2003, she sent letters to the relevant officials (17th Annual Activity Report, para 31); in December 2005, Mozambique ratified the Women's Protocol.

[140] AU Doc ACHPR/Res.103(XXXX)06, 'Resolution on the Situation of Women in the Democratic Republic of Congo', adopted on 29 November 2006.

[141] As at 31 December 2006 the position was held by Commissioner Alapini-Gansou (a national of Benin).

[142] Resolution on the Protection of Human Rights Defenders in Africa, establishing this position, at the Commission's 35th session, 21 May–4 June 2004.

[143] Appeals sent by Commissioner Johm to the Presidents of Sudan and Zimbabwe (18th Activity Report, AU Doc EX/CL.199(VII), para 27); no information is available about follow-up actions.

Special Rapporteur on Refugees, Asylum Seekers, and Internally Displaced Persons in Africa

The Special Rapporteur on Refugees, Asylum Seekers, and Internally Displaced Persons in Africa is mandated to examine the situation of persons falling within its mandate, to 'act upon information', to undertake fact-finding missions to refugee and IDP camps, to assist states in developing appropriate legal and policy frameworks, to raise awareness about the plight of these vulnerable groups, and to promote the implementation of the relevant standards.[144] Among its activities, the Special Rapporteur conducted a 'fact-finding' mission to Senegal,[145] and joined the AU's Humanitarian and Security Assessment Mission to the Darfur Region of Sudan.[146] In response to the eviction and demolition caused by the Zimbabwean government's Operation Murambatsvina, the Special Rapporteur directed an urgent appeal to the government.[147] At the request of the AU Commission, he undertook a 'fact-finding' mission to Zimbabwe. Upon his arrival in Zimbabwe, and after negotiations aimed at enabling the Special Rapporteur to carry out his mission had failed, the Zimbabwean government asked him to leave the country.[148] As a consequence, the Special Rapporteur did not accomplish his mission.

Special Rapporteur on Freedom of Expression in Africa

The Special Rapporteur on Freedom of Expression in Africa, who represents an institutional continuation of the Working Group on Freedom of Expression,[149] was established to monitor state compliance with the Declaration of Principles on Freedom of Expression in Africa.[150] When reports of massive violations of the right to freedom of expression are received, the Special Rapporteur may undertake investigative missions to a particular country. When any other relevant case is brought to the Special Rapporteur's attention, he or she may make 'public interventions' in the form of press releases and 'urgent appeals'. Promotional activities, including country missions, may be undertaken as well. Benefiting from her presence in that country, the Special Rapporteur discussed the issue of freedom of expression in The Gambia with government officials.

The effectiveness of these mechanisms has been constrained largely due to a lack of resources, a lack of state consent for visits, and inadequate publicity given to their activities.

[144] The decision to establish the position and to appoint Commissioner Nyanduga was taken at the Commission's 35th session; the mandate was adopted at its 36th session, 'Resolution on the Mandate of the Special Rapporteur on Refugees, Asylum Seekers and Internally Displaced Persons in Africa', 7 December 2004. At the Commission's 39th session, the mandate was extended to cover migrant issues (20th Activity Report, para 7).

[145] Aimed at investigating the situation of Mauritanian refugees in Senegal, 19th Activity Report, para 42). [146] ibid, para 37.

[147] ibid, para 38. [148] ibid, para 39.

[149] Established at the Commission's 30th session, it was composed of members of the Commission, staff members of the Secretariat and of Article 19, a NGO working on freedom of expression in Africa.

[150] Established at the 36th session by the 'Resolution on the Mandate and Appointment of a Special Rapporteur on Freedom of Expression in Africa', 7 December 2004; as at 31 December 2006, Commissioner Tlakula (a South African national) occupied the position.

2 Working Groups

The Commission has also established a number of working groups.[151] Working groups differ from Special Rapporteurs in their establishment, mandate, and composition. While Special Rapporteurs are based on a formal and detailed mandate adopted by the Commission, working groups function on a more ad hoc basis and without an extended mandate. While Special Rapporteurs investigate specific issues with a view to making recommendations, working groups are more exploratory and research-directed, focusing on emerging issues or matters internal to the Commission's functioning. Thus far, members of the Commission were appointed as Special Rapporteurs, while the membership of working groups is more varied, consisting of NGOs and individual experts.

The first working group to be established, dealing with the rights of 'indigenous or ethnic communities in Africa', was set up at the Commission's 28th session.[152] It consists of two Commissioners and four experts in the field of human rights or indigenous issues.[153] Its mandate is to examine the concept of indigenous people and communities in Africa, and to report to the Commission. The establishment of the Working Group follows on the initial appointment of three Commissioners as a committee to study this issue. Its major accomplishment is the drafting of a comprehensive document, the 'Report of the African Commission's Working Group of Experts on Indigenous Populations/Communities', on the human rights situation of indigenous peoples and communities in Africa.[154] The African Commission adopted this report in November 2003,[155] and it was published in book-form in 2005. The Working Group, often not comprising a member of the Commission, also conducted fact-finding visits.[156]

Following a seminar in Dakar in 1999, organized by the Commission and the NGO Interights, a Working Group on Fair Trial was established at the Commission's 27th session, in November 1999. This Working Group drafted recommendations on fair trial and legal assistance, presented to the Commission at its 31st session. After the adoption of the Robben Island Guidelines on Torture in 2002,[157] the Working Group was reconstituted as the Follow-Up Committee on the Implementation of the Robben Island Guidelines.[158]

Another three working groups have been established. One of these, the Working Group on Specific Issues Relevant to the Work of the African Commission, occupies

---

[151] Rules of Procedure, r 28.
[152] 23 October–6 November 2000; see 14th Annual Activity Report, Annex IV.
[153] As at 31 December 2006, the Commissioners represented on the Working Group were Rezag-Bara, Bitaye, and Malila.   [154] <http://www.iwgia.org.sw163.asp> (30 November 2006).
[155] At the Commission's 34th session (17th Annual Activity Report, para 41).
[156] To eg Botswana, Namibia, Niger, Burundi, the Republic of Congo, Libya, and Uganda.
[157] Reprinted in Heyns and Killander (n 12 above) 236.
[158] The Working Group subsequently, in 2003, adopted the 'Principles and Guidelines on the Right to a Fair Trial and Legal Assistance in Africa'; reprinted in Heyns and Killander (n 12 above) 240. As at 31 December 2006, Commissioner Monageng was represented on the Working Group.

itself with the improvement of the internal procedures of the Commission.[159] The other two study substantive aspects arising from the Charter. As part of her mandate as SRP, Commissioner Chirwa drew attention to the issue of the death penalty in Africa.[160] As a result of this new focus, a Working Group on the Death Penalty in Africa was established.[161] The Working Group on Economic, Social and Cultural Rights in Africa aims to prepare 'draft principles and guidelines on economic, social and cultural rights', to elaborate revised guidelines for state reporting on socio-economic rights, and to undertake 'studies and research on specific social, economic and cultural rights'.[162] In its resolution establishing the Working Group, the Commission made a broader call to all Commissioners and special mechanisms to 'pay particular attention' to social, economic, and cultural rights in the discharge of their functions.[163]

C Promotional Visits

Giving effect to the pertinent call for 'promotion' in the African Charter, the African Commission is alone among regional human rights bodies in undertaking 'promotional visits'. On a continent where many states still frown upon the inspection of their internal affairs, promotional visits may be an important first step to securing some form of engagement. Consent is required for visits,[164] and states are more likely to permit non-confrontational and non-investigative visits. Constructive dialogue with non-compliant states is probably achieved best in this way, allowing a Commissioner to sensitize high-ranking government officials to the role and importance of the African Charter, encouraging them to ratify outstanding treaties and to submit state reports. However, as 53 AU member states are shared between only 11 Commissioners, 'promotional visits' to countries occur infrequently.[165]

---

[159] As at 31 December 2006, consisting of Commissioners Melo and Tlakula, serving with representatives of three NGOs (Interights, Open Society Initiative, African Institute for Human Rights and Development). Commissioner Babana was also a founding member.

[160] By expressing 'satisfaction' about the moratoriums on execution in Kenya and Zambia, she made her position clear; see also the Commission's 'Resolution Urging the States to Envisage a Moratorium on the Death Penalty' (1999).

[161] As at 31 December 2006, consisting of Commissioners Hassan and Nyanduga, and five independent experts. So far, the activities of this Working Group have been limited owing to a lack of funds (20th Activity Report, para 37).

[162] 'Resolution on Social, Economic and Cultural Rights in Africa' (AU Doc ACHPR/Res.73 (XXXVI)04), established at the Commission's 36th session, 23 November–7 December 2004; as at 31 December 2006, members of this Working Group were Commissioners El Hassan and Melo. See also the Declaration of the Pretoria Seminar on Economic, Social and Cultural Rights in Africa, reprinted in (2005) 5 *AHRLJ* 182, which served as the impetus for the resolution above. In its resolution, the Commission also 'adopted' the Declaration and called for its wide dissemination.

[163] As above, para 3.

[164] In 2005, a promotional visit planned for Zimbabwe was cancelled when the Zimbabwean government withdrew its consent (19th Activity Report, para 35).

[165] For the current allocation of countries to Commissioners, see the Commission's 19th Activity Report, Annex II; one of the Commissioners with the largest number of allocated states (six),

The lack of adequate financial resources has been a further constraining factor.[166] For these reasons, promotional visits should not be scheduled as a matter of routine, but principally to ensure the engagement of states which never attend the Commission's sessions, to encourage states that are lagging behind with their obligations under the Charter, or to monitor situations of uncertainty or conflict.[167]

Although Commissioners are not assigned to countries of which they are nationals, they often play an important part in promoting and reinforcing their own country's obligations under the Charter. A striking example is the submission of the first Zambian state report in 2006, soon after Commissioner Malila (the Chair of the Zambian Human Rights Commission) was sworn in as a member of the African Commission in November 2005.

D Resolutions

Early on the Commission may have adopted resolutions that served a *rightorical* culture, but it later employed them much more imaginatively and productively. Resolutions are generally concisely and clearly articulated, and adequately substantiated.[168] Elaborating in greater detail on substantive rights barely mentioned in the Charter, a number of the Commission's resolutions play a role similar to that of 'General Comments' adopted by UN human rights treaty bodies.[169] These resolutions are important normative tools that inform the obligations of states, and the promotional and protective mandate of the Commission. The Commission adopted not only thematic, but also country-specific resolutions. Resolutions directed at particular states in which pertinent human rights violations are addressed, may serve a quasi-protective function, especially in the absence of individual communications against those states.

The adoption of country-specific resolutions in 2006 become a primary site of contestation, demonstrating a greater awareness on the part of states of the activities of the Commission, but also the uneasy relationship between states and the NGO community and the sensitivity of states to criticism of their human rights

Commissioner Babana, last attended the Commission's 38th session. His disengagement from the Commission left the important states of Sudan and Côte d'Ivoire without an assigned Commissioner.

[166] In the 20th Activity Report, it is reported that 'most' promotional visits could not take place 'due to a lack of funds' (para 22).

[167] It is encouraging to note that some of the more recent visits took place to countries that lacked compliance: Seychelles (not sending a representative to present its state report); Botswana (non-compliance with interim orders, never reported); Guinea-Bissau (disengaged state); and to states that recently experienced some transition or turmoil (Burundi, Mauritania) (19th Activity Report; agenda of the Commission's 38th session).

[168] In fact, the PAP could take a leaf out of the Commission's book in this regard—see Ch 5 above.

[169] See eg Declaration of Principles on Freedom of Expression in Africa (2002); Guidelines and Measures for the Prohibition and Prevention of Torture, Cruel, Inhuman or Degrading Treatment of Punishment in Africa ('Robben Island Guidelines'); and Principles and Guidelines on the Right to a Fair Trial and Legal Assistance in Africa (2003), reprinted in Heyns and Killander (n 12 above) 231–63.

record.[170] These debates also sharpened the Commission's insight into the importance of accurate fact-finding.[171]

Despite the failure of the Ugandan government to protect its nationals against the atrocities of the Lord's Resistance Army (LRA), no communications have been submitted against Uganda in this regard.[172] Nevertheless, in a resolution addressing the issue, adopted at its 38th session, the Commission called upon the LRA to free women and children and to demobilize its combatants.[173] Directing itself directly to the state, the Commission called on Uganda to guarantee the independence of the judiciary and to amend laws that allow civilians to be tried before military courts. The resolution is worded in terms reminiscent of a recommendation following a finding of a violation in an individual communication. Uganda, when given the opportunity to comment on this resolution at the time its publication was being withheld as part of the 19th Activity Report, denied that it ever threatened the independence of the judiciary, while at the same time advising the Commission about a constitutional challenge to civilian trials before military courts and an ongoing process of law reform.[174] It finally requested that parts of the resolution 'not based on facts' be 'expunged' and assured the Commission of its willingness to continue a 'constructive dialogue'.[175]

On the same occasion, country-specific resolutions were also adopted on Eritrea, Ethiopia, Sudan, and Zimbabwe. With the exception of Eritrea, which did not respond at all, the other three states took issue with various aspects of these resolutions.

In response to the seven-paragraph resolution, deploring the killing of civilians 'during confrontations with security forces', and requesting the release of arbitrarily detained political prisoners, Ethiopia submitted a 37-page response, concluding with a call that the 'ill-conceived' resolution should be excluded from the Activity Report.[176] The government expressed the view that the resolution did not take into account 'the environment in which Ethiopia's freest and most democratic election has taken place'. Although it conceded that 35 civilians were killed,

---

[170] Inspired by the 'brave new world' of human rights under the AU, the Commission at its 38th session adopted 17 resolutions, only to be faced with a backlash of resistance by states.

[171] Report of the Brainstorming Meeting on the African Commission: 9–10 May 2006, Banjul, the Gambia (Brainstorming Meeting) para 58(b) (NGOs should provide accurate information in their draft resolutions and the Commission should set up a verification mechanism).

[172] The single communication submitted against Uganda deals with a complaint by a Zaïrian national (*Buyingo v Uganda* (2000) AHRLR 320 (ACHPR 1995) (Eighth Annual Activity Report); a communication has, however, been submitted to the Committee of Experts on the Rights of the Child regarding the LRA (see Ch 5 above).

[173] 'Resolution on the Human Rights Situation in Uganda', adopted on 5 December 2005, 20th Activity Report, Annex III.

[174] Executive Summary of Uganda's Response to the African Commission Resolution on the Human Rights Situation in Uganda, presented at the 39th session of the African Commission, Banjul, The Gambia, 18 May 2006, 20th Activity Report, Annex III, paras 6–8.   [175] As above, 'prayer'.

[176] Submission by Ethiopia in accordance with Resolution EX/CL/Dec.257(VIII) concerning the 16th Activities Report (*sic*) of the African Commission, 20th Activity Report, Annex III (Ethiopian Submission) para 11.

the government blamed their deaths on action instigated by the opposition, the Coalition for Unity and Democracy (CUD).[177] Replying to the issue of arbitrary detention, the government further provided details of the applicable legal framework and of ongoing trials. As for the Commission's procedures, the government identified similarities between the Commission's resolution and that adopted by the NGO Workshop prior to the session as an indication that the Commission adopted the NGO proposal without 'further scrutiny and assessment'.[178] It also objected to the fact that the Commission placed the full text of the resolution on its web-site immediately after its adoption.

Ethiopia's argument that resolutions are confidential until their publication has been authorized by the Assembly, based on rules 77 and 79 of the Commission's Rules of Procedure,[179] is ill-conceived. The relevant provision of the Charter, article 59(1), does not require the Assembly's authorization prior to the publication of resolutions, because they are not 'measures taken' under the Commission's protective mandate. Rule 77 deals with inter-state communications and is not applicable; rule 79 does not detract from article 58(1) but merely stipulates that the Chairperson of the Commission must ensure that the Activity Report is published after the Assembly has 'considered' it.

The resolution on Darfur provides an example of the Commission reinforcing calls made at the global level, in this instance, by the UN Security Council.[180] In response to this resolution, the Sudanese government reiterated that it 'takes all necessary measures to promote human rights in the Sudan', while at the same time striving to 'preserve its political sovereignty and territorial integrity'.[181]

Invoking grounds similar to those invoked by Ethiopia, Zimbabwe called for the exclusion of the resolution on Zimbabwe.[182] The government criticized the Commission for relying on a draft resolution submitted by Amnesty International, and for pre-judging the 13 communications against Zimbabwe pending before the Commission. It proposed that the Commission amends its procedure of adopting resolutions by allowing 'equity and fair play during the exercise of the right response in the public sessions'.[183] This last suggestion is valid, and should lead to a 'verification' process; however, it should not be used as a mechanism to delay the publication of resolutions. It is essential that the Commission is not intimidated; reverting to a situation where it adopts resolutions but withholds them from the public eye until such time as their content no longer matters. Invoking article 59(1) of the Charter, it also objected to what it considered the premature publicity

---

[177] ibid, para 5.   [178] ibid, para 2.3. See also Ch 5.B above.   [179] ibid, para 2.4.

[180] 'Resolution on the Situation of Human Rights in the Darfur Region of Sudan', adopted on 5 December 2005, 20th Activity Report, Annex III, para 2(d).

[181] Comments of the Sudan on the Decision of the African Commission concerning Darfur during its 38th session, 20th Activity Report, Annex III.

[182] Response of Zimbabwe to the Resolution of the African Commission adopted during its 38th session, 20th Activity Report, Annex III (Zimbabwean Response).

[183] Zimbabwean Response (n 182 above) para 4.2.

given to the resolution. As in the case of Ethiopia, this argument misconstrues the Charter.

Illustrating how the resolutions of the Commission may play a role at the national level, an opposition MP tabled a motion commending the Commission for its adoption of the resolution on Zimbabwe.[184] This action not only provoked a debate in Parliament, but also led to publicity being given to the Commission's work in the targeted country.

E Seminars and Conferences

The Commission's agendas and Activity Reports contain many references to its intention of hosting seminars on a variety of topics.[185] A positive feature of the relatively small number of workshops and seminars organized by NGOs, with the Commission as nominal co-organizer, is their resonance with other aspects of the Commission's mandate. Far from being mere talk-shops, these meetings led to the adoption of normative frameworks supplementing the Charter, and paved the way for the appointment of special mechanisms. One such example is a seminar on socio-economic rights, held in September 2004, which spearheaded a process towards the adoption of a 'general comment' on socio-economic rights and guidelines on state reporting pertaining to these rights.[186]

F Publication and Dissemination of Information

The publication and dissemination of information, aimed at education and greater visibility, form a central part of the Commission's promotional mandate. In an electronic age, the primary dissemination tool of the Commission is the Internet. Although the Commission has a functioning web-site, it is not updated and contains only a very limited number of the documents that are in the public domain.[187] Information is also distributed electronically to NGOs enjoying observer status with the Commission.[188] The Commission has never systematically published

---

[184] L Guma, 'War of Words in Parliament over African Commission Report', <http://www.swradioafrica.com>, 14 February 2006 (27 February 2006).

[185] eg seminars on refugees and contemporary forms of slavery have been envisaged for 2005 and 2006 (18th Activity Report, para 40; 19th Activity Report, para 20).

[186] S Khoza, 'Promoting Economic, Social and Cultural Rights in Africa: The African Commission Holds a Seminar in Pretoria' (2004) 4 *AHRLJ* 334; and 'Statement on Social, Economic and Cultural Rights' (2005) 5 *AHRLJ* 182.

[187] The last Activity Report on the web-site is the 16th (omitting five later reports); the latest final communiqué is that of the 36th session (omitting the last four). Important legal texts, such as the Guidelines for National Periodic Reports and reports of special mechanisms, are not accessible on the web-site.

[188] This information is also very limited, and mostly consists of agendas for meetings and final communiqués adopted after sessions.

information about its two main functions, the examination of state reports and the consideration of communications, either on its web-site or in print form.[189]

An Information and Documentation Centre (IDOC) has been established at the Secretariat, and is overseen by a Documentation Officer.[190] The IDOC prepares and distributes information and documentation at the Commission's sessions. These documents include, for example, the 'Status of submission of state reports' and versions of Protocols in discussion or adopted. The Commission also produces a few in-house publications: its Activity Reports, resolutions, the *Review of the African Commission on Human and Peoples' Rights*, and the *Bulletin of the Commission*, and other booklets and brochures. However, these publications appear irregularly, are not up to date, and often leave much to be desired in their content and quality.[191]

The Commission alone cannot give adequate publicity to the African Charter and the work of the Commission. Local and pan-African media, working with NGOs, must step in to support the Commission's efforts. Sustained publicity about the Commission's activities in Zimbabwe provides an example of successful engagement of local and international media.[192] Increasingly, NGOs are framing domestic human rights issues with reference to the African Charter.[193]

G Relationship between Commission and NGOs

The Commission grants observer status to NGOs, entitling them to address the Commission during its public sessions. The participation of NGOs has increased significantly over the years,[194] making them by far the most visible presence at

---

[189] Transcripts of the examination of reports at the 9th to the 14th session have been published (Danielson and Harrington (n 1 above)); although the Commission does not publish a law report series, other reports fulfil that function (such as the African Human Rights Law Reports (AHRLR)).

[190] This position has been vacant since early 2006.

[191] The first to tenth Annual Activity Reports were published in 1998, identified as 'volume 1', but this remains the only volume. The 13th Annual Activity Report was published separately, but without an annex containing communications. *Resolutions* are published and updated from time to time; but they are not very user-friendly, merely listing the resolutions without providing any background or context. The *Review* last appeared in 2000, and the *Bulletin* in December 2000. These publications do not reach a wide audience.

[192] See eg N Sandu, 'African Commission to Hear APPIA Challenge' the *Independent*, <http://www.theindependent.co.zw>, 24 March 2005 (29 March 2005); UN Integrated Regional Information Networks (IRIN), 'Zimbabwe: AU Slams Human Rights Record', <http://www.allafrica.com> 3 January 2006 (5 January 2006); A Meldrum, 'African Leaders Break Silence over Mugabe's Human Rights Abuses', the *Guardian* (digital edn), <http:// www.guardian.co.uk>, 4 January 2006 (5 January 2006).

[193] See eg Reporters sans Frontières, 'Two Imprisoned Journalists Continue to be Detained in Run-Up to Elections', <http://allafrica.com>, 21 March 2005 (23 March 2005); D Andoor, 'Ugokwe Sues FG over Rights Violation' *This Day*, <http://www.thisdayonline.com>, 4 February 2006 (6 February 2006).

[194] The Commission started admitting NGOs as observers at its third session in 1988, when three NGOs were admitted. Attendance grew from three in 1988 to 137 in 2004, at the 36th session. By the 1990s, after its sixth session, 16 NGOs had obtained observer status. By the end of 2006, the number of NGOs with observer status had grown to 370 (21st Activity Report, AU Doc EX.CL/322(X), para 15).

these sessions. With more than a hundred NGOs represented at each session, the NGO community embodies the Commission's most tangible constituency.[195] Apart from being formally accountable to the AU, in practice the Commission is held accountable more consistently by NGOs.

NGOs have been crucial in the growth and consolidation of the Commission.[196] They were instrumental in the drafting of the Charter and subsequent standards, in the submission of communications, and the development of the communications procedure. They have brought to the Commission's attention human rights problems on the continent, also as part of the state reporting procedure; they have proposed resolutions; they took the initiative in establishing and providing support to special mechanisms; they facilitated missions of the Commission; lobbied governments to comply with their obligations under the Charter; and contributed to education on and dissemination of the Charter. Increasingly regarded as 'partners', NGOs have engaged critically with the Commission on its working methods, and played an important role in its working groups.

Most importantly, the prospect that NGOs may use the Commission's public sessions to 'mobilize shame' against states has brought an increasing number of states to the table. Often, these public sessions not only provide a platform for NGOs to speak to a broader international audience, but also provide a forum for dialogue with the state that may be absent domestically. Faced with criticism from home-grown NGOs, states have difficulty in persuasively raising the convenient defences of 'uninformed meddling by foreigners' or 'Westerners'. It is the challenge of NGOs that unmasks the *rightorics* in the declarations by government delegates, prompting them to invoke their 'right to reply'. At times, when NGOs and the state posit mutually exclusive factual versions, 'dialogue' is replaced by denial. At the Commission's 40th session, for example, by labelling allegations of the Ethiopian Human Rights Council as 'false and outrageous', the Ethiopian government precluded debate on the issues raised. Responding to averments by FIDH, the government of the Central African Republic implicitly placed that NGO's good faith in question by stating that FIDH 'knows very well' that the cause of violations is external, being due to attacks from 'outside' and to 'manipulations of the former regime'.

In recent times, two countries (Sudan and Zimbabwe) have featured prominently in public sessions. Usually, a minimum of five well-prepared Zimbabwean NGOs would fire a barrage of well-directed criticisms against the government. These are met by a mixture of outrage, denial, and questioning of the credentials of the NGOs. However, the tone of the responses has changed. At the 40th session, the government adopted a conciliatory stance, pointing to recommendations in the Commission's 2002 Report which had been implemented, and conceding

[195] The number of NGOs represented at the 36th–39th sessions stood at 137, 110, 135 and 128. NGOs are often represented by more than one individual (Final Communiqués of these sessions).
[196] For a comprehensive overview, see A Motala, 'Non-Governmental Organisations in the African System' in Evans and Murray (n 2 above) 246–79.

that some had not (yet) been given effect. By insisting that the extent of progress made should be appreciated, the government (at least implicitly) acknowledged that violations had occurred and that they required rectification.

To be granted 'observer status' with the Commission, NGOs must work 'in the field of human rights', and their objectives must be in 'consonance with' those of the AU Constitutive Act and African Charter.[197] The formal criteria for the written application of NGOs wishing to be granted observer status are as follows: the NGO must show proof of its 'statutes', 'legal existence', membership, sources of funding, its last financial statement, and its programme of activities. The requirement that an application must be submitted three months before the session at which it is to be considered has not been applied rigorously.

At each session, the Commission devotes a considerable period of time to the consideration of applications for observer status. As this consideration consists mainly of the mechanical yet almost comically incoherent application of technical requirements,[198] it should best be dealt with administratively by the Secretariat. Applications almost exclusively fail on formal grounds, and are deferred for the provision of supplementary documentation. Only on very rare occasions did the Commission reject applications for observer status on substantive grounds. In one notable example, the Commission rejected the application of the Project for International Courts and Tribunals (PICT), mainly due to the difficulty of locating this trans-institutional academic research centre based outside Africa within the existing criteria, leading to calls by Commissioners for a new 'categorization' of such 'NGOs'. However, at the 40th session, without any change to the criteria, the Commission granted observer status to two similarly situated institutions.[199]

The Commission's practice of granting observer status fluctuates between legalistic formalism and substance-based flexibility. This tension is illustrated by the requirement that an applicant presents a certificate of registration to show proof of 'legal existence'. In its consideration of applications from NGOs denied domestic registration, for example in Nigeria during the Abacha period and in Mauritania during 1997,[200] the Commission adopted a flexible approach to admission. At its 40th session, the Commission granted observer status to Lawyers for Human Rights Swaziland (LHR—Swaziland), despite the fact that it had not been registered officially as an NGO in Swaziland. Although it lodged an application according to Swaziland's domestic requirements for legal status in 2003, LHR—Swaziland's application was still pending in 2006. As proof of its legal existence, LHR—Swaziland submitted to the Commission a letter from the Swaziland Department

---

[197] Criteria for the Granting of and for Maintaining Observer Status with the African Commission on Human and Peoples' Rights, ch 1.2.

[198] The goalposts on issues such as the 'authentication' of financial statements, the date of the last financial statements, the scope of activities, and membership lists seem to shift depending on the approach of the Commissioner responsible for the applicant's file.

[199] Feinstein International Law Center, at Friedman School of Nutrition Science and Policy, based at Tufts University, and the Center for Reproductive Rights, both based in the USA.

[200] Motala (n 196 above) 250.

of Taxes, indicating that it had been paying taxes since 2003. Some Commissioners expressed anxiety about the precedent-setting nature of their finding (in the process displaying their ignorance of existing precedents). It was also suggested that LHR—Swaziland should await formal notification; and in the case of rejection, should lodge a petition for judicial review. Fortunately, a more flexible approach won the day, and LHR—Swaziland was accorded observer status. None of the Commissioners linked the unreasonable governmental delay in granting LHR—Swaziland official acceptance to the fact that that NGO had brought the only communication ever against Swaziland to the African Commission.[201]

From the outset, and to this day, INGOs—especially those based outside Africa—have played a dominant role within the NGO community. These organizations often have the advantages of broad membership, greater access to funding, an established institutional record, and a supportive environment. One of these INGOs, the International Commission of Jurists, based in Geneva (ICJ—Geneva), played a crucial role in the fledgling years of the Commission. Under the leadership of the Senegalese, Adama Dieng, ICJ—Geneva became one of the first three NGOs to obtain observer status, and initiated the organization of NGO Workshops immediately preceding the Commission sessions. Probably more than any other factor, the support given by ICJ—Geneva to a substantial number of NGOs, enabling them to attend these Workshops and the subsequent Commission session, saved the Commission from isolation and insularity.[202] Between 1990 and 1994, the Banjul-based African Centre for Democracy and Human Rights Studies (African Centre) collaborated with ICJ—Geneva in this endeavour. Since 2000, the African Centre has been facilitating the participation of NGOs in the 'Forum on the Participation of NGOs' prior to the sessions of the Commission. Resolutions by the NGO Forum are formally proposed to the Commission for its consideration during the session subsequent to the Forum.

Other INGOs based outside Africa, such as Amnesty International, Interights, PRI, and the International Work Group for Indigenous Affairs (IWGIA), have all made crucial contributions to the work of the Commission.[203] Although the majority of NGOs enjoying observer status with the Commission are African-based, they are less visible, often do not engage the Commission on its working methods, and mostly do not comply with the obligations attached to observer status. There are some notable exceptions, illustrated by the determined approach of NGOs in Nigeria during the Abacha era.[204] While African NGOs should

---

[201] Communication 251/2002, *Lawyers for Human Rights v Swaziland*, 18th Activity Report, Annex III.

[202] The ICJ—Geneva was also at the forefront of the move towards the establishment of an African Human Rights Court, see Ch 11 below.

[203] In many instances, the presence of Africans within particular INGOs was the driving force propelling the institutional focus towards the African regional human rights system (see eg Dieng in ICJ–Geneva, Ahmed Motala in Amnesty International, Ibrahima Kane and Chidi Odinkalu in Interights).

[204] See OC Okafor, *Legitimizing Human Rights NGOs: Lessons from Nigeria* (Trenton: Africa World Press, 2006).

increasingly be empowered to participate meaningfully in the Commission's activities, the role of INGOs in raising concerns and submitting communications is undeniable, especially where local NGOs are reluctant or unable to do so. Branding INGOs as 'Western NGOs', 'which use their financial contributions to the African Commission budget to unduly influence African Commission decisions in pursuit of the agendas of Western countries'[205] is a device by which governments seek to deflect attention away from their human rights record. A welcome development is the formation of NGO coalitions, involving African NGOs and INGOs, such as the Coalition for an Effective African Court.[206]

The involvement of IWGIA in the activities of the African Commission provides a blueprint for an effective engagement with the African regional human rights system.[207] A membership-based INGO with its secretariat in Denmark, established in 1968 in response to reports about the genocide of Indians in the Amazon, IWGIA was already well established by the time it extended its focus to include Africa.[208] Not only did it have a good track record, it also had and continues to have easy access to donor funding. As a role-player igniting the global imagination on the rights of indigenous peoples, resources have been forthcoming, enabling IWGIA to sustain attention on this topical issue.

IWGIA obtained observer status with the African Commission in 1993,[209] but only started working actively in this arena in 1999, when it organized a conference on indigenous peoples with a Tanzanian NGO, the Pastoralists Indigenous Non-Governmental Organizations Forum (PINGOS Forum).[210] Since then, IWGIA has maintained a consistent presence in Africa, reflecting its sustained commitment to the issue of indigenous peoples' rights. Its representatives are consistently present and visible at the Commission's sessions, and make informed and informative contributions from the floor.

From the outset, IWGIA worked at establishing a network of African-based indigenous groups, underscoring the simultaneous global and local dimensions of the international indigenous rights movement. In so far as it pushed its own agenda, it did so through and with local NGOs. This approach gave it legitimacy,

[205] The Response of the Government of Zimbabwe to the Resolution Adopted at the Commission's 38th session, 20th Activity Report of the Commission, Annex III, para 3.6.

[206] See <http://www.africancourtcoalition.org> (30 November 2006).

[207] The discussion of IWGIA is informed by an interview with Marianne Jensen, African Project Officer, IWGIA, at the Commission's 38th session, November 2005, Banjul, The Gambia, and a perusal of the IWGIA web-site. Other INGOs have also obtained observer status with the Commission and also play a significant role in the promotion of indigenous rights in Africa. They include the International Network for Indigenous Affairs (obtaining observer status at the 14th session); Survival International (at the 29th session); Minority Rights Group (at the 30th session); and the Forest Peoples Programme (at the 37th session).

[208] See <http://www.iwgia.org> (30 September 2006). Before it included Africa in its focus, IWGIA worked in the Arctic and in areas of Latin America and with North American Indians.

[209] Observer status granted at the Commission's 14th session, Addis Ababa, December 1993.

[210] IWGIA, *Indigenous World (2001–2002)*, <http://www.iwgia.org/graphics/Synkron-Library/Documents/publications/Downloadpublications/IndigenousWorld/YB02.pdf> (30 November 2006) 453.

derived from being at least partially rooted in the concerns of indigenous Africans at the grassroots level. IWGIA provided financial and technical support to individuals and organizations in African countries to enable them to attend sessions. After regional representation had been assured, and realizing that the acceptance of indigenous peoples' issues depends on their articulation by African voices, IWGIA assisted NGOs working in this field to obtain observer status.[211] All these voices served to sensitize other NGOs, Commissioners, and states about the plight of indigenous peoples and the importance of the inclusion of their rights as a constant discussion point on the Commission's agenda.

Premising its activities on the importance of institutionalizing efforts within the mandate of the African Commission, IWGIA and its partners lobbied one of the Commissioners to commit to their cause, and advocated the adoption of a thematic resolution by the Commission.[212] Commissioner Pityana, who took on this role, become the very able, articulate, and enthusiastic spokesperson for indigenous affairs in Africa. He did not hesitate to raise pertinent issues, put this aspect permanently on the Commission's agenda, and assisted in overcoming initial resistance from within the Commission. As a result, indigenous issues were further institutionalized within the Commission's mandate. For the first time deviating from the model of establishing a single Commissioner as Special Rapporteur, and following the precedent of similar UN institutions, the Commission was persuaded to establish a Working Group of Experts on Indigenous Populations/Communities, comprising both Commissioners and outside experts. The inclusion of non-Commissioners was a very significant step, given the Commission's persistent objection to the appointment of 'outsiders' as Special Rapporteurs. Although initially Commissioner members (Pityana and Rezag-Bara) formally retained control, they were outnumbered by and allowed the experts greater latitude in making their contributions. IWGIA continues to assist the Working Group with technical expertise and resources.

One of the reasons for resistance from governments was the lack of a clear normative commitment to indigenous peoples' rights in the Charter. Supplementary to lobbying efforts and institutional reforms, the elaboration of a normative framework was an important part of the strategy. Acting under its mandate, and based on a concept paper by IWGIA, the Working Group of Experts on Indigenous Populations/Communities elaborated a comprehensive report linking the position of indigenous peoples in Africa to the African Charter and the potential role of the African Commission. Part of IWGIA's (and the Working Group's) success is its

---

[211] African NGOs active in the domain of indigenous peoples' rights and which have obtained observer status are: Centre for Minority Rights Development (CEMIRIDE, at the 33rd session); Ogiek Welfare Council (at the 37th session); Indigenous Movement for Peace Advancement and Conflicts Transformation (at the 37th session); Mbororo Social and Cultural Development Association of Cameroon (at the 38th session); *Unissons-nous pour la Promotion des Batwa* (UNIPOBRA) (at the 40th session).

[212] Commissioner Pityana attended the 1999 conference and 'brought up the issue' at the Commission's sessions in Rwanda and Algeria (IWGIA, n 210 above, 453).

combination of solid research with activism. Appropriated by local NGOs at the national level, this report became a tool for lobbying. During 2005, the Working Group's report was, for example, employed as an important lobby instrument as a coalition of Kenyan indigenous organizations cooperated on a key advocacy activity. Three advertisements—two in English and one in Swahili—were published in three major Kenyan newspapers. These advertisements publicized the recently adopted report, and constructively drew the general public's attention to indigenous peoples' human rights. The advertisements contributed to a process of awareness-raising with regard to indigenous issues and human rights in Kenya.[213]

H Relationship between Commission and National Human Rights Institutions (NHRIs)

At the time the African Charter was drafted, the idea of a national human rights institution had not been popularized. However, the Charter pre-empted this development by obliging state parties to 'allow the establishment' of 'appropriate national institutions entrusted with the promotion and protection' of human rights.[214] On the basis of this formulation, the Commission recommended that states establish institutions to conduct 'studies and research'.[215] This narrow interpretation leaves some room for uncertainty about the type of institution envisaged, as the 'proposed' mandate falls far short of the current understanding of the mandate of NHRIs.

Nudged on and supported by donors and the UN, NHRIs flourished in Africa during the 1990s. Although the NHRIs from Ghana, South Africa, and Uganda (and to a lesser extent those from Malawi and Senegal) gained legitimacy and started functioning independently and effectively, most were 'formed by governments with dismal human rights records, weak state institutions, and no history of autonomous state bodies',[216] and often appeared to serve the largely *rightorical* role of deflecting international criticism of serious human rights abuses. As these criticisms about the independence of African NHRIs indicate, the phenomenon of Government NGOs (GONGOs) is not altogether unrelated to the growth of NHRIs in Africa.

As NHRIs were established in Africa, some started attending the sessions of the African Commission. Often sandwiched between states and NGOs, their role and contribution were never clearly defined. Based on a decision taken at its 24th session, the Commission from its 27th session onwards started granting a special

---

[213] African Commission: an IWGIA Briefing on the Process and Current Status, October 2006 <http://www.iwgia.org/graphics/Synkron-Library/Documents/InternationalProcesses/ACHR/ACHPRstatusOct2006.htm> (30 November 2006). [214] African Charter, art 26.

[215] 'Resolution on the Establishment of Committees on Human Rights or Other Similar Organs at National, Regional or Subregional Level' and 'Recommendation on Some Modalities for Promoting Human and Peoples' Rights' para (iii), Second Annual Activity Report, Annexes VIII & IX.

[216] Human Rights Watch, 'Protectors or Pretenders Government Human Rights Commissions in Africa', <http://www.hrw.org/reports/2001/africa/> (11 November 2006); summary.

status to NHRIs, termed 'affiliate status'.[217] The major requirement for 'affiliate status' is that the NHRI 'should conform' to the UN Principles relating to the Status of National Institutions (the Paris Principles).[218] The term 'affiliate status' does not define the role of NHRIs any more clearly, though, as it is merely required that these institutions 'will assist the Commission in the promotion and protection of human rights at national level'.[219] Similar to 'observer status', the affiliate status of NHRIs entitles them to be invited to, be present at, and to participate 'without voting rights' in the Commission sessions.

Half of the states in Africa have established a national human rights institution.[220] By the end of 2006, affiliate status had been granted to 19 of them.[221] With little tangible benefit to them or clarity about their role, a dwindling number of these institutions attend the Commission's sessions.[222] Especially those NHRIs that are truly 'protectors' rather than 'pretenders'[223] are more likely to prioritize available human and other resources to fulfil their very demanding mandates than to 'waste' time at the Commission's sessions.[224] These institutions already meet at 'Conferences of African Human Rights Institutions'.

On the occasion of the celebration of 25 years since the adoption of the Charter, prior to the Commission's 39th session, a second AU Conference on NHRIs was held to discuss the role of NHRIs in the African Commission.[225] This event brought 19 NHRIs together, but it remains to be seen whether the recommendations that were adopted will be implemented leading to greater engagement between the Commission and NHRIs.

---

[217] The hand of Commissioner Rezag-Bara, at the time chairing the Algerian national human rights institution, is discernible from the location where this status was granted for the first time (Algiers) and from the inclusion of the Observatoire Nationale des Droits de l'Homme d'Algrie amongst the first three NHRIs obtaining that status. He also introduced the topic when he presented a 'paper' at the 21st session, and together with Commissioner Pityana he was assigned the task of preparing a subsequent resolution.

[218] Resolution on Granting Observer [Affiliate] Status to National Human Rights Institutions in Africa, adopted at the Commission's 24th session, Banjul, the Gambia, 22–31 October 1998, para 4(a).

[219] Resolution on Granting Observer [Affiliate] Status to National Human Rights Institutions in Africa, adopted at the Commission's 24th session, Banjul, the Gambia, 22–31 October 1998.

[220] According to the Danish Human Rights Institute, National Human Rights Institutions Forum: Algeria, Benin, Burkina Faso, Cameroon, Chad, Congo, DRC, Egypt, Gabon, Ghana, Kenya, Madagascar, Malawi, Mauritania, Mauritius, Namibia, Niger, Nigeria, Rwanda, Senegal, South Africa, Tanzania, Togo, Tunisia, Uganda, Zambia, <http://www.nhri.net> (11 November 2006).

[221] 21st Activity Report, AU Doc EX/CL/322(X) para 12.

[222] A high-water mark of attendance was reached at the Commission's 28th session, when 10 NHRIs attended; the number declined to eight by the 31st session, reached seven by the 33rd session, and six by the 37th session.

[223] Human Rights Watch, 'Protectors or Pretenders Government Human Rights Commissions in Africa', <http://www.hrw.org/reports/2001/africa/> (11 November 2006), in which the Uganda Human Rights Commission is held out as a 'strong example for other human rights commissions in the region'.

[224] See eg the Uganda Human Rights Commission, Annual Report 2005, indicating that it received 1,208 complaints during 2005, and finalized 974 investigations in 2004 and 2005 <http://www. uhrc.org> (30 November 2006).   [225] 20th Activity Report, para 18.

10

The African Commission: An Assessment

In light of the three preceding chapters, a balance sheet that offsets the accomplishments of the African Commission in implementing the African Charter against its failures to accomplish that goal is now attempted. In the process, not only the Commission's role, but also that of the AU, member states, individuals, and NGOs is assessed.

During its life span of almost 20 years, the Commission has made significant progress and has taken initiatives that exceeded initial expectations. The Commission started off well when it dispelled doubts about whether its mandate included the consideration of individual communications. It subsequently resisted arguments that the complaints mandate of the Commission is restricted to cases of massive or serious violations. When the Assembly failed to respond to findings of massive violations under article 58 of the Charter, the Commission adapted its practice by treating these cases as individual communications. However, by never filling the lacuna left by the Assembly's inaction, the Commission remains without a coherent strategy to deal with urgent cases.[1] Still, the possibilities presented by an efficient collaborative relationship with the AU Peace and Security Council hold some promise for improvement.[2]

The Commission also interpreted the Charter progressively and generously, relaxing traditional standing requirements, minimizing the effect of the 'claw-back' clauses and the domestic remedies requirement, and 'reading into' the Charter some important socio-economic rights. By adopting 'general comments' elaborating the substantive provisions of the Charter, it further expanded the scope of the Charter. Compared to most other international human rights bodies, it declared a high percentage of cases admissible. It also found violations in almost all admissible cases, in the process building up a sizeable jurisprudence. Even if its practice in this regard remains inconsistent, the Commission sometimes directed detailed remedies at offending states. Formally, its decisions evolved from one-line statements into reasoned and more fully substantiated findings. Its recent decision to require states to supply information about the implementation of its findings, and to include

---

[1] Nothing much has transpired since the Commission adopted an 'Early Intervention Mechanism in Cases of Massive Human Rights Violations' at its 24th session, October 1998 (DOC/05/52(XXIV)).

[2] See Ch 5 above.

this information in its Activity Reports, is a giant leap towards a more effective complaints mechanism.

On the downside, the Commission has failed to deal effectively with complaints. Multiple postponements and long delays have characterized its procedure, leading to situations in which final decisions were taken long after the event in a less-charged political environment where the immediate impact of the decision was lost. The impression is created that the Commission postponed decisions when they were too politically charged. A narrow interpretation of its mandate for long caused the Commission to take only negligible steps in ensuring follow-up on its decisions. Its reasoning is sometimes incoherent, and inconsistencies in its application of the communications procedure are at times difficult to explain.

Based on open-ended aspects of its mandate, the Commission mandated on-site protective and other fact-finding missions. These missions have been plagued by a lack of clear procedure and by uncertainty about their aim, plunging the Commission into controversy. Delays in the adoption and publication of mission reports further undermined the impact of this procedure. In some instances, apparently due to government pressure, reports were never adopted and made public.

The Commission took it upon itself to examine reports submitted by states. However, it failed to establish a credible practice for examining these reports. The main problem is the lack of a real dialogue between the Commission and states. This is due to the examinations procedure used and a failure to consistently adopt publicly accessible concluding observations on these reports. Effective action has also not been taken against states that have never submitted reports or those that lag far behind in submitting reports. In this respect, also, the Commission has too often adopted a deferential attitude towards states, allowing them to evade from accountability.

Given the limited success of its country-specific communications and state reporting procedures, the Commission went beyond its explicit mandate when it adopted a more thematic approach to the accomplishment of its mandate by establishing special thematic mechanisms. While these mechanisms are important promotional tools, they confront states with allegations of specific violations only to a limited extent. Again, delays and the failure to adopt reports by these mechanisms, their omission from the Commission's Activity Reports, and the lack of dissemination of these reports are major impediments to their effectiveness and impact.

Even if on the whole the Commission has failed in respect of its protective mandate, it might be expected that it would be more successful at accomplishing its largely non-confrontational promotional mandate. Underscoring its promotional role, the Commission undertakes promotional visits and adopts resolutions. Drawing on the insight that it cannot by itself promote an awareness of the Charter on a continent-wide scale, the Commission has enlisted the support of NGOs and NHRIs. Still, as in many of the instances highlighted above, the dissemination of information has been lacking. Despite some recent advances, the question must be asked as to how information about the Commission's activities could be expected to permeate the public domain if the main authoritative source of its activities, its Activity Report, is (for years after its adoption) not even accessible on the Commission's own web-site. To a large extent, the Commission has performed its activities in splendid isolation from the rest of the continent, including the AU organs. While budgetary constraints account for some of these failings, they do not explain outdated information or failure to adopt and make public its numerous reports.

As far as the role of the AU, as a collective of states, is considered, discrepancies abound between AU decisions and actions. The AU's schizophrenic attitude of praising the Commission for its accomplishments, yet starving it of resources, suggests that the AU does not wish to see the Commission become more effective and forceful. The AU's failure, over many years, to answer the needs of the Commission displays a cynical satisfaction with the Commission's minimal success.

It is ironic that the advent of the AU, with its unequivocal commitment to human rights, has witnessed a reversal of some of the Commission's gains. With the AU Executive Council taking on the role of debating the Commission's Activity Reports, the Commission's activities have become much more closely scrutinized. Closer scrutiny by their peers has prompted states (in particular Ethiopia and Zimbabwe) to question the established procedures of the Commission, to contest the accuracy of the Commission's fact-finding and to delay the publication of the whole or parts of the Commission's Activity Reports. As human rights become an integral part of regional politics and inter-state relations, states that are called upon to confront these concerns have to defend their actions as being human rights-compliant. In doing this, they subscribe to human rights, as they do not want to be seen to be out of step with the demands of the changed environment, but they often use human rights language in support of pseudo-legal arguments about procedure and other technicalities.

As democratization took hold in Africa after 1990, undemocratic governments made room for more representative and accountable governments. The improved engagement of African states with the African Commission reflects the changing nature of most of these states. Today, it is the rule, rather than the exception, for states to cooperate with the Commission's communications procedure. States are more often represented at hearings and regularly submit responses to communications. States' initial reluctance to submit reports and their submission of inadequate reports have been replaced by an increasing trend in submission and an improvement in the quality of reports. Better attendance at Commission sessions by government delegations is another indication that the regional human rights system has become entrenched in the affairs of state.[3]

However, states continue to place obstacles in the way of the Commission. As constituent members of the AU, individual states share responsibility for the indefensible neglect of the material and human resource needs of the Commission. 'Invitations' for visits by the Commission's special mechanisms are rarely given, or,

---

[3] Although attendance fluctuates, it reached 36 at the 39th session.

as in the case of Zimbabwe, they may even be withdrawn. A sizeable number of states still neglect their reporting obligations. Willingness to host the Commission's sessions has also waned over the last two years. States further remain ambivalent and often uncooperative when it comes to the implementation of decisions, recommendations, or requests for information. From this perspective, even state attendance at sessions should be viewed with circumspection, as it may represent attempts by states to neutralize criticism.[4]

Even if NGOs and individuals have largely become the backbone of the African Commission, the committed involvement of African NGOs has been lacking. Only a handful is represented at Commission sessions; and few submit communications or present 'shadow' reports to the Commission. While it is understandable that local NGOs devote their limited resources to addressing more immediate concerns at the national level, and recognizing that the Commission's track record does not inspire confidence, it is up to these NGOs to fully unlock the potential of the regional system. By way of example, the experience of indigenous peoples shows that the benefits of engaging the Commission may be most significant when domestic protection is at its most precarious.

The question remains whether the Commission has focused its attention productively on the situation of poverty in Africa. Despite the prominence given in the African Charter to socio-economic rights, they have been conspicuous in their absence from the Commission's promotional activities and resolutions. In two general resolutions about the 'human rights situation in Africa', adopted in 1994 and 1999, for example, the Commission expressed its concern only about 'civil and political' rights. The Commission's preoccupation with these rights may be ascribed to the immediacy of those violations in Africa, but also to the limited agendas of NGOs involved in the Commission's work. Its two prominent decisions on socio-economic rights, the *Ogoniland* and the *Gambian Mental Health* cases, the Declaration of the Pretoria Seminar on Social, Economic and Cultural Rights in Africa, and the establishment of a Working Group to deal with these rights are largely the result of a shift in NGO activism. To its credit, the Commission gave a progressive interpretation to socio-economic rights in the two cases mentioned above, and has subsequently integrated these rights into its mandate. However, the impact of the two decisions has been negligible, and the Commission's other efforts have come far too late.

---

[4] Support for this suspicion may be found in a perusal of attending states and the number of persons in their delegations. At the height of criticism against Mauritania, this government was consistently represented by a sizeable high-level delegation; the same applies to states such as Ethiopia, Sudan, and Zimbabwe.

11

The African Court on Human and Peoples' Rights

Across the globe, including in Africa, 'political' questions have over the last decade become more and more judicialized. Africa has witnessed the creation of an international and a quasi-international criminal tribunal, the International Criminal Tribunal for Rwanda (ICTR) and Special Court for Sierra Leone (SCSL), the institution of national constitutional courts, and the establishment of the African Court on Human and Peoples' Rights (African Human Rights Court).[1] African states have also accepted judicial resolution, by way of international and national

---

[1] OAU Doc OAU/LEG/MIN/AFCHPR/PROT(I)Rev.2, adopted on 10 June 1998, and entered into force on 25 January 2004; see <http://www.africa-union.org> (30 November 2006) and C Heyns (ed), *Human Rights Law in Africa* (vol 1) (Leiden: Martinus Nijhoff, 2004) 170. On the Protocol and Court generally, see N Krisch, 'The Establishment of an African Court on Human and Peoples' Rights' (1998) 58 *Zeitschrift für ausländisches öffentliches Recht und Völkerrecht* 713; EK Quashigah, 'The African Court of Human Rights: Prospects, in Comparison with the European Court of Human Rights and the Inter-American Court of Human Rights' (1998) 10 *ASICL Proc* 59; GJ Naldi and KD Magliveras, 'Reinforcing the African System of Human Rights: The Protocol on the Establishment of a Regional Court of Human and Peoples' Rights' (1998) 16 *NQHR* 431; M Mutua, 'The African Human Rights Court: A Two-Legged Stool?' (1999) 21 *HRQ* 342; NJ Udombana, 'Towards the African Court on Human and Peoples' Rights: Better Late than Never' (2000) 3 *Yale Human Rights Development LJ* 45; F Ouguergouz, *The African Charter on Human and Peoples' Rights. A Comprehensive Agenda for Human Dignity and Sustainable Democracy in Africa* (The Hague: Martinus Nijhoff, 2003) (*Ouguergouz: African Charter*) 687–754; IA El-Sheikh, 'The Future Relationship between the African Court and the African Commission' (2002) 2 *AHRLJ* 252; J Harrington, 'The African Court on Human and Peoples' Rights' in MD Evans and R Murray (eds), *The African Charter on Human Rights. The System in Practice, 1986–2000* (Cambridge: Cambridge University Press, 2002) 305; F Viljoen, 'A Human Rights Court for Africa, and Africans' (2004) 30 *Brooklyn J of Intl L* 1; F Ouguergouz, 'The Establishment of an African Court of Human and Peoples' Rights: A Judicial Premiere for the African Union' (2005) *AYBIL* 79 (*Ouguergouz: African Court*); F Viljoen (ed), *Judiciary Watch Report: The African Human Rights System: Towards the Co-existence of the African Commission on Human and Peoples' Rights and African Court on Human and Peoples' Rights* (Nairobi: Kenyan Section of the International Commission of Jurists, 2006) (*Judiciary Watch Report*).

adjudication, of contentious issues ranging from border disputes and armed incursions to disputed elections and the constitutionality of the death penalty.[2] While these processes may represent 'the continuation of politics by other means',[3] it is also true that legal argument and reasoned judgments may place significant constraints on political bargaining and arbitrary decision-making by the executive. In this chapter, a background is given to the African Human Rights Court, before an assessment is made of the challenges it faces, among others in addressing the tension between law and politics.

A Historical Background to the Court's Establishment

The drafters of the African Charter on Human and Peoples' Rights (African Charter) did not follow the European and Inter-American human rights systems' precedents of creating a regional court, but opted to establish a quasi-judicial body, the African Commission on Human and Peoples' Rights (African Commission).[4] As a quasi-judicial body, the African Commission is only able to make 'recommendations' to the AU Assembly of Heads of State and Government (AU Assembly),[5] and performs not only protective, but also conciliatory and promotional functions.[6]

The movement towards establishing an African human rights court may be traced back to 1961, when African jurists assembled in Lagos, Nigeria, for an African

[2] See Section-below, cases cited in nn 236 and 237, and nn 275–8 in I.1 below, and eg the ruling of the Supreme Court of Justice of Guinea-Bissau on the constitutionality of the naming of a Prime Minister (afrolNews,'Guinea-Bissau Supreme Court to Decide on Naming of PM', <http://www.afrol.com>, 5 December 2005 (5 December 2005)); the Swaziland High Court upholding a ban on opposition parties (IRIN, 'Swaziland: Court Upholds Ban on Opposition Parties', <htttp://www.irinnews.org>, 24 March 2005 (30 March 2005)); and numerous election-related petitions (eg against the 2003 presidential elections in Nigeria; concerning the right of jailed opposition politician Roy Bennett to contest parliamentary elections in Zimbabwe; challenging President Mugabe's 2002 victory in the Zimbabwean presidential election; and the contestation of presidential election results in Madagascar and the DRC; and on the constitutionality of the death penalty, see eg *Mbushuu and Another v Tanzania* [1995] 1 LRC 216 (Tanzania), *S v Makwanyane* (1995) 3 SA 391 (CC) (South Africa), *S v Ntesang* (1995) 4 BCLR 436 (Botswana), *Klau v State* (1998) 13 NWR 531 (Nigeria), and *Susan Kigula and others v The Attorney General* [2006] 3 LRC 388 (Uganda), Constitutional Petition No 6 of 2003, judgment delivered in June 2005 (Uganda).

[3] LR Helfer and AM Slaughter, 'Towards a Theory of Effective Supranational Adjudication' (1997) 107 *Yale L J* 273, 389. The downside of 'judicialization of politics' is the use of judicial means to silence or constrain political opponents (see eg the treason charges against the leaders of the opposition in eg Malawi, Uganda, Zambia, and Zimbabwe).

[4] Given the alternatives in existence at the time, African states opted for a solution midway between a minimalist type of institution (as exemplified by the Convention on the Elimination of Racial Discrimination Committee) and a maximalist institution (such as the European Court of Human Rights). As Ouguergouz observes, the OAU opted for the 'prince' (the medium of diplomacy and politics) rather than the 'sage' (judicial means) (F Ouguergouz, *La Charte Africaine des Droits de l'Homme et des Peuples* (Paris: Presses Universitaires de France, 1993) 75). I Österdahl, *Implementing Human Rights in Africa* (Uppsala: Iustus Förlag, 2002) points to the similarities between the Charter system and the 1503 procedure under the UN Charter (39–43).

[5] African Charter, arts 52, 53, 58(2).

[6] ibid, art 45 and eg UO Umozurike, *The African Charter on Human and Peoples' Rights* (The Hague: Martinus Nijhoff, 1997) 81. See also Chs 8 and 9 above.

'Conference on the Rule of Law'. The resolution adopted by the Conference, which subsequently became known as 'The Law of Lagos', urged African governments to 'study the possibility of adopting an African Convention on Human Rights' and 'the creation of a court of appropriate jurisdiction'.[7] However, these efforts came to naught, as the OAU Charter was adopted in 1963 without either a human rights framework or any human rights mechanism whatsoever.

The issue of a judicial implementation mechanism was raised again during the deliberations immediately preceding the adoption of the African Charter in 1981.[8] A proposal introduced by Keba M'Baye omitted the institution of a court, explaining that it is 'thought premature to do so at this stage'.[9] Prophetically, it added that the 'ideal is, no doubt, a good and useful one which could be introduced in future by means of an additional protocol to the Charter'.[10] At the ministerial meeting in Banjul, Guinea proposed that a tribunal to judge crimes against humanity and to protect human rights should be created.[11] This proposal was (at least implicitly) directed at the situation in South Africa, which had become a burning issue after the 1976 uprising in Soweto.[12]

It took almost four decades for the idea of an African Human Rights Court to ripen into the Protocol to the African Charter on the Establishment of an African Court on Human and Peoples' Rights (Court Protocol or Protocol), adopted by the OAU Assembly on 9 June 1998, in Ouagadougou, Burkina Faso.[13] The number of NGOs enjoying observer status with the African Commission had by then grown substantially,[14] and the regular pre-session workshops provided a forum to raise support for the establishment of a court.[15] In 1994, as a window of opportunity opened up in Africa, following the end of the Cold War, the OAU Assembly mandated the drafting process. Democratization swept across the continent, by the middle of the decade leading to multi-party elections resulting in political

---

[7] International Commission of Jurists, *African Conference on the Rule of Law* (1961) 11.

[8] See Ch 4 above.

[9] Fourth para of 'Introduction' of M'Baye Draft African Charter on Human and Peoples' Rights, OAU Doc CAB/LEG/67/1, prepared for the Meeting of Experts, Dakar, Senegal, 28 November–8 December 1979, reprinted in C Heyns (ed), *Human Rights Law in Africa 1999* (The Hague: Kluwer Law International, 2002) 65–77 (M'Baye proposal).   [10] ibid.

[11] Meeting of 7–19 January 1981; quoted in Ouguergouz (n 4 above) 72.

[12] The Rapporteur (M'Baye) gave the following summary of the resulting discussion: 'It should be mentioned that a delegation proposed an amendment according to which the meeting was to draft a text establishing an African Court on Human and Peoples' Rights to judge crimes against mankind and violations of human rights. The participants took note of this amendment but were of the opinion that it was untimely to discuss it' (Council of Ministers 37th ordinary session, OAU Doc CM/1149(XXXVII) (1981) para 117).

[13] On the drafting history of the Protocol, see eg B Kioko, 'The Road to the African Court on Human and Peoples' Rights' (1998) 10 *ASICL Proc* 70.

[14] By the end of 1994, some 140 NGOs had been granted observer status with the African Commission.

[15] Among numerous NGOs, the International Commission of Jurists, headquartered in Geneva (ICJ—Geneva) was very influential in this regard. It produced the first draft, tabled at Cape Town. The ICJ's Secretary-General at the time, Adama Dieng, was a prominent figure in the process.

change and the establishment of, and greater reliance on, domestic constitutional courts. This paved the way for the acceptance of a continental court. The end of the Cold War also resulted in a flourish of new international judicial mechanisms, linking the adoption of the Court Protocol to a global trend.

Government experts, mainly lawyers, meeting in Cape Town in 1995, adopted the first draft Protocol (Cape Town draft).[16] The Cape Town draft made the acceptance of direct access to the Court by individuals an automatic consequence of ratification.[17] After discussing it, the OAU Council of Ministers referred this draft back to a further meeting of government experts. This meeting, which took place in Nouakchott, Mauritania, during 1997, adopted the 'Nouakchott draft'.[18] This draft amended the Cape Town draft in two significant respects. First, the number of ratifications required for the entry into force of the Protocol was increased from 11 to 15.[19] Secondly, the Nouakchott draft made state acceptance of the Court's competence to receive petitions directly from individuals dependent on an optional declaration, rather than an automatic consequence of ratification.[20]

A third meeting of government legal experts, this time enlarged to include diplomats, took place in Addis Ababa, culminating in the 'Addis Ababa draft'. Both the changes mentioned above were retained in the Addis Ababa draft. The Addis Ababa draft was submitted to a Conference of Ministers of Justice and Attorneys-General, which effected a minor amendment.[21] The OAU Assembly then endorsed it without any further amendment.[22]

Soon after the adoption of the Protocol, the Commission urged member states to ratify the Protocol 'within the shortest possible time'.[23] However, by 1998, only two states (Burkina Faso and Senegal) had ratified the Protocol. For the next four years, the pace of ratification dropped to one country per year (The Gambia in 1999, Mali in 2000, Uganda in 2001 and South Africa in 2002). The year 2003 saw an acceleration, with nine states (Algeria, Burundi, Comoros, Côte d'Ivoire, Lesotho, Libya, Mauritius, Rwanda, and Togo) depositing their instruments of ratification. In 2004 five more states (Ghana, Kenya, Mozambique, Niger, and Nigeria) became state parties to the Protocol, and in 2005 and 2006

---

[16] OAU Doc OAU/LEG/EXP/AFC/HPR(I). For an in-depth discussion of this draft, see GJ Naldi and K Magliveras, 'The Proposed African Court of Human and Peoples' Rights: Evaluation and Comparison' (1996) 8 *RADIC* 944. The Cape Town meeting was organized by OAU General Secretariat, together with the African Commission and 'with the support of the International Commission of Jurists' (Report of the Government Experts Meeting on the Establishment of an African Court of Human and Peoples' Rights, OAU Doc OAU/LEG/EXP/AFC/HPR/RPT(I)Rev.1, repr in Heyns (n 9 above) 245. The draft tabled for discussion in Cape Town was prepared by Vasak at the request of the ICJ (Harrington (n 1 above) 308).

[17] Cape Town draft, art 6, allowing 'individuals, non-governmental organisations and groups of individuals' to bypass the Commission on 'exceptional grounds'.

[18] OAU Doc OAU/LEGAL/EXP/AFCHPR/PRO (2), repr in Heyns (n 9 above) 259.

[19] ibid, art 33(3).   [20] ibid, art 6.

[21] See art 34(3) and 34(6) of the Addis Ababa draft.   [22] n 1 above.

[23] 'Resolution on the Ratification of the Additional Protocol on the Creation of an African Court on Human and Peoples' Rights', adopted at the Commission's 24th session, October 1998.

two more, Mauritania and Tanzania. By the end of 2006, the number of state parties stood at 23.

Factors that may have precipitated this accelerated adoption are as follows: The African Commission persisted in prodding states to ratify, as evidenced by a call in May 2002 urging 'all OAU member states to ratify or accede as soon as possible to the Protocol'.[24] In the late 1990s, human rights promotion and protection received strong backing from the OAU Assembly and Secretary-General. The OAU's first Ministerial Conference on human rights in Africa was held in 1999, followed by a second (the first under AU auspices) in May 2003, in Kigali, Rwanda. The Kigali Declaration, adopted thereafter, noted 'with concern' that only nine states had ratified the Protocol, and 'appealed' to other states to follow suit—in particular 'to enable [the Protocol] to come into force by July 2003 as required by AHG/Dec. 117 (XXXVIII)'.[25] The sudden surge in acceptance may also be indicative of a spirit of greater commitment to African unity and the development of the AU and its institutions, more generally. A sense of enthusiasm inspired by the 'new era' of the AU was exemplified by the speed with which a simple majority of member states ratified the Protocol establishing the Peace and Security Council, and the Protocol to the Treaty establishing the African Economic Community relating to the Pan-African Parliament:[26] the former entered into force about a year and a half after its adoption,[27] and the latter just short of three years after its adoption.[28] The institution of the first inter-state communication procedure before the African Commission caused governments to take note of the African human rights system—it is more than coincidental that all three respondent states have ratified the Protocol.[29] On a more cynical note, some states may have been propelled into action by the prospect of bidding to host the Court, an avenue open only to state parties to the Protocol. To some extent, African enthusiasm and participation in establishing the International Criminal Court (ICC), and the entry into force of its Statute in 2002, also left their mark on the parallel process of putting the African Human Rights Court in place.[30]

---

[24] 'Resolution on the Ratification of the Protocol to the African Charter on Human and Peoples' Rights on the Establishment of an African Court on Human and Peoples' Rights', adopted at the Commission's 31st session, 2–16 May 2002, Pretoria, South Africa (15th Annual Activity Report, Annex IV).

[25] Kigali Declaration, para 26, AU Doc MIN/CONF/HRA/Decl.1(I) (8 May 2003).

[26] For their texts, see <http://www.africa-union.org> (30 November 2006).

[27] It was adopted on 9 July 2002, in Durban, South Africa, and entered into force on 26 December 2003, in accordance with art 22(5) of the Peace and Security Council Protocol.

[28] It was adopted on 2 March 2001, in Sirte, Libya, and entered into force on 14 December 2003, in accordance with art 22 of the Pan-African Parliament Protocol.   [29] See Ch 8 above.

[30] African participation in the creation of the ICC has been significant (S Maqungo, 'The African Contribution towards the Establishment of an International Criminal Court' (2000) 8 *AYBIL* 333). As the ICC Statute and Protocol both opened for ratification in 1998, the relative acceptance by African states is revealing: By 31 December 2006, 29 AU members had ratified the ICC Statute, slightly more than the 23 Protocol ratifications. Eight states (Burkina Faso, The Gambia, Lesotho, Mali, Mauritius, Senegal, South Africa, and Uganda) have ratified both, thus leaving 21 states that have ratified the ICC Statute but not the Protocol.

B The Court as Judicial Complement to the Quasi-judicial Mandate of the African Commission

The overarching aim of the Court is to supplement the Commission's individual communications procedure.[31] The question may therefore be posed whether the Court will be able to overcome the problems thus far experienced by the Commission in dealing with these communications. Seven difficulties associated with the Commission's efforts, mostly resulting from its status as a quasi-judicial body, are discussed below, and the potential of the African Court to rectify these deficiencies is investigated.

1 Nature of the Findings: From Recommendatory to Binding

The Commission's findings (or 'reports') are not regarded as final: they merely are 'recommendations' to the political body that had given life to the Commission, the OAU/AU Assembly, and lately, the AU Executive Council. These findings become 'final' only once they are contained in the Commission's Activity Report and are approved by the OAU/AU Assembly, or Executive Council.[32] This has weakened the impact of the findings of the Commission by inhibiting state compliance with findings. During the drafting process, the Chairman of the Committee of Experts (M'Baye) drew attention to 'the essentially technical terms of reference of the African Commission'.[33] His aim apparently was to appease disconcerted states by reassuring them about the limited intrusion allowed by the Charter. Rembe points out that one of the draw-backs of the Commission is the lack of a mandate to make final binding decisions[34] and suggests that 'a court with final decision making power be set up'.[35]

Under the Protocol, the decisions of the Court are final.[36] They are not subject to appeal (to any other judicial institution) or to political confirmation (by any

---

[31] In terms of art 2 of the Court Protocol, the Court 'shall ... complement the protective mandate of the African Commission ... '. Thus far, the exercise of this mandate has been directed almost exclusively at individual communications. Art 8 of the Protocol stipulates that the Rules of Procedure of the Court have to bear in mind the 'complementarity between the Commission and the Court'.

[32] This 'finality' introduces the question whether the 'adoption' of these findings by the OAU/AU 'converts' them into legally binding decisions. The answer to this question depends on the legal force of the OAU/AU decisions themselves. While the situation under the OAU Charter was unclear, decisions of the AU amounting to 'regulations' and 'directives' are legally binding (see r 33 of the AU Assembly's Rules of Procedure, <htttp://www.africa-union.org>).

[33] Annex to Report of the Secretary-General on the Draft African Charter, para 13 of the Rapporteur's report.

[34] NS Rembe, *The System of Protection of Human Rights under the African Charter: Problems and Prospects* (Rome, Lesotho: Institute for Southern African Studies, University of Lesotho, 1991) 44.

[35] ibid; see also interview with Commissioner Amega (1996) (October–December) *AFLAQ* 43.

[36] Court Protocol, art 28(2). The only exception is that the Court may review its own decision 'in the light of new evidence' (art 28(3)). This exception is allowed for in other international courts' rules,

body of the AU). The consequence is that these decisions are unequivocally bind-ing on state parties. State parties not only 'undertake to comply with the judgment in any case to which they are parties', but also to 'guarantee its execution'.[37]

2 Remedies: From Uncertainty to Clarity

Complainants who approach the African Commission are required to have exhausted domestic remedies before their complaints may be considered. The lack of remedies at the national level is the most important reason for the existence and necessity of supranational recourse. Consequently, the underlying idea is that, should a state fail to provide effective remedies, the Commission will step in. Although it has taken encouraging and innovative steps, the Commission has not been able to provide effective remedies, or to oversee their implementation. In this regard its efforts have been erratic, constituting inconsistent, *ad hoc* practices. This is hardly surprising, given the Charter's silence about any form of remedy following a find-ing of violation.[38] In fact, the Charter mentions this concept only as an obstacle, in the form of the general rule that 'domestic remedies' have to be exhausted before the Commission will consider a communication.[39] As far as the sufficiency of the remedies recommended by the Commission is concerned, three categories may be distinguished: no remedy, a very open-ended remedy,[40] and a specific and detailed remedy.[41] Omitting to order a remedy or recommending an open-ended remedy does not make it clear to states what they are required to do, thus impeding fol-low-up or implementation as the form and nature of the remedy are bound to be contested. An example is *Media Rights Agenda and Others v Nigeria*, where the respondent state was urged 'to bring its laws in conformity with the provisions of

see eg r 120 (Request for Review) of the ICTR Rules of Procedure and Evidence, and the ICTR Appeal Chamber decision in *Jean Bosco Barayagwiza v The Prosecutor* (*Prosecutor's Request for Review or Reconsideration*), ICTR-97-19-AR72 (31 March 2000).

[37] Court Protocol, art 30.

[38] This function is not explicitly provided for by the Charter, but a generous and purposive inter-pretation of art 45(2) can include the ordering of appropriate remedies. This sub-section mandates the Commission to 'ensure the protection of the human and peoples' rights', but adds that this has to be done 'under conditions laid down by the present Charter'. This qualification complicates matters and makes a broadened interpretation unlikely.

[39] African Charter, arts 50 and 56; where 'redress' is mentioned, it refers to 'redress already given' by a state, something which may be relevant in a state's explanation of a violation as part of the inter-state communications procedure (art 47 of the Charter).

[40] Examples of relatively recent instances where the Commission found violations of the Charter, but left the issue of an appropriate remedy totally open (that is, by not stipulating a remedy), are Communication 225/98, *Huri-Laws v Nigeria* (2000) AHRLR 273 (ACHPR 2000) (14th Annual Activity Report), and Communication 223/98, *Forum of Conscience v Sierra Leone* (2000) AHRLR 293 (ACHPR 2000) (15th Annual Activity Report).

[41] Examples are found in Communication 155/96, *Social and Economic Rights Action Centre and Another v Nigeria* (2001) AHRLR 60 (ACHPR 2001) (15th Annual Activity Report) (*Ogoniland* case), and in Communications 54/91, 61/91, 98/93, 164/97–196/97, 210/98 (joined), *Malawi African Association and Others v Mauritania* (2000) AHRLR 149 (ACHPR 2000) (13th Annual Activity Report).

the Charter'.[42] The failure of the African Commission to define the conditions of 'conformity' is likely to have contributed to Nigeria's non-compliance with this recommendation.

In contrast, there is a clear legal basis in the Court Protocol for the provision of remedies, allowing the African Court to make 'appropriate orders to remedy the violation'.[43] Although the provision does not provide an exhaustive list of remedies, it stipulates some specific examples of possible remedies. Further elaboration will be guided by the 'appropriateness' of a particular remedy to attain the purpose of 'restoring the victim in his or her rights' (according to the principle of *restitutio in integrum*).

3 Implementation: From an Ad Hoc Practice to a Comprehensive System

Given the non-binding nature of findings and the weak legal basis of remedies under the Charter, it is hardly surprising that the implementation (or enforcement) of remedies has been weak. The Commission has not instituted a follow-up system geared towards gathering information about steps taken by states in response to findings by the Commission. Without the required information base, the Commission has remained passive in respect of the consequences of its findings. For some time, no systematic follow-up of decisions of the Commission has been in place. This aspect does not feature explicitly in either the African Charter or in the Commission's Rules of Procedure. In practice, some Commissioners have undertaken limited follow-up on an ad hoc basis. Questions have been posed about the implementation of decisions on individual communications during the examination of state reports.[44] The Commission has also included recommendations in its findings on the merits that the state party should report in its periodic report about the implementation of that finding.[45] Some of the remedies ordered also imply a system of follow-up.[46] Sometime after setting a time-limit within which an offending state had to report back directly to the Commission on implementation in one communication,[47] the Commission adopted a resolution allowing

[42] Communications 105/93, 128/94, 130/94, 152/96 (joined), *Media Rights Agenda and Others v Nigeria* (2000) AHRLR 200 (ACHPR 1998) (14th Annual Activity Report).

[43] Court Protocol, art 27(1).

[44] As was done by Commissioner Johm, in respect of the state reports of Mauritania, examined during the Commission's 31st session, held in Pretoria, May 2002 (notes on file with author).

[45] See Communication 211/98, *Legal Resources Foundation Centre v Zambia* (2001) AHRLR 84 (ACHPR 2001) (14th Annual Activity Report), remedy ordered.

[46] See eg the remedy in the *Ogoniland* case (n 41 above) where the Commission urged the government of Nigeria to keep the Commission informed of the outcome of the work of the Ministry of the Environment addressing environmental issues particularly in Ogoniland, and about the outcome of the Judicial Commission of Inquiry investigating human rights violations. These requests imply a continuous monitoring role on the part of the Commission.

[47] Communication 251/2002, *Lawyers for Human Rights v Swaziland* (18th Annual Activity Report).

states 90 days to indicate how recommendations have been implemented in all cases.[48]

State parties to the Court Protocol specifically undertake to implement the findings of the Court (including remedies ordered).[49] Institutional or systematic control over 'enforcement' is provided for: the Executive Council must be notified of judgments, and must monitor their execution on behalf of the Assembly. In its annual report to the Assembly, the Court must also specify instances of non-compliance by states.[50] Non-compliance may lead to an AU decision, which in turn may lead to sanctions envisaged under the AU Constitutive Act.[51] Findings of a court can be implemented effectively as they are binding. This will lead to real sanctions and remedies, and not recommended courses of action.[52] The perception must be established firmly that ordinary Africans stand to benefit from the African Charter and its institutions. Human rights and democracy are closely connected—if not in practice, then in people's minds. Once the concept of human rights has become important to members of civil society, they have an added incentive to ensure continued democratic governance in their country. In this way, the Court may, through its pronouncements, indirectly strengthen democratic values and help consolidate fragile African democracies.

4 Accessibility: From Secrecy to Openness

Confidentiality obscures the protective work of the Commission. Under the Charter, 'all measures taken' by the Commission have to remain confidential until they are approved by the Assembly. The term 'all measures taken' was interpreted to include the Commission's finding and reasoning in all communications.[53] Once authorized, the Commission's decisions were not made accessible enough and were not disseminated widely. There is also no systematic official publication of the Commission's decisions.[54] Excessive confidentiality is one of the factors contributing to a very low media profile and awareness of the African Commission in Africa.

---

[48] See Ch 8.A.9 above, where the implications of the Commission's resolution, adopted in November 2006, are discussed.   [49] Court Protocol, art 30.

[50] ibid, art 31.

[51] See the term 'other measures of a political and economic nature' in art 23(2) of the AU Constitutive Act.

[52] See eg observations made by Commissioner Kisanga in (1996) (October–December) *AFLAQ* 31.

[53] African Charter, art 59(1).

[54] The most recent decisions may be accessed in the Annual Activity Reports of the Commission, available at the Commission's web-site, <http://www.achpr.org> (up to the 18th Annual Activity Report) and at <http://www.chr.up.ac.za> (up to the 21st Activity Report). The Institute for Human Rights and Development, an NGO based in Banjul, The Gambia, published a 'Compilation of Decisions on Communications of the African Commission on Human and Peoples' Rights' (1st edn 2000, 1994–99; 2nd edn 2002, 1994–2001); and the Centre for Human Rights, University of Pretoria, publishes the 'African Human Rights Reports', 2000–4.

Court proceedings are usually open to the press and public. The African Court is no different.[55] Although there is an exception to the principle of openness, it should only be applied to protect witnesses in situations where individuals (complainants or witnesses) are seriously threatened. A reasoned judgment has to be 'read in open court'.[56] Not only the parties to the case, but all AU members have to be notified of decisions.[57] The Court's decisions should be made accessible on its web-site.

5 Urgent Cases: From Inadequacy to Efficiency?

The Commission has been ineffective in dealing with urgent matters that require interim relief. The African Charter does not provide for the adoption of interim (or provisional) measures. The Commission's Rules of Procedure fill this lacuna, by providing that the Commission may inform a state party on the 'appropriateness of taking provisional measures to avoid irreparable damage being caused to the victim of the alleged violation'.[58] Such measures may be 'indicated' by the Commission, or when it is not in session or in cases of urgency, by the Chair, in consultation with other members of the Commission.[59] The Chair may take 'any necessary action' in urgent cases, but must report back to the Commission about action taken, at the next session.[60] The Commission's use of interim measures was met with disregard by targeted states, as in the case involving Ken Saro-Wiwa. Ambivalence about the legal status of decisions on interim measures further undermined the Commission's ability to deal effectively with urgent cases.[61] The regular procedure before the Commission is not attuned to deal with communications of an urgent nature. The Commission's 'Early Warning Mechanism' is unclear and unknown.

Under the Court Protocol, the Court has a wide mandate to adopt 'such provisional measures as it deems necessary' in cases 'of extreme gravity and urgency, and when necessary to avoid irreparable harm to persons'.[62] The question may be posed whether the 'adopted measures' are 'judgments' that the parties have undertaken to execute, and that the AU Executive Council will monitor on behalf of the Assembly. In one possible interpretation, those 'measures' include: 'findings' in article 27 (a finding of a violation, a remedy, or a provisional measure), the dispositive *parts of* the 'judgment'. The terms 'finding' and 'judgment' are not mutually exclusive. The Court could clarify this apparent uncertainty by denoting its 'finding' on provisional measures as a 'judgment', an avenue followed in the other

---

[55] Court Protocol, art 10(1). The Rules of Procedure may clarify under which circumstances *in camera* proceedings may take place. 'Proceedings' should be interpreted broadly so as to include court documents, such as pleadings, which should be publicly accessible on the Court's web-site, see also R Murray, 'A Comparison between the African and European Courts of Human Rights' (2002) 2 *AHRLJ* 195, 215.   [56] Court Protocol, art 28(5).
[57] ibid, art 29(1).   [58] Commission's Rules of Procedure, r 111(1).   [59] R 111(2).
[60] R 111(3).   [61] See Ch 8 above.   [62] Court Protocol, art 27(2).

regional systems. It should therefore follow that these measures are binding on state parties.[63]

6 Profile: From Obscurity to Visibility?

Considering the vastness of the African continent and the frequency of human rights reports and allegations, very few communications have reached the Commission.[64] At the domestic level, many factors accounted for this, among them illiteracy, political instability or war, absence of civil society, lack of legal aid, lack of access to justice, onerous local remedies, dysfunctional court systems, and corruption. Factors at the level of the Commission also contributed, though. Not exploiting the possibilities of media exposure, the Commission has not been very effective in disseminating information about its existence and its case-law.

Does the mere existence of a Court signify greater media interest and exposure? To some extent, it does. A continental Court is bound to have a much clearer identity in the mind of Africans. Ultimately, though, the Court itself will have to move beyond symbolism and earn its legitimacy by securing a high profile through accessible and transparent procedures, the quality of its judgments, and the fairness of its findings. In his speech at the opening of the meeting of experts in Cape Town, the South African Minister of Justice, Dullah Omar, remarked that the precise impact of the Court is unpredictable, but expressed his conviction that 'its establishment will raise awareness in the field of human rights generally'.[65]

7 Pace of the Process: From Delayed to more Immediate Justice?

Another serious problem experienced so far is that of the delay in finalizing communications.[66] Often, when the Commission eventually reaches a finding and recommends a remedy, a change of government has already taken place. In the

---

[63] See also *LaGrand (Germany v United States of America)* [2001] ICJ Rep 466 (27 June 2001) para 109, where the ICJ found that interim measures under art 41 of its Statute are binding. This matter may also be clarified in the Court's Rules of Procedure. See also *Mamatkalov and Another v Turkey*, European Court of Human Rights (6 February 2003).   [64] See Ch 8.A above.

[65] Photocopy of speech at 8.

[66] See, generally, D Shelton, 'Ensuring Justice with Deliberate Speed: Case Management in the European Court of Human Rights and the United States Courts of Appeals' (2000) 21 *Human Rights L J* 337. Institutional delay was one of the main justifications for the transformation of the European human rights system into a single judicial system (under Protocol 11), and is behind the further attempts to streamline the system, as foreseen in Protocol 14 to the Convention for the Protection of Human Rights and Fundamental Freedoms, Amending the Control System of the Convention (Protocol 14). The Explanatory Report to Protocol 11, establishing a single European Court of Human Rights, describes the extent of the problem: 'The backlog of cases before the Commission is considerable. At the end of the Commission's session in January 1994, the number of pending cases stood at 2,672, more than 1,487 of which had not yet been looked at by the Commission. It takes on average over 5 years for a case to be finally determined by the Court or the Committee of Ministers. Also, whereas up to 1988 there were never more than 25 cases referred to the Court in one year, 31 were referred in 1989, 61 in 1990, 93 in 1991, 50 in 1992 and 52 in 1993, and it is probable that the

Ogoniland case, the delay between the receipt of the communication and the finalization thereof was five years and seven months (March 1996 to October 2001), illustrating the problem of delay and the confluence of various factors causing delay. The delay may to a very limited extent be attributed to the state party and its obstruction of the Commission's planned on-site mission to Nigeria. The complainant also contributed to the delay, as one postponement was made 'pending the receipt of written submissions from the complainants'.[67] However, the delays mostly emanated from the Commission itself: the discussion of the Nigeria mission report and the 'lack of time' are cited as reasons why the case was postponed on two occasions.[68] More disconcerting, and more difficult to interpret, are the numerous unexplained postponements, which merely refer to a decision to 'postpone' or 'defer' the final consideration.[69]

Recourse to the African Court may mean more—rather than fewer—delays. The supplementary nature of the Court necessitates some duplication.[70] Both the Commission and the Court are mandated to deal with admissibility and substantive questions,[71] unless a case is submitted directly to the Court, bypassing the Commission.[72] This last possibility requires that an optional declaration be made by states, something proving to be the exception rather than the rule. As is argued below, the Protocol should be interpreted to minimize the danger of two sets of arguments and two findings before two institutions (the Commission and the Court), especially when (numerous) domestic courts have dealt with the issue already, or when it is an urgent matter. Once the Court has deliberated on a judgment, it must 'render' its written opinion within three months (90 days).[73] The undertaking of state parties to comply with the Court's judgment 'within the time stipulated by the Court' also implies that the Court will set time-frames for compliance and that states must abide by them.[74] Excessive delay was one of the reasons

---

number will increase even more in the next few years... ' (para 21, available at <http://conventions. coe.int/Treaty> (accessed 30 November 2006). However, with the enlargement of membership, the Court continued to be the victim of its own success. While under the two-tier system 38,389 cases were completed in 45 years, the new Court finalized 61,633 cases in the first five years of its existence, but continued to lag further and further behind in dealing with an escalating case-load, which in 2002 saw 34,546 new applications, compared to 5,279 new applications in 1990 (Council of Europe, Explanatory Report to Protocol 14, 2005 <http://www.coe.int> (31 January 2007)). Protocol 14 provides for a simplified procedure that allows (i) a single judge to rule a case inadmissible; (ii) a panel of three judges to deal with 'repetitive' cases on the basis of established case-law; and (iii) the Court to declare a case inadmissible on a new ground, namely, that the applicant did not suffer a 'significant disadvantage', provided that the subject-matter of the case was properly considered domestically. By the end of 2006, the non-ratification of only one member state, Russia, was preventing the entry into force of Protocol 14.

[67] Para 16 of the decided case (n 41 above).

[68] Paras 18 and 19 of the decided case (n 41 above). The mission took place from 7 to 14 March 1994; no final report has been adopted, see F Viljoen, 'Introduction to the African Commission and the Regional Human Rights System' in Heyns (n 1 above) 385, 461–2.

[69] This happened from the 24th to the 29th sessions—see paras 21 to 32 of the decided case.

[70] This argument was crucial in the transformation of the European human rights machinery into a single judicial institution.   [71] Court Protocol, arts 2, 3, and 6.

[72] ibid, art 34(6).   [73] ibid, art 28(1).   [74] ibid, art 30.

for the merger of the European Commission and Court into one institution. This may well be the long-term solution for the African system if the simultaneous existence of the Commission and the Court produces similar or even longer delays in finalizing cases than had been the case when the Commission acted alone.

C Organization and Functioning of the Court

1 Judges

The Court consists of 11 judges, elected for six-year terms.[75] Unlike the European system, each state party is not represented on the Court. The limited number of judges makes the process of election all the more important. After their election, judges choose their own President (and Vice-President), for a once-renewable term of two years.[76] As the only judge serving on a full-time basis and residing at the seat of the Court,[77] the President is likely to play a very important role in establishing and running the Court.

The phases of nominating and electing judges should be distinguished. Only state parties to the Protocol (23 states at this stage) may nominate candidates. Each state that is a member at the time when the Chairperson of the AU Commission calls for nominations may provide three names, two of whom must be nationals of that state.[78] They may thus also nominate candidates from AU member states that have not accepted the Protocol. A list of these names is sent to the members of the Assembly 30 days before its next session.[79]

The election of judges is in the hands of the Assembly: the 53 states together determine the judges in respect of the 23 states that have ratified the Protocol. This may at first glance seem inappropriate.[80] However, leaving the decision to the AU as a whole makes sense from the point of view that any of the other AU member states may within six years (the general term of tenure for the judges) become a state party to the Protocol, and therefore should have some say in the composition of the Court.[81] The election of judges by the Assembly may also

---

[75] ibid, art 15. To ensure continuity, only three judges of the initial group will serve the full six-year term. Four will serve only two years, and the other four will serve four years. Judges are allocated terms in accordance with lots drawn by the Chairperson of the AU Commission (previously the OAU Secretary-General). Judges may be re-elected once, thus permitting at maximum a 12-year term.

[76] Court Protocol, art 21(1).   [77] ibid, art 21(2).   [78] ibid, art 12(1).

[79] ibid, art 13(2). At its third ordinary session, the AU decided to hold sessions twice a year in the future (AU Doc Assembly/AU/Dec.53(III)).

[80] See eg E De Wet, 'The Present Control Machinery under the European Convention on Human Rights: Its Future Reform and Possible Implications for the African Court on Human Rights' (1996) 26 *CILSA* 357–8, who argues that only ratifying states should be allowed to vote, as that would encourage ratification and eliminate the anomaly of non-ratifying states appointing judges to the Court. It may also be argued that states that do not intend to ratify are able, through the election process, to manipulate or weaken the system.

[81] In the Inter-American system, state parties to the American Convention (so, not the bigger pool of the OAS Assembly, but also not the smaller pool of the states that have accepted the Court's

encourage AU member states to ratify the Protocol.[82] Furthermore, the Court is an AU institution, and the AU takes political responsibility for its functioning and the enforcement of its judgments: The Court is dependent on the AU for its budget,[83] the AU Assembly has the final say over the removal of judges from office,[84] it determines and may change the Court's seat,[85] the Court reports annually to the Assembly, specifying instances of non-compliance,[86] and the monitoring of judgments is the Assembly's responsibility.[87] It could thus be argued that the Assembly has a vested political and financial interest in, and responsibility for, the Court. In any event, this method of election is also followed in respect of members of the African Commission.[88]

The process of election is governed by two main guidelines, the personal appropriateness of the candidate, and the more general need for balance. As for personal attributes, candidates must be AU nationals (not necessarily of state parties), they must be 'jurists' by profession, with specific and demonstrated human rights expertise and experience ('competence and experience in the field of human rights'), and they should be 'of high moral character'.[89] As for balance, there must be 'adequate gender representation' (not 'equal', which is in any event impossible in a court of 11 judges),[90] and representation of geographical areas and Africa's 'principal legal traditions'.[91] Regional representation has been a recurring problem experienced in the election of members to the African Commission, occasionally leading to an overrepresentation or non-representation of a region. The Protocol correctly links geographic concerns to varying legal traditions. It will not, for instance, make sense to ensure proportional representation for the West African region by electing two judges from anglophone/common law countries. It is suggested that the requirement of regional representation is met if each of the five

---

compulsory jurisdiction) nominate and elect the judges (American Convention, art 53). In Europe, members of the Council of Europe nominate, and the Council of Europe's Parliamentary Assembly elects judges (one judge in respect of each state) (European Convention, art 22).

[82] A Dieng, 'Introduction to the African Court on Human and Peoples' Rights' (2004) 15 *Interights Bulletin* 3, 4.   [83] Court Protocol, art 32.

[84] ibid, art 19(2).   [85] ibid, art 25.   [86] ibid, art 31.

[87] ibid, art 29(2); the AU Executive Council monitors the execution of judgments '*on behalf of* the Assembly' (emphasis added).

[88] As all 53 AU members have since 1999 been state parties to the Charter, this distinction no longer matters in that context.   [89] Court Protocol, art 11(1).

[90] ibid, art 14(3); art 12(2) of the Protocol requires 'due consideration' to this factor in the nominations process. See also art 4(l) of the AU Constitutive Act, defining the promotion of gender equality as one of the AU's principles. Women over the years have been under represented in international *fora*, including international judicial bodies. As of the beginning of 2003, there were 11 women out of a total of 43 judges on the European Court (see Interights, *Judicial Independence: Law and Practice of Appointments to the European Court of Human Rights* (London: Interights, 2003) 25) and never more than one woman out of seven judges on the Inter-American Court. It seems that female participation in quasi-judicial bodies is more generally accepted—the African Commission has seen its female representation increase from none out of 11 in 1993, to five out of 11 in 2003, which include its Chairperson (Commissioner Sawadogo). The Inter-American Commission had two women members out of seven at the beginning of 2003 (<http://www.cidh.org> (30 November 2006)).

[91] Court Protocol, art 14(2).

regions is 'represented' by at least one judge on the Court.[92] Greater attention should be paid to assuring that each of the legal traditions is covered, being the Islamic/Shari'ah-based system, the common law system, the civil law system, African customary law (in as much as the variety of customary systems show some common characteristics), and the particular brand of mixed 'Roman-Dutch law' in Southern Africa. Reference should also be made here to the personal profile of candidates so as to ensure that expertise in traditional African customary law and tradition is included.

The Protocol determines that the position of judge is incompatible with 'any activity that might interfere with the independence or impartiality' of judges.[93] On 5 April 2005, the AU Commission issued a *note verbale*, in which it cites the following from an early opinion of the Advisory Committee of Jurists concerning the eligibility criteria for appointment to the Permanent Court of International Justice:[94] 'a member of government, a Minister or under-Secretary of State, a diplomatic representative, a Director of a ministry, or one of his subordinates, or the legal advisor to a foreign office . . . are certainly not eligible for appointment as judges upon our Court'. States are called upon to observe this guideline in the nomination process. As for the process, the following are advised: (1) The procedure for nomination should 'at the minimum' be 'that for appointment to the highest judicial office' in a particular country. (2) States should encourage civil society participation in the domestic selection process. (3) The domestic nomination process should be 'transparent and impartial . . . in order to create public trust in the integrity' of that process.

Individuals thus have a role in the domestic nomination process and the AU's election process. NGOs and individuals should involve themselves by nominating competent persons or by challenging incompetent or inappropriate candidates at the domestic level. For this to be possible there should be openness and a free flow of information about the domestic nomination process. These efforts should extend to the process of election, which should be supported by civil society in all AU member states. It is important that the process is as transparent as possible, with the curriculum vitae of a candidate being subjected to public scrutiny.

Initially, June 2004 was set as the date for the election of judges. However, due to an inadequate number of nominations and the decision on the merger of the two Courts, elections did not take place. After re-opening nominations, the election of judges eventually took place in January 2006.[95] Of the 21 nominees, five were women. Candidates were nominated by 16 countries: four from Northern Africa; five from the East; two from Central Africa; two from the South; and eight from the West. As part of the election process at the AU Executive Council, each

---

[92] The 23 ratifying states cover the five regions—North (3), West (9), East (6) (including the island states Comoros and Mauritius, as well as Rwanda), Central (2), and South (3).
[93] Court Protocol, art 18. See also Court Protocol, art 8.   [94] See Ch 5 above.
[95] AU Doc Assembly/AU/Dec.100(VI).

nominating state was requested to reduce its list of candidates to one. This process left 16 nominees, of whom only two were female.

The following judges were elected:[96] Mr Gerard Niyungeko (Burundi) (professor of law, incumbent of the UNESCO Chair in Education for Peace and Conflict Resolution at the University of Burundi; serving for six years), who was also elected as the Court's President; Mr Modibo Tounty Guindo (Magistrate in the Ministry of Justice, Mali) (six years), who will serve as the Vice-President; Mr Fatsah Ouguergouz (Secretary of the International Court of Justice, Algeria) (four years); Mr Jean Emile Somda (member of the Constitutional Court, Burkina Faso) (two years); Ms Sophia Akuffo (Supreme Court judge, Ghana) (two years); Mrs Kelello Justina Masafo-Guni (High Court judge, Lesotho) (four years); Mr Hamdi Faraj Fanoush (Supreme Court judge, Libya) (four years); Mr Jean Mutsinzi (Supreme Court judge, Rwanda) (six years); Mr El Hadji Guisse (advocate, member of the UN Sub-Commission on the Promotion and Protection of Human Rights, serving as its Special Rapporteur on the right to drinking water supply and sanitation, Senegal) (four years); Mr Bernard Ngoepe (High Court Judge-President, South Africa) (two years); and Mr George Kanyiehamba (Supreme Court judge, Uganda) (two years). While there is wisdom in the Court's decision to elect as its 'bureau' two judges who will serve six-year terms, it is unfortunate that they are both from civil law jurisdictions. This not only leads to a formal underrepresentation of other legal systems, but may also undermine efforts to fuse different legal approaches in the Court's operational procedures and methods.

As the experience of the African Commission demonstrates, much of the success of the Court depends on the activism and jurisprudential approach of its members. The presence of some judges inspires some optimism. The Court's first President, Gerard Niyungeko, is an accomplished jurist, who combines a very solid grounding and exceptional academic career in international law with considerable experience at the domestic level (as judge on the Constitutional Court of Burundi) and on the international plane (as legal counsel before the ICJ). One of the most prolific writers on the African regional human rights system,[97] and a senior member of the staff of the ICJ's Registry, Judge Ouguergouz brings along a valuable combination of theoretical insight and practical experience about the functioning of an international court. The experience of Judge Mutsinzi as the Chief Legal Advisor of the OAU, and as the Secretary to the African Commission between 1989 and 1994 may be invaluable, provided he proves able to transcend the relatively restrictive approach to human rights that characterized his contribution during that epoch. Judge Kanyeihamba has published widely in the fields of constitutional law, the rule of law, and human rights.[98] Judge Guisse served the UN Sub-Commission

[96] For biographical data on the Judges, see <http://www.pict-pcti.org/courts/ACHPR_judg_bio.html> (30 September 2006).

[97] See eg *Ouguergouz: African Charter* and *Ouguergouz: African Court* (n 1 above).

[98] See eg GW Kanyeihamba, *Constitutional and Political History of Uganda: From 1984 to the Present* (Kampala: Centenary Publishing House, 2002). He also chaired the Legal and Drafting Committee of

on the Promotion and Protection of Human Rights in numerous capacities, and was a member of the Working Group on Indigenous Populations. In at least one significant case before the Supreme Court of Ghana,[99] Judge Akuffo found herself among a slender majority declaring unconstitutional legislation that allowed for 'extensive ministerial control' in the process of regulating 'registered associations', including political parties.[100]

Question marks hang over some of the other judges. It is disappointing that Burkina Faso, the one state to have accepted the right of individuals to petition the Court directly, nominated someone closely associated with the executive. Judge Somela previously held the position of legal advisor to the Minister of Justice. Before holding judicial office, Judge Faraij Fanoush was a diplomat. For 13 years, he served as the Libyan Ambassador to Cameroon. In an interview after his election, he stated that Libya 'has the best human rights situation in Africa' and expressed the hope that it 'remains that way'.[101]

With the exception of Judge Ouguergouz, all the other members of the Court have served on domestic courts. In comparison, academics dominated the membership of the Inter-American Court. No doubt, the high domestic judicial positions held by most of the judges on the African Court endow that institution with prestige. At the same time, though, these judges may experience as challenges their lack of familiarity with the African human rights system and international human rights more generally, and may find it difficult to adapt to the role of international 'constitutional' judge on an ad hoc basis as they continue to fulfil their full-time roles in 'criminal' or 'civil' judicial proceedings.

As only two women were elected, it can hardly be said that the AU ensured 'adequate gender representation' in the election process. Following subregional ratification patterns, the Court's regional representation tilts towards Western Africa, with four judges; Northern Africa, Eastern Africa, and Southern Africa have two judges each; while Central Africa is represented by one judge. The main legal traditions seem to be represented. As far as language and other colonial legacies are concerned, no Lusophone country is represented, due in part to the fact that the one Lusophone state party, Mozambique, did not put forward a candidate.

Attempts have been made to insulate judges from political pressure and interference. Judges act independently, as expert jurists, and not as delegates of their countries. When they take office, they publicly commit themselves to adjudicate

---

the Constituent Assembly, which drafted the 1995 Ugandan Constitution (see his profile on the website of the Courts of Judicature, <http://www.judicature.go.ug/supreme> (31 January 2007)).

[99] *New Patriotic Party v Attorney-General* (*CIBA* case) [1997] ICHRL 24 (12 March 1997), and <http://www.worldlii.org/int/cases/IHRCL/1997/24.html> (30 April 2007).

[100] On the crucial issue of standing, she found that 'artificial legal persons' are entitled to invoke the right to freedom of association, granted to 'all persons' (ibid, 338d).

[101] 'Coalition for an effective African Court on Human and Peoples' Rights', *E-bulletin*, June 2006, <http://www.africancourtcoalition.iorg> (accessed 31 July 2006) and I Anaba, 'AU will Enforce Judgments of Human and Peoples' Rights Court' *Vanguard*, Lagos, Nigeria (2 June 2006).

impartially.[102] They enjoy the same immunities and privileges that diplomats enjoy under international law,[103] and cannot be held liable for any decision.[104] Judges are also not allowed to sit in a case involving the state of which he or she is a national. The reverse applies in other international courts, such as the European Court of Human Rights, the Inter-American Court, and the ICJ, where nationals are not barred from hearing cases involving their own states. In the latter two courts, an ad hoc judge may be appointed from a state party to a dispute that is not represented.[105] The African political reality weighed heavier than the ideal of representation and other possible operational advantages that a judge familiar with a particular national system could bring to the Court.

2 Seat of the Court

The seat of the Court is not determined in the Protocol. Rather, it was left to the AU Assembly to select a seat once the Protocol had entered into force.[106] The Protocol requires that the Court's seat is 'from among state parties' to the Protocol.[107] Given the difficulties associated with Banjul as the seat of the Commission,[108] The Gambia was never a serious contender to host the Court. Having assigned new AU institutions to other regions, the AU Assembly decided that the Court should be located in the Eastern region.[109] Mauritius showed clear signs of interest in hosting the Court, but the eventual choice fell on Tanzania, and more specifically, Arusha, where the ICTR had been located since 1995. The actual establishment of the Court in Arusha is complicated due to the fact that the activities of the ICTR are set to be wound up only by the end of 2008.[110]

3 Adoption of Rules of Procedure

In terms of the Protocol, the Court 'shall draw up its Rules and determine its procedures'.[111] Because the Rules of Procedure of the Court should be harmonized with those of the African Commission, the Court is required to 'consult' with

---

[102] Court Protocol, art 16.   [103] ibid, art 17(3).   [104] ibid, art 17(4).

[105] American Convention, art 55(2); ICJ Statute, art 31(2).   [106] Court Protocol, art 25.

[107] This requirement may have been the reason why the decision about the Court's seat was not taken simultaneously with the election of the judges of the Court, as the preferred candidate, Tanzania, had at that stage not become a state party to the Protocol. Almost immediately after the session when the judges had been elected (January 2006), Tanzania deposited its instrument of ratification (10 February 2006).   [108] Ch 7.B above.

[109] AU Doc Assembly/AU/Dec.64(IV), assigning African Central Bank to the Western region, the African Investment Bank to the Northern region, the African Monetary Fund to the Central region, and the Court of Justice to the Eastern region. The Pan-African Parliament had already been assigned to the Southern region.

[110] At its eighth session, in January 2007, the AU Assembly requested the AU Commission to actively engage Tanzania 'with a view to securing the swift installation' of the Court in Arusha ('Decision on the Activity Report of the African Court on Human and Peoples' Rights for 2006', AU Doc Assembly/AU/Dec.144(VIII) para 5).   [111] Court Protocol, art 33.

the Commission as it determines its Rules.[112] As is indicated in the discussion below, these Rules may go a long way to strengthen (or weaken) individual access to the Court. At the same time, the revision of the Commission's Rules needs to be informed by the Statute and Rules of the Court.

D Relationship between the Court and the African Commission

As the Court has been established to complement only the 'protective' mandate of the Commission, the Commission retains its very important and extensive 'promotional' role, including the examination of state reports and the work of its special mechanisms. Some commentators have called for the Court to completely take over the protective mandate under the Charter, leaving the Commission to focus on promotion.[113]

As far as its protective mandate is concerned, the Commission remains the only mechanism of redress for individuals in states not party to the Protocol, which at the moment still represents a majority of states. For states to the Protocol that do not allow direct access, the Commission also remains the first port of call for individual complainants. In cases where the Commission shares jurisdiction with the Court, the Commission may sometimes still be the most appropriate mechanism to deal with complaints. In situations of large-scale violations, for example, an on-site mission by the Commission, providing the opportunity for direct discussion and intervention with government officials, may provide a better prospect of success than contentious litigation.

In deciding how best to give effect to the complementarity of the two institutions, the addition of the Court should not place an undue burden of delay on applicants. For this reason, the Rules of Procedure of the Commission and those of the Court should be harmonized to allow at least some cases to proceed to the Court even before the Commission has dealt with them on the merits. If this does not happen, in the majority of cases the delay may undermine the legitimacy of the new body.

The potential for duplication should be minimized. An example of potential overlap is the capacity of the Commission to 'interpret' the Charter,[114] and the Court's advisory competence. Although the Commission and the Court cannot consider the same matter simultaneously,[115] the Court would in principle be able to adopt an advisory opinion after the Commission had given an 'interpretation'. There is nothing in the Protocol to suggest that the Court should consider such a

---

[112] ibid.
[113] Mutua (n 1 above) 360–1; VOO Nmehielle, *The African Human Rights System: Its Laws, Practice, and Institutions* (The Hague: Martinus Nijhoff, 2001) 307.
[114] African Charter, art 45(3), echoing the wording of the Protocol.
[115] According to the *lis alibi pendens* principle (literally, a matter pending elsewhere), enshrined in the Protocol, art 4(1).

matter as *res judicata*. Since the Commission has never used this competence in almost 20 years, the actual danger of overlap seems unlikely.

Given the limited acceptance of direct access to the Court, most individual complaints are likely to proceed first to the Commission, and thereafter, possibly, to the Court.[116] The complementary relationship between the Commission and Court should not allow the Court to apply the doctrine of *res judicata* in respect of cases finalized (or 'settled') by the Commission.

Questions are also bound to arise about the appropriate value that the Court should attach to the Commission's sizeable body of jurisprudence. One of the essential consequences of the 'complementary' relationship between the two bodies is that the Court is competent to overrule the Commission's findings. If the Court cannot be bound to follow the Commission's finding in a specific case, it is also not compelled to follow the Commission's 'precedents'. However, the Court would be wise to take note of and allow itself to be persuaded by the Commission's progressive interpretation of the Charter, especially regarding the 'exhaustion of local remedies'-requirement, socio-economic and fair trial rights, its approach to 'limitations', and by its thematic resolutions ('general comments').[117]

It is not clear to what extent the Court will rely on fact-finding by the Commission. Given that the independence of many African judiciaries is suspect and that even in urban areas judiciaries do not function effectively, the likelihood is great that the Court will have to deal with matters that have not been canvassed by domestic courts. This may pose problems, and will require reliable fact-finding by either the Commission or Court.

Following the example of the Inter-American Commission and the Court of Human Rights, regular meetings between the African Court and the Commission should be organized.

A discussion of the Court's contentious and advisory jurisdiction follows.

E Contentious Jurisdiction

1 Standing to Bring a Matter before the Court

In terms of article 5(1) of the Protocol, the following entities may submit contentious cases to the Court: '(a) The Commission; (b) The state party which has lodged a complaint to the Commission; (c) The state party against which the complaint has been lodged at the Commission; (d) The state party whose citizen is a victim of human rights violation; (e) African intergovernmental organizations'. In addition, article 5(3) provides as follows: 'The Court may entitle relevant NGOs

---

[116] See also Section E.1.2 below.

[117] See Chs 8 and 9 above. However, as noted in Ch 8.A.6 above, the Commission's jurisprudence has not always been consistent, making reliance by the Court problematic in such instances.

with observer status before the Commission, and individuals, to institute cases directly before it, in accordance with article 34(6) of this Protocol'. Article 34(6) stipulates that '[a]t the time of the ratification of this Protocol or any time thereafter, the state shall make a declaration accepting the competence of the Court to receive cases under article 5(3) . . . '.

Thus, two avenues are open to individuals. The main road goes through the Commission; individuals are not allowed to lift the barrier (by 'submitting cases') that separates Commission and Court. Their onward journey is primarily dependent upon the Commission and the respondent state, who are acting as the Court's gatekeepers. The road 'less travelled' leads directly to the Court, bypassing the Commission. Only after permission has been granted by the state in terms of article 34(6), may this road be used. So far, only Burkina Faso has made such a declaration. Given that the optional declaration accepting the right of direct access to the Court is the exception rather than the rule, most cases eventually reaching the Court are likely to start as communications before the Commission. Once a case is before the Commission, individuals lose the capacity to further determine its fate and, as a consequence, to impact upon setting the Court's agenda.

If the rationale behind the African Court is the strengthening of the complaints mechanism by providing an institution (the Court) to redress the deficiencies inherent in the Commission's findings, then the Court should be allowed to play as far-reaching a role as is possible.[118] Put differently, as many communications as are possible should reach the Court (at least initially). One cannot help but wonder about the suitability of relying on those states against which complaints have been lodged (respondent states), and on the Commission, to set the process in motion.

1.1 Respondent States—Article 5(1)(c)

It is unlikely that the potential of the Court will be unlocked if reliance is placed upon respondent states. If it is accepted that the Commission finalizes communications (either by declaring them admissible or by reaching a finding on the merits) before giving consideration to article 5, and if the Commission finds in favour of individual complainants, states may decide to 'appeal' to the Court against the Commission's findings (that they had violated the Charter). If this should happen in *all* cases where a violation was found, eventually most matters will be referred to the Court on the initiative of respondent states. However, states are likely to be hesitant to submit cases due to their weariness of the very reasons grounding the supplementary existence of the Court, such as the binding nature and the extensive exposure of its decisions. States may very well prefer the *certainty* of a *non-binding* finding above the *possibility* of a *binding* decision against them. In addition, there is little incentive for states that had 'won' before the

---

[118] See also Murray (n 55 above) 213, arguing that the Court should be supplied with 'a regular list of cases'.

Commission to submit such cases to the Court where they could only be 'worse off' should the Court find that there had indeed been a violation.

1.2 The Commission—Article 5(1)(a)

As in most cases the individual (or NGO) who had submitted the complaint has no competence to refer the matter any further, and states are unlikely to do so, it is mainly the Commission that is able or likely to refer the matter to the Court. The Inter-American system, where a similar two-tier system operates, illustrates the risk of relying on the Commission to refer cases to the Court: although the Inter-American Court was established in 1980, it received its first contentious case only in 1986,[119] and its second in 1990.[120]

Since the Protocol does not explicitly require the Commission to make a finding on the admissibility and merits of a case before submitting the case to the Court, three possibilities present themselves:[121] (i) The Commission may submit a case to the Court without dealing with it *at all*. Such an approach, which would ensure that delay is reduced to the minimum, would reduce the Commission to a mere conduit in respect of its protective mandate. It may be argued that this avenue should be followed at least in the most urgent cases, because a binding judicial decision will be reached without exhausting the lengthy process before the Commission. (ii) The Commission may also submit a case after it had dealt with it *partially*, for example, after it had made a finding of fact, a finding on admissibility, or after unsuccessfully trying to reach a friendly settlement.[122] In support of this approach, it may be contended that a quasi-judicial body (such as the Commission) is better placed than a judicial body (the Court) to deal with fact-finding and friendly settlement. While this may in principle be correct, the African Commission's practice in this regard has not inspired confidence, and needs to be improved for this possibility to become more feasible. (iii) Lastly, the Commission may submit a case to the Court after *finally disposing* of the case by finding on the merits or by reaching a friendly settlement. Although most commentators seem to accept that this option is most likely,[123] this is by no means a foregone conclusion. My position is that the first two alternatives would allow for the most effective complementarity between Commission and Court, as they both allow for a system of referral that does not further compound delay.

However, with its focus on state compliance, the approach adopted in the Inter-American system also invites itself as a suitable model. Once the Inter-American Commission has made a finding of violation (in accordance with the third of the options discussed above), it allows the violating state three months to comply with

[119] *Velásquez Rodríguez v Honduras* (18 April 1986), Series L/V/II 68, Doc. 8 Rev. 1.

[120] DJ Padilla, 'An African Human Rights Court: Reflections from the Perspective of the Inter-American System' (2002) 2 *AHRLJ* 185, 191.

[121] For a more detailed discussion, see Viljoen (n 1 above)

[122] See RW Eno, 'The Jurisdiction of the African Court on Human and Peoples' Rights' (2002) 2 *AHRLJ* 223, 228.   [123] See eg Harrington (n 1 above) 330.

its finding. After the expiry of that period, the Commission adopts its final report.[124] If a state has by then not complied with the Commission's report, a rebuttable presumption of referral to the Inter-American Court kicks in.[125]

1.3 State Party Citizen-Victim—Article 5(1)(d)

A state may also submit a case when one of its citizens 'is a victim of a human rights violation'.[126] The formulation raises a number of questions: it does not require the citizen to have 'lodged a complaint' at the Commission, as the other two sub-articles dealing with state submission do. The word 'is' (rather than 'is *allegedly* a victim') implies an 'objective truth'.

According to one possible interpretation, this 'objective truth' is the view of the state of which the 'victim' is a national. Interpreted in this way, the provision opens the door for states to submit cases directly to the Court, that is, bypassing the Commission, if the rights of its citizens are, *in its opinion*, violated by another state. This would mean that some inter-state complaints, namely those involving citizens, are privileged above those not involving the citizens of the complaining state. If this argument holds true, the inter-state complaints system provided for under the Charter is overridden.

An interpretation that better accounts for the use of 'is a victim' is that the Commission must have made a finding in this regard. But this is not satisfactory, as it would allow the state to submit a case *only when the Commission has found a violation*, and not when none had been found. It may even be more important for such a state to refer the matter when the Commission had not found a violation, on the basis of the complaint lodged by its national.

Perhaps the intention of the drafters was only to emulate the position under the European two-tier system, which allowed a state to submit a case to the European Court after the European Commission had found that its national was a victim of a violation.[127] *Soering v UK* presents a typical illustration of its application.[128] The applicant, a German national, lodged a complaint against the UK, where he was resident at the time of the complaint. After the Commission's final report had been adopted and transferred to the Committee of Ministers, the Commission, the respondent state (the UK), *and the German government* (on the basis of the complainant's nationality) in quick succession referred the case to the Court.[129]

---

124 Rules of Procedure of the Inter-American Commission, r 45.

125 ibid r 44(1) (the Commission 'shall refer the case to the Court, unless there is a reasoned decision by an absolute majority of the members of the Commission to the contrary'). In arriving at its decision, the Commission is guided by the need to obtain justice in the particular case, and the following factors: 'the position of the petitioner; the nature and seriousness of the violation; the need to develop or clarify the case-law of the system; the future effect of the decision within the legal systems of the member states; and the quality of the evidence available' (r 44(2)).   126 Court Protocol, art 5(1)(d).

127 On the basis of European Convention, art 33 (formerly art 24).

128 Series A No 161 (7 July 1989).

129 On 25 January, 30 January, 3 February 1989, respectively. See L Clements, *European Human Rights: Taking a Case under the Convention* (1994) 74. Communication 40/90, *Njoku v Egypt* (2000)

1.4 African Intergovernmental Organizations—Article 5(1)(e)

'African intergovernmental organizations' may also submit cases to the Court. One such 'organization' is the African Committee of Experts on the Rights and Welfare of the Child,[130] the implementing body of the African Charter on the Rights and Welfare of the African Child (African Children's Charter). After it has finalized a case, it has the competence, under this provision, similar to that of the African Commission, to refer a case to the Court. Another possibility is that other organizations falling into this category, such as regional economic communities, or even the AU itself, may 'submit' cases directly to the Court under this provision without first instituting them before the Commission. Arguably, this provision enables the AU to submit a case against any AU member state for allegedly breaching the African Charter in the course of applying AU law, or in any respect whatsoever (such as applying domestic law), on the material basis of the human rights treaties ratified by that state. In this way, the AU may access any one of the two courts that will eventually fall under its auspices, depending on the subject-matter in dispute: the African Human Rights Court, if a human rights matter is pivotal, or the African Court of Justice, on more general matters related to economic integration and politics.[131]

1.5 Direct Access—Article 5(3)

Government consent, taking the form of a declaration under article 34(6), is a prerequisite for embarking on the road 'less travelled', allowing those who do so to bypass the Commission and present cases directly to the Court.[132] The fact that only one of the ratifying states has made such a declaration is not as hopeless as it may seem—state parties may make such declarations 'at any time' subsequent to ratification.[133]

AHRLR 83 (ACHPR 1997) (11th Annual Activity Report), a communication finalized by the African Commission in 1997, illustrates a situation in which the possibility could have been useful in the African context. A Nigerian national who was arrested while in the 'transit zone' of Cairo Airport, and who was charged, convicted, and sentenced to life imprisonment on a drug-related offence in Egypt, directed a complaint to the Commission. Reluctant to interfere with the factual findings of the Egyptian courts, the Commission concluded that there was no violation of the African Charter (para 60 of the finding). Under these circumstances, it is unlikely that the Commission, and very unlikely that Egypt, would have submitted the case to the Court, but possible that Nigeria might have used article 5(1)(d) of the Protocol, had it been in place.

[130] Hereinafter the African Children's Committee; about its first meeting in 2002, see A Lloyd, 'The First Meeting of the African Committee of Experts on the Rights and Welfare of the Child' (2002) 2 *AHRLJ* 320.   [131] See Section H below.

[132] Plain language advocates take issue with 'shall', arguing that it is often unclear whether 'shall' is used to denote future or compulsion. Art 34(6) provides as follows: 'At the time of ratification . . . or any time thereafter, the State shall make a declaration'. This 'shall' cannot be read to express compulsion, as the declaration is *optional*. To some extent it refers to the future, but in essence 'shall' here expresses a discretionary competence.

[133] Court Protocol, art 34(6). It has been suggested that the provision allows ad hoc declarations for the purpose of a particular case, or for a fixed period. It is difficult to conceive of a situation in

The standing of individuals under the Charter, as developed by the Commission, is quite wide, dispensing with the victim-requirement of, for example, the International Covenant on Civil and Political Rights (ICCPR) or the European Convention,[134] and allowing a broad range of individuals, groups, or NGOs to lodge communications.[135] These requirements obviously remain in place for cases that reach the Court after first having been submitted before the Commission. In so far as cases instituted directly before the Court are concerned, the Protocol does not restrict access to victims, and should not be interpreted as restricting access to victims.

Direct access is restricted to NGOs 'with observer status before the Commission'.[136] In terms of the system of granting observer status to NGOs, the Commission has granted such status to 360 NGOs, both African and international.[137] Most cases submitted to the Commission have been submitted by NGOs that enjoy observer status. In the few instances in which an NGO endeavouring to submit a case does not have observer status, the case can always be instituted in the name of an 'individual', as allowed for by the Protocol.

Article 5(3) provides that the Court 'may entitle' individuals to submit cases directly before it in terms of article 34(6). This phrase should not be read as introducing an additional discretion to the Court to disallow a case submitted under that provision. Granting the Court a discretionary power of refusal would be placing an unduly heavy burden on individuals, as they would be required to pass the hurdle of the state's acceptance of the optional mechanism under article 34(6), only to meet the second barrier of the Court's approval. The formulation seems to be rooted in the drafting history of the Protocol—it initially was introduced, when direct access was made exceptional, but could be granted at the discretion of the Court (the Court 'may entitle').[138] When direct access became subject to an optional state declaration, the formulation was left intact. This formulation should thus be interpreted to place authorization under these circumstances 'within the sole domain' of state parties.[139]

which a state makes a case-specific declaration. The direct submission of cases depends on the initiative of the individual, who is only able to institute a case if the state had already made the declaration. A state making a declaration for a specific case implies foresight about the intention of individuals to present such a case. Case-specific declarations thus imply situations where the cart pulls the horses. Period-specific declarations should be discouraged, as they invite regression and uncertainty into the system.

[134] See eg the Human Rights Committee's finding in Communication 187/1985, *JH v Canada*, UN Doc A/40/40 (12 April 1985), 230 (declaring the communication inadmissible due to a lack of any indication that 'the author himself had been adversely affected') and P Leach, *Taking a Case to the European Court of Human Rights* (Oxford: Oxford University Press, 2nd edn, 2005) 124–33, who shows that the strict 'victim'-requirement in art 33 of the European Convention has been extended to include 'potential' and 'indirect' victims.   [135] Similar to art 44 of the American Convention.
[136] Court Protocol, art 5(3).   [137] See Ch 9 above.
[138] See ICJ draft, art 20(1), the Cape Town draft, art 6(1) and Nouakchott draft, art 6.
[139] *Ouguergouz: African Charter* (n 1 above) 724.

Another respect in which the Protocol allows a restriction is its failing to extend the competence to bring cases to groups, especially in the light of the 'peoples'-concept in the African Charter. If the golden thread running through the Charter is the rights of individuals and peoples, then the Court's standing requirements must reflect that. This aspect should be clarified in the Court's Rules of Procedure.

2 Substantive Jurisdiction in Contentious Cases

Article 3, dealing with 'Jurisdiction', delineates the Court's jurisdiction to include the Charter, the Protocol, and 'other relevant human rights instruments ratified by the states concerned'. While the inclusion of the first two (the Charter and the Protocol) is hardly surprising, the third certainly is. The extended jurisdiction of the Court relates to the subject-matter of cases, and not only to the use of these instruments as interpretative guides.[140] With its substantive jurisdiction stretching beyond the African Charter, the African Human Rights Court will have a much wider substantive scope than the Inter-American and European Courts of Human Rights.[141] At first glance, this provision seems to enlarge the subject-matter of the Court in contentious cases to include *all other human rights instruments*. However, there are certain limits to this extension in the qualifiers 'relevant', 'ratified', 'human rights', and 'by the state concerned'.

The most important qualifier is 'ratified', implying that the instruments referred to are treaties—not merely declarations or other non-binding legal texts or instruments. Thus, these human rights treaties first of all refer to other African human rights treaties, such as the 1969 OAU Convention governing the Specific Aspects of Refugees Problems in Africa (OAU Refugee Convention),[142] the 1990 African Children's Charter,[143] and the 2003 Protocol to the African Charter on the Rights of Women in Africa.[144] Indeed, the Nouakchott version of the Court Protocol restricted these 'other treaties' to exactly this group of treaties by including the word 'African' before 'human rights instruments'.[145] In so far as they are all adopted under the auspices of the same body, the OAU/AU, and are in any event ratified by the states concerned, their inclusion in the Court's jurisdictional scope is not problematic. As for the OAU Refugee Convention, the lack of a dispute settlement

---

[140] A clear distinction, therefore, has to be drawn between art 3 of the Court Protocol and arts 60 and 61 of the African Charter.

[141] The European Court's jurisdiction does not include other human rights instruments adopted by the Council of Europe, such as the European Social Charter and the European Convention for the Prevention of Torture and Inhuman or Degrading Treatment or Punishment. With the exception of a limited number of instances allowed for under the Protocol of San Salvador (dealing with social, economic, and cultural rights), cases alleging violations of OAS human rights instruments other than the American Convention may not be adjudicated by the Inter-American Court.

[142] Repr in eg (1969) 8 ILM 1288; and in Heyns (n 1 above) 122.

[143] Repr in eg Heyns (n 1 above) 143.

[144] OAU Doc CAB/LEG/23.18; adopted in July 2003, Maputo, Mozambique, requiring 15 ratifications to enter into force (art 29(1) of the Protocol). By 31 January 2004, there had been no ratifications (<http://www.africa-union.org>).   [145] Nouakchott draft, art 3(1).

mechanism has in any event been one of its weaknesses.[146] The African Children's Committee has a mandate very similar to that of the African Commission. As this Committee may reasonably be expected to suffer from the same institutional and functional weaknesses as the African Commission, it seems only logical to supplement and reinforce its protective mandate by introducing the Court as a judicial body with competence (and the final say) over its provisions as well. African human rights instruments such as the 1976 Algiers Universal Declaration on the Rights of Peoples, the Kampala Declaration on Prison Conditions in Africa, and the numerous resolutions of the African Commission are, as instruments not open to ratification, excluded from serving as a basis for a contentious case.

Reliance is further restricted to 'human rights' treaties. Some treaties adopted under OAU auspices have a significant bearing on human rights, but are not human rights instruments in the narrow sense of the phrase. In one of its advisory opinions, the Inter-American Court distinguished 'modern human rights treaties', whose object is 'the protection of the basic rights of individual beings irrespective of their nationality', from 'multilateral treaties of the traditional type' that are 'concluded to accomplish the reciprocal exchange of rights for the mutual benefit of the contracting State'.[147] The main dividing line is that states assume obligations 'towards all individuals within their jurisdiction' when they ratify human rights treaties, and not merely 'in relation to other States'.[148] Applying this interpretation, AU treaties such as the 1968 African Convention on the Conservation of Nature and Natural Resources and the 1977 Convention for the Elimination of Mercenarism in Africa, may not be included under article 3. It may be argued that, although these treaties place obligations upon states that have important *human rights implications*, they do not provide for human rights in the sense of direct entitlements or 'rights' available to individuals. The question may also be posed whether the AU Constitutive Act, the Treaty establishing the African Economic Community (AEC Treaty), or even the treaties of regional economic groupings, such as ECOWAS, qualify as 'human rights' treaties, in particular in so far as they make adherence to the African Charter part of their aims and objectives.[149] The principal preoccupation of these treaties is economic and political integration, as well as institutional development to attain this objective. While these arrangements consider human rights in the formulation and application of their policies,

---

[146] On the OAU Refugee Convention generally, see G Okoth-Obbo, 'Thirty Years On: A Legal Review of the 1996 OAU Refugee Convention' (2000) 8 *AYBIL* 3; R Ramcharan, 'The African Refugee Crisis' (2000) 8 *AYBIL* 119 argues that refugee rights should be re-conceptualized as human rights violations, and that the African human rights machinery should be improved to deal with such cases.

[147] *The Effect of Reservation on the Entry into Force of the American Convention (Advisory Opinion)*, OC-2/28, Inter-American Court of Human Rights (24 September 1982) para 29.

[148] ibid.

[149] On the AU, see eg E Baimu, 'The African Union: Hope for Better Protection of Human Rights in Africa?' (2001) 1 *AHRLJ* 299. Of all the African RECs, ECOWAS—with its explicit human rights mandate—most seriously challenges the contention that REC treaties are not 'human rights' treaties; see Ch 12 below.

this fact alone cannot transform them into human rights organizations (or their founding treaties into human rights instruments). Such a conclusion is supported by the fact that judicial institutions have already been—or are being—established to settle disputes arising from these treaties.[150]

As African states do not qualify to become state parties to the other regional human rights treaties, the omission of 'African' implies that the door is further opened for the Court to adjudicate on UN human rights treaties to which AU members (that are also UN members) are party. In one interpretation of the phrase 'by the states concerned', an individual communication may be directed to the Court on the basis of a UN human rights treaty if the state complained against had ratified it.[151] The problems arising from this expansion in jurisdictional scope are legion. It would imply that a communication under the ICCPR, for example, may in principle be submitted to either the Human Rights Committee (HRC) or the African Court. This may lead to divergence in jurisprudence, and to forum shopping, where quasi-judicial and judicial institutions are compared and played off against one another.[152] No other regional human rights system 'enforces' the treaties of another regional or the UN system. As Österdahl notes, it 'may be a delicate matter for the African Court to apply an international convention to which non-African states are also parties, and to render judgments on how the Convention should be interpreted on a particular point'.[153] Even more strikingly, a state that had not accepted optional individual complaints procedures under UN treaties may find that the Court usurps jurisdiction against it on the basis of article 3. The Protocol does not require that the state had accepted the optional individual complaints mechanism, if such exists, before they may invoke the treaty provisions.[154] To this may be added the far-reaching implication that individuals in state parties to the Protocol may submit cases alleging violations of UN treaties (such as the International Covenant on Economic, Social and Cultural Rights (ICESCR) and the Convention on the Rights of the Child (CRC)) to a court, while individuals in state parties to those treaties may not even submit an individual communication to the applicable UN quasi-judicial body. A solution to curb such

---

[150] Most notably, the AU Assembly adopted a Protocol establishing an African Court of Justice (see Section G below).

[151] See eg C Heyns, 'The African Regional Human Rights System: In Need of Reform?' (2001) 1 *AHRLJ* 167, pointing to the danger of states being inhibited from ratifying the Protocol and UN treaties as a result. Heyns also warns that 'even the pretence' of regional specificity will be lost with the erosion of a uniquely African conception of human rights.   [152] See Section H below.

[153] I Österdahl, 'The Jurisdiction *Ratione Materiae* of the African Court of Human and Peoples' Rights: A Comparative Critique' (1998) 7 *Review of the African Commission on Human and Peoples' Rights* 132.

[154] Consider a concrete example involving a state party that has accepted the right of direct individual access to the court: Burkina Faso is a state party to the African Charter and the Convention against Torture (CAT). It has ratified the Protocol, but has not made the optional declaration under CAT allowing individuals to submit communications to the CAT Committee. Under art 3 of the Protocol, an individual may submit a contentious case, alleging a violation of CAT by the Burkinabe government, to the African Court, while that individual may not do so under CAT itself.

jurisdictional inroads is to interpret the term 'states concerned' as *all the state parties to the Protocol*, and not only the state against which the complaint is brought. Such a reading would, at least, restrict the African Court's jurisdiction in contentious cases to UN treaties ratified by all state parties to the Protocol.[155] The word 'relevant' may provide another interpretative 'way out' to the Court: In order to eliminate consequences tending towards the absurd (such as the ICESCR and CRC examples above), the Court may hold that such a treaty is not 'relevant' (in the sense of being 'appropriate') for the purpose of establishing jurisdiction under article 3. Others see less of a problem, and support a broad interpretation of article 3, as binding judgments by the Court would 'expose those states that took ratification as a public relations exercise'.[156]

However, the problems raised may be more apparent than real, at least for the time being. As was mentioned, of the 23 states that have so far ratified the Charter, only one has made a declaration in terms of article 34(6) of the Protocol. Only against that state may individual cases be submitted directly to the Court, therefore also on the basis of the extended jurisdiction allowed for under article 3 of the Protocol. Most cases still are to be presented to the Commission first, in terms of the normative legal framework applicable to the Commission, which is the African Charter: only violations of the African Charter may be brought before the Commission.[157] Even if those cases are referred to the Court (either before, during, or after the Commission's consideration), it may be argued that referral from the Commission should be restricted to the legal basis of the finding before the Commission. Arguably, referral of the case does not extend the initial legal basis on which the case has been submitted. The extended basis, with its concomitant problems, will therefore only arise in a relatively small percentage of cases.

Far-reaching as they are as interpretative guides, articles 60 and 61 of the Charter do not extend the legal basis on which complaints may be brought.[158] The conclusion is however inescapable that an individual instituting a case *directly before the Court* has a much wider array of substantive rights to invoke than had been the case under the Charter.[159]

---

[155] But this does not solve the problem, as illustrated by the fact that the Convention on the Rights of the Child has been ratified by all the state parties to the Protocol.

[156] Eno (n 122 above) 228. This view also finds support in the fact that some self-executing international human rights treaty provisions are justiciable in at least some African states.

[157] African Charter, art 56(2). However, see the Commission's finding in Communication 224/98, *Media Rights Agenda v Nigeria* (2000) AHRLR 262 (ACHPR 2000) (14th Annual Activity Report), in which the Commission 'holds' a violation by the state of numerous Charter provisions, as well as of 'Principle 5 of the UN Basic Principles on the Independence of the Judiciary', and the discussion in Ch 8.A.6.2 above.

[158] See eg Österdahl (n 153 above) 137, who draws a distinction between arts 60 and 61, which entitle the Commission to *draw inspiration*, and art 3, which provides a legal basis for *application*.

[159] Unfortunately, the *travaux préparatoires* of the Protocol do not provide an explanation for the expansive jurisdiction, leaving one to speculate that it may have been influenced by (a misreading of?) arts 60 and 61 of the Charter, and by the idea that all possible means should be brought to bear on states to ensure that their human rights obligations are observed, emphasizing the interconnectedness of human rights using a very holistic approach.

3 Proceedings before the Court

3.1 Friendly Settlement

The Court may also 'try to reach an amicable settlement in a case pending before it in accordance with the provisions of the Charter'.[160] This formulation invites some uncertainty about the application of the Court's conciliatory jurisdiction in individual communications. Although the Commission has *by way of its jurisprudence* extended the 'friendly settlement' procedure to individual communications, the Charter itself allows for this possibility only in respect of inter-state communications.[161] The stipulation in the Protocol therefore seems to suggest that the conciliatory jurisdiction of the Court is limited to those cases in respect of which an amicable settlement is envisaged between states.

Should the friendly settlement be extended to individual cases, it may either be used when a case has been referred by the Commission or when it comes directly before the Court. As Ouguergouz points out, in both instances the Court may be in a better position than the Commission to persuade a respondent state to 'soften its position' in the shadow of an 'unfavourable judicial decision'.[162] The Court's Rules of Procedure should spell out the practical details about which information needs to be included in settlement agreements, and should also stipulate the principle that settlements must be 'in accordance with human rights'.[163]

3.2 Admissibility

To be admitted before the Court, the standard requirements set out in article 56 of the African Charter have to be 'taken into account'.[164] This wording allows for a departure from the rigid application of the conditions, as there is no prescription that each of them has to be complied with. An analysis of the drafting history reveals that an initial requirement that article 56 must be 'applied' was altered to this more open-ended formulation, allowing the Court more leeway. The Court also has a discretion, most likely when it has been approached directly, to request the opinion of the Commission on the admissibility of a case.[165]

3.3 Role of Individuals before the Court

The African Commission's Rules of Procedure obliges the Commission to request the respondent state and the author of a communication to submit written 'information and observations' on admissibility and the merits of the case, thus allowing

---

[160] Court Protocol, art 9.   [161] African Charter, art 48.

[162] *Ouguergouz: African Court* (n 1 above) 130.

[163] See American Convention on Human Rights, art 48(1)(f) and European Convention for the Protection of Human Rights and Fundamental Freedoms, art 38. This aspect is provided for in respect of inter-state communications under the Charter (art 52), allowing for the construction of an analogous argument with respect to individual communications.

[164] Court Protocol, art 6(2).   [165] ibid, art 6(1).

the complainant's arguments to be taken into account as part of the Commission's consideration.[166] Although the Charter does not allow for that possibility, the Commission has developed a practice of allowing individuals (or NGOs) to be present at hearings or to be represented before it during the consideration of communications lodged by that individual (or NGO).[167] No provision has, however, been made for legal aid or for awarding costs by either the Charter or the Rules of Procedure.

An individual who lodges a case directly before the Court is entitled, as a 'party to a case', to be represented by a legal representative of their choice.[168] But what about individuals who have lodged communications with the Commission, and whose cases are then submitted to the Court, either by the Commission or the state? It is submitted that, under such circumstances, the individual remains 'a party' to the case. When the Commission decides to submit the case to the Court, the Commission itself does not become a party to the case, but rather acts to initiate proceedings between the parties before the Court. In the dual European system, before the Court became the single monitoring mechanism, the Commission saw its function before the Court primarily as that of clarifying and justifying (defending) its own opinion, and of ensuring that all the relevant information was placed before the Court.[169] The contention that the individual remains a 'party' is supported by the possibility that one of the parties to the case, the state, may refer the case to the Court. It would be anomalous to accept that the individual loses the status of 'party' when the case is submitted, as that would mean that there is only one party left—the state. As a result, individuals, as 'parties' to the case, are also 'entitled to be represented by a legal representative' of their choice when cases involving them are submitted to the Court by either a state or the Commission.

Such an interpretation is in keeping with developments under the other two major human rights systems. Initially, under both the European and Inter-American systems, the individual was not, as a matter of principle, able to be present, to be represented, or to make representations to the Court, once his or her case had been referred.[170] Gradually, though, the role of the individual increased, allowing them to be present, allowing lawyers to represent them, and thus allowing them to make submissions directly before the Court. In all but name, they were 'parties' to the case.

When it was adopted the European Convention did not establish a role for complainants in the process before the Court. Initially, the Commission allowed individual complainants on a discretionary basis, as 'assistants' to the Commission's lawyers. In its very first case, the European Court of Human Rights ruled that the

---

[166] Rr 117 and 119.

[167] R Murray, 'Evidence and Fact-Finding by the African Commission' in Evans and Murray (n 1 above) 100, 104–6.   [168] Court Protocol, art 10(2).

[169] See Clements (n 129 above) 75.

[170] In terms of r 1 of the Rules of Court, an applicant was explicitly excluded as a 'party'.

Court should be informed of the applicant's views.[171] Ten years later, the Court ruled that the applicant's lawyer may act as 'assistant' to the Commission's delegates, but 'always subject to the control and responsibility of the Delegates'.[172] When amended Rules of Court came into effect in 1983, the Commission was legally obliged to inform applicants of that fact and to invite them to be represented at the hearing in their own right. In 1994, when Protocol 9 entered into force, NGOs and individuals could decide to refer cases to the Court; and since 1998, when Protocol 11 took effect, they could submit cases directly to the Court.[173]

The Inter-American system adopted a similar pragmatic approach in terms of which the complainant's lawyer was allowed to be part of the Commission's legal team, and 'may present the petitioner's argument in that capacity, though only under the control of the Commission'.[174] Serving as an 'assistant' on the Commission's team, however, is not ideal, as the interests and approach of the Commission 'as guardian of the Convention assisting the Court' and those of the complainant do not always coincide.[175] A 1996 amendment to the Rules of Court allows the representatives of victims to present autonomous arguments 'at the stage of reparations'.[176] The following anomaly is thus presented: the complainant may lodge a case before the Commission, that is, be in complete control at *the beginning* of the case; may make presentations at the reparations phase before the Court, at *the end* of the case; but does not have autonomous standing *during* the proceedings before the Court.[177]

Perhaps one's view of the importance of the presence and participation of the individual boils down to one's understanding of the function of the Commission and one's faith in it. It has been suggested that the role of the Commission in litigation before the Court is 'not litigious: it is ministerial'.[178] It does not fall to the Commission to defend the individual's case 'as such', or the Commission's opinion

---

[171] *Lawless v UK (Preliminary Objections and Questions of Procedure)* Series A No 1 (14 November 1960) 16. Neither the applicant nor his representative appeared—the Commission's delegate presented these views as part of his oral submission at the Court's hearing. See P Mahoney, 'Developments in the Procedure of the European Court of Human Rights: The Revised Rules of Court' (1983) 3 *Ybk of Eur L* 127, 129.

[172] *De Wilde, Ooms and Versyp v Belgium (Question of Procedure)* Series A No 12 (18 November 1970) 8.

[173] Rr 30(1) and 33(3)(d); see also MW Janis, RS Kay, and AW Bradley, *European Human Rights Law: Text and Materials* (Oxford: Oxford University Press, 2nd edn, 2000) 67–8.

[174] D Harris, 'Regional Protection of Human Rights: The Inter-American Achievement' in DJ Harris and S Livingstone (eds), *The Inter-American System of Human Rights* (Oxford: Clarendon Press, 1998) 1, 25 (*The Inter-American System*) (stating that the Commission may 'hide a petitioner's lawyer under its skirts'). Padilla (n 120 above) 185 describes the implication of being allowed a 'legal advisor' in the following terms: 'This permits the victim a place at the table alongside' the Commission and 'allows the victim to actively participate in the litigation of the case', for example by cross-examining witnesses (192).

[175] AAC Trinidade, 'The Inter-American Human Rights System at the Dawn of the New Century: Recommendations for Improvement of its Mechanisms of Protection' in *The Inter-American System* (n 174 above) 395, 415.   [176] Rules of Court, r 23.

[177] See Trinidade in *The Inter-American System* (n 174 above) 416.

[178] This is the view of Sir Humphrey Waldock, who appeared for the European Commission in the *Lawless* case before the European Court, quoted in Janis *et al* (n 173 above) 67.

'as such', but to place the relevant elements of the case before the Court. This role should be juxtaposed with that of individuals and their representatives. Rejecting an early challenge to their presence at a hearing, the European Court remarked that the Commission, in its role as 'defender of the public interest', must 'make known the applicant's views to the Court as a means of throwing light on the points at issue', 'even if it does not share them'.[179] Because 'the whole of the proceedings before the Court are upon issues which concern the Applicant', the Court held that it is 'in the interests of the proper administration of justice that the Court should have knowledge' of the individual's contentions.[180] In order to ensure a 'genuine hearing of both sides in contention',[181] the African Court should interpret the Protocol to allow individuals to be represented in all hearings before it. While taking part in the hearing, the Commission's role then evolves into that of the guardian of the public interest. Given the limited human and financial resources available to the African Commission, it probably would be unwise to burden the Commission and its Secretariat with the task of preparing and presenting legal arguments before the Court. Parties should at least be given the option of engaging their own counsel or appear on their own behalf, with the Commission playing a formal facilitating role.

3.4 Legal Aid

Although the Protocol provides that parties to the case may be represented by lawyers of their choice, it also takes into account that this 'choice' may not be available to all individuals or NGOs.[182] Taking the case to the Court is bound to be an expensive exercise, including the cost of a senior lawyer and travel expenses. It therefore adds that free legal representation 'may be provided where the interests of justice so require'.[183] The use of the passive form in this phrase seems very deliberate, avoiding the identification of both the subject and the object of such legal aid. Legal aid, provided by the Court, is yet another contender for meagre resources within the ambit of the AU. Perhaps a special fund may be established, or perhaps the responsibility may fall to the states, a possibility not excluded from the Protocol. It is suggested here that the Court itself should administer a system of legal aid, with funds forming a regular part of its budget. As long as the right of individuals to access the Court remains restricted, and assuming that the Commission itself will litigate the cases before the Court 'on behalf of' complainants, the need for legal aid will be limited.

The need will be much greater, though, if free legal representation should extend to the exhaustion of local remedies. Due to the lack of legal aid in most African states, especially in civil law and human rights matters, many potential litigants

---

[179] *Lawless v UK* (n 171 above) 16.   [180] ibid 15.

[181] P Mahoney, 'Developments in the Procedure of the European Court of Human Rights: The Revised Rules of Court' (1983) 3 *Ybk of Eur L* 127, 131.

[182] Court Protocol, art 10(2).   [183] ibid.

will be unable to access domestic courts. It is suggested that the Court should consider indigence as a ground for exempting litigants from the exhaustion of local remedies.[184]

The passive formulation in article 10(2) leaves open the possibility that (resource-constrained) states may also benefit from legal aid. This should certainly only be applied in exceptional cases, as states normally have their own legal staff, based in the ministries of justice or in the legal sections of departments of foreign affairs, who may be assigned to represent the state.

Other aspects to be addressed are: At what stage of the proceedings should such an application be made? Is it made to the judges, or the Registrar acting in terms of guidelines adopted by the Court? What are the factors that constitute 'interests of justice'? Questions regarding the awarding of cost of proceedings also come into play. Individuals should not be expected to pay the costs incurred by governments.[185] These aspects need to be clarified in the Rules of Procedure, or in an addendum thereto, as in the case with the European Court.[186]

3.5 Judgment

Under the Protocol, seven judges make up a quorum. A judge may not hear cases involving the state of which he or she is a national.[187] After hearing the case the judges deliberate. The Court must issue a judgment within 90 days of their deliberations.[188] A written, reasoned judgment has to be prepared. Judgments are taken by majority vote, but individual judges may deliver separate or dissenting opinions.[189] The judgment has to be read in an open court.[190]

The 90-day time-limit within which the Court must deliver its judgments is of value, but its formulation leaves room for manoeuvre: the 90-day period starts running when the Court has completed 'its deliberations' and not after the parties have presented their cases. This leaves open the possibility of the 'deliberations' commencing only at some later date, or of incomplete deliberations being deferred *sine die*. Such an interpretation should be avoided. 'Deliberations' are part of the proceedings and follow directly after the parties have presented their case. Only in highly exceptional cases should the proceedings be postponed for later deliberation.

---

[184] In this regard, see the Inter-American Court's opinion OC-11/90, *Exceptions to the Exhaustion of Domestic Remedies in Cases of Indigence or Inability to Obtain Legal Representation because of a Generalized Fear within the Legal Community*, Advisory Opinion of 10 August 1990. See also the discussion on exhaustion of local remedies before the African Commission, Ch 8.A above.

[185] See eg Murray (n 55 above) 214.

[186] Legal aid under the European system has been described as 'very limited and means-tested at state level' (Murray (n 55 above) 214–15).

[187] Court Protocol, art 22. This 'exclusion' of judge-nationals from hearings also differs from the appointment of ad hoc judges from states involved in disputes before the ICJ (under art 31 of the ICJ Statute). In Krisch's view (n 1 above) 713, 717), the Protocol position improves the perception of impartiality, and may 'represent a reaction to the problems of the Commission in this respect'. Their impartiality is further underscored by art 11(1) (they are 'elected in an individual capacity') and art 16 of the Protocol (they make an oath of office to 'discharge their duties impartially and faithfully').

[188] Court Protocol, art 28(1).   [189] ibid, art 28(7).   [190] ibid, art 28(5).

3.6 Remedial Orders

The Court's remedial competence, allowing it the broad discretion to choose from an open-ended list of 'appropriate remedies', is more akin to that of the Inter-American than the European Court.[191] The Inter-American Court has taken the following range of remedial steps:[192] (i) It awarded reparation to 'victims' and an extended group of people falling within the category 'next of kin'; (ii) it ordered injunctive relief by for example ordering that a victim be freed or retried; (iii) and it ordered the violating state to remedy the consequences of the violation, for instance by investigating the facts giving rise to the violation; punishing those responsible; amending, adopting, or repealing domestic law of judicial decisions; ordering the state to refrain from a particular course of action; and by demanding that the state issues an apology.

The African Court, like both the Inter-American and European Courts, may also provide interim relief in the form of 'provisional measures'.[193] It has been suggested that the Court should not only make use of this competence when cases are already before it, but also when cases are still pending before the Commission.[194]

3.7 Enforcement

States 'undertake to comply' with judgments issued against them.[195] Depending on the remedy ordered, compliance may take numerous forms, and may require a combination of legal and political action. Although the AU Assembly is ultimately responsible for ensuring that states comply with judgments, it is the Executive Council that is tasked with following up the implementation on a continuous basis.[196] It is not clear what this entails. At a minimum, it should involve 'keeping a mere record of judgments' implementation in the internal legal orders of recalcitrant states'.[197] In line with other regional systems, the Executive Council should inscribe the issue of implementation by a particular state on its agenda until that state complies. In the process, the Council may take a decision reiterating the state's obligation to abide by the Court's decision. Such decisions are also binding and non-compliance exposes a state to the imposition of sanctions and 'other measures of a political and economic nature to be determined by the Assembly'.[198]

In fulfilling its duty to 'report' annually to the Assembly about its activities, including non-compliance by states, the Court should cooperate closely with the

---

[191] ibid, art 27(1) corresponds closely with American Convention, art 63(1). The European Convention has a much narrower remedial competence, limited to affording 'just satisfaction' to injured parties (European Convention, art 41).

[192] JM Pasqualucci, *The Practice and Procedure of the Inter-American Court of Human Rights* (Cambridge: Cambridge University Press, 2003) 233–80.   [193] Court Protocol, art 27(2).

[194] GJ Naldi, 'Interim Measures of Protection in the African System for the Protection of Human and Peoples' Rights' (2002) 2 *AHRLJ* 1, 9.   [195] Court Protocol, art 30.

[196] ibid, arts 29 and 30.   [197] Naldi and Magliveras (n 16 above) 963.

[198] AU Constitutive Act, art 23(2).

Executive Council. The Court should keep itself informed and its follow-up work should reinforce that of the Council.

F Advisory Jurisdiction

1 Standing to Request Advisory Opinions

Even if an advisory opinion is not binding on the party requesting it, it may have profound persuasive force and a wide ripple effect.[199] While a judgment in a contentious case provides an outcome to the dispute between, and only binds specific parties, the influence of an advisory opinion may reach much more widely. Advisory opinions have been used extensively and to significant effect in the Inter-American system. During its fledgling years, the Inter-American Court dealt with many more advisory than contentious cases, due mainly to the reluctance of the Commission and respondent states to submit contentious cases to the Court. In Buergenthal's view, this development was fortunate, providing the Court with a chance to consolidate itself, seeing that governments in 'fragile emerging democracies' will 'find it easier to give effect to an advisory opinion than to comply with a contentious decision in a case they lost'.[200] The relevance of this sentiment for Africa, where democracy is still seeking a strong foothold, is clear.[201] Providing a less confrontational avenue to approach the Court than the contentious route, the possibility of advisory opinions may be an effective way of effecting domestic changes without 'embarrassing' African states as 'human rights violators'.

Three categories (states, the AU and its organs, and a broader and undefined group of 'African organizations') may request advisory opinions, and can thus claim standing before the Court.[202] This position allows wider standing than any other international court allowing for advisory opinions.[203]

All AU member states may make such requests, as there is no requirement that the requesting state must have ratified the Protocol, thereby opening this aspect of the jurisdiction to non-state parties. In the Americas, states and the Inter-American Commission have mainly approached the Inter-American Court for advisory opinions. Under that system, the executive branch of the government (for example, represented by the Minister of Foreign Affairs) is considered to be the appropriate

---

[199] See generally AP Van der Mei, 'The Advisory Jurisdiction of the African Court on Human and Peoples' Rights' (2005) 5 *AHRLJ* 27.

[200] T Buergenthal, 'The European and Inter-American Human Rights Courts: Beneficial Interaction' in P Mahoney, F Matscher, H Petzold, and L Wildhaber (eds), *Protecting Human Rights: The European Perspective. Studies in Honour of Rolv Ryssdal* (Cologne: Heymann, 2000) 123, 131.

[201] See also Österdahl (n 153 above) 141, noting that the 'softer less obliging channel of advisory opinions' may be more applicable outside a 'well-functioning democratic environment characterised by the rule of law'.   [202] Court Protocol, art 4(1).

[203] UN Charter, art 96; European Convention of Human Rights, art 47(1); American Convention, art 64.

entity to make a request on behalf of a state.[204] Despite being part of national state institutions, domestic courts are not allowed to direct requests for advisory opinions to the Inter-American Court.[205] Given their vulnerability to executive interference and insufficient infrastructure, domestic courts in Africa should be allowed to refer matters (such as a question about the compliance of legislation with the African Charter) to the Court for its advice.[206] Such referrals would serve the principle of subsidiarity, and may enable a domestic court to base its finding on the views of an independent African judicial body, thus escaping charges of political bias.

The AU and any of its organs may also request advisory opinions from the Court. Although the African Commission is not listed as an AU 'organ', it has been recognized as a 'functional AU organ', and should be allowed standing in this category. This competence may for example be utilized by the AU Assembly to request an opinion on the interpretation of the term 'peace and security' in article 4(j) of the AU Constitutive Act, or by the African Commission to solicit a clarification of the competence of the Executive Council to bar the publication of its resolutions.

Any 'African organization recognized by the AU' may also request an advisory opinion from the African Human Rights Court. The question should be asked as to which bodies qualify as 'African organizations'. In other provisions of the Protocol, the terms 'African intergovernmental organization' and 'NGOs with observer status before the Commission' have been used.[207] The word 'organization' is thus a generic term, and encompasses both intergovernmental and non-governmental bodies. However, the organizations are qualified as 'African'. An 'African organization' is therefore a narrower group than NGOs enjoying observer status with the African Commission, because members of that group need not be African, but may, for example, have headquarters outside Africa or operate internationally. The organization also needs to be 'recognized by the AU'. It is suggested that all African NGOs that enjoy observer status with the African Commission, a form of recognition by AU, qualify, so should civil society organizations represented on ECOSOCC, and regional economic arrangements, such as ECOWAS and SADC. Other African organizations should also qualify, in so far as they work in association with the AU or AEC.

Granting standing before the Court to NGOs to request advisory opinions will necessarily entail the risk of NGOs using the procedure to bring contentious disputes against states that had not accepted the Court's contentious jurisdiction in the name of advisory requests, 'through the back door' so to speak.[208] However, this risk also exists in relation to states or other AU organs,[209] and should not be

---

[204] Proposed Amendments to the Naturalization Provisions of the Constitution of Costa Rica, Advisory Opinion OC-4/84, para 12.　　　　　　　　　　　[205] Pasqualucci (n 192 above) 41.

[206] In line with eg the Treaty Establishing the European Economic Community, art 234.

[207] Court Protocol, art 5(1)(e) and 5(3).　　　　　　　　　[208] Van der Mei (n 199 above) 36.

[209] When the Inter-American Commission requested an advisory opinion about constitutional provisions dealing with the death penalty in Peru, that country accused the Commission of trying to

overstated, especially in the light thereof that the final judgment of the Court is 'advisory', thus remaining non-binding.

No mention is made in the Protocol of the possibility that the Court may itself—*mero motu*—set its advisory jurisdiction in motion. Although none of the other international courts are endowed with such authority, the benefits of this option have been debated in the Inter-American context. Some of these suggested advantages, such as the potential contribution to 'clarity and consistency',[210] are also applicable in Africa. Especially if the Court receives no or few cases (including requests for advisory opinions), it should explore this option.

2 Substantive Basis of Advisory Opinions

As for subject-matter jurisdiction, advisory opinions may be requested on a legal matter relating to the Charter or 'any other relevant human rights instruments'.[211] Omitted is the qualification 'ratified by the states concerned' that had been put in place for contentious cases, thus broadening the pool to include any human rights 'instrument', both non-binding and declaratory. Any conceivable human rights document may be invoked, as long as the one threshold requirement—relevance—is met. Similar problems as those in respect of the material jurisdiction of the Court (such as divergence and forum-shopping) may occur here. However, even though the subject-matter of the Court's advisory jurisdiction is much broader than its contentious jurisdiction, it is, in light of the non-binding nature of the Court's advisory findings, less likely to be as controversial.

G Merger with the African Court of Justice

Two distinct but co-existing processes, economic integration and democratization, characterize both African and European integration. In Europe, separate institutions (the EU and the Council of Europe) are responsible for the two objectives, and two separate judicial institutions have been set up to resolve disputes—the European Court of Justice (based in Luxembourg) and the European Court of Human Rights (based in Strasbourg). To some extent inspired by this dualism, the African system set up the framework for two similar courts.[212] Already when the African Economic Community (AEC) was founded, in 1991, a Court of Justice was foreseen as one of its institutions. Supplementing the African Human Rights

---

'obtain indirectly' what it 'is prevented from achieving directly', as it was precluded from bringing a contentious case against Peru (International Responsibility for the Promulgation and Enforcement of Laws in Violation of the Convention, Advisory Opinion OC-14/94, para 1).

[210] Pasqualucci (n 192 above) 37.   [211] Court Protocol, art 4(1).

[212] F Viljoen and E Baimu, 'Courts for Africa: Considering the Co-existence of the African Court on Human and Peoples' Rights and the Court of Justice' (2004) 22 *NQHR* 241.

Court, which had already in 1998 been instituted under the OAU, the AU reiterated that a Court of Justice would be established.[213] The AU Constitutive Act did not provide much detail about the nature of the Court of Justice, since it was envisaged that a separate detailed protocol defining its statute, composition, and functions would be adopted in future.[214] From the Protocol of the African Court of Justice of the African Union (ACJ Protocol), adopted in 2003,[215] it is clear that the African Court of Justice was mandated to administer matters of interpretation arising from the application or implementation of the AU Constitutive Act.[216] However, pending the establishment of the African Court of Justice, this task was to be handled by the AU Assembly.[217] Under the ACJ Protocol, the AU Assembly appoints African Court of Justice judges.[218] As of 31 December 2006, 12 states have become party to the ACJ Protocol—three short of the required number to ensure its entry into force.

In 2003, during the drafting of the ACJ Protocol, the possibility of merging the African Human Rights Court and the Court of Justice was raised and considered, but rejected.[219] During its 2nd session in July 2003, the AU Assembly encouraged states to ratify the ACJ Protocol as soon as possible,[220] while taking note of the Executive Council's decision that the African Human Rights Court 'shall remain a separate and distinct institution from the Court of Justice of the African Union'.[221] However, when the Assembly met again in July 2004, and without prior consultation or notice, the Chairperson of the Assembly suggested that the 'operationalization' of the Human Rights Court should be stalled, to allow for a process of merging the two Courts.[222] This should be done, the Chairperson explained, due to 'the danger of not having enough funds to do what we should do and just proliferating organs'.[223] Without any debate, the Assembly mandated a dramatic departure from the previous AU position by deciding that 'the African Court on

[213] Constitutive Act, art 18.   [214] ibid, art 18(2).

[215] The AU Assembly adopted the Protocol on the Court of Justice of the African Union (see <http://www.africa-union.org>) on 11 July 2003 (for an early discussion of such a court, provided for under the AEC Treaty, see CM Peter, 'The Proposed African Court of Justice—Jurisprudential, Procedural, Enforcement Problems and Beyond' (1993) 1 *East African J of Peace and Human Rights* 117. By the end of 2006, 12 states had ratified the Protocol, which requires 15 deposited ratifications to enter into force. On this duality, see also NJ Udombana, 'An African Human Rights Court and an African Union Court: A Needful Duality or a Needless Duplication?' (2003) 28 *Brooklyn J of Intl L* 811.

[216] Constitutive Act, art 26.   [217] ibid.   [218] ibid, art 9(1)(h).

[219] The 'Decision on the Draft Protocol of the Court of Justice' (AU Doc EX/CL/59 (III), para 2) reflects the consensus that the African Court on Human and Peoples' Rights 'shall remain a separate and distinct institution from the Court of Justice of the African Union'.

[220] AU Doc Assembly/AU/Dec.25(II) (Decision on the Draft Protocol of the Court of Justice of the African Union) para 3.

[221] AU Doc EX/CL/Dec.58(III) (Decision on the Draft Protocol of the Court of Justice) para 2.

[222] Peter (n 215 above) 123–30, in 1993 called for the expansion of the mandate of the African Court of Justice to include eg the protection of human rights and combating mercenarism.

[223] Summary read out by President Obasanjo, quoted by B Kioko, 'The African Union and the Implementation of the Decisions of the African Court on Human and Peoples' Rights' (2004) 15 *Interights Bulletin* 7, 8; and Udombana (n 215 above) 812.

Human and Peoples' Rights and the Court of Justice should be integrated into one Court'.[224]

This decision set in motion a process that is still ongoing, running parallel to the establishment of the African Human Rights Court. On the basis of a draft prepared by a previous President of the ICJ, Bedjaoui, the Algerian Ministry of Foreign Affairs submitted a proposed 'Draft of the Single Judicial Instrument (African Court of Justice and Human Rights)'. An amended version[225] of this proposal was discussed at a meeting of the PRC and legal experts from member states, held in May 2006, at the AU headquarters. The meeting came up with an amended draft (the 'Draft Protocol on the Statute of the African Court of Justice and Human Rights'), which was submitted to the Executive Council in June 2006.[226] Progress towards consensus has been significant, leaving only five clauses unresolved. The Executive Council subsequently referred this draft to a meeting for Ministers of Justice and Attorneys-General from member states 'for finalization and submission of a report to the next Ordinary Session of the Executive Council, in January 2007'.[227] However, this matter did not feature on the agenda of the Executive Council's January 2007 session, and by mid-2007 was still unresolved.

Under the latest version of the draft Merging Protocol, a single judicial institution, the 'African Court of Justice and Human Rights', will be established. The new Court will occupy the seat and take over the assets, rights, and obligations of the African Human Rights Court. The Merging Protocol will enter into force either when 15 states have ratified it, or after that number of states have signed both the pre-existing Protocols.[228] Once the Merging Protocol has entered into force it will replace and abrogate both existing Protocols.

It seems certain that the new Court will consist of 15 judges, sitting in two 'sections'—the General Affairs Section, composed of eight members, and the Human and Peoples' Rights Section, composed of seven judges. Although it constitutes a numerical minority, the Human Rights Chamber has sufficient autonomy: It alone has jurisdiction over matters 'concerning human and/or peoples' rights issues';[229] and it decides when it is 'necessary' to refer a case for consideration by

---

[224] AU Doc Assembly/AU/Dec.45(III) para 4.

[225] Following a Working Group meeting in Algiers, in November 2005.

[226] Annex II to AU Doc EX.CL/253(IX) (Report on the Draft Single Legal Instrument on the Merger of the African Court on Human and Peoples' Rights and the Court of Justice of the African Union). The Annex consists of two instruments, the 'Protocol on the Statute of the African Court of Justice and Human Rights' and, attached thereto, the 'Statute of the African Court of Justice and Human Rights'.

[227] AU Doc EX.CL/Dec.283(IX), Decision on the Single Legal Instrument on the Merger of the African Court on Human and Peoples' Rights and the Court of Justice of the African Union; endorsed by the Assembly: AU Doc Assembly/AU/Dec.118(VII). The Executive Council did not adopt any decision on this matter in January 2007.

[228] Protocol on the Statute of the African Court of Justice and Human Rights, n 226 above, proposed art 8.   [229] ibid, proposed art 17(1).

the 'Full Bench'.[230] The regional composition of the Court was one of the unresolved issues.[231]

The draft Merging Protocol leaves a further important issue unresolved. It proposes that wording similar to article 34(6) of the Human Rights Court Protocol be omitted, but that a general clause be inserted into the Merging Protocol, allowing states explicitly to enter reservations that are compatible with the Protocol's object and purpose.[232] The acceptance of this proposal will reverse the current position which specifically requires states to 'opt in' to accept direct individual access to the Human Rights Court. Under the amended procedure, the fall-back position will be that states accept direct access to the Court, unless they 'opt out' by entering a reservation to that effect.

Provided that the autonomy of the Human and Peoples' Rights Section is guaranteed, the merger of the two courts is supported. Emulating the European example, which derives its dual nature from the fact that each of the Courts exists under a separate political institution, is not called for in Africa, where both Courts will function within the ambit of the same institution—the AU.

H Co-existence of the Court with Quasi-judicial and Other Judicial Bodies

It is a truly post-modern judicial landscape that the African Court enters into: a landscape of apparent institutional proliferation, imitation, and duplication. However, the drafters of the Court Protocol did not seek to insulate the African Court from this uncertain world, but rather seem to have celebrated these complexities when it framed article 3(1) of the Protocol so expansively. The co-existence of the African Court with other international judicial and quasi-judicial bodies postulates the possibility of overlapping jurisdictions, forum-shopping, and conflicting interpretations.[233] These possibilities only become significant problems if another tribunal shares two crucial features with the African Court—its substantive (human rights) mandate; and the possibility of (direct and indirect) individual access.

Some international courts, notably the ICC and ad hoc criminal tribunals (such as the ICTR and SCSL), are often misunderstood as sharing with the African

---

[230] As above, proposed art 18.

[231] Northern states, arguing in favour of strict numerical equality, advocated a 3-3-3-3-3 representation per subregion; while most other states preferred a 4-3-3-3-2 equation, with the West (with 16 members) and North (with five members) represented according to the weight of their AU membership. Currently, the African Human Rights Court, roughly following regional representation, consists of four judges from West Africa, two each from the North, East and South, and one from Central Africa.

[232] Protocol on the Statute of the African Court of Justice and Human Rights, n 226 above, proposed art 8(4).

[233] See generally Y Shany, *The Competing Jurisdictions of International Courts and Tribunals* (Oxford: Oxford University Press, 2003).

Courts the goal of fighting individual impunity. While the ICC, ICTR, and SCSL indeed concern themselves with individual criminal responsibility, the African Court has no penal jurisdiction.[234] In so far as it also deals with impunity, the African Court directs itself at the state and its responsibility to investigate atrocities and prosecute offenders.

The very expansive general international law scope of the International Court of Justice (ICJ) comprises the more specific human rights focus of the African Court.[235] This overlap is clearly illustrated by the two separate but substantially similar cases instituted concerning armed activities on the territory of the DRC: one before the ICJ,[236] and one before the African Commission.[237] In both these instances, the tribunal found violations of the African Charter.[238] However, because only states may approach the ICJ, the extent of concurrent jurisdiction with the African Court will be limited to inter-state complaints, and will not cover the more pervasive possibility of individual complaints.

Regional and subregional arrangements primarily aimed at political and economic integration have also established courts.[239] The jurisdiction-conferring provisions of the founding treaties establishing these courts relate mainly to their objectives (political and economic integration) and trade-related aspects. Each of these courts has a specialized field of jurisdiction, concerning itself with the interpretation and application of each of these founding treaties. However, there clearly are human rights dimensions to economic and political integration, and to trade. This is even more so when the founding treaties explicitly include human rights protection as part of their aims and objectives. With the exception of SADC, the other regional economic communities (RECs) all invoke the African Charter as part of

---

[234] In answer to questions posed at the ministerial meeting drafting the African Charter, M'Baye, as Chairman of the Committee of Experts, explained that 'an international penal court' was already provided for under the Convention on the Elimination and the Suppression of the Crime of Apartheid, and that the UN 'is considering at the present time a project with a view to establishing an international court to repress crime against mankind' (Rapporteur's report (OAU Doc CAB/LEG/67/DraftRapt.Rpt(II)Rev.4), Annex II to Report of the Secretary-General on the Draft African Charter on Human and Peoples' Rights (OAU Doc CM/1149(XXXVII) para 13, report reprinted in Heyns (n 9 above) 94–105). From this may be deduced that the question of a court was raised, but mainly as a possible instrument to punish crimes against humanity, including apartheid. At some later point during the deliberations, an unnamed delegation proposed the establishment of a court 'to judge crimes against mankind and violations of human rights' (para 117), thus extending the possible material jurisdiction of such a court. The meeting was of the opinion 'that it was untimely to discuss it' (para 117).

[235] ICJ Statute, art 36(1): 'The jurisdiction of the Court comprises all cases which the parties refer to it and all matters specifically provided for in the Charter of the United Nations or in treaties or conventions in force'; and art 36(2), extending the ICJ's jurisdiction to the 'interpretation of a treaty' and 'any question of international law'.

[236] *Armed Activities on the Territory of the Congo (DRC v Uganda)* (19 December 2005).

[237] Communication 227/99, *DRC v Burundi, Rwanda and Uganda* (2004) AHRLR 19 (ACHPR 2004) (20th Activity Report), see Ch 4 above.

[238] (n 236 above) para 219; (n 237 above) final para. A further dimension of the overlapping jurisdiction is that the one state involved in both proceedings, Uganda, was required to pay compensation twice.   [239] Ch 12.D.4 below.

their foundational principles, making it an appropriate basis for the development of a continental human rights *jus commune*.[240]

In my view, this overlap is generally more apparent than real. Even if human rights feature in them, these treaties are not—as such—human rights treaties. Individuals also sometimes lack standing before these courts. When the African Charter is relied upon, it will serve as interpretative guidance to these courts *in interpreting and applying their founding treaties*. Consider the following example. In a case decided on 27 November 2006 by the East African Court of Justice, a group of individuals contested the nomination, by the Kenyan government, of Kenyan representatives to the East African Legislative Assembly (EALA).[241] Although the human right to participate in representative institutions underlies this challenge,[242] the Court indicated that the matter stood to be decided under article 50 of the EAC Treaty, which provides that 'each national Assembly shall elect' its representatives.

When the determination of a human rights matter (under the African Charter) is pertinent to the outcome of the case before a subregional court, such courts could adopt a procedure of referral, similar to that in place when a national court refers a matter for a preliminary ruling to the European Court of Justice,[243] and similar to referrals provided for under the African RECs.[244] These courts may use the existing possibility under the Protocol of requesting an advisory opinion to approach the African Court on the human rights aspect—based on the African Charter—of the case before them, and should then decide the matter in line with the African Court's determination (or 'preliminary ruling'). Such an approach, which will minimize conflicting jurisprudence and increase regional judicial convergence, will also ensure that judicial developments do not take place in negation of the fact that the subregional units, including their courts, are the building blocks of closer union within the AU.[245]

The Court's substantive mandate most clearly overlaps with that of UN human rights treaty bodies. With five of these treaty bodies allowing for individual complaints,[246] questions may arise about the choice of forum, and the sequence to be

---

[240] See Ch 12.D.3 below.

[241] *Anyang' Nyong'o and Others v Attorney General of Kenya and Others*, Reference No 1 of 2006, EAC Court (27 November 2006).

[242] The African Charter's protection in this regard is equivocal, see art 13(1).

[243] EC Treaty, art 234 (formerly art 177): 'The Court of Justice shall have jurisdiction to give preliminary rulings concerning (a) the interpretation of this treaty . . . where such a question is raised before any court or tribunal of a Member State, that court or tribunal may, if it considers that a decision on the question is necessary to enable it to give judgment, request the Court of Justice to give a ruling thereon. Where any such question is raised in a case pending before a court or tribunal of a Member State against whose decisions there is no judicial remedy under national law, that court or tribunal shall bring the matter before the Court of Justice' See also art 35 of the Treaty of the EU which makes preliminary referral of issues related to the 'third pillar' (freedom, security, and justice) optional on member states.

[244] See eg EAC Treaty, art 34, SADC Treaty, art 16, COMESA Treaty, art 30; and Ch 12 below.

[245] The ECOWAS Court of Justice, with its clear human rights mandate and allowing direct individual access without stipulating that domestic remedies need to be exhausted, may pose the greatest challenge to this approach (see Ch 12.D.5 below). [246] See Ch 3 above.

followed when more than one forum—including the African Court—may be approached. Choice of forum depends on a number of factors, including: (i) the most appropriate substantive provision(s) to be invoked; (ii) the prospect of success, based on the jurisprudential approach of each potential tribunal or body, as reflected in its precedents; and (iii) the nature of the finding reached within each forum. With respect to the last factor, the binding nature of the African Court's decision should heavily favour it as complainants' tribunal of choice. Three main possibilities (*lis alibi pendens*, *res judicata*, and a combination of the first two) come into play when multiple proceedings are set in motion, and should guide complainants to choose the sequence in which to stagger their applications.[247]

First, the body that is approached may refuse to consider any matter that is pending (that 'is being considered') before another international dispute resolution mechanism (the '*lis alibi pendens*' principle). Adopting this approach, the HRC refuses to entertain a matter if it is *pending* before another international tribunal, but considers matters that have been *finalized* by another tribunal.[248] The same approach applies to the African Court's advisory jurisdiction in so far as it may not be exercised when the same question is pending before the African Commission.[249]

Secondly, the body that is approached may refuse to entertain matters that have been finalized ('settled') in other international fora. This principle is enshrined in article 56(7) of the African Charter, which disallows communications before the African Commission if they 'have been settled' under another international dispute settlement mechanism.

Thirdly, and essentially combining the first two approaches, the tribunal that is approached may dictate that only one route may be selected. Once a particular course is chosen, the complainant precludes all other possibilities of redress. This approach for example applies under the Convention against Torture.[250]

In a practical application of these principles before the African Human Rights Court had been established, Garreth Prince, a Rastafarian lawyer, found himself in the dilemma of having to choose between his religion and his professional career path.[251] After exhausting his local remedies—he 'lost' five–four at the South African Constitutional Court—he had to decide which international tribunal or body he should approach. Substantively, the African Charter and the ICCPR provided the best possibilities. Procedurally, it made most sense to approach the African Commission first, because the HRC could thereafter still be approached. Had he submitted his complaint first to the HRC, the matter—on the basis of the *res judicata* principle followed by the Commission—would not have been considered by the African Commission. It is suggested that the African Court should follow a similar approach in all contentious cases, given the inherent logic and general

---

[247] Shany (n 233 above) 212–26.   [248] ibid, 218; OPI, art 5(2).
[249] Court Protocol, art 4(1).
[250] CAT, art 22(5)(a): The CAT Committee 'shall not consider any communication' unless it has been ascertained that 'the same matter has not been, and is not being, examined under another procedure of international investigation or settlement'.   [251] See Ch 8.A.7 above.

acceptability of the *res judicata* principle. Once the Court has delivered a judgment, the matter is, according to article 28(2) of the Protocol, not 'subject to appeal'. This formulation seems wide enough to preclude the HRC (as well as other UN treaty bodies, and REC Courts) from entertaining matters that have been finalized by the African Human Rights Court.

I The Court's Challenges

Apart from merely addressing the weaknesses of the African Commission, the Court may have a much broader impact. An effective regional court is likely to strengthen local courts. Decisions of the African Human Rights Court may enable courts in states without a human rights tradition to take risky and courageous steps by relying on a continental jurisprudence. At the same time, the Court is by no means a panacea for human rights in Africa. Many challenges and obstacles remain, some of which are now assessed.

1 The Court May Lack Universal Regional Acceptance

The question remains whether all AU member states will accept the Protocol and whether more states will accept direct individual access to the Court. To ensure the maximum effect of the Court as regional institution, there should be universal regional acceptance of its jurisdiction.[252] As long as this objective has not been attained, the African regional human rights system will operate differently for different states, thereby undermining the development of common institutions and norms. Two factors that may inhibit acceptance of the Court's jurisdiction are: (i) reliance on national sovereignty, linked to disquiet about the disruption of national legal orders; and (ii) a professed 'African' suspicion of judicial settlement of disputes.

The main reason for states' reluctance to accept international supervision and access to individuals relates to the principle of national 'sovereignty'. The creation of the African Court represents an inroad into a state party's exercise of judicial sovereignty, and may even impact on its executive and legislative sovereignty. A supra-national court, by its very nature, acquires jurisdiction over the treatment of individuals within the borders of participating states. 'State sovereignty', supported by the principle of non-interference in the domestic affairs of member states, is frequently invoked as a barrier against international inspection of internal affairs. Conscious of the frailty of their 'sovereign' states, African leaders have sought refuge in the classical view of this concept, which postulates that 'states hold essentially unfettered powers within their frontiers'.[253] When the African

[252] Pasqualucci (n 192 above) 340–2.
[253] CE Welch, 'The Organisation of African Unity and the Promotion of Human Rights' (1991) 29 *J of Modern African Studies* 535; see also 1963 OAU Charter, art 2(1)(c).

Charter was drafted in the 1970s, one of the overriding principles was that it 'should not exceed what African states may be willing to accept'.[254]

However, state parties have, by the very act of ratifying the African Charter and other UN and African human rights treaties, already forfeited exclusive jurisdiction of matters regulated by the treaties they have ratified.[255] In this respect, the time-honoured principle that states are bound by their explicit prior agreement to the terms of a treaty should be invoked.[256] In any event, all African states have, as parties to the Charter, already accepted the competence of the African Commission to decide inter-state and individual complaints.[257] In addition, the Protocol itself endeavours to accommodate considerations of political sovereignty by making direct access to the Court optional. Under the Protocol, states do not automatically accept the right of individuals to bring cases directly to the Court,[258] but are required to make an optional declaration indicating their acceptance of that possibility.[259]

In an era where the protection of human rights has become accepted as an integral part of governance, the very notion of 'state sovereignty' has taken on a different meaning.[260] It is now understood that the source of sovereignty is no longer 'the sovereign', but the 'people'; and that its purpose is to ensure that individuals prosper and that their rights are realized. Even in Africa sovereignty is no longer sacrosanct. Evidence of a people-centred understanding of sovereignty is found in numerous African constitutions,[261] and in the AU Constitutive Act, which accepts the right of the Union to use military force in member states in order to restore grave human rights violations.[262] In other words, AU states have accepted the principle that individual rights may have to be protected against the abuse of state sovereignty.

Unease may also be based on a lack of a proper understanding of the relationship between the African Court and domestic courts. The fear has been expressed

[254] R Sock, 'The Case for an African Court of Human and Peoples' Rights' (1994) 2 *African Topics* 9.
[255] African Charter, art 1.   [256] The principle of *pacta sunt servanda*.
[257] Welch has noted the importance of the Commission's role in undermining claims based on sovereignty: 'The establishment and functioning of the OAU's newest subsidiary organization, the African Commission on Human and Peoples' Rights, challenges a basic principle of positivist international law on which the OAU has long based its policies: the sovereign domestic control of member States' (CE Welch, 'The Organisation of African Unity and Human Rights: Regional Promotion of Human Rights' in Y El-Ayouty (ed), *The Organization of African Unity after Thirty Years* (Westport, Conn: Praeger, 1994) 53).   [258] Court Protocol, art 34(6).
[259] Optional provisions in the other regional human rights instruments are of a different nature, as they do not relate to 'direct access' to the relevant Court, but to the competence of the Commission (and, therefore, the Court) to consider individual or inter-state complaints. In the African system, those initial obstacles do not exist.
[260] T Meron, *The Humanization of International Law* (Leiden: Martinus Nijhoff, 2006) 93 ('sovereignty is now being attenuated by the heightened impact of human rights law and acceptance of the principle that human rights are a matter of international concern').
[261] In particular constitutions of 'Francophone' countries, which, following the French constitutional tradition, declare that 'sovereignty belongs to the people', and is exercised on their behalf by elected representatives (see eg Chad Constitution 1996, art 3; Congo Constitution 2001, art 3; and Burundi Constitution 2004, art 7).   [262] AU Constitutive Act, art 4(h).

that states may be reluctant to ratify the Protocol in order to avoid 'the disruption of their domestic legal orders' resulting from the Court's judgments.[263] Pityana counters this apprehension by pointing out that the African Court is not able to 'directly annul or repeal any judgment by a court of law', but concedes that the 'offending' state has to 'implement the decision within its national legal system'.[264] It is not entirely convincing merely to shift the responsibility to respond to the judgment from the legal to the political arena. Pityana may have shown that a fear of judicial 'disruption' is overstated, but he may not have dispelled fears that the legal system needs to be reformed in line with the African Court's decisions. While it is correct that the state's accountability to the AU plays itself out in the domain of international relations, the ultimate resolution of conflicts between the African Court and domestic courts lies at the national level, and may require legal reform. One answer to fears of contradictions between the African Court and domestic courts is that domestic courts should pre-emptively avoid them by following the jurisprudence of the Commission and the Court.[265] At the moment domestic courts would find limited guidance, but this situation should change in the future.

Another reason why states may be apprehensive about accepting the competence of the African Human Rights Court is an alleged 'African preference' for non-judicial methods of resolving disputes, in which dialogue and conciliation are emphasized.[266] While it is correct to state that many traditional African societies avoided conflict resolution that ended in 'open-confrontation-type win/lose' modes of adjudication,[267] such a statement does not sufficiently account for the 'public law' nature of human rights conflicts and for the position in more centralized societies, even in traditional Africa. In 'public law' disputes, for example involving grave misconduct that threatens the security of the whole community, the presiding traditional official or group acted more rigidly, by imposing the appropriate penalty prescribed by custom.[268] Further, the argument pertaining to traditional Africa on the whole does not apply neatly to modern African states.[269] The argument

---

[263] A Stemmet, 'A Future African Court for Human and Peoples' Rights and Domestic Human Rights Norms' (1998) 23 *SAYIL* 233, 238.

[264] NB Pityana, 'Hurdles and Pitfalls in International Human Rights Law: The Ratification Process of the African Charter on the Establishment of the African Court on Human and Peoples' Rights' (2003) 28 *SAYIL* 110, 122.   [265] ibid 123.

[266] See eg K M'Baye, *Les Droits de l'Homme en Afrique* (Paris: Pedone, 1992) 164–5, who gives this 'philosophical' reason for the omission of a Court, referring to the '*palabres*' where conflicts were discussed and underscoring that African justice is essentially conciliatory. Decisions to intervene in a situation are generally based on consensus. See also the arguments cited by Sock (n 254 above) 9.

[267] P Amoah, 'The African Charter on Human and Peoples' Rights—An Effective Weapon for Human Rights?' (1992) 4 *RADIC* 226, 238.

[268] C Ebo, 'Indigenous Law and Justice: Some Major Concepts and Practices' (1979) 76 *Vierteljahresberichte* 139, 142, 146.

[269] The powerful rhetorical line of questioning by E Bondzie-Simpson, 'A Critique of the African Charter of Human and Peoples' Rights' (1988) 31 *Howard L J* 643, 663, merits full quotation (albeit only in a footnote): 'What did the framers want to suggest? That traditional African states had no courts? If so, they were wrong. That litigation was alien to traditional Africa? If so, they are wrong. That courts engender violations of human rights and that in the absence of courts these violations are

that traditional Africa preferred reconciliatory resolution of disputes, while logical and conceptually attractive, does not sufficiently take the reality of present-day African society into account.[270] With the impersonal nation state replacing relations of tribal kinship, several factors such as increasing urbanization, acculturation and population concentration have contributed to the disintegration of traditional authority. In principle, each newly independent state created a formal judicial system, consisting of courts at various levels. In most instances, traditional court structures were also incorporated and integrated with common or civil law rules and principles. Codes of civil and criminal procedure, based on colonial examples, were retained after independence.

The argument that courts are not of great importance in post-colonial African states further suffers from the weakness that it relates to the national, rather than the international, sphere. There are some indications of African preference for non-adjudicatory resolution of disputes also in respect of international affairs. The best and most apt illustration in this regard is the initial creation of a commission, and not a court, to supervise the African Charter. Mediation and other non-judicial means of resolving disputes are exemplified by the 1969 OAU Convention Governing the Specific Aspects of Refugee Problems in Africa, which provides that 'any dispute between State signatories... relating to its interpretation or application, which cannot be settled by other means, shall be referred to the Commission for Mediation, Conciliation and Arbitration' of the OAU.[271] In contrast, disputes between state parties about the application and interpretation of the UN Convention on Refugees that cannot be settled by other means 'shall be referred to the International Court of Justice at the request of any one of the parties to the dispute'.[272] The reservations entered by a number of African states when ratifying CERD, which also provides for the ICJ to settle disputes, are also indicative of reluctance to accept international adjudication.

However, there are many more recent indications of acceptance by African states of judicial mechanism on the international plane. Acceptance by African states of the ICJ's jurisdiction has been an important feature of international law after 1966.

eschewed, or better redressed? If so, then again, they are wrong'. See also P Tigere, 'State Reporting to the African Commission: The Case of Zimbabwe' (1994) 339 *JAL* 64, 66, who referred to the drafters' preference for 'a romanticized traditional African dispute resolution mechanism'.

[270] Adopting a law and literature approach, one may also point to the extent to which the concept of a 'trial' has been highlighted in prose works and dramas written in independent Africa. I mention five titles in which the 'reality' of court structures feature to varying degrees: CO Ancholonu, *The Trial of the Beautiful Ones* (Owerri, Nigeria: Total, 1985), B Abdallah, *The Trial of Mallam Ilya and other Plays* (Accra: Woeli Publishing Services, 1987), AA Mazrui, *The Trial of Christopher Okigbo* (Oxford: Heinemann, 1971), S Samkange, *On Trial for my Country* (Oxford: Heinemann, 1966), and N wa Thiong'o and MG Mugo, *The Trial of Dedan Kimathi* (Oxford: Heinemann, 1976).

[271] OAU Refugee Convention, art IX. Weis makes the following observation in relation to the OAU Refugee Convention: 'This is in accordance with the Charter of the Organisation of African Unity and reflects the known reluctance of many African States to accept the compulsory jurisdiction of the International Court of Justice' (P Weis, 'The Convention of the Organisation of African Unity governing the Specific Aspects of Refugee Problems in Africa' (1970) 3 *Revue des Droits de l'Homme* 449, 462).   [272] UN Refugee Convention, art 38.

African unease about the domination of Western jurisprudence was replaced with an active exploitation of the system in cases such as the frontier and territorial disputes between Burkina Faso and Mali,[273] between Libya and Chad,[274] between Botswana and Namibia,[275] and more recently, between Nigeria and Cameroon and between Benin and Niger;[276] the submission by the DRC of disputes against Uganda, Rwanda, and Belgium;[277] and the disputes submitted by Congo and Djibouti against France.[278] A number of regional courts have been established under regional arrangements and have started issuing judgments.[279]

The evolving practice of the African Commission further indicates a predilection for a more accusatorial, adjudicating function.[280] The tendency of African states to enter reservations to the competence of the ICJ to hear disputes without the consent of both parties (as exemplified in CERD) has changed for the better with regard to later treaties (such as CAT), in that African states had generally not made similar declarations. A later human rights instrument, the African Children's Charter, also challenges the assumption that conciliatory methods are preferable in Africa. In contrast to the UN Convention on the Rights of the Child, its African equivalent provides for individual complaints by way of a litigation-based approach. The status of ratification of the two regional courts, the African Human Rights Court and the Court of Justice, and the Rome Statute, as well the establishment of numerous subregional courts, also contradict arguments that courts are inappropriate in an African context. A previous member of the African Commission, Umozurike, remarked that 'with Courts working in the national system, there is no basis for concluding that they would not, as in Europe and America, work at the inter-African level'.[281]

2 Addressing Poverty: Systemic Violations of Socio-economic Rights

Can the Court be a vehicle to improve the lives of downtrodden and materially deprived Africans? Will it be able to realize its potential to adjudicate not only on

---

[273] [1986] ICJ Rep 554.   [274] See (1995) ILR 1.

[275] *Case concerning the Kasikili/Sedudu Island (Botswana/Namibia)* (13 December 1999) (Court finding that Kasikili/Sedudu Island forms part of the territory of Botswana).

[276] *Case concerning the Land and Maritime Boundary between Cameroon and Nigeria (Cameroon v Nigeria, judgment of 10 October 2002) (case concerning the Bakassi Peninsula); Case concerning the Frontier Dispute (Benin/Niger)* (12 July 2005), finding that the island of Lété Goungou belongs to Niger.

[277] See *Armed Activities on the Territory of the Congo (DRC v Uganda)*, judgment of 19 December 2005; *Armed Activities on the Territory of the Congo (New Application: 2002) (Democratic Republic of the Congo v Rwanda)*, judgment of 3 February 2006 (finding that the Court lacks jurisdiction) and *Case concerning the Arrest Warrant of 11 April 2000 (DRC v Belgium)*, judgment of 14 February 2002.

[278] *Case concerning Certain Criminal Proceedings in France (Republic of the Congo v France); Certain Questions of Mutual Assistance in Criminal Matters (Djibouti v France)* submitted on 9 January 2006; France accepted the jurisdiction of the ICJ in this matter on 9 August 2006, ICJ Press Release, <http://www.icj-cij.org/icjwww/idocket/idfj/idjfframe.htm> (30 September 2006).

[279] Ch 12.D.4 below.   [280] See Ch 8.A above.

[281] In C Theoderopoulos (ed), *Human Rights in Europe and in Africa: A Comparative Analysis* (Athens: Hellenic University Press, 1992) 111.

individual 'civil and political rights' violations, but also on violations on a massive scale and of a socio-economic nature?

It is often stated that courts present an inappropriate forum for the resolution of disputes about economic matters because judges are not equipped to take decisions on these matters. In addition, it has been argued that the judicial focus on these rights is 'a sophistication, a Western imposition and a bane to development',[282] and that economic development should precede the judicialization of these rights.[283] Development 'automatically promotes or will lead to the realisation of democracy and respect for human rights'.[284] However, the African Charter includes socio-economic rights as justiciable guarantees, and the Commission has some time ago, in the *Ogoniland* and the *Gambian Mental Health* findings, buried the spectre of 'unenforceability'.[285] These decisions illustrate that the realization of socio-economic rights involves different nuances, ranging from the primary obligation to *respect* these rights, the secondary obligation to *protect* them, to the tertiary obligation to *promote* and *fulfil* these rights.[286] In *Gambian Mental Health*, the Commission went even further when it accepted that the right to health also entails the obligation to fulfil the right to health.[287] This is one area in which the Court should pay particular attention to the African Commission's jurisprudence.

'Poverty' claims are likely to be brought by groups or to have collective implications. A court may be an ideal forum to provide effective remedies to an individual complaining against a state that has infringed an identifiable right. However, human rights violations in Africa often occur on a 'massive' scale, involving numerous victims and the simultaneous violation of manifold rights, which are serious in nature, and reveal systematic or institutionalized patterns of disregard for human rights. Because courts give findings on the facts of individual cases presented to them, their findings are directed at relief for individual litigants, making them ill-equipped to address situations involving numerous victims. Cases are usually brought by a small number of victims, and not by all affected persons. Only those victims who are able to gain access to the court are granted remedies. The *Velásquez Rodríguez* case,[288] decided by the Inter-American Court, presents an example of this disadvantage. From 1991 to 1994, between 100 and 150 persons were 'disappeared'

---

[282] AE-O El-Obaid and A-A Appiagyei-Atua, 'Human Rights in Africa—A New Perspective on Linking the Past to the Present' (1996) 41 *McGill L J* 853.

[283] Writing in 1974, OC Eze ('Prospects for International Protection of Human Rights in Africa' (1974) 4 *The African Rev* 79, 90) argued that only a 'recommendatory' human rights body was at that stage feasible in Africa, and added: 'In the meantime the war against illiteracy, disease and want should be relentlessly waged because victory over these represents the backbone to a meaningful protection of human rights both at national and international levels'.   [284] ibid.

[285] See Ch 6.A.1 above.

[286] See P De Vos, 'Pious Wishes or Directly Enforceable Human Rights? Social and Economic Rights in South Africa's 1996 Constitution' (1997) 13 *South African J on Human Rights* 67, 79–91; A Eide 'Economic, Social and Cultural Rights as Human Rights' in A Eide, *Economic, Social and Cultural Rights: A Textbook* (Dordrecht: Martinus Nijhoff, C Krause and A Roses 1995) 21, 37–9; H Shue, *Basic Rights: Subsistence, Affluence and US Foreign Policy* (Princeton: Princeton University Press, 1980) 5.

[287] See Ch 6.A.1 above.   [288] Series C No 4 (29 July 1988).

in Honduras.[289] The Inter-American Commission was inundated with a flood of individual complaints, but only 'one or two of these cases' could 'be sent to the Court, which sits part-time'.[290] In terms of the American Convention, remedies were ordered primarily in respect of the parties to the dispute before the Court. However, by relying on the approach of some national courts, such as that of the South African Constitutional Court,[291] on the possibility of 'class actions',[292] and on the experience of the European system,[293] the African Human Rights Court may yet overcome this limitation.

3 Can the Court Bridge Intra-continental Divides?

Legal, cultural, religious, economical, political, and many other differences within and between African states abound. Even before considering factors causing regional diversity, one has to pause and consider the internal fragmentation of many states and the resulting lack of national integration. Due to the imposition of colonial borders, often many diverse linguistic and cultural groups have been compacted into one territorial unit. Within most African states, the urban–rural divide overlaps with difference in political governance (traditional versus democratic), legal culture (unwritten, customary, and informal versus written, rule-based, and formal) and economic conditions (subsistence versus market opportunities).

Africa has a rich diversity of ethnic, cultural, and linguistic groups, making the invocation of an 'African' legal system or approach to law a fallacy. Legal traditions and the language of law differ across Africa.[294] Post-independence African legal systems may be divided into two main groups: the civil law[295] and the common law[296] traditions. To this one should add localized African customary law, religious

---

[289] See discussion by JM Pasqualucci, 'Victim Reparations in the Inter-American Human Rights System: A Critical Assessment of Current Practice and Procedure' (1996) 18 *Michigan J of Intl L* 1, 23.

[290] ibid. [291] See Ch 14.C.1 below.

[292] On the *actio popularis* before the African Commission, see Ch 8.A.3 above.

[293] One of the reasons for the increased caseload of the European Court of Human Rights is the huge number of cases brought subsequent to a finding relating to the same structural cause of the initial finding of violation. Under Protocol 14 (n 66 above), the European Court devised a simplified procedure of dealing with 'repetitive' cases on the basis of established jurisprudence. See also n 313 below.

[294] This is an update and reworking of data in AK Mensah-Brown, *Introduction to Law in Contemporary Africa* (New York: Conch, 1976) 8–16.

[295] While countries under the common law umbrella show some coherence, civil law traditions are by no means homogeneous. They differ according to the colonial power responsible for their introduction. Most of the civil law countries in Africa (19 of them) were under French rule (Algeria, Benin, Burkina Faso, Chad, Central African Republic, Comoros, Congo, Djibouti, Gabon, Guinea, Côte d'Ivoire, Madagascar, Mali, Mauritania, Morocco, Niger, Senegal, Togo and Tunisia). Burundi, Rwanda, and the DRC became 'civil law' countries through Belgian influence. Portuguese codes were introduced in Angola, Cape Verde, Guinea-Bissau, Mozambique, and São Tomé e Príncipe. Spanish colonial rule in Equatorial Guinea and the Western Sahara brought these territories into the civil law 'cluster'. Brief periods of Italian occupation introduced Libya and Somalia to this legal tradition.

[296] Common law-based legal systems are found in eg The Gambia, Ghana, Kenya, Malawi, Nigeria, Sierra Leone, Sudan, Liberia, Tanzania, Uganda, and Zambia.

law (particularly Islam or Shari'ah-based systems[297] and Indian customs),[298] (formerly) Soviet law,[299] and Roman-Dutch legal systems.[300] This co-existence of different traditions creates legal pluralism, or at least, legal dualism, in most sub-Saharan African states. The values underlying states and societies within states in Africa are radically divergent. In terms of religion-based values, differentiation runs along the Christian-Muslim-animist divide. These values obviously impact on constitutional matters, for example the position that women have in a particular society and under the local constitution. Differences about the interrelationship between law and religion are also fundamental, as they determine to what extent law and religion are regarded as separate, and separable. Against this background, the question is posed whether these centrifugal forces will prevent the Court from exercising its mandate effectively.

On the one hand, it may be argued that the Court, threatened by the deep-seated differences alluded to above, will be unable to realize the ideal of uniform human rights law across Africa. Perhaps the expectations of 'unification' suggested by this line of argument are too high, and should be attenuated. The 'Africanization' of law through the influence of the African Charter (and African Human Rights Court) should not be equated with the total equalization of legal systems. Under the Council of Europe, 'Europeanization' has been given two meanings. It may indicate a tendency to cooperate and to harmonize laws, or it may denote, in a looser sense, 'the coming together of legal systems, inspired as much by an internal drive towards reform and improvement as by the exigencies of European politics'.[301] An analysis of the European Court of Human Rights case-law on criminal procedure found, for instance, that the Court 'does not insist on any type of procedure, accepting each system in its own right, provided the end result is compatible with Article 5 and 6 of ECHR'.[302] The general conclusion of the analysis was that a

---

[297] In an extreme form eg in Sudan: see report of Commission's mission to Sudan (see Ch 8.C above).

[298] eg Zanzibar.

[299] In eg Benin and Congo; but since 1990 becoming increasingly irrelevent.

[300] Roman-Dutch law differs fundamentally from the civil law tradition. It is not based on the Napoleonic Code, or any other code. It is based on the writings of 17th to 19th century Dutch authors, decisions of Dutch courts of the 17th century, and legislation adopted at the Cape. When the British occupied the Cape in the early 19th century, they left the legal system intact. Today the legal systems of Botswana, Lesotho, Namibia, South Africa, Swaziland, and Zimbabwe show strong influences of this system. However, all these countries (except Namibia) were under British rule for a substantial period. This caused Roman-Dutch law to be influenced by common law, giving rise to 'mixed' legal systems in these countries. The extent of the impact and influence of English law differs in these states, creating greater diversity. A combination of civil and common law accounts for 'mixed' legal systems in Cameroon, Egypt, Mauritius, and Somalia. In a category of its own, defying easy definition, is Ethiopia, and Eritrea states Eritned in which no colonial legal order was imposed. In both these countries, the system is codified and has characteristics of the civil law system.

[301] C Harding, B Swart, N Jörg, and P Fennell, 'Conclusion: Europeanization and Convergence: The Lessons of Comparative Study' in P Fennell, C Harding, N Jörg, and B Swart (eds), *Criminal Justice in Europe: A Comparative Study* (Oxford: Clarendon Press, 1995) 379, 380.

[302] See N Jorg, S Field, and C Brants, 'Are Inquisitorial and Accusatorial Systems Converging?' in Fennell *et al* ((n 301 above) 41, 56, where the case of *Barberà v Spain* (ECHR Series A No 146 (December 1988)) is quoted as an illustration of the point. In this case the European Court of Human Rights held Spain to its own, inquisitorial guarantees.

different legal system cannot be (and has not been) transported into other systems without taking national tradition and outlook into consideration. A key element of success in the development of any regional legal system lies in allowing for 'sensitive and mutually-understood local diversity, regulated ultimately by shared policy objectives in the relevant field of activity',[303] which is also the goal of the 'margin of appreciation' doctrine. In essence, the African Human Rights Court provides guidance about minimum human rights standards on the continent, and does not purport to bring about uniformity to Africa's diverse legal systems.

On the other hand, it may be argued that, if the Court is to succeed, it will do so only by subordinating some of these fundamentally different values and principles to others.[304] Paradoxically, a single court's success will be built on the domination of certain core values over others. In other words, the suitability of the posited ideal of legal unification and harmonization, even if it is restricted to the domain of human rights, is called into question. However, the premise of this argument, namely that the establishment of a supra-national court aims at creating greater legal uniformity between legal systems, has itself increasingly been questioned in the post-modern age, rendering suspect notions of one legally uniform continental monolith. Previously, Western conceptions of the law have almost exclusively concentrated on formal law, exercised through formal institutions, based on a centralized legal instrument. In this view, which has been influenced especially by the codification movement, law is regarded as part of the institutions of and indispensable to the indirect control exerted by the modern nation-state. It should not be surprising that this model has gained much less currency in Africa, where everyday life is influenced too markedly by a plurality of legal systems. This plurality is integrated into the reality of all African societies and the consciousness of most individuals living in Africa, and is likely to stifle attempts at establishing legal uniformity. Given that legal unity still eludes most domestic legal systems, the notion of an 'African' human rights jurisprudence should be approached with realism and modesty.

Cultural and historical differences will remain, and will no doubt lead to conflicting views about the resolution of disputes. However, it should be kept in mind that the Court's finding in a case binds the parties to the case, and does not automatically apply to all other ratifying states. Although the divisiveness of diversity in Africa should not be downplayed, it should also not be elevated to become an insurmountable obstacle in the quest for better human rights protection in Africa.

4 Will the Court's Decisions be Implemented and Enforced Domestically?

A supra-national court presupposes domestic courts that are independent from executive domination and interference, perceived to be legitimate and operating

---

[303] Harding *et al* in Fennell *et al* (n 301 above) 379, 386.
[304] See K Hopkins, 'The Effect of an African Court on the Domestic Legal Orders of African States' (2002) 2 *AHRLJ* 234.

and accessible to ordinary nationals. It is particularly when domestic courts are found wanting that the African Human Rights Court will be approached. When that Court orders a remedy, domestic judicial enforcement may be required. Both domestic exhaustion and enforcement become problematic in the absence of a functioning domestic legal system. The reality that the executive often disregards both domestic and international judicial decisions underlines that the enforcement of judicial remedies remains contingent upon political will.

Judicial decisions, including those concerning human rights, do not impact on a void or function in a vacuum. They are directed at and interact with a specific society. Ghai used Weber's typology to postulate a theory of the African state, drawing a distinction between the rational-legal and the patrimonial state.[305] In the rational-legal state, legality is the underlying principle and principal source of legitimacy. It derives from rules, or overriding principles. In independent African states, the constitution is the foundation of authority; in the regional context, it is the African Charter. As allegiance is not owed to any individual person, authority becomes impersonalized.[306] The patrimonial state, on the other hand, is characterized by 'highly personal rule'. In the ruler, in his discretion and personality, one finds the source of authority. This distinction corresponds with the differentiation between the *Gemeinschaft* and *Gesellschaft* constructs of society and social values.[307] *Gemeinschaft* (or 'community') denotes social relationships of solidarity based on affection and kinship, such as the relationship between members of a family. *Gesellschaft* (or 'society'), on the other hand, refers to social relationships based on division of labour and 'contractual relations between isolated individuals'. In a context where patrimonial states are still heavily based on *Gemeinschaft* values, the rational-legal system of judicial review is limited, as is illustrated by a series of events taking place in Swaziland during the early 1970s. In terms of Swazi legislation, one Ngwenya was declared a prohibited immigrant. Shortly thereafter, the Swazi legislature passed the Immigration Amendment Act.[308] In terms of the amendment a new tribunal was established to decide all matters concerning citizenship. None of the new tribunal's decisions could be subjected to judicial review. Ngwenya sought judicial relief, arguing that the amendment was unconstitutional. This contention found little favour with the Swaziland High Court. A final appeal lay to the Swaziland Court of Appeal. This Court had replaced the Swaziland Privy Council, and consisted of South African judges. Judge of Appeal Schreiner wrote the Court of Appeal's judgment, in which the amendment was found to be in violation of the Swaziland Constitution. This was followed by a unanimous resolution passed by the Swaziland Parliament, stating that the Constitution was

---

[305] YP Ghai, 'Constitutions and Governance in Africa: A Prolegomenon' in S Adelman and A Paliwala (eds), *Law and Crisis in the Third World* (New York: H Zell, 1993) 63–4.   [306] ibid, 64.
[307] See also the distinction drawn by AV Dicey, *Introduction to the Study of Law of the Constitution* (London: Macmillan, 1959) between the 'rule of law' and the 'exercise by persons in authority of wide, arbitrary, or discretionary powers of constraint' (188).   [308] Act 22 of 1972.

unworkable.[309] The King proceeded to suspend the Constitution by radio broadcast and assumed all legislative, executive, and judicial authority in his person.

Although most African states adopted multi-party electoral systems in the 1990s, their conversion to democratic values was only partial. Ultimately, public opinion is the means through which pressure may be exerted on states to ensure compliance. Even the holding of multi-party elections in Africa since 1990 does not necessarily mean the institution of liberal democracy. A lack of a political culture of tolerance and democratic values is still evident even where formal democracies are in place. However, the AU has strengthened the institutional support for democracy, reflected in its suspension from the AU of governments that come to power through unconstitutional means.

Human rights disputes are often very politically charged. By their very nature, individual complaints are directed at the authority exercised by the state. As members of the AU, states subscribe to democratic principles and the 'rule of law'. An essential component of adherence to the 'rule of law' is the resolution of political disputes and conflicts through judicial means. By depoliticizing conflict, the African Human Rights Court may provide solutions that states may feel more comfortable abiding by. Politicized disputes may be addressed on at least three levels: at the political level, by a political body; through mediation or settlement, usually undertaken by a quasi-judicial body; or by resolution of a judicial tribunal. It is suggested that overly politicized issues often are not efficiently addressed by diplomacy, mediation or friendly settlement. Judicial and political decisions are different in nature. Courts, including international or regional courts, use juridical concepts, their criteria are standards of legality, and their methods are enquiries into legal proof. The tests of validity and the basis of decision 'are naturally not the same as they would be before a political or executive organ of the United Nations'.[310] The resolution of some of these conflicts by a court may be preferable to a resolution through pressure and coercion.[311] It has been suggested that states would sometimes submit disputes for decision by an impartial tribunal when they do not want those disputes to be resolved in more 'political' dispute resolution settings. These would be situations where a state would not want to be seen to give in to a political settlement or to make a politically costly concession. Judicial decisions require at least the articulation of a rational basis. The Court considers all the relevant evidence and must then decide the case *on the basis of the evidence*, and not on the basis of extraneous (political) factors that have not been placed before it.[312]

Ultimately, the mere fact that conflict has been reduced to a judicial decision does not guarantee that states will adhere to the Court's decisions. To a significant extent, the 'political will' of the state will be determined by domestic factors such

[309] J Hund, 'Aspects of Judicial Review in Southern Africa' (1982) 15 *CILSA* 276, 282.

[310] Judge Weeramantry in the *Lockerbie* case [1992] ICJ Rep 56, 166.

[311] RB Bilder, 'Possibilities for Development of New International Judicial Mechanisms' in L Henkin and JL Hargrove (eds), *Human Rights: An Agenda for the Next Century* (Washington, DC: The American Society of International Law, 1994) 328.   [312] Court Protocol, art 26(2).

as the system of government, by its inter-state relations, and the institutional pressure brought to bear by the AU on that state.[313] However, as the European experience suggests, part of the answer may also lie in further 'judicializing' enforcement.[314]

5 The Court, like the Commission, Depends on Support from the AU

Even if the African Commission and Court on Human and Peoples' Rights are not mentioned in the AU Constitutive Act, these institutions were set up by and function under the auspices of the AU. Support by the AU in the form of financial resources and political commitment is required to ensure the success of the Court.

The establishment of the Court comes at a time of competing claims to limited resources. To a large extent, the AU Constitutive Act is only a framework document, allowing for the adoption of detailed 'Protocols' to establish the institutional organs. Since its launch in 2002, the AU set up the Peace and Security Council, the Pan-African Parliament, and the Economic, Social and Cultural Council.

A functional treaty body develops through phases. The last and crucial phase of 'operationalization' is sometimes neglected. Devoid of personnel, paper, printers, buildings, and an infrastructure, institutional mechanisms will remain empty shells. A meagre allocation of resources undermines independence. For many years the OAU has suffered problems of inadequate financing. Despite numerous calls by the OAU/AU Assembly that the necessary resources should be allocated to the African Commission, funds for its activities and resources are still lacking.[315] Whatever modalities of co-existence are worked out, the fact remains that the Court's progress depends on a well-resourced and functional Commission. It should be recalled that, although the African Children's Committee has been launched, it has not yet been provided with a functional Secretariat. Where institutional proliferation makes financial demands, there are bound to be casualties.

It is just as important that the AU ensures a transparent and legitimate election process and engages in a thorough and critical discussion of the Court's annual report, in which the status of state compliance will be contained. As it is a judicial

---

[313] See Ch 8.A.9 above.

[314] Under Protocol 14 (n 66 above), amending art 46 of the European Convention, the competence of bringing a case ('infringement proceedings') against a state that does not comply with the European Court's judgment is added to the supervisory powers of the Committee of Ministers. The Committee may also approach the Court with a request to 'interpret' a judgment. The need to do so arises from the lack of clarity in the remedial orders of the Court, which causes 'repetitive' cases to be lodged because states do not undertake structural or general reforms.

[315] See Ch 3 above. There are some early indications that, with an allocation of US$2,373,750 for 2007, the African Human Rights Court may receive more resources from the AU (AU Doc Assembly/AU/Dec.154(VIII)). One hopes that the African Commission will not remain the lesser endowed part of the two-tier system. Especially given its extensive promotional mandate, the Commission in fact has a solid claim for a bigger budgetary allocation than the Court. See also Ch 7.C above, where some developments giving the Comission more say in its own budget are mantioned.

institution, judgments of the Court will not be subject to the objection by states (raised previously in respect of the Commission) that they be given an opportunity to provide their views before the report may be adopted. At the regional level, the AU represents a significant departure from the OAU, signalling the prospect of greater commitment in the future.

Enthusiasm for the Court should be tempered by the track record of the African Commission. The reasons for the failings of the Commission, for almost 20 years the primary human rights institution in the AU, should be analysed. It is more than likely that the same weaknesses will be visited upon the Court. Concerns raised by the 'gradualists' at the start of the drafting process that culminated in the Court Protocol are just as valid today as they were then.[316]

6 Expectations and Misunderstandings

The burden of expectation on the Court is very high, driven primarily by frustration about the weaknesses of domestic courts and the African Commission. To a great extent, the tone will be set by the first judges who serve on the Court. In order to fully exploit the 'window of expectation', it is important that the Court's effective operationalization is not unduly delayed, that the Commission starts referring cases to the Court without delay, that individuals make use of the limited direct access possibilities, and that the Court's advisory jurisdiction is explored. In addition, the on-going reform of the judicial landscape, which will see the merger of the African Human Rights Court with the Court of Justice in the not too distant future, should be communicated to the people of Africa as clearly as possible to avoid confusion and misunderstanding.

[316] See E Ankumah, *The African Commission on Human and Peoples' Rights: Practice and Procedures* (The Hague: Martinus Nijhoff, 1996) 195.

PART IV
THE SUBREGIONAL LEVEL

12

The Realization of Human Rights in Africa through Subregional Institutions

A Introduction

Institutionally, the AU ensured the continuation of pre-existing OAU political organs such as the Assembly, albeit in a new guise, and also established new ones, such as the Peace and Security Council. Economic integration and development did not share centre stage in the transformation of the OAU/AEC into the AU. In fact, the extent to and way in which the AEC was integrated into the AU are still not very clear.[1] Although the newcomer NEPAD received much publicity, for long its relationship with the AU remained ambivalent and elusive. At the same time, the AU committed itself to the accelerated socio-economic integration of Africa.[2] However, serious economic convergence requires more than political posturing and occasional high-level meetings. A period of relative growth in most of colonial Africa after the attainment of political freedom in the 1960s and 1970s was in the

---

[1] See Ch 5 below.   [2] AU Constitutive Act, art 3(c).

1980s followed by economic deprivation and negative growth. Although the new millennium brought some cause for optimism and at least some increase in growth rates and economic development,[3] Africa remains by a substantial margin the poorest continent. Economic matters should therefore receive increased focus in the process of integration, starting at the subregional level.

Political declarations, abstract neo-liberal economic theory, and Eurocentric modelling have largely driven the African integrationist project. In the process, politicians did not seek or muster popular support and often did not back up rhetoric with tangible political will, economic realities were ignored or wished away, and institutions in the image of the successful European 'other' proliferated.[4] Political and economic dictates foreclosed a discussion in which the relevance of historical, sociological, and anthropological considerations could be debated. In this chapter, the process of economic integration at the subregional level and its potential influence upon human rights are reviewed. Thus far, the social dimension of subregional integration, generally, and its human rights aspect more particularly, have received inadequate attention.[5] The underlying question remains: What is the effect of closer cooperation and integration upon the eradication of poverty in each region?

Scepticism about the political and economic unification of Africa is best countered by pointing out that, on the short to medium term, the aim is to achieve subregional integration in different parts of the continent. The magnitude of the task to achieve integrated economic growth and development in Africa should not inspire an impasse, but should rather highlight the fact that efforts must be directed at the subregional level as a logical and necessary starting point, in line with both the AU Constitutive Act and AEC Treaty. This more modest dimension of unification provides a much more likely setting for a success story. Some proponents of African integration and unity view the re-drafting of the Berlin-brokered boundaries as an important step towards a new beginning. Rather than re-imagining Berlin, though, and playing a reconfiguring numbers game, it should be accepted

---

[3] According to the Organization for Economic Co-operation and Development's *African Economic Outlook 2005/2006*, economic activity in Africa is estimated to have risen by nearly 5% in 2005, and is estimated at 5.8% and 5.5% in 2006 and 2007, respectively. Oil-exporting countries, however, are outpacing others by a substantial margin.

[4] See eg C Jackson, 'Constitutional Structure and Governance Strategies for Economic Integration in Africa and Europe' (2003) 13 *Transnational L and Contemporary Problems* 139, 176 (observing that the AEC and AU Treaties strike 'several cords of similarity with the Treaty of Rome in terms of structure and aspirations'). The AU web-site <http://www.au2002.gov.za/docs/background/oau_to_au.htm> (31 July 2006) underlines the tension between the home-grown and the 'foreign': 'During the Lusaka Summit several references were made to the African Union being loosely based on the European Union model, in which respect it was said that Africa "should not re-invent the wheel". However, it was agreed that the African Union should be something new, with the emphasis on being an African experience'.

[5] See F Viljoen, 'The Realization of Human Rights in Africa through Sub-regional Institutions' (2001) 7 *AYBIL* 186; SF Musungu, 'Economic Integration and Human Rights in Africa: A Comment on Conceptual Linkages' (2003) 3 *AHRLJ* 88 and EK Quashigah, 'Human Rights and Integration' in R Lavergne (ed), *Regional Integration and Cooperation in West Africa: A Multidimensional Perspective* (Trenton: African World Press, 1997) 259.

that a few dominant regional economic communities (RECs) will eventually be the constitutive elements of a new pan-African statehood. More than mere building blocks, they should in the short term form the focus and the end point of the evolution of what is feasible and possible, leaving unity on a pan-African scale as a much more remote prospect.

For now, the emphasis should be on solidifying subregional convergence, not on pursuing prematurely grandiose continental utopias.[6] Close trade and other economic links, more likely to be developed at the subregional level, may serve as a guarantee of respect for commonly agreed standards, including human rights. The threat of exclusion from membership only becomes real if tangible consequences are likely to follow non-membership. The scale of the subregional is smaller than that of the continental level: It has greater geographic proximity, allowing for strategic closeness. It also has greater potential for trade links, increasing the immediacy of mutual incentives, presenting closer linguistic and cultural ties, and holding the promise of greater effectiveness in implementation and enforcement, for example through trade boycotts or other sanctions.[7] As members of a subregion often share a common legal tradition, such as the 'civil law' tradition of Central African states, the harmonization of laws will be easier. By contrast, integration on an Africa-wide scale is extremely ambitious, considering that the most expansive continental arrangement in existence, the European Union (EU), serves a population of approximately 460 million in 25 countries.[8] This contrasts dramatically with the more than 916 million people and 53 states on the African continent.[9]

Africa's model should be Latin America, where the subregional aspect enjoys pride of place. The modest Latin American Integration Association (ALADI) was set up in 1980 to coordinate the 'gradual and progressive establishment of a Latin American common market'.[10] Four smaller subregional groupings exist, and membership does not overlap. Already in the early 1960s, the General Treaty on Central American Integration (CACM) brought together Costa Rica, El Salvador, Guatemala, Honduras, and Nicaragua. The Treaty Establishing the Caribbean Community and Common Market (CARICOM) was adopted in 1973, and today comprises all 15 Caribbean states. The most powerful of the four is the Common Market of the Southern Cone (MERCOSUR), established in 1991 between Argentina, Brazil, Paraguay, and Uruguay. The Andean countries (Bolivia, Colombia, Ecuador, Peru, and Venezuela) have already in 1969 adopted the Cartagena Agreement, and are in

---

[6] A 'bottom-up', rather than a 'top-down' approach to integration should be followed. Attempts to superimpose continent-wide integration in the absence of a subregional basis are likely to falter, as the lethargy in implementing the AU Executive Council's decision of free movement of persons illustrates (AU Doc EX.CL/Dec.337(X)).

[7] Fifteen ECOWAS members, for example, imposed an economic blockade against Koroma in 1997, after he had taken power in Sierra Leone, also an ECOWAS member (RE Mshomba, *Africa in the Global Economy* (Boulder, Colo: Lynne Reinner Publishers, 2000) 191).

[8] Jackson (n 4 above) 176: 'The fact that Africa, with its practical limitations, is attempting what Europe really only almost did in a comparable period of time is a matter of concern'.

[9] <http://www.internetworldstats.com/africa.htm> (31 July 2006) (estimate for 2006).

[10] 1980 Montevideo Treaty establishing the ALADI, art 1.

the process of establishing the Andean Community. In Latin America, political agendas are distinctly separate from economic pursuits, and take place under the auspices of the Organization of American States (OAS).

Similarly, the Association of Southeast Asian Nations (ASEAN) has a very limited membership.[11] Formed in 1967 as a bulwark against the perceived threat of Communism from Vietnam and subregional Communist expansionism, ASEAN initially comprised Indonesia, Malaysia, the Philippines, Thailand, and Singapore, Brunei Darussalam join in 1984. In the changed political context of the post-Cold War 1990s, Vietnam, Laos, Myanmar, and Cambodia joined. Having ensured political stability and eliminated conflict between members, ASEAN was able to embark on an economic agenda. So far, it has accomplished a free trade area.

Efforts to forge unity and commonality in an important area, that of law, have for some time manifested themselves especially in Southern Africa.[12] Even before the establishment of SADC, a subregional jurisprudence started developing among the states of this subregion. This case-law already provides a starting point for a common subregional human rights jurisprudence. The process has been facilitated by the common issues faced by these states, by a common historical[13] and legal background,[14] the fact that all countries have not only Bills of Rights, but also similar provisions, by an exchange of judicial officers,[15] by geographic proximity and linguistic homogeneity,[16] and by the existence of a common law report series.[17] In later years, this trend has been reinforced by the fact that the judiciary faces

---

[11] <http://www.aseansec.org> (31 July 2006).

[12] On West African legal diversity and the emergence of a harmonized ECOWAS common law beyond commercial law, see A Bajulo, 'Sources of the Law of the Economic Community of West African States (ECOWAS)' (2001) 45 *JAL* 73, 96.

[13] Like all of Africa, these countries have suffered under colonialism. In Southern Africa, however, colonialism took a singular form as initial trading contacts were followed by substantive settling of Dutch, English, Portuguese, and Germans communities. The presence of the non-indigenous groups in Southern Africa lasted longer than in most of Africa. Colonialism lasted longest in this region, and led to the severest national liberation campaigns, including armed struggles. Angola and Mozambique gained independence in 1975. Zimbabwe became independent only in 1980; Namibia even later, in 1990. A democratic government was installed in South Africa in 1994.

[14] See the quote from *S v Williams* (1995) 3 SA 632 (CC) para 31: 'The decisions of the Supreme Courts of Namibia and of Zimbabwe are of special significance. Not only are these countries geographic neighbours, but South Africa shares with them the same English colonial experience which has had a deep influence on our law; we of course also share the Roman-Dutch legal tradition'.

[15] The regional exchange of judicial officers is exemplified in the person of late judge Mahomed, who was Chief Justice of Namibia and judge (and later Deputy President) of the South African Constitutional Court, before becoming that country's Chief Justice. Another example is the previous Chief Justice of Zimbabwe, Dumbutshena, who acted as judge in the Namibian Supreme Court. Also, since the latter part of 1994, judge Mtambanengwe has been seconded from the Zimbabwean to the Namibian High Court (see eg his judgment in *Kauesa v Minister of Home Affairs* (1996) 4 SA 965 (NmS)). In other instances, judicial exchanges underscore the regional hegemony of South Africa, as in respect of South African judges sitting on the highest courts of Botswana, Lesotho, and Swaziland.

[16] All these countries, except Angola and Mozambique, have English as an official language. After its admission to the Commonwealth, English has gained ground in Mozambique.

[17] For example, the South African Law Reports series includes cases from Namibia and Zimbabwe; the South African Constitutional Law Reports series includes cases from Namibia, Swaziland, and Zimbabwe. In one of the latest issues of the Butterworths Constitutional Law Reports (BCLR) series

similar issues in these countries, such as the constitutionality of corporal punishment,[18] and of the death penalty,[19] the prohibition on alien husbands residing in the country of their wives' citizenship,[20] matters related to criminal procedure such as 'reverse onus' provisions,[21] and balancing vested property rights with programmes of land reform and redistribution.[22]

This chapter investigates the extent to which these subregional arrangements have been—and in future may be—vehicles for the improvement of human rights on the African continent. Many of these arrangements provide for an institution in the form of a court or tribunal to resolve conflicts arising from the application and interpretation of the founding treaty. These judicial institutions are the central focus and introduce more general observations on courts in a supra-national, but subregional setting.

B Background to Regional Economic Integration in Africa

1 Phases of Integration

It is accepted that regional integration usually evolves through five phases:[23]

(1) Fledgling integration takes the form of a *preferential trading arrangement* (or preferential trade area), where lower tariffs on imports apply to members compared

(1997(8)), cases from Lesotho have also been included. Previously, cases from eg Namibia, Zimbabwe, and Botswana have also been included in the BCLR series.

[18] See eg the references to the Namibian case *Ex parte A-G, Namibia: In re Corporal Punishment* (1991) 3 SA 76 (NmS) and the Zimbabwean cases *S v Ncube* (1988) 2 SA 702 (ZS) and *S v A Juvenile* (1990) 4 SA 151 (ZS) by Langa J in the South African case *S v Williams* (1995) 3 SA 632 (CC) (in particular at para 31).

[19] See the reference to *Mbushuu v The Republic* (Tanzania Court of Appeal, Criminal Appeal 142 of 1994, 30 January 1995) in *S v Makwanyane* (1995) 3 SA 391 (CC) at paras 114–15.

[20] See *Dow v A-G* [1992] LRC (Const) 623 (Botswana CA) followed in *Rattigan v Chief Immigration Officer, Zimbabwe* (1995) 2 SA 182 (ZS). See also *Salem v Immigration Officer* [1994] 1 LRC (Const) 355; (1995) 4 SA 280; (1995) 1 BCLR 78 (ZS). An earlier case dealing with this issue is the UN Human Rights Committee decision in *Aumeeruddy-Cziffra v Mauritius* (1981) 62 ILR 255. The question arises whether this island state is or may become part of a Southern African human rights vanguard. In terms of its human rights record, it may fit, but cultural differences may inhibit such a development. Mauritius has a mixed or hybrid system.

[21] See eg the Malawian case *Jumbe and Another v Attorney-General*, Constitutional case 1 and 2 of 2005, High Court of Malawi, judgment of 21 October 2005 (on file with author), in which both the majority and the minority placed heavy reliance on the decisions of the South African Constitutional Court.

[22] See the thoughtful discussion by T Roux, 'Constitutional Property Rights in Southern Africa: The Record of the Zimbabwe Supreme Court' (1996) 8 *RADIC* 755, in which reference is made to cases on this issue in the following SADC member states: Botswana, Namibia, South Africa, Tanzania, Zambia, Zimbabwe (see especially n 44 at 762). The author could also have included case-law from Mauritius. See also *Leite v The Government of Seychelles*, Constitutional case 9 of 2001, Constitutional Court of Seychelles, judgment of 11 June 2002 (constitutionality of intended acquisition of property, on file with author).

[23] The discussion follows B Balassa, *The Theory of Economic Integration* (Homewood, Ill: Richard D Irvine, 1961).

to non-members. Going one step further, a free trade area establishes an arrangement in which all tariffs on imports from members are abolished, thus making possible free trade between the members. This may be done for all or for certain specified products. In both these types of arrangements, members may set their own tariffs and barriers for exports from non-members. This opens the door to 'trans-shipment', allowing a non-member state to export to a member with low tariffs, only to re-export from there to another member of the arrangement that has a higher external tariff structure. These arrangements therefore usually have a 'rules of origin' provision, stipulating that goods must be imported directly from the producing country.

(2) In a *customs union*, members adopt a common commercial policy with respect to non-members. The most important measure is the imposition of tariffs on imports from all non-members (a 'common external tariff').

(3) Taking the customs union one step further, a *common market* in addition provides for the free movement of goods and services and the factors of production (capital and labour) across the borders of its members.

(4) A common market becomes an *economic union* when its members further harmonize economic policies, for example by agreeing on a common monetary and fiscal policy. When a common currency is instituted, a monetary union is achieved. When a single, 'unified' economy is achieved, total economic integration is attained.

(5) As total economic integration necessitates political integration,[24] the pinnacle of regional integration finds its form in a *political union*. In this arrangement, states cede their sovereignty over economic and social policies to a supra-national, rather than an intergovernmental, authority. Common legislative and judicial institutions are established.

2 Rationale for Integration

Integration should not be pursued for integration's sake. Although these aims relate to both subregional and broader (continental) integration, the former is highlighted below.[25]

Importantly, regional cooperation aims at undoing the balkanization of Africa that not only separated members of one ethnic group from one another, but also severed resources in one country from human capital in another. At the subregional level, greater cohesiveness and a shared historical tradition should be exploited to undo the damage done by colonialism in particular. In a subregional arrangement, states may work together, allowing resources such as water, oil, or agricultural products of one country to be shared by others, and allowing for the distribution

[24] SKB Asante, *Regionalism and Africa's Development: Expectations, Reality and Challenges* (New York: St Martin's Press, 1997) 26.
[25] See Economic Commission for Africa (ECA), *Assessing Regional Integration in Africa* (Addis Ababa: ECA, 2004) (2004 ECA Study) 10–24 for a discussion of these rationales.

of benefits derived from academic institutions or production capacity located in one country.

Due to their small population size and low incomes, many African states have small domestic markets. This presents an impediment to their global competitiveness. As part of a regional economic arrangement, these countries become part of an economy of scale, in the process strengthening their competitiveness and making them more attractive to foreign investment. These markets are more feasible between countries in immediate proximity to each other.

Being part of a regional arrangement may also enhance the international economic bargaining power and visibility of smaller states, enabling them to strike better bargains with developed countries. This power may be greater if more states form a common bulwark. However, given the difficulties of a common position among the 53 states, it has to start on a smaller scale.

Most African countries launched economic (and political) reforms in the 1990s. However, in many instances the initial economic and political reforms have not been developed, often due to a lack of capacity or expertise. In a regional arrangement, there are likely to be both the institutional capacity and political incentives required to entrench reforms more effectively. Existing links between states and relative homogeneity at the subregional level provide the best chance of attaining this objective.

3 Obstacles to Integration

There is always a danger that the weaker and more fragile a state, the more tenaciously it may cling to its political and economic sovereignty. Conversely, it is often assumed that strong and consolidated states are more likely to relinquish part of their political sovereignty to intergovernmental or supra-national institutions. Inherent dysfunctionality may inform much of the lack of political will on the part of states. Misplaced 'economic nationalism' may also present an obstacle. The progress made in ECOWAS, in a region where weak mini-states proliferated, to some extent contradicts these assumptions.

One of the main obstacles to meaningful integration has been the lack of political will to implement and give effect to treaty provisions and ideals at the national level.[26] A by-product of authoritarian rule in Africa has been a lack of public participation in decision-making and a lack of transparency and accountability in governance. In such an atmosphere, leaders often committed states to elaborate arrangements that were never implemented. Such a lack of political will still persists in Africa, giving rise to concerns that there is insufficient 'political will to convert words into action'.[27] Concrete action may also be absent due to the lack of know-how and technical expertise, often embedded in the weakness of state structures

---

[26] Mshomba (n 7 above) 194–5.   [27] 2004 ECA Study (n 25 above) 33.

and the absence of an enabling legal environment. Appropriate legal rules are often non-existent at the national level, not to mention a framework regulating trans-border transactions and trade. The regional effort to rationalize business law in Francophone Africa, the Organization for the Harmonization of Corporate Law in Africa (*Organisation pour l'Harmonisation en Afrique du Droit des Affaires* (OHADA)), provides a notable exception. Many African countries also lack an effective and functional economic and financial infrastructure on which regional efforts may be built. Financial systems are often underdeveloped and administrative difficulties abound.

The reluctance of states (and leaders) to take regionalism seriously may derive from a fear that the benefits of integration may be distributed unevenly. Huge discrepancies in the economies of potential partners, especially different levels of development in the manufacturing sector, put paid to the apprehension that those states with a more developed production capacity sector (such as South Africa, Ghana, Nigeria, and Cameroon) stand to benefit more. These apprehensions are well-founded: In each of the main RECs, the economies of one or two states make up the bulk of intra-regional exports.[28] In order to equalize benefits, it is possible that more developed countries could assist lesser developed countries in the region, indirectly, by making bigger contributions to REC institutional development and support. These efforts may still be doomed to failure if corruption or inefficiencies are prevalent in member states, as is often the case in Africa.[29]

One of Africa's colonial legacies is its dependence on industrialized states as trade partners. Intra-African trade is limited, as states in the past opted to export raw materials to and import manufactured products from former colonial powers. The increasing presence of China may see the skewed trade relations change direction from the European Union to the East, but will make little difference to the dearth of meaningful and sustained trade between African states.

Socio-political and cultural factors may also pose obstacles to economic integration. Internal political instability and border conflicts paralyse integration efforts and cause resources and attention to be diverted to peace-keeping and conflict resolution. Linguistic, cultural and ideological heterogeneity may drive the ideal of integration, but they are also potential drawbacks.

At the subregional level, the main obstacles are overlapping institutional membership, the lack of a sound resource base to enable the effective functioning of the REC, and a tendency towards grandiose plans and programmes that defy realistic implementation.[30]

---

[28] In SADC, South Africa and Zimbabwe; in ECOWAS, Côte d'Ivoire and Nigeria; in ECCAS, Cameroon; in COMESA, Kenya and Zimbabwe; and in EAC, Kenya (see Mshomba (n 7 above) 187, 189, 191, 183).   [29] See eg Mshomba (n 7 above) 199.

[30] W Kennes, 'African Regional Economic Integration and the European Union' in DC Bach (ed), *Regionalism in Africa: Integration and Disintegration* (Oxford: James Currey, 1999) 27, 30.

C Africa's Main Regional Economic Communities (RECs)

Africa currently has at least 14 subregional integration groupings, with two or more in each subregion. The increasing acceptance of neo-liberal economic policies and the force of 'globalization' converted Africa to the benefits of closer integrated markets. Although membership of RECs defies neat categorization into subregional compartments, it mostly centres around a particular subregion. Four subregions will be discussed: (i) North, (ii) Eastern and Southern, (iii) West, and (iv) Central Africa. As part of a process to harmonize RECs, the AU Assembly has officially recognized eight:[31] ECOWAS, COMESA, ECCAS, SADC, IGAD, UMA, CEN-SAD, and the EAC. In the discussion that follows, an overall picture is provided, after which the focus falls on the potential to advance human rights through these eight institutions.

As the institutional structures of these arrangements are broadly similar, they are not discussed for each REC. Usually, the supreme institution is an Assembly or Council of Heads of State and Government which has policy-making authority. Tasked with informing the policy agenda and sessions of the main body, a Council of Foreign Affairs or Trade Ministers prepares its sessions, meeting more frequently and increasingly engaging in policy implementation. There may also be follow-up committees or other inter-sectoral ministerial meetings to implement resolutions and decisions. Much of the success depends on an effective secretariat, which also exists in each of the RECs.

1 North Africa

Until the Community of Sahel-Saharan States (CEN-SAD) emerged, North Africa hosted only the Arab Maghreb Union (UMA). However, CEN-SAD and a third REC functioning in this subregion, the Euro-Mediterranean Free Trade Area (EU-MEFTA), straddle other economic communities and subregions.

1.1 *Arab Maghreb Union (UMA)*

The Treaty of Marrakesh, establishing the Arab Maghreb Union (*Union du Maghreb Arabe* in French, hence UMA), was concluded in 1989 between Algeria, Libya, Mauritania, Morocco, and Tunisia.[32] The main aims of the Union are to create viable regional economic integration, to form a North African Common Market, and to develop trade and other links with the European Union. After some initial progress and activity, its activities have slowed down considerably since 1995. A free trade area has not yet been achieved. The UMA is one of two African regional blocs

---

[31] AU Doc Assembly/AU/Dec.112(VII) (July 2006).
[32] <http://www.maghrebarabe.org> (31 July 2006). See, in general, on the Maghreb Arab Union, A El Kadiri, 'L'Union du Maghreb Arabe' (1994) 2 *AYBIL* 141.

that comprises a non-AU member (Morocco). Although the Saharawi Arab Democratic Republic (SADR) is not a member, it has been a source of debilitating dispute, especially between Algeria and Morocco, stunting subregional progress.

1.2 Community of Sahel-Saharan States (CEN-SAD)

More recently, in 1998, following the Conference of Leaders and Heads of States held in Tripoli, another REC, the Community of Sahel-Saharan States (CEN-SAD), was established in the Sahel and Sahara region, spanning North, West, and Central Africa.[33] This REC is aimed at addressing common problems, the integration of various sectors, a free trade area, and strengthening peace, security, and stability in the region. Numerous ministerial sectoral meetings have taken place. At the beginning of 2007, its current membership stood at 23: Benin, Burkina Faso, Central African Republic, Chad, Côte d'Ivoire, Djibouti, Egypt, Eritrea, The Gambia, Ghana, Guinea-Bissau, Liberia, Libya, Mali, Morocco, Niger, Nigeria, Senegal, Sierra Leone, Somalia, Sudan, Togo, and Tunisia.

1.3 Euro-Mediterranean Free Trade Area (EU-MEFTA)

Three North African states (Egypt, Morocco, and Tunisia) also participate in the Euro-Mediterranean Free Trade Area (EU-MEFTA). This area comprises states around the Mediterranean and aims to create a free trade area in the Middle East by 2010.[34] The 2004 Agadir Agreement established a free trade agreement between Jordania, Tunisia, Egypt, and Morocco as a first building block in the EU-MEFTA. Once a free trade agreement is in place, a single free trade area is to be formed, which will include the European Union.

2 Eastern and Southern Africa

Eastern and Southern Africa share six regional economic communities: the Southern African Customs Union (SACU), the East African Community (EAC), the Inter-Governmental Authority on Development (IGAD), the Common Market for Eastern and Southern Africa (COMESA), the Southern African Development Community (SADC), and the Indian Ocean Commission (IOC).

2.1 Southern African Customs Union (SACU)

The Customs Union Agreement, signed in 1969, entering into force in 1970 and amended in 2002, established the Southern African Customs Union (SACU) between South Africa, Botswana, Lesotho, Namibia, and Swaziland—five states with close economic ties and sharing a common colonial history.[35] SACU replaced the Customs Union Agreement of 1910. It aims at maintaining the free interchange

[33] <http://www.cen-sad.org> (31 July 2006).
[34] <http://ec.europa.eu/comm/external.relations/euromed/free_trade_area.htm> (31 July 2006).
[35] <http://www.dfa.gov.za/foreign/Multilateral/africa/sacu.htm> (31 July 2006).

of goods between members. SACU members have agreed on a common external tariff and a common excise tariff. Customs and excise collected in the common customs area are paid into South Africa's national Revenue Fund, which is then shared among members according to a revenue-sharing formula as described in the SACU Agreement.

2.2 East African Community (EAC)

The East African Community (EAC) is the most recently established, and with only three members, the smallest REC in Africa. The Treaty establishing the EAC was adopted in 1999 and entered into force in 2000. Its membership comprises Kenya, Tanzania, and Uganda.[36] After a verification mission had been sent to Burundi and Rwanda, and acknowledging the level of political stability achieved, the EAC decided to expand its membership to five. At the beginning of 2007 accession by Burundi and Rwanda was pending.

This union is a revival of a similar arrangement that became defunct in 1977. Its earlier roots may be traced to strides taken by the British colonial administration towards subregional unity in East Africa, which included an East African Court of Appeal.[37] In 1967, soon after Kenya, Tanzania, and Uganda had gained independence, the East African Community (EAC) was established.[38] The Treaty of East African Cooperation provided for cooperation in various fields. The Court of Appeal of East Africa was retained in its previous form as one of the institutions of the Community. The Community, and with it the Court, were abolished in 1977.[39]

The reasons for the Community's demise are varied. Businessmen in Kenya pressurized the government to withdraw, because the Court's appellate jurisdiction had affected their financial and commercial interests, even though Kenya benefited from an inequitable distribution of benefits.[40] Differences in economic policies and political approaches also constituted important reasons for failure. In Tanzania, and to a lesser extent in Uganda, a socialist state and state-controlled economic structure were being developed. This was in clear conflict with the broadly capitalist economic approach of Kenya. Tanzania became reluctant to submit all

---

[36] The official web-site is <http://www.eac.int> (31 July 2006); see also R Ajulu (ed), *The Making of a Region: The Revival of the East African Community* (Midrand: Institute for Global Dialogue, 2005).

[37] SEA Mvungi, *Constitutional Questions in the Regional Integration Process: The Case of the Southern African Development Community with References to the European Union*, D Iur Thesis (Hamburg: Institut für Internationale Angelegenheiten, 1994), points out that trade networks, political dynamism, and social mingling had over centuries succeeded in establishing a common cultural identity and a 'non-tribal common language', known as Kiswahili (108).

[38] By the Treaty of East African Cooperation signed at Kampala, and which entered into force in December 1967. It took over the assets and liabilities of the East African Common Services Organization (EACSO), which was established in 1962. EACSO was established to take over from the British East Africa High Commission (see TO Elias, *Africa and the Development of International Law* (Dordrecht: Martinus Nijhoff, 2nd edn, 1988) 26).

[39] On its demise, see Mvungi (n 37 above) 118.

[40] See AEC Secretariat, 'Important Aspects of the Treaty for the Establishment of the East African Community' (2002).

civil matters to the jurisdiction of a Court dominated by lawyers with a liberal-capitalist world-view. In Uganda, Idi Amin took power by military means in 1971, causing a breakdown of civil and state institutions, and leading to animosity between Amin and Tanzanian President Nyerere.[41] Amin's gross human rights violations presented the Tanzanian President with an ideal opportunity to disband the East Africa Community. In any event, when Tanzanian forces invaded Uganda, little prospect remained of political and judicial unity, causing the collapse of the EAC in 1977.[42]

Still, at least on paper, the prospects for cooperation in East Africa looked promising. Factors uniting the three states are geographic proximity, institutional links,[43] a shared colonial history, broad knowledge of one language, Swahili, and ethnic ties across borders, for example the presence of Luos in all three states. It comes as no surprise, then, that the same three states re-launched the EAC in 1999. So far, the EAC has been able to make significant progress regarding a free trade area. A common market is envisaged for 2010.[44]

2.3 Intergovernmental Authority on Development (IGAD)

Kenya and Uganda are also members of another REC in East Africa, the Intergovernmental Authority on Development (IGAD).[45] IGAD's membership further includes Djibouti, Eritrea, Ethiopia, Somalia, and Sudan. Initially called the Intergovernmental Authority on Drought and Development (IGADD), it was at first directed towards issues concerning the environment and drought in the region but later extended its scope to include issues such as conflict management and prevention, and health. IGAD's headquarters are in Djibouti. However, progress has been hampered by intra-state and inter-state conflict in the Horn of Africa.

2.4 Common Market for Eastern and Southern Africa (COMESA)

Both Kenya and Uganda, as well as all the other IGAD members (with the exception of Somalia), are also members of the regional body in Africa with the broadest scope—the Common Market for Eastern and Southern Africa (COMESA). Its membership extends as far north as Egypt and as far south as Swaziland; and from Angola in the west to the Comoros in the east. COMESA was established in 1993,[46] with the aim of enhancing economic development in the region.[47] COMESA was established to replace the Preferential Trade Area of Eastern and Southern African

41 See Republic of Uganda, 'The Report of the Commission of Inquiry into Violations of Human Rights' (1994) 24.

42 See United Republic of Tanzania, 'Tanzania and the War against Amin's Uganda' (1979) 2.

43 For a recent manifestation of these links, see 'The Establishment of the Lake Victoria Fisheries Organisation between Kenya, Tanzania and Uganda' (1997) 36 ILM 667.

44 Communiqué, Seventh Summit of Heads of State of the EAC, 5 April 2006.

45 See <http://www.igad.org> (31 July 2006).

46 See (1994) 33 ILM 1067; <http://www.comesa.int> (31 July 2006).

47 COMESA Treaty, art 3.

States (PTA) of 1981.[48] The scope of COMESA is much broader than that of the PTA, though. Despite its name, COMESA is not (yet) a 'common market'.[49]

2.5 Southern African Development Community (SADC)

In 1993, the Treaty of the Southern African Development Community (SADC) transformed the pre-existing Southern African Development Coordination Conference (SADCC) into a new institution.[50] SADCC was founded in 1980, mainly as a bulwark against the then minority South African government's stated policy of establishing a 'constellation' of Southern African states. Aimed at regional peace and security, at cooperation in a number of sectors, and at integrating regional economies, SADC's ideals are much more ambitious than those of SADCC. Adopted in August 2001, and entering into force upon signature of all the member states, the Agreement Amending the Treaty of SADC brought about some important substantive and institutional changes to the SADC Treaty. Its current membership stands at 14 (Angola, Botswana, the Democratic Republic of Congo, Lesotho, Madagascar, Malawi, Mauritius, Mozambique, Namibia, South Africa, Swaziland, Tanzania, Zambia, and Zimbabwe)[51] and its headquarters are in Gaborone, Botswana.

2.6 Indian Ocean Commission (COI)

The Indian Ocean Commission, known as the *Commission de l'Océan Indien* in French (hence, COI) is an intergovernmental organization that joins the four AU island member states located in the Indian Ocean (Comoros, Madagascar, Mauritius, and Seychelles) with two French-dependent islands in the region (Mayotte and Réunion). The COI, which was launched in January 1984, aims to encourage cooperation among its six members.[52]

3 West Africa

In West Africa, the West African Economic and Monetary Union (UEMOA), the Mano River Union (MRU), the Liptako-Gourma Authority, and the West African

---

[48] The PTA wound itself up on 5 November 1993 and established COMESA in its place. The PTA comprised 23 countries in East and Southern Africa ((1994) New African Market Bulletin 23).

[49] Mshomba (n 7 above) 183.

[50] The SADC Treaty appears at (1993) 32 ILM 116 and (1993) 5 *RADIC* 418. On SADC generally, see its web-site <http://www.sadc.int> (31 July 2006); JP Barosso, 'Profile of the Southern African Development Community' in C Heyns (ed), *Human Rights Law in Africa* (vol 1) (Leiden: Martinus Nijhoff, 2004) 675 and GH Oosthuizen, *The Southern African Development Community: The Organisation, its Policies and Prospects* (Johannesburg: Institute for Global Dialogue, 2006).

[51] In September 1997, the Summit of Heads of State and Government approved the applications for membership of the Democratic Republic of Congo (the former Zaire) and the Seychelles. Due to the high cost of membership, compared to the limited benefits derived from membership, the Seychelles withdrew from SADC in 2003.

[52] <http://www.governpub.com/CIA-Abbreviations-H-I/Indian_Ocean_Commission.php> (31 July 2006).

Monetary Zone co-exist with the Economic Community of West African States (ECOWAS). Contrary to expectations, the highest degree of regional integration was accomplished here, in the subregion with the weakest and poorest states. West Africa is home to some of the world's poorest countries (such as Burkina Faso, The Gambia, Guinea-Bissau, and Mali), some of the smallest populations, markets, and geographic territory (for instance, The Gambia and Togo). The lowest-ranked five states on the UNDP Development Index are located in this region.[53] As Asante observes, if boundaries in Africa are in general 'artificial and arbitrary', then they are 'absurd and capricious' in West Africa.[54]

3.1 Economic Community of West African States (ECOWAS)

The Economic Community of West African States (ECOWAS) was formed in 1975.[55] Its aim is to promote economic development in Western Africa by establishing a common market, harmonizing economic policies, including agriculture, industrial development, and monetary policies. In 1993 the original Treaty was amended.[56] By early 2007, 16 states in West Africa, comprising anglophone, francophone and lusophone countries, had become members. They are Benin, Burkina Faso, Cape Verde, Côte d'Ivoire, The Gambia, Ghana, Guinea, Guinea-Bissau, Liberia, Mali, Mauritania, Niger, Nigeria, Senegal, Sierra Leone, and Togo.

3.2 West African Economic and Monetary Union (UEMOA)[57]

Established in 1994 among former French colonies, and sharing the use of the CFA currency, the West African Economic and Monetary Union (UEMOA) is also aimed at enhancing economic cooperation between the members to their advantage. The current members, all non-anglophone members of ECOWAS, are Benin, Burkina Faso, Côte d'Ivoire, Mali, Niger, Senegal, Togo, and Guinea-Bissau.[58]

3.3 Manu River Union

The Manu River Union was set up in 1973, with the aim of facilitating integration in multiple sectors between three neighbouring states situated around the Manu River: Guinea, Sierra Leone and Liberia.[59] Due to conflicts involving these

---

[53] Guinea-Bissau, Burkina Faso, Mali, Sierra Leone, and Niger take up positions 173 to 177 of states included in the survey (<http://www.undp.org/hdr2006> (31 January 2007)).

[54] SKB Asante, *The Political Economy of Regionalism in Africa: A Decade of the Economic Community of West African States (ECOWAS)* (New York: Praeger, 1986) 37.

[55] <http://www.ewcowas.int> (31 July 2006). Treaty reproduced in (1975) 14 ILM 1200, entered into by Côte d'Ivoire, Dahomey, The Gambia, Ghana, Guinea, Guinea-Bissau, Liberia, Mali, Mauritania, Niger, Nigeria, Senegal, Sierra Leone, Togo, and Upper Volta. See generally CA Odinkalu, 'Profile of the Economic Community of West African States' in Heyns (n 50 above) 644.

[56] See (1996) 35 ILM 660. The revised Treaty was agreed at Cotonou, Benin, 24 July 1993 (see (1996) 8 *RADIC* 187).

[57] The abbreviation follows the French, *L'Union économique et monétaire de l'Afrique de l'ouest.*

[58] <http://www.uemoa.int> (31 July 2006).

[59] See generally <http://www.uemoa.int> (31 July 2006).

countries, the objectives of the Union could not be achieved. However, in 2004, the Union was reactivated at a summit of the three leaders of the Manu River Union States.

3.4 Liptako-Gourma Authority

The Liptako-Gourma Authority is a regional organization to develop the contiguous areas of Mali, Burkina Faso, and Niger. Created in 1970, the Authority has as its goal the promotion of the area's mineral, energy, hydraulic, and agricultural resources within a regional framework. This zone is composed entirely of the semi-arid Sahel region. The dominant economic activity of the region is agriculture and livestock herding, but the zone has considerable energy, hydraulic, and mining potential.[60]

3.5 West African Monetary Zone (WAMZ)

The West African Monetary Zone is a group of five countries in ECOWAS that plan to introduce a common currency, the Eco, by the year 2009. The five member states are The Gambia, Ghana, Guinea, Nigeria, and Sierra Leone. Liberia (also a member of ECOWAS), has expressed an interest in joining.[61]

4 Central Africa

With a membership of eight, the Economic Community of Central African States (ECCAS) forms the main grouping in this region. Its members also belong to two sub-groups, the Central African Economic and Monetary Community (CEMAC) and the Economic Community of Great Lakes Countries (CEPGL).

4.1 Economic Community of Central African States (ECCAS)

Eight states in Central Africa and around the Great Lakes founded the Economic Community of Central African States (ECCAS),[62] which was formed in 1983 to establish and enhance economic cooperation and to accomplish full economic union between them. Its present member states are Angola, Burundi, Cameroon, CAR, Chad, Congo, Equatorial Guinea, Rwanda, Gabon, and São Tomé e Príncipe. Persistent civil strife and conflict (especially Angolan and Rwandan involvement in the DRC) presented a serious impediment to regional integration. Other priorities fade fast if internal security is threatened. Political conflict in several member countries hampered progress between 1992 and 1997, but after its re-launch in 1998, advances have been made towards a trade

---

[60] <http://en.wikipedia.org/wiki/Liptako-Gourma_Authority> (31 July 2006).

[61] <http://en.wikipedia.org/wiki/West_African_Monetary_Zone> (31 July 2006).

[62] See <http://www.ceeac-eccas.org> (31 July 2006). 'CEEAC' refers to the name of the organization in French (*Communauté Economique des Etats de l'Afrique Centrale*).

tariff reduction programme. ECCAS is aimed at realizing a Central African common market.

4.2 Economic Community of Great Lakes Countries (CEPGL)

The Economic Community of Great Lakes Countries (CEPGL), founded in 1976, is the oldest regional arrangement in the region.[63] It is aimed at forming a full economic union between the states located around Lake Victoria: Burundi, the DRC, and Rwanda. Although preferential trade arrangements have been signed, integration came to a standstill in 1994 due to political conflict arising from the Rwandan genocide. The extent of conflict between these states has been evidenced in a case before the International Court of Justice, as well as one individual and one inter-state communication submitted to the African Commission.[64]

4.3 Central African Economic and Monetary Community (CEMAC)

The roots of the third REC in Central Africa, the Central African Economic and Monetary Community (CEMAC), lie in a customs union formed in 1964 between states that had gained their independence from France.[65] CEMAC is a monetary union, with the CFA franc as common currency. CEMAC also aims at full economic union. Its current members are Cameroon, CAR, Chad, Congo, Equatorial Guinea, and Gabon.

D Human Rights in RECs

1 Realizing Human Rights has become Integral to the Goals of RECs

From the point of view of nationals, ceding sovereignty to intergovernmental arrangements has value only if it results in an improvement in their material well-being and if the subregional space allows human rights to prosper in ways that were impossible in the nation state. As indicated above, RECs have not been set up primarily to foster human rights, but to facilitate a process of economic convergence through closer economic and financial cooperation and harmonization of policies and programmes. However, even if the RECs are in the first place aimed at increased trade and improved economic links, and not at good governance and

---

[63] See generally <http://en.wikipedia.org/wiki/Economic_Community_of_the_Great_Lakes_Countries> (31 July 2006). 'CEPGL' refers to the name of the organization in French (*Communauté Economique des Pays des Grands Lacs*).

[64] *Case Concerning Armed Activities on the Territory of the Congo* (*Democratic Republic of Congo v Rwanda*), judgment of 3 February 2006, see <http://icj-cij.org/icjwww/idocket/icrw/icrwframe.htm> (31 July 2006); *Association pour la Sauvegarde de la Paix (ASP-Burundi) v Kenya and Others* (Communication 157/96, Seventeenth Activity Report (2003) ACHPR 111 (ACHPR 2003)) and Communication 227/1999, *DRC v Burundi, Rwanda and Uganda* (*Great Lakes* case) (20th Activity Report). [65] See generally <http://www.cemac.net/> (31 July 2006).

sustaining or improving human rights within states or across state borders, there is an obvious link between one of the main objectives of regional integration—improving the welfare of the people in the participating countries—and the realization of socio-economic rights. Increasingly, calls are being made to bridge the schism between the 'trade' and 'human rights' regimes, and to emphasize the 'ethics' of economic integration.[66] The heart of subregional integration would beat in vain if it does not provide a lifeline to those living in poverty. Even if, or especially because, the rights that can affect their situation most directly—socio-economic rights—are rarely protected effectively under national constitutional law,[67] it is up to the RECs to put policies in place that are of relevance to the realization of socio-economic rights.

Poverty is the greatest threat to, and source of, human rights violations in Africa. Even if this is not always clearly acknowledged, regional economic integration is not a goal in itself, but is a means to an end—the eradication of poverty. The 2001 amendments to the SADC Treaty, which introduced the requirement that 'poverty eradication' must form part of all SADC activities and programmes,[68] provide some evidence of a growing appreciation of the instrumental role of regional integration in addressing poverty. The SADC Summit in 2003 also adopted a Charter of Fundamental Social Rights in SADC.[69] Acknowledging that the creation of an economic union and free trade areas is not an end in itself, the founding treaties of these institutions include the improvement of 'living conditions' and 'self-sustained development' among their aims or objectives.[70] In so far as the right to development is a conglomerate consisting of numerous rights to the basic necessities of life, the developmentalist imperative that drives the project of regional integration is closely linked to socio-economic rights.

Not only socio-economic rights, but also 'civil and political' rights are inherent in economic integration. When integration reaches the phase of a common market, especially 'civil and political' rights such as free movement of persons, come into play. Most of the subregional treaties refer to free movement of persons, the right to residence, and to 'establishment'.[71]

These freedoms are the furthest developed and defined in West Africa, where informal trading has been a long-standing feature of transboundary relationships. Already in 1979, ECOWAS adopted the Protocol A/P.1/5/79 Relating to Free Movement of Persons, the Right of Residence and Establishment. A three-phase implementation is envisaged: first, the right to entry and abolition of visas; secondly, the right to residence; and thirdly, the right to establishment. The first case

---

[66] See eg P Alston and M Robinson (eds), *Human Rights and Development: Towards Mutual Reinforcement* (Oxford: Oxford University Press, 2005).   [67] See Ch 14.C.1 below.

[68] 2001 SADC Treaty, art 5(1)(j).

[69] Angola and Botswana were by July 2006 still to sign this Charter.

[70] ECCAS Treaty, art 60 provides that member states must use their human resources fully and rationally for the development of the community.

[71] Eg IGAD Agreement, art 13A(o) and EAC Treaty, art 104.

submitted to the ECOWAS Court also invoked this freedom.[72] These aims are further elaborated in Protocols supplementary to the one mentioned above. Migrants and members of their families are for example protected against collective or arbitrary expulsion from a partner country.[73]

Other REC treaties also deal with free movement of persons, services, and the right of establishment and residence.[74] In the ECCAS region, where four landlocked countries depend on river ways and the ports of other states, free movement takes on an increased importance. Building on the provisions in its Treaty,[75] ECCAS adopted a Protocol on freedom of movement and the right of establishment. Community passports are also phased in under CEMAC. The Treaty of another West African REC, UEMOA, at least formally recognizes freedom of movement and the right of establishment of citizens within member states, and the principle of non-discrimination on the grounds of nationality.[76] All nationals within member states are free to move between member states and have the right to seek employment on a par with nationals of member states.[77] Like the EC Treaty, the SADC Treaty guarantees equal treatment and non-discrimination in member states and by SADC and its institutions.[78]

In theory, a free trade area provides access to a supply of products at the lowest cost. As few of the RECs have attained even the first stage of a fully functional free trade area, it is difficult to assess the 'welfare-enhancing gains from trade'[79] and other benefits to member countries and, more particularly, nationals of these countries.

2 Human Rights are Increasingly being Recognized as Part of the Principles and Activities of RECs

In the earliest founding legal texts of RECs there is no reference to human rights, as such, as part of the institutions' foundational values. However, as the winds of democracy swept authoritarianism and militarism from the continent in a post-Cold War world, and with the OAU being eclipsed by the AU, human rights became mainstreamed into all forms of subregional cooperation. Apart from setting out their objectives or aims, the founding treaties of the RECs also contain fundamental principles. Although human rights, the rule of law, and good governance do not feature as *goals* of the RECS, these aspects form part of the way in

---

[72] Section D.5 below.

[73] Supplementary Protocol A/SP.1/7/86 on the Second Phase (Right of Residence) on the Protocol on Free Movement of Persons, the Right of Residence and Establishment, art 13; see also UNESCO, 'The Rights of Migrant Workers and their Families: Nigeria' (2003) (Doc SHS/2003/MC/7).

[74] See eg the EAC Treaty, art 104 and the Protocol on the Facilitation of Movement of Persons in SADC, signed in 2005 but not yet in force. [75] ECCAS Treaty, art 40(1).

[76] UEMOA Treaty, art 91. [77] UEMOA Treaty, art 93.

[78] SADC Treaty, art 6(2) and 6(3).

[79] A Scott, 'Theories of Regional Economic Integration and the Global Economy' in J Gower (ed), *The European Union Handbook* (London: Fitzroy Dearborn, 2002) 103, 105.

which the goals have to be attained in a *principled* way. Developments within the EAC and ECOWAS are most strikingly illustrative of this change, on the basis of comparing earlier and more recent founding texts.

A concern for human rights is made an integral part of the 1999 EAC regime, departing from the initial silence about human rights and constitutionalism in the 1967 Treaty. In contrast to the original founding text, the new one includes good governance, respect for the rule of law, and for human rights among its fundamental principles.[80] More significantly, the prerequisite for admission to the EAC is made contingent on 'adherence to universally acceptable principles of good governance, democracy, the rule of law, observance of human rights and social justice'.[81] These factors have been part of the process of considering the applications of Burundi and Rwanda to join the EAC.

Similarly, there was no explicit reference to human rights in any of the articles forming the body of the original 1975 ECOWAS Treaty. When the Treaty was amended in 1993, the principle of adherence to human rights was given increased prominence.[82] A limited number of provisions in the initial treaty, such as freedom of movement and residence,[83] had human rights implications, but did not extend the jurisdiction of the ECOWAS Court to human rights matters as such. A shift in emphasis has been brought about by the ratification by ECOWAS member states of the African Charter, and a regional movement towards greater democratization in the period between 1975 and 1993. This development also provides a clear example of the increased importance attached to the African Charter in African political life. It remains to be seen whether these changes are largely cosmetic, occasioned by the rhetorical demands of international relations, or whether human rights concerns will be integrated meaningfully within the activities of ECOWAS. Human rights concerns further culminated in treaties dealing with vulnerable persons such as child soldiers, and with the issue of human trafficking.[84]

Other RECs that have been established in the 1990s (particularly SADC and COMESA) display a similar shift towards greater recognition of human rights.

Set up against the background of democratization processes across Southern Africa, reference to human rights is found in the SADC Treaty. It declares that the member states are 'mindful of the need to involve peoples of the Region centrally' in development and integration, 'particularly through the guarantee of democratic rights, observance of human rights and the rule of law'.[85] One of the five groups of principles in accordance with which SADC acts is 'human rights, democracy and the rule of law'.[86] The inclusion of human rights may be explained by reference to

---

[80] EAC Treaty, arts 6(d) and 7(2).   [81] EAC Treaty, art 3(3)(b).
[82] CA Odinkalu identifies the inclusion of 'fundamental principles' as one of the 'most far-reaching consequences' of the 1993 review ('Profile of the Economic Community of West African States' in Heyns (n 50 above) 644).   [83] ECOWAS 1975 Treaty, art 27.
[84] The ECOWAS Declaration on the Fight against Trafficking in Persons is repr in Heyns (n 50 above) 666–9.   [85] ibid, art 5.
[86] ibid, art 4.

the fact that the countries in Southern Africa have suffered a denial of human rights for a longer period than other African countries. An increased concern for human rights is also reflected in the amendment of the admission criteria for admission to SADC. In 2003, the Summit amended the admission criteria adopted in 1995 by adding the requirement that there should be a commonality of 'observance of the principles of democracy, human rights, good governance and the rule of law in accordance with the African Charter'.[87] Playing an almost inevitable hegemonic role in the region, a post-1994 democratic South Africa has reinforced concerns for human rights within SADC. This region has already started (and is well positioned) to produce a subregional human rights jurisprudence.

As is the case with other RECs, COMESA is not in the first place aimed at realizing any specific aim in the field of human rights. However, as the Treaty establishing COMESA suggests, issues pertaining to human rights cannot be divorced totally from its functioning. In its Preamble, reference is made to 'the principles of international law governing relations between sovereign states, and the principles of liberty, fundamental freedoms and the rule of law'. This formulation may be read as an attempt at reconciling the sanctity of the state with attempts to protect human rights within the state. This initial hesitance is supplemented by an unequivocal adherence to human rights as part of the organization's fundamental principles. These principles include the promotion and sustenance of a democratic system of governance in each member state,[88] the recognition and observance of the rule of law,[89] and the recognition, promotion, and protection of human and peoples' rights in accordance with the African Charter.[90] The inclusion of human rights as part of COMESA's fundamental principles and the possibility of applications by individuals make this a system full of potential for human rights realization.

Well-founded optimism about the actual realization of human rights may be further grounded on the omission of territorial integrity and non-interference in the internal affairs of members as aims or principles of all four of these communities.[91]

However, human rights are not accorded an equally significant place in all the regional arrangements. Predating the 1990s, the Treaty establishing UMA refers to human rights as those of 'member societies' rather than of individuals. Mirroring the OAU Charter, the 1983 ECCAS Treaty prioritizes 'non-interference in internal affairs' above human rights concerns.[92] Despite this, and assisted by the active role played by the permanent UN Consultative Committee in security issues in Central Africa, ECCAS too has taken some steps towards giving human rights a more prominent place. At a ministerial meeting in 1994, for example, a declaration

---

[87] Quoted in Oosthuizen (n 50 above) 135.   [88] COMESA Treaty, art 6(h).
[89] ibid, art 6(g).   [90] ibid, art 6(e).
[91] See arts 3 and 4 of the 1993 ECOWAS Treaty; arts 5, 6, and 7 of the 1999 EAC Treaty; arts 4 and 5 of the 1992 SADC Treaty; arts 3 and 6 of the 1993 COMESA Treaty; contrasting with art 3(2) and 3(3) of the OAU Charter and arts 3(b) and 4(g) of the AU Constitutive Act.
[92] ECCAS Treaty, art 3.

was adopted that acknowledged the need to improve security and stability to promote respect for human rights and democracy. Calls for a subregional human rights centre under the aegis of UN, which the UN General Assembly subsequently approved,[93] called on the Secretary-General and the OHCHR to establish a subregional centre for human rights in Central Africa.

3 The African Charter is becoming the Basis of a Common Subregional Human Rights Standard

Once it is accepted that human rights play (or should play) an important role in the RECs, the question arises whether, and on what basis, a common standard should be determined to enable possible future consolidation. This standard could be derived from common international law standards at the global or regional level. Although UN human rights instruments enjoy wide acceptance across subregions, none of them has been ratified by all states.

It is preferable that the African Charter, to which all AU member states are party, should serve as a common standard. The development of distinct subregional human rights standards, such as the SADC Charter of Fundamental Social Rights, is likely to enhance and accentuate differences, undermining the movement towards African unity and legal integration. The option of creating subregional human rights charters will further take time and effort, requiring member states to agree on a common standard. While it may be contended that subregional charters will be able to raise the human rights standard set out in the African Charter, the same aim can be attained if the African Charter is interpreted and applied creatively by activist REC courts. This argument is strengthened by the envisaged merger of the RECs with the AEC/AU.

The African Charter is the most representative and legitimate source of reference to ensure subregional judicial harmonization. With the exception of Morocco, all African states are party to the African Charter. This explains why most of the subregional treaties make reference to the 'recognition, promotion and protection of human and peoples' rights in accordance with the African Charter' as a 'fundamental principle' guiding the accomplishment of their objectives.[94] Predictably, the UMA Treaty does not include that incantation, presumably because Morocco is one of its constituent members. Predating the entry into force of the African Charter, the ECCAS Treaty is also silent about the African Charter. Less predictable, though, is the omission of any explicit reference to the African Charter from the SADC Treaty and the Protocol on the SADC Tribunal, allowing the Tribunal to

---

[93] Resolution 53/78 of 8 November 1998.

[94] See eg the similar wording in art 4(g) of the 1993 ECOWAS Treaty, art 6(d) of the 1999 EAC Treaty and art 6A of the IGAD Agreement; mirroring the preambular formula of the domestic Constitutions of its members, the UEMOA Treaty reaffirms the institution's commitment to the Universal Declaration and African Charter (art 3 of the UEMOA Treaty).

'develop its own Community jurisprudence having regard to applicable relevant treaties, principles and rules of general international law and any rules and principles of the law of states'.[95] The reason for this omission is not clear.

Even if not all the existing subregional arrangements invoke the African Charter, it could serve as part of the general principles of subregional law. Writing in 2003, Msungu raises the following expectation:[96]

Direct reference to the African Charter in the various economic treaties in Africa would, at least in theory, mean that the courts of justice and tribunals are bound to directly apply human rights rules in determining trade disputes and interpreting the agreements. In that sense, the African Charter could be seen as a kind of bill of rights for the African regional human rights system.

Developments in Europe serve as an analogy. Judgments of the Court of Justice of the European Communities illustrate a trend towards increasingly introducing human rights into Community law by recognizing the European Convention as a source of 'general legal principles' of European Community law.[97] In 1996 the Court of Justice of the European Communities observed as follows:[98]

[I]t is well settled that fundamental rights form an integral part of the general principles of law whose observance the Court ensures. For that purpose, the Court draws inspiration from the constitutional traditions common to the Member States and from the guidelines supplied by international treaties for the protection of human rights on which the Member States have collaborated or of which they are signatories. In this regard, the Court has stated that the Convention has special significance.

In the absence of a judicially integrated Africa, the problem of divergent interpretations of one normative source by different judicial bodies is undeniable. The numerous subregional courts will co-exist with each other and with the African Court on Human and Peoples' Rights (or the future AU Court of Justice or merged African Court of Justice and Human Rights). If all these judicial bodies adjudicate on the basis of the African Charter, a cohesive jurisprudence could—but need not—develop. While these overlapping jurisdictions may lead to cross-fertilization and could strengthen both institutions, the inverse may also be true, leading to a cacophony of divergent interpretations. This eventuality could be curbed if subregional courts follow the African Court's interpretation, when such an interpretation

---

[95] SADC Tribunal Protocol, art 22(b).   [96] Musungu (n 5 above) 93.

[97] See eg *Nold v Commission* [1974] ECR 491, *Rutili v Minister of the Interior* [1975] ECR 1219, and *Hauer v Land Rheinland-Pfalz* [1979] ECR 37727. See also *Kremzow v Austrian State* [1996] ECR I-2637: '... where national legislation falls within the field of application of Community law the Court, in a reference for a preliminary ruling, must give the national court all the guidance as to interpretation necessary to enable it to assess the compatibility of that legislation with the fundamental rights—as laid down in particular in the Convention—whose observance the Court endures. However, the Court has no such jurisdiction with regard to national legislation lying outside the scope of Community law' (para 15).

[98] Opinion 2/94 (Accession by the Communities to the Convention for the Protection of Human Rights and Fundamental Freedoms) [1996] ECR I-1759, para 33.

exists, by working out a system of referral to the African Court, for interpretive guidance in other cases.[99]

A further disadvantage of a multiplicity of courts is the possibility of forum-shopping. A consequence of the duplication of REC membership is the possibility that a litigant may choose the institution to which he or she addresses a complaint or application. One way of curbing this possibility is that each of the subregional tribunals may apply the principle of *res judicata* in relation to other subregional tribunals. However, the same approach should not be followed with respect to the African Human Rights Court. In principle, further recourse from REC Courts should be allowed to the African Court. It seems that, in respect of the ECOWAS Court, this will not be the case, as that Court's Protocol, in articles 19(2) and 22(1), provides for the finality of judgments by the ECOWAS Court.

The ECOWAS Court has taken some tentative steps towards judicial acceptance of the African Charter as such a common standard. Under the ECOWAS Court Protocol, the Court examines disputes in accordance with the ECOWAS Treaty and the Protocol and, if necessary, article 38 of the ICJ Statute. In a case brought concerning the legality of a domestic electoral process, the ECOWAS Court clarified that the inclusion of the African Charter in the Treaty 'behoves on the Court ... to bring in the application of those rights catalogued in the African Charter'.[100] Although these remarks do not form part of the *ratio* of the decision, they represent a clear and logical acceptance that the African Charter forms an integral part of the Court's substantive scope. However, in its jurisprudence, the ECOWAS Court has so far not made reference to specific provisions of the Charter or to the findings of the African Commission—despite applicants explicitly invoking the Charter at least once.[101] Instead, the Court tended to explore and rely on case-law of the ICJ, as far as international tribunals are concerned, and on the precedents of Nigerian and English courts. One rather obvious reason for the omission of reliance on the Charter is the fact that most matters have thus far been decided on purely procedural grounds.

4 Subregional Tribunals may Contribute towards the Realization of Human Rights

In so far as they contain provisions pertaining to human rights, the REC treaties should put in place procedures and mechanisms to adjudicate allegations that human rights have been violated in their 'application and interpretation'. Traditionally,

---

[99] eg requesting advisory opinions from the Court: see art 4(1) of the Protocol to the African Charter on the Establishment of an African Court on Human and Peoples' Rights, allowing 'African organizations' recognized by the AU to submit such requests.

[100] *Ugokwe v Nigeria and Others*, Case ECW/CCJ/APP/02/05, Community Court of Justice of ECOWAS, 7 October 2005, para 13.

[101] In *Lijadu-Oyemade v Executive Secretary of ECOWAS and Another*, Case ECW/CCJ/APP/01/05, Community Court of Justice of ECOWAS, 10 October 2005, para 26.

RECs have opted for arbitration and other non-judicial means of resolving disputes, and have set up courts to resolve disputes arising from closer economic and political union, rather than human rights violations. Now, most of the subregional arrangements provide for a judicial body to adjudicate disputes,[102] and to give binding judgments. With jurisdiction essentially limited to their founding treaties, these courts are still principally concerned with subregional economic integration. However, even if they concern themselves mainly with disputes arising from the process of economic and legal integration, these courts are also called upon to consider the human rights implications of economic policies and programmes. With the extension of the mandate of RECs to include human security, subregional courts may even become vehicles to initiate intervention to curb human rights violations.

Subregional courts may be divided into three categories: fully functional, fledgling and future courts. First, there are three fully functional Courts, those established under ECOWAS, COMESA, and the EAC. The ECOWAS Community Court of Justice, based in Abuja, Nigeria, has been the most active of the subregional courts. The ECOWAS Court was provided for in the 1975 ECOWAS Treaty to 'ensure observance of law and justice'.[103] Disputes arising from the application of the Treaty had to be resolved by the states among themselves, and in amicable settlement 'by direct agreement'.[104] Failing such a settlement, any of the parties involved could refer the matter to the Court. In 1991, due to the 'scope and degree of regional integration ECOWAS had embarked on',[105] a Protocol setting up the ECOWAS Court was adopted. It entered into force in 1996. By the end of 2006, the Court had finalized some ten cases.

The jurisdiction of the Court extends to disputes about the interpretation, application, and legality of ECOWAS laws, the 'failure by Member States to honour their obligations' under ECOWAS law, vicarious liability of ECOWAS officials, and employer–employee relations within ECOWAS.[106] Going further than any of the other treaties, the Protocol states in no uncertain terms that the Court also has jurisdiction to 'determine cases of violation of human rights that occur in any Member State'.[107]

A functional court also exists within COMESA. Like other subregional courts, the COMESA Court does not have a general mandate, but has to ensure 'the adherence to law in the interpretation and application' of the Treaty.[108] The COMESA Authority appoints seven judges for a once-renewable term of five years.[109] No

---

[102] On these tribunals, see <http://www.aict.ctia.org> (31 July 2006).

[103] ECOWAS 1975 Treaty, art 11(1).   [104] ibid, art 56.

[105] Final Communiqué of the 14th Session of the Authority of Heads of State and Government, Abuja, July 1991 contained in (1991) 19 Official J of ECOWAS 62. The Protocol is reprinted at (1996) 8 *RADIC* 28.   [106] 2005 Supplementary Protocol, art 9.

[107] The new art 9(4) of the Protocol on the Community Court of Justice (see art 3 of the Supplementary Protocol A/SP.1/11/04).   [108] COMESA Treaty, art 19.

[109] ibid, arts 20, 21.

two nationals from a specific member state may hold judicial office simultaneously. The Court has contentious and advisory jurisdiction.[110] The Court's judgments are binding and member states undertake to implement them without delay.[111] The Court may also grant appropriate interim orders.[112] In 2006, the seat of the Court was shifted from Lusaka, Zambia, to its permanent seat in Khartoum, Sudan. It is reported that the Court has not been sitting since 2004, due in part to a hiatus between the expiry of judges' terms and new judicial appointments, and due more recently to deficiencies in infrastructure.[113] Going by the information on its web-site, the Court has dealt with seven cases, in some instances delivering numerous judgments on one case.

The Court may decide on the compliance *with Community law* of any act, directive or decision adopted by COMESA bodies or by member states. Both member states and individuals may institute such cases before the Court. National courts have concurrent jurisdiction with the COMESA Court on COMESA law, unless jurisdiction has been conferred on the COMESA Court.[114] However, deci-sions of the COMESA Court have precedence over national court decisions.[115] When the Court considers that 'questions' raised before it concerning the appli-cation or interpretation of the Treaty are 'necessary' to enable it to 'give judgment', all domestic courts *may* and the highest court *must* 'refer' that 'question' to the COMESA Court for its determination.[116] The resulting decision of the COMESA Court will guide the domestic court in finalizing the case.

The East African Court of Justice (EAC Court) must ensure 'adherence to law in the interpretation and application of and compliance with the Treaty'.[117] The Court, seated in Arusha, Tanzania, became operational in 2001. Six ad hoc judges have been elected. An intra-institutional dispute, concerning the legislative author-ity of the EAC Legislative Assembly and its relationship with the EAC Council of Ministers, led to the Court's first judgment.[118] The Court does not have a clear human rights mandate, as appears from the fact that the jurisdiction of the Court may be extended to human rights matters at some time in the future, when the members adopt a Protocol to this effect.[119] However, to the extent that the Treaty itself already contains references to human rights—including the African Charter—current law does not foreclose individual referrals on the basis of human rights.

Domestic courts may request a preliminary ruling from the EAC Court before it decides on an issue involving the application of the Treaty.[120] As the experience of the European Court of Justice demonstrates, the potential effect of such referrals

---

[110] Advisory jurisdiction is regulated by COMESA Treaty, art 32.   [111] ibid, art 34(3).
[112] ibid, art 35.
[113] 'COMESA Court faces logistical, funding woes' *The East African* (28 March 2006).
[114] COMESA Treaty, art 29(1).   [115] ibid, art 29(2).   [116] ibid, art 30.
[117] EAC Treaty, art 23.
[118] 'EAC Law Makers go to Court over AG's "Interference" in Assembly' *The East African* (18 December 2005): see *Mwatela and Others v EAC*, Application No 1 of 2005, EAC Court (October 2006).   [119] EAC Treaty, art 27.
[120] ibid, art 34.

is significant. Members undertake to enforce judgments on the basis that the Court's order for execution appended to the judgment of the Court 'shall require only the verification of the authenticity of the judgment by the Registrar, where-upon the party in whose favour execution is to take place, may proceed to execute the judgment'.[121] This is an innovative procedure that eases the process of domestic enforcement of supra-national court orders.

Orders of both the ECOWAS and COMESA Courts may be executed domestically, according to domestic rules of civil procedure.[122] Once a Court's enforcement order has been verified, it must be enforced. In both systems, priority is given to judgments that impose financial obligations on members: The COMESA Treaty provides that judgments imposing a 'pecuniary obligation' must be enforced according to the rules of civil procedure. The ECOWAS Protocol states, in article 19(2), that all the ECOWAS Court's judgments are 'immediately enforceable'.

The SADC Tribunal, which has been set up but is yet to become fully operational, falls into the second category of 'fledgling courts'. The SADC Tribunal is one of six organs established under the SADC Treaty.[123] It can adjudicate disputes or give advisory opinions.[124] Its decisions will be final and binding.[125] The Heads of State and Government of SADC adopted a Protocol granting the SADC Tribunal jurisdiction over (a) the interpretation and application of the Treaty; (b) the interpretation, application or validity of SADC law, and acts of SADC organs; (c) any other mandate-specific matter.[126] With its seat in Windhoek, Namibia, the SADC Tribunal since its inauguration in 2001, and the election of judges in 2005, has not heard a single case. One of the reasons for the dearth of cases may be the requirement that disputes arising from the interpretation and application of the SADC Treaty should in the first place be settled amicably through a process of friendly settlement.[127] Only if a dispute cannot be settled amicably, is it to be referred to the SADC Tribunal.

The inclusion of human rights in the mandate of the SADC Tribunal was considered, but eventually rejected. A panel of experts, mandated to draft a proposal for an SADC Tribunal in 1997,[128] proposed that individuals should be granted the right to seize the future Tribunal. The panel noted that the SADC Treaty imposes the obligation on states not to discriminate on certain grounds, and concluded that this makes individual access imperative.[129] Noting that SADC has a more general human rights mandate,[130] the panel concluded that the Tribunal could be 'given a more general jurisdiction in relation to human rights'. It continued: 'In the event of a separate instrument being drawn up, setting up the scope of the human rights to be protected, jurisdiction should be conferred on the Tribunal'.

---

[121] ibid, art 44.

[122] See COMESA Treaty, art 40 and ECOWAS Court Protocol, as amended, art 24.

[123] SADC Treaty, art 9.   [124] ibid, art 16.   [125] ibid, art 16(5).

[126] SADC Tribunal Protocol, art 15.   [127] SADC Treaty, art 32.

[128] The SADC Tribunal, dated 18 February 1997. This document, and the Record of the First Legal Experts Meeting, were supplied to me by Mr André Stemmet, from the South African Department of Foreign Affairs.   [129] See art 6(1) and 6(2) of the SADC Treaty.

[130] In terms of SADC Treaty, art 4.

The third category comprises a number of subregional courts that exist only on paper. A Maghreb Court of Justice, consisting of two judges from each member state, has formally been instituted. Its function is to adjudicate on disputes relating to the interpretation and application of the Treaty and other agreements within the ambit of the UMA.[131] Its seat is to be established at Nouakchott, Mauritania. The Court will have contentious and advisory jurisdiction. In the latter capacity, the Maghreb Court of Justice will provide advice to the Presidential Council.[132] Courts of Justice are also provided for under UEMOA and ECCAS, but have not yet become operational.

If the limited record of the two operational Courts is anything to go by, Africa's materially deprived and downtrodden will wait in vain for the transformative agency of Community law. Out of six contentious cases decided by the ECOWAS Court, only one dealt with any issue of substance. The other cases ground to a halt at the procedural stage due to a lack of individual standing, the failure to engage in friendly settlement efforts, the lack of retrospective effect of the Supplementary Protocol, and non-observance of time-limits. There is a discrepancy between the Court's invocation of an approach eschewing 'mere technicality to defeat the substance of the case' and its reasoning, which dwells at length on procedural aspects in a very formalistic way. It would be wrong to blame the Court alone. Legal counsel certainly contributed to the staid approach. The Court expressed criticism of counsel in at least two cases (albeit implicitly), based on counsel's failure to indicate why the Supplementary Protocol should have retrospective effect or why the Protocol is procedural rather than substantive in nature, and on the non-observance of clearly prescribed amicable settlement procedures.

Similarly, the COMESA Court's jurisprudence to date teems with procedural matters and intricate legal arguments. In one case, no fewer than six 'interlocutory applications' were brought, ranging from challenges to the jurisdiction of the Court, stays of proceedings, and suspension of orders.[133] In other cases, issues of the standing and citation of parties occupied the Court's attention, rather than the substantive guarantees of COMESA law.[134] It is hardly surprising that cases are settled out of court.[135]

5 Individual Access to Subregional Courts is a Prerequisite to Addressing Human Rights Violations

Traditionally, international courts resolved disputes between the main role players in international law—states. This position is reflected in most of the REC Courts.

---

[131] Marrakesh Treaty, art 13(2).   [132] See El Kadiri (n 32 above) 146.

[133] See the numerous judgments in *PTA Bank and Michael Gondwe v Martin Ogang*, references 1A/2000, 1B/2000 and 1C/2000.

[134] See eg *Kenya and Another v Coastal Aquaculture*, Reference 3/2001, judgment of 26 April 2002 and *Standard Chartered Financial Services Limited and Others v Kenya*, reference 4/2002, judgment of 20 November 2002.

[135] See eg *Building Design Enterprise v COMESA*, reference 1/2002, order of 18 October 2002 and *Bilika Harry Simamba v COMESA*, reference 3/2002, order of 25 October 2002.

As the experience of human rights bodies shows, the role of the individual is often crucial to unlocking the potential beyond the surface of formal human rights provisions. In general, however, individuals may not refer cases to, and do not have standing before, subregional judicial institutions, making it impossible for them to raise human rights concerns in these fora.

The importance of individual access is illustrated in the ECOWAS experience. After the adoption of the Protocol on the ECOWAS Court in 1991, and its entry into force in 1996, the Court lay dormant until 2004, when a Nigerian businessman, Mr Olajide Afolabi, brought a case before the Court. Afolabi alleged that the unilateral closure by Nigeria of the border with neighbouring Benin in August 2003 constituted a violation of his right to free movement as enshrined in the ECOWAS Treaty, the Protocol on Free Movement of Persons and Goods, and the African Charter.[136] Due to the limitation in the ECOWAS Court Protocol that only a state on behalf of its nationals could institute actions before it, the Court decided to forego the first chance of exercising its mandate. Conscious of the implications of its finding, the Court requested that, in the light of the 'great interest and importance to all member States', these states should all be notified of the judgment date.

An analysis of the arguments presented shows that an activist Court could have viewed the matter differently. Because the Protocol does not stipulate in so many words that only states can appear before the Court, the applicant argued that the door was open for an interpretation allowing individuals standing. If only states have standing, a case involving a dispute about non-conformity with Community law by a member would require that member state to bring a suit as applicant against itself as respondent. To overcome this absurdity, the argument continued, and to observe 'equity', individuals should be allowed to have standing before the Court. Adopting a different line of argument, the respondent argued that it was a matter of jurisdiction rather than standing, and warned that the Court should not usurp the legislative function of redrafting the clear provisions of the Protocol.

Against this background, the Protocol relating to the ECOWAS Court was amended in 2005 to broaden access to the Court to individuals and corporate bodies 'in proceedings for the determination of an act or inaction of a Community official that violates the rights' of the individual or corporate body, and, more broadly, for 'relief for violations of their human rights'.[137]

As the situation stands, individuals may also submit cases directly to the COMESA, EAC, and SADC tribunals. Individuals may refer the legality of any act, regulation, directive, or decision of the Community or any member state to

---

[136] *Olajide Afolabi v Nigeria*, Suit no ECW/CCJ/APP/01/03, judgment of 27 April 2004. See also 'ECOWAS Court hears First Case Thursday' *Panapress* (22 January 2004).

[137] New art 10(c) and (d) of the Protocol (see Supplementary Protocol, art 4).

each of these judicial organs, arguing that it is unlawful or an infringement of the founding treaty.[138]

Under the Protocol establishing the SADC Tribunal, this Tribunal has jurisdiction over inter-state disputes, as well as those between natural or legal persons and states.[139] More importantly, natural or legal persons may refer individual disputes to the Tribunal.[140] This provision is in line with the SADC Treaty, which already provides for the full involvement of individuals and NGOs in the process of regional integration.[141] When a question concerning the application and interpretation of the SADC Treaty is raised before a national court, that court must refer the matter to the SADC Tribunal for its 'preliminary ruling'. The matter is then referred back, and the national court must finalize the matter in accordance with the Tribunal's ruling.

Under most international law systems, individuals are granted standing only if they have fulfilled some preconditions, which usually include the requirement that local remedies must have been exhausted.[142] A mechanical application of this condition led the COMESA Court to dismiss the following application:[143] Coastal Aquaculture, a Kenyan company, sought an injunction from the COMESA Court to restrain the Kenyan authorities from acquiring some of its property without first making advance payment of adequate compensation. The legal basis of this application was the Kenyan Constitution, which provides for prompt compensation in cases of the compulsory acquisition of property, and the Kenyan Land Acquisition Act. The applicant alleged that it had been constrained in its operations since 1993, due to three acquisition attempts, none of which involved compensation being paid. For eight years, the applicant has unsuccessfully tried to follow the 'simple legal procedures laid down in the Land Acquisition Act to their logical conclusion'. In 1996, the applicant instituted proceedings before Kenyan courts, but withdrew that action just before starting the proceedings before the COMESA Court, presumably in 2001. Although the Court expressed some sympathy for the applicant's frustration, it held that domestic remedies had not been exhausted because the action was not 'persecuted to finality'. By presenting its conclusion in such unproblematic terms, the Court leaves no room for reading in grounds of exemption, as the African Commission on Human and People's Rights has done, in cases where domestic remedies are not effective or available in practice. Although the wording of the Treaty does not allow specifically for exemptions to the exhaustion-rule, the Court could have used its 'inherent power' to find solutions that 'meet the ends of justice' as a basis to investigate that possibility.[144]

---

[138] COMESA Treaty, art 26; EAC Treaty, art 30; SADC Tribunal Protocol, art 18.
[139] ibid, art 16.   [140] ibid, art 18.
[141] SADC Treaty, art 23(2).
[142] See eg COMESA Treaty, art 26; SADC Tribunal Protocol, art 15(2).
[143] *Kenya v Coastal Aquaculture*, reference 3/2001, judgment of 26 April 2004.
[144] See Rules of the COMESA Court, r 36(2.

Exhaustion of domestic remedies does not feature as a prerequisite for standing before the ECOWAS Court. On the one hand, it may be argued that this omission derives from the status of Community law, which is regarded as superior and integral to the law of member states. In *Ugokwe v Nigeria and Others*,[145] the ECOWAS Court stated that 'the distinctive feature' of the ECOWAS legal order is that it 'sets forth a judicial monism of first and last resort in Community law'. Even if domestic courts are needed to implement Court decisions, the relationship between national and supranational courts is not 'vertical'. These remarks should be understood within the context of the case, in which the applicant submitted that the annulment of his election as Nigerian Member of Parliament violated ECOWAS law. The main contention on his behalf was that the Nigerian Tribunal and Appeal Court violated his right to a fair trial in the process of annulment. The Court made the observations quoted in the excerpt above to underline that it is not a court of appeal or cassation, and that 'appealing against the decision of the national Courts of member states does not form part of the powers of the Court'. It consequently lacks competence, the Court concluded.

This finding is correct if the matter before the Court is construed as an 'electoral dispute', over which the Court lacks jurisdiction. However, in my view even an electoral matter may give rise to human rights violations, as the applicant alleged in this case. From this perspective, the Court missed the point by misconstruing its responsibility. While it is correct that the ECOWAS Court is not a court of appeal on issues related to national law (in this instance, section 36 of the Nigerian Constitution, which guarantees the right to fair trial), it shirks from its responsibility if it does not deal with allegations that member states do not comply with Community law (the right to fair trial in the African Charter). If Nigeria violated Community law in the process of annulling the applicant's election, the Court should find that Nigeria was in breach of its treaty obligations.

It may also be accepted, on the other hand, that this requirement should be 'read into' the treaty. Under article 38(1)(b) and (c) of the ICJ Statute, which it is entitled to apply, the ECOWAS Court may rely on customary international law and 'general principles of law'. Both these sources provide a basis to argue that domestic remedies are required. Such a course of action will be analogous to the requirement that an individual staff member of ECOWAS may not approach the Court before he or she has exhausted internal appeal processes.[146]

Unsuccessful efforts to settle the dispute amicably may also be posed as a condition for direct access, thus impeding and delaying individual access.[147] Attempts

---

[145] Case no ECW/CCJ/APP/02/05, judgment of 7 October 2005.

[146] 2005 Protocol, art 10(e). Such an approach will also be in line with art 56(5) of the African Charter. See also ECOWAS Protocol on Democracy and Good Governance of 2001, art 39, which provides that the Court Protocol 'shall be reviewed' to allow the Court to hear cases 'relating to violations of human rights, after all attempts to resolve the matter at the national level have failed'. While the first aspect (the Court's competence to hear human rights matters) was taken up in the Supplementary Protocol, the second (the requirement of exhaustion of domestic remedies) was not.

[147] 1993 ECOWAS Treaty, art 76.

towards a friendly settlement should precede submission of a case to the ECOWAS Court, but must be 'without prejudice to the provisions' of the ECOWAS Treaty. In a dispute between the Parliament and Council of Ministers, the ECOWAS Court declined to make a decision on the substantive issues on the ground that it is compulsory for parties first to 'have recourse to amicable settlement'.[148] It consequently ordered that the applicant must fulfil this formality, and indicated that in its pleadings. So far, this requirement has for example not featured in the *Ugokwe* case, which was submitted by an individual alleging a violation of his human rights.

Treaties may also provide for other prerequisites. Applications brought to the ECOWAS Court must for example not be anonymous, and must not have been submitted for adjudication before any other international court.[149]

6 The Standards and Institutions of RECs have been Extended to Cover Specific Human Rights Themes

Some human rights issues, such as the HIV and AIDS pandemic, movement and treatment of refugees, and trafficking of persons, never concern only a single state in isolation. Based on the premise that they lend themselves particularly well to subregional responses, African RECs have acted upon these and other human rights-related matters. Substantively their involvement has taken the form of declarations and protocols. Institutionally, committees and other monitoring bodies have been set up.

6.1 HIV and AIDS

Pandemics such as AIDS confront societies on all fronts. With the highest HIV prevalence in the world, sub-Saharan Africa, and particularly Southern Africa,[150] forms the epicentre of global HIV and AIDS cases. Given the well-established link between mobility and the spread of HIV, factors such as intra-regional trade, immigration, and trans-boundary employment accentuate the regional dimension of the problem. However, not only the problem, but also its solution should have a subregional dimension. For example, states in a subregion may develop common prevention strategies, devise common positions on intellectual property issues, share examples of successful interventions, and formulate 'model legislation'.

Having remit for the part of the world most affected by HIV and AIDS, SADC has done the most, even if its response came too late to stem the epidemic. One of the amendments to the SADC Treaty, adopted in 2001, made the combating of

---

[148] *Parliament of the Community of West African States represented by Chief F O Offia v Council of Ministers of ECOWAS and Another*, Suit no ECW/CCJ/APP/03/05, judgment of 4 October 2005, para 13.   [149] New art 10(d) of the Protocol.

[150] According to UNAIDS, the 2005 HIV prevalence rate in Swaziland was 33.4%, in Botswana 24.1% and in Lesotho 23.2% of the adult population. The highest number of infected people live in South Africa.

HIV/AIDS and 'other deadly and communicable diseases' an objective of SADC.[151] The SADC Protocol on Health, adopted in 1999 and having entered into force in August 2004,[152] requires state parties to harmonize HIV/AIDS policies, to standardize surveillance systems and to exchange information.[153] State parties must also 'endeavour to provide high-risk and trans-border populations with preventative and basic curative services for HIV/AIDS/STDs'.[154]

SADC member states are also party to numerous other normative frameworks. These include the SADC Code of HIV/AIDS and Employment, as developed by the Employment and Labour Sector; the Health Sector Policy Framework Document, as developed by the SADC Health Ministers; the 2003 SADC Declaration on HIV/AIDS; and the SADC Declaration on Gender and Development. Although it lacks binding force, the 2003 Declaration provides a comprehensive framework for action. Emphasizing the urgent need for intervention, it calls for initiatives that 'would increase the capacities of women and adolescent girls to protect themselves from the risk of HIV infection', for 'regional regimes to ensure the availability of technologies and drugs at affordable prices', and establishes a regional Fund to implement the SADC HIV/AIDS Strategic Framework.[155] Since 2000, SADC has had an HIV and AIDS Strategic Framework in place, the most recent spanning 2003 to 2007. The Plan sets out a number of time-bound activities for directorates in a reorganized SADC Secretariat.[156]

Institutionally, the SADC Secretariat has established an HIV and AIDS Unit within its Department of Strategic Planning, Gender and Policy Harmonization. The mandate of the HIV and AIDS Unit is to 'lead, coordinate and manage SADC's response to the epidemic through the operationalization of the HIV and AIDS Strategic Framework (2003–2007) and the Maseru Declaration'.[157] The Unit has four core staff members and additional project staff.[158]

Not only SADC, but other RECs in East and Central Africa took measures to address HIV and AIDS. Numerous activities of the EAC have a bearing on human rights in the context of HIV and AIDS. States undertake to take steps for the prevention and control of communicable diseases such as HIV/AIDS.[159] EAC partner states are also called upon to take joint action and to cooperate in addressing diseases such as HIV and AIDS and to ensure greater inclusion of marginalized groups in social welfare. An East African Integrated Diseases Surveillance Network (EIDSNet) has been established. In 2004, ECCAS Heads of State reiterated that HIV and AIDS programmes should be prioritized at the national level, and committed themselves to establishing a regional fund and to adhere to

---

[151] SADC Treaty, art 5(i).
[152] At the time of writing, nine of the 14 SADC member states are parties to the Protocol.
[153] SADC Protocol on Health, art 10(1).   [154] ibid, art 10(2).
[155] Repr in (2004) 5 *Development Update*, which also brings together a number of essays on HIV and AIDS in Southern Africa.   [156] ibid, 20–32.
[157] SADC, 'HIV and AIDS Business Plan' (2004) 12.   [158] ibid.
[159] EAC Treaty, art 118(a).

the allocation of 15 per cent of their budgets to health. In an example of sub-regional cooperation, 11 Central African countries applied jointly to the Global Fund for HIV/AIDS, tuberculosis, and malaria.[160]

6.2 Refugees

One of the most persistent problems in the Eastern and Horn areas of Africa is that of refugees and internally displaced people. It is estimated that 30 per cent of the global figure of displaced persons find themselves in this region.[161] IGAD Ministers held a conference on this issue in February 2006, culminating in the Nairobi Declaration, in which states committed themselves to strengthening the IGAD Secretariat to ensure its active and effective role, and calling for part-nerships between IGAD and other role players such as the UNHCR, the AU, and the UN.[162]

6.3 Human Trafficking

Human trafficking has affected West Africa in particular. In 2001, the ECOWAS Protocol on Democracy and Good Governance identified the need for special national and Community laws against child trafficking and child prostitution. Simultaneously, the ECOWAS Declaration on the Fight Against Trafficking in Persons was adopted, calling on members to take practical steps to combat human trafficking in West Africa.[163] In the Declaration, states further committed them-selves to criminalizing human trafficking, to setting up anti-trafficking law enforce-ment units, and to sensitizing and training government officials dealing with trafficking. The Declaration also calls on states to ratify the African Children's Charter.

6.4 Women's Equality and Gender Issues

Shunned by their governments, and frustrated domestically, women reached out to a broader sisterhood, formed multinational civil society structures, and made use of more sympathetic public fora at the subregional level. As a consequence, local women's organizations and their campaigns have been strengthened by the inclusion of their agenda points within a wider movement.

The SADC response has been particularly significant. SADC has gone beyond the provisions of its founding treaty, which proclaims its commitment to the prin-ciple of non-discrimination on the basis of sex. Institutionally, a SADC Gender Unit was set up in 1998 to promote gender equality and to advise SADC structures

---

[160] <http://www.theglobalfund.org/programs/news_summary> (31 July 2006).

[161] IGAD Strategy, Djibouti, October 2003.

[162] Adopted 21 February 2006, by the Ministerial Conference on refugees, returnees, and internally displaced persons in the IGAD region, <http://www.igad.org/psd/nairobi_refugees_conf_decl.htm> (31 July 2006).   [163] Repr in Heyns (n 50 above) 666.

on matters pertaining to gender.[164] A non-binding declaration and addendum thereto have been adopted. Departing from and inspired by international precedents, such as the Beijing Declaration and Platform of Action, the SADC Declaration on Gender and Development was adopted in 1997.[165] This wide-ranging Declaration aims to 'mainstream gender in the process of community building'. It also establishes a policy aimed at ensuring at least 30 per cent women in political and decision-making structures by 2005. Although only Mozambique and South Africa (both with 33 per cent female parliamentarians) had reached this goal by mid-2006, women's representation approximated the target in some other member states.[166] As it was considered that the pertinent problem of violence against women 'merited particular attention',[167] an addendum to the Declaration was drafted, focusing on the 'prevention and eradication of violence against women and children'. Discussions about the conversion of the Declaration into a binding treaty are ongoing.

Other RECs have also taken steps to put women's equality and gender issues on the agenda. In the ECOWAS Protocol on Democracy and Good Governance, the close link between women's welfare, on the one hand, and peace and development, on the other, is recognized. More recently, a Gender Division has been established in the ECOWAS Secretariat, and a Gender Policy has been adopted. The more recent EAC Treaty is much more explicit about the obligation of states to act upon gender discrimination and prejudice and to mainstream gender into development and decision-making than is the case with other founding treaties. EAC members are required to ensure women's increased participation in development, decision-making, and commit themselves to abolish discriminatory laws and customs.[168] Also, UEMOA passed a resolution on women's rights in 1999.

6.5 Children's Rights

ECOWAS has been most active in the elaboration of specific human rights instruments dealing with children, such as the Declaration on the Decade of a Culture of the Rights of the Child in West Africa[169] and a declaration on child soldiers adopted by ministers of foreign affairs in 1999. The problem is that these instruments have limited legal value, being non-binding declarations. However, they may serve as a normative basis for further elaboration and may be the first step towards relevant binding standards.

---

[164] 2004 ECA Study (n 25 above) 214–15.
[165] F Banda, *Woman Law and Human Rights in Africa: An African Perspective* (Oxford: Hart, 2005) 54–5.
[166] The corresponding figures in Tanzania and Namibia stood at 28% and 24%. See <http://www.sadc.int/news/news_details.php?news_id=628> (31 July 2006). At 11%, Botswana had the lowest level of representation.   [167] Banda (n 165 above) 55.
[168] 1999 EAC Treaty, arts 118, 120, and 121.
[169] Declaration A/DCL.1/12/01, adopted in Dakar on 20–1 December 2001.

7 Not only Human Rights, but also Democratization has been Accepted as Part of the Goals of RECs

The political advantages of subregionalism have gradually gained importance alongside its initial aim of effective economic integration. Especially after 1990, with the advent of democracy at the national level, most RECs unequivocally proclaimed an attachment to democracy and good governance. Over time, the mandates of RECs were extended pragmatically to include issues intimately related to economic progress and human rights, such as democracy, peace and security and conflict resolution. Aimed at consolidating the gains of democracy, election monitoring also became a function of a number of RECs.

A supplement to the 1999 ECOWAS Conflict Prevention Protocol, on 'Democracy and Good Governance', was adopted in 2001, representing the clearest acknowledgement that the objectives of ECOWAS have shifted far beyond the initial devotion to economic integration. Since 1975, most ECOWAS states have experienced at least one *coup d'état*, and a period of military rule. Against this background of militarized politics, the Protocol sets some significant principles of 'constitutional convergence': Armies need to be subordinated to civilian government. Not only does the Protocol reiterate the commitment of the partner states to the African Charter, but it also emphasizes that an individual should have legal recourse to an appropriate institution to ensure protection of his or her rights. In a far-reaching provision, the Protocol adds: 'In the absence of a court of special jurisdiction, the ... Protocol shall be regarded as giving the necessary powers to common or civil law judicial bodies'.[170] Political instability usually detracts from regional integration, but here it seems to have been a factor enhancing integration. It remains important that the main ECOWAS role players, such as Senegal and Ghana, and later Nigeria, have been stable, even if they have not always been totally democratic.

Manipulations of the Togolese Constitution to ensure the succession of President Gnassingbé Eyadema by his son, Faure Gnassingbé, provoked ECOWAS to action. ECOWAS denounced the violation of the Constitution, imposed sanctions on Togo, and exerted pressure on Faure not to take office and to ensure that free elections were held.[171] ECOWAS election observers also subsequently monitored the April 2005 presidential elections, and provided moral support during the ongoing negotiations, culminating in the August 2006 Comprehensive Political Agreement.[172] In June 2005, ECOWAS observers also monitored the presidential elections in Guinea-Bissau.[173]

---

[170] 2001 Protocol on Democracy and Good Governance, art 1(h).
[171] SJ Schnalby 'The OAS and Constitutionalism: Lessons from Recent West African Experience' (2005) 33 *Syracuse J of Intl L and Commerce* 263.
[172] ECOWAS, 'ECOWAS Expresses Satisfaction with the Signing of the Comprehensive Political Agreement in Togo' <http://news.ecowas.int> (8 September 2006).
[173] 'ECOWAS Electoral Observers Arrive in Guinea-Bissau' *Panapress* (18 June 2005).

An effective way of increasing the likelihood of human rights adherence among members is to make membership conditional on a proven track-record in this respect. At least one of the African RECs, the EAC, in its 1999 Treaty included a substantive threshold requirement of adherence to 'good governance, democracy, the rule of law, the observance of human rights and social justice' for admission.[174] In forging a common foreign and security policy, the EAC partner states must, similarly, aim to consolidate democracy, the rule of law, and a respect for human rights.[175]

The currents of democratic change also pulled SADC towards a clearer democratic commitment. In 2001, SADC amended its founding Treaty in a number of important respects. Where the original Treaty directed SADC towards the promotion of 'peace and security', the amended version adds the maintenance of democracy into the mix.[176] Another noteworthy addition is the qualification that 'common political values' are those associated with 'institutions which are democratic, legitimate and effective'.[177]

Building on its legal and policy instruments and on OAU/AU principles and guidelines,[178] SADC in 2004 adopted SADC Principles and Guidelines governing Elections. Both SADC and the SADC Parliamentary Forum (SADC PF) engaged in election monitoring. SADC PF has since the 1990s been observing most elections in the region, and in 2001, adopted its own Norms and Standards for Elections in the SADC region. In respect of the Zimbabwean elections, the SADC PF Observer Mission concluded that the 'climate of insecurity obtaining in Zimbabwe since the 2000 parliamentary elections was such that the electoral process could not be said to adequately comply with the Norms and Standards for Elections in the SADC region'.

Also under ECCAS, a Central African Parliamentarians' Network, and a Human Rights and Democracy Centre have been established.

8 Peace and Security have been Accepted as Prerequisites for Development and Economic Integration

Breaches in political stability and peaceful co-existence are obstacles to a respect for human rights. Negative economic growth rates in countries experiencing conflict and political instability also underline the close link between political stability and economic growth. Although African RECs were principally designed as subregional organizations for the pursuit of economic and social goals, their founding treaties either mention the aim of promoting 'security and stability' or later introduce

---

[174] 1999 EAC Treaty, art 3(3)(b).   [175] ibid, art 123(23).

[176] Contrast art 5(1)(c) of the original and revised SADC Treaties.

[177] 2001 SADC Treaty, art 5(1)(b).

[178] OAU/AU Declaration on the Principles Governing Democratic Elections in Africa—AHG/DECL.1(XXXVIII) and the AU Guidelines for African Union Electoral Observation and Monitoring Missions—EX/CL/35(III) Annex II.

supplements thereto that have gradually extended their mandates to clearly embrace these objectives.[179] With the establishment of the OAU Mechanism for Conflict Prevention, Management and Resolution (in 1993) and the AU Peace and Security Council (in 2003), regional arrangements have increasingly echoed the continental approach in this area. RECs increasingly act in concert with and under authorization of the PSC,[180] underscoring the primacy of reliance on subregional security arrangements.

Even before the ECOWAS Treaty was amended in 1993, two protocols, supplementary to the 1975 Treaty, illustrate this shift. One is the 1978 Protocol on Non-Aggression, which seeks to ensure respect for territorial integrity and independence of member states, and the other is the 1981 Protocol on Mutual Assistance in Defence,[181] under which member states pledge to assist each other against armed threats or aggression.[182] In 1978, a meeting of Heads of State and Government also adopted a declaration calling for a moratorium on the importation, exportation, and manufacture of light weapons in ECOWAS member states. Under the 1999 Protocol relating to the Mechanism for Conflict Prevention, Management, Resolution, Peace-Keeping and Security, ECOWAS set up an infrastructure in the form of a Defence and Security Commission, an Early Warning System, Council of Elders, supplement to ECOMOG. ECOWAS also adopted a Moratorium on Small Arms in West Africa.

In 2001, SADC adopted the Protocol on Politics, Defence and Security Cooperation (OPDS Protocol), which entered into force in 2004.[183] Its mandate includes human rights matters.[184] Due to tensions within SADC, it has not been invoked on a consistent basis.

---

[179] See eg the Agreement establishing IGAD (art 18A), which provides that 'member countries shall act collectively to preserve peace, security and stability, *which are essential prerequisites for economic development and social progress*' (emphasis added).

[180] See eg Communiqué of the 24th meeting of the PSC, AU Doc PSC/PR/Comm(XXIV) 7 February 2005, para 3, authorizing the deployment of an IGAD Peace Support Mission in Somalia; and Communiqué of the 25th meeting of the PSC, AU Doc PSC/PR/Comm(XXV) 25 February 2005, paras 4 and 5, mandating ECOWAS to 'take all such measures as it deems necessary to restore constitutional legality in Togo' and endorsing the sanctions imposed by ECOWAS on the *de facto* Togolese authorities.

[181] Repr in full by M Weller, *Regional Peace-Keeping and International Enforcement: The Liberian Crisis* (Cambridge: Cambridge University Press, 1994) 18–24.

[182] Protocol relating to Mutual Assistance in Defence, arts 2 and 3.

[183] The OPDS Protocol establishes the SADC Organ on Politics, Defence and Security Cooperation (OPDS), which, amongst other objectives, is aimed at encouraging the observance of international human rights by member states. For a background to security issues in the sub-region and a call for its establishment, see Amnesty International, *Southern Africa: Policing and Human Rights in SADC* <http://web.amnesty.org/library/index/ENGAFR030021997?open&of=ENG-390>, 1 April 1997 (30 April 2007). By 31 July 2006, Angola, the DRC, Swaziland and Zambia were yet to ratify the OPDS Protocol.

[184] One of its objectives is to 'promote and enhance the development of democratic institutions and practices within member states, and to encourage the observance of universal human rights as provided for in the Charters and Conventions of the OAU and United Nations' (see Amnesty International (n 183 above) 10). See also 'The Birth of Sahringon' *African Topics* (April–May 1997) 22.

The need to expand economic objectives to include peace and security concerns was most acute in Central Africa. Reflecting the common understanding of REC at the time, the 1983 Treaty did not make specific mention of pace and security. Having been plagued by inter- and intra-state conflict, the ECCAS Heads of State and Government in 1994 adopted a Non-aggression Pact, and in 1999 established a Central African Council of Peace and Security (*Conseil de Paix, de Sécurité et de Stabilité de l'Afrique Centrale* (COPAX)) under its Declaration on Peace, Security and Stability in Central Africa. Under COPAX, a Defence and Security Commission, a Central African Multinational Force (FOMAC), and a Central African Early Warning Mechanism (MARAC) have been set up. FOMAC may be involved in peace-keeping, the restoration of peace, humanitarian intervention 'following a humanitarian disaster', and enforcing sanctions. MARAC is responsible for collecting and analysing data in order to forestall conflict. While ECCAS was involved in solving conflict in Chad and São Tomé e Príncipe,[185] it has been less successful in the DRC where three of its members have been involved. Another Central African REC, CEMAC, has been maintaining a peace-keeping mission in the CAR since 2000.[186]

The EAC has not developed any specific institution, but is committed to the promotion of peace, security, and stability in the region.[187]

Two African countries most ridden with conflict, Somalia and the Sudan, are IGAD members. It should therefore come as no surprise that IGAD embraced peace and security concerns in its mandate.[188] IGAD has involved itself in the peace processes in the Sudan and Somalia.[189] Its attempts contributed to the eventual Comprehensive Peace Agreement of 2005 in Sudan, but its efforts in Somalia have largely been foiled by the persistence of the power struggle between warring parties. It is also in this region of Africa that the threat of terrorism has been most pronounced. Although the issue of terrorism may be overplayed and manipulated in the 'Global War on Terror', it is undeniable that terrorism may lead to violence and the deprivation of the basic rights to life and bodily security of populations. Responding to these issues, members of IGAD in 2004 adopted the Khartoum Declaration on Terrorism and Transnational Organized Crime.

Conflict casts its shadow over the IGAD area. Not only the situation in Somalia and Sudan, but also the aftermath of the inter-state war between two members (Ethiopia and Eritrea) and a great number of endemic cross-border pastoralist conflicts, have given rise to the adoption of the Conflict Early Warning and Response Mechanism (CEWARN). This has been done as a Protocol to the IGAD agreement and entered into force after four ratifications. Under the aegis of IGAD, an East African Brigade has been created as part of the AU Standby Force established

---

[185] 'La CEEAC va aider à résoudre la crise gouvernementale a Sao Tome' *Le Regard Africain* (14 March 2004).   [186] Oosthuizen (n 50 above) 92.

[187] EAC Treaty, art 5(3)(e).   [188] IGAD Charter, art 7(g).

[189] See eg A Alao, 'The Role of African Regional and Subregional Organizations in Conflict Prevention and Resolution' <http://www.jha.ac/~articles/uo23.htm> (30 April 2007).

in terms of the Protocol establishing the AU Peace and Security Council. This force will interface with the AU, and can act on the instructions of the AU Peace and Security Council. The office of its coordinating body is in Addis Ababa.

9 RECs have become Involved in Maintenance of Peace and Humanitarian Intervention

Two RECs, ECOWAS and SADC, have gone further than other RECs by converting the commitment towards peace and security into an involvement in peace-keeping, peace enforcement, and humanitarian intervention.

9.1 ECOWAS

Inter-state conflicts between Burkina Faso and Mali (in 1987) and between Mauritania and Senegal (in 1989), as well as the internal conflict in one of the ECOWAS member states, Liberia, prompted the ECOWAS Summit to establish the ECOWAS Mediation Standing Committee in 1990.[190] As far as Liberia is concerned, initial attempts at a cease-fire and a national coalition failed. In 1991 the Yamoussoukrou agreement was reached, providing for a cease-fire and elections. ECOWAS imposed sanctions on the National Patriotic Front of Liberia (NPFL) when they failed to keep to the agreement. ECOWAS efforts were supplemented by the UN, when the Security Council endorsed these decisions by ECOWAS, and the UN Observer Mission in Liberia (UNOMIL) was established.

A military force, the ECOWAS Cease-Fire Monitoring Group (ECOMOG),[191] consisting of troops from member states, was also set up. Not all the ECOWAS member states approved of the decision of the Mediation Standing Committee to undertake military action in Liberia. Some regarded the establishment of ECO-MOG as an interference in the domestic affairs of a member state. However, its establishment finds legal support in the subsequent approval by the ECOWAS Authority of Heads of State and Government of the Committee's decisions.

The establishment of ECOMOG is significant, in particular as far as human rights issues are concerned, for the following reasons: It marks a shift in the activities of ECOWAS away from economic integration towards the promotion of human rights. The intervention was directed not only at securing lives by ending the massacres, but ultimately at the restoration of democratic governance and institutions.[192] ECOMOG, as the first regional peace-keeping initiative on the African continent,[193] may be regarded as indicative of an emerging trend in which Africa endeavours to solve its own problems. Strict adherence to notions of state sovereignty would have made these efforts impossible. This operation is premised on the

[190] A/DEC.9/5/90; see also the later ECOMOG force in Sierra Leone.
[191] On ECOMOG, see Weller (n 181 above) 94; F Ouguergouz, 'Liberia' (1994) 2 *AYBIL* 208; and E Kwakwa, 'Internal Conflicts in Africa: Is there a Right of Humanitarian Intervention?' (1994) 2 *AYBIL* 9.   [192] See sources in Weller (n 181 above) xxii.
[193] El Kadiri (n 32 above) 146

assumption that internal events in one state are of concern to other states and may allow them, under certain circumstances, to interfere. The UN force, UNOMIL, was deployed as the first UN peace-keeping mission undertaken in cooperation with a peace-keeping operation already established by another international organization.[194] This illustrates the extent to which the interests of the UN and African subregional organizations may coincide.

ECOMOG also intervened in Sierra Leone in 1997 to restore peace and to provide humanitarian assistance in the aftermath of the overthrow of the Kabbah government. The intervention and attempts to reinstate Kabbah arguably were justified on the basis of consent, under article 58 of the ECOWAS Treaty, and on the ground that human rights abuses against civilians were to be curbed.[195] In any event, the UN Security Council subsequently approved the intervention.[196]

Although the contribution of ECOWAS in curbing the conflict is undeniable, it is not without controversy. Dominated by Nigerian troops and financially dependent on Nigerian resources, in the eyes of many the Sierra Leone effort became an extension of Nigerian foreign policy. It even became personalized, as the Nigerian leader, Abacha, himself a dictator and persistent human rights violator, was perceived to be manipulating the events in Sierra Leone to sanitize himself in international eyes. On the ground, troops committed atrocities and were implicated in illegal mining and trade in alluvial diamonds.[197]

Consolidating peace-keeping efforts and retrospectively providing an unequivocal legal basis for ECOMOG interventions, ECOWAS in 1999 adopted the Protocol relating to the Mechanism for Conflict Prevention, Management, Resolution, Peace-Keeping and Security (Conflict Prevention Protocol). A Mediation and Security Council was established to oversee humanitarian assistance and peace-building and to monitor ECOMOG's role in both. This body is guided by a respect for human rights and humanitarian law, as embodied in the African Charter.[198] The greatest significance of this Protocol is that it formally establishes and provides a legal basis for ECOMOG intervention.[199] Neither the initial nor the revised ECOWAS Treaty allows for humanitarian or other intervention in a member state. Under this Protocol, ECOWAS may intervene to alleviate human suffering, and the Mechanism may be triggered by serious and massive human rights violations and when a democratically elected government has been overthrown.[200] Institutionally, there is an evolution away from the sanctity of territorial integrity foregrounded in

[194] Ouguergouz (n 191 above) 208.

[195] J Levitt, 'Humanitarian Intervention by Regional Actors in Internal Conflicts: The Case of ECOWAS in Liberia and Sierra Leone' (1998) 12 *Temple Intl and Comparative L J* 363.

[196] Resolution 1289 S/RES/1289 (2000).

[197] TM Shaw, 'The Future of New Regionalism in Africa: Beyond Governance, Human Security/ Development and Beyond' in JA Grant and F Söderbaum (eds), *The New Regionalism in Africa* (Ashgate: Aldershot, 2003) 203.

[198] 1999 Protocol relating to the Mechanism for Conflict Prevention, Management, Resolution, Peace-Keeping and Security, art 2.   [199] See ibid, art 17.

[200] ibid, art 25.

the 1978 Protocol on Non-aggression, to the inroads in to sovereignty that the Conflict Resolution Protocol allows.

Since the adoption of the Conflict Prevention Protocol, ECOMOG was deployed in Guinea-Bissau, in order to maintain peace and oversee the transition to a government of national unity,[201] and also in Côte d'Ivoire. In its 2004 Resolution on Côte d'Ivoire, the African Commission noted the 'laudable role of ECOWAS in its efforts to bring peace to Côte d'Ivoire'.[202]

9.2 SADC

Given the circumstances of its birth, SADC from the outset foresaw for itself a role in the defence of peace and security.[203] It still took many years to agree on an institutional mechanism to deal with peace and security. In the meantime, violence erupted in Lesotho when the opposition's protest against the outcome of the 1998 elections, alleging fraud and asking for an annulment, fell on deaf ears. Allied forces from two SADC states, Botswana and South Africa, intervened to restore order and support the newly-elected government. This intervention remains shrouded in controversy, for two reasons. First, Was the authority requesting intervention legitimate? This question arose because it was the newly (re)instated government, rather than the head of state (the President), that requested intervention. Secondly, did SADC mandate the intervention? This question arises because only two members intervened. Much more controversial is the intervention by Zimbabwe, followed by Angola and Namibia, in the DRC, on the request of Zimbabwe, motivated by a search for subregional hegemony and resource riches. The intervention, initially not authorized by SADC, led to a stand-off between South Africa and Zimbabwe, which was eventually resolved when President Mandela announced that SADC unanimously supported the intervention.[204]

Much in the same way as with ECOWAS, the SADC Protocol on Politics, Defence and Security Cooperation entitles SADC to undertake 'enforcement action' as a matter of last resort. Rather euphemistically, the Protocol mandates the Organ on Politics, Defence and Security to 'seek to resolve' significant inter-state and intra-state conflict in SADC members. Significance arises from situations that threaten regional peace and security and amount to gross human rights violations.

On the record of these two RECs, the question must be posed whether it is appropriate and feasible to extend the mandate of these arrangements to include peace-enforcement and peace-keeping. As Van Nieuwkerk argues, the immediate past experience and inherent expectations show that the 'politics of power' and the 'politics of greed' are likely to frustrate the functioning of fully-fledged regional

---

[201] See SC Resolution 1216 (1998), adopted unanimously, asking the UN Secretary-General to Make Recommendations on Possible UN Role in Peace Process in Guinea-Bissau.

[202] ACHPR /Res.67(XXXV)04: Resolution on Côte d'Ivoire.

[203] SADC Treaty, arts 4(b) and 5(1)(c).

[204] N Patel, 'Conflict Resolution through Regional Organisations in Africa' in E Moloka (ed), *A United States of Africa?* (Pretoria: Africa Institute of South Africa, 2001) 354.

security arrangements.[205] Factors such as the likelihood of the exercise of hegemonic power outside legal constraints, the dubious effect of troops on the ground, bureaucratic hurdles and financial strains all point to the difficulties that may arise when RECs take on security concerns. A more feasible approach would be to focus on containing and preventing conflict at the subregional level, and to defer to UN or AU intervention when required. Only when that fails, should subregional military forces be deployed. So far, military force has been used too easily, but at the same time also too haphazardly.

10 Integration Processes are Increasingly being Democratized by Establishing Regional Parliaments and through the Involvement of Civil Society

Regional integration not only entails closer institutional links between states, but also between people. In a relentless top-down approach, a small political elite dictates how the contours of integration develop, leaving ordinary Africans with little sense that this grand project serves the public good. National Parliaments have played a minimal role and are often sidelined in the process of adopting subregional legal instruments. The human face, or 'social dimension', of integration has so far hardly been visible. At both the continental and subregional level, nationals have been marginalized in the process of integration—despite the impact of liberalizing trade on labour and other aspects of the lives of ordinary citizens. Citizens are conscripted into the project of subregional integration without an underlying process of socialization. Even the occasional reference to the objective of enhancing 'long-standing historical, social and cultural links among the peoples of the region'[206] is little more than a meaningless wants.

Without popular buy-in, the process will be perceived as an elitist imposition. Information about these institutions has not been integrated into educational curricula. Their visibility and access to them by the general public are further constrained by the geographic centralization of bodies in one or a few states.[207]

10.1 Subregional Parliaments

As a pluralistic and open deliberative space, subregional parliaments present fora for general greater awareness, public debate, and broad participation. The number of subregional parliaments has grown steadily. At the moment, three RECs (SADC, EAC, and ECOWAS) have functioning community parliamentary structures, while others have seen the emergence of some fledgling institution or

[205] A Van Nieuwkerk, 'Regionalism into Globalism? War into Peace? SADC and ECOWAS Compared' (2001) 10 *African Security Rev* <http://www.iss.co.za/pubs/ASR/10No2/Vannieuwkerk. html> (31 July 2006).   [206] 2001 SADC Treaty, art 5(1)(h).
[207] See the call by the Zanzibar Chief Minister that sub-offices of the EAC should be established in each member state: *People's Daily Online* <http://english.people.com.cn> (24 July 2006).

at least allow for such a possibility.[208] Under ECCAS, for example, a more informal network of central African Parliamentarians has been established.

Although not provided for under the SADC Treaty, the SADC Parliamentary Forum (PF) was launched in 1996 as a separate but intimately related institution. Its membership is open to national parliaments of the SADC member states.[209] Each parliament must ensure the fair representation of women, and all political parties to the Forum. The Forum has its seat in Windhoek, Namibia. Organs of the SADC PF are a plenary assembly, an executive committee, the office of the Secretary-General, and standing committees. Although the Forum is mandated not only to promote economic cooperation, but also to advance democracy, the rule of law, and human rights in the subregion, its competences remain very limited. SADC PF conducts election monitoring, using its own set of guidelines (the 2001 Norms and Standards for Elections in the SADC Region) and not that of SADC. The relationship between SADC and the SADC PF is sometimes strained, as exemplified in its criticism of the 2000 and 2002 elections in Zimbabwe. More clarity is therefore required about the relationship between SADC and the SADC PF, especially in this respect.

The newly constituted EAC Treaty of 1999 introduced the East African Legislative Assembly as the main legislative organ of the East African Community.[210] Apart from its legislative functions, the Assembly aims at enhancing cooperation with the legislatures of partner states on matters of common interest. The Assembly is also responsible for approving the budgets of the Community. However, before approving the budgets, the Assembly has to examine and evaluate the annual reports of the Community. Another function of the Assembly is discussing all the affairs of the Community, and forwarding the recommendations to the Council of Ministers. It is also one of the functions of the Assembly to recommend nominees for the position of the Secretary-General and other officers of the Community.

The ECOWAS Community Parliament, established under the Revised ECOWAS Treaty and a separate Protocol relating to the Parliament,[211] started operating in 2001 with its headquarters in Abuja, Nigeria. In principle, members of the ECOWAS Parliament are elected through direct universal suffrage by citizens of ECOWAS member states. However, states are allowed a period of grace to put such measures in place, pending which National Assemblies of member states assign members from among themselves.[212] It lacks 'legislative' powers, as it is left to national parliaments to decide whether they will give domestic effect to the Parliament's advisory or recommendatory resolutions (or 'bills').

---

[208] eg a treaty to establish an UEMOA Parliament was signed in 2003, and a founding Protocol for an ECCAS Network of Parliamentarians was adopted in 2002.

[209] The account of the Parliamentary Forum is based on information in (1997) 34 *Africa Research Bulletin* 12636.   [210] EAC Treaty, art 49.

[211] ECOWAS Protocol A/P2/8/94, 9 August 1994; signed in 1994 and entered into force in 2002.

[212] <http://www.ecowas.int/> (31 July 2006). ECOWAS Protocol, A/P2/8/94, n 211 above, art 7(1). See also the ECOWAS Parliament's Resolution relating to Enhancement of the Powers of the Community Parliament', 13 September 2002, in which it called on the Heads of State and Government

The potential role of these institutions in giving a meaningful voice to Africa's people and in advancing human rights is constrained by three factors. These constraints relate to the *composition* of these Parliaments, their *mandates*, and the *status of the outcomes* of their deliberations.

Members of an REC parliament may be elected directly, as is now the case in the European Parliament, or may be selected from among sitting national MPs. So far, membership of subregional Parliaments in Africa has not been by way of direct elections, but has been derived from existing membership of the legislatures of the participating countries. This indirect form of representation hinders popular participation and hampers institutional legitimacy, especially where a culture of democratic elections has not taken root at the national level.

The mandates of these Parliaments are not concerned explicitly with human rights or with normative oversight. However, in so far as reference is made to them among the guiding principles, human rights may play a role. These institutions are still embryonic, and need more clearly to define and develop their roles to include executive oversight and the promotion and protection of human rights.

At the national level, there is no doubt that parliaments adopt binding legislation. The same certainty does not exist at the subregional level. Generally, the outcomes of parliamentary debates do not bind member states. At the moment, the EAC Legislative Assembly is the only subregional Parliament that has a law-making mandate. The outcomes of the debates of other subregional Parliaments are advisory. As Quashigah points out, advisory powers are insufficient 'for the regional parliaments to act as the vanguard of human rights as we hope they can become'.[213] Over time, however, advisory powers may and should develop into binding legislative competences. Even under the European system, the European Parliament did not initially (in 1951) have binding powers. Over time, the Parliament was first given the power to reject the draft budget of the Council of Ministers, and later the competence effectively to veto legislation introduced by the Council.[214]

10.2 Involvement of Civil Society

At both the national and supra-national levels, political or economic reform driven by political elites lacks legitimacy and will remain superficial. Proponents of the 'new regionalism in Africa' have argued against a formalistic state-centred approach to regional integration, emphasizing instead the role of non-state actors as civil societies in regionalism.[215] Civil society participation will enhance the social and political legitimacy of integration.[216] Unfortunately, the involvement of NGOs in establishing subregional norms and institutions has been extremely limited.

---

to fix a terminal date... for the transitional period' (<http://www.afrimap.org/english/inages/treaty/file423afdfd15036.pdf> (30 April 2007)).

[213] n 5 above.

[214] TC Salmon, 'The Structure, Institutions, and Powers of the EU' in J Gower (ed), *The European Union Handbook* (London: Fitzroy Dearborn, 2002) 16, 26.   [215] Shaw (n 197 above) 197.

[216] F Jonyo, 'The Role of Civil Society in Regional Integration' in Ajulu (n 36 above) 111, 121.

The structure and functioning of the RECs leave little possibility of interfacing with civil society. Some openings exist and tentative steps have been taken, though. For example, the EAC recognizes explicitly, as part of its first operational principle, the importance of 'people-centred co-operation'.[217] However, elsewhere the EAC Treaty expands on the contribution of non-state market-associated actors (the 'private sector') rather than that of social role players (CBOs).[218] IGAD established and has taken some steps towards the establishment of the IGAD-NGO/ CSO Forum. The West African Civil Society Forum, consisting of the executive secretary of ECOWAS, national human rights institutions, and NGOs, meets annually on a rotational basis in member states to discuss human rights issues of relevance to the region.[219] ECOWAS has further formalized the status of NGOs,[220] and created the ECOWAS Economic and Social Council, composed of 'various categories of economic and social activity',[221] but whose role in the ECOWAS institutional framework is not clear.

However, some tension between the state's and the institution's role in 'conscripting' or 'ensuring' NGO involvement, on the one hand, and the spontaneous involvement and ownership of the process of including civil society, on the other, will continue. At the subregional level, NGOs and civil society organs spanning the region and targeting wider interests than narrow national interests, are required. Despite an initial shortage, subregional NGOs or national NGOs with a subregional or pan-African focus are starting to take root.

Efforts to secure the place of human rights within the activities of SADC have depended largely on NGOs. For this reason, the creation of the Southern African Human Rights NGO Network (SAHRINGON) is important. This entity was established between over 60 NGOs in the region. The objectives of the Network include 'forming a platform to lobby SADC members to prioritise human rights issues'.[222] Other subregional NGOs include *Rencontre africaine pour la defense des droits de l'Homme* (RADDHO) in West Africa, and the Arab Organization for Human Rights (in North Africa). A more rare phenomenon is a pan-African NGO, such as the *Union Inter-africaine des droits de l'Homme* (UIDH).

NGOs working on gender issues and regional women's associations advocate the inclusion of women in the process of integration and women's equality and development. In Central Africa, for example, the *Réseau pour les femmes de l'Afrique*

---

[217] EAC Treaty, art 7(1)(a).   [218] EAC Treaty, art 127.

[219] African Network on Debt and Development, Open Society Initiative for Southern Africa, and Oxfam GB, 'Towards a People-Driven African Union: Current Obstacles and New Opportunities' (2007) <http://www.afrimap.org> (31 January 2007) 27–8 (indicating that the Forum is a membership organization, and not an organ of ECOWAS, and that it had held three annual forums).

[220] Decision A/DEC.9/8/94 establishing regulations for granting to Non-Governmental Organizations the status of observer within the institutions of ECOWAS.

[221] <http://www.iss.co.za/Af/RegOrg/unity_to_union/ecowasprof.htm> (31 July 2006); this body has not yet been established.

[222] On its establishment, see 'The Birth of Sahringon' (n 184 above) 22.

Centrale (RESEFAC) have brought into the spotlight issues of capacity building and 'gender mainstreaming'.[223]

Effective civil society participation suffers from a lack of mechanisms institutionalizing its role and from the predominance of commercial aspects of integration at the expense of a 'social agenda' in the architecture of RECs.

E Towards a Future Merger

In the grand scheme of the AU/AEC and NEPAD, the RECs are building blocks for full integration in the future. They must be strengthened and consolidated with a view to their merging into a single institution, as the borders between the subregional blocs fade away over time. Already in 1998, the AEC and some RECs concluded a Protocol to strengthen and promote closer cooperation between RECs.[224] However, overlapping membership constrains this ideal. Many African countries are members of more than one regional grouping. Of the 53 AU member states, 30 belong to two RECs, and 16 to three.[225] One country, the DRC, for example belongs to four RECs, namely CEPGL, COMESA, ECCAS, and SADC. In AU Chairperson Konaré's words, this 'leads to wasteful duplication of effort, increases the burdens imposed on member governments, and diminishes our collective success'.[226]

For some time, however, rather than fading away, RECs have asserted their independence and showed some intolerance towards consolidation. In the 1990s, for example, PTA/COMESA's efforts at merger with SADC were rebuffed,[227] culminating in even greater regional rivalry, and in the expansion of the mandate of IGAD. The problem with proliferation is that states may have varying obligations in respect of integration. Such duplication may increase benefits, but it is also more costly. Consolidating membership will also mean that mandates of institutions such as REC Courts will be harmonized, establishing legal certainty for investors and Community citizens alike.

Conscious of this proliferation, the AU/AEC assigned five pillar RECs, with four sub-groups. These pillars are UMA, ECOWAS (with UEMOA and WAMZ as sub-groups), ECCAS (with CEMAC as sub-group), COMESA, and SADC (with SACU as sub-group). The AU Assembly has taken further steps to address this problem. In July 2006, after it had recognized eight RECs, the AU Assembly placed a moratorium on the recognition of further RECs within the framework of

---

[223] 2004 ECA Study (n 25 above) 7.

[224] Protocol on the relationship between the African Economic Community and the Regional Economic Communities, repr in (1998) 10 *RADIC* 157–69.

[225] Economic Commission for Africa, 'Defining Priorities for Integration', Third African Development Forum 3–8 March 2002, ECA Addis Ababa.

[226] 'Foreword' to 2004 ECA Study (n 25 above) x.   [227] Mshomba (n 7 above) 186.

the AU.[228] Following the first conference of African Ministers in charge of integration earlier in 2006, the Assembly further decided that such meetings should take place at regular intervals of at least one year.[229]

The challenge is to bridge rhetorical commitment and the reality on the ground. There should be an increased focus on the way in which the process of integration affects the lives of ordinary Africans. National parliaments and civil society organs should be involved in law-making, public debate, and awareness-raising. Referendums should, for example, be held to ensure broad acceptance and legitimacy of closer integration. States should be prepared increasingly to cede sovereignty to RECs, in preparation for eventually giving up sovereignty to African-wide institutions. Cession of sovereignty must progressively extend to the heart of regionalism— the treatment of Africa's people, and the promotion and protection of their human rights.

The post-Westphalian nation state, premised on the notion of a culturally distinct population, almost inevitably displays coercive homogenizing tendencies.[230] When independent Africa in the 1960s saw the rise of centrifugal forces, sometimes occasioning internecine conflict, international law provided the newly independent states with the lifeline of *uti possidetis*, forged in the context of bloody conquest and nation formation in Europe. African diversity and difference were perceived as threats to relentless processes of establishing insular nation states acceptable to the international community of states.

Subregional arrangements provide a feasible option of 'disaggregating' the problematic structures of the inherited colonial state in Africa.[231] Multinational statehood could create a space in which a strengthened central locus of functionality and legitimacy supplements greater tolerance and respect for diversity. Paradoxically, the loss of state power to a supra-national institution may coincide with greater empowerment of the sub-national sphere. The very essence of the subregional is that it brings together multiple 'nations', all of which are part of the new arrangement without preconditions of amalgamation or homogenization. The more prominent role human rights can play in this process, as an integral and not separate part of subregional integration, the more likely it is that the economic benefits and advances of integration may be given a more solid footing in genuine human rights-based democracies.

---

[228] Decision on the Institutionalization of the Conference of African Ministers in Charge of Integration Doc EX.Cl/282 (IX)Assembly/AU/Dec.112(VII).

[229] Decision on the Institutionalization of the Conference of African Ministers in Charge of Integration, Assembly/AU/Dec.113(VII) (July 2006).

[230] See eg OC Okafor, 'After Martyrdom: International Law, Sub-state Groups, and the Construction of Legitimate Statehood in Africa' (2000) 41 *Harvard Intl L J* 503.

[231] M Mutua, 'Putting Humpty Dumpy Back Together Again: The Dilemma of the Post-Colonial African State' (1995) 21 *Brooklyn J Intl L* 520, 536.

PART V

THE NATIONAL LEVEL

13

Domestication of International Human Rights Law

The ultimate test of international human rights law is the extent to which it takes root at the national level, and its ability to flourish in the soil of states and to bear fruit in the lives of people. Throughout this work it has been acknowledged that the national sphere is the pre-eminent domain of concern. In this chapter, the process of bringing home international law is first mapped in general terms, by looking at the constitutional framework of African states, and specifically at the domestic application of the African Charter. The focus in the next chapter (Chapter 14) switches to poverty, one of the bleakest features in the African landscape, and the role (and potential role) in its eradication played by justiciable socio-economic rights in the domestic law of African states. As these rights have been articulated as justiciable in the African regional, but only to a very limited extent in the global, human rights system, their domestic justiciability is both a reflection and an extension of international human rights law. In Chapter 15, the national legal response of African states to HIV and AIDS is assessed as a supplement to international law's hesitant contribution to this most pressing issue of our time.

The ratification of international human rights treaties is of significance only if their provisions have an impact at the national level. Usually, the main obligation of a state party is to *recognize* the rights in the treaty and to *give effect* to them by adopting *legislative* and *other measures*.[1] Three questions are posed to ascertain the extent to which international human rights law has been domesticated in African states: (1) Are international human rights norms part of domestic law? (2) If so, where do international human rights norms feature in the hierarchy of the municipal national legal order? (3) Have domestic courts 'applied' international human rights norms in their decisions? Answers to these three questions are now attempted.

A Are International Human Rights Norms Part of Domestic Law?

According to international law theory, the extent to which the provisions of international human rights treaties have become part of a particular country's domestic law correlates with the status enjoyed by international law in that domestic legal system.

As far as international treaties are concerned, they are expected to become an integral part of national law upon ratification in states following the monist tradition. Dualist states should in theory be clearly distinguishable, because international norms, in principle, need to be domesticated before they become part of national law. However, as the discussion below illustrates, this rigid distinction is not played out in practice.[2]

As the norms of customary international human rights law are by and large contained in the constitutions of African states,[3] the discussion that follows does not delve into their status under domestic constitutional orders. Suffice it to state that, under the monist theory, customary international law also forms an 'automatic' part

---

[1] See eg African Charter, art 1.

[2] O Tshosa, *National Law and International Human Rights Law. Cases of Botswana, Namibia and Zimbabwe* (Aldershot: Ashgate, 2001) 270 notes a 'lack of consistency, regularity and uniformity in the application of these theories'.

[3] See Ch 1 above for a 'listing' of these rights, and C Heyns (ed), *Human Rights Law in Africa* (vol 2) (Leiden: Martinus Nijhoff, 2004), in which the constitutional provisions dealing with human rights of African states are contained.

of national law,[4] but that the position in dualist countries is less certain. With a few exceptions, the constitutions of countries in the latter category do not stipulate what the status of customary international law is,[5] but it may be assumed that, following the common law tradition, custom automatically becomes part of national law.

1 Monism is as Monism Does: The Fallacy of Immediate Direct Incorporation

In 'monist' states, following French constitutional law,[6] once a treaty has been ratified and published 'externally', it becomes part of internal law. At least in theory, no legislative action is needed to lower the second storey level of international law norms to the ground floor level of national law. In line with this tradition, international human rights law is 'directly incorporated' into and made an 'integral part' of national law in most of civil law Africa, either in the Preamble to,[7] or elsewhere in the Constitution.[8]

---

[4] Cape Verde Constitution 1992, art 11(1) refers to 'international law . . . in force', thus encompassing customary international law, as being an 'integral' part of the legal system.

[5] Among the exceptions are the South African Constitution 1996, s 231(4); and the Malawi Constitution 1995, s 211; see also J Dugard, *International Law: A South African Perspective* (Cape Town: Juta, 3rd edn, 2005), who shows strong support for the monist approach to customary international law among South African courts (51).

[6] The Constitution of France 1958, art 53 requires that treaties need to be approved or ratified by a law (*loi*) before they 'take effect'. Art 55 provides as follows: 'Treaties or agreements duly ratified or approved prevail over Acts of Parliament, subject, in regard to each agreement or treaty, to its application by the other party'. Art 54 provides for a mechanism to determine whether there is a conflict between any part of a treaty and the Constitution. If the *Conseil Constitutionnel* holds that a conflict exists, authorization to ratify or approve the treaty may only be given after a revision of the Constitution has been undertaken. After an amendment in 1974, the question whether such a conflict exists may be referred to the *Conseil Constitutionnel* not only by a limited number of powerful individuals, but also by 60 members of the National Assembly or 60 members of the Senate (see D Maus, 'The Birth of Judicial Review of Legislation in France' in E Smith (ed), *Constitutional Justice under Old Constitutions* (The Hague: Kluwer, 1995) 113; J Bell, S Boyron, and S Whittaker, *Principles of French Law* (Oxford: Oxford University Press, 1998) 152–4).

[7] See eg Madagascar Constitution 1992, Preamble, which invokes the African Charter, the ICCPR, the ICSECR, CEDAW, and CRC in its Preamble as an 'integral part' of its law; the Preamble to the Constitution of Benin 1990 reaffirms a commitment to the principles of participatory democracy and human rights as defined in the UN Charter, the Universal Declaration, and the African Charter, adding that those provisions 'make up an integral part of this present Constitution and of Benin law and have a value superior to the internal law'; Burkina Faso 1991 Constitution, Preamble; Central African Republic Constitution 1995, Preamble (affirming international human rights treaties but not making them part of the Constitution or internal law); Chad Constitution 1996, Preamble; Guinea Constitution 1990, Preamble (also not integrating the Preamble into the Constitution); Mali Constitution 1992, Preamble (not made part of the Constitution); Niger Constitution 1999, Preamble (Preamble not made part of Constitution); and the Togo Constitution 1992, Preamble.

[8] eg Constitution of Niger 1999, art 132 (treaties ratified have superior authority to that of legislation once ratified), and similar provisions in the Constitution of Burundi 2004, art 292 and the Constitution of Cameroon 1996, art 45. For a non-francophone civil law country, see Constitution of Cape Verde 1992, art 12(2) (treaties 'shall be in force' upon ratification, and all 'general or common international law shall be an integral part' of its judicial system). When there is a formal requirement

The question may be posed as to the legal implications of invoking international instruments, such as the 1789 Declaration of the Rights of Man and the Citizen or the African Charter, as part of a constitution's preamble, as Gabon for example has done.[9] The answer is tied closely to developments under French constitutional law. Despite the inclusion of the Declaration and a set of fundamental rights in the Preamble to the 1958 French Constitution, and not in its 'body', the *Conseil Constitutionnel* did not engage in judicial review on the basis of a violation of human rights until 1971, when it declared a law unconstitutional for the first time. Only then was the principle settled that 'constitutional review involves taking into consideration the "fundamental rights" inherited from 1789 and strengthened in 1946'.[10] This reasoning elevated the hortatory status of preambular human rights in the 1958 French Constitution to enforceable guarantees. By providing for human rights only in its Preamble, while at the same time stipulating that the Preamble is an integral (and thus presumably enforceable) part of the Constitution, the 1996 Cameroon Constitution reflects the French position. The judiciaries of other civil law states have not, however, followed the precedent of French law or the principle in the Cameroon Constitution.[11]

Is the situation different when the status of international human rights law is determined in the body of the Constitution, rather than in the Preamble? To answer this question, one may consider the practical application of the monist theory as set out in the Senegalese Constitution 2001, which mirrors the 1958 French Constitution, in the following words:[12] 'Treaties or agreements duly ratified shall, upon their publication, have an authority superior to that of the laws, subject, for each treaty and agreement, to its application by the other party'. In 1986, Senegal ratified the Convention against Torture and Other Cruel, Inhuman or Degrading Treatment or Punishment (CAT). In theory, then, CAT's provisions form an integral part of Senegalese law, and should therefore be 'directly enforceable' in Senegalese courts. If there is a conflict, international law prevails over ordinary law, but appears to be inferior to the Senegalese Constitution.

However, the Senegalese judiciary's involvement in drawn-out efforts to prosecute Hissène Habré for atrocities committed in Chad when he was that country's

---

of 'publication', as is required by art 147 of the Constitution of Benin 1990, judicial reliance on treaty provisions is not possible until that prerequisite has been met. In Décision DCC 03-009 of 19 February 2003, the Constitutional Court of Benin held that the Convention on the Rights of the Child was not part of the 'positive law' of Benin because it has not been published.

[9] Constitution of Gabon 1991, Preamble (affirming its 'adherence' to human rights as set out in, amongst other instruments, the 1789 Declaration); on the status of fundamental rights declared in a preamble, see *Re Akoto* (1961) GLR 523 (in Ghana, the Court found that it imposes a moral obligation on the President) and *Société United Docks v Government of Mauritius* [1985] CLR (Constitutional and Administrative Law Reports) 801 (where the Preamble was regarded as an 'enacting section' and was given effect in Mauritius).

[10] Maus (n 6 above) 142; see also J Bell, *French Constitutional Law* (Oxford: Clarendon Press, 1992) 273–4.

[11] See the example of Gabon (n 9 above).

[12] Art 98.

head of state demonstrates that formal adherence to monism does not necessarily guarantee 'direct enforcement'.[13] After fleeing Chad, Habré was charged in a Senegalese court with complicity in crimes against humanity, acts of torture, and barbarity. It was argued on behalf of Habré that the prosecution did not 'cite any legal text' that renders torture 'committed by a foreigner outside of the territory regardless of the nationality of the victims' criminal under Senegalese law.[14] As a state party to CAT, Senegal is, according to article 5, under an obligation to 'take such measures as may be necessary to establish its jurisdiction' over offences of torture 'where the alleged offender is present in any territory under its jurisdiction and it does not extradite him'.[15] However, relying on article 4 of CAT, requiring state parties to 'ensure that all acts of torture are offences under its criminal law', the *Cour de Cassation* held that the 'enforcement of the Convention makes it necessary for Senegal to take prior legislative measures'.[16] Despite being a 'monist' country, legislative enactment is thus required for provisions that domestic courts do not automatically regard as part of domestic law.

The conclusion is inescapable: The monist tradition promises more than it delivers.[17] Despite the constitutional promise that international human rights law is an integral part of national law, occupying a place above ordinary legislation in the hierarchy, internal measures (such as legislation) still need to be enacted to make the provisions of the treaty applicable, unless the provisions are deemed to be 'self-executing'.[18] Almost without fail, African 'monist' states have not adopted the required enactments. By glibly referring to constitutional provisions as proof of the 'integration' of treaty norms into national law, as these states often do when they submit state reports,[19] they brush over this contradiction. Consider the following

---

[13] *Guengueng and Others v Habré* (2002) AHRLR 183 (SeCC 2001).

[14] As above, paras 11, 38.

[15] CAT, art 5(2).

[16] *Guengueng and Others v Habré* (n 13 above) para 38.

[17] See, however, C Courtis, 'Socio-economic Rights before the Courts in Argentina' in F Coomans (ed), *Justiciability of Economic and Social Rights, Experience from Domestic Systems* (Antwerp: Intersentia, 2006) 309, 314–15, who draws a distinction between the issue of 'incorporation', which is resolved by domestic constitutional law, and the 'so-called "self-executing character" of international treaties', which is an 'independent' question to be determined with reference to the generality of a specific provision. Still, the question may be asked what the value and importance of 'incorporation' is if it does not allow for the domestic invocation of that treaty.

[18] PF Gonidec, 'Droit International et Droit Interne en Afrique' (1996) 8 *RADIC* 789, 794. This approach seems to be adopted by the Madagascar *Chambre Adminstrative*, in case 101/79—*ADM et autres, Recueil de Jurisprudence de la Chambre Administrative de 1977 à 2003*, 112, 146, where the *Chambre* stated that the right to strike is incorporated into the internal legal order ('*incorporé à l'ordre juridique interne malgache*') by virtue of the country's ratification of ICESCR and despite its omission from the 1975 Constitution. At the same time, though, the right to strike 'can only be exercised in conformity with local law' ('*ne peut être exercé que conformément à l'ordonnance*'). On the position regarding custom, see T Maluwa, 'The Incorporation of International Law and its Interpretative Role in Municipal Legal Systems in Africa: An Exploratory Survey' (1998) 23 *SAYIL* 45, 50.

[19] See eg the second report (combining the eighth and ninth reports) of Mauritania, submitted to the African Commission in January 2005, para 35: Without citing any specifics, the report states that the Constitution and the jurisprudence of the *Conseil Constitutionnel* 'make the Charter an integral part' of Mauritanian law and can 'for this reason' 'be relied on before national jurisdictions for direct

example: Although formally 'monist', an admission on the part of the Malian state representative that the Convention on the Rights of All Migrant Workers and the Members of their Families cannot be applied domestically 'because it has not yet been incorporated into national legislation' prompted the recommendation that Mali has to take steps 'to ensure that the Convention can be applied in the Malian legal system'.[20] Failure to take such measures diminishes human rights treaties to declarations without effect and contributes to the largely 'ideological' nature of African international law in these states.[21]

The unhelpful and deceptive label of 'monism' should therefore be discarded in favour of an approach identifying whether treaty provisions may serve as grounds for independent legal action in the absence of domestic enactments 'grounding' these treaties. In other countries, starting in the USA and taking root in Europe, a conceptual and terminological distinction is drawn between 'self-executing' and 'non-self-executing' treaty provisions. Treaty provisions in the first category do not require legislation to make them private rights of action, while those in the second do. The Constitution of the Republic of South Africa 1996 also incorporates this terminology. In general, the 'dualist' approach is affirmed, in that external ratification of human rights treaties has to be followed by the approval of the National Assembly and Council of Provinces,[22] and the treaty provisions have to be enacted into national legislation before it becomes law.[23] However, if the treaty provision is 'self-executing' and it is not inconsistent with the Constitution or other act of Parliament, it becomes part of national law upon Parliament's mere approval of the external ratification even in the absence of any domesticating enactment as such.[24] Some Constitutions, such as those of Burundi, Senegal, and Togo, seem implicitly to make use of the concept of 'self-execution'. Under these Constitutions, the content of treaties determines whether legislation is required to effect ratification. Treaties dealing with, amongst other aspects, the status of persons, have to be 'ratified only by virtue of a law'.[25] This provision has apparently not been applied in respect of international human rights treaties.

These experiences underscore that attention should be deflected from the comfort of the 'monist' label, to the challenge of determining whether a treaty provision is 'self-executing'. Some guidance exists on determining the 'self-executing' nature of a treaty provision. Although the requirements mentioned below need to be

---

enforcement'. This claim is based on the Constitution of Mauritania 1991, art 80 (treaties ratified 'shall have an authority superior to that of laws').

[20] UN Doc CMW/C/MLI/CO/1 (31 May 2006) para 13.

[21] PF Gonidec, 'Existe-t-il un Droit International Africain?' (1993) 3 *RADIC* 243.

[22] Constitution of South Africa 1996, s 231(2).

[23] ibid, s 231(4).

[24] As above; and ME Olivier, 'Exploring the Doctrine of Self-Execution as Enforcement Mechanism of International Obligations' (2002) 12 *SAYIL* 99, 117–18 (containing a critique of the South African position).

[25] Constitution of Burundi 2004, art 290; Constitution of Senegal 2001, art 96; Constitution of Togo 1992, art 138.

understood in the context of a particular legal system, they shed some light on the concept more generally. Some of the factors that determine whether a treaty provision permits a 'self-executing' private right of action are as follows:[26] the intention of the parties; the subject-matter of the treaty; the nature of the obligations imposed by the treaty, as reflected in its wording; the availability and feasibility of alternative enforcement mechanisms; the necessity for the adoption of legislation; the capacity of judges to adjudicate the matter; the inclusion of individuals' rights as justiciable 'entitlements'; and the language of the provision (is it drafted in sufficiently precise and detailed language to be applied directly to a dispute, or in language indicating a general government programme or broad policy objective?).[27]

In a very significant decision in 2005, the Kenyan Court of Appeal indicated that the rigid distinction between the monist and dualist theories, respectively associated with civil and common law jurisdictions, is no longer tenable.[28] The Court asserted that the 'current thinking on the common law theory is that both international customary law and treaty law can be applied by state courts where there is no conflict with existing state law, even in the absence of implementing legislation'.[29] However, by 'applying' the equality provision in CEDAW to the succession dispute before it, the Court disregarded section 82(4) of the Constitution, which insulates 'devolution of property on death' from the constitutional protection against discrimination on the ground of sex. The Court found that the lower court's 'devolution of property' of an estate, which was skewed in favour of the deceased's sons, did not 'resonate with the noble notions enunciated in our Constitution and international laws', and therefore discriminated against female heirs. By substituting the lower court's determination, the Court in effect directly applied the unqualified equality provision of CEDAW to arrive at a decision apparently at odds with domestic law, thereby giving CEDAW 'self-executing' effect in a nominally 'dualist' constitutional order.

2 The Road Less Travelled: The Paucity of Transformation or Incorporation

In Commonwealth Africa, which on the whole is following the dualist theory, treaties do not become part of domestic law merely by virtue of their ratification. The explanation for this lies in the British constitutional tradition. The ratification

---

[26] See generally *Frolova v Union of Soviet Socialist Republics* 761 F.2d 370, 373–6 (7th Cir 1985); CM Vásquez, 'The Four Doctrines of Self-Executing Treaties' (1995) 89 *AJIL* 695, 711; MCR Craven, 'The Domestic Application of the International Covenant on Economic, Social and Cultural Rights' (1993) 40 *NILR* 367; Olivier (n 24 above).

[27] *Banque de Crédit Internationale v Conseil d'Etat du Canton de Genève, Chambre de Droit Administratif* (13 October 1972), cited in Craven (n 26 above) 388.

[28] *Mary Rono v Jane Rono and Another*, Civil Appeal 66 of 2002, Court of Appeal at Eldoret, judgment of 29 April 2005 (on file with author).

[29] ibid 11–12 of typed judgment.

of a treaty which binds the state at the international level ('external ratification') is a prerogative of the Crown. Once ratified, treaties have to be incorporated explicitly into the domestic legal system. This is in line with the system of parliamentary sovereignty, which has been developed as a cherished bulwark against the exercise of executive prerogatives. In terms of the long-standing principle of checks and balances, and of the more recent symbolical functions of the Crown, such 'external' ratification does not automatically bind domestic courts:

> If... the provisions of a treaty made by the Crown were to become operative within Great Britain automatically and without any specified act of incorporation, this might lead to the result that the Crown would alter the British municipal law or otherwise take some important step without consulting Parliament or obtaining Parliament's approval.[30]

Following this tradition, the position in most Commonwealth African states is that international law does not become part of domestic law, unless explicitly incorporated by an Act of Parliament.[31] International law may be incorporated into these 'dualist' legal systems in one of two ways: directly, through incorporation, or indirectly, through a process of reception ('transformation').[32] Incorporation entails the 'wholesale' enactment, as part of domestic legislation, of an international agreement. Explicit reference is usually made to the international instrument. Reception (or 'transformation') takes place if the provisions of an international agreement are reflected in parts of national legislation; or if pieces of national legislation are amended or repealed to conform with international norms, usually without explicit reference to the source of these norms.

The only dualist state that has clearly incorporated (domesticated) the African Charter is Nigeria, when it adopted the African Charter on Human and Peoples' Rights (Ratification and Enforcement) Act.[33] In its Preamble, the Act states that it is 'necessary and expedient to make legislative provisions for the enforcement in Nigeria' of the Charter 'by way of an Act of the National Assembly'. The domesticating provision of the Act stipulates that the provisions of the African Charter, which are attached in a schedule to the Act, 'have force of law in Nigeria and shall be given full recognition and effect and be applied by all authorities and persons exercising legislative, executive or judicial powers in Nigeria'.[34]

---

[30] IA Shearer, *Starke's International Law* (London: Butterworths, 11th edn, 1994) 70.

[31] Malawi Constitution 1994, s 211(1) provides that agreements ratified by Parliament 'shall form part of the law of the Republic if so provided for in the Act of Parliament ratifying the agreement'. While this formulation leaves some uncertainty about the process of international ratification, it seems clear that the municipal law cannot be altered without 'the democratic participation of the legislature' (T Maluwa, 'The Role of International Law in the Protection of Human Rights under the Malawi Constitution' (1995) 3 *AYBIL* 53, 74). After an amendment in 1993, the Zimbabwean Constitution contains the general rule that no international treaty or agreement forms part of the law of Zimbabwe unless 'incorporated' into domestic law by an 'Act of Parliament' (s 111B(1)(b) of the Constitution, as amended by Act 4 of 1993 (see (1993) 3 *Bulletin of Zimbabwean L* at 26–7).

[32] See Ch 1.C.2 above.

[33] Laws of the Federation, 1990, ch 10.

[34] ibid, art 1.

Most states are also able to point to 'reception' by way of legislation that gives effect to rights in UN and AU human rights treaties.[35] This may range from the trite (murder is punishable as a crime, giving effect to the right to life), to the potentially more controversial (elections are conducted in terms of the Constitution and Electoral Act).[36] It is obviously difficult to determine conclusively which laws have been enacted or amended *as a result of (and consequent to)* the adoption of an international instrument. Indications of such a causal link could conceivably be found in official press statements, parliamentary debates, and memoranda attached to draft legislation, or in the legislative provisions themselves. However, not only is such a search difficult to undertake on a continent-wide scale, often such material does not exist in domestic African systems. When states include such information in their state reports under UN and AU treaties, they also fail to draw any causal link. In any event, this omission is understandable, as it is the eventual guarantee of the particular rights that is of importance, and not the route or causal chain that brought them there.

As far as could be ascertained, the African Charter has played a very limited role in this sense. Of the UN treaties, it is especially the CRC that has inspired domestic legislation. As the UN treaty enjoying the most universal acceptance and having been ratified by most African states for some time, the CRC provides an appropriate instrument to gauge the 'impact' of international law upon domestic legal regimes.[37] At least one African Constitution explicitly refers to the CRC.[38] Others contain children's rights that in significant respects mirror those contained in the CRC.[39] As for domestic legislation, there are some clear indications that the CRC has served as inspiration and provided guidance to juvenile justice reform processes.[40] In some instances CRC provisions are taken

---

[35] States often do so in the reports submitted in terms of their treaty obligations: They often show that their Constitutions contain rights corresponding with relevant Charter provisions (see eg Lesotho's 'Initial Report on the Implementation of the African Charter on Human and Peoples' Rights' (August 2000) (on file with author, Lesotho's Initial Report), citing s 4(1) of its Constitution as reflective of art 2 of the Charter (non-discrimination), s 5 as being in conformity with art 4 (life), and s 8 as giving effect to art 5 (torture)); and further invoke national legislation and case-law as evidence of national 'transformation' (see eg Lesotho's Initial Report, in which case-law is cited to show that the right to life is honoured by criminal investigation and prosecution of killings by police officers, and legislation such as the Labour Code Order, 1992 and the Children's Act 6 of 1980 are cited).

[36] As indicated in the second Namibian Report, considered at the Commission's 29th session (23 April–7 May 2001, on file with author).

[37] See also P Alston and J Tobin (with M Darrow), 'Laying the Foundations for Children's Rights: An Independent Study of some Key Legal and Institutional Aspects of the Impact of the Convention on the Rights of the Child' (Florence: UNICEF Innocenti Research Centre, 2005).

[38] Constitution of Senegal 2001, Preamble.

[39] See eg Constitution of Cape Verde 1992, art 73; Constitution of Ethiopia 1994, art 36; Constitution of Malawi 1994, art 23 (which contrasts with CRC and the African Children's Charter by defining a child as anyone under 16 years of age); Constitution of South Africa 1996, s 28; Constitution of Uganda 1995, art 34.

[40] OG Odhiambo, 'The Domestication of International Law Standards on the Rights of the Child with specific Reference to Juvenile Justice in the African Context' (unpublished LL D thesis, University of the Western Cape, October 2005), reviews child law reform in six African States

over in full;[41] in other instances the influence of the CRC may be discerned from the principled acceptance of, for example, a separate juvenile system or diversion as a preferred strategy,[42] from provisions outlawing child marriages and recruitment of children into the armed forces,[43] or the recognition of the right to basic education.[44]

B What is the Place of International Human Rights Law in the Municipal Hierarchy of Laws?

It is only when an international human rights treaty has become part of national law, either as a 'self-executing' provision or as an enactment in domestic law, that the question of its position in the domestic legal hierarchy arises. There are three options: (i) international law may be accorded a status above all national law, including the Constitution; (ii) its status may be equal to that of the Constitution, but superior to all ordinary national laws; or (iii) it may have a position in the legal hierarchy equal to that of ordinary national laws. Although theoretically international law may also have an even lower place on the ladder, below ordinary national law, this possibility would negate totally the potential role of international law, and is not found in any of the African constitutions.

In most francophone constitutional regimes in Africa a clear distinction is drawn between the status of international law in relation to the Constitution (on the one hand), and in relation to other laws (on the other hand). International law may be superior to both the Constitution and other laws, or only to ordinary laws and not the Constitution. In the latter case, potential conflict with the Constitution must be pre-empted and resolved before ratification is confirmed. In this respect, the French Constitution of 1958 is followed.[45] The Central African Republic is an example of a country in which the Constitution has superiority over international treaties, while international law has superior authority over all other laws.[46] Should there be a conflict between the Constitution and a provision of a treaty, Parliament may approve ratification only once the Constitution has

(Ghana, Kenya, Namibia, Lesotho, South Africa, and Uganda) from the late 1990s, and reaches the well-substantiated conclusion that reforms in the following areas show significant reliance on the CRC: determination of ages of criminal capacity; diversion, provision for a separate system for juveniles at pre-trial and trial stages; and the introduction of alternative sentencing regimes.

[41] J Sloth-Nielsen, 'The Role of International Human Rights Law in the Development of South Africa's Legislation on Juvenile Justice' (2001) 5 *Law, Democracy and Development* 59, 73.

[42] ibid 74–9.

[43] Nigeria Child's Rights Act 2006, ss 21 and 34.

[44] See eg Kenya's Child Act 2001, referred to by K Singh, 'Right to Basic Education: International Obligations and Regional Normative Action in Africa' (2004) 12 *AYBIL* 437, 460 (also showing links with the African Children's Charter).

[45] Art 54.

[46] Constitution of Central African Republic 1995, art 68.

been revised to bring it into line with the provision.[47] In another civil law country, Cape Verde, a similar distinction is made, in that international law takes precedence 'over all laws and regulations below the constitutional level'.[48]

Some other francophone African states proclaim the superiority of international law in more general terms, without drawing a distinction between the relative status of the Constitution and other laws. In Tunisia, treaties 'duly ratified' have an authority superior to laws in general.[49] Once again reflecting the French constitutional approach,[50] the Constitutions of Chad, Congo, Mali, and Democratic Republic of Congo (DRC) introduce the principle of reciprocity, in formulations such as: 'Treaties... have, as soon as they are published, a higher authority than that of law; provided that each treaty... is approved by the other party'.[51]

The South African Constitution presents an example of a system where domestic law is superior in status to international law—not only the Constitution, but other local legislation as well. 'Self-executing' treaty provisions become part of national law once Parliament has assented to the executive's decision to ratify a human rights treaty only if these provisions are *consistent with the Constitution and any other act of Parliament*.[52] The subordination of international law to domestic law is tempered by the duty placed on courts to 'prefer any reasonable interpretation... that is consistent with international law' over any alternative interpretation that is inconsistent with international law, when interpreting legislation.[53] In terms of the Namibian Constitution, international law forms 'part of the law of Namibia' unless 'otherwise provided by this Constitution or Act of Parliament'.[54] In South Africa and Namibia the superiority of the Constitution is in a sense predictable, as in these two countries a system of 'constitutional supremacy' is followed.[55]

In Nigeria, the only country that has domesticated the African Charter, the domesticating enactment does not expressly stipulate what 'rank' the Charter

---

[47] The Constitutional Court determines whether a conflict exists. Determination of such an issue is required if the President of the Republic, the President of the National Assembly, or a third of the members of the National Assembly seizes the Constitutional Court.

[48] Constitution of Cape Verde 1992, art 11(4).

[49] Constitution of Tunisia 1959, art 32.

[50] Constitution of France 1958, art 55.

[51] Constitution of Chad 1996, art 222; Constitution of Congo 2002, art 184; Constitution of Mali 1992, art 116; Constitution of the Democratic Republic of Congo 2006, art 184.

[52] Constitution of South Africa 1996, s 231(4).

[53] ibid, s 233.

[54] Constitution of Namibia 1991, s 144. See also *Kauesa v Minister of Home Affairs* (1995) 1 SA 51 (NmHC) at 86J–87A: 'The specific provisions of the Constitution of Namibia, where specific and unequivocal, override provisions of international agreements which have become part of Namibian law. In [such] cases the provisions of the international agreements must at least be given considerable weight in interpreting and defining the scope of the provisions contained in the Namibian Constitution' (emphasis in original). See also, however, *Namibia v Mwilima and Others* 2002 NR 223, 271A–B, where O'Linn AJA held that the provisions of the ICCPR should be understood as supplementary to (in the sense of extending the content of) the Constitution.

[55] Constitution of South Africa 1996, s 2 and Constitution of Namibia 1990, art 1(6).

enjoys within the municipal legal order. In *Abacha v Fawehinmi*,[56] the Supreme Court held that the Charter is superior to ordinary legislation, but apparently not to the Constitution.[57] Such an approach would defeat the impact of the Charter, especially in respect of justiciable socio-economic rights, which are contained in the Charter but do not form part of the Nigerian constitutional order.[58]

C Have African Courts 'Applied' International Human Rights Law, and in particular the African Charter?

The choice of the rather ambiguous term 'apply' in the question above is deliberate, as it entails both 'direct enforcement', and reliance on international law for 'interpretive guidance'. A distinction has to be drawn between judicial reliance on an international treaty as the basis of a remedy, allowing the international agreement to be 'treated as part of domestic law for purposes of adjudication' in a domestic court ('direct enforcement'),[59] and the use of international agreements as 'an aid to interpretation' of domestic constitutions or ordinary laws ('interpretative guidance').[60] To a large extent the judicial application of an international treaty also depends on the status that international human rights norms enjoy in a local legal system. It is unlikely that judicial institutions will, for example, base findings on provisions of the African Charter if the Charter is not regarded as part of domestic law, either because its provisions are not 'self-executing' or because they have not been domesticated explicitly. Focusing on these two manifestations of 'judicial application' rather than on notions of 'monism' and 'dualism' may lead to a more nuanced and informative discussion.

Judicial decisions in Nigeria and Benin speak to the possibility of direct enforcement. Given the legislative domestication of the African Charter, an international treaty entered into by the Nigerian government 'does not become binding until enacted into law by the National Assembly'.[61] Once domesticated in this way, courts have the jurisdiction to 'construe or apply' the Charter and any aggrieved party may 'resort to its provisions to obtain redress in our domestic

---

[56] *Abacha v Fawehinmi* (2001) AHRLR 172 (NgSC 2000). (*Abacha*-AHRLR, judgment of ogundare JSC) (the full judgment is at <http://www.chr.up.ac.za/centre_publications/ahrlr/docs/fawehinmi.doc> (30 April 2007) and also [2002] 3 LRC 296 (Nigeria) (*Abacha*-LRC).

[57] Ogundare JSC, *Abacha*-AHRLR, para 15; *Abacha*-LRC, 309f–h. However, see Achike JSC, who argues that, as the Charter has been incorporated by domestic legislation, it stands on a par with other domestic laws, (*Abacha*-LRC, 339a).

[58] See also Communication 155/96, *Social and Economic Rights Action Centre and Another v Nigeria* (2001) AHRLR 60 (ACHPR 2001) (15th Annual Activity Report) (*Ogoniland* case).

[59] *Gwebu v Rex* (2002) AHRLR 229 (SwCA 2002) para 17.

[60] ibid, para 15; *Attorney-General v Dow* (2001) AHRLR 99 (BwCA 1992); see also (1992 BLR 119) (*Unity Dow* case).

[61] *Abacha v Fawehinmi* (n 56 above), Ogundare JSC, *Abacha*-AHRLR, para 12; *Abacha*-LRC, 308h.

courts'.[62] The Nigerian Supreme Court also held that the aggrieved party may use the usual constitutional procedures for enforcing fundamental rights, such as an action commenced by a writ, thus rejecting arguments aimed at invoking proced-ural obstacles to 'impede the attainment of justice'.[63] Even in cases where ratified treaties automatically form an 'integral' part of national law, their 'direct invoca-tion' 'by citizens before a court' depends on the 'self-executing nature of each individual treaty right'.[64] In at least one case, the Benin Constitutional Court directly 'applied' a provision of the African Charter without embedding it in or invoking it in conjunction with a provision of the Benin Constitution,[65] by implication finding the particular provision to be 'self-executing'.

However, much more frequently courts look to international human rights law for interpretive guidance, thereby providing for a non-legislative measure to 'give effect' to the treaty. The basis for using international human rights law as a source of interpretive guidance is sometimes found in national law. Exceptionally, reliance on international law to guide interpretation may be mandated by the Constitution;[66] it may also be stipulated in ordinary legislation;[67] or it may be a rule of statutory interpretation that enjoys acceptance within the particular legal system.[68] Quite frequently, courts do not locate their interpretive reliance on any explicit legal basis, but refer to international law texts 'seamlessly, without noting or explaining the binding nature or level of persuasive authority' of their

[62] ibid, Ejiwunmi JSC, *Abacha*-LRC, 378d.

[63] ibid, Achike JSC, *Abacha*-LRC, 341e.

[64] F Coomans, 'Some Introductory Remarks on the Justiciability of Economic and Social Rights in a Comparative Constitutional Context' in Coomans (n 17 above) 1, 7.

[65] *Okpeitcha v Okpeitcha* (2002) AHRLR 33 (BnCC 2001) para 11.

[66] The South African Constitution 1996 affirms that, in interpreting the bill of rights, courts 'must consider international law', and 'may consider foreign law' (Constitution of South Africa 1996, s 39(1)). When they interpret 'any legislation', South African courts must 'prefer any reasonable inter-pretation' that is consistent with international law (Constitution of South Africa 1996, s 233). The Constitution of Malawi echoes the South African 1993 Constitution, where it provides that courts 'shall, where applicable, have regard to current norms of public international and comparable foreign case law' (Constitution of Malawi 1994, s 11(2)). The Constitution of the Seychelles not only instructs courts to interpret the Chapter on Fundamental Rights consistently with the country's international human rights obligations, but also allows judicial notice of international instruments, reports, and views adopted by UN and regional human rights treaty bodies, and the decisions of for-eign, regional, and international courts (Constitution of Seychelles 1993, art 48).

[67] eg the Interpretation Act of Botswana, s 24(1): 'For the purposes of ascertaining that which an enactment was made to correct and as an aid to the construction of the enactment a court may have regard to any text-book or other work of reference, to the report of any commission of enquiry into the state of the law, to any memorandum published by authority in reference to the enactment or to the Bill for the enactment, to any relevant international agreement or convention and to any papers laid before the National Assembly in reference to the enactment or to its subject matter, but not to the debates of the Assembly' (emphasis added).

[68] In common law jurisdictions, the presumption of statutory interpretation implies that a statute will not be interpreted so as to violate a rule of international law or international obligations. This rule was for example applied productively in South Africa before the 1993 and 1996 Constitutions (see eg GE Devenish, *Interpretation of Statutes* (Cape Town: Juta, 1992) 212–15; and J Dugard, 'International Human-Rights Norms in Domestic Courts: Can South Africa Learn from Britain and

provisions.[69] Widespread judicial reliance on foreign and international sources in the absence of explicit domestic authority testifies to the emergence of a 'general principle of law' in this regard. Due to the imprecision of international law, decisions and resolutions of the relevant quasi-judicial and judicial bodies are often more helpful in the interpretive process than the treaties themselves. However, these potentially useful sources are not often invoked.

What follows is an attempt to gauge the extent to which domestic African courts have 'applied' international human rights instruments, and in particular the African Charter, and to assess the significance thereof.[70] This is not a comprehensive survey of the application of the African Charter by all domestic courts around Africa, as the exposition is sometimes very brief, and the relevant sources are generally quite inaccessible. Although this discussion covers only 14 countries, it extends across subregional divides and includes the major legal systems on the continent. Although comparable foreign case-law may also steer interpretation and is increasingly being used in Africa and elsewhere,[71] it is excluded from this overview.

1 Benin

Following the adoption of a democratic Constitution in 1990,[72] a Constitutional Court was established in Benin in 1991.[73] In terms of the Benin Constitution, treaties have 'an authority superior to that of laws' once ratified.[74]

Soon after the Constitution entered into force on 22 May 1991, a trade union leader seized the Court.[75] He claimed that the legislation of 26 September 1988 contravened articles 17 and 22 of the Benin Constitution, as well as article 7(1) of the African Charter. In its very brief decision (less than two typed pages), citing article 7(1)(a) to (c) of the African Charter, the Court found that the '*loi*' conformed with the Constitution. In a subsequent case, one Madame Bagri invoked the right

the United States?' in E Kahn (ed), *Fiat Iustitia: Essays in Memory of Oliver Deneys Schreiner* (Cape Town: Juta, 1993) 221, 234–9).

[69] ME Adjami, 'African Courts, International Law, and Comparative Case Law: Chimera or Emerging Human Rights Jurisprudence?' (2002) 24 *Michigan J Intl L* 103, 165–6. See also I Brownlie, *Principles of Public International Law* (Oxford: Oxford University Press, 6th edn, 2003) 46, noting that since 1974, English courts have, with 'variable consistency', relied on international human rights instruments for interpretative guidance.

[70] This discussion is an update and reworking of F Viljoen, 'Application of the African Charter on Human and Peoples' Rights by Domestic Courts in Africa' (1999) 43 *JAL* 1; see also the contributions in J Flauss and E Lambert-Abelgawad (eds), *L'Application Nationale de la Charte Africaine des Droits de l'Homme et des Peuples* (Antwerp: Bruylant, 2004).

[71] See eg RB Ginsburg, 'Looking beyond Our Borders: The Value of a Comparative Perspective in Constitutional Adjudication' (2003–4) 40 *Idaho L R* 1, for an account of the change in the 'lone ranger' attitude of the courts of the USA.

[72] The Constitution of Benin was adopted on 11 December 1990.

[73] Pursuant to '*Loi Organique sur la Cour Constitutionnelle*' Loi 91–009 of 4 March 1991.

[74] Constitution of Benin 1990, art 147.

[75] Decision DDC (2 June 1991).

to work, as guaranteed in both the Benin Constitution and the African Charter,[76] before the Constitutional Court.[77] The Court, remarking that the complaint related to the application of rules of the 'Statuts de la Fonction Publique', found that the actions taken to dismiss Madame Bagri were not unconstitutional.

The first cases in which the Benin Constitutional Court declared government action unconstitutional date from 1994.[78] In one case a decree by the Minister of the Interior, Security and Territorial Administration had to be scrutinized for constitutional compatibility.[79] The decree declared that only one developmental association shall be registered per administrative entity. Associations that had previously existed and whose applications for registration had been refused had to cease all activities and be liquidated.[80] The Court observed that, in making this decree, the Minister had encroached upon the domain reserved to the law in terms of the Benin Constitution and article 10 of the African Charter.[81] Article 10 of the Charter declares that 'every individual shall have the right to free association provided that he abides by the law'.

Commentators have speculated about the interpretation of the term 'provided that he abides by the law' in the African Charter. Some have criticized the African Charter as draconian, as they reasoned that every legal response by a government would qualify as 'law'. Others have suggested that 'law' should and could be interpreted restrictively, requiring an essential minimum moral content before government fiat is elevated to law. It is quite clear that the President of the Court, Elisabeth Pognon, and her five male colleagues adopted the latter approach. The mere fact that a Minister has issued a decree does not mean that it becomes impossible to invoke the right to freely associate in article 10 of the Charter. According to the Benin Constitutional Court there is 'a domain reserved to law', upon which the executive may not encroach. The implications of the decision should not be overstated. It was an executive law-making activity that came under scrutiny, not an ordinary law of a law-making body, such as Parliament. The meaning of 'law' in French constitutionalism must also be taken into account. The decision says that '*loi*' should be distinguished from an '*arrêté*'.

In another case decided by the Benin Constitutional Court in 1994, the Court heard an application to have certain appointments to the Communications Authority declared unconstitutional.[82] Interfering to a very limited extent with the executive decree, the Court referred to the African Charter as an integral part of the Constitution of 11 December 1990.[83] Article 10 of the African Charter was

---

[76] Specifically art 13(2), which guarantees equal access to the public service.
[77] Decision DDC-03-93 (28 October 1993).
[78] Based on a personal perusal of the Court's records in Cotonou, Benin, during April 1995.
[79] Decision DCC 16-94 (27 May 1994).
[80] Decree 260/MISAT/DC/DAI/SAAP of 22 November 1993.
[81] The Minister '*a empiété sur le domaine réservé à la loi par les articles 25 et 98 de la Constitution et 10 de la Charte Africaine des Droits de l'Homme et des Peuples*'.
[82] Decision DCC 10-94 (9 May 1994).
[83] '*partie intégrante*'.

cited as an interpretive tool, providing confirmation of the freedom to associate set out in article 25 of the Benin Constitution.

Although not consistently followed, a trend has emerged from subsequent decisions: The Constitutional Court invokes the African Charter in its reasoning, but bases its decisions on the Constitution when the Charter merely amplifies existing constitutional provisions.[84] When the Charter provides a legal basis that does not exist at national level, the Court has on occasion gone one step further by basing its decisions on the Charter, rather than the Constitution.[85]

2 Botswana[86]

The question whether discrimination based on sex was unconstitutional arose in the case *Attorney-General of Botswana v Unity Dow (Unity Dow* case).[87] The lower court relied on international human rights treaties ratified by Botswana to inform its conclusion that the omission of the word 'sex' from the list of prohibited grounds in the Botswana Constitution does not imply that discrimination based on sex is constitutionally tolerable. One of these treaties was the African Charter. Article 2 of the Charter guarantees the enjoyment of the rights recognized therein without distinction on the basis of, amongst other factors, sex. At the Court of Appeal, the appellant raised an objection against the lower court's reliance on these international instruments. Amissah JP rejected these objections. However, the international norms were applied not as 'enforceable rights', but as 'an aid to the construction of an enactment' such as a 'difficult provision of the Constitution'.[88] In relation to the African Charter, Amissah JP made the following observations: 'Botswana is a signatory to this Charter. Indeed it would appear that Botswana is one of the credible prime movers behind the promotion and supervision of the Charter'.[89] The judge conceded that the Charter is not binding law 'as legislation passed by its Parliament', but that domestic legislation should be interpreted so as not 'to conflict with Botswana's obligations under the Charter'.[90]

The facts of the case concerned the constitutionality of provisions in the Citizenship Act of 1982, in terms of which children had to adopt the nationality of their fathers. This meant that if a female Botswana citizen married a non-Botswana

[84] See eg Decision DCC 05-137 (28 October 2005), where the Court invokes the African Charter, art 6(2) in conjuction with the corresponding provisions of the Constitution of Benin, art 16(1), and finds a violation of the Constitution.

[85] See eg Decision DCC 05-114 (20 September 2005), where the Court finds a violation of the African Charter, art 7(1)(a) and (d) (dealing with the right to a trial within a reasonable time) in the absence of a corresponding provision in the national Constitution.

[86] See in general the discussion by L Lindholt, *Questioning the Universality of Human Rights: The African Charter on Human and Peoples' Rights in Botswana, Malawi and Mozambique* (Aldershot: Ashgate, 1997) chs 6 and 7.

[87] *Unity Dow* case (n 60 above).

[88] ibid, para 108.

[89] ibid.

[90] ibid.

citizen, their children would not have Botswana nationality.[91] It was argued that this provision amounted to discrimination against women and was in conflict with article 15 of the Botswana Constitution.[92] However, the state contended that article 15 was not applicable, as it did not refer to 'sex' or 'gender' as explicit grounds in its definition of 'discrimination'. Basing itself on the international law obligations of the state, including article 2 of the African Charter, a majority of the Botswana Court of Appeal found a violation of the Botswana Constitution.[93]

As a direct consequence of this decision,[94] and a clear manifestation of judicial and legislative 'effect' being given to the Charter, the Botswana Parliament amended the Citizenship Act, so that the relevant section now provides that a person 'shall be a citizen of Botswana... if, at the time of his birth, his father *or mother* was a citizen of Botswana'.[95] The Court of Appeal continued its progressive improvement of women's rights when it declared unconstitutional regulations that forced female students to leave college upon becoming pregnant.[96] This sequence of events stands as testimony to the undeniable effect of global and regional human rights norms in a domestic legal system.

A finding of the Botswana Industrial Court illustrates a growing tendency on the part of judges to shed the light of international law on the issue at hand, only to leave everyone in the dark about the value and role of these norms in the interpretive process and outcome.[97] In this case, a relatively simple question presented itself: Is the dismissal of a female employee on the basis that she cannot work late-night shifts unfair? The Court found that it is substantively unfair, as it contravened the Employment Act, which stipulates that an employee's employment may not be terminated on the basis of 'sex'.[98] In the course of its judgment, the Court referred to CEDAW and two ILO Conventions, and stated the following: 'Botswana being a member of the ILO, and the Industrial Court, being a court of equity,... follows international labour standards and applies the conventions and recommendations of

[91] On the investigation of the Botswana Law Reform Commission and its conclusions see Lindholt (n 86 above) 199.

[92] Art 15(1) prohibits laws which are discriminatory 'either in itself or in its effect'.

[93] Art 2 of the Charter includes 'sex' as one of the grounds on which the guarantees of the Charter may not be denied to any individual. The other grounds are 'race, ethnic group, language, religion, political or any other opinion, national and social origin, fortune, birth or other status'. The list in the Botswana Constitution is restricted to 'race, tribe, place of origin, political opinions, colour or creed' (art 15(3)).

[94] Although the amendment came several years after the *Unity Dow* judgment (n 60 above), it is clear from the memorandum accompanying the amendment that it was adopted in reaction to the judgment (Memorandum on Citizenship (Amendment) Bill 9 1995, which quotes the *Unity Dow* case). See Lindholt (n 86 above) 200. For a background to the pressure on the government, see also EK Quansah, 'Is the Right to Get Pregnant a Fundamental Human Right in Botswana?' (1995) 39 *JAL* 97, 102.

[95] Emphasis added.

[96] *Student Representative Council, Molepolole College of Education v A-G of Botswana*, Civil Appeal 13 of 1994 (31 January 1995). For a discussion of the case, see Quansah (n 94 above) 97. See also Lindholt (n 86 above) 209.

[97] *Moatswi v Fencing Centre* (2002) 1 BLR 262 (IC); (2004) AHRLR 131 (BWIC 2002).

[98] Botswana Employment Act of 1982, amended in 1992, s 23.

546 Domestication of International Norms

the ILO'.[99] However, it then proceeded to juxtapose the relevant ILO Convention with national law, finding the employer in violation of the Employment Act. The Court's 'application' of international standards amounts to little more than a parallel being drawn between the local law, which is 'applied', and the international law, which hovers about but does not find a foothold in the judgment.

3 Congo

Some time ago, one of the previous Commissioners of the African Commission on Human and Peoples' Rights, Mrs Ondziel-Gnelenga, herself a lawyer in her home country, Congo, sketched the following bleak picture: 'Personally, I have invoked in some cases, certain provisions of the Charter, but this has only served as additional information to the cases in question. The judges and magistrates have not taken into account these provisions when making decisions or formulating opinions'.[100]

4 Ghana

In an article published in 1991, a previous member and Chairperson of the African Commission, EVO Dankwa, a Ghanaian, made a plea for the incorporation of international human rights treaties into domestic law in Ghana.[101] He lamented the fact that none of the nine international treaties ratified by Ghana had been made part of local law. This had the effect that the provisions of these instruments could not be asserted in Ghanaian courts. He proceeded to indicate the practical implications of one of these instruments, the African Charter. He argued that PNDC Law 4 (the Preventative Custody Law, 1982) and PNDC Law 91 (*Habeas Corpus* (Amendment) Law, 1984) cannot stand in the face of article 6 of the African Charter.[102] Furthermore, he expressed his doubts whether PNDC Law 211 (the Newspaper Licensing Law) 'can stand by virtue of the combined effect of Articles 9 and 7(1) of the same Charter'.[103] This decree provides that anyone intent on publishing a newspaper in Ghana must first obtain a licence, which may be withdrawn at the discretion of the PNDC Secretary for Information. The legislation does not provide for review of or appeal against this decision.

The Ghana Public Order Decree 1972 came under scrutiny in *New Patriotic Party v Inspector-General of Police, Accra*.[104] The measures of this Decree included giving the

[99] n 97 above, para 24.

[100] Interview in (1996) (October–December) *AFLAQ* 34.

[101] EVO Dankwa, 'Implementation of International Human Rights Instruments: Ghana as an Illustration' (1991) 3 *ASICL Proc* 57.

[102] ibid.

[103] Dankwa (n 101 above) 63.

[104] [2000] 2 HRLRA 1 (see also (2001) AHRLR 138 (GhSC 1993) for excerpts from the judgment). Neither in his discussion of the case, nor elsewhere where he deals with constitutional

Minister of the Interior the power to prohibit the holding of public meetings or processions for a specific period in a specified area,[105] and a requirement that any meeting to celebrate a traditional custom be subject to prior permission.[106] The Supreme Court of Ghana found section 7 to be in violation not only of the Ghanaian Constitution,[107] but also of the mirror-provision in the African Charter.[108] Archer CJ added the following remarks to the leading judgment of Hayfron-Benjamin J:

> Ghana is a signatory to this African Charter and Member States of the Organization of African Unity and parties to the Charter are expected to recognize the rights, duties and freedoms enshrined in the Charter and to undertake to adopt legislative and other measures to give effect to the rights and duties. I do not think that the fact that Ghana has not passed specific legislation to give effect to the Charter, the Charter cannot be relied upon. On the contrary, Article 21 of our Constitution has recognized the right to assembly mentioned in Article 11 of the African Charter.[109]

This does not necessarily form a pattern in judicial interpretation. In another decision handed down on the same day, *New Patriotic Party v Ghana Broadcasting Corporation*,[110] pertaining to the right to information, for example, no reference is made to the African Charter.[111]

5 Lesotho

Faced with a constitutional challenge against the legislative introduction of an electoral quota system that set aside one-third of local council seats for women, the Lesotho Court of Appeal relied heavily on international law in its interpretation of the Lesotho Constitution.[112] The challenge was based on a formal view of equality, with the applicant arguing that the quota system infringes male candidates' right to

interpretation does Bimpong-Buta refer to the African Charter or other international human rights law (SY Bimpong-Buta, *The Law of Interpretation in Ghana (Exposition & Critique)* (Accra: Advanced Legal Publications, 1995) 307–26).

[105] Ghana Public Order Decree 1972, s 7.

[106] ibid, s 8.

[107] Constitution of Ghana 1992, s 21, which guarantees freedom of assembly including freedom to take part in processions and demonstrations.

[108] African Charter, art 11, dealing with freedom of assembly.

[109] *New Patriotic Party v Inspector-General of Police, Accra* (n 104 above) 63.

[110] Writ 1/93, Supreme Court, judgment of 22 July 1993, [1992–3] GLR 522, SC *per* Archer CJ, Francois J, Sekyi J, Aitkins J, Wirebu J, Bamford-Addo J, and Hayfron-Benjamin J.

[111] The Ghanaian Court referred to the fact that the Constitution demands that a broad and Liberal spirit of a democratic and pluralist society should prevail in the country (paras 26, 58, and 59). Art 21(1)(f) of the Constitution of Ghana provides that all persons have the right to information, subject to such qualifications as are necessary in a democratic society. The Court chose to seek the spirit referred to in Ghanaian law, rather than in art 9(1) or 9(2) of the Charter. Art 9(1) of the Charter grants an unqualified right to receive information. Art 9(2) has a claw-back clause: Everyone may express their opinions 'within the law'. It is perhaps understandable that the Court did not seek to find the embodiment of a democratic and pluralist spirit in these two provisions of the Charter.

[112] *Tšepe v Independent Electoral Commission and Others*, Case C of A (Civ) 11/05, judgment of 30 June 2005 (on file with author).

equality before the law. Finding support in Lesotho's obligations under UN treaties for the adoption of a substantive approach to equality, which allows for 'temporary special measures',[113] and which does not require 'identical treatment in every instance',[114] the Court upheld the constitutionality of the quota system. Although reference was made to standards at the regional level (contained in the African Charter), they were not sufficiently clear on the issue to provide guidance.[115] However, the Court found unambiguous support in the Declaration on Gender and Development adopted under SADC,[116] making this judgment a rare example of judicial reliance on subregional standards on human rights.

In its application for the recusal of the Chief Justice, the Basotho National Party questioned the compliance of domestic standards for judicial appointment with international standards and requested the High Court to order the 'government' to enact legislation to give effect to international treaties, including the African Charter and the ICCPR.[117] Clearly departing from a dualist stance, the Court held that those instruments do not form part of Lesotho's municipal law unless and until incorporated into municipal law by legislative enactment. The Court declined to order the legislature to enact the relevant legislation on the basis that it was the legislature's 'prerogative' to do so. However, this is too deferential an attitude: It can hardly be termed 'interference' in the legislative process if a court reminds an organ of state of an unequivocal international law obligation.

6 Malawi

Through negotiation a new Constitution was adopted in Malawi in 1994, and signed into law by the President in 1995. Not long before this, under the previous constitutional dispensation, a rare occasion presented itself to the Malawi Supreme Court of Appeal when the African Charter was invoked. Malawi had already ratified the African Charter on 17 November 1989.[118]

In the case, *Chafukwa Chichana v The Republic*, the appellant was sentenced after a conviction for the importation and possession of seditious materials.[119] It was argued that certain of the appellant's fundamental rights, enshrined in the Universal Declaration, had been violated by the state. The Court agreed, holding

---

[113] CEDAW, art 4, quoted and discussed in the judgment, para 19.

[114] ICCPR, art 26, elucidated in General Comment 18 on 'Non-Discrimination' of the UN Human Rights Committee (10 November 1989), quoted with approval by the Court, para 18.

[115] Reference was made to arts 2 and 18(3) (para 20); the Protocol to the African Charter on the Rights of Women in Africa is much more pertinent to the issue (see Ch 6.C above), but was not relied upon because the case was decided before its entry into force.

[116] Judgment, para 21; on this Declaration, see Ch 12 D.6.4 above.

[117] *Basotho National Party v Government of Lesotho* (2005) 11 BCLR 1169 (LesH).

[118] On the potential effects of the African Charter on Malawi law, see Lindholt (n 86 above) chs 6 and 7.

[119] Discussed by Maluwa (n 31 above) 65–9.

that the content of the Universal Declaration had been incorporated into Malawi law by virtue of the 1966 Constitution.[120]

Counsel for the applicant further argued that the applicant's rights were protected also under the African Charter, to which Malawi was a party. Based on the fact that no specific legislation had been passed to incorporate the Charter into domestic law, Banda CJ rejected this contention:

> This Charter, in our view, must be placed on a different plane from the UN Universal Declaration of Human Rights. Whereas the latter is part of the law of Malawi the African Charter is not. Malawi may well be a signatory to the Charter but until Malawi takes legislative measures to adopt it, the Charter is not part of the municipal law of Malawi and we doubt whether in the absence of any local statute incorporating its provisions the Charter would be enforceable in our Courts.[121]

Maluwa agrees with this conclusion. He points out that the Court did not address in any depth the relevance of international law in protecting and interpreting human rights domestically. He suggests a different line of argument, not based on the constitutional incorporation of the Universal Declaration into Malawi law, but on it having become binding customary international law. In so far as the rights in the African Charter resemble the Universal Declaration (as binding customary international law), they may be applied by municipal courts. As Maluwa concedes, this argument remains premised and dependent on the status of the Universal Declaration—not the African Charter.[122] It appears as if a similar conclusion would have been reached under the provisions of the 1995 Constitution.[123]

7 Namibia

Namibia ratified the African Charter on 30 July 1990, not long after its independence on 21 March 1990. In a subsequent case, the Namibian High Court in *Kauesa v Minister of Home Affairs*[124] referred to various articles of the African Charter.[125] Quoting articles 143[126] and 144[127] of the Namibian Constitution, the Court made the following general statement: 'The Namibian government has,

---

[120] The 1966 Constitution, then in force, provided in s 2(1)(iii) that the 'Government and the people of Malawi shall continue to recognise the sanctity of the personal liberties enshrined in the United Nations' Universal Declaration of Human Rights...'.

[121] Cited by Maluwa (n 31 above) 68.

[122] See ibid 68–9.

[123] Constitution of Malawi 1994, s 211(1).

[124] (1995) 1 SA 51 (NmHC); [1994] 2 CLR 263 (Namibia, HC).

[125] Noting that the provision for non-discrimination in the African Charter does not allow for any exception (86D; 302I).

[126] 'All existing international agreements binding on Namibia shall remain in force, unless and until the National Assembly, acting under article 63(2)(d) hereof, otherwise decide.'

[127] 'Unless otherwise provided by this Constitution or act of parliament, the general rules of public international law and international agreements binding on Namibia under this Constitution shall form part of the law of Namibia.'

as far as can be established, formally recognised the African Charter in accordance with article 143 read with article 63(2)(d) of the Namibian Constitution. The provisions of the Charter have therefore become binding on Namibia and form part of the law of Namibia in accordance with article 143, read with article 144 of the Namibian Constitution'.[128] On this basis the Court rejected arguments that certain hate speech provisions and a regulation criminalizing unfavourable comment about the armed forces were unconstitutional.[129]

The Namibian Immigration Selection Board's decision to refuse a permanent residence permit to a German national (Erna Frank) was the issue before the Namibian Supreme Court in *Chairperson of the Immigration Selection Board v Frank*.[130] Frank is a lesbian and had been involved in a long-standing relationship with another lesbian, a Namibian citizen. They indicated that they would have married if legally able to do so. On behalf of Frank it was argued, amongst other things, that her and her partner's right to family life was infringed by denying Frank a permanent residence permit. In delineating the scope of the right to family life, the majority of the Court referred to articles 17(3), as well as 18(1) and 18(2) of the African Charter. After also invoking the Universal Declaration and the ICCPR, the majority concluded as follows:[131]

The 'family institution' of the African Charter, the United Nations Universal Declaration of Human Rights, the International Covenant on Civil and Political Rights and the Namibian Constitution, envisages a formal relationship between male and female, where sexual intercourse between them in the family context is the method to procreate offspring and thus ensure the perpetuation and survival of the nation and the human race.

In another case, reference was made to international human rights law, but not to the African Charter. A number of escaped prisoners who were put in 'chains' after their recapture, applied for an order directing the prison authorities to remove the irons, as such mechanical restraints violated their right to dignity and not to be subjected to torture or to cruel, inhuman or degrading treatment or punishment. Finding in the prisoners' favour, the Namibian Supreme Court in *Namunjepo v Commanding Officer, Windhoek Prison*[132] referred to the 'contemporary aspirations, norms, expectations and sensitivities of the Namibian People'.[133] Remarking that

---

[128] At 86G-H; 303D. In its decision reversing the court *a quo's* finding, the Namibian Supreme Court did not make reference to the African Charter: *Kauesa v Minister of Home Affairs* (1996) 4 SA 965 (NmSC).

[129] Racial Discrimination Prohibition Amendment Act, s 11(1)(b) and reg 58(32) made in terms of the Police Act (RSA) 7 of 1958.

[130] *Chairperson of the Immigration Selection Board v Frank* 2001 NR 107 (NmSC).

[131] As above, 146G; see also 156C. Although the majority refused to 'read into' the Constitution or the Immigration Act protection of homosexual long-term partners, it referred the matter back to the Immigration Selection Board to apply the *audi alteram partem* principle. It noted that the Board's wide discretion allows for the 'special relationship' between Frank and her long-term partner to be taken into account as one of the factors in the Board's determination.

[132] *Namunjepo v Commanding Officer, Windhoek Prison* [2000] 3 LRC 360 (NmSC).

[133] ibid 372.

Parliament is an important source of these values, the Court continued: 'Therefore the accession of Parliament to both the Convention against Torture and other Cruel Inhuman or Degrading Treatment or Punishment and the ICCPR on 28 November 1994 is significant'. No reference is made to article 5 of the African Charter, in which inherent dignity is guaranteed and torture, cruel, inhuman or degrading treatment or punishment is prohibited in unqualified terms. The reason for this oversight is perhaps explained by the fact that counsel explicitly referred to the other two instruments and apparently not to the Charter.[134]

In a case involving a German national living in Namibia who married a Namibian citizen and wanted to adopt his wife's surname, the relevant legislation provides that wives may adopt their husband's surnames, but that husbands have to follow an administrative process to reverse a presumption of illegality attached to the use of the wife's surname.[135] Finding that the provision does not violate the constitutional guarantee against discrimination of sex,[136] the Supreme Court dismissed the argument for reliance on CEDAW by stating that this Convention is 'of course subject to the Constitution and cannot change the situation'.[137] However, international human rights law still had the last say in this matter, when the UN Human Rights Committee found that the government had violated the ICCPR, and the complainant was awarded individual redress.[138]

8 Nigeria

It is ironic, but perhaps predictable, that the clearest illustration of the potential effect of the African Charter upon domestic law is found in Nigeria during a military regime at a time of severe repression[139] following the nullification of the results of the elections held on 12 June 1993.[140] This is a clear example of the incorporation of the Charter by explicit reference.

Nigeria ratified the African Charter on 22 June 1983. In addition to the African Charter on Human and Peoples' Rights (Ratification and Enforcement) Decree, chapter 4 of the 1979 Constitution, as amended, also protects human rights in Nigeria. In some of the cases to be discussed, the operation of the chapter 4 rights has been suspended explicitly. However, the operation of Charter rights has

---

[134] ibid 371.
[135] Aliens Act, s 9.
[136] Constitution of Namibia 1990, art 10.
[137] *Müller v President of Namibia* 1999 NR 190, 205F.
[138] This case was subsequently submitted to the UN Human Rights Committee, see Ch 3.B above, also on the government's 'compliance' in respect of the specific case.
[139] This fact is also reflected in the proliferation of 'non-official' human rights case reports, such as those published in the *Journal of Human Rights Law and Practice*.
[140] The Nigerian courts were also approached on bases other than the African Charter. In some judgments, judges showed a willingness to stand up to executive conduct, such as Judge Akinsanya in *Abiola v National Electoral Commission* (1993) 1 NLPR 42, in which the High Court of Lagos State ruled that the previous President Babangida lacked the authority to annul the elections and instate an interim government.

never been suspended, leaving the door open for the judicial application of the Charter.[141]

During the previous military regime some judges took tentative steps to ameliorate the eroding impact of military rule on fundamental rights in Nigeria. Eleven youths were convicted and sentenced to death by an 'armed robbery tribunal' in 1988. The fundamental issue to be decided by Longe J in *Garba v Lagos State Attorney-General*[142] was whether the jurisdiction of the High Court of Lagos State was ousted by section 10(3) of the Robbery and Firearms (Special Provisions) Decree 5 of 1984, which reads as follows: 'The question whether any provision of Chapter VI of the Constitution of the Federal Republic of Nigeria 1979 has been, is being or would be contravened by anything done in pursuance of this Decree shall not be inquired into in ... any Court of Law'. As the applicants relied on the right to life contained in that chapter of the Constitution, the respondent argued that the Court lacked jurisdiction to hear the matter. In deciding that it had jurisdiction, the Court referred to the African Charter: 'The African Charter on Human and Peoples' Rights, of which Nigeria is a signatory is now made into our law by African Charter Act 1983, cited by the learned counsel for the applicants. Even if its aspect in our Constitution is suspended or ousted by any provision of our local law, the international aspect of it cannot unilaterally be abrogated'.

Not all Nigerian judges adopted this approach. In *Wahab Akanmu v Attorney-General of Lagos State*,[143] the Court rejected the applicants' request for an order restraining the government from carrying out their execution pending the determination of a communication directed to the African Commission. In this instance, the Court held that Decree 5, quoted in the preceding paragraph, precluded it from considering the application. The Court rejected the contention that the African Charter was part of and enforceable in Nigerian law, remarking as follows: 'As for the African Charter on Human Right (*sic*), this cannot override the Laws of the Land ... The applicants are Nigerians residing in Nigeria. They were charged in Nigeria for Armed Robbery and were convicted and sentenced to death by a Competent Tribunal on the Law of the Land'.[144]

In 1993 the following facts came before the High Court of Lagos State in *The Registered Trustees of the Constitutional Rights Project v President of Nigeria*.[145] Six

[141] See CC Nweze, 'Human Rights and Sustainable Development in the African Charter: A Judicial Prolegomenon to an Integrative Approach to Charter Rights' (1997) 1 *Abia State U L J* 1, 11–12.

[142] *Garba v Lagos State A-G* Suit ID/599M/91 (31 October 1991); see F Falana, 'Application of Fundamental Rights in Nigeria' (1994) 7 (of typed manuscript, unpublished paper presented at workshop on Law, Legal Institutions and Human Rights in Nigeria, held in Lagos, Nigeria, 24–5 November 1994).

[143] *Wahab Akanmu v A-G of Lagos State* Suit M/568/91 (High Court of Lagos State, 31 January 1992).

[144] Quoted in A Lester, L Tedeschini, and B Byfield, 'The Potential Relevance of the European Convention on Human Rights' in Commonwealth Secretariat, *Developing Human Rights Jurisprudence* (vol 4) (London: Commonwealth Secretariat, 1992) 136, 152.

[145] *The Registered Trustees of the Constitutional Rights Project v President of Nigeria* Civil suit M/102/92 (5 May 1992).

persons had been convicted and sentenced to death by a 'Disturbance Tribunal', set up pursuant to the Civil Disturbances (Special Tribunal) Decree 2 of 1987. The State wanted to proceed with their execution. An application had at that stage already been lodged on their behalf with the African Commission.[146] In that application the contention was that the applicants did not receive a fair trial, as required by the African Charter. The application before the domestic court was directed at preventing the government from carrying out the applicants' execution pending the final determination of the communication by the African Commission. When the African Commission finally decided the case (in October 1994, at its 16th session), it found that articles 7 and 26 of the Charter had been violated and recommended that the complainants should be freed.[147] This must stand as one of the clearest examples of how the Charter (and the Commission) has materially affected the destiny of Africans, in that the death sentences have not been enforced.[148]

In the High Court of Lagos the respondents argued that the jurisdiction of the Court to hear the application was excluded by virtue of certain decrees. Section 8(1) of the Civil Disturbances (Special Tribunal) Decree 2 of 1987 provides: 'The validity of any decision, sentence, judgement, conformation, direction, notice or order given or made as the case may be or any other thing whatsoever done under this Act shall not be inquired into in any court of law'. To avoid any doubt, Decree 55 of 1992 was also invoked in their argument. Section 3(1) of that Decree determines that no 'civil proceedings shall lie or be instituted in any court or tribunal for or on account of or in respect of any act, matter or thing done or purported to be done under or pursuant to this Decree by or on behalf of the Military Government'. The respondent argued that the African Charter, by being incorporated into domestic law, lost its status as international law. The Court (*per* Onalaja J) held that the Human and Peoples' Rights (Ratification and Enforcement) Act[149] is also a 'decree' for the purposes of Decree 55 of 1992, but 'it is a Decree with a difference being a Decree to enable effect to be given in the Federal Republic of Nigeria to the African Charter'.[150] The African Charter is a treaty ratified by the Nigerian government.

Since the government was still a member of the OAU (now the AU), Chapter 10 of the federal laws was binding on the government. Assuming that the Human and Peoples' Rights (Ratification and Enforcement) Act is an ordinary decree, the Court was presented with a conflict between it and the ouster clauses. With reference to existing case-law, the Court applied the principle that international law

---

[146] See Communication 87/93, *Constitutional Rights Project (in respect of Lekwot and Others) v Nigeria* (2000) AHRLR 183 (ACHPR 1995) (Eighth Annual Activity Report) (*Lekwot* case).

[147] ibid, para 15.

[148] At its 17th session the Commission decided to bring the file to Nigeria for a planned mission 'in order to make sure that the violations have been repaired'. This mission took place from 7 to 14 March 1997, but the mission report has not yet been submitted (see Tenth Annual Activity Report, paras 21, 22).

[149] Laws of the Federation of Nigeria 1990, ch 10.

[150] *The Registered Trustees of the Constitutional Rights Project v President of Nigeria* (n 145 above) 40 of the typed judgment.

obligations 'prevail over the rules of domestic law when they are incompatible with the latter'.[151] In the light thereof, the Court found that its jurisdiction was preserved by the African Charter, as provisions of the Charter override the ouster clauses.

The judge introduced his judgment with a statement on the significance of the decision: 'This is a case of great constitutional landmark and significance not only for Nigeria but also for member states of OAU as it touches the interpretation of African Charter due to paucity of cases that involved the said Charter. This case opens a novel point with its uniqueness in the approach for the enforcement of the African Charter... with the guide to the courts of member states where there is conflict between the municipal or domestic law of the member state and the said charter...'.[152] This illustrates the leading role of the Nigerian judiciary in making the Charter guarantees effective.

In *Akinnola v General Babangida*[153] the same Court (*per* Hunponu-Wusu J) went a step further. The applicant in this case sought an order declaring the Newspaper Decree 43 of 1993 in violation of the 1979 Nigerian Constitution and contrary to the African Charter. In terms of the Newspaper Decree newspapers had to comply with new registration guidelines. The applicant argued that these guidelines infringed the applicant's freedom of expression, as guaranteed in both the 1979 Constitution and the African Charter.

Again the state party raised jurisdiction as a preliminary objection, arguing that enactments in the Constitution Suspension and Modification Act (similar to those in the *Lekwot* case above) ousted the jurisdiction of the courts. The Court relied on the judgment previously given by Onalaja J, extending it to apply to cases brought under the Nigerian Constitution and the African Charter in the domestic courts: 'Since the Courts have held that the African Charter is like an enactment of the Federal Government like a decree, it follows that if there is a conflict between an enactment ousting the jurisdiction of the Court and another which does not, the Court should lean more on the one that preserves the jurisdiction of the Court'. The judge also referred to the proceedings of the Judicial Colloquium held in Bangalore in 1988, in which Chief Justice Helfen of Pakistan said: 'The International human rights norms are in fact part of the constitutional expression of liberties guaranteed at the national level. The domestic Courts can assume the task of expanding these liberties'.

Counsel for the state in *Nemi v The State*[154] argued that a lacuna exists in Nigerian law for the enforcement of the rights in the Charter. A particular enforcement procedure was enacted in the 1979 Constitution[155] to provide for a process of enforcing fundamental rights guaranteed in that Constitution. Similar

---

[151] ibid, 44 of the typed judgment.　　　　[152] ibid, 1 of the typed judgment.

[153] *Akinnola v General Babangida* judgment reprinted in (1994) 4 *J of Human Rights L and Practice* 250.

[154] *Nemi v The State* [1994] 1 LRC 376 (Nigeria, SC).

[155] Constitution of Nigeria 1979, s 42.

provision was not made in the African Charter or the Ratification and Enforcement Act. Rejecting this argument, Bello CJ continued: 'Since the Charter has become part of our domestic law, the enforcement of its provisions like all our other laws fall (*sic*) within the judicial powers of the courts as provided by the Constitution and all other laws relating thereto'.[156]

Another case in which reference was made to the African Charter is *Agbakoba v Director State Security Services*.[157] The passport of the applicant in this case was impounded by a state security official without giving any reasons. The High Court held that a passport was the property of the government and could be withdrawn at any time. Allowing an appeal against the judgment, the Court of Appeal found that the seizure of the passport constituted a violation of the right to freedom of movement. The Court observed that the right (particularly the right not to be refused entry to or exit from one's country) was recognized in the African Charter.

In two cases dealing with the occupation and closure of newspaper premises the government was found to have violated the Constitution.[158] Although the findings were not based on the African Charter, both applications made reference to the violation of rights protected in the Charter.

The Court of Appeal affirmed the status of the Charter as superior to that of ordinary legislation in *Fawehinmi v Abacha*.[159] In this case, the appellant was arrested without a warrant and detained by members of the state security services. He sought relief on the basis that his rights guaranteed in both the 1979 Constitution and under Chapter 10 (incorporating the African Charter) had been violated. The state argued that the members of the state security forces had been granted immunity and that the jurisdiction of the Courts had been ousted in terms of various military decrees. The Court of Appeal found that the provisions of the African Charter, as incorporated into Chapter 10, were superior to national legislation. It reasoned as follows: 'Cap 10 of the Laws of the Federation are provisions in a class of their own. While the Decrees of the Federal Military Government may over-ride other municipal laws, they cannot oust the jurisdiction of the court whenever properly called upon to do so in relation to matters pertaining to human rights under the African Charter. They are protected by the International Law and the Federal Military Government is not legally permitted to legislate out of its obligations'.[160] Despite this finding, the Court concluded that the trial court was correct in declining jurisdiction, because the appellant had adopted the wrong procedural route.[161]

---

[156] *Nemi v The State* (n 154 above) para 385C–D.

[157] *Agbakoba v Director State Security Services* [1994] 6 Nigeria Weekly L Rep 475; [1996] 1 CHRD. 89.

[158] *Punch Nigeria Ltd v A-G* (1996) 1 CHRD 46 and *Concord Press of Nigeria Ltd v A-G* (1996) 1 CHRD 47.

[159] *Fawehinmi v Abacha* (1996) 9 NWLR (Pt 475) 710.

[160] ibid 747, quoted by E Ojukwa, 'Is *Fawehinmi v Abacha* a Correct Decision?' (1997) 1 *Legal Practice Notes: Human Rights LJ* 21.

[161] For criticism of this finding, see Ojukwa (n 160 above) n 77.

Commissioner Umozurike, when interviewed about the domestic invocation of the Charter, referred to the 'latest case *Fawehinmi v Attorney-General*' in which it was held 'in an important *ratio decidendi* that the African Charter has priority over any decree by government and cannot be excluded from application by decree'.[162] Despite the importance of this finding, it has not served to benefit the individual who sought relief.

9 Senegal

When questioned about the Charter's domestic application in Senegal, a previous Chairperson of the African Commission, Youssoupha Ndiaye, referred in vague terms to 'a decision stating that the African Charter and international treaties have direct applicability in the courts of Senegal'.[163] Ndiaye may be referring to the case in which the Senegalese Constitutional Court declared certain provisions of the Electoral Code unconstitutional on the basis of its conflict with rights in the Constitution, but also with article 3 of the African Charter.[164] To Ouguergouz, the importance of this decision is that the African Charter was taken together ('*en bloc*') with the constitutional provisions as a yardstick for 'constitutionality'.[165] To him, this seems to conflict with article 79 of the Constitution, which gives international agreements a status above 'law', but not the Constitution. He ascribes the 'elevation' of the African Charter to a status equal with the Constitution to the influence of Ndiaye, who was at the time both President of the Court and a member of the African Commission.

10 South Africa

When South Africa became a democracy in 1994, its Constitution for the first time included a justiciable Bill of Rights, of which the newly established Constitutional Court became the final arbiter. The African Charter, to which South Africa acceded in 1996, has been invoked in numerous judgments, but mostly as a mere confirmation of existing constitutional provisions.

Even before accession, in a decision declaring capital punishment unconstitutional,[166] Chaskalson P made a footnoted reference to the African Charter in his leading judgment, emphasizing that the Charter prohibits the arbitrary deprivation of life.[167] O'Regan J referred to the same provision of the Charter, contrasting it with the open-ended formulation of the 1993 Constitution, which protected

---

[162] Interview reported in (1996) (October–December) *AFLAQ* 47.
[163] See ibid 39.
[164] Decision 3-C-98 of 3 March 1998.
[165] F Ouguergouz, 'L'Application de la Charte Africaine des Droits et des Peuples par les Autorités Nationales en Afrique Occidentale' in Flauss and Lambert-Abdelgawad (n 70 above) 161, 202–3.
[166] *S v Makwanyane* (1995) 3 SA 391 (CC).
[167] ibid, para 36 n 52.

life as such.[168] In *S v Williams*,[169] also decided prior to South Africa becoming a state party, the Court declared juvenile whipping unconstitutional. Article 5 of the African Charter helped Langa J to substantiate the assertion that section 11(2) of the 1993 Constitution, which outlawed cruel, inhuman, and degrading treatment or punishment, corresponds with most international human rights instruments.[170] However, the judge seems to have gone beyond referring to the African Charter as an interpretative tool when he mentioned that Mozambique had abolished corporal punishment in 1989 '*in accordance with* the country's obligations under the African Charter'.[171]

A critical issue in *Ferreira v Levin NO*[172] was the interpretation of the right to freedom and security of the person in the 1993 Constitution.[173] Relying on, amongst others, the philosophers Berlin and Kant, as well as Canadian, American, and German case-law, Ackermann J opted for a broad interpretation of the right. Chaskalson P, with whom the majority agreed, adopted a narrow interpretation. Support for an interpretation limiting 'freedom and security of the person' to a context relating to detention or other physical constraints was found in public international law, including the African Charter.[174] In another case predating South Africa's accession to the Charter, involving the possession of indecent material, Mokgoro J found the African Charter unequivocal in its providing for the right to receive information.[175]

Since South Africa became a state party to the Charter, this tendency has changed very gradually. In *AZAPO v President of the RSA*,[176] the South African Constitutional Court had to consider the constitutionality of a provision in the Promotion of National Unity and Reconciliation Act,[177] which precluded the civil and criminal liability of persons granted amnesty under the Act. The argument on behalf of the applicants was that such a preclusion of liability flies in the face of the constitutional guarantee of victims to have justiciable disputes settled by a court of law.[178] Finding against the applicant, the Court held that the right of access to courts had been qualified by the 'post-amble'[179] of the 1993 Constitution, in terms of which Parliament was required to adopt amnesty legislation. The Court referred to the four 1949 Geneva Conventions and the two 1977 Protocols thereto, but not to the African Charter. Having exhausted local remedies, the

---

[168] ibid, para 324 n 221.
[169] *S v Williams* (1995) 3 SA 632 (CC).
[170] ibid, para 21 n 24.
[171] ibid, para 40 n 58 (emphasis added).
[172] *Ferreira v Levin NO* (1996) 1 SA 984 (CC).
[173] Constitution of the Republic of South Africa 1993, s 11(1).
[174] *Ferreira v Levin NO* (n 172 above) para 170.
[175] See *Case v Minister of Safety and Security* (1996) 3 SA 617 (CC) at para 29 n 41, referring to art 9 of the African Charter.
[176] *AZAPO v President of RSA* (1996) 4 SA 671 (CC).
[177] Promotion of National Unity and Reconciliation Act 34 of 1995, s 20(7).
[178] Constitution of the Republic of South Africa 1993, s 22.
[179] Titled 'National Unity and Reconciliation'.

applicants could therefore have availed themselves of the protection under article 7(1) of the African Charter which states as follows: 'Every individual shall have the right to have his cause heard', comprising 'the right to an appeal to competent national organs against acts of violating his fundamental rights'.[180] Why did this not happen? Were the applicants (and their lawyers) unaware of this possibility? Were they by then too exhausted? Was it due to a lack of confidence in the African human rights system? The most plausible explanation may be that South Africa acceded to the Charter on 9 July 1996, sometime after the Act was adopted, and that the judgment in the case was delivered on 25 July 1996, only two weeks after South Africa had become a state party to the Charter. Still, in my view the denial of the article 7(1)(a) guarantee constituted a 'continuous violation' and could have been adjudicated under the African Charter.

Neglect of the African Charter is striking in the *First Certification* case,[181] where extensive reference is made to other constitutions and international instruments,[182] while the African Charter is mentioned only twice: once as part of some background on developments in international human rights,[183] and once to support the proposition that a right to intellectual property is rarely recognized in regional human rights conventions.[184] Disregard for the African Charter appears from the *Second Certification* case,[185] where the Court for example did not include the Charter in its survey of freedom of trade under foreign and international law.[186]

The relatively minimal role of the African Charter in these cases may be explained by the fact that South Africa's accession did not enjoy extensive media coverage and was not preceded by discussions in legal circles. However, the limited degree to which South African judges have relied upon the African Charter in subsequent years remains disappointing, and is a reminder that the professional training of both judges and senior counsel dates from a period when the African regional human rights system was absent from legal studies.[187]

Due to their open-ended formulation, the rights in the Charter may lead to diverging interpretations, especially when the Commission has not given them more concrete content in resolutions or decisions. Used as an interpretive tool, international law may be invoked not only to protect, but also to restrict litigants' benefits under the Constitution. In *Volks NO v Robinson*,[188] for example, the question before the Constitutional Court was whether the Maintenance of

[180] Art 7(1)(a).
[181] *Ex p Chairperson of the Constitutional Assembly: In re Certification of the Constitution of the Republic of South Africa 1996* (1996) 4 SA 744 (CC), judgment of 6 September 1996.
[182] ibid, eg paras 71 and 73.
[183] ibid, para 50 n 46.
[184] ibid, para 75n 67.
[185] *Ex p Chairperson of the Constitutional Assembly: In re Certification of the Amended Text of the Constitution of the Republic of South Africa 1996* (1997) 2 SA 97 (CC).
[186] ibid, paras 18–21.
[187] For an incorrect reference to the African Charter as the 'United Nations' Charter on Human and Peoples' Rights', see *Matukane v Laerskool Potgietersrus* [1996] 1 All SA 468 (T), 476b.
[188] *Volks NO v Robinson* (2005) 5 BCLR 446 (CC) paras 82–5.

Surviving Spouses Act was constitutional in so far as it allowed surviving spouses, and not partners in a permanent life partnership, to benefit from the estate of his or her spouse. In support of his reasoning that the state had a duty to protect the institution of marriage and therefore could afford protection to married persons that is not afforded to others (such as long-term unmarried partners), the Court relied on the emphasis placed on the family under the African Charter, and the right to marry provided for in the ICCPR. However, this interpretation is disputable. The concept of 'family' under the African Charter is not defined, and arguably leaves room for the inclusion of 'heterosexual life partners', especially given that the Charter does not include a 'right to marry'.

Clearly contextualized in a broader African framework, *Kaunda v President of South Africa*,[189] which interrogated whether the South African government has a duty to ensure the right to a fair trial in another African country of nationals who were alleged mercenaries, invoked the African Charter more pertinently. While the majority mentions the Charter, fleetingly, in support of its conclusion that diplomatic protection is not regarded as a human right, the minority places much stronger reliance on and gives more prominence to the Charter in support of its finding that the alleged mercenaries' extradition would lead to an unfair trial. Similarly, in *Doctors for Life International v Speaker of the National Assembly*,[190] both the majority and minority cited international law in support of their conclusions about the scope of public participation that is required for law-making. The majority, which requires substantial direct participation, found support for its reasoning in the ICCPR and the African Charter.[191] In contrast, the minority found support in 'all' international instruments for its conclusion that indirect public participation 'without any direct component' is sufficient for valid law-making.[192]

Other AU and UN treaties are also invoked as interpretive sources. In *Bhe v Magistrate, Khayelitsha*,[193] the South African Constitutional Court declared unconstitutional and invalidated the rule of male primogeniture as it applied to the African customary law of inheritance. Making reference to provisions of the CRC, ICCPR, and the African Charter on the Rights and Welfare of the Child (African Children's Charter), the Court emphasizes that it does so 'in interpreting' the relevant provision of the South African Constitution.[194] In a number of other judgments, the African Children's Charter was referred to, often as confirmation of the 'best interests of the child' principle in the South African Constitution,[195] but sometimes more purposively.[196]

---

[189] (2005) 4 SA 235 (CC).
[190] (2006) 12 BCLR 1399 (CC).
[191] ibid 1433–4, the African Charter, arts 9, 13, and 25 are cited.
[192] ibid 1505H-I.
[193] *Bhe v Magistrate, Khayelitsha* (2005) 1 BCLR 1 (CC).
[194] ibid, para 55.
[195] See eg *B v M* (2006) 9 BCLR 1034 (W), para 137.
[196] See eg *Centre for Child Law v Minister of Home Affairs* (2005) 6 SA 50 (T), in which CRC and the African Children's Charter are referred to as sources of the right to education and health care of

While South African courts from time to time relied on 'General Comments' on UN treaties, and on the jurisprudence of UN and other regional human rights bodies, they did not make use of the African Commission's resolutions and decisions. The judgment in *City of Johannesburg v Rand Properties and Others* provides an example of a missed opportunity to do so.[197] In the judgment, Jajbhay J noted that the Charter does not include a right to housing, but argued that the right to life and to health 'provide a basis for the assertion' of such a right. This very line of reasoning informed the Commission's decision in the *Ogoniland* case,[198] and could have been cited in support of the judge's finding.

11 Tanzania

From a perusal of Maina Peter's authoritative collection of Tanzanian case-law, entitled *Human Rights in Tanzania: Selected Cases and Materials*,[199] it would appear that the African Charter had not featured in any way before Tanzanian courts. The following two cases, nonetheless, deserve mention.

Equality of the sexes was the issue in *Ephrahim v Pastory*,[200] a decision of the Tanzanian High Court. A woman inherited clan land from her father. In old age, the woman decided to sell the land. The willing buyer happened to be someone not belonging to the clan. A male clan member filed a suit to declare the sale void, as females do not have the power to sell clan land. The relevant codification of customary law (of the Haya group) indeed provides that clan land shall not be sold by female members of the clan. In terms of an amendment to the Tanzanian Constitution, a bill of rights was introduced.[201] In terms thereof a court must construe existing law 'as may be necessary to bring it into conformity with' the provisions of the bill of rights.[202] Article 13(4) of the bill of rights prohibits discrimination against women. In interpreting article 13(4), the Court referred to similar provisions in the Universal Declaration of Human Rights and the ICCPR, and to the fact that Tanzania ratified the Convention on the Elimination of All Forms of Discrimination against Women. Mwalusanya J continued:

That is not all. Tanzania has also ratified the African Charter on Human and Peoples' Rights which in art 18(3) prohibits discrimination based on account of sex... The principles

---

children (para 24). After noting that South Africa subscribes to the principles in these treaties, De Vos J warned that 'all these lofty ideas become hypocritical nonsense if the policies and sentiments are not translated into action' (para 30).

  [197] (2006) 6 BCLR 728 (W). But see also *Modderklip v President, RSA* (2003) 6 BCLR 638 T 681–2.
  [198] n 58 above.
  [199] CM Peter, *Human Rights in Tanzania: Selected Cases and Materials* (Cologne: Rudiger Koppe Verlag, 1997).
  [200] *Ephrahim v Pastory* [1990] LRC (Constitutional and Administrative L Rep) 757; (2001) AHRLR 236 (TzHC 1990).
  [201] By means of the Constitution (Consequential, Transitional and Temporal Provisions) Act 16 of 1984, which took effect in March 1988.
  [202] Constitution (Consequential, Transitional and Temporal Provisions) Act, s 5(1).

enunciated in the above-named documents are a standard below which any civilised nation will be ashamed to fall. It is clear ... that the customary law under discussion flies in the face of our Bill of Rights as well as the international conventions to which we are signatories.[203]

As a result, he found the Haya customary rule to be inconsistent with the Bill of Rights and ordered that the Constitution should prevail.[204]

In *DPP v Pete*,[205] Tanzania's highest court, the Court of Appeal, heard an appeal against a judgment of Mwalusanya J.[206] Sub-sections 148(4) and 148(5) of the Criminal Procedure Act 1985 were declared unconstitutional by him in the lower court. The first sub-section provided that bail had to be denied if the Director of Public Prosecutions issued a certificate to the effect that the release of a detained person would be prejudicial to the safety of the Republic. The second made it impossible for courts to grant bail in respect of certain categories of offences, including offences in which possessing a firearm was an element. In the course of interpreting the bill of rights, the Court found support for its interpretation in the African Charter: 'Tanzania signed the Charter on 31 May, 1982 and ratified it on 18 February, 1984. Since our Bill of Rights and Duties was introduced into the Constitution under the Fifth Amendment in February 1985, that is, slightly over three years after Tanzania signed the Charter, and about a year after ratification, account must be taken of the Charter in interpreting our Bill of Rights and Duties'.[207] The Court referred to the Preamble to the Charter and concluded: 'It seems evident in our view that the Bill of Rights and Duties embodied in our Constitution is consistent with the concepts underlying the African Charter on Human and Peoples' Rights as stated in the Preamble to the Charter'.[208] The Court consequently affirmed the decision of the lower court, holding that provisions of the Criminal Procedure Act violated the individual's right to personal freedom.[209]

12 Uganda

Reference is made to a Ugandan case in which the African Charter could have been invoked, but was not: *Attorney General v Abuki*.[210] The respondent had been convicted on a charge of practising witchcraft. Part of his sentence was an order under section 7 of the Witchcraft Act that he be banished 'from that home' for ten years after completion of his 22 months' imprisonment. Departing from the

---

[203] *Ephrahim v Pastory* (n 200 above) 763a–c; para 10.

[204] ibid 770c; para 42.

[205] *DPP v Pete* [1991] LRC (Constitutional and Administrative L Rep) 553.

[206] For a comment on the case, see S Coldham, 'Case Notes (*Ephrahim v Pastory; DPP v Pete*)' (1991) 35 *JAL* 205.

[207] *DPP v Pete* (n 205 above), 565 *per* Nyalali CJ, Makame, and Ramadhani JJA.

[208] ibid, 566.

[209] ibid, 568. The violation could also not be 'saved' under ss 30 or 31 of the bill of rights, because the provision was over-broad (at 572).

[210] *A-G v Abuki* [2001] 1 LRC 63 (Ug SC).

premise that such an exclusion order had the effect of excluding the offender from his home and land for ten years, the Court declared section 7 unconstitutional. The majority based its decision on the right not to undergo cruel, inhuman, or degrading punishment. The African Charter contains a similar prohibition. It also provides for the right to property, which may only be encroached upon under circumscribed circumstances.[211]

In *Kigula v Attorney General*,[212] a majority of the Ugandan Supreme Court found that the *mandatory* imposition of the death penalty and the exclusion of the right to appeal against such sentences constituted cruel, inhuman, and degrading punishment contrary to the Ugandan Constitution. No reference was made to the Charter, or, more pertinently, to the Commission's resolution urging states to ensure that persons accused of crimes carrying the death penalty as a possible sentence should be 'afforded all the guarantees' of the Charter (which includes the right to appeal),[213] and to limit the imposition of the death sentence to the 'most serious offences'. One of the judges referred to the African Charter in his opinion concurring with the Court's finding that the death sentence, as such, does not conflict with the right to life or any other provision of the Ugandan Constitution.[214]

13 Zambia

Counsel in *Longwe v Intercontinental Hotels*[215] referred to international human rights documents, including the African Charter. The Zambian High Court (*per* Musumali J) made some remarks about the effect of international treaties ratified by Zambia:

It is my considered view that ratification of such documents by a nation state without reservations is a clear testimony to the willingness by that state to be bound by the provisions of such a document. Since there is that willingness, if an issue comes before this Court which would not be covered by local legislation but would be covered by such international document, I would take judicial notice of that treaty or convention in my resolution of the dispute.[216]

The African Charter was cited explicitly as a treaty with such an effect.[217] By allowing for 'judicial notice' to be taken of international treaties in resolving disputes, the

---

211 African Charter, art 14.

212 [2006] 3 LRC 388 (Uganda).

213 ACHPR/Res.42(XXVI)99, Resolution Urging the States to Envisage a Moratorium on the Death Penalty, adopted at the Commission's 26th session, 15 November 1999. On the right to appeal, the majority would also have found support in the Commission's decision in eg Communications 137/94, 139/94, 154/96, 161/97 (joined), *International Pen and Others (on behalf of Saro-Wiwa) v Nigeria* (2000) AHRLR 212 (ACHPR 1998) (12th Annual Activity Report).

214 *Kigula v Attorney General* (n 212 above), 403i (Byamugisha JA referring to the African Charter to illustrate that international law still recognizes that the death penalty does not necessarily conflict with the right to life).

215 *Longwe v Intercontinental Hotels* [1993] 4 LRC (Constitutional and Administrative L Rep) 221.

216 ibid, 233.   217 ibid.

Court seems to suggest an approach that amounts to the treaty provisions being considered as 'self-executing'.

14 Zimbabwe

Zimbabwe ratified the African Charter on 30 May 1986. The Zimbabwean Constitution was silent on the status of international law until a clear dualist position was introduced in 1993.[218] Under each of the three Chief Justices since 1986, Dumbutshena, Gubbay, and Chidyausiku,[219] judicial reliance had been placed on international human rights treaties—presumably based on the common law presumption of statutory interpretation referred to earlier. However, in doing so, one finds scant reference to the African Charter. In two significant decisions dealing with corporal punishment, the activist Dumbutshena Supreme Court even looked beyond treaties ratified by Zimbabwe to find anchors for its progressive interpretations of the Constitution, but did not refer to the African Charter.[220]

The African Charter was referred to as one of a number of international instruments containing a right to freedom of movement and travel, supporting the High Court's judgment in *Chirwa v Registrar-General*.[221] In a case concerning the refusal of a licence to operate a mobile cellular telephone service, the Supreme Court ruled that such a refusal violated the applicant's freedom of expression.[222] Referring to its inclusion in a number of international human rights instruments, the Court held that this right is an indispensable condition for a free and democratic society.[223]

In its 2000 judgment, *S v Banana*,[224] a majority of the Zimbabwean Supreme Court found the criminalization of sodomy to be in line with the Constitution. Neither the majority nor the minority made any reference to the African Charter in arriving at their conclusions. The majority held that the Court should not strain itself to interpret constitutional provisions in order 'to modernise the social mores' of a conservative society.[225] This argument could arguably have been bolstered by references to the values of the 'African civilization', referred to in the

---

[218] Constitution of Zimbabwe 1979, as amended in 1993, s 111B(1), which stipulates that an international treaty 'shall not form part of the law of Zimbabwe unless it has been incorporated into the law by or under an Act of Parliament'. The 1993 amendment sees much further than an amendment introduced in 1987, which requires Parliament to 'ratify' international agreements that 'impose fiscal obligations on Zimbabwe'. In fact, this provision has been retained in the Constitution when it was amended in 1993. The 'ratification' by Parliament relates to the validity of the agreement, and not to its domestic effect.

[219] Dumbutshena CJ and Gubbay CJ served during the 'golden era of human rights litigation' from 1985 to mid-2001 (see A De Bourbon, 'Human Rights Litigation in Zimbabwe: Past, Present and Future' (2003) 3 *AHRLJ* 195, 206). The current Chief Justice, Chidyausiku, took office in mid-2001.

[220] *S v Ncube* (1988) 2 SA 702 (ZS) (see the reference also to US courts at eg 718) and *S v A Juvenile* (1990) 4 SA 151 (ZS).

[221] *Chirwa v Registrar-General* (1993) 1 ZLR 1 (H).

[222] *Retrofit v Telecommunications Corporation* (1996) 1 SA 847 (ZS).

[223] One of these references is to the African Charter, art 9 (ibid, 856).

[224] *S v Banana* (2000) 3 SA 885 (ZSC).

[225] ibid, 935.

Preamble to the Charter and the explicit duty on state parties to protect the family which is the custodian of 'morals and traditional values recognized by the community'.[226] On the other hand, the minority[227] could have made much of the guarantee of non-discrimination in the open-ended listed grounds in article 2.[228] Instead, the Court relied on interpretations based on the European Convention and the South African Constitution. The availability, accessibility, and relevance of these two instruments do not justify a total negation of the African Charter, and the subsequent non-submission of the case to the African Commission.

In this instance, the non-submission may have been motivated by the history of a communication previously submitted to the Commission. In this communication, the complaint alleged that the Zimbabwean legislation criminalizing male, but not female, consensual homosexual sex infringes the Charter's non-discrimination provision. Although the complaint was withdrawn, Ankumah quotes the Commissioner who acted as rapporteur as saying the following:

> Because of the deleterious nature of homosexuality, the Commission seizes the opportunity to make a pronouncement on it. Although homosexuality and lesbianism are gaining recognition in certain parts of the world, this is not the case in Africa. Homosexuality offends the African sense of dignity and morality and is inconsistent with positive African values.[229]

A case decided in the Chidyausiku era, *Kachingwe and Others v Minister of Home Affairs and Another*,[230] highlights the important role of legal counsel in arguing on the basis of international human rights law. Confronted with an argument that the African Charter and the ICCPR have become integrated into Zimbabwean law without 'explicit [domesticating] legislation', the Court observed that it had 'no doubt that, in all probability' this contention was correct.[231] In other words, the Court seems to accept that treaties ratified before the 1993 amendment need not have been domesticated to be the source of domestic remedies. However, it held that the determination of that particular issue was not necessary, because the relevant international law provisions are 'almost identical' to those in the Zimbabwean Constitution. On the facts of the case, the Court held that the conditions of detention in which the applicants found themselves violated article 15(1) of the Zimbabwean Constitution (the prohibition of inhuman and degrading treatment). In arriving at this conclusion the Court held three findings of the African Commission, to which counsel had referred it, to be of 'persuasive' value.[232] Although the Court found the government

---

226 African Charter, art 18(2).
227 Gubbay CJ and Ebrahim JA.
228 African Charter, art 2 ends in 'or other status'.
229 EA Ankumah, *The African Commission on Human and Peoples' Rights: Practice and Procedures* (The Hague: Martinus Nijhoff, 1996) 174.
230 [2006] 1 All SA 412 (ZS).
231 ibid, 425j; there seems to be some confusion about the requirements for approval (s 111B(2)) and domestication (s 111B(1), n 218 above).
232 ibid, 426c; these three findings (referred to as 'reports' in the case) are Communication 255/98, *Huri-Laws v Nigeria* (2000) AHRLR 273 (ACHPR 2000) (14th Annual Activity Report): Communication 151/96, *Civil Liberties Organisation v Nigeria* (2000) AHRLR 243 (ACHPR 1999)

in violation of the Constitution, and by implication of its international law obligations, the remedial orders were very narrow in that they related only to the toilet facility, toilet paper, and washing basin in the police cells of two specific police stations, and not to conditions of overcrowding and to the situation in other places of detention.

D Conclusion

International human rights law does not form an effective part of domestic law in Africa. It is rarely used on its own as the source of an enforceable right. Courts much more frequently invoke international human rights standards as interpretative guides, alongside constitutional provisions, to underscore or support a particular interpretation. Using the Charter as an interpretative guide is the most likely first step in extending the sphere of influence of the Charter, in line with the African Commission's resolution, adopted at its 19th session, urging judges and magistrates in African states to 'play a greater role in incorporating the Charter and future jurisprudence of the Commission' in their judgments.[233] Although some cases illustrate their role as interpretative guides and as support to legitimate a court's reasoning, very often international human rights norms are invoked merely as an afterthought not linked to the outcome of the case.

As far as the African Charter, in particular, is concerned, it has been noted that in many cases where interpretative reliance could have been placed on the Charter, this was not done. Particularly in the corporal punishment cases decided by Southern African courts (Namibia, South Africa and Zimbabwe), the European rather than the African system was referred to. An obvious explanation for this preference is the fact that the abstract norm 'cruel, inhuman and degrading punishment' has been given concrete content in European jurisprudence.[234] In one instance the African Charter had not yet been ratified at the time the case was instituted or decided.[235] These reasons do not explain why a Cameroonian court relied on the Universal Declaration of Human Rights to come to its decision, when reliance on a corresponding provision in the African Charter was possible.[236]

(13th Annual Activity Report); and Communication 232/99, *Ouko v Kenya* (2000) AHRLR 135 (ACHPR 2000) (14th Annual Activity Report).

[233] Resolution on the Role of Lawyers and Judges in Integration of the Charter and Enhancement of the Commission's Work in National and Sub-regional Systems, Ninth Annual Activity Report, Annex VII.

[234] See eg the remarks by Gubbay, a past Chief Justice of Zimbabwe: '... we have looked to precedential judicial decisions emanating from those jurisdictions whose reputation for human rights is highly regarded and, of course, the opinions of the European Court of Human Rights' (1997) 19 *HRQ* 277, 253.

[235] This justifies the omission in the Namibian case *Ex p A-G, Namibia: In re Corporal Punishment by Organs of State* (1991) 3 SA 76 (NmS).

[236] The *People v Nya Henry and Others*, case BA/236C/01-02, Court of First Instance of Bamenda, judgment of 29 October 2001; (2005) 1 Cameroon Common Law Rep Part 10, 61, 65.

One possible reason is a desire for international legitimation.[237] A further reason why African courts have not relied explicitly on the Charter, even as an interpretative guide, is that local courts primarily interpret and apply national law. In some instances, where the provisions of the Charter have been 'transformed' into domestic law, the international and national systems overlap, causing judicial application of national law to become a simultaneous (albeit implicit) application of the Charter's provisions. Although this may not be stated explicitly, the Charter has effectively been applied under such circumstances. Even if the Charter had been domesticated, it is still possible for domestic courts to make reference to the findings of the African Commission especially in cases where the African Commission case-law provides a clear and useful precedent.[238]

A growing judicial awareness of the African Charter has been experienced since the 1990s, in some instances following the creation of new domestic institutions for the enforcement of constitutional rights, as exemplified by the case-law emanating from Benin and South Africa. There is also some evidence of a cumulative or domino effect. Once a single case has been decided on the basis of the African Charter, others follow, as in the case of Nigeria. The awareness of a single judge may have a disproportionate impact, underscoring how different matters could have been if more had followed this example. The lone voice of Mwalusanya J of the Tanzanian High Court epitomizes the singular resolve of one judge to convert the guarantees of a bill of rights into reality.

As some South African cases in particular illustrate, due to their vague and open-ended character international human rights standards may be interpreted differently by different judges. It is therefore important that judicial reliance is placed on the resolutions and decisions of the Commission, and not on the Charter alone.

As some recent case-law illustrates, the frequent and innovative use of the Charter by the local judiciary is closely linked to arguments forwarded by legal counsel.[239] For this reason, not only judges, but lawyers more generally should be exposed to training programmes on the Charter. In this, NGOs and law societies in the different countries will have to play an active role.[240]

---

[237] The Judge reiterated that the decision confirms that Cameroon is a 'state of law', and ordered that copies of the judgment should be served not only on the head of state, but also a number of foreign ambassadors and INGOs based in Cameroon.

[238] See eg *Jonah Gbemre v Shell Petroleum Development Company Nigeria Ltd and Others*, suit FHC/B/CS/53/05, High Court of Nigeria Benin Judicial Division, 14 November 2005 (on file with author), in which the Court omitted any reference to the *Ogoniland* case (also see Ch 4 above).

[239] See eg the remarks by Onalaja J in *The Registered Trustees of the Constitutional Rights Project v The President of Nigeria* (n 145 above) at 46–7 of the typed judgement: 'Let me put on record that the ingenuity in the quintessence manner and dexterity of the learned counsel for the applicant/respondent has shed a new light and horizon on African Charter on Human and Peoples' Rights in African jurisprudence (*sic*). It has reflected the law and lawyer in the words of Dean Roscoe Pound as social engineers'.

[240] See also the African Commission's recommendation at its 19th session in which it urged bodies in civil society 'to initiate specialised and comprehensive training for judicial officers, lawyers at national and sub-regional level' (Ninth Annual Activity Report, Annex VII).

Many of the examples above illustrate that constitutional prescriptions do not guarantee favourable outcomes. On the contrary, activist courts with a limited legal mandate have sometimes allowed international law to play a pronounced role and reached progressive outcomes. It is not so much the legal position as the awareness, attitude, and judicial activism that allows international human rights law to flourish domestically.

One should neither overestimate nor undervalue the potential role of international human rights law in the domestic system. There is enough evidence to support a claim that domestic judicial reliance on international law has become accepted as a general principle of law. As a source of interpretation, international human rights law—not so much treaties, but treaty interpretations—may steer and soften interpretations of existing national law. When international standards fill a gap by supplementing existing domestic remedies, the question should not be whether the national legal system is 'monist' or 'dualist'. Instead, the focus should fall on the 'self-executing' nature of the applicable treaty provision. By ratifying a treaty a state becomes bound to give effect to its provisions. If a treaty provision allows for direct 'enforcement' as a source of a domestic remedy, it should be applied in that way—irrespective of the legal tradition that prevails in a particular country.

14

Justiciability of Socio-economic Rights at the Domestic Level

A Justiciability as Accountability

Africa is a rich continent. It is abundant in natural resources, such as oil and gas; in minerals, such as cobalt, vanadium, manganese, phosphate, and bauxite; in iron ore; in precious metals, such as gold and silver; and in diamonds.[1] With the

---

[1] In 1998, out of 103 minerals, Africa held the most estimated reserves of 24 (or 23%), second most of 7 (7%), and third most of 21 minerals (20%). It also held more than 50% of cobalt, gold, diamonds, vanadium, manganese, phosphate, platinum, chromium, and iridium reserves. It held most of the world's iron and copper ore; and third most of the world's bauxite (M Alemayehu, *Industrializing Africa: Development Options and Challenges for the 21st Century* (Trenton: Africa World Press, 2000) 93–8. Estimates are that Guinea has 27% of the world's bauxite; together, South Africa and Gabon have 80% of the world's manganese; that more than half the phosphate reserves are located in Morocco (F Maury, 'Ces Richesses que l'Afrique Laisse Echapper' (2006) 2377 *Jeune Afrique* 70).

world's greatest surviving tropical rain forests, it is rich in timber. Even its animal kingdom contributes to its riches, providing the dubious promise of ivory.[2]

Tell that to Africa's impoverished. Too often the hardship of eking out a livelihood leaves them unaware of the profitable goings-on in enclaves of exploitation, of forests that disappear overnight, of railway lines carrying tons of iron ore to waiting ships. Experience has shown that resource abundance is most frequently a curse, leading to 'rentier states' that are highly dependent on 'external rents produced by a few economic actors'.[3] With the stakes so high and the involvement of civil society so small, political power becomes increasingly centralized and authoritarian. Accountability wanes and corruption holds sway. An insightful study concludes that higher levels of natural resources are 'associated with higher levels of government consumption and worse government performance'.[4] Despite recent growth rates in many African states,[5] inequality spirals.[6] Even in states with fewer resources, there is a gulf between the masses and the few who have direct or indirect access to resources. In whatever way it is measured, impoverishment is rife in Africa.

Converting these 'needs' and 'services' into entitlements ('justiciable socio-economic rights')[7] may play some part in ensuring that diamonds, oil, and ore are not only the incumbent regime's best friends, but benefit the people of African countries as well. The justiciability of socio-economic rights does not provide a simple or one-dimensional solution. To have a meaningful effect, justiciability has to go hand in hand with a respect for the rule of law; an independent, functioning

---

[2] As a rapacious scramble for Africa met the desperation of a politically and economically side-lined country, Zimbabwe sold 30 tons of ivory to China (RW Johnson, 'China's Empire-Builders Sweep up African Riches' *The Sunday Times* (16 June 2006), <http://www.timesonline.co.uk/tol/news/world/article688292.ece> (30 April 2007).

[3] N Jensen and L Wantchekon, 'Resource Wealth and Political Regimes in Africa' <www.nyu.edu/gsas/dept/politics/faculty/wantchekon/research> (31 July 2006); UN Security Council, 'Report of the Panel of Experts on the Illegal Exploitation of Natural Resources and Other Forms of Wealth of the Democratic Republic of Congo', UN Doc S/2001/357 (2001).

[4] ibid.

[5] The real per capita GDP growth in Africa stood at around 1% in 2000, and peaked at 3% in 2004 (African Development Bank, 'Selected Statistics on African Countries', 2006) Figure 1.2, 21 (<http://www.afdb.org>).

[6] See the Gini coefficient figure, measuring the degree of equality in societies, and which should ideally be 0, of eg relatively resource-blessed countries such as Botswana (63), Sierra Leone (62.9) South Africa (57.8), Guinea-Bissau (56.2), and Nigeria (50.6). This contrasts with the Gini coefficient of some resource-poorer countries such as Mozambique (39.6) and Tanzania (38.2). In general, though, this figure is much higher in most African states (see eg Namibia (70.7) compared with other regions of the world (see eg India (32.5), Sweden (25), and Japan (24.9)), UNDP, 2005 Human Development Report, <http://hrd.undp.org/reports/global/2005> (31 July 2006).

[7] Thus adopting a 'violations-based approach' in the words of A Chapman, 'A "Violations Approach" to Monitoring Economic, Social and Cultural Rights' (1996) 23 *HRQ* 181, when it comes to the allocation of resources, the essence of such an approach would be to 'review' policy choices rather than to formulate them; see E Mureinik, 'Beyond a Charter of Luxuries: Economic Rights in the Constitution' (1992) 8 *South African J on Human Rights* 464, 472 (citing the example of a government deciding to build another St Peter's or a nuclear submarine before delivering on the promise of the constitutional right to education).

and respected judiciary; and the availability of at least some resources. Used effectively, justiciable socio-economic rights may go as far as to expose the distortion in a state's financial (budgetary) priorities. Its application may be most incisive where a state does not allocate its available resources to realize socio-economic rights.[8] Now that Africa's growth in GDP has been sustained since 1980, reaching a high of around 5 per cent in most recent figures,[9] priority should be given to making socio-economic rights justiciable as part of a strategy to hold states accountable for 'trickling down' the benefits of growth to the socially and economically excluded. At the same time it should be kept in mind that the material dimension of impoverishment is often a manifestation of social exclusion and discrimination—aspects that may and should also be addressed in a broader rights-based framework.[10] This focus does not deny the fact that many additional factors, ranging from the geopolitical and macroeconomic[11] to 'disease, physical isolation, climate stress, environment degradation, and ... extreme poverty itself',[12] may derail the efforts of willing and committed states.

Acknowledging that the potential of human rights to act as agents of social change should not be overestimated, the discussion turns to the possibility of making socio-economic rights justiciable in the domestic courts of African states.[13] The basis for justiciability is sought first in ordinary legislation, and, secondly, in the constitutional provisions of African states.

B Ordinary National Legislation as a Source of Justiciable Socio-economic Rights

In the national legal order, justiciable rights may either be found in ordinary legislation or in constitutions. Doing a disservice to the discourse on socio-economic

---

[8] According to the 2004 Human Development Report, Nigeria, for example, devoted only 0.8% of its total budget to health (and São Tomé e Príncipe, one of the new oil-rich countries, only 1.5%), compared with 4.9% and 4% in Tunisia and Mozambique, respectively, UNDP, 2004 Human Development Report, <http://hrd.undp.org/reports/global/2004> (31 July 2006).

[9] World Bank Development Indicators 2006, <http://devdata.worldbank.org/wdi2006/contents/section4.htm> (30 April 2007).

[10] H Maander, 'Rights as Struggle—Towards a More Just and Humane World' in P Gready and J Ensor (eds), *Reinventing Development? Translating Rights-Based Approaches from Theory to Practice* (London: Zed Books, 2005) 233, 238.

[11] See *Armed Activities on the Territory of the Congo (DRC v Uganda)*, ICJ judgment of 19 December 2005, paras 222–50, in which the ICJ found Uganda in violation of international human rights and humanitarian law for allowing its military forces to engage in looting, plundering, and exploitation of the DRC's natural resources; also see the discussion on globalization and human rights in Ch 2 above.

[12] J Sachs, *The End of Poverty* (London: Penguin, 2005) 19.

[13] Although the literature increasingly abounds with texts on socio-economic rights and their justiciability, scant attention has been devoted to African practice north of the Limpopo River (see eg two recent overviews, F Coomans (ed), *Justiciability of Economic and Social Rights: Experience from Domestic Systems* (Antwerp: Intersentia, 2006), including only South Africa, and R Gargarella, P Domingo, and T Roux (eds), *Courts and Social Transformation in New Democracies: An Institutional*

rights, too many commentators prioritize international standards and their potential implementation. Participants in the debate about justiciability should devote less attention to the development of an optional protocol to the ICESCR, for example, and more time to the infinitely more immediate and pressing concern of ensuring justiciability at the national level by way of national norms.[14]

In its General Comment 9 (1998), the UN Committee on Economic, Social and Cultural Rights emphasizes that it is desirable that socio-economic rights be translated into national law, thus allowing individuals to invoke them directly in national courts. In many ways ordinary legislation is a better source of justiciable rights than a constitution. Because domestic legislation is a relatively accessible source of possible redress or a remedy, it provides an important first port of call for the realization of socio-economic or cultural rights.[15] Domestic legislation may be invoked before any court, significantly increasing the immediate potential of access to a remedy. Legislation tends to be more clearly and precisely formulated than constitutional standards, thus overcoming the argument that vagueness implies non-justiciability. To the extent that courts keep their decisions about the 'fulfilment' of socio-economic rights within the interpretative confines of national law, allegations of political legitimacy or about the separation of powers are also less likely to arise. Enacted as subjective rights by national parliaments, domestic justiciable socio-economic rights will at least overcome some of the 'deficit in democracy and accountability'.[16]

A few examples of national law giving effect to the right to health are provided. In South Africa, constitutional guarantees are sometimes converted to legislation, as in the National Health Act,[17] which in section 5 provides as follows: 'A health care provider, health worker or health establishment may not refuse a person emergency medical treatment'. By defining the term 'health establishment' to include 'the whole or part of a … private institution … that is operated or designed to provide … health services', this Act goes beyond the constitutional provision (worded similarly to section 5),[18] thus putting to bed any controversy about the 'horizontal' application of the right. An example from Djibouti demonstrates

Voice for the Poor? (Aldershot: Ashgate, 2006), dealing with socio-economic rights in South Africa and principally with judicial restructuring in Angola.

[14] MJ Dennis and DP Stewart, 'Justiciability of Economic, Social and Cultural Rights: Should there be an International Complaints Mechanism to Adjudicate the Rights to Food, Water, Housing, and Health?' (2004) 98 *AJIL* 462, 515, who do not reject out of hand the notion that 'some economic and social rights may be domestically justiciable', but who do not consider that a new international complaints mechanism under ICESCR 'would help bridge the still growing gap between human rights commitment and concrete action'.

[15] F Viljoen, 'National Legislation as a Source of Justiciable Socio-Economic Rights' (2005) 6 *ESR Review* 6.

[16] Y Ghai and J Cottrell, 'The Role of the Courts in Implementing Economic, Social and Cultural Rights' in Y Ghai and J Cottrell (eds), *Economic, Social and Cultural Rights in Practice: The Role of Judges in Implementing Economic, Social and Cultural Rights* (London: Interights, 2004) 88.

[17] National Health Act 61 of 2003.

[18] Constitution of South Africa 1996, s 27(2).

the legislature enacting (seemingly) justiciable socio-economic rights in the absence of any constitutional imperative. Notwithstanding the omission of all socio-economic rights from its 1992 Constitution, in 1999 Djibouti introduced legislation that provides for the right to health in the following formulation:[19] 'The nation (state) declares that everyone has the right to health'.[20] It is one of the state's 'essential duties' to guarantee this right and to set up 'the means that are necessary to perform this duty'.[21] To this end, the state must put in place, progressively, a system that allows an increasing number of people to recover at least part of their health expenses.[22] The Benin Law on Sexual Health and Reproduction provides, amongst other things, that every individual and couple has the right to benefit from the best possible quality health care that is 'certain, effective, accessible, acceptable, and affordable'.[23]

Other socio-economic rights are also provided for in domestic legislation. Under another piece of South African legislation, an occupier of land has the right 'not to be denied or deprived of access to water', and 'not to be denied or deprived of access to educational or health services'.[24] In the Water Services Act,[25] the right of 'everyone' to 'access to basic water supply and basic sanitation' is guaranteed. As in the previous South African example, this provision gives legislative effect in a particular and concrete way to already justiciable constitutionalized guarantees.[26] Social security legislation in Burundi,[27] South Africa,[28] and Namibia[29] provides further evidence of domestic accessibility to internationally recognized socio-economic rights. The internationally recognized right to education has also been translated into national legislation, as exemplified by the Nigerian Act on Compulsory Free Universal Education (2004).[30]

Not all legislation dealing with socio-economic benefits will give rise to justiciable rights as understood here. A distinction may usefully be drawn between subjective

---

[19] *Loi* (law) 48/AN/99/4ème L (Establishing the Direction of Health Policy: *'portant Orientation de la Politique de Santé'*) <http://www.presidence.dj/page392.html> (31 July 2006).

[20] ibid, art 2: *'La nation proclame le droit à la santé pour tous'*.

[21] ibid, art 2: *'La garantie de ce droit est une mission essentielle de l'État, qui adopte les principes et met en place les moyens nécessaires à l'accomplissement de cette mission'*.

[22] ibid, art 3: *'A cette fin, l'État met en place de façon graduelle un système de participation élargi à l'ensemble des bénéficiaires pour permettre de recouvrer, en partie, les coûts de la santé'*.

[23] Law 2003–04 of 3 March 2003 (*Loi Relative à la Santé Sexuelle et à la Reproduction*) art 6: *'Tout individu, tout couple a le droit de bénéficier des soins de santé de la meilleure qualité possible et de services sûrs, efficaces, accessibles, acceptables et à des coûts abordables'*). See also art 12 of the Burkinabe *Loi* 049-2005 (*en portant santé de la reproduction*) of 9 February 2006, which emulates the Benin example in crucial respects: *'Tout individu, tout couple a le droit de bénéficier des soins de santé de la meilleure qualité possible et de ne pas être exposé à des pratiques qui nuisent à sa santé'*.

[24] Extension of Security of Tenure Act 62 of 1997, s 5(3)(e)–(f).

[25] Act 108 of 1997, s 3(1).

[26] Constitution of South Africa 1996, ss 27(1) and 29.

[27] *Loi 1-010 du 16 juin 1999 portant Code de la Sécurité Sociale.*

[28] Social Assistance Act 13 of 2004.   [29] Social Security Act 34 of 1994.

[30] This Act corresponds with the provisions of the African Children's Charter, see K Singh, 'Right to Basic Education: International Obligations and Regional Normative Action in Africa' (2004) 12 *AYBIL* 437, 461.

rights (usually formulated as 'the right to...') and legislative commands (for example, couched as 'the Minister shall...') embodied in legislation.[31] A breach of the former entitles the individual to approach a court directly for a remedy, without further legislative action being required. Yet, the latter, such as a legislated duty on states to adopt a housing scheme, does not necessarily give rise to a directly enforceable right but rather requires the adoption of (mostly legislative) measures by the government.

It is precisely this kind of 'domestication' that shows the downside of a sole reliance on legislation. For all its potential advantages, legislative transformation may distort the nature and scope of an internationally guaranteed right when it is enacted domestically. At the same time, a challenge to a domestic enactment is made more difficult because the domestic provision has been sugar-coated with its apparent reliance on international law. Constitutional provisions for socio-economic rights should therefore retain their place in the normative framework of a supreme constitution as important assurances against the domestic erosion of internationally agreed guarantees.

C Constitution as Source of Justiciable Socio-economic Rights

1 Constitutional Inclusion of Justiciable Socio-economic Rights

Geographically, the reach of justiciable socio-economic rights in Africa is already quite wide. For example, Algeria (an arabophone country with an Islam-based legal tradition), Benin and Burkina Faso (francophone countries belonging to the civil law family), Cape Verde and Mozambique (lusophone countries also part of the civil law family), and South Africa (an anglophone 'common law' country) all include numerous socio-economic rights in their constitutions.

Thematically, the reach of these rights is much more restricted. More than half the constitutions of African states in some form include the right to education, health, and social security; but only a handful contain any provision on housing, food, or water. In one, the Constitution of Burkina Faso, almost all these rights are provided for in one wide-ranging and sweeping statement:[32] 'Education, instruction, formation, work, social security, housing, sport, leisure, health, protection of motherhood and of infancy, assistance to the aged or handicapped persons and in social cases, artistic and scientific creation, constitute social and cultural rights recognized by the present Constitution which aims to promote them'.

---

[31] See eg the South African Social Assistance Act, s 4, which requires the 'Minister' to 'make available' certain forms of social assistance such as child support grants, care dependency grants, and disability grants, but does not grant any 'rights' to these forms of assistance.

[32] Constitution of Burkina Faso 1991, art 18.

As far as the right to education is concerned, the Constitution of Cape Verde provides very elaborate protection:[33]

1. Everyone shall have the right to education.
2. Education, carried out through the school, the family and other agents, shall:

   (a) Be integral and contribute towards human, moral, social, cultural and economic promotion of the citizens;
   (b) Prepare and equip all citizens to exercise a professional activity, to partake at civic and democratic level in active life and to fully exercise the rights of citizenship;
   (c) Promote the development of the scientific spirit, scientific creation and research, as well as technological innovation;
   (d) Contribute to equal opportunities in access to material, social and cultural resources;
   (e) Stimulate the development of personality, autonomy, entrepreneurial spirit and creativity, as well as artistic sensibility and interest for knowledge and know-how;
   (f) Promote the values of democracy, the spirit of tolerance, of solidarity, responsibility and participation.

Mostly, the right to health is provided for in vague and open-ended terms. Algeria and Cape Verde provide examples of greater precision, and correspondingly an increased expectation of state compliance. The Algerian Constitution requires that the state 'assures the prevention of and the fight against epidemic and endemic diseases'.[34] Adopting much more detailed wording, the Constitution of Cape Verde tabulates the following state obligations as being part of the right to health:[35]

(a) To assure the existence and functioning of a national health system;
(b) To encourage the community's participation at the various levels of health services;
(c) To assure the existence of public health care;
(d) To encourage and support private initiative in the rendering of preventive, curative and rehabilitative health care;
(e) To promote the socialization of the costs of medical care and medication;
(f) To regulate and supervise the activity and quality of health care services;
(g) To regulate and control the production, commercialization and use of pharmacological products, and other means of treatment and diagnosis.

A constitution may also contain internal modifiers or 'claw-back clauses'. Under the Mozambican Constitution, for example, 'all citizens shall have the right to medical and health care, *within the terms of the law*, and shall have the duty to promote and preserve health'.[36]

Included among an extensive list of justiciable socio-economic rights in the 1993 Constitution of the Seychelles is the right to social security, which recognizes

---

[33] Constitution of Cape Verde 1992, art 77.
[34] Constitution of Algeria 1979, art 54.
[35] Constitution of Cape Verde 1992, art 70(3).
[36] Constitution of Mozambique 1990, art 94 (emphasis added).

the right of every 'citizen' to a 'dignified existence' and compels the government to 'maintain a system of social security'.[37] The 1996 South African Constitution provides for a right of 'access to' social security, alongside the right of access to 'health care services', and 'sufficient food and water'.[38]

The most comprehensive provision for housing is found in the 2005 Mozambican Constitution:[39]

1. All citizens shall have the right to a suitable home, and it shall be the duty of the State, in accordance with national economic development, to create the appropriate institutional, normative and infra-structural conditions.
2. The State shall also be responsible for funding and supporting the initiatives of the local communities, the local authorities and the people, in order to promote private and co-operative construction as well the accessibility of home ownership.

Despite the plethora of provisions, there has been a dearth of judgments in these legal systems. For all the volumes its decisions fill, the Constitutional Court of Benin can point to no clear instance of a 'socio-economic right' (as understood here) that it rendered 'justiciable'. This is so despite the obligation on the state to assure 'equal access to its citizens' to health, water, and education.[40] The Court's jurisprudence concerns itself almost exclusively with 'civil and political' rights such as the rights to freedom of assembly and association, the right to vote, and the guarantees against arbitrary detention and torture. Two categories of rights of a social and economic nature have successfully been invoked before the Court—the right to property and workers' rights.[41]

The African constitution that goes the furthest in providing—both in theory and practice—for justiciable socio-economic rights is that of South Africa. Once these rights had been included in the final (1996) Constitution, justiciability became a non-issue,[42] and the focus shifted to the application (or 'enforcement') of these rights in concrete cases on a contextual basis, allowing a flexibility in respect of remedial orders. Textual differences between provisions are important. The main difference lies between those rights that are formulated as 'rights to . . .' and those that are formulated as 'rights of access to . . .'. Compare, on the one hand, the right of children to 'basic nutrition, shelter, basic health care services and social services'[43] or the right 'to basic education',[44] to the right of 'access to

---

[37] Constitution of Seychelles 1993, art 37.

[38] Constitution of South Africa 1996, s 27(1).

[39] Constitution of Mozambique 2005, art 91.

[40] Constitution of Benin 1990, art 8.

[41] ibid, arts 22 and 30–3; see eg Decision DCC 00–032 of 28 June 2000, in which an expropriation was found to have violated art 22 of the 1990 Constitution.

[42] *Ex p Chairperson of the Constitutional Assembly: In re Certification of the Amended Text of the Constitution of the Republic of South Africa, 1996 (Second Certification judgment)* (1997) 2 SA 97 (CC) para 78.

[43] Constitution of South Africa 1996, s 28(1)(c).

[44] ibid, s 29(1)(a).

adequate housing' or 'access to health care services',[45] on the other hand. A second category of rights, 'indirect' or 'access' rights, has been the subject of three major South African Constitutional Court judgments, in which the Court accepted that the state is obliged to comply with its positive (or 'fulfilment') obligations under sections 26 and 27 of the South African Constitution.

The Constitutional Court devised a 'reasonableness test', which operates according to a 'sliding scale'.[46] Three important principles that the Court lays down are the following: First, when a court considers 'reasonableness', it does not 'enquire whether other more desirable or favourable measures could have been adopted, or whether public money could have been better spent. The question is whether the measures that have been adopted are reasonable'.[47] Secondly, programmes have to address the needs of 'those desperately in need of access' to the particular right.[48] Thirdly, effective implementation is part of the question of justiciability. The formulation of a programme is only the first step: 'The programme must also be reasonably implemented. An otherwise reasonable programme that is not implemented reasonably will not constitute compliance with the state's obligations'.[49]

Socio-economic rights may also be relied upon for purposes other than that of founding causes of action. On one occasion, the right to education, guaranteed under the Namibian Constitution, was for example invoked—not to serve as a justiciable right, but as a factor relevant to determining an appropriate sentence in a criminal case.[50]

2 Constitutional Inclusion of Directive Principles of State Policy (DPSP)

When socio-economic 'rights' are included as Directive Principles of State Policy (DPSP), they are not justiciable as such, but they serve as a guide to the executive or legislature in the exercise of its functions,[51] or as a guide to the judiciary on the interpretation of the Constitution and other laws. Nigeria, Lesotho, and Sierra Leone provide examples.

---

[45] ibid, ss 26(1) and 27(1)(a).

[46] D Brand, 'Socio-economic Rights and Courts in South Africa: Justiciability on a Sliding Scale' in Coomans (n 12 above) 207, 227.

[47] *Government of the Republic of South Africa and Others v Grootboom and Others (Grootboom case)* (2001) 1 SA 46 (CC), (2000) 11 BCLR 1169 (CC) para 41.

[48] ibid, para 95.   [49] ibid, para 42.

[50] In *S v Namseb* (1991) 1 SACR 233 (SWA), the judge reduced the sentence imposed for stock theft imposed on a father in the light of, amongst other factors, the fact that the right to education of children has been made a fundamental human right, and that parents must be placed as far as possible in a position that enables them to support their children.

[51] See the earliest precedent, art 45 of the 1937 Irish Constitution, which stipulates that the 'Directive Principles of Social Policy' are intended as general guidelines for the legislature; and art 37

The Nigerian Constitution presents the paradoxical situation of solemn constitutional commitments that are explicitly excluded from judicial scrutiny. An extensive list of DPSP is preceded by the statement that it is the 'duty and responsibility' of all organs of government to 'conform to, observe and apply' these principles.[52] At the same time, the same document stipulates that courts have no jurisdiction to inquire if conduct or legislation conforms with the DPSP.[53] Although DPSP are clearly non-justiciable, their inclusion in the Constitution must still have some meaning. In *Morebishe v Lagos State House of Assembly*,[54] the Lagos State High Court reiterated the non-justiciability of the DPSP, but added that they remain pillars of guidance and the focus of attention for all tiers of government. Principally based on the Nigerian bill of rights, and thus indirectly on the European Convention, the Constitutions of Lesotho and Sierra Leone do not provide for any justiciable socio-economic rights, but both include non-justiciable DPSP.

A failed attempt to bring these DPSP to life is illustrated in a case from Lesotho, which was decided against the following background: Insufficient access to markets inhibits surplus production in much of rural Africa. Coming to cities to trade even small surplus production is both a quest for markets and an imperative of survival. More concerned with the appearance of orderly urban planning than with the interests of the rural poor, the neo-colonial state often consigns informal markets to invisible urban spaces. Is there a role for human rights law in such circumstances?

In answering this question, the Lesotho Court of Appeal in *Khathang Tema Baitsokoli and Another v Maseru City Council and Others*[55] had to respond to arguments contending for an extended reading of the right to life in the light of the DPSP in the Lesotho Constitution. The facts of the case were as follows: A group of Basotho traders whose economic needs drew them from rural areas to the Lesotho capital, Maseru, were selling foodstuffs in stalls along the city's main thoroughfare. Acting under Lesotho's Urban Government Act, the Maseru City Council forcibly removed these traders to an alternative site, some 200 metres away. The Court accepted that, as a consequence, the livelihood of the traders had been put at risk. The evidence of one trader was, by way of an example, that gross daily sales reduced from 300 Maluti to 'hardly anything', resulting in him 'slowly starving to death'.[56]

of the Indian Constitution of 1949, which calls the DPSP fundamental in the 'governance of the country' and 'in making laws'.

[52] Constitution of Nigeria 1999, art 13.

[53] ibid, art 6(6)(c).

[54] *Morebishe v Lagos State House of Assembly* [2000] 3 WRN 134, 150.

[55] *Khathang Tema Baitsokoli and Another v Maseru City Council and Others* Lesotho Court of Appeal, Case (CIV) 4/05, CONST/C/1/2004 (20 April 2004); *Baitsokoli and Another v Maseru City Council and Others* (2004) AHRLR 195 (LeCA 2004).

[56] ibid, para 2.

The traders challenged the constitutionality of the exercise of discretion under the relevant legislation, and not the legislation as such. This challenge could only succeed, the Court of Appeal reasoned, if the exercise of discretion violated a 'justiciable right'. On behalf of the traders it was argued that this 'justiciable right' is the right to life, provided for under section 5 of the Bill of Rights in the Lesotho Constitution, and that the right to life encompasses the right to livelihood, one of the DPSP contained in the Constitution. The Court rejected this contention, finding that the right to life does not encompass a right to livelihood.

The Court adopted a very formal textual analysis to arrive at the conclusion that it could not undo the Constitution's deliberately constructed dichotomy of justiciable and non-justiciable guarantees. The rights to life and to livelihood are in fact both explicitly provided for, the Court observed, but in two separate parts: The right to life as a justiciable guarantee, in the Bill of Rights, and the right to a livelihood as a non-justiciable DPSP. To interpret the right to life provision as encompassing a right to livelihood would therefore be a 'tautology, inconsistency and anomaly'.[57]

However, the Court's construction does not take into account the proper function of the DPSP, which are to serve as 'part of public policy' to guide the 'authorities and agencies of Lesotho' to achieve these principles progressively 'by legislation or otherwise'. Only the 'enforcement', not the use as interpretative inspiration by courts of DPSP, is outlawed. Many aspects of the DPSP are in some way already reflected in the Bill of Rights.[58] This measure of overlap does not mean that the DPSP lose their role as normative goals.

In its judgment, the court itself remarked that recourse may be had to the Courts to ensure that the principles 'find implementation' in 'appropriate circumstances and in appropriate ways'.[59] The Court therefore seems to leave the door open for instances where the substantive content of the principle is not already contained in the Bill of Rights, in which case a 'socio-economic right' in the DPSP may be successfully invoked before the Courts.

Would an 'appropriate circumstance' for example be the invocation of the right to health, which is explicitly contained in the DPSP, but which is not mentioned in the Bill of Rights? It seems not to be the case, because the principle would, on the Court's reasoning, still be non-justiciable, on the following three-step reasoning: (1) Only the rights in the Bill of Rights are justiciable. (2) For the non-justiciable 'principle' concerning health to be justiciable, it has to be invoked as an *element of* a justiciable right such as 'life' or 'dignity' (and not the 'right to health' as such). (3) However, invoking the relevant DPSP as the basis of a right already assumes that the particular right 'contains' the right to health. Such an interpretation is

[57] ibid, para 20.
[58] See eg the right to freedom from discrimination (Lesotho Constitution 1993, s 18; and the DPSP on 'equality and justice', s 26).
[59] *Khathang Tema Baitsokoli and Another v Maseru City Council and Others* (n 55 above) para 19.

therefore once again open to the Court's criticism that the right to health would, in effect, be provided for twice, once implicitly (for example, in the right to life) and another time explicitly (in the DPSP).

But surely the Court's statement that the DPSP may sometimes 'find application' must have some meaning, and surely the inclusion of the DPSP must serve some purpose? At the very least, they should serve as guides to the interpretation of a constitution and of ordinary legislation. In the present case, the Court does not pay any attention to this aspect. Like the Maseru City Council, the Court should have interpreted the Urban Government Act and its regulations in the light of the DPSP. There is no mention of this possibility in its judgment. Still, the question may be posed as to the difference between a constitutional challenge of executive conduct (at stake in the *Baitsokoli* case) and a contention that a principle was not accorded the requisite weight in the exercise of executive authority. The Court's logic would therefore never allow any of the DPSP to 'find application' as a justiciable right, because socio-economic rights are set out only in the DPSP and will always depend for their justiciability on that of the civil and political right in which they are subsumed.

In its efforts to create a firewall between the Bill of Rights and DPSP, the Lesotho Court of Appeal also draws a distinction between the present case and the Indian case of *Tellis v Bombay Municipality* (*Tellis* case).[60] In that case, the Indian Supreme Court under analogous circumstances held that the right to life encompasses the right to a livelihood. The Lesotho Court of Appeal dismissed the Indian Court's reasoning on the basis that the Indian Court did not consider the arguments about tautology, on which the Lesotho Court founded its judgment. These remarks illustrate the difference between the Indian Court's purposive and generous approach and the Lesotho Court's narrow textual approach to interpretation. By suggesting that its approach is superior or 'logically correct', the Lesotho Court of Appeal displays an arrogant lack of insight into the contingency of its own finding.

The Lesotho Court also pointed out that the *Tellis* case ultimately deals with a 'procedural irregularity in slum clearance', and is therefore not direct authority in the present case. This distinction does not correspond with reality. In both the *Tellis* and *Baitsokoli* cases, the state's obligation to 'respect', rather than to 'fulfil', is at stake. The two cases are therefore analogous, as the claim in the Lesotho case is about a forced removal of a business, without taking account of the severity of its impact on those affected by it. In the *Tellis* case, the remedy was that the eviction of the dwellers was suspended. Similarly, in *Baitsokoli*, the traders merely wanted to return to their initial trading space. In fact, the Lesotho case essentially requires *less* government involvement and regulation—a classical case of the need for the government to 'respect' the rights of the traders.

---

[60] *Tellis v Bombay Municipality* [1987] LRC 351.

A further ground for rejecting the applicant's contention also derives from a literal reading of the constitutional text. This ground relates to the constitutional limitation allowed to the right of life. In the Court's view, the type of limitation allowed for under section 5 is consistent with a narrow construction of the right to life. Because the limitations do not relate to a broad understanding encompassing 'livelihood', the Court argues that the inclusion of 'livelihood' in the right to life would not be subject to any limitation. In other words, the Court regarded the absence of considerations such as 'reasonable measures' and 'available resources' in the limitations provision as an indication that the right to life cannot conceivably include the right to 'livelihood'. However, this reasoning focuses on the governmental obligation to 'fulfil' aspects of a person's 'livelihood'. As far as the obligation to 'respect' is concerned, the limitations of 'arbitrary deprivation' or 'necessary force' provide a sufficient basis for limiting the right to livelihood. For example, forced eviction or deprivation of existing sources of livelihood are allowed, provided it does not amount to 'arbitrary' measures or constitute 'unnecessary force'.

3 Combined Constitutional Inclusion of Justiciable Socio-economic Rights and DPSP

The Constitutions of a number of African states contain a combination of justiciable socio-economic rights and DPSP. Under the Ghanaian Constitution,[61] a limited number of socio-economic rights, including the right to free basic education and the progressive introduction of free secondary education,[62] co-exist with an elaborate set of DPSP, including one on education.[63] Uganda's Constitution contains a similar overlap,[64] but as far as the DPSP are concerned, its scope extends much wider to include health services and other basic necessities such as 'clean and safe water, decent shelter, adequate clothing, food security and pension'.[65] The Gambian Constitution also provides for a justiciable right to education, juxtaposed with DPSP that do 'not confer legal rights' and are not 'enforceable in any court'. These DPSP are framed in terms very similar to those in the Ugandan Constitution.[66]

Under the Ethiopian Constitution, there is no specified individual right to health, education, or social services, but the state's obligation to 'allocate ever increasing resources to provide to the public health, education and other socials services' is clearly included as part of the chapter on 'Fundamental Rights'.[67] In a separate chapter, containing 'National Policy, Principles and Objectives', the state

---

[61] The 'National Objectives and Directive Principles of State Policy', following the Preamble to the Uganda Constitution of 1995.

[62] Constitution of Ghana 1992, art 25(1)(a) and (b).

[63] Art 38.   [64] Constitution of Uganda 1995, DPSP XVIII and art 30.

[65] ibid, DPSP XIV.

[66] Constitution of The Gambia 1996, art 216(4).

[67] Ethiopian Constitution 1994, art 41(4).

policy of aiming 'to provide all Ethiopians access to public health and education, clean water, housing, food and social security' is proclaimed.[68]

Even as non-justiciable DPSP, socio-economic goals are often already weakened or curtailed. The laudable Ethiopian social objectives, referred to in the previous paragraph, are qualified by the extent to which 'the country's resources permit'.[69] When even their role as mere guidelines is made conditional upon 'practical measures' or upon what is 'to the greatest extent feasible', the potential contribution of DPSP to 'fulfil' socio-economic rights is further minimized.

Under the Ghanaian and Ugandan Constitutions, the President is required to report to Parliament at least once a year about the realization of the DPSP.[70] In respect of Ghana, the requirement to report relates to 'policy objectives contained in this Chapter [dealing with DPSP]', specifically to the right to 'good health care'. On closer inspection, the promise of reporting on health issues is eroded, as the right to health extends only as far as requiring the state to 'safeguard the health . . . of all persons in employment'.[71]

An obligation on the executive occasionally to report about DPSP does not go very far. Inserted in parliamentary systems where oversight is generally lacking, presidential compliance with obligations to report about DPSP has been sparse. The reporting process has not led to greater accountability; it generated little, if any, public discussion on the importance of DPSP; it has not enhanced visibility about governments' efforts in this regard; and it has not ensured greater government commitment to uphold DPSP.

4 Domestic Enforcement of Socio-economic Rights contained in International Human Rights Treaties

When a monist country ratifies an international treaty such as the ICESCR, it should in principle be possible to base a justiciable claim on the provisions of that treaty.[72] In practice, this happens very infrequently. Although the ICESCR is in principle 'part and parcel' of the law of Benin,[73] for example, the Committee on

---

[68] Art 90(1).   [69] ibid.

[70] Constitution of Ghana 1992, art 34(2); Constitution of Uganda 1995, DPSP I(ii).

[71] Not only the judiciary, but also the South African Human Rights Commission, has an oversight function over the socio-economic rights under the South African Constitution 1996 (s 184(3)). This function has not been performed very effectively, in part due to the lack of involvement by the legislature. (See DG Newman, 'Institutional Monitoring of Social and Economic Rights: A South African Case Study and New Research Agenda' (2003) 19 *South African J on Human Rights* 189, and also the Human Rights Commission's latest report, http://www.sahrc.org.za/sahrc_cms/publish/article_215.shtml (30 April 2007).)

[72] See the cases from the Dutch Supreme Court, finding ICESCR, arts 8(1)(d) (state parties 'undertake to ensure the right to strike') and 13(1) (state parties 'recognize the right of everyone to education'), cited and discussed by Craven (MCR Craven, 'The Domestic Application of the International Covenant on Economic, Social and Cultural Rights' (1993) 40 *NILR* 367, 393).

[73] Constitution of Benin 1990, Preamble, art 7.

Economic, Social and Cultural Rights in its concluding observations on Benin's initial report 'strongly urges the State party to ensure that the Covenant is fully taken into consideration in the formulation and implementation of all measures relating to economic, social and cultural rights and that, *in practical terms*, legal proceedings may be brought on the basis of its provisions'.[74]

In dualist countries, reliance on international law as a directly enforceable claim is only possible if the treaty provisions have been domesticated. As has been shown, this is not often the case. In the isolated instance of Nigeria, the right to health under the African Charter has been invoked as a substantive basis to ensure medical treatment for prisoners.[75] The High Court held that the African Charter entrenches the socio-economic rights of a person and considered itself enjoined to ensure that they are observed. Denying medical treatment to persons awaiting trial for longer than two years violated the Charter guarantee, which is part of the Nigerian constitutional order. Although the Court 'appreciated' the 'economic cost of embarking on medical provision', it made an order for the relocation of the applicants to a designated government hospital for proper medical attention.

In practical terms, the use of international law as a tool in litigation is dependent on whether the particular provision is self-executing. And this decision depends on judicial discretion. In General Comment 3, the Committee on Economic, Social and Cultural Rights listed a number of ICESCR provisions that are capable of immediate application.[76] Even when socio-economic rights in international treaties (especially the ICESCR) have been made self-executing at the national level, courts have been reluctant to give 'direct effect' to them.[77] Instead, courts have mainly made 'reference' to international treaties as interpretative guides, even in the context of socio-economic rights.[78]

5 No Socio-economic Rights Provided for in the Constitution: Reliance on 'Civil and Political' Rights

Surprisingly, only a relatively small number of African constitutions, notably those of Botswana, Tunisia, Zambia, and Zimbabwe, contain neither explicit guarantees of socio-economic rights[79] nor DPSP.[80]

---

[74] UN Doc E/C.12/1/Add.78 (Concluding Observations) 5 June 2002 (emphasis added) para 28.
[75] *Odafe v A-G*, Federal High Court of Nigeria, Port Harcourt, Suit FHC/PH/CS/680/2003, judgment of 23 February 2003 (unreported, on file with author); reported as *Odafe and Others v Attorney-General and Others* (2004) AHRLR 205 (NgHC 2004).
[76] General Comment 3, on 'The Nature of States Parties Obligations' (1990) para 5, listing eg arts 3 (non-discrimination), 7(a) (conditions of work), 8 (trade union rights), 10(3) (protection of children), 13(2)(a) (primary education), 15(3) (freedom of scientific research).
[77] See eg the discussion by BCA Toebes, *The Right to Health as a Human Right in International Law* (Antwerp: Intersentia-Hart, 1999) 194–200 (about the position in the Netherlands).
[78] See eg the *Grootboom* case (n 47 above) (paras 28–31).
[79] Both constitutions include the right to property, which is here not considered as a socio-economic right.
[80] For reprinted versions of the human rights provisions of all African states, see C Heyns (ed), *Human Rights Law in Africa* (vol 2) (Leiden: Martinus Nijhoff, 2004); see also eg DM Chirwa, 'A Full

The status of Botswana as one of Africa's few long-standing democracies largely insulated it from the democratic upheavals of the early 1990s and the concomitant constitution-rewriting conferences. As a result, the Botswana Constitution is still the one adopted at independence in 1966, omitting all reference to socio-economic rights. History explains this anachronism: The Botswana Constitution was modelled on the European Convention, which at the time (before later substantive extensions) did not contain any socio-economic rights. Starting in Nigeria, this model found its way into many African independence constitutions.[81] This model also found its way to Zambia and Zimbabwe, where it served as the model for the 1964 and 1979 Constitutions, respectively. Neither the 1991 redrafted Zambian Constitution, nor the numerous amendments to the Zimbabwean Constitution served as opportunities to provide for the inclusion of socio-economic rights in these two constitutions. Relative stability and continuity also explains why the independence Constitution of 1959 remained on place in Tunisia. Written in the late 1950s, the 1959 Constitution predates many advances in the human rights discourse and predictably does not include socio-economic rights.

In these instances, the existing framework of civil and political rights has to be exploited to secure benefits of a socio-economic nature through the avenues of the law. Most African constitutions contain the right to respect for dignity, life and a guarantee against discrimination, all examples of 'cross-cutting' rights which 'straddle, underlie or facilitate' the exercise of socio-economic as well as 'civil and political' rights.[82] It must be possible to convince domestic courts that the right to dignity, alone, but preferably in conjunction with an equality guarantee, by necessity includes crucial constituent parts of a dignified existence (such as the right of access to drinkable water and to health care).[83] The right to just administrative action also holds possibilities of indirectly protecting socio-economic rights, for example when employment (entailing the right to work) is terminated without reasons being given for such termination.[84] The possibility of invoking 'civil and political' rights such as the right to life as including socio-economic entitlements has not often arisen without supporting arguments derived from the existence of DPSP.[85]

Loaf is Better than Half: The Constitutional Protection of Economic, Social and Cultural Rights in Malawi' (2005) 49 *JAL* 207–41.

[81] C Heyns, 'African Human Rights Law and the European Convention' (1995) 11 *South African J on Human Rights* 252.

[82] C Odinkalu, 'Implementing Economic, Social and Cultural Rights' in M Evans and R Murray (eds), *The African Charter on Human and Peoples' Rights: The System in Practice, 1986–2000* (Cambridge: Cambridge University Press, 2002) 178, 188.

[83] A Chaskalson, 'The Third Bram Fischer Lecture: Human Dignity as a Foundational Value of the Constitutional Order' (2000) 16 *South African J on Human Rights* 193 (who argues that respect 'for human dignity is a value implicit in almost all the rights enumerated in the Universal Declaration'); see also Communication 155/96, *Social and Economic Rights Action Centre (SERAC) v Nigeria* (2001) AHRLR 60 (ACHPR 2001) (15th Annual Activity Report) (*Ogoniland* case).

[84] See Chirwa (n 80 above) 232, referring to Malawian case-law illustrating this point.

[85] See also eg the Indian case *Unni Kkrishnan J P v State of Andhra Pradesh* (1993) 1 SCC 645 (SC).

Courts have demonstrated that the issues of resource allocation and of delineating governmental obligations to 'fulfil' a right do not only arise in respect of socio-economic rights, but also when interpreting civil and political rights. The South African case of *August v Electoral Commission*[86] illustrates that a classical civil and political right, the right to vote, also has resource implications. Prisoners were not formally excluded from voting in the 1998 elections. However, prior to the election, the Electoral Commission did not make any arrangements enabling prisoners to register and to vote. In a case brought on behalf of some prisoners, the Constitutional Court held that such omissions would disenfranchise prisoners. As the right to vote 'by its very nature imposes positive obligations upon the legislature and the executive',[87] the state has the obligation to 'take reasonable steps to create the opportunity to enable eligible prisoners to register and vote'.[88]

One of the classical civil rights, the right to a trial within a reasonable period, also clearly necessitates resource allocation for its realization. Concluding that a delay of some three years and five months in a criminal prosecution was unreasonable, the Botswana High Court found that the state 'had at its disposal the necessary resources to have acquitted itself infinitely more credibly than what in fact turned out to be the case'.[89] In its judgment, the Court addressed the government's defence based on the country's level of socio-economic development. Refusing to situate Botswana on a continuum of 'levels of socio-economic development', the Court concluded that the steps taken by the state in the particular case did not meet what it did not specifically earmark, but which essentially amounts to a standard of reasonableness.

Although the Nigerian Constitution provides for DPSP, these were not invoked in a case brought by prisoners to secure 'proper medical treatment'.[90] Instead, the applicants based their claim on 'civil and political' rights such as the right to dignity, the prohibition against discrimination and against cruel, inhuman and degrading treatment or punishment. All these rights are contained in the justiciable part of the Nigerian Constitution. Even if the High Court dealt with other aspects of the claim, it appears that the claim would have been resolved on the issue of 'torture' alone. Relying on precedent that 'torture' includes 'mental torture',[91] the Court held that the HIV-positive prisoners' continued detention in overcrowded conditions amongst other inmates who might at any moment attack them, as well as the failure of the state to provide medical treatment to those diagnosed 'as HIV/AIDS carriers', amounted to torture and therefore constituted a violation of the Nigerian Constitution.

[86] *August v Electoral Commission* (1999) 3 SA 1 (CC).
[87] ibid, para 16.
[88] ibid, para. 22.
[89] *Ntwa v State* (2001) 2 BLR 212 (HC) 220.
[90] *Odafe* case (n 75 above).
[91] *Uzoukwu v Ezeonu* (1991) 6 NWLR 200.

D Conclusion

Africa has great economic potential. As the preceding discussion shows, there are equally vast yet unexplored judicial means to assist in unlocking this potential to the advantage of the people of Africa.

Sometimes the potential lies in unimplemented legislation. In a surprising number of instances, the potential lies in justiciable constitutional guarantees that have never been invoked. DPSP may, at the very least, be used as interpretive tools. Even in the absence of all these possibilities, it is possible to exploit 'civil and political' rights to become a vehicle for responding to claims that are essentially socio-economic in nature.

The possibilities discussed above may also overlap. In a Nigerian case dealing with the detrimental effects of oil exploration in the Niger Delta,[92] the High Court at Benin City held that the 'continued flaring of gas' violates not only 'civil and political' rights guaranteed under the Constitution (the right to life and to dignity), but was also inconsistent with provisions of the African Charter,[93] which had been domesticated into Nigerian law. Although it could have used one of the DPSP to support its interpretation,[94] the Court did not do so.

Although different strategies are suggested on the basis of the legal status enjoyed by socio-economic rights under national law, the analysis in this chapter reveals that effective judicial enforcement is contingent more upon the degree of judicial activism than on the 'legal' status or nature of any particular right.

---

[92] In a case brought against Shell of Nigeria and the Nigerian National Petroleum Company, the Nigerian High Court found that the right to life and dignity—reinforced by the right to health and to a favourable environment provided for in the African Charter—includes 'the right to clean poison-free, pollution-free and healthy environment' (*sic*): *Jonah Gbemre v Shell Petroleum Development Company Nigeria and Others* Suit FHC/B/CS/53/05.

[93] African Charter, arts 4, 16, and 24.

[94] Nigerian Constitution 1999, art 20 ('The state shall protect and improve the environment and safeguard the water, air and land, forest and wildlife of Nigeria').

15

Lack of a Human Rights-based
Approach to HIV and AIDS

HIV/AIDS is as much a disease of society as it is a disease of the body. Not only does it invade the body's immune system, but it feeds off and further exacerbates pre-existing human rights violations in society such as gender inequality and socio-economic exclusion and deprivation. Devastating the social fabric through high levels of death and illness, HIV and AIDS have taken hold particularly in Southern and Eastern Africa, which have become the global epicentre of HIV and AIDS.[1]

A Beyond Policy: The Need for Human Rights-based
Legislation and Litigation

A human rights-based approach to HIV and AIDS depends on the availability of justiciable guarantees, secured through constitutions and legislation, rather than

---

[1] See UNAIDS 2006 Report on the Global Aids Epidemic <http://www.unaids.org> (31 July 2006) (the average prevalence rate in sub-Saharan Africa among adults aged 15–49 is more than 6%, and more than 24 million people are estimated to live with HIV and AIDS in this region).

on discretionary ad hoc policies.[2] To date, though, such a human rights-based approach has formed only a minimal part of Africa's response to HIV and AIDS. Although policy documents (such as strategic plans, programmes of action, and declarations) on HIV and AIDS abound, and do have an important role to play as non-binding guides, few African countries have adopted comprehensive legislation to secure a consistent and clear framework for the protection of human rights. The lack of a legislative response may be ascribed to underlying weaknesses in sub-Saharan African legal formulation and drafting systems. Legal reform institutions (such as law reform commissions) in Africa often do not function effectively, and law-making processes are often cumbersome and underdeveloped.

A similar trend towards non-binding standards at the international level serves to reinforce these domestic responses. No binding UN instrument has been adopted in response to the AIDS epidemic. UN human rights treaty bodies have issued General Comments to show the relevance to HIV and AIDS of existing human rights instruments,[3] but while they add some clarity and direction to their parent instruments, they do not constitute new binding standards in their own right.[4] The international community has contributed mostly at the level of policy and the issuing of declarations. An important example is the International Guidelines on HIV/AIDS and Human Rights,[5] adopted in 1996 by a consultative meeting convened by two UN entities, UNAIDS and the Office of the High Commissioner for Human Rights. Despite being adopted by only a limited group of 35 governmental, non-governmental, and academic experts, these Guidelines have attained a high level of persuasion as a benchmark for government action.[6] One of the Millennium Development Goals (MDGs) aims to halt and begin reversing 'the spread of HIV/AIDS' by 2015.[7] Although the MDGs are not contained in a binding treaty format, it is possible to argue that at least some of them— including goal 6—have attained the status of customary international law.[8] However, as it is formulated in terse terms, goal 6 does not provide much guidance to states intent on adopting a human rights-based approach.[9]

---

[2] See eg L Gostin and JM Mann, 'Towards the Development of a Human Rights Impact Assessment for the Formulation and Evaluation of Public Health Policies' (1994) 1 *Health and Human Rights* 58; C Kissoon, M Ceasar, and T Jithoo, 'Whose Right?' *AIDS Review 2002* (Pretoria: Centre for the Study of AIDS, University of Pretoria, 2002) 13–19.

[3] See eg General Comment 14 on the ICESCR (The right to the best attainable standard of health), General Comments 24 (Women and Health), on CEDAW and General Comment 3 on the CRC (HIV/AIDS and the rights of the child).

[4] See Ch 1 above.

[5] UN Doc E/CN.4/1997/37.

[6] Two reasons in particular explain the high level of acceptance: The Guidelines were subsequently 'welcomed' by the UN Commission on Human Rights (Resolution 1997/33), and were translated and widely disseminated.

[7] Goal 6.

[8] P Alston, 'Ships Passing in the Night: The Current State of the Human Rights and Development Debate Seen Through the Lens of the Millennium Development Goals' (2005) 27 *HRQ* 755, 774.

[9] In 2001, the UN General Assembly Special Session (UNGASS) went further by adopting the Declaration of Commitment on HIV/AIDS, which provides for time-bound targets. Quantifiable targets such as the following have been set: 'By 2003, enact, strengthen or enforce, as appropriate, legislation, regulations and other measures to eliminate all forms of discrimination against and to

The AU (and its predecessor, the OAU) adopted a number of declarations pertaining to HIV and AIDS. Perhaps the most significant of these is the 2001 Abuja
Declaration on HIV/AIDS, Tuberculoses and Other Related Infectious Diseases.[10]
Highlighting the importance of resources and of budgetary priorities, the Heads
of State and Government pledged 'to set a target of allocating at least 15% of
[their] annual budget[s] to the improvement of the health sector'.[11] AU organs
have stressed the importance of legal measures, though. In its Solemn
Declaration on Gender Equality in Africa, the AU Assembly called for an accelerated implementation of gender specific legal measures to combat HIV and AIDS,[12]
and the Pan-African Parliament recommended that states adopt legislation dealing with HIV and AIDS.[13] Although the African Charter does not refer explicitly
to HIV or AIDS, many of its provisions are of potential relevance in the context of
HIV and AIDS. However, no HIV-related case has thus far been submitted to the
African Commission.[14] Adopted in 2003, the Protocol to the African Charter on
the Rights of Women in Africa (Women's Protocol) became the first binding international human rights instrument to specifically mention HIV and AIDS.[15]

In response to the undeniable presence of HIV/AIDS in Southern African
states in the mid- to late 1980s, policies were soon put in place.[16] These initial policies were often directed at containment and control, focusing primarily on the
blood supply. One explanation for the preference of governments for policies over
laws is that the indirect effect and non-binding nature of policies make them more
acceptable to governments.

The limitation of a policy-based approach is illustrated by the following example.
The Industrial Court of Botswana had the opportunity to pronounce on the legal

---

ensure the full enjoyment of all human rights and fundamental freedoms by people living with
HIV/AIDS and members of vulnerable groups...' (para 58 of Declaration of Commitment on
HIV/AIDS, UNGA Res S-62/2, 27 June 2001).

[10] <http://www.onusida-aoc.org/Eng/Abuja%Declaration.html> (31 July 2006). See also the
2001 Abuja Declaration and Plan of Action to Roll Back Malaria; and the 2003 Maputo Declaration
on HIV/AIDS, Tuberculosis and Other Infectious Diseases in Africa.

[11] Para 26. The AU also established AIDS Watch Africa (AWA), located in the Department of
Social Affairs.

[12] Para 1.

[13] 'Malaria, Tuberculoses and HIV/AIDS' (AU Doc PAP-Rec 005/06).

[14] See generally S Gumedze, 'HIV/AIDS and Human Rights: The Role of the African
Commission on Human and Peoples' Rights' (2004) 4 *AHRLJ* 181. At its 23rd session (23 April–7
May 2001), the African Commission adopted a resolution ('Resolution on the HIV/AIDS
Pandemic—Threat against Human Rights and Humanity'), identifying HIV/AIDS as a 'human
rights issue' and calling on states to 'ensure human rights protection for those living with HIV/AIDS
against discrimination'.

[15] Women's Protocol, art 14(1); also see discussion below about 'shared confidentiality'; and
Ch 6.D above.

[16] eg Swaziland, which introduced its first HIV/AIDS Plan in 1987, followed by subsequent
strategic plans and the Swaziland Strategic Plan for HIV/AIDS 2000–2005; and the 1986 National
AIDS Prevention and Control Programme of Zambia. See 'HIV/AIDS and Human Rights in
Swaziland' and 'HIV/AIDS and Human Rights in Zambia' (Pretoria: Centre for the Study of AIDS
and Centre for Human Rights, 2004); <http://www.csa.za.org/filemanager/list/10/> (31 July 2006).

status of Botswana's National Policy on HIV/AIDS (National Policy), which discourages pre-employment HIV testing, when it was faced with the question whether a private employer's pre-employment HIV testing policy was legal.[17] Although it made clear its moral disapproval of HIV testing of employees, the Court emphasized that 'law' and 'policy' operate at different levels and explained that courts apply binding law and not policy, which 'carry[ies] only persuasive authority'.[18] It was held, therefore, that the National Policy could not be found to legally ban pre-employment testing in Botswana.

The South African *TAC* case also speaks to this point.[19] When the TAC's attempts at negotiating an extension in the limited reach of the South African government's prevention of HIV infection from mother-to-child (PMTCT) 'rollout' policy failed, the courts provided an avenue of last resort. The Constitutional Court found that the government's policy did not give effect adequately to the justiciable right of 'everyone' to have access to health care and of every child to 'basic health care services'.[20] Subsequent difficulties to ensure implementation of an amended policy in respect of PMTCT, and the protracted struggle to guarantee access to ARVs for all who need them, were partially due to the fact that the constitutional commitments of access to health care have not been translated into legislation containing unequivocal and easily accessible entitlements.[21]

A human rights-based approach not only needs to manifest itself in legislation, but also in the actual application and interpretation of the law in disputed cases. Aside from South Africa, which has seen some important public interest litigation in the realm of HIV and human rights,[22] the weakness of many other African legal systems has resulted in a sparseness of case-law in Africa. Human rights have not become tools for litigation and for combating government inaction. The primary reasons may be the mistrust of the administration of justice, the minimal role of the formal legal system in the lives of the majorities in these states, and a lack of access to justice. But the lack of a clear legislative basis to some extent also accounts for this failure. It may be true that human rights litigation could still be brought

---

[17] *Rapula Jimson v Botswana Building Society* Case IC 35/05, Industrial Court of Botswana, Gaborone, judgment of 30 May 2003 (on file with author).

[18] Judgment, 17 (typed).

[19] *Minister of Health v Treatment Action Campaign (TAC)* (2002) 5 SA 721 (CC). The TAC is a South African-based NGO campaigning in particular for improved access to treatment for people living with HIV.

[20] South Africa's 1996 Constitution, arts 27(1)(a) and 28(1)(c).

[21] As has eg been done in Brazil, where a series of court challenges emanated in the adoption of Law 9313/96 (*Lei dispõe sobre a distribuição gratuita de medicamentos aos portadores do HIV e doentes de AIDS*), which provides that everyone in need of ARVs has the right to acquire them at state expense, and that the state has the obligation to finance the provision of the appropriate medications at all levels of government.

[22] See eg *Van Biljon v Minister of Correctional Services* (1997) 4 SA 441 (C); *Hoffmann v South African Airways (SAA)* (2001) 1 SA 1 (CC) and *EN and Others v Government of South Africa and Others* (2007) 1 BCLR 84 (D); case 4576/2006, High Court Durban and Coast Local Division, judgment of June 2006 <http://www.tac.org.za/westville.html> (31 July 2006).

on the basis of the Constitution, even though no explicit reference to HIV has been made. This was done in South Africa, as far as the rights to health, to medical care, privacy, and non-discrimination are concerned.[23] The outcome of litigation depends on judicial officers, who are also members of societies, and who are likely to reflect some of the views of that society. As is illustrated below, especially when the epidemic first appeared on the continent, the lack of information bolstered stigma. Sexual taboos, fear of death in the face of an epidemic with no cure, and even a belief in witchcraft reinforced stigma in the early years.

Litigation thus has its limits, as the *Rapula Jimson* case also illustrates.[24] In that case, the Industrial Court of Botswana found that the *way in which* the Botswana Building Society introduced HIV testing for all prospective employees in June 2002 was illegal. Jimson, an employee of the Botswana Building Society, was unfairly treated because a new condition (an HIV test) was added after he had already entered into a contract of employment. However, the Court did not go beyond the individual litigant, finding that the post-June 2002 HIV testing was in conformity with the law. A private employer, such as the Botswana Building Society, could therefore require pre-employment HIV testing as long as there was no 'legal stipulation forbidding the making of that policy'.[25] Although the Court leaves no doubt that it views the policy as prejudicial to individuals, it adopted a deferential approach by holding that it does not fall to judicial organs to create a new law outlawing HIV testing, but to the legislature: 'The courts can only fill the gaps, clear doubts or give meaning where there is lack of clarity'.[26]

B A Human Rights-based Critique of the Legal Response of African States to HIV and AIDS

Often, even when legislation is adopted, it hinders rather than helps attempts to stem the spread of the disease. To date, laws passed in response to HIV have mostly been reactive and not proactive, and have, therefore, failed to address the root causes that are responsible for or 'drive' HIV.

1 Institution-Creation as Bureaucratic Response

States have put in place institutional mechanisms such as national AIDS councils to oversee the development and implementation of government HIV and AIDS policies. Although the coordination of national efforts is important, these attempts too often allow governments to be 'seen to be doing something' rather than actually doing something. Also, they are limited in their sustainable impact

---

[23] See cases cited above.   [24] n 17 above.
[25] ibid, judgment, 18 (typed).
[26] ibid, judgment, 19 (typed).

by factors such as their composition and mandate. An institution that could play a more pronounced role is an HIV/AIDS multi-sectoral parliamentary oversight committee, by monitoring through parliamentary oversight the management of HIV and AIDS by the legislature and the executive.

2 Prioritizing the Valuable

So far, most legislation adopted in response to discrimination on the basis of HIV in African societies has targeted the employment sphere. In a number of states, pre-employment screening for HIV and discrimination against HIV-positive employees have been outlawed.[27] By covering formal—and not informal—employment relationships, these laws provide increased protection to the small minority already enjoying relative privilege in African societies. In this respect African legislatures mustered their law-making powers in aid of those most valued in economic and political terms and most like them—privileged males.[28]

3 Lack of Comprehensive Protection against Discrimination and Stigma

Very little HIV-specific anti-discrimination protection has been put in place to ensure that discrimination against persons living with the virus is held in check.[29] This is both a great weakness and a missed opportunity to harness the significant symbolism of a constitutional injunction against stigma and discrimination. As many of the continent's constitutions date from Africa's 'third wave' of democratization that began in 1989, well after the manifestation of HIV and AIDS, the lack of any clear constitutional commitment to non-discrimination on the basis of HIV status is disappointing. The Burundi Transitional Constitution became a notable exception. Adopted in 2001 in a country where HIV infection rates and AIDS deaths were soaring,[30] the Constitution includes 'being a carrier of HIV/AIDS' as one of the listed grounds on which discrimination may not take place.[31]

The pitfalls of omitting HIV as a prohibited ground for discrimination is illustrated in a Nigerian case, instituted by four prisoners against Nigerian prison

---

[27] See eg the South African Employment Equity Act 55 of 1998, s 7; Decree Law 1/037 of Burundi, art 6; Act 5 of 2002 of Mozambique.

[28] The UN Statistics Division places the percentage of parliamentary lower house seats held by women in sub-Saharan Africa at 14.2%; the corresponding figure in Northern Africa is 8.5%, while the global average percentage is 15.9%, which is up from 12.4% in 1990. <http://millenniumindictoars.un.org> (31 July 2006).

[29] International Guideline 5 requires states to 'enact or strengthen anti-discrimination and other protective laws that protect vulnerable groups'.

[30] The estimated number of people living with HIV in Burundi in 2003 was 250,000; the estimated HIV infection rate in young pregnant women (aged 15–24) was 13.6% in 2001 (UNAIDS Report on the Global AIDS Epidemic (2004) 190, 194).

[31] Constitution of Burundi 2001, art 23; this position was confirmed in the 2004 Constitution, art 22 (the quoted phrase was rephrased as 'because they are suffering from HIV/AIDS').

authorities for the refusal of appropriate medical attention based upon their HIV positive status.[32] The prisoners alleged that the denial of care was impermissible discrimination under the Nigerian Constitution. Rejecting their claim on this particular issue, the Federal High Court ruled that the right to non-discrimination guaranteed by the Constitution does not include discrimination based on an illness, virus, or disease.[33] This stands in contrast to the constitutional jurisprudence from South Africa and Botswana discussed previously, which demonstrates that HIV status may be included as a ground analogous to those usually included in constitutions.[34]

Even when constitutions contain general non-discrimination provisions, the implications of such provisions on the horizontal plane, affecting relationships between non-state actors, have not been spelt out. There is therefore a clear need for anti-discrimination legislation that goes beyond the vague and open-ended commitments contained in many constitutions. In South Africa, where anti-discrimination legislation exists, HIV is not an explicit ground for non-discrimination.[35] The reported introduction in 2006 of comprehensive anti-discrimination legislation in Nigeria, banning amongst other things discrimination on the basis of HIV status in the enjoyment of social services, is commendable,[36] even if it comes late in the day.

Non-discrimination on the basis of HIV status may also be included in legislation dealing principally with other aspects, as exemplified by the laws on sexual reproduction in Benin and Burkina Faso. Under these laws, persons living with HIV and AIDS have the right to enjoy their civil, political, and social rights, such as housing, education, employment, health and social assistance, without any discrimination.[37]

In the absence of specific legal guarantees against HIV discrimination, a Nigerian judge in 2001 seemed to have adopted prevailing stigma and stereotypes by ordering that a woman be denied the chance to present evidence in a State High Court

---

[32] *Odafe v A-G*, Federal High Court of Nigeria, Port Harcourt, Suit FHC/PH/CS/680/2003 (2004) AHRLR 205 (NgHC 2004).

[33] The guarantee of non-discrimination contained in art 42 of the Constitution forbids discrimination based on 'particular community, ethnic group, place of origin, sex, religion or political opinion'. In a ruling that discrimination based on illness or HIV status is not barred by this clause, the Court has construed the word 'community' narrowly. It is plausible that subsequent decisions could read 'community' in such a way as to include the social group formed by those infected with HIV.

[34] *Hoffmann v SAA* (n 22 above) paras 28 and 41; *Makuto v State* [2000] 5 LRC 183 (Botswana), where the Botswana Court of Appeal noted that the framers of the 1966 Constitution did not consider the categories of discrimination in s 15(3) to be closed, and held that different treatment on the sole basis of HIV status amounted to discrimination under the Constitution (187–9).

[35] Promotion of Equality and Prevention of Unfair Discrimination Act 4 of 2000, s 34(1) (containing 'directive principles' on HIV and AIDS).

[36] F Akinwumi, 'Bill against HIV/AIDS discrimination passed' *Nigerian Tribune* (13 June 2006) <http://www.tribune.com.ng/13063\2006/news/news6.html> (31 July 2006).

[37] Art 18 of Benin's Law 2003–04 of 3 March 2003 (Sexual Health and Reproduction Law) and art 14 of the Burkina Faso Law 049-2005/AN Regarding Reproductive Health of 9 February 2006, which echo their Benin predecessor word for word: 'Anybody infected with a Sexually Transmitted Disease (STD), especially the Human Immunodeficiency Virus/Acquired Immunodeficiency Syndrome (HIV/AIDS), should benefit, without discrimination, from civil, political and social

due to her HIV-positive status.[38] The woman had been dismissed from work and denied health care based on her HIV status. An appeal of the decision was dismissed on technical grounds. The case has subsequently been re-listed in the High Court.

A Kenyan case also illustrates that despite the theoretical cloak of impartiality, judicial officers are not necessarily free from societal prejudices.[39] After learning about his wife's HIV-positive status, a husband filed for divorce on the basis that his wife was 'endangering' his 'life'. Pending the finalization of the divorce proceedings, the High Court granted an order expelling the wife from the matrimonial home and consigning her to live under 'traumatising and dehumanising conditions in the unfurnished and incomplete servant's quarter of her own house'.[40]

In an application to the Court of Appeal, the wife asked for and was granted a 'stay of execution' of this order. In granting her application, the Court of Appeal found that the lower court ignored the fact that the wife was still healthy and strong, still worked and paid the mortgage on the house, and that it was in the interest of the two children of a 'tender age' to be with their mother. The Court seems to have been swayed particularly by the last factor, the 'welfare of the children', which it regarded as 'the paramount consideration'.[41] It added that it would be 'morally wrong' for the husband to 'desert' his wife before a divorce has been granted. However, the Court expressed sympathy for the husband's contention that his wife 'poses a grave risk to his life'.[42] Departing from an assumption that the wife is the 'vector' through which HIV penetrates an idyllic and HIV-free home environment, this inappropriate remark shows that the Court did not consider that the wife might have contracted HIV from her husband in the safety of her own home. A question mark should have been raised about the trajectory of blame, especially since the husband's HIV status was 'not revealed'.[43]

4 Criminalization as Legal Response

Criminal law is another field in which reactive legislation has been adopted. Criminal measures send the message that HIV is an external danger and source of deviance that threatens an HIV-free society.

On the whole, existing laws provide ample possibilities to prosecute wilful HIV transmission. Upholding the rights of victims of rape, for example, serves the right

---

rights: housing, education, employment, health and social welfare'. <http://www.wildaf-ao.org/fr/rubrique=autrenouvelles_afrique.php3?id_rubrique=63#129> (31 July 2006).

[38] *Ahamefule v Imperial Medical Centre* Suit ID/1627/2000. See 'High Court Judge Denies Person Living with HIV/AIDS Access to Court' (2001) July *SERAC@Work* 1.

[39] *Midwa v Midwa* (2003) AHRLR 189 (KeCA).

[40] Ibid, para 34.   [41] Ibid, para 9.

[42] Ibid, para 10.   [43] Ibid, para 3.

to bodily integrity and security of the person. Notwithstanding, in many countries
laws were adopted to codify or clarify the current statutory or common law position.[44] In addition, criminalization efforts resulted in the creation of new offences,
such as HIV exposure or negligent transmission.[45] However, the danger always
lurks that these measures may target those already at the greatest risk and 'blamed'
for the spread of HIV, such as women and migrants.

In a number of African states, sentences for HIV-positive perpetrators of sexual
offences (including rape) were also increased.[46] Deterring transmission of HIV
through rape is aimed at upholding the human rights of bodily integrity and
security. Nevertheless, these legislative provisions have human rights implications
also in their formulation. In Botswana, for example, a minimum sentence of 15
years applies if an accused is convicted of rape and it is shown that he was HIV
positive at the time of conviction, even if he had been *unaware* of this fact when he
committed the offence.[47] If, on a balance of probabilities it is shown that he had
been *aware* of his status at the time, the minimum sentence is 20 years.[48] The
Court of Appeal held the first of these provisions, article 142(2)(a), to be unconstitutional, as its discriminatory effect could not be justified in light of the possibility that the suspect tested positive after the commission of the offence, or that
he may even have contracted the infection during his commission of the
offence.[49] The constitutionality of the second provision, article 142(2)(b), was
upheld on the basis that it constituted a reasonable limitation serving the purpose
of deterrence.

The feasibility of imposing criminal sanctions in the realm of HIV and their
contribution to addressing the root causes of the increases in HIV prevalence is
questionable. It appears that legislative intervention is directed at symbolical issues
such as public outrage at isolated events rather than at the real factors that drive
the HIV epidemic in the region. In the absence of anything more than a handful
of prosecutions, these penal measures remain mostly symbolical. Criminal measures are often not used due to the social cost of lodging a complaint, problems of
proof, and generally dysfunctional criminal justice systems. However, given that
all these inhibiting factors were foreseeable when the relevant laws were adopted,
the laws serve only to further demonize and stigmatize HIV and to legitimize
social opprobrium and even violence against HIV-positive people. Highly

---

[44] See eg Burkina Faso's Law 049-2005/AN regarding Reproductive Health of 9 February 2006
which provides that HIV infection resulting from a failure to use condoms may constitute the existing offences of voluntary homicide, and, if death ensues, murder (art 18).
[45] See eg the Law No 049-2005/AN Regarding Reproductive Health of 9 February 2006 of
Burkina Faso, where willful exposure to HIV (ie not taking the necessary precautions during sexual
intercourse) is made an offence (art 18).
[46] Botswana Penal Code (Amendment) Act 5 of 1998; Lesotho Sexual Offences Act (2003); the
Zimbabwe Sexual Offences Act (8 of 2001); see also the Kenyan Sexual Offences Act (approved in
July 2006), s 27 and its HIV/AIDS Prevention and Control Bill (2006).
[47] Penal Code (Cap 08.01) art 142(2)(a).   [48] Penal Code (Cap 08.01) art 142(2)(b).
[49] *Makuto v State* (n 33 above) 188–94.

symbolical and largely unenforced, most of the criminal laws adopted in response to HIV may be categorized as HILs (highly ineffectual laws).[50]

Nonetheless, the criminal law may have a positive contribution to make. The Mauritius HIV and AIDS Act provides an example of a rights-based criminal law provision that addresses stigma.[51] This Act makes it an offence for any person to treat 'any other person or his relative unfairly, unjustly' or with 'hatred, ridicule or contempt' on account of 'being, or being perceived as being, infected with HIV'.[52] Other positive roles of criminal law are manifested in the criminalization of marital rape, as is the case in South Africa,[53] the criminalization of female circumcision and of sexual harassment.[54] Although these measures may also be consigned to HILs if they remain unenforced, they are not merely symbolic, but address the root causes of HIV infection, which this chapter now proceeds to investigate more fully.

5 Failure of the Law to Address the Root Causes and Protect those Rendered most Vulnerable

People who are already at a disadvantage in a society are also those who are most vulnerable to HIV and AIDS. In Africa, as in many other societies, cultural traditions and modern law conspire to marginalize women, especially girls, and to silence children. Impoverished people, especially in rural areas, live on the margins of social life without access to nutrition, health care, and education. The latent vilification of sex work, which, though formally illegal, is allowed to continue, surfaces when scapegoats are sought. At the best of times, intravenous drug users are shunned. Men who have sex with men (MSM) are denied their very existence, as the mere possibility of consensual sex between men is questioned. 'Foreigners' are blamed for society's ills. Prisoners are victims of society's unconcern. Feeding off the combination of inequality, social exclusion, and denial, and targeting the vulnerabilities of these groups, the tremor of HIV and AIDS not only runs along existing fault lines, but further deepens them. The discussion now turns to three groups inhabiting these fault lines: women, MSM, and prisoners.

Women
Women's inferior position in tradition and law has made them more vulnerable to HIV and AIDS. Traditional practices that predispose women to infection include polygamy, the precarious position of widows (through wife inheritance or practices

---

[50] M Kirby, 'The Never-Ending Paradoxes of HIV/AIDS and Human Rights' (2004) 4 *AHRLJ* 163, 167.
[51] Adopted 22 December 2006, not yet in force.
[52] Art 18(3)(a); on conviction, a maximum fine of 5000 rupees may be imposed.
[53] Domestic Violence Act 113 of 1993, s 5.
[54] See eg the Kenyan Sexual Offences Act, ss 23 and 31.

allowing for sex with a widow by the deceased's brother), early marriages, initiation practices (allowing for sexual initiation of girls), and female genital mutilation (FGM). In many African states, violence against women is not only rife, but also left unpunished. The legal position in respect of marriage, divorce, property, and such matters further exacerbates women's precarious position. Legislation is needed to address these issues, which are linked to one of the major root causes of the spread of HIV in Africa—the inequality of women.[55]

An awareness of the challenges posed by HIV and AIDS appears at least in part to have informed the Benin legislation on reproductive health, and the law that outlaws the practice of female genital mutilation, adopted in 2003.[56] Principles that are reinforced in these two enactments include: free consent of both prospective spouses to marriage; the right to information about reproductive choices; non-discrimination on the basis of sex and marital status; the prohibition of sexual violence; and the criminalization of FGM.

Across the continent, a number of legislative designs aimed at eradicating sex and gender inequalities have been or are in the process of being adopted. Although some of them are reactive in nature, there are signs that legislatures are increasingly engaging with those structural issues that are driving the epidemic. After pending for a long time, the Kenyan HIV/AIDS Prevention and Control Act was adopted at the end of 2006. Examples of bills that aim to ensure greater equality between men and women are the Lesotho Legal Capacity of Married Persons Act, 2006; the Ugandan Domestic Relations Bill (which has been before the Ugandan Parliament for over a decade but has not yet been passed); and the Malawi Protection against Domestic Violence Act (5 of 2006). The delay and inertia may be ascribed to cumbersome legislative procedures, a lack of technical expertise, contending priorities, a deep-seated disregard for the role of legislation, and the stigma attached to the subject-matter.

While it is encouraging to note that legislation has been put in place in a number of countries to address the position of women in the HIV/AIDS epidemic and that steps to do so are being taken in others, it remains disappointing that more than a decade into the African HIV/AIDS epidemic so little action has been taken. Ironically, should a human rights-based approach place the spotlight on the deeper causes of HIV infection and AIDS progression, AIDS could leave in its wake a legacy of a more equal, just, and tolerant society. As much as this focus requires reconfigured international trade and the redress of global inequalities, it

---

[55] This was acknowledged by the AU in its adoption of a Continental Policy Framework for the Promotion of Sexual and Reproductive Health and Rights in Africa, which implores states to develop 'linkages between sexual and reproductive rights' in their health care programmes (EX.CL/Dec.249(VIII), Decision on the Continental Policy Framework for the Promotion of Sexual and Reproductive Health and Rights in Africa).

[56] Benin's Law 2003–04 of 3 March 2003, arts 4, 5, 19 (Sexual Health and Reproduction Law) and arts 2 and 4 of Law 2003–03 of 3 March 2003 on the Prohibition of the Practice of Female Genital Multilation (*Loi portant Repression dans la Pratique des Multilations Génitales Féminines en République du Bénin*).

also demands of African political elites that they grasp the opportunity to reshape gender relations in their societies.

Men who have Sex with Men (MSM)

Although consensual sexual contact between members of the same sex was not uncommon in early and pre-colonial Africa, of more recent origin is the use of sexual orientation to mark a preferred lifestyle, or its acceptance as an identity marker.[57] Although in practice few prosecutions take place, colonial codes which criminalize consensual same sex are still in force in most African countries. A clear exception is South Africa, where, based on the constitutional guarantee against non-discrimination on the grounds of sexual orientation, consensual same sex intercourse has been decriminalized.[58]

In *Kanane v The State*,[59] the Botswana Court of Appeal and High Court considered the constitutionality of provisions of the Penal Code criminalizing sex between consenting adult males. Neither in the course of the court proceedings, nor in the High Court's judgment, was the case contextualized against the background of the HIV/AIDS epidemic. At no time was the argument raised that the denial of such sexual practices merely stigmatizes, drives underground, leads to self-hate and denial, and most importantly in the context of HIV/AIDS, exposes MSM to a greater risk of exposure to HIV. The only reference to AIDS was the High Court judge's remark about the moral decay of countries in which 'sodomy' had been decriminalized. Quoting a book by one Dobson entitled *When God Does not Make Sense*, the judge points to the consequence of 'one million Americans [being] infected with HIV (and 110 million worldwide)' and that '[e]very one of these unfortunate people will die of AIDS eventually, barring the improbable development of a cure'.[60] The Court of Appeal dissociated itself 'completely' from those remarks, but it took judicial notice of the 'incidence of HIV' to support the extension of sodomy (and other acts 'against the order of nature') as a criminal offence, to cover not only sex between men but also between men and women.[61]

---

[57] See eg various essays in D Constantine-Simms (ed), *The Greatest Taboo: Homosexually in Black Communities* (Los Angeles: Alyson Books, 2001) and P De Vos, 'The Constitution Made Us Queer' in C Stychin and D Herman (eds), *Sexuality in the Legal Arena* (London: Athlone Press, 2000) 194.

[58] *National Coalition for Gay and Lesbian Equality v Minster of Justice* (1999) 1 SA 6 (CC). The inclusion of the constitutional protection of gays and lesbians in South Africa is informed by the role of gay people in an inclusive ANC struggle against apartheid. See eg N Hoad, K Martin, and G Reid (eds), *Sex and Politics in South Africa* (Cape Town: Double Story, 2005), which contains the address by Mosinoa Lekota, a South African cabinet minister, at the funeral of Simon Nkoli. In this address, the influential role of Nkoli and other gay ANC activists is highlighted.

[59] 1995 BLR 94 (High Court); Criminal Appeal 9 of 2003, [2003] 2 BLR 67 (Court of Appeal) (*Kanane* case); see KN Bojosi, 'An Opportunity Missed for Gay Rights in Botswana: *Utjiwa Kanane v The State*' (2004) 20 *South African J on Human Rights* 466.

[60] *Kanane* case, High Court judgment (typed), 25.

[61] *Kanane* case, Court of Appeal judgment, 21, 25.

Sex between men has also been criminalized for example in Nigeria under the Criminal Code Act of 1990, which considers it an 'offence against morality'.[62] There is no move in Nigeria to decriminalize homosexual sex or to provide treatment and education to homosexuals (or MSM) on how to prevent the spread of HIV. Instead, in 2006 a Bill was introduced in Parliament which is aimed at rendering illegal not only marriages between persons of the same sex but also the formation of associations advocating gay and lesbian rights.[63]

An important consequence of the non-recognition of the existence of MSM, and of the denial of their rights is that—despite their increased biological vulnerability—they are excluded from HIV prevention strategies, educational campaigns, and other sex education. This may foreclose the possibility of those at risk having access to HIV education and prevention, placing them at risk of infection, further reinforcing internalized stigma, and thus in turn placing them at greater risk of HIV infection. As long as they are compelled by law to hide their sexuality, they will not be in a position to mobilize as a group, and may be forced to suppress their sexual identity.

Prisoners

The issue of MSM also pertains to prisoners, as sex between men takes place most visibly in prisons. MSM are particularly at risk of HIV infection in prisons. Criminalization leads to the denial of any form of sex between men, and consequently to the exclusion of MSM from awareness and educational programmes about the risk of HIV. Sexual acts between men in enclosed environments such as prisons may arise from coercion, but often is either a pragmatic or preferred form of sexual expression.

It has been acknowledged officially that sex between men occurs in African prisons. The high incidence of HIV and the high death toll due to AIDS in prisons are at least to some extent due to the infection of prisoners while they are in prison. In a report by the African Commission's Special Rapporteur on Prison Conditions in Africa (SRP) to Malawi, cases of STDs and peri-anal abscess which 'could only have been contracted within the prison through anal intercourse', as well as 'confessions' about sexual 'behaviour' were reported.[64] Following the Special Rapporteur's visit to prisons in Malawi, the Malawian Commissioner of Prisons remarked as follows: 'While it is undeniable that homosexuality may exist in our Prisons, it is very difficult to prove when it happens, as it is done in the absence of Prison Officers and behind curtains'.[65] Despite this reality, the SRP's report is silent about the provision of condoms in prisons and about the implications of the lack of such provision.

---

[62] S 214 of the Act reads, in part 'Any person who (a) has carnal knowledge of any person against the order of nature; . . . or (c) permits a male person to have carnal knowledge of him or her against the order of nature; is guilty of a felony, and is liable to imprisonment for fourteen years'.

[63] A Bill for an Act to Make Provisions for the Prohibition of Sexual Relationships between Persons of the Same Sex, Celebration of Marriage by them and for Other Matters Connected therewith, clauses 4 and 7.   [64] On the SRP, see Ch 9.B.1 above.

[65] Attachment to report, 51. Report of visit 17–28 June 2001 (OAU Prisons in Malawi Series, 2001, IV no 9).

Usually the consensual nature of such sex in prisons is underplayed, and forceful and non-consensual forms are emphasized. Although rape in prison cannot be denied, consensual sex also occurs systematically and frequently. Despite this reality, and even in the face of official recognition, governments refuse to allow the distribution of condoms in prisons. Their main argument is that it would be illegal to provide condoms to prisoners, as this would amount to aiding or assisting the commission of an offence. As a matter of formal logic, this reasoning is difficult to fault. However, the underlying reason why condoms are not provided can only be addressed by decriminalizing consensual sex between adults (in the form of 'sodomy' or 'unnatural acts'). If a particular society is not yet 'ready' to accept such decriminalization, at the very least the risk of HIV infection in prisons should be regarded as a state of emergency or necessity,[66] allowing prisoners access to condoms under specified circumstances.

In this respect, South Africa may be held out as a case of 'best practice'. In his report on South Africa, the SRP merely mentions that homosexuality and lesbianism are 'common in most prisons' and adds that most prisons 'distribute condoms for those who want to use them'. If the report had explored the matter further, it would have found that government policy allows for condom distribution in South African prisons 'on the same basis as condoms are provided in the community'.[67]

Other factors increase prisoners' vulnerability to HIV and AIDS. Prisons in Africa are often overcrowded, inhospitable, and unhygienic relics of colonial times. The standard justification of these conditions—the lack of resources—reflects society's lack of concern towards prisoners generally. Add to the equation the high rate of HIV prevalence among prisoners and it becomes evident that HIV-positive prisoners are rendered vulnerable due to a 'double stigma': stigma resulting from their incarceration and stigma resulting from their HIV status.

In some instances, litigation has been successful in securing one of the most basic needs of prisoners; that is, access to effective HIV treatment. In South Africa, the Constitution served as a basis to compel prison authorities to provide ARVs to prisoners to whom they were medically prescribed.[68] Given the low level of access to ARVs in the country as a whole at that stage, as well as the fact that it was decided by a provincial High Court, the case did not serve as a precedent for universal access to ARVs in prisons. However, it did provide a useful precedent in the Court's rejection of the government's argument about budgetary constraints. Along with the state's 'decision' to keep HIV-positive persons in custody under conditions which

---

[66] As a ground excluding the perceived unlawfulness of distributing condoms in prisons.

[67] See <http://www.plusnews.org/webspecials/HIV-in-prisons/SouthAfrica.asp> (31 July 2006). However, the implementation of even this 'best practice' is flawed. Before receiving a condom, a prisoner needs to undergo counselling regarding AIDS, the use of condoms and the dangers of 'high risk behaviour'. The fact of the counselling has to be reflected in the prisoner's medical file. These facts impede the accessibility of condoms, as prisoners may be wary of stigma and prison officials' moral condemnation. The alternative is to provide condoms freely—that is, in condom dispensers that may be accessed in private.

[68] *Van Biljon v Minister of Correctional Services* (n 22 above).

increase their vulnerability to opportunistic infections, in turn causing them to progress more rapidly to AIDS, comes the responsibility to provide them with a level of care that is higher than that in the community on the 'outside'. The decision reiterates the long-standing principle that inroads into a prisoner's rights should be restricted to those consequent upon the deprivation of liberty.

With the acceptance of the South African Operational Plan for Comprehensive HIV and AIDS Care, every HIV-positive person with a CD4 count of less than 200 qualifies for the provision of ARVs by the state. The limited implementation of this Plan in prisons caused a group of HIV positive prisoners to approach the Durban High Court to 'remove all obstacles' preventing them from accessing treatment.[69] In this case, budgetary constraints were not in issue, but instead the reasonableness of measures. The access of prisoners to ARVs was restricted because only one hospital was assigned as a 'designated site', allowing only four detainees per week to access the relevant service. Finding these measures unreasonable, the Court ordered that the applicants—as well as all similarly situated prisoners in the particular prison—be granted immediate access to ARVs in accordance with the Plan.

C Challenges to a Human Rights-based Approach to HIV and AIDS

In the last few years, the human rights-based response to HIV and AIDS has increasingly been questioned, not only from a public health perspective but also from 'within' the human rights movement. Two particular issues, both questioning the traditional wisdom of applying a human rights-based approach, have been raised, namely, shared confidentiality or compulsory disclosure to sexual partners or even to family members, and routine testing. Criticizing the approach followed so far as 'HIV and AIDS exceptionalism',[70] which allowed HIV and AIDS to be exempted from traditionally proven public health tenets, it is argued that the disclosure of HIV status and test results should correspond as far as possible to that of other diseases.[71]

1 Disclosure

The scale of the epidemic prompted an erosion of the right to privacy and confidentiality. 'Privacy' may be defined as the 'state or condition of being withdrawn

---

[69] *EN and Others v Government of South Africa and Others* (n 22 above).

[70] See eg R Bayer, 'Public Health Policy and the AIDS Epidemic' (1991) 324(21) *New England J of Medicine* 1500, 1503 who predicted that, as medicine advances, 'the effort to sustain a set of policies treating HIV infection as fundamentally different from all other public health threats will be increasingly difficult', and that, inevitably, 'HIV exceptionalism will be viewed as a relic of the epidemic's first years'.

[71] KM De Cock, D Mbori-Ngacha and E Marum, 'Shadow on the Continent: Public Health and HIV/AIDS in Africa in the 21st Century' (2002) 360 *The Lancet* 67, also available at <http://www.thelancet.com/journal/journal.isa> (31 July 2006).

from the society of others . . . '.[72] The right to privacy, accordingly, is an individualistic right, the ultimate right 'to be left alone', indicating an individual self separated from collective identity and rooted in personal preferences. The right to privacy is often associated with claims pertaining to 'nobody's business but mine',[73] which may include the possession of pornography[74] or decisions concerning sexual relationships.[75] Its very definition and its application in case-law posit the right to privacy in opposition to the collective concerns of society.

In the era of HIV and AIDS, other notions of privacy have been advanced. These depart from a premise of a collective interest or stake in private knowledge, and give rise to the notion of 'shared confidentiality'. In terms of a World Health Organization Fact Sheet, 'shared confidentiality' is 'confidentiality that is shared with others', such as family members, loved ones, care-givers and trusted friends.[76] According to the Fact Sheet, sharing confidentiality is in the discretion of a person who has been tested for HIV. The notion of 'shared confidentiality' is premised on the view that confidentiality, as 'a one-on-one exchange between the healer and the patient', rarely exists in traditional African culture.[77] However, the effect of this understanding of privacy is that it undermines the rights of HIV-positive persons, exposing them to discrimination and even violence in societies where stigma is rife.

A practical illustration of shared confidentiality is found in Botswana's National Policy on HIV. It proposes 'shared confidentiality' as an ideal, but stresses that consent should be obtained from the HIV-positive person before the information is divulged. Ideally, 'those who need to know' in order to provide appropriate health and social assistance should be told about a person's HIV status. This policy flows from the premise that the individual is inextricably linked to a family and a community. The family is, therefore, encouraged to be involved from the pre-testing phase, as a support structure, and not as a potential threat. According to this vision, HIV or AIDS is regarded not as 'a matter of placing blame but of drawing together to cure'.[78]

A more extreme form of 'shared confidentiality' has found its way into the Botswana Medical Council (Professional Conduct) Regulations 1988,[79] allowing doctors to 'share' confidential information about the HIV status of patients.[80] The amended regulations provide that 'a person taking care of, living with or otherwise coming into regular close contact with the patient shall be informed

---

[72] *The New Shorter Oxford English Dictionary.*

[73] *Case v Minister of Safety and Security* (1996) 3 SA 165 (CC), per Didcott J (para 91).

[74] ibid.

[75] *National Coalition for Gay and Lesbian Equality v Minister of Justice* (n 56 above) eg para 23.

[76] See <http://www3.who.int/whosis/factsheets> (31 July 2006) Fact Sheet 1.

[77] EM Ankrah and LO Gostin, 'Ethical and Legal Considerations of the HIV Epidemic in Africa' in M Essex *et al* (eds), *AIDS in Africa* (New York: Raven Press, 1994) 547, 550.

[78] S Bockie, *Death and the Invisible Powers* (Bloomington, Ind: Indiana University Press, 1993) 39.

[79] After amendment in 1999.

[80] A Zuyderduin and I Melville, 'Shared Confidentiality—An Ethical Dilemma in Botswana' paper prepared for XIII AIDS Conference, Durban, 5 July 2000, available at <http://www.ditshwanelo.org.bw> (31 July 2006).

about such patient's medical condition' should the patient be HIV positive. By not
requiring the patient's consent for such a disclosure, the notion of shared confidentiality has been extended. The broad category of people to whom the information may be disclosed (even including those with whom the patient has 'regular
close contact'), and also the fact that none of them is under an obligation to keep
the information confidential, led Zuyderduin and Melville to conclude that these
regulations are unconstitutional.[81]

The African Union's major normative framework dealing with the rights of
women, the Protocol to the African Charter on Human and Peoples' Rights on
the Rights of Women in Africa (the Protocol), also invokes notions of shared confidentiality.[82] Provisions included under the heading '[h]ealth and reproductive
rights' require that a state party ensures that its legal system provides for the right
'to be informed on one's health status and on the health status of one's partner,
particularly if affected with sexually transmitted infections, including HIV/AIDS,
in accordance with internationally recognized standards and best practices'.[83]

Internationally recognized standards protect the confidential relationship
between doctor and patient as part of the right to privacy.[84] In general, confidentiality regarding all medical information has to be guaranteed, including HIV status. An exception to the general rule may be invoked only when predetermined
guidelines have been followed, allowing as a matter of last resort disclosure to a
specific person at immediate and clearly demonstrated risk of infection.[85] Such an
approach, derived from the principle that all rights may be limited by the rights of
others (such as the right to life), is more in line with international standards than
the vague notion of 'shared confidentiality'.

2 Routine Testing

The urgency of placing millions of people on ARV treatment in a short time has
led some to argue that traditional safeguards such as pre- and post-test counselling,
confidentiality, and voluntariness should not stand in the way of widespread HIV
testing.[86] Widespread testing, it is argued, will both facilitate increased access to
HIV treatment and prevent new HIV infections by bringing more people into the
health care system, enabling the provision of information on how to prevent HIV

[81] ibid.
[82] Adopted in July 2003, in Maputo, Mozambique; the Protocol entered into force in November
2005 (see Ch 6.D above).
[83] Art 14(1)(e) of the Protocol.
[84] International Guideline 5; ICCPR, art 17.
[85] See the discussion of the South African Health Professions Council's Guidelines (F Viljoen,
'Disclosing In an Age of AIDS: Confidentiality and Community in Conflict?' in F Viljoen (ed),
Righting Stigma: Exploring a Rights-Based Approach to Addressing Stigma (Pretoria: AIDS and Human
Rights Research Unit, University of Pretoria, 2005) 64, 74–90 and the American case of *Tarasoff v
Regents of the University of California* (551 P 2d 334 (Cal 1976)).
[86] KM De Cock, 'HIV Testing in an Era of Treatment Scale-Up' (2005) 8 *Health and Human
Rights* 31.

transmission. In addition, widespread testing is thought by many to reduce HIV-related stigma and discrimination by 'normalizing' the disease: as more people learn their HIV status, it is argued, AIDS will come to be perceived as yet another chronic, manageable illness such as cancer or heart disease. These arguments are raised particularly with reference to Africa, where the discrepancy between HIV infection rates and individual knowledge of HIV status is at its starkest.[87]

Even if 'routine offer' or 'opt-out' testing and not compulsory testing is proposed, there are still human rights issues involved.[88] Although routine testing is 'advertised' as 'voluntary', because it allows patients to refuse, the routine nature of the offer in the context of an unequal power relationship between unsophisticated 'patients' and health care workers impedes individual agency. In addition, the proposed guidelines and most proponents accept the inevitability, occasioned by an increase in numbers, of 'scaled down' pre-test counselling. The form of consent required by UNAIDS/WHO under routine testing is 'simplified informed consent'.[89] In the UNAIDS/WHO 2004 *Policy Statement on HIV Testing*, informed consent is 'simplified' by being reduced to the following elements: a review of the clinical and prevention benefits of testing, the right to refuse, follow-up services, and the importance of informing someone (a partner) at risk if the test is positive. A 'full education and counselling session' is not required, as voluntary counselling and testing (VCT) services are 'adapted to simply ensure informed consent, without a full education and counselling session'.[90]

International human rights law recognizes the individual right to withhold consent to medical treatment, including diagnostic tests.[91] This right derives from the principle of individual autonomy, which has its roots in the inherent dignity of every individual.[92] Testing for HIV without informed consent represents an involuntary intrusion into bodily integrity, which is protected by the right to liberty and security of the person in article 9 of the International Covenant on Civil and Political Rights (ICCPR).[93]

---

[87] It is estimated that only some 10 per cent of people living with HIV in Africa are aware of their status. This low level is attributable to many factors, some of which are cultural, some related to stigma, and some related to the low level of access to HIV testing and counselling (see eg Report of the UNAIDS/WHO/USA Government Consultative Meeting on HIV Testing and Counselling in the Africa Region (15–17 November 2004, Johannesburg, South Africa), in which it is estimated that less than 10 per cent of people in Africa have access to these services).

[88] J Csete, R Schleifer, and J Cohen, ' "Opt-out" Testing for HIV in Africa: A Caution' (2004) 363 *The Lancet* 493.

[89] An example of the use of simplified guidelines could be the following: A patient that has a cold, and may be informed that blood will be drawn, so that an HIV test can be done, and may be asked if 'that is ok'.   [90] UNAIDS/WHO Policy Statement, point 3.

[91] See eg Committee on Economic, Social and Cultural Rights, The Right to the Highest Attainable Standard of Health: CESCR General Comment 14, UN Doc E/C.12/2000/4 (8 November 2000) para 8: 'The right to health contains both freedoms and entitlements. The freedoms include the right to control one's health and body, including . . . the right to be free from interference, such as the right to be free from . . . non-consensual medical treatment and experimentation'.

[92] Universal Declaration of Human Rights, arts 1 and 3.

[93] See eg Universal Declaration of Human Rights, arts 1 and 3; ICCPR, arts 9 and 10.

Under international law (as well as under some domestic constitutions), rights may only be limited by way of laws of general application that pursue a legitimate aim responding to a pressing social need, and that are proportionate to that aim.[94] In addition, governments must use the least restrictive means possible to achieve those aims.[95] Under the same legal regime, the onus of showing that an inroad into rights is justified rests with the party introducing the encroachment.

To meet this standard of persuasion, proponents of routine testing have argued that some curtailment of the right to informed consent may be justified to ensure that new medical advances, particularly ARV treatment, will reach people living with HIV on a large scale.[96] They all accept, as do the WHO Guidelines, that the availability of treatment must serve as a prerequisite for testing. However, in reality in most of Africa there is no guarantee that the tested person will indeed receive ARVs, due to the unavailability of these medications in many African settings.[97] Even if ARVs are available, there is no guaranteed benefit to the tested person, due to the general requirement that only HIV-positive people with a CD4 count of less that 200 qualify for ARV treatment. Thus, it cannot be assumed that the trade-off being proposed—universal treatment in exchange for a reduction in individual rights—even exists. While appropriate treatment may become increasingly available, the present drive towards routine testing is premature. Less restrictive means, such as increasing access to VCT, have to be exhausted before this radical departure from the rights-based approach can be supported.

Other justifications are premised on similarly shaky ground. Some proponents of routine testing argue that an increase in the number of people who are tested for HIV, thus learning their status, will lead to a decrease in stigma and discrimination. In this sense, proponents of routine testing depart from the school of AIDS 'exceptionalism', which argues that AIDS is a uniquely stigmatized disease requiring specific human rights protection.

It is true that access to ARVs could contribute to the de-stigmatization of AIDS by reducing the prevalence of 'body marks' associated with opportunistic infections, such as wasting or Kaposi's sarcoma. Once HIV is perceived as a chronic but treatable condition, one of the factors that amplifies stigma—fear of contagion and inevitable death—is lessened. However, stigma is much more than fear of contagion. It is also related to the perception that HIV infection results from 'immoral'

---

[94] See eg the Siracusa Principles on the Limitation and Derogation Provisions in the ICCPR; ICCPR, arts 12(3) and 18(1); Arab Charter on Human Rights, art 4(a).

[95] See eg Universal Declaration, art 29; Siracusa Principles on the Limitation and Derogation Provisions in the ICCPR; Canadian Constitution, s 1; Constitution of South Africa, s 36.

[96] See eg AD Paltiel *et al*, 'Expanded Screening for HIV in the United States—An Analysis of Cost-Effectiveness' (2005) 352(6) *New England J of Medicine* 586, who find—on the basis of a computer simulation—that one-time screening improved the survival rate of HIV-infected patients.

[97] eg: the UN Special Rapporteur on Health reports as follows about the situation in Mozambique: 'Very few Mozambicans—less than 1 per cent of those in need—are receiving treatment for HIV/AIDS, although progress is now possible owing to a major drop in the cost of anti-retroviral (ARV) drugs and the political will to deliver treatment through the public sector' (UN Doc E/CN.4/2005/51/Add.2, 4 January 2005) para 22.

behaviour such as extra-marital sex, homosexuality, prostitution, or injection drug use. While 'downgrading' HIV to the status of a 'manageable disease' may go some distance towards addressing HIV/AIDS-related stigma, it is unlikely on its own to alter deeply rooted perceptions of the moral stature of people living with AIDS. On the contrary, information about a person's status may be dangerous or even deadly, exposing him or her not only to stigma, but also to its physical manifestations such as violence. Without a greater guarantee that such attitudes will be addressed, individuals should not be expected to trade away their individual right to informed consent for the meagre prospect of a stigma-free world or even treatment. Because treatment does not guarantee that HIV-positive persons become non-infectious, the fear of infection remains—as does the need for safe sex and prevention programmes.

The only justification that does merit serious consideration is that an HIV test 'empowers' a patient to make more rational choices. Far from being a means of 'empowerment', routine testing and possible disclosure may make the position of women much more precarious. Not only is there a likelihood that the confidentiality of test results could be breached,[98] but as women are more likely than men to come into contact with the health system (largely because of antenatal services), routine testing may reinforce stereotypes about women being the principal carriers of HIV infection. Women may thus suffer very greatly from the consequences of routine testing—emotionally, physically, and economically. Unless tests are offered in an environment in which efforts are made to establish what ongoing support the woman will need, what kind of support is available to the woman, and, in the absence of family or community support, who she can turn to—the basic fundamentals of good pre-test counselling—she should not be offered the test. In addition, for many women the option of 'opting out' of HIV testing in the face of pressure from a medical professional is not realistic.

D Conclusion

The obligations of governments in respect of human rights may be classified into four categories: the duty to *promote*, respect, protect, and fulfil rights. These four aspects require increasing tiers of government commitment.

In most African countries governments have, on the whole, complied with the obligation to promote rights by adopting policy statements and embarking on educational and sensitization campaigns to prevent and curtail the spread of HIV. However, these policies, themselves, have not been disseminated systematically or comprehensively, and their effectiveness has been seriously questioned.

---

[98] See eg Viljoen (ed) (n 85 above) ch 1 ('A Report of the Tswelopele Research Project of the Centre for the Study of AIDS on Stigma and Human Rights in the Peri-urban Community of Hammanskraal, South Africa' (interviews indicating that health care workers are sometimes the cause of information about HIV status becoming public knowledge)).

Governments in most of the African countries under investigation have in the main *respected* the rights of those infected and affected by HIV. Initial responses that had to be formulated at the end of the 1980s were informed by the 'civil liberties/human rights' approach to HIV/AIDS adopted in the USA and Europe. In Africa the initial approach was certainly reinforced by a perception that HIV/AIDS was not the continent's priority, and by a failure to foresee the eventual profound impact of AIDS on African society. The initial response generally did not involve compulsory testing, isolation, quarantine, or travel restrictions. There are some exceptions, however, such as compulsory testing for HIV and exclusion on the basis of positive results from serving in the military.

Governments have been less diligent in adhering to their obligation to *protect* the rights of those infected, affected, or potentially infected or affected from encroachment by non-state actors, including neighbours and family members. One of the clearest examples of governments' omission to 'protect' human rights is their failure to challenge and curb the discriminatory practices of insurance companies. Governments' most prominent intervention has been in the criminal sphere. This reveals either a high degree of trust in the criminal justice system, or a need for clear symbolic action. Penal measures include the compulsory testing of rape suspects or convicts, fixed minimum sentences, and the denial of bail. Governments have also mostly adopted legislative or other measures to protect HIV-positive employees from discrimination in private employment. Legal reforms to protect vulnerable groups, especially women and prisoners, from infection by partners and fellow prisoners, have been less pronounced. Nominal efforts have been made to address the underlying causes of gender equality which expose women to abuse in the family sphere.

The last, and most cumbersome duty of governments, that of *fulfilling* rights, has been left mostly unfulfilled. The level of non-compliance is linked to the inability of governments to mobilize resources and political will to prioritize spending on HIV/AIDS. Many other factors may have a negative impact on the fulfilment of rights, such as political instability, drought, and poverty. In Zimbabwe, for example, an AIDS levy of 3 per cent (on the taxable income of all formally employed persons and of companies) is used to fund AIDS programmes. The current economic crisis has also had a negative impact on this effort.

Governments have by and large been in dereliction of duty in respect of their most obvious obligation—that of fulfilling the right to health care—which flows from the inherent responsibility of governments to their subjects, and the right to life recognized in all constitutions. Two exceptions are Botswana, and to some extent South Africa. This is perhaps not surprising, given the resources available to these two governments.

The human rights response of countries should move beyond mere rhetoric and policy to legislation—the basis of a human rights-based approach. Such a response could, for example, take the form of a comprehensive statute, a Human Rights and HIV/AIDS Act. This Act might spell out government's duty to *promote* the rights of all affected, by placing a legal duty on government to widely disseminate its policies and to embark on effective awareness-raising campaigns; the duty to prevent, by addressing the legal rules underlying gender inequality, such as those related to divorce law, the inheritance of property, and the status of women; the duty to fulfil, by converting social security benefits and health care into legal entitlements.

With the increased 'medicalization' of HIV and AIDS,[99] focus falls on the medical dimension of the solution. While treatment is a core issue, and undeniably supports the important rights to life and health, it should not blind us to the social and human rights dimensions of both the problem and its ultimate resolution.

---

[99] S Kippax, 'Medicalisation of Prevention', paper presented at the Australasian Society of HIV Medicine (ASHM) Conference, Canberra, Australia, 4 September 2004 (on file with author).

PART VI

CONCLUSION

16

Conclusion

In the discussions and conclusions of the chapters above, some of the questions posed at the outset of this book have been addressed. Instead of revisiting and summarizing those answers, a few of the most salient features of the overview of international human rights law in Africa are canvassed here.

The discussion of international human rights law is located within an *institutional* framework. Functioning at three levels (the UN, globally, the AU, regionally, and various RECs, subregionally), these international organizations all claim to pursue the goals of human development, security, and the protection of human rights. However, political and economic agendas sometimes trump human rights principles. Despite their prominence in the UN and AU, human rights are not sufficiently integrated into their institutional functioning. One of the major problems is the lack of integration of the multiplicity of human rights bodies and mechanisms. (Streamlining, for example by integrating the mandate of the African Children's Committee with that of the African Commission, has been suggested earlier.) This lack of integration spills over into the relationship between UN and AU bodies and mechanisms. Closer collaboration between the global and regional levels is clearly required.

Institutions consist of people. The study highlights the importance of individual leaders, of members of human rights bodies, their support staff, and the management of these bodies. Domestic nomination processes should therefore be democratized to ensure more people-responsive representation, and UN appointments should better reflect Africa's diversity.

Central to this book stands the nation state, as it does in the international human rights discourse generally. 'National sovereignty' and 'non-interference' remain smokescreens behind which human rights violations are hidden and are used as devices to silence critics. The debilitating consequences of the nation-building imperative imposed by the retention of colonial borders in Africa are made most visible in the denial of the existence of the rights of Africa's indigenous peoples and in the stifling of cultural diversity, more generally.

African integration, gradually eroding the nation state as the primary site of contestation about human rights, is spearheaded by a closer collaboration within and between RECs. Institutional integration for economic purposes has an inevitable legal dimension, leaving room for the greater convergence and stronger implementation of human rights. Even if the nation state is not (yet) disappearing, the real prospect of weakening national sovereignty within subregional entities has to take place in a context that reinforces adherence to international human rights law. Closer ties and deeper bonds should not only serve to create successful trade blocs and viable economic units, but should also be the basis for common human rights standards and effective implementation by way of moral and material sanctions. In the long term, when the RECs have been consolidated and have reached their AEC Treaty targets, and when the PAP has full legislative powers, the AU Court of Justice and Human Rights is up and running, and AU directives apply directly in the legal orders of member states, the AU will have grown from an intergovernmental to a supra-national organization. The role and place of human rights within the RECs and the AU are therefore all the more important, as these institutions will play an increasingly important part in the lives of every African.

Of the three regional human rights systems in the world, Africa's is the weakest. While there is a clear preference for the regional systems, there has been limited interest in and only a trickle of cases to the African Commission. The reasons for the small number of cases are multifaceted. One of these reasons is that individuals may not value legal recourse highly if they are faced with immense and deep-seated structural problems to which the solutions are perceived to be 'political'. Although there are high hopes for the African Human Rights Court, these expectations have to be tempered if regard is had to the experience so far.

As far as international human rights *norms* and the *procedures* for their implementation and enforcement are concerned, seven layers of state commitment are identified below. Starting with standard-setting and ending with enforcement, these layers represent mounting levels of commitment required. Reference is made to the UN, AU, subregional, and national dimensions, as appropriate.

(1) International human rights law is mostly formalized through the *elaboration and adoption* of human rights treaties. The extent, scope, and nature of treaties differ according to the 'level' at which they operate. It may be assumed, for example, that the detail and specificity with which norms may be articulated increase from the global through to the national level. Starting with the Convention on the Prevention and Punishment of the Crime of Genocide (in 1948) and CERD (in 1965), an elaborate network of treaties has been established under UN auspices. Despite its significant membership of the organization, African involvement in UN standard-setting has been minimal. This, together with the failure of UN treaties to resonate sufficiently with concerns particular to Africa, gave rise to the OAU/AU adopting norms supplementing UN treaties. As a consequence, some regional treaties speaking to clear African specificities have been adopted. However, as a result of the homogenizing effect of international law and of international pressure, other African treaties largely resemble those adopted at the global level. So far, the potential of subregional organizations to articulate human rights-related norms with more precision lies unexplored, and still needs to be

incorporated into subregional economic integration and development. Despite various constitutional transitions in most African countries, African domestic legal systems largely still reflect the law—including the constitutional law—of erstwhile colonial powers, and lack features associated with 'African' legal thinking such as collective (peoples') rights and the principle that human rights are indivisible.

(2) The next step is the *formal acceptance* of the treaty norms. In ascending order of commitment, formal acceptance by states may consist of (i) signing a treaty; (ii) ratifying it with reservation; and (iii) ratifying it without reservation. On the whole, African states have been exemplary in ratifying without reservation treaties adopted under the aegis of both the UN and AU. In respect of six of the seven major UN human rights treaties, the percentage of African ratifying states is higher than the corresponding global percentage. (For the seventh, CRC, the difference is marginal.) Even in respect of treaties under which reservations have been entered by African states, in particular CEDAW, Africa is a lesser culprit. Manifesting a promising trend, African state parties to the AU's Women's Protocol have been less likely to enter reservations to that treaty than to CEDAW. There are also indications that international and national pressure may persuade states into withdrawing reservations, as exemplified by the withdrawal of the Malawi and Lesotho reservations to CEDAW, and of the extensive Gambian reservation to the Women's Protocol. With the exception of the African Charter, regional standards enjoy more limited acceptance by African states than those in UN treaties. In respect of the Women's Protocol, this may be explained by the more recent adoption of the African instrument. The same explanation does not hold true for the African Children's Charter, though. However, the slow pace of ratification and the smaller number of state parties to the African Children's Charter hold an important lesson. Initial hesitance to accept a treaty encompassing regional imperatives and a comparatively strong implementation procedure has gradually made way for acceptance and meaningful domestication. This experience shows that the impact of international human rights law may, in the long run, be enhanced if higher standards, and not the lowest common denominator, guide the drafting process.

In some instances, notably that of the OPII to the ICCPR, on the abolition of the death penalty, African ratification lags behind the global percentage. In line with global trends, a modest number of African state parties has accepted OPII subsequent to undertaking domestic legal reform. The ratification of OPII therefore serves as confirmation of a *fait accompli*. If OPII exerts influence on a state, it does so *in anticipation of* ratification, and not *as a result of ratification*. One of the major reasons why states ensure compatibility with this treaty prior to ratifying it, and not with most other treaties, is the starkly demonstrable nature of (non-)compliance with its obligations: either a state refrains from applying capital punishment and abolishes the death penalty, or it does not. Given the attachment to the death penalty of most African states, at the very least as a symbol of state authority, few have ratified OPII. In respect of other treaties, a state can at least argue that its formal legal order is in line with the relevant treaty even if state practice does not conform to it. The impossibility of doing so makes the application of *rightoric* in respect of OPII impractical. The 'starkly demonstrable' nature of the specificities in regional treaties such as the Women's Protocol and the African Children's Charter also renders their ratification problematic, and accounts for the lack of enthusiasm among African political elites for throwing their weight behind these regional pendants to global treaties.

(3) The basic *obligation* arising from treaty ratification is *to submit timely state reports*. African state reporting has been erratic. Under CERD, for example, states initially reported regularly, but as it became clear that the treaty deals with problems of ethnicity within their states, and not only with apartheid in other states, their enthusiasm waned. More recently, state reporting has improved under treaties perceived to be 'non-political' (notably CEDAW and CRC). All 52 African state parties to CRC have submitted at least one report—for a number of states, this remains the only treaty under which they have ever reported. This stands in distinct contrast to the African Children's Charter, under which only two states have submitted reports. While African states have scorned their obligation to report under ICESCR, they have taken a leadership role with reporting under the CMW. The reason for this difference is perhaps not too hard to find: while the CMW concerns an issue that is viewed as 'external' to Africa, the dereliction of socio-economic rights is too embarrassingly close to home. Reporting under the African Charter has improved gradually, with only 15 failing to submit a single report. Curiously, a number of states that remain disengaged the regional system are active participants in the global system.

(4) Formal norm-acceptance is mere *rightoric* if it is not complemented by (formal) acceptance of treaty procedures where there is an *option* to do so. Moving up the commitment scale from 'protection' to 'prevention', states may (i) accept optional individual complaints mechanisms provided for in the treaty; (ii) accept ad hoc visits from special mechanisms; (iii) issue a standing invitation to special mechanisms; and (iv) accept inquiry procedures. In respect of all five optional individual complaints procedures under UN treaties, the African rate of acceptance is significantly lower than global acceptance rates. However, African acceptance of the most prominent procedure, which allows the HRC to consider individual communications under the ICCPR, is the least discrepant. Still, the number of complaints against African states represents a mere trickle. In a small number of findings of violations (48), this mechanism has been used to some positive effect. Although the acceptance of individual complaints is a necessary consequence of ratifying the African Charter, the number of complaints leading to a finding of violation under that procedure (57) is only slightly higher. Some of the reasons for the small number of complaints to treaty bodies are the lack of visibility and awareness at the national level; their perceived inaccessibility; the track-record of these bodies, especially when it comes to the 'enforcement' of their decisions; the weakness of domestic legal recourse; and the shortage of legal aid at the national

level. A reluctance to allow direct individual access to the African Human Rights Court is another example of halfway measures by states.

While some African states have accepted visits by special mechanisms, especially the UN's thematic rapporteurs, only Sierra Leone and South Africa have extended 'standing invitations' to UN special mechanisms. One may also mention NEPAD's APRM here. Almost half of all African states have accepted this voluntary procedure, which allows an independent inspection of governance, including human rights, of the visited country. Even if states subscribe to the APRM in order to benefit from foreign funding, it is significant that they allow themselves to be subjected to scrutiny. Greater visibility and the political backing of political leadership make the APRM an exciting vehicle for the improvement of human rights in Africa. African acceptance of OP-CAT, which allows for independent inspections of places of detention to prevent torture, is very low, and compares unfavourably with global acceptance. African states also stand out among CAT state parties for opting out of its inquiry procedure, and Egypt earned notoriety for its constructive refusal to allow the CAT Committee to conduct an inquiry on its soil.

(5) A prerequisite for national relevance is the *domestication* of norms, which traditionally has been regarded as largely dependent on the way the domestic legal order views the relationship between international and national law. As the study shows, however, both 'dualist' and 'monist' legal systems may act as gatekeepers to the free passage of international law. As the case of Habré and other examples illustrate, the 'monist' nature of legal systems is often invoked as subterfuge, while in practice some form of 'transformation' of international law is required to make it an effective part of national law. With a few exceptions, African states have done very little to domesticate international human rights law. However, its role as an interpretative source in judicial decision-making cannot be ignored. An international human rights treaty should be used as a direct source of a domestic remedy if the treaty provision allows for direct application (that is, if it is 'self-executing'), irrespective of its constitutional status within a ratifying state.

(6) It is not enough for states to conform with their formal obligations. They must also *implement* the conclusions of treaty bodies, in particular concluding observations adopted after the examination of state reports. Although it is difficult to accurately assess compliance in this regard, the repetition of similar recommendations from one report to another is clear evidence of non-compliance. While examples of non-implementation are abundant, there are some indications that states make efforts to respond to concluding observations. The response of Kenya to the HRC's concluding observations on its second periodic report provides an encouraging example of constructive engagement with a treaty body's recommendations. Largely due to the African Commission's inconsistent and secretive practice, an assessment of the implementation of its concluding observations cannot be accomplished. Given the accessibility of its documentation and the involvement of civil society, the APRM process may lead to better implementation, or, at least, better monitoring of implementation. The goal of 'implementation' is only

wholly accomplished if not only states (government officials), but also ordinary people, do not act out of self-interest or fear of sanctions, but because international norms have been internalized as part of the culture of governance and way of life. Internalization presupposes that 'the law has a central place in the affected individual's world'. This assumption may ring true for formally employed urbanized persons and civil servants, but is likely to be exposed as a fallacy in the lives of those closer to their rural roots. Culture and tradition cannot be changed by enactment alone. To achieve internalization in many areas of life, education and sensitization have to go hand-in-hand with efforts to enhance the legitimacy of law as a meaningful agent for social change. It should be recalled that African states have also been reluctant to regard the HIV and AIDS pandemic as presenting an opportunity and an obligation to address the major societal fault-line of gender inequality.

(7) '*Enforcement*', in the sense of giving domestic effect to a 'view' or 'recommendation' of a treaty body in respect of an individual communication, represents the pinnacle of compliance. Treaty bodies have shifted their attention to this aspect. Although enforcement is certainly not the rule, numerous exceptions of decisions adopted under both OPI and the African Charter show that states may at least in isolated instances move beyond *rightoric*. Judgments by international courts are generally effectively enforced, as is illustrated by compliance with decisions of the ICJ and imprisonment following the decisions of the ICTR. The binding judgments of the African Human Rights Court will likewise make recourse to compliance-avoiding stratagems more difficult. In some instances, the decisions of international bodies supplement those of domestic courts (as in the *Müller* case against Namibia); sometimes one quasi-judicial body reinforces the decision of a similar body (such as the *Forum of Conscience/Mansaraj* case against Sierra Leone); and sometimes an international judicial decision adds weight to that of an international quasi-judicial body (as was the case with the inter-state case concerning the Great Lakes before the African Commission and the ICJ).

The history of the *Habré* case, which brings different aspects of the seven identified layers into play, should go some distance towards convincing the Thomases doubting the significance of international human rights law. In the absence of CAT and other human rights law, the matter could have been resolved with reference only to domestic law and international politics. Because Senegal is a state party to CAT (and leaving aside customary international law arguments), Chadian 'victims' could invoke judicial means to further secure Habré's prosecution. Senegalese attempts to evade its responsibility met with an adverse reaction from the CAT treaty body, which found Senegal in violation of its treaty obligations. The AU, too, was spurred into action. Because the AU had unequivocally embraced human rights as part of its mandate (in itself reflecting the influence of international human rights law), it insisted that Habré should be tried by Senegal 'on behalf of Africa'. In its decision, the AU Assembly made specific reference to the fact that Senegal had ratified CAT. Although protracted in nature, the process illustrates that persistence and a modicum of goodwill and political resolve may achieve human rights-compliant outcomes.

With the arrival of the twenty-first century, poverty has increasingly taken centre stage in global and regional institutions. As important as macro-economic factors, such as debt relief, foreign aid and investment, neo-colonial resource-driven 'engagement', equitable trade arrangements, the attainment of the MDGs, and the regulation of MNCs are, human rights law has a significant contribution to make. Aimed at the realization of socio-economic rights, the programmes of NEPAD show promise in their conception, but questions about their fulfilment are still unanswered. Deliberations and declarations are not enough. Good governance, linked to a respect for 'civil and political' rights, together with justiciable 'socio-economic' rights, may create a basis to address poverty through the workings of the law. Departing from the premise that it is people who are poor, and not states, the law can become an instrument in the re-direction of state resources by challenging the reasonableness of government programmes. Such arguments are all the more cogent now that Africa is experiencing a period of relative economic growth, supplemented by significant debt relief in those countries that have LDC status. Some of the states with very high GDPs are also countries in which social indicators reveal that government-spending priorities are misplaced. Gabon, for example, has one of Africa's highest GDPs.[1] Despite an HIV prevalence rate of 7.9 per cent of the adult population, its health expenditure made up only 1.8 per cent of GDP in 2002.[2] The rights discourse may be useful to argue (or even litigate) for appropriate social allocations in countries such as Gabon, and also in countries where oil has recently been discovered.

The effective implementation and enforcement of 'socio-economic' rights are the Achilles' heel of international human rights law at the global level. Discussions about making these rights justiciable have been going on for many years. In the meantime, state reporting by African states under ICESCR has been farcical. With at least some 'socio-economic' rights contained in the African Charter, and the concrete example of their application in the *Ogoniland* and *Gambian Mental Health* cases, the African regional system provides a clear contrast to the UN system. It is on this foundation, as well as on the possibilities in their own constitutions, that lawyers and judges in African states should build in order to ensure the domestic justiciability of 'socio-economic' rights. Such a development should strengthen developments at the global level, which may eventually reflect rather than guide domestic African practice.

The book did not start off with a focus on civil society. However, the repeated references to the 'levels' on which international human rights law operates do not imply that this study is concerned with places, and not with people. Although a

---

[1] US$5,280, see IMF, Gabon: Country Brief <www.imf.org> (31 December 2006).

[2] This is a very low percentage, compared to eg Mozambique's 4.1% and Norway's 8%. See UNDP, Human Development Report 2005, Human Development Indicators, Table 6 <http://hdr.undp.org> (31 December 2006).

people-centred approach was always implied in its focus on the national level and the 'homecoming' of international law, the crucial role of civil society actors in whatever progress has been achieved should be celebrated. The information provided may be insufficient, but the little information provided in the pages above underscores the crucial nature of their contribution. Despite being less developed in many African states, this sector has been prominent—stepping into the void left by weak or dysfunctional states; and becoming the only means of unmasking the *rightoric* of autocratic governments. It falls to NGOs, and civil society more broadly, to bring the international human rights system home. This can be done by informing and educating nationals about the content of international human rights, while linking these norms to national law; by raising awareness of the status of human rights treaties, for example about non-acceptance of optional complaints mechanisms; by drawing attention to the state's overdue reports; by dissemination of and advocacy on the basis of concluding observations; and by assisting in follow-up arising from individual communications. At the same time, much more could have been and still needs to be accomplished. Civil society organizations and Africans themselves must shoulder at least part of the blame for the scarcity of cases that have been submitted to the Commission. While there may be valid reasons that explain their reluctance—such as the long delay before any recourse would be possible, and the nature of the (non-binding) eventual remedy—it remains their responsibility to explore all available avenues and to help foment a viable regional human rights system.

Hopefully, this work will serve as the foundation for some further investigation. More research has to be undertaken, especially about the role and impact of international human rights law at the national level. At best, the study highlights examples from national jurisdictions, but it cannot provide a complete picture and it does not do justice to the diversity and complexity of national legal responses in Africa. Three possibilities for further research are highlighted: (i) Further research needs to be conducted on the role and impact of international human rights law in national legal orders and within states. As they are best placed to undertake empirical surveys and to arrive at critical understandings, local multidisciplinary research teams should trace trends, thereby supplementing the insights so far gained from researchers taking 'snap shots', or through reliance on data such as that of the US State Department and Freedom House. (ii) Opportunities for empirical research in international human rights law should be explored, in order to arrive at rigorous comparisons between the experiences under the UN and the AU systems. So, for example, may the nature of state reporting by African states under the UN treaty bodies be compared with that under the African Charter and other AU treaties, and the reasons for the differences investigated. (iii) A thorough analysis should be undertaken of the reasons why some states remain consistently disengaged from both the global and regional human rights systems. Attention should in particular be given to the role of factors such as a recent involvement in civil or external conflict, population size, and colonial tradition.

As the content of this book shows, the potential of international human rights law in Africa has only to a very limited extent been realized. It is my hope that not only future research, but also education, training and academic writing on international human rights law will be characterized by a closer integration of multidisciplinary approaches as a means to ensure a more meaningful role for the elaborate network of human rights promotion and protection that has developed on the continent.

Bibliography

Abdallah, B, *The Trial of Mallam Ilya and other Plays* (Accra: Woeli Publishing Services, 1987)

Adedeji, A, 'Comparative Strategies of Economic Decolonization in Africa' in AA Mazrui (ed), *General History of Africa VIII: Africa since 1935* (Glosderry: New Africa Books, 2003) 401

Adjami, ME, 'African Courts, International Law, and Comparative Case Law: Chimera or Emerging Human Rights Jurisprudence?' (2002) 24 *Michigan Journal of International Law* 103

Ajala, A, *Pan-Africanism: Evolution, Progress and Prospects* (London: André Deutsch, 1974)

Ajulu, R (ed), *The Making of a Region: The Revival of the East African Community* (Midrand: Institute for Global Dialogue, 2005)

Akende, JO, *Introduction to the Nigerian Constitution* (London: Sweet and Maxwell, 1982)

Akinnusi, AO, 'The Bamako and Basel Conventions on the Transboundary Movement and Disposal of Hazardous Waste: A Comparative and Critical Analysis' [2001] *Stellenbosch Law Review* 306

Alfredsson, G and R Ring (eds), *The Inspection Panel of the World Bank: A Different Complaints Procedure* (The Hague: Martinus Nijhoff, 2001)

Alemayehu, M, *Industrializing Africa: Development Options and Challenges for the 21st Century* (Trenton: Africa World Press, 2000)

Alston, P, 'The Committee on Economic, Social and Cultural Rights' in P Alston (ed), *The United Nations and Human Rights: A Critical Appraisal* (Oxford: Clarendon Press, 1992) 504

—— 'The Purposes of Reporting' in United Nations, *Manual on Human Rights Reporting* (Geneva: United Nations, 1997) 19

—— 'Ships Passing in the Night: The Current State of the Human Rights and Development Debate Seen through the Lens of the Millennium Development Goals' (2005) 27 *HRQ* 755

—— and M Robinson (eds), *Human Rights and Development: Towards Mutual Reinforcement* (Oxford: Oxford University Press, 2005)

—— and J Tobin (with M Darrow), 'Laying the Foundations for Children's Rights: An Independent Study of some Key Legal and Institutional Aspects of the Impact of the Convention on the Rights of the Child' (Florence: UNICEF Innocenti Research Centre, 2005)

—— and JHH Weler, 'An "Ever Closer Union" in Need of a Human Rights Policy: The European Union and Human Rights' in P Alston (ed), *The EU and Human Rights* (Oxford: Oxford University Press, 1999) 3

Alting van Geusau, FAM, 'Recent and Problematic: The Imposition of Sanctions by the UN Security Council' in WJM Van Genugten and GA De Groot (eds), *United Nations Sanctions: Effectiveness and Effects, Especially in the Field of Human Rights: A Multidisciplinary Approach* (Antwerp: Intersentia, 1999) 1

Amerasinghe, CF, *Local Remedies in International Law* (Cambridge: Cambridge University Press, 2nd edn, 2004)

Amoah, P, 'The African Charter on Human and Peoples' Rights—An Effective Weapon for Human Rights?' (1992) 4 *RADIC* 226

Anaya, SJ, *Indigenous Peoples in International Law* (Oxford: Oxford University Press, 2nd edn, 2004)

Ancholonu, CO, *The Trial of the Beautiful Ones* (Owerri, Nigeria: Totan, 1985)

Andemicael, B, *The OAU and the UN: Relations between the Organization of African Unity and the United Nations* (New York: Africana Publishing, 1976)

—— 'Organisation of African Unity—UN Relations in a Changing World' in Y El-Ayouty (ed), *The Organisation of African Unity after Thirty Years* (Westport, Conn: Praeger, 1994) 119

Ankrah, EM and LO Gostin, 'Ethical and Legal Considerations of the HIV Epidemic in Africa' in M Essex, S Mboup, PJ Kanki, MR Kalengayi, and PJ Brewer (eds), *AIDS in Africa* (New York: Raven Press, 1994) 547

Ankumah, E, *The African Commission on Human and Peoples' Rights: Practice and Procedures* (The Hague, Martinus Nijhoff, 1996)

An Na'im, AA, 'Human Rights in the Muslim World: Socio-political Conditions and Scriptural Imperatives' (1990) 3 *Harvard Human Rights Journal* 13

Appiagyei-Atua, K, 'Bumps on the Road: A Critique of How Africa Got to NEPAD' (2006) 6 *AHRLJ* 524

Appiah, KA, 'Pan-Africanism' in KA Appiah and HL Gates (eds), *Africana: The Encyclopedia of the African and African American Experience* (New York: Basic Civitas Books, 1999) 1484

Arakai-Takahashi, Y, *The Margin of Appreciation Doctrine and the Principle of Proportionality in the Jurisprudence of the ECHR* (Antwerp: Intersentia, 2002)

Arambulo, K, *Strengthening the Supervision of the International Covenant on Economic, Social and Cultural Rights: Theoretical and Procedural Aspects* (Oxford: Hart, 1999)

Arboleda, E, 'Refugee Definitions in Africa and Latin America: The Lessons of Pragmatism' (1991) 3 *International Journal of Refugee Law* 185

Asante, SKB, *The Political Economy of Regionalism in Africa: A Decade of the Economic Community of West African States (ECOWAS)* (New York: Praeger, 1986)

—— *Regionalism and Africa's Development: Expectations, Reality and Challenges* (New York: St Martin's Press, 1997)

Bailey, SD, *The United Nations Security and Human Rights* (London: St Martin's, 1994)

Baimu, E, 'The African Union: Hope for Better Protection of Human Rights in Africa?' (2001) 1 *AHRLJ* 299

—— 'Human Rights in NEPAD and its Implications for the African Human Rights System' (2002) 2 *AHRLJ* 301

—— and K Sturman, 'Amendments to the African Union's Right to Intervene: A Shift from Human Security to Regional Security?' (2003) 12 *African Security Review* 37

Bajulo, A, 'Sources of the Law of the Economic Community of West African States (ECOWAS)' (2001) 45 *JAL* 73

Balanda, ML, 'African Charter on Human and Peoples' Rights' in K Ginther and W Benedek (eds), *New Perspectives and Conceptions of International Law: An Afro-European Dialogue* (Vienna: Springer-Verlag, 1983) 134

Balassa, B, *The Theory of Economic Integration* (Homewood, Ill: Richard D Irvine, 1961)

Banda, F, *Women, Law and Human Rights: An African Perspective* (Oxford: Hart, 2005)
—— 'Blazing a Trail: The African Protocol on Women's Rights Comes into Force' (2006) 50 *JAL* 72
Banton, M, 'Decision-Taking in the Committee on the Elimination of Racial Discrimination' in P Alston and J Crawford (eds), *The Future of UN Human Rights Treaty Monitoring* (Cambridge: Cambridge University Press, 2000) 55
Baricako, G, 'La Mise en Oeuvre des Décisions de la Commission Africaine des Droits de l'Homme et des Peuples par les Autorités Nationales' in J Flauss and E Lambert-Abdelgawad, *L'application Nationale de la Charter Africaine des Droits de l'Homme et des Peuples* (Brussels: Bruylant, 2004) 207
Barosso, JP, 'Profile of the Southern African Development Community' in C Heyns (ed), *Human Rights Law in Africa* (vol 1) (Leiden: Martinus Nijhoff, 2004) 675
Barsh, R, 'The Draft Convention on the Rights of the Child: A Case of Eurocentrism in Standard Setting' (1989) 58 *Nordic Journal of International Law* 24
Bayefsky, AF, 'Making the Human Rights Treaties Work' in L Henkin and JL Hargrove (eds), *Human Rights: An Agenda for the Next Century* (Washington, DC: The American Society of International Law, 1994) 269
—— *The UN Human Rights Treaty System: Universality at the Crossroads* (The Hague: Kluwer Law International, 2001)
Bayer, R, 'Public Health Policy and the AIDS Epidemic' (1991) 324(21) *New England Journal of Medicine* 1500
Bekker, G, 'The Social and Economic Rights Action Center and the Center for Economic and Social Rights/Nigeria' [2003] *JAL* 126
Bell, J, *French Constitutional Law* (Oxford: Clarendon Press, 1992)
—— S Boyron, and S Whittaker, *Principles of French Law* (Oxford: Oxford University Press, 1998)
Benedek, W, 'The 9th Session of the African Commission on Human and Peoples' Rights' (1993) 12 *HRLJ* 216
Benneh, EY, 'The United Nations and Economic Sanctions: Towards a New World Order?' (1993) 5 *ASICL Proc* 241
Bernhardt, R and JA Jolowicz (eds), *International Enforcement of Human Rights* (Berlin: Springer-Verlag, 1987)
Bilder, RB, 'Possibilities for Development of New International Judicial Mechanisms' in L Henkin and JL Hargrove (eds), *Human Rights: An Agenda for the Next Century* (Washington, DC: The American Society of International Law, 1994) 328
Bimpong-Buta, SY, *The Law of Interpretation in Ghana (Exposition & Critique)* (Accra: Advanced Legal Publications, 1995)
Blay, SKN, 'Changing African Perspectives on the Right to Self-Determination in the Wake of the Banjul Charter on Human and Peoples' Rights' (1985) 29 *JAL* 143
Bockie, S, *Death and the Invisible Powers* (Bloomington, Ind: Indiana University Press, 1993)
Boekle, H, 'Western States, the UN Commission on Human Rights and the "1235 Procedure": The "Question of Bias" Revisited' (1995) 13 *NQHR* 367
Bojosi, KN, 'An Opportunity Missed for Gay Rights in Botswana: *Utjiwa Kanane v The State*' (2004) 20 *South African Journal on Human Rights* 466
—— and GM Wachira, 'Protecting Indigenous Peoples in Africa: An Analysis of the Approach of the African Commission on Human and Peoples' Rights' (2006) 6 *AHRLJ* 382, 393–406.

Bondzie-Simpson, E, 'A Critique of the African Charter of Human and Peoples' Rights' (1988) 31 *Howard Law Journal* 643

Botha, C, 'Soldiers of Fortune or Whores of War: The Legal Position of Mercenaries with Specific Reference to South Africa' (1993) 15 *Strategic Review of Southern Africa* 75

Boutros-Ghali, B, 'Introduction' in United Nations, *The United Nations and Human Rights 1945–1995* (New York: UN Department of Public Information, 1995) 112

Bowden, B, 'The Colonial Origins of International Law, European Expansion and the Classical Standard of Civilization' (2005) 7 *Journal of the History of International Law* 1

Bradlow, D, 'The World Bank, the IMF and Human Rights' (1996) 6 *Transnational Law and Contemporary Problems* 48

Brand, D, 'Socio-economic Rights and Courts in South Africa: Justiciability on a Sliding Scale' in F Coomans (ed), *Justiciability of Economic and Social Rights: Experience from Domestic Systems* (Antwerp: Intersentia, 2006) 207

Bratton, M, 'Zambia Starts Over' (1992) 3 *Journal of Democracy* 81

Brody, R, 'UN Peace-Building and Human Rights' (1994) 53 *The Review: International Commission of Jurists* 1

Brownlie, I, *Principles of Public International Law* (Oxford: Clarendon, 4th edn, 1990)
—— *Principles of International Law* (Oxford: Oxford University Press, 6th edn, 2003)

Buergenthal, T, *International Human Rights in a Nutshell* (St Paul, Minn: West Publishing, 2nd edn, 1995)
—— 'A Court and Two Consolidated Treaty Bodies' in A Bayefsky (ed), *The UN Human Rights Treaty System in the 21st Century* (The Hague: Kluwer Law International, 2000) 299
—— 'The European and Inter-American Human Rights Courts: Beneficial Interaction' in P Mahoney, F Matscher, H Petzold, and L Wildhaber (eds), *Protecting Human Rights: The European Perspective: Studies in Honour of Rolv Ryssdal* (Cologne: Heymann, 2000) 123
—— 'Proliferation of International Courts and Tribunals: Is it Good or Bad?' (2001) 14 *Leiden Journal of International Law* 267
—— 'The UN Human Rights Committee' (2001) 5 *Max Planck Yearbook of United Nations Law* 341
—— and D Shelton, *Protecting Human Rights in the Americas: Cases and Materials* (Kehl: NP Engel, 1995)

Burgers JH and H Danelius, *The United Nations Convention against Torture* (Dordrecht: Martinus Nijhoff, 1988)

Burgstaller, M, *Theories of Compliance with International Law* (Leiden: Martinus Nijhoff, 2005)

Byrnes, AC, 'The "Other" Human Rights Treaty Body: The Work of the Committee on the Elimination of Discrimination against Women' (1989) 14 *Yale Journal of International Law* 1
—— 'The Committee against Torture' in P Alston (ed), *The United Nations and Human Rights: A Critical Appraisal* (Oxford: Clarendon Press, 1992) 532
—— and M Graterol, 'Violence against Women: Private Actors and the Obligation of Due Diligence' (2006) 15 *Interights Bulletin* 156

Calderisi, R, *The Trouble with Africa: Why Foreign Aid is Not Working* (New Haven, Conn: Yale University Press, 2006)

Caron, DD, 'The Legitimacy of the Collective Authority of the Security Council' (1993) 87 *AJIL* 552

Cassese, A, 'Political Self-Determination—Old Conceptions and New Developments' in A Cassese (ed), *UN Law/Fundamental Rights: Two Topics in International Law* (Alphen aan den Rijn: Sijthoff and Noordhoff, 1979) 141

—— 'The General Assembly: Historical Perspectives 1945–1989' in P Alston (ed), *The United Nations and Human Rights: A Critical Appraisal* (Oxford: Clarendon Press, 1992) 25

Castellino, J and S Allen, *Title to Territoriality in International Law: A Temporal Analysis* (Aldershot: Ashgate, 2003)

Cervenka, Z, *The Unfinished Quest for Unity: Africa and the OAU* (New York: Africana, 1977)

Chanda, A, 'The Organization of African Unity: An Appraisal' (1989–92) 21–4 *Zambian Law Journal* 1

Chapman, AR, 'A New Approach to Monitoring the International Covenant on Economic, Social and Cultural Rights' (1995) 55 *The Review: International Commission of Jurists* 23

—— 'A "Violations Approach" for Monitoring the International Covenant on Economic, Social and Cultural Rights' (1996) 18 *HRQ* 23

Chaskalson, A, 'The Third Bram Fischer Lecture: Human Dignity as a Foundational Value of the Constitutional Order' (2000) 16 *South African Journal on Human Rights* 193

Cheyne, I, 'Africa and the International Trade in Hazardous Waste' (1994) 6 *RADIC* 493

Chime, C, *Integration and Politics among African States* (Uppsala: Scandinavian Institute for African Studies, 1977)

Chirwa, DM, 'A Full Loaf is Better than Half: The Constitutional Protection of Socio-economic Rights in Malawi' (2005) 49 *JAL* 207

Chongwe, R, 'The Commonwealth and the New World Order—Safeguarding Civil Society' (1992) 4 *RADIC* 962

Cilliers, J and P Mashele, 'The Pan-African Parliament: A Plenary of Parliamentarians' (2004) 13 *African Security Review* 78

—— and K Sturman, 'Challenges Facing the AU's Peace and Security Council' (2004) 13 *African Security Review* 97

Clapham, A, *Human Rights Obligations of Non-state Actors* (Oxford: Oxford University Press, 2006)

Clapham, C, 'Boundaries and States in the New African Order' in DC Bach (ed), *Regionalism in Africa: Integration and Disintegration* (Oxford: James Currey, 1999)

Clark, DL, 'The World Bank and Human Rights: The Need for Greater Accountability' (2002) 15 *Harvard Human Rights Journal* 205

Claude, IL, *Swords into Ploughshares: The Problems and Progress of International Organization* (New York: Random House, 1974)

Clements, L, *European Human Rights: Taking a Case under the Convention* (London: Sweet and Maxwell, 1994)

Coldham, S, 'Case Notes (Ephrahim v Pastory; DPP v Pete)' (1991) 35 *JAL 205*

Condé, VH, *A Handbook of International Human Rights Terminology* (Lincoln, Nebr: University of Nebraska, 2004)

Constantine-Simms, D (ed), *The Greatest Taboo: Homosexuality in Black Communities* (Los Angeles: Alyson Books, 2001)

Coomans, F (ed), *Justiciability of Economic and Social Rights: Experience from Domestic Systems* (Antwerp: Intersentia, 2006)

Coomans, F (ed), 'Some Introductory Remarks on the Justiciability of Economic and Social Rights in a Comparative Constitutional Context' in F Coomans (ed), *Justiciability of Economic and Social Rights: Experience from Domestic Systems* (Antwerp: Intersentia, 2006) 1

Cotran, E (ed), *Readings in African Law* (London: Cass, 1970)

Cotright, DC and GA Lopez, *Sanctions and the Search for Security* (Boulder, Colo: Lynne Rienner, 2002)

Council of Europe, *Treaty Making: Expression of Consent to be Bound by Treaty* (The Hague: Kluwer Law International, 2001)

Courtis, C, 'Socio-economic Rights before the Courts in Argentina' in F Coomans (ed), *Justiciability of Economic and Social Rights: Experience from Domestic Systems* (Antwerp: Intersentia, 2006) 309

Craven, MCR, 'The Domestic Application of the International Covenant on Economic, Social and Cultural Rights' (1993) 40 *NILR* 367

—— *The International Covenant on Economic, Social and Cultural Rights: A Perspective on its Development* (Oxford: Clarendon Press, 1995)

Csete, J, R Schleifer, and J Cohen, ' "Opt-out" Testing for HIV in Africa: A Caution' (2004) 363 *The Lancet* 493

Danielsen, A, *The State Reporting Procedure under the African Charter* (Copenhagen: Danish Centre for Human Rights, 1994)

—— and J Harrington (eds), *Examination of State Reports* (vols 1–5) (Copenhagen: Danish Centre for Human Rights and African Commission on Human and Peoples' Rights, 1995)

Dankwa, EVO, 'Implementation of International Human Rights Instruments: Ghana as an Illustration' (1991) 3 *ASICL Proc* 57

—— C Flinterman, and S Leckie, 'Commentary to the Maastricht Guidelines on Violations of Economic, Social and Cultural Rights' (1998) 20 *HRQ* 705

Danňň, R 'The Legal Aspects of the World Bank's Work on Human Rights: Some Preliminary Thoughts' in P Alston and M Robinson (eds), *Human Rights and Development: Towards Mutual Reinforcement* (Oxford: Oxford University Press, 2005) 509

Davidson, B, *Africa in History: Themes and Outlines* (London: Paladin, 1974)

—— *Modern Africa* (New York: Longman, 1987)

De Bourbon, A, 'Human Rights Litigation in Zimbabwe: Past, Present and Future' (2003) 3 *AHRLJ* 195

De Cock, KM, 'HIV Testing in an Era of Treatment Scale-Up' (2005) 8 *Health and Human Rights* 31

—— D Mbori-Ngacha, and E Marum, 'Shadow on the Continent: Public Health and HIV/AIDS in Africa in the 21st Century' (2002) 360 *The Lancet* 67

De Feyter, K, 'The International Financial Institutions and Human Rights: Law and Practice' in F Gómez Isa and K De Feyter (eds), *International Protection of Human Rights: Achievements and Challenges* (Bilbao: University of Deusto, 2005) 561

—— and F Gómez Isa, 'Privatisation and Human Rights: An Overview' in K De Feyter and F Gómez Isa (eds), *Privatisation and Human Rights in the Age of Globalisation* (Antwerp: Intersentia, 2005) 1

De Vos, P, 'Pious Wishes or Directly Enforceable Human Rights? Social and Economic Rights in South Africa's 1996 Constitution' (1997) 13 *South African Journal on Human Rights* 67

—— 'The Constitution Made Us Queer' in C Stychia and D Herman (eds), *Sexuality in the Legal Arena* (London: Athlane Press, 2000) 194

—— 'A New Beginning? The Enforcement of Social, Economic and Cultural Rights under the African Charter on Human and Peoples' Rights' (2004) 8 *Law, Democracy and Development* 1

De Wet, E, 'The Present Control Machinery under the European Convention on Human Rights: Its Future Reform and Possible Implications for the African Court on Human Rights' (1996) 26 *CILSA* 357

Deng, FM, 'Human Rights in the African Context' in K Wiredu (ed), A *Companion to African Philosophy* (Oxford: Blackwell, 2004) 499

Dennis, MJ and DP Stewart, 'Justiciability of Economic, Social and Cultural Rights: Should there be an International Complaints Mechanism to Adjudicate the Rights to Food, Water, Housing, and Health?' (2004) 98 *AJIL* 462

Dersso, SA, 'The Jurisprudence of the African Commission on Human and Peoples' Rights with Respect to Peoples' Rights' (2006) 6 *AHRLJ* 358

Dicey, AV, *Introduction to the Study of the Law of the Constitution* (London: Macmillan, 1959)

Dieng, A, 'Introduction to the African Court on Human and Peoples' Rights' (2004) 15 *Interights Bulletin* 3

Donelly, J, 'The Virtues of Legalization' in S Meckled-García and B Çali (eds), *The Legalization of Human Rights: Multidisciplinary Perspectives on Human Rights and Human Rights Law* (London: Routledge, 2006) 67

Douzinas, C, *The End of Human Rights* (Oxford: Hart, 2000)

Drinan, RF, *Mobilization of Shame: A World View of Human Rights* (New Haven, Conn: Yale University Press, 2001)

Dugard, J, 'International Human-Rights Norms in Domestic Courts: Can South Africa Learn from Britain and the United States?' in E Kahn (ed), *Fiat Iustitia: Essays in Memory of Oliver Deneys Schreiner* (Cape Town: Juta, 1993) 221

—— *International Law: A South African Perspective* (Cape Town: Juta, 3rd edn, 2005)

Du Plessis, M and C Gevers, 'Into the Deep End—The International Criminal Court and Sudan' (2006) *African YB on International Humanitarian Law* 88

Duxbury, A, 'Rejuvenating the Commonwealth—the Human Rights Remedy' (1977) 46 *ICLQ* 344

Ebo, C, 'Indigenous Law and Justice: Some Major Concepts and Practices' (1979) 76 *Vierteljahresberichte* 139

Economic Commission for Africa (ECA), *Assessing Regional Integration in Africa* (Addis Abada: ECA, 2004)

Eide, A 'The Right to an Adequate Standard of Living including the Right to Food' in A Eide, C Krause, and A Rosas (eds), *Economic, Social and Cultural Rights: A Textbook* (Dordrecht: Martinus Nijhoff, 1995) 89

Elias, TO, *Africa and the Development of International Law* (Dordrecht: Martinus Nijhoff, 2nd edn, 1988)

El Kadiri, A , '*L'Union du Maghreb Arabe*' (1994) 2 *AYBIL* 141

El-Obaid, AE and A Appiagyei-Atua, 'Human Rights in Africa—A New Perspective on Linking the Past to the Present' (1996) 41 *McGill Law Journal* 819

El-Sheikh, IA, 'The Future Relationship between the African Court and the African Commission' (2002) 2 *AHRLJ* 252

Eno, RW, 'The Jurisdiction of the African Court on Human and Peoples' Rights' (2002) 2 *AHRLJ* 223

Evans, MD, T Ige, and R Murray, 'The Reporting Mechanism of the African Charter on
Human and Peoples' Rights' in MD Evans and R Murray (eds), *The African Charter on
Human and Peoples' Rights: The System in Practice, 1986–2000* (Cambridge: Cambridge
University Press, 2002) 36

—— and R Murray, 'The Special Rapporteurs in the African System' in M Evans and
R Murray, *African Charter on Human and Peoples' Rights: The System in Practice,
1986–2000* (Cambridge: Cambridge University Press, 2002) 280

Ewi, M and K Aning, 'Assessing the Role of the African Union in Preventing and Combating
Terrorism in Africa' (2006) 15(3) *African Security Review* 32

Eze, OC, 'Prospects for International Protection of Human Rights in Africa' (1974) 4 *The
African Review* 79

Fitzpatrick, J, 'Human Rights Fact-Finding' in AF Bayefsky (ed), *The UN Human Rights
Treaty System in the 21st Century* (The Hague: Kluwer Law International, 2000) 65

Flauss, J, 'Notule sur les Mesures Provisoires devant la Commission Africaine des Droits de
l'Homme et des Peuples' in G Cohen-Jonathan and J Flauss (eds), *Mesures Conservatoires
et Droits Fondamentaux* (Brussels: Bruylant, 2005) 213

Evans, MD and E Lambert-Abelgawad (eds), *L'Application Nationale de la Charte Africaine
des Droits de l'Homme et des Peuples* (Antwerp: Bruylant, 2004)

Foltz, WJ and J Widner, 'The OAU and Southern African Liberation' in Y El-Ayouty and
IW Zartman (eds), *The OAU after Twenty Years* (New York: Praeger, 1984)

Forsythe, DP, *Human Rights in International Relations* (Cambridge: Cambridge University
Press, 2nd edn, 2006)

Freeman, M, *Human Rights: An Interdisciplinary Approach* (Cambridge: Polity, 2002)

Fukuyama, F, *State Building, Governance and World Order in the Twenty-First Century*
(London: Profile Books, 2005)

Gaer, FD, 'First Fruits: Reporting by States under the African Charter on Human and
Peoples' Rights' (1992) 10 *NQHR* 29

Gaparayi, IP, 'Justice and Social Reconstruction in the Aftermath of the Genocide in
Rwanda: An Evaluation of the Possible Role of the *Gacaca* Tribunals' (2001) 1 *AHRLJ* 78

Gargarella, R, P Domingo, and T Roux (eds), *Courts and Social Transformation in New
Democracies: An Institutional Voice for the Poor?* (Aldershot: Ashgate, 2006)

Gathii, J, 'A Critical Appraisal of the NEPAD Agenda in Light of Africa's Place in the
World Trade Regime in an Era of Market Centred Development' (2003) 13 *Transnational
Law and Contemporary Problems* 179

Geiss, I, *The Pan-African Movement* (London: Methuen, 1974)

Ghai, YP, 'Constitutions and Governance in Africa: A Prolegomenon' in S Adelman and
A Paliwala (eds), *Law and Crisis in the Third World* (New York: H Zell, 1993) 63

—— and J Cottrell, 'The Role of the Courts in Implementing Economic, Social and
Cultural Rights' in Y Ghai and J Cottrell (eds), *Economic, Social and Cultural Rights in
Practice: The Role of Judges in Implementing Economic, Social and Cultural Rights*
(London: Interights, 2004) 88

Ghazi, B, *The IMF, the World Bank Group and the Question of Human Rights* (Ardsley:
Transnational Publishers, 2005)

Ginsburg, RB, 'Looking beyond Our Borders: The Value of a Comparative Perspective in
Constitutional Adjudication' (2003–4) 40 *Idaho Law Report* 1

Gittleman, R, 'The Banjul Charter on Human and Peoples' Rights: A Legal Analysis' in
CE Welch and RE Meltzer (eds), *Human Rights and Development in Africa* (Albany, NY:
State University of New York Press, 1984) 152

Gómez Isa, F, 'Globalisation, Privatisation and Human Rights' in K De Feyter and F Gómez Isa (eds), *Privatisation and Human Rights in an Age of Globalisation* (Antwerp: Intersentia, 2005) 9

Gonidec, PF, 'Existe-t-il un Droit International Africain?' (1993) 3 *RADIC* 243

—— 'Droit International et Droit Interne en Afrique' (1996) 8 *RADIC* 789

Gostin, L and JM Mann, 'Towards the Development of a Human Rights Impact Assessment for the Formulation and Evaluation of Public Health Policies' (1994) 1 *Health and Human Rights* 58

Grant, JA and F Söderbaum (eds), *The New Regionalism in Africa* (Aldershot: Ashgate, 2003)

Gumedze, S, 'HIV/AIDS and Human Rights: The Role of the African Commission on Human and Peoples' Rights' (2004) 4 *AHRLJ* 181

—— 'The NEPAD and Human Rights' (2006) 22 *South African Journal on Human Rights* 144

Gutto, SBO, 'The New Mechanism of the Organisation of African Unity for Conflict Prevention, Management and Resolution, and the Controversial Concept of Humanitarian Intervention in International Law' (1996) 113 *South African Law Journal* 314

—— 'Beyond Justiciability: Challenges of Implementing/Enforcing Socio-Economic Rights in South Africa' (1998) 4 *Buffalo Human Rights Law Review* 94

—— 'The Reform and Renewal of the African Regional Human and Peoples' Rights System' (2001) 1 *AHRLJ* 175

Hammouda, HB, SN Karingi, AE Njuguna, and MS Jallab, 'Africa's (Mis)fortunes in Global Trade and the Continent's Diversification Regimes' (2006) 7 *Journal of World Investment and Trade* 587

Hamrell, S, 'Introduction' in S Hamrell (ed), *Refugee Problems in Africa* (Uppsala: Scandinavian Institute of African Studies, 1967) 9

Hansungule, M, 'Access to Panel: The Notion of Affected Party, Issues of Collective and Material Interest' in G Alfredsson and R Ring (eds), *The Inspection Panel of the World Bank: A Different Complaints Procedure* (The Hague: Martinus Nijhoff, 2001) 143

Harding, C, B Swart, N Jörg, and P Fennell, 'Conclusion: Europeanization and Convergence: The Lessons of Comparative Study' in P Fennell, C Harding, N Jörg, and B Swart (eds), *Criminal Justice in Europe: A Comparative Study* (Oxford: Clarendon Press, 1995) 379

Harrington, J, 'Special Rapporteurs of the African Commission on Human and Peoples' Rights' (2001) 1 *AHRLJ* 247

—— 'The African Court on Human and Peoples' Rights' in MD Evans and R Murray, *The African Charter on Human and Peoples' Rights: The System in Practice, 1986–2000* (Cambridge: Cambridge University Press, 2002) 305

Harris, D, 'Regional Protection of Human Rights: The Inter-American Achievement' in DJ Harris and S Livingstone (eds), *The Inter-American System of Human Rights* (Oxford: Clarendon Press, 1998) 1

Hartmann, H, 'US Human Rights Policy under Carter and Reagan, 1977–1981' (2001) 23 *HRQ* 402

Hathaway, OA, 'Do Human Rights Treaties Make a Difference?' (2002) 112 *Yale Law Journal* 1935

Heiman, MRA, 'The Drive towards Regionalisation in Southern Africa: Fictional Reality' (1997) 9 *RADIC* 639

Helfer, LR and AM Slaughter, 'Towards a Theory of Effective Supranational Adjudication' (1997) 107 *Yale Law Journal* 273

Herndl, K, 'Recent Developments Concerning United Nations Fact-finding in the Field of Human Rights' in M Nowak, D Steurer, and H Tretter (eds), *Fortschritt im Bewuβtsein der Grund- und Menschenrechte: Festschrift für Felix Ermacora (Progress in the Spirit of Human Right)* (Kehl: NP Engel, 1988) 9

Heyns, C, 'African Human Rights Law and the European Convention' (1995) 11 *South African Journal on Human Rights* 252

—— (ed), *Human Rights Law in Africa 1996* (The Hague: Kluwer Law International, 1996)

—— 'The African Regional Human Rights System: In Need of Reform?' (2001) 1 *AHRLJ* 167

—— 'Civil and Political Rights in the African Charter' in MD Evans and R Murray (eds), *The African Charter on Human and Peoples' Rights: The System in Practice, 1986–2000* (Cambridge: Cambridge University Press, 2002) 137

—— (ed), *Human Rights Law in Africa 1999* (The Hague: Kluwer Law International, 2002)

—— (ed), *Human Rights Law in Africa* (vol 1) (Leiden: Martinus Nijhoff, 2004)

—— (ed), *Human Rights Law in Africa* (vol 2) (Leiden: Martinus Nijhoff, 2004)

—— 'A "Struggle Approach" to Human Rights' in C Heyns and K Stefiszyn (eds), *Human Rights, Peace and Justice in Africa: A Reader* (Pretoria: Pretoria University Law Press, 2006)

—— and M Killander, 'The African Regional Human Rights System' in F Gómez Isa and K de Feyter (eds), *International Protection of Human Rights: Achievements and Challenges* (Bilbao: University of Deusto, 2006) 509

—— (eds), *Compendium of Key Human Rights Documents of the African Union* (Pretoria: Pretoria University Law Press, 2006)

—— D Padilla, and L Zwaak, 'A Schematic Comparison of Regional Human Rights Systems' in F Gómez Isa and K De Feyter, *International Protection of Human Rights: Achievements and Challenges* (Bilbao: University of Deusto, 2006) 545

—— and W Kagnongo, 'Constitutional Human Rights Law in Africa' (2006) 22 *South African J on Human Rights* 673

—— and F Viljoen, *The Impact of the United Nations Human Rights Treaties on the Domestic Level* (The Hague: Kluwer Law International, 2002)

Higgins, R, 'Africa and the Covenant on Civil and Political Rights during the First Five Years of the *Journal*: Some Facts and Some Thoughts' (1993) 5 *RADIC* 55

—— *Problems and Process: International Law and How to Use It* (Oxford: Clarendon, 1994)

Hitchcock, R and D Vinding, 'Indigenous Peoples' Rights in Southern Africa: An Introduction' in R Hitchcock and D Vinding (eds), *Indigenous Peoples' Rights in Southern Africa* (Copenhagen: IWGIA, 2004) 8

Hoad, N, K Martin, and G Reid (eds), *Sex and Politics in South Africa* (Cape Town: Double Story, 2005)

Hodgson, DL, 'Introduction: Comparative Perspectives on the Indigenous Rights Movement in Africa and the Americas' (2002) 104 *American Anthropologist* 1037

Hopkins, K, 'The Effect of an African Court on the Domestic Legal Orders of African States' (2002) 2 *AHRLJ* 234

Horta, K, 'Rhetoric and Reality: Human Rights and the World Bank' (2002) 15 *Harvard Human Rights Journal* 227

Hüfnerk, K, *Agenda for Change: New Tasks for the United Nations* (Opladen: Leske and Bundrich, 1995)

Hund, J, 'Aspects of Judicial Review in Southern Africa' (1982) 15 *CILSA* 276

Huntington, SP, *The Third Wave: Democratization in the Late Twentieth Century* (Norman, Okla: University of Oklahoma Press, 1991)

Hydén, H, 'Implementation of International Conventions as a Socio-legal Enterprise: Examples from the Convention on the Rights of the Child' in J Grimheben and R Ring (eds), *Human Rights Law: From Dissemination to Application* (Leiden: Martinus Nijhoff, 2006) 375

Ibhawoh, B, 'Between Culture and Constitution: Evaluating the Cultural Legitimacy of Human Rights in the African State' (2000) 22 *HRQ* 856

Interights, *Judicial Independence: Law and Practice of Appointments to the European Court of Human Rights* (London: Interights, 2003)

Jackson, C, 'Constitutional Structure and Governance Strategies for Economic Integration in Africa and Europe' (2003) 13 *Transnational Law and Contemporary Problems* 139

Janis, MW, RS Kay, and AW Bradley, *European Human Rights Law: Text and Materials* (Oxford: Oxford University Press, 2nd edn, 2000)

Johnson, D, 'Cultural and Regional Pluralism in the Drafting of the UN Convention on the Rights of the Child' in M Freeman and P Veerman (eds), *The Ideologies of Children's Rights* (Dordrecht: Martinus Nijhoff, 1992) 95

Jonah, JOC, 'The Organization of African Unity: Peace-Keeping and Conflict Resolution' in Y El-Ayouty (ed), *The Organization of African Unity after Thirty Years* (Westport, Conn: Praeger, 1994) 1

Jones, S, 'Regional Institutions for Protecting Human Rights in Asia' (1996) 50 *Australian Journal of International Affairs* 269

Jonyo, F, 'The Role of Civil Society in Regional Integration' in R Ajulu (ed), *The Making of a Region: The Revival of the East African Community* (Midrand: Institute for Global Dialogue, 2005) 111

Jörg, N, S Field, and C Brants, 'Are Inquisitorial and Accusatorial Systems Converging?' in P Fennell, C Harding, N Jörg, and B Swart (eds), *Criminal Justice in Europe: A Comparative Study* (Oxford: Clarendon Press, 1995) 41

Kaime, T, 'From Lofty Jargon to Durable Solutions: Unaccompanied Refugee Children and the African Charter on the Rights and Welfare of the Child' (2004) 16 *International Journal of Refugee Law* 336

Kamminga, MT, 'Lessons Learned from the Exercise of Universal Jurisdiction in respect of Gross Human Rights Violations' (2001) 23 *HRQ* 940

Kane, I, 'The African Commission on Human and Peoples' Rights and the New Organs of the African Union' in L Wohlgemuth and E Sall (eds), *Human Rights, Regionalism and the Dilemmas of Democracy in Africa* (Dakar: CODESRIA, 2006) 154

Kannyo, E, 'The Banjul Charter on Human and Peoples' Rights: Genesis and Political Background' in CE Welch and RI Meltzer (eds), *Human Rights and Development in Africa* (Albany, NY: State University of New York, 1984) 128

Kanyeihamba, GW, *Constitutional and Political History of Uganda: From 1984 to the Present* (Kampala: Centenary Publishing House, 2002)

Kato, LL, 'The Court of Appeal for East Africa: From a Colonial Court to an International Court' (1971) 7 *East African Law Journal* 1

Keal, P, *European Conquest and the Rights of Indigenous Peoples: The Moral Backwardness of International Society* (Cambridge: Cambridge University Press, 2003)

Keith, LC, 'The United Nations International Covenant on Civil and Political Rights: Does it Make a Difference in Human Rights Behavior?' (1999) 36 *Journal of Peace Research* 95

Kennes, W, 'African Regional Economic Integration and the European Union' in DC Bach (ed), *Regionalism in Africa: Integration and Disintegration* (Oxford: James Currey, 1999) 27

Kenrick, J and J Lewis, 'Indigenous Peoples' Rights and the Politics of the Term "Indigenous"' (2004) 20 *Anthropology Today* 4

Khoza, S, 'Promoting Economic, Social and Cultural Rights in Africa: The African Commission Holds a Seminar in Pretoria' (2004) 4 *AHRLJ* 334

Killander, M, 'Communications before the African Commission on Human and Peoples' Rights 1998–2002' (2006) 10(1) *Law, Democracy and Development* 101

—— 'Confidentiality versus Publicity: Interpreting Article 59 of the African Charter on Human and People's Rights' (2006) 6 *AHRLJ* 572

Kindiki, K, 'The Normative and Institutional Framework of the African Union relating to the Protection of Human Rights and the Maintenance of International Peace and Security: A Critical Appraisal' (2003) 3 *AHRLJ* 97

Kingsbury, B, ' "Indigenous Peoples" in International Law: A Constructivist Approach to the Asian Controversy' (1998) 92 *AJIL* 414

—— 'Reconciling Five Competing Conceptual Structures of Indigeous Peoples' Claims in International and Comparative Law' in P Alston (ed), *Peoples' Rights* (Oxford: Oxford University Press, 2001) 69

Kioko, B, 'The Road to the African Court on Human and Peoples' Rights' (1998) 10 *ASICL Proc* 70

—— 'The African Union and the Implementation of the Decisions of the African Court on Human and Peoples' Rights' (2004) 15 *Interights Bulletin* 7

Kirby, M, 'The Never-Ending Paradoxes of HIV/AIDS and Human Rights' (2004) 4 *AHRLJ* 163

Kissoon, C, M Ceasar, and T Jithoo, 'Whose Right?' *AIDS Review 2002* (Pretoria: Centre for the Study of AIDS, University of Pretoria, 2002)

Kiwanuka, RN, 'The Meaning of "People" in the African Charter on Human and Peoples' Rights' (1988) 82 *AJIL* 80

Kjǿrum, M, 'Article 14' in G Alfredsson and A Eide (eds), *The Universal Declaration of Human Rights: A Common Standard of Achievement* (The Hague: Kluwer Law International, 1999) 279

Klabbers, J, 'Some Problems Regarding the Object and Purpose of Treaties' (1997) 8 *Finnish Yearbook of International Law* 138

Kleffner, J and L Zegveld, 'Establishing an Individual Complaints Procedure for Violations of International Humanitarian Law' (2000) 3 *Yearbook of International Humanitarian Law* 384

Koechler, H, 'The United Nations Security Council and the New World Order' in F Barnaby (ed), *Building a More Democratic United Nations* (New York: Frank Cass, 1991) 238

Kokott, J, 'The Protection of Fundamental Rights under German and International Law' (1996) 8 *RADIC* 347

Koraytem, T, 'Arab Islamic Developments on Human Rights' (2001) 16 *Arab Law Quarterly* 256

Koskenniemi, M, *From Apology to Utopia* (Helsinki: Finnish Lawyers' Publishing, 1989)

Kotecha, KC and RW Adams, *African Politics: The Corruption of Power* (Washington, DC: University Press of America, 1981)

Krisch, N, 'The Establishment of an African Court on Human and Peoples' Rights' (1998) 58 *Zeitschrift für ausländisches öffentliches Recht und Völkerrecht* 713

Kuper, A, 'The Return of the Native' (2003) 44 *Current Anthropology* 389

Kwakwa, E, 'Internal Conflicts in Africa: Is there a Right of Humanitarian Intervention?' (1994) 2 *AYBIL* 9

Langley, W, 'The Rights of, Women, the African Charter, and the Economic Development of Africa' (1987) 7 *Boston College Third World Law Journal* 215

Lawyers Committee for Human Rights, *African Exodus: Refugee Crisis, Human Rights and the 1969 OAU Refugee Convention* (New York: Lawyers Committee for Human Rights, 1995)

Leach, P, *Taking a Case to the European Court of Human Rights* (Oxford: Oxford University Press, 2nd edn, 2005)

LeBlanc, LJ, *The Convention on the Rights of the Child: United Nations Lawmaking on Human Rights* (Lincoln, Nebr: University of Nebraska Press, 1995)

Lee, RS, 'The Rwanda Tribunal' (1996) 9 *Leiden Journal of International Law* 37

Lempinen, M, *The United Nations Commission on Human Rights and the Different Treatment of Governments* (Abo: Abo Akademi Forlag, 2005)

Lerner, N, *The UN Convention on the Elimination of All Forms of Racial Discrimination* (Alphen aan den Rijn: Sijthoff and Noordhoff, 1980)

Lester, A, L Tedeschiimi, and B Byfield, 'The Potential Relevance of the European Convention on Human Rights' in Commonwealth Secretariat, *Developing Human Rights Jurisprudence* (vol 4) (London: Commonwealth Secretariat, 1992)136

Levitt, J, 'Humanitarian Intervention by Regional Actors in Internal Conflicts: The Case of ECOWAS in Liberia and Sierra Leone' (1998) 12 *Temple International and Comparative Law Journal* 363

—— and L Louw, 'Considering the Interpretation and Implementation of Article 24 of the African Charter on Human and Peoples' Rights in the Light of the *SERAC* Communication' (2003) 3 *AHRLJ* 167

Lindholt, L, *Questioning the Universality of Human Rights: The African Charter on Human and Peoples' Rights in Botswana, Malawi and Mozambique* (Aldershot: Ashgate, 1997)

Lijnzaad, L, *Reservations to UN-Human Rights Treaties: Ratify and Ruin?* (Dordrecht: Martinus Nijhoff, 1995)

Lloyd, A, 'The First Meeting of the African Committee of Experts on the Rights and Welfare of the Child' (2002) 2 *AHRLJ* 320

—— 'Report of the Second Ordinary Session of the African Committee of Experts on the Rights and Welfare of the Child' (2003) 3 *AHRLJ* 329

—— 'How to Guarantee Credence: Recommendations and Proposals for the African Committee of Experts on the Rights and Welfare of the Child' (2004) 12 *International Journal of Children's Rights* 21

—— 'The Third Ordinary Session of the African Committee of Experts on the Rights and Welfare of the Child' (2004) 4 *AHRLJ* 139

—— and R Murray, 'Institutions with Responsibility for Human Rights Protection under the African Union' (2004) 48 *JAL* 165

Luhmann, N, *A Sociological Theory of Law* (London: Routledge and Kegan Paul, 1985)

Lyster, S, *International Wildlife Law: An Analysis of International Treaties Concerned with the Conservation of Wildlife* (Cambridge: Grotius Publications, 1985)

Maander, H, 'Rights as Struggle—Towards a More Just and Humane World' in P Gready and J Ensor (eds), *Reinventing Development? Translating Rights-Based Approaches from Theory to Practice* (London: Zed Books, 2005) 233

MacDonald, RW, *The League of Arab States* (Princeton, NJ: Princeton University Press, 1965)

McGoldrick, D, *The Human Rights Committee: Its Role in the Development of the International Covenant on Civil and Political Rights* (Oxford: Clarendon Press, 1991)

McGrory, G, 'Reservations of Virtue? Lessons from Trinidad and Tobago's Reservation to the First Optional Protocol' (2001) 23 *HRQ* 769

Magnarella, PJ, 'Some Milestones and Achievements at the International Criminal Tribunal for Rwanda: The 1998 *Kambanda, Akayesu* Cases' (1998) 11 *Florida Journal of International Law* 517

Mahoney, P, 'Developments in the Procedure of the European Court of Human Rights: The Revised Rules of Court' (1983) 3 *Yearbook of European Law* 127

Maloka, E (ed), *A United States of Africa?* (Pretoria: Africa Institute of South Africa, 2001)

Maluwa, T, 'The Domestic Implementation of International Refugee Law: A Brief Note on Malawi's Refugee Act of 1989' (1991) 1 *International Journal of Refugee Law* 503

—— 'The Role of International Law in the Protection of Human Rights under the Malawi Constitution' (1995) 3 *AYBIL* 53

—— 'The Incorporation of International Law and its Interpretive Role in Municipal Legal Systems in Africa: An Exploratory Survey' (1998) 23 *SAYIL* 45

—— 'International Law-Making in the Organisation of African Unity' (2000) 12 *RADIC* 201

—— 'Reimagining African Unity: Some Preliminary Reflections on the Constitutive Act of the African Union' (2002) 8 *AYBI Law* 28

Mamashela, MP, 'The Significance of the Convention on the Elimination of All Forms of Discrimination against Women for a Mosotho Woman' (1993) 5 *ASICL Proc* 153

Manby, B, 'The African Union, NEPAD and Human Rights: The Missing Agenda' (2004) 26 *HRQ* 983

Maqungo, S, 'The African Contribution towards the Establishment of an International Criminal Court' (2000) 8 *AYBIL* 333

Marks, SP, 'Social and Humanitarian Issues' in J Tessitore and S Woolfson (eds), *A Global Agenda: Issues before the 51st General Assembly of the United Nations* (Boulder, Colo: Rowman and Littlefields Publishers, 1996) 203

Masolo, DA, 'Western and African Communitarianism: A Comparison' in K Wiredu (ed), *A Companion to African Philosophy* (Oxford: Blackwell, 2004) 483

Mathews, K, 'The Organization of African Unity' in D Mazzeo (ed), *African Regional Organizations* (Cambridge: Cambridge University Press, 1984) 49

Maury, F, 'Ces Richesses que l'Afrique Laisse Echapper' (2006) 2377 *Jeune Afrique* 70

Maus, D, 'The Birth of Judicial Review of Legislation in France' in E Smith (ed), *Constitutional Justice under Old Constitutions* (The Hague: Kluwer, 1995) 113

Mazrui, AA, *The Trial of Christopher Okigbo* (Oxford: Heinemann, 1971)

—— and M Tidy, *Nationalism and New States in Africa from about 1935 to the Present* (Nairobi: Heinemann, 1984)

Mazzeo, D (ed), *African Regional Organizations* (Cambridge: Cambridge University Press, 1984)

M'Baye, K, *Les Droits de l'Homme en Afrique* (Paris: Pedone, 1992)

—— and B Ndiaye, 'The Organization of African Unity' in K Vasak and P Alston (eds), *The International Dimension of Human Rights* (Westport, Conn: Greenwood Press, 1982) 583

Mbazira, C, 'A Path to Realising Economic, Social and Cultural Rights in Africa? A Critique of the New Partnership for African's Development' (2004) 4 *AHRLJ* 35

—— 'Enforcing the Economic, Social and Cultural Rights in the African Charter on Human and Peoples' Rights: Twenty Years of Redundancy, Progression and Significant Strides' (2006) 6 *AHRLJ* 333

Meckled-García, S and B Çali, 'Lost in Translation: The Human Rights Ideal and International Human Rights Law' in S Meckled-García and B Çali (eds), *The Legalization of Human Rights: Multidisciplinary Perspectives on Human Rights and Human Rights Law* (London: Routledge, 2006) 11

Mensah-Brown, AK, *Introduction to Law in Contemporary Africa* (New York: Conch, 1976)

Meron, T, 'On a Hierarchy of International Human Rights' (1986) 80 *AJIL* 1

—— *The Humanization of International Law* (Leiden: Martinus Nijhoff, 2006)

Mezmur, BD, 'The African Committee of Experts on the Rights and Welfare of the Child: An Update' (2006) 6 *AHRLJ* 549

Motala, A, 'Non-Governmental Organisations in the African System' in MD Evans and R Murray (eds), *African Charter on Human and Peoples' Rights: The System in Practice, 1986–2000* (Cambridge: Cambridge University Press, 2002) 246

Mourning, PW, 'Leashing the Dogs of War: Outlawing the Recruitment of and Use of Mercenaries' (1981/2) 22 *Virginia Journal of International Law* 589

Mshomba, RE, *Africa in the Global Economy* (Boulder, Colo: Lynne Reinner Publishers, 2000)

Msungu, SF, 'Economic Integration and Human Rights in Africa: A Comment on Conceptual Linkages' (2003) 3 *AHRLJ* 93

Mubiala, M, 'L'Operation des Nations Unies pour les Droits de l'Homme au Rwanda' (1995) 3 *AYBIL* 277

—— *Le Système Régional Africain de Protection des Droits de l'Homme* (Brussels: Bruylant, 2005)

Mugwanya, GW, *Human Rights in Africa: Enhancing Human Rights through the African Regional Human Rights System* (Ardsley: Transnational, 2003)

Murdoch, J, 'The European Convention for the Prevention of Torture and Inhuman or Degrading Treatment or Punishment: Activities in 2001' (2002) 27 *European Law Review* 47

Mureinik, E, 'Beyond a Charter of Luxuries: Economic Rights in the Constitution' (1992) 8 *South African Journal on Human Rights* 464

Murithi, T, *The African Union: Pan-Africanism, Peacebuilding and Development* (Aldershot: Ashgate, 2005)

Murray, R, 'Massive or Serious Violations under the African Charter on Human and Peoples' Rights: A Comparison with the Inter American and European Mechanisms' (1999) 17 *NQHR* 109

—— *The African Commission on Human and Peoples' Rights and International Law* (Oxford: Hart, 2000)

—— 'The Human Rights Act: The End of the Privy Council and Death Penalty Cases?' (2001) 6 *Journal of Civil Liberties* 35

—— 'A Comparison between the African and European Courts of Human Rights' (2002) 2 *AHRLJ* 195

Murray, R, 'Evidence and Fact-Finding by the African Commission' in MD Evans and R Murray (eds), *The African Charter on Human and Peoples' Rights: The System in Practice, 1986–2000* (Cambridge: Cambridge University Press, 2002) 100

—— *Human Rights in Africa: From the OAU to the African Union* (Cambridge: Cambridge University Press, 2004)

—— 'Women's Rights and the Organization of African Unity and African Union: The Protocol on the Rights of Women in Africa' in D Buss and A Manji (eds), *International Law: Modern Feminist Approaches* (Oxford: Hart, 2005) 252

—— and M Evans (eds), *Documents of the African Commission on Human and Peoples' Rights* (Oxford: Hart, 2001)

Murungi, J, 'The Question of an African Jurisprudence: Some Hermeneutical Reflections' in K Wiredu (ed), A *Companion to African Philosophy* (Oxford: Blackwell, 2004) 519

Musungu, SF, 'Economic Integration and Human Rights in Africa: A Comment on Conceptual Linkages' (2003) 3 *AHRLJ* 93

Mutangi, T, 'Fact-Finding Missions or Omissions? A Critical Analysis of the African Commission on Human and Peoples' Rights' (2006) 12 *East African Journal of Peace and Human Rights* 1

Mutharika, PM, 'The Role of International Law in the Twenty-First Century: An African Perspective' (1994–95) 18 *Fordham International Law Journal* 1706

Mutua, M, wa, 'The African Human Rights System in a Comparative Perspective' (1993) 3 *Review of the African Commission on Human and Peoples' Rights* 5

—— 'Why Redraw the Map of Africa: A Moral and Legal Inquiry' (1994–5) 16 *Michigan Journal of International Law* 113

—— 'Putting Humpty Dumpy Back Together Again: The Dilemma of the Post-colonial African State' (1995) 21 *Brooklyn Journal of International Law* 520

—— 'The Banjul Charter and the African Cultural Fingerprint: An Evaluation of the Language of Duties' (1995) 35 *Virginia Journal of International Law* 339

—— 'The African Human Rights Court: A Two-Legged Stool?' (1999) 21 *HRQ* 342

Mvungi, SEA, *Constitutional Questions in the Regional Integration Process: The Case of the Southern African Development Community with References to the European Union* (Hamburg: Institute für Internationale Angelegerheiten, 1994)

Naldi, G, 'The Organization of African Unity and the Sahara Arab Democratic Republic' (1982) 26 *JAL* 152

—— *The Organization of African Unity: An Analysis of its Role* (London: Mansell, 1989)

—— *The Organization of African Unity: An Analysis of its Role* (London: Mansell, 2nd edn, 1999)

—— 'Interim Measures of Protection in the African System for the Protection of Human and Peoples' Rights' (2002) 2 *AHRLJ* 1

—— and K Magliveras, 'The Proposed African Court of Human and Peoples' Rights: Evaluation and Comparison' (1996) 8 *RADIC* 944

—— —— 'Reinforcing the African System of Human Rights: The Protocol on the Establishment of a Regional Court of Human and Peoples' Rights' (1998) 16 *NQHR* 431

Nifosi, I, *The UN Special Procedures in the Field of Human Rights* (Antwerp: Intersentia, 2005)

Nkot, PF, *Usages Politiques du Droit en Afrique: Le Cas du Cameroon* (Brussels: Bruylant, 2000)

Nkrumah, K, *Africa Must Unite* (New York: Praeger, 1963)

Nmehielle, VOO, *The African Human Rights System: Its Laws, Practice, and Institutions* (The Hague: Martiuus Nijhoff, 2001)

Noble, P, 'Refugees, Law and Development in Africa' (1982) *Michigan Yearbook of International Legal Studies* 255

Novogrodsky, N and M Goldstein, 'Small Steps: Prosecuting the Recruitment of Child Soldiers—The Case of *Sam Hinga Norman*' (2006) 15 *Interights Bulletin* 148

Nowak, M, 'The Activities of the UN Human Rights Committee: Development from 1 August 1989 through 31 July 1992' (1993) 14 *HRLJ* 9

—— 'The Activities of the UN Human Rights Committee: Developments from 1 August 1992 through 31 July 1995' (1995) 16 *HRLJ* 377

—— 'The International Covenant on Civil and Political Rights' in R Hanski and M Suksiy (eds), *An Introduction to the International Protection of Human Rights: A Textbook* (Abo: Abo Akademi University, 1997) 79

—— *Introduction to the International Human Rights Regime* (Leiden: Martinus Nijhoff, 2003)

—— *UN Covenant on Civil and Political Rights (CCPR) Commentary* (Kehl: NP Engel, 2nd edn, 2005)

Nsibirwa, M, 'A Brief Analysis of the Draft Protocol to the African Charter on Human and Peoples' Rights on the Rights of Women' (2001) 1 *AHRLJ* 40

Nweze, CC, 'Human Rights and Sustainable Development in the African Charter: A Judicial Prolegomenon to an Integrative Approach to Charter Rights' (1997) 1 *Abia State University Law Journal* 1

Odinkalu, CA, 'The Individual Complaints Procedures of the African Commission on Human and Peoples' Rights: A Preliminary Assessment' (1998) 8 *Transnational Law and Contemporary Problems* 359

—— 'Implementing Economic, Social and Cultural Rights' in MD Evans and R Murray (eds), *The African Charter on Human and Peoples' Rights: The System in Practice, 1986–2000* (Cambridge: Cambridge University Press, 2002) 178

—— 'Back to the Future: The Imperative of Prioritizing for the Protection of Human Rights in Africa' (2003) 47 *JAL* 1

—— 'Profile of the Economic Community of West African States' in C Heyns (ed), *Human Rights Law in Africa* (vol 1) (Leiden: Martinus Nijhoff, 2004) 644

—— and A Christensen, 'The African Commission on Human and Peoples' Rights: The Development of its Non-state Communications Procedures' (1998) 20 *HRQ* 235

—— Y Tadesse, and P Lumumba, 'The Work of the UN Human Rights Committee on Individual Communication from Africa: An Overview (1994) 8 (3) *Interights Bulletin* 67

O'Flaherty, M, *Human Rights and the UN* (London: Sweet and Maxwell, 1996)

Ojukwa, E, 'Is *Fawehinmi v Abacha* a Correct Decision?' (1997) 1 *Legal Practice Notes: HRLJ* 21

Okafor, OC, 'After Martyrdom: International Law, Sub-state Groups, and the Construction of Legitimate Statehood in Africa' (2000) 41 *Harvard International Law Journal* 503

—— *Legitimizing Human Rights NGOs: Lessons from Nigeria* (Trenton: Africa World Press, 2006)

Okogbule, NS, 'The Legal Dimensions of the Refugee Problem in Africa' (2004) 10 *East African Journal of Peace and Human Rights* 176

Okoth-Obbo, G, 'Thirty Years On: A Legal Review of the 1996 OAU Refugee Convention' (2000) 8 *AYBIL* 3

Olinga, AD, 'The Embargo against Burundi before the African Commission on Human and Peoples' Rights (Note on Communication 157/96, *Association pour la Sauvegarde de la Paix au Burundi v Kenya, Rwanda, Tanzania, Uganda, Zaire and Zambia*') (2005) 5 *AHRLJ* 424

Oliver, ME, 'Exploring the Doctrine of Self-Execution as Enforcement Mechanism of International Obligations' (2002) 27 *SAYIL* 99

Oloka-Onyango, J, 'Human Rights, the OAU Convention and the Refugee Crisis in Africa: Forty Years after Geneva' (1991) 3 *International Journal of Refugee Law* 453

—— 'Beyond the Rhetoric: Reinvigorating the Struggle for Economic and Social Rights in Africa' (1995) 26 *California Western International Law Journal* 1

—— 'The Plight of the Larger Half: Human Rights, Gender Violence and the Legal Status of Refugee and Internally Displaced Women in Africa' (1995–6) 24 *Denver Journal of International Law and Policy* 349

—— 'Who's Watching "Big Brother"? Globalization and the Protection of Cultural Rights in Present Day Africa' (2005) 27 *HRQ* 1245

—— and S Tamale, ' "The Personal is Political" of why Women's Rights are Indeed Human Rights: An African Perspective on International Feminism' (1995) 17 *HRQ* 691

O'Neill, WB Rutinwa, and G Verdirame, 'The Great Lakes: A Survey of the Application of the Exclusion Clause in the Central African Republic, Kenya and Tanzania' (2000) 12 *International Journal of Refugee Law* 135

Oosthuizen, GH, *The Southern African Development Community: The Organisation, its Policies and Prospects* (Johannesburg: Institute for Global Dialogue, 2006)

Österdahl, I, 'The Jurisdiction *Ratione Materiae* of the African Court of Human and Peoples' Rights: A Comparative Critique' (1998) 7 *Review of the African Commission on Human and Peoples' Rights* 132

—— *Implementing Human Rights in Africa* (Uppsala: Iustus Förlag, 2002)

Ouguergouz, F, *La Charte Africaine des Droits de l'Homme et des Peuples* (Paris: Presses Universitaires de France, 1993)

—— 'The Bamako Convention on Hazardous Waste: A New Step in the Development of the African Environmental Law' (1993) 1 *AYBIL* 195

—— 'Liberia' (1994) 2 *AYBIL* 2108

—— *The African Charter on Human and Peoples' Rights: A Comprehensive Agenda for Human Dignity and Sustainable Democracy in Africa* (The Hague: Martinus Nijhoff, 2003)

—— 'L'application de la Charte Africaine des Droits et des Peuples par les Autorités Nationales en Afrique Occidentale' in JF Flauss and E Lambert-Abdelgawad, *L'application Nationale de la Charte Africaine des Droits de l'Homme et des Peuples* (Antwerp: Bruylant, 2004) 161

—— 'The Establishment of an African Court of Human and Peoples' Rights: A Judicial Premiere for the African Union' (2005) 13 *AYBIL* 79

Packer, CAA, *Using Human Rights to Change Tradition: Traditional Practices Harmful to Women's Reproductive Health in Sub-Saharan Africa* (Antwerp: Intersentia, 2002)

—— and D Rukare, 'The New African Union and its Constitutive Act' (2002) 96 *AJIL* 365

Padilla, DJ, 'An African Human Rights Court: Reflections from the Perspective of the Inter-American System' (2002) 2 *AHRLJ* 185

Pakenham, T, *Scramble for Africa: 1876–1912* (New York: Random House, 1991)

Paltiel, AD *et al*, 'Expanded Screening for HIV in the United States—An Analysis of Cost-Effectiveness' (2005) 352(6) *New England Journal of Medicine* 586

Partsch, KJ, 'The Committee on the Elimination of Racial Discrimination' in P Alston (ed), *The United Nations and Human Rights* (Oxford: Clarendon Press, 1992) 339

—— 'The Committee on the Elimination of Racial Discrimination' in P Alston and J Crawford (eds), *The Future of UN Human Rights Treaty Monitoring* (Cambridge: Cambridge University Press, 2000) 339

Pasqualucci, JM, 'Victim Reparations in the Inter-American Human Rights System: A Critical Assessment of Current Practice and Procedure' (1996) 18 *Michigan Journal of International Law* 1

—— *The Practice and Procedure of the Inter-American Court of Human Rights* (Cambridge: Cambridge University Press, 2003)

Patel, N, 'Conflict Resolution through Regional Organisations in Africa' in E Moloka (ed), *A United States of Africa?* (Pretoria: Africa Institute of South Africa, 2001) 354

Pedersen, MP 'Standing and the African Commission on Human and Peoples' Rights' (2006) 6 *AHRLJ* 407

Peter, CM, 'The Proposed African Court of Justice—Jurisprudential, Procedural, Enforcement Problems and Beyond' (1993) 1 *East African Journal of Peace and Human Rights* 117

—— *Human Rights in Tanzania: Selected Cases and Materials* (Cologne: Rüdiger Koppe Verlag, 1997)

Pinder, J, 'The EU of the Future: Federal or Intergovernmental?' in J Gower (ed), *The European Union Handbook* (London: Fitzroy Dearborn, 2002) 369

Pires, MJM, 'Profile of the Community of Portuguese Speaking Countries', in C Heyns (ed), *Human Rights Law in Africa* (vol 1) (Leiden: Martinus Nijhoff, 2004) 744

Pityana, NB, 'Hurdles and Pitfalls in International Human Rights Law: The Ratification Process of the African Charter on the Establishment of the African Court on Human and Peoples' Rights' (2003) 28 *SAYIL* 110

Quansah, EK, 'Is the Right to Get Pregnant a Fundamental Human Right in Botswana?' (1995) 39 *JAL* 97

Quashigah, EK, 'Human Rights and Integration' in R Lavergne (ed), *Regional Integration and Cooperation in West Africa: A Multidimensional Perspective* (Trenton: Africa World Press, 1997) 259

—— 'The African Court of Human Rights: Prospects, in Comparison with the European Court of Human Rights and the Inter-American Court of Human Rights' (1998) 10 *ASICL Proc* 59

—— 'The African Charter on Human and Peoples' Rights: Towards a More Effective Reporting Mechanism' (2002) 2 *AHRLJ* 261

Quinn, J, 'The General Assembly into the 1990s' in P Alston (ed), *The United Nations and Human Rights: A Critical Appraisal* (Oxford: Clarendon Press, 1992) 55

Ramcharan, BG, 'The *Travaux Préparatoires* of the African Commission on Human Rights' (1992) 13 *HRLJ* 307

Ramcharan, R, 'The African Refugee Crisis' (2000) 8 *AYBIL* 119

Ratner, SR, 'Drawing a Better Line: *Uti Possidetis* and the Borders of New States' (1996) 90 *AJIL* 590

Rehman, J, *International Human Rights Law: A Practical Approach* (London: Longman, 2003)

Rembe, NS, *The System of Protection of Human Rights under the African Charter: Problems and Prospects* (Roma, Lesotho: Institute for Southern African Studies, University of Lesotho, 1991)

Republic of Uganda, *The Report of the Commission of Inquiry into Violations of Human Rights* (Kampala: Republic of Uganda Printers, 1994)

Rishmawi, M, 'The Arab Charter of Human Rights: A Comment' (1996) 10 *Interights Bulletin* 8

Robertson, AH and JG Merrils, *Human Rights in the World* (Manchester: Manchester University Press, 1977)

Roberts-Wray, K, *Commonwealth and Colonial Law* (London: Stevens and Sons, 1966)

Rodley, N, 'United Nations Human Rights Treaty Bodies and Special Procedures of the Commission on Human Rights—Complementarity of Competition?' in N Ando (ed), *Towards Implementing Universal Human Rights: Festschrift for the Twenty-Fifth Anniversary of the Human Rights Committee* (Leiden: Martinus Nijhoff, 2004) 3

Roux, T, 'Constitutional Property Rights in Southern Africa: The Record of the Zimbabwe Supreme Court' (1996) 8 *RADIC* 755

Rudolf, B, 'The Thematic Rapporteurs and Working Groups of the United Nations Commission on Human Rights' (2000) 4 *Max Planck Yearbook of United Nations Law* 297

Rwelamira, M, 'The 1969 Convention on the Specific Aspects of Refugee Problems in Africa' (1989) 1 *International Journal of Refugee Law* 557

Sacco, S, 'A Comparative Study of the Implementation in Zimbabwe and South Africa of the International Law Rules that Allow Compulsory Licensing and Parallel Importation of HIV/AIDS Drugs' (2005) 5 *AHRLJ* 105

Sachs, J, *The End of Poverty* (London: Penguin, 2005)

Salmon, TC, 'The Structure, Institutions, and Powers of the EU' in J Gower (ed), *The European Union Handbook* (London: Fitzroy Dearborn, 2002) 16

Samkange, S, *On Trial for my Country* (Oxford: Heinemann, 1966)

Scanlon, H, 'The Human Rights Council: From Human Rights to Responsibility?' in A Adebajo and H Scanlon (eds), *A Dialogue of the Deaf: Essays on Africa and the United Nations* (Auckland Park: Centre for Conflict Resolution, 2006) 131

Schermers, HC and NM Blokker, *International Institutional Law: Unity within Diversity* (The Hague: Martinus Nijhoff, 1995)

Schnalby, SJ, 'The OAS and Constitutionalism: Lessons from Recent West African Experience' (2005) 33 *Syracuse Journal of International Law and Commerce* 263

Schrijver, NJ, 'The Future of the Charter of the United Nations' (2006) 10 *Max Planck Ybk of United Nations Law* 1

Schwelb, E, 'The International Convention on the Elimination of All Forms of Racial Discrimination' (1966) 15 *ICLQ* 996

Scott, A, 'Theories of Regional Economic Integration and the Global Economy' in J Gower (ed), *The European Union Handbook* (London: Fitzroy Dearborn, 2002) 103

Scott, C and P Macklem, 'Constitutional Ropes of Sand or Justiciable Guarantees? Social Rights in a New South African Constitution' (1992) 141 *University of Pennsylvania Law Review*

Selassie, AG, 'Ethnic Identity and Constitutional Design for Africa' (1992–3) 29 *Stanford Journal International Law* 1

Shany, Y, *The Competing Jurisdictions of International Courts and Tribunals* (Oxford: Oxford University Press, 2003)

Shaw, TM, 'The Future of New Regionalism in Africa: Beyond Governance, Human Security/Development and Beyond' in JA Grant and F Söderbaum (eds), *The New Regionalism in Africa* (Ashgate: Aldershot, 2003) 203

Shearer, IA, *Starke's International Law* (London: Butterworths, 11th edn, 1994)

Shelton, D, 'Ensuring Justice with Deliberate Speed: Case Management in the European Court of Human Rights and the United States Courts of Appeals' (2000) 21 *HRLJ* 337

Shivji, I, *The Concept of Human Rights in Africa* (London: CODESRIA, 1989)

Shue, H, *Basic Rights: Subsistence, Affluence and US Foreign Policy* (Princeton, NJ: Princeton University Press, 1980)

Singh, K, 'Right to Basic Education: International Obligations and Regional Normative Action in Africa' (2004) 12 *AYBIL* 437

Sinjela, M, 'The UN and Internal Conflicts in Africa: A Documentary Survey' (1995) 3 *AYBIL* 318

Skogly, SI, 'The Position of the World Bank and the International Monetary Fund in the Human Rights Field' in R Hanski and M Suksi (eds), *An Introduction to the International Protection of Human Rights: A Textbook* (Turku: Abo Akademi University, 2nd edn, 1999) 231

Sloth-Nielsen, J, 'The Role of International Human Rights Law in the Development of South Africa's Legislation on Juvenile Justice' (2001) 5 *Law, Democracy and Development* 59

Smith, J, 'Legitimacy and Democracy in the EU' in J Gower (ed), *The European Union Handbook* (London: Fitzroy Dearborn, 2002) 64

Smith, RM, *Textbook on International Human Rights* (Oxford: Oxford University Press, 2003)

Sock, R, 'The Case for an African Court of Human and Peoples' Rights' (1994) 2 *African Topics* 9

Stefiszyn, K, 'The African Union: Challenges and Opportunities for Women' (2005) 5 *AHRLJ* 358

Stemmet, A, 'A Future African Court for Human and Peoples' Rights and Domestic Human Rights Norms' (1998) 23 *SAYIL* 233

Stiglitz, J, *Globalization and its Discontents* (London: Penguin, 2002)

Stultz, NM, 'Evolution of the United Nations Anti-Apartheid Regime' (1991) 13 *HRQ* 1

Syed, MH, *Human Rights in Islam: The Modern Approach* (New Delhi: Anmol, 2003)

Sylvian, R, ' "Land, Water, Truth": San Identity and Global Indigenism' (2002) 104 *American Anthropologist* 1074

Taulbee, JL, 'Myths, Mercenaries and Contemporary International Law' (1985) 15 *California Western International Law Journal* 339

Tavernier, P, 'International Organisation of the Francophonie: Profile of the Francophonie' in C Heyns (ed), *Human Rights Law in Africa* (Leiden: Martinus Nijhoff, 2004) 746

Tehindrazanarivelo, DL, 'Les sanctions de l'Union africaine contre les coups d'etat et autres changements anticonstitutionnels de gouvernement: potentialités et mesures de renforcement' (2004) 12 *AYBIL* 255

Theoderopoulos, C (ed), *Human Rights in Europe and in Africa: A Comparative Analysis* (Athens: Hellenic University Press, 1992)

Thompson, B, 'Economic Integration Efforts in Africa: A Milestone — The Abuja Treaty' (1993) 5 *RADIC* 743

Thiong'o, N wa and MG Mugo, *The Trial of Dedan Kimathi* (Oxford: Heinemann, 1976)

Tigere, P, 'State Reporting to the African Commission: The Case of Zimbabwe' (1994) 339 *JAL* 64

Tladi, D, 'The Quest to Ban Hazardous Waste Import into Africa: First Bamako and Now Basel' (2000) 33 *CILSA* 210

Toebes, BCA, *The Right to Health as a Human Right in International Law* (Antwerp: Intersentia-Hart, 1999)

Tomuschat, C, *Human Rights between Idealism and Realism* (Oxford: Oxford University Press, 2003)

Touval, S, *The Boundary Politics of Independent Africa* (Cambridge, Mass: Harvard University Press, 1972)

Trinidade, AAC, 'The Inter-American Human Rights System at the Dawn of the New Century: Recommendations for Improvement of its Mechanisms of Protection' in DJ Harris and A Livingstone (eds), *The Inter-American System of Human Rights* (New York: Oxford University Press, 1998) 395

Tshosa, O, *National Law and International Human Rights Law: Cases of Botswana, Namibia and Zimbabwe* (Aldershot: Ashgate, 2001)

Tuttle, K, 'Perry, Ruth' in KA Appiah and HL Gates (eds), *Africana: The Encyclopedia of the African and African American Experience* (New York: Basic Civitas Books, 1999)

Udombana, NJ, 'Towards the African Court on Human and Peoples' Rights: Better Late than Never' (2000) 3 *Yale Human Rights Development Law Journal* 45
—— 'A Harmony or a Cacophony? The Music of Integration in the African Union Treaty and the New Partnership for Africa's Development' (2002) 13 *Indiana International and Comparative Law Report* 185
—— 'An African Human Rights Court and an African Union Court: A Needful Duality or a Needless Duplication?' (2003) 28 *Brooklyn Journal of International Law* 811

Umozurike, UO 'The African Commission on Human and Peoples' Rights: An Introduction' (1991) 1 *Review of the African Commission on Human and Peoples' Rights* 5
—— *Five Years of the African Commission on Human and Peoples' Rights* (Ile-Ife: Obafemi Awolowo University, 1992)
—— *The African Charter on Human and Peoples' Rights* (The Hague: Kluwer Law International, 1997)

United Nations, *The United Nations and Human Rights 1945–1995* (New York: UN Department of Public Information, 1995)

United Republic of Tanzania, *Tanzania and the War against Amin's Uganda* (Dar es Salaam: Government Printer, 1979)

Uriz, GH, 'To Lend or Not to Lend: Oil, Human Rights, and the World Bank's Internal Contradictions' (2001) 14 *Harvard Human Rights Journal* 197

Van Hoof, GJH, 'The Legal Nature of Economic, Social and Cultural Rights: A Rebuttal of Some Traditional Views' in P Alston and K Tomasevski (eds), *The Right to Food* (Utrecht: Martinus Nijhoff, 1984) 97

Vandenhole, W, *The Procedure before the UN Human Rights Treaty Bodies* (Antwerp: Intersentia, 2004)

Van Boven, T, 'The Petition System under the International Covenant on the Elimination of All Forms of Racial Discrimination: A Sobering Balance Sheet' (2000) 4 *Max Planck Yearbook of United Nations Law* 271

Van der Linde, M, 'A Review of the African Convention on Nature and Natural Resources' (2002) 2 *AHRLJ* 33

Van de Mei, AP 'The Advisory Jurisdiction of the African Court on Human and Peoples' Rights' (2005) 5 *AHRLJ* 27

Van Dijk, P and GJH Van Hoof, *Theory and Practice of the European Convention on Human Rights* (The Hague: Kluwer Law International, 3rd edn, 1998)

Van Nieuwkerk, A, 'Regionalism into Globalism? War into Peace? SADC and ECOWAS Compared' (2001) 10(2) *African Security Review* 7

Vásquez, CM, 'The Four Doctrines of Self-Executing Treaties' (1995) 89 *AJIL* 695

Veber, H and E Waehle, '... Never Drink from the Same Cup' in H Veber, J Dahl, F Wilson, and E Waehle (eds), ... *Never Drink from the Same Cup: Proceedings of the Conference on Indigenous Peoples in Africa, Tune, Denmark, 1993* (Copenhagen: IWGIA and Centre for Development Research, 1993) 9

Vierdag, F, 'The Nature of the Rights Granted by the International Covenant on Economic, Social and Cultural Rights' (1987) 9 *NYBIL* 69

Viljoen, F, 'Supra-national Human Rights Instruments for the Protection of Children in Africa: The Convention on the Rights of the Child and the African Charter on the Rights and Welfare of the Child' (1998) 31 *CILSA* 199

—— 'Application of the African Charter on Human and Peoples' Rights by Domestic Courts in Africa' (1999) 43 *JAL* 1

—— 'The Realisation of Human Rights in Africa through Sub-regional Institutions' (1999) 7 *AYBIL* 185

—— 'State Reporting under the African Charter on Human and Peoples' Rights: A Boost from the South' (2000) 44 *JAL* 110

—— 'The African Charter on the Rights and Welfare of the Child' in CJ Davel (ed), *Introduction to Child Law in South Africa* (Cape Town: Juta, 2000) 214

—— 'Admissibility under the African Charter on Human and Peoples' Rights' in MD Evans and R Murray (eds), *The System in Practice 1986–2000* (Cambridge: Cambridge University Press, 2002) 61

—— 'A Human Rights Court for Africa, and Africans' (2004) 30 *Brooklyn Journal of International Law* 1

—— 'Fact-finding by UN Human Rights Complaints Bodies—Analysis and Suggested Reforms' (2004) 8 *Max Planck Yearbook of United Nations Law* 49

—— 'Introduction to the African Commission and the Regional Human Rights System' in C Heyns (ed), *Human Rights Law in Africa* (vol 1) (Leiden: Martinus Nijhoff, 2004) 385

—— 'Recent Developments in the African Regional Human Rights System' (2004) 4 *AHRLJ* 344

—— 'The African Charter on Human and Peoples' Rights: The *Travaux Préparatoires* in the Light of Subsequent Practice' (2004) 25 *HRLJ* 313

—— 'Disclosing in an Age of AIDS: Confidentiality and Community in Conflict?' in F Viljoen (ed), *Righting Stigma: Exploring a Rights-Based Approach to Addressing Stigma* (Pretoria: AIDS and Human Rights Research Unit, University of Pretoria, 2005) 64

—— 'Hate Speech in Rwanda as a Test Case for International Human Rights Law' (2005) 38 *CILSA* 1

—— 'National Legislation as a Source of Justiciable Socio-Economic Rights' (2005) 6 *ESR Review* 6

Viljoen, F, (ed), *Righting Stigma: Exploring a Rights-Based Approach to Addressing Stigma* (Pretoria: AIDS and Human Rights Research Unit, University of Pretoria, 2005)

—— 'The Special Rapporteur on Prisons and Conditions of Detention in Africa: Achievements and Possibilities' (2005) 27 *HRQ* 125

—— (ed), *Judiciary Watch Report: The African Human Rights System: Towards the Co-existence of the Africa Commission on Human and Peoples' Rights and African Court on Human and Peoples' Rights* (Nairobi: Kenya Section of the International Commission of Jurists, 2006)

—— 'Promising Profiles: An Interview with the Four New Members of the African Commission on Human and Peoples' Rights' (2006) 6 *AHRLJ* 237

—— and E Baimu, 'Courts for Africa: Considering the Co-existence of the African Court on Human and Peoples' Rights and the Court of Justice' (2004) 22 *NQHR* 241

—— and L Louw, 'The Status of the Findings of the African Commission: From Moral Persuasion to Legal Obligation' (2004) 48 *JAL* 1

—— —— 'State Compliance with the Recommendations of the African Commission on Human and Peoples' Rights, 1993–2004' (2007) 101 *AJIL* 1

—— 'Communications under the African Charter: Procedure and Admissibility' in MD Evans and R Murray (eds), *The African Charter on Human and Peoples' Rights: The System in Practice* (Cambridge: Cambridge University Press, 2007) Ch 3

Weis, P, 'The Convention of the Organization of African Unity governing the Specific Aspects of Refugee Problems in Africa' (1970) 3 *Revue des Droits de l'Homme* 449

—— 'Towards Relative Normativity in International Law?' (1983) 77 *AJIL* 413

Weisfelder, RF, 'Human Rights and Majority Rule in Southern Africa: The Mote in Thy Brother's Eye' in CE Welch and RI Meltzer (eds), *Human Rights and Development in Africa* (Albany, NY: State University of New York Press, 1984) 90

Welch, CE, 'The Organisation of African Unity and the Promotion of Human Rights' (1991) 29 *Journal of Modern African Studies* 535

—— 'The African Commission on Human and Peoples' Rights: A Five Year Report and Assessment' (1992) 14 *HRQ* 43

—— 'The Organisation of African Unity and Human Rights: Regional Promotion of Human Rights' in Y El-Ayouty (ed), *The Organisation of African Unity after Thirty Years* (Westport, Conn: Praeger, 1994) 53

—— *Protecting Human Rights in Africa: Strategies and Roles of Non-Governmental Organizations* (Philadelphia: University of Pennsylvania, 1995)

Weller, M (ed), *Regional Peacekeeping and International Enforcement: The Liberian Crisis* (Cambridge: Cambridge University Press, 1994)

Wembou, MD, 'A Propos du Nouveau Mécanisme de l'OUA sur les Conflits' (1993) 5 *RADIC* 725

Whittaker, DJ, *United Nations in Action* (London: University College London Press, 1995)

Wiessner, S, 'Rights and Status of Indigenous Peoples: A Global Comparative and International Legal Analysis' (1999) 12 *Harvard Human Rights Journal* 57

World Bank, *Development and Human Rights: The Role of the World Bank* (Washington, DC: World Bank, 1998)

—— *Can Africa Claim the 21st Century?* (Washington, DC: World Bank, 2000)

Young, C, 'Africa: An Interim Balance Sheet' (1996) 7 *Journal of Democracy* 53

Zarate, JC, 'The Emergence of a New Dog of War: Private International Security Companies, International Law, and the New World Disorder' (1998) 34 *Stanford Journal of International Law* 75

Zeleza, PT, 'The Struggle for Human Rights' in PT Zeleza and PJ McConnaughag (eds), *Human Rights, the Rule of Law, and Development in Africa* (Philadelphia: University of Pennsylvania Press, 2004) 1

Index